Jesus Speaks
to Seven of His Churches

A Historical and Exegetical Commentary on the Messages to the Seven Churches in Revelation

An Examination of the Graeco-Roman local references and the Hebraic-Semitic covenant lawsuit influences

David E. Graves, Ph.D.

Toronto, Canada

2017

Unless otherwise indicated, all Scripture quotations are from the *ESV*® Bible (*The Holy Bible, English Standard Version*®), copyright © 2001 by Crossway Bibles, a publishing ministry of Good News Publishers. Used by permission. All rights reserved. Italics within Scripture quotations indicate emphasis added.

EB Garamond Font was used for the Greek and Hebrew text. This Font Software is licensed under the SIL Open Font License, Version 1.1. http://scripts.sil.org/OFL

Jesus Speaks to Seven of His Churches: A Historical and Exegetical Commentary on the Messages to the Seven Churches in Revelation. An examination of the Graeco-Roman local references and the Hebraic-Semitic covenant lawsuit influences.
Includes bibliographic references and indexes.
Copyright © 2017 by David E. Graves
Revision May 19, 2017; August 29, 2017
Published by Electronic Christian Media
Toronto, Ontario, Canada M2J 4T4

Permission is granted to copy, distribute and/or modify public domain photographs under the terms of the GNU Free Documentation License, Version 1.2.

ISBN-13: 978-0-9948060-8-6
1. Bible. N.T. Revelation II–III–Criticism, interpretation, etc. 2. Seven Churches. 3. Turkey–Church history. I Graves, David E. II. Title. ECM. 2017.

Interior Book Design: David E. Graves
Cover Design: David E. Graves

Front page background and top of spine – Temple of Artemis and Byzantine Church in Sardis. Photography by David E. Graves. Spine bottom – Mosaic from the sidewalk in Ephesus. Courtesy of David E. Graves.

For information about books and resources for Christian leaders, and all new releases available from Electronic Christian Media, visit our web site: http://smyrnaean.blogspot.ca/2016/10/ecm-company.html

Online Companion website: http://jesusspeaks7.blogspot.ca/

All rights reserved. No portion of this publication may be reproduced, stored in a retrieval system, or transmitted in any form (i.e., electronic, scanning, photocopy or recording) without the written permission of the publisher. The only exception is brief excerpts for reviews.

Printed by CreateSpace in the United States of America.

To my supervisor and mentor
I. Howard Marshall

and in honor of the pioneering work of
Sir. William M. Ramsay

who both taught at my alma mater
the University of Aberdeen

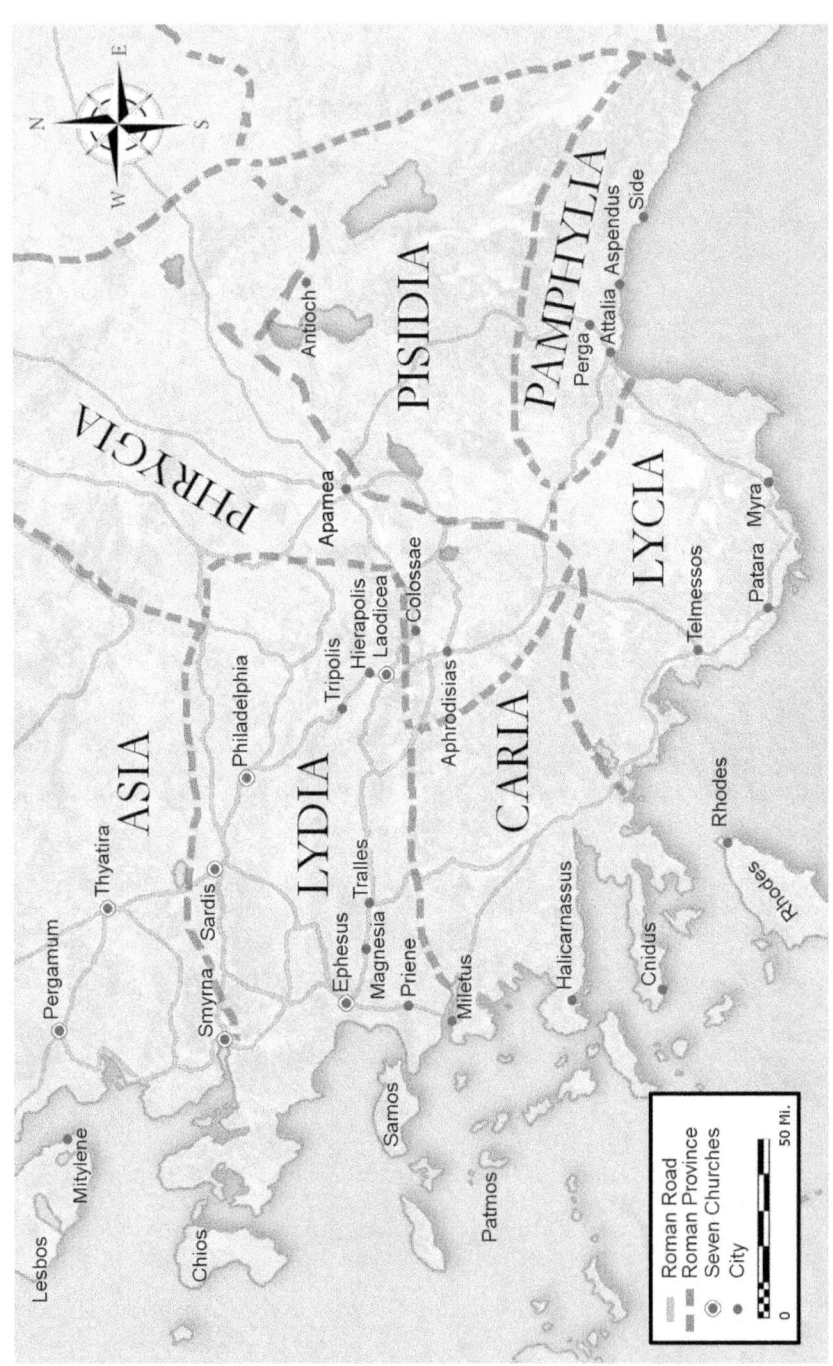

Seven Churches of Asia Minor.

Table of Contents

INDEX OF IMAGES XII
ABBREVIATIONS XVII
   OLD TESTAMENT XVII
   NEW TESTAMENT XVIII
   DEAD SEA SCROLLS XVIII
   ANCIENT AND MODERN SOURCES XIX
PREFACE XXXIX
THE LITERARY CONTEXT OF THE BOOK OF REVELATION 42
   THE AUTHORSHIP OF REVELATION 42
   THE OCCASION OF REVELATION 43
   THE LOCATION OF WRITING 44
   THE DATE OF WRITING 46
   THE QUESTION OF GENRE 48
      The genre of the seven messages 49
THE CULTURAL BACKGROUND OF THE SEVEN MESSAGES 52
   LOCAL REFERENCES IN THE SEVEN MESSAGES 52
      Proponents 52
      Arguments for the use of local references 53
      A balanced use of local references 54
   THE CULTURAL ISSUES IN THE SEVEN MESSAGES 55
      External problems 55
      Internal problems 64
THE COVENANTAL FRAMEWORK OF THE SEVEN MESSAGES 65
   RESPONSE TO THE CRITICS 69
   THE MESSENGER'S COMMISSION 71
      Angels defined as messengers 71
      Three categories of interpretation 72
      The angels' function 75
      Messengers from an ANE perspective 76
   MESSENGER PREAMBLE FORMULA 79
   HISTORICAL PROLOGUE 82
   FORMAL ETHICAL STIPULATIONS 84
   SANCTIONS 85
      Benediction 88
      Malediction 88
   PROCLAMATION WITNESSES FORMULA 91
   DEPOSIT AND PUBLIC READING 94
   METHODOLOGY 97
      The influence of the OT 97

Historical churches *97*
Unity *98*
Hebraic-Semitic and Graeco-Roman presence *99*
John, in the OT prophetic tradition *99*

ELEGANT EPHESUS 100

THE GEOGRAPHY OF EPHESUS 100
THE HISTORY OF EPHESUS 101
THE POPULATION OF EPHESUS 102
AN IMPORTANT COMMERCIAL CENTER 104
The commercial harbour *104*
The road system *106*
The commercial agora *106*
AN IMPORTANT POLITICAL CENTER 107
A free city *107*
The judicial circuit of Ephesus (Assize) *109*
The panionian games *109*
The theater of Ephesus *110*
The library of Celsus *112*
AN IMPORTANT RELIGIOUS CENTER 112
The imperial cult and the keeper of the temples (neōkoros) *112*
Augusteion temple *122*
A city of immorality and superstition *122*
The Jewish community *125*
The Christian community *126*

EXTINCT EPHESUS 128

MESSENGER PREAMBLE FORMULA—2:1 128
Description of the suzerain *129*
The omnipotent suzerain holds the seven stars—2:1a *129*
The suzerain walks among the churches—2:1b *130*
HISTORICAL PROLOGUE—2:2–4 130
The suzerain knows their works—2:2a *131*
The suzerain knows they have tested false apostles—2:2b *132*
The suzerain knows their patient endurance—2:3 .... *134*
The suzerain knows they have abandoned their first love—2:4 .... *134*
ETHICAL STIPULATIONS—2:5A 135
First imperative: Remember—2:5a *136*
Second imperative: Repent—2:5a *136*
Third imperative: Repeat—2:5a *137*
SANCTIONS: CURSE—2:5B,C 137
The curse of the suzerain's visit—2:5b *137*
The curse of a removed lampstand—2:5c *138*
HISTORICAL PROLOGUE II—2:6 141
The suzerain knows they hate the works of the Nicolaitans—2:6 .... *141*
PROCLAMATION WITNESS FORMULA—2:7A 143

    Hearing formula 2:7a *143*
  SANCTIONS: BLESSING—2:7B,C 145
    The blessing of eating of the tree of life—2:7b *146*
    The blessing of the paradise of god—2:7c *148*
  CONCLUSION 149

SUPREME SMYRNA 151

  THE ORIGIN OF THE NAME 151
  THE GEOGRAPHY OF SMYRNA 153
  THE HISTORY OF SMYRNA 153
    The ancient period *153*
    The Archaic period: old Smyrna *154*
    The Alexandrian period: new Smyrna *154*
    The Roman period *155*
    The Byzantine period *155*
  THE POPULATION OF SMYRNA 157
  SMYRNA: FIRST IN ASIA 158
  A GREAT TRADE CITY 160
  A BEAUTIFULLY CULTURED CITY 160
    The aqueduct *161*
    The gymnasium *161*
    The stadium *162*
    The theater *162*
  A PROMINENT POLITICAL CITY 163
    Homonoia coins *163*
    The state agora *163*
  A THRIVING RELIGIOUS CITY 166
    A city of the imperial cult *166*
    A city of temples *169*
    The Jewish community *170*
    The Christian community *177*
    The martyrs of Smyrna *178*

STEADFAST SMYRNA 180

  MESSENGER PREAMBLE FORMULA—2:8 180
    Description of the Suzerain *181*
    The transcendent Suzerain is the first and the last—2:8b *181*
    The Suzerain: dead and has come to life—2:8c *183*
  HISTORICAL PROLOGUE—2:9 188
    The suzerain knows their afflictions—2:9a *189*
    The suzerain knows their poverty and riches—2:9b *190*
    The suzerain knows the enemy—2:9c *193*
    Summary *200*
  ETHICAL STIPULATIONS—2:10 200
    First imperative: do not fear—2:10a *201*
    Second imperative: be faithful to death—2:10b *209*

- SANCTIONS: BLESSINGS—2:10C, 11B 211
  - *The blessing of the crown of life—2:10c* 211
  - *The blessing of no second death—2:11b* 221
  - *Summary* 223
- PROCLAMATION WITNESS FORMULA—2:11A 223
- CONCLUSION 224

POLYTHEISTIC PERGAMUM 225

- THE GEOGRAPHY OF PERGAMUM 225
- THE HISTORY OF PERGAMUM 227
  - *Under Seleucid control* 227
  - *Under Pergamene control* 227
  - *Under Roman control* 228
- THE POPULATION OF PERGAMUM 231
- THE IMPORTANT BUILDINGS OF PERGAMUM 231
  - *Famous for her library* 231
  - *Famous for her Asclepeion* 235
  - *Famous for her theater* 238
- FAMOUS FOR HER RELIGIOUS WORSHIP 239
  - *The great altar of Zeus* 240
- FAMOUS FOR THE IMPERIAL CULT 242
  - *The Trajaneium* 243

PRAISED PERGAMUM 244

- MESSENGER PREAMBLE FORMULA—2:12A 244
  - *Description of the suzerain who has a sword—2:12b* 244
- HISTORICAL PROLOGUE—2:13–15 247
  - *The suzerain knows where Satan has his throne—2:13a* 247
  - *The suzerain knows they have remained faithful—2:13b* 254
  - *The suzerain knows of Antipas' death—2:13c* 254
  - *The suzerain knows people who hold to the teaching of Balaam—2:14* ... 256
  - *The suzerain knows those who hold to the teaching of the Nicolaitans—2:15* ... 258
- ETHICAL STIPULATIONS—2:16A 260
  - *Imperative: Repent —2:16a* 260
- SANCTIONS: CURSES—2:16B–C 261
  - *The curse of the suzerain's presence—2:16b* 261
  - *The curse of the suzerain's war against them—2:16c* 262
- PROCLAMATION WITNESS FORMULA—2:17A 262
- SANCTIONS: BLESSINGS—2:17B 263
  - *The blessing of hidden manna—2:17c* 263
  - *The blessing of a new name—2:17d* 265
- CONCLUSION 274

TIRELESS THYATIRA 276

- THE GEOGRAPHY OF THYATIRA 276
- THE HISTORY OF THYATIRA 277

The population of Thyatira	279
The important buildings of Thyatira	281
The commerce of Thyatira	283
The trade guilds	*283*
The dyers guild	*285*
The slave trade	*297*
The religious community of Thyatira	297
The gods of Thyatira	*297*
The imperial cult	*298*
The Jewish community	*299*
The Christian community	*300*

THREATENED THYATIRA 302

Messenger preamble formula—2:18	302
Description of the suzerain	*302*
The transcendent suzerain: Son of God—2:18b	*303*
The transcendent suzerain: Eyes like a flame of fire—2:18c	*305*
The transcendent suzerain: Feet like burnished bronze—2:18d	*306*
Historical prologue—2:19–21	307
The suzerain knows their works—2:19	*307*
The suzerain knows that you tolerate Jezebel—2:20	*309*
The suzerain knows that Jezebel refuses to repent—2:21	*312*
Sanctions—2:22–23	313
The curse of thrown on a sickbed—2:22a	*313*
The curse of great tribulation—2:22b	*314*
The curse of dead children—2:23a	*315*
The curse of receiving according to their works—2:23b	*316*
Ethical stipulations—2:24–25	317
First imperative: No other burdens—2:24b	*319*
Second imperative: Hold fast to what you Have—2:25	*319*
Sanctions: blessing—2:26–28	320
The blessing of authority over the nations—2:26b	*320*
The blessing of an iron rule—2:27	*321*
The blessing of the morning star—2:28	*322*
Proclamation witness formula—2:29	323
Conclusion	324

STALWART SARDIS 325

The geography of Sardis	325
The history of Sardis	326
Under Lydian control (1200–546 BC)	*326*
Under Persian control (547–334 BC)	*328*
Under Macedonian control (334–323 BC)	*329*
Under Seleucid control (312–189 BC)	*330*
Under Pergamese control (189–133 BC)	*330*
Under Roman control (133 BC–AD 660)	*331*

  Under Byzantine control (AD 661–716) *333*
 THE POPULATION OF SARDIS 333
 THE IMPORTANT BUILDINGS OF SARDIS 335
  The bath-gymnasium complex *337*
  The temple of Artemis *338*
  The Jewish synagogue *341*
 THE COMMERCE OF SARDIS 344
  The invention of coins *345*
  The slave trade *347*
  Textile industry of Sardis *347*
 THE RELIGIOUS COMMUNITY OF SARDIS 348
  The gods of Sardis *348*
  The imperial cult *352*
  The Jewish community *353*
  The Christian community *355*

SEDATE SARDIS 356

 MESSENGER PREAMBLE FORMULA—3:1B 356
 HISTORICAL PROLOGUE—3:1 359
  The suzerain knows their works—3:1c *359*
  The suzerain knows their reputation—3:1d *359*
  The suzerain knows they are dead—3:1e *360*
 ETHICAL STIPULATIONS—3:2–3A 360
  First imperative: Be vigilant—3:2a *361*
  Second imperative: Strengthen what remains—3:2b *361*
  Third imperative: Bear in mind what you received—3:3a *362*
  Fourth imperative: Keep it or pay attention—3:3b *363*
  Fifth imperative: Repent—3:3c *363*
 SANCTIONS 364
  Curses—3:3d-e *364*
  Blessings—3:4–5 .... *368*
 PROCLAMATION WITNESS FORMULA—3:6 377
 CONCLUSION 377

PROSPEROUS PHILADELPHIA 379

 THE GEOGRAPHY OF PHILADELPHIA 379
 THE HISTORY OF PHILADELPHIA 380
  Ancient Philadelphia *380*
  Roman Philadelphia *382*
  Byzantine Philadelphia *382*
  Modern period *383*
 THE POPULATION OF PHILADELPHIA 384
 AN INDUSTRIOUS CITY 385
  Fertile land *385*
  Textile and leather *386*
 A CULTURED CITY 387

The aqueduct	387
The theater	387
The stadium	388
The temples	388
A POLITICAL CITY	389
A RELIGIOUS CITY	390
The gods of Philadelphia	390
The imperial cult	396
Neōkoros	396
The Jewish community	397
The Christian community	397

FAITHFUL PHILADELPHIA 399

MESSENGER PREAMBLE FORMULA—3:7	399
Description of the suzerain—3:7	399
The transcendent suzerain is the holy one—3:7b	400
The transcendent suzerain is the true one—3:7c	400
The transcendent suzerain has the key of David—3:7d	401
The transcendent suzerain opens and shuts doors—3:7d	402
HISTORICAL PROLOGUE—3:8–9	403
The suzerain knows their works—3:8a	403
The suzerain knows they have little strength—3:8b	405
The suzerain knows they have kept his word—3:8c	405
The suzerain knows they have not denied his name—3:8d	406
The suzerain knows the enemy—3:9a	407
Forced to come and grovel at your feet—3:9b	408
The suzerain knows they are loved—3:9c	409
The suzerain knows they have kept his word—3:10a	410
SANCTIONS: BLESSINGS—3:10A	411
Blessing of being kept from the hour of trial—3:10b	411
Blessing of the suzerain's soon coming—3:11a	413
ETHICAL STIPULATIONS—3:11B	415
Imperative: Hold fast what you have—3:11b	415
SANCTIONS: BLESSINGS—3:12	416
Blessing of becoming a temple pillar—3:12a	417
Blessing of never leaving the temple of God—3:12b	421
Blessing of wearing the name of God—3:12c	421
Blessing of wearing the name of the new Jerusalem—3:12d	422
Blessing of wearing God's new name—3:12e	423
PROCLAMATION WITNESS FORMULA—3:13	424
CONCLUSION	424

LUXURIOUS LAODICEA 426

THE GEOGRAPHY OF LAODICEA	426
THE HISTORY OF LAODICEA	429
Under Seleucid control	429

JESUS SPEAKS TO SEVEN OF HIS CHURCHES

    Under Pergamene control *430*
    Under Roman control (133 BC–AD 660) *430*
    Under Byzantine control *435*
  THE POPULATION OF LAODICEA 436
  THE IMPORTANT BUILDINGS OF LAODICEA 437
    The city gates (no. 1, 2, 3, 32) *438*
    The north state agora *439*
    The water system *439*
    The nymphaeums *444*
    The stadium (no. 4) *446*
    The temples *447*
    Temple A, AD 26–60 (no. 18) *447*
    The theaters *448*
    The bouleuterion (no. 7) *450*
    The south bath-gymnasium complex (no. 5) *451*
    Cental baths (no. 16) *452*
    The necropolis *452*
  THE COMMERCE OF LAODICEA 452
    Medical center and ophthalmology *452*
    Textile industry and wool *456*
    The financial world at Laodicea *460*
  THE RELIGIOUS COMMUNITY OF LAODICEA 462
    The gods of Laodicea *462*
    The imperial cult *468*
    The Jewish community *470*
    The Christian community *471*

LUKEWARM LAODICEA **474**

  MESSENGER PREAMBLE FORMULA— 3:14B 474
    Description of the suzerain *475*
    The preexistent suzerain: the amen—14b *475*
    The preexistent suzerain: faithful and true—14c *476*
    The preexistent suzerain: the beginning of God's creation—14d *477*
  HISTORICAL PROLOGUE—3:15–16A 478
    The suzerain knows their works—3:15a *478*
    The suzerain knows they are neither cold nor hot—15b *479*
    The suzerain knows they are lukewarm—3:16a *483*
  SANCTIONS: CURSES—3:16B–17 484
    The curse of being spit out of his mouth—3:16b *484*
    The curse of prosperity—17a *485*
    The curse of not realizing that they are a pititful wretch—17b *486*
    The curse of not realizing that they are poor—17b *487*
    The curse of not realizing that they are blind—17b *487*
    The curse of not realizing that they are naked—17b *487*
  ETHICAL STIPULATIONS—3:18–19 488
    First imperative: Buy from the suzerain—3:18a *488*

Second imperative: Buy gold to become rich—18b *488*
Third imperative: Buy white garments to hide your nakedness—18c *489*
Fourth imperative: Buy salve to anoint your eyes—18d *490*
Fifth imperative: Be zealous—19a *491*
Six imperative: Repent—19b *492*
SANCTIONS: BLESSING—3:20–21 493
The blessing of the suzerain who knocks—20a *493*
The blessings of a communion meal—20b *495*
The blessings of sitting with Christ on his throne—21 .... *500*
Conclusion *502*
PROCLAMATION WITNESS FORMULA—3:22 502
CONCLUSION 503

CONCLUSION 504

THE SOCIAL SETTING 504
BLESSINGS FOR OVERCOMERS 505

APPENDIX A – THE GRAECO-ROMAN LITERARY CONTEXT 506

GLOSSARY 521

BIBLIOGRAPHY 532

PRIMARY SOURCES 532
SECONDARY SOURCES 555

CREDITS AND PERMISSIONS 635

Photographs *635*
Drawings *638*
Maps and charts *638*

INDEX OF SUBJECTS 639

INDEX OF FOREIGN WORDS 653

INDEX OF GREEK WORDS 658

INDEX OF SCRIPTURE AND ANCIENT WRITINGS 662

Index of Images

1. The island of Patmos where John received his vision of Revelation. — 44
2. Bust of Julius Claudius Caesar. — 47
3. The statue of Romulus and Remus, the founders of Rome. — 56
4. Marcus Aurelius and members of the Imperial family offer sacrifice — 57
5. A round altar used in the imperial cult. — 58
6. Portrait of a priest who served in the temple of the imperial cult. — 59
7. The Sebasteion or Augusteum, in Aphrodisias. — 59
8. Coin of Nero with the goddess Roma holding Victory in her right hand. — 60
9. Papyrus document of a certificate of sacrifice (*libellus*). — 61
10. *Apotheōsis* of Antoninus Pius and Faustina. — 62
11. Marble Statue of Trajan in armor. — 63
12. The Treaty of Kadesh discovered at Boğazköy, Turkey. — 67
13. Stone carving of the winged angel Nike, the goddess of victory, Ephesus. — 71
14. Fragment of a Hittite tablet. — 82
15. The Nash Papyrus. — 92
16. Replica of the Ark of the Covenant. — 95
17. Woman holding wax tablets in the form of the codex and stylus. — 96
18. Urban plan of the city of Ephesus. — 103
19. Main road called the Sacred Way, leading from Ephesus to Magnesia. — 106
20. Market Square of the commercial agora, Ephesus. — 107
21. Ephesian *Boulētarion* or *Odeon*. — 108
22. The theater in Ephesus with The Arcadian Way leading down to the now silted harbour. — 111
23. The library of Celsus and Gate of Macaeus and Mithridates in Ephesus. — 112
24. Recreation of the Artemision, Temple of Artemis, as it would have looked at Ephesus. — 113
25. The remains of the Temple of Artemis in Ephesus. — 114
26. Artemis, the goddess of hunting, as portrayed in Cyrene. — 115
27. "The Great Artemis" from the Prytanaeum of Ephesus. — 115
28. Ephesian coin with the head of Claudius and cult statue of Artemis within a tetrastyle temple. — 116
29. Ephesian *neokorōn* coin struck under Nero with the Temple of Artemis. — 116
30. Ephesian coin with the head of Augustus and the altar of Artemis with two deer. — 117
31. Bust of Roman emperor Domitian. — 118
32. Colossal statue of Emperor Titus (not Domitian) from the Temple of Sebastoi, Ephesus. — 119
33. Temple of Hadrian on Curetes Street, Ephesus. — 120
34. Coin from Thyatira with the bust of Athena and Tyche standing. — 121
35. Marble statue of Dionysus. — 123
36. A sign etched in the marble pavement in Ephesus, pointing the way to the brothel. — 124
37. Menorah inscribed into a step of the second cent. AD Library of Celsus. — 125
38. Restored Library of Celsus, Ephesus. — 126
39. Silver coin with the bust of Domitian and Domitia's deified infant son, with seven stars. — 129
40. Arch of Titus, Rome, depicting the menorah from the temple in Jerusalem (70 AD). — 138
41. Woman lighting an oil lamp on a lampstand. — 139

42. Ephesian coin struck under Archidamos with a bee, and stag in front of the sacred palm tree.	147
43. Bust of Emperor Tiberius Caesar Augustus.	155
44. Harbor of Izmir (Smyrna) from Mount Pagus, surrounded by the modern city.	161
45. *Homōnoia* coin from Smyrna with three temples to Tiberius, Roma and Hadrian.	162
46. The Corinthian columns of the stao of the commercial agora, Smyrna.	163
47. Arch in the western stoa of the state agora in Smyrna with a portrait of Faustina the Younger.	165
48. Faustina the Younger, wife of Marcus Aurelius (second cent. AD).	166
49. Priest of the imperial cult at Smyrna (30 BC–AD 395).	168
50. Stained glass window depicting Polycarp (St. John Anglican Church, Izmir).	172
51. Painting of the martyrdom of Polycarp, St. Polycarp Roman Catholic Church, Izmir.	174
52. Small reliefs of the mother goddess Cybele/Tyche.	183
53. Painting of a phoenix from the Musicians Cave, Israel.	185
54. Silver coin from Smyrna with the Anatolian goddess Tyche/Cybele wearing a turreted crown.	214
55. Bronze statue of a runner wearing the laurel wreath awarded to the winner.	218
56. Acropolis of Pergamum, with the Hellenistic theater with a capacity of ca. 10,000 citizens.	226
57. A Hellenistic portrait of the king of Pergamum, Attalus I.	228
58. A model of the acropolis of the ancient Greek city of Pergamum.	230
59. The acropolis library at Pergamum.	232
60. Asclepeion complex and the north stoa viewed from the theater.	233
61. Map of the Pergamum Asclepion, the santuary of Asclepios Soter.	234
62. Statue of Galen of Pergamum.	236
63. Pergamum coin with a basket used for housing sacred snakes (Lat. *cista mystica*).	237
64. Hellenistic Pergamum theater with a capacity of ca. 10,000 citizens.	239
65. The Great Altar of Pergamum, now in the Pergamum museum in Berlin, Germany.	240
66. The remains of the Altar of Zeus.	241
67. The partially restored Trajaneium in Pergamum.	243
68. Replica of the Pompeii gladius sword.	245
69. Reconstruction of Mycenaean replica swords, the left one being a machaira-type sword.	246
70. Column in the courtyard of the entrance (*propylon*) of the Asclepion, Pergamum.	250
71. Statue of Asclepius, exhibited in the Museum of Epidaurus Theater.	251
72. Drawing of the opening section of the Balaam text from Tell Deir 'Alla.	257
73. Artist's depiction of a high priest.	265
74. Ostracon found at Masada bearing the name Eleazar ben Ya'ir, the leader of the Zealots.	267
75. A small white tessera and a replica of an ivory or bone token used as a theater ticket.	268
76. Bone or ivory tessera (*tesserae nummulariae*) seal.	269
77. Roman *tessera frumentaria* (left) compared to a Euro cent coin (right).	270
78. Egyptian scarab beetle with an inscription.	272
79. A white stone pillar at Pergamum with names inscribed on it.	273
80. Bronze bust of Seleucus I Nicator from Herculaneum.	278
81. The ancient ruins of Thyatira among the modern city.	281
82. *Homonoia* coin from Thyatira with Pergamum in Mysia with Asclepius Apollo and Tyrimnaeus.	282
83. Principal Mediterranean molluscan species, (a) trunculus; (b) brandaris; and (c) haemastoma.	289

84. Romand fresco from Fullonica with workers putting up clothes for drying. 291
85. Purple dye shellfish from the western Mediterranean, *hexaplex trunculus*, and *haustellum brandaris*. 292
86. Coin from Thyatira, struck under Marcus Aurelius with Apollo Tyrimnaeus, holding a *bipennis*. 298
87. Coin from Thyatira with the bust of Domitian and the goddess Nike or Victory. 299
88. Coin from Thyatira with the head of Augustus Denarius and a comet with eight rays. 304
89. Coin from Thyatira with the bust of the magistrate and Hephaestus and Athena. 306
90. Coin from Thyatira with the head of Apollo and a *labrys* (double axe) with a bow. 307
91. Votive relief showing a funerary banquet. Lying on a *kliné*, holding a "*kylix*" in his hand. 314
92. Plaster reproduction of the Law Code of Hammurabi. 317
93. Coin from Aphrhodisias with the bust of Hadrian with statue of Venus (Aphrodite) and Cupid. 323
94. An Attic red-figure amphora depicting Croesus prepared to burn on the *pyre*. 327
95. Coin from Sardis with the head of Heracles wearing a lion's skin and *Zeus Aëtophoros*. 330
96. Gold coin from Seleukeia with the head of Antiochus III "the Great" and *Apollo Delphios*. 331
97. Coin from Rome with head of Tiberius and inscription "Cities of Asia restored." 331
98. Coin from Sardis with Tiberius and Tyche, also Livia, the goddess Demeter, with ears of grain. 332
99. Urban plan of the city of Sardis. 334
100. Ruins of the Byzantine era shops at Sardis along the marble avenue. 335
101. The Bath-gymnasium complex at Sardis, late section dates to the early third cent. AD. 336
102. Floor plan of the Bath-Gymnasium Complex at Sardis. 337
103. Marble column from the Temple of Artemis at Sardis. 339
104. The Temple of Artemis in Sardis. 340
105. The *bēma* of the third cent. AD synagogue in Sardis with lion statues and carved eagles. 342
106. The Torah shrine (*aediculae*) used in worship in the synagogue. 343
107. A electrum coin from Sardis minted by King Alyattes with head of a lion. 345
108. Marble statue of Cybele enthroned, with lion, cornucopia and mural crown. 349
109. Coin from Sardis with the head of Hadrian and cult image of Kore wearing a high head-dress. 351
110. Painting titled "The Frigidarium" (1890) by Lawrence Alma-Tadema. 371
111. Coin from Hispania (Spain), with the head of Tiberius and the prefect's name removed. 375
112. Stone relief of Attalus II (second cent. BC). 380
113. Coin from Neocaesarea with the head of Gallienus. A prize urn and three-legged table. 381
114. Coin from Philadelphia with the head of Vespasian and the name *Flavi* and image of Zeus. 382
115. Basilica of St. John in *Alaşehir* (ancient Philadelphia). 383
116. Map of the Greek Orthodox Metropolises in Asia Minor (Anatolia) ca. 1880. 384
117. Coin from Philadelphia with bust of Augusta and a bunch of grapes. 385
118. Urban plan of the city of Philadelphia (modern *Alaşehir*). 386
119. Coin from Philadelphia with the head of Trajan and an eagle standing within a distyle temple. 387
120. The overgrown remains of the theater in Philadelphia. 387
121. Coin from Philadelphia with head of Domitian and statue of goddess *Artemis Ephesia*. 388
122. Coin from Philadelphia with head of Demos, with Aphrodite holding an apple. 391
123. Coin from Philadelphia with portrait of Julia Domna and tetrastyle temple with Aphrodite. 392
124. Coin from Philadelphia with head of Demos with Athena holding a figure of *Artemis Anaitis*. 393
125. *Homonoia* coin from Philadelphia with Ephesus and head of Trajan Decius and Tyche with Dioskuri in the temple. 394

Index of Images

126.	Coin from Philadelphia with head of Zeus Koryphaeos with Aphrodite holding an apple.	394
127.	Coin from Philadelphia with bust of Artemis, with quiver and arrows with Apollo.	395
128.	*Neōkoros* coin from Philadelphia with head of Caracalla with a tetrastyle temple with Helios.	396
129.	Drawing of the locking mechanism found at a palace in Khorsabad (Nineveh).	401
130.	House keys. Cave of the Letters, Nahal Hever (AD 132–135).	402
131.	Black Obelisk depicting the Israelite King Jehu prostrate, before King Shalmaneser III.	409
132.	The Caryatid Porch of the Erechtheion, Athens, 421–407 BC.	418
133.	Greek inscription on a pillar in the Capernaum synagogue.	419
134.	Map of the modern area around Hierapolis, Laodicea, and Colossae.	427
135.	Coin from *Laodicea ad Lycum* with the head of Polemon, the son of Zenon. Tripod *lebes* (cauldron) surmounted by a serpent.	432
136.	Coin from *Laodikeia ad Lycum*, with Dioskourides and Zeus standing holding an eagle.	433
137.	Map of the urban plan for the city of Laodicea.	436
138.	The Frontinus Gate at Hierapolis built during the time of Domitian.	438
139.	The north state agora in Laodicea.	439
140.	Water distribution tower (*castellum aquae*), terminal 1 at Laodicea.	440
141.	Map of the modern area around Laodicea identifying the cold and thermal springs.	441
142.	Closeup of the water distribution tower (*castellum aquae*), terminal 1 at Laodicea.	442
143.	Ground level aqueduct at Laodicea.	443
144.	The nymphaeum (AD 130–150) of Perga, located 113 miles (182 km) southeast of Laodicea.	445
145.	The overgrown Ladoicean stadium.	446
146.	The restored Temple A dedicated to Apollo with 19 columns restored and raised.	447
147.	West theater looking toward the Lycus Valley with the white traverstine cliffs of Hierapolis.	449
148.	The north theater in 1838, when the stage building still indicated three rows of blocks.	450
149.	The south Bath-Gymnasium complex arches at Laodicea.	451
150.	The Central Bath complex looking across the Lycus Valley to Hireopolis.	452
151.	Coin from *Laodikeia ad Lycum* with the head of Augustus and Zeus holding an eagle.	453
152.	Reconstruction of a vertical loom with genuine loom weights and string heddles.	456
153.	The tomb of Flavius Zeuxis at Hierapolis.	460
154.	Votive Stele of Zeus Ktesios Patrios from Laodicea holding a shepherd's staff.	461
155.	The middle wreath on column A with the relief of Laodicea (Fortuna/Tyche).	463
156.	Coin from *Laodikeia ad Lycum* with bust of Demos with *Zeus Laodiceus* holding an eagle.	463
157.	Marble altar to *Zeus Ktesios Patrios*.	464
158.	Coin from *Laodicea ad Lycum* with bust of Domitian with Hera facing *Zeus Laodiceus*, and Athena.	464
159.	The third cent. AD votive stele of Zeus Laodikeus portrayed as a shepherd.	465
160.	Column B from Temple A. Displays relief of Apollo, two griffins, and Fortuna or Tyche.	466
161.	*Neōkoros* coin of *Laodicea ad Lycum* with Ailios Pisoneinos, Asiarch. Tyche is facing an octostyle temple with a statue of Minerva.	467
162.	Coin from *Laodicea ad Lycum* with bust of Caracalla, with three tetrastyle temples, each containing one of the statues of Caracalla, Zeus and Asclepius.	467
163.	*Neōkoros* coin of *Laodicea ad Lycum* with bust of Caracalla him in a chariot driving four of lions.	468
164.	Column from Laodicea with an inscribed menorah, *lulav*, shophar and a cross.	470

165. Hierapolis' (modern Pamukkale, Turkey) travertine terrace pools. 480
166. A bronze cylindical device (authepsa) for heating water to mix with wine. 481
167. Thermopolium in Herculaneum. 482
168. Roman bronze wine-strainer. 482
169. Oil painting of *The Light of the World* by William Holman Hunt (1851–1856). 493
170. Reproduction of a triclinium (dining room, Lat. *lectus triclinaris*) with two couches. 497
171. The marble Lansdowne throne of Apollo. 499
172. Special armchair of honor (*poedria*) at ground level in the theater of Priene. 500
173. Roman cameo of Gemma Augustea with Augustus and Dea Roma seated on a bisellium. 501

Abbreviations

This work will conform to the abbreviations for ancient and modern sources and general format conventions set out by *The SBL Handbook of Style: For Biblical Studies and Related Disciplines*. 2nd ed. Alexander, Patrick, James Eisenbraun, and Billie Jean Collins, eds. (Atlanta, Ga.: SBL Press, 2014). Unless otherwise indicated the references to the works of classical authors reflect the Loeb Classical Library (LCL) numbering system, translations and Latin abbreviations. Following the classical author the Latin title is given with an English translation followed by the LCL number. The source for the other primary sources are indicated at the end of each abbreviation. Unless otherwise indicated, all Scripture quotations are from the ESV® Bible (*The Holy Bible, English Standard Version*®), copyright © 2001 by Crossway Bibles, a publishing ministry of Good News Publishers. Used by permission. All rights reserved. Italics within Scripture quotations indicate emphasis added. The *Septuagint* is based on *Septuaginta* edited by Alfred Rahlfs, Copyright © 1935 by the Württembergische Bibelanstalt / Deutsche Bibelgesellschaft (German Bible Society), Stuttgart. Greek translations are my own unless otherwise indicated and based on the Greek text of the 27th ed. edition of *Nestle-Aland, Novum Testamentum Graece* in cooperation with the Institute for New Testament Textual Research, Münster/Westphalia. ed., Kurt Aland, et al., Stuttgart, Germany: Deutsche Bibelgesellschaft, 1993 unless otherwise indicated. Used by permission. Philological work is based on Michael S. Bushell, Michael D. Tan *BibleWorks*™ Version 8 (1992–2008). Where no book is cited before the reference this will refer to a citation from the book of Revelation and has been removed to simplify the text (example: 3:5; 2:6). Apart from the biblial abbreviations and Dead Sea Scrolls the ancient and modern sources have been combined to make it easier to locate the abbreviation. General abbreviations are used sparingly however, I utilize the following:

OLD TESTAMENT

Gen	Genesis	Prov	Proverbs
Exod	Exodus	Eccl	Ecclesiastes
Lev	Leviticus	Isa	Isaiah
Num	Numbers	Jer	Jeremiah
Deut	Deuteronomy	Lam	Lamentations
Judg	Judges	Ezek	Ezekiel
Josh	Joshua	Dan	Daniel
1–2 Sam	1–2 Samuel	Obad	Obadiah
1–2 Kgs	1–2 Kings	Jonah	Jonah
1–2 Chr	1–2 Chronicles	Mic	Micah
Neh	Nehemiah	Nah	Nahum
Esth	Esther	Hab	Habakkuk
Job	Job	Zeph	Zephaniah
Ps/Pss	Psalms	Mal	Malachi

New Testament

Matt	Matthew	1–2 Tim	1–2 Timothy
Rom	Romans	Phlm	Philemon
1–2 Cor	1–2 Corinthians	Heb	Hebrews
Gal	Galatians	Jas	James
Eph	Ephesians	1–2 Pet	1–2 Peter
Phil	Philippians	1–2–3 John	1–2–3 John
Col	Colossians	Rev	Revelation
1–2 Thess	1–2 Thessalonians		

Dead Sea Scrolls

11Q19	11QT^a, *Temple Scroll^a* from Qumran Cave 11 (Yadin, *Temple Scroll,* 1985)
1Q26	*Instruction* or *Widsom Apocryphon* from Qumran Cave 1, pls. XXX–XXXI (eds. Strugnell et al., *DJD* 34, 1999)
1QH	*Hodayot* or *Thanksgiving Scroll* from Qumran Cave 1 (Sukenik, *DSSHU,* 1955)
1QM	*Milchamah* or *War Scroll* from Qumran Cave 1 (Sukenik, *DSSHU,* 1955)
1QpHab	*Pesher Habakkuk,* from Qumran Cave I, 156-57 (Trevor, *SQC,* 1974)
1QS	*Serek ha-Yahad* or *Rule of the Community, Manual of Discipline* from Qumran Cave 1 (Trever, *SQC,* 1974)
1QSa	1Q28a, *Rule of the Congregation* from Qumran Cave 1. Appendix a to 1QS (Trever, SQC, 1974)
4Q158	4QRPa; *Reworked Pentateuch, BibPar* from Qumran Cave 4 (Allegro, *DJD* 5, 1968)
4Q174	4QFlor (*MidrEschata*); *Florilegium* also *Midrash on Eschatologya,* from Qumran Cave 4 pls. XIX–XX (Allegro, *DJD* 5, 1968)
4Q175	4QTest; *Testimonia* from Qumran Cave 4 (Allegro, *DJD* 5, 1968)
4Q246	*psDand Puech* from Qumran Cave 4: pl. XI. (Brooke et al., *DJD* 22, 1996)
4Q369	*Prayer of Enosh* or *Prayer Concerning God and Israel?* from Qumran Cave 4 (Attridge et al., *DJD* 13, 1995)
4Q375	*Apocryphon of Moses* from Qumran Cave 4: pl. XIV (Strugnell et al., *DJD* 19, 1995)
4Q381	*Non-Canonical Psalms B* from Qumran Cave 4: pls. IX–XV (Schuller et al., *DJD* 11, 1998)
4Q382	*Pap paraKings* from Qumran Cave 4. Olyan, pls. XXXVIII–XLI (Attridge et al., *DJD* 13, 1995)
4Q405	*ShirShabb^f* from Qumran Cave 4. Newsom, pls. XXII–XXX (Schuller et al., *DJD* 11, 1998)
4Q415–418	*Instruction* from Qumran Cave 4. pls. I–XXIX (eds. Strugnell et al., *DJD* 34, 1999)
4Q423	*Instruction_g* (*olim* Sap. Work A^e and E; *olim,* Tree of Knowledge) from Qumran Cave 4. Elgvin, pls. XXX–XXXI (eds. Strugnell et al., *DJD* 34, 1999)
4Q504	*Qumrân Grotte 4.III* (4Q482–4Q520). (ed. Baillet, *DJD* 7, 1982)
4Q521	*4QMessianic Apocalypse* from Qumran Cave 4 (ed. Puech, *DJD* 25, 1998)
4QEnGiants^a	*Book of Giants from Qumran* by Stuckenbruck (ed. Pfann, Qumran Cave 4, *DJD* 36. 2000)
4QpNah	*Pesher Nahum* from Qumran Cave 4 (ed. Allegro, *DJD* 5, 1968)
DJD	*Discoveries in the Judaean Desert*
DSSHU	*The Dead Sea Scrolls of the Hebrew University* (Sukenik, 1955)
SQC	*Scrolls from Qumran Cave I* (Trever, 1974)

ABBREVIATIONS

ANCIENT AND MODERN SOURCES

§	section
1 Apoc. Jas.	First Apocalypse of James, ANT
1 Apol.	Justin Martyr. Apologia I, First Apology. ANF 1
1 Clem.	1 Clement, APF 1
1 En.	1 Enoch (Ethiopic Apocalypse), OTP
1 Esd	1 Esdras, APOT
1 Macc	1st Book of Maccabees, APOT
2 Apoc. Bar.	2 Baruch (Syriac Apocalypse), OTP
2 Apol.	Justin Martyr. Apologia II, Second Apology. ANF 1
2 Apol. Apologia ii Second Apology	
2 Bar.	2 Baruch (Syriac Apocalypse), OTP
2 Clem.	2 Clement, ANF 1
2 En.	2 Enoch (Slavonic Apocalypse), OTP
2 Esd	2 Esdras, APOT
2 Macc	2nd Book of Maccabees, APOT
3 Bar.	3 Baruch (Greek Apocalypse), OTP
3 En.	3 Enoch (Hebrew Apocalypse), OTP
3 Macc.	3 Maccabees, OTP
4 Esd	A Latin Apocalypse of Esdras, OTP
4 Ezra	4 Ezra, OTP
4 Macc.	4 Maccabees, OTP
AA	Archaeologischer Anzeiger
AB	The Anchor Bible
abbr.	abbreviation
ABD	The Anchor Yale Bible Dictionary (6 vols. eds. Freedman et al., 1996)
Abr.	Philo. De Abrahamo, On the Life of Abraham. LCL 289
ABRL	Anchor Bible Reference Library
ABSA	Annual of the British School of Athens
ABul	The Art Bulletin
Ach.	Aristophanes. Acharnians. LCL 178
ACNT	Augsburg Commentary on the New Testament Series
ACT	Ancient Christian Texts
Acts John	Acts of John. ANF 8
Acts Phil.	Acts of Philip. ANT (trans. Bovon and Matthews, 2012)
Acts Thom.	Acts of Thomas. ANT
AD	Anno Domini (Lat.) in the year of our Lord.
ad Aen.	Servius Maurus Honoratus. Ad Aeneidam, In Vergilii Aeneidem commentarii, Commentary on the Aeneid of Vergil (trans. Thilo and Hagen, 2011)
Adv. nat.	Arnobius. Adversus nationes, Against the Pagans. ANF 6
AE	L'Année épigraphique (Merlin, 1909-2010)

Aen.	Virgil. *Aeneid.* LCL 63, 64
AESM	Archaeological Exploration of Sardis Monograph
AESR	Archaeological Exploration of Sardis Reports
AESR	Archaeological Exploration of Sardis Reports
Aeth.	Heliodorus of Emesa. *Aethiopica, An Ethiopian Romance* (trans. Hadas. 1999)
Ag.	Aeschylus. *Agamemnon. Agamemnon.* LCL 146
Ag. Ap.	Josephus. *Contra Apionem, Against Apion.* LCL 186
AGRW	*Associations in the Greco-Roman World* (eds. Ascough, Harland, and Kloppenborg, 2012)
AJ.	Sophocles, Oedipus Tyrannus. *Ajax.* LCL 20
AJA	*American Journal of Archaeology*
AJEC	Ancient Judaism and Early Christianity
AKZ	*Ausgewählte Koptische Zaubertexte* (ed. Kropp, 1930-1931)
Alex.	Plutarch. *Lives: Alexander, Life of Alexander.* LCL 99
Alex.	Lycophron. *Alexandra.* LCL 129
Am.	Ovid. *Amores.* LCL 41
Amic.	Cicero. *De amicitia, On Friendship.* LCL 154
AMStud.	Asia Minor Studien
Anab.	Xenophon. *Anabasis.* LCL 90
Anab.	Arrian. *Anabasis of Alexander.* LCL 236
Anat. Admin.	Galen. *De anatomicis administrationibus, On Anatomical Procedures* (trans. Singer 1956)
AnBib	*Analecta biblica*
ANE	ancient Near East (Eastern)
ANET OT	*The Ancient Near Eastern Texts Relating to the Old Testament* (3rd ed. ed. Pritchard, 1969)
ANEVT	ancient Near Eastern vassal treaty (-ies)
ANF	*The Ante-Nicene Fathers* (eds. Roberts et al., 10 vols, 1994)
Ann.	Tacitus. *Histories and Annales, Annals.* LCL 111, 249, 312, 322
ANRW	*Aufstieg und Niedergang der römischen Welt: Geschichte und Kultur Roms im Spiegel der neueren Forschung* (eds. Haase and Temporini, 1972–1995)
ANT	*The Apocryphal New Testament* (ed. Elliott, 2005)
Ant.	Plutarch. *The Life of Marcus Antonius, Marc Antony, Mark Anthony.* LCL 101
Ant.	Josephus. *Antiquitates judaicae, Jewish Antiquities.* LCL 242, 265, 281, 489, 410, 433, 456, 490
Antichr.	Hippolytus of Rome. *De antichristo, On Christ and the Antichrist.* ANF 5
AÖAW	Anzeiger der Österreichischen Akademie der Wissenschaften
Ap. John	II,1 *Apocryphon of John.* NHC
APAACS	American Philological Association American Classical Studies
APF	*The Apostolic Fathers* (ed. Lightfoot, 2007)
Apoc.	*Apocalypsis*, Revelation
Apoc. Ab.	*Apocalypse of Abraham.* OTP
Apoc. El.	*Apocalypse of Elijah.* OTP
Apoc. Mos.	*Apocalypse of Moses.* OTP
Apoc. Zeph.	*Apocalypse of Zephaniah.* OTP
Apol.	Tertullian. *Apologeticus, Apology.* ANF 3; LCL 250

ABBREVIATIONS

Apol.	Aristides. *Apologia, Apology.* ANF 9
Apol.	Justin Martyr. *Apologia, Apology.* ANF 1
Apos. Con.	*Apostolic Constitutions and Canons*, commonly called the *Clementine Liturgy.* ANF 7
APOT	*The Apocrypha and Pseudepigrapha of the Old Testament.* 2 vols. (ed. Charles, 1913)
App.	Ausonius. *Appendix to Ausonius.* LCL 115
Arch.	Cicero. *Pro Archia.* LCL 158
Arch.	Vitruvius. *De architectura, The Ten Books on Architecture.* LCL 251, 280
Argo.	Flaccus, C. Valerius. *Argonautica.* LCL 286
AS	*Anatolian Studies*
As. Mos.	*Assumption of Moses.* OTP
ASES	American Society for the Excavation of Sardis
Astron.	Manilius. *Astronomica.* LCL 469
Att.	Cicero. *Epistulae ad Atticum, Letters to Atticus.* LCL 7
Aug.	Suetonius Tranquillus, Gaius. *Lives of the Caesars: Augustus.* LCL 31
AUSS	*Andrews University Seminary Studies*
Autol.	Theophilus of Antioch. *Apologia ad Autolycum, Apology to Autolycus.* ANF 2
AvP	*Die Inschriften von Pergamon* (Fränkel, Fabricius, and Schuchhardt 1890)
AYBC	*The Anchor Yale Bible Commentaries* (40 vols. eds. Freedman et al., 1996)
b.	(before *rabb.* txt.) *Babylonian Talmud,* (ed. Rodkinson, 1918)
b. Bar.	Babylonian Talmud tractate *Barakot* (Goldwurm, 1990)
b. Ḥagigah	Babylonian Mishnaic tractate *Ḥagigah*
b. Sanh.	Babylonian Talmud tractate *Sanhedrin* (Goldwurm, 1990)
b. Yoma	Babylonian Talmud tractate *Yoma* (Kippurim, Goldwurm, 1990)
BA	*The Biblical Archaeologist*
BABesch	Bulletin antieke beschaving Supplement
Bacch.	Euripides. *Bacchae, Bacchanals.* LCL 495
Bacch.	Plautus. *Bacchides, The Two Bacchises.* LCL 60
BAFCS	Book of Acts in Its First-Century Setting Series
Bar	Baruch. APOT
BAR	*Biblical Archaeology Review*
BARI	British Archaeological Reports International Series
Barn.	Barnabas. ANF 1
BASOR	*Bulletin of the American Schools of Oriental Research*
BBR	*Bulletin for Biblical Research*
BC	Before Christ
BCH	*Bulletin de correspondance hellénique*
BDAG	Bauer, Danker, Arndt, and Gingrich. *Greek-English Lexicon of the New Testament and Other Early Christian Literature* (3rd ed., 1999)
BDB	Briggs, Driver, and Brown. *A Hebrew and English Lexicon of the Old Testament* (1996)
BDF	Blass, and Debrunner. *A Greek Grammar of the New Testament and Other Early Christian Literature* (trans. Funk 1961)
BECNT	Baker Exegetical Commentary on the New Testament

BEFAR	Bibliothèque des Écoles Françaises d'Athènes et de Rome
Bell. civ.	Appian of Alexandria. *Bella civilia, Civil Wars*. LCL 5
Bell. gall.	Julius Caesar. *Bellum gallicum, Gallic War*. LCL 39
BETL	Bibliotheca ephemeridum theologicarum lovaniensium
BI	*Biblical Illustrator*
BJRL	*Bulletin of the John Rylands University Library of Manchester*
BJS	*Brown Judaic Studies*
BM	British Museum
BMC Ionia	*Catalogue of the Greek Coins of Ionia in the British Museum* (Head, Vol. 16, 1892)
BMC Lydia	*Catalogue of the Greek Coins in the British Museum: Lydia* (Head, Vol. 22, 1902)
BMC Phrygia	*Catalogue of the Greek Coins in the British Museum: Phrygia* (Head, Vol. 25, 1906)
BMC	British Museum Catalogue
BN	*Biblische Notizen*
BNTC	Black's New Testament Commentaries
BR	*Biblical Research*
BrillPauly	*Brill's Encyclopaedia of the Ancient World New Pauly* (28 vols. eds. Landfester, Manfred, and Gentry. Trans. Salazar and Gentry, 2007)
BrillPaulyA	*Brill's New Pauly, Antiquity Volumes Online* (22 vols. eds. Cancik, and Schneider. Trans. Salazar and Gentry, 2006)
BS	*Bible and Spade*
BSac	*Bibliotheca sacra*
BSCS	Bible Study Commentary Series
BST	The Bible Speaks Today
BT	*The Bible Translator*
BTB	*Biblical Theology Bulletin*
Byz.	Byzantine
BZ	*Biblische Zeitschrift*
C. Rom. Hist.	Paterculus, Marcus Velleius. *Historiarum Libri Duo, Compendium of Roman History*. LCL 152
ca.	*circa* (Lat.) "around, about, approximately"
CAD	*The Assyrian Dictionary of the Oriental Institute of the University of Chicago* (eds. Oppenheim and Erica Reiner, 1956–)
Caecin.	Cicero. *Pro Caecina, On behalf of Aulus Caecina*. LCL 198
Caes.	Plutarch. *Lives: Caesar*. LCL 99
CAH	Cambridge Ancient History
Cal.	Suetonius Tranquillus. *Caligula*. LCL 31
Cant.	*Canticum canticorum*, Song of Songs
CB	*The Classical Bulletin*
CBQ	*Catholic Biblical Quarterly*
CBR	*Currents in Biblical Research*
CBSC	The Cambridge Bible for Schools and Colleges
CCS	*Cincinnati Classical Studies*
CE	*The Catholic Encyclopedia* (19 vols., eds. Herbermann, Pace, Pallen, Shahan, and Wynne, 1913)

Cels.	Origen of Alexandria. *Contra Celsum, Against Celsus*. ANF 4	
cent.	century	
cf.	*conferre* (Lat.); conferer (French), compare	
ch. / chs.	chapter and chapters	
Char.	Lucian of Samosata. *Charon or The Inspectors*. LCL 54	
Char.	Theophrastus. *Characters*. LCL 225	
Cher.	Philo. *De cherubim, On the Cherubim*. LCL 227	
ChrEg	*Chronique d'Égypte*	
Chron.	Pamphilus Eusebius. *Chronicon, Chronicle* (ed. Fotheringham, 2012)	
CIG	*Corpus inscriptionum graecarum* (4 vols., eds. Böeckh et al., 1828–1877)	
CIJ	*Corpus inscriptionum judaricarum* (3 vols., ed. Frey, 1936)	
CIL	*Corpus inscriptionum latinarum* (20 vols., ed., Mommsen, 1974)	
Civ.	Augustine of Hippo. *De civitate Dei, The City of God*. NANF[1]	
CJ	*Classical Journal*	
Cl.	Suetonius. *Lives of the Caesars: Divus Claudius, The Deified Claudius*. LCL 38	
ClQ	*Classical Quarterly*	
CNT	Commentary on the New Testament Series	
Cogn.	Galen. *Libellus de cognoscendis curandisque animi morbis, On the affections of the mind* (trans. Coxe, 1846)	
Col.	Aristotle. *de Coloribus, On Colours*. LCL 307	
Comm. Apoc.	Andrew of Caesarea. *Commentary on the Apocalypse* (Constantinou, 2011)	
Comm. Apoc.	Victorinus of Petovium. *Commentary on the Apocalypse* (ed. Weinrich, 2012); *ANF* 7	
Comm. Dan.	Hippolytus of Rome. *Commentarium in Danielem, Commentary on Daniel*. ANF 5	
Comm. Gen.	Origen of Alexandria. *Commentary on Genesis*. ANF 9	
Comm. in Ep. Paul	Jerome. *Commentary on Epistles of Paul*, APNF[2]	
Comm. Isa.	Basil the Great. *Commentary on Isaiah*. NPNF[2] 8	
Comm. Job.	Origen of Alexandria. *Commentary on Job*. ANF 9	
Comm. Matt.	Origen of Alexandria. *Commentary on Matthew*. ANF 9	
Comm. Mich.	Jerome. *Commentariorum in Michaeum libri II, Commentary on Micah*. APNF[2] 6	
Comp. Doct.	Marcellus, Nonius. *De compendiosa doctrina libros* 20 (3 vols. ed. Lindsay, 1903)	
Comp. Med.	Galen. *De Compositione Medicamentorum Secundum Locus, On the Composition of Drugs (Medical Compounds) according to Places* (ed. Kühn, *Claudii Galeni Opera Omnia*, 1964)	
Comp. Phil. Flam.	Plutarch. *Comparatio Philopoemenis et Titi Flaminini, A Comparison of Philopoemen and Titus Flamininus*. LCL 102	
Contempl.	Philo. *De vita contemplativa, On the Contemplative Life*. LCL 363	
Contin.	Augustine, *De continentia, Continence*. NPNF[1] 3	
Cor.	Demosthenes. *De corona, On the Crown*. LCL 155	
Cor.	Plutarch. *Lives: Marcius Coriolanus*. LCL 80	
Cor.	Tertullian. *De corona militis, The Crown*. ANF 3	
COS	*The Context of Scripture* (3 vols., eds. Hallo and Younger, 1997–2002)	
CP	*Classical Philology*	
CPJ	*Corpus papyrorum judaicorum* (3 vols. ed. Tcherikover, 1957–1964)	
CQ	*Church Quarterly*	

CRAI	Comptes rendus de l'Académie des inscriptions et belles-lettres
CRINT	Compendia Rerum Iudaicarum Ad Novum Testamentum
CSCA	California Studies in Classical Antiquity
Ctes.	Aeschines. *In Ctesiphonem, Against Ctesiphon*. LCL 106
CTJ	*Calvin Theological Journal*
CTQ	*Concordia Theological Quarterly*
CTSJ	*Chafer Theological Seminary Journal*
Curc.	Plautus, Titus Maccius. *Curculio*. LCL 61
Cyr.	*Cyranides* or *Kiranides* (Waegeman, 1987)
Cyr.	Xenophon. *Cyropaedia, The Education of Cyrus*. LCL 52
d.	died
DACL	*Dictionnaire d'archéologie chrétienne et de liturgie* (eds. Cabrol and Leclercq. 15 vols. Paris, 1907–1953)
DAW	Denkschriften der Kaiserlichen Akademie der Wissenschaften in Wien, Philosophisch-Historische Klasse
DBib	*A Dictionary of the Bible* (5 vols., eds. Hastings and Selbie, 1911)
DBSup	*Dictionnaire de la Bible: Supplément* (ed. Pirot and Robert, 1928–)
De Herod.	Plutarch. *De Herodoti malignitate, On the Malice of Herodotus*. LCL 426
De nat. anim.	Aelian, Claudius. *De natura animalium, On the Nature of Animals*. LCL 449
De or.	Cicero. *De oratore, On the Orator*. LCL 348
De Urb.	Stephanus of Byzantium. *De Urbanus, Urban* (ed. de Pinedo, 1678)
Deipn.	Athenaeus. *Deipnosophistae, The Learned Banqueters*. LCL 204, 208, 224, 327
Dem. ev.	Eusebius. *Demonstratio evangelica, Demonstration [or proof] of the Gospel* (trans. Ferrar, 2001)
Descr.	Pausanias. *Graeciae description, Description of Greece*. LCL 93, 188, 272, 297
DGRA	*Dictionary of Greek and Roman Antiquities* (2 Vols, ed. Smith, Wayte, and Marindin, 1890–1891)
Dial.	Justin Martyr. *Dialogus cum Tryphone, Dialogue with Trypho the Jew*. ANF 1
Dial. d.	Lucian of Samosata. *Dialogi deorum, Dialogues of the Gods*. LCL 431
Dial. meretr.	Lucian. *Dialogues of the Courtesans*. LCL 431
Diatr.	Arrian. *Epicteti Diatribai, Epictetus Discourses or Dissertations*. LCL 131, 218
Did.	*Didache*. APF
Dig.	Ulpian. *Digest of Justinian* (ed. Watson, 1998)
Diogn.	*Epistle to Diognetus*. ANF
DJD	Discoveries in the Judaean Desert
DJG	*Dictionary of Jesus and the Gospels* (eds. Green, McKnight, and Marshall, 1992)
DNTB	*Dictionary of New Testament Background* (eds. Evans and Porter, 2000)
Dom.	Cicero. *De domo suo, For Himself*. LCL 158
Dom.	Suetonius. *Lives of the Caesars: Domitianus, Domitian*. LCL 38
DSS	Dead Sea Scrolls
DSSHU	*The Dead Sea Scrolls of the Hebrew University* (Sukenik, 1955)
e.g.	*exempli gratia* (Lat.) for example.
EA	*Epigraphica Anatolica*
EBC	The Expositor's Bible Commentary
ECAM	Early Christianity in Asia Minor

Eccl.	Aristophanes. *Ecclesiazusae, Women of the Assembly.* LCL 180
Ecl.	Clement of Alexandria. *Eclogae propheticae, Extracts from the Prophets.* ANF 8
ECM	Electronic Christian Media
ECR	*Eastern Churches Review*
ed(s).	editor(s), edited by
ed.	edition
EDB	*Eerdmans Dictionary of the Bible* (eds. Freedman, Myers, and Beck, 2000)
EDEJ	*The Eerdmans Dictionary of Early Judaism* (eds. Collins and Harlow, 2010)
Edict. Diocl.	*Edict of Diocletian* (Graser, 1975).
EDNT	*Exegetical Dictionary of the New Testament* (3 vols., eds. Balz, and Schneider, 1990-1993)
EDRL	*Encyclopedic Dictionary of Roman Law* (ed. Berger, 1953)
EDT	*Evangelical Dictionary of Theology* (ed. Elwell, 2001)
EGGNT	*The Exegetical Guide to the Greek New Testament*
EGT	The Expositor's Greek Testament
Eleg.	Propertius, Sextus. *Elegies.* LCL 18
Ep Jer	Epistle of Jeremiah. *APOT*
Ep.	Augustine, *Epistulae, Letters of St. Augustin.* NPNF[1]
Ep.	Bacchylides. *Epinicians, Victory Odes.* LCL 461
Ep.	Cyprian of Carthage. *Epistulae, Letters.* ANF 5
Ep.	Hieronymus (Jerome). *Epistulae, Letters.* NPNF[2] 6
Ep.	Horace. *Epodes.* LCL 33
Ep.	Pliny the Younger. *Epistulae, Letters.* LCL 55, 59
Ep.	Sidonius Apollinaris. *Epistulae, Letters.* LCL 420
Ep. Arist.	*The Letter of Aristeas, OTP*
Ep. Mor.	Seneca the Younger. *Ad Lucilium Epistulae Morales, Moral Letters to Lucilius.* LCL 75, 76, 77
Eph. Tale	Xenophon of Ephesus. *The Ephesian Tale of Anthia and Habrocomes.* LCL 69
Epig.	Martial, Marcus Valerius. *Epigrammata, Epigrams,* LCL 94, 95, 480
Epit.	Justinus, Marcus Junianus. *Epitome of the Philippic, History of Pompeius Trogus* (ed. Clauss, 1994)
ÉPRO	Études préliminaires aux religions orientales dans l'empire romain
EQ	*The Evangelical Quarterly*
Eq.	Aristophanes. *Equites, The Knights.* LCL 178
ESV	English Standard Version
et al.	*et alii* (Lat.), and others
etc.	*et cetera,* and the rest
Eth. eud.	Aristotle. *Ethica eudemia, Eudemian Ethics.* LCL 285
Eth. nic.	Aristotle. *Ethica nichomachea Nichomachean Ethics.* LCL 73
ETL	*Ephemerides theologicae lovanienses*
ETS	Evangelical Theological Society
Eum.	Aeschylus. *Eumenides.* LCL 146
EvQ	*The Evangelical Quarterly*
ExpTim	*The Expository Times*

f.	following (verse or page)
Fab.	Hyginus, Gaius Julius. *Fabulae in The Myths of Hyginus* (ed. Grant, 1960)
Facs.	Facsimile
Fals. leg.	Aeschines, *De falsa legatione, False Embassy (Speeches)*. LCL 106
Fam.	Cicero. *Epistulae ad familiars, Letters to Friends*. LCL 205, 216
Fas.	Ovid. *Fasti*. LCL 253
Fem.	Feminine
ff.	following (verses or pages).
FiE	*Forschungen in Ephesos*
Flac.	Cicero. *Pro Flacco, Valerius Flaccus, In Defense of Lucius*. LCL 324
Fort.	Cyprian of Carthage. *Exhortation to Martyrdom: Addressed to Fortunatus*. ANF 5
Fr. Ps.	Origen. *Fragmenta in Psalmos 1–150, Fragments of the Book of Psalms*, ANF 4
Fr.	French
Frag.	Eumelus. *Fragments*. (West) LCL 497
Frag.	Hipponax of Ephesus. *Fragments*. LCL 259
Frag.	Sappho. *Fragments*. LCL 142
Frag.	Sophocles. Oedipus Tyrannus. *Fragments of Known Plays*. LCL 483
FrgPol.	*Fragments on Polycarp* (Weidmann, 2010)
FRLANT	Forschungen zur Religion und Literatur des Alten und Neuen Testaments
ft.	feet
Fug.	Philo. *De fuga et inventione, On Flight and Finding*. LCL 275
Galb.	Suetonius. *The Lives of The Twelve Caesars: Galba*. LCL 38
Galen.	Galen on the Passions and Errors of the Soul.
GDBS	Gorgias Dissertations Biblical Studies
GELNT	*Greek-English Lexicon of the New Testament* (eds. Gesenius, Tregelles, and Thayer, 1987)
Gen. Rab.	*Rabbah on Genesis* (ed. Freedman, 1992)
Geogr.	Strabo. *Geographica, Geography*. LCL 49, 50, 182, 196, 211, 223, 241
Ger.	German
GIBM	*Collection of Greek Inscriptions in the British Museum* (5 vols. ed. Newton 1874–1916)
Gk. Apoc. Ezra	*Greek Apocalypse of Ezra*. OTP
GNB	Good News Bible
Gos. Mary	BG, 1 *Gospel of Mary*, NHC
Gos. Thom.	II,2 *Gospel of Thomas* NHC
Gr.	Greek
GTCEC	The Greek Testament: A Critical and Exegetical Commentary
GTJ	*Grace Theological Journal*
HA Carin.	*The Historia Augusta: Carinus* (trans. Magie) LCL 263
HA Comm.	*The Historia Augusta: Commodus* (trans. Magie) LCL 139
HA Elag.	*The Historia Augusta: Elagabalus* (trans. Magie) LCL 140
ha.	hectare
Haer.	Augustine. *De haeresibus, Heresies*. NANF[1]

Haer.	Hippolytus of Rome. *Refutatio omnium haeresium (Philosophoumena), Refutation of All Heresies.* ANF 5
Haer.	Irenaeus. *Adversus haereses, Against Heresies.* ANF 1
HALOT	*The Hebrew and Aramaic Lexicon of the Old Testament* (4 vols., eds. Koehler, Baumgartner, and Stamm, 1994–1999)
Hamm.	*The Code of Hammurabi* (trans. Harper, 1904)
HDB	*Dictionary of the Bible* (4 vols., eds. Hastings et al., 1899–1911)
HDR	Harvard Dissertations in Religion
Hell.	Xenophon. *Hellenica, Hellenic Writings.* LCL 88
Her.	Ovid. *Heroides.* LCL 41
Her.	Philo. *Quis rerum divinarum heres sit, Who Is the Heir?* LCL 261
Hist.	Herodotus. *Historiae, The Histories of the Persian Wars.* LCL 117–119
Hist.	Polybius. *Historiae, The Histories or The Rise of the Roman Empire.* LCL 128, 138, 159–161
Hist.	Thucydides. *Histories, History of the Peloponnesian War.* LCL 109
Hist. An.	Aristotle. *Historia Animalium History of Animals; Natural History of Animals.* LCL 438
Hist. eccl.	Eusebius, Pamphilus. *Historia ecclesiastica, Ecclesiastical History.* NPNF² 1
Hist. Her.	Memnon. *History of Heracleia* (trans. Jacoby)
Hist. Lib.	Diodorus Siculus. *Bibliotheca historica, Library of History.* LCL 375, 389, 409, 422, 423
Hist. Rom.	Dio Cassius. *Historia Romana, Roman History.* LCL 66, 83, 175–177
Hist. Rome	Livy or Titus Livius Patavinus. *Ab Urbe Condita, History of Rome.* LCL 172, 295, 301, 313, 332
Hist.	Marcellinus. *History.* LCL 300
HKNT	Handkommentar zum Neuen Testament
HNT	Handbuch zum neuen Testament
HNTC	Harper's New Testament Commentaries
Hom. Luc.	Origen. *Homiliae in Lucam, Homilies on Luke* (Trans. Lienhard, 1996)
Hom. Num.	Origen. *Homiliae in Numeros, Homilies on Numbers* (trans. Scheck, 2009)
Hom. Od.	Eustathius, Archbishop of Thessalinica. *Commentarii Ad Homeri Iliadem et Odysseam, Commentaries On Homer's Iliad and Odyssey* (4 vols. ed. Stallbaum, 1970)
HSCP	*Harvard Studies in Classical Philology*
HTR	*Harvard Theological Review*
HTS	*Harvard Theological Studies*
HUCA	*Hebrew Union College Annual*
Hymn. Apoll.	Callimachus. *Hymnus in Apollinem, Hymn to Apollo.* LCL 129
Hymn. Dian.	Callimachus. *Hymnus in Dianam, Hymn to Diana or Artemis.* LCL 129
i.e.	*id est* (Lat). that is
I.Eph.	*Die Inschriften von Ephesos, Inscriptions of Ephesus* (8 vols. ed. Wankel et al., 1979–1984)
I.Ias.	*Die Inschriften von Iasos* (2 vols. ed. Blümel, 1985)
I.Laod.	*Die Inschriften von Laodikeia am Lykos* (ed. Corsten, 1997)
I.Perg.	*Die Inschriften von Pergamon* (2 Vols. Fränkel, Fabricius, and Schuchhardt. 1890–1895)
I.Phil.	*Tituli Lydiae Linguis Graeca et Latina Conscripti: Fasciculus III, Philadelpheia et Ager Philadelphenus.* TAM V,3. (ed. Petzl, 2007)
I.Philipp.	*Philippi. Band II. Katalog der Inschriften von Philippi* (2 vols. Pilhofer, 2009)
I.Sard.	*Sardis: Greek and Latin Inscriptions* (eds. Buckler and Robinson, 1932).

I.Smyr.	*Die Inschriften von Smyrna* (2 vols. ed. Petzl, 1987–1990)
I.Thyat.	*Inscriptions from Thyatira*, in *Tituli Lydiae Linguis.* TAM V, 2. (ed. Hermann 1989)
Icar.	Lucian of Samosata. *Icaromenippus, The Sky-man.* LCL 54
ICC	International Critical Commentary Series
IDB	*The Interpreter's Dictionary of the Bible* (4 vols., ed. Buttrick, 1984)
IEJ	*Israel Exploration Journal*
IG II	*Inscriptiones graecae II: Inscriptiones Atticae: Editio minor* (8 vols. eds. Kirchner, Gaertingen, and Hiller, 1923)
IG IX,1	*Inscriptiones graecae IX.1: Inscriptiones Phocidis, Locridis, Aetoliae, Acarnaniae, insularum maris Ionii* (Vol. 1. ed. Dittenberger, 1897)
IG V,1	*Inscriptiones graecae V.1: Inscriptiones Laconiae et Messeniae* (Vol. 1. ed. Kolbe, 1967)
IG X 2.1	*Inscriptiones graecae X: Inscriptiones Epiri, Macedoniae, Thraciae, Scythiae. Pars II, fasc. 1: Inscriptiones Thessalonicae et viciniae* (2 vols. ed. Edson, 1972)
IG XII 2	*Inscriptiones graecae XII: Inscriptiones Insularum Maris Aegaei Praeter Delum: 2. Inscriptiones Lesbi, Nesi, Tenedi* (ed. Paton, 1899)
IG XIV	*Inscriptiones graecae XIV: Inscriptiones Siciliae et Italiae, additis Galliae, Hispaniae, Britanniae, Germaniae inscriptionibus* (ed. Kaibel, 1890)
IGLAM	*Voyage archéologique en Grèce et en Asie Mineure, Tome III: Inscriptions grecques et latines recueillies en Asie Mineure* (Le Bas, Waddington, Landron, and Foucart, 1870)
Ign. *Eph.*	Ignatius. *To the Ephesians.* ANF
Ign. *Magn.*	Ignatius. *To the Magnesians.* ANF
Ign. *Phld.*	Ignatius. *To the Philadelphians.* ANF
Ign. *Pol.*	Ignatius. *To Polycarp.* ANF
Ign. *Smyrn.*	Ignatius. *To the Smyrnaeans.* ANF
IGR	*Inscriptiones graecae ad res romanas pertinentes* (4 vols., eds. Lafaye, Toutain, Henry, and Cagnat, 1911–1927) Vol 1: (nos. 1–1518; ed. Cagnat, Toutain, and Jouguet, 1911); Vol 2: never published; Vol 3: ed. Cagnat and Lafaye,1906); Vol. 4: Asia (nos. 1–1764; ed. Lafaye, 1927)
IGSK	Inschriften griechischer Städte aus Kleinasien
IJC	*Israel Journal of Chemistry*
IJO	*Inscriptiones Judaicae Orientis* (3 vols. eds. Noy and Bloedhorn, 2004)
Il.	Homer. *Iliad.* LCL 170, 171
ILS	*Inscriptiones latinae selectae* (3 vols. in 5 parts. Dessau, 1892–1916).
ILydiaHoz	*Die lydischen Kulte im Lichte der griechischen inschriften.* AMStud. 36. (ed. Hoz, 1999)
ILydiaKP	*Bericht über eine Reise in Lydien und der südlichen Aiolis* (eds. Keil, and Premerstein, Vol 1. 1908; Vol 2. *Bericht über eine zweite Reise in Lydien,* 1911)
Imhoof *KM*	*Kleinasiatische Münzen* (2 vols. Imhoof-Blumer, 1901)
Inst.	Lactantius. *Divinarum institutionum libri VII, The Divine Institutes.* ANF 7
Int	*Interpretation*
Introd.	Pseudo-Galen. *Oeuvres, III. Le Médecin. Introduction.* (ed. Petit, 2009)
Ion	Euripides. *Ion, Romantic Drama.* LCL 10
Iph. taur.	Euripides. *Iphigenia taurica, Iphigeneia at Tauris.* LCL 495
ISBE	*The International Standard Bible Encyclopedia* (4 vols. Fully Revised ed. Bromiley, 1995)
It.	Italian

IVP	Inter-Varsity Press
IVPBD	The IVP Bible Dictionary Series
J.W.	Josephus. *Bellum judaicum, Jewish War.* LCL 203, 210, 487
JAC	*Jahrbuch für Antike und Christentum*
JANES	*Journal of the Ancient Near Eastern Society of Columbia University*
JATS	*Journal of the Adventist Theological Society*
JBL	*Journal of Biblical Literature*
JBR	*Journal of Bible and Religion*
JDAI	Jahrbuch des kaiserlich-deutschen archäologischen Instituts
Jdt	Judith. *APOT*
JETS	*Journal of the Evangelical Theological Society*
JHS	*Journal of Hellenic Studies*
JJS	*Journal of Jewish Studies*
JNES	*Journal of Near Eastern Studies*
JÖAI	*Jahreshefte des Österreichischen archäologischen Instituts*
Jos. As.	Joseph and Asenath, OTP
JPS	The Jewish Publication Society Torah Commentary Series
JR	*Journal of Religion*
JRA	*Journal of Roman Archaeology*
JRASC	*Journal of the Royal Astronomical Society of Canada*
JRGS	*Journal of the Royal Geographical Society of London*
JRH	*Journal of Religious History*
JRS	*Journal of Roman Studies*
JRSM	*Journal of Roman Studies Monographs*
JSJ	*Journal for the Study of Judaism in the Persian, Hellenistic, and Roman Periods*
JSJSup	Supplements to the Journal for the Study of Judaism
JSNT	*Journal for the Study of the New Testament*
JSNTSup	Journal for the Study of the New Testament: Supplement Series
JSOT	*Journal for the Study of the Old Testament*
JSOTSup	Journal for the Study of the Old Testament: Supplement Series
JSP	*Journal for the Study of the Pseudepigrapha*
JSQ	*Jewish Studies Quarterly*
JTS	*Journal of Theological Studies*
JTVI	*Journal of the Transactions of the Victoria Institute, or Philosophical Society of Great Britain*
Jub.	Jubilees. *APOT*
Jul.	Suetonius. *Divus Julius, The Lives of the Caesars: The Deified Julius Caesar.* LCL 31
KAI	*Kanaanäische und aramäische Inschriften* (Donner and Röllig. 5th ed., 1966–2002)
KJV	King James Version
KST	*Kazi Sonuçlari Toplantisi*
KZNT	Kommentar Zum Neuen Testament
L&N	*Greek-English Lexicon of the New Testament: Based on Semantic Domains* (2nd ed., eds. Louw and Nida, 1989)

L.A.B.	Pseudo-Philo. *Liber Antiquitatum Biblicarum, Book of Biblical Antiquities.* OTP
Lacae.	Plutarch. *Moralia: Lacaenarum Apophthegmata, Sayings of Spartan Women.* LCL 245
Lanz	*Numismatik Lanz München, Auction Catlogues* (Lanz, 2010)
Laps.	Cyprian of Carthage. *De lapsis, Concerning the Lapsed.* ANF 5
Lat.	Latin
LBW	*Inscriptions Grecques et Latines Recueillies En Asie Mineure* (Le Bas, and Waddington, 1972)
Leg.	Cicero. *De legibus, On the Laws.* LCL 213
Leg.	Philo. *Legum allegoriae I, II, III, Allegorical Interpretation 1, 2, 3.* LCL 226
Leg.	Plato. *Leges, Laws.* LCL 192
Legat.	Philo. *Legatio ad Gaium, On the Embassy to Gaius.* LCL 379
Let.	Apollonius of Tyana. *Letters.* LCL 458
Leuc. Clit.	Tatius, Achilles, *Leucippe et Clitophon, The Adventures of Leucippe and Cleitophon.* LCL 45
Lex.	Lucian of Samosata. *Lexiphanes.* LCL 302
LHSOT	The Library of Hebrew Bible/Old Testament Studies
Lib.	Apollodorus. *The Library.* LCL 121
Lib. Mem.	Ampelius, Lucius. *Liber Memorialis, Memorial Book* (trans. Assmann, 1935)
Life	Josephus. *Vita, The Life.* LCL 186
LIMC	*Lexicon iconographicum mythologiae classicae* (8 vols. eds. Ackerman and Gisler, 1981–1997)
Ling.	Varro, Marcus Terentius. *De lingua latina, On the Latin Language.* LCL 233
lit.	literal, or literally.
LNTS	The Library of New Testament Studies
LSJ	Liddell, Henry G., Robert Scott, H. S. Jones, *A Greek-English Lexicon* (10th ed., 1940)
LTQ	*Lexington Theological Quarterly*
Lucil.	Seneca, Lucius Annaeus, the Younger. *Epistulae morales ad Lucilium, Moral Epistles to Lucilius.* LCL 77
LXX	The Septuagint Version of the Bible (the Greek OT)
m	meter
m.	*The Mishnah* (ed. Lipman)
m. Pir. 'Abot	Mishnah tractate *Pirqe 'Abot, Sayings of the Jewish Fathers* (ed. Lipman)
m. Sanh.	Mishnah tractate *Sanhedrin* (ed. Lipman)
Macc.	*Macchabaei,* Maccabees
MAMA 4	*Monumenta Asiae Minoris Antiqua: Monuments and Documents from Eastern Asia and Western Galatia* (vol. 4. eds. Buckler, Calder, and Guthrie, 1933)
MAMA 6	*Monumenta Asiae Minoris Antiqua: Monuments and Documents from Phrygia and Caria* (vol. 6. eds. Buckler, Calder, and Guthrie, 1939)
Mand.	Shepherd of Hermas. *Mandate.* ANF
Marc.	Tertullian. *Adversus Marcionem, Against Marcion,* ANF 3
Mart. Asc. Isa.	*Martyrdom and Ascension of Isaiah.* OTP
Mart. Carp.	*Martyrdom of Carpus* (Musurillo, 1972)
Mart. Perp.	*Martyrdom of Perpetua* (Musurillo, 1972)
Mart. Pionii	*Martyrdom of Pionius* (Musurillo, 1972)
Mart. Pol.	*Martyrdom of Polycarp.* APF (Musurillo, 1972)
MBAH	*Marburger Beiträge zu antiken Handels-, Sozial- und Wirtschaftsgeschichte*

MDAI	*Mitteilungen des Deutschen archäologischen Instituts*
Med.	Celsus, Aulus Cornelius. *De medico, On Medicine.* LCL 292
Med.	Seneca, Lucius Annaeus. *Medea.* LCL 62
Medi.	Aëtius Amidenus. *Aetii medici graeci contractae ex veteribus medicinae sermones 16* (1553)
Mem.	Xenophon of Ephesus. *Memorabilia.* LCL 168
Menaÿ.	*Menaÿot,* Talmudic tractate of *Menahot*
Mens.	Ioannes Lydus. *De mensibus, On the Months* (Bandy, 2013)
Merc. cond.	Lucian of Samosata. *De mercede conductis, Salaried Posts in Great Houses.* LCL 130
Metam.	Apuleius. *Metamorphoses, The Golden Ass.* LCL 44, 453
Metam.	Ovid. *Metamorphoses.* LCL 42, 43
Meth. Med.	Galen of Pergamum. *De Methodo Medendi, On the Method of Medicine.* LCL 516–18
Midr. Rab.	Rabbinic writing, *Midrash Rabbah* (10 vols. eds. Freedman and *Simon,* 1992)
Mionnet Supp.	*Description de médailles antiques, grecques et romaines: Supplément.* (16 vols. Mionnet, 1807
Mionnet	*Description de médailles antiques, grecques et romaines, avec leur degré de rareté et leur estimation* (15 vols. ed. Mionnet, 1807–1837)
Mir.	Aristotle. *de Mirabilibus Auscultationibus, On Marvellous Things Heard.* LCL 307
Mith.	Appian of Alexandria. *Mithridatic Wars, The Foreign Wars* (trans. White)
MM	Moulton, J. H., and G. Milligan. *The Vocabulary of the Greek Testament* (1930. Reprint, 1997)
MNTC	The Moffatt New Testament Commentary
Mor.	Plutarch. *Moralia, Moral Essays.* LCL 245, 305, 306, 424
Mos.	Philo. *De vita Mosis I, II, On the Life of Moses 1, 2.* LCL 289
MS	Manuscript
MSJ	*The Master's Seminary Journal*
MSS	Manuscripts
MT	Masoretic Text
n.p.	no page; proper name; no place; no publisher
NAB	New American Bible
NANF[1]	*Nicene and Post-Nicene Fathers, Series 1* (eds. Roberts, Donaldson, Schaff, and Wace. 14 vols., 1994)
NASB	New American Standard Bible
Nat. d.	Cicero. *De natura deorum, On the Nature of the Gods.* LCL 268
Nat. quaest.	Seneca, Lucius Annaeus. *Naturales Quaestiones, Natural Questions.* LCL 450
Nat.	Pliny the Elder. *Naturalis historia, Natural History.* LCL 330, 352, 353, 370, 392–394, 418, 419
NBC	*New Bible Commentary: 21st Century Edition* (eds. Carson, France, and Motyer, 1994).
NBD	*New Bible Dictionary* (eds. Marshall et al., 3rd ed. 1996)
NCB	New Century Bible Commentary
NDSB	The New Daily Study Bible
NDT	*New Dictionary of Theology* (eds. Wright, Ferguson, and Packer, 1988)
NEASB	*Near Eastern Archaeology Society Bulletin*
NedTT	*Nederlands theologisch tijdschrift*
Neot	*Neotestamentica*
Nero	Suetonius. *Lives of the Caesars, Nero.* LCL 38
NES	Near Eastern Studies

NewDocs	*New Documents Illustrating Early Christianity* (10 vols. eds. Horsley, and Llewelyn, 1981–2012)
NHC	*Nag Hammadi Codices* (eds. Meyer, and Robinson, 2009)
NIBC	New International Biblical Commentary
NICNT	New International Commentary on the New Testament
NICOT	New International Commentary on the Old Testament
NIDNTT	*New International Dictionary of New Testament Theology* (ed. Brown, 4 vol. 1975–1986)
NIGTC	New International Greek Testament Commentary
NIV	New International Version
NIVAC	New International Version Application Commentary
no(s).	number (s)
Nov.	Theodosius II. *Novellae, Novel* (Pharr, 2001)
NovT	*Novum Testamentum*
NovTSup	Novum Testamentum Supplements
NPNF¹	*Nicene and Post-Nicene Fathers*, Series 1 (eds. Roberts et al. 14 vols. 1994)
NPNF²	*Nicene and Post-Nicene Fathers*, Series 2 (eds. Roberts et al., 14 vols. 1994)
NRSV	New Revised Standard Version
NT	New Testament
NTC	New Testament Commentary
NTCC	The New Testament in Context Commentaries
NTG	New Testament Guides
NTOA	Novum Testamentum et Orbis Antiquus
NTS	*New Testament Studies*
ÖAI	Österreichischen Archäologischen Instituts, Austrian Archaeological Institute
ÖAW	Österreichischen Akademie der Wissenschaften
Obv.	Obverse (see Glossary)
OCD	*The Oxford Classical Dictionary* (eds. Hornblower and Spawforth, 2003)
OCM	*Oxford Classical Monographs*
Oct.	Marcus Minucius Felix. *Octavius*. LCL 250
Od.	Homer, *The Odyssey*. LCL 104, 105
Odes	Horace. *Carmina, Odes*. LCL 33
Odes Sol.	*Odes of Solomon*, OTP
OEAGR	*The Oxford Encyclopedia of Ancient Greece and Rome* (7 vols. ed. Gagarin, 2010)
OEANE	*The Oxford Encyclopedia of Archaeology in the Near East* (5 vols. ed. Meyers, 1997)
OGIS	*Orientis graeci inscriptiones selectee, Supplementum Sylloges Inscriptionum Graecarum* (4 vols. eds. Dittenberger et al. 1915)
Ol.	Pindar. *Olympionikai, Olympian Odes*. LCL 56
Oneir.	Artemidorus. *Oneirocritica, The Interpretation of Dreams* (ed. White, 1975)
Onom.	Pollux, Julius. *Onomasticon* (ed. Dindorf, 1824)
op. cit.	Lat. *opere citato*, in the work cited
OPBIAA	Occasional Publications of the British Institute of Archaeology at Ankara
Opif.	Philo. *De opificio mundi, On the Creation of the World*. LCL 226
Or. Bas.	Gregory of Nazianzus or Nazianzen. *Orationes, Oratio in Iaudem Basilii, Orations*, NPNF² 7

or. Graec.	Tatian. *Oratio ad Graecos, Address to the Greeks.* ANF 2
Or.	Dio Chrysostom. *Orations, Discourses.* LCL 257, 339, 358, 376, 385
Orat.	Aelius Aristides. *Orations* (2 Vols. trans. Behr 1981, 1986). LCL 533
OSRE	Oxford Studies on the Roman Economy
OT	Old Testament
ÖTKNT	Ökumenischer Taschenbuch-kommentar zum Neuen Testament
OTP	*Old Testament Pseudepigrapha* (ed. Charlesworth. 2 vols. 1983)
𝔭	papyrus
Passim	here and there
P.Oxy.	*The Oxyrhynchus Papyri* (75 vols. trans. Grenfell and Hunt, 2009)
P.Ryl.	*Ryland Papyri.* LCL 282 (trans. Hunt, 1934)
Paed.	Clement of Alexandria. *Paedagogus, Christ the Educator or Tutor.* ANF 2
Pan.	Epiphanius of Salamis. *Panarion (Adversus haereses), Refutation of All Heresies* (trans. Williams, 1993)
Pat.	Cyprian of Carthage. *De bono patientiae, The Advantage of Patience.* ANF 5
Pax	Aristophanes. *Pax, Peace.* LCL 488
PD	Public Domain
PDM	Papyri demoticae magicae. Demotic texts in PGM corpus as collated in *The Greek Magical Papyri in Translation, including the Demotic Spells* (ed. Betz, 1996)
PECS	*Princeton Encyclopaedia of Classical Sites* (eds. Stillwell, MacDonald, and McAllister, 1976)
PEQ	*Palestine Exploration Quarterly*
Per.	Ctesias. *Persica* (trans. Stronk, 2010)
Per.	Livy. *The Periochae* (ed. Jal, 1984)
Peric.	Plutarch. *Lives: Pericles and Fabius Maximus.* LCL 65
Pers.	Persian
Pers.	Aeschylus. *The Persians.* LCL 145
Pesiq. Rab.	*Pesiqta Rabbati* (ed. Ulmer 2002)
PGM	*Papyri graecae magicae, Great Magical Papyri* (ed. Betz, 1996)
Phar.	Lucan. *Pharsalia or The Civil War.* LCL 220
PHI	Packard Humanities Institute numbers for Greek inscriptions. Cornell University and Ohio State University. http://epigraphy.packhum.org/inscriptions
Phil.	Cicero. *Orationes philippicae, The Philippic Speeches: Consisting of 14 tirades against Mark Anthony (Antonian Orations).* LCL 189, 507; (Yonge, 1913)
Phil.	Sophocles. *Oedipus Tyrannus, Philoctetes.* LCL 21
Philop.	Lucian. *Philopseudes, Lover of Lies or Cheater.* LCL 130
Phoen.	Lactantius. *de Ave Phoenice, The Phoenix* (ed. Fitzpatrick, 1933)
Pirqe R. El.	*Pirqe Rabbi Eliezer* (trans. Friedlander, 1916)
Pist. Soph.	*Pistis Sophia.* (trans. Mead, 2006)
pl.	plural
Plant.	Philo. *De plantatione Noe, Concerning Noah's Work as a Planter.* LCL 247
pls.	plates
Pneum.	Heron of Alexandria. *Pneumatica* (Schmidt 1976)
PNTC	Pillar New Testament Commentary Series

Pol.	Aristotle. *Politics.* LCL 264
Pol.	Xenophanes of Colophon. *Pollux.* (see Tyrtaeus) LCL 258
Pol. *Phil.*	Polycarp. *To the Philippians.* ANF
Praec. ger. publ.	Plutarch. *Praecepta gerendae rei publicae, Precepts of Statecraft.* LCL 321
Praep. Ev.	Eusebius. *Praeparatio evangelica, Preparation for the Gospel* (ed. Gifford 1981)
Praescr.	Tertullian. *De praescriptione haereticorum, Prescription against Heretics.* ANF 3
Prob.	Philo. *Quod omnis probus liber sit, Good Person That Every Good Person is Free.* LCL 363
Prop.	Galen. *De Propriorum Animi Cuiuslibet Affectuum Dignotione et Curatione (Aff. Dig.) V:40-1, The Passions and Errors of the Soul* (trans. Riese, 1963).
Pseud. Clem. Rec.	Pseudo-Clementine *Recognitions.* ANF 8
Pss. Sol.	*Psalms of Solomon,* OTP
PTMS	Princeton Theological Monograph Studies
Pud.	Tertullian. *De pudicitia, Modesty.* ANF 4
PW	*Pauly's Realencyclopädie der classischen Altertumswissenschaft* (New edition. 49 vols. eds. Georg Wissowa, et al. 1980)
QE	Philo. *Quaestiones et solutiones in Exodum I, II, Questions and Answers on Exodus 1, 2.* LCL 401
Quaest. conv.	Plutarch. *Quaestionum convivialium libri IX, Moralia, Table-Talk.* LCL 425
Quaest. rom.	Plutarch. *Quaestiones romanae et graecae (Aetia romana et graeca), Roman and Greek Questions.* LCL 305
r.	ruled
Rab.	*Rabbah,* rabbinic writing usually on one of the books of the Pentateuch (i.e., Genesis Rabbah)
RAC	*Reallexikon für Antike und Christentum* (10 vols. ed. Klauser et al. 1950–78)
RB	*Revue biblique*
RBL	*Reveiw of Biblical Literature*
RBPH	*Revue belge de philologie et d'histoire*
RCT	*Revista catalana de teología*
RE Supp	Realencyklopädie für protestantische Theologie und Kirche Supplement
Re. Nat.	Lucretius. *De Rerum Natura, On the Nature of Things.* LCL 181
REA	*Revue Des études Anciennes*
Recog.	Pseudo-Clementines. *Recognitions.* ANF 8
Res.	Tertullian. *De Resurrectione Carnis, The Resurrection of the Flesh.* ANF
Resp.	Plato. *Respublica, Republic.* LCL 237
Rev.	Reverse (see Glossary)
RevExp	*Review and Expositor*
RHR	*Revue de l'histoire des religions*
RIC	*Roman Imperial Coinage* (13 Vols. ed. Mattingly et al. 1923)
RivB	*Rivista biblica italiana*
RNT	Regensburger Neues Testament
Rom. Hist.	Eutropius. *Abridgment of Roman History* (trans. Watson, 1886)
Rom. Hist.	Herodian. *History of the Roman Empire.* LCL 455
Rosc. Amer.	Cicero. *Pro Sexto Roscio Amerino, For Sextus Roscius of Ameria.* LCL 240
RPC	*Roman Provincial Coinage* (9 Vol. ed. Burnett, 2003)
RSA	*Religion in South Africa*

RSC	*Rivista di studi classici*
RSR	*Recherches de science religieuse*
RSV	Revised Standard Version
Rud.	Plautus. *Rudens, The Rope.* LCL 260
Rufin.	Claudian. *In Rufinum, Against Rufinus 1 and 2.* LCL 135
Rust.	Varro, Marcus Terentius. *Res Rustica or Rerum Rusticarum, Concerning Agriculture.* LCL 283
Sacr.	Philo. *De sacrificiis Abelis et Caini, On the Sacrifices of Cain and Abel.* LCL 227
San. Tu.	Galen. *De Sanitate Tuenda, On the Preservation of Health* (trans. Green, 1951)
Sanh.	Sanhedrin
Sat.	Horace. *Satirae, Satires.* LCL 194
Sat.	Juvenal. *Satire.* LCL 91
Sat.	Petronius. *Satyricon, Satyrica.* LCL 15
SBL	Society for Biblical Literature
SBLDS	Society of Biblical Literature Dissertation Series
SBLSP	Society of Biblical Literature Seminar Papers
SBLSS	Society of Biblical Literature: Resources for Biblical Study
SBLWAW	Society of Biblical Literature Writings from the Ancient World series
SBT	Studies in Biblical Theology 2nd Series
SCJS	Studies in Christianity and Judaism Series
Scorp.	Tertullian. *Scorpiace, Antidote for the Scorpion's Sting.* ANF 3
SDB	Smith's *Dictionary of the Bible* (4 vols. ed. Hackett, 1883)
SEÅ	*Svensk exegetisk årsbok*
SEG	*Supplementum epigraphicum graecum* (eds. Chaniotis, Corsten, Papazarkadas, and Tybout, 1923–)
Sert.	Plutarch. *Lives: Sertorius.* LCL 100
SFSHJ	South Florida Studies in the History of Judaism
Shem.	*Shemoth Rabbah* on Exodus (ed. Freedman, 1992)
Sib. Or.	*Sibylline Oracles, APOT*
sic	"so, thus, in this manner" meaning the error was in the original
Sifre	Classical Jewish legal Biblical exegesis, based on the biblical books of Devarim (Deuteronomy).
SIG	*Sylloge inscriptionum graecarum* (4 vols., ed. Dittenberger, 3rd ed. 1915–1924)
Silv.	Statius. *Silvae.* LCL 206
Sim.	Shepherd of Hermas. *Similitude. ANF*
Sir	Sirach, Ecclesiasticus, *APOT*
SJLA	Studies in Judaism in Late Antiquity
SJT	*Scottish Journal of Theology*
SMR	seven messages of Revelation
SMRVT	*The Seven Messages of Revelation and Vassal Treaties: Literary Genre, Structure, and Function* (Graves, 2009)
Smyrn.	Ignatius. *To the Smyrnaeans. ANF*
SNG BnF	*Sylloge Nummorum Graecorum, France, Cabinet des Médailles, Bibliothéque Nationale* (eds. Nicolet, Delepierre, and Le Rider, 1983– 2001)=SNG France, SNG Paris, SNG BN
SNG Cop.	*Sylloge Nummorum Graecorum, Denmark, The Royal Collection of Coins and Medals, Danish National Museum* (7 vols. ed. Breitenstein, and Schwabacher. Copenhagen, 1942)

SNG Kayhan	*Sylloge Nummorum Graecorum: Turkey 1, The Muharrem Kayhan Collection Part 2.* (Tekin, Ozdizbay, and Koray, 2015)
SNG Lewis	*Sylloge Nummorum Graecorum, Great Britain VI, Corpus Christi College Cambridge, The Lewis Collection Part I: The Greek and Hellenistic Coins (with Britain and Parthia)* (ed. Carradice, 1972)
SNG München	*Sylloge Nummorum Graecorum, Deutschland: Staatliche Münzsammlung München* (Franke, and Küthmann, 1968)
SNG Righetti	*Sylloge nummorum graecorum Schweiz II. Katalog der Sammlung Jean-Pierre Righetti im Bernischen Historischen Museum II* (ed. Kapossy, 1993)
SNG Tübingen	*Sylloge Nummorum Graecorum, Deutschland, Münzsammlung Universität Tübingen* (6 vols. ed. Mannsperger, 1981–1998)
SNGvA	*Sylloge Nummorum Graecorum: Collection of Greek Coins from Asia Minor* (4 vols. Von Aulock. ed. Kleiner, 1957-1967, 1987)
SNR	*Schweizerische Numismatische Rundschau*
SNT	Studien zum Neuen Testament
SNTS	Society for New Testament Studies Monograph Series
Sobr.	Philo. *De Sobrietate, On Sobriety.* LCL 247
Somn.	Philo. *De somniis, On Dreams.* LCL 275
Song (Cant.)	Song of Songs (Song or Solomon, or Canticles)
Soph. Jes. Chr.	*Sophia of Jesus Christ,* NHC
SPAW	Sitzungsberichte der Preußischen Akademie der Wissenschaften
SPDI	Studi pubblicati dall' Istituto Italiano per la Storia Antica
Spec.	Philo. *De specialibus legibus, On the Special Laws.* LCL 320
SPS	Sacra Pagina Series
SQC	*Scrolls from Qumran Cave I* (Trever, 1974)
SR	*Studies in Religion/Sciences religieuses*
SSEJC	Studies in Early Judaism and Christianity
StABH	Studies in American Biblical Hermeneutics
StBL	Studies in Biblical Literature
Strat.	Polyaenus. *Strategemata, Stratagems of War* (trans. Shepherd 1793)
Strom.	Clement of Alexandria. *Stromata, Miscellanies or Patchwork. ANF*
STTJ	Studies of the Texts of Thedesert of Judah
Sull.	Plutarch. *Lives: Sulla.* LCL 80
SUNT	Studien zur Umwelt des Neuen Testaments
Sus	Susanna, *APOT*
T. Ab.	*Testament of Abraham,* OTP
T. Benj.	*Testament of Benjamin,* OTP
T. Dan	*Testament of Dan,* OTP
T. Job	*Testament of Job,* OTP
T. Jud.	*Testament of Judah,* OTP
T. Levi	*Testament of Levi,* OTP
T. Mos.	*Testament of Moses,* OTP
TAD	*Türk Arkeoloji Dergisi*

TAM III	*Tituli Asiae Minoris, III* (Heberdey, 1941)
TAM V	*Titula Asiae Minoris, V* (Vol. 1, nos. 1-825; Vol. 2, nos. 826-1414, ed. Hermann 1989)
TDNT	*Theological Dictionary of the New Testament* (10 vols. eds. Kittel and Friedrich, Trans. Bromiley 1964–1985)
TDOT	*Theological Dictionary of the Old Testament* (8 vols. eds. Botterweck, and Ringgren, trans. Willis, Bromiley, and Green, 1974–)
Teach. Silv.	*VII, 4 Teachings of Silvanus. NHC*
Test.	Cyprian of Carthage. *Ad Quirinum testimonia adversus Judaeos, To Quirinius: Three Books of Testomonies against the Jews, ANF* 5
Tg. Isa.	*Targum of Isaiah* (Chilton 1987)
Tg. Jer.	*Targum of Jeremiah.* Aramaic Old Testament
Tg. Neof.	*Targum Neofiti.* Aramaic Old Testament
Tg. Onq.	*Targum Onqelos*
Tg. Pal.	*The Palestinian Targum.* The Western Targumim on the Torah
Tg. Ps.-J.	*Targum Pseudo-Jonathan* (Etheridge, 1862)
Tg.	*Targum*
Theb.	Statius. *Thebais, Thebaid.* LCL 207
Theog.	Hesiod. *Theogonia, Theogony.* LCL 57
ThS	*Theological Studies*
Tib.	Suetonius. *The Lives of the Caesars: Tiberius.* LCL 31
Tim. Frag.	Theopompus. *Timaei Fragmenta* (Müller, 1841)
TJ	*Trinity Journal*
TNTC	The Tyndale New Testament Commentary
Tob	Tobias, Tobit, *APOT*
TP	*Theologie und Philosophie*
TPINTC	Trinity Press International New Testament Commentaries
Trist.	Ovid. *Tristia, Sorrows.* LCL 151
TSAJ	Texte Und Studien Zum Antiken Judentum
TSK	*Theologische Studien und Kritiken*
TU	Texte und Untersuchungen zur Geschichte der altchristlichen Literatur
TWNT	*Theologisches Wörterbuch zum Neuen Testament* (10 vols. eds. Kittel and Friedrich, 1932–1979)
TynBul	*Tyndale Bulletin*
UF	*Ugarit-Forschungen*
Var. hist.	Aelian, Claudius. *Varia historia, Historical Miscellany.* LCL 486
VC	*Vigiliae Christianae*
ver. vs.	verse, verses.
Verr.	Cicero. *In Verrem, Against Gaius Verres, or The Verrines.* LCL 293
Vir. ill.	Jerome. *De viris illustribus, On Illustrious Men.* NPNF[1] 3
Vis.	Shepherd of Hermas. *Vision. ANF*
vit.	vita
Vit. Aes.	Aesop. *Vita Aesopi, Vita G or Perriana* (2 vol. ed. Perry, 1952)
Vit. Apoll.	Philostratus, Flavius. *De Vita Apollonii, Life of Apollonius of Tyana.* LCL 16, 17

Vit. Phil.	Diogenes Laertius. *Vitae philosophorum, Lives of Eminent Philosophers*. LCL 184, 185
Vit. Polyc.	Pionius. *Vita Polycarp, The Life of Polycarp, APF*
Vit. Soph.	Philostratus, Lucius Flavius. *Vita Sophistarum, The Lives of the Sophists*. LCL 134
VÖAW	Verlag der Österreichischen Akademie der Wissenschaften
vol.	volume.
VT	*Vetus Testamentum*
VTSup	Vetus Testamentum Supplements
Waddington	*Inventaire Sommaire de La Collection Waddington Acquise Par L'état En 1897 Pour Le Département Des Médailles et Antiques de La Bibliothèque Nationale, Rédigé Par Ernest Babelon* (Waddington, 1898).
WBC	Word Biblical Commentary
Wis	Wisdom of Solomon, *APOT*
WMANT	Wissenschaftliche Monographien zum Alten und Neuen Testament
WTJ	*Westminster Theological Journal*
WUNT	Wissenschaftliche Untersuchungen zum Neuen Testament
ZAW	Zeitschrift für die alttestamentliche Wissenschaft
ZBK	Zürcher Bibelkommentare
ZEB	*Zondervan Encyclopedia of the Bible* (Revised, Full-Colour ed. 5 vols. eds. Tenney and Silva eds. 2009)
ZECNT	Zondervan Exegetical Commentary on the New Testament
ZIBBC	Zondervan Illustrated Bible Backgrounds Commentary
ZNW	*Zeitschrift für die neutestamentliche Wissenschaft und die Kunde der älteren Kirche*
ZPE	*Zeitschrift für Papyrologie und Epigraphik*
ZPEB	*The Zondervan Pictorial Encyclopedia of the Bible* (eds. Tenney and Silva, 5 vols. 2009)
ZRGG	*Zeitschrift für Religions- und Geistesgeschichte*

Preface

There have been so many excellent works on this mysterious book of the NT, one might wonder, why another commentary on Revelation? The reality, however, is that of all the works written on Revelation and the Seven Churches no commentary, to this point, has examined all the messages to the seven churches considering the ancient Near Eastern Vassal treaty (ANEVT) structure. The notion of the influence of the ancient Near Eastern vassal treaty structure was not new to me, but goes back over 35 years to when I was an undergraduate student and reading about Meredith Kline's work on this subject in relation to the OT. Then during the research for my Ph.D. dissertation, David Aune suggested that the seven messages were influenced by Imperial Edicts. While this intrigued me, it never truly satisfied my impression that they were first and foremost influenced by the OT Torah. The vassal treaty structure common to both the OT and what I believed to be evident in the messages to the churches in Revelation, naturally lent itself to further investigation. This present commentary has been fifteen years in the works.

This volume is an outworking of my Ph.D. dissertation completed at Highland Theological College and the University of Aberdeen under the supervision of Professors I. Howard Marshall, Jamie Grant, and Alistair Wilson. My original dissertation "The Influence of Ancient Near Eastern Vassal Treaties on the Seven Prophetic Messages in Revelation with Special Reference to the Message to Smyrna" was defended in 2008 and published shortly thereafter in 2009 by Gorgias Press under the title *The Seven Messages of Revelation and Vassal Treaties: Literary Genre, Structure, and Function* in the Gorgias Dissertations Biblical Studies Series 41. In my dissertation, the message to the city of Smyrna was examined, and included in this commentary with the kind permission of Gorgias Press, but left the six remaining messages to the churches to be dealt with in this fashion.

David Chilton did write a commentary on the entire book of Revelation called *The Days of Vengeance* (1987), using the ANEVT structure as the five divisions of his work. According to Chilton the structure of the seven messages of Revelation (SMR) "follows the same general pattern" and "each message itself recapitulates the entire five-part covenant structure" (p. 85). But Chilton considered the SMR as the *Historical Prologue* element of the overall ANEVT structure he used for his commentary. Ray R. Sutton in Appendix 5 of his work, *That You May Prosper: Dominion by Covenant* (1987), outlines the book of Revelation using the ANEVT structure and describes the structure in the messages using Ephesians as his example identical to Chilton (p. 253). They only dealt with the elements of the ANEVT structure in the message to Ephesus, and neglected the remaining cities. While they contribute to the discussion of the ANEVT structure and the book of Revelation, their material on the SMR needed further development.

So with only Smyrna and Ephesus treated according to the ANEVT structure, this volume was written to consider all of the SMR in light of the covenantal lawsuit motif following the ANEVT structure. This, it is hoped, will shed new light on the text and bring the messages to light for the reader in a new way.

Several trips were undertaken to visit the ruins of the cities of the seven churches in Turkey and to explore the museums that now house many of their remains. Then early in my research for my dissertation my supervisor, I. Howard Marshall, encouraged me to pursue a defence of William Ramsay's work of identifying local references in the text which was taken up by Collin Hemer, but I was too far along in my research on the ANEVT structure to give it my attention at that time. In subsequent years, I published several articles on the local references in the SMR[1] and have included the essence of the material here with the kind permission of the editor of *Bible and Spade* and with new developments in archaeology added. This work will combine the historical references and the vassal treaty structure in one commentary achieving in part what I. Howard Marshall had requested. My only regret is that he did not live to see the finished commentary, passing away one year before its completion.

The purpose of this volume is not only to provide the reader with exegetical and background information on the messages to the seven churches of Asia Minor, but to help the reader analyze the genre, structure and function of these proclamations. Therefore, there is a great deal of interdisciplinary data in the book that is becoming increasingly necessary in academic research. Although this commentary is based on the Greek text of Revelation, I have usually provided a transliteration and English translation in parenthesis after the Greek words or phrases in order that those who are not proficient in Greek would be able to benefit from reading the commentary. Also, primary sources, of three entries or more, were moved to a footnote to aid in the readability of the text.

This book owes a great debt of gratitude to many friends and family whose profession and passion for the Bible have contributed to its completion. First is the late I. Howard Marshall who challenged me to write a defence of William Ramsay for my dissertation but was unable to take up the challenge during that time because of previous research on the covenant. It was his inspiration that propelled me into this present project.

Second is my good friend and editor Glen Ruffle. He has tirelessly laboured on the initial manuscript through its several versions and provided helpful comments and suggestions along the way. His eye to detail and prompt attention to editorial issues is much appreciated. This work has benefitted greatly from his expertice.

I also wish to thank Kimberly Day, the resource sharing librarian, at the Jerry Falwell Library, Liberty University, for her help in locating journal articles and books for my research. It is not always easy to do research from a distance so it is with gratitude that I wish to thank the Library department at Liberty for their quick response to my endless requests for obscure articles and books.

---

[1] David E. Graves, "Local References in the Letter to Smyrna (Rev 2:8–11), Part 1: Archaeological Background," *BS* 18, no. 4 (2005): 114–23; "Local References in the Letter to Smyrna (Rev 2:8–11), Part 2: Historical Background," *BS* 19, no. 1 (2006): 23–31; "Local References in the Letter to Smyrna (Rev 2:8–11), Part 3: Jewish Background," *BS* 19, no. 2 (2006): 41–47; "Local References in the Letter to Smyrna (Rev 2:8–11), Part 4: Religious Background," *BS* 19, no. 3 (2006): 88–96; "Jesus Speaks to Seven of His Churches, Part 1," *Bible and Spade* 23, no. 2 (Spring 2010): 46–56; "Jesus Speaks to Seven of His Churches, Part 2," *Bible and Spade* 23, no. 3 (Summer 2010): 66–74.

I also wish to express my gratitude to the Classical Numismatic Group, Todd Bolen, Ferrell Jenkins, Mark Wilson, and others for their permission to use their professional work in photographs, and images to enhance the readers experience.

Lastly, I wish to express my thankfulness to my loving wife Irina for her helpful comments, deep love, care, and patience during the long hours of writing and editing this work. Her editing skills and keen eye to detail along with here companionship are deeply appreciated.

The online *Jesus Speaks* companion website is free for everyone and accessible through this link http://JesusSpeaks7.blogspot.com. The website provides photos from the book, enlarged and in color, external web links, and an extended bibliography for research, along with additional bonus material that could not be put into the book due to space limitations and to keep the cost down for students.

My hope and prayer is that this research will lead not only to a deeper understanding of the seven messages to the church, but also that it will enrich our understanding of the covenant relationship between Christ and his church.

David E. Graves, Ph.D.
Toronto, Canada
April 12, 2017

1

The Literary Context of the Book of Revelation

Revelation is perhaps the least understood and most misrepresented book in the NT. The title for Revelation comes from the first sentence which, as in many other ancient books, provides the title for the work along with the content and the name of the author. The book begins with the phrase "The revelation (Ἀποκάλυψις, *apokalypsis*) of Jesus Christ" (1:1), referring to John simply as the author. *Apocalypse*[1] means "to disclose," "unveiling" or "revealing,"[2] but for most readers the book tends to hide rather than reveal its message, as much of its interpretation is argued over by scholars.

THE AUTHORSHIP OF REVELATION

Scholars also hotly debate the authorship of the Book of Revelation and several prominent scholars such as Kiddle, Beale, Aune, Beasley-Murray, Michaels, and deSilva[3] conclude that determining the identity of *John* is a hopeless endeavor.[4] Kiddle sums up the view comments,

---

[1] For the study of genre and apocalyptic literature and the book of Revelation, see E. Frank Tupper, "The Revival of Apocalyptic in Biblical and Theological Studies," *Review and Expositor* 72, no. 3 (1975): 279–303; Jan Lambrecht, "The Book of Revelation and Apocalyptic in the New Testament," in *L'Apocalypse Johannique et L' Apocalyptique Dans Le NouveauTestament*, ed. Jan lambrecht (Leuven: Leuven University Press, 1980), 18; David Hellholm and Kungl Vitterhets, *Apocalypticism in the Mediterranean World and the Near East: Proceedings of the International Colloquium on Apocalypticism, Uppsala, August 12–17, 1979* (Tübingen: Siebeck, 1989); David E. Aune, "The Apocalypse of John and the Problem of Genre," in *Early Christian Apocalypticism: Genre and Social Setting*, Semeia 36 (Atlanta, Ga.: Scholars Press, 1986), 65–69; John M. Court, *The Book of Revelation and the Johannine Apocalyptic Tradition* (Sheffield, U.K.: Sheffield Academic, 2000).

[2] Richard J. Bauckham, "Apocalyptic," ed. Sinclair B. Ferguson, David F. Wright, and James I. Packer, *NDT* (Downers Grove, Ill.: InterVarsity, 1988), 34.

[3] DeSilva describes it as a "seemingly insoluble question of authorship". David A. DeSilva, "The Social Setting of the Revelation to John: Conflicts Within, Fears Without," *WTJ* 54, no. 2 (1992): 282.

[4] Martin Kiddle, *The Revelation of St. John*, ed. James Moffatt, MNTC 17 (London, U.K.: Hodder & Stoughton, 1952), 33; George R. Beasley-Murray, *The Book of Revelation*, NCB 23 (Grand Rapids, Mich.: Eerdmans, 1992), 36–37; David E Aune, "The Prophetic Circle of John of Patmos and the Exegesis of Revelation 22:16," *JSNT* 37 (1989): 103–16; J. Ramsey Michaels, *Interpreting the Book of Revelation*, Guides to New Testament Exegesis (Grand Rapids, Mich.: Baker, 1992), 27–29; Gregory K. Beale, *The Book of Revelation: A Commentary on the Greek Text*, NIGTC 12 (Grand

"The authorship of Revelation may prove the one mystery of the book which will be never revealed in this world."[5] It is best to simply use *John* as the name for the author of Revelation, although the apostle John, the son of Zebedee, is widely held to be the main candidate for the author, especially among conservative scholars. For this, they relying heavily on the external evidence of the early church fathers (Justin *Dial.* 81).[6] It appears that this John was so well known that no further identification was necessary, and although there were other John's of note (i.e., John the Elder, John the Baptist), only the Apostle John carried enough recognition to go simply by the name of "John".[7]

THE OCCASION OF REVELATION

The letter of Revelation was written as an individual message, to seven real churches, in the Asia Minor cities of Ephesus, Smyrna, Pergamum, Thyatira, Sardis, Philadelphia, and Laodicea. The seven cities were located on what Ramsay considered a circular postal route.[8] Each church had their own set of problems and issues, and the message of Revelation sought to address, reprimand and provide encouragement to them. It was thus designed to be read aloud in each one of the seven churches.[9]

The letter of Revelation, which presents the triumph of Christ over evil, was meant to be a source of encouragement to these suffering churches, dealing with the crisis of persecution from Rome (see below under "External Problems"; Eusebius *Chron.* 19.551–52; *Hist. eccl.* 3.23.3–4) and the Jewish community (see below under "Internal Problems").[10]

Rapids, Mich.: Eerdmans, 1998), 35–36.

[5] Kiddle, *Revelation*, 33.

[6] Herman Hoeksema, *Behold, He Cometh! An Exposition of the Book of Revelation*, 2nd ed. (Grand Rapids, Mich.: Reformed Free Publishing Association, 1974), 2; Beasley-Murray, *Revelation*, NCB, 36; Stephen S. Smalley, "John's Revelation and John's Community," *BJRL* 69 (1987): 564–65; Robert H. Mounce, *The Book of Revelation*, Revised, NICNT 17 (Grand Rapids, Mich.: Eerdmans, 1997), 15; Simon J. Kistemaker, *Exposition of the Book of Revelation*, NTC 12 (Grand Rapids, Mich.: Baker Academic, 2001), 18–24; Smalley, "John's Revelation," 2.

[7] Robert L. Thomas, *Revelation 1–7 Commentary* (Chicago, Ill.: Moody, 1992), 2–19; David E. Aune, *Revelation 1–5*, WBC 52A (Dallas, Tex.: Word Books, 1997), xlvii–lvi; Grant R. Osborne, *Revelation*, BECNT (Grand Rapids, Mich.: Baker Academic, 2002), 2–6.

[8] William M. Ramsay, *The Letters to Seven Churches: Updated*, ed. Mark W. Wilson (Peabody, Mass.: Hendrickson, 1994), 183.

[9] Graves, "Jesus Speaks to Seven of His Churches, Part 1"; "Jesus Speaks to Seven of His Churches, Part 2"; "Local References in the Letter to Smyrna (Rev 2:8–11), Part 1: Archaeological Background"; "Local References in the Letter to Smyrna (Rev 2:8–11), Part 2: Historical Background"; "Local References in the Letter to Smyrna (Rev 2:8–11), Part 3: Jewish Background"; "Local References in the Letter to Smyrna (Rev 2:8–11), Part 4: Religious Background."

[10] Thompson and Yarbro Collins have argued that the message was *creating* the feeling of a "perceived crisis" rather than *responding* to one. Leonard L. Thompson, *The Book of Revelation: Apocalypse and Empire* (New York, N.Y.: Oxford University Press, USA, 1997), 27–28; Adela Yarbro Collins, *Crisis and Catharsis: The Power of the Apocalypse* (Louisville, Ky.: Westminster/Knox, 1984), 84.

Jesus Speaks to Seven of His Churches

1. The island of Patmos where John received his vision of Revelation.

The Location of Writing

John received his vision *(Apocalypse)* on the island of Patmos (in modern Greece; Rev 1:9), located in the Aegean Sea southeast of Miletus (in modern Turkey; see Fig. 1). Eusebius, referencing Irenaeus, states that in the fourteenth year of Domitian's reign, during a persecution of Christian, "the apostle John is banished to Patmos and sees his Apocalypse" *(Chron.* 19.551–52; *Hist. eccl.* 3.23.3–4).

Presumably John was banished to Patmos because of his faith (1:9). Scholars speculate that the island was used by Rome as a place to exile criminals and political prisoners. This is based on Tacitus' mention of three other islands in the Aegean (Donusa, Gyarus and Amorgus) where the Romans exiled political prisoners (Tacitus *Ann.* 3.69; see *Quotes from Antiquity*).[11]

There is evidence of continual

> **Quotes from Antiquity**
>
> An old tradition based on Origen and recorded by Victorinus of Pettau (d. *ca.* AD 304), states that:
>
> When John saw this revelation, he was on the island of Patmos, having been condemned to the mines by Caesar Domitian. There, it seems, John wrote the Revelation, and when he had already become aged, he thought that he would be received into bliss after his suffering. However, when Domitian was killed, all of his decrees were null and void. John was, therefore, released from the mines, and afterward he disseminated the revelation that he had received from the Lord. *(Comm. Apoc.* 10.3 [Weinrich])

---

[11] Henry Barclay Swete, *Commentary on Revelation*, reprint 1906 (Eugene, Oreg.: Wipf & Stock, 1999), 12; Robert H. Charles, *A Critical and Exegetical Commentary on the Revelation of St John*, ICC (Edinburgh, U.K.: T&T Clark, 1963), 1:21; Ernst Lohmeyer, *Die Offenbarung Des Johannes*, HNT 16 (Tübingen: Siebeck, 1926), 15; Eduard Lohse, *Die Offenbarung Des Johannes*, Das Neue Testament Deutsch 11 (Göttingen: Vandenhoeck & Ruprecht, 1993), 19; Heinrich Kraft, *Die Offenbarung Des Johannes*, HNT 16a (Tübingen: Siebeck, 1974), 40.

occupation during the time when John lived there, showing that the island was not deserted or just used as a Roman penal colony[12] (Pliny *Nat.* 4.12.69; Tacitus *Ann.* 4.30).[13] There is no evidence from ancient writers that Patmos ever had mines or quarries on it.[14] Tertullian (*Praescr.* 36; AD 220), Origen (*Comm. Matt.* 16.6 on Matt 20:22–23; AD 254), and Eusebius (AD 313) state that John was "exiled to an island" (*Hist. eccl.* 3.18.1), using language of banishment and condemnation for John's removal. However, the biblical text only states: "I, John, your brother and partner in the tribulation and the kingdom and the patient endurance that are in Jesus, was on the island called Patmos on account of the word of God and the testimony (μαρτυρίαν, *martyrian*[15] meaning "witness") of Jesus (Rev 1:9)."[16]

Scholars note that the modern idea of martyrdom for this term *martyrian* did not develop until much later.[17] Perhaps, John was carrying out missionary (witnessing) activities on Patmos when he received his vision,[18] although scholars speculate that surely he would have chosen a larger and more populated island as a location to engage in evangelism.[19]

During the Hellenistic period, Patmos was part of Miletus, and along with two other islands, formed the "fortresses" of Miletus to protect its harbour on the Gulf of Latmique. By the second century BC these three islands were populated by a Milesian garrison.[20] A second century AD inscription mentions the presence of the cult of Artemis flourishing on the island, including the existence of a temple to Artemis which is now under the Christian basilica.[21] Between the seventh and eleventh century Patmos was deserted due to pirates. However, as

---

[12] For more details on Roman law, see Adolf Berger, *Encyclopedic Dictionary of Roman Law*, Reprint of the 1953 edition, Transactions of the American Philosophical Society V. 43, Pt. 2. (The Lawbook Exchange, Ltd., 2002), 633; David E. Aune, *Revelation 1–5*, WBC 52A (Nashville: Nelson, 1997), 79.

[13] Otto F. A. Meinardus, *St. John of Patmos and the Seven Churches of the Apocalypse*, In the Footsteps of the Saints (New York, N.Y.: Caratzas, 1979), 13.

[14] Brian M. Rapske, "Exiles, Islands, and the Identity and Perspective of John in Revelation," in *Christian Origins and Greco-Roman Culture: Social and Literary Contexts for the New Testament*, ed. Stanley E. Porter and Andrew W. Pitts, Texts and Editions for New Testament Study: Early Christianity in Its Hellenistic Context 1 (Leiden: Brill, 2012), 311–46.

[15] Scholars note that the modern idea of martyrdom for this term *martyrian* did not develop until much later. Boudewijn Dehandschütter, "The Meaning of Witness in the Apocalypse," in *L'Apocalypse Johannique et L' Apocalyptique Dans Le Nouveau Testament*, ed. Jan Lambrecht (Gembloux, Belgium: Louvain University Press, 1980), 283–88.

[16] Perhaps, John was carrying out missionary (witnessing) activities on Patmos when he received his vision, although scholars speculate that surely he would have chosen a larger and more populated island as a location to engage in evangelism. Kistemaker, *Revelation*, 91; John R. Yeatts, *Revelation*, Believers Church Bible Commentary (Harrisonburg, VA: Herald, 2003), 40.

[17] Dehandschütter, "The Meaning of Witness in the Apocalypse."

[18] Rapske, "Exiles, Islands, and the Identity and Perspective of John in Revelation," 311.

[19] Kistemaker, *Revelation*, 91; Yeatts, *Revelation*, 40.

[20] H. D. Saffrey, "Relire l'Apocalypse À Patmos," *RB* 82 (1975): 388–91.

[21] Aune, *Rev 1–5*, 77; Saffrey, "Relire l'Apocalypse À Patmos," 399–407; Werner Peek, "Die Hydrophore Vera von Patmos," *Rheinisches Museum Für Philologie*, 1964, 315–25; Clyde E. Fant and Mitchell G. Reddish, *A Guide to Biblical Sites in Greece and Turkey* (Oxford, U.K.: Oxford University Press, 2003), 93.

mentioned earlier, the island was definitely not deserted or a Roman penal colony in John's day (Pliny *Nat.* 4.12.69; Tacitus *Ann.* 4.30).

In 1088, Emperor Alexios I Comnenos granted Christodoulos Latrenus, a Nicaean monk, permission to build the Monastery of St. John the Theologian on Patmos over the Christian basilica and the temple of Artemis (see Figs. 24, 28, 29). Near the Grotto or cave of the Apocalypse, which was supposedly the place where John received his vision, he built the Chapel of St. Anne, named either after the virgin Mary or the mother of Alexios I Comnenos.[22]

Today the monastery holds a collection of valuable manuscripts, including the sixth cent. AD Codex Purpureus Petropolitanus (a copy of the Gospel of Mark), and an eighth cent. AD book of Job. Also, the museum houses a fourth cent. BC marble inscription stating that "Orestes (son of Agamemnon and Clytemnestra) visited Patmos and established a temple to Artemis on the island, supposedly in the same location as the Monastery of St. John."[23]

THE DATE OF WRITING

Scholars vigorously debate the date of Revelation's composition. There are three periods put forth: the reign of Nero (AD 54–68), the reign of Domitian (AD 81–96), and the reign of Trajan (AD 98–117).

The early date is after Nero's reign around AD 54–68.[24] It was popular with scholars in the nineteenth cent., but also promoted by several scholars from the twenty-first century.[25]

The late date, during, either the reign of Domitian or Trajan, is supported by Irenaeus, bishop of Lyons in Gaul, and disciple of Polycarp, bishop of Smyrna (writing in AD ca. 175–195), who places the date of the work of Revelation "near the end of Domitian's reign" (Eusebius *Hist. eccl.* 5.8.5). Irenaeus, a second-generation church father, is quoted by Eusebius saying that Revelation was written "no long time ago, but almost in our own day, towards the end of Domitian's reign" (Irenaeus *Haer.* 5.30.3 [Roberts]). Irenaeus is widely quoted by the church fathers (Victorinus *Comm. Apoc.* 10.11; 17.10; Jerome *Vir. ill.* 9) propagating the tradition of the late date.

However, in two other places, Eusebius contradicted himself, claiming that John the apostle lived during the time of Domitian's successor Trajan in AD 98–117 (Irenaeus *Haer.* 2.22.5; 3.3.4).[26] Church tradition since the time of Irenaeus stated that the apostle John returned

---

[22] Frank Leslie Cross and Elizabeth A. Livingstone, eds., *The Oxford Dictionary Of The Christian Church* (Oxford, U.K.: Oxford University Press, 2005), 1024.

[23] Fant and Reddish, *Guide to Biblical Sites*, 98.

[24] For an extensive discussion, cf. Kenneth L. Gentry Jr., *Before Jerusalem Fell: Dating the Book of Revelation* (Powder Springs, GA: American Vision, 1998), 68–85; Beale, *Revelation,* 20–26.

[25] Albert A. Bell, Jr., "The Date of John's Apocalypse: The Evidence of Some Roman Historians Reconsidered," *NTS* 10, no. 1 (1978): 93; David Hill, *New Testament Prophecy*, Marshall's Theological Library (London, U.K.: Marshall, Morgan & Scott, 1979), 218–19; J. Christian Wilson, "The Problem of the Domitianic Date of Revelation," *NTS* 39, no. 4 (1993): 587; Gentry, *Before Jerusalem Fell*, 68–85.

[26] Both passages are quoted in Eusebius *Hist. Eccl.* 3.23.3–4; *contra* Irenaeus *Haer.* 5.30.3.

2. Bust of Julius Claudius Caesar (AD 41–54) discovered in Nikomedia.

to Ephesus after being released from prison with other political prisoners under the reign of Nerva (AD 96–98) following the death of Domitian (Eusebius *Hist. eccl.* 3.17–20) and survived into the reign of Trajan (Eusebius *Hist. eccl.* 2.22.5; 3.3.43; 3.23.1–3). The Trajanic date would reconcile statements by Irenaeus who writes in Book 2 and 3 of his *Against Heresies* about John's presence in Ephesus "until the time of Trajan" (Eusebius *Hist. eccl.* 3:21; 3.23.1, 6; Irenaeus *Haer.* 2.33; 3.3).[27]

However, Epiphanius of Salamis contradicts this tradition, stating that John left Patmos during the reign of Claudius Caesar (AD 41–54, see Fig. 2, 28) when John was over ninety years old (*Pan.* 51.12.1–2). Aune points out that there is some confusion over Claudius's name, as he was also known as Nero Claudius Caesar,[28] and, according to the Syriac Apocrypha, John's exile took place under "Nero, the unclean and impure and wicked king."[29]

One could use either an early or a late date for first-century suffering and persecution. While the immediate circumstances would be different, the general issue of the threat of the imperial cult and Jewish antagonism is present in both periods. Wilson argues that "the persecution of 95 and 96 was the creation of Eusebius and Lightfoot, not of Domitian".[30]

Beale argues for a later persecution under Domitian's reign (Rev 12–16).[31] Yarbro Collins questions the "widespread view that apocalyptic literature is crisis literature"[32] and hypothesizes for a "perceived crisis" in Asia Minor toward the end of Domitian's reign.[33] However, as Loren

---

[27] For the Trajanic date, cf. Austin M. Farrer, *The Revelation of St. John the Divine: Commentary on the English Text* (Oxford, U.K.: Clarendon, 1964), 37; F. Gerald Downing, "Pliny's Prosecutions of Christians," *Journal for the Study of the New Testament* 34 (1988): 105–23; Martin Hengel, *The Johannine Question*, trans. John Bowden (Philadelphia, Pa.: Trinity, 1989), 80–81; DeSilva, "The Social Setting of the Revelation to John: Conflicts Within, Fears Without," 280; Steven J. Friesen, *Imperial Cults and the Apocalypse of John: Reading Revelation in the Ruins* (Oxford, U.K.: Oxford University Press, 2001), 150.

[28] Aune, *Rev 1–5*, 77–78.

[29] William Wright, *Apocryphal Acts of the Apostles* (London, U.K.: Williams & Norgate, 1871), 2:55.

[30] Wilson, "Problem of the Domitianic Date," 605.

[31] Duane Warden, "Imperial Persecution and the Dating of First Peter and Revelation," *NTS* 34, no. 2 (1991): 203–12.

[32] Adela Yarbro Collins, "Dating the Apocalypse of John," *BR* 26, no. 1 (1981): 42.

[33] Collins, *Crisis and Catharsis*, 84–110.

T. Stuckenbruck points out, this "recent doubt cast on the notion of an organized persecution of Christians during the latter part of Domitian's reign... does not require a Neronian date".[34]

THE QUESTION OF GENRE

Despite the volume of genre studies already conducted,[35] when it comes to the book of Revelation as a whole, genre is an "elusive" question.[36] While some scholars point to a specific genre of apocalypse (Ἀποκάλυψις, *apokalypsis* Rev 1:1), prophecy (προφητεία, *propheteia* Rev 1:3), and epistle (ἐκκλησίας γράψον, *ekklesias graphon*),[37] most acknowledge that the book of Revelation is composed in a mixed genre (Lat. *mixtum compositum*).[38] Robert M. Royalty questions the exegetical value of a mixed genre,[39] while Aune allows for the mixed genre designation of "prophetic edicts."[40] It is complicated in that there appears to be several kinds of literature packaged together into one document. One of the key elements in understanding the genre of Revelation is to recognize that there are more OT allusions in Revelation than any other NT book. As Keener points out:

> Revelation mixes elements of Old Testament prophecy with a heavy dose of the apocalyptic genre, a style of writing that grew out of elements of Old Testament prophecy. Although nearly all its images have parallels in the biblical prophets, the images most relevant to late-first-century readers, which were prominent in popular Jewish revelations about the end time, are stressed most heavily.[41]

However, Aune and others point out that the book of Revelation itself opens (1:4–5) and closes (22:21) with "a formal epistolary framework,"[42] indicating a single circulating document.[43]

---

[34] Loren T. Stuckenbruck, "Revelation," in *Eerdmans Commentary on the Bible*, ed. James D. G. Dunn and John W. Rogerson (Grand Rapids, Mich.: Eerdmans, 2003), 1536.

[35] Tupper, "The Revival of Apocalyptic in Biblical and Theological Studies," 279–303; Lambrecht, "The Book of Revelation," 18; Hellholm and Vitterhets, *Apocalypticism in the Mediterranean World and the Near East: Proceedings of the International Colloquium on Apocalypticism, Uppsala, August 12–17, 1979*; Aune, "The Apocalypse of John and the Problem of Genre," 65–69; Court, *The Book of Revelation*.

[36] James L. Blevins, "The Genre of Revelation," *RevExp* 77, no. 3 (1980): 393.

[37] Rev 1:11; 2:1, 8, 12, 18; 3:1, 7, 14; 14:13; 19:9; 21:5.

[38] Gerhard von Rad, *Theologie Des Alten Testaments*, 6th ed. (Munich: Auflage, 1975), 2:331; David Mathewson, "Revelation in Recent Genre Criticism: Some Implications for Interpretation," *TJ* 13 (1992): 206; Beale, *Rev*, 37, 39, 356; Donald A. Carson and Douglas J. Moo, *An Introduction to the New Testament* (Grand Rapids, Mich.: Zondervan, 2009), 479.

[39] Robert M. Royalty Jr., *The Ideology of Wealth in the Apocalypse of John* (Macon, Ga.: Mercer University Press, 1998), 157 n. 18.

[40] David E. Aune, "The Form and Function of the Proclamations to the Seven Churches," *NTS* 36 (1990): 183 n. 6.

[41] Craig S. Keener, *The IVP Bible Background Commentary: New Testament*, 2nd ed. (Downers Grove, Ill.: InterVarsity, 2004).

[42] Aune, *Rev 1–5*, lxxii.

[43] Martin Karrer, Die Johannesoffenbarung Als Brief: Studien Zu Ihrem Literarischen, Historischen Und Theologischen Ort, vol. 1, FRLANT 140 (Göttingen: Vandenhoeck & Ruprecht, 1986), 20–21.

In addition, the blessing-and-curse attachments at the beginning (1:3) and end (22:18) imply that the church was to read the whole book from beginning to end as a single message (Eusebius *Hist. eccl.* 7.25.9–10).

THE GENRE OF THE SEVEN MESSAGES

Essential to understanding the genre of Revelation is to divide the *internal* genre-structure inside chapter 2 and 3 from the *external*, contextual genre-matrix in the whole book of Revelation.[44] Chapters two and three of Revelation contain messages written to seven churches in Asia Minor. Scholars are divided over the proper designation of their genre. However, the necessity of working with the internal genre-structure *in situ* alone[45] has not barred scholars from proposing distinct genre-structures for chapters 2 and 3. Proposals come in three main types: letters,[46] prophetic messages[47]/oracles,[48] and imperial edicts.[49]

It is well documented in Scripture that letters were circulated to more than one church (1 Pet 1:1; Col 4:13). Aune has documented non-biblical prophetic literature in the form of letters from Mari and Hellenistic Egypt,[50] and letters communicating divine revelation (i.e., oracles or prophecies) with examples from the ancient Near East.[51] Prophetic letters are also found in the OT, particularly Jeremiah, and early Jewish writings.[52] Mazzaferri claims the early Christian prophets, following the OT prophets, wrote their letters in place of delivering the prophetic message in person.[53] This has justified Berger calling this style of writing *prophetic* or *oracular letters*.[54]

---

[44] David E. Graves, The Seven Messages of Revelation and Vassal Treaties: Literary Genre, Structure, and Function, GDBS 41 (Piscataway, N.J.: Gorgias, 2009), 49.

[45] John Joseph Collins, "Introduction: Towards the Morphology of a Genre," in *Apocalypse: The Morphology of a Genre*, ed. John Joseph Collins, vol. 14, Semeia 294 (Atlanta, Ga.: SBL, 1979), 14.

[46] Ramsay, Letters: Updated, 11–24; Michaels, Interpreting the Book of Revelation, 30–31.

[47] Richard J. Bauckham, The Climax of Prophecy: Studies on the Book of Revelation, New Ed (Edinburgh, U.K.: T&T Clark, 1999), 2; Stephen S. Smalley, The Revelation to John: A Commentary on the Greek Text of the Apocalypse (Downers Grove, Ill.: InterVarsity, 2005), 47; Elisabeth Schüssler Fiorenza, The Book of Revelation: Justice and Judgment, ed. Gerhard A. Krodel, PC (Minneapolis, Minn.: Fortress, 1998), 165; J. H. Roberts, "A Letter to Seven Churches in the Roman Province of Asia," in Reading Revelation, ed. J. E. Botha, P. G. R. Villiers, and J. Engelbrecht (Pretoria: Van Schaik Uitgewers, 2004), 17–35.

[48] John T. Kirby, "The Rhetorical Situation of Revelation 1–3," *NTS* 34, no. 2 (1988): 197–207.

[49] Aune, *Rev 1–5*, 126; "Form and Function," 183.

[50] Aune, *Rev 1–5*, lxxiii; Herbert B. Huffmon, "Prophecy in the Mari Letters," *BA* 31 (1968): 101–24; T. C. Skeat and E. G. Turner, "An Oracle of Hermes Trismegistos at Saqqara," *Journal of Egyptian Archaeology* 54 (1968): 199–208.

[51] Aune, *Rev 1–5*, lxxiii–lxxiv, 125; David E. Aune, *Prophecy in Early Christianity and the Ancient Mediterranean World* (Grand Rapids, Mich.: Eerdmans, 2002), 72–73.

[52] 2 Chr 21:12–15; Jer 29:4–32; Ep Jer 6:15–7:4; 7:24–35; *2 Bar.* 77:17–19; 78–87; *1 En.* 91–108; Meindert Dijkstra, "Prophecy by Letter (Jeremiah 29:24–32)," *Vetus Testamentum* 33 (1983): 319–22; Dennis Pardee, *Handbook of Ancient Hebrew Letters*, SBLSBS 15 (Atlanta, Ga.: Scholars Press, 1982), 175–78, 181.

[53] Frederick David Mazzaferri, The Genre of the Book of Revelation from a Source Critical Perspective (Berlin: de Gruyter, 1989), 133–34; Paul S. Minear, I Saw a New Earth: An Introduction to the Visions of the Apocalypse

If the genre of prophetic letter existed, were the messages in Revelation constructed using it? Are the seven messages of Revelation (SMR) individually composed in the *letter* genre, as individual prophetic oracles, or part of a single oracle addressed to the corporate church?[55] Although several commentators use the term *letter* to describe these messages collectively,[56] this would have to mean that John employed a very specialized sevenfold form of letter.

Paul's letters are typically characterised with personal salutations and postscripts. These are not the characteristics of the messages in Revelation chapters 2 and 3. If a letter is defined by its distinctive introductory salutation and ending, and has its key themes inserted in-between, the seven messages can, at most, be a form of excerpts from a letter—where the excerpt itself changes the discourse genre. These messages contain structured, disciplined, and formal content, not personal, spontaneous correspondence. Court concludes that these documents are "further removed from the type of the 'true letter' than any other New Testament composition."[57] As Michaels points out: "to speak of letters within a letter does not make sense, and there is no textual evidence that these messages were ever separated so that each congregation received only the communication bearing its name."[58]

John addresses his messages to individual churches he knew well with a preliminary message from Christ, before communicating a general message that each church was to read publicly. The plural addresses in the refrain "let him hear what the Spirit says to the churches" (2:7, 11, 29; 3:6, 13, 22) are a strong indication that all the churches were to read the document.

Thus, it is best to use the term messages, oracles or proclamations, but not letters for these seven messages to the churches. This is not to say that the book of Revelation itself is not structured as a letter.[59] This has led Bauckham to conclude that the book as a whole is a letter, while the messages to the churches are *prophetic oracles* within this singular letter, read from seven different perspectives.[60] Aune makes a strong, two-part case that: "the *literary genre* or *kind* to which the seven proclamations belong is that of the *royal* or *imperial edict*, while the *mode* is that of the prophetic form of speech called the *paraenetic salvation-judgment oracle*."[61]

(Washington, D.C.: Corpus Books, 1968), 5; Aune, Prophecy in Early Christianity and the Ancient Mediterranean World, 275.

[54] Klaus Berger, "Apostelbrief Und Apostolische Rede: Zum Formular Frühchristlicher Briefe," *Zeitschrift Für Die Neutestamentliche Wissenschaft Und Die Kunde Der Älteren Kirche* 65 (1974): 190–231.

[55] John M Court, *Myth and History in the Book of Revelation* (Louisville, Ky.: Westminster/Knox, 1979), 21.

[56] Ramsay, *Letters: Updated*, 25–35; Berger, "Apostelbrief Und Apostolische Rede: Zum Formular Frühchristlicher Briefe," 212–19; Karrer, *Johannesoffenbarung*, 1:49–66; Adela Yarbro Collins, *The Combat Myth in the Book of Revelation*, HDR 9 (Atlanta, Ga.: Scholars Press, 1976), 5–8.

[57] Court, Myth and History, 21.

[58] Michaels, Interpreting the Book of Revelation, 32.

[59] Prologue 1:1–8; a body 1:9–22:9; and the epilogue 22:6–21.

[60] Richard J. Bauckham, *The Theology of the Book of Revelation*, New Testament Theology (Cambridge, U.K.: Cambridge University Press, 1993), 14; *Climax of Prophecy*, 16.

[61] Aune, "The Form and Function of the Proclamations to the Seven Churches," 183; See also David E. Aune, *Prophecy in Early Christianity and the Ancient Mediterranean World* (Grand Rapids: Eerdmans, 2002), 326; *Revelation 1–5*, 119,

As this author has argued before: "Aune's comparison of the main elements of imperial edicts with the SMR [seven messages of Revelation] shows a number of similarities with the elements of the ANEVT [ancient Near Eastern vassal treaties], including a prominent functional parity between them."[62] The conclusion, "John wrote his messages to the seven churches in Revelation using a prophetic oracle genre in the tradition of OT prophets."[63]

126; *The New Testament in Its Literary Environment*, 242; Beale, *Revelation*, 228.
[62] Graves, *SMRVT*, 55.
[63] Ibid., 123.

2

The Cultural Background of the Seven Messages

U nderstanding the political, religious, and historical context, of the Book of Revelation is essential to unraveling the message of the book. Some have called these cultural allusions, *local references*.

LOCAL REFERENCES IN THE SEVEN MESSAGES

It is believed there are several allusions to *local references* within the message to the seven churches (Rev 2–3), by which allusions to local geographical, historical or cultural features is meant.

PROPONENTS

One of the foremost proponents of the *local reference* approach was Sir William Ramsay (d. 1939) who began as an historical skeptic following the views of the Tübingen School,[1] but after visiting Asia Minor in 1880 testified to the reliability of Luke and John's writings. He wrote of his trips:

> I began with a mind unfavorable to it [the reliability of Acts] . . . but more recently I found myself often brought into contact with the Book of Acts as an authority for the topography, antiquities, and society of Asia Minor. It was gradually borne in upon me that in various details the narrative showed marvelous truth.[2]

His most famous work on Revelation is *The Letters to the Seven Churches* which is updated by Colin Hemer in his *Letters to the Seven Churches of Asia in their Local Setting*. Both scholars document numerous allusions, commonly known as "local references," in the seven messages (2–3) to the churches in Anatolia (modern day Turkey). They, along with other scholars, draw these "allusions" from geography, history and culture, illustrating this by referring to evidence

---

[1] William M. Ramsay, "Exploration of Asia Minor: As Bearing on the Historical Trustworthiness of the New Testament," *JTVI*, 1907, 204–5.

[2] William M. Ramsay, *St. Paul the Traveler and Roman Citizen: Updated*, ed. Mark W. Wilson, Reprinted of 1897 (Grand Rapids, Mich.: Baker, 2001), 8; *The Bearing of Recent Discovery on the Trustworthiness of the New Testament* (London, U.K.: Hodder & Stoughton, 1915), 39–52.

from archaeology, museum artifacts, coins (numismatics), and inscriptions.[3] This only makes sense, if as Ramsay points out, "the letters were written by one who was familiar with the situation, the character, the past history, the possibilities of future development, of those seven cities."[4]

According to de Lassus, the presence of local references "increases the realism and impact of the message of the letters on their recipients."[5] For example, the warning about being lukewarm would have a deeper significance to Laodicea then to another city due to the unique qualities of the Laodicean water system.

Out of the possible fifty "allusions" which Ramsay documents (Hemer accepts approximately thirty), one must not be too dogmatic about all associations,[6] as it is impossible to know what was going through John's mind during the process of inspiration.[7]

Although Thompson disagrees with Hemer's "tenuous connections" and "over controlled"[8] parallels, Scobie has pointed out that of Hemer's proposed thirty-five allusions, only two or three solid cases need demonstration within the first century contemporary culture to make a solid case for the overall principle of the existence of local allusions in the text.[9] Scobie answers those who doubt the exegetical methodology of local allusions when he argues: "If only two or three local references can be convincingly demonstrated this would be sufficient to uphold the theory of local references."[10] The combined weight of two or three, rather than any one example, is all that is needed to set the precedent of the practice of using local reference as a legitimate method.

ARGUMENTS FOR THE USE OF LOCAL REFERENCES

Beale, commenting on Hemer, cautiously lays out the parameters under which exegetes could use local reference when he states:

> Hemer recognizes that some of his suggestions may appear as special pleading in support of an overriding presupposition since the evidence is sometimes circumstantial and fragmentary.

---

[3] Ramsay, *Letters: Updated*; Colin J. Hemer, *The Letters to the Seven Churches of Asia in Their Local Setting*, The Biblical Resource Series (Grand Rapids, Mich.: Eerdmans, 2001); Charles H. Scobie, "Local References in the Letters to the Seven Churches," *NTS* 39, no. 4 (1993): 616–17; Peter Wood, "Local Knowledge of the Letters of the Apocalypse," *ExpTim* 73, no. 9 (1962): 263–64; Stanley E. Porter, "Why the Laodiceans Received Lukewarm Water (Rev 3:15–18)," *TynBul* 38 (1987): 143–49; Philip A. Harland, "Imperial Cults within Local Cultural Life: Associations in Roman Asia," *Ancient History Bulletin* 17, no. 1–2 (2003): 85–107.

[4] Ramsay, Letters: Updated, 28.

[5] Alain-Marie de Lassus, "Le Septénaire Des Lettres de L'apocalypse de Jean: De La Correction Au Témoignage Militant" (Ph.D. diss., University of Strasbourg, 2005), 112.

[6] Edwin M. Yamauchi, "Ramsay's View on Archaeology in Asia Minor Reviewed," in *The New Testament Student and His Field*, ed. John Skilton (Phillipsburg, N.J: P & R Press, 1982), 27–40.

[7] Hemer, Letters to the Seven Churches, 210.

[8] Thompson, Apocalypse and Empire, 203–4.

[9] Scobie, "Local References," 608.

[10] Ibid., 616–17.

Nevertheless, he urges that the ancient readers would have been more familiar with some of these than the modern interpreter. Certainly all would agree, but this does not make his more tenuous arguments any more compelling.[11]

Certainly Beale's point, concerning the perception of the ancient reader, is a valid one. Just because the connection with the first century social-cultural setting appears strange to us today does not mean that it was unusual to the first recipients. As Malina points out, "The goal is to understand the document in terms that would have made sense to a first-century AD audience. Only such a historical approach can be considered fair and adequate to the prophet's concern about 'anyone taking away from the utterances of the scroll of this prophecy'" (21:19).[12]

A BALANCED USE OF LOCAL REFERENCES

It is possible that local conditions and settings around John transported his mind to the OT, helping guide his selection of OT passages. Looking at the clear OT references ("tree of life" 2:7; "crown" 2:10; 3:11; and "book of life" 3:5) within the messages, these local allusions may provide a relationship between the Graeco-Roman and Hebrew-Semitic backgrounds. The identification of Graeco-Roman *local references* is useful for interpreting the Hebraic-Semitic prophetic oracles. Johnson captures something of the balance necessary when he reasons:

> If we begin our inquiry with the assumption that God intended first-century believers to get the message of Revelation,[13] we read its visions against the backdrop of OT imagery rather than forcing them into the template of twenty-first-century technologies or politics. This principle also encourages us to understand Revelation in the context of the cultural and intellectual forces that were affecting the churches of first-century Asia: religious institutions, political structures, military conflicts, natural disasters, and even, perhaps, the symbolic vocabulary of Jewish apocalyptic literature or pagan myth. God is so much the sovereign of history that he can use every dimension of his people's experience to communicate his word.[14]

Doubtless these details would have been clearer to the local audience. Not only are many of these references prominent historical details, but assist the original readers in remembering the spiritual lessons.[15]

Certainly, each element of the text must be examined on its own merits to determine if the evidence is indeed circumstantial and fragmentary or if it makes sense in a first-century context.

---

[11] Gregory K. Beale, "Review of Colin J. Hemer, The Letters to the Seven Churches of Asia in Their Local Setting," *Trinity Journal* 7, no. 2 (1986): 110.

[12] Bruce J. Malina, On the Genre and Message of Revelation: Star Visions and Sky Journeys (Peabody, Mass.: Hendrickson, 1995), 10.

[13] Steven J. Friesen, "Revelation, Realia, and Religion: Archaeology in the Interpretations of the Apocalypse," *HTR* 88, no. 3 (1995): 297; Ramsay, *Letters: Updated*, xiii, 62–67, 289, 362; Osborne, *Revelation*, 110; Roland H. Worth, Jr., *The Seven Cities of the Apocalypse and Greco-Asian Culture* (New York, N.Y.: Paulist, 2002), 67; Robin Scroggs, "The Sociological Interpretation of the New Testament: The Present State of Research," *NTS*, Sociological Interpretation of the NT, 26, no. 2 (1980): 179.

[14] Dennis E. Johnson, *Triumph of the Lamb: A Commentary on Revelation* (Phillipsburg, N.J.: P&R, 2001), 20–21.

[15] David L. Barr, "The Apocalypse of John as Oral Enactment," *Interpretation* 40, no. 3 (1986): 245–46 n. 9; Hemer, *Letters to the Seven Churches*, 210; Worth, Jr., *Greco-Asian Culture*, 67.

But with the combined weight of the numerous allusions, there is a solid body of evidence that cumulatively tips the scales in favor of the use of local references as a hermeneutical tool.[16]

THE CULTURAL ISSUES IN THE SEVEN MESSAGES

In this regard a variety of cultural issues are addressed in John's messages to each church. They may be categorized into the external and internal problems.

EXTERNAL PROBLEMS

Several problems affected the churches from their external cultural surroundings.

JEWISH PERSECUTION

Firstly, the Christians in Asia Minor were experiencing persecution from the side of the Jews. The Jews were granted an exemption from worshiping the emperor because of their distinctive religion, and for a period in the first cent. the Christians were permitted to participate in this exemption.[17] But the Jews became jealous and pointed out that the Christians were not Jews and worshiped a Messiah the Jews did not recognise, and began turning in the Christians to the Roman authorities. This led to pockets of persecution by the Romans.

The Roman authorities did not care who their citizens worshiped as long as they obeyed the Roman edicts and worshiped the imperial cult as well (Pliny *Ep*. 10.96). The general polytheistic populace had no problem in worshiping their own gods and offering sacrifices to Roma, however the Christians could not do this as they were exclusive in their worship, so they were punished for disobeying the Roman law (Pliny *Ep*. 10.96). The Jews were often instrumental in getting the Christians in trouble, as is evident from the martyrdom of two bishops of Smyrna: Polycarp (*Mart. Pol.* 1.13; 12.2; *FrgPol.* 64.23; see Figs. 50, 51) and Pionius (AD 250; *Mart. Pionii* 2.1; 3.6; 4.2, 8; 13.1; 14.1).[18] Two churches, Smyrna and Philadelphia, speak of the Jewish elements in their cities as the "synagogue of Satan" (2:9; 3:9). The synagogue in Smyrna is also mentioned in the second cent. in the account of the martyrdom of Pionius (*Mart. Pionii* 13.1).

While some scholars doubt Jewish involvement,[19] others point out that the Jews gathered wood on the Sabbath and ventured into the stadium to watch Polycarp burn (see Fig. 51),

---

[16] See Appendix A-*The Graeco-Roman Literary Context for the Seven Messages of Revelation* for the analysis of unlikely, possible and likely local references.

[17] James S. Jeffers, The Greco-Roman World of the New Testament Era: Exploring the Background of Early Christianity (Downers Grove, Ill.: InterVarsity, 1999), 102.

[18] Graves, *SMRVT*, 245–46.

[19] Judith M. Lieu, "Accusations of Jewish Persecution in Early Christian Sources, with Particular Reference to Justin Martyr and the Martyrdom of Polycarp," in *Tolerance and Intolerance in Early Judaism and Christianity*, ed. Graham N. Stanton and Gedaliahu A. G Stroumsa (Cambridge, U.K.: Cambridge University Press, 1998), 285–6; Hebert Musurillo, ed., *The Acts of the Christian Martyrs*, trans. Hebert Musurillo (Oxford, U.K.: Clarendon, 1972), 11 n. 16.

arguing for the viability of Jewish hostility.[20] While Aune, with others, questions the historical reliability of the account,[21] Lightfoot affirms that: "the story is told with a good deal of restraint, and may be judged to provide a generally reliable, and certainly very moving, account of Polycarp's martyrdom."[22]

TRADE GUILDS

Secondly, there were trade guilds that focused on a particular trade or guild, like tanners, dyers (Thyatira; Acts 19:10), shoemakers, clothiers, bakers, potters, slave traders, and copper smiths, but which also participated in various religious ceremonies.[23] Although membership was voluntary and not directly connected to business activities, few could perform business activities without membership. Members typically participated in cultic rituals, which included offering imperial cult sacrifices to the guild god when they attended the guild meetings (see Figs. 4, 5).[24] While the Roman authorities were apathetic over religious practices and did not normally apply economic sanctions against their citizens,[25] trade guilds were different. Refusal to participate in their respective trade guild may have led to poverty and financial ruin (Rev 2:9).[26]

3. The iconic statue of Romulus and Remus, the founders of Rome, being suckled by a wolf. While traditional scholarship holds that the figure of the wolf is Etruscan (fifth cent. BC), with the figures of Romulus and Remus being added later

---

[20] E. J. Banks, "Smyrna," ed. Geoffrey W. Bromiley, *ISBE* (Grand Rapids, Mich.: Eerdmans, 1995), 4:8183; William H. C. Frend, "The Persecutions: Some Links between Judaism and the Early Church," *JEH* 9 (1958): 157; Alan James Beagley, *The "Sitz Im Leben" of the Apocalypse With Particular Reference to the Role of the Church's Enemies* (Berlin: De Gruyter, 1987), 179– 80; Beale, *Rev*, 25 nn. 127, 31 15.

[21] Aune, with others, believes that this entire account is "historically tendentious as well as strikingly anti-Jewish, consciously formulated in an attempt to replicate the Gospel narratives of the passion of Jesus." Aune, *Rev 1–5*, 162; Musurillo, *Acts of the Christian Martyrs*, xiv; Boudewijn Dehandschütter, "The Martyrium Polycarpi: A Century of Research," ed. Wolfgang Haase and Hildegard Temporini, *Aufstieg Und Niedergang Der Römischen Welt: Geschichte Und Kultur Roms Im Spiegel Der Neueren Forschung* 27, no. 2 (1993): 485–522.

[22] Joseph B. Lightfoot, *The Apostolic Fathers: Greek Texts and English Translations*, ed. Michael W. Holmes, trans. J. R. Harmer, 2nd ed. (Grand Rapids, Mich.: Baker Academic, 1989), 133.

[23] David Magie, *Roman Rule in Asia Minor to the End of the Third Century After Christ*, ed. T. James Luce, Roman History (New York, N.Y.: Arno, 1975), 1:48; 2:812 n. 78; A. H. M. Jones, *The Greek City: From Alexander to Justinian* (Oxford, U.K.: Clarendon, 1940), 83; Colin J. Hemer, "Unto the Angels of the Churches," *Buried History* 11 (1975): 110.

[24] David E. Aune, *Revelation 6–16*, WBC 52B (Dallas, Tex.: Word Books, 1998), 768.

[25] George B. Caird, *The Revelation of St. John the Divine*, HNTC (Peabody, Mass.: Hendrickson, 1987), 173.

[26] Aune, *Rev 1–5*, 161; Charles, *Revelation*, 1:56; Caird, *Revelation*, 35; Hemer, *Letters to the Seven Churches*, 68;

IMPERIAL CULT

Thirdly, the imperial cult created a problem for the early Christians.[27] This problem centerd on the worship of the Roman emperor and Roma, the spirit of Rome ("sharp, double-edged sword"; "throne of Satan" Rev 2:13). This practice goes back to the Roman Senate deifying Julius Caesar upon his death. This flourished in the East of the Empire, where the worship of a hero or leader was encouraged, while initially in the West it was discouraged by the emperors. However, the practice of paying homage to an Emperor as god soon found widespread favour with the emperors as a means of unifying the empire and demonstrating loyalty to Rome. Those who sacrificed to the emperor received a certificate (Lat. *libellus*) to confirm their practice (see *Quotes from Antiquity*). Christians of course would not sacrifice to the Roman god Roma (see Fig. 173) and thus were persecuted for their disobedience to Rome.

4. Emperor Marcus Aurelius (AD 161–180) and members of the Imperial family offer sacrifice in gratitude for success against Germanic tribes. In the backgrounds stands the Temple of Jupiter on the Capitolium (this is the only extant portrayal of this Roman temple). Bas-relief from the Arch of Marcus Aurelius, Rome.

Osborne, *Revelation*, 151–52.

[27] Allen Brent, The Imperial Cult and the Development of Church Order: Concepts and Images of Authority in Paganism and Early Christianity Before the Age of Cyprian (Leiden: Brill, 1999), 178–90.

5. A round altar (Lat. *ara*) used in the imperial cult from the second or third cent. AD. Altars were usually decorated with the works of the most notable artists of the day. Most altars were erected outside in the open air and in sacred groves.

The imperial cult[28] was well-established in Asia minor and represented in all seven cities of Revelation, each with an imperial temple. Thompson reports that: "Five of the seven cities had imperial altars (all but Philadelphia and Laodicea), six had imperial temples (all but Thyatira),[29] and five had imperial priests (all but Philadelphia and Laodicea)."[30] Evidence of it exists in Smyrna (c. 23–26 AD; Tacitus *Ann.* 4.15), Pergamum (by the provincial council κοινόν, *koinon*)[31] of Asia in 29, BC), in Ephesus (where it dedicated the temple of *Sebastoi* in 89–90 AD), Thyatira (*I.Thyat.* 902; 980; *I.Sard.* 8.99); including a temple (*I.Thyat. 1098*), Philadelphia (*I.Phil.* 1428, 1434, 1472; 1484), and Laodicea[32]. Temples dedicated to the worship of Rome were common in the Roman Empire, but the temple of the *Sebastoi* (Gr. "venerable one") was more particular in that they only venerated the family of the emperor (the family of Vespasian, Titus and Domitian; see Fig. 7).[33] Nicolas of Damascus was Augustus' (63 BC–AD 14) chief orator and he had this to say about the emperors' deification:

Because mankind addresses him thus [as *Sebastos*] in accordance with their estimation of his honour, they revere him with temples and sacrifices over islands and continents, organized in cities and provinces, matching the greatness of his virtue and repaying his benefactions towards them.[34]

Price documents priests of Augustus in 34 Asia Minor cities, priests of Tiberius in 11 cities, 35 cities using the title temple warden (νεωκόρος, *neōkoros*, Acts 19:35), and at least 80 cities with

---

[28]For a survey of research on the imperial cult and Revelation see Naylor's thorough article. Michael Naylor, "The Roman Imperial Cult and Revelation," *CBR* 8, no. 2 (2010): 207–39; Thompson, *Apocalypse and Empire*, 158–64.

[29] There was a temple dedicated by Xenon in Thyatira (*I.Thyat.* 1098).

[30] Thompson, Apocalypse and Empire, 159.

[31] Thompson, *Apocalypse and Empire*, 160.

[32] *BMC Phrygia* 307.181; 185; 308.187–188; 314.217, 221; 315.225; 316.226–227; *I.Laod.* 45.

[33] Joyce Reynolds, "New Evidence for the Imperial Cult in Julio-Claudian Aphrodisias," *ZPE* 43 (1981): 317–27; Geraldine Thommen, "The Sebasteion at Aphrodisias: An Imperial Cult to Honor Augustus and the Julio-Claudian Emperors," *Chronika* 2 (2012): 82–91.

[34] S. R. F. Price, *Rituals and Power: The Roman Imperial Cult in Asia Minor*, Reprint (Cambridge, U.K.: Cambridge University Press, 1985), 1; Felix Jacoby, ed., *Die Fragmente Der Griechischen Historiker*, trans. Felix Jacoby, Part 2 Zeitgeschichte: A: Universalgeschichte Und Hellenika (Leiden: Brill Academic, 2004), 90 F125.

6. Portrait of a priest who served in the temple of the imperial cult. This statue comes from Ephesus and dates from the second cent. AD. The priesthood of the emperor cult was usually held by the local aristocracy, providing them with political status and a means of social advancement.

7. The Sebasteion (σεβαστός, *Sebastós* = Lat. *Augustus*, AD 5) or Augusteum, in Aphrodisias (in modern Turkey) was jointly dedicated, according to a first cent. inscription on its propylon, "to Aphrodite, the Divine Sebastoi [Augusti] and the municipalities" (Ἀφροδίτηι, θεοῖς Σεβαστοῖς, τῶι δήμωι; Joyce Maire Reynolds, "Further Information on the Imperial Cult at Aphrodisias," *Studii Clasice* 24 (1986): 111). The temple was used by the imperial cult to honor Augustus.

priests servicing *Sebastoi* (see Fig. 7)[35] The wealthy citizens of the city would "bid for the honor of becoming priests in the imperial cult" (Suetonius *Cal.* 22.3).[36] Friesen points out that:

> It has long been recognized that the worship of the emperors in some way constituted an important aspect of the relationships between the emperor and the cities of the Roman province of Asia. The importance of imperial cults in Asia is reflected in the city titles that permeate the epigraphic record. These titles tend to focus on the word νεωκόρος *(neōkoros)*, which is often translated into English as 'temple warden,' because the term began as the titles for an official who had special responsibilities related to the precincts of a deity. During the Roman imperial period, however, *'neōkoros'* took on a specialized meaning. It became the technical term for a city where a provincial temple of the emperors was located. Thus, in the secondary literature the words *'neōkoros'* and *'neōkorate'* have become synonymous with provincial imperial cults.[37]

The book of Acts mentions several technical terms related to the imperial cult in Ephesus and the cult of Artemis: "And when the town clerk [γραμματεύς, *grammateus*, Thucydides *Hist.* 7.10] had quieted the crowd, he said, "Men of Ephesus, who is there who does not know that

---

[35] Price, *Rituals and Power*, 58, 66–67.

[36] Craig S. Keener, *Acts: An Exegetical Commentary: 15:1–23:35*, vol. 3 (Grand Rapids, Mich.: Baker Academic, 2014), 3:2871.

[37] Steven J. Friesen, "The Cult of the Roman Emperors in Ephesos: Temple Wardens, City Titles, and the Interpretation of the Revelation of John," in *Ephesos Metropolis of Asia: An Interdisciplinary Approach to Its Archaeology, Religion, and Culture*, ed. Helmut Koester, HTR 41 (Valley Forge, PA: Trinity, 1995), 229.

8. Bronze sestertius coin (AD 65) of Nero (AD 54–68). Obv.: Laureate head of Nero. *NERO CLAVD CAESAR AVG GER P M TR P IMP P P*. Obv.: The goddess Roma helmeted in military dress and seated left on a cuirass with her foot on a helmet, holding Victory in her right hand while resting her left hand on a dagger (Lat. *parazonium*), surrounded by weaponry on the ground behind.

the city of the Ephesians is temple keeper [νεωκόρος, *neōkoros*] of the great Artemis, and of the sacred stone that fell from the sky?" (Acts 19:35–38).

LIBELLUS

The *libelli* (pl. certificates of sacrifice)[38] were documents instituted in AD 249 by Emperor Decius (AD 249–251) to help unify the Roman Empire and return it to its old traditions.[39] Origen noted that the political problems being experienced in his day were due to the increased number of Christians (*Cels*. 3.15; see also Cyprian *Ep*. 55.9).[40] The Roman authorities required a *libelli* from Roman citizens to verify that they had offered a pagan sacrifice to the ancestral gods to demonstrate their allegiance to Rome.[41] As Potter points out, "failure to sacrifice could result in exile, the confiscation of property, prison, or death."[42] Nobbs describes the creation and relevance of the *libellus*. Potter explains that it was to:

> show the solidarity of all Romans behind their ancestral gods and sacrifices, every household was obliged to appear on a fixed day, veiled and crowned, and submit a *libellus* (certificate) declaring

---

[38] However, as Leadbetter points out, technically: "the libellus is not a certificate of sacrifice, meaning a document issued by the state upon the completion of a prescribed act, but rather a request from the sacrificer asking for confirmation of an act publicly performed." W. L. Leadbetter, "Libellus of the Decian Persecution," in *NewDocs* 2:181.

[39] J. B. Rives, "The Decree of Decius and the Religion of Empire," *JRS* 89 (1999): 135–54.

[40] G. E. M. de Ste. Croix, "Aspects of the 'Great' Persecution," *HTR* 47, no. 2 (1954): 73–113; "Why Were the Early Christians Persecuted?," *Past and Present* 26 (1963): 1–38; "Christianity's Encounter with the Roman Imperial Government," in *The Crucible of Christianity: Judaism, Hellenism and The Historical Background to the Christian Faith*, ed. Arnold Toynbee (New York, N.Y.: Thames & Hudson, 1969), 345–46.

[41] Graeme Wilber Clarke, "The Persecution of Decius," in *The Letters of St. Cyprian*, ed. Graeme Wilber Clarke, vol. 1, Ancient Christian Writers 43 (New York, N.Y.: Newman, 1984), 103–14; Paul Keresztes, "The Decian Libelli and Contemporary Literature," *Latomus* 34, no. 3 (1975): 761–81; John R. Knipfing, "The Libelli of the Decian Persecution," *HTR* 16, no. 4 (1923): 345–90; W. L. Leadbetter, "Libellus of the Decian Persecution," in *NewDocs*, ed. G. H. R. Horsley, vol. 2 (Liverpool, U.K.: Liverpool University Press, 1982), 180–84; Paul McKechnie, "Roman Law and the Laws of the Medes and Persians: Decius' and Valerian's Persecutions of Christianity," in *Thinking Like a Lawyer: Essays on Legal History and General History for John Crook on His Eightieth Birthday*, ed. J. A. Crook and Paul McKechnie, Mnemosyne, Bibliotheca Classica Batava Supplementum 231 (Leiden: Brill Academic, 2002), 253–69; Rives, "Decree of Decius," 135–54.

[42] David S. Potter, "Persecution of the Early Church," ed. David Noel Freedman et al., *ABD* (New York, N.Y.: Doubleday, 1996), 233.

participation in the sacrifice. The requirement to produce documentary witness to the act of sacrifice was novel. The obligation to retain a personal copy indicated that this proof of religious piety had ongoing significance and implications for the civil identity of those concerned.[43]

Four examples of *libelli* have been identified in the papyrus documents discovered at Oxyrhynchus, Egypt (P.Oxy. 4.658;[44] 12.1464;[45] 41.2990;[46] 58.3929[47] [see Fig. 9].[48] *Libelli* have also been discovered outside of Egypt, including at Carthage, Smyrna, Rome, and Spain.[49] A comparison of forty-six extant *libelli* texts indicates that there was a standard format used for all *libelli*.[50]

A Greek *libellus* (P.Oxy. 58.3929; see Fig. 9) from the Decian persecution (AD 250, June 25–July 24) translates into English as:

> [first hand] To the commissioners of sacrifices of the village of Thosbis, from Aurelius Amois styled as the son of his mother Taamois from the village of Thosbis. Always have I continued to sacrifice and pour libations to the gods, and since now too in your presence in accordance with the orders I sacrificed and poured a libation and tasted the sacrificial meats together with my mother Taamois and my sister Taharpaesis, I request that (you) subscribe to this fact for me. Year 1 of imperator Caesar Gaius Messius Quintus Traianus Decius, Pius Felix Augustus, Epeiph ... [second hand] 1, Aurelius

9. This papyrus document, found in Oxyrhynchus in Egypt, is a certificate of sacrifice (*libellus*) from the Decian persecution (AD 250). Papyrology Room, Ashmolean Museum, Oxford (P.Oxy. 58.3929).

---

[43] Alanna M. Nobbs, "Christians in a Pluralistic Society: Papyrus Evidence from the Roman Empire," *International Journal of New Perspectives in Christianity* 1, no. 1.7 (2009): 52.

[44] AD 250. Presently housed in the Beinecke Library, Yale University, New Haven, Conneticut.

[45] AD 250, June 27. Presently housed in the Department of Manuscripts, British Museum, London.

[46] AD third century. Presently housed in the Papyrology Rooms, Sackler Library, Oxford.

[47] AD 250, June 25–July 24. Presently housed in the Papyrology Room, Ashmolean Museum, Oxford.

[48] Olivier Joram Hekster and Nicholas Zair, *Rome and Its Empire: Ad 193–284* (Edinburgh, U.K.: Edinburgh University Press, 2008), 130; Knipfing, "The Libelli of the Decian Persecution," 386–87.

[49] Knipfing, "The Libelli of the Decian Persecution," 352, 354.

[50] AnneMarie Luijendijk, *Greetings in the Lord: Early Christians and the Oxyrhynchus Papyri* (Cambridge, Mass.: Harvard University Press, 2009), 167.

Amois, have delivered [the petition]. 1, Aurelius ... ion, wrote on his behalf [On the back, along the fibers first hand?] Registration of Amoitas. mother Taarnois [Luijendijk].[51]

During the Valerian persecution, several official documents (AD 259–260; P.Oxy. 43.3119; 42.3035) mention the arrest of Christians, one of which is the oldest mention of the word "Christian" in a papyrus document.[52]

While not intentionally directed at Christians, having a *libellus* became proof that the person in possession was not a Christian, and thus exempted them from persecution. Cyprian, the bishop of Carthage in North Africa, addressed the question at length in his *Concerning the Lapsed* (*Laps*. 15–21), of what to do with Christians who either sacrificed (Lat. *sacrificati*) or bought certificates (Lat. *libellatici*). Should they be readmitted into the church? This led to a controversy, which Cyprian sought to address, but which was finally settled at the Council of Carthage (AD 251), where it was determined that repentant *libellatici* should have their church membership restored, but those who actually sacrificed must do penance for the rest of their lives. Several bishops died as a result of the Decian persecution, including Fabian, bishop of Rome (AD 250), the bishop of Alexandria, and the bishop of Jerusalem.

While these documents date later than the NT and the book of Revelation, they illustrate the result of the growing issues that were being created by the Christians in first cent. Rome.

DEIFICATION OF EMPERORS

Evidence of the deification of emperors or the belief that emperors were transformed into gods (ἀποθέωσις, *apotheōsis*) is clearly supported by ancient texts and archaeology.

Deification of Domitian

Domitian (Lat. *Titus Flavius Caesar Domitianus Augustus* AD 81–96), the son of Vespasian, succeeded his brother Titus in AD 81 and gradually acquired despotic powers, demanding that public worship should be given to him as Lord and God (Lat. *dominus et Deus*). Suetonius states that Domitian requested his correspondence sent out in the name of "Our Lord and God" (Lat. *dominus et dues noster*) and that "the custom arose of henceforth addressing him in no other way even in writing or in

10. *Apotheōsis* of Antoninus Pius and Faustina. The basis of the Campo Marzio Colonna Antonina, relief on the front face of the pedestal of the Antoninus Pius' column, three-quarter view AD 161.

---

[51] Ibid., 165–66.
[52] J. E. G. Whitehorne, "P. Oxy. XLIII 3119: A Document of Valerian's Persecution?," *ZPE* 24, no. 1 (1977): 187–96; Lincoln H. Blumell, *Lettered Christians: Christians, Letters, and Late Antique Oxyrhynchus*, NTTS 39 (Leiden: Brill Academic, 2012), 252 n.61.

conversation" (Suetonius *Dom.* 13.2 [Rolfe], see also Cassius *Hist. Rom.* 67.4.7; 67.13.4).[53]

Deification of Antoninus Pius

A statue of Antoninus Pius (ca. AD 161), now displayed in the Vatican Museum (see Fig. 10) depicts the ἀποθέωσις (*apotheōsis*, "transformed into a god") of Antoninus Pius and his wife Faustina, as they are carried to heaven by the genius "eternity," a winged spirit that protected nature. The female figure saluting them (right side) personifies Rome, holding a shield depicting the legendary founders of Rome—Romulus and Remus—being suckled by a wolf (see also Fig. 3). The nude figure (left side) is believed to be the personification of the Roman Field of Mars (Lat. *Campus Martius*), where imperial funerals took place.[54]

Pliny the Younger

11. Marble Statue of Trajan (Imperator Marcus Ulpius Trajanus, AD 98–117) in armor.

The first recorded mention of Christians in the Roman imperial record is in a letter written to Emperor Trajan (ca. AD 111; see Fig. 11) by Pliny the Younger, the governor of Bithynia, a province north of the seven churches of Revelation. In his letter, Pliny asks Trajan for "advice on how to handle cases where citizens have pressed charges against individuals suspected of being Christians" (Pliny *Ep.* 10.96–97, see *Quotes from Antiquity*).[55] It is also the first time that Christianity is officially recognized as a separate religion from Judaism and begins the persecution of Christians in the second and third centuries.

Pliny is presented with a number of Christians who have had charges laid against them, and is unsure whether he should prosecute them or not. It appears that this is a new dilemma for them both. He decided, in spite of the fact that they appeared harmless to him, to execute them if they did not recant their faith. Uncertain of the legality of his actions, he sought the advice of the emperor.[56] See *Quotes from Antiquity*.

---

[53] Contra, see Thompson, *Revelation*, 105.

[54] Lise Vogel, *The Column of Antoninus Pius* (Cambridge, Mass.: Harvard University Press, 1973), 32–55.

[55] J. Nelson Kraybill, Apocalypse and Allegiance: Worship, Politics, and Devotion in the Book of Revelation (Grand Rapids, Mich.: Brazos Press, 2010), 75.

[56] Downing, "Pliny's Prosecutions of Christians."

> **Quotes from Antiquity**
>
> Trajan replied:
>
> You have followed the right course of action, my dear Secundus [i.e., Pliny], in your examination of the cases of those who have been charged with being Christians. For it is impossible to lay down a general rule in something like a fixed formula. They [the Christians] must not be hunted out; if they are brought before you and convicted, they must be punished, excepting, however, anyone who denies that he is a Christian and makes this fact clear, by offering prayers to our gods, he is to be pardoned as a result of his repentance, however suspect his past conduct may be. But pamphlets (*libelli*) circulated anonymously ought to have no part in any accusation. For they are the worst sort of precedent (*exemplum*) and are not in keeping with the spirit of our age. (Pliny *Ep.* 10.97 [Radice])

What is clear from this exchange of letters is that although the growth of Christianity had spread throughout the cities and villages of Asia Minor, even affecting the sale of sacrifices for the temple and number of worshipers of the imperial cult, Trajan ordered that no official persecution of Christians be carried out by Pliny.

INTERNAL PROBLEMS

Several internal issues were addressed in the seven messages. Various heresies (Nicolaitans, 2:6, 15) identified with OT figures (Balaam, 2:14; Jezebel, 2:20) had arisen in several churches. Closely connected with their teaching was the practice of eating food sacrificed to idols and sexual immorality (2:14; 20). John recorded these events by describing the Ephesian church as having forsaken their first love (2:4), while the Laodicean church was lukewarm (3:16). What is clear is that there are more external tensions described in the messages than internal problems within the local congregations.

3

The Covenantal Framework of the Seven Messages

Over[1] the past eighty-years scholars have documented multiple similarities between *ancient Near Eastern vassal treaties* (ANEVT) and various other documents including the biblical testaments,[2] Homer's *Iliad,* the *Odyssey,* and the *Hippocratic Oath*.[3]

The research in ANEVT structure has its origins in Mendenhall and Bickerman, who detected the presence of the ANEVT structure in the OT covenant relationship with Israel.[4] Based on research by Korošec,[5] Mendenhall identified six elements in the suzerainty treaty[6]

---

[1] This section is reproduced with minor corrections, with permission of Gorgias Press, from Graves, *SMRVT,* 125–91.

[2] This is only representative of a larger body of material. George E. Mendenhall, "Covenant Forms in Israelite Tradition," *BA* 17 (1954): 50–76; *Law and Covenant in Israel and the Ancient Near East* (Pittsburgh: Biblical Colloquium, 1955), 53–70; "Covenant," ed. G. A. Buttrick and Keith R. Crim, *IDB* (Nashville, Tenn.: Abingdon, 1962), 714; Donald J. Wiseman, "The Vassal-Treaties of Esarhaddon," *Iraq* 20 (1958): 3; F. Charles Fensham, "Maledictions and Benedictions in Ancient Near Eastern Vassal–Treaties and the Old Testament," *ZAW* 74 (1962): 1–9; "Clauses of Protection in Hittite Vassal-Treaties and the Old Testament," *VT* 13 (1963): 133–43; John A. Thompson, *The Ancient Near Eastern Treaties and the Old Testament* (Wheaton, Ill.: Tyndale, 1964), 1–39; Delbert R. Hillers, *Treaty-Curses and the Old Testament Prophets,* Biblica et Orientalia 16 (Rome: Pontifical Biblical Institute, 1964), 6; Kenneth A. Kitchen, *Ancient Orient and Old Testament* (Wheaton, Ill.: Tyndale, 1966), 91–99; *On the Reliability of the Old Testament* (Grand Rapids, Mich.: Eerdmans, 2003), 283–94; Moshe Weinfeld, *Deuteronomy and the Deuteronomic School* (Oxford, U.K.: Clarendon, 1983), 283–94; "Covenant Terminology in the Ancient Near East and Its Influence on the West," *JAOS* 93, no. 2 (1973): 190–99; "Ancient Near Eastern Patterns in Prophetic Literature," *VT* 27 (1977): 175–95; Dennis J McCarthy, *Treaty and Covenant: A Study in the Ancient Oriental Documents and in the Old Testament,* AnBib 21 (Rome: Biblical Institute, 1981), 51–81, 152–53; Gary N. Knoppers, "Ancient Near Eastern Royal Grants and the Davidic Covenant: A Parallel?," *JAOS* 116, no. 4 (1996): 670 n. 2.

[3] Peter Karavites, *Promise-Giving and Treaty-Making Homer and the Near East* (Leiden: Brill, 1992), 82–107; John Pairman Brown, *Ancient Israel and Ancient Greece Religion, Politics, and Culture* (Minneapolis, Minn.: Augsburg Fortress, 2003), 254; Gerald K. Gresseth, "The 'Gilgamesh Epic and Homer," *CJ* 70 (1975): 1–18; David E. Graves, "Influence of the Ancient Near Eastern Vassal Treaties on the Hippocratic Oath," *NEASB* 57 (2012): 27–45; *SMRVT,* 71–72.

[4] Mendenhall, "Covenant Forms," 50–76; *Law and Covenant*; Elias Bickerman, "Couper Une Alliance," *Archives D'histoire Du Droit Oriental* 5 (1951 1950): 133–56; Fensham, "Maledictions and Benedictions," 1–9; "Clauses of Protection," 133–43; Thompson, *ANE Treaties,* 1–39; Hillers, *Treaty-Curses,* 6; McCarthy, *Treaty and Covenant,* 51–81; Knoppers, "Ancient Near Eastern Royal Grants and the Davidic Covenant: A Parallel?," 670 n.2.

[5] E. Von Schuler questions Korošec's uniform structure of the Hittite treaties. Viktor Korošec, *Hethitische*

which form a *functional* structure. These elements are the *preamble*,[7] *historical prologue*,[8] *stipulations*,[9] *blessing and cursing*,[10] *witness*,[11] and *deposit/public reading*.[12] The components fluctuate in number and order throughout the various ANEVTs (Hittite, Assyrian, Aramean, etc.); however, according to

---

Staatsverträge: Ein Beitrag Zu Ihrer Juristischen Wertung (Leipzig: Weicher, 1931), 12–14; E. Von Schuler, "Sonderformen Hethitischer Staatsverträge," *Jahrbuch Für Kleinasiatische Forschung* 2 (1965): 224–64; Gary M. Beckman, "Hittite Treaties and the Development of Cuneiform Treaty Tradition," in *Beihefte Zur Zeitschrift Für Die Alttestamentliche Wissenschaft Die Deuteronomistischen Geschichtswerke: Redaktions– Und Religionsgeschichtliche Perspektiven Zur 'Deuteronomismus'–Diskussion in Tora Und Vorderen Propheten*, ed. Marku Witte et al., BZAW 365 (Berlin: de Gruyter, 2006), 184 n.25. Gary M. Beckman believes that the narrow set of texts available for his research primarily from the reign of king Muršili II misled Korošec.

[6] While Mendenhall identifies four different types of secular covenants as suzerainty, parity, patron, and promissory, he argues that the biblical model fits best with the suzerainty treaties. Mendenhall, "Covenant," 1:716–23.

[7] Ibid.; John H Walton, *Ancient Israelite Literature in Its Cultural Context: A Survey of Parallels between Biblical and Ancient Near Eastern Texts*, 2nd ed., Library of Biblical Interpretation (Grand Rapids, Mich.: Zondervan, 1990), 101; Julien Harvey, "Le 'RIB-Pattern', Réquisitoire Prophétique Sur La Rupture de L'alliance," *Biblica* 43, no. 2 (1962): 186; McCarthy, *Treaty and Covenant*, 51, 67; James Du Preez, "Ancient Near Eastern Vassal Treaties and the Book of Revelation: Possible Links," *RSA* 2, no. 2 (1981): 33–34. McCarthy and James Du Preez, following Korošec, used the term *Titulary*, a replacement of the Germanism *titulature*.

[8] John Bright used the term *historical recital*, while McCarthy simply used *the history* or *historical narrative* and Pritchard used the title *Historical Introduction*. John Bright, *Covenant and Promise: The Prophetic Understanding of the Future in Pre-Exilic Israel* (Philadelphia, Pa.: Westminster/Knox, 1976), 37; McCarthy, *Treaty and Covenant*, 51, 53; James Bennett Pritchard, *Ancient Near Eastern Texts Relating to the Old Testament with Supplement*, 3rd ed. (Princeton, N.J.: Princeton University Press, 1969), 203.

[9] McCarthy used the term *stipulations*, but prefers *clause* or *terms* as he believed they are better suited to the idea of the "prescriptions of treaties." Beckman primarily used the term *provisions*. but also made use of *stipulations*. McCarthy, *Treaty and Covenant*, 51 n.3; Gary M Beckman, *Hittite Diplomatic Texts*, ed. Harry A Hoffner, 2nd ed., SBLWAW 7 (Atlanta, Ga.: Scholars Press, 1999), 3.

[10] Harvey used the French terms *Malédictions et bénédictions*. These terms are used interchangeably with *cursing and blessing* by many writers. Muse preferred the German term *Weckruf*, literally *wake up, watch or hear* for the curse. Schüssler Fiorenza translated *Weckruf* as "exhortation to watch" and as *Siegerspruch* for *benediction* and translated it as a "conqueror's saying." Mazzaferri used the German term *Weckformel* literally *waking formula* for the curse. Harvey, "RIB-Pattern," 186; Robert L. Muse, "Revelation 2–3: A Critical Analysis of Seven Prophetic Messages," *JETS* 29, no. 2 (1986): 160; Elisabeth Schüssler Fiorenza, *Revelation: Vision of a Just World*, ed. Gerhard A. Krodel, PC (Minneapolis, Minn.: Fortress, 1991), 47; Mazzaferri, *Genre of Revelation*, 121.

[11] Harvey uses the French phrase *Invocation des dieux*, while Meredith G. Kline uses *Invocation of Witnesses*. Harvey, "RIB-Pattern," 186; Meredith G. Kline, *Treaty of the Great King: The Covenant Structure of Deuteronomy: Studies and Commentary* (Grand Rapids, Mich.: Eerdmans, 1963), 15.

[12] The *deposit* and *public reading* portion of the treaties are perpetuity instructions made by the vassal and are not part of the treaties literary structure. Harvey uses the French term *Détails techniques* while, Beckman prefers the term *depositions*. Du Preez and McCarthy prefer the term *Document Clause*, as they combine the element of public reading with preservation. Mendenhall, "Covenant Forms," 59–60; Korošec, *Hethitische Staatsverträge*, 12–14; Beckman, "Hittite Treaties," 3; Harvey, "RIB-Pattern," 186; Du Preez, "Ancient Near Eastern Vassal Treaties and the Book of Revelation: Possible Links," 38; McCarthy, *Treaty and Covenant*, 52–63; Graves, *SMRVT*, 130.

López, "scholars have come to a consensus that the six elements"[13] form a single, basic, uniform treaty formulary used throughout the ANE as a "*typical pattern.*"[14]

Tigay, while pointing out the dangers of "parallelomania,"[15] provides criteria for identifying parallels between ANE documents and the scriptures. He indicates that, "In the case of the Hebrew scriptures and the rest of the ancient Near East, frequent contacts between pre-Israelite Palestine and the Israelites, on the one hand, and Egypt, Mesopotamia, and Syro-Palestinian states on the other hand, provide sufficient channels to make borrowing in principle likely" (see Fig. 12)[16]

12. The Treaty of Kadesh (1274 BC), discovered at Boğazköy, Turkey. Peace treaty made after the Battle of Kadesh between Ancient Egyptians, under Rameses II and the Hittites, under Muwatalli II (see Hattusilis II who finalized the treaty).

The primary criteria for borrowing are set out by Albright in a shared complexity "forming a pattern."[17] This pattern of six elements identified as the ANEVT structure will form the outline for the following exegetical commentary on each of the messages to the seven churches.

Kline in passing comes close to identifying the ANEVT structure within the SMR when describing the analogy in Revelation. He states:

---

[13] René A. López, "Israelite Covenants in the Light of Ancient Near Eastern Covenants: Part 2," *CTSJ* 10, no. 4 (2004): 72; "Israelite Covenants in the Light of Ancient Near Eastern Covenants: Part 1," *CTSJ* 9, no. 4 (2003): 92–111.

[14] McCarthy agrees with Lopez and states that "in spite of variations in different times and places, variations even of some importance, there is a fundamental unity in the treaties. And this unity goes back beyond the Hittite examples unto the third millennium." Weeks cautions that "there is no fixed treaty form, even within one society at one particular time. Rather there is a clustering around a *typical pattern*: but that clustering includes, if we take the Hittites as example, grants, decrees, instructions and other sorts of texts" [emphasis added]. McCarthy, *Treaty and Covenant*, 80; Noel Weeks, *Admonition and Curse the Ancient Near Eastern Treaty/Covenant Form as a Problem in Inter-Cultural Relationships*, JSOTSup 407 (Edinburgh, U.K.: T&T Clark, 2004), 174.

[15] Samuel Sandmel, "Parallelomania," *JBL* 81, no. 1 (1962): 1–13.

[16] Jeffrey H. Tigay, "On Evaluating Claims of Literary Borrowing," in *The Tablet and the Scroll: Near Eastern Studies in Honor of William W. Hallo*, ed. Mark E. Cohen, Daniel C. Snell, and David B. Weisberg (Bethesda, Md.: Capital Decisions Ltd, 1993), 251.

[17] William F. Albright, From the Stone Age to Christianity: Monotheism and the Historical Process (La Vergne, Tenn.: Lightning Source, 2008), 67.

> Once again from the *New Testament Apocalypse* the lines can be traced through the *Old Testament prophets* to the eschatological curses and blessings of the sanctions section of the treaties. *The Book of Revelation* is replete with treaty analogues from its opening preamble-like identification of the awesome Lord Christ; through the *letters to the churches,* administering Christ's covenantal lordship after the manner of the ancient *lawsuit;* on through the elaborately expounded prophetic sanctions which constitute the major part of the book; and down to the closing documentary clause and canonical curse [emphasis added].[18]

For the purposes of consistency and clarity, the term *messenger preamble formula* will be used rather than *preamble,* the term *sanctions* will combine *blessing and cursing,* and *proclamation witness formula* will replace *divine witnesses.* These are used to reflect a more precise identification of the inherent structural elements within the text. Occasionally synonyms will be used for some terms: i.e., *threat* or *malediction* for curses; *clauses* or *terms* for stipulations; and *benediction* for blessing.

Campbell performs what he calls a covenant *audit* on the material using a *covenant findings* methodology.[19] He locates the elements of the covenant structure present within the messages, which the king then uses to audit the covenant faithfulness of the churches. A similar method of investigation is followed here to identify the ANEVT structure.

The evidence for this ANEVT, covenantal approach to the seven churches has been put forth by Lohse, Du Preeze, Shea, and others,[20] and defended in the Ph.D. dissertation by this author, published under Gorgias Press, entitled *The Seven Messages of Revelation and Vassal Treaties.* Although space does not permit the repeating of the various arguments here,[21] perhaps the most obvious argument for the ANEVT structure in the SMR is the presence of the Deuteronomic structure, as influenced by the ANEVT, clearly delineated in the SMR. Lohse also sees in the letters (*Die Briefe*) an OT covenant schema similar to Exodus 19:3–8, Deuteronomy 24:3–7,[22] and Joshua 24.[23]

---

[18] Meredith G. Kline, *Structure of Biblical Authority* (Grand Rapids, Mich.: Eerdmans, 1972), 73–74.

[19] Gordon Campbell, "Findings, Seals, Trumpets, and Bowls: Variations upon the Theme of Covenant Rupture and Restoration in the Book of Revelation," *WTJ* 66 (2004): 79 nn. 34; 76–77.

[20] Lohse, *Offenbarung*, 24; James Du Preez, "Mission Perspective in the Book of Revelation," *EvQ* 42 (1970): 152–67; "Ancient Near Eastern Vassal Treaties and the Book of Revelation: Possible Links," 33–43; Kline, *Structure of Biblical Authority*, 74; William H. Shea, "The Covenantal Form of the Letters to the Seven Churches," *AUSS* 21 (1983): 77–84; "A Further Note on the Covenantal Form in the Book of Revelation," *AUSS* 21 (1983): 251–64; David Chilton, *The Days of Vengeance: An Exposition of the Book of Revelation* (Fort Worth: Dominion, 1987), 85–86; Ray R. Sutton, *That You May Prosper: Dominion by Covenant* (Tyler, Tex.: Institute for Christian Economics, 1987), 85–86; R. Dean Davis, "The Heavenly Court Scene of Revelation 4–5" (Ph.D. diss., Andrews University, 1986); *The Heavenly Court Judgment of Revelation 4–5* (Lanham, Md.: University Press of America, 1992); Beale, *Revelation,* 37, 227; Campbell, "Findings, Seals, Trumpets, and Bowls," 78 n.2979.

[21] For a defence of this approach see, Graves, *SMRVT*, 1–224.

[22] Ibid., 13.

[23] Lohse, *Offenbarung*, 24; Graves, *SMRVT*, 20.

RESPONSE TO THE CRITICS

In 2014 Ryan Hansen responded with three arguments against the covenant lawsuit approach arguing that it is unconvincing.[24] Firstly, he adopted Michael De Roche argument that because in a lawsuit there are three parties (plaintiff, judge, and accused) seeking the resolution of an accusation and because the biblical covenant portrays one party (Yahweh) functioning as both judge and plaintiff, that the term covenant lawsuit should be dropped.[25] However, within the biblical context, God operates as both plaintiff and judge.[26] According to G. Ernest Wright the biblical imagery of lawsuit is used as a metaphor evoking the forensic nature of the courtroom to depict the nature of God's justice and does not require an exact parallel.[27] However, as De Roche admits, this does "not mean that the prophets never drew upon images and forms from the realm of the courts."[28]

Secondly, Hansen argued that "apocalyptic rhetorolect"[29] does not "focus on confrontation within a kingdom" and differentiates this from "prophetic rhetorolect, which confronts those within a kingdom who are not living according to the righteousness of the king."[30] However, it is clear that there is "prophetic rhetorolect" within the Apocalpyse especially in the seven messages where five of the seven churches (except Smyrna and Philadelphia) are reprimanded for not living according to the stipulations of the king. These exhortations to the churches function in the same way as the stipulations in a covenant, conveying the new covenant obligation of faithfulness to their king.[31] Hanson argues "since God is acting in the cycles with the ultimate goal of de-creation and new creation, the emphasis falls squarely on transformation[32]—regime change—rather than confrontation intended to bring

---

[24] Ryan Leif Hansen, *Silence and Praise: Rhetorical Cosmology and Political Theology in the Book of Revelation*, Emerging Scholars (Minneapolis, Minn.: Fortress, 2014), 75–76. Other opponents are dealt with in Graves, *SMRVT*, 25–28.

[25] Ibid., 75; Michael De Roche, "Yahweh's Rîb against Israel: A Reassessment of the So-Called 'Prophetic Lawsuit' in the Pre-Exilic Prophets," *JBL* 102, no. 4 (1983): 563–74.

[26] Kirsten Nielsen, *Yahweh as Prosecutor and Judge: An Investigation of the Prophetic Lawsuit (Rîb-Pattern)* (Sheffield, U.K.: University of Sheffield, 1978); Graves, *SMRVT*, 40 n.38.

[27] George Ernest Wright, "The Lawsuit of God: A Form-Critical Study of Deuteronomy 32," in *Israel's Prophetic Heritage: Essays in Honor of James Muilenberg*, ed. Bernhard W. Anderson and Walter Harrelson (New York, N.Y.: Harper & Row, 1962), 26–67.

[28] De Roche, "Yahweh's Rîb against Israel: A Reassessment of the So-Called 'Prophetic Lawsuit' in the Pre-Exilic Prophets," 571; Claus Westermann, *Basic Forms of Prophetic Speech*, trans. Hugh Clayton White (Louisville, Ky.: Westminster/Knox, 1991), 199–200.

[29] A rhetorolect is "a form of language variety or discourse identifiable on the basis of a distinctive configuration of themes, topics, reasonings, and argumentations." Vernon K. Robbins, *The Invention of Christian Discourse: From Wisdom to Apocalyptic*, Rhetoric of Religious Antiquity 1 (Dorset: Deo, 2008), 7.

[30] Hansen, *Silence and Praise*, 76; see also 34–49.

[31] Shea, "Covenantal," 75.

[32] On the issue of transformation versus confrontation, Robbins says, "God's activities of transformation are not limited to the abilities or efforts of humans to transform themselves through repentance and obedience, nor are they limited to the abilities or efforts of humans to transform themselves during their time of life on earth . . . The processes of transformation come from the realm of God and concern God's transformation of humans, the world and time

subjects into obeisance."[33] However, confrontation by the king in the prophetic oracles is initiated by the king to produce repentance and transformation. The two elements are not mutually exclusive. The ANEVT structures within the SMR are appropriate for prophetic oracles that call the churches to repentance and covenantal faithfulness. Another functional element of the SMR is the paraenetic (παραίνεσις, *parainesis*, "to exhort") aspect of the oracles. While relatively rare in Jewish apocalyptic literature[34] and in Revelation 4–21, it is an important component of 2–3 and 22:10–21.[35] Hill points out the value of this analysis: "For the illumination it brings to the question of the prophet's purpose: clearly he spoke to warn, judge, appeal (for repentance) and to encourage."[36]

Thirdly, Hanen argued that the book of revelation is liturgical[37] and that:

> the participatory nature of the work is not to condemn but to redirect — from false worship to true. If the audience is participating in worship by performing the Apocalypse, they are keeping covenant; they are holding the spirit of prophecy by worshiping God and keeping the testimony of Jesus.[38]

Hahn argued that covenant-making is a cultic, liturgical act, as much as a legal and ethical one.[39] This last point has not been well-studied, but it is critical to see the unity of Scripture and liturgy in the establishment, renewal, and maintenance of God's covenant relationship with his people. For both Christians and Jews, the scriptural texts were originally enacted in the liturgy for the purposes of remembering and ritualizing the divine saving events, and renewing the people's covenant relationship with God.[40] From Hahn's perspective, "Covenants have not only legal but social, ethical, familial and cultic-liturgical aspects."[41]

---

itself into 'heaven-like' personages and spaces, and into eternal 'non-time.'" Robbins, *The Invention of Christian Discourse*, 343.

[33] Hansen, Silence and Praise, 76.

[34] Collins, "Introduction," 6–8; Aune, *Rev 1–5*, lxxxvii.

[35] Minear identifies eight paraenetic literary forms including the SMR. Minear, *I Saw a New Earth*, 215–21.

[36] Hill, *NT Prophecy*, 84; Édouard Cothenet, *Le Prophétisme Dans Le Nouveau Testament*, ed. Louis Pirot et al., DBSup 8 (Paris: Letouzey et Ané, 1972), col. 1325.

[37] Ugo Vanni, "Liturgical Dialogue as a Literary Form in the Book of Revelation," *NTS* 37, no. 3 (1991): 348–72; Paulo Augusto de Souza Nogueira, "Celestial Worship and Ecstatic-Visionary Experience," trans. Leslie Milton, *JSNT* 25, no. 2 (2002): 165–84; Jean-Pierre Ruiz, "Betwixt and Between on the Lord's Day: Liturgy and the Apocalypse," in *The Reality of Apocalypse: Rhetoric and Politics in the Book of Revelation*, ed. L. Barr David, SBLSS 39 (Atlanta, Ga.: Scholars Press, 2006), 221–41; Stanley P. Saunders, "Between Blessing and Curse: Reading, Hearing and Performing the Apocalypse in a World of Terror," in *Shaking Heaven and Earth: Essays in Honor of Walter Brueggemann and Charles B. Cousar*, ed. Christine Roy Yoder et al. (Louisville, Ky.: Westminster John Knox, 2005), 141–55; "Revelation and Resistance: Narrative and Worship in John's Apocalypse," in *Narrative Reading, Narrative Preaching: Reuniting New Testament Interpretation and Proclamation*, ed. Joel Green and Michael Pasquarello III (Grand Rapids, Mich.: Baker, 2009), 117–50.

[38] Hansen, Silence and Praise, 77.

[39] Scott W. Hahn, "Canon, Cult and Covenant: The Promise of Liturgical Hermeneutics," in *Canon And Biblical Interpretation*, ed. Scott W. Hahn et al., Scripture and Hermeneutics Series 7 (Grand Rapids, Mich.: Zondervan, 2006), 211.

[40] On the liturgical aspect of the covenant, see Jon D. Levenson, *Sinai and Zion* (New York, N.Y.: HarperOne,

The audience participating in the worship and praise would be only those from the churches who had repented and overcome. Those guilty of breaking the covenant and unrepentant would not be involved in the liturgical worship of the king. Hansen's criticism is misdirected to a "staw man" argument.

Since the ANEVT structure may be new to some readers, a brief description of each element will be provided here.

THE MESSENGER'S COMMISSION

One of the characteristics of apocalyptic literature is the presence of a mediating messenger who functions as *angelus interpres*, 'interpreting angel'[42] (Ezek 40–48; Zech 1–6; Dan 7–12). Such an angel is mentioned in Revelation 1:1 and 22:6; and each church has a corresponding angel (2:1; 8; 12; 18; 3:1; 7; 14) with mediatorial angels scattered throughout the book (17:1–18; 21:9–22:5). The concept of mediatorial angels has roots in both the Hebraic-Semitic and Graeco-Roman world.

13. Stone carving of the winged angel Nike, the goddess of victory, Ephesus.

ANGELS DEFINED AS MESSENGERS

In Revelation, there was a need for someone (a messenger) to deliver the king's royal messages to the seven churches. Thus, in Revelation 1:11, 19, John is commissioned to write (γράψον, *grapson*) and commanded to deliver the messages, by the *messenger* (τῷ ἀγγέλῳ, *tō angelō*, 2:1, 8; 12; 18; 3:1; 7; 14) of the churches (see Fig. 13). This shows that John is distinguished from the messenger, and the article τῷ, (*tō*) distinguishes between the messengers of the individual churches.[43] An ἄγγελος (*angelos*, "angel") is defined as an envoy dispatched to deliver a message; thus, the term refers to a *messenger* or angel.[44]

1987), 80–81; Albert Vanhoye, *Old Testament Priests and the New Priest*, Revised (Herefordshire England: Gracewing, 2009), 181–82.

[41] Scott W. Hahn, "Covenant in the Old and New Testaments: Some Current Research (1994–2004)," *CBR* 3, no. 2 (2005): 285.

[42] Michael Mach, *Entwicklungsstadien Des Jüdischen Engelglaubens in Vorrabbinischer Zeit*, TSAJ 34 (Tübingen: Mohr Siebeck, 1992), 142–44; Hansgünter Reichelt, *Angelus Interpres-Texte in Der Johannes-Apokalypse* (Frankfurt: Peter Lang, 1994), 34–136.

[43] Thomas, *Rev 1–7*, 126–27; John F. Walvoord, *Revelation*, ed. Roy B. Zuck (Wheaton, Ill.: Victor, 1983), 53.

[44] The cognate verb ἀγγέλω (*angellō*, "I announce") and noun ἀγγελία (*angelia*, "message") convey this meaning. See BDAG, 7.

THREE CATEGORIES OF INTERPRETATION

The difficulty, as Thomas points out, in identifying ἄγγελοι *(angeloi,* "angels") is partially due to the fact that they can be "used of both human envoys (cf. Luke 9:52) and spirit beings (cf. Luke 1:11), of good angels (cf. Heb 1:13–14) and evil spirits (cf. Jude 6; 2 Pet 2:4)."[45] In addition, each view has its own difficulties.[46] Thus, the identity of the ἄγγελος *(angelos,* "angel") is disputed, and has led to three main categories of interpretation.

UNFALLEN ANGELS

The most popular view is unfallen angels,[47] who are heavenly personifications,[48] or counterparts,[49] and guardians of the churches[50]. Originally, Ulrich B. Müller held that the angels were a "literary fiction" created by John to deal with his lack of knowledge regarding the ecclesiological structure of the Asia Minor churches,[51] but ultimately, Müller settled on

---

[45] Thomas, *Rev 1–7*, 127.

[46] For detailed treatments of the problem, cf. Loren T. Stuckenbruck, *Angel Veneration and Christology: A Study in Early Judaism and the Christology of the Apocalypse of John*, WUNT, 2/70 (Tübingen: Mohr Siebeck, 1995), 232–38; Hemer, *Letters to the Seven Churches*, 32–34; Kraft, *Offenbarung*, 50–52; Ulrich B. Müller, *Prophetie Und Predigt Im Neuen Testament: Formgeschichtliche Untersuchungen Zur Urchristlichen Prophetie*, SNT 10 (Gütersloh: Mohn, 1975), 87–89; Karrer, *Johannesoffenbarung*, 1:1:169–86; Aune, *Rev 1–5*, 108–12.

[47] Hans Bietenhard, "ἄγγελος," *NIDNTT* 1:103; Walter Grundmann, "ἄγγελος," *TDNT* 1:74.

[48] Isbon T. Beckwith, *The Apocalypse of John* (New York, N.Y.: MacMillan, 1919), 445–46; James Moffatt, *The Revelation of St. John the Divine*, ed. W. Robertson Nicoll, vol. 5, EGT (London, U.K.: Hodder & Stoughton, 1910), 348; Leon L. Morris, *The Revelation of St. John*, TNTC 20 (Grand Rapids, Mich.: Eerdmans, 1975), 57; Kiddle, *Revelation*, 17:17; Mounce, *Revelation*, 63.

[49] James H. Moulton, "It Is His Angel," *JTS* 3, no. 12 (1902): 514–16; Ramsay, *Letters: Updated*, 50; Charles, *Revelation*, 34–35; Beasley-Murray, *Revelation*, NCB, 69; Pierre Prigent, *L'Apocalypse de saint Jean*, Commentaire du Nouveau Testament (Lausanne: Delachaux et Niestlé, 1981), 34; Alan F. Johnson, "Revelation," in *Hebrews-Revelation*, ed. Tremper Longman and David E Garland, Revised, EBC 13 (Grand Rapids, Mich.: Zondervan, 2006), 430; Lohmeyer, *Offenbarung*, 18–20; Gerhard A. Krodel, *Revelation*, ACNT (Minneapolis, Minn.: Augsburg Fortress, 1989), 103; Beale, *Rev*, 217; Osborne, *Revelation*, 98–99. Osborne prefers a combination of literal angel and heavenly counterpart.

[50] Ps 34:7; 91:11; Dan 10:13–21; Matt 18:10; Acts 12:15; Heb 1:14; Karrer, *Johannesoffenbarung*, 1:185–86; Banks, "Smyrna," 4:8183; Hill, *NT Prophecy*, 406; Roland H. Worth, Jr., *The Seven Cities of the Apocalypse and Roman Culture* (New York, N.Y.: Paulist, 2002), 111; William M. Ramsay, *The Letters to Seven Churches of Asia and Their Place in the Plan of the Apocalypse* (London, U.K.: Hodder & Stoughton, 1904), 50; Charles, *Revelation*, 1:34–35; Caird, *Revelation*, 24; Lohmeyer, *Offenbarung*, 20; Michael Wilcock, *The Message of Revelation: I Saw Heaven Opened*, BST (Downers Grove, Ill.: InterVarsity, 1975), 41; Johnson, "Revelation," 430; Beasley-Murray, *Revelation*, NCB, 69–70; Henry Barclay Swete, *The Apocalypse of St. John*, 3rd ed. (London, U.K.: MacMillan & Co., 1917), 73; Moffatt, *Revelation*, 5:348. Moffatt, *Revelation*, 348. The *Ascension of Isaiah* speaks of "the descent of the angel of the Christian Church, which is in the heavens" (3:15). This view was also common in the writings of the early church fathers (Gregory *Or. Bas.* 42; Origen *Hom. Luc.* 23; *Hom. Num.* 20.3; Jerome *Comm. Mich.* 6:1, 2; Basil *Comm. Isa.* 1.46; Hippolytus *Antichr.* 59).

[51] Ulrich B. Müller, Zur Frühchristlichen Theologiegeschichte. Judenchristentum Und Paulinismus in Kleinasien an Der Wende Vom Ersten Zum Zweiten Jahrhundert Nach Christus (Gütersloh: Mohn, 1976), 33–34.

accepting the counterpart theory.[52] Variations on this theme include Swete who identified a Persian parallel of heavenly bodies[53] with earthly communities as counterparts.[54] Also, Enroth and others, appealing to 22:16, propose that ἄγγελοι *(angeloi,* "angels") refers to "visionary counterparts of the other prophets in the community,"[55] rather than to the churches themselves. A case could be made that ἄγγελος *(angelos,* "angel") is a heavenly being who typifies each church (1:20) as being in God's protection (1:16) and thus personifies the church,[56] but it functions as the means through whom Christ conveys his word to the church.[57] This view would be compatible with the notion of messengers delivering a message to the churches on behalf of the suzerain (king).[58]

HUMAN CHURCH LEADERS

A second category is human messengers (angels), who represent untitled church leaders,[59] ecclesiastical bishops/elders,[60] or Christian prophets.[61] While Schüssler Fiorenza argues that this lacks support from the text,[62] it must be pointed out that all positions are deficient in this area.

---

[52] Ulrich B. Müller, *Die Offenbarung Des Johannes,* ÖTKNT 19 (Gütersloh: Mohn, 1984), 88.

[53] Wojciechowski believes that the seven churches, represented by the seven stars, are to be identified with the sun, the moon and five planets. Michael Wojciechowski, "Seven Churches and Seven Celestial Bodies (Rev 1,16; Rev 2–3)," *BN* 45 (1988): 48–50.

[54] Swete, *Apocalypse,* 22; Caird, *Revelation,* 25.

[55] Anne-Mart Enroth, "The Hearing Formula in the Book of Revelation," *NTS* 36, no. 4 (1990): 604; Elisabeth Schüssler Fiorenza, "Apokalypsis and Propheteia: The Book of Revelation in the Context of Early Christian Prophecy," in *The Book of Revelation: Justice and Judgment,* ed. Gerhard A. Krodel, 2nd ed., PC (Minneapolis, Minn.: Fortress, 1999), 145–46; *Revelation: Vision,* 52–53; David E. Aune, "The Social Matrix of the Apocalypse of John," *Biblical Research* 26 (1981): 23; Beale, *Revelation,* 217.

[56] See Karrer's documented case from the *Book of Giants* from Qumran (4QEnGiants[a] fragment 8) of Enoch writing to a fallen angel. Karrer, *Johannesoffenbarung,* 1:57–59, 172.

[57] Stuckenbruck points out that the parallel with Revelation breaks down as Enoch appears "otherworldly" in the text, and the angel is clearly fallen. However, as Stuckenbruck cautions, there is no "one angel-one congregation correspondence" in either first-century Christian or Jewish literature. Stuckenbruck, *Angel Veneration & Christology,* 236–37.

[58] Stuckenbruck argues persuasively that given the "admonitory tone" of the associated messages the "author's representation of angels in the seven letters involves a demotion from views of angelic functions held by the intended readers" Ibid., 238. However, this would not necessarily undercut the church's understanding of angels as messengers sent from God.

[59] This could mean men who are moral representatives of each church but are without a unique leadership function. Thomas proposes Epaphroditus (Phil 2:25; 4:18) and Epaphras (Col 4:12) as examples of church representatives who helped Paul while in prison (*Rev 1–7,* 117–18, 127). See David S Clark, *The Message from Patmos: A Postmillennial Commentary on the Book of Revelation* (Grand Rapids, Mich.: Baker, 1989), 30.

[60] Richard C. Trench, *Commentary on the Epistles to the Seven Churches in Asia: Revelation 2, 3,* 2nd ed. (London, U.K.: Parker, Son & Bourn, 1862), 53–58, 78, 82; Hugh Martin, *The Seven Letters: Christ's Message to His Church* (Philadelphia, Pa.: Westminster, 1956), 56; William H. Brownlee, "The Priestly Character of the Church in the Apocalypse," *NTS* 5, no. 3 (1959): 224–25; Müller, *Prophetie,* 101; Richard C. H. Lenski, *The Interpretation of St. John's Revelation,* CNT (Minneapolis, Minn.: Augsburg Fortress, 1963), 97; Hoeksema, *Behold, He Cometh!,* 41–42; Beasley-Murray, *Revelation,*

According to Thomas, ἄγγελος *(angelos,* "angel") represents men of the church "without a unique leadership function."[63] He argues that it is easier to answer the objections of this view, than it is to answer the objections of the "heavenly angels" argument. Müller suggests that "John addresses the seven messages to 'angels' because he does not want to mention the official local leaders of the churches."[64] Müller bases his argument on the apparent struggle between bishops and prophets in Asia Minor at this time. Banks also argues that the messengers are human, equating them with bishops: "the seven angels of the seven churches (1:20) received seven letters, figurative letters, and therefore it would seem that the seven angels are also figurative and may refer to the seven bishops who presided over the seven churches of Asia."[65]

SOME ELUSIVE MEANING

Hemer provides the possibility of some kind of mysterious meaning for the angels, although he does not give it much weight.[66] He does raise the similarities of this view of the angels with several obscure Anatolian cultural practices. Hemer notes one similarity: "a pagan expression of the idea of a guardian of the individual reappears in Aelius Aristides, writing of an experience in Smyrna" (Aristides *Orat.* 26 [Dindorf]).[67] While an understanding of the angels that stresses the role of a guardian is unlikely, Hemer believes that these obscure allusions in Aristides make the mysterious idea of the angel "less strange than it appears."[68] Thus Hemer argues for a view that incorporates meanings that encompass "complex and elusive ways or at differing levels, so that we cannot expect to assign it a lexical equivalent that tells the whole story."[69]

CONCLUSION

The major dilemma in understanding the symbolism focuses on the antithesis between the meaning of heavenly beings and human leaders. Central to this is the role of messengers bringing proclamations from the suzerain, and that this role does not require one to specify with

---

NCB, 69; William Hendriksen, *More than Conquerors* (Grand Rapids, Mich.: Baker, 1982), 58 n.1; Philip Edgcumbe Hughes, *The Book of the Revelation: A Commentary*, PNTC 16 (Grand Rapids, Mich.: Eerdmans, 1990), 30–31; Kistemaker, *Revelation*, 103, 111; Banks, "Smyrna," 4:8183. and others.

[61] Friedrich Spitta, *Die Offenbarung des Johannes* (Halle: Waisenhaus, 1889), 38–39; W. D. Davies, "A Note on Josephus, Antiquities 15:136," *HTR* 47, no. 3 (1954): 135–40; Kraft, *Offenbarung*, 50–52; Hill, *NT Prophecy*, 30; George T. Montague, *The Apocalypse: Understanding the Book of Revelation and the End of the World* (Ann Arbor, Mich.: Servant, 1992), 56.

[62] Schüssler Fiorenza, "Apokalypsis," 105; Swete, *Apocalypse*, 22. Swete dispels this view as "this person was in no sense a Church-ruler, and offers no true analogy."

[63] Thomas, *Rev 1–7*, 118.
[64] Müller, Frühchristlichen, 34.
[65] Banks, "Smyrna," 4:8183.
[66] Hemer, Letters to the Seven Churches, 32.
[67] Ibid., 33.
[68] Ibid., 32.
[69] Ibid.

precision the identity of the messenger. Whether the messenger is of human or heavenly origin does not affect their roles as royal envoys. Within the context of Revelation, the angels could be heavenly beings typifying each church (1:20), protected by the hand of God (1:16), and thus could be said to personify the church; but which are functioning as messengers to convey Christ's message to the church.

THE ANGELS' FUNCTION

Whether the seven angels are heavenly angels or earthly angels, they function similarly to John and the other prophets, namely to communicate the prophetic message of the resurrected Lord.[70] Revelation 1:20 differentiates between the angels and the churches. The message of Christ is written to the angels (messengers) as representatives of the churches, despite the fact that they are separate. However, it is clear that the message is meant to be conveyed to the churches by the angels associated with each church. This would also be consistent with understanding the angels' function as messengers (i.e., messenger to the church).[71] According to Aune, the angels should be interpreted as messengers:

> [The angels] should be regarded as prophetic messengers rather than guardian angels or church officials, it would appear that John is functioning as a kind of master prophet in transmitting revelatory messages to the churches under his (real or assumed) jurisdiction through local prophetic messengers. But this is purely hypothetical and incapable of demonstration.[72]

The identity of the angels may be impossible to determine with certainty; however, the context seems to indicate that the angels of the churches (1:20) are representing either the churches or standing as themselves, as heavenly beings. Either way, they function as messengers carrying a divine message to the churches. While Roloff argues against the idea of angels as messengers, presenting that, in the ancient world, messengers only delivered messages,[73] his argument does not take into consideration that in order to deliver a message, one must first receive it. The messages to the churches were delivered to ἄγγελοι *(angeloi,* "angels") who in turn communicated them to the churches (22:16).

---

[70] Schüssler Fiorenza, "Apokalypsis," 120.

[71] It is unclear whether the angel in 22:16 is to be identified with the seven angels of the churches; however, the function is similar in that "I, Jesus, have sent my angel (messenger) to give you [ὑμῖν, *humin*] this testimony for the churches" (22:16). Regardless of the identity of the ὑμῖν *(humin,* "you"), the message is mediated. Note also the forensic tone of to "testify" (22:18, 20) as in a lawsuit. For the possible meaning for ὑμῖν *(humin,* "you"), see Beale, *Revelation*, 1143–48.

[72] Aune, *Prophecy in Early Christianity and the Ancient Mediterranean World*, 197; Thomas, *Rev 1–7*, 118. Thomas maintains that these church representatives were "without a unique leadership function."

[73] Jürgen Roloff, *The Revelation of John*, trans. John E. Alsup, CC (Minneapolis, Minn.: Fortress, 1993), 39.

Messengers from an ANE Perspective

Messengers within OT Prophets

The concept of ἄγγελοι (*angeloi*, angels) delivering divine oracles is prevalent throughout the first century Graeco-Roman and Hebrew-Semitic world.[74] The OT LXX uses ἄγγελοι (*angeloi*, angels) to represent prophets (מלאך, *mlan*)[75] who convey the message received from the Lord.[76] Aune identifies angels as interpreters, stating:

> One characteristic feature of apocalyptic literature is the presence of a stock literary figure who functions as a supernatural mediator, *angelus interpres*, "interpreting angels," who begins to appear in late OT prophecy (Ezek 40–48; Zech 1–6; Dan 7–12). This *angelus interpres* may have developed by analogy to revelatory dialogues between God and a human recipient of revelation, i.e., passages in which God himself provides an interpretation of a vision (Jer 1:11–13; Job 38–42:6).[77]

The use of ἄγγελοι (*angeloi*, "angels") for prophets and priests is occasionally found in the LXX.[78] The ἄγγελος (*angelos*, "angel") may be connected to the Hebrew מלאך (*mlan*, "prophets") as it is translated by the LXX in Mal 2:7 (ἄγγελος κυρίου παντοκράτορος (*angelos kuriou pantokratopos*, "the messenger of the LORD of hosts") where it refers to the Jewish priests (Mal 2:1).

In addition to this Jewish context, the Johannine usage could be broadened to include the prophetic office and administration. The plural מלאכיו, (*mlakyw*, "messenger") in Isaiah 44:26 is rendered τῶν ἀγγέλων (*tōn angelōn*, "the angels") in the LXX and appears to refer to prophets earlier in the verse. Second Chronicles 36:15–16 also uses messengers (LXX τοὺς ἀγγέλους, *tous angelous*, "the angels") and prophets[79] interchangeably from the practice of God's prophets being his messengers.[80]

Another phrase of interest is *Messenger of the Covenant* (ומלאך קימא, *wmlan qyma*, LXX ὁ ἄγγελος τῆς διαθήκης, *o angelos tēs diathēkēs*, "Covenant-Angel")[81] in Malachi 3:1.[82] Calvin makes

---

[74] Johann Michl, "Engel I–IX," *RAC* 5 (1962): 53–60.

[75] 1 Kgs 19:2; 2 Kgs 5:10; Ezek 23:40; Hag 1:13.

[76] While in the SMR the proclamations were sent to the angels of the church, possibly as representatives. The message was meant to be passed onto the churches (1:11; 22:8, 16) and publicly read (1:3; cf. *the hearing formula* 2:7, etc., 22:18). The messages did not stop with the angels.

[77] Aune, *Rev 1–5*, 16; John S. Holladay, "Assyrian Statecraft and the Prophets of Israel," *HTR* 63, no. 1 (1970): 30–33; Hemer, *Letters to the Seven Churches*, 34. Hemer believes the angel imagery is a "concept developed under Jewish influence."

[78] Davies, "Note on Josephus," 138.

[79] ß omits προφήτης (*prophētēs*) but as Davies speculates, "It may well be that ß regards the reference to *angelous* as sufficient to indicate prophets." Ibid., 139.

[80] Davies points out that the "phrase 'rising up early and sending' is associated with God's sending of the prophets" in Jer 29:19; 26:5; 35:14. Ibid., 138.

[81] This phrase is found nowhere else in Scripture.

[82] Dempster argues for the ban inaugurated by the Messenger of Yahweh in Malachi upon covenant violators. Stephen G. Dempster, "The Prophetic Invocation of the Ban as Covenant Curse: A Historical Analysis of a Prophetic Theme" (Th.M. diss., Westminster Theological Seminary, 1978), 134–37.

the following statement about this term: "He called John the Baptist at the beginning of this verse a messenger, the messenger of Jehovah; and now he calls Christ a messenger, but he is the messenger of the covenant; for it was necessary that the covenant should be confirmed by him."[83]

MESSENGERS WITHIN JUDAISM

Several scholars find a parallel with *synagogue messenger* (שליח צבור, *slyḥ ṣbwr*),[84] who represented the entire congregation in prayer.[85] In first-century Judaism one of the roles of the leader of the synagogue (ἀρχισυνάγωγος, *archisynagōgos*, Mark 5:22, 35–38; Luke 8:49; 13:14; Acts 13:15; 18:8, 17) was to rotate among the members of the congregation the responsibility for prayer (*messenger of the congregation*).[86] Yamauchi points out that from Luke 13:10–17 and Acts 18:1–17, "we can infer that such an officer [ἀρχισυνάγωγος, *archisynagōgos*, "synagogue leader"] was responsible for keeping the congregation faithful to the Torah,"[87] a role John could be emulating here in Revelation. Billerbeck believed that שליח (*slyḥ*, "messenger") was widely accepted as the *authorized person* equivalent to an apostle or angel. Therefore, he concludes that in John's day it could have been equal to "angel of the church," and widely used for leader of the congregation.[88] However, Beasley-Murray points out that "the seven letters, although addressed to the angels of the churches, have in view the congregations themselves, not simply their leaders."[89] Aune believes that "such a subordinate position cannot seriously be proposed for the role of the ἄγγελος [*angelos*, "angel"]."[90] In addition, the congregation, rather than God's appointed messenger, appoints the office. Nevertheless, the concept of a messenger within the synagogue was familiar to the first century Jewish Christian.[91]

---

[83] John Calvin, *Commentaries on The Twelve Minor Prophets* (Grand Rapids, Mich.: Baker, 1979), 15:569; Carl F. Keil, *The Twelve Minor Prophets*, ed. Carl F. Keil and Franz Delitzsch, trans. James Martin, Commentary on the OT (Grand Rapids, Mich.: Eerdmans, 1977), 10:459.

[84] Paul Billerbeck and Hermann L. Strack, *Kommentar Zum Neuen Testament Aus Talmud Und Midrasch* (Munich: C. H. Beck, 1922), 3:790–2; John Lightfoot, *Horæ Hebraicæ et Talmudicæ*, trans. Robert Gandell (Oxford, U.K.: Oxford University Press, 1859), 2:90–95.

[85] Richard Watson, *A Biblical and Theological Dictionary* (New York, N.Y.: Waugh & Mason, 1833), 940.

[86] Shemuel Safrai and Menahem Stern, "The Synagogue," in The Jewish People in the First Century: Historical Geography, Political History, Social, Cultural and Religious Life and Institutions, ed. Shemuel Safrai, vol. 2 (Assen: Van Gorcum, 1987), 2:915; Kaufmann Kohler, The Origins of the Synagogue and the Church (New York, N.Y.: MacMillan, 1929), 66. See BDAG, 952.27.

[87] Edwin M. Yamauchi, "Synagogues," ed. Joel B. Green, Scot McKnight, and I. Howard Marshall, *DJG* (Downers Grove, Ill.: InterVarsity, 1992), 782.

[88] Billerbeck and Strack, Kommentar Zum Neuen Testament Aus Talmud Und Midrasch, 3:790–2.

[89] Beasley-Murray, *Revelation*, NCB, 69.

[90] Aune, *Rev 1–5*, 112.

[91] The use of *messenger* for ἄγγελος (*angelos*, "angels") is also documented in late Jewish apocalyptic literature (*Apoc. Ab.* 20–31; *2 Bar.* 22:1–30:5; 39:1–43:3; 50:1–51:16; *4 Ezra* 8:27–9:25; 13:20–56). However, an ἄγγελος (*angelos*, "angels") is a human or heavenly messenger according to the context. The specialised biblical meaning does not eliminate the other usage. For more details, see Mach, *Entwicklungsstadien*, 142–44; Reichelt, *Angelus Interpres*, 34–136.

MESSENGERS WITHIN GRAECO-ROMAN CULTURE

In Graeco-Roman culture, the πάρεδρος δαίμων (*paredros daimōna*, "divine being") was also known as an ἄγγελος and served in the role of a prophetic medium and assistant messenger. The Greeks used the terms θεός, δαίμων, and ἄγγελος interchangeably in their magical incantations.[92] In one Greek magical papyri it states:

> He [πάρεδρος δαίμων, *paredros daimōn*] will tell you what things will happen both when and at what time of the night or day. And if / anyone asks you "What do I have in mind?" or "What has happened to me?" or even "What is going to happen?," question the angel [ἄγγελος], and he will tell you in silence. But you speak to the one who questions you as if from yourself (*PGM* 1.167–77 [Betz]).

The angel serves as an assistant "who will reveal everything to you clearly and will be your [companion and] will eat and sleep with you" (*PGM* I.1–3).

MESSENGERS WITHIN THE ANEVT

Within the ANEVT context, there was a continual flow of professional royal *messengers*[93] linking the courts of the suzerain with his vassals. A line in the letter of Hattusili III to the Babylonian king, Kadashman-Enlil II, states, "[Only if two kings] are hostile do their messengers not travel continually between them" (No. 23, §6).[94] According to Beckman, "in order that the partner could be certain that the envoy was presenting his master's position accurately, he was also given a dispatch in Akkadian (see No. 2, §59; cf. No. 22F, §§10–14)."[95] Holladay describes the activity of the *messenger* in receiving the message from the suzerain (sent *to* the messenger) and then delivering it to the vassal, as that of being a regal representative of the Great King:

> The royal messenger stood in the court of the Great King, participated in the deliberative processes of the court, received the declaration of the king's wishes from the king's own mouth, and then carried the tablet or sealed roll of papyrus to its destination—in the case of imperial state administration, to the court of the vassal king. Here, received in the manner befitting a representative of the Great King, he would break the seals, hold up the letter, and proclaim: "To PN$_1$, thus (says) PN$_2$: I am well, may your heart be at peace. Now concerning the matter of. . . ."[96]

SUMMARY

Just as the king would send a messenger to the vassal to warn of the offenders' coming judgment and the enforcement of the covenant sanctions, John is instructed to send a similar

---

[92] A. Abt, *Die Apologie Des Apuleius von Madaura Und Die Antike Zauberei* (Giessen: Töpelmann, 1908), 253–57. See *PGM* 1, which contains spells for acquiring a πάρεδρος δαίμων (*paredros daimōn*, in which they equate the term θεός (*theos*, "god" lines 40, 77, 86, 88, 89, 90, 92, 93), with ἄγγελος (*aggelos*, "angel" lines 76, 78, 87, 172, 176).

[93] Akk. *ālikūtu* (function of) "messenger"; *āliku* "he who goes"; *ālikum* "one who goes with a message"; also *šapru* "one who sends or carries a message" (Oppenheim and Reiner (ed), "*ālikūtu*," *CAD*, 1:375). Cf. Beckman, *Hittite Diplomatic Texts*, 5.

[94] Ibid.
[95] Ibid.
[96] Holladay, "Assyrian Statecraft," 31.

message of covenant unfaithfulness to the angels (messengers), who in turn deliver the message to the churches (1:11; 22:8, 16) where they were to be publicly read (1:3; see also the hearing formula 2:7 etc.; 22:18). Enroth, following Schüssler Fiorenza, argues: "the angel of each community may be the prophet of the community and probably belongs to the same group as John and his followers who are prophets."[97]

The responsibility of these messengers for the actions of the churches points to their leadership position and raises their functions as messenger to new levels.[98] This prophetic/angelic messenger receives and delivers the suzerain's message in a typical prophetic formula (2:1b),[99] reminiscent of the ANE messengers.

While the term "angel" is predominantly used to describe heavenly angels in Revelation, this usage is still closely connected with the sinful earthly church which is held responsible and accountable for its actions; the message of Revelation is mediated to the churches by this special angelic messenger. Regardless of whether this angel is of divine origin or a human envoy from within the churches, its function remains the same – a recipient (2:1; etc.) and deliverer of the divine message of John. The Spirit's message reaches the churches (2:7; etc.) through the meditating work of the angels (2:1; etc.). This is precisely the role of the messenger in the ANEVT's: a messenger who carries/ delivers the royal message of the suzerain (king).

MESSENGER PREAMBLE FORMULA

The message carried by the messenger (ἄγγελος, *angelos*, "angel") is comprised of six elements, the first of which is commonly called *the preamble* and was "attested in all periods in all locations"[100] in the ANE. Normally these are the opening *words* (LXX λέγει, *legei*; Akk. *awāte*)[101] of the suzerain identifying his name, title, attributes and occasionally his genealogy.[102] Persian kings employed the formula τάδε λέγει Ω (*tade legei omega*, "these are the words") in the introduction of their royal decrees (imperial edicts[103]; Josephus *Ant.* 11.26),[104] followed by the identification of the suzerain or king.[105] The primary function of the preamble within the ANEVT was to identify the character of the suzerain/king who established the covenant.

---

[97] Enroth, "Hearing Formula," 604; Schüssler Fiorenza, *Book of Revelation*, 145–46.

[98] Thomas, *Rev 1–7*, 604; Henry Alford, *Hebrews-Revelation*, ed. Everett F. Harrison, vol. 4, GTCEC (Chicago, Ill.: Moody, 1968), 560.

[99] Muse, "Rev 2–3," 147–61.

[100] Walton, *Ancient Israelite Literature*, 102; John A. Thompson, "The Near Eastern Suzerain-Vassal Concept in the Religion of Israel," *JRH* 3 (1964): 4.

[101] J. Wijngaards, *Vazal van Jahweh* (Baarn: Bosch & Keuning, 1965), 153.

[102] Mendenhall, "Covenant Forms," 59; Kline, *Treaty of the Great King*, 50; Kitchen, *Ancient Orient*, 92; Walton, *Ancient Israelite Literature*, 101.

[103] For the similarities between the Imperial Edicts and the ANEVT's, see Graves, *SMRVT*, 54.

[104] See BDAG, 553; Aune, *Rev 1–5*, 126–29; Aune, "Form and Function," 187. This has led Aune to compare the messages to imperial edicts. However, the close proximity of the τάδε λέγει Ω (*tade legei*, "these are the words") formula with the other ANEVT elements argues for their inclusion as part of the ANEVT package.

[105] This messenger formula was also found in a prophetic speech of the Mari letters. Aune, *Prophecy in Early*

Throughout the OT, τάδε λέγει Ω (*tade legei omega*, "these are the words") was also used to convey a royal message through a messenger.[106] Various endings are added to the prophetic formula, such as *Lord God of Israel*;[107] *Sovereign Lord*;[108] *of the Hebrews*;[109] *of David*;[110] and *the Lord Almighty*.[111] Thus, this recognized pattern of τάδε λέγει Ω, followed by a royal title, constitutes a messenger formula introducing a prophetic oracle.

The OT prophetic uses of the τάδε λέγει Ω (*tade legei omega*, "these are the words") formula brings to bear the covenant lawsuit against the disobedient people of God to return to their covenant pledge (Amos 2:4; Zech 1:3). The messenger formula is not only deeply prophetic but also an integral part of the covenant relationship of the suzerain, who speaks "Thus says the Lord" to his vassal,[112] which is repeated in the Ten Commandments in the preamble "I am the Lord your God" (Exod 20:2).

Given the proliferation of the τάδε λέγει Ω (*tade legei omega*, "these are the words") formula in the OT,[113] with over 424 occurrences in the OT prophets,[114] the early church would clearly understand this as a prophetic term.[115]

It appears that the preamble is multilayered in the message of Revelation as it is a complex montage of prophetic messages set in the broader context of the covenant lawsuit message of the book itself.[116] The classic OT *prophetic messenger formula*,[117] τάδε λέγει Ω (*tade legei omega*, "these

---

Christianity and the Ancient Mediterranean World, 89.

[106] Exod 5:10; 1 Kgs 2:30; 20:2, 5; 2 Kgs 1:11; 18:19, 29; Isa 36:4, 14, 16; 1 Esd 2:2; Jdt 2:5; Beale, *Rev*, 229; Bauckham, *Theology of Revelation*, 5; Hill, *NT Prophecy*, 81–82; Alan S. Bandy, *The Prophetic Lawsuit in the Book of Revelation*, NT Monograph 29 (Sheffield, U.K.: Sheffield Phoenix, 2010), 207; Westermann, *Basic Forms*, 35, 82.

[107] Used 20 times e.g., Ezek 34:18; Jer 7:3; Isa 17:6.

[108] Used 7 times exclusively in Isa 7:7; 10:24; 14:24; 17:3; 19:4; 22:15, 25.

[109] Used in Exod 9:1; 10:3.

[110] Used in 2 Chr 21:12; Isa 38:5.

[111] "Lord Almighty" is used 28 times primarily in Zechariah and Haggai (e.g., Zech 1:3). Only this last name phrase is used nine times in Revelation (1:8; 4:8; 11:17; 15:3; 16:7, 14; 19:6, 15; 21:22).

[112] Matitiahu Tsevat, "The Neo-Assyrian and Neo-Babylonian Vassal Oaths and the Prophet Ezekiel," *JBL* 78, no. 3 (1959): 199–204; Harvey, "RIB-Pattern," 180–88; Thompson, "Near Eastern Suzerain-Vassal," 12.

[113] Hebrew כה אמר יהוה (*kh amn yhwh*, LXX τάδε λέγει κύριος, *tade legei kurios*, "these are the words of the Lord") is used 34 times in the Minor Prophets, 64 times in Jeremiah, 26 times in Isaiah, and 127 times in Ezekiel. Of the six prophetic formula classifications identified by Aune the message formula, "Thus says Yahweh," is the formula employed by John in Revelation. Aune, *Prophecy in Early Christianity and the Ancient Mediterranean World*, 89–90; Beale, *Revelation*, 111.

[114] The statistics were calculated using the Hebrew order of the prophetic books. Representative examples, of the 424 occurrences of τάδε λέγει, include Amos 1:6; Mic 2:3; Obad 1:1; Hag 1:2; Zech 1:3.

[115] See BDAG, 553.

[116] Bandy, *Prophetic Lawsuit*, 362–63; Kenneth A. Strand, "A Further Note on the Covenantal Form in the Book of Revelation," *AUSS* 21 (1983): 251–64; Sutton, *That You May Prosper*, 253–67; Chilton, *Days of Vengeance*, 15.

[117] Osborne, *Revelation*, 128; Müller, *Prophetie*, 47–49. Müller identifies τάδε λέγει (*tade legei*, "these are the words. . .") within Revelation as a "messenger formula of Old Testament prophecy," he goes further to identify the messages to the churches as eschatological *sermons*, unlike the OT judgment speeches.

are the words. . .", lit. "thus says" or some variation cf. LXX Isa 56:1; Jer 4:27; Amos 1:6; et al.) is repeatedly used in the SMR to introduce what the king *(Ω)* will say to each church (2:1, 8, 12, 18; 3:1, 7, 14).[118] According to Kirby, this section is designed "to establish the *ethos* of the Christ of the vision (1:10–20) so that he is then able to administer praise and blame with the authority accorded to divinity."[119] As Campbell has argued, "The covenant mechanism provides the logic for such credibility and authority."[120] The various titles of Christ[121] found in the SMR, which are drawn from chapter 1 of Revelation (1:17–18; see also 1:8; 10–20),[122] can be identified with the suzerain[123] in the preamble of the ANEVT.[124]

The use of the τάδε λέγει Ω (*tade legei*, "these are the words") formula in the messages reveals that Jesus is speaking in the role of Yahweh, and John stands in the role of Yahweh's prophet with divine/prophetic authority.[125] Aune recounts how the word τάδε (*tade*, "these") was obsolete in first-century Koine Greek[126] and thus conveys a sense of archaism,[127] arguing for John re-employing an ancient prophetic form.

---

[118] Beale, *Revelation*, 229.

[119] Kirby, "The Rhetorical Situation of Revelation 1–3," 201; Aune, *Prophecy in Early Christianity and the Ancient Mediterranean World*, 115. Aune points out that "the messenger formula, and the more comprehensive commission formula not only reflect the OT prophets' view of themselves as messengers, but also and more importantly they are formulaic means of affirming the divine origin and truth of the prophetic message."

[120] Campbell, "Findings, Seals, Trumpets, and Bowls," 79 n.33.

[121] Various titles for Jesus Christ are recorded throughout Revelation as in *Lamb* (ἀρνίον, *arnion* used 30 times only in Rev), and *King of kings and Lord of Lords* (19:16) just to mention a few. Bengel points out that the phrase "who is and who was and who is to come" in 1:4, 8 recalls the covenant name for Yahweh, "I am who I am," used in Exod 3:14. Johann Albrecht Bengel, *New Testament Word Studies*, trans. John H Vincent and Charlton T. Lewis, Kregel Reprint Library (Grand Rapids, Mich.: Kregel, 1971), 2:413.

[122] Revelation 1:12–20. There are parallels with the opening verses of Revelation (1:1) and Deuteronomy (Deut 1:3) with Moses and John (and angel) both given a revelation from the transcendent God. Sutton, *That You May Prosper*, 255.

[123] The title "King of king and Lord of lords" (19:16) presents Christ as the Great King of the covenant who speaks as the suzerain.

[124] In the biblical accounts, the message of the suzerain is communicated through human agents; i.e., Moses, Joshua, and John. This should not be taken to mean that the human agents were the kings, but indicates their role as spokesman through their prophetic office. Significantly, the authority of the divine message of the King is in no way diminished simply because it passes through the prophetic offices. For example, in Exodus 7:1–2 Moses is as God to Aaron, Aaron is Moses' prophet or messenger, and Pharaoh is the recipient of the prophetic word. Peter C. Craigie, *The Book of Deuteronomy*, ed. R. K. Harrison, NICOT 5 (Grand Rapids, Mich.: Eerdmans, 1976), 38; O. Palmer Robertson, *The Final Word: A Biblical Response to the Case for Tongues and Prophecy Today* (Carlisle, Pa.: Banner of Truth, 1993), 6.

[125] Osborne, *Revelation*, 111 n.5; Muse, "Rev 2–3," 147–61; Mark W. Wilson, "A Pie in a Very Bleak Sky? Analysis and Appropriation of the Promise Sayings in the Seven Letters to the Churches in Revelation 2–3" (D.Litt., University of South Africa, 1997), 12.

[126] Aune, "Form and Function," 187; *Rev 1–5*, 121.

[127] Aune, "Form and Function," 187.

Τάδε λέγει Ω (*tade legei*, "these are the words") is only found once in the NT outside of Revelation, but also within the context of the NT prophet Agabus (Acts 21:11).[128] The use of this phrase by Agabus and John indicates that it is part of the continuation of the inspired OT prophetic method.

Minear points out the strong emotional impact of the formula: "This conventional formula, simple and direct, would conjure up in a worshiping congregation the fear and trembling associated with standing before God and hearing his awesome words of judgment and warning (Exod 19:5–25; Deut 5:2–5)."[129]

John, therefore, adopts τάδε λέγει Ω (*tade legei omega*, "these are the words") as his prophetic messenger formula or "oracular preamble"[130] to introduce the suzerain/King who would judge the church in classic OT prophetic prescription and to make the message understandable to a first-century reader with a Jewish background. This address carries with it all the awesomeness of Sinai, together with the legitimate prophetic authority necessary to carry Christ's word to the Christian community.

HISTORICAL PROLOGUE

The second element of the covenant structure is called *the historical prologue*[131] because the king, who enters into covenant with his subjects, acknowledges the historical intimacy of their relationship as a historical summary.[132] The historical context of the suzerainty treaty lists the suzerain's knowledge as designating a "mutual legal recognition on the part of the suzerain and vassal,"[133] particularly of the vassal's past relationship to the Great King.[134]

The historical prologue, characteristic of the Hittite treaties of the second millennium (see Fig. 12, 14), is noticeably absent from the

14. Fragment of a Hittite tablet.

---

[128] Hill, *NT Prophecy*, 77.

[129] Minear, I Saw a New Earth, 43.

[130] Hill, *NT Prophecy*, 77.

[131] For an extensive treatment of the "historical prologue" in the Hittite treaties, see Amnon Altman, *The Historical Prologue of the Hittite Vassal Treaties an Inquiry into the Concepts of Hittite Interstate Law*, Bar-Ilan Studies in Near Eastern Languages and Culture. (Ramat-Gan: Bar-Ilan University Press, 2004).

[132] Joshua A. Berman, "Histories Twice Told: Deuteronomy 1–3 and the Hittite Treaty Prologue Tradition," *JBL* 132, no. 2 (2013): 232.

[133] Herbert B. Huffmon, "The Treaty Background of Hebrew Yāda'," *BASOR* 181 (1966): 31–37.

[134] Mendenhall, "Covenant Forms," 59; Thompson, *ANE Treaties*, 16; Thompson, "Near Eastern Suzerain-Vassal," 4; Walton, *Ancient Israelite Literature*, 102.

Assyrian treaties of the first millennium BC.¹³⁵ Weinfeld speculates that the historical prologue's absence in the Assyrian documents is "not that it was unknown to the Assyrians but, more likely, a matter of principle."¹³⁶ Nicholson¹³⁷ also points out that Deuteronomy is missing the "designation of Yahweh as king," although it is likely that Yahweh is called king in Deuteronomy 33:5.¹³⁸ Fink highlights several important characteristics of the historical prologue in Hittite letters:

> (1) in most letters, it directly follows the opening formula; (2) it is abbreviated in order to conform to letter conventions; (3) the father or ancestors of the correspondent and of the addressee are in many cases the focal point of the prologue; and (4) frequently, the historical prologue, which at first glance seems merely nostalgic, in fact provides justification and legitimization for a significant request or demand presented by the sender later on in the letter.¹³⁹

Thompson concludes that: "it provided the *raison d'être* for the establishment of the treaty,"¹⁴⁰ it revealed formal terms that keep recurring. Huffmon is the first to indicate that the Near Eastern suzerain used the verb *to know* (Hebrew ידע, *yd'*; Hittite *šak*; Akk. *idû*) "in two technical legal senses: to recognize as legitimate suzerain or vassal, and to recognize treaty stipulations as binding."¹⁴¹ Hillers points out the adapted use of the common verb "to know" in the ANE and its implications for the prophets: "thus verbs meaning "to know" in ordinary contexts were used for "to recognize," "be loyal to," in the vocabulary of international relations over a wide range of the ancient world, and the reader will anticipate the significance of this for the prophets."¹⁴²

Mendenhall points out another formal characteristic of ANEVT in "the 'I–Thou' form of address. Since the Hittite king is the author of the covenant, he speaks in the first person directly to the vassal."¹⁴³

---

¹³⁵ Ernest W. Nicholson, God and His People: Covenant and Theology in the Old Testament. (Oxford, U.K.: Clarendon, 1988), 66.

¹³⁶ Weinfeld, Deuteronomic School, 68.

¹³⁷ For a critical evaluation of Nicholson, see Kenneth A. Kitchen, "The Fall and Rise of Covenant, Law and Treaty," *TB* 40 (1989): 118–35.

¹³⁸ Nicholson, *God and His People*, 71 n.31; Berman, "Histories Twice Told," 229–50. Yahweh is the king who in the Ten Commandments identifies himself as the one "who brought you out of the land of Egypt, out of the house of slavery" (Exod 20:2). Berman deals with the absence of prologue history in Deuteronomy.

¹³⁹ Amir Sumaka'i Fink, "The Historical Prologue in a Letter from Šuppiluliuma II to 'Ammurapi', King of Ugarit (RS 18.038)," in "I Will Speak the Riddles of Ancient Times:" Archaeological and Historical Studies in Honor of Amihai Mazar on the Occasion of His Sixtieth Birthday, ed. Aren M. Maeir and Pierre de Miroschedji, vol. 2 (Winona Lake, Ind.: Eisenbrauns, 2006), 2:682–83.

¹⁴⁰ Thompson, "Near Eastern Suzerain-Vassal," 4.

¹⁴¹ Delbert R. Hillers, *Covenant: The History of a Biblical Idea* (Baltimore: Johns Hopkins University Press, 1969), 121; Huffmon, "Treaty Background," 31–37; Herbert B. Huffmon and Simon B. Parker, "A Further Note on the Treaty Background of Hebrew Yāda'," *BASOR* 184 (1966): 36–38.

¹⁴² Hillers, *Covenant*, 122.

¹⁴³ Mendenhall, "Covenant Forms," 59.

The first person perspective is also identifiable in the SMR. Immediately following the τάδε λέγει Ω (*tade legei*, "these are the words"), each of the SMR begins with the classic prophetic οἶδα (*oida*, "to know"; ידע, *ydṣ*) phrase,[144] which Hillers identifies as a "literary pattern known as the lawsuit of God."[145] The king, who enters into covenant with his subjects, acknowledges his historical intimacy with their circumstances so that we are justified in calling this section "a historical prologue."[146] The historical prologues within the seven churches all convey Jesus' knowledge (οἶδα, *oida*, "I know") of the deeds (ἔργα, *erga*) of the vassals and indicate previous knowledge and past relationship.[147]

Five of the messages use the phrase οἶδά σου τὰ ἔργα (*oida sou ta erga*, "I am aware of the deeds"), while Ephesus and Pergamum record a variation of the phrase (οἶδα τὰ ἔργα σου, *oida ta erga sou*, "I am aware of the deeds of you"). This still does not negate the historical nature of the prologue and the suzerain's knowledge of each church, but it demonstrates the intimate history between the two parties. The dissimilarities in phrasing are consistent with the ANEVT influence and do not weaken it.

Formal Ethical Stipulations

Within the ANEVT context, this section sets forth the covenant "obligations[148] imposed upon and accepted by the vassal."[149] Baltzer distinguishes between basic and detailed stipulations.[150] Walton identifies stipulations formulated in the precative, imperative, and conditional forms.[151]

Mendenhall observed that a key element of the Hittite treaty[152] is that: "the parity between the vassals, created by the Hittite king must not be changed. One cannot be a slave or

---

[144] Lars Hartman, "Form and Message: A Preliminary Discussion of 'Partial Texts' in Rev 1–3 and 22, 6ff," in *L'Apocalypse Johannique et L' Apocalyptique Dans Le NouveauTestament*, ed. Jan Lambrecht (Leuven: Leuven University Press, 1980), 143.

[145] Hillers, *Covenant*, 120.

[146] Baltzer uses *antecedent history*, while Aune identifies this as the *narratio* section. Klaus Baltzer, *The Covenant Formulary in Old Testament, Jewish, and Early Christian Writings*, trans. David E. Green (Oxford, U.K.: Basil Blackwell, 1971), 20–24; Aune, *Rev 1–5*, 121.

[147] de Lassus, "Le Septénaire," 41; Bandy, *Prophetic Lawsuit*, 217. Bandy points out a distinction between the ANEVT, where the historical prologue was meant to "rehearse the prior relationship between the two parties," and the oracle which "merely recounts the deeds of the churches". However, there is a previous historical knowledge that God is involved in, as he "walks among the lampstands" (2:1), holds the seven stars (3:1), and where Pergamum "remains true to my name" (2:13). This history cannot be denied in both situations and creates a functional equivalence with the ANEVT.

[148] The vassal-treaties of Esarhaddon list thirty-three stipulations, which follow the divine witnesses, and are to be kept by the vassal. Simo Parpola and Kazuko Watanabe, *Neo-Assyrian Treaties and Loyalty Oaths*, State Archives of Assyria 2 (Helsinki, Finland: Helsinki University Press, 1988), nos. 1–6, 46–57; Wiseman, "Vassal-Treaties," 23–24.

[149] Mendenhall, "Covenant Forms," 59; "Covenant," 1:714; Shea, "Covenantal Form," 72; Bright, *Covenant and Promise*, 37; Thompson, "Near Eastern Suzerain-Vassal," 4; McCarthy, *Treaty and Covenant*, 51 n.3.

[150] Baltzer, *Covenant Formulary*, 20, 22–24.

[151] Walton, Ancient Israelite Literature, 103.

[152] For the similarities with the stipulations of the king of Mari see, J. R. Kupper, "Zimri-Lim et Ses Vassaux," in

dependant of another. Every hostile action against a co-vassal is hostility against the king himself."[153]

The dominant theme of the ANEVT stipulations was the vassal's loyalty and faithfulness, with all controversies to be settled by the suzerain.[154] Loyalty to the suzerain would ensure protection and avoid punishment and possible attack.[155] What is more, Altman points out that "the vassal's obligations, as well as the suzerain's undertakings, were backed by a ceremonial oath taken by both of them before the images of the gods."[156]

Within the SMR, the transition to ethical stipulations is indicated by the imperative verbs, and presented in terms of commands:[157] *repent* (2:5, 16, 21, 22, 3:3, 19), *remember* (2:5; 3:3), *do not be afraid* (2:10), *be faithful* (2:10, 13; 3:14), *wake up* (3:2, 3), *hold fast* (3:11), and *be earnest* (3:19).[158] The stipulations are connected with the blessing and cursing as given in the OT covenant stipulations of Deuteronomy 30:19.[159] All churches are exhorted to repent,[160] except Smyrna and Philadelphia; these churches are exhorted to continue in faithfulness. These exhortations to the churches function in the same way as the stipulations in a covenant, conveying the new covenant obligation of faithfulness to their king.[161]

SANCTIONS

The structure moves from ethical stipulations and legal requirements to the sanctions set out for obedience or disobedience. Walton makes a subtle distinction between the curses and blessings when he states that: "this section entails not the specifics of what the suzerain will do in the event of either faithfulness to or violation of the treaty, but rather, the actions of the gods either for or against the vassal."[162]

Marchands, Diplomates et Empereurs: Études Sur La Civilisation Mésopotamienne Offertes À Paul Garelli, ed. Dominique Charpin and Francis Joannès (Paris, France: Recherche sur les civilisations, 1991), 179–84.

[153] Mendenhall, "Covenant Forms," 59.

[154] Thompson, *ANE Treaties*, 16.

[155] Lucas argues for the gracious nature of the stipulations as "the vassal keeps the stipulations of the covenant not to earn favour but as a response of gratitude for the overlord's benefactions." E. C. Lucas, "Covenant, Treaty, and Prophecy," *Themelios* 8, no. 1 (1982): 23. However, Lucas misses the element of threat and obligation in his comments.

[156] Amnon Altman, "Rethinking the Hittite System of Subordinate Countries from the Legal Point of View," *Journal of the American Oriental Society* 123, no. 4 (2003): 748; "Who Took an Oath on a Vassal Treaty: Only the Vassal King or Also the Suzerain?—the Hittite Evidence," *Zeitschrift Für Altorientalische Und Biblische Rechtgeschichte* 9 (2003): 178–84. *contra* Beckman, *Hittite Diplomatic Texts*, 2.

[157] Aune identifies the central sections of each proclamation as *dispositio*, which means "arrangement," not marked by any characteristic phrase but imperative verbs. Aune, *Rev 1–5*, 122.

[158] Aune identifies the formulae "let him hear what the Spirit says to the churches" and "the one who overcomes" as stipulations or injunctions, though they are more implicit. Ibid., 126.

[159] Within the Ten Commandments the stipulations are described in negative terms "You shall not . . ." (Exod 20:3–17).

[160] Thyatira is to change its ways.

[161] Shea, "Covenantal Form," 75.

[162] Walton, Ancient Israelite Literature, 104.

A standard characteristic of the ANEVT is the regularity of the list of *blessings and curses* (also reads *oaths*) along with the stipulations (*binding*), which are the most important elements of the structure.[163] Weinfeld points out that sanctions were:

> included not only in treaty texts but in all types of official legal settlements: judicial arrangements in connection with border conflicts, grants and land transactions, the imposition of a system of laws upon the people, imposing an oath in connection with succession, and assuring the loyalty of officials, soldiers, and craftsmen.[164]

This feature is consistent within the OT (Amos 1–2), and "form[s] the core of the prophetic message."[165] Within the Ten Commandments the blessings and curses are best identified in verse 5 and 6: "You shall not bow down to them or serve them, for I the Lord your God am a jealous God, visiting the iniquity of the fathers on the children to the third and the fourth generation of those who hate me, but showing steadfast love to thousands of those who love me and keep my commandments" (Exod 20:5–6).

In the context of the prophetic sanctions (Amos 1–2),[166] the vassal is cursed (*maledictions*) for disobedience (dishonors the treaty), and blessed (*benedictions*) for obedience to the stated stipulations (honors the treaty).[167]

As Mendenhall points out, sanctions surrounding the stipulations, mirrored in the OT, were usually identified in terms of "destruction, sterility, misery, poverty, plague, famine. The blessings conversely are divine protection, continuity of the vassal's line, health, prosperity, and peace"[168] (Lev 26:1–13; Deut 27–28). Walton makes a subtle distinction between the curses and blessings, observing that: "this section entails not the specifics of what the suzerain will do in the event of either faithfulness to or violation of the treaty, but rather, the actions of the gods either for or against the vassal."[169]

The two elements of blessing and curses are also central in the new covenant book of Revelation (1:3; 22:18, 19) and, in particular, the SMR.[170] The book of Revelation opens with a blessing (1:3) for those who publicly read and hear the words of the prophecy, while it closes with a maledictory oath for the preservation and transmission of the covenant text to the

---

[163] Beckman, Hittite Diplomatic Texts, 2; Rich Lowry, Admonition and Curse (London, U.K.: T&T Clark, 2004), 55–98; Noel Weeks, Admonition and Curse: The Ancient Near Eastern Treaty/Covenant Form as a Problem in Inter-Cultural Relationships (New York, N.Y.: T&T Clark, 2004).

[164] Weinfeld, *Deuteronomic School*, 61–62.

[165] Fensham, "Maledictions and Benedictions," 8 n. 48.

[166] Fensham loosely translates the German as *Salvation-Damnation* and points out that "the '*Heil-Unheil*'-prophecies form the core of the prophetic message." Ibid., 8 n.48.

[167] Mendenhall, "Covenant Forms," 60; Thompson, *ANE Treaties*, 17; Thompson, "Near Eastern Suzerain-Vassal," 4; Beckman, *Hittite Diplomatic Texts*, 3.

[168] Mendenhall, "Covenant," 1:715.

[169] Walton, Ancient Israelite Literature, 104.

[170] Graves, *SMRVT*, 266–81; Shea, "Covenantal Form," 74, 77–78; Strand, "Note on the Covenantal Form," 264; Hill, *NT Prophecy*, 79. Hill identifies the presence of blessings and curses in "seven beatitudes" (1:3, 14:13; 16:15; 19:9; 20:6; 22:7 and 22:14) and "seven woe-sentences" (8:13; 9:12; 11:14; 12:13; 18:10, 16, 19).

churches (22:18–19). The sanctions[171] pronounced upon the oral prophetic transmission within the book of Revelation further solidify the authority of the suzerain/king within the churches.[172]

This feature is also present in other early church documents (*Ap. John* II,1.35). There are similar prophetic oracles within the Synoptic tradition. The phrase ὁ ἔχων οὖς ἀκουσάτω [*o echōn ous akousatō*, "The one having ears to hear let him hear"] can be found with a similar structure in Matt 11:15, 12:9, 43, among the eschatological parables.[173]

Barr suggests that these words "function in the situation of extended orality as a control on the reader to faithfully reproduce the words of the prophecy."[174] The covenant message must be guarded because it comes from the King of the church.

The sanctions are clearly aligned with the faithfulness of the church (2–3) and result in the blessing of the new creation (no more curses 22:3, 7, 14) or with unfaithfulness and the curse (absence of the blessings 20:12–15).[175] However, the messages within the new covenant focus on the blessings[176] and the promise of salvation, in contrast with the OT and ANEVT pattern.[177] Because of this change in order, de Lassus argues that the SMR are inconsistent with the ANEVT.[178]

However, the ANEVT were also inconsistent in the use of malediction and benediction.[179] Hillers notes "That a few Assyrian inscriptions contain only a blessing, promised to those who will care for the memorial, and no curse."[180] The fact that two of the churches are missing a curse is consistent with the ANEVT pattern.

---

[171] Campbell prefers the term sanctions "since the issue is ratification of the covenant" and prefers "a designation which covers both eventualities" of blessing and curse. Campbell, "Findings, Seals, Trumpets, and Bowls," 80 n.40.

[172] Muse, "Rev 2–3," 156–59.

[173] Fensham also mentions this in a footnote: "the idea of breach of covenant is very important in the writings of Qumran." Fensham, "Maledictions and Benedictions," 6 n.37; Hillers, *Treaty-Curses*, 3.

[174] Barr, "The Apocalypse of John as Oral Enactment," 251.

[175] Du Preez, "Mission Perspective in the Book of Revelation," 154.

[176] Shea prefers the order *blessing* then *cursing*, since the messages focus on blessings. Shea, "Covenantal Form," 74. Note that in the OT blessings precede curse in Lev 26 and are definitely evident in Deuteronomy 27–30.

[177] Alan S. Bandy, "Patterns of Prophetic Lawsuits in the Oracles to the Seven Churches," *Neot* 45, no. 2 (2011): 194; Wiseman, "Vassal-Treaties," 27.

[178] de Lassus, "Le Septénaire," 44.

[179] Weinfeld explains the absence of the blessing in the Assyrian treaties in that "the Hittites felt it necessary not only to justify their demands for loyalty but also to give promises of help in time of danger, as well as to bestow divine blessings for loyal service. The Assyrian treaties neither gave promises to the vassal nor bestowed blessings, but, on the contrary, they increased and expanded the list of threats and curses in order to terrorize him." Weinfeld, *Deuteronomic School*, 68.

[180] Hillers, *Treaty-Curses*, 6 n.18; Graves, *SMRVT*, Inconsistent Pattern, 212.

BENEDICTION

All seven churches mention a blessing, while only six of the churches mention curses,[181] leaving Philadelphia (3:10) without a malediction. The OT provides the framework for a biblical understanding of the benediction and malediction, which may shed light on the covenantal pattern evident in the messages to the churches. Within the OT covenant structure, one of the ways the consequences of the blessings and curses are reflected in the covenant relationship is via the inheritance of land (longevity or exile). Those displaying covenant faithfulness would live long in the land and be established by God and not destroyed (חרם *ḥāram* or *ḥērem*, "destruction").[182] Longevity of life is central to the covenant blessing in the OT.

McCarthy explains that some of the ANEVT included a land grant.[183] Wijngaard states that the promise of the land was considered one of the greatest gifts of the suzerain to the vassal.[184] For Israel, the gift of land was first understood as Canaan (Gen 12:7; 15:18; Deut 1:8), then as the Davidic Kingdom (2 Sam 7), and ultimately as the new heaven and the new earth (Ps 37:11; Isa 65:17; Rev 5:10; 21:1–22:5). Thus, the consummation of the covenant promises to those who overcome is understood eschatologically. Within the NT context, the promise of the inheritance of the land is fulfilled in the inheritance of the kingdom of God,[185] which according to Holwerda "embraces all nations, the entire creation, and even the cosmos itself" (1 Cor 3:21–3; Rom 8:17–25; John 6:39, 44, 54).[186]

Is it possible that the temporal land grant is also promised to the faithful obedience and repentance of the churches (removal or establishment of the lampstand [church 1:20] from its place [2:5]) as a precursor of better things to come? Noticeable is the promise of longevity for those faithful to the covenant (21:7), to be understood or reinterpreted in a certain way (as is very deliberately done in *1 En.* 102:4–104:8).

MALEDICTION

Curses were common in the treaties of the Hittite Empire, Old Babylonian, Assyrian, Egyptian, and other periods.[187] As Wiseman points out, the idea of the curse or divine retribution was "an integral part of religious belief throughout the ancient Near East at all periods".[188] Weinfeld points out that sanctions were

---

[181] The curse is present in Ephesus 2:5b; Smyrna 2:10a; Pergamum 2:16b; Thyatira 2:22–23; Sardis 3:3b; and Laodicea 3:16 while absent in Philadelphia.

[182] Exod 22:20; Deut 4:1, 4; 8:1–4, 18–20; 11:9; 16:20; 28:9; Graves, *SMRVT*, Malediction, 160.

[183] McCarthy, Treaty and Covenant, 73.

[184] Wijngaards, *Vazal van Jahweh*, 150.

[185] Hester argues that inheritance was an important part of Paul's argument even though there is no specific mention of it in his letters. James D. Hester, *Paul's Concept of Inheritance: A Contribution to the Understanding of Heilsgeschichte*, SJTOP 19 (Edinburgh, U.K.: Oliver & Boyd, 1968), 82.

[186] David E. Holwerda, *Jesus and Israel: One Covenant or Two?* (Grand Rapids, Mich.: Eerdmans, 1995), 104.

[187] For an analysis of the role of imprecation in the ANE as protectors of the law, see Jan Assman, "When Justice Fails: Jurisdiction and Imprecation in Ancient Egypt and the Near East," *JEA* 78 (1992): 149–62.

[188] Wiseman, "Vassal-Treaties," 27.

included not only in treaty texts but in all types of official legal settlements: judicial arrangements in connection with border conflicts, grants and land transactions, the imposition of a system of laws upon the people, imposing an oath in connection with succession, and assuring the loyalty of officials, soldiers, and craftsmen.[189]

Further, in a broad sense within the ANEVT, the entire household is affected by the curse.[190]

Fensham identifies the curse-clause within the Akkadian texts of Ugarit, vassal-treaty of Sefire, but the benediction is absent from the vassal-treaties of Esarhaddon. He explains that: "this may be explained by the rigid attitude of the Assyrians against their vassals or by the mutilated state of the tablets. Where the benediction is used, it is couched in the casuistic style like the malediction-clauses."[191]

The idea of *curse* is not a foreign concept in Revelation as it is found in Revelation 22:3 (κατάθεμα, *katanathama*, "accursed thing") as the fulfilment of Zechariah 14:11 (חרם *ḥêrem*, "destruction"; LXX ἀνάθεμα, *anathema*, "cursed") and Isaiah 34:1–2 (חרם; LXX ἀπόλλυμι, *apollumi*, "destroy" or "ruin"). The curse is removed by the redemptive work of the Lamb.[192] It is rooted in the ancient idea of the *ḥāram* or *ḥêrem* (חרם *ḥêrem*, "destruction"), defined by *BDB* as: "ban, devote, exterminate... most often of devoting to destruction cities of Canaanites and other neighbours of Isr., *exterminating* inhabitants, and destroying or appropriating their possessions."[193] The חרם (*ḥêrem*, "destruction") or curse was pronounced on people (Canaanites) as a result of sin; thus, it was understood as a form of punishment within the Torah (Lev 27:19, 28–29; Num 21:2; Deut 13:16–17; Josh 6:21; 10:28; see also Isa 11:15).[194] If the five cursed cities in Revelation had been destroyed, then this would follow the characteristic archetype of the OT חרם (*ḥêrem*, "destruction"). According to Aune, the curse's connection with Zechariah 14:11 leads to the possibility for the removal of suffering and persecution, resulting in absolute protection in the New Jerusalem.[195] This would culminate in the ultimate fulfilment of the covenant blessings, and by antithesis the final completion of the malediction in eternal punishment.

---

[189] Weinfeld, *Deuteronomic School*, 61–62.

[190] Moshe Weinfeld, "The Common Heritage of Covenantal Traditions in the Ancient World," in *I Trattati Nel Mondo Antico-Forma, Ideologia, Funzione (Saggi Di Storia Antica)*, ed. Luciano Canfora, Mario Liverani, and Carlo Zaccagnini, vol. 2 (Roma: L'Erma, 1990), 187–88.

[191] Fensham, "Maledictions and Benedictions," 6; Mendenhall, "Covenant Forms," 60; Barr, "The Apocalypse of John as Oral Enactment," 243–56; Thompson, *ANE Treaties*, 17; Thompson, "Near Eastern Suzerain-Vassal," 4; Beckman, *Hittite Diplomatic Texts*, 3; David J. Bederman, *International Law in Antiquity*, Cambridge Studies in International and Comparative Law (Cambridge, U.K.: Cambridge University Press, 2001), 144–46.

[192] Rev 5:6; 5:12; 7:14, 17; 12:11; 17:14; 22:3; Beale, *Revelation*, 1112. D. Müller, "ἀνάθεμα," *NIDNTT* 1:414.

[193] Francis Brown et al., eds., "חרם," *BDB* 355–56. *HALOT* defines חרם "to dedicate something to Y. [Yahweh] by the ban [to devote to destruction] and thus rule out redemption" (Ludwig Koehler et al., eds., "חרם," *HALOT* 1:354). See Dempster, "Prophetic Invocation of the Ban," 134–37.

[194] Philip D. Stern, *The Biblical Ḥērem a Window on Israel's Religious Experience*, Brown Judaic Studies 211 (Atlanta, Ga.: Scholars Press, 1991), 89–121; Hyung Dae Park, *Finding Herem?: A Study of Luke-Acts in the Light of Herem*, ed. Mark Goodacre, 1st ed., LNTS 357 (London, U.K.: T&T Clark, 2007), 8–17; Beale, *Rev*, 1112; Osborne, *Revelation*, 773.

[195] Aune, *Rev 1–5*, 1179.

The Deuteronomic covenant stresses that the "fruit of your womb will be cursed, and the crops of your land, and the calves of your herds and the lambs of your flocks" (Deut 28:18). Within the New Covenant there appears to be a more individualistic responsibility (Jer 31:27–30) which moves away from the idea of communal responsibility. Certainly there is no mechanical/magical execution of the curse as symbolized by the imagery of the melting wax.[196]

However, in contrast to the ANEVT, there is the possibility of the curse being turned into a blessing through repentance.[197] For writers of the documents in the NT, Christ (the Lamb) fulfils the stipulations of the old covenant through his perfect obedience and by taking upon himself the curse of (κατάθεμα, *katathema*, *accursed thing*) the covenant (22:3). The work of Christ enables the believer to appropriate the blessings of forgiveness and eternal life (2:10c) by Christ himself bearing the curse (κατάρα, *katara*, "curse") on the cross (Deut 21:22–23; Gal 3:13). Strand interprets the work of Christ in covenantal terms:

> the Suzerain's own infinite sacrifice was made in order to establish the covenant relationship and is the fundamental standard by which to measure the crucial significance of that relationship. It is a relationship so vitally important that it must also be safeguarded by the vassal's own death, if need be (2:13; 12:11; 14:12–13; etc.).[198]

Revelation points to the consummation of the covenant through the work of the Lamb (*suzerain*) by permanently removing the curse (κατάθεμα, *katathema*, *accursed thing*, 22:3). The Lion/King (5:5) triumphs by humbling himself to become the suffering lamb (5:6, 8) turning the suzerain/vassal motif upside down.

How then, do the sanctions function within the seven oracles? Earlier scholars identified the blessings and curses as "dynamic," automatically working in themselves with inherent effectual power of their own, as when Isaac blesses Jacob and is unable to retract his blessing once it is given (Gen 27:35).[199] However, Thiselton has refuted this view with several effective arguments:[200]

1. God's pronouncement of his word is the issue in question. The power of the blessing and the curse resides within the deity, not the words.[201]

2. The blessings and curses are "effective, in most cases, only when performed by the appropriate person in the appropriate situation."[202]

---

[196] Moshe Weinfeld, "Covenant Making in Anatolia and Mesopotamia," *The Ancient Near Eastern Society of Columbia University* 22 (1992): 138; "The Loyalty Oath in the Ancient Near East," *UF* 8 (1976): 400–401.

[197] F. Charles Fensham, "Common Trends in Curses of the Near East: Treaties and Kudurru Inscriptions Compared with Maledictions of Amos and Isaiah," *ZAW* 75 (1963): 158, 173–74.

[198] Strand, "Note on the Covenantal Form," 264.

[199] Gerhard von Rad, *Old Testament Theology* (New York, N.Y.: Harper & Row, 1962), 2:80ff.; O. Prochsch, "λέγω," *TWNT* 4:89–100.

[200] Anthony C. Thiselton, "The Supposed Power of Words in the Biblical Writings," *JTS* 25, no. 2 (1974): 283–99.

[201] George B. Caird, *The Language and Imagery of the Bible* (London, U.K.: Duckworth, 1980), 22; Thiselton, "Power of Words," 290–99.

Lucas draws an important theological implication of the blessings and curses within covenant law. He sees the obedience of the vassals as a response of gratitude to the gracious act of the suzerain. He believes that the Hittite treaties were not legal contracts but gracious gifts of the overlords:

> The Hittite treaties are not contracts. They are gifts of grace given by the overlord to define and confirm an existing relationship (hence the historical prologue). . . . The point of the blessings and curses is that the faithful vassal continues to enjoy these benefactions, whereas persistent infidelity (which in the context of the treaty is seen as an expression of gross ingratitude) effectively puts an end to the relationship expressed by the covenant. However, the end is not necessarily definitive. The overlord could exercise mercy and renew the relationship with a repentant vassal.[203]

This call to repentance over the breached covenant is precisely what is found in the seven oracles. Since the blessing and curse are central to the ANEVT and Deuteronomic covenant structure,[204] along with the covenant lawsuit of the prophetic message, it is fair to argue that their presence in the SMR provides a clue to their genre and helps substantiate their covenantal/prophetic character.[205] The combination of the covenant structure in the SMR that is also found in Deuteronomy (the Torah) are founded on the ANEVT, and the blessing/curse elements central to the covenant lawsuit of the prophets, provide John's messages with evidence that they are prophetic hybrid oracles.

PROCLAMATION WITNESSES FORMULA

With the distribution of the stipulations, along with blessings and curses, it was customary for ancient treaty and oath documents to be sealed with a list of divine witnesses.[206] This common, although not universal, feature of the ANEVT invoked a list of gods of the suzerain and vassal as witnesses[207] to the covenant agreement.[208] Also, there were natural witnesses[209] of "mountains, rivers, springs, the great sea, heaven and earth, winds and clouds"[210] called upon as guarantors against disobedience. During the Roman period, a will (*Praetorian Testament*) was

---

[202] Thiselton, "Power of Words," 294.

[203] Lucas, "Covenant, Treaty, and Prophecy," 22–23; McCarthy, *Treaty and Covenant*, 79. Fensham seems to take exception to this idea when he states that "The mechanical, magical execution of the treaty-curse if stipulations of a legal document should be broken, stands in glaring contrast to the ego-theological approach of the prophetic writings." Fensham, "Common Trends in Curses," 173.

[204] Mendenhall, "Covenant Forms," 60; Thompson, *ANE Treaties*, 17.

[205] Shea does not connect the covenant blessing and cursing with the prophetic office; however, he focuses on the interpretation of the text, not genre. Shea, "Covenantal Form," 83.

[206] The divine witnesses were also listed in the vassal-treaties of Esarhaddon (672 BC), Bar-ga'ayah (8th cent. BC), Aššur-nirari VI of Assyria (753–746 BC; Wiseman, "Vassal-Treaties," 22–23), and Old Babylonian Syria. André Finet, "Les Dieux Voyageurs En Mésopotamie," *Akkadica* 21 (1981): 1–13.

[207] Harvey identifies this development within the treaty as *Invocation des dieux*. Harvey, "RIB-Pattern," 186.

[208] Mendenhall, "Covenant Forms," 60; Thompson, *ANE Treaties*, 16–17; Thompson, "Near Eastern Suzerain-Vassal," 4; McCarthy, *Treaty and Covenant*, 52, 63; Harvey, "RIB-Pattern," 186; Finet, "Les Dieux Voyageurs," 1–13.

[209] See the calling of meteorological and natural phenomena as witnesses, e.g., in *1 En.* 101.

[210] Mendenhall, "Covenant," 1:715.

sealed with seals from seven witnesses to attest to the validity of the will (AD 439; Theodosius *Nov.* 16.6; 21.4). Perhaps these seven messages represent the seven witnesses that seal the divine document.

In the OT, the witness in the ANE treaty sense is noticeably absent.[211] As Gaffney points out, the Decalogue (Ten Commandments, see Fig. 15) does not possess the divine witnesses "for the obvious reason that this would be completely inconsistent with the stipulation of monotheism embedded in the first commandment."[212] However, within the Decalogue, the divine witness may be identified as God himself in the natural phenomena connected with the event (Exod 20:18). This view is also argued by Philo who states: "For our conception of an oath is an appeal to God as a witness on some disputed matter. But nothing is uncertain or open to dispute with God.... Truly He needs no witness, for there is no other god to be His peer" (*Sacr.* 91–92 [Colson and Whitaker]).

Mendenhall and Herion earlier pointed out this same view that: "the list of gods as witnesses was of course incompatible with the monotheistic community, and so the members of the community themselves became the witnesses"[213] (see also Josh 24:22).[214] Under the OT prophetic court, the witness, called upon to observe the covenant, was either God himself, or at times the natural elements. Weinfeld explains, "in the biblical covenant we are obviously not to expect any [divine witnesses] but the one God who is party to the covenant, however natural forces

15. The Nash Papyrus, a collection of four papyrus fragments acquired in Egypt by W. L. Nash and first described by Stanley A. Cook in 1903. The fragments were the oldest Hebrew fragments known at that time which contained a portion of the biblical pre-Masoretic text, specifically the Ten Commandments and the Shema Yisrael prayer.

---

[211] Kitchen points out that "the gods of paganism were excluded, so the god-lists of the Ancient Oriental covenants are not found in the biblical ones." Kitchen, *Ancient Orient*, 97.

[212] Edward McGlynn Gaffney, Jr., "Of Covenants Ancient and New: The Influence of Secular Law on Biblical Religion," *Journal of Law and Religion* 2, no. 1 (1984): 125; Herbert B. Huffmon, "The Covenant Lawsuit in the Prophets," *JBL* 68, no. 4 (1959): 285–95.

[213] Harvey also proposes that the vassals themselves are witnesses (Josh 24:22; Exod 24:8; Deut 26:16–19; 1 Sam 12:20–25), abandoning the polytheistic term "heaven and earth." Julien Harvey, *Le Plaidoyer Prophétique, Contre Israël Après La Rupture de L'alliance: Étude D'une Formule Littéraire de l'Ancien Testament* (Paris: Bruges, 1967), 107.

[214] George E. Mendenhall and Gary A. Herion, "Covenant," ed. David Noel Freedman et al., *ABD* (New York, N.Y.: Doubleday, 1996), 1:1184.

are invoked as witnesses: heaven and earth,[215] and in prophecy, mountains and hills (Mic 6:1–2)."[216] Huffmon explores the role of the mountains, rivers, heaven, earth, sea, winds and clouds as witnesses to the covenant lawsuit in Isa 1:2–20, Mic 6:1–8, Jer 2:4–13, Deut 32:1, and Pss 50:1–15.[217] In addition, with both biblical and Near Eastern covenants, the community-at-large gathered to witness the covenant (2 Kgs 23:1–3). The monotheistic nature of the Hebrew witness in contrast with Hittite Polytheism could also explain why the order is reversed from blessings–curses–witness to witness–curses–blessing in the OT.[218]

The absence of an expressly stated list of divine witnesses in the SMR is not an argument against the ANE influence on the SMR,[219] but indicates the superiority of the biblical suzerain, where the Spirit of Christ himself is the divine witness in the theistic NT covenant context. Since there is a change in the situation from the ANEVT, there is a change of form in the NT.[220]

However, witness language is found in rich use throughout Revelation; from the mentioning of the heavens and earth (12:12),[221] to the formal witnesses' role of angels, John (1:2), the church, the spirit, and Christ (22:7b; 16–20; see also Deut 4:26). The Greek family of μάρτυς—μαρτυρία (*martus—marturia*, "witness—testimony") are found nine times in Revelation.[222] The witness is assumed in the SMR, but the witness signature attached to each oracle[223] indicates that the Spirit of Christ[224] is like an independent voice underlining what the

---

[215] Deut 4:26; 30:19; 31:28; Isa 1:2–20; Hos 2:21–22; Weinfeld mentions another witness in the great stone which Joshua placed in the Shechem sanctuary. Weinfeld, *Deuteronomic School*, 62.

[216] Weinfeld, "Loyalty Oath in the ANE," 395; Walther Eichrodt, "Prophet and Covenant: Observations on the Exegesis of Isaiah," in *Proclamation and Presence: Old Testament Essays in Honour of Gwynne Henton Davies*, ed. John I. Durham and J. Roy Porter (Louisville, Ky.: Westminster/Knox, 1970), 175. *contra* Eichrodt writes, "It is equally questionable whether we are on sure ground when the calling of heaven and earth as witnesses or judges (as in Isa 1.2 but also in Micah 6.1f.; Jer 2.12; Deut 32.1; Ps 50.4) is taken to be regular part of the covenant formula on the basis of similar appeals in the Hittite treaties" (ibid). However, Eichrodt gives no evidence for his doubts.

[217] Huffmon, "Covenant Lawsuit," 285–95.

[218] Kitchen, *Ancient Orient*, 97.

[219] Graves, *SMRVT*, Inconsistent Pattern, 212. Despite this, some commentators like de Lassus use this inconsistency to argue against ANEVT influence. He argues, "It is debatable to interpret this formula as if the Spirit was a witness of a covenant between Christ and the Churches. As regards the joint mention of the heaven and earth in 12:12, apart from the fact that it occurs separately from the group of seven letters and that the sea is associated with the earth (which is not the case in the covenant form), it contains nothing that pertains to witness" (de Lassus, "Le Septénaire," 43–44 [Graves]).

[220] The Monotheistic nature of the Hebrew witness in contrast with Hittite Polytheism could also explain why the order is reversed from blessings–curses–witness to witness–curses–blessing in the OT. See Kitchen, *Ancient Orient*, 97; Bright, *Covenant and Promise*, 37.

[221] Heaven and earth are connected in at least six occurrences. de Lassus, "Le Septénaire," 42.

[222] Rev 1:2, 9; 6:9; 11:7; 12:11, 17; 15:4; 19:10; 20:4.

[223] Rev 2:7; 11; 17; 29; 3:6; 13; 22; see also 22:18.

[224] The debate over the speaker in 22:18 leans toward the Spirit of Christ, rather than John, given the context that Jesus is the speaker in both verse 16 and 2. Osborne, *Revelation*, 794. The phrase is also found in 13:9, and a variation of it can be found in 13:18.

message says.[225] The Spirit of Christ is functionally equivalent to the witness formula, but it is conveyed in a different form of expression.

Not only does the phrase "He who has an ear, let him hear what the Spirit says to the churches" (2:7, etc.) serve as a divine witness,[226] but it also serves as a "proclamation formula . . . i.e., as an injunction to an audience to pay very close attention to the message that it accompanies."[227] It not only identifies the speaker, but, according to Aune, "when the proclamation formula concludes an oracle, it functions as a *prophetic signature*."[228] This formula witnesses to the divine nature of the message spoken by the prophet; the prophetic message introduced by the divine Spirit of Christ is the faithful witness (1:5; 3:14). Since the message is preceded and followed by words of Christ, it appears that the Lord (Christ) is the actual speaker of the formula. Christ identifies his words with the voice of the Spirit speaking to the churches. It is as though Christ authenticates John's message by the witness formula, and by so doing, calls the church to pay attention to the message. This is different from an independent Spirit-borne message and fits the context where no external ratification is needed.

As Aune points out, this formula has "no close verbal parallels in ancient literature with the exception of the parable tradition found in the Synoptic Gospels and in some apocryphal gospels".[229] There appears to be a paraenetic function connected with this formula.[230]

However, there is a partial variation on this formula in Ezekiel 3:27. As demonstrated by Aune, this formula has its roots in the legal courtroom or in the introduction of legal instruction.[231] They witnessed to the authentication of the divine author as an incentive to listen to the message. This proclamation witness formula calls the churches to hear the proclamation of the divine witness and to heed the message by the Spirit who spoke it. Thus, this repeated phrase of the messenger functions as a proclamation witness formula, calling the churches to hear the proclamation of the divine witness, as authenticated by the voice of Christ and inspired by the Spirit.

Deposit and Public Reading

Within the ANE, the covenant or suzerainty treaty document was perpetuated through the deposit of the document in a safe place (temple), and its periodic public reading[232] in a covenant

---

[225] de Lassus, "Le Septénaire," 42.
[226] Bandy, *Prophetic Lawsuit*, 218 n.120.
[227] Aune, *Rev 1–5*, 123.
[228] Ibid.
[229] Ibid.; Matt 11:15; 13:9, 43; Luke 8:8; 14:35; 1 Cor 14:37–38; *Odes Sol.* 3:10–11.
[230] Graves, *SMRVT*, Parabolic Revealing/Concealing, 303.
[231] Mic 6:2; Jer 2:4–5; Isa 49:1; 51:4; Aune, *Rev 1–5*, 123.
[232] Harvey uses the term "technical details" (*détails techniques*) to describe the "conservation of the documents" while, Beckman prefers the term *depositions*. Du Preez and McCarthy prefer the term *Document Clause*, as they combine the element of public reading with preservation. Mendenhall, "Covenant Forms," 59–60; Korošec, *Hethitische Staatsverträge*, 12–14; Beckman, "Hittite Treaties," 3; Harvey, "RIB-Pattern," 186; Du Preez, "Ancient Near Eastern

renewal ceremony.²³³ The covenant was considered "a sacred act and object"²³⁴ and thus it was deposited in the temple under the protection of the gods. This practice is mentioned, for example, in the treaty between Shattiwaza of Mittanni and Suppiluliuma I of Hatti and reads: "[A duplicate of this tablet is deposited] in the land [of Mittanni before the Storm-god, Lord of Kurinnu of Kahat. It shall be read repeatedly, for ever and ever], before the king of the land [of Mittanni and before the Hurrians]."²³⁵

It was also incorporated as law in the legislation of the kingdom and kept in a safe place for future public readings anywhere "from one to four times a year."²³⁶

The protection and public reading of the treaty are not considered part of the formal structure of the treaty, but they are functional elements that accompany the treaties, and demonstrate solidarity with the elements of the ANEVT formulary and provide a delivery mechanism for perpetuity.

The OT describes the practice of the deposit and public reading of the covenant²³⁷ and understood it in terms of *covenant renewal* ²³⁸ and what scholars call the *perpetuation of the covenant* relationship.²³⁹ Although early in Israel's history there was no temple to deposit their covenants, the Decalogue was placed in the Ark of the Covenant (see Fig. 16) in the holy of holies for safe keeping (Exod 25:16; 40:20; Josh 24:26). Millard believes that: "the deposit of the stone tablets in the Ark, which was then placed

16. Replica of the Ark of the Covenant.

Vassal Treaties and the Book of Revelation: Possible Links," 38; McCarthy, *Treaty and Covenant*, 52–63; Graves, *SMRVT*, 130.

²³³ Mendenhall, "Covenant Forms," 60; "Covenant," 1:715; Thompson, "Near Eastern Suzerain-Vassal," 4.

²³⁴ Mendenhall and Herion, "Covenant," 1181.

²³⁵ Beckman, *Hittite Diplomatic Texts*, 51.

²³⁶ Mendenhall and Herion, "Covenant," 1181.

²³⁷ Exod 25:16; 40:20; Deut 10:1–5; 31:9–13, 24–26; Josh 24:26; see also 2 Kgs 23:1–3.

²³⁸ Campbell calls this formula the *inheritance questions,* but it is more appropriate as a blessing given to the overcomer. Chilton prefers using *succession arrangements,* and Sutton prefers *continuity*. Campbell, "Findings, Seals, Trumpets, and Bowls," 80; Chilton, *Days of Vengeance*, 16–20; Sutton, *That You May Prosper*, 96.

²³⁹ Larry L. Walker, "Deuteronomy," ed. Merrill C. Tenney and Moises Silva, *ZEB* (Grand Rapids, Mich.: Zondervan, 2009), 2:124; John I. Durham, *Exodus*, WBC 3 (Dallas, Tex.: Word Books, 1987), 414.

in the holiest part of the Tabernacle, is exactly like the deposit of ancient treaty texts in the presence of the gods."[240] Public reading was carried out by Moses who "took the Book of the Covenant and read it in the hearing of the people" (Exod 24:7–8; see also Exod 23:17 and Deut 27:11–26).

Lucas and Weinfeld observed that the liturgy of the covenant renewal ceremony could have been the way the suzerainty treaty form was passed down to the later prophetic generation.[241] This ratification ceremony was also closely connected with the documentary clause and the words of the prophets.[242]

17. Woman holding wax tablets in the form of the codex (book) and stylus (so-called *Sappho*). Letters were first written on wax tablets for easy correction before being copied to scrolls. Fresco from Pompeii, ca. 55–79 AD. (inv. no. 9084).

Even this element of the ANEVT mechanism is evident in the book of Revelation. Instructions in Revelation to read the covenant publicly and deposit it in the churches are also present through Christ's directions that these prophetic oracles should be circulated and heard (implies reading) in the churches (1:11; 2:7, 11 etc.). Thus, the instruction given to John to "*write* on a scroll what you see and *send* it to the seven churches" (1:11, see Fig. 17) functions as the deposit and the call formula (call to hear the messages), perpetuating the covenant.

The repeated phrase "He who has an ear, let him hear what the Spirit says to the churches"[243] (2:7, 11, 17, 29, 3:6, 13, 22) implies that these oracles were to be read publicly in the churches (1:3; 11; 19; 22:16, 18), so the members could hear and not forget the Spirit's message. Since these messages are to be treated as a whole, the *deposit/public reading* element is functionally present as similar instructions for the perpetuity of the messages.[244]

---

[240] Allen R. Millard, "The Tablets in the Ark," in *Reading the Law: Studies in Honour of Gordon J. Wenham*, ed. J. Gordon McConville and Karl Möller, LHSOT 461 (New York, N.Y.: T&T Clark, 2007), 265.

[241] Lucas, "Covenant, Treaty, and Prophecy," 22; Weinfeld, *Deuteronomic School*, 51–58; 158–78.

[242] A similar situation is established in *The Shepherd of Hermas* when Hermas is asked, "'Can you report these things to God's elect?' I said to her, 'Madam, I cannot remember so many things; but give me the little book, so that I can copy it.' . . . Hermas is to take this book back and give it to the "elders" to be read in church and send it abroad to others to do likewise" (*Vis.* 2.1.3; 2.2.2–3 [Lightfoot]). Barr, "The Apocalypse of John as Oral Enactment," 251 n.20.

[243] Technically the *proclamation messenger formula* combines the two features of the divine witness and the public reading.

[244] Weinfeld, "Common Heritage," 189. The remembrance of the covenant messages by the churches is also

Barr makes this conclusion about the deposit and public readings:

> [The deposit and oral readings] serve as limits on oral invention. On the other hand, as words read before the assembly they function to increase the status and power of the reading. By guaranteeing the integrity of the presentation, they increase the power of the oral message. The hearers are assured that they hear the "very word of John," so to speak. In hearing the voice of John, they hear far more, . . . the prophet as surrogate for Jesus.[245]

The delivery and public reading of the SMR in the churches are functionally equivalent to the deposit and public reading of the ANEVT.

METHODOLOGY

The core of the methodology employed in this commentary will involve the integration of historical, theological, and literary analysis to arrive at the meaning of the text.[246] Therefore, this work will incorporate an interdisciplinary set of hermeneutical tools.

THE INFLUENCE OF THE OT

Most scholars acknowledge the influence of the OT prophets in the Book of Revelation.[247] Bandy has traced the background of the "literary phenomenon signaling a motif intentionally woven into the tapestry of John's vision echoing the pattern of prophetic lawsuits"[248] back to the OT, and it is probable that the OT may also hold the key to the theological significance and literary structure of the SMR.

HISTORICAL CHURCHES

Most scholars also agree that John wrote the seven prophetic messages to historical first-century churches in Asia Minor. Therefore, this work will interpret the messages on the assumption that John was addressing his contemporary Christian readers[249] in a prophetic manner, and like Scripture generally, Revelation has a permanent and lasting message for subsequent readers.[250]

---

functionally equivalent to the covenant renewal ceremony in the Lord's Supper as words of institution are read publicly (1 Cor 11:23–26).

[245] Barr, "The Apocalypse of John as Oral Enactment," 251.

[246] N. T. Wright, *The New Testament and the People of God: Christian Origins and the Question of God* (Minneapolis: Fortress Press, 1992), 31–144; Adolf Schlatter, *The History of the Christ: The Foundation of New Testament Theology*, trans. Andreas J. Köstenberger (Grand Rapids, Mich.: Baker Academic, 1997), 17–20.

[247] Ferrell Jenkins, *The Old Testament in the Book of Revelation* (Grand Rapids, Mich.: Baker, 1976); Bauckham, *Climax of Prophecy*, 143–57; Steve Moyise, "The Language of the Old Testament in the Apocalypse," *JSNT* 22, no. 76 (2000): 97–113; *The Old Testament in the Book of Revelation*, JSNTSup 115 (Sheffield, U.K.: Sheffield Academic, 1995); Gregory K. Beale, *John's Use of the Old Testament in Revelation*, LNTS (New York, N.Y.: Bloomsbury, 2014).

[248] Bandy, "Patterns of Prophetic Lawsuits," 179; *Prophetic Lawsuit*, 24–58.

[249] Beale maintains that there are no specific prophesied historical events in Revelation except "2:10, 22 and 3:9–10 which are unconditional prophecies to be fulfilled imminently in the specific local churches of Smyrna, Thyatira, and Philadelphia". Beale, *Revelation*, 48 n.16.

[250] According to Bauckham, Paul's messages were "addressed to specific churches as representative of all the

This is evident from the proclamation witness formula[251] attached to each of the messages: "he who has an ear, let him hear what the Spirit says to the churches" (2:7, 11, 17, 29; 3:6, 13, 22).[252]

UNITY

It will be assumed that the messages in Revelation fit within the larger corpus as a literary unity. Although Aune cautions that the "literary unity and coherence of Revelation have been exaggerated, though they certainly exist in some levels of composition,"[253] the scholarly consensus argues for the literary unity of the entire book of Revelation and the SMR as part of the whole.[254] Hahn observes that scholarly consensus has abandoned the notion of seven independent proclamations; instead, "the letters represent an integral part of the apocalyptic design." [Graves][255] Therefore, scholars treat the SMR as a unity within the context of the vision of Revelation.[256] As Graves concluded in his dissertation:

> This unity does not obliterate the individual elements within each church, evident in the unique local references and messages to each church. Revelation 2 and 3 are a coherent *literary unity*. These chapters contain seven mutually inter-related parts that are individually, cumulatively, and

---

churches." Bauckham, *Theology of Revelation*, 16; Beale, *Revelation*, 204; Alan F. Johnson et al., *Hebrews - Revelation*, ed. Tremper Longman III and David E. Garland, Revised, EBC 13 (Grand Rapids, Mich.: Zondervan, 2006), 420; André Feuillet, *The Apocalypse*, trans. T. E. Crane (New York, N.Y.: Alba, 1965), 50; Robert L. Thomas, "The Chronological Interpretation of Revelation 2–3," *BSac* 124, no. 496 (1967): 327; Kistemaker, *Revelation*, 12, 108.

[251] Graves, *SMRVT*, Proclamation Witnesses Formula, 170.

[252] It is conceded that this phrase could refer to each church individually as it is repeatedly addressed to each church. But as Ramsay points out, "those others [cities] were not much in the writer's mind: he was absorbed with the thought of that one city: he saw only death before it. But the other cities which were connected with it may be warned by its fate; and he that overcometh shall be spared and honoured". Ramsay, *Letters: Updated*, 28.

[253] Aune, *Rev 1–5*, cx–cxxxiv; Adela Yarbro Collins, "The Book of Revelation," in *The Encyclopedia of Apocalypticism*, ed. John Joseph Collins, Bernard McGinn, and Stephen J. Stein (New York, N.Y.: T&T Clark, 2000), 389. Collins states that, "It is now generally accepted that the author of the book of Revelation used sources, but not as many or as extensive ones as some source critics have argued."

[254] See Modeste for a comprehensive review and defence of the literary unity (style and grammar) of Revelation, arguing for strong coherence in both the content and from the situational, compositional, and theological unity concluding that, above all, "the letters and visions… are united by their common focus on Christ and his judgment and salvation" Rakoto E. Modeste, "Unity of the Letters and Visions in the Revelation of John" (Ph.D. diss., Lutheran School of Theology, 1991), 64; Gerard Mussies, *The Morphology of Koine Greek, As Used in the Apocalypse of St. John: A Study in Bilingualism*, NovTSup 27 (Leiden: Brill, 1971), 351; Stephen S. Smalley, *Thunder and Love: John's Revelation and John's Community* (Milton Keynes, England: Wood, 1994), 97–101; C. H. Parez, "The Seven Letters and the Rest of the Apocalypse," *JTS* 12, no. 46 (1911): 284–86; Collins, *Combat Myth*, 32–40; Ramsay, *Letters: Updated*, 27–28.

[255] Ferdinand Hahn, "Die Sendschreiben Der Johannesapokalypse: Ein Beitrag Zur Bestimmung Prophetischer Redeformen," in *Tradition Und Glauben: Das Frühe Christentum in Seiner Umwelt*, ed. Karl Georg Kuhn et al. (Göttingen: Vandenhoeck & Ruprecht, 1971), 362; André Feuillet, *The Apocalypse*, trans. T. E. Crane (New York, N.Y.: Alba, 1965), 48; Beasley-Murray, *Revelation*, NCB, 71; Kistemaker, *Revelation*, 109; Krodel, *Revelation*, 100.

[256] Luverne C. Tengbom, "Studies in the Interpretation of Revelation Two and Three" (Ph.D. diss., Hartford Seminary, 1976), 84–88.

collectively embedded within the larger text, to which they both reciprocally contribute to the whole message.[257]

HEBRAIC-SEMITIC AND GRAECO-ROMAN PRESENCE

This exegetical study, of each of the seven messages in Revelation, will recognize the interrelationships between the ANEVT schema of the prophetic oracles (Hebraic-Semitic) and the imperial edicts with local references (Graeco-Roman).

JOHN, IN THE OT PROPHETIC TRADITION

John came to these troubled churches in the tradition of the OT prophets (Moses, Jeremiah, Ezekiel, and Daniel) to exhort (παραίνεσις, *paraenesis*) them to repentance and know God's covenant blessing. This was the classic prophetic message for times of persecution and suffering. To guard the message from the Roman authorities, John concealed his message using OT symbols and obscure cultural clues. This cryptic methodology (conceal/reveal Mark 4:10–12) is evident from the same parabolic formula (2:7, 11, 17, 29; 3:6, 13, 22) used by Jesus, where he taught in parables: "he who has ears to hear, let him hear" (Mark 4:9, 23; see *Quotes from Antiquity*).[258]

Quotes from Antiquity

Jesus explains parables:

And he [Jesus] said to them, "To you has been given the secret of the kingdom of God, but for those outside everything is in parables, so that "they may indeed see but not perceive, and may indeed hear but not understand, lest they should turn and be forgiven." (Mark 4:11–12; Isa 6:9–10)

---

[257] Graves, *SMRVT*, 44.
[258] Beale, *Revelation*, 234, 236–39.

4

Elegant Ephesus

The History of the City

*I*n order to understand the message to glorious and elegant Ephesus, it is helpful to examine both the cultural (Graeco-Roman) history of Ephesus, as well as the (Hebraic-Semitic) OT theological roots of the message.[1] This chapter will examine the historical background to the city of Ephesus.

THE GEOGRAPHY OF EPHESUS

Ephesus (Ἐφέσος, modern *Selçuk*; coordinates: 37:56:28 N 27:20:30 E)[2] was an ancient Greek city built on the Aegean coast by Greek colonizers[3] in ca. 1100 BC[4] over *Apaša*, the royal Hittite city of greater Arzawa.[5]

Τῷ ἀγγέλῳ τῆς ἐν Ἐφέσῳ ἐκκλησίας γράψον·

"To the angel [*messenger*] of the church in Ephesus write:" (Rev 2:1a)

---

[1] While Thompson is highly critical of Hemer's (including Ramsay's) referentiality as a primary way to interpret a text (*Apocalypse and Empire*, 202–203), Thompson sees the apocalypse as "grounded in first-century Asian life and [believes that it] necessarily entangles itself in all power structures in all dimensions of human society." Thompson's aversion is to social stereotypes of "upheaval and crisis" when he argues that it is "not class-specific or status-specific." Thompson, *Apocalypse and Empire*, 196–97.

[2] For an extensive treatment of Ephesus, see Ludwig Bürchner, "Ephesos," in *Paulys Realencyclopädie Der Classischen Altertumswissenschaft*, ed. August Friedrich Pauly, Georg Wissowa, and S. Kroll, 5th ed., vol. 2 (Stuttgart, Germany: Metzler, 1905), 2773–2822; Ramsay, *Letters to Seven Churches*, 151–71; Josef Keil, *Zur Topographie Und Geschichte von Ephesos*, JÖAI 21–22 (Vienna: ÖAI, 1922), 21–22; George E. Bean, *Aegean Turkey: An Archaeological Guide* (New York, N.Y.: Praeger, 1966), 160–84; Hemer, *Letters to the Seven Churches*, 35–41; Worth, Jr., *Greco-Asian Culture*, 9–68; Richard Oster, *A Bibliography of Ancient Ephesus* (Dorst: Scarecrow, 1987).

[3] Mehmet Fatih Yavuz, "Ephesus," in *OEAGR*, ed. Michael Gagarin, vol. 3 (New York, N.Y.: Oxford University Press, 2010), 78.

[4] Sjef Van Tilborg, *Reading John in Ephesus*, NovTSup 83 (Leiden: Brill Academic, 1997), 33–35.

[5] John Garstang and Oliver Robert Gurney, *The Geography of the Hittite Empire*, OPBIAA 5 (London, U.K.: British Institute of Archaeology at Ankara, 1959), 88; J. David Hawkins, "The Arzawa Letters in Recent Perspective," *British Museum Studies in Ancient Egypt and Sudan* 14 (2009): 76; Gregory McMahon and Sharon R. Steadman, eds., *The Oxford Handbook of Ancient Anatolia* (Oxford, U.K.: Oxford University Press, 2011), 366, 608.

According to Greek legend the Amazons[6] established the city (Strabo *Geogr.* 11.5.3–4) along with the cult of Artemis (Callimachus *Hymn. Dian.* 3.233)[7] as one of the twelve cities of the Ionian league.[8]

THE HISTORY OF EPHESUS

The city was captured by Croesus, King of Lydia, in ca. 555 BC (Herodotus *Hist.* 1.26), only to be taken by Cyrus the Persian in ca. 546 BC.[9] Following the Persian wars, Ephesus was a member of the Delian League (an Athenian maritime confederacy), only to revolt in ca. 412 and side with the Spartan's during the Peloponnesian war (431–404 BC). Following the liberation of Ionia from the Persians by Alexander the Great in 334 BC, Ephesus fell under Hellenistic rule. Following Alexander's death (323 BC), Lysimachus controlled the area around Ephesus (Pausanias *Descr.* 1.9.7) and in 287 BC moved the city to a new location and enlarged it by building a six-mile long wall around the city (Strabo *Geogr.* 14.1.21). With the defeat of Antiochus the Great in 190 BC, Ephesus passed into the control of the Seleucids under the Pergamene rulers until 133 BC, when it passed into the control of the Romans.[10] Pergamum remained the capital of Asia[11] until Emperor Augustus[12] declared Ephesus its capital in ca. 29

---

[6] The Amazons were a female tribe of warriors ruled by a Queen, who settled in central Asia Minor (Cappadocia). Adrienne Mayor, *The Amazons: Lives and Legends of Warrior Women across the Ancient World* (Princeton, N.J.: Princeton University Press, 2014), 34–36.

[7] Burkert points out that the Artemis cult originated prior to the Greek colonization of Ionia. Walter Burkert, *Greek Religion* (Cambridge, Mass.: Harvard University Press, 1985), 149–52; Andrew E. Hill, "Ancient Art and Artemis: Toward Explaining the Polymastic Nature of the Figurine," *JANES* 21 (1992): 92.

[8] Pliny *Nat.* 34.53; Strabo *Geogr.* 8.71; Pausanias *Descr.* 7.2.6; Richard E. Oster, "Ephesus as a Religious Center Under the Principate, I: Paganism Before Constantine," *ANRW* 18, no. 3 (1990): 1720–21.

[9] Ekrem Akurgal, *Ancient Civilizations and Ruins of Turkey from Prehistoric Times until the End of the Roman Empire*, trans. John Whybrow and Mollie Emre, 2nd ed. (Istanbul: Mobil Oil Turk A. S., 1985), 142.

[10] Ibid., 143.

[11] Gallusz points out "Scholarly opinion is divided concerning the identity of the capital of Asia Minor at the time of the writing of Revelation. The prevailing consensus is that the capital was in Pergamon when Rome took over the province. It is also generally accepted that the centre was moved to Ephesus a few centuries later. However when the capital was located during the first and second centuries CE is controversial." Laszlo Gallusz, *The Throne Motif in the Book of Revelation*, LNTS (New York, N.Y.: Bloomsbury, 2013), 204; Worth, Jr., *Roman Culture*, 159–62 nn.24–34. See Worth for a list of scholars on either side of the debate.

[12] Osborne, following Ramsay, reports "that Pergamum was the capital until Hadrian made Ephesus capital in AD 129." Osborne, *Revelation*, 108 n.2; William M. Ramsay, "Pergamus or Pergamum," in *DBib*, ed. James Hastings, Frederick C. Grant, and Harold. H. Rowley, vol. 3 (New York, N.Y.: Scribner's Sons, 1909), 751; E. J. Banks, "Ephesus," ed. James Orr and Melvin Grove Kyle, *ISBE* (Grand Rapids, Mich.: Hendrickson, 1915), 961.

BC.[13] Ephesus then competed with Smyrna and Pergamum for official honors, temples, and recognition from Rome, given in the form of "political concord" (ὁμόνοια, *homonoia*).[14]

THE POPULATION OF EPHESUS

Apollonius of Tyana (AD ca. 15–100) quoted by Philostratus (AD ca. 172–250) states that:

> Ephesus grew in size beyond all other cities of Ionia and Lydia, and stretched herself out to the sea, on the promontory over which she is built, and is filled with studious people, both philosophers and rhetoricians, thanks to whom the city owes her strength, not to her cavalry, but to the tens of thousands of her inhabitants in whom she encourages wisdom." (Philostratus *Vit. Apoll.* 8.7.8 [Conybeare])

Ephesus grew to became the fifth largest city in the Roman Empire (after Rome,[15] Antioch [Syria], Alexandria Troas and Sardis),[16] and held a prominent place in Asia Minor (third largest) as a "commercial center," (ἐμπόριον, *emporion;* Strabo *Geogr.* 14.1.24). In the first cent. AD, according to Hanson, Ephesus had a population of between 33,600 and 56,000,[17] although most scholars in the past,[18] based on Beloch's assessment,[19] have placed the size much higher, at between 200,000 and 250,000,[20] with a few as high as 300,000 to 500,000.[21] Bagnall and Warden

---

[13] Paul R. Trebilco, "Asia," in *The Book of Acts in Its Graeco-Roman Setting*, ed. David W. Gill and Conrad H. Gempf, vol. 2, Book of Acts in Its First Century Setting 2 (Grand Rapids, Mich.: Eerdmans, 1994), 304; Monte A. Shanks, *Papias and the New Testament* (Eugene, Oreg.: Wipf & Stock, 2013), 97.

[14] John Paul Lotz, "The Homonoia Coins of Asia Minor and Ephesians 1:21," *TynBul* 50, no. 2 (1999): 173–88; Ursula Kampmann, "Homonoia Politics in Asia Minor," in *Pergamon-Citadel of the Gods: Archaeological Record, Literary Description, and Religious Development*, ed. Helmut Koester (Harrisburg, Pa.: Morehouse, 2002), 385.

[15] According to Storey, Rome had a population of 450,000 in the Roman period. Glenn R. Storey, "The Population of Ancient Rome," *Antiquity* 71, no. 274 (1997): 966–78.

[16] Krodel considers Ephesus the fourth largest city of the Roman Empire, but according to Hanson, Sardis had a larger population than both Ephesus and Alexandria Troas. Krodel, *Revelation*, 104; J. W. Hanson, "The Urban System of Roman Asia Minor and Wider Urban Connectivity," in *Settlement, Urbanization, and Population*, ed. Alan Bowman and Andrew Wilson, OSRE (Oxford, U.K.: Oxford University Press, 2011), 254.

[17] Hanson, "Urban System," 252–57.

[18] See Worth for a detailed breakdown of which scholars hold what date. Worth, Jr., *Greco-Asian Culture*, 11–12, 222–24.

[19] Julius Beloch, *Die bevölkerung der griechisch-römischen welt*, Historische Beiträge Zur Bevölkerungslehre 1 (Duncker & Humblot, 1886), 230–31; T. R. S. Broughton, "Roman Asia Minor," in *An Economic Survey of Ancient Rome: Africa, Syria, Greece, Asia Minor*, ed. Tenney Frank, vol. 4 (Baltimore, Md.: John Hopkins University Press, 1975), 4:812–16; Richard P. Duncan-Jones, *The Economy of the Roman Empire: Quantitative Studies* (Cambridge, Mass.: Cambridge University Press, 1974), 260–61 n.4; Magie, *Roman Rule in Asia Minor*, 1:585; 2:1446 n.50. Magie reduces the population slightly to 200,000.

[20] Bean, Aegean Turkey, 164; Edwin M. Yamauchi, New Testament Cities in Western Asia Minor: Light from Archaeology on Cities of Paul and the Seven Churches of Revelation (Eugene, Oreg.: Wipf & Stock, 2003), 79; Smalley, "John's Revelation," 59; Trebilco, "Asia," 307; Ben Witherington III, Revelation (Cambridge, U.K.: Cambridge University Press, 2003), 59. and others

[21] Lubbertus Selles, *The Book of Revelation: A Series of Outlines for Societies and Bible Study Clubs*, vol. 1 (London, Ont.: Interleague Publication Board of Canadian Reformed Societies, 1972), 14; Francis E. Peters, *The Harvest of Hellenism: A*

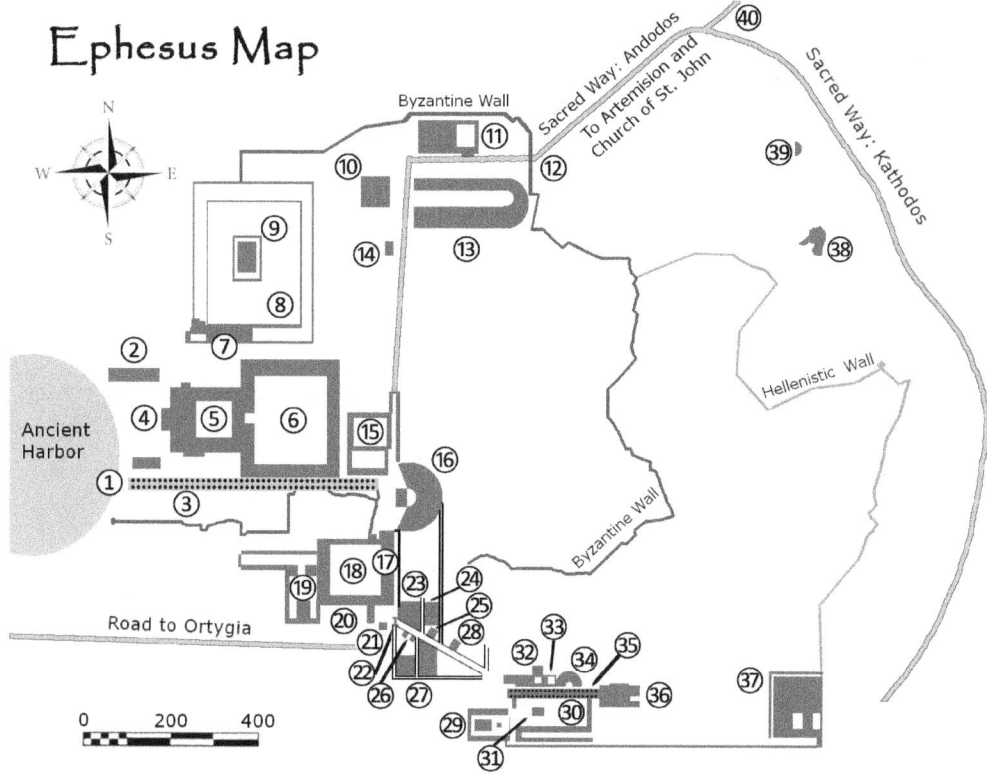

18. Urban plan of the city of Ephesus. 1). Harbour gate; 2). Warehouses; 3). Street of Arcadius; 4). Harbour baths; 5). Harbour gym; 6). Xystol of the Harbour gym; 7). Church of Mary; 8). Stoa of the Olympieion; 9). Temple of Hadrian Olympios; 10). Macellum; 11). Vedius gym; 12). North gate; 13). Stadium; 14). Fountain; 15). Theater Gym; 16). Theater; 17). Hall of Nero; 18). Commercial agora; 19). Sarapeion; 20). Library of Celsus; 21). Altar of Artemis; 22). Hadrian's gate; 23). Latrine; 24). Scholastikia baths; 25). Temple of Hadrian; 26). Heroon of Androklos and Arsinoë IV; 27). Slope Houses; 28). Fountain of Trajan; 29). Temple of Domitian [Flavian Sebastoi]; 30). State agora; 31). Temple of Divius Julius and Deo Roma [Temple of Isis?]; 32). Prytaneion; 33). Peristyle; 34). Odeon or Bouleuterion; 35). Baslike Stao; 36). Upper gym; 37). East gym; 38). Seven Sleepers; 39). Kybele Sanctuary; 40). Road to Artemision and Church of St. John.

propose that Beloch misinterpreted an inscription that supposedly mentions 40,000 males (*I.Eph.* 3.951), upon which these large populations are based.[22] Hanson concludes that:

> At Ephesus, such estimates [of 225,000] are clearly not possible, since the scope of extramural settlement is limited by the inland mountain range, the ancient coastline, and the region's quarries;

History of the Near East from Alexander the Great to the Triumph of Christianity (New York, N.Y.: Barnes & Noble, 1996), 517; MacKendrick, *The Greek Stones Speak: The Story of Archaeology in Greek Lands*, 2nd ed. (New York, N.Y.: Norton & Company, 1983), 466; Alfons Wotschitzky, "Ephesus: Past, Present and Future of an Ancient Metropolis," *Archaeology* 14, no. 3 (1961): 212.

[22] According to Bagnall the inscription should read 1,040 as a gigantic number. Preston Duane Warden and Roger S. Bagnall, "The Forty Thousand Citizens of Ephesus," *CP* 83, no. 3 (1988): 220–23.

even allowing for some suburban settlement, the total population figure could not be increased to anything like estimates of 225,000.[23]

To date, Hanson has done the most extensive analysis of the population of Asia Minor cities and his recent calculations "reduce these figures to a probable range with a minimum of 50,000 [250/ha.] and a maximum of 90,000 [400/ha.]."[24]

For a city to grow to this size it is clear that it was an important city. Dio Cassius records that by 29 BC, Ephesus had "attained chief place in Asia" (*Hist. Rom.* 51.20.6–7 [Cary and Foster]). Strabo considered it second only to Rome in importance (*Geogr.* 14.1.24).

AN IMPORTANT COMMERCIAL CENTER

Several infrastructure features lead to Ephesus becoming an important commercial center. Its large harbour, efficient road system and agora all played an important role in Ephesus's prosperity.

THE COMMERCIAL HARBOUR

Mark Antony assembled his fleet in the port of Ephesus as he prepared for his battle against Octavian (later, Caesar Augustus) at the battle of Actium (31 BC). However, the silting up of the harbour[25] with alluvium from the Cayster river (Küçük Menderes) has played a significant role in the history and several relocations of the city of Ephesus.[26] It has often been repeated, based on Strabo's comments about the silting of the harbour and need for dredging (*Geogr.* 6.41), that in the first cent. the city was in commercial decline due to the problem of a build-up of alluvium deposits from the Cayster River blocking the harbour.[27] This has led Horsley to propose that Paul used the port at Miletus (Acts 20:17) because the harbour at Ephesus was silted.[28] Wendel suggested that the earthquake of 17 AD (Pliny *Nat.* 2.200; Tacitus *Ann.* 2.47)[29] shifted the landmass and blocked the harbour for a period of time.[30] It does seem strange that Paul called

---

[23] Hanson, "Urban System," 258.

[24] Ibid.

[25] Other Asia Minor cities such as Troy, Miletus, and Priene on the Aagean coast faced the same problem. Clarence A. Wendel, "Land Tilting or Silting? Which Ruined Ancient Aegean Harbors?," *Archaeology* 22, no. 4 (1969): 322.

[26] Clive Foss, "Appendix III: The Silting of the Harbor of Ephesus," in *Ephesus After Antiquity: A Late Antique, Byzantine and Turkish City* (Cambridge, Mass.: Cambridge University Press, 2010), 185–87.

[27] Ramsay, *Letters: Updated*, 165; Chilton, *Days of Vengeance*, 96–97; Hemer, *Letters to the Seven Churches*, 53; Worth, Jr., *Greco-Asian Culture*, 63; Ben Witherington III, *New Testament History: A Narrative Account* (Grand Rapids, Mich.: Baker, 2003), 280.

[28] G. H. R. Horsley, "The Inscriptions of Ephesos and the New Testament," *NovT* 34, no. 2 (1992): 134–35.

[29] For the addition of Ephesus and Cibyra to the list of cities in Tacitus, see Emanuela Guidoboni, Alberto Comastri, and Giusto Traina, *Catalogue of Ancient Earthquakes in the Mediterranean Area Up to the 10th Century* (Rome: Istituto nazionale di geofisica, 1994), 184.

[30] Wendel, "Land Tilting or Silting?," 322–24.

the Ephesian elders to the port at Miletus to depart Asia Minor and not the port at Ephesus (Acts 20:17).

However, Trebilco documents several explanations put forth by other scholars for why Paul used the port at Miletus, noting that if Paul had been in a hurry, then why did he spend five days there?[31] First, the only vessel available from Troas was bound for Miletus and not Ephesus.[32] Second, Paul was carrying the financial collection for the suffering Christians in Jerusalem (Acts 11:25–30; Rom 15:26), and felt safer in the smaller city of Miletus.[33] Third, Paul did not want to get involved in protracted apostolic work by returning to Ephesus.[34] And finally, Paul did not want to face the silversmiths which he had upset just months earlier,[35] or he had been banned from the city because of his conduct.[36]

However, as Oster mentions, literary (Tacitus *Ann.* 16.23) and epigraphic documents (*I.Eph.* 1.23, 2.274, 6.2061, 7.3066, 7.3071) indicate that the dredging operations were successful (dredged in AD 62), allowing ships to dock and carry on trade during the first century.[37] Prior to AD 62, the harbour experienced many difficulties, resulting in the order for it to be dredged.[38] In the second cent. AD Aristides testified that the harbour was still commercially used (*Orat.* 23.24) and did not become unusable until the Byzantine period.[39] There is no doubt that today the harbour is completely silted in, as Ephesus is now some 6 miles (10 km) inland and inaccessible by sea (see Fig. 22).[40]

---

[31] Paul Trebilco, *The Early Christians in Ephesus from Paul to Ignatius* (Grand Rapids, Mich.: Eerdmans, 2007), 173–74.

[32] Colin J. Hemer, *The Book of Acts in the Setting of Hellenistic History*, ed. Conrad H. Gempf, WUNT 49 (Winona Lake, Ind.: Eisenbrauns, 1990), 125; "The Speeches of Acts: I. The Ephesian Elders at Miletus," *TynBul* 40, no. 1 (1989): 77–85; F. F. Bruce, *The Book of Acts*, New International Commentary on the New Testament (Grand Rapids, Mich.: Eerdmans, 1988), 387.

[33] Ernst Haenchen, *The Acts of the Apostles: A Commentary* (Hoboken, N.J.: Wiley & Sons, 1971), 588; C. K. Barrett, "Paul's Address to the Ephesian Elders," in *God's Christ and His Peopl E, Studies in Honour of Nils Alstrup Dahl*, ed. J. Jervell and W. A. Meeks (Oslo: Univer sitetsforlaget, 1977), 108; *A Critical and Exegetical Commentary on the Acts of the Apostles: Introduction and Commentary on Acts XV–XXVIII*, vol. 2 (Edinburgh, U.K.: T&T Clark, 1998), 2:960.

[34] Jan Lambrecht, "Paul's Farewell-Address at Miletus, Acts 20, 17–38," in *Les Actes Des Apôtres: Traditions, Rédaction, Théologie*, ed. Jacob Kremer, BETL 48 (Gembloux: Duculot, 1979), 331–32; David W. Gill and Conrad H. Gempf, eds., *The Book of Acts in Its Graeco-Roman Setting*, vol. 2, Book of Acts in Its First Century Setting 2 (Grand Rapids, Mich.: Eerdmans, 1994), 362; Justin Taylor, *Les Actes Des Deux Apôtres VI: Commentaire Historique (Act. 18,23–28,31)*, Etudes Bibliques 30 (Paris, France: Gabalda, 1996), 93–94.

[35] Luke Timothy Johnson, *The Acts of the Apostles*, ed. Daniel J. Harrington, SPS 5 (Collegeville, Minn.: Liturgical, 1992), 352.

[36] Hans Conzelmann, *Acts of the Apostles: A Commentary on the Acts of the Apostles*, Hermeneia (Philadelphia, Pa.: Fortress, 1987), 167.

[37] Richard E. Oster, "Ephesus (Place)," ed. David Noel Freedman et al., *ABD* (New York, N.Y.: Doubleday, 1996), 2:543.

[38] Keener, *Acts: 15:1–23:35*, 3:3:2341.

[39] Foss, "Silting of the Harbor," 186.

[40] Wotschitzky, "Ephesus," 206–7.

THE ROAD SYSTEM

In the Roman provinces, there were short roads which linked cities together, but Ephesus was well connected to the rest of Asia Minor by three main roads (Lat. *viae*) that led to Colossae/Laodicea, Sardis, and south to the Meander valley (see Fig. 19). Ephesus was the Rome of Asia Minor and it was well serviced by the three main roads as well as its large harbour. While there was no public postal service, personal messengers would have delivered important messages between cities using the existing road system.[41]

19. Main road (Lat. *Viae*), called the Sacred Way, leading from Ephesus to Magnesia.

Paying for the building of roads (Lat. *curator*) often produced political results, with many of those who used their own money later being elected to political power.[42] The roads around Ephesus became an important political and commercial enterprise.

THE COMMERCIAL AGORA

The Market Square commercial agora (τετράγωνος, *tetragōnos*; Rev 21:16; 111 m/364 ft.; see Fig. 20) was the main shopping area of the city and was surrounded on all four sides with a stoa, consisting of shops under a covered colonnade. Located next to the library of Celsus, the agora was built in the Hellenistic period, but remodelled under Augustus. Nero added a second story to the basilica on the east side of the agora between AD 54 and 59. The center square had a sundial and water-clock (Ὡρολόγιον, *horologion*) feature to add to its beauty. The gate at the south end of the agora bears the bronze bilingual[43] inscription:

> To the Emperor Caesar Augustus son of a god, the high priests, twelve times consul, twenty times tribune, and Livia, wife of Caesar Augustus, to Marc Agrippa, son of Lucius, three times consul, emperor, six times tribune and daughter of Julio Caesar Augustus, our patrons Mazeus and Mythridates [dedicate this arch]. (*I.Eph.* 3006 [Wilson]).[44]

---

[41] William M. Ramsay, "Roads and Travel (in NT)," in *DBib*, ed. James Hastings, Frederick C. Grant, and Harold. H. Rowley, vol. 5 (New York, N.Y.: Scribner's Sons, 1909), 5:375–402; M. P. Charlesworth, *Trade-Routes and Commerce of the Roman Empire*, 2nd ed. (New York, N.Y.: Cooper Square, 1970), 86.

[42] Pliny *Ep.* 5.15; Plutarch *Caes.* 5; Cicero *Leg.* 3.3; Ray Laurence, *The Roads of Roman Italy: Mobility and Cultural Change* (New York, N.Y.: Routledge, 1999), 41.

[43] William A. Johnson and Holt N. Parker, eds., *Ancient Literacies: The Culture of Reading in Greece and Rome: The Culture of Reading in Greece and Rome* (Oxford, U.K.: Oxford University Press, 2009), 72.

[44] Mark W. Wilson, Biblical Turkey: A Guide to Jewish and Christian Sites of Asia Minor (Istanbul: Ege Yayinlari, 2010), 217.

20. Market Square of the commercial agora, Ephesus.

Ephesus had more bilingual, Greek and Latin, inscriptions than any other city in Asia Minor indicating that it was an important cultural crossroad.[45] There was easy access to the harbour through the West Gate where goods from all over the Mediterranean were unloaded and sold in the local market. It is very possible that chapter 18 of Revelation is describing the activity of the agora in Ephesus.[46] It reads:

> And the merchants of the earth weep and mourn for her, since no one buys their cargo anymore, cargo of gold, silver, jewels, pearls, fine linen, purple cloth, silk, scarlet cloth, all kinds of scented wood, all kinds of articles of ivory, all kinds of articles of costly wood, bronze, iron and marble, cinnamon, spice, incense, myrrh, frankincense, wine, oil, fine flour, wheat, cattle and sheep, horses and chariots, and slaves, that is, human souls. (18:11–13)

It has been suggested that the commercial agora was where Paul worked in tent making and leatherwork with Priscilla and Aquila (Acts 18:2–3; 20:34). Also, it has been suggested that this was where Demetrius, the Silversmith, who crafted the statues of Artemis (Acts 19:23–41), had his shop.[47] Eight inscriptions, mentioning "the association of silversmiths",[48] have been located in Ephesus, one of which (*I.Eph.* 2.547) was located on a column along Arcadian Way (Harbour Street) near the theater, beside the commercial agora.[49]

AN IMPORTANT POLITICAL CENTER

Ephesus was not only an important commercial center, but also an important political center for Asia Minor.

A FREE CITY

Cities were not all the same in the Roman Empire as there were various types of settlement. There was the colony (Lat. *coloniae*), municipalities (Lat. *municipia*), and various types of settlements called prefectures (Lat. *praefecturae*), forums (Lat. *fora*) and rural settlements (Lat. *conciliabula*).[50] Cities (Lat. *coloniae*) were comprised of either colonies settled by Roman citizens or

---

[45] Johnson and Parker, *Ancient Literacies*, 70.
[46] Farrer, *Revelation*, 188.
[47] Wilson, *Biblical Turkey*, 218; Keener, *Acts: 15:1–23:35*, 3:2870.
[48] *I.Eph.* 2.425.10; 2.585; 2.586; 3.636; 6.2212; 6.2441; *NewDocs* 4:7–8.
[49] Horsley, "Inscriptions of Ephesos," 142–43.
[50] Ray Laurence and Gareth Sears, *The City in the Roman West, C. 250 BC–C. AD 250* (Cambridge, Mass.: Cambridge University Press, 2011), 65.

21. Ephesian *Boulētarion/Odeon* (concert hall), not to be confused with the larger theater/stadium.

army veterans loyal to Rome, or municipalities which had found themselves taken over by the Roman expansion. Colonies could be comprised not just of colonists but resident aliens (Lat. *incolae*), guests (Lat. *hopites*), and visitors (Lat. *atuentores*).[51] In the East, Augustus permitted the cities a certain degree of autonomy to protect and govern themselves while still being integrated into a larger provincial and national Roman government.[52] When Augustus became emperor in 27 BC, Ephesus was granted the right of self-government as the capital of proconsular Asia and never suffered the indignity of having Roman troops posted there.[53]

Ephesus had its own magistrates called *strategoi* (later *exactor*),[54] originally a term for a Greek general, but by NT times it had developed into a political office of *praetor* (Acts 16:20).[55] The city had a democratically elected government body called the βουλή *(boulē)* or γερουσία *(gerousia,* literally "body of old men")[56] that met in a small theater, also called a βουλευτήριον *(bouleutērion,* see Fig. 21). In secular Graeco-Roman society the assembly of citizens who gathered for political activities was called the ἐκκλησία *(ekklēsia,* "called out"), which was adopted as the term for the Christian church (Acts 19:39).[57]

The **state agora**, to the south of the city, was the governmental district and was not used for commercial trade (that was in the commercial agora). Here is where the *bouleutērion/odeum* (Ὠδεῖον, *ōideion* "school of music"; Lat. "concert hall") was located, along with the state agora baths and temple of Domitian and the temple of Isis, sacred precinct (τέμενος, *temenos*) dedicated to Dia Roma (see Fig. 173) and Divus Julius (Dio Cassius *Hist. Rom.* 51.20.6–7), Prytaneion, where the perpetual sacred (Εστία, *Hestia*) flame of the city burned (*I.Eph.* 4.1058, 4.1060,

---

[51] Ibid., 72.

[52] Ibid., 64.

[53] Arjan Zuiderhoek, "Cities, Roman Empire (East)," in *The Encyclopedia of Ancient History*, ed. Roger S. Bagnall et al., vol. 1 (Malden, Mass.: Wiley-Blackwell, 2012), 1:1516–20.

[54] J. David Thomas, "Strategos and Exactor in the Fourth Century: One Office or Two?," *ChrEg* 70 (1995): 230–39.

[55] Peter Daniel MacDearmon Witt, "The Judicial Function of the Strategos in the Roman Period" (Ph.D. diss., Duke University, 1977).

[56] As Bailey points out "Ephesus alone accounts for almost 30% of the approximately three hundred and sixty references to the *gerousia* in the inscriptions of Asia Minor." Colin Bailey, "The Gerousia of Ephesus" (Ph.D. diss., The University of British Columbia, 2006), 1.

[57] Gerhard Kittel and Gerhard Friedrich, eds., *Theological Dictionary of the New Testament*, trans. Geoffrey W. Bromiley, Abridged (Grand Rapids, Mich.: Eerdmans, 1985), 3:513.

4.1070) and the city magistrate (πρύτανις, *prutanis* or Ἀσιάρχης, *Asiarch*) carried out his responsibilities, all necessary institutions for the function of Roman government.

One of their main functions was the *grammateus* which Luke mentions in Acts 19:35 ("town clerk" NIV), but also kept the city archives handling all correspondence for the city as well as presenting the business of the *boulē* to the Roman provincial officials, as well as depositing money in the temple of Artemis (see Figs. 24, 28, 29).

THE JUDICIAL CIRCUIT OF EPHESUS (ASSIZE)

Pliny considered Ephesus "the light of Asia" (Lat. *Lumen Asiae*, Pliny *Nat.* 5.31 [Rackham]) and an *assize* (Lat. *conventus*) town (Gr. Ἀγορά δικῶν, *agora dikōn*; Josephus *Ant.* 14.10.21),[58] under the proconsul's jurisdiction, from where justice was dispensed during the reign of Emperor Augustus to sixty-seven ethnic communities from ten *conventus* or districts (διοίκησις, *dioceseis*) in Asia Minor, which included Ephesus, Alabanda, Smyrna, Pergamum, Sardis, Adramytteum, Apamea, Cibyra, Snynnada and Philomelium (Pliny *Nat.* 5.29).[59] As Ephesus was the first port of entry into the region,[60] the Roman governor would travel to the surrounding cities, known as the judicial circuit of Ephesus,[61] and hold regular court sessions.[62] In the first cent. AD, Ephesus was also the official residence of the Roman proconsul of Asia.[63]

Thus during certain times of the year Ephesus would experience the pageantry of the arrival of the Roman governor and his entourage at its port. It was certainly the most important city of those John addressed, and perhaps this was the reason it was addressed first.[64] In the first cent., the Ephesian Christians had to live in a city with fourteen additional deities, each with its own temple.[65]

THE PANIONIAN GAMES

The Panionia festival (πανήγυρις, *panegyris*, "gathering")) was moved from the Panionium[66] near Mount Mycale (Strabo *Geogr.* 14.1.20) to Ephesus because of war (Diodorus *Hist. Lib.* 15.49.1;

---

[58] G. P. Burton, "Proconsuls, Assizes and the Administration of Justice under the Empire," *JRS* 65 (1975): 92–106.

[59] Christian Habicht, "New Evidence on the Province of Asia," *JRS* 65 (1975): 70.

[60] Appian *Hist. rom.* 12.3; 12.9; 12.17; by royal decree, Ulpian *Dig.* 1.16.4.5; Burrell, *Neokoroi*, 59.

[61] Beale, *Revelation*, 228–29.

[62] George Long, "Ephesus," in *Dictionary of Greek and Roman Geography*, ed. William Smith (London, U.K.: Murray, 1878), 836; William Barclay, *The Revelation of John: Chapters 1 to 5*, vol. 1, NDSB (Louisville, Ky.: Westminster/Knox, 2004), 59.

[63] Steven M. Baugh, "Paul and Ephesus: The Apostle among His Contemporaries" (Ph.D. diss., University of California-Irvine, 1990), 47–49.

[64] Mounce, *Revelation*, 66; Smalley, *Revelation*, 59.

[65] Mark W. Wilson, Revelation, ZIBBC (Grand Rapids, Mich.: Zondervan, 2007), 18; Trebilco, Early Christians in Ephesus; Helmut Koester, ed., Ephesos Metropolis of Asia: An Interdisciplinary Approach to Its Archaeology, Religion, and Culture, HTS 41 (Cambridge, Mass.: Harvard Divinity School, 1995).

[66] Herodotus *Hist.* 1.148; Strabo *Geogr.* 8.7.2; Pausanias *Descr.* 7.24.

Thucydides *Hist.* 3.104).[67] The Panionia festival was a combination of business, sport and religion. [68] The sacred games for the various festivals were arranged by the "*Asiarch*[69] of the temples in Ephesos" (*I.Eph.* 7.1.3017; also used in Acts 19:31) who coordinated the gladiators, "procuring the proper sacrifices, and often" led the "rituals sacrifices",[70] along with arranging the agenda for the games. The Panionian games were comparable to the Olympic games, but held in the spring, in the month of Artemesion,[71] the sacred month of Artemis (*I.Eph.* 7.1.24).[72]

THE THEATER OF EPHESUS

The theater/stadium of Ephesus, the largest in Asia Minor (154 m in width), with a capacity of ca. 24,000 people,[73] was the site of the famous riot against the preaching of Paul, which had negatively affected the businesses of the craftsmen of Artemis, led by Demetrius the Silversmith (Acts 19:23–41).[74] An inscription mentioning the "place of the silversmiths" (ἀργυροκόπων, *argurokopōn I.Eph.* 2.547.1)[75] has been located near the theater beside the commercial agora.

---

[67] Alexandros, son of Menodoros, is honoured for winning the wrestling (Gr. *palēn*) competition at Ephesus during the Panionian games (*I.Eph.* 4.1123). Dieter Knibbe and Helmut Engelmann, "Aus Ephesischen Skizzenbuchern," *JÖAI* 52 (1980): 35 n.40; Clinton E. Arnold, *Ephesians: Power and Magic: The Concept of Power in Ephesians in Light of Its Historical Setting*, SNTS 63 (Cambridge, Mass.: Cambridge University Press, 1989), 116, 205 n.46.

[68] Leonhard Schmiz and George Elden Marindin, "Panionia," in *DGRA*, ed. William Smith (London, U.K.: Murray, 1891), 861–62.

[69] The prevailing view that *asiarch* was a title for the priesthood of the imperial cult, has been disproven by Friesen. Magie, *Roman Rule in Asia Minor*, 2:198–99 n.61; Steven J. Friesen, " Asiarch," *ZPE* 126 (1999): 275–90; Rosalinde A. Kearsley, "Asiarchs," in *The Book of Acts in Its Graeco-Roman Setting*, ed. David W. Gill and Conrad H. Gempf, vol. 2, Book of Acts in Its First Century Setting 2 (Grand Rapids, Mich.: Eerdmans, 1994), 362–76; "Asiarchs," ed. David Noel Freedman et al., *ABD* (New York, N.Y.: Doubleday, 1996), 1:495–97.

[70] Friesen, "Asiarchs," 286.

[71] Joachim Ebert, "Zur Stiftungsurkunde Der Leukophryena in Magnesia Am Mäander," *Philologus* 126 (1982): 212; Kent J. Rigsby, *Asylia: Territorial Inviolability in the Hellenistic World* (Oakland, Calf.: University of California Press, 1997), 181 n.12.

[72] Newton suggests the month of March, while Barclay records that the games were held in the month of May and Murphy-O'Connor states April. Charles Thomas Newton, *The Collection of Ancient Greek Inscriptions in the British Museum*, ed. E. L. Hicks (Oxford, U.K.: Clarendon, 1874), 145; William Barclay, *Letters to the Seven Churches* (Louisville, Ky.: Westminster John Knox, 2001), 3; Jerome Murphy-O'Connor, *St. Paul's Ephesus: Texts and Archaeology* (Minneapolis, Minn.: Liturgical, 2008), 175.

[73] Horsley, "Inscriptions of Ephesos," 110 n.15; Margarete Bieber, *The History of the Greek and Roman Theater* (Princeton, N.J.: Princeton University Press, 1961); Mary T. Boatwright, "Theaters in the Roman Empire," *BA* 53, no. 4 (1990): 184–92.

[74] Kreitzer concludes that: "These coins, which coincide remarkably well with recent attempts to establish Pauline chronology in relation to the Ephesian ministry, suggest that the Empress's syncretistic association with the goddess Artemis/Diana (as implied by the coins) could help explain the surge of popular fervour and support for the temple cultus which occurs in reaction to Paul's ministry in Ephesus." L. Joseph Kreitzer, "A Numismatic Clue to Acts 19:23–41: The Ephesian Cistophori of Claudius and Agrippina," *JSNT* 9, no. 30 (1987): 59–70.

[75] Erol Atalay, "Die Kurudağ-Höhle [Bei Ephesos] Mit Archäologischen Funden," *JÖAI* 52 (1980 1978): 40, no. 56a.

The theater was an important institution during the Graeco-Roman period and was the location for much more than just plays. The city assembly regularly met here in the spring, during the month of Artemision,[76] and it was also used as a gathering place to hear imperial edicts read (*SIG* 3.883. 26–27) and for civic festivals called *Artemisia*,[77] which were all accompanied by sacrifices and prayers to the gods (*SIG* 3.1003.15–17). A statue base bore the following inscription in honor of Artemis. It read: "Therefore, it is decreed that the entire month of Artemision be sacred for all its days, and that on the same (days) of the month, and throughout the year, feasts and the festival and the sacrifices of the Artemisia are to be conducted, inasmuch as the entire month is dedicated to the goddess [Artemis]" (*NewDocs* 4:75–76).

22. The theater in Ephesus with the colonnaded street, The Arcadian Way, leading down to the now silted harbour.

Thus, it is not surprising that during the Acts 19 demonstration the masses congregated in the theater (see Fig. 22), where for two hours they chanted "Great is Diana (Artemis) of the Ephesians" (Acts 19:32–34).[78] During the festivals of Artemis, the statue of Artemis (see Figs. 27) was carried from the temple into the city, and set on nine pedestals in the theater, only to be returned to the temple after the festival.[79] It is possible that the statue of Artemis was present in the theater during the crowd's demonstration in Acts 19.

The theater was built in the first half of the third cent. BC, into the side of Mount Pion, and enlarged under Emperor Claudius (AD 41–54, see Fig. 2, 28), with more renovations during Nero and Trajan. The Arcadian Way (Street), that leads to the harbour (see Fig. 22), was lined on both sides with shops and colonnades.

---

[76] *I.Eph.* 1.28.9–10; 1.29.19–20; Dio Chrysostom *Or.* 7.24; 40.6; Tacitus *Ann.* 2.80; Cicero *Flac.* 16; Josephus *Ant.* 14.150; Newton suggests the month of March, while Barclay records that the games were held in the month of May and Murphy-O'Connor states April. Newton, *Ancient Greek Inscriptions*, 145; Barclay, *Letters*, 3; Murphy-O'Connor, *St. Paul's Ephesus*, 175.

[77] *I.Eph.* 4.1452.3; 1457.4; Xenophon *Eph. Tale* 1.1–3.

[78] Sherman E. Johnson, "The Apostle Paul and the Riot in Ephesus," *LTQ* 14 (1979): 179–88.

[79] *SIG* 3.1003.15–17; *I.Eph.* 2.202–208; 3.145; 4.1457; Xenophon *Eph. Tale* 1.2–3; Guy Maclean Rogers, *The Sacred Identity of Ephesos: Foundation Myths of a Roman City*, Routledge Revivals (New York, N.Y.: Routledge, 2014), 83–85.

THE LIBRARY OF CELSUS

The famous library of Celsus and Gate of Macaeus and Mithridates (see Figs. 23, 38) were only constructed in 135 AD and not present when John was in the city.[80]

AN IMPORTANT RELIGIOUS CENTER

The importance of Ephesus was attested in many ways, but one was viewed by all of Asia Minor as significant. Cities, during the Roman imperial period, were honored by being selected as sites for the erection of temples to patron deities (e.g., Serapis, Artemis, etc.)[81] and the imperial cult,[82] and were granted the honor of the title, *neōkoros* (νεωκόρος, "temple-keeper").[83]

THE IMPERIAL CULT AND THE KEEPER OF THE TEMPLES (*NEŌKOROS*)

23. The library of Celsus and Gate of Macaeus and Mithridates in Ephesus (modern Selçuk, Turkey). The library was built in honour of Roman Senator Tiberius Julius Celsus Polemaeanus and completed by his son in 135 AD. The library held 12,000 scrolls, but was destroyed by an earthquake with all of its contents in 262 AD. Note the *aediculae* (shrine niche) in the front of the building.

What began as a title for the person responsible for overseeing the cult in the temple, later evolved into a civic title under the Ephesian Cult of the Sebastoi.[84] By the third cent., several cities had several *neōkorates* and rival cities boasted of their numbers with coins displaying their temples and accompanying legends such as "of the Ephesians, alone, first of all to have four *neōcorates*" (*SNG* Cop. 442; *BMC Ionia* 92, no. 307).[85] Ephesus was given the unusual privilege of *civitas neōkora* ("city temple-keeper", the official term by the second cent. AD) four times, identified with temples to Domitian (the temple of Sebastoi; see Fig. 7), Hadrian (see Fig. 33, 93, 109), Elagabalus, and Caracalla's (AD 198–217; see Figs. 128, 162, 163), with a fifth *neōkoros* associated with the temple of Artemis.[86]

---

[80] On the library of Celsus, see George W. Houston, *Inside Roman Libraries: Book Collections and Their Management in Antiquity* (Raleigh, NC: University of North Carolina Press, 2014), 189–94.

[81] For a general treatment of religion at Ephesus, see Oster, "Ephesus as a Religious Center," 1661–1728.

[82] For a comprehensive treatment of the Imperial Cult in Ephesus from numismatic and epigraphic remains, see chapter 4. Ephesos in Ionia (Nero) in Barbara Burrell, *Neokoroi: Greek Cities and Roman Emperors*, CCS 9 (Leiden: Brill, 2004), 59–85.

[83] *SIG* 3.867; *I.Eph.* 2.212; *SEG* 37.886; *CIG* 2972; and Acts 19:35; Today this term is used for a custodian in the Greek Orthodox church. Literally it comes from the Greek νεώς (*neōs*) "temple") + κορέω (*koreō*) "to sweep", thus literally a "temple-sweeper."

[84] Steven J. Friesen, *Twice Neokoros: Ephesus, Asia and the Cult of the Flavian Imperial Family* (Leiden: Brill Academic, 1993), 56.

[85] Ann Johnston, "The Provinces After Commodus," in *The Oxford Handbook of Greek and Roman Coinage*, ed. William E. Metcalf (Oxford, U.K.: Oxford University Press, 2012), 456–57 fig. 24.12.

[86] The *neōkoros* of the temple of Atremis (Acts 19:35) was not directly connected to the imperial cult, which gave it

THE TEMPLE OF ARTEMIS (550 BC)

The temple of Artemis (see Figs. 24, 28, 29) provided Ephesus with the prestigious title of "temple-keeper or warden" (νεωκόρος, *neōkoros*)[87] of the goddess Artemis,[88] a designation usually reserved for temples to the imperial cult.[89] It was the first to be named νεωκόρον (*neōkorōn*, "temple-keeper"), a deduction made from the term appearing on their coins from the reign of Nero (AD 54–68), likely representing the temple of Artemis[90] and not the temples dedicated to the imperial cult.[91] However, under Elagabalus (AD 218–222), Ephesus was again made "four times *neōkoros*"[92] by including the temple of Artemis.[93]

24. Recreation of the Artemision, Temple of Artemis, as it would have looked at Ephesus. This model is at Miniatürk Park, Istanbul, Turkey.

The primacy between cities is evident from the rivalry over first, second, or third rank *neōkoros* as the site for the provincial imperial temple (Philostratus *Vit. Soph.* 1.25.10; AD 172?). Artemis (Lat. *Diana*) was a popular mythical Greek goddess worshiped throughout the Roman Empire (Acts 19:27; Pausanias *Descr.* 4.31.8), but particularly in Asia Minor and Ephesus.[94] She

---

a distinctive honor.

[87] *SIG* 3.867; *I.Eph.* 2.212; *SEG* 37.886; and *CIG* 2972; "Temple-keeper of Artemis" Acts 19:35; Friesen, *Twice Neokoros*, 56–59; Gregory Stevenson, *Power and Place: Temple and Identity in the Book of Revelation* (Berlin: de Gruyter, 2001), 95. See also BDAG, 670.

[88] Friesen, *Twice Neokoros*, 58; Rick Strelan, *Paul, Artemis, and the Jews in Ephesus* (Berlin: de Gruyter, 1996), 47.

[89] Ramsay, *Letters: Updated*, 168–69.

[90] Josef Keil, "Die Erste Neokorie von Ephesos," NZ 48 (1919): 125–30; Price, *Rituals and Power*, 65 n.47.

[91] RPC states: "But the argument that it cannot refer to a provincial temple of Nero at Ephesus is not very strong; it is based on coins of Domitian which refer to a second *neōcorate* at Ephesus. As a *neōcorate* for Nero would not have been included in the numbering because of his *damnatio memoriae*, it is argued, the first *neōcorate* must refer to something else." Andrew Burnett, Michael Amandry, and Ian Carradice, *Roman Provincial Coinage: From Vespasian to Domitian (AD 69–96)*, vol. 2 (London, U.K.: British Museum Press, 1999), 433.

[92] Ramsay, *Letters: Updated*, 168.

[93] Hans Willer Laale, *Ephesus (Ephesos): An Abbreviated History from Androclus to Constantine XI* (Bloomington, Ind.: WestBow, 2011), 269; Barclay Vincent Head, *Catalogue of the Greek Coins of Ionia in the British Museum*, ed. Reginald Stuart Poole (Oxford, U.K.: Oxford University Press, 1892); Burrell, *Neokoroi*, 59–85.

[94] Lynn R. LiDonnici, "The Images of Artemis Ephesia and Greco-Roman Worship: A Reconsideration," *HTR* 85, no. 4 (October 1992): 389–415; Trebilco, "Asia," 332–36; Murphy-O'Connor, *St. Paul's Ephesus*, 120–31; C. L. Brinks, "'Great Is Artemis of the Ephesians': Acts 19:23–41 in Light of Goddess Worship in Ephesus," *CBQ* 71, no. 4 (2009): 776–94; Zynep Aktüre, "Reading into the Mysteries of Artemis Ephesia," in *Curating Architecture and the City*, ed. Sarah Chaplin and Alexandra Stara (New York, N.Y.: Routledge, 2009), 145–63; Morna D. Hooker, "Artemis of Ephesus," *JTS* 64, no. 1 (2013): 37–46.

was the virgin goddess of the hunt, wild animals, childbirth, virginity, and thus associated with various animals such as lions, bulls, rams, deer (see Fig. 30) and bees (see Figs. 26, 42). [95]

She is often depicted with a short skirt carrying a bow and arrow (Ovid *Metam.* 3.251) and accompanied with a hunting dog or deer (see Figs. 26, 30). Homer describes Artemis "of the Wilds" (Ἀγροτέρα, *Agrotera*, "the huntress") and "Mistress of Animals" (Ἡ Πότνια Θηρῶν, *Ho Potnia Therōn*; *Il.* 21.470). In Greek mythology she was the daughter of Zeus and twin sister of Apollo (Hesiod *Theog.* 918–20). [96]

During the excavations of the Prytaneion (city hall) in Ephesus, four cult statues of Artemis were excavated by Franz Miltner in 1956. [97] They depicted a fertility goddess with unique features (see Figs. 27) to those of typical Hellenistic huntress statues (see Fig. 26). [98] Two large marble statues of Artemis and two smaller copies were discovered. [99] The Ephesian depiction of Artemis was unique, [100] with what appears to be multiple breasts (Felix *Oct.* 22.5; Jerome *Comm. in Ep. Paul*), [101] or, as variously identified by

25. This single, remaining column of the original 127, and this foundation, are all that remains of the Temple of Artemis in Ephesus, one of the seven wonders of the ancient world. Originally it measured 67 meters (220 ft.) wide by 130 meters (425 ft.) long and was 18 meters (60 ft.) high. In the background: Isa Bey Camii, fortress of Ayasoluk and (behind the column) ruins of St. John's Cathedral.

---

[95] Fifty-five Ephesian Drachma coins (*ca.* 202–133 BC) represent the Artemesian priestess as a bee, with a stag standing under a tree on the obv., representing the sacred grove of Artemis. Christine Sourvinou-Inwood, "Artemis," ed. Simon Hornblower and Anthony J. S. Spawforth, *OCD* (Oxford, U.K.: Clarendon, 2003), 176–77; Marjatta Nielsen, "Diana Efesia Multimammmia: The Metamorphoses of a Pagan Goddess from the Renaissance to the Age of Neo-Classicism," in *From Artemis to Diana: The Goddess of Man and Beast*, ed. Tobias Fischer-Hansen and Birte Poulsen, AH 12 (Copenhagen: Museum Tusculanum, 2009), 455–96.

[96] William K. C. Guthrie, *The Greeks and Their Gods*, Ariadne Series (Boston, Mass.: Beacon, 1950), 99ff.; Burkert, *Greek Religion*, 149–52.

[97] Peter Scherrer, ed., *Ephesus: The New Guide* (Turkey: Ege Yayinin, 2000), 86; Murphy-O'Connor, *St. Paul's Ephesus*, 191.

[98] Frederick E. Brenk, "Artemis of Ephesos: An Avant Garde Goddess," *Kernos* 11 (1998): 157–71; Aktüre, "Reading into the Mysteries," 145.

[99] The "Great Artemis" (inv. no. 712; see Figs. 27) was discovered fallen in the courtyard likely toppled by an earthquake in the 4th cent. or pushed over by Christians. The "Beautiful Artemis" (inv. no. 718) was found purposefully buried in a side room (no. 5) of the Prytaneion. The "Small Artemis," along with its copy, were discovered in the vestibule of the stoa and the courtyard of the Prytaneion. They have been dated to AD 150–200. Guy MacLean Rogers, *The Mysteries of Artemis of Ephesos: Cult, Polis, and Change in the Greaeco-Roman World* (New Haven, Conn.: Yale University Press, 2012), 180–83.

[100] Hooker, "Artemis," 37–46.

[101] Edward Falkener, *Ephesus, and the Temple of Diana* (London, U.K.: Day & Son, 1862), 290; Oster, "Ephesus as a

scholars, bulls' scrota,[102] pomegranates,[103] eggs,[104] ostrich eggs[105] or bee ova.[106] Until recently, most scholars suggested that whatever they are, they are linked to fertility in some way.[107] However, the general consensus now is that she retained her role as the virgin huntress and protector of young women, rather than becoming an Anatolian sex and fertility goddess.[108]

The "Great Artemis" statue (inv. No. 712; see Figs. 27) is depicted wearing a three-level headdress with the top level depicting the temple of Artemis (see Figs. 24, 28, 29). Sadly, both of her arms are missing. She is wearing a long cloak of various

26. Artemis, the goddess of hunting, as portrayed in Cyrene (second cent. AD). She was originally holding a bow in her hand. In Ephesus, her statues show her with many breasts or eggs (see Fig. 27).

27. Ephesian Greek goddess Artemis (Roman goddess *Diana*) from the Prytanaeum (city hall) of Ephesus. This statue is known as "the Great Artemis" (inv. no. 712).

Religious Center," 1725–26.

[102] Gérard Seiterle, "Artemis–Die Grosse Göttin von Ephesus," *Antike Welt* 10, no. 3 (1979): 3–16; Robert Fleischer, "Neues Zu Kleinasiastischen Kultstatuen," *AA* 98 (1983): 86; Lilian Portefaix, "The Image of Artemis Ephesia–A Symbolic Configuration Related to Her Mysteries?," in *100 Jahre Österreichische Forschunge in Ephesos*, ed. Herwig Friesinger and Friedrich Krinzinger, Archäologische Forschungen 1 (Wien: VÖAW, 1999), 611–17.

[103] Yulia Ustinova, The Supreme Gods of the Bosporan Kingdom: Celestial Aphrodite and the Most High God (Leiden: Brill, 1999), 62; Bernard Saftner, Punctuated Equilibrium Featuring The Proepistrephomeniad (Bloomington, Ind.: Xlibris, 2008), 210.

[104] Jack Finegan, The Archeology of the New Testament: The Life of Jesus and the Beginning of the Early Church, Revised (Princeton, N.J.: Princeton University Press, 2014), 156.

[105] Christoph Briese, "Ostrich Eggs," in *BrillPauly*, vol. 10 (Leiden: Brill, 2007), 10:290.

[106] Stefan Karweise, "Ephesos," *RE Supp* 12 (1970): 323–26; Gerard Mussies, "Pagans, Jews, and Christians at Ephesus," in *Studies on the Hellenistic Background of the New Testament*, ed. Pieter Wilhelm van der Horst and Gerard Mussies, Utrechtse Theologische Reeks 10 (Utrecht: Theological Faculty Utrecht University, 1990), 117–94; Robert Fleischer, *Artemis von Ephesos: und verwandte Kultstatuen aus Anatolien und Syrien*, ÉPRO 35 (Leiden: Brill, 1973), 1–136.

[107] Clinton E. Arnold, Ephesians: Power and Magic : The Concept of Power in Ephesians in Light of Its Historical Setting, SNTS 63 (Cambridge, Mass.: Cambridge University Press, 1989), 25; Fant and Reddish, Guide to Biblical Sites, 205–06.

[108] Ramsay, *Paul the Traveler: Updated*, 212; Keener, *Acts: 15:1–23:35*, 3:3:2875; Gerard Mussies, "Artemis," in *Dictionary of Deities and Demons in the Bible*, ed. Karel van der Toorn, Bob Becking, and Pieter Willem van der Horst, 2nd ed. (Grand Rapids, Mich.: Eerdmans, 1999), 91–97.

28. Ephesian Cistophoric Tetradrachm coin. Obv.: The bare head of Claudius (*ca.* AD 41–54). *TI CLAVD CAES AVG*. Rev.: *DIAN EPHE*. The cult statue of Artemis (Diana) of Ephesus within a tetrastyle temple set on a four-tiered base (*RPC* I 2222; *BMC* 229; *RSC* 30).

29. Ephesian coin struck under Nero (AD 54–68). Rev.: four column ionic temple in three-quarter view, likely the Temple of Artemis. It is inscribed with the first occurance of the term *NEOKORΩN* (*neokorōn*, "Keeper of the Temple") on a coin (*RPC* 2626; Waddington 1620).

animals, including bees and bulls. Bulls were often sacrificed to Artemis, and some suggest that this is connected to fertility symbolism.[109]

The "Beautiful Artemis" (inv. no. 718), dates to the second cent. AD. The headdress is missing on this statue, but she does retain both of her hands. She is situated between two deer and two beehives. The necklace is also encrusted with the signs of the Zodiac.[110] According to Eustathius, the Archbishop of Thessalonica, the incantations of the mysterious "Ephesian letters" (Ἐφέσια Γράμματα, *Ephesia grammata*) were inscribed on the feet, girdle and crown of some of the statues of Artemis (*Hom. Od.* 19.247).[111] There seemed to be similar attributes with Cybele (or Tyche Τύχη; an Anatolian mother goddess, see Figs. 52, 54, 98, 108), including being served in the temple by female slaves, young virgins, and eunuch priests (Strabo *Geogr.* 14.1.23).[112]

The Ephesian goddess Artemis (Lat. *Diana*, see Figs. 27, 121) was worshiped in a magnificent temple (Acts 19:27; built by Croesus, the rich King of Lydia in 550 BC over a period of 120 years. See Figs. 29, 24, 23), known as the Artemision (Aristides *Orat.* 23.25) just outside of Ephesus (modern Selçuk), considered one of the seven wonders of the ancient world.[113] In 356 BC the temple of Artemis (see Figs. 28, 29, 24) was destroyed by arson. A man

---

[109] Nielsen, "Diana Efesia Multimammmia: The Metamorphoses of a Pagan Goddess from the Renaissance to the Age of Neo-Classicism," 455–96.

[110] Rogers, *Mysteries of Artemis*, 180–83.

[111] Alberto Bernabé, "The Ephesia Grammata: Genesis of a Magical Formula," in *The Getty Hexameters: Poetry, Magic, and Mystery in Ancient Selinous*, ed. Christopher A. Faraone and Dirk Obbink (Oxford, U.K.: Oxford University Press, 2013), 73–74; Strelan, *Paul, Artemis, and the Jews in Ephesus*, 88.

[112] LiDonnici, "Images of Artemis," 389–415.

[113] Pausanias *Descr.* 4.31.8; 7.5.4; Pliny *Nat.* 16.79; 36.21; Antipater of Sidon *Gr. Ant.* 9.58; Kai Brodersen, "Seven Wonders," in *OEAGR*, ed. Michael Gagarin, vol. 6 (New York, N.Y.: Oxford University Press, 2010), 289; Bluma L. Trell, "The Temple of Artemis at Ephesos," in *The Seven Wonders of the Ancient World*, ed. Peter A. Clayton and Martin Price (New York, N.Y.: Routledge, 2013), 78–99.

by the name of Herostratus, set fire to the wooden roof-beams, seeking fame. For this outrage, the Ephesians sentenced the perpetrator to death and forbade anyone from mentioning his name; but historian Theopompus later noted it (*Tim.Frag.* 137).[114] In Greek and Roman historical tradition, the temple's destruction coincided with the birth of Alexander the Great (around 20/21 July 356 BC). Plutarch remarked that Artemis was too preoccupied with Alexander's delivery to save her burning temple (*Alex.* 1.3.5).

30. Tetradrachm coin mined in Ephesus (*ca.* 25–20 BC). Obv.: Head of Augustus (r. 27 BC–14 AD). AVGVSTVS Rev.: The altar of Artemis (Diana) with two deer, animals sacred to Ephesus, facing each other (*RPC* 1:2215).

The temple to Artemis is the place where the incident in the book of Acts over the Artemis statues (*I.Eph.* 3.961; 6.2212) produced by Demetrius, the silversmith (Acts 19:23–42; ἀργυροκόπος, *argurokopos*; *I.Eph.* 2.547) took place, and also for the account in Second Timothy of Alexander the coppersmith (2 Tim 4:14; *NewDocs* 4:7–10).[115] Demetrius, the silversmith (Acts 19:23–41), feared that Paul's preaching against idols would affect his business of producing miniature idols of Artemis.[116]

The Artemision[117] was one of the largest Greek temples ever built and the first temple to be constructed out of marble.[118] Originally it measured 67 metres (220 ft.) wide by 130 metres (425 ft.) long and was 18 metres (60 ft.) high with some 127 columns.[119] It was also the most important financial institution in Asia Minor, widely known as being a secure place to deposit money.[120]

The foundation of the temple's altar was discovered outside the temple in 1965.[121] According to the apocryphal work *Acts of John* (42), the temple was destroyed by John the

---

[114] Karl Müller, Theodor Müller, and Victor Langlois, *Fragmenta historicorum graecorum* (Paris, France: Ambrosio Firmin Didot, 1841).

[115] Horsley, "Inscriptions of Ephesos," 142–45.

[116] Richard E. Oster, "The Ephesian Artemis as an Opponent of Early Christianity," *JAC* 19 (1976): 24–44; Strelan, *Paul, Artemis, and the Jews in Ephesus*, 135–37.

[117] Ulrike Muss, "The Artemision at Ephesos: From Paganism to Christianity," in *Mustafa Büyükkolancı'ya Armağan: Essays in Honour of Mustafa Büyükkolancı*, ed. Celal Şimşek, Bahadır Duman, and Erim Konakçi (Istanbul: Yayinlari, 2015), 413–22.

[118] Oster, "Ephesus (Place)," 2:545–46.

[119] Pliny *Nat.* 36.21.95ff; Vitruvius *Arch.* 3.2.7; 10.2.11–12.

[120] Dio Chrysostom *Or.* 31.54–55; Appian *Bell. civ.* 3.33; Plautus *Bacchides* 312; Aristides *Orat.* 42.522; *CIG* 2:2953b; Trebilco, "Asia," 325.

[121] Oster, "Ephesus (Place)," 2:545.

apostle, though the final temple on this site was in fact destroyed by the Goths in AD 262 and never reconstructed.[122] All that remains today of the once magnificent Artemision is a single column from the fifth temple built on the site (see Fig. 25),[123] along with the great altar (see Fig. 30),[124] although many of the sculptured sections of the temple, excavated by Wood and Hogarth,[125] were shipped to the British Museum.[126]

THE TEMPLE OF SEBASTOI (DOMITIAN AD 89)

In AD 26, the Ephesians appealed before Emperor Tiberius (see see Figs. 43, 97, 111), together with eleven other Asian cities, for the honor of establishing a second temple in the city in honor of the emperor. Each city presented their arguments based on their loyalty and support for Rome. However, Tiberius turned down the Ephesian request because they were considered "fully occupied" with the cult of Artemis (Tacitus *Ann.* 4.55).

However, by the second cent., Ephesus was considered "twice temple keeper" (νεωκόρος, *neōkoros*) as identified on her coins (*BMC Phrygia* 234).[127] The temple of *Sebastoi* (lit. "venerable ones" see Fig. 7, Greek form of the Roman imperial title "Augustus") was originally identified with Domitian (see Fig. 31), but transferred to Vespasian following Domitian's *damnatio memoriae* (see Fig. 111, and called the temple of *Sebastoi* from that time on, being dedicated to the

31. Bust of Roman emperor Domitian. Antique head, body added in the 18th century. Musée du Louvre (Ma 1264), Paris.

---

[122] Ibid.

[123] W. R. Lethaby, "The Earlier Temple of Artemis at Ephesus," *JHS* 37 (1917): 1–16.

[124] Hemer, Letters to the Seven Churches, 138.

[125] For the details of the excavations of the temple of Artemis by John T. Wood and David G. Hogarth, see John Turtle Wood, *Discoveries at Ephesus: Including the Sites and Remains of the Great Temple of Diana* (London, U.K.: Longmans, Green & Company, 1877); David George Hogarth, *Excavations at Ephesus: The Archaic Artemisia* (London, U.K.: Longmans & Co., 1908); Steven J. Friesen, "Ephesus: Key to a Vision in Revelation," *BAR* 19, no. 3 (1993): 24–37; David E. Graves, *Biblical Archaeology: An Introduction with Recent Discoveries That Support the Reliability of the Bible*, vol. 1 (Toronto, Ont.: Electronic Christian Media, 2017), 210–14.

[126] W. R. Lethaby, *The Sculptures of the Later Temple of Artemis at Ephesus* (London, U.K.: The Society for the Promotion of Hellenic Studies, 1913).

[127] T. C. Mitchell, *Biblical Archaeology: Documents from the British Museum* (Cambridge, U.K.: Cambridge University Press, 1988), 99.

veneration of the Flavian dynasty.[128] The temple of *Sebastoi* was unique in its focus on the imperial family (Vespasian, Domitian [see Fig. 31], possibly Domitia, and Titus)[129] and excluded Roma and the Senate. Domitian granted Ephesus the honor of having the first Roman temple dedicated (AD 89–90) to the imperial cult of the Flavian dynasty.[130]

The temple of *Sebastoi* was the location of an annual festival, first held in Smyrna (*I.Smyr.* 2.1.635; *IGR* 4.824), accompanied by sacrifices, drama, poetry, music and athletics, called the Ephesian Olympics (AD 90; *I.Ias.* 1.108),[131] held in the sacred month of *Artemesion* (*I.Eph.* 1.24).[132] The games were discontinued after Domitian's death and reinstituted in the second cent. to honor Hadrian Zeus Olympios (*I.Eph.* 2.267–271a).[133]

32. Parts of the colossal statue from the Temple of Sebastoi, Ephesus Museum, in Selçuk, Turkey. The head is over 1.18 m high. Originally identified as Emperor Domitian (AD 81–96), but has since been identified as Emperor Titus.

While the temple of *Sebastoi* was not mentioned by ancient writers, its existence was confirmed by the discovery of archaeological remains in 1930 on the side of Mount Korressos,[134] and thirteen inscriptions on statue bases scattered around the cities of Asia, which mentioned "Asia's common[135] temple of the *Sebastoi* in Ephesos" (*I.Eph.* 2.233 from Aphrodisias).[136]

While the remains of a large statue five meters tall (16.4 ft.; see Fig. 32), uncovered beneath the *cryptoporticus* of the temple, was once identified as Domitian,[137] it has since been identified as

---

[128] Friesen, *Twice Neokoros*, 44–49; Friesen, *Imperial Cults*, 43–55, 232 n.35.

[129] Augustus and Tiberius were not included as they were venerated in other imperial cult temples in Asia Minor. Nero, Gaius and Claudius were beyond veneration at this point.

[130] Friesen, *Twice Neokoros*, 44–49.

[131] Luigi Moretti, *Iscrizioni agonistiche greche*, SPDI 12 (Rome: Angelo Signorelli, 1953), 181–83 #66; Friesen, *Imperial Cults*, 52; *Twice Neokoros*, 119–23; J. Nelson Kraybill, *Imperial Cult and Commerce in John's Apocalypse*, JSNTSup 132 (Sheffield, U.K.: Sheffield Academic, 1999), 28.

[132] Newton, *Ancient Greek Inscriptions*, 145; Barclay, *Letters*, 3; Murphy-O'Connor, *St. Paul's Ephesus*, 175.

[133] Wilhelm Alzinger and Dieter Knibbe, *Ephesos Vom Beginn Der Römischen Herrschaft in Kleinasien Bis Zum Ende derPrincipatzeit*, ed. Hildegard Temporini, ANRW, II 7.2 (Berlin: De Gruyter, 1980), 785; Friesen, *Twice Neokoros*, 117–21.

[134] Josef Keil, E. Reisch, and F. Knoll, *Die Marienkirche in Ephesos*, FiE, 4.1 (Wien: ÖAI, 1932), 53–61.

[135] As the *neōkoros* Ephesus was merely the caretaker of the temple for the collective cities of Asia Minor.

[136] Joyce Maire Reynolds and Kenan T. Erim, *Aphrodisias and Rome*, JRSM (London, U.K.: Society for the Promotion of Roman Studies, 1982), 167–68 #42; Friesen, *Imperial Cults*, 44–45.

[137] Keil, Reisch, and Knoll, *Die Marienkirche*, 59–60; Jale Inan and Elisabeth Rosenbaum, *Roman and Early Byzantine Portrait Sculpture in Asia Minor* (Oxford, U.K.: Oxford University Press, 1966), 67, 16 #1.

Emperor Titus.[138] It would have stood inside the temple and Titus originally would have held a spear or javelin in his hand. Today it is displayed in the Ephesus Museum, in Selçuk Turkey.[139]

THE TEMPLE OF HADRIAN (AD 138)

The third *neōkoros*, and second dedicated to the imperial cult, was "the temple of the god Hadrian" (*I.Eph.* 2.428, 921; AD 138)[140] or the temple of Hadrian Olympios or simply the *Olympieion*[141] situated on Curetes Street in Ephesus (see Fig. 33). It was built by P. Quintilius Valens Varius and dedicated to Hadrian (r. AD 117–138; see Figs. 93, 109), the goddess Artemis and the *demos* of Ephesus, likely when Hadrian (see Fig. 93, 109) visited the city between 123 and 131. Burrell reports that: "In 124 he [Hadrian] listened as the *ephēbos* [ἐφηβη, adolescent boys] sang his praises in the theater (*I.Eph.* 1145); and perhaps it was on his way back from his last trip in 131 that he called in at Ephesos and awarded that city its second provincial imperial temple."[142]

33. Temple of Hadrian on Curetes Street, Ephesus. The pillar bases were for the statues of the Emperors Diocletian, Maximian, Constantius I, and Galerius (AD 293–305). The outside facade of the temple displays four Corinthian columns supporting a curved arch. In the center there was a relief of Tyche (Cybele), goddess of victory.

A statue base from Ephesus records the accomplishments of "[Tiberius Cl]audius Piso Diophantos, who was chief priest of the two temples in Ephesos, under whom the temple of the god Hadrian was consecrated, who first asked for (it) from the god Hadrian and obtained (it)." (*I.Eph.* 2.428)[143]

Following Ephesus receiving its second temple of the imperial cult (for Hadrian), it acquired the official civic title (with variations) of "The First and Greatest Metropolis of Asia and Twice Temple-warden of the Sebastoi, City of Ephesus" (*I.Eph.* 1a.24B).[144]

---

[138] Georg Daltrop, Ulrich Hausmann, and Max Wegner, *Die Flavier: Vespasian, Titus, Domitian, Nerva, Julia Titi, Domitilla, Domitia* (Berlin: Mann, 1966), 26, 38, 86, and pl. 15b.

[139] Krodel, *Revelation*, 105.

[140] Also called "the temple of Lord Hadrian Caesar" (*I.Eph.* 814). Burrell, *Neokoroi*, 61 n26; Magie, *Roman Rule in Asia Minor*, 2:1432–34. Contra. Friesen, *Twice Neokoros*, 34.

[141] Trebilco, *Early Christians in Ephesus*, 35.

[142] Burrell, *Neokoroi*, 66–67.

[143] Ibid., 67.

[144] See, also *I.Eph.* 2.282D, 2.438; 3.611, 3.613A, 3.649, 3.661, 3.686, 3.985–86; Cecil J. Cadoux, *Ancient Smyrna: A History of the City from the Earliest Times to 224 A.D.* (Oxford, U.K.: Basil Blackwell, 1938), 291; Barclay, *Revelation*, 1:65; Stevenson, *Power and Place*, 95.

Just inside the front door, the hall was lined with friezes depicting the founders of Ephesus, including Amazons, Dionysus (see Fig. 35), Androclus, Apollo (see Figs. 86, 90, 96), Athena (see Figs. 34, 124), Artemis (Diana, see Figs. 26, 27, 121, 124, 127), Tyche (Τύχη or Cybele, see Figs. 52, 54, 98, 108, 160), and Herakles.[145] The friezes onsite in modern Ephesus

34. Coin from Thyatira (third cent. AD). Obv.: The bust of Athena, wearing a crested Corinthian helmet and *aegis*, holding a spear over the shoulder. Rev.: ΘΥΑΤΙΡΗΝΩΝ, *Tyche Soterios (Fortuna Redux)* standing (*SNG Cop.* 581 = *BMC* 34 = *SNGvA* 2.3206).

are copies, as the originals are displayed in the Ephesus Museum. Following Hadrian's mysterious death, Emperor Antoninus also had him deified (AD 139) and a temple was built in his honor on the *Campus Martius* in Rome.

THE TEMPLE OF ELAGABALUS (AD 218–222)

Ephesus gained its fourth *neōkorate* under Emperor Marcus Aurelius Antoninus (who took the name Elagabalus after his god, Gr. *Heliogabalus*) a fact supported by coins (*SNG* Cop. 442; *BMC Ionia* 307) depicting four temples.[146] According to Laale, "the city may have lost the honor of being four-times *neōkorate* when all memory of Elagabalus was subsequently erased from inscriptions as part of a process of *damnatio memoriae* [see Fig. 111]."[147]

The *Elagabalium* was dedicated to the controversial sun cult of *Deus Sol Invictus*, with the emperor himself serving as the high priest.[148] When Emperor Antoninus (Elagabalius) came to power in AD 218, he expanded the temple and rededicated it to the god El-Gabal, the patron god of his Syrian hometown (Herodian *Rom. Hist.* 5.5),[149] and took the title *Deus Invictus Sol Elagabalus* from AD 218 to 222. *Deus Sol Invictus* was represented on several coins[150] as a conical black stone, identified by most as a piece of a meteorite (Herodian *Rom. Hist.* 3.5).[151] It was relocated from Rome to the temple of Emesa in Syria after Antoninus' death.

---

[145] Laale, Ephesus (Ephesos), 234.
[146] Johnston, "Provinces After Commodus," 456–57 fig. 24.12.
[147] Laale, *Ephesus (Ephesos)*, 269; Burrell, *Neokoroi*, 59–85.
[148] Gaston H. Halsberghe, *The Cult of Sol Invictus* (Leiden: Brill Archive, 1972), 36.
[149] Ibid., 62; Françoise Lenormant, "Sol Elagablus," *RHR* 3 (1881): 310.
[150] Robert Turcan, *Héliogabale et le sacre du soleil* (Paris: Michel, 1986), Chapter 3 #18.
[151] Pierre M. Bellamare, "Meteorite Sparks a Cult," *JRASC* 90 (1996): 287–91.

AUGUSTEION TEMPLE

There were other temples in Ephesus that celebrated the imperial cult but not given the status of *neōkoros*. The Augusteion was built in AD 11–13 near the state agora in Ephesus, financed by one of the leading individuals in Ephesus, G. Sextilius Pollio.[152] An inscription on the basilica (βασιλική, *basilikē*, Lat. *basilicam*) states that it was dedicated "to Ephesian Artemis; to Emperor Caesar Augustus, son of god; to Tiberius Caesar, son of Augustus; and to the Dēmos of the Ephesians" (*I.Eph.* 2.404; see Figs. 26, 27, 121, 124, 127).[153]

Even though several of the νεωκόρος (*neōkoros*) temples were built after the first cent. the cult of emperor worship was still thriving during Paul's visit and John's writing of Revelation, during which Ephesus hosted temples dedicated to Artemis (or Diana), Sebastoi, and Augustus.

A CITY OF IMMORALITY AND SUPERSTITION

Ephesus, as most Roman cities (i.e., Pompeii,[154] Corinth [1 Cor 5, 6], Rome,[155] etc.), was known for its immorality (from Lat. *mores* but the idea is closer to the Lat. *impudicitia*, "sexual vice")[156] and idolatry. Oster lists some of the gods and goddesses attested in literature, coins, epigraphy and monuments from Ephesus which include: Aphrodite (see Figs. 93, 122, 123, 126), Apollo (see Figs. 86, 90, 96), Asclepius (see Fig. 71), Athena (or Diana, see Figs. 34, 124), Cabeiri, Cybele (Gr. *Magna Mater*, "great mother"; or Tyche Τύχη; see Figs. 52, 54, 98, 108, 160), Demeter (see Fig. 98), Dionysus (see Fig. 35), Egyptian Cults, Ge, Gods Most High, Hestia, Hecate, Hephaestus, Hercules, Pluto (Πλούτων, Ploutōn), Poseidon, and Zeus (see Figs. 95, 115, 126, 151, 154, 156).[157] The noble Ephesian philosopher Heraclitus (540–480 BC) accused the Ephesians of grossness, beastliness (86, 111) and immorality (124).[158]

However, it is a modern myth to project orgiastic or sexual behavior upon the Artemis cult,[159] and little connection has been made with the Cybele cult (Tyche, Τύχη, see Figs. 52, 54,

---

[152] Trebilco, *Early Christians in Ephesus*, 35.

[153] Veronika Mitsopoulos-Leon, Die Basilika Am Staatsmarkt in Ephesos – Kleinfunde. 1. Teil: Keramik Hellenistischer Und Römischer Zeit, FiE, 9.2.2 (Wien: Schindler, 1991), 13.

[154] Antonio Varone, *Erotica Pompeiana: Love Inscriptions on the Walls of Pompeii*, trans. Ria P. Berg (Rome: Di Bretschneider, 2003).

[155] Catharine Edwards, *The Politics of Immorality in Ancient Rome* (Cambridge, U.K.: Cambridge University Press, 1993); Thomas A. J. McGinn, *Prostitution, Sexuality, and the Law in Ancient Rome* (Oxford, U.K.: Oxford University Press, 2003); Rebecca Langlands, *Sexual Morality in Ancient Rome* (Cambridge, U.K.: Cambridge University Press, 2009).

[156] Edwards points out the lack of an equivalent for our term "immorality" in ancient Rome, but they often used the Latin term *mores*. Edwards, *The Politics of Immorality in Ancient Rome*, 3–4.

[157] Oster, "Ephesus (Place)," 2:548.

[158] Heraclitus of Ephesus, *The Fragments of the Work of Heraclitus of Ephesus on Nature*, trans. Ingram Bywater and G. T. W. Patrick (London, U.K.: Murray, 1889), 58.

[159] Sharon Hodgin Gritz, Paul, Women Teachers, and the Mother Goddess at Ephesus: A Study of 1 Timothy 2:9–15 in Light of the Religious and Cultural Milieu of the First Century (Washington, D.C.: University Press of America, 1991); Lewis Richard Farnell, The Cults of the Greek States, Cambridge Library Collection – Classics (Cambridge, U.K.: Cambridge University Press, 2010), 481; H. Wernicke, "Artemis," in PW, ed. A. F. Pauly and Georg

98, 108, 160). Strelan points out that "the orgiastic behaviour came from the Dionysian festivals and rituals and not from the Artemis cult."[160] Also Strabo mentions the practice of sacred prostitution in the Aphrodite (see Figs. 93, 122, 123, 126) temple during the classical period and there was still a temple to Aphrodite in the Roman Period (*Geogr.* 8.6.20).[161]

35. Marble statue of Dionysus, second cent. AD (arms and legs were heavily restored in the eighteenth cent.), found in Italy. Louvre MR 73.

Dionysus (see Fig. 35) was the god of fertility and wine and his festival was held in the spring, in the month of Lenaeon at Ephesus, when the vines were young.[162] Dillon describes the immoral practices during the Roman period of: "sexually unrestricted Dionysiac groups, in which sexual intercourse, cultic or otherwise, may have been a feature, but there is no evidence of large-scale promiscuity, though it was alleged in hostile sources (leading to the banning of Dionysiac worship in Rome in 186 BC)."[163]

Otto points out that according to the tradition on the celebration of Anthesteria (Ἀνθεστήρια, *Anthestēria*), Dionysus appears in the temple of Dionysus in a ship on wheels and takes as his own, the wife of an earthly official. The Dionysus (see Fig. 35) celebrations was different from all other festivals "because of their physical immediacy, so there is no precedent in the history of [the] cult[s] for the rite of sexual intercourse with the queen"[164] that ends with the appearance of Dionysus at the end of the precession during the feast.

Wissowa, New, vol. 2 (Munich: Buchhandlung, 1895), 2:1373; Anne Ley, "Artemis," in BrillPauly, vol. 2 (Leiden: Brill, 2007), 2:145–46; Oster, "Ephesus (Place)," 2:548.

[160] Strelan, *Paul, Artemis, and the Jews in Ephesus*, 92.

[161] What Strabo does not mention is if the practice of Prostitution also continued into the Roman period. Strabo Ben Witherington III, "Not So Idle Thoughts About Eidolothuton," *TynBul* 44, no. 2 (1993): 149 n.27.

[162] Strelan, *Paul, Artemis, and the Jews in Ephesus*, 122–25.

[163] John M. Dillon, "Dionysus (Deity)," ed. David Noel Freedman et al., *ABD* (New York, N.Y.: Doubleday, 1996), 202.

[164] Walter Friedrich Otto, *Dionysus: Myth and Cult*, trans. Robert B. Palmer (Bloomington, Ind.: Indiana University Press, 1965), 85.

However, Baugh has pointed out that immorality was not connected to the practice of cult prostitution (Lat. *hetairai*).[165] Van Der Toorn documents that there was "prostitution that was profitable to, and at times organized by, the temple and its administration," but "there is no need to postulate the existence of sacred prostitution in the service of a fertility cult."[166]

Next to the latrine, part of the Scholastica Baths, is an inscription on a peristyle house, that some identify as a brothel (παιδικοιν, *paidikoin*; *SEG* 16.719), due to the statue of the god Priapus (Pausanias *Descr.* 9.31.2), with an oversize penis displaying a permanent erection that was found in the house,[167] although the exact location of the brothel is debated.[168] A street sign is believed by some to be indicating the direction of the establishment (see Fig. 36), and Tacitus (*Ann.* 6.1) derived the term for a male prostitute (Lat. *sellarii*; Suetonius *Tib.* 43.1) from the public latrine (Lat. *sallarium*), the place where they congregated.[169] The location of the brothel near the latrine at Ephesus is customary. As Hubbard documents:

36. A sign etched in the marble pavement in Ephesus, believed by some to be pointing the way to the brothel.

> There is also considerable evidence of sexual promiscuity associated with bathing. Mixed bathing was common, as was complete nudity. Martial takes for granted that bathing was *au naturel* and provided an opportunity to meet sexual partners, whatever one's sexual orientation.[170]

---

[165] Steven M. Baugh, "Cult Prostitution in New Testament Ephesus: A Reappraisal," *JETS* 42, no. 3 (1999): 443–60.

[166] Karel van der Toorn, "Cultic Prostitution," in *ABD*, ed. David Noel Freedman et al., vol. 5 (New York, N.Y.: Doubleday, 1996), 5:510, 512.

[167] Fant and Reddish, *Guide to Biblical Sites*, 204. The small Priopus statue and statue of the god Bes are displayed in the Ephesus Museum.

[168] Werner Jobst, "Das 'Öffentliche Freudenhaus' in Ephesos," *JÖAI* 51 (1976): 69; Thomas A. J. McGinn, *The Economy of Prostitution in the Roman World: A Study of Social History and the Brothel* (Ann Arbor, Mich.: University of Michigan Press, 2004), 255; Allison Glazebrook and Madeleine M. Henry, eds., *Greek Prostitutes in the Ancient Mediterranean, 800 BCE–200 CE* (Madison, Wisc.: University of Wisconsin Press, 2011), 55 n.3.

[169] John Younger, *Sex in the Ancient World from A to Z* (New York, N.Y.: Routledge, 2005), 164.

[170] Martial *Epig.* 1.23, 96; 3.57, 72, 87; 9.33; 11.47, 63, 95; Moyer V. Hubbard, *Christianity in the Greco-Roman World: A Narrative Introduction* (Peabody, Mass.: Hendrickson, 2010), 136; Garrett G. Fagan, *Bathing in Public in the Roman World* (Ann Arbor, Mich.: University of Michigan Press, 2002), 34–36. *PGM* 2:36.69–75; 2:127.1–12.

Ephesus was also the center of pagan superstition, connected to the worship of Hestia, where people came for charms and spells contained in the famous "Ephesian letters" ('Εφέσια Γράμματα, *Ephesia grammata*),[171] used for various incantations, from safe childbirth to successful business. Their cryptic parchments were "unintelligible[172] formulae used in the practice of magic",[173] thought to carry enchanting powers to bring success to those who purchased them. Plutarch commented on the power of the Ephesian letters for those under the power of demons (δαιμόνιον, *daimonion*), stating "sorcerers advise those possessed by demons to recite and name over to themselves the Ephesian letters" (*Quaest. conv.* 9.5 [Minar]).[174] (See *Quotes from Antiquity*)

While cultic prostitution cannot be associated with Artemis and only a limited amount of sexually explicit material has been collected from Ephesus to paint the city as immoral, Christians would certainly have had a problem with the idolatry celebrated in their polytheistic festivals and the superstition, made famous by the Ephesian letters, and general immoral culture of the city.

> ### *Quotes from Antiquity*
>
> Pausanias in the *Rhetorical Lexicon* says that the Ephesian letters were words encompassing in themselves the natural sense of warding off evil. He also says that Croesus spoke these on the pyre, and that such letters seem to have been inscribed unclearly and enigmatically on the feet and girdle and crown of (i.e., the statue of Ephesian) Artemis (Eustathius, archbishop of Thessalonica *Hom. Od.* 19.247 [Bernabé]).

THE JEWISH COMMUNITY

In the second cent., Ephesus was home to a large number of Jews, particularly after the Bar-Kochba revolt in Judea. Following the uprising, some Jews took refuge in Ephesus (Irenaeus *Haer.* 3.23).[175] Inscriptions testify to a synagogue in Ephesus,[176] although no archaeological remains have yet been discovered.[177] Further evidence of a Jewish community is found in a

---

[171] For the nine ancient texts and translations, where the "Ephesian Letters" are mentioned, see, Bernabé, "Ephesia Grammata," 71–96.

[172] Bernabé concludes that "The *Ephesia Grammata* ['Εφέσια Γράμματα] evolve from a completely comprehensible Greek narrative text, originally composed in dactylic hexameters." Ibid., 77.

[173] Everett Ferguson, *Demonology of the Early Christian World*, Symposium 12 (New York, N.Y.: Mellen, 1984), 54. Clement of Alexandria provided the words in his texts (*Strom.* 5.8.45.2).

[174] Murphy-O'Connor, *St. Paul's Ephesus*, 51.

[175] A. Thomas Kraabel, "Judaism in Western Asia Minor under the Roman Empire, with a Preliminary Study of the Jewish Community in Sardis, Lydia" (Ph.D. diss., Harvard University, 1968), 52.

[176] *I.Eph.* 4.1251; *I.Eph.* 4.1676 = *CIJ* 2.746; *I.Eph.* 4.1677 = *CIJ* 2.745; *NewDocs* 3:116; 4:113, 215 n.23; Horsley, "Inscriptions of Ephesos," 121–22; Mussies, "Pagans, Jews, and Christians at Ephesus," 186. Mussies argues from evidence in the Targum to demonstrate the large number of Jewish residents in the city at a later period.

[177] Meinardus suggests that the synagogue was located near the harbour in order to have easy access to water for

menorah cut into one of the steps of the second cent. library of Celsus (see Figs. 23, 37) and several oil lamps discovered in the "Cemetery of the Seven Sleepers," which also displayed a menorah and *shofar*.[178] Another oil lamp was discovered in a basilica-like structure north of the theater gymnasium.[179]

THE CHRISTIAN COMMUNITY

The Christian faith came to Ephesus in about AD 53 when Paul left Aquila and Priscilla there, heading for Antioch via Corinth (Acts 18:18–22). During Paul's second missionary journey, he stayed in Ephesus for two years (Acts 19:8, 10), and later Timothy ministered there (1 Tim 1:3).

Paul's missionary activity of two-to-three years (Acts 20:31; about AD 52–55) reached its high point in this city, and according to Luke "all the residents of Asia heard the word of the Lord, both Jews and Greeks" (Acts 19:10)[180]; Timothy apparently lived there for some time (1 Tim 1:3), and according to Irenaeus, the Fourth Gospel was written in Ephesus, though he may have confused the fourth evangelist with the author of Revelation. . . indeed, the Pastoral Epistles and the first and longest letter of Ignatius, together with later traditions, reflect the importance of the church in Ephesus in early Christianity. Some manuscripts even refer to Ephesus in the prescript of Ephesians (Eph 1:1), though the better manuscripts omit this reference.[181] It is also believed that Paul's correspondence to the Corinthian and Roman churches was written from Ephesus.

37. Menorah inscribed into a step of the second cent. Library of Celsus.

---

their purification rituals. Meinardus, *John of Patmos*, 36–37; Clive Foss, *Ephesus After Antiquity: A Late Antique, Byzantine and Turkish City* (Cambridge, Mass.: Cambridge University Press, 2010), 49. Foss places the synagogue as possibly next to the theater gymnasium.

[178] *Jahreshefte des Österreichischen Archäologischen Institutes in Wien*, vol. 26 (Wien: ÖAI, 1930), B41; Keil, Reisch, and Knoll, *Die Marienkirche*, 99 n.30; Otto F. A. Meinardus, "The Christian Remains of the Seven Churches of the Apocalypse," *BA* 37, no. 3 (September 1, 1974): 71–72; Foss, *Ephesus After Antiquity*, 45.

[179] Foss, *Ephesus After Antiquity*, 48; E. Praschniker, F. Miltner, and H. Gerstinger, *Das Coemeterium Der Sieben Schläfer*, FiE, 4.2 (Baden: Rohrer, 1937), 187 n.159.

[180] See, also 1 Cor 15:32; 16:9; Acts 20:29–30.

[181] Krodel, *Revelation*, 105.

Ignatius of Antioch also wrote a letter to the Ephesians (Ign. *Eph*. 1:3; 6:2) while traveling through Asia Minor on his way to Rome (ca. AD 110). Onesimus was the Bishop of Ephesus at the time, who some believe was the same runaway slave that Paul mentions in his letter to Philemon (Phil 10).[182]

The details are less clear when it comes to the apostle John's relationship with Ephesus. While the Book of Revelation was written from the island of Patmos just off the coast from Ephesus, second cent. Christian sources place John in Ephesus for the later part of his life, as he survived into Trajan's reign (AD 98–117).[183] The fact that two John's are mentioned in Ephesus further complicates the sorting of fact from tradition.

Church tradition also places Mary, the mother of Jesus, in Ephesus, the traditional location of her grave (according to Breviarius of Jerusalem, AD 395). However, later Christian writers such as Epiphanius of Salamis, Gregory of Tours, Isidore of Seville, Modest, Sophronius of Jerusalem, German of Constantinople, Andrew of Crete, and John of Damascus, place her burial site in Jerusalem. Timothy is mentioned as the first bishop of Ephesus.[184] The Christian apologist, Justin Martyr, carried out his dialogue with Tryho the Jew here in Ephesus (*Dial*. 2–8; Eusebius *Hist. eccl.* 4.18.6).

38. Restored Library of Celsus, Ephesus. The relief in the foreground is reminiscent of the elements of armor mentioned in Ephesians 6:13–17, including the belt, breastplate, greaves for the feet, shield, helmet and sword. While the Library was only completed in 135 AD and was not present in Paul's day, the relief may have existed earlier.

---

[182] John Knox, *Philemon among the Letters of Paul* (Chicago, Ill.: University of Chicago Press, 1960), 51–56; F. F. Bruce, *The Epistles to the Colossians, to Philemon, and to the Ephesians*, 2nd ed., NICNT (Grand Rapids, Mich.: Eerdmans, 1984), 200–202. Bruce concludes: "That Onesimus did become bishop of Ephesus is not improbable."

[183] Eusebius *Hist. eccl.* 3:21; 3.23.1, 6; Irenaeus *Haer.* 2.33; 3.3.4; see chapter 1, *The Date of Writing*.

[184] Eusebius *Hist. eccl.* 3.4.5; 1 Tim 1:3; Titus 1:5.

5

Extinct Ephesus

Commentary on Revelation 2:1–7

This chapter will examine the extinct love of the Ephesians and their message in the light of the proposed covenant background and structure found in Revelation 2:1–17. On the commission to write (γράψον, *graphon* 3:7a) and the role of angels (ἄγγελος, *angelos*) as mediating messengers, see chapter 3, *The Messenger's Commission*.

> Τῷ ἀγγέλῳ τῆς ἐν Ἐφέσῳ ἐκκλησίας γράψον.
>
> "To the angel [*messenger*] of the church in Ephesus write:" (Rev 2:1a)

MESSENGER PREAMBLE FORMULA—2:1

> Τάδε λέγει ὁ κρατῶν τοὺς ἑπτὰ ἀστέρας ἐν τῇ δεξιᾷ αὐτοῦ, ὁ περιπατῶν ἐν μέσῳ τῶν ἑπτὰ λυχνιῶν τῶν χρυσῶν.
>
> "*The words* of him who holds the seven stars in his right hand, who walks among the seven golden lampstands." (Rev 2:1)

John begins each message to the churches with τάδε λέγει Ω (*tade legei omega*, "These are the words" 2:1, 8,12,18; 3:1a, 7, 14), setting the context for the suzerain/King who will speak to the churches.[1] He proceeds to describe Christ as an echo from Revelation chapter 1 (vs.13, 16) in a format familiar to the Christian community. Within the OT prophetic structure[2] this prophetic *messenger preamble formula*[3] τάδε λέγει Ω, (*tade legei omega*, "These are the words") introduces the sovereign's message. On the prophetic *messenger preamble formula* see the discussion under "The Messenger's Commission" in chapter 1.

---

[1] Beale, *Revelation*, 229.
[2] Num 22:15–16; Judg 11:14–15; 1 Kgs 2:30; 2 Chr 36:23; Ezra 1:2.
[3] Graves, *SMRVT*, 141–47; Osborne, *Revelation*, 111.

DESCRIPTION OF THE SUZERAIN

The imagery here harkens back to chapter 1 where Christ appears in the vision to John "in the midst of the seven lampstands One like the Son of Man, clothed with a garment down to His feet ... He had in His right hand seven stars" (1:13, 16). The message begins with a reminder that it is the sovereign Christ who is the head of the church in Ephesus, and it is he who speaks to his church, and these are his words.

THE OMNIPOTENT SUZERAIN HOLDS THE SEVEN STARS—2:1A

ὁ κρατῶν τοὺς ἑπτὰ ἀστέρας ἐν τῇ δεξιᾷ αὐτοῦ,

"him who holds the seven stars in his right hand," (Rev 2:1a)

The description of the suzerain is made even more emphatic than the earlier vision in chapter 1 by using the synonym κρατῶν (*kratōn*; κράτος , "grasp" 2:1b) in place of ἔχων (*echōn*, "hold" 1:16; 2:11). There is also an echo of this description of the suzerain in the second half of the message to the church in Sardis "who has (ἔχων, *echōn*, "hold") ... the seven stars" (2:11).

Various interpretations of what these seven stars represented have been offered by commentators.[4] Ramsay argues that the seven stars in the right hand represent Ephesus as the leading city in Asia, compared with Sardis which was the ancient capital of Lydia and whose suzerain also holds (ἔχων, *echōn*) seven stars.[5]

Beale has suggested John had the OT in mind, deriving his allusion to seven stars from Daniel 12:3 and the seven lamps from Zechariah chapter 4.[6] However, John may also have been aware of the early Jewish tradition that symbolically connected the seven lamps in the temple with seven planets.[7]

However, there may also have been a numismatic connection, as seen in the coinage of the deified Domitian. A silver denarius coin from AD 82–83 features Domitian's deified infant son, seated on a globe[8] surrounded by seven stars (see Fig. 39). The child has been identified as the Empress Domitia Longinas' son (AD 82–96 left), T. Flavius

39. Silver denarius coin (AD 82–83) of Domitian. Obv.: *DOMITIA AVGVSTA IMP DOMIT*, draped bust of Domitian. Rev.: *DIVVS CAESAR IMP DOMITIANI F*, Domitian and Domitia's deified infant son, seated on a globe reaching out to seven stars. (*RIC* 153; 213; *RSC* 11; *BMC* 63) CNG

---

[4] Strangely Aune is silent on the meaning of the "seven stars" or "right hand". Aune, *Rev 1–5*, 141–42.

[5] Ramsay, *Letters: Updated*, 172–75.

[6] Beale, *Revelation*, 211–13.

[7] See Josephus *Ant*. 3.145; *J.W.* 5.217; Philo *Mos*. 2.102–5; *Her*. 45.221–25; *QE* 2.73–81; *Tg. Pal*. Exod. 40:4; *Midr. Rab*. Num 12:13; see also Clement of Alexandria *Strom*. 5.6; Aune, *Rev 1–5*, 97–98; Beale, *Rev*, 212; Wojciechowski, "Celestial Bodies," 48–50.

[8] The globe suggests that the Romans believed the earth was a sphere, although Eratosthenes (276–194 BC) of

Caesar,[9] who was born in AD 73 and died young (Suetonius *Dom.* 3.1).[10] The inscription on the coin reads: *DIVVS CAESAR IMP DOMITIANI*, which translates as "The Deified Caesar, Son of the emperor Domitian."[11] The seven stars symbolize the child's divine status, perhaps connected to the seven hills[12] of Rome.[13]

Beale and others have suggested that the reference in Revelation may be "a polemic against the imperial myth of an emperor's son who dies and becomes a divine ruler over the stars of heaven, since the title 'ruler of the kings of the earth' in 1:5 likely also has such a polemical connotation."[14]

Revelation interprets the seven stars as "the angels of the seven churches" (1:20), so the suzerain is one who securely holds the messengers of the churches in his right hand of power and control with a sense of security (John 10:28), contrasted with the power and control of the Roman Emperors, who only offered a sense of false security to their loyal subjects, and no security to the church.

THE SUZERAIN WALKS AMONG THE CHURCHES—2:1B

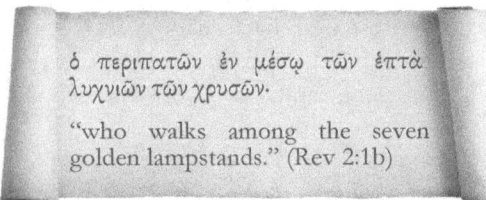

ὁ περιπατῶν ἐν μέσῳ τῶν ἑπτὰ λυχνιῶν τῶν χρυσῶν·

"who walks among the seven golden lampstands." (Rev 2:1b)

Oil lamps were placed on a metal stand to provide light for the dwelling. Revelation interprets the seven lampstands (τῶν ἑπτὰ λυχνιῶν, *tōn epta luchniōn*) as "the seven churches" (1:20), and therefore, the king is walking in the midst of the seven churches, no doubt trimming the wick of the lamps and replenishing the oil to maintain their light. He is a king who cares for his churches and is involved in their shining testimony (1 John 2:8).

HISTORICAL PROLOGUE—2:2–4

Within the ANEVT structure, following the preamble it was customary for the suzerain to highlight the past relationship between the suzerain and the vassal. The first person οἶδα (*oida*, "I

Cyrene (modern Libya) was the first to discover that the earth is round. Mary Gow, *Measuring the Earth: Eratosthenes and His Celestial Geometry* (Berkeley Heights, N.J.: Enslow, 2009), 6.

[9] Jean-Lu Desnier, "Divus Caesar Imp. Domitiani F.," *REA* 81 (1979): 64.

[10] John Garthwaite, "Martial, Book 6, on Domitian's Moral Censorship," *Prudentia* 22 (1990): 16–17; Eric R. Varner, "Domitia Longina and the Politics of Portraiture," *AJA* 99, no. 2 (1995): 188; Olivier Hekster, *Emperors and Ancestors: Roman Rulers and the Constraints of Tradition*, OSACR (Oxford, U.K.: Oxford University Press, 2015), 57.

[11] Harold B. Mattingly and Edward Allen Sydenham, eds., *The Roman Imperial Coinage: Vespasian to Hadrian (69–138)*, vol. 2 (London, U.K.: Spink & Son, 1926), 209a.

[12] Grant Heiken, Renato Funiciello, and Donatella de Rita, *The Seven Hills of Rome: A Geological Tour of the Eternal City* (Princeton University Press, 2013), ix.

[13] Virgil *Aen.* 6.782; Martial *Epig.* 4.64; Cicero *Att.* 6.5; see also Rev 17:9.

[14] Beale, *Revelation,* 211; Caird, *Revelation,* 15; Lohmeyer, *Offenbarung,* 18.

know") was a common feature of the ANEVT's,[15] as it is in the SMR. Christ has an intimate knowledge of the churches, as well as an ongoing covenant relationship.[16] However, οἶδα (*oida*, "I know") conveys more than mere knowledge (γινώσκω, *ginōskō*, "know" 2:23, 24; 3:3, 9)[17] of the facts about the Ephesian church in its use throughout Revelation for Christ's knowledge of the churches. It conveys the idea of an intimate and intuitive knowledge[18] and "emphasizes better the absolute clearness of mental vision which photographs all the facts of life as they pass."[19]

THE SUZERAIN KNOWS THEIR WORKS—2:2A

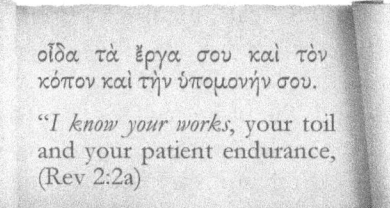

οἶδα τὰ ἔργα σου καὶ τὸν κόπον καὶ τὴν ὑπομονήν σου.

"*I know your works*, your toil and your patient endurance, (Rev 2:2a)

Because Christ is in the midst of the churches (lampstands; 1:13, 20), he knows their works or deeds (ἔργα, *erga*). The two epexegetical καί appositives following ἔργα (*erga*, "works" or "deeds") convey more than their good words, conveying their whole Christian walk as deeds that involved effort and endurance and can rightly be translated as "namely, your toil and endurance."[20] The elements of their conduct embrace many of the deeds contained in their letter. It refers to the hard work and patient endurance involved as they discerningly resisted evil.

The Ephesians had laboured to the point of exhaustion (κόπος, *kopos*, "wearisome toil") on several fronts. Worthy and Chilton have suggested that the *deeds, hard work and perseverance* are pictured "manifesting similar virtues in keeping the harbour" from silting up.[21] However, the labour referred to here is more likely to be understood against the backdrop of the Christian community who patiently persevered against a hostile culture that was at odds with their Christian values (see "enduring patiently and bearing up for my name's sake," 2:3). While the temple to Artemis (see Figs. 24, 25) is not mentioned in Revelation, it no doubt played a role in the perseverance and endurance of the Ephesian Christians. Acts 19:23–42 illustrates the kind of perseverance and obstacles the Ephesian Christians had to endure over the Artemis statues (*I.Eph.* 3.961; 6.2212) produced by Demetrius the silversmith (19:23–42; ἀργυροκόπος, *argurokopos*) and the account in Second Timothy of Alexander the coppersmith (4:14; *NewDocs*

---

[15] Hartman, "The Book of Revelation," 143; Baltzer, *Covenant Formulary*, 20–24; Aune, *Rev 1–5*, 121. Aune identifies this as the *narratio* section.

[16] Gregg R. Allison, *Sojourners and Strangers: The Doctrine of the Church* (Wheaton, Ill.: Crossway, 2012), 76–78.

[17] Joseph B. Lightfoot, *St. Paul's Epistle to the Galatians*, 6th ed. (London, U.K.: MacMillan, 1880), 171. Lightfoot's opinion that οἶδα refers to absolute facts while γινώσκω refers to attained knowledge is rejected by most scholars.

[18] *EDNT* 2:494; MM 439; A. T. Robertson, *Word Pictures in the New Testament* (Nashville, Tenn.: B&H, 1998), 6:297; Mounce, *Revelation*, 68.

[19] Swete, *Apocalypse*, 24.

[20] Osborne, *Revelation*, 112; Charles, *Revelation*, 1:59; Thomas, *Rev 1–7*, 133; Aune, *Rev 1–5*, 143; Lohmeyer, *Offenbarung*, 21–22.

[21] Worth, Jr., *Greco-Asian Culture*, 63; Chilton, *Days of Vengeance*, 96–97.

4:7–10).[22] The exalted Christ (suzerain) was familiar with all of these works, as well as with their failures.

THE SUZERAIN KNOWS THEY HAVE TESTED FALSE APOSTLES—2:2B

> καὶ ἐπείρασας τοὺς λέγοντας ἑαυτοὺς ἀποστόλους καὶ οὐκ εἰσὶν καὶ εὗρες αὐτοὺς ψευδεῖς
>
> "and you put to the test those calling themselves apostles and are not, and found them to be false (liars)." (Rev 2:2b [Graves])

The suzerain knows that the Ephesians have not only worked hard to persevere against those outside the church, but also those within its walls. The Ephesians had no tolerance for those who are evil (κακούς, *kakous*, "evil men") and have tested those among them who call themselves apostles (Ign. *Eph.* 6:2; 9:1; see *Quotes from Antiquity*), but who were found to be false (ψευδεῖς, *pseudeis* "liars") apostles and therefore evil.[23] The term "apostles" (ἀπόστολος, *apostolos*, "person sent forth or messenger sent by another person") refer to the twelve disciples of Jesus[24] who were used to organize the church and spread the gospel.[25] To qualify as an apostle one must have been a witness of the risen Christ[26] and called by Jesus to this office (Luke 6:13; Gal 1:1).[27] It is unlikely that these false apostles could claim they had been eyewitnesses of the resurrection and it is likely that they may have met Jesus or been in a crowd, but exaggerated their claim to make it sound as if they had been personally appointed by Christ. Caird identified these apostles as those from the outer circle, "claiming to belong to that group of apostles of Christ which was wider than the Twelve, and which included James the Just, Barnabas, Paul, Silas, Andronicus, and Junias."[28] The sign of apostolic authority was the ability to perform miracles,[29] but these could also be imitated by false prophets.[30] Thus John earlier warned that it was necessary to "test the

> **Quotes from Antiquity**
>
> "I have learned that some from elsewhere who have evil teaching stayed with you, but you did not allow them to sow it among you, and stopped our ears, so that you might not receive what they sow." (Ign. *Eph.* 9:1)

---

[22] Horsley, "Inscriptions of Ephesos," 142–45.

[23] As Thomas has pointed out these were more than just backslidden Christians as Lenski has proposed. Thomas, *Rev 1–7*, 135.

[24] Matt 10:1–5; Mark 3:14; 6:7; Luke 6:13; 9:1.

[25] Matt 10:2–4; Mark 3:16; Luke 6:14; Acts 1:13.

[26] John 15:27; Acts 1:21, 22; 1 Cor 9:1; Acts 22:14, 15.

[27] The apostolic fathers refer only to the recognized NT apostles and the church fathers understood that the special NT apostolic office ceased to function with the close of the apostolic age. Alan F. Johnson et al., *Hebrews – Revelation*, ed. Tremper Longman III and David E. Garland, Revised, EBC 13 (Grand Rapids, Mich.: Zondervan, 2006), 613.

[28] 1 Cor 20:7; Gal 1:19; Acts 14:1; 1 Thess 2:6; Rom 16:7; Caird, *Revelation*, 30; Beale, *Revelation*, 229.

[29] Mark 16:20; Acts 2:43; 1 Cor 12:8–11; 2 Cor 12:12; Heb 2:4.

[30] Mark 13:22; 2 Thess 2:9; 2 Tim 3:8; Rev 13:13–14.

spirits to see whether they are from God, for many false prophets have gone out into the world" (1 John 4:1).

Thomas points out that the participle λέγοντας (*legontas*, "saying"), is timeless and does not just refer to the past state of the so-called apostles, meaning the sentence can equally be translated: "they were not apostles in the past and are not now, nor will they be in the future."[31] The suzerain was intimately familiar with their handling of false apostles.

Aune points out that a pun (παρονομασία, *paronomasia*, "one name") is used in the sentence, with two aorist verbs used in close proximity to one another (βαστάσαι, *bastasai* and ἐβάστασας, *ebastasas*), one used negatively and the second positively.[32] The suzerain knows that the Ephesians cannot "endure" evil men, but are "enduring" (also John 20:15) for the sake of the suzerain.

Earlier Jesus had warned of false prophets in terms of "wolves in sheep's clothing" (Matt 7:15). Then Paul warned about similar false prophets within the church in Ephesus in his farewell speech to the Ephesian elders in Miletus: "I know that after my departure fierce wolves will come in among you, not sparing the flock; and from among your own selves will arise men speaking twisted things, to draw away the disciples after them" (Acts 20:29). John indicates that the Ephesians have been discerning and testing false apostles (including Nicolaitans 2:6). The vigilant practice of inner purity is reported to have continued, as Ignatius of Antioch (AD ca. 35 or 50–98 to 117)[33] heard from Onesimus, the bishop of Ephesus (d. ca. AD 68), that the Ephesians closed their ears to any false teaching, so that no sect could claim a foothold in Ephesus (Ign. *Eph.* 6:2; 7:1; 9:1).

These apostles have been variously identified as: Judaizers sent from Jerusalem (2 Cor 11:13–23);[34] as the disciples of Paul or even Paul himself;[35] as the Nicolaitans (2:6 the Balaam group);[36] or any self-appointed apostles among those in the church.[37] This last option seems the more likely.

---

[31] Thomas, *Rev 1–7*, 138.
[32] Leonard L. Thompson, *Revelation* (Nashville, Tenn.: Abingdon, 1998), 49; Aune, *Rev 1–5*, 143.
[33] David Hugh Farmer, *The Oxford Dictionary of Saints*, 5th ed. (Oxford, U.K.: Oxford University Press, 2011), 220.
[34] Spitta, *Offenbarung*, op. cit.
[35] Heinrich Julius Holtzmann, *Evangelium, Briefe und Offenbarung des Johannes*, ed. R. A. Lipsius, 2nd ed., Hand-Commentar Zum Neuen Testament (Halle: Gebauer & Schwetschke, 1906), op. cit.
[36] Wilhelm Bousset, *Die Offenbarung Johannis* (Göttingen: Vandenhoeck & Ruprecht, 1906); Charles, *Revelation*, 1:50; Wilfrid J Harrington, *Revelation*, ed. Daniel J Harrington, SPS 16 (Collegeville, Minn.: Liturgical, 2008), 57; Beale, *Revelation*, 229; Pierre Prigent, *Commentary on the Apocalypse of St. John*, trans. Wendy Pradels (Tübingen: Siebeck, 2004), 158. This is unlikely, as the Nicolaitan's were antinomians (anti-law) rather than legalists (Judaizers). Thomas, *Rev 1–7*, 137; Mounce, *Revelation*, 87.
[37] Caird, *Revelation*, 30.

THE SUZERAIN KNOWS THEIR PATIENT ENDURANCE—2:3

> ἀλλὰ ἔχω κατὰ σοῦ ὅτι τὴν ἀγάπην σου τὴν πρώτην ἀφῆκες.
>
> "But I have this against you, that you have abandoned the love you had at first." (Rev 2:4 [Graves])

The same phrase "for my name's sake" is used in Matthew 10:22 and 24:9 where the persecuted followers of Christ are involved in spreading the gospel. The Ephesians are patiently enduring persecution for the name of Christ; something the suzerain is aware of. This is evident in their resistance of the artisans of Artemis (Acts 19:32–38) and Paul's persecution by Alexander the coppersmith (2 Tim 4:14).[38] The suzerain knows that in spite of their perseverance, they have not grown weary.

THE SUZERAIN KNOWS THEY HAVE ABANDONED THEIR FIRST LOVE—2:4

> καὶ ὑπομονὴν ἔχεις καὶ ἐβάστασας διὰ τὸ ὄνομά μου καὶ οὐ κεκοπίακες.
>
> "and you are bearing up and enduring patiently and because of my name you have toiled and you have not faltered." (Rev 2:3 [Graves])

The suzerain has an issue with the Ephesian Christians (Charles sees a parallel with Matt 5:23; Mark 11:25).[39] Although the Ephesians were known for their steadfast perseverance and zealous testing of those calling themselves "apostles", the suzerain was aware of one fatal flaw; they had "let go" (ἀφῆκας, *aphēkas*, "you have given up" or "leave," John 4:3; 10:12; 16:28) of their "first love" (ἀγάπην σου τὴν πρώτην, *agapēn sou tēn prōtēn*)—not their first or primary love, but the love they had in the beginning. Osborne puts it this way: "They had lost the first flush of enthusiasm and excitement in their Christian life and had settled into a cold orthodoxy with more surface strength than depth."[40]

While several interpretations have been put forward for their "first love," the majority of commentators propose that it means their love for one another (Acts 20:35; Eph 1:15),[41] rather than forsaking their love for God,[42] although a growing number of commentators acknowledge

---

[38] Andrew Tait, The Messages to the Seven Churches of Asia Minor: An Exposition of the First Three Chapters of the Book of the Revelation (London, U.K.: Hodder & Stoughton, 1884), 136.

[39] Charles, *Revelation*, 1:51.

[40] Osborne, *Revelation*, 115.

[41] Kiddle, *Revelation*, Moffatt's translation 21; George Eldon Ladd, *A Commentary on the Revelation of John* (Grand Rapids, Mich.: Eerdmans, 1972), 39; Johnson et al., *Hebrews – Revelation*, 2006, 613; Mounce, *Revelation*, 69; George R. Beasley-Murray, *Revelation: Three Viewpoints* (Nashville: Baptist Sunday School Board, 1981), Ray R. Robbins 160; Beasley-Murray, *Revelation, NCB*, 75; Roloff, *Revelation*, 45; Witherington III, *Revelation*, 96.

[42] John Stott, *What Christ Thinks of the Church: An Exposition of Revelation 1–3* (Grand Rapids, Mich.: Baker, 2003), 27; Alford, *Revelation*, 4:4:563; Prigent, *Apocalypse*, 159; John F. Walvoord, *The Revelation of Jesus Christ* (Chicago, Ill.: Moody, 1989), 55; Hughes, *Revelation*, op. cit.; Stauffer *TDNT* 1:53.

that love to God and love for others are both connected and neither eliminates the other.[43] Beale departs from both arguing that "The idea that they no longer expressed their former zealous love for Jesus *by witnessing to him in the world.*"[44] He supports his argument by pointing to Christ (the suzerain) standing in the midst of the church[45] and that "their primary role in relation to their Lord should be that of a light of witness to the outside world"[46] (compared with "the love of many will grow cold." Matt 24:12–14).[47] Harrington, points out that "sadly, later Christian history has too many instances of unholy zeal in the pursuit of 'truth.' Orthodoxy is no substitute for orthopraxis [correct practice]; it surely cannot replace the praxis of love."[48]

Kiddle suggests that *giving up loving one another as they did at first* was, according to Apollonius of Tyana (AD ca. 15–100), recognized as a fault of the ordinary citizens of Ephesus involved in trade guilds and commerce, though he fails to provide any references supporting this claim.[49] However, Philostratus (AD ca. 172–250) records in one of Apollonius of Tyana's (AD ca. 15–100) speeches in Ephesus that: "he dissuaded and discouraged them [the Ephesians] from other pursuits, and urged them to fill Ephesus with real study rather than with idleness and *revelry* such as he found around him there" (Philostratus, *Vit. Apoll.* 4.1–4 [Conybeare]).

Ethical Stipulations—2:5a

The loyalty of the churches (vassals) to the suzerain is demonstrated through obedience to stated ethical stipulations. While two of the churches, Smyrna and Philadelphia, are called to continued faithfulness, five churches are called to correct their deficiencies. The stipulations surrounding the Ephesian message are given in terms of three imperatives—remember (μνημόνευε, *mnēmoneue*), repent (μετανόησον, *metanoēson*), and repeat (ποίησον, *poiēson*, do).[50] Johnson argues that "the three imperatives are all part of a single action designed to keep the Ephesians from the judgment of Christ, which would effectively remove them as his representatives in the world."[51] Smalley points out that these could represent the "three stages in the history of conversion. . . all three commands, in the life of the Christian and the church, require an obedient response which is constant."[52]

---

[43] Hemer, *Letters to the Seven Churches*, 41; Krodel, *Revelation*, 107; Craig S. Keener, *Revelation*, ed. Terry C. Muck, NIVAC 20 (Grand Rapids, Mich.: Zondervan, 2000), 106; Thomas, *Rev 1–7*, 140–41; Johnson, "Revelation," 613.

[44] Beale, *Revelation*, 230.

[45] Keener does not believe Beale's argument appears clear in the text. Keener, *Revelation*, 106–7 n.12.

[46] Beale, *Revelation*, 230.

[47] John Gill, *Exposition of the New Testament: Galatians to Revelation*, vol. 3 (Philadelphia, Pa.: Woodward, 1811), 705; John P. M. Sweet, *Revelation*, TPINTC (Valley Forge, PA: Trinity Press International, 1990), 79; Krodel, *Revelation*, 107.

[48] Harrington, *Revelation*, 57.

[49] Kiddle, *Revelation*, 23.

[50] Merrill C. Tenney, *Interpreting Revelation* (Grand Rapids, Mich.: Eerdmans, 1988), 57.

[51] Johnson et al., *Hebrews – Revelation*, 2006, 614.

[52] Smalley, *Revelation*, 61–62; Sweet, *Revelation*, 27.

First Imperative: Remember—2:5a

> μνημόνευε οὖν πόθεν πέπτωκας καὶ μετανόησον καὶ τὰ πρῶτα ἔργα ποίησον.
>
> "*Remember* therefore from where you have fallen; *repent*, and *do* the works you did at first." (Rev 2:5)

The Ephesians are called to remember (μνημόνευε, *mnēmoneue*), a present imperative in this case directed at their memory of the past, as "keep on remembering".[53] They must not simply bring it to mind, but they are called to act upon what they have remembered. Aune points out that both the OT and NT use "remember" to "recapture earlier moral and spiritual standards"[54]. It is also used in Graeco-Roman literature for paraenetic lessons (Dio Chrysostom *Or.* 17.2; 78.39; Seneca *Ep. Mor.* 94.21). The suzerain calls the church to remember their earlier works of fervent love (see also Sardis 3:3) and compare them with their present situation, in order to realise "how far you have fallen" (πόθεν πέπτωκας, *pothen peptōkas*).[55] As Aune points out, remembering implies "that the author [suzerain] had a lengthy acquaintance with the history of each of these congregations."[56]

Second Imperative: Repent—2:5a

The suzerain calls the Ephesians to "repent" (μετανόησον, *metanoēson,* aorist imperative "totally turn") from their ways (see the prodigal son in Luke 15:17–18). The imperative to repent is placed on both sides of the judgment, in order to powerfully reinforce that this is the way to escape from the said judgment. Lunde defines it as "the radical 'turning away' from anything which hinders one's wholehearted trust in God. As such, the notion of 'turning to' God in love and obedience is most often included."[57] Mounce describes repentance as "a radical redirection of one's entire life."[58] Smalley reminds us that repentance demands a "change of heart, leading to loving conduct":[59] in other words, a 180–degree-turn was required from the Ephesians away from their former conduct.

---

[53] Kistemaker, *Revelation*, 115.

[54] Aune, *Rev 1–5*, 147. Deut 5:15; 7:18; 8:18–19; Isa 44:21; 46:8–9; 57:11; Mic 6:5; Rom 15:15; Gal 1:6–9; 3:2–3; 1 Thess 1:5–10; 2:13–14; 4:1–2; see also *1 Clem.* 53:1.

[55] Krodel and Roloff maintain that because "you have fallen" is singular, it refers to the angel of the church and conveys the common apocalyptic idea of the fall of angels (e.g., *1 En.* 6–18; 64–69; *Jub.* 5; Rev 1:20; 12:4). Osborne does not believe the angel has fallen literally, but is fallen for "rhetorical effect." Krodel, *Revelation*, 108; Roloff, *Revelation*, 45; Osborne, *Revelation*, 117.

[56] Beale, *Revelation,* 147.

[57] Jonathan M. Lunde, "Repentance," ed. Joel B. Green, I. Howard Marshall, and Scot McKnight, *DJG* (Downers Grove, Ill.: InterVarsity, 1992), 669.

[58] Mounce, *Revelation*, 70.

[59] Smalley, *Revelation*, 62.

THIRD IMPERATIVE: REPEAT—2:5A

The Ephesians were required to "*do* [redo] the works [you did] at first" (τὰ πρῶτα ἔργα ποίησον, *ta prōta erga poiēson*). The aorist imperative here marks a state of urgency, thus can be translated as "start doing those works which characterized your church at its earliest stage of existence, do it at once!"[60]

In a secular sense, several commentators suggest that this may have been a call to act now on the problem of the Cayster River silting up, as it was prone to doing and had done repeatedly in the past.[61] This hardly makes sense in the context, although the language may have resonated with the Ephesians who were continually dredging the harbour.

SANCTIONS: CURSE—2:5B,C

Within the ANEVT structure the ethical imperatives are followed with divine sanctions of curses and blessings.[62] In like manner, the Ephesians are warned that if they do not repent they will experience the curses of Christ's visit in judgment and their lampstand will be removed.

THE CURSE OF THE SUZERAIN'S VISIT—2:5B

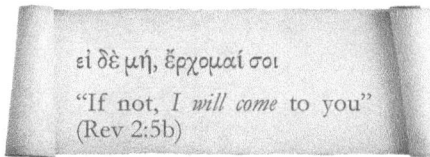

"If not, *I will come* to you" (Rev 2:5b)

Christ's visit to the church can be understood as a curse since he is coming in judgment. Aune points out that verbs meaning "come" (ἔρχομαί, *erchomai* and ἥκειν, *ekein*) are used five times in Revelation 2 and 3 (2:5, 16, 25; 3:3, 11). He notes that "three times they are used in the negative sense of Christ's coming to judge a community (2:5, 16; 3:3) and twice in the very different and positive sense of the Parousia of Christ (2:25; 3:11)."[63] The coming of the suzerain is accompanied by sanctions. "I come" (ἔρχομαί, *erchomai*) is in the present tense, while "I will remove" (κινήσω, *kinēsō*) is in the future indicative, meaning that "the threat is not a possibility but a certainty."[64]

The phrase "I am coming" (ἔρχομαί, *erchomai* present tense) has been understood in several ways. First, it has been understood to mean Christ's second coming for universal judgment.[65] But as Caird notes, the coming is conditional on their repentance, and thus is not referring to the second coming.[66] Secondly, it is a special "coming in judgment" that is just for the Ephesian

---

[60] Thomas, *Rev 1–7*, 143; Lenski, *Revelation*, 1963, 87; Tenney, *Revelation*, 57.

[61] Worth, Jr., *Greco-Asian Culture*, 63; Chilton, *Days of Vengeance*, 96–97. Richard E. Oster, "Ephesus," ed. David Noel Freedman et al., *ABD* (New York, N.Y.: Doubleday, 1996), 2:543. See *The Commercial Harbour*.

[62] See chapter 3, *Sanctions*.

[63] Aune, *Rev 1–5*, 147.

[64] Kistemaker, *Revelation*, 115; Beale, *Revelation*, 231.

[65] Krodel, *Revelation*, 109; Thomas, *Rev 1–7*, 144–47; Moffatt, *Revelation*, 5:5:352; Robert W. Wall, *Revelation*, ed. W. Ward Gasque, NIBC 18 (Peabody, Mass.: Hendrickson, 2002), 70–71; Muse, "Rev 2–3," 153–54; Aune, "Form and Function," 192; Frederick David Mazzaferri, "Martyria Iesou Revisited," *BT* 39, no. 1 (1988): 119.

[66] Caird, *Revelation*, 32.

church, and prior to the second coming.[67] The fact that it mentions the removal of just one lampstand on which the lamps were hung (see Fig. 41), instead of seven in a fixed candelabrum, argues for the local meaning and judgment of Ephesus alone.[68] Osborne argues that it is not "either-or" but "both-and."[69] Others suggest that his coming is also connected to a Eucharistic emphasis, where Parousia and judgment are constantly anticipated (1 Cor 11:28–32).[70] As Beale states "in the Eucharist believers experience in the present repeated anticipations of the judicial and salvific effects of Christ's final coming."[71]

THE CURSE OF A REMOVED LAMPSTAND—2:5C

καὶ κινήσω τὴν λυχνίαν σου ἐκ τοῦ τόπου αὐτῆς, ἐὰν μὴ μετανοήσῃς.

" and *remove your lampstand* from its place, unless you repent." (Rev 2:5c)

If the vassal refuses to repent, Christ, the suzerain, will visit in judgment and bring to bear the sanction of removing (κινήσω, *kinēsō*, to move or remove) their lampstand (λυχνία, *lychnia*). Aune suggests that the lamp imagery is taken from 1 Kings 7:49 where the term "lamp" (נר, *ner*) is used for the tribe of Benjamin.[72] Most commentators associate the lampstand with the Jewish seven-branched lampstand or menorah (מנורה *mĕnōrâ*, Exod 25, 37; Num 8; Zech 4:2; Rev 1:12, 20; 11:4),[73] which stood in the tabernacle, and the First and Second Temple. The lampstands (note the plural) were removed several times over the history of the temple. They were looted by the Babylonians prior to the temple's destruction in 586 BC (2 Chr 36:7, 10, 18; Ezra 1:7; Dan 1:2; Jer 52:19). Then the lampstands were taken by Antiochus IV in 170 BC (1 Macc 1:21; Josephus *Ant.* 12.250. Josephus speaks of lampstands in the plural.).

Then finally in 70 AD the lampstand was taken from the temple by the Romans (Josephus *J.W.* 7.148; see Fig. 40). The Jewish community in

40. Relief on the arch of Titus, Rome, depicting the removal of the menorah or lampstand from the temple in Jerusalem following its destruction in 70 AD by the Romans.

---

[67] Ibid.; Beasley-Murray, *Revelation*, NCB, 75; Smalley, *Revelation*, 62; Lenski, *Revelation*, 1963, 89; Kistemaker, *Revelation*, 116; Ladd, *Revelation*; Mounce, *Revelation*, 70; Beale, *Rev*, 231–32.

[68] Mounce, *Revelation*, 89; Smalley, *Revelation*, 62.

[69] Osborne, *Revelation*, 118.

[70] C. F. D. Moule, "The Judgment Them in the Sacraments," in *The Background of the New Testament and Its Eschatology*, ed. William David Davies and D. Daube (Cambridge, U.K.: Cambridge University Press, 2009), 464–81; Sweet, *Revelation*, 41–42; Beale, *Revelation*, 233.

[71] Beale, *Revelation*, 233.

[72] Aune, *Rev 1–5*, 147.

[73] Ibid., 88–90; Osborne, *Revelation*, 99; Johnson, "Revelation," 605; Beale, *Revelation*, 206.

Ephesus would have remembered these three removals of the lampstands from the temple. All Ephesians would have been aware of the looting of the temple in 70 AD, as it was commemorated on a bronze Sestertius coin of Vespasian (AD 69–79) depicting the victory of Vespasian and Titus over the Jews (issued in AD 71). In Latin it reads *IVDAEA CAPTA*, which translates as "Judea captured".[74] The author of 4 Ezra records, following the plundering of the temple by the Romans, that "the light of our lampstand has been put out" (10:22), indicating that their worship life in the temple had ended. Beale points out that the lampstand (מנורת, *menorat, menorah*)[75] in Zechariah 4:2–6 "with its seven [separate] lamps is a figurative synecdoche: part of the temple furniture stands for the whole temple, which by extension also represents faithful Israel (see also Zech 4:6–9)".[76] Beale concludes that "Rev. 11:1–13 confirms that the lampstands represent the church as the true temple and the totality of the people of God witnessing [light bearers] in the period between Christ's resurrection and his final coming."[77] The church represented by the lampstand bears the light of the gospel to a world in darkness.

In addition, every household would have had a lampstand to hold the oil lamps that would provide light for the house (see Figs. 37, 41). Revelation 1:12 indicates that there were seven golden lampstands with Christ walking among them and identifies the seven lampstands with the seven churches (1:20). The curse on the unrepentant Ephesians would be either the moving of its ecclesiastical authority[78] or destruction[79] (closing the church), as in the loss of their status as a

41. Woman lighting an oil lamp on a lampstand.

---

[74] Some coins carried the words *Judaea devicta* meaning "Judea defeated". H. Porter, "Money," ed. Geoffrey W. Bromiley, *ISBE* (Grand Rapids, Mich.: Eerdmans, 1995), 3:2080; Ya 'akov Meshorer, *Jewish Coins of the Second Temple Period* (Tel Aviv, Israel: Am Hassefer and Masada, 1967), 107–8; A. Thomas Kraabel, J. Andrew Overman, and Robert S. MacLennan, eds., *Diaspora Jews and Judaism: Essays in Honor Of, and in Dialogue With, A. Thomas Kraabel* (Atlanta, Ga.: Scholars Press, 1992), 302–3. On the left is the laureate head of Vespasian with the words IMP CAES VESPASIAN AVG P M TR P P P COS III. The right depicts Vespasian, holding a spear and standing with his left foot on a helmet over a Jewess who is mourning over the destruction of Jerusalem.

[75] Klaus Gamber, *Das Geheimnis Der Sieben Sterne* (Regensburg: Pustet, 1987), 24–26.

[76] Beale, *Rev*, 206–7. *Midr. Rab.* Num 13:8; 15:10; *Midr. Rab.* Ps 16.12; *Midr. Rab.* Lev 30.2; 32:8; *Midr. Rab.* Cant. 4:7; *Midr. Rab.* Eccl. 4:1; *Sifre* Deut 10; *Pesiq. Rab.* 7.7; 8.4; 51.4; See Beale for an extended treatment of the Jewish writer's view of the lampstand.

[77] Ibid., 207.

[78] Some understand the phrase *Remove your lampstand from its place* to mean that the primacy of the Ephesus

church (single lampstand).[80] Some have understood the reference to the removal of the lampstand as an allusion to the relocation of the city of Ephesus, caused by the problem of the Cayster River silting up,[81] but the sanction is directed at the church and not the city as a whole. However, Osborne reminds us that the language of loss would certainly have resonated with the Ephesians. He states: "like the city fighting for its life against silting of the harbor, the church was fighting for its life against the loss of its status as a church before God."[82]

According to Hemer, the danger for both city and church was it "would be moved back under the deadening power of the temple"[83] of Artemis due to the city being severed from its maritime commerce. Beale and Johnson see the meaning of the lampstand (λυχνία, *luchnia*) directly connected to witnessing,[84] and the removal of the lamps for not shining their light.[85] Beale suggests that: "among the warnings of judgment in the letters this one is unique to the letter to Ephesus and is especially suited in a *lex talionis* manner to their role as light-bearers: if they will not exercise their call to be a lamp of witness, then their lamp will be removed, as with Israel in the OT."[86] It may be that a second generation of Ephesians had lost their zeal for witnessing, and if not recovered, this would lead to the church ceasing to exist.

However, Ignatius indicated that the Ephesians had repented and responded positively to John's message, stating that they were "righteous in nature, according to faith and love in Christ" (Eph 1:1), thus meaning that the early church did not understand the "coming" tied to the second coming (Eph 9:1; 11:2).[87]

Beale points out that both the "removing" and the "coming" are conditional[88] and that "the actual wording 'I will remove your lampstand *from its place*' indicates removal of it *before*

---

ecclesiastical Holy See will be moved. The head of the Ephesus church is now at the city of Magnesia ad Sipylum (modern Manisa, Turkey), only surpassed in importance by the Holy See of Smyrna. Also, over time the citizens of Ephesus have relocated to Kirkindje. Ramsay, *Letters: Updated*, 177. Hemer comments that where the city moved to is debatable and that this interpretation "may be open to some doubt." Hemer, *Letters to the Seven Churches*, 53, 37.

[79] Perhaps through the closing of the harbor and the destruction of the entire city of Ephesus which did eventually happen.

[80] Beckwith, *Apocalypse*, 260; Mounce, *Revelation*, 70; Hughes, *Revelation*, 37; Krodel, *Revelation*, 109.

[81] Ramsay, *Letters: Updated*, 169–70; Worth, Jr., *Greco-Asian Culture*, 63; Chilton, *Days of Vengeance*, 96–97; Oster, "Ephesus (Place)," 2:543. See *The Commercial Harbour*.

[82] Osborne, *Revelation*, 119.

[83] Hemer, Letters to the Seven Churches, 53.

[84] Rev 11:3–7, 10; Mark 4:21–25; Luke 8:16–18.

[85] Beale, *Revelation*, 232; Johnson, "Revelation," 614.

[86] Beale, *Revelation*, 231.

[87] Ibid., 232.

[88] Beale *Revelation*, 232; contra Richard Bauckham, "Synoptic Parousia Parables and the Apocalypse," *NTS* 23, no. 2 (1977): 173–74; Traugott Holtz, *Die Christologie Der Apokalypse Des Johannes*, 2nd ed., TU 85 (Berlin: Akademie-Verlag, 1971), 207; Akira Satake, *Die Gemeindeordnung in Der Johannesapokalypse*, WMANT 21 (Neukirchener: Neukirchen-Vluyn, 1966), 153; Krodel, *Revelation*, 109; Thomas, *Rev 1–7*, 143–47, 154.

HISTORICAL PROLOGUE II—2:6

THE SUZERAIN KNOWS THEY HATE THE WORKS OF THE NICOLAITANS—2:6

Christ's final coming, since the churches' witness is a relevant activity only before the final advent,[89] not afterward."[90]

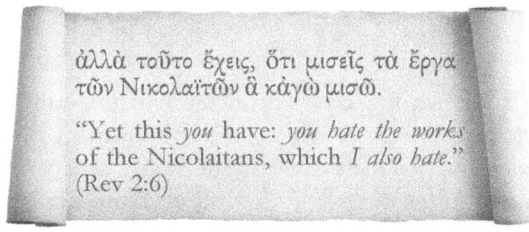

ἀλλὰ τοῦτο ἔχεις, ὅτι μισεῖς τὰ ἔργα τῶν Νικολαϊτῶν ἃ κἀγὼ μισῶ.

"Yet this *you* have: *you hate the works of the Nicolaitans, which I also hate.*" (Rev 2:6)

The suzerain and vassal relationship is deepened by referring to the shared history between them, selecting the fact that they both hate the works of the Nicolaitans (Νικολαϊται, *Nikolaitai*).[91] There is a transition here to a new thought with the use of the adversative term ἀλλά (*alla*, "but"). Aune suggests that this indicates that the Nicolaitans are not to be identified with the false apostles of verse 2.[92] But who were these Nicolaitans? Little is known about them other than what is mentioned in Revelation 2:6 and 15 and from post-apostolic writers (Irenaeus, Hippolytus, Clement of Alexandria, Tertullian and others), leading scholars to propose several possibilities, none of which are certain.[93]

3. The Nicolaitans are "a minority group of Christians [outside the Ephesian church] trying to gain a hearing and a more extensive following in the Ephesian church,"[94] but who where rejected by the Ephesians (also found in the church in Pergamum (15) and Laodicea).[95]

---

[89] While Thomas sees the removal of the lampstand as an indication of loss of witness, he still insists that the judgment is connected with the second coming when there would be no need for witnessing. Thomas, *Rev 1–7*, 146–47.

[90] Beale, *Revelation*, 232.

[91] For the exegesis of these verses, and more details on Balaam and the Nicolatians see the messages to Pergamum (2:14–15) and Thyatira (2:20–24).

[92] Aune, *Rev 1–5*, 147.

[93] For a survey of the interpretations of the Nicolaitans see, Ibid., Excursus 2A: The Nicolaitans, 148–49; Colin J. Hemer, "Nicolaitan," ed. Colin Brown, *NIDNTT* (Grand Rapids, Mich.: Zondervan, 1976), 2:676–78; *Letters to the Seven Churches*, 87–94; Alford, *Revelation*, 4:4:563–4; Tait, *Messages to the Seven Churches*, 157–58; Smalley, *Revelation*, 62–63; Duane F. Watson, "Nicolaitans," ed. David Noel Freedman et al., *ABD* (New York, N.Y.: Doubleday, 1996), 1106–7; Schüssler Fiorenza, *Book of Revelation*, 114–32.

[94] Aune, *Rev 1–5*, 147.

[95] Helmut Koester, "Ephesos in Early Christian Literature," in *Ephesos Metropolis of Asia: An Interdisciplinary Approach to Its Archaeology, Religion, and Culture*, ed. Helmut Koester, Harvard Theological Studies 41 (Cambridge, Mass.: Harvard Divinity School, 1995), 132; Kenneth A. Fox, "The Nicolaitans, Nicolaus and the Early Church," *SR* 23, no. 4 (1994): 496; Ian Boxall, "'For Paul' or 'For Cephas,'" in *Understanding, Studying and Reading: New Testament Essays in Honour of John Ashton*, ed. Christopher Rowland and Crispin H. Fletcher-Louis (New York, N.Y.: A&C Black, 1998), 202; Trebilco, *Early Christians in Ephesus*, 309; Bruce J. Malina and John J. Pilch, eds., *Handbook of Biblical Social Values* (Grand Rapids, Mich.: Baker Academic, 2009), 52; Farrer, *Revelation*, 74.

4. The practice of the Nicolaitans is identified with the Balaamites (Num 31:16; 25:1–3), based on a similar etymology (see also 2:14; Acts 15:20), which seems to be a Graecized derogatory term for Balaamite.[96] The etymology of the name means "to conquer the people" (Νικολαΐται, *Nikalaitai*), similar to the meaning of Balaam (vs. 14–15), "master of the people" (Heb. *ba'al'am*).[97] In addition, following Balaam's utterance of a blessing instead of a curse on Israel (Num 22–24), the Israelites participated in sexual immorality with the Moabite women and worshiped their gods and ate their sacrifices (Num 25:1–2), which are the two faults attributed to the Nicolaitans (2:14–15; 20, 24).

5. The practice of the Nicolaitans is connected to the second cent. gnostic sect of the same name[98] that Irenaeus (*Haer*. 1.26.3; 3.9.1), Hippolytus (*Haer*. 7.24; 7.36.3), and Clement of Alexandria (*Strom*. 2.20) traced back to Nicolaus of Antioch, one of the seven deacons mentioned in Acts 6:1–6, but quickly died (Eusebius *Hist. eccl.* 3:29).[99] Tertullian distinguishes the contemporary gnostics, which he calls Nicolaitans (similar to the Gaian heresy, *Praescr.* 33), from the Nicolaitans of Revelation, which he identified as a Satanic sect (*Marc*. 1.29; *Praescr*. 33; see also *Pud*. 19).[100] However, Aune points out that the Gnostic texts do not mention the practice of sexual promiscuity or eating meat sacrificed to idols (2:14; 20).[101]

6. The Nicolaitans were libertine Gentiles who were granting the Christians permission to participate in their syncretistic pagan society of the imperial cult, and burn incense to the emperor as a deity.[102] From the message to Pergamum (2:14–15) and Thyatira (2:20, 24 Jezebel) we learn that the Nicolaitans permitted the eating of meat sacrificed to idols (contra to the Jerusalem Council in Acts 15:29) along with fornication (πορνεύω, *porneuō*).[103] Some

---

[96] Tait, *Messages to the Seven Churches*, 159–60; Barclay, *Letters*, 23–24; Beale, *Rev*, 251; Watson, "Nicolaitans," 4:1107; Edward M. Blaiklock, "Nicolaus, Nicolaitans," in *NBD*, ed. I. Howard Marshall et al., 3rd ed. (Downers Grove, Ill.: InterVarsity, 1996), 823; Charles, *Revelation*, 1:63–64.

[97] For the use of similar wordplays based on Balaam see *t. b. Sanh.* 105a; Philo *Cher*. 32.

[98] Elisabeth Schüssler Fiorenza, "Apocalyptic and Gnosis in the Book of Revelation and Paul," *JBL* 92 (1973): 570; A. Von Harnack, "The Sect of the Nicolaitans and Nicolaus, the Deacon of Jerusalem," *JR* 3 (1923): 413–22; Barclay Moon Newman, *Rediscovering the Book of Revelation* (Valley Forge, Penn.: Judson, 1968), 11–30. See Newman who sees the entire book of Revelation as an anti-Gnostic polemic.

[99] For the testimony of the church Fathers to the gnostic character of the Nicolaitans see Smalley, *Thunder and Love*, 88.

[100] Fiorenza, "Apocalyptic and Gnosis," 565–81; Fox, "Nicolaitans," 485–96; Heikki Räisänen, "The Nicolaitans: Apoc. 2; Acts 6," *ANRW* II, 26.2 (1996): 1602–44; Alberto Ferreiro, "Priscillian and Nicolaitism," *VC* 52, no. 4 (1998): 382–92.

[101] Aune, *Rev 1–5*, 195.

[102] Swete, *Apocalypse*, 37; Ramsay, *Letters: Updated*, 220; Aune, *Rev 1–5*, 148–49; David A. deSilva, "The Revelation to John: A Case Study in Apocalyptic Propaganda and the Maintenance of Sectarian Identity," *Sociological Analysis* 53, no. 4 (1992): 384.

[103] Smalley argues that they were likely "guilty of religious infidelity more than sexual license." Smalley, "John's Revelation," 63.

have identified the practice of the Nicolaitans with the prostitution cult of the priestesses of Artemis and the holiday festivals.[104] While some suggest that the charge of fornication is to be taken figuratively as idolatry,[105] within the context of the first cent. culture, "sexual immorality" was widely practiced in Greece and Asia Minor.[106] Durant explains that "at the beginning of April, various cities in Greece celebrated [Aphrodite's] great festival, the Aphrodisia; and on that occasion, for those who cared to take part, sexual freedom was the order of the day."[107]

What is known of the Nicolaitans gathered from these clues indicates that elements of all of these theories could be part of this mysterious heretical gnostic group. They were Christians within the church who were seeking to influence the faithful to participate in the sacrificial offerings in the imperial cult, granting license to revelers to participate in the festive immorality. The OT Balaamites became identified with them because of their similar practice. The suzerain shared the Ephesian church's hatred of this gnostic group.

PROCLAMATION WITNESS FORMULA—2:7A

The witnesses to the ANEVT were traditionally the suzerain/vassal's pantheon of gods.[108] Since there is a change in the situation in the NT, because God is speaking as his own witness, there is a change of form from the polytheistic context of the ANE culture. The Spirit is the judge presiding over the covenant case. This proclamation witness or hearing formula, repeated in each of the messages to the churches (2:7; 11, 17, 29, 3:13, 22), calls the churches to hear the proclamation of the divine witness[109] and to heed the message of the Spirit[110] who spoke it.

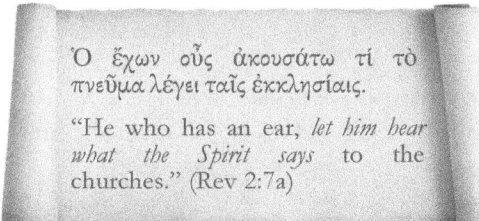

Ὁ ἔχων οὖς ἀκουσάτω τί τὸ πνεῦμα λέγει ταῖς ἐκκλησίαις.

"He who has an ear, *let him hear what the Spirit says* to the churches." (Rev 2:7a)

HEARING FORMULA 2:7A

The Spirit is continually speaking to the churches, as the term λέγει (*legei*, "is saying") is in the present tense. However, while the messages are addressed to the churches at large as well as in Ephesus, the phrase Ὁ ἔχων οὖς (*ho echōn ous*, "anyone who has

---

[104] Johnson, "Revelation," 614. Little evidence however has surfaced to support the wide spread practice of an prostitution cult. See *An Important Religious Centre—A City of Immorality and Superstition*.

[105] Num 25:1–2; Isa 1:21; Ezek 23:37; Ralph P. Martin and Peter H. Davids, eds., *Dictionary of the Later New Testament and Its Developments*, IVPBD (Downers Grove, Ill.: InterVarsity, 1997), 26; Smalley, *Revelation*, 63.

[106] See "Ephesus: A City of Immorality and Superstition" for more evidence.

[107] Will Durant, *The Story of Civilization, Part II: The Life of Greece* (New York, N.Y.: Simon & Schuster, 1966), 75, 185.

[108] See the *Introduction—Proclamation Witness Formula*.

[109] There are echoes of the OT phrase "hear the word of the Lord" (e.g. Isa 1:10; Jer 2:4; Hos 4:1; Amos 7:16).

[110] This is the first explicit occurance in the apocalypse to the Spirit (although see also 1:4, 10). Stephen S. Smalley, "The Paraclete: Pneumatology in the Johannine Gospel and Apocalypse," in *Exploring the Gospel of John: In Honor of D. Moody Smith*, ed. R. Alan Culpepper and C. Clifton Black (Louisville, Ky.: Westminster/Knox, 1996), 289–300.

an ear") is in the singular and thus individuals are called to hear the message of the suzerain. There are clear parallels with the sayings of Jesus in Matthew 11:15; 13:9, 43; Mark 4:9; Luke 8:8; and 14:35.[111] According to Vos, John adapted "the current sayings of Jesus as a mediatory means for the expression of his prophecy."[112] This has led Hahn and Dibelius to argue that the formula originated in the early church.[113] However, there is evidence for its OT roots and as Burkill points out, "It is quite unnecessary and even erroneous to attribute this view of history to the early Christian community alone."[114] However, Aune argues that they were not direct allusions but "drawn from the distinctive modes of speech that entered into Christian discourse from both the Gospel texts themselves and the oral traditions within which such texts were transmitted."[115]

The hearing formula, "He who has an ear, let him hear," is identified by most scholars as a warning designed to call God's people to repentance and not in the full force of a *verdict* (ban, *hêrem*, *rîb*)[116] to destroy his people. Parallels with the ANEVT structure are identified in the works of Nielsen, following Julien Harvey, who argues for a specific type of ANE treaty, *Rîb B*, which he identifies as closest to the OT treaty, and which also appears to be used in the covenant lawsuits of the seven oracles in Revelation in a restorative rather than punitive sense.[117] Nielsen observes this about the treatment of the prophetic lawsuit in the OT:

> [It is] understood as a form of paranesis; this is most evident in the species of the *Rîb* which Harvey designates *Rîb B*, in which the verdict is replaced by a warning. According to Harvey, we should seek the background of this phenomenon in the type of letter which a Hittite suzerain would send his vassal when the latter had broken the covenant, but when the suzerain had not yet decided to send a declaration of war. As long as the suzerain felt that it was still possible to preserve the relationship, he could be content to issue a warning. . . . The specific phrasing and structure of the lawsuit thus contribute to the emphasizing of Yahweh's salvatory intent, in spite of his role as prosecutor and judge.[118]

Enroth likewise argues for a *paraenetic* interpretation of the *hearing formula* (*Weckformel* or *Weckruf*) and concludes that "the HF [*hearing formula*] is positive, for it does not contain the idea

---

[111] See parallels in 1 Cor 14:37–38; *Odes Sol.* 3:10–11. The *hearing formula* is also found in the Gnostic texts. *Gos. Thom.* 8.21, 24, 63, 65, 96; *Gos. Mary* 7.10, 8.16; *Pist. Soph.* 1.17, 19, 33, 42, 43; 2.68, 86, 87; 3.124, 125; *Soph. Jes. Chr.* 98, 105, 107.

[112] Louis A. Vos, *The Synoptic Traditions in the Apocalypse* (Kampen, Netherlands: Kok, 1965), 224.

[113] Hahn, "Sendschreiben," 378; Martin Dibelius, "Wer Ohren Hat Zu Hören, Der Höre," *TSK* 83 (1910): 471.

[114] T. Alec Burkill, "The Hidden Son of Man in St. Mark's Gospel," *ZNW* 52, no. 3–4 (1961): 206.

[115] Aune, *Rev 1–5*, 265.

[116] See introduction—Malediction.

[117] Beale proposes that the role of the hearing formula, present in each of the SMR (2:7; etc.), was developed from the parabolic nature of the OT prophets in hardening and blinding (Isa 6:9–10). Gregory K. Beale, "The Hearing Formula and the Visions of John in Revelation," in *Vision for the Church*, ed. Markus N. A. Bockmuehl and Michael B. Thompson, Studies in Early Christian Ecclesiology (Edinburgh, U.K.: T&T Clark, 1997), 167–80; *Revelation*, 236–39.

[118] Nielsen, *Yahweh as Prosecutor*, 75; Harvey, *Le Plaidoyer*, 153–57; Berend Gemser, "The Rîb-or Controversy-Pattern in Hebrew Mentality," in *Wisdom in Israel and in the Ancient Near East*, ed. Martin Noth and David Winton Thomas, VTSup 3 (Leiden: Brill, 1955), 128–33.

of judgment or of hardening. On the contrary, it underlines the promise and the possibility of salvation."[119]

Consequently, the *call to hear* is employed as a *Rîb B* covenant-warning document. Rather than a declared verdict,[120] one observes a warning given to produce repentance within the seven churches of Asia Minor. The courtroom motif allows for the tension between God as Judge and prosecutor.[121]

Scott points out that "Let him hear" and "give ear" introduces the complaint in the prophets and "calls for the attention of witnesses."[122] Huffmon comments on the role of the witnesses:

> The source of the literary appeal to the natural elements is no doubt actual court procedure, either an appeal to the judges to hear the case or to witnesses to attend the trial. Mixed by the prophets with the covenant form, in which the natural phenomena is invoked as witnesses, the two different settings have been merged into a literary type used as a means of religious communication by the prophets in order to express indictment and trial of Israel because of unfulfilled covenant obligations.[123]

Yahweh, the judge, appeals to the heavens and the earth to hear (שמע, *sm'*) the case of the lawyer/prophet for the plaintiff.[124] In Revelation, through John, God is the one who testifies by use of a lawsuit against the churches. A blessing is promised to those who hear the words of the testimony (μαρτυρία, *marturia*) of the witnesses delivered through the messengers of the churches:

> John, who *testifies* (μαρτυρέω, *martureō*) to everything he saw–that is, the word of God and the *testimony* (μαρτυρία, *marturia*) of Jesus Christ. *Blessed* is the one who reads the words of this prophecy, and blessed are those who hear it and take to heart what is written in it, because the time is near. . . . And from Jesus Christ, *who is* the faithful *witness* (Ἰησοῦ Χριστοῦ ὁ μάρτυς ὁ πιστός, *Iēsou Christou ho martus ho pistos*), and the first begotten of the dead, and the prince of the kings of the earth (1:1–3, 5 Emphasis added).

SANCTIONS: BLESSING—2:7B,C

Blessings are promised to the those who conquer or overcome (τῷ νικῶντι, *tō nikōnti*). This is a common Johannine athletic and military metaphor in a work that promises the victory of the suzerain and the vassal over their enemies.[125] For the Ephesians, victory is identified as conquest

---

[119] Enroth, "Hearing Formula," 601.

[120] Nielsen maintains, "It was not the curse-clauses of the covenant which were automatically activated, as von Waldow thought, but Yahweh who, after conducting a trial against his people, decided to punish them" Nielsen, *Yahweh as Prosecutor*, 77.

[121] Ibid.

[122] R. B. Y. Scott, "The Literary Structure of Isaiah's Oracles," in *Studies in Old Testament Prophecy*, ed. Harold. H. Rowley (Edinburgh, U.K.: T&T Clark, 1950), 179; Nielsen, *Yahweh as Prosecutor*, 77.

[123] Huffmon, "Covenant Lawsuit," 293.

[124] Ibid., 286.

[125] Rev 2:7, 17, 26; 3:5; 5:5; 12:11; 17:14; 21:7; John 16:33; 1 John 2:13–14; 4:4; 5:4–5; Osborne, *Revelation*, 122.

"over doctrinal error and imperial persecution"[126] (1 John 5:4). Each message contains a blessing to the overcomers that uses a different synonym for eternal life.

THE BLESSING OF EATING OF THE TREE OF LIFE—2:7B

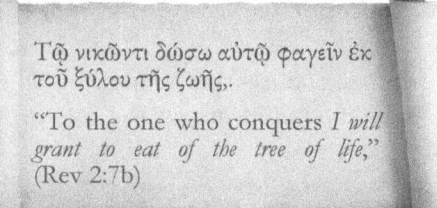

Τῷ νικῶντι δώσω αὐτῷ φαγεῖν ἐκ τοῦ ξύλου τῆς ζωῆς,.

"To the one who conquers *I will grant to eat of the tree of life*," (Rev 2:7b)

The blessing of eternal life promised to the overcomers at Ephesus is "to eat of the tree of life [2:7; 22:2, 14, 19], which is in the paradise of God" (2:7). It clearly recalls the Garden of Eden in the OT.[127] It was also a Jewish eschatological concept.[128] This phrase is a clear metaphor for eternal life given by God to the overcomers. Osborne points out that "the curse of the first Eden is reversed and eternal 'life' is now given to God's people. . . [it] pictures the reinstatement of the original Edenic paradise in the last days."[129]

The tree of life may also be understood against the Graeco-Roman background of the Artemision royal gardens (παράδεισος, *paradeisos*) outside Ephesus. These sacred gardens were believed to be the traditional birthplace of Artemis, and were stocked with deer and edible fruit (Strabo *Geogr.* 14.1.5, 20).[130] The sacred groves are depicted on fifty-six Ephesian coins with, on one side, a sacred palm tree (tree-shrine) with a stag, and a bee depicting the Artemision priestess on the other (see Fig. 42).[131] The *tree of life* is reminiscent of the sacred palm tree on the Ephesian coins.

Two inscriptions quoted by Hemer describe the foundations of the sacred temple of Artemis as a tree-shrine (see Figs. 24, 25).[132] After six years of excavations searching for the

---

[126] Smalley, *Revelation*, 64.

[127] Gen 2:9; 3:23–24; Ezek 31:2–9; see also 1QH 6:14–19; 7:24; See Aune for a full development of the OT background. Aune, *Rev 1–5*, 152–54.

[128] *1 En.* 25:5; *3 En.* 23:18; *T. Levi* 18:11; *Apoc. Mos.* 28:4; *Apoc. El.* 5:6; Benedikt Otzen, "The Paradise Trees in Jewish Apocalyptic," in *Apocryphon Severini: Presented to Søren Giversen*, ed. Pia Guldager Bilde, H. K. Nielsen, and J. Podemann Sørensen (Aarhus, Denmark: Aarhus University Press, 1993), 141; Eibert J. C. Tigchelaar, "Eden and Paradise: The Garden Motif in Some Early Jewish Texts (1 Enoch and Other Texts Found at Qumran)," in *Paradise Interpreted: Representations of Biblical Paradise in Judaism and Christianity*, ed. Gerard P. Luttikhuizen, Themes in Biblical Narrative 2 (Leiden: Brill, 1999), 37–62; Peter T. Lanfer, "Allusion to and Expansion of the Tree of Life and Garden of Eden in Biblical and Pseudepigraphal Literature," in *Early Christian Literature and Intertextuality: Thematic Studies*, ed. Craig A. Evans and H. Danny Zacharias, vol. 1, LNTS (London, U.K.: T&T Clark, 2009), 1:96–108.

[129] Osborne, *Revelation*, 124.

[130] Darice E. Birge, "Sacred Groves in the Ancient Greek World" (Ph.D. diss., University of California-Berkely, 1982), 27; Osborne, *Revelation*, 124; Ramsay, *The Letters to Seven Churches*, 246–9; Hemer, *The Letters to the Seven Churches*, 41–47; Gordon Franz, "Propaganda, Power and the Perversion of Biblical Truths: Coins Illustrating the Book of Revelation," *BS* 19, no. 3 (2006): 80; Ford, *Revelation*, 388; Earl F Palmer, *1, 2, 3 John; Revelation* (Atlantia, Ga.: Nelson, 1982), 130; Worth, Jr., *Greco-Asian*, 68.

[131] Hemer, *Letters to the Seven Churches*, 46; Mark Rakicic, "The Bees of Ephesos," *The Celator* 8, no. 12 (1994): 6–12.

[132] Hemer, Letters to the Seven Churches, 44–45.

EXTINCT LOVE OF EPHESUS – COMMENTARY

42. The Ephesian tetradrachm coin struck under Archidamos (*ca.* 340–325 BC). Obv.: E-Φ, A bee depicting the Artemision priestess. Rev.: *ARCIDAMOS*, A stag in front of the sacred palm tree (tree-shrine) depicting the sacred groves. (*BMC* 34, see also 28–51).

temple of Artemis (see Figs. 28, 29, 24), in 1869 John Turtle Wood identified the Artemision, but failed to reach its lower levels.[133] David G. Hogarth later penetrated to the bottom in 1887–1888 and found evidence of a tree-shrine.[134] Successive structures were built upon this sacred tree foundation.[135] The reference to the tree of life would have resonated with the Ephesians, as they would have been familiar with the Artemision's sacred tree, understanding what it meant, as it also provided sanctuary and protection for criminals seeking asylum.[136]

Several commentators have suggested that the *tree of life* is associated with the cross of Christ[137] that also gives life (Irenaeus *Haer.* 5.17.3).[138] They trace the usage of ξύλον (*zulon*, "tree") in earlier Greek literature, as well as in the NT,[139] to demonstrate that the recipients of Revelation would have recalled the cross of Christ. Proponents of this view also find parallels with the cross and the pagan tree-shrine (temple) of the goddess Artemis (see Figs. 26, 27, 121, 124, 127, used as an asylum for criminals. Hemer points out that the tree-shrine, like the cross, provided "the means of salvation."[140] Starke reminds us that "unlike its pagan imitation, the true Tree of Life provides soteriological asylum to the faithful."[141]

However, Wong points out that the common occurrence of OT imagery in the seven messages[142] points to the Garden of Eden in Genesis 2:9 as the source for the imagery.[143]

---

[133] Wood, *Discoveries at Ephesus*; Friesen, "Ephesus: Key to a Vision," 24–37.

[134] Hogarth, *Excavations at Ephesus*; Friedrich Krinzinger, *Ephesos: Architecture, Monuments and Sculpture*, ed. Ahmet Ertuğ and Sabine Ladstätter (Istanbul: Ertuğ & Kocabıyık, 2007).

[135] Hemer, *Letters to the Seven Churches*, 45. There is an ancient tradition that a wooden statue of the goddess artemis fell from the sky into a thicket and placed into a thicket, and planted itself into the trunk of a tree in a grove of trees near Ephesus. The hollow cedar tree was the foundation of the first temple of Artemis.

[136] Ibid., 44, 51, 55; Charles Homer Giblin, *The Book of Revelation: The Open Book of Prophecy*, GNS 34 (Collegeville, Minn.: Liturgical, 1991), 54.

[137] Hemer, *Letters to the Seven Churches*, 42, 44 51, 55; J. Schneider, "Ξύλον," ed. Gerhard Kittel and Gerhard Friedrich, trans. Geoffrey W. Bromiley, *Theological Dictionary of the New Testament* (Grand Rapids, Mich.: Eerdmans, 1985), 5:40; Richard Roberts, "The Tree of Life (Rev 2:7)," *ExpTim* 25, no. 7 (1914): 332; Kraft, *Offenbarung*, 59; Charles Brütsch, *Die Offenbarung Jesu Christi*, ZBK 18 (Zürich: Zwingh, 1970), 1:127; Osborne, *Revelation*, 124; Beale, *Rev*, 235; Giblin, *Revelation*, 54.

[138] Irenaeus states that the cross as "the tree of life" contrasts with "the tree of knowledge of good and evil," through which the human race fell in sin.

[139] Acts 5:30; 10:39, 13:29; Gal 3:13; 1 Pet 2:24.

[140] Hemer, Letters to the Seven Churches, 44, 51, 55; Giblin, Revelation, 54.

[141] Robert Starke, "The Tree of Life: Protological to Eschatological," *Kerux* 11, no. 2 (2010): 10.

[142] i.e., the lampstand, 2:5 and Exod 25:31–40; 27:21–22; Jer 52:19; paradise, 2:7 and Gen 2:8, 15; 3:23; Balaam and

What is clear from all the biblical references is that the fall has been reversed, with the tree of life at the center of the heavenly city at the end of Revelation (21–22). The tree of life in apocalyptic literature also conveyed a reward following judgment (*1 En.* 2:44–25:7; *T. Levi* 18:10–14). Certainly, the Ephesian citizens would have known the Artemision royal gardens and the use of the temple as an asylum, but this only accentuates the predominant imagery found in the OT allusion of the Garden of Eden in Genesis 2:9 and paradise regained in the New Earth (22:1–5).

THE BLESSING OF THE PARADISE OF GOD—2:7C

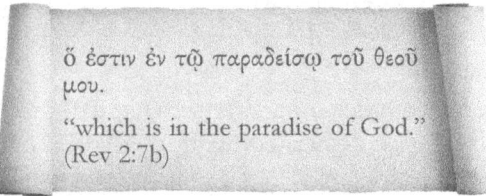

ὅ ἐστιν ἐν τῷ παραδείσῳ τοῦ θεοῦ μου.

"which is in the paradise of God." (Rev 2:7b)

The term paradise (παράδεισος, *paradeisos*) comes from the Median *paridaeza* and Old Persian *paridaida* meaning a "enclosure wall"[144] and was used in the LXX for "garden" (of Eden, Gen 2:8, 15, et al.).[145] Hemer elaborates that it is "an enclosed garden, especially a royal park . . . planted with fruit trees, laid out regularly, and often stocked with animals of the chase,"[146] where the suzerain would stroll.[147] Jewish literature commonly understood the "Garden of Eden" and "paradise" as referring to the dwelling of the righteous.[148] There was a παράδεισος (*paradeisos*), "large, fine, and thick with all kind of trees," situated in Babylon near the Tigris river (Xenophon *Anab.* 2.4.14, 16). There was also a *paradeisos* near Sardis (Herodotus *Hist.* 7.31; Aelian *Var. hist.* 2.14). As Beasley-Murray states:

> In Jewish literature 'Garden of Eden' and 'paradise' were both used for the dwelling of the righteous in the future life. Jewish teachers therefore spoke of the paradise of Adam, the paradise of the blessed in heaven and the paradise of the righteous in the coming kingdom of God. It is the last of these meanings which is in mind in this promise. Adam and Eve lost access to the tree of life and were driven from the garden (Gen 3:22–23); the believer who shares his Lord's victory is promised that both blessings will be restored (see 22:2). A frequent term for the cross of Jesus in the NT is 'tree' (especially on the lips of Peter; see Acts 5:30; 10:39; 1 Pet. 2:24). The temple of Artemis was built on a tree shrine, and a tree frequently symbolized Ephesus or its goddess.

Balak, 2:14 and Num 22–24; Deut 23:4; Josh 13:22; manna, 2:17 and Exod 16:4, 7, 15; Deut 8:3, 16; Jezebel, 2:20 and 1 Kgs 16:31; 18:4; 19:1; the rod of authority, 2:26–27 and Pss 2:8–9; the morning star, 2:28 and Num 24:17; the book of life, 3:5 and Ps 69:28; Dan 12:1; and the pillar in the temple, 3:12 and 1 Kgs 7:21; Jer 52:17.

[143] Daniel K. K. Wong, "The Tree of Life in Revelation 2:7," *BSac* 155, no. 618 (1998): 216.

[144] Jan N. Bremmer, "Paradise: From Persia, via Greece, into the Septuagint," in *Paradise Interpreted: Representations of Biblical Paradise in Judaism and Christianity*, ed. Gerard P. Luttikhuizen, Themes in Biblical Narrative 2 (Leiden: Brill, 1999), 1–2; Colin Brown, ed., *New International Dictionary of New Testament Theology*, trans. Colin Brown (Grand Rapids, Mich.: Zondervan, 1986), 2:760.

[145] It also occurs in the reference to the Jordan Valley (Heb. *kikkār*), which was well watered "like the garden of the Lord" (Gen 13:10; cf. Joel 2:3).

[146] Hemer, Letters to the Seven Churches, 50; Beasley-Murray, Revelation, NCB, 79–80.

[147] Xenophon *Anab.* 1.2.7; 1.3.14; 2.4.14; Josephus *J.W.* 4.467; 6.6; *Ant.* 7.347; 8.186.

[148] Aune, *Rev 1–5*, 152–54.

> Whereas the Ephesian believers once viewed the tree of Artemis as the seat of divine life and the intermediary between that life and human nature, they now learn that life eternal in the paradise of God was theirs through the cross of him who died and rose.[149]

Undoubtedly the Ephesian citizens would have recognized the relevance of the imagery of eating fruit from paradise's sacred groves, and the cultic worship of Artemis around the sacred tree. But as Beale reminds us: "What paganism promised only Christianity as the fulfillment of OT hope could deliver."[150] The Artemis "paradise" pales in comparison with the paradise granted the overcomer in the New Jerusalem (21:16–18; 22:2).

Conclusion

Seven unmistakable essential elements of the ANEVT, constituting a structure, are identified within the prophetic message to convey a covenant lawsuit message of encouragement to the overcomers within the church of Ephesus. The order is slightly altered here in that the blessings are listed at the end reather than with the curses, likely due to presenting an encouraging message for the Ephesian church.

Firstly, the preamble, marked by the prophetic oracular formula τάδε λέγει Ω, calls attention to what the suzerain, identified here as the sovereign omnipotent and omniscient "who holds the seven stars and walks among the churhces," will say to Ephesian church.

Secondly, the historical prologue is characterized by the omniscient suzerain's intimate knowledge of Ephesian's works. He knows that they have tested false Apostles and found them to be liars. He aknowledges their patient endurance and because of the suzerain's name they have been faithful. But the suzerain also knows that they have abandoned their love for him.

Thirdly, the Great King sets out the Ephesian stipulations in terms of three imperatives— *Remember, Repent* and *Repeat*.

Fourthly, the suzerain declared two curses against their actions if they do not repent. The suzerain will visit them in judgment and remove their lampstand. The curse will remind the churches of the omniscience of the suzerain and that he gives to each according to their works.

Fifthly, the Great King returns to the historical prologue and mentions that he knows that they hate the works of the Nicolaitants.

Sixthly, acting as his own witness in the court case, the Spirit-Judge calls the Ephesian congregation to hear what he has to say to the conduct of the churches.

---

[149] George R. Beasley-Murray, "Revelation," in *NBC*, ed. D. A. Carson, R. T. France, and J. A. Motyer, 4th ed. (Downers Grove, Ill.: InterVarsity, 1992), 1428.

[150] Beale, *Revelation*, 236.

Finally, two blessings are promised to the faithful vassals. The eschatological *macarism* for the overcomers' obedience to the stipulations will result in the King's gracious pledge of eternal preservation (eternal life) metaphorically conveyed by the eating of the tree of life and the promise of participation in the paradise of God.

6

Supreme Smyrna

The History of the City

*I*n order to understand the message to Smyrna, who prided themselves in being supreme as the "first of Asia", it is helpful to examine both the cultural (Graeco-Roman) history of Smyrna, as well as the (Hebraic-Semitic) OT theological roots of the message. This chapter will examine the historical background to the city of Smyrna.

THE ORIGIN OF THE NAME

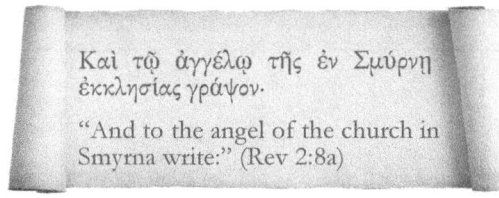

"And to the angel of the church in Smyrna write:" (Rev 2:8a)

The origin and meaning of the name Smyrna is concealed by ancient mythology and legends. There is also debate over the linguistic connection between Smyrna the city and myrrh (מֹר, *mōr*; LXX σμύρνα, *smurna*) the spice.[1] Harris identifies Smyrna and Myra (Acts 27:5) with the spice[2] arguing that "the existence of a trade in spices and frankincense and myrrh between S. Arabia and the Mediterranean"[3] led to the naming of Smyrna, Myra and Adramyttion (Ἀδραμύττιον)[4] after "the products which were the stock-in-trade of the first settlers"[5] during the pre-Hellenic era.[6] This becomes a plausible theory given that western Asia Minor does not produce myrrh on its own and the common practice of colonists identifying the name of a place with either a product or import from their homeland.[7]

---

[1] Strabo indicates that part or all of Ephesus was also called Smyrna, which could lead to further confusion (*Geogr.* 6.14.1.4).

[2] J. Rendel Harris, "The Early Colonists of the Mediterranean," *BJRL* 10, no. 2 (1926): 330, 340.

[3] Ibid., 340.

[4] *Hazarmaveth* (Hebrew, "village of death"), son of Shemite Joktan, (Gen 10:26).

[5] Harris, "Early Colonists," 330.

[6] Cadoux, *Ancient Smyrna*, 31 n.2. However, Cadoux states, if there is a connection between the substance of myrrh and the city, it "remains an unsolved mystery."

[7] Many cities are given names from a connection with their past i.e., New England, New South Wales, Philippi,

The ancient Semitic root for "myrrh" is רוֹם (*mōr;* LXX σμύρνα, *smurna*),[8] used 21 times in the OT denoting a sacred oil and perfume extracted from the gum in the bark of the Balsamodendron Myrrh tree or shrub found in Somaliland, Arabia and Ethiopia.[9] The Hebrew word for myrrh (רוֹם, *mōr*) is derived from the Hebrew root *mrr* meaning "to be bitter".[10] The physical taste is bitter, hence the term "bitter" (רוֹם, *mōr*) arose for its name.[11]

The city later developed the name Smyrna[12] from its trading connections with myrrh. The term myrrh is used three times in the NT, excluding the name of the city.[13] It was one of the expensive gifts brought to the infant Christ by the Magi (Matt 2:11, LXX σμύρνα, *smurna*). Again, at the close of Christ's ministry, myrrh was mixed with wine (σμυρνίζω, *smurnidzō*) to hide the bitter taste of the wine (Mark 15:23).[14] Myrrh's antiseptic properties were also used in embalming the body of Christ (John 19:39, σμύρνης, *smurnēs*). The use of myrrh (σμύρνα, *smurna*) in the NT was connected with the humiliation and suffering of Christ, and is consistent with the theme of martyrdom. Hemer concludes that the symbolism of myrrh points to the suffering and death of Christ. He states: "as it has been used in death and burial, in the expectation of an after-life, so Christ himself had died and lived again. The themes of suffering, death and resurrection pervade every verse of our letter".[15] The name of Smyrna is, therefore, indeed appropriate for a city which would come to know significant suffering (2:10).

---

etc. Harris, "Early Colonists," 330.

[8] J. Hausmann, "*mōr,* Myrrh," *TDOT,* 8: 557–60.

[9] Exod 30:23; Ruth 1:13; 1 Sam 15:32; 22:2; Pss 45:9; 64:4; Prov 7:17; 27:7; Eccl 7:26; Cant. 4:14; Isa 5:20; 33:7; 38:15, 17; Jer 4:18; Lam 1:4; Ezek 3:14; 27:31; Amos 8:10; Zeph 1:14; Gus W. van Beek, "Frankincense and Myrrh in Ancient South Arabia," *JAOS* 78, no. 3 (1958): 141–52; "Frankincense and Myrrh in Ancient South Arabia," *BA* 23 (1960): 70–95; Nigel Groom, *Frankincense & Myrrh: A Study of the Arabian Incense Trade* (London, U.K.: Longman, 1981); Philip J. King and Lawrence E. Stager, *Life in Biblical Israel* (Louisville, Ky.: Westminster/Knox, 2001), 347–48. Pliny describes several different kinds of myrrh, each identified by the region of origin: "Minaean in Main, Astramitic in Hadhramaut, Gebbanitic in Qataban, Ausaritic in Ausan, Sambracene in southern Tihama and two other types from unidentified location" (*Nat.* 12:35.69).

[10] The Hebrew term *marar* is used 19 times in the OT (*BDB,* 600; Wilhelm Michaelis, "Σμύρνα," ed. Gerhard Kittel and Gerhard Friedrich, trans. Geoffrey W. Bromiley, *TDNT* (Grand Rapids, Mich.: Eerdmans, 1985), 7:457.

[11] Ibid.

[12] The Greek form *Smurna* is occasionally used on coins and in inscriptions. Georg Petzl, *Die Inschriften von Smyrna,* vol. 1, AÖAW 23–24 (Bonn: Habelt, 1982), 10.657.

[13] Hemer, *Letters to the Seven Churches,* 58–59, 76; Thomas, *Rev 1–7,* 158; W. A Criswell, *Expository Sermons on Revelation* (Grand Rapids, Mich.: Zondervan, 1975), 92.

[14] Thayer states that: "since the ancients used to infuse myrrh into wine in order to give it a more agreeable fragrance and flavor, we must in this matter accept Matthew's account (Matt 27:34, viz. 'mingled with gall') as by far the more probable." Joseph Henry Thayer, *Thayer's Greek-English Lexicon of the New Testament. Complete and Unabridged* (Grand Rapids, Mich.: Baker, 1889), §4669.

[15] Hemer, Letters to the Seven Churches, 59.

The Geography of Smyrna

Smyrna (Σμύρνα, modern *İzmir;* coordinates: 38:25:07 N 27:08:21 E) is a major seaport on the Aegean, about 40 miles (65 km) north of Ephesus (320 stadia, Strabo *Geogr.* 14.1.2; 14.2.29), and the fourth largest city in Asia Minor (see *The Population of Smyrna* below). In antiquity, Smyrna, along with the other seven cities of Revelation, formed a circular mail route, placing Smyrna as the second letter delivered on the route.

The History of Smyrna

The Ancient Period

The history of Smyrna,[16] one of the most important cities in Asia Minor, covers two successive locations and spans some 5000 years. The site was traditionally believed to have been founded by the Amazons,[17] but the recent excavations at Yeşilova Höyük (discovered in 2003), one of the oldest settlements of Izmir, has confirmed that Smyrna is "one of the oldest settlement area[s] in Western Anatolia"[18] dating back to between the seventh to fourth millennium BC.[19]

By ca. 1500 BC, Old Smyrna had fallen under the influence of the Central Anatolian Hittite Empire. The original site of the city of Smyrna, before the city moved across the Gulf of İzmir, was known as the Bayraklı Höyük settlement, and was excavated in the 1960's by Ekrem Akurgal. Excavations indicated that the early history of Smyrna made it comparable with the city of Troy.[20]

In the 13th cent. BC, the Balkans invaded Central and Western Anatolia and Smyrna became part of the collapse of the Bronze Age (the Anatolian Dark Ages).

---

[16] There are five extant works by Aristides regarding the city of Smyrna (*Orat.* 17, 18, 19, 20, 21). The first "Smyrnaean Oration 17," is a sort of guided tour of the city for visiting dignitaries, and provides one of the best descriptions of ancient Smyrna that exists. For the historical background of Smyrna consult the following: Richard Chandler, *Travels in Asia Minor, and Greece: Or An Account of a Tour Made at the Expense of the Society of Dilettanti*, 2 vols. (London, U.K.: Booker & Priestley, 1817); Cadoux, *Ancient Smyrna*, 23–170; J. M. Cook, *The Greeks: In Ionia and the East*, ed. Glyn Daniel, Ancient Peoples and Places 31 (New York, N.Y.: Praeger, 1963), 68–74; Ramsay, *Letters: Updated*, 182–94; Akurgal, *Ancient Civilizations*, "Smyrna," ed. Richard Stillwell, William L. MacDonald, and Marian Holland, *PECS* (Princeton, N.J.: Princeton University Press, 1976), 847–48; David S. Potter, "Smyrna," ed. David Noel Freedman, *ABD* (New York, N.Y.: Doubleday, 1996), 6:73–5; Graves, "Local References in the Letter to Smyrna (Rev 2:8–11), Part 2: Historical Background."

[17] Known as the ancient Hittites, Strabo *Geogr.* 11.5.4; 12.3.21; Pliny *Nat.* 10:5.118.

[18] Zafer Derin, "Yeşilova Höyük Excavations," *Ege University*, December 12, 2015, n.p., http://www.yesilova.ege.edu.tr/eng/.

[19] Zafer Derin, "Yeşilova Höyük," *Actual Archaeology Magazine* 2 (2012): 108–20; Zafer Derin and T. Caymaz, "İzmir'in Prehistorik Yerleşimi, Yeşilova Höyüğü 2012 Yılı Kazı Çalışmaları," *Kazı Sonuçları Toplantısı* 35, no. 1 (2014): 419–33.

[20] Akurgal, *Ancient Civilizations*; Crawford H. Greenewalt, Jr., "Ekrem Akurgal, 1911–2002," *AJA* 109, no. 3 (2005): 561–63.

THE ARCHAIC PERIOD: OLD SMYRNA

According to Aristides, Smyrna was founded no less than three times, once by Tantalus (Pelops), then by Thesus, and finally by Alexander the Great.[21] The Greek walled settlement of Old Smyrna (the Archaic period) was located at Tepekule, Bayraklı.[22] Pottery from the excavations indicate the settlement was occupied in ca. 1000–700 BC.[23] According to Herodotus, the Greek Aeolian city was seized by Ionians and made part of the Ionian league.[24]

Old Smyrna was destroyed in 600 BC by the Lydian King, Alyattes (*Hist.* 1.14.1);[25] then reduced from a city (πόλις, *polis*) to a village system, in which it remained for over 250 years (Strabo *Geogr.* 6.14.1.37; See *Quotes from Antiquity*).[26] This was the period when the temple of Athena (see Figs. 34, 124) appeared (ca. 640–580 BC). Old Smyrna came to an end with the invasion of the Persian Empire in 545 BC.

> **Quotes from Antiquity**
>
> After Smyrna had been raised by the Lydians, its inhabitants continued for about 400 years to live in villages. Then they were reassembled into a city by Antigonus, and afterwards by Lysimachus, and their city is now the most beautiful of all (Strabo *Geogr.* 6.14.1.37 [Jones]).

THE ALEXANDRIAN PERIOD: NEW SMYRNA

In about 340 BC, Alexander the Great is said to have refounded the city at a new location beyond the Meles River (Pausanias *Descr.* 7.5.2),[27] located on the slopes of Mount Pagus (modern Kadifekale, "Velvet Castle"; Strabo *Geogr.* 14.1.37). Alexander is shown on coins dreaming under a palm tree at the foot of Mount Pagus, across the Sacred Meles, where he is said to have been told in the dream to build the city (Pausanias *Descr.* 7.5.1).

Aristides called Smyrna a crown[28] due to its prominence on the top of Mount Pagus. This was a much larger area than Old Smyrna and allowed the city to expand and provide room for a growing population. Smyrna emerged again in the third cent. BC as an influential commercial

---

[21] Aristides *Orat.* 17.3–5; 18.2; 21.3–4; Pausanias *Descr.* 7.5.1–3.
[22] Wilson, *Biblical Turkey*, 310, 312.
[23] Akurgal, Ancient Civilizations.
[24] Herodotus *Hist.* 1.16.1–2; Strabo *Geogr.* 6.14.1.4; Pausanias *Descr.* 7.5.1.
[25] Magie speculates that Smyrna was destroyed by King Alyattes in about 575 BC. Magie, *Roman Rule in Asia Minor*, 2:876, n.66.
[26] William M. Calder, "Smyrna as Described by the Orator Aelius Aristides," in *Studies in the History and Art of the Eastern Provinces of the Roman Empire*, ed. William Mitchell Ramsay (Aberdeen, Scotland: Aberdeen University, 1906), 103; Howard Carroll, "Polycarp of Smyrna: With Special Reference to Early Christian Martyrdom" (Ph.D. diss., Duke University, 1946), 8. Strabo overestimates the time to be more than 400 years (*Geogr.* 6.14.1.37).
[27] Strabo suggests that it was the Hellenistic rulers Antigonus and Lysimachus who were responsible for the refounding of the second city *ca.* 290 BC (*Geogr.* 14.1.37).
[28] Aristides *Orat.* 15, 20–22, 41; see also Philostratus *Vit. Apoll.* 1.4.7; 1.8.24.

and cultural urban center.[29] Following the preliminary work done at Smyrna in 288/287 BC, the city expanded rapidly over the next century.[30]

THE ROMAN PERIOD

Eumenes III bequeathed his kingdom, which included Smyrna, to the Roman Republic in 133 BC, and after the defeat of the Seleucid king Antiochus III (r. 222–187 BC; see Fig. 96) in 189 BC, Rome granted Smyrna the status of a free city and entered a period of prosperity. In 195 BC, it was declared the first temple to *dea Roma* (Lat. "goddess Roma"; see Fig. 173) in Asia Minor.

During the insurrection against the Romans in first cent. BC, Smyrna allied itself with Mithridates. Following his defeat by the Romans (42 BC), it lost its status as a free city. In AD 26 Emperor Tiberius (see Figs. 43, 97, 111) granted Smyrna the privilege of temple-keeper (νεωκόρος, *neōkoros*) for Asia's second imperial cult temple over eleven other applicants.

43. Emperor Tiberius Caesar Augustus (42 BC–AD 37). In AD 26, Tiberius granted Smyrna the right to build a second temple to the the *dea Roma* (Lat. "goddess Roma"; Tacitus *Ann.* 4.55–56).

It was during these periods that the letter mentioned in Revelation was written and delivered to the Christian church in Smyrna. In AD 177 or 178, the city was devastated by an earthquake (Aristides *Orat.* 18, 19), followed by another in 180, but the city was rebuilt with the contributions of Emperor Marcus Aurelius. Many of the ruins still visible today were the result of this rebuilding of the city.

THE BYZANTINE PERIOD

In the fifth cent. AD, Meinardus described how "the Christian community grew in strength and numbers and Smyrna became one of the more important archbishoprics in Asia Minor".[31] During the Byzantine era, Smyrna was under the control of Emperor John II Ducas Vatatzes of Nicaea, who refortified and beautified the city. In 1097 a Turkish fleet of sailors under the leadership of Tzach murdered 10,000 Smyrnaeans. It is unknown how many of these citizens were Christians. A Turk called Morbassan attacked Smyrna around 1332, laying siege to it for three months, and eventually slaughtering all the Christians living there.[32] It was taken back by

---

[29] Ramsay, *Letters: Updated*, 182–94; Hemer, *Letters to the Seven Churches*, 62–63; Barr, "The Apocalypse of John as Oral Enactment," 245 n.9.

[30] Cadoux, *Ancient Smyrna*, 94–141; Ramsay, *Letters: Updated*, 182.

[31] Meinardus, *John of Patmos*, 68.

[32] Francis Vyvian J. Arundell, A Visit to the Seven Churches of Asia with an Excursion into Pisidia (London, U.K.: Rodwell, 1828), 381.

the Knights of St. John in 1344, only to be captured in the fourteenth cent. by the Arabs.[33] Meinardus states:

> in 1402 Tamerlane sent a message to the Knights summoning them to embrace Islam and threatening them with death if they refused. The Knights rejected the ultimatum and Tamerlane besieged the city, capturing it on December 17, 1402. The Knights escaped with their galleys, but the Smyrnaean Christians were massacred.[34]

The Moslems occupied Smyrna in the 13th cent. causing the church to lose its "power and prestige," but not its presence. Meinardus indicates that, "we have no record of a metropolitan of Smyrna after 1389 but the church survived the conquest by Tamerlane and appears in the 15th century catalogue of metropolitan sees".[35]

Among the first missionaries to settle in Smyrna were the Franciscans, Jesuits, Anglicans, and Dutch Reformed in the fifteenth and sixteenth centuries.[36] McDonagh explains, "according to Kinglake it was called *Glaour Izmir* ('Infidel Smyrna') by the Turks because of the large number of foreigners who lived and worked here".[37]

One of the first Western travellers to provide us with a description of medieval Smyrna is Father Pacifique. In 1622 he listed one or two Greek churches, one small Catholic church, one synagogue, and four mosques.[38] In 1671 Thomas Smith witnessed that the Greeks had two churches, and retained the dignity of the Metropolitical seat, two Jewish synagogues, and 13 mosques.[39] There was an increase in Muslim and Jewish buildings, but not Christian churches. In 1694 the Turks sat in the Gulf of Smyrna ready to take all Smyrnaean Christians as hostages. Through diplomatic intervention of the British, French and Dutch consuls, the Turks were persuaded to leave. In 1770 Russia called on the Greeks to revolt and the Turks took revenge, killing more than 10,000 Greeks in Smyrna alone.[40]

In 1797, a fire swept through Smyrna destroying 4500 homes. During this period, many Christians lost their lives. They have been identified as the "New Martyrs" and commemorated by the Greek Orthodox church.[41] According to Vailhé, "in 1818 Pius VII established the

---

[33] Vailhé records that: "the Latin See of Smyrna was created by Clement VI in 1346 and had an uninterrupted succession of titulars until the seventeenth century. This was the beginning of the Vicariate Apostolic of Asia Minor, or of Smyrna, of vast extent" Siméon Vailhé, "Smyrna," in *CE*, ed. Charles George Herbermann, trans. Mario Anello, vol. 14 (New York, N.Y.: Appleton & Company, 1913), 14:60.

[34] Meinardus, *John of Patmos*, 69; Vailhé, "Smyrna," 60; Arundell, *Visit to the Seven Churches*, 383. Arundell states that: "Tamerlane is reported to have beheaded a thousand of the prisoners, and to have built, as a monument of his victory, a wall or tower composed of stones and their heads intermixed."

[35] Meinardus, *John of Patmos*, 69.

[36] Ibid.

[37] Bernard McDonagh, *Blue Guide: Turkey*, 3rd ed. (London, U.K.: A & C Black, 2001), 174.

[38] Meinardus, *John of Patmos*, 70.

[39] Thomas Smith, Remarks upon the Manners, Religion and Government of the Turks: A Survey of the Seven Churches of Asia, as They Now Lye in Their Ruines., Early History of Travel and Geography (London, U.K.: Pitt, 1678), 270.

[40] Meinardus, *John of Patmos*, 73.

[41] Ibid.

Archdiocese of Smyrna, at the same time retaining the vicariate Apostolic, the jurisdiction of which was wider...The archdiocese had 17,000 Latin Catholics, some Greek Melchites, called Alepi, and Armenians under special organization".[42] There were 26 priests in the archdiocese, four of which were in Smyrna at this time.[43] Arundell reports in 1822, "The Greeks have three churches; the Armenians one; the Latins two; the Protestants two".[44]

Prior to a massacre in 1922, in which as many as 50,000 Christians were killed,[45] "Smyrna was a predominately Christian city with 135,000 Greeks, 11,175 Catholics, 8,500 Armenians".[46] The Greeks maintained over 55 churches and before 1922 the Armenians built the Cathedral of St. Stephen, one of the most beautiful churches in Turkey.[47] There were over 100,000 Christians in Smyrna at that time. Several Christian congregations have survived to the present day.[48]

THE POPULATION OF SMYRNA

In Paul's day, Cadoux estimated that Smyrna had a population of about 250,000 and developed into an important commercial center.[49] Pfeiffer is more cautious, placing the population at nearly 200,000,[50] while Aune is even more conservative, maintaining that the population was 100,000.[51] Thompson proposed that the population was over 100,000 during the first cent. BC.[52]

Strangely, Hanson does not list Smyrna among the 39 cities he works with in determining the populations of cities from Roman Asia Minor. Perhaps it is because the modern city of Izmir sits atop the ancient ruins of Smyrna and no site plan exists for the ancient site. However, Hanson does state: "far from seeing populations of up to 225,000 in the case of Pergamum, Ephesus, and Smyrna, we can in fact reduce these figures to a probable range with a minimum of 50,000 and a maximum of 90,000."[53] The realistic size would likely be about 33,000–55,000 in the Roman period making it the fourth largest city in Asia Minor in the first cent. AD.

---

[42] Vailhé, "Smyrna," 14:60.

[43] Ibid.

[44] Arundell, Visit to the Seven Churches, 415.

[45] Meinardus, *John of Patmos*, 75.

[46] Ibid.

[47] Ibid.

[48] The Cathedral of St. John the Evangelist, two other catholic churches, and The Anglican Church of St. John. McDonagh, *Blue Guide: Turkey*, 272; A. T. Robertson, *A Grammar of the Greek New Testament in the Light of Historical Research* (Nashville, Tenn.: Broadman, 1934), 6:30. There are other Christian churches in Izmir today.

[49] Cadoux, *Ancient Smyrna*, 23–170; Akurgal, "Smyrna," 848; Potter, "Smyrna," 73–75; Graves, "Local References in the Letter to Smyrna (Rev 2:8–11), Part 2: Historical Background," 23–41.

[50] Charles F. Pfeiffer, ed., *The Biblical World: A Dictionary of Biblical Archaeology* (Nashville, Tenn.: Broadman, 1976), 543; Merrill F. Unger, *Archaeology and the New Testament* (Grand Rapids, Mich.: Zondervan, 1975), 281.

[51] Aune, *Rev 1–5*, 159.

[52] Thompson, *Revelation*, 68.

[53] Hanson, "Urban System," 258.

SMYRNA: FIRST IN ASIA

Although Smyrna classifies herself on her coins[54] as πρώτη τῆς Ἀσίας (*prōtē tēs Asias*, "First of Asia"),[55] this honor was contested by Ephesus and Pergamum.[56] All three could be classified as first in some area.[57] Pergamum classified herself as πρώτη καί Μητρόπολις[58] (*prōtē kai mētropolis*, "First and Metropolis"),[59] and Ephesus called herself ’ο πρώτη καί μαγίστη Μητρόπολις τῆς Ἀσίας (*ho prōtē kai magiste metropolis tēs Asias*, "The First and Greatest Metropolis of Asia" (*I.Eph.* 1a.24B),[60] leaving Smyrna the honor of πρώτη τῆς Ἀσίας κάλλει καί μεγέθει (*prōtē tēs Asias kallei kai megathi*, "First of Asia, in Beauty and Size (greatness)" (AD 193; *OGIS* 2.514.3–4; *I.Smyr.* 637; 665.2–4).[61] The race for primacy between cities is evident from the rivalry over first, second, or third rank *neōkoros* as the site for the provincial imperial temple (Philostratus *Vit. Soph.* 1.25.10; ca. AD 172). It is also evident in an inscription in the agora Basilica in Smyrna. It reads "the first of Asia" (Ἀσίας πρώτοις, 11 cm high; T9.1) with an additional inscription in a smaller hand with

---

[54] "The name of the city appears either completely written out in the genitive plural *SMURNAION* '(coin) of Smyrna' or shortened, usually to *SMUR*, more rarely also to *SMU* or *SM*. The nominative singular *SMURNA* stands only for the designation of the busts of the Amazone Smyrna. As a spelling both 'Smyrna' and 'Zmyrna' occur. In the third century BC the usual spelling was with sigma, then from the second century BC until the time of Hadrian (before 130 AD) with very few exceptions after the end of Nero's time, (V 8. 18 and R 15) the form with Z predominates. Since the issue of Polemon under Hadrian the old form of 'Smyrna' again becomes generally accepted. In the inscriptions both letters occur (141 times with S, 64 times with Z [Cadoux, *Ancient Smyrna*, 31]), without a chronological development being apparent as is the case with the coins [*IGR* 4.1418 (Time of the first Neokorie, before Hadrian) and *IGR* 4.1444 (Time of Augustus) with *S*, *IGR* 4.1415 (after 212?) with Z]. With the exception of the honour name Hadrian on some coins from the time of the Antoninus Pius (XIII 1, 1 ff., V 1–2) Smyrna still has no titles on the coins in the time before Caracalla, on inscriptions there were only individual titles without a particular order [The titles *NEWKOROS, LAMPROTATH* and *PROTH ASIAS* come into inscriptions isolated already before 212 onwards (*IGR* 4.1388, 4.1418, 4.1428, 4.1482 F; *CIG* 3179; 3851), but there still is no fixed title with certain order of the titles]" Dietrich O. A. Klose, *Die Münzprägung Von Smyrna in Der Römischen Kaiserzeit* (Berlin: de Gruyter, 1987), 40.

[55] Head, *BMC Ionia*, nos. 405, 423–24. All coins are from the period of Caracalla's reign (r. AD 211–217).

[56] Magie, Roman Rule in Asia Minor, 2:635–36.

[57] Ramsay points out that: "similar quarrels between rival claimants to the title 'First City' occurred very frequently: Tarsos vied with Anazarbos, Ephesos with Smyrna and Pergamos, Nikomedeia with Nikaia, Philippi with Amphipolis; and in such cases, each claimant aimed at cumulating titles on itself, inventing new ones and appropriating those invented by its rival." William M. Ramsay, *Cities and Bishoprics of Phrygia* (Oxford, U.K.: Clarendon, 1895), 2:632.

[58] Also, this title was claimed by Nikomedia. Burrell, *Neokoroi*, 165.

[59] Pergamum was also the first city to be *Twice Temple-Warden*. Magie, *Roman Rule in Asia Minor*, 2:636. Also claimed by Nikomedia. Burrell, Barbara. *Neokoroi: Greek Cities and Roman Emperors*. CCS 9. Leiden: Brill, 2004. 165

[60] See, also *I.Eph.* 2.282D, 438; 3.611, 613A, 649, 661, 686, 985–86; The full inscriptions reads "The First and Greatest Metropolis of Asia and Twice Temple-Warden of the Sebastoi, City of Ephesus." Cadoux, *Ancient Smyrna*, 291; Trebilco, "Asia," 306; L. Michael White, "Urban Development and Social Change in Imperial Ephesos," in *Ephesos Metropolis of Asia: An Interdisciplinary Approach to Its Archaeology, Religion, and Culture*, ed. Helmut Koester, HTS 41 (Cambridge, Mass.: Harvard Divinity School, 1995), 34; Mussies, "Pagans, Jews, and Christians at Ephesus," 178.

[61] Barclay Vincent Head, *Historia Numorum: A Manual of Greek Numismatics*, 2nd ed. (Oxford, U.K.: Clarendon, 1911), 593; Klose, *Münzprägung*, 40–43; Ramsay, *Cities and Bishoprics*, 2:632; Magie, *Roman Rule in Asia Minor*, 2:635–37.

the word Ἐφεσίοις "to the Ephesians" clearly an attempt at hijacking Smyrna's claim to being the first of Asia.[62]

During the reign of Antoninus Pius (AD 138–161) the enmity between Ephesus and Smyrna was addressed in a letter to the *Council and People of Ephesus* in which the emperor urges the Ephesians to:

> overlook the Smyrniots' failure to refer to Ephesus in the proper manner. He also admonished them, when addressing their rival, to use the titles which Smyrna had the right to bear; for if they did so, it was hoped, the latter "would in the future be willing to adopt a conciliatory attitude".[63]

Under Antoninus' successor, Smyrna's contest with Pergamum was successful and "the city obtained a share in the position of primacy hitherto held by Ephesus".[64] Smyrna celebrated her fame by inscribing on some of her coins, "Smyrna, first of Asia in beauty and size (greatness)" (Σμυρναιων πρώτων Ἀσίας . . . κάλλει καί μεγαθι, *Smurnaiōn prōtōn Asias. . . kallei kai megathi*), as her claim to prominence.[65] The full phrase as found in numerous inscriptions reads "first of Asia in beauty and size, and the most brilliant, and Metropolis *[Capital]* of Asia, and thrice Temple-Warden [νεωκόρος, *neōkoros*][66] of the Augusti, according to the decrees of the most sacred Senate, and ornament of Ionia".[67]

Even though this phrase does not appear on coinage until the reign of Caracalla (r. AD 211–217; see Figs. 128, 162, 163),[68] the sentiments were well entrenched in the Smyrnaean mind long before they became impressed in currency. However, as Klose observes, this title was too long for coins and was shortened.[69] In addition, a partial or late appearance on Smyrna's coins does not indicate the inception of primacy but a formalizing of a deep-rooted belief within the

---

[62] Roger S. Bagnall, "Christianity," in *Graffiti from the Basilica in the Agora of Smyrna*, ed. Roger S. Bagnall et al., Institute for the Study of the Ancient World (New York, N.Y.: New York University Press, 2016), 47.

[63] Magie, Roman Rule in Asia Minor, 2:636.

[64] Ibid. Pergamum was content to bear the title "Metropolis of Asia and the first city to be Twice Temple-Warden"

[65] Klose, *Münzprägung*, 40; Cadoux, *Ancient Smyrna*, 291; Magie, *Roman Rule in Asia Minor*, 2:636; Ramsay, *Letters: Updated*, 185.

[66] The titles ΝΕΩΚΟΡΟΣ (Gr. *neōkoros*) and ΠΡΩΤΗ ΑΣΙΑΣ (Gr. *prōtōn Asias*) are found on inscriptions prior to AD 212: IGR 4.1388, 1418, 1428; Klose, *Münzprägung*, 40; Burrell, *Neokoroi*, 289.

[67] Klose, *Münzprägung*, 40; Cadoux, *Ancient Smyrna*, 291; Magie, *Roman Rule in Asia Minor*, 2:637, 685; Burrell, *Neokoroi*, 289. CIG 3202; IGR 4.1420. Variant readings follow: "and the most brilliant, and Metropolis, and thrice Temple-Warden of the Augusti, according to the decrees of the most sacred Senate, and ornament of Ionia" (CIG 3204; 2.3205; 2.3206A; cf. IGR 4.1419A; 4.1421); "First of Asia in beauty and size, and the most brilliant, and Metropolis of Asia, and thrice Temple-Warden of the Augusti, and ornament of Ionia, according to the decrees of the most sacred Senate" (CIG 3191; cf. IGR 4.1424; OGIS 2.514); "and the most brilliant, and Metropolis, and thrice Temple-Warden of the Augusti, according to the decrees of the most sacred Senate" (CIG 3197; cf. IGR 4.1426); "First of Asia, and the most brilliant, and Metropolis, and thrice Temple-Warden of the Augusti, according to the decrees of the most sacred Senate"(IGR 4.1425); "First of Asia"(CIG 3851; cf. IGR 4.541); "First of Asia and most brilliant" (CIG 3179d; cf. IGR 4.1482).

[68] Klose, *Münzprägung*, 40.

[69] Ibid.

citizens of Smyrna.[70] This formalizing is evident from the use of the shorter words ΠΡΩΤΗ ΑΣΙΑΣ (*prōtn Asias*) on her coins prior to AD 212.

A GREAT TRADE CITY

It was an important seaport on the Aegean with two harbours (Strabo *Geogr.* 6.14.1.37),[71] one of which could be closed for security and defensive purposes, but which had silted up by the early nineteenth century.[72] The harbors facilitated the trade and commerce that developed Smyrna into a major commercial metropolis.[73] Smyrna was known for its fine wine, luxury and wealth (Strabo *Geogr.* 14.1.15). The temple of Artemis (see Figs. 28, 29, 24) was used as a bank.

A BEAUTIFULLY CULTURED CITY

One of the notable features of Smyrna is her beauty,[74] celebrated by a long literary and rhetorical tradition.[75] Numerous inscriptions and coins record Smyrna's distinction as the "first of Asia in beauty and size, and the most brilliant, and Metropolis [*Capital*] of Asia, and thrice Temple–Warden [νεωκόρος, *neōkoros*] of the Augusti, according to the decrees of the most sacred Senate, and ornament of Ionia."[76] It was a beautiful metropolis with purposely-symmetrical streets through which cool breezes off the Mediterranean cooled the citizens on hot summer nights.[77] Cicero (first cent. BC) spoke of Smyrna as ἄγαλμα τῆς Ἀσίας (*agalma tēs Asias*, "The ornament of Asia" (*Arch.* 7.8.19).

---

[70] The ὁμόνοια (Gr. *homonia*, "concordance") coins minted during this time between Ephesus, Pergamum, and Smyrna "probably celebrated the settlement of this dispute." Cadoux, *Ancient Smyrna*, 264, 263 n.5.

[71] Cook, *The Greeks*, 17; Charles F. Pfeiffer, ed., *Wycliffe Dictionary of Biblical Archaeology* (Peabody, Mass.: Hendrickson, 2000), 542; Calder, "Smyrna," 100.

[72] George Horton, The Blight of Asia: An Account of the Systematic Extermination of Christian Populations by Mohammedans and of the Culpability of Certain Great Power; with the True Story of the Burning of Smyrna (Indianapolis, Ind.: Bobbs-Merrill, 1953), 101.

[73] Ramsay, Cities and Bishoprics, 2:571.

[74] Ramsay, *Letters: Updated*, 185–88; Cadoux, *Ancient Smyrna*, 171–73; Hemer, *Letters to the Seven Churches*, 59–60.

[75] Philostratus *Vit. Apoll.* 4.7; Aristides *Orat.* 41.19; 42.770–76; Anna Heller, *Les bêtises des Grecs: Conflits et rivalités entre cités d'Asie et de Bithynie à l'époque romaine (129 AD.–235 AD)*, SA 17 (Bordeaux, France: Ausonius, 2006), 326ff; Pierre Destrée and Penelope Murray, *A Companion to Ancient Aesthetics* (Hoboken, N.J.: Wiley & Sons, 2015), 135.

[76] Klose, *Münzprägung*, 40; August Böeckh et al., *Corpus Inscriptionum Graecarum* (Berolini, Italy: Officina academica, 1877), 2: no. 3202; Georges Lafaye et al., eds., *Inscriptiones Graecae Ad Res Romanas Pertinentes* (Paris: Leroux, 1901), 4: no. 1420; Donald F. McCabe, *Smyrna Inscriptions: Texts and List*, ed. Tad Brennan and R. Neil Elliott (Princeton, N.J.: Princeton Institute for Advanced Study, 1988), 150, 156, 171–72.

[77] Strabo *Geogr.* 14.1.37; Aristides *Orat.* 41.19; 42.770–76; *Mart. Pionii* 4.2; Pionius *Vit. Polyc.* 30.4; Hemer, *Letters to the Seven Churches*, 59; Calder, "Smyrna," 95–116.

Smyrna was a cultured metropolis known for its famous poets, orators, scientists, doctors and theologians (Strabo *Geogr.* 12.8.20) including Homer,[78] Aristides,[79] Irenaeus,[80] Ignatius of Antioch,[81] Pionius, and Polycarp (see Figs. 50, 51). The church of Smyrna was placed in the midst of this thriving cultural setting.

THE AQUEDUCT

The ruins of the aqueduct built by Trajan's father date back to AD 79–80.[82] Inscriptions describing repairs to the aqueduct by Proconsul L. Baebius Tullus between AD 102 and 112 have been identified.[83] These aqueducts still supply water to the city of Izmir and can be located along the road to Ephesus.[84]

44. Harbor of Izmir (Smyrna) from Mount Pagus, surrounded by the modern city. The ruins of the second cent. state agora (market) are visible on the left side of the photo.

THE GYMNASIUM

The gymnasium (γυμνάσιον, *gumnasion*) in the first cent. AD was a place where youths met for exercise (1 Tim 4:8) and philosophical discussion in the nude (γυμνός, *gumnos*).[85] The gymnasium of Smyrna is reported to be the most beautiful in Asia. Strabo mentions it in passing when he describes the location of the city "near the gymnasium" (*Geogr.* 14.1.37). Hadrian (r. AD 117–38;

---

[78] Strabo *Geogr.* 6.14.1.37; Aristides *Orat.* 328; Cicero *Arch.* 7.8.19; Plutarch *Sert.* 1.3; Bean, *Aegean Turkey*, 45. Smyrna also laid claim to being the birthplace of Homer, author of the famous *Iliad and Odyssey*. His original name was Melesigenes ("born of Meles") which is the name of the river that flows through the city.

[79] Charles A. Behr, *Aelius Aristides and the Sacred Tales* (Amsterdam: Hakkert, 1968), 1, 4 n.5; Cook, *The Greeks*, 202.

[80] Beckwith, *Apocalypse*, 338; Collins, *Crisis and Catharsis*, 26.

[81] Frederick C. Grant, "Smyrna," in *DBib*, ed. James Hastings, Frederick C. Grant, and Harold. H. Rowley, vol. 4 (New York, N.Y.: Scribner's Sons, 1909), 927.

[82] Pfeiffer, *Biblical World*, 543; Yamauchi, *NT Cities*, 58; Cornelius C. Vermeule, *Roman Imperial Art in Greece and Asia Minor* (Cambridge, U.K.: Harvard University Press, 1968), 252, 468; Magie, *Roman Rule in Asia Minor*, 578.

[83] Vermeule, *Roman Imperial Art*, 252, 468; Cadoux, *Ancient Smyrna*, 254.

[84] McDonagh, *Blue Guide: Turkey*, 179; Wilson, *Biblical Turkey*, 312.

[85] Fikret K. Yegül, "The Bath-Gymnasium Complex in Asia Minor During the Imperial Roman Age" (Ph.D. diss., Harvard University, 1975); Roger Chambers, "Greek Athletics and the Jews: 165 BC–AD 70" (Ph.D. diss., Miami University, 1980).

see Figs. 93, 109) was a benefactor of Smyrna, according to his good friend Polemon, who had given "a million in one day" to Smyrna to build both a corn market and the gymnasium.[86]

THE STADIUM

The stadium (amphitheater) was the location of the martyrdom of Pionius (*Mart. Pionii* 21.1). This was also the location of the periodic festivals held in honor of Augustus[87] and the public games celebrating the *Olympia Hadriana* (Pausanias *Descr.* 6.14.1).[88] Two altars to Hadrian have been discovered, along with a statue of Hadrian as Olympian, near the hieron of Dionysus at the foot of Mount Pagus.[89] About 30 to 40 years ago the stadium and the theater could still be seen, but today they are covered by the growing city of Izmir.[90]

THE THEATER

On the northwest slopes of Mount Pagus sat a 16,000–20,000 spectator theater.[91] Little remains of the theater today,[92] although parts of the *cavea* and *spolia* can still be seen built into modern buildings.[93] Vermeule points out Claudius (see Fig. 2, 28) may have rebuilt or renovated the theater after the earthquake of AD 178, but the evidence is based solely on the name Claudius in a doubtful and lost inscription.[94] Bean states regarding the architecture of the theater, "the joggled arch technique was no doubt adopted as a precaution against further shocks".[95]

45. *Homōnoia* (Gr. "political concord") coin from Smyrna. Obv.: Three temples to Emperor Tiberius, the goddess Roma and the emperor Hadrian at Smyrna, minted by Caracalla (AD 211–217). *Homōnoia* coins from Smyrna were prevalent during the reigns of Marcus Aurelius, Commodus, Faustina, Caracalla, and Gordian (*ca.* AD 160–249). Smyrna had the closest *homōnoia* relationship with Laodicea, Thyatira and Philadelphia.

---

[86] *CIG* 3114; Vermeule, *Roman Imperial Art*, 468; Magie, *Roman Rule in Asia Minor*, 1513.
[87] Swete, *Apocalypse*, lxi.
[88] Vermeule, *Roman Imperial Art*, 468.
[89] Ibid.
[90] Wilson, *Biblical Turkey*, 312.
[91] Banks, "Smyrna," 2818.
[92] Akurgal, "Smyrna," 848; *Ancient Civilizations*, 122; Bean, *Aegean Turkey*, 51.
[93] Wilson, *Biblical Turkey*, 312.
[94] Vermeule, Roman Imperial Art, 468; Magie, Roman Rule in Asia Minor, 1401.
[95] Bean, *Aegean Turkey*, 51.

A PROMINENT POLITICAL CITY

The prominence of Smyrna as a political city is well known as it competed with Ephesus and Pergamum to be "the first in Asia."[96]

HOMONOIA COINS

The rivalry between cities in Asia Minor is also evident from the "political concord" (ὁμόνοια, *homonoia*)[97] coins (Plutarch *Praec. ger. publ.* 824E; see Fig. 45, 82).[98] Dio Chrysostom provided the most comprehensive discussion of *homonoia* as a political virtue.[99] As Lotz points out:

> The *homonoia* coins of Asia Minor offer us in [*sic.* an] important insight into the tensions and vicissitudes of city politics in late first century Asia Minor, and help broaden our understanding of the sociopolitical background and context that Paul and his disciples spoke to. . . . and how these speak to the persistent struggle to achieve peace and concord in the cities of the Greek East under the Roman "peace".[100]

Smyrna had developed a complex network of alliances with other cities that had uniquely set her apart from the other seven cities.[101] This was demonstrated in the ὁμόνοια (*homonoia*, political concord or alliance) coins which Smyrna had encouraged as a mutual acknowledgment of religious practices with the surrounding cities. The height of the coins' popularity was during the time of Domitian.[102]

THE STATE AGORA

The agora dates from the Roman period of Marcus Aurelius (AD 161–180), who rebuilt it following the earthquake of AD 178.[103] Although it has no bearing on NT events,[104] it does have relevance to the period of the early church. The state agora is different to the commercial agora, which is situated near the harbor. It is perhaps one of the best preserved agoras in all of Anatolia.[105] The state agora was an impressive complex occupying an area of ca. 260 x 390 ft.

---

[96] Ramsay, Cities and Bishoprics, 2:632; Magie, Roman Rule in Asia Minor, 2:635–36.

[97] Nicholas Purcell defines *homonoia* as "Concordia: The cult of personified harmonious agreement within the body politic of Rome" Purcell, "Concordia," *OCD* 375.

[98] Kampmann, "Homonoia Politics," 373–93.

[99] Christopher P. Jones, *The Roman World of Dio Chrysostom* (Cambridge, Mass.: Harvard University Press, 1978), 94.

[100] Lotz, "The Homonoia Coins of Asia Minor and Ephesians 1:21," 173.

[101] Ramsay, *Letters: Updated*, 193.

[102] During the Gordian period Smyrna minted ὁμόνοια coins with eight cities and the *Koinon* of Asia. The *Koinon* were the provincial council of the Asian cities. This indicates a sudden intensification of diplomatic activity. Klose, *Münzprägung*, 46, 50; Martin J. Price and Bluma L. Trell, *Coins and Their Cities: Architecture on the Ancient Coins of Greece, Rome, and Palestine* (Detroit, Mich.: Wayne State University Press, 1977), 32.

[103] Bean, *Aegean Turkey*, 52.

[104] Pfeiffer, *Biblical World*, 543.

[105] Wilson, *Biblical Turkey*, 313.

46. The Corinthian columns of the stao of the commercial agora, Smyrna.

(80 x 120 m). It had two-story colonnades divided into three sections, with two rows of Corinthian columns (see Fig. 46; Strabo *Geogr.* 14.1.37).[106] Akurgal adds:

> There is also a magnificent vaulted basement beneath the north colonnade, still in splendid condition. The north aisle in the basement was composed of shops, which must have opened onto a street in Roman times. Court cases were heard in an *exedra* in the west part of the north colonnade. The stoa on the south side, not yet excavated, must also have had two stories with a nave and two aisles.[107]

Between 1932 and 1942, German and Turkish archaeologists excavated the agora under the direction of Numan, Kantar and Miltner.[108] Excavations were resumed in 2002 by the Izmir Archaeology Museum under the direction of the Museum's director, Mehmet Taslialan. Excavations in the northern and western portions of the civic basilica have revealed many sculptures and architectural pieces. A portion of the basilica and part of the west stoa are being restored to a height of two stories.[109] According to Taslialan,

> The inscriptions on stone provide information about civic life and the Roman government of the Province of Asia, and very numerous graffiti, preserved on the plaster which covers the north wall and many of the pillars of the lower story of the Basilica, constitute a Greek counterpart to the Latin graffiti of Pompeii, unique in the Roman East. [110]

Thomas Derwbear, a tablet expert, was brought in by Taslialan to help decipher the graffiti, tablets and inscriptions discovered in the agora. Derwbear states that "Smyrnian youth ornamented the walls with everything about their daily life. Gladiator figures describing a fight with lions, comedians on stage, and other graffiti about sport and health were found".[111] Some of the messages used *gematria*, a secret code similar to that used in Revelation 13:18 for the number 666, to convey their messages of love, sex and religion. One inscription from the agora Basilica, that was an example of Isopsephism (*gematria*) from Smyrna, states: "equal in value:

---

[106] McDonagh, *Blue Guide: Turkey*, 178, fig. 3.

[107] Akurgal, "Smyrna," 848; Akurgal, *Ancient Civilizations*, 122.

[108] McDonagh, *Blue Guide: Turkey*, 178.

[109] Mehmet Taslialan, "New Excavations and Restorations in the Agora of Smyrna," in *Paper Presented at Institut Für Archäologie, Abt. Archäologie Des Mittelmeerraumes* (University of Berne, Institute of Archaeology, University of Berne, Institute of Archaeology, June 24, 2004), n.p.

[110] Ibid.

[111] Thomas Derwbear, "Secret of Ancient Graffiti," *Turks.US Daily EU News, July 22,* 2003, n.p., www.turks.us/article.php?story = 20030722090305725.

lord, 800; faith 800" (TP100.3 = *SIG* 3.973).[112] Three female names, in the same building, are identified representing 616. One reads "I love a woman whose number is 616" (T22.1).[113]

> Wilson reports that:
>
>> One example provides perhaps the earliest Christian graffiti yet discovered. It reads *o dedwkwj pneuma*: "the one who has given the Spirit," that is, the Lord (*kurios*) Jesus. The function of this graffito was apparently to announce that there were Christians in the city with whom other believers could fellowship and worship.[114]

47. Arch in the western stoa (*portico*) of the state agora in Smyrna (second cent. AD). At the top of the arch is a portrait of Faustina the Younger (see Fig. 48), honored for financing the rebuilding of the city.

According to Aristides, in the center of the agora, surrounded by colonnades, stood "a large altar dedicated to Zeus" (see Figs. 95, 115, 126, 151, 154, 156).[115] In addition, Demeter (see Fig. 98) and Poseidon are depicted standing next to each other on a relief along with other gods.[116] They are now on display in the Izmir Archaeological Museum. Akurgal postulates, "[I]t may well be that placing these deities side by side was intended to demonstrate that Smyrna at that time dominated commerce by both land and sea".[117] Vermeule mentions that a statue of Trajan was also located in the agora.[118]

The area around the agora altar was no doubt the place mentioned in the *Martyrdom of Pionius*, where Polemon was leading Pionius to make his sacrifice (see *Quotes from Antiquity*). On the second arch in the colonnade of the agora is a portrait of Faustina the Younger, wife of Marcus Aurelius (see Fig. 48), honoring her contribution to the rebuilding of the agora following the AD 178 earthquake (see Fig. 47).

> **Quotes from Antiquity**
>
> Come then to the market-place [Gr. *agora*]; there you will change your minds. . . . As they came into the forum, by the eastern Stoa and the double gate, all the forum and the upper storeys of the porches were crowded with Greeks, Jews, and women (*Mart. Pionii* 3.3, 4 [Musurillo]).

---

[112] Bagnall, "Christianity," 46.

[113] Roger S. Bagnall, "Isopsephisms of Desire," in *Graffiti from the Basilica in the Agora of Smyrna*, ed. Roger S. Bagnall et al., Institute for the Study of the Ancient World (New York, N.Y.: New York University Press, 2016), 50, 226.

[114] Wilson, *Biblical Turkey*, 315.

[115] McDonagh, *Blue Guide: Turkey*, 178.

[116] Bean, *Aegean Turkey*, 52.

[117] Akurgal, Ancient Civilizations, 848.

[118] Vermeule, *Roman Imperial Art*, 252.

A THRIVING RELIGIOUS CITY

The city of Smyrna was also home to other religions, with temples to "Sipylene Cybele[119] and the local Zeus" (see Figs. 95, 115, 126, 151, 154, 156),[120] and Asclepius (see Fig. 71).[121] Other temples to the *neōkorate*, Nemesis[122] and Tyche (Τύχη or Cybele; see Figs. 52, 54, 98, 108, 160) are depicted on the coinage of Smyrna.[123] In the account of the martyrdom of Pionius, Sabina and others "throw themselves on the ground to avoid being dragged to the temple" (εἰδώλαιον, *eidōlaion*, "idol temple"; *Mart. Pionii* 15.7 [Musurillo]). Pagan temples provided a climate of clashing worldviews and set the stage for persecution of the Christians in Smyrna.

A CITY OF THE IMPERIAL CULT

The worship of the emperor (imperial cult) was an important part of Smyrna's culture from early on in Rome's rise to power.[124] Kistemaker writes that to make the spirit of Rome concrete throughout the empire, "Romans presented the emperor as its embodiment, and thus worship of the emperor arose. Although some of the first emperors disparaged this worship, the population energized it to the point that the emperor was considered to be divine".[125]

48. Faustina the Younger, wife of Marcus Aurelius (second cent. AD).

ORIGIN OF THE IMPERIAL CULT

The origin of the goddess *Roma cultus* (see Fig. 173), the deification of Rome,[126] can be traced in the Greek world to the city of Smyrna, because of her need to invent and maintain a relationship with Rome.[127] Smyrna was a faithful ally of Rome going back first to 43 BC when

---

[119] Giulia Sfameni Gasparro, *Soteriology and Mystic Aspects in the Cult of Cybele and Attis*, ÉPRO 103 (Leiden: Brill Academic, 1985), 71–72.

[120] Swete, *Apocalypse*, lxi.

[121] Pausanias *Descr.* 2.36.9; 7.5.9; Tacitus *Ann.* 3.63; 4.55–56.

[122] Wilson reports that archaeologists may have discovered the ruins of the temple of Nemesis under the Hürriyet Anadolu Lisesi (high school) building near the agora. Wilson, *Biblical Turkey*, 310.

[123] Klose, *Münzprägung*, 38; Price and Trell, *Coins and Their Cities: Architecture on the Ancient Coins of Greece, Rome, and Palestine*, 215, 268.

[124] For a comprehensive treatment of the Imperial Cult in Smyrna from numismatic and epigraphic remains, see chapter 2. Smyrna in Ionia (Tiberius) in Burrell, *Neokoroi*, 38–54.

[125] Kistemaker, *Revelation*, 121.

[126] Livy *Hist. Rome* 33.38.3; 34.59.4; 35.17.1; Polybius *Hist.* 18.52.1.

[127] Potter, "Smyrna," 6:74; Ronald Mellor, *Thea Rhōmē: The Worship of the Goddess Roma in the Greek World*, Hypomnemata 42 (Göttingen: Vandenhoeck & Ruprecht, 1975), 14–15.

Cicero declared that they were "our most faithful and most ancient allies" (*Phil.* 11.2.5 [Yonge]) and even farther back to 195 BC when Smyrna was the first Ionian city to establish a *templum urbis Romae* (Lat. "temple to Roma"), in honor of *dea Roma* (Lat. "goddess Roma"; Tacitus *Ann.* 4.37–8, 56; see Fig. 173),[128] the center of the imperial cult. The temple of Roma appears on several Smyrna coins through the third cent. AD as a tetrastyle (four column) temple.[129] Mellor is uncertain if this is a depiction of the original temple of 195 BC or its replacement.[130] Another bronze coin may portray an altar connected with the temple.[131] Mellor points out that "after more than two centuries, the temple of Roma at Smyrna still served its original function: to flatter Rome and thereby secure favors for Smyrna".[132] Smyrna's city calendar also conveyed an allegiance to Rome as "the month from late February to March was named *Philosebastos* [φιλοσέβαστος], "friend to the emperor")".[133]

In AD 26, according to Tacitus, the provincial council (Lat. *Commune Asiae*) decreed a second temple (Tacitus *Ann.* 4.56) to the goddess of Rome (Lat. *dea Roma*),[134] resulting in envoys from 11 Asia Minor cities vying for the privilege of construction. Emperor Tiberius Tiberius (see Figs. 43, 97, 111) heard the arguments (see *Quotes from Antiquity*) and narrowed the decision down to Sardis and Smyrna (Tacitus *Ann.* 4.55–56).[135] Upon hearing the arguments, Tiberius granted Smyrna the right to construct and become keeper (νεωκόρος, *neōkoros*) of the second

> ### *Quotes from Antiquity*
> The envoys from Smyrna, after tracing their city's antiquity back to such founders as either Tantalus, the son of Jupiter, or Theseus, also of divine origin, or one of the Amazons, passed on to that on which they chiefly relied, their services to the Roman people, whom they had helped with naval armaments, not only in wars abroad, but in those under which we struggled in Italy. They had also been the first, they said, to build a temple in honour of Rome, during the consulship of Marcus Porcius Cato, when Rome's power indeed was great, but not yet raised to the highest point, inasmuch as the Punic capital was still standing and there were mighty kings in Asia. They appealed too to the testimony of Lucius Sulla, whose army was once in terrible jeopardy from a severe winter and want of clothing, and this having been announced at Smyrna in a public assembly, all who were present stript their clothes off their backs and sent them to the legions. And so the Senate, when the question was put, gave the preference to Smyrna. (Tacitus *Ann.* 4.56)

---

[128] Ramsay, *Letters: Updated*, 184; Aune, *Rev 1–5*, 160; Burrell, *Neokoroi*, 38–39.

[129] Head, *BMC Ionia* 268. nos. 266–68; 286, no. 389 (*Julia Domna*); 288, no. 403, and: 289, no. 410 (*Caracalla*); 293, no. 434 (*Julia Mammaea*); 299, no. 467 (*Gallienus*).

[130] Mellor, *Thea Rhōmē*, 51, 135; Friesen, *Twice Neokoros*, 18 n.52; Klose, *Münzprägung*, 1.

[131] Head, *BMC Ionia* 268, nos. 263–65.

[132] Mellor, *Thea Rhōmē*, 14.

[133] Robin Lane Fox, *Pagans and Christians* (New York, N.Y.: HarperCollins, 1988), 476–77; Rogers, *Mysteries of Artemis*, 158–62.

[134] Cadoux, *Ancient Smyrna*, 239.

[135] Mellor, *Thea Rhōmē*, 14; Friesen, *Twice Neokoros*, 15–16; Aune, *Rev 1–5*, 160; Cadoux, *Ancient Smyrna*, 239.

imperial cult temple in Asia (Tacitus *Ann.* 4:56). Unfortunately, no archaeological evidence for this temple has yet been discovered.[136] Smyrna dedicated this temple[137] to Emperor Tiberius (see Figs. 43, 97, 111) together with his mother Julia and took pride in boasting that she was the first city to construct a temple to emperor worship.[138] The fact that Smyrna was chosen over other cities demonstrates the wealth and status of this city.[139]

ROLE OF THE IMPERIAL CULT

The presence of a provincial cult within a city would indicate that a close relationship existed between that city and Rome, providing a sense of unity in the Empire and promoting the *pax Romana* (Lat. "Roman Peace"). When Pionius, the Bishop of Smyrna (died AD 250) was first asked and refused to sacrifice to the gods ("the golden image," *Mart. Pionii* 4.24; 5.2 [Musurillo]), Poleman the temple warden (νεωκόρος, *neōkoros*), asked him to "make a sacrifice at least to the emperor" (*Mart. Pionii* 7.2 [Musurillo]). For

49. Priest of the imperial cult at Smyrna (30 BC–AD 395).

Poleman, a leading pagan in Smyrna, to use the term "at least" indicates that the emperor was not on the same level as the gods. Certainly, the cult of the emperor was present in Smyrna, "but not even the prosecutors saw it as the most divisive issue. It was a cult, they felt, which allowed a compromise. Unlike the other pagan gods, a living emperor had no divine anger, no power to cause droughts or tremors".[140] However, for Christians, the worship of both gods and emperors was unthinkable (*Mart. Pionii* 7.2; 8.4).

The imperial cult (see Fig. 49) may well have played a significant role in the mistreatment of Smyrnaean Christians by Jews. The Roman authorities slowly began to understand that Christians did not fit under Judaism's exemption from the ban on religious practices outside of the cult of the emperor, and this led to the persecution of the Christians.[141] Kiddle provides an

---

[136] Yamauchi, *NT Cities*, 55–62; Potter, "Smyrna," 6:73–75.

[137] Mellor thinks that "this temple was probably converted from the earlier temple of Roma built in 195 B.C." Mellor, *Thea Rhōmē*, 135 n.10; Wilson, "Pie in a Very Bleak Sky," 41–42; Cadoux, *Ancient Smyrna*, 239.

[138] Banks, "Smyrna," 4:2818.

[139] Friesen, *Twice Neokoros*, 19. Without a social welfare system the contrast between the wealthy and poor would be evident (2:9).

[140] Lane Fox, Pagans and Christians, 477.

[141] Osborne, *Revelation*, 131; Adela Yarbro Collins, "Vilification and Self-Definition in the Book of Revelation," *HTR* 79 (1986): 313.

excellent overview of the historical background for the role of the imperial cult in the persecution of Christians in Smyrna:

> And in cities like Smyrna, where the Imperial cult had been enthusiastically fostered for many years, it must have been an easy matter to urge the authorities to action. It was part of the Imperial policy to respect the religion of its subjects' nation, the Jews, who were legally excused from actual worship of the emperor on condition that intercession was offered for him in synagogues. But Christians had no national name to protect them, and consequently no legal privileges. Once disowned by Judaism, of which to the casual eye of the pagan they might seem merely an eccentric and troublesome sect, they were at the mercy of the prejudices of local administrators. And certain Jews were not content with disowning and ridiculing their opponents; there is reason to believe that they would on occasion traduce them, laying malicious accusations at their charge—accusations, for example, of disloyalty and positive sedition.[142]

The Jews would have sought "to dissociate themselves from the Christian movement, and, on the other hand, to enlist and support local authorities in the removal of this threat to the status quo".[143] Jewish persecution is the context within which the Jewish synagogue in Revelation is to be understood as a "synagogue of Satan." Grant points out that "The historical context for this animosity is best understood before the Jewish revolt of 66–70 AD, after which the Romans removed the special status of the Jews and the Jews, themselves, faced persecution from the Romans".[144]

A CITY OF TEMPLES

Certainly if Smyrna could not claim a special cult like Ephesus (Artemis, or Diana, see Figs. 26, 27, 121, 124, 127), it celebrated a number of temples, including Sipylene Cybele (Tyche, Τύχη, see Figs. 52, 54, 98, 108, 160), Apollo (see Figs. 86, 90, 96), Asclepius (see Fig. 71), Aphrodite (see Figs. 93, 122, 123, 126), and Zeus (see Figs. 95, 115, 126, 151, 154, 156).[145] The temples of Smyrna were beautifully decorated as is evident from Pliny's reference to them as "consecrated mirrors" (*Nat.* 10:33.9). Even though they were built from private revenue and managed by priests, the temples were seen as public buildings or, more correctly, the property of the gods.[146] They were protected by local authorities that bore the name Crown-Wearer (see Fig. 54, 55), assisted by an independent city priest.[147]

---

[142] Kiddle, *Revelation*, 27.
[143] M. Robert Mulholland, *Revelation: Holy Living in an Unholy World* (Grand Rapids, Mich.: Asbury, 1990), 360.
[144] Grant, "Smyrna," 927.
[145] Barclay, *Letters*, 15–16; Akurgal, *Ancient Civilizations*, 848; Cadoux, *Ancient Smyrna*, 202.
[146] In the account of the martyrdom of Pionius (*Mart. Pionii* 15.7 [Musurillo]), Sabina and the others throw themselves on the ground to avoid being dragged to the temple (Gr. *eidoleion*), "a temple which houses an idol," as in 1 Cor 8:10.
[147] *IGR* 4.1393a (AD 80); 4.1386, 4.1420 (AD 200); 1431, 4.1435, 4.1449 (AD 135); Cadoux, *Ancient Smyrna*, 26 n.10; Klose, *Münzprägung*, 38.

THE JEWISH COMMUNITY

There was a considerable Jewish population in Smyrna[148] which was hostile to the early church but on relatively good terms with the Roman government.[149] They opposed the early Christians and encouraged persecution of Christians (2:9–10). In the Revelation to John, they are described as calling themselves Jews, but really belonging to the synagogue of Satan. As Walvoord points out, the Christian persecutors were not only pagans, who naturally would be offended by the peculiarities of the Christian faith, but also hostile Jews and Satan himself.[150]

JEWISH PRESENCE IN SMYRNA

The source of the Jewish presence in Asia Minor can be traced back to the time of the Seleucids, as early as 200 BC when Antiochus the Great (261–248 BC) imported 2,000 Jewish families from Babylon to improve his grip on this territory (Josephus *Ant.* 12.125).[151] These Jews were given land, guaranteed privileges,[152] and a separate government. It has also been documented that there was a large Jewish population from the time of Cicero settling in every city in Asia and particularly in western Asia Minor (Cicero *Flac.* 68; Philo *Leg.* 1.245).[153] By the first cent. the Jewish population in Asia Minor perhaps reached in excess of one million.[154] From these data, Ramsay rightly concludes that, "we cannot doubt that this large Jewish population exercised a great influence on the development of the district and of the cities".[155] Persecution of Christians by the Jews during the first two centuries was frequent[156] and also

---

[148] *CIJ* 2:742.29; 2.749–43; *IGR* 4:1431.29; *CIG* 2:3148; *NewDocs* 3:52, §17; McCabe, *Smyrna Inscriptions*, 54; William H. C. Frend, *Martyrdom and Persecution in the Early Church: A Study of a Conflict from the Maccabees to Donatus* (Oxford, U.K.: Blackwell, 1965), 148 n.47; Hemer, "Unto the Angels of the Churches," 62; E. Mary Smallwood, *The Jews Under Roman Rule: From Pompey to Diocletian: A Study in Political Relations*, SJLA 20 (Leiden: Brill, 1981), 234 nn.59, 507; A. Thomas Kraabel, "The Roman Diaspora: Six Questionable Assumptions," *JJS* 33 (1982): 455; Kraybill, *Imperial Cult and Commerce in John's Apocalypse*, 170–94; Elizabeth Leigh Gibson, "Jews in the Inscriptions of Smyrna," *JJS* 56, no. 1 (2005): 66–79.

[149] Claudia J. Setzer, *Jewish Responses To Early Christians* (Minneapolis, Minn.: Fortress, 1994), 114; Keener, *Revelation*, 115.

[150] Walvoord, *Revelation*, 61.

[151] Ramsay, *Cities and Bishoprics*, 2:668 n.4; Eisig Silberschlag, "The Earliest Record of Jews in Asia Minor," *JBL* 52, no. 1 (1933): 67. Silberschlag points out that "the origin of Jews in Asia Minor is still a matter of conjecture" and goes on to trace the roots of the Jews back to a fragment from Clearchus's book *On Sleep* (Περὶ ὕπνου *peri hupnou*) recorded by Josephus (*Ag. Ap.* 1.176–83).

[152] Ramsay recounts how the Jews were granted the special privilege of buying their own oil following the protest against the Gentile privilege of manufacturing their own oil. Ramsay, *Cities and Bishoprics*, 2:668.

[153] Smallwood, Jews Under Roman Rule, 121.

[154] Pieter Willem van der Horst, "Jews and Christians in Aphrodisias in the Light of Their Relations in Other Cities of Asia Minor," *NedTT* 43 (1989): 106–7. While van der Horst's article deals with Aphrodisias, many of his arguments can also apply to Smyrna, as the lack of direct evidence is similar in both cities, and his use of indirect evidence applies to other cities in the region.

[155] Ramsay, Cities and Bishoprics, 2:668.

[156] Acts 6:9–15; 9:23, 29; 12:1–3; 13:45–50; 14:1–5, 19; 17:5, 13; 18:6; 12; 19:33; 20:3; 21:27; 22:30; 23:12; 24:9; 25:7–15; 26:7.

> **Quotes from Antiquity**
>
> Though they [Jews] read, do not understand what is said, but count us foes and enemies; and, like yourselves, they kill and punish us whenever they have the power, as you can well believe. For in the Jewish war which lately raged, Barchochebas, the leader of the revolt of the Jews, gave orders that Christians alone should be led to cruel punishments, unless they would deny Jesus Christ and utter blasphemy. . . . And this the Jews who possessed the books of the prophets did not understand, and therefore did not recognise Christ even when He came, but even hate us who say that He has come, and who prove that, as was predicted, He was crucified by them. (Justin *1 Apol.* 31.5–6, 36.36)

present in Smyrna (2:10).[157] Frend points out that "In the persecutions which were to wrack Asia in the reign of Marcus Aurelius, the Jew was often in the background".[158] Lieu challenges this view in her article on Jewish persecution, stating that it is easy to show that the Jewish persecution of Christians must "rely more on rhetoric than on wealth of evidence".[159] She argues away the predominance of Jewish involvement stating, that it was less fact than the Christians' imagination. Her major premise focuses on the illusion of persecution:

> What is beyond dispute is that Christians perceived and presented themselves as persecuted. . . . That Justin was seriously convinced of Jewish hostility to Christians is not to be doubted; however, the frequent repetition of the theme owes as much to its function within one (or more than one) theological schema, as it does to its historical primacy.[160]

However, even given Lieu's best efforts to argue away the evidence, there appears to be sufficient justification for claiming a predominant Jewish influence in early Christian persecution.[161] Frend goes so far as to say that, "In the last resort, the troubles of the early church were due as much to the virulence of the Christian-Jewish controversy as to any other cause".[162]

Waal also recognizes that "the great dispute in Revelation is between *ecclesia* and *synagoga*; it is there that the antithesis lies".[163] There is sufficient evidence to support the claim of a significantly hostile Jewish community in Smyrna in the first and second century.

---

[157] Kraabel, "Judaism in Western Asia Minor," 32–40.

[158] Frend, *Martyrdom and Persecution*, 259.

[159] Lieu, "Accusations of Jewish Persecution," 279, 287. Lieu concludes that: "The charge of Jewish involvement in persecution is deeply implicated in Christian apologetics of self-identity, and, considering the dialectical relationship with Judaism within those apologetics, claiming their antiquity and heritage while denying their legitimacy, we may be surprised that it is not found more frequently."

[160] Ibid., 280, 282–83.

[161] See *Quotes from Antiquity*; Justin *Dial.* 16.4; 17.1; Irenaeus *Haer.* 4.21.3; Origen *Cels.* 6.27; Hippolytus *Comm. Dan.* 1.13–5; Eusebius *Hist. eccl.* 2.23.11, 18; 5.16.12; *Mart. Pol.* 13.1; 17.2–18.1; *Mart. Pionii* 3.6; Cyprian *Pat.* 21; Tertullian *Apol.* 7.3; *Scorp.* 9.2; *Cor.* 10.9; Frend, *Martyrdom and Persecution*, 157.

[162] Ibid., 156.

[163] Cornelis van der Waal, *The Covenantal Gospel*, ed. H. DeJong, trans. G. L. Bertram (Alberta: Inheritance, 1990), 125. Waal also identifies this same contrast in the gospel of John along with a dominating paschal style.

JEWISH INVOLVEMENT IN THE MARTYRDOM OF POLYCARP

Although there is evidence for a Jewish community in first and second century Smyrna, it was not until the middle of the second cent. that the Jews of Smyrna made an "impact on recorded history"[164] when they joined with the residents of Smyrna against the Christians to martyr Polycarp, Bishop of Smyrna (see Figs. 50, 51; *Mart. Pol.* 1.13)[165] and Pionius (*Mart. Pionii*).[166] While martyrdom was a very real possibility within the early church, it is significant that when Polycarp died (according to the *Martyrdom of Polycarp*) eleven Christians from Philadelphia died as martyrs alongside him (*Mart. Pol.* 19.1).

Polycarp was the bishop of Smyrna for many years. Polycarp (Πολύκαρπος, *polycarpos*)[167] means "fruitful," evident through his life's work. According to Pionius, Polycarp was an orphan raised by a woman named Callisto, who was directed by an angel to purchase him and raise him. Pionius tells us that he was "a native of the East. . . . during the time of Bucolus" (*Vit. Polyc.* 1.3 [Lightfoot]).[168] With the death of Polycarp in ca. AD 155,[169] under the governance of Statius

50. Stained glass window depicting Polycarp (St. John Anglican Church, Izmir).

---

[164] Smallwood, Jews Under Roman Rule, 507.

[165] Musurillo views the Martyrdom of Polycarp as guilty of an "undisguised anti-semitism", although it is more likely just stating the events as they happened in the church at Smyrna. Musurillo, *Acts of the Christian Martyrs*, xiv; Alford, *Revelation*, 4:4:566; Swete, *Apocalypse*, 31.

[166] James William Parkes, The Conflict of the Church and the Synagogue: A Study in the Origins of Antisemitism (New York, N.Y.: Meridian, 1964), 136–40.

[167] According to Foster, Polycarp was rarely used as a man's name. The name Polycarp is recorded by Irenaeus (*Haer.* 3.3.4) and repeated by Tertullian (*Praeser.* 32). Foster makes a connection between Polycarp's name and *karpon polun* (Gr. "much fruit") in John 15:5. John Foster, "Note on St. Polycarp," *ExpTim* 77 (1966): 319.

[168] However, most scholars do not consider *The Life of Polycarp* historically accurate. Lightfoot says of this document, "if it contains any grains of truth, we have not means of sifting them from the huge heap of falsehood". J. B. Lightfoot, *The Apostolic Fathers (APF)*, ed. J. R. Harmer, 2nd ed. (London, U.K.: Macmillan, 1898), 1:435–36; Kenneth Berding, "Historical Connections to John but Literary Connections to Paul: Can We Resolve a Dilemma in Our Understanding of Polycarp of Smyrna?," in *Paper Presented at the First International Symposium on Ancient Smyrna* (Izmir, Turkey, 2003), 2; Leslie W. Barnard, "In Defense of Pseudo-Pionius' Account of Polycarp's Martyrdom," in *Kyriakon Festschrift Johannes Quasten*, ed. Josef A. Jungman and Patrick Granfield, vol. 1 (Münster: Aschendorff, 1970), 192–204. See Barnard for a defense of the historicity of Pionius.

[169] Potter, "Smyrna," 6:75; William M. Ramsay, "The Date of St. Polycarp's Martyrdom," *JÖAI* 27 (1932): 245–58; Behr, *Aelius Aristides and the Sacred Tales*, 99 n.15; Paul Hartog, *Polycarp and the New Testament: The Occasion, Rhetoric, Theme, and Unity of the Epistle to the Philippians and Its Allusions to New Testament Literature*, WUNT, 2.134 (Tübingen: Siebeck, 2002), 30–31. There is some debate over the exact date of Polycarp's martyrdom. Following Behr's examination of the evidence found in the *Letter on the Martyrdom of Polycarp* he concludes "Polycarp died on a Christian Festival, on Saturday February 23, 166 AD, under the Governor Statius Quadratus and the High priest of Asia C. Julius Philippus of Tralles,

Quadratus,[170] he won the martyr's crown[171] of immortality (Eusebius *Hist. eccl.* 4.15.40, 45). The martyrdom of Polycarp bore much fruit, as is evident from the advice he was called upon to give to the Philippian[172] church 300 miles (483 km) away[173] and the churches named in his honor still in existence today.[174]

The account of his martyrdom recalls how in his old age as he stood before the proconsul he was given the choice of cursing Jesus' name and living, or confessing his name and dyeing. Polycarp (see Fig. 50, 51) replied: "86 years have I served Christ, and he has never done me wrong. How can I blaspheme my King who saved me?" (Eusebius *Hist. eccl.* 4.15.25 [Lightfoot and Harmer]). At this point the proconsul sentenced him to die by being burned at the stake. The record indicates that the Jews were foremost in gathering wood for the fire. Even though it was the Sabbath, they deliberately carried burdens of wood and transgressed the law (*Mart. Pol.* 8.1; 13.1). When the persecution broke out in Smyrna in this period, the Jews were not directly involved initially (*Mart. Pol.* 3.2), but the Jews became involved when the focus was placed upon Polycarp:

> Gentiles as well as Jews living in Smyrna, cried out with uncontrollable anger and with a loud shout: "This is the teacher of Asia [*or* of impiety],[175] the father of the Christians, the destroyer of our gods, who teaches many not to sacrifice, or worship (*Mart. Pol.* 12.2 [Lightfoot and Harmer]).

Lieu doubts that Jews spoke these words, arguing:

> These we cannot pursue except to note that it is irrelevant, albeit true, that the words are unlikely to have been found on Jewish lips—they would not have claimed the city gods as "theirs" nor ventured to accuse someone else of avoiding their worship without running the risk of having the same charge turned against themselves. It is equally pointless to allocate the cries to the groups involved, so that the Jews contribute only the first two affirmations, or to debate the "orthodoxy" of the Jews involved or the official nature of their involvement. From the point of view of the

---

just after the games of the Provincial Assembly, which were held that year in Smyrna". Hartog has suggested a new date for the martyrdom of Polycarp at AD 161.

[170] Behr, *Aelius Aristides and the Sacred Tales*, 98.

[171] Stewart points out that "In this first appearance of crown and prize and athletic contest in a martyrological setting the figurative language is already well developed and the terminology extensive. It is clear that by this date, but perhaps not very long before, Christians were picturing their martyrs as victorious athletes." Zeph Stewart, "Greek Crowns and Christian Martyrs," in *Mémorial André-Jean Festugière: Antiquité Païenne et Chrétienne*, ed. E. Lucchesi and H. D. Saffrey (Geneva: Cramer, 1984), 122.

[172] Peter Pilhofer, "The Early Christian Community of Smyrna—Smyrna in the New Testament and Beyond," in *Paper Presented at the First International Symposium on Ancient Smyrna* (Izmir, Turkey, 2003), 53–56; Kenneth Berding, *Polycarp and Paul: An Analysis of Their Literary and Theological Relationship in Light of Polycarp's Use of Biblical and Extra-Biblical Literature* (Leiden: Brill, 2002), 416; Hartog, *Polycarp and the NT*. Berding and Pilhofer raise concerns over Hartog's research on Polycarp and Philipi questioning how he can "'concur with Goodspeed and Grant' that Polycarp writes as a bishop (p. 50) when the prologue to Pol. *Phil.* simply reads, 'Polycarp and the elders with him…'?"

[173] Pilhofer, "Early Christian Community of Smyrna," 9.

[174] St. Polycarp Roman Catholic Church and St. John Anglican Church, with her beautiful stained glass windows, both stand today commemorating Polycarp's martyrdom.

[175] Lieu points out that: "all the Greek manuscripts except M[oscow] read 'teacher of impiety'; 'of Asia' has the support of M, Eusebius and the Latin translation." Lieu, "Accusations of Jewish Persecution," 293 n.20.

51. Painting of the martyrdom of Polycarp on the ceiling of the St. Polycarp Roman Catholic Church, the oldest Catholic Church in Izmir. He was burned to death after refusing to deny Christ, saying "86 years I have served Him and He never did me any injury, how then can I blaspheme my King and my Savior?" (Mart. Pol. 9:5). Permission to build a chapel to Polycarp was granted in 1520 by Suleyman the Magnificent, sultan of the Ottoman Empire 1520–1566.

narrative Polycarp's clear testimony must have a universal audience and he himself must stand alone against the gathered forces of the opposition.[176]

Musurillo ascribes the Jews' remarks to different groups in the crowd.[177] Regardless of the suspected motives, evidence of Jewish involvement in persecution of the early church is found throughout the Acts[178] and in the accounts of the early church fathers to indicate that this was not out of character in Smyrna.

Beagley argues "that Jews, not primarily Rome, were the main opponents to Christians throughout Revelation."[179] Banks demonstrates this by pointing out how deeply rooted the

---

[176] Ibid., 285–86.
[177] Musurillo, Acts of the Christian Martyrs, 11 n.16.
[178] Acts 6:9–15; 9:23, 29; 12:1–3; 13:45–50; 14:1–5, 19; 17:5, 13; 18:6; 12; 19:33; 20:3; 21:27; 22:30; 23:12; 24:9; 25:7–15; 26:7.
[179] Beagley, *"Sitz Im Leben" of the Apocalypse*, 179–80; Beale, *Revelation*, 25 n.27; 31 n.15; Unger, *Archaeology and the New Testament*, 282; Frend, *Martyrdom and Persecution*, 157. Frend states: "The conflict, however, at the end of the first

convictions of the Jews were in their actions against Polycarp (see Figs. 50, 51). He states, "it seems that the Jews of Smyrna were more antagonistic than were the Romans to the spread of Christianity, for it is said that even on Saturday, their sacred day, they brought wood for the fire in which Polycarp was burned".[180] Ramsay points out that "many who would abhor to appear as spectators of the games on a Sabbath would feel justified in putting to death an enemy of their faith on that day".[181] Smallwood observes that,

> even if common hostility rather than positive friendship lay behind this possibly temporary alliance, the part played by the Jews in the story and the fact that the day of the martyrdom is given in Jewish terms as "a great Sabbath" speaks for the Jews' importance in Smyrna at the time.[182]

The consensus of scholars favors the Jewish community playing a significant role, even if they did not instigate the attack on Polycarp (*Mart. Pol.* 12–18).

JEWISH INVOLVEMENT IN THE MARTYRDOM OF PIONIUS

Pionius was a priest of Smyrna who, according to the *Acts of Pionius*, was martyred in about AD 250. The *Acts of Pionius* is generally accepted by most scholars as historically accurate in most of its content.[183] It is filled with historical details that collectively point toward a historically "reliable document".[184] Meinardus gives the account that, "Euktemon, the bishop of Smyrna, apostasised and surrendered to the demands of the government and offered sacrifices to the gods. Pionius, however, remained true to his faith and died a martyr's death".[185] The *Martyrdom of Pionius* states the time of his martyrdom (see *Quotes from Antiquity*).

The Ides of March mentioned in *Mart. Pionii* 23.1 would be March 12, 250, if the account is accurate. While some understand Eusebius' statement to mean that Pionius was martyred "about the time of Polycarp's death" (see Figs. 50, 51; *Hist. eccl.* 4.15.46) during the reign of Marcus Aurelius (AD 161–180; Eusebius *Hist. eccl.* 4.15.46–47), most scholars question Eusebius

---

century was less with the Roman Empire than with the 'synagogue of Satan'".

[180] Banks, "Smyrna," 2818.
[181] Ramsay, *Letters: Updated*, 199.
[182] Smallwood, *Jews Under Roman Rule*, 507.
[183] Sergio Zincone, "Smyrna," in *Encyclopedia of the Early Church*, ed. Angelo Di Berardino, trans. Adran Walford, vol. 2 (Oxford, U.K.: Oxford University Press, 1992), 2:688–89; Lane Fox, *Pagans and Christians*, 460; Darrell J. Doughty, "Persecution and Martyrdom in Early Christianity," 2003, http://courses.drew.edu/FA2001/bibst-720s-001. Doughty points out their weakness and observes that "the presence of 'color and detail' is not necessarily a mark of authenticity, but may simply characterize a good forgery."
[184] Frank Leslie Cross and Elizabeth A. Livingstone, eds., "Pionius, St.," in *The Oxford Dictionary Of The Christian Church*, Revised (Oxford, U.K.: Oxford University Press, 2005), 1298; Lane Fox, *Pagans and Christians*, 468; Doughty, "Persecution and Martyrdom." Lane Fox points out that Decius is mentioned as Emperor; Trajan, Polemon, Nemeseis, Sabina, Polita, and Rafinius are also mentioned, indicating a period document (*Mart. Pionii* 2.1). He concludes "these individuals vindicate the martyrdom's details, date it to 250, and refute Eusebius's view." Doughty sees the martyrdom of Pionius as "an embellished version of Eusebius' account of Polycarp's martyrdom, which in an indirect way now extends the celebration of Polycarp's martyrdom."
[185] Meinardus, *John of Patmos*, 68.

> **Quotes from Antiquity**
>
> His martyrdom took place when Julius Proculus Quintillian was proconsul of Asia, under the consulship of Emperor Gaius Messius Quintus Trajan Decius Augustus for the second time and Vettius Gratus, on the fourth day before the Ides of March according to the Roman calendar, and according to the Asiatic reckoning on the 19th day of the sixth month, Saturday, at the tenth hour. (*Mart. Pionii* 23.1 [Musurillo])

and place Pionius' execution in AD 250 under the reign of Decius (*Mart. Pionii* 23.1).[186] Maier adds the footnote in his work that "Pionius was indeed martyred at Smyrna, but on the anniversary of Polycarp's martyrdom a century later. Evidently Eusebius included him here thematically rather than chronologically".[187] This would make sense given the internal evidence within the account of the *Martyrdom of Pionius*.[188]

The attitude of Jews toward Christians can be further illustrated from the trial of Pionius, a priest in Smyrna, during the Decian persecution in AD 250.[189] In a public *apologia*, Pionius directs his defense speech to the Jewish community when he addresses "Greeks, Jews and women" (*Mart. Pionii* 3.6 [Musurillo]). Pionius specifically refers to Jews when he says, "those among this audience who are Jews, listen while I make my brief discourse" (*Mart. Pionii* 4.2 [Musurillo]). He refers to the Jews again, and notes their ridicule of those who deserted the faith: I understand that you [Jews] laughed and rejoiced at those who deserted and considered as a joke the error of those who voluntarily offered sacrifice (*Mart. Pionii* 4.3). Then he addresses the men of Judea and appeals to Moses and Solomon, quoting from Deuteronomy 22:4 and Proverbs 24:17 (*Mart. Pionii* 4.4–6). During his discourse, Pionius "mentions Jewish proselytizing efforts among Christians and attempts to discredit Christian doctrine"[190]. According to Smallwood, this would indicate an active community of Jews, "enjoying good relations with their gentile neighbours and considerable freedom of action".[191] Pionius acknowledged that, even if, as they [Jews] claim, we are their enemies, we are at any rate men, and men who have been treated unjustly (*Mart. Pionii* 4.8). Pionius indicates a strong hostility between the Jews of Smyrna and the Christian community, whom the Jews call their enemies. Lane Fox makes several conclusions from the evidence in Martyrdom of Pionius. His first conclusion stated that there was, "a Jewish community of some size and rank."[192] Second, that Jews and gentiles lived in close proximity to each other. Third, the Jews had "contacts in the

---

[186] Potter, "Smyrna," 6:75; Zincone, "Smyrna," 2:688–89; Doughty, "Persecution and Martyrdom," n.p.

[187] Eusebius, *Eusebius: The Church History*, trans. Paul L. Maier (Grand Rapids, Mich.: Kregel Academic & Professional, 2007), 135 n.24; Cross and Livingstone, "Pionius, St.," 1298.

[188] Louis Robert, ed., *Le Martyre de Pionios Pretre de Smyrne* (Washington, D.C.: Dumbarton Oaks Research Library and Collection, 1994), 1–9.

[189] Potter, "Smyrna," 6:75; Zincone, "Smyrna," 2:688–89.

[190] Smallwood, *Jews Under Roman Rule*, 508. *Mart. Pionii* 2.1; 3.6; 4.2; 13.1; 14.1.

[191] Ibid.

[192] Lane Fox, *Pagans and Christians*, 481–82.

city's life."[193] Finally, "the Christian church was a poor relation to the strong Jewish community".[194] Even Doughty, who challenges most of Lane Fox's conclusions, agrees to at least these conclusions.[195] The historical evidence from the martyrdoms of Polycarp (see Figs. 50, 51) and Pionius concurs with the statement about Jewish persecution in Revelation 2:9.

PERSECUTION BY JEWS OF JEWISH CHRISTIANS

Ramsay argues that the Jews expressed their strongest hatred against converted Jews: "It was the Jewish Christians, and not the pagan converts, whom the national Jews hated so violently".[196] The Jews had no interest in converted pagans, but focused on those who owned strong convictions in leaving Judaism, like the apostle Paul.[197] The animosity from the Jewish quarter within Smyrna may additionally be based on Christianity winning God fearers from the synagogue.[198]

THE CHRISTIAN COMMUNITY

The city of Smyrna has had a long and illustrious history of Christian presence. Christian figures such as Clement of Rome (active AD 90–100) and Ignatius of Antioch (died AD 110) wrote letters to Smyrna. Irenaeus, bishop of Lyons, was born in Smyrna, while Polycarp and Pionius, bishops of Smyrna, were martyred there. As a result, perhaps no other city has contributed so much to our understanding of the early church other than Rome and possibly Jerusalem.[199]

According to Charles, "the Church in Smyrna was not founded till 61–64 AD at earliest" (Pol. *Phil.* 2).[200] The majority of the information on the early church of Smyrna is derived from letters written by Ignatius to the church at Smyrna and Polycarp, bishop of Smyrna (see Figs. 50, 51). He wrote to them in Troas a few days after leaving Smyrna, on his way from Antioch to Rome. While the exact length of time Ignatius spent in Smyrna is not known, it was not a brief stay.[201]

Devout Jews from the province of Asia were at the feast of Pentecost in Jerusalem when the Holy Spirit was poured out (Acts 2:9). Some of these may have come from Smyrna and taken the gospel back to their hometown. When Paul came to Ephesus in the early AD 50's, he or his associates may have instituted the church in Smyrna. Polycarp's letter to the church at Philippi may indicate that the knowledge of Christ had not yet come to Smyrna when Paul in AD 62 wrote his letter to the Philippians: "for we did not yet know him [Christ]" (Pol. *Phil.* 11).

---

[193] Ibid.
[194] Ibid.
[195] Doughty, "Persecution and Martyrdom," n.p.
[196] Ramsay, *Letters: Updated*, 198.
[197] Ibid.; Grant, "Smyrna," 927.
[198] McDonagh, *Blue Guide: Turkey*, 245.
[199] Massey H. Shepherd, Jr., "Smyrna in the Ignatius Letters," *JR* 20 (1940): 141.
[200] Charles, *Revelation*, 1:xlviii.
[201] Shepherd, Jr., "Smyrna in the Ignatius Letters," 141–42.

The size of the congregation in Smyrna is also not known, but as Shepherd concludes, the Christian population in Smyrna at the time of Ignatius' visit was too numerous to be congregated in its entirety at any given assembly. Or perhaps it would be more correct to say that it does not appear from our sources that the Christians had only one invariable place of meeting at regular, stated times.[202] Perhaps they met in house churches of local believers, like Tavia and the widow Epitropos that Ignatius mentioned by name in his writings (Ign. *Smyrn.* 12.2; Ign. *Pol.* 8.2).[203]

THE MARTYRS OF SMYRNA

The central message to the church in Smyrna is centerd on suffering and martyrdom (2:9–10). While much of the suffering that has taken place in Smyrna has forever been lost to time, there are a number of famous martyrs who have suffered for their faith, both ancient and modern. While the two most famous martyrs were Polycarp (ca. AD 155; see Figs. 50, 51) and Pionius (AD 250 see *Jewish Involvement in the Martyrdom of Polycarp* and *Pionius* above), there were many more in modern times.

MODERN MARTYRS OF SMYRNA

It is impossible to list the names of all the Christians of this city who laid down their lives for their commitment to Christ following the example of St. Polycarp, but the Greek Orthodox Church commemorates many. Most of these "New Martyrs" were poor people who had embraced Islam for various reasons, but later repented and publicly proclaimed their faith in Jesus Christ. Athanasius of Attalia (January 7), who lived most of his life in Smyrna, was said to have embraced Islam, but in 1653 when he returned to his Christian faith he was decapitated. In 1675 Nicholas of Karaman (December 6), in a moment of anger, swore he would become a Muslim. When he refused to fulfill this oath he was hanged. Dioscorus of Smyrna (May 11) experienced a similar fate. Demus of Smyrna (April 10) was accused by his Turkish master of insulting Islam and was beheaded in 1763. Alexander of Salonica (May 26) had even become a *hodja*,[204] but as he preached the crucified Christ he was martyred in Smyrna in 1794. Other new martyrs of Smyrna include Procopius the New Martyr (June 25), who was killed in 1810; Agathangelus the New Martyr (April 19), who suffered martyrdom in 1818; and Nektarius the New Martyr (July 11) who was hanged in 1820.[205] Athanasios of Smyrna was martyred in 1819.[206]

---

[202] Ibid., 148.
[203] Ibid.
[204] One who had made the pilgrimage to Mecca.
[205] Meinardus, *John of Patmos*, 73–74.
[206] Richard Clogg, "Little Known Orthodox Neo-Martyr, Athanasios of Smyrna (1819)," *ECR* 5 (1973): 28–36.

SUPREME SMYRNA – HISTORY

MARTYRDOM OF ST. CHRYSOSTOM AD 1922

On September 9, 1922, St. Chrysostom, Greek Metropolitan of Smyrna, was tortured, mutilated, and killed by a Turkish mob in front of the military headquarters.[207] Turkish General Noureddin had requested the prelate's presence, but then refused to shake his hand. Instead, he sent Chrysostom into the hands of the waiting crowd, shouting from the balcony, "Treat him as he deserves!"[208] The crowd dragged him down the street to a Jewish barber and demanded, "Give him a shave!"[209]

> They tore out the Prelate's beard, gouged out his eyes with knives, cut off his ears, his nose, and his hands. A dozen French marines who had accompanied Chrysostomos to the government house were standing by, beside themselves. Several of the men jumped instinctively forward to intervene, but the officer in charge forbade them to move. "He had his hand on his gun, though he was trembling himself," one of the men said later, "so we dared not lift ours. They finished Chrysostomos there before our eyes." The Archbishop's murder was reported to Admiral Dumesnil aboard the French flagship. He shrugged his shoulders: "He got what was coming to him," he said.[210]

---

[207] Horton, The Blight of Asia: An Account of the Systematic Extermination of Christian Populations by Mohammedans and of the Culpability of Certain Great Power; with the True Story of the Burning of Smyrna, 99; Marjorie H. Dobkin, Smyrna 1922: The Destruction of a City (New York, N.Y.: Newmark, 1988), 133; Edward Hale Bierstadt, The Great Betrayal: A Survey of the Near East Problem (Pontian Greek Society of Chicago, 2008), 24–25.

[208] According to Dobkin, based on a folder of sworn accusations against him "a revolutionary tribunal in Angora had already condemned Chrysostomos to death. 'There is nothing left but for the people to give their judgment,' he shouted. 'Now get out of my sight!'" Dobkin, Smyrna 1922: The Destruction of a City, 133.

[209] Ibid., 260 n.133.

[210] Dobkin quotes Dumesnil from a letter to the Secretary of State, September 18, 1922: "when the massacre of Chrysostomos was reported to Admiral Dumesnil of the French Navy, he replied, sardonically, with a French idiom which means exactly 'He got what was coming to him'." Ibid., 134, 260 nn.133–34, 127.

7

Steadfast Smyrna

Commentary on Revelation 2:8–11

This chapter[1] will examine the steadfast faithfulness of the Smyrna in the message to Smyrna found in Revelation 2:8–11, especially in the light of the proposed covenant background and structure.[2] On the commission to write (γράψον, *graphon* 3:7a) and the role of angels (ἄγγελος, *angelos*) as mediating messengers, see chapter 3, *The Messenger's Commission*.

MESSENGER PREAMBLE FORMULA—2:8

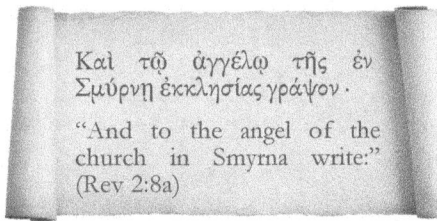

Καὶ τῷ ἀγγέλῳ τῆς ἐν Σμύρνῃ ἐκκλησίας γράψον·

"And to the angel of the church in Smyrna write:" (Rev 2:8a)

John begins each message to the churches with τάδε λέγει Ω (*tade legei omega*, "These are the words"[3]), setting the context for the suzerain/King who will speak to the churches.[4] He proceeds to describe Christ as an echo from Revelation chapter 1 (vs. 13, 16) in a format familiar to the Christian community. Within the OT prophetic structure[5] this prophetic *messenger preamble formula*[6] τάδε λέγει Ω, (*tade legei omega*, "These are the words") introduces the suzerain's message. On the prophetic *messenger preamble formula* see the discussion under "The Messenger's Commission" in chapter 1. Here in the message to Smyrna the king is described as "the first and the last, who died and came to life'" (2:8a).

---

[1] This section on the theological commentary of Smyrna is reproduced with the permission of Gorgias Press with minor corrections from Graves, *SMRVT*, 225–86.

[2] The Historical background of this chapter is reworked from the following four articles and used with permission from *Bible and Spade*. Graves, "Local References in the Letter to Smyrna (Rev 2:8–11), Part 1: Archaeological Background"; "Local References in the Letter to Smyrna (Rev 2:8–11), Part 2: Historical Background"; "Local References in the Letter to Smyrna (Rev 2:8–11), Part 3: Jewish Background"; "Local References in the Letter to Smyrna (Rev 2:8–11), Part 4: Religious Background."

[3] Rev 2:1, 8, 12, 18; 3:1a, 7, 14.

[4] Beale, *Revelation*, 229.

[5] Num 22:15–16; Judg 11:14–15; 1 Kgs 2:30; 2 Chr 36:23; Ezra 1:2.

[6] Graves, *SMRVT*, 141–47; Osborne, *Revelation*, 111.

DESCRIPTION OF THE SUZERAIN

As Sutton indicates, the preamble highlights the "Creator-creature" relationship, which he identifies as one of "transcendence."[7] This arises from the description of Christ in terms of eternity and victory over death through the resurrection (2:8). Transcendence is precisely the doctrinal concept conveyed by *the first and the last*. Beale captures the spirit of the text when he states, "He [Christ] is the sovereign God of history who alone possesses the attribute of eternity."[8] What better attribute to encourage those about to experience suffering and persecution?

THE TRANSCENDENT SUZERAIN IS THE FIRST AND THE LAST—2:8B

Τάδε λέγει ὁ πρῶτος καὶ ὁ ἔσχατος,

"'The words of the first and the last,'" (Rev 2:8a)

The description clearly echoes the earlier usage in Revelation 1:17–18a, and ties this description of the King of the covenant to that of the One "like the son of man"[9] described there. The parallels are unmistakable as the following comparison illustrates in Table 1.

Revelation 1:17–18a	Revelation 2:8b
ἐγώ γἰμι ὁ πρῶτος καὶ ὁ ἔσχατος	τάδε λέγει ὁ πρῶτος καὶ ὁ ἔσχατος
καὶ ὁ ζῶν[10]	
καὶ ἐγενόμην νεκρὸς	ὃς ἐγένετο νεκρὸς
καὶ ἰδού	
ζῶν εἰμι εἰς τοὺς	καὶ ἔζησεν·
αἰῶνας τῶν αἰώνων	

Table 1. Comparison of First and Last in Rev 1:17–18 and Rev 2:8b.

The messenger preamble formula is used to stimulate divine confidence in a church threatened with suffering and martyrdom.[11]

However, Christ's πρῶτος *(prōtos)* declaration could also be understood antithetically with Smyrna's early struggle for pre-eminence within Asia Minor (see *Smyrna—First in Asia*).[12] The citizens of Smyrna would have been familiar with this claim of primacy from the well-known rivalry with Ephesus and Pergamum over first, second, or third rank *neōkoros* as the site for the

---

[7] Sutton, *That You May Prosper*, 21–40, 282; Beale, *Revelation*, 213.
[8] Beale, *Revelation*, 239.
[9] The passage in Rev 2:8 may be a quote from Dan 8:18; 10:10, 12, or it may be a mere coincidence in language.
[10] Omitted by a few MSS possibly because of the parallel in Revelation 2:8.
[11] Swete, Apocalypse, 31; Hemer, Letters to the Seven Churches, 213.
[12] Klose, *Münzprägung*, 44.

provincial imperial temple (Philostratus *Vit. Soph.* 1.25.10; AD 172?), evident on some of Smyrna's coins that read πρώτη τῆς Ἀσίας (*prōtē tēs Asias*, "First of Asia"; AD 193; *OGIS* 2.514.3–4; *I.Smyr.* 637; 665.2–4).[13] While Smyrna promoted itself as πρώτη τῆς Ἀσίας (*prōtē tēs Asias*, "First of Asia,"),[14] Christ declared that he is ὁ πρῶτος καὶ ὁ ἔσχατος[15] (*ho prōtos kai ho eschatos*, "the First and the Last" 2:8),[16] providing a superior foundation for security as the eternal savior.[17] While affiliation with Smyrna's prominence is not necessarily the primary purpose for John using ὁ πρῶτος καὶ ὁ ἔσχατος (*ho prōtos kai ho eschatos*, "the First and the Last"),[18] the fact that Smyrna was πρώτη τῆς Ἀσίας (*prōtē tēs Asias*, "first of Asia") was such a celebrated idea that it would later be used on Smyrna's coinage. This demonstrates that the primacy of Smyrna in Asia was already a deep-seated ideology among her citizens by the first cent. AD.

The security derived from him who is called *the first and the last* is further strengthened by the concept of eternity. Two distinct aspects of eternity, past and future, are connected by καί (*kai*, "and") in the expression ὁ πρῶτος καὶ ὁ ἔσχατος (*ho prōtos kai ho eschatos*, "the First and the Last") to express the God/King as eternal.[19] This title is picked up from 1:17 and, in addition, it is used alongside the title *the Alpha and the Omega* in Revelation 22:13 to strengthen the eternity of Christ. The appellation *the first and the last* [20] is used of Yahweh by the prophet Isaiah (Isa 41:4; 44:6; 48:12).[21] Nielsen observes that Yahweh's court speeches against the nations in Isaiah 40–55 function as *cosmic lawsuits*[22] "in which Yahweh and his witnesses are placed on one side and the gods of the nations and their supporters on the other."[23] Lincoln observes that "Yahweh is both prosecuting witness and judge. . . . When there is no reply, Yahweh asserts that Yahweh is 'first, and will be with the last.'"[24] Delitzsch, commenting on Isaiah 48:12, gives one of the motivations for listening to Jehovah:

---

[13] Head, *BMC Ionia* nos. 405, 413–4; Ramsay, *Cities and Bishoprics*, 2:632; *Letters: Updated*, 185; Magie, *Roman Rule in Asia Minor*, 2:635–6; Klose, *Münzprägung*, 40; Cadoux, *Ancient Smyrna*, 291.

[14] Ramsay, Cities and Bishoprics, 2:632; Magie, Roman Rule in Asia Minor, 2:635–6.

[15] Worth links the allusion to the *last* with the historical setting of Smyrna but wonders, "If Jesus is *first* in the debated Pergamon-Ephesian-Symranaian sense of 'primary' or 'of most importance,' in what sense would Jesus be regarded as *last?*" Worth, Jr., *Greco-Asian Culture*, 75.

[16] Ramsay makes no comment about the title "the first and the last". Ramsay, *Letters: Updated*, 196.

[17] Krodel understands *first of Asia* as "mocked in Christ's self-designation." Krodel, *Revelation*, 110.

[18] Moyise argues that this title derives from Isaiah 44:6; 48:12 making it "remarkable that a statement concerning the eternity of God is juxtaposed with a statement about Christ's death and resurrection. The profundity of this combination weakens the case for supposing that it originated from a desire to allude to Smyrna's history." Moyise, *OT in Revelation*, 30–31.

[19] Thomas, *Rev 1–7*, 161 n.13; Swete, *Apocalypse*, 30–31.

[20] This is believed to be the only allusion to an OT passage in the letter to Smyrna.

[21] Charles, Revelation, 1:31; Hemer, Letters to the Seven Churches, 61; Beale, Revelation, 199; Moyise, OT in Revelation, 30–31.

[22] Andrew T. Lincoln, *Truth on Trial: The Lawsuit Motif in the Fourth Gospel* (Peabody, Mass.: Hendrickson, 2000), 39.

[23] Nielsen, *Yahweh as Prosecutor*, 25.

[24] Lincoln, *Truth on Trial*, 39.

the fact that Jehovah is אוּה (ever since Deut 32:39, the fundamental clause of the Old Testament *credo*), i.e., the absolute and eternally unchangeable One, the Alpha and Omega of all history, more especially of that of Israel, the creator of earth and heavens. . . . at whose almighty call they stand ready to obey, with all the beings they contain.[25]

The controversial law suit God has with his creation is held in the transcendent court of the covenant-making and covenant-keeping judge.

This primacy appellation in the SMR functions similarly because John, like Isaiah, demonstrates the transcendent claim of Yahweh throughout history in context of a covenant lawsuit.[26] Campbell argues, "The covenant mechanism provides the logic for such credibility and authority."[27] There is an elimination of any competition from either the emperor cult or the Cybele religion (Tyche, Τύχη, see Figs. 52, 54, 98, 108, 160; *Mart. Pionii* 15.7).[28] Yahweh transcends all others as *the first and the last*. Thus, the message to Smyrna opens with a classic transcendent statement for its preamble. Christ, in his role as the God/King, is described in terms of eternal transcendence, and his pre-eminence is contrasted with Smyrna's struggle for her own pre-eminence within Asia Minor.[29]

THE SUZERAIN: DEAD AND HAS COME TO LIFE—2:8C

The description of the suzerain continues with the phrase ὃς ἐγένετο νεκρὸς καὶ ἔζησεν, (*hos egeneto nekros kai ezēsen*) which is literally, *who became dead and lived again*. (2:8c).[30] This phrase, used alongside ὁ πρῶτος καὶ ὁ ἔσχατος

52. Small reliefs of the mother goddess Cybele/Tyche. Her image frequently appeared on the coins of Smyrna. The worship of Cybele was introduced to Rome as *Magna Mater* (Gr. "great mother") because the Romans believed that Aenaes, a member of the Trojan royal family, was their ancestor (30 BC–AD 395, from various sites in Western Anatolia).

---

[25] Franz Delitzsch, *Isaiah*, COT 7 (Grand Rapids, Mich.: Eerdmans, 1977), 251.

[26] For Isaiah, God's sovereignty was displayed in the raising up of Cyrus (Isa 44:28). Lincoln, *Truth on Trial*, 39; Weinfeld, "Common Heritage," 183.

[27] Campbell, "Findings, Seals, Trumpets, and Bowls," 79 n.33.

[28] Smyrna was home to a number of temples, particularly Sipylene Cybele and Zeus with other temples to the *Neokorie* and the temple of the *Tyche* depicted on the coinage of Smyrna. See *A Thriving Religious City*. Klose, *Münzprägung*, 38; Swete, *Apocalypse*, lxi; Akurgal, "Smyrna," 848; Cadoux, *Ancient Smyrna*, 202; Rousas John Rushdoony, *Thy Kingdom Come: Studies in Daniel and Revelation* (Vallecito, Calif.: Ross House, 2001), 107.

[29] Mulholland, *Revelation*, 99.

[30] Thomas explains that "the aorist ἔζησεν [Gr. *exēsen*] is ingressive and focuses on the beginning of life. Christ 'began to live' after death." Thomas, *Rev 1–7*, 161 b,14; Buist M. Fanning, *Verbal Aspect in New Testament Greek*, ed. J. Barton, Oxford Theology and Religion Monographs (Oxford, U.K.: Oxford University, 1990), 251–53. See BDAG, 336.

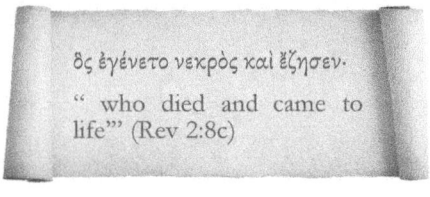

"ὃς ἐγένετο νεκρὸς καὶ ἔζησεν· 'who died and came to life'" (Rev 2:8c)

(*ho prōtos kai ho eschatos*, "the first and the last," 1:17; 2:8; 22:13), identifies Christ the suzerain and refers back to the description of the power of *the son of man* over death (1:18)[31]. Strand argues that the sovereignty of the transcendent Christ is demonstrated in his overcoming of death by the power of the resurrection to live again.[32] It unmistakably recalls the *resurrection* event. [33]

Commentators have identified several connections with the first cent. culture and the city of Smyrna around the idea of the resurrection.[34] Allusions to the resurrection may be found in the first cent. symbolic use of the phoenix, the building of the second city in 287 BC by Lysimachus (Strabo *Geogr.* 14.1.37; see *The History of Ephesus*), and the restoration of the city following its destruction by earthquake in AD 178 (Aristides *Orat.* 2.18; 2.19).

THE TRADITION OF THE PHOENIX

Some commentators see a comparison with the phrase *who died and came to life* with the resurrection of the phoenix bird (see Fig. 53).[35] This ancient Greek myth recounts how the phoenix bird dies, in flames or simply decomposing, before being reborn.[36] The tradition[37] of the phoenix bird[38] was legendary among classical writers,[39] and among the first cent. Jewish apocalyptic literature.[40] The phoenix was then adopted by some church fathers to illustrate the resurrection (*1 Clem.* 25; see *Quotes from Antiquity*; Tertullian *Res.* 13).[41]

---

[31] See, also Isa 41:4; 44:6; 48:12.
[32] Strand, "Note on the Covenantal Form," 261.
[33] Aune, *Rev 1–5*, 161; Lenski, *Revelation*, 1963, 96; Osborne, *Revelation*, 128.
[34] Hemer, *Letters to the Seven Churches*, 62; Scobie, "Local References," 609.
[35] Hemer, *Letters to the Seven Churches*, 63–64; 231 n.28; Beale, "Review of Colin J. Hemer," 110. Beale agrees that this view is possible but argues that it is not necessary as the connection with death and resurrection is made in the context.
[36] Roelof Van den Broek, The Myth of the Phoenix: According to Classical and Early Christian Traditions, trans. I. Seeger (Leiden: Brill, 1972), 146.
[37] Peck point out that: "similar stories of marvellous birds are found in Persian literature (of the bird Simorg) and in Sanskrit literature (of the bird Semendar)." Harry Thurston Peck, *Harper's Dictionary of Classical Literature and Antiquities* (New York, N.Y.: Harper & Brothers, 1898), 1246.
[38] Herodotus describes the appearance of the phoenix close to the shape and size of an eagle (*Hist.* 2:73.2) while How states that it "was represented on the monuments as a heron." Walter W. How and Joseph Wells, eds., *A Commentary on Herodotus: With Introduction and Appendices*, vol. 2 (Oxford, U.K.: Oxford University Press, 1990), 1:203.
[39] Herodotus *Hist.* 2:73.1–5; Plutarch *Mor.* 415c; Tacitus *Ann.* 2:6.20, 28; Pliny *Nat.* 10:2.3–5; Ovid *Metam.* 15.392–407; Ovid *Am.* 2.6.52; Achilles Tatius *Leuc. Clit.* 3.25; Philostratus *Vit. Apoll.* 3.49; Artemidorus *Oneir.* 4:47; Dio Cassius *Hist. Rom.* 58.27.1; Lactantius *Phoen.* 20.
[40] *2 En.* 12.1; 15.1; 19.3; *3 Bar.* 6.11; 7:5; *Sib. Or.* 8.39. The resurrection theme was not as prominent until later Christian writers. 2 Enoch identifies the phoenix in the company of the Cherubim and Chalkydri as "other flying elements of the sun" (*2 En.* 12:1; 15:1; 19:3) while 3 Baruch describes the phoenix beside the angel coming down from heaven (*2 Bar.* 6:11; 7:5) as the "guardian of the earth" protecting the earth from rays of the sun using its wings (*2 Bar.*

53. Painting of a phoenix from the Musicians Cave, part of the Sidonian caves, Beit Guvrin-Maresha National Park, Israel.

The legend was popular enough to travel through the centuries and leave an impression on the early church. To find biblical justification for its use, the first cent. church fathers incorrectly identified the Greek word φοῖνιξ (*phoinix;* Lat. *phoenix*), in Psalm 92:12 (LXX 91:12; *phoinix* = palm tree) and Job 29:18 with the phoenix bird.[42] The legend is best described by Clement (see the *Quotes from Antiquity*).

While there is no direct connection between the use of Σμύρνα (*smurna*) in the text of *1 Clements* 25:1–5 and the city of Smyrna, it is interesting to see the centrality of myrrh in the tradition of the phoenix.[43] Hemer confesses "its use in 1 Clement is rather puzzling, for it seems a very imperfect expression of the Christian idea".[44] The popularity of the legend of the phoenix throughout antiquity may explain Clement and Tertullian's (see *Quotes from Antiquity*) inclination to use it to illustrate the resurrection.[45]

Quotes from Antiquity

Let us observe the remarkable sign which is seen in the regions of the East, that is, the vicinity of Arabia. There is a bird, which is named the phoenix. This bird, the only one of its species, lives for 500 years. When the time of its dissolution and death arrives, it makes for itself a coffinlike nest of frankincense and myrrh [Gr. *smurna*] and the other species, into which, its time being completed, it enters and dies. But as the flesh decays, a certain worm is born, which is nourished by the juices of the dead bird and eventually grows wings. Then when it has grown strong, it takes up the coffinlike nest containing the bones of its parent, and carrying them away, it makes its way from the country of Arabia to Egypt, to the city called Heliopolis. There, in broad daylight in the sight of all, it flies to the altar of the sun and deposits them there, and then it sets out on its return. The priests then examine the public records of the dates, and they find that it has come at the end of the 500th year. (*1 Clem.* 25.1–5 [Lightfoot and Harmer 1989])

6:5–6).

[41] This Egyptian symbol of the rising sun also depicted the resurrection. According to Porphyry, Herodotus derived the idea from Hecataeus. Heliopolis was where the phoenix was specially revered (*1 Clem.* 25.3).

[42] Lightfoot, *The Apostolic Fathers*, 43 n.66.

[43] Herodotus *Hist.* 2:73, 86; Tacitus *Ann.* 6:20; Ovid *Metam.* 15.402; *1 Clem.* 25.1–5; Lactantius *Phoen.* 11, 20.

[44] Hemer, *Letters to the Seven Churches*, 63–64.

[45] Ibid., 23, ln. 25.

> **Quotes from Antiquity**
>
> Then take a most complete and unassailable, symbol of our hope, for it shall be an animated being, and subject alike to life and death. I refer to the bird which is peculiar to the East, famous for its singularity, marvelous from its posthumous life, which renews its life in a voluntary death; its dyeing day is its birthday, for on it it departs and returns; once more a phoenix where just now there was none; once more himself, but just now out of existence; another, yet the same. What can be more express and more significant for our subject; or to what other thing can such a phenomenon bear witness? God even in His own Scripture says: 'The righteous shall flourish like the phoenix;'(1) that is, shall flourish or revive, from death, from the grave—to teach you to believe that a bodily substance may be recovered even from the fire. Our Lord has declared that we are 'better than many sparrows:'(2) well, if not better than many a phoenix too, it were no great thing. But must men die once for all, while birds in Arabia are sure of a resurrection? (Tertullian *Res.* 13 [Holmes])

Aristides makes the connection between the phoenix and Smyrna in a speech before P. Cluvius Baximus Paullinus of Smyrna March 3, AD 157, that exalts Smyrna's beauty, entitled the *Smyrnaean Oration* (*Orat.* 2.18–21).[46] During his speech, delivered to recognize the restoration of Smyrna following the AD 178 earthquake, Aristides focuses on the theme of renewed life utilizing numerous resurrection terms (*Orat.* 2.18–21).[47] In his last speech Aristides compares the phoenix to Smyrna, causing Hemer to observe that "the successive reincarnations of the bird are likened to the successive refoundations of the city of Theseus and Alexander".[48]

As Aristides compares Smyrna with the phoenix to make a point of resurrection, so John uses a similar comparison with the resurrection of Christ and Smyrna. In addition, as Hemer points out, "most accounts of the phoenix, including that of Clement, emphasize the use of myrrh in its burial and reincarnation"[49] (*1 Clem.* 25.2). Hemer draws a connection between myrrh and Christ's burial when he writes that "later patristic interpreters read an allegory of the burial of Christ into the mention of myrrh in the Psalms and Canticles". [50] As mentioned earlier, myrrh was used in the humiliation and suffering of Christ, and for the Jew it may have had an indirect association for the preparation of the body as a prerequisite for the resurrection. Hemer speculates that Smyrnaeans may have known "the Gospel tradition in some of the several areas which linked myrrh with the resurrection of Jesus".[51]

---

[46] Behr, *Aelius Aristides and the Sacred Tales*, 91.

[47] Aristides uses the Greek terms *anegeiresthai* ("to wake up, raise"), *anabiwnai* ("a reviving"), *egregorsis* ("raise up, bring into being; wake, rouse"), and *anistanai* ("raise" [of the dead]), to apply to the city of Smyrna (*Orat.* 2.18–21).

[48] Hemer, *Letters to the Seven Churches*, 62–63; 230 n.19. Aristides makes similar connection with Smyrna and the phoenix throughout his speeches (*Orat.* 2.17.2; 2.18.9; 2.20.19).

[49] Ibid., 64.

[50] Ibid., 231 n.28.

[51] Ibid., 65.

The Resurrection of the City

A second cultural allusion to the resurrection may be found in the civic death/rebirth phenomena in the phrase "died and came to life again" (2:8).[52] Ramsay and Hemer both see in this phrase a connection with Smyrna's history; however, they see the connection in varying degrees.[53] Ramsay, following Strabo, holds that Smyrna lay in ruins for four centuries (*Geogr.* 6.14.1.37). Old Smyrna was destroyed in 600 BC by King Alyattes;[54] then reduced from a city (πόλις, *polis*) to a village system,[55] and it remained such for over 250 years (Herodotus *Hist.* 1.16.1–2).[56] Then Smyrna was resurrected from the dead to new life in the third cent. BC.[57] The Jewish community,[58] according to a second cent. inscription (*CIG* 3148.30), contributed 10,000 denarii toward a project to enhance the beauty of the city.[59] Smyrna's primacy as a city was enhanced by maritime trade which turned it into a commercial metropolis and increased the population[60] in John's day.[61] Calder could say as late as 1906 that Smyrna was "still one of the loveliest sights in the Levant".[62] However, the fire of 1922 destroyed most of the dwellings in the Greek section.[63] But it could not remove her beautiful setting on the water framed by Mount Pagus.

According to Ramsay, "died and came to life again" perfectly describes Smyrna's history so that "all Smyrnaean readers would at once appreciate the striking analogy to the early history of their own city which lies in that form of address".[64] Hemer is more guarded; he calls Ramsay's analysis "unnecessarily pedantic," but still agrees in principle with his assessment.[65] Moyise

---

[52] Moyise believes that this allusion is "extremely unlikely", but based on insufficient historical evidence. Steve Moyise, "Does the Author of Revelation Misappropriate the Scriptures?," *AUSS* 40, no. 1 (2002): 3–21.

[53] While Hemer questions the details of Ramsay's evidence for Smyrna's desolation, he still supports the basic thesis on more recent evidence. Ramsay, *Letters: Updated*, 251–52, 269–70; Hemer, *Letters to the Seven Churches*, 60–64, 76; Franz, "Propaganda, Power and the Perversion," 80; Sweet, *Revelation*, 651; Johnson, "Revelation," 438; Steve Gregg, *Revelation: Four Views: A Parallel Commentary* (Nashville, Tenn.: Nelson, 1997), 66; Barr, "The Apocalypse of John as Oral Enactment," 245 n.9; Mulholland, *Revelation*, 97–99.

[54] See *The History of Smyrna*.

[55] This is mentioned in a fragment of Pinder about 500 BC and in an inscription of 388 BC. Cadoux, *Ancient Smyrna*, 36.

[56] Calder, "Smyrna," 103; Aune, *Rev 1–5*, 160; Carroll, "Polycarp," 8; Magie, *Roman Rule in Asia Minor*, 876 n.66.

[57] Ramsay, *Letters: Updated*, 184; Hemer, *Letters to the Seven Churches*, 62–63; Barr, "The Apocalypse of John as Oral Enactment," 245 n.9.

[58] The Jewish Community was called "the Quondam Jews" (*CIG* 3148.30), whom Ramsay and Hemer identify as ordinary citizens of Smyrna. Ramsay, *Letters: Updated*, 198; Hemer, *Letters to the Seven Churches*, 9, 66.

[59] Ramsay, *Letters: Updated*, 198; Kistemaker, *Revelation*, 121; Barclay, *Revelation*, 1:1:92.

[60] See *The Population of Smyrna*.

[61] Barclay, *Letters*, 26; Kistemaker, *Revelation*, 121.

[62] Calder, "Smyrna," 97.

[63] Dobkin, Smyrna 1922: The Destruction of a City.

[64] Ramsay, *Letters: Updated*, 196.

[65] Moyise represents Hemer as more opposed to Ramsay than Hemer admits, when Hemer writes that we "must recognize that in fact Smyrna had a more nearly continuous history than Ramsay and his followers have allowed."

challenges the priority of the historical reference made by Ramsay and Hemer as "extremely unlikely," and agrees that "Smyrna's history is insufficient to explain the deliberate linking of a title for God ('First and the Last') and testimony to Christ's death and resurrection ('I was dead, and behold, I am alive forever and ever,' Rev 1:18)".[66] While there is reason to be cautious, there does appear to be sufficient historical evidence to argue that Smyrna would have been aware of her own historical rebirth leading to a deeper understanding of the "died and came to life again" phrase.

The risen Christ is encouraging news for a church about to experience suffering. Beale states that Smyrnaeans "could take comfort in their suffering because just as Christ had likewise suffered and overcome it, so too would they."[67] The risen Christ had been victorious over death; likewise, Smyrnaeans could face suffering and martyrdom knowing that their faithfulness would be rewarded with the crown of life.[68] Beckwith and Swete point out the implications for the Smyrnaean church: by remembering "that Christ himself, the eternal one, shared the martyr's death, but revived again,"[69] "so will his martyrs triumph over death" (2 Tim 2:8.[70] In the genealogical preamble, the God/King is identified as the eternal, transcendent, resurrected Christ, the alpha and omega, who was crucified and raised to life. The preamble functions in the same way as in the ANEVT in announcing the King.

Historical prologue—2:9

Christ is in the midst (μέσος, *masos*) of the churches (lampstands 1:13, 20); therefore, he is so intimately familiar with their circumstances (1:12–13) that he knows their afflictions, poverty, and slander as part of their "fellowship of his sufferings" (Phil 3:10). The relationship that Christ has with the churches is reflected in the covenant relationship with their God, and is central to their relationship with the King.

Within the ANEVT and after the preamble, the historical context is listed. This is where the suzerain records his knowledge of the past relationships with his vassals.[71] As indicated in the introduction, an important feature of the historical prologue is the notable similarity between the ANEVT and the prophetic message in terms of their use of the first person.[72] As in the ANEVT, the message to Smyrna also begins with the first person singular; οἶδά (*oida*) recounting the God/King's intimate knowledge of the churches.

Hemer, *Letters to the Seven Churches*, 78, 61–62; Moyise, OT in Revelation, 30.

[66] Moyise, OT in Revelation, 36.
[67] Beale, "Review of Colin J. Hemer, The Letters to the Seven Churches," 110.
[68] Mounce, *Revelation*, 76.
[69] Beckwith, *Apocalypse*, 453.
[70] Swete, *Apocalypse*, 31; Mounce, *Revelation*, 74.
[71] Thompson, *ANE Treaties*, 16.
[72] See chapter 3, *Historical Prologue*.

The Suzerain Knows Their Afflictions—2:9a

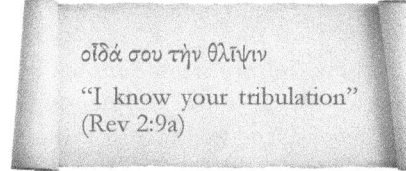

"I know your tribulation" (Rev 2:9a)

The omniscient God/King intimately knows the afflictions of the church of Smyrna: *I know of your afflictions* (οἶδά σου τὴν θλῖψιν, *oida sou tēn thlipsin* 2:9; never γινώσκω, *ginōskō*).[73] Huffmon and Boyle explain the common use of the term *know* (LXX οἶδα, *oida*, ידע, *'ry*) as a technical legal term by the Hittite and Akkadian treaties that is paralleled in the OT prophets (Amos 3:2; Hos 13:4–5).[74] They speculate that ידע (*'ry* "know") may "refer to mutual legal recognition on the part of the suzerain and vassal and may serve as a technical term for recognition of the treaty stipulations as binding."[75]

Early in Israel's history οἶδα (*oida*) was used to refer to an omniscient God who noticed the afflictions of his children in Egypt under taskmasters. This is why God states, "*I know* their sufferings" (Exod 3:7; οἶδα γὰρ τὴν ὀδύνην αὐτῶν, *oida gar tēn odunēn autōn* LXX).[76] Because God is omniscient, he knows the condition of the vassals; however, the use of the term *know* in the OT goes beyond a simple *care for* or *knowledge of*, it conveys the sense of covenant relationship (Hosea 2:22; 4:1; 5:4). Amos makes this clear when he states: "you only have I *chosen* (lit. *known* ידע, *'ry*) among all the families of the earth; therefore, I will punish you (*covenant curse*) for all your iniquities" (Amos 3:2). Harrelson acknowledges the technical covenantal usage of *know* in Amos, who "uses the verb 'to know' in the sense of the covenant relationship."[77] Harrelson also points out that in some passages *know* "refers to the vassal's 'knowing' the suzerain, i.e., to Israel's recognizing Yahweh as its (sole) legitimate God."[78] This indicates the reciprocal covenant relationship between Yahweh and Israel. The covenantal use of *know* is also an integral part of the New Covenant in Jeremiah: "I will give them a heart to *know* (ידע, *'ry;* οἶδα, *oida* LXX) me, that I am the LORD. They will be my people, and I will be their God, for they will return to me with all their heart" (Jer 24:7), and "No longer will a man teach his neighbour, or a man his

---

[73] οἶδα (*oida*) is used of the churches in three areas: "I know your works" (2:2, 19; 3:1, 8, 15), "I know your tribulation" (2:9), and "I know where you live" (2:13). It appears that this is conveying the clarity of the prophetic vision. Bandy, dependant on Mazzaferri, states that "judgment is clearly implied with the repeated οἶδα." Alan S. Bandy, "Word and Witness: An Analysis of the Lawsuit Motif in Revelation Based on the Witness Terminology," in *Unpublished Paper Presented at the Evangelical Theological Society*. (Valley Forge, Penn. November 17, 2005), 12; Mazzaferri, *Genre of Revelation*, 244.

[74] According to Huffmon the word *know* is used in both the sense of the god(s) recognizing "the king as a legitimate ruler" and "recognition of the treaty stipulations as binding." Huffmon and Parker point out a similar usage in the Akkadian text found at Mari and a Ugaritic text from Ras Shamra. Huffmon, "Treaty Background," 31, 33; Marjorie O'Rourke Boyle, "The Covenant Lawsuit in the Prophet Amos: III 1–IV 13," *VT* 21, no. 3 (1971): 344–45; Huffmon and Parker, "Further Note," 36–38.

[75] Boyle, "Covenant Lawsuit," 244; Huffmon, "Treaty Background," 34.

[76] For the use of οἶδα (Gr. *oida*) by Balaam in the Torah; cf. Graves, *SMRVT*, 193.

[77] Walter J. Harrelson, *Interpreting the Old Testament* (New York, N.Y.: Holt, Rinehart & Winston, 1964), 346; Bruce Vawter, *The Conscience of Israel; Pre-Exilic Prophets and Prophecy* (New York, N.Y.: Sheed & Ward, 1961), 95. On the silence of the prophetic use of the term *covenant*, see Mendenhall, *Law and Covenant*, 46.

[78] Huffmon, "Treaty Background," 35.

brother, saying, '*Know* the LORD,' because they will all *know* (ידע; *ry;* οἶδα, *oida* LXX) me" (Jer 31:34). The use of οἶδα (*oida*) is central both to the ANEVT as well as to the covenant relationship between God and his people.

Thompson argues that "a myriad of qualities, behavioural traits, religious commitments, psychosocial understandings, and social, political interactions coalesce into a term like 'tribulation.'"[79] Christ knows the history of *afflictions* (θλίβω, *thlibō*) experienced by the Smyrnaean church and endured at the "hands of its Jewish and heathen persecutors and oppressors."[80] Morris understands the tribulation to mean "the burden that crushes."[81] The omniscience of the God/King alone is great comfort for those facing afflictions,[82] but add to this the covenant relationship (*I know*) of the King with his subjects, and there is momentous encouragement. The evidence of local references in Smyrna and the other churches reinforces the fact that their King, who stands in the midst of the lampstands, is intimately knowledgeable of the afflictions that *crush the Smyrnaeans*.[83]

THE SUZERAIN KNOWS THEIR POVERTY AND RICHES—2:9B

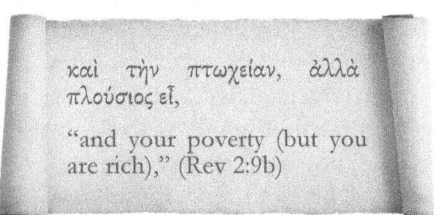

"and your poverty (but you are rich)," (Rev 2:9b)

The sovereign Lord also knows their poverty.[84] Osborne develops the special role of poverty within the old covenant. He states:

> Since the land belonged to Yahweh and has been given in trust to his people as a whole, there should not be poverty (cf. Deut 8:9; 15:1–18; 24:14–22). The prophets see the presence of poverty as a special proof of the apostasy of the nation as a whole, and 'the poor' becomes a semitechnical term for the remnant of Israel as persecuted by the rebellious nation (e.g., Isa 41:17; 51:21–23; 54:11). Both in the OT and the NT the poor have a special relationship to God as their protector.[85]

---

[79] Leonard L. Thompson, "A Sociological Analysis of Tribulation in the Apocalypse of John," in *Early Christian Apocalypticism: Genre and Social Setting*, ed. Adela Yarbro Collins, Semeia 36 (Decatur, Ga.: SBL, 1986), 170.

[80] Trench, *Commentary on Seven Churches*, 136. 1 Thess 3:4; Heb 11:37; Acts 20:23; Rev 1:9, etc.

[81] Leon L. Morris, *Revelation* (Downers Grove, Ill.: Intervarsity, 2007), 63.

[82] Lenski, *Revelation*, 1963, 97.

[83] Paul Gardner, "Review of Colin J. Hemer, The Letters to the Seven Churches of Asia in Their Local Setting," *Churchman* 101, no. 3 (1987): 279–80.

[84] The Qumran Scrolls often represent "poverty" (מחסור, *mhswr*) as a pious virtue (4Q415–418, 4Q423, 1Q26), however in the contest of the message to Smyrna it is contrasted with the loss of wealth, suggesting real suffering. Benjamin G. Wright III, "The Categories of Rich and Poor in the Qumran Sapiential Literature," in *Sapiential Perspectives: Wisdom Literature in Light of the Dead Sea Scrolls: Proceedings of the Sixth International Symposium of the Orion Center for the Study of the Dead Sea Scrolls and Associated Literature, 20–22 May, 2001*, ed. John Joseph Collins, Gregory E. Sterling, and Ruth A. Clements, STTJ 51 (Leiden: Brill Academic, 2004), 101–23.

[85] Osborne, *Revelation*, 130; Moffatt, *Revelation*, 5:355. The covenant is integrated into the identification of the martyrs in the Latin Apocalypse 4 *Esdras*: "Look not at the deeds of the impious but at those who have kept Thy covenants amid affliction" (4 *Esd* 8:27; i.e., the martyrs).

Malina points out that compared with modern economic arrangements, poverty took on a different meaning in antiquity, "Determined by the social structure considered primary in the culture in question."[86] Mullin makes this point about the label *poor*:

> [The term poor] applied, in particular, to the vast majority of the people in any city-state who, having no claim to the income of a large estate, lacked that degree of leisure and independence regarded as essential to the life of a gentleman. . . . "the poor" as recipients of a wealthy man's benevolence would primarily be unfortunate members of his own class. . . . "some ought to be poor" (Aristotle) and . . . . "deserve misfortune" (Cicero).[87]

Malina argues that the "cultural criteria of the day had the word 'poor' pointing to the socially impotent, while the label 'rich' or 'wealthy' attached to the greedy and avaricious." [88] If Malina's evaluation of NT social norms is correct, then the term *poverty* in this context may mean that these Christians were culturally and socially *impotent*. As a result of their Christian status the Smyrnaeans were adversely affected economically.

There is some debate over the meaning of πτωχεία (*ptōcheia*) in the NT. Trench distinguishes between πτωχός (*ptōchos*, having *nothing at all*) and πένης (*penēs*, having *nothing superfluous*).[89] However, Osborne argues that since πένης (*penēs*) – a quote from the LXX, and only found in 1 Corinthians 9:9 – the NT writers "make no such distinction."[90] But while the distinction may not be as sharp in the NT, the use of the term by the Greek writers indicates that it was understood to mean *utter destitution* in the culture of the day[91] and justified the use of πτωχεία (*ptōcheia*) as a life of extreme destitution and poverty, possibly leading to a life of beggary.[92]

The obvious question is "why was this church so poor in such a prosperous city" (Strabo *Geogr.* 6.14.1.15)?[93] Aune perceptively mentions that "the fact that no mention is made of the economic poverty of the other six Christian communities suggests that the situation of this congregation is unusual."[94] Smyrna's strong ties to Rome and the imperial cult (Tacitus *Ann.* 4.55–56),[95] combined with a significant Jewish population,[96] are factors which would cause

---

[86] Bruce J. Malina, "Wealth and Poverty in the New Testament and Its World," *Interpretation* 41 (1987): 360; Gildas H. Hamel, *Poverty and Charity in Roman Palestine, First Three Centuries C.E.*, NES 23 (Berkeley, Calf.: University of California Press, 1990).

[87] Redmond Mullin, *The Wealth of Christians* (Maryknoll, N.Y.: Orbis Books, 1984), 17; Royalty Jr., *Ideology of Wealth*, 175. According to Royalty, when Christ speaks of *wealth* he speaks in terms of a "Stoic philosopher . . . devaluing wealth and extolling the virtue of poverty" (*Ideology of Wealth*, 175). However, Christ is not promoting stoic philosophy; rather, he is acting as the sovereign protector.

[88] Malina, "Wealth and Poverty," 367.

[89] "πτωχός," LSJ 1550; "πτωχεία," GELNT 557.

[90] Osborne, *Revelation*, 129 n.2.

[91] "πτωχεία," GELNT 557; "πτωχός," LSJ 1550.

[92] "πτωχεία," TDNT 6:911.

[93] Johnson, "Revelation," 438; Cadoux, *Ancient Smyrna*, 228–29; Carroll, "Polycarp," 20; Ramsay, *Letters: Updated*, 193.

[94] Aune, *Rev 1–5*, 161.

[95] Johnson, "Revelation," 438.

difficulty for Christians.[97] Witherington suggests that their poverty "was possibly based in the guild system. To work at a particular trade one had to be a member of a guild, but the latter required participation in various pagan religious ceremonies."[98]

Hemer summarizes the possible causes for the poverty of Smyrna into four categories:[99] (1) Christians were the poorest class of society (1 Cor 1:26; Jas 2:5);[100] (2) the generosity of the Christians' gifts;[101] (3) their possessions are confiscated or stolen by aggressive neighbours (Heb 10:34);[102] and (4) persecution from the Jews and Romans resulting in the loss of their jobs (2 Cor 6:10; 8:2).[103] Most commentators combine one or more of these causes.[104] Several commentators combine Jewish and Roman persecution with confiscation of property and looting by hostile mobs. However, Thompson argues that the tribulation and suffering mentioned associated with Smyrna is future oriented and does not appear to refer to "present social distress."[105] This is certainly true of the future suffering in verse 10 (ἃ μέλεις πάσχειν, *ha melleis paschein*), but the afflictions and suffering of verse 8 are not connected to time (οἶδα, *oida*, perfect tense).[106]

By contrast, the God/King *parenthetically*[107] acknowledges the true character of the Smyrnaean overcomers. Even though the church members were poor socio-economically, God knows the real condition of his people. He states, *but you are rich* (ἀλλὰ πλούσιος εἶ, *alla plousios ei*). Rich is used in a metaphorical sense as treasure laid up in heaven[108] in Matthew 6:19–21 = Luke

---

[96] See *The Historical Setting of Smyrna*.

[97] Witherington III, *Revelation*, 98; Smalley, *Revelation*, 65.

[98] Witherington III, *Revelation*, 98; Schüssler Fiorenza, *Revelation: Vision*, 56.

[99] Hemer, *Letters to the Seven Churches*, 68.

[100] While Deissmann has been credited for the view that early Christians were predominantly from the lower social classes, the general consensus today is that Christians represented all strata within society. Gustav Adolf Deissmann, *Light from the Ancient East*, trans. Lionel R. M. Strachan (New York, N.Y.: Harper & Brothers, 1927); Edwin Arthur Judge, "The Social Pattern of Christian Groups in the First Century: Some Prolegomena to the Study of New Testament Ideas of Social Obligation," in *Social Distinctives of the Christians in the First Century: Pivotal Essays by E. A. Judge*, ed. David M. Scholer (Grand Rapids, Mich.: Baker Academic, 2007), 1–56; Scroggs, "The Sociological Interpretation of the New Testament: The Present State of Research," 168–71.

[101] Acts 2:45; 1 Cor 16:3; 2 Cor 8:2–5; Aune believes that this is "improbable." Aune, *Rev 1–5*, 161; Swete, *Apocalypse*, 32.

[102] Beale, *Rev*, 240; Caird, *Revelation*, 35; Mounce, *Revelation*, 74; Osborne, *Revelation*, 130; Robertson, *Word Pictures*, 6:302; William H. Simcox, *The Revelation of St. John the Divine*, CBSC (Cambridge, U.K.: Cambridge University Press, 1890), 13; Swete, *Apocalypse*, 31; Morris, *Revelation*, 64; Aune, *Rev 1–5*, 161; Trench, *Commentary on Seven Churches*, 136; Walvoord, *Revelation*, 61; Beckwith, *Apocalypse*, 453. Beckwith states that while this is "without intimation here," it is "conceivable."

[103] Charles, Revelation, 1:56; Caird, *Revelation*, 35; Hemer, *Letters to the Seven Churches*, 68.

[104] Ladd, *Revelation*, 42; Mounce, *Revelation*, 74; Trench, *Commentary on Seven Churches*, 136; Johnson, "Revelation," 438.

[105] Thompson, "Sociological Analysis," 149.

[106] Robertson, *Grammar*, 357.

[107] Robertson, *Word Pictures*, 6:302; Trench, *Commentary on Seven Churches*, 136; Lenski, *Revelation*, 1963, 97.

[108] Aune, *Rev 1–5*, 161.

12:33–34; Luke 6:20 = Matthew 5:3; Luke 12:21; 1 Corinthians 1:5; 2 Corinthians 6:10.[109] In a similar way, James employs the same Greek words referring to "those who are poor (πτωχός, *ptōchos*) in the eyes of the world to be rich (πλούσιος, *plousios*) in faith" (Jas 2:5).[110] Trench explains that John employs "a very beautiful parenthesis, declaring as they [these verses] do the judgment of heaven concerning this church of Smyrna, as contradistinguished from the judgment of earth."[111]

The Smyrnaeans were the opposite of the Laodiceans. Smyrna is intentionally contrasted with the *wealth* of Laodicea (3:17); the Laodiceans were spiritually poor, while the poor church in Smyrna was spiritually *rich*.[112] Despite Smyrna's physical suffering and poverty, the church's real condition was one of riches toward God.[113] That God is their sovereign and protector is a wealth of encouragement to an impoverished people. The God/King is not only protector but also preserver of impoverished Christians. Christ vindicates the poor in his interpretation of the Torah in the Beatitudes as they "inherit the kingdom of God" (Matt 5:3; Luke 6:20; compared with "inherit the crown of life" 2:10). Here, the God/King instead recognizes the rich spiritual value of his covenant people, and it is he who defines their true value.

THE SUZERAIN KNOWS THE ENEMY—2:9C

> καὶ τὴν βλασφημίαν ἐκ τῶν λεγόντων Ἰουδαίους εἶναι ἑαυτοὺς καὶ οὐκ εἰσὶν ἀλλὰ συναγωγὴ τοῦ σατανᾶ.
>
> "and the slander of those who say that they are Jews and are not, but are a synagogue of Satan." (Rev 2:9c)

Not only are the vassals known to the King, but the conduct of their enemies is also laid bare before his omniscient gaze. This gaze recognizes "*the slander* (βλασφημία, *blasphēmia*) *of those who say they are Jews and are not, but are a synagogue of Satan*" (2:9). Most lexicons define βλασφημία (*blasphēmia*) as reviling or railing in the sense of "'defaming God' . . . by claiming some kind of equality with God. Any such statement was regarded by the Jews of biblical times as being harmful and injurious to the nature of God."[114] Thayer defines this term as "impious and reproachful speech injurious to the divine majesty."[115] However, is the activity of βλασφημία (*blasphēmia*) directed solely at the Messiah, or is it also directed at Christians? Several commentators suggest that slander against God's people is essentially blasphemy against God and that they are difficult to separate.[116]

---

[109] Ibid.; Osborne, *Revelation*, 130. The Stoics also used wealth figuratively (Seneca *Ep. Mor.* 62:3; Philo *Somn.* 1:179; *Plant.* 69; *Sobr.* 56; *Fug.* 17).

[110] Walvoord, *Revelation*, 61.

[111] Trench, Commentary on Seven Churches, 136; Robertson, Word Pictures, 6:302.

[112] Beale, *Revelation*, 305; Robertson, *Word Pictures*, 6:302.

[113] Rom 8:32; Col 2:3; 1 Tim 6:18; Matt 6:20; 19:21; Luke 12:21; 2 Cor 8:9.

[114] "βλασφημέω; βλασφημία," *L&N* 33.400, 434; Robertson, *Word Pictures*, 6:302; Kiddle, *Revelation*, 27.

[115] "βλασφημία, βλασφημίας," *GELNT* 102; Eduard Lohse, "Synagogue of Satan and Church of God," *SEÅ* 58 (1993): 119.

[116] Osborne, *Revelation*, 131; Mulholland, *Revelation*, 101; Simcox, *Revelation*, 13; Lenski, *Revelation*, 1963, 97–98.

Lambrecht argues that *blasphemy* should not be understood theologically, as is the case elsewhere in Revelation (13:1, 5, 6; 16:11, 21; 17:3), but rather as Jewish slander[117] before pagan magistrates during court proceedings in Smyrna.[118] Following Roman law,[119] Lambrecht argues that "these Jews must have been *delatores* [Lat. "informers"],[120] [as] they formulate an *accusatio* [Lat. "accusation"]."[121] The context of imprisonment (2:10), as well as NT examples,[122] supports the forensic nature of this interpretation. The early church also recounts Jewish cursing and blaspheming against Christians,[123] including those in Smyrna (*Mart. Pol.* 12.2–3; 13:1; Ign. *Smyrn.* 1.2).[124]

This historical account provides evidence of the blasphemy against the church vocalized by enemies of the King of kings (see also 17:12–14). Polycarp (see Figs. 50, 51) interprets blasphemy in this light when he declares to the Roman authorities "How can I blaspheme my King who saved me?" (Eusebius *Hist. eccl.* 4.15.25 [Lightfoot and Harmer]). From the perspective of a theocracy, this slanderous language could be interpreted as treason toward the Great King (see also Ps 2). In the context of a covenant relationship, a word of slander against God's people is equivalent to an attack on the King (see imprecations Pss 69; 109; 137).[125]

However, within Revelation, Christ's Kingship as the "lion of Judah" (5:5) is radically redefined as the suffering/slain Lamb (5:6, 12; 13:8; see also Isa 53:7). The suzerain/vassal image is turned upside down and redefined in terms of Lamb Christology, which raises the suzerain/vassal relationship to a new level of significance. The vassal (Lamb) is the new suzerain standing in the center of the throne (5:6), ruling in humility and strength, worthy to open the

---

Justin recounts how "Barchochebas, the leader of the revolt of the Jews, gave orders that Christians alone should be led to cruel punishments, unless they would deny Jesus Christ and utter blasphemy" (*1 Apol.* 31.5–6 [Roberts]).

[117] Mark 15:29; Rom 38; 1 Cor 10:30; 1 Pet 4:4.

[118] John J. O'Rourke, "Roman Law and the Early Church," in *The Catacombs and the Colosseum: The Roman Empire as the Setting of Primitive Christianity*, ed. Stephen Benko and John J. O'Rourke (Valley Forge, Penn.: Judson, 1971), 179.

[119] Keener, *Revelation*, 116.

[120] William J. O'Neal, "Delation in the Early Empire," *CB* 55 (1978): 24–28; Judge, "The Social Pattern of Christian Groups in the First Century: Some Prolegomena to the Study of New Testament Ideas of Social Obligation," 71; Gary J. Johnson, "De Conspiratione Delatorum: Pliny and the Christians Revisited," *Latomus* 47, no. 2 (1988): 417–22.

[121] Berger, "*Accusatio*," *EDRL* 340; Jan Lambrecht, "Jewish Slander: A Note on Revelation 2:9–10," *ETL* 75, no. 4 (1999): 423; Philip L. Mayo, *Those Who Call Themselves Jews: The Church and Judaism in the Apocalypse of John*, PTMS 60 (Eugene, Oreg.: Pickwick, 2006), 62–63; Bandy, *Prophetic Lawsuit*, 220 n.127; Aune, *Rev 1–5*, 163.

[122] Mark 14:12–14; Matt 27:22–23; Luke 23:20–23; John 19:6–7, 14–15; Acts 13:5–12; 13:45; 18:13–17; 22:30; 23:25–30; 24:1–22; 25:1–27; 26:1–7, 11.

[123] Irenaeus *Haer.* 26.2; Tertullian *Scorp.* 10.10; Justin *Dial.* 16.2; 47.4,15, etc.

[124] Thompson points out that "Josephus says that Jews aren't inclined to 'blaspheme' (*Ag. Ap.* 236–7). One person's *blasphemia* is, of course, another person's confession of faith (cf. Artemis at Acts 19:37; Jesus on the cross at Matt 27:39; Gentiles at 1 Pet 4:4)." Thompson, *Revelation*, 68.

[125] N. John Day, "The Imprecatory Psalms and Christian Ethics" (Ph.D. diss., Dallas Theological Seminary, 2001), 201.

scroll (5:9). By contrast, those who were previously vassals (redeemed) will also reign as suzerain's with the Lamb (5:10; 7:9).[126]

ACTUAL JEWS

The God/King (suzerain) was aware of the deepest roots of treason in Satan's activity against God's rule in the Jewish synagogue. There is more than a resistance to the offence of the gospel; there is open hostility to the Christians in Smyrna by Jews ('Ιουδαίους, *Ioudaious*) who are vilified as belonging to Satan (2:9, 3:9). However, who were these Jews, identified with the Synagogue of Satan? Several proposals have been offered for their identification including: a "hybrid Jewish-pagan cult,"[127] Jewish proselytes,[128] Gentile Judaizers,[129] a Christian gnostic group within the church,[130] and Nicolaitans.[131] However, the general consensus of commentators is that

---

[126] Donald MacLeod, "The Lion and the Lamb," *PSB* 44, no. 3 (1950): 61–62; Loren L. Johns, *The Lamb Christology of the Apocalypse of John: An Investigation into Its Origins and Rhetorical Force*, WUNT 167 (Tübingen: Siebeck, 2003); Matthias Reinhard Hoffmann, *The Destroyer and the Lamb: The Relationship Between Angelomorphic and Lamb Christology in the Book of Revelation*, WUNT 203 (Tübingen: Siebeck, 2005); George Heyman, "Review of Loren L. John's The Lamb Christology of the Apocalypse of John: An Investigation into Its Origins and Rehetorical Force," *RBL* 2 (2005): 1–4; Robert M. Royalty Jr., "Review of Loren L. Johns The Lamb Christology of the Apocalypse of John: An Investigation into Its Origins and Rehetorical Force," *RBL* 8 (2006): 571–75; David J. MacLeod, "The Lion Who Is a Lamb: An Exposition of Revelation 5:1–7," *BSac* 164, no. 655 (2007): 323–40.

[127] Turner describes them as "some Judaeo-Gnostic sect." Cuthbert H. Turner, *Studies in Early Church History: Collected Papers* (Oxford, U.K.: Oxford University Press, 1912), 202, 225; Worth, Jr., *Greco-Asian Culture*, 84; Martin Hengel, *Judaism and Hellenism: Studies in Their Encounter in Palestine During the Early Hellenistic Period*, trans. John Bowde (Eugene, Oreg.: Wipf & Stock, 2003), 308; W. W. Tarn, *Hellenistic Civilization*, 3rd ed. (London, U.K.: Arnold & Co., 1952), 225.

[128] Pilhofer, "Early Christian Community of Smyrna," 6; David H. Stern, *Jewish New Testament Commentary* (Chandler, Ariz.: Messianic Jewish Resources International, 1992), 795–96; J. Ramsey Michaels, *Revelation* (Downers Grove, Ill.: InterVarsity, 1997), 74.

[129] Based on Ignatius (*Phld.* 6.1), Irenaeus (*Haer.* 1.30.15) and Hippolytus (*Haer.* 5.12). Marshall maintains that they were "Gentile Christians who had 'Judaized', that is, who adopted Jewish ways or even converted to Judaism, perhaps to avoid persecution by the Romans." John W. Marshall, *Parables of War: Reading John's Jewish Apocalypse*, ed. Peter Richardson, SCJS 10 (Waterloo, Ont.: Wilfrid Laurier University Press, 2001), 132–34; Stephen G. Wilson, "Gentile Judaizers," *NTS* 38, no. 4 (1992): 613–15; John C. Gager, *The Origins of Anti-Semitism* (Oxford, U.K.: Oxford University Press, 1983), 132; Kraft, *Offenbarung*, 60–61; Prigent, *L'Apocalypse*, 47–48; David Frankfurter, "Jews or Not? Reconstructing The 'other' in Rev 2:9 and 3:9," *HTR* 94, no. 4 (2001): 423.

[130] Newman, proposes a connection with the Gnostic sects, particularly the Ophites connected with serpent worship. Newman, *Rediscovering the Book of Revelation*, 48–49; A. Thomas Kraabel, "Impact of the Discovery of the Sardis Synagogue," in *Sardis from Prehistoric to Roman Times: Results of the Archaeological Exploration of Sardis, 1958–1975*, ed. George M. A. Hanfmann, William E. Mierse, and Clive Foss (Cambridge, Mass.: Harvard University Press, 1983), 180; John J. Pilch, "Lying and Deceit in the Letters to the Seven Churches: Perspectives from Cultural Anthropology," *Biblical Theology Bulletin* 22, no. 3 (1992): 131.

[131] Grys and Koester connect the *Synagogue of Satan* with the Nicolaitans arguing that the dispute was internal in the church. Alan Le Grys, "Conflict and Vengeance in the Book of Revelation," *ExpTim* 104, no. 3 (1992): 77; Helmut Koester, "GNOMAI DIAPHORAI: The Origin and Nature of Diversification in the History of Early Christianity," in *Trajectories through Early Christianity*, ed. James McConkey Robinson and Helmut Koester (Philadelphia: Fortress Press,

Ἰουδαίους (*Ioudaious*) refers to anti-Christian ethnic Jews[132] outside the church[133] who converted to Judaism to avoid Roman persecution, based on the evidence of the text and the historical context.[134] The parallel passage to the church in Philadelphia indicates that these Jews lie (ψεύδομαιν, *pseudomain* 3:9), either about their identity as Jews or the slander they perpetrate against the churches. Revelation 3:9 indicates a group outside the church, as the synagogue group would "come and fall down at your [Christ's] feet" (3:9). It may also imply that those faithful to God in the churches are true Jews. To the early Christians, these were Jews in name only.[135] Paul and Clement both put forth this view (Rom 2:28–29; Clement, *Recog.* 5.34), demonstrating that this idea was a general perception in the early church. In all probability these were local ethnic Jews who, though religious, had rejected Jesus and their true "Jewishness" in Him, and who were jealous of the Christians' exemption from participation in the imperial cult, and antagonistic to those in the church.[136]

HISTORICAL CONTEXT

The evidence for Jews living in Smyrna in the first and second century is persuasive.[137] In addition, Jewish persecution of Christians in the early church is well documented in Acts (6:9–15; 9:23, 29; 12:1–3; etc.) and the early church fathers. [138] In the accounts of the martyrdom of both Polycarp, bishop of Smyrna (see Figs. 50, 51; *Mart. Pol.* 1.13; 12.2; *FrgPol.* 64.23), and Pionius, priest in Smyrna (AD 250; *Mart. Pionii* 2.1; 3.6; 4.2, 8; 13.1; 14.1), the Jews had a hand in both acts (see *The Jewish Involvement in the Martyrdom of Polycarp and Pionius*).[139]

1971), 148–49.

[132] Trench, *Commentary on Seven Churches*, 137; Friedrich Düsterdieck, *Critical and Exegetical Handbook to the Revelation of John*, trans. Henry E. Jacobs, 3rd ed. (New York, N.Y.: Funk & Wagnalls, 1887), 138; Simcox, *Revelation*, 14; Robertson, *Word Pictures*, 6:302; Charles, *Revelation*, 1:57; Lenski, *Revelation*, 1963, 97; Gregg, *Revelation: Four Views*, 67; Alford, *Revelation*, 4:4:566; Joseph S. Exell, *Revelation*, BI 23 (Grand Rapids, Mich.: Baker, 1978), 137; Keener, *Revelation*, 115; Setzer, *Jewish Responses*, 101; Hemer, *Letters to the Seven Churches*, 67.

[133] Matt 3:9; John 8:33; Rom 2:28–29; 2 Cor 11:22; Gal 6:15 and Phil 3:4; *Pseud. Clem. Rec.* 5.34.

[134] Collins, "Vilification," 314; Beagley, *"Sitz Im Leben" of the Apocalypse*, 179; Beale, *Rev*, 25 nn.127, 31 15; Aune, *Rev 1–5*, 162; Osborne, *Revelation*, 131 n.4; Schüssler Fiorenza, *Book of Revelation*, 118; Hemer, *Letters to the Seven Churches*, 65–68; Düsterdieck, *Revelation*, 138; Thompson, *Revelation*, 68–69; Adela Yarbro Collins, "Persecution and Vengeance in the Book of Revelation," in *Apocalypticism in the Mediterranean World and the Near East: Proceedings of the International Colloquium on Apocalypticism, Uppsala, August 12–17, 1979*, ed. David Hellholm (Tübingen: Mohr Siebeck, 1983), 739.

[135] See Matt 3:9; John 8:33; 2 Cor 11:22; Phil 3:4ff.

[136] Hemer, *Letters to the Seven Churches*, 65–68, 76; Osborne, *Revelation*, 131; Collins, "Vilification," 313; Kiddle, *Revelation*, 27; Grant, "Smyrna," 927; Mulholland, *Revelation*, 360.

[137] Cicero *Flac.* 68; Philo *Legat.* 245; Josephus *J.W.* 2.398; 7.43; *Ant.* 14.115; *Sib. Or.* 3.271; Augustine *Civ.* 6.11; See chapter 6, *The Jewish Community*.

[138] Frend, Martyrdom and Persecution, 259.

[139] Although an argument from silence, Thompson points out that "Ignatius does not mention any conflict between Jews and Christians in his letter to either Smyrna or Polycarp." Thompson, *Revelation*, 70.

Lieu and others attempt to argue away the predominance of Jewish involvement in persecution, stating that it was an *illusion* of persecution, more Christian imagination than fact.[140] However, even given Lieu's best efforts to argue away the evidence, there appears to be sufficient justification for claiming a predominantly Jewish influence in early Christian persecution. Frend captures the argument well when he states that: "the troubles of the early Church were due as much to the virulence of the Christian-Jewish controversy as to any other cause" (see also Tertullian *Scorp.* 9.2; 10.6).[141] Thompson accounts for the conflict in this way:

> [the] conflict with the synagogue probably arises for John because, on the one hand, Christians had lost their 'Jewish shelter' in dealing with the Romans, and on the other hand, Asian Jews participated fully in the social and political [*sic*] structures of Roman life.[142]

Although συναγωγή *(synagōgē,* "synagogue") is used only once in the NT outside of Revelation (Jas 2:2), here it is used to distinguish the Jewish community from the Christian church and identify the Jews as the agent of persecution.[143] This is even more significant when it is remembered that John was also a Jew. The church in Smyrna was not understood as opposing Judaism generally but as opposing a specific group in the synagogue in Smyrna.

That the phrase *Synagogue of Satan* refers to some of those in the local Jewish synagogue (συναγωγή, *synagōgē*) at Smyrna (and Philadelphia),[144] and not the Christian church (ἐκκλησία, *ekklēsia*), is indicated from the distinctive use in Scripture of these Greek terms, and their polemical tone.[145] Although no synagogue has yet been discovered in Smyrna,[146] several

---

[140] Aune, following Hare, posits that "the suffering of Christians was in part a theological convention in Christian apologetics requiring little or no evidence." Aune, *Rev 1–5*, 163; Douglas R. A Hare, *The Theme of Jewish Persecution of Christians in the Gospel According to St. Matthew*, SNTS 6 (Cambridge, U.K.: Cambridge University Press, 2005); Lieu, "Accusations of Jewish Persecution," 279.

[141] Frend, *Martyrdom and Persecution*, 156–57; Beagley, *"Sitz Im Leben" of the Apocalypse*, 179; Peder Borgen, "Polemic in the Book of Revelation," in *Anti-Semitism and Early Christianity: Issues of Polemic and Faith*, ed. Craig A. Evans and Donald A. Hagner (Minneapolis, Minn.: Fortress, 1993), 199–211; Friedrich W. Horn, "Zwischen Der Synagoge Des Satans Und Dem Neuen Jerusalem: Die Christlich-Jüdische Standortbestimmung in Der Apokalypse Des Johannes," ZRGG 46, no. 2 (1994): 143–62; Steven J. Friesen, "Sarcasm in Revelation 2–3: Churches, Christians, True Jews, and Satanic Synagogues," in *The Reality of Apocalypse: Rhetoric and Politics in the Book of Revelation*, ed. L. Barr David, SBLSS 39 (Atlanta, Ga.: Scholars Press, 2006), 127–46; Paul B. Duff, "The 'Synagogues of Satan': Crisis Mongering and the Apocalypse of John," in *The Reality of Apocalypse: Rhetoric and Politics in the Book of Revelation*, ed. L. Barr David, SBLSS 39 (Atlanta, Ga.: Scholars Press, 2006), 147–68; Smallwood, *Jews Under Roman Rule*, 508.

[142] Thompson, "Sociological Analysis," 149; cf. 159–62.

[143] Trench, *Commentary on Seven Churches*, 139. Polemical remarks were also found within the Qumran community (1QM 15:9; 1:2; 4:9; 1QH 2:22).

[144] It is not the Synagogue *per se* that is spoken of in a derogatory fashion, but its connection with Satan.

[145] Some commentators argue for confusion of the two terms. However, Simcox points out that "the distinction between the two words is not always maintained: Israel is called "the Church" in Acts vii. 38, and the assembly of *Christian* Jews is called a "synagogue" in St James ii. 2, and almost in Heb X. 25." Simcox, *Revelation*, 14; Ladd, *Revelation*, 44; Trench, *Commentary on Seven Churches*, 139; Düsterdieck, *Revelation*, 138. *contra* Le Grys, "Conflict and Vengeance," 77. John Marshall takes exception to the distinction between synagogue and church and translates them respectively as *a group led together* and *assembly* with συναγωγή τοῦ Σατανα, translated *gathering of the adversary* (*Parables of War*, 83–87, 133).

[146] Because the modern city of Izmir stands over the ancient ruins of Smyrna the fact that no synagogue has been

inscriptions verify the presence of a Jewish synagogue.[147] An inscription dating from around AD 60–80 refers to a Jewess by the name of Rufina who was "head of the Synagogue" in Smyrna (*CIJ* 2.740–741, 743), indicating that, according to Jewish law, women were holding improper offices in the Synagogue.[148] In the account of Pionius' martyrdom, Jewish rulers (ἄρχων, *archon*; *Mart. Pionii* 13.2) and the synagogue (Ἰουδαῖοι καλοῶσιν εἰς συναγωγάς; *ioudaioi kalousin eis synagōgas*; *Mart. Pionii* 13.1) are mentioned as located in Smyrna.

Fox makes several conclusions from the evidence in *Mart. Pionii*. First, there was "a Jewish community of some size and rank."[149] Second, Jews and Gentiles lived in close proximity to each other. Third, the Jews had "contacts in the city's life."[150] Fourth, there was a "strong Jewish community" in Smyrna.[151] The historical evidence from the martyrdoms of Polycarp (see Figs. 50, 51) and Pionius concurs with the statement about Jewish persecution in Revelation 2:9; there is sufficient evidence to support the claim of a significantly hostile Jewish community in Smyrna in the first and second centuries. Perhaps the purported Jewish persecution in 2:9 reflects a hostility that betrays the closeness between the Christians (who are true Jews) and the non-Christian Jews (who are not true Jews).

ROLE OF THE IMPERIAL CULT

The imperial cult played a significant role in the Jewish treatment of Smyrnaean Christians.[152] Judaism benefited from legal exemptions (Lat. *religio licita*),[153] and the Christians were considered by many in the first cent. to be a sect within Judaism (Josephus *Ag. Ap.* 2.6; Philo *Legat.* 349–67).[154] Jealousy over this privileged status soon festered among the Jews, with many then

---

discovered does not carry a lot of weight. P. W. van der Horst uses the same argument for the absence of a synagogue in Aphrodisias. Horst, "Jews and Christians," 112.

[147] Hemer, "Unto the Angels of the Churches," 62; Lane Fox, *Pagans and Christians*, 481; Ramsay, *Letters: Updated*; Unger, *Archaeology and the New Testament*, 284.

[148] Bernadette J. Brooten, *Women Leaders in the Ancient Synagogue: Inscriptional Evidence and Background Issues*, BJS (Atlanta, Ga.: Scholars Press, 1982), 5; Trebilco, *Jewish Communities in Asia Minor*, 104–13; Worth, Jr., *Greco-Asian Culture*, 82–84. The inscription is from the second century and may not be reflective of conditions in the first century.

[149] Lane Fox, Pagans and Christians, 481.

[150] Ibid.

[151] Ibid., 482.

[152] The imperial cult was not the only influence on the Christian church as Thompson well documents. Thompson points out that "some of the fundamental elements contributing to the reality of tribulation and oppression were the Christian gospel of the crucified King, faithful behavior as imitation of Christ, social-political relations in the cities of Asia, and the affirmation of Christian separatism from the Roman world." Thompson, "Sociological Analysis," 170.

[153] Kraabel recounts how many Jews in Asia Minor still had the right to observe Sabbath along with other Jewish rites. Kraabel, "Judaism in Western Asia Minor," 6, 52, 136.

[154] Bandy, *Prophetic Lawsuit*, 122; Beale, *Revelation*, 8, 240; Osborne, *Revelation*, 131; Collins, "Vilification," 313; Ford, *Revelation*, 393; Shimon Applebaum, "The Legal Status of the Jewish Communities of the Diaspora," in *The Jewish People in the First Century*, ed. Shemuel Safrai and Y. Aschkenasy, vol. 2, CRINT (Assen: Van Gorcum, 1987), 420–63; Price, *Rituals and Power*, 220–21.

slandering the Christians.¹⁵⁵ Also, many of the Christians were converted Jews who lost their special Jewish status after AD 70, when the Romans removed their national status for Christians who converted, and Jewish leaders accused Christians of sedition before the magistrates.¹⁵⁶ Kiddle envisages the process for the persecution of Christians in Smyrna in this passage:

> In cities like Smyrna, where the Imperial cult had been enthusiastically fostered for many years, it must have been an easy matter to urge the authorities to action. . . . Once disowned by Judaism, of which to the casual eye of the pagan they might seem merely an eccentric and troublesome sect, they were at the mercy of the prejudices of local administrators. And certain Jews were not content with disowning and ridiculing their opponents; there is reason to believe that they would on occasion traduce them, laying malicious accusations at their charge—accusations, for example, of disloyalty and positive sedition.¹⁵⁷

It is probable that Jewish persecution is the context within which the Jewish synagogue in Revelation is to be understood as a *synagogue of Satan* (ἀλλὰ συναγωγὴ τοῦ σατανᾶ, *alla synagōgē tou satana*), and this reference sets the stage for the anticipated suffering in 10a. John aligns the activity of the synagogue with that of the great accuser Satan, the enemy of the Great King.¹⁵⁸

This is not an anti-Semitic¹⁵⁹ statement within the context of the NT setting; it is an accurate statement of the *Sitz im Leben* of the social climate in Smyrna. Ellul places the proper emphasis on the attack of the Jews when he states that they "are not condemned as Jews but as Persecutors."¹⁶⁰ As Bauckham explains, Jews were persecuting fellow Jews: "[The conflict was] an intra-Jewish dispute. This is not the Gentile church claiming to supersede Judaism, but a rift like that between the temple establishment and the Qumran community, who denounced their fellow-Jews as 'an assembly of deceit and a congregation of Belial'"¹⁶¹ (1QH 2:22).¹⁶²

---

¹⁵⁵ Mark 15:29; Rom 3:8; 1 Cor 10:30; 1 Pet 4:4.

¹⁵⁶ Justin *Dial.* 16.4; 47.4; 93.4; 95.4; 96.2; 108.3; 133.6; 137.2; Thompson, "Sociological Analysis," 149.

¹⁵⁷ Kiddle, *Revelation*, 27; Osborne, *Revelation*, 130; Beale, *Revelation*, 240; Mulholland, *Revelation*, 360.

¹⁵⁸ Trench, *Commentary on Seven Churches*, 139; Caird, *Revelation*, 35; J. L. Campbell, *The Patmos Letters* (London, U.K.: Morgan & Scott, 1898), 89. Campbell points out that the phrase *throne of Satan* is used in Pergamum "when the hostility was enforced by the heathen."

¹⁵⁹ Some scholars have claimed that John reflects the anti-Semitic attitudes of the early church fathers like Chrysostom. Jocelyn Hellig, *The Holocaust and Antisemitism: A Short History* (Oxford, U.K.: One World, 2003), 205–9; Sander L. Gilman, Steven T. Katz, and Moshe Lozer, eds., "The Lamb and the Scapegoat: The Dehumanization of the Jews in Medieval Propaganda Imagery," in *Anti-Semitism in Times of Crisis* (New York, N.Y.: New York University Press, 1993), 38–80. Friesen also charges Hemer with "anti-Semitic stereotypes." "Revelation, Realia, and Religion" 305. *contra* Rushdoony, *Thy Kingdom Come*, 107–8; Trench, *Commentary*, 139. According to Aune, the term Ἰουδαίους (Gr. *Ioudaios*) here is not meant to condemn Jews generally "but only those associated with synagogues in Smyrna and Philadelphia." Aune, Revelation 1–5, 162.

¹⁶⁰ Jacques Ellul, *Apocalypse: The Book of Revelation*, trans. George W. Schreiner (New York, N.Y.: Seabury, 1977), 130.

¹⁶¹ *Synagogue of Satan* is understood against the parallel in the assembly of Belial and the syncretistic worship of Zeus in the Jewish synagogues in Mysia and Delos. Ford, *Revelation*, 393; W. O. E. Oesterley and T. H. Robinson, *A History of Israel* (Oxford, U.K.: Oxford University Press, 1932), 424.

¹⁶² Bauckham, *Theology of Revelation*, 124.

Stuckenbruck points out that the persecution may have been in the form of verbal attacks: "Some form of social or political persecution is, however, not a necessary inference from the text. The 'slander' may, more generally, presuppose a situation of mutual conflict among members of both religious communities who traded accusations in accordance with their respective interests."[163]

As several scholars point out, persecution in the first cent. was not a widespread phenomenon,[164] and the Synagogue dispute is only mentioned in Smyrna (2:9) and Philadelphia (3:9).

SUMMARY

God, the Great King, is familiar with the Smyrnaean plight, and intimately aware of their afflictions, their poverty, and the schemes of their enemy. The persecution by the Jewish elements in their community led to affliction and may have contributed to their poverty. The King is not only protector, but also preserver of impoverished vassals. He pronounces them spiritually rich toward God. In this passage, the suzerain/King recognizes the rich spiritual value of the covenant people and the suzerain's protection of the vassals[165] against the slanderous behavior of Satan's instrument, the Jewish synagogue. There is history between God and his children, evident from the similar message to Philadelphia where the King declares that he has loved (ἠγάπησά, ēgapēsa) them (3:9). The message to Smyrna is not God entering into a covenant relationship with his people, but a demonstration of a historical covenant relationship rooted in love. The lawsuits were brought against a people who already had a covenant relationship with a covenant-making and covenant-keeping God (Deut 5:10; 7:12–13). There is evidence of a strong history between Yahweh and his children (suzerain/vassal). Verse 9 functions in the same way as the historical prologue of the ANEVT and Deuteronomy because it acknowledges God's relationship with his people by describing their suffering and poverty and preserving them as spiritually rich toward God.

ETHICAL STIPULATIONS—2:10

The loyalty of the churches is called for through obedience to stated ethical stipulations. While the stipulations for most of the churches involved correction of deficiencies, Smyrna and Philadelphia were called to continued faithfulness. The stipulations surrounding Smyrna are given in terms of two imperatives—*Do not fear*, and *Be faithful*—and in response the king pledges to give *the crown of life*.

---

[163] Stuckenbruck, "Revelation," 1541; Thompson, *Apocalypse and Empire*, 126.

[164] Most scholars do not accept Eusebius' accounts of widespread persecution (*Hist. eccl.* 3.17–20; 5.8.6); cf. Sweet, *Revelation*, 26; Collins, "Dating," 33; Thompson, "Sociological Analysis," 153.

[165] The role of the suzerain in protecting the vassals from their enemies is evident in Deuteronomy (7:23; 23:14; 31:5; 32:29) and the ANEVT. "Treaty between Mursilis II and Tuppi-Teshshup of Amurru" Beckman, *Hittite Diplomatic Texts*, 61 §§8, 9. There is a functional equivalence in the way the historical prologue is used in the SMR to express protection and assurance for the suffering church.

Within the ANEVT context, the loyalty of the vassals to the suzerain was also demonstrated by their obedience to the obligations of the stated stipulations.[166] In addition, Thompson observes that the treaty stipulations were the "invention of the suzerain alone, without any consulting with the vassal who was merely bound by oath to render obedience."[167]

Strand points out striking similarities between Revelation and the ANEVT:

> The whole concept of vassal obligations within the covenant relationship is built upon the prior goodness of the suzerain. . . . Obedience to the covenant stipulations—summarized in the book of Revelation as "the commandments of God" and "the testimony of Jesus" (12:17; cf. 14:12)—represents the Christian's obligation of love that stems from Christ's own prior love.[168]

The stipulations are framed in covenant terms as obligations for God's people to be faithful. In the message to Smyrna God grants the crown of life by grace and not due to any inherent right of the vassal.

Thompson also observes that there is "no evidence that the suzerain bound himself by any kind of oath, although, no doubt, the treaty relationship was intended to protect the vassal from capricious attack by the suzerain."[169] Obviously, this point breaks down with God the suzerain, as God is unchangeable, long-suffering, and gracious. Christ the king "holds the keys of death and Hades" (1:18); thus, he secures the "crown of life" (2:10), and provides protection from "the second death" (2:11) for his vassals. In addition, in the covenant, God binds himself in oath to his vassals through the cutting of the animals (Gen 15:9–18a), symbolizing the consequences in the event of God's non-compliance (Jer 39:18). Similarly, in Revelation's Lamb Christology, the cutting (slaying) of the Lamb[170] played a central role (5:6, 12; 7:14; 12:11; 13:8) in God's redemptive work. Christ binds himself to his people through the redemptive work of the cross. This demonstrates how much better God's covenant is compared to the ANEVT.

First Imperative: Do Not Fear—2:10a

The stipulations begin with the suzerain's first imperative: "do not fear the things which you are about to suffer" (μηδὲν φοβοῦ ἃ μέλλεις πάσχειν, *mēden phobou a melleis paschein* 2:10). The phrase is emphatic according to Osborne, who translates it "don't be afraid of anyone."[171] Beale paraphrases it this way:

> they are "not to fear" the imminent trial because their lives and destiny are in the hands of the eternal Pantokrator of history, who has already experienced persecution, even to death, and yet overcame it through resurrection.[172]

---

[166] Mendenhall, "Covenant Forms," 59; Shea, "Covenantal Form," 72; Thompson, *ANE Treaties*, 16.
[167] Thompson, *ANE Treaties*, 13; Mendenhall, "Covenant Forms," 60.
[168] Strand, "Note on the Covenantal Form," 264.
[169] Thompson, *ANE Treaties*, 13.
[170] See Weinfeld for the details in the ANEVT of killing a sacrificial lamb to ratify the treaty. Weinfeld, *Deuteronomic School*, 102–4.
[171] Osborne, *Revelation*, 132.
[172] Beale, *Revelation*, 242.

> μηδὲν φοβοῦ ἃ μέλλεις πάσχειν. ἰδοὺ μέλλει βάλλειν ὁ διάβολος ἐξ ὑμῶν εἰς φυλακὴν ἵνα πειρασθῆτε καὶ ἕξετε θλῖψιν ἡμερῶν δέκα. γίνου πιστὸς ἄχρι θανάτου,
>
> "Do not fear what you are about to suffer. Behold, the devil is about to throw some of you into prison, that you may be tested, and for ten days you will have tribulation." (Rev 2:10a)

A similar logical argument is put forth in Revelation chapter 1 where the great motivation against fear is the eternal victory of the King: "Fear not (μηδὲν φοβοῦ, *mēden phobou*); I am the first and the last" (ver. 17).[173]

Swete points out the need to be reminded of the victorious accomplishments of the King as "there were worse things in store than πτωχεία [*ptōcheia*, "Poverty"] or even βλασφημία [*blasphēmia*, "slander"]; imprisonment, perhaps death, might await the faithful at Smyrna"[174] (2:10). Cyprian states, "In the Apocalypse, divine protection is promised to our sufferings. 'Fear nothing of these things,' it says, 'which thou shalt suffer'" (*Fort.* 11.76 [Roberts]). The divine protection of the Great King is the greatest comfort for the believer in times of suffering.

THE SUZERAIN'S ADVERSARY—THE DEVIL

The Smyrnaean church must contend with more than prison and torture; the spiritual world is active with more than mortals. The devil (ὁ διάβολος, *ho diabolos*)[175] is also at work behind the scenes, affecting disorder:[176] the sentence "about to throw some of you into prison" (2:10 ἰδοὺ μέλλει βάλλειν[177] ὁ διάβολος ἐξ ὑμῶν εἰς φυλακὴν, *idou mellei ballein ho diabolos ex humōn eis phulakēn*). Job (1:2), along with other biblical accounts,[178] provides a similar heavenly perspective from which to view this activity. However, as in the book of Job (Job 1:12; 2:6), Satan's activities are restricted by the sovereign King.[179] The devil's schemes are not to be feared for behold (ἰδού, *idou*, "behold"),[180] they are used by God to bring about his sovereign purposes (Acts 2:23, 36; 4:10).[181]

---

[173] Robertson, *Word Pictures*, 6:301.

[174] Swete, *Apocalypse*, 32; Robertson, *Word Pictures*, 6:301.

[175] The reason for John's change of the title "Satan" in 2:9 to "Devil" here is unclear. Osborne's suggestion that it "is probably for emphasis" is unsatisfactory since there is no support and because the LXX uses the terms synonymously. Osborne, *Revelation*, 133.

[176] Ellul, Apocalypse, 131; Tait, Messages to the Seven Churches, 199.

[177] *Keep on casting.* According to Thomas, "the durative idea of the present tense of βάλλειν [*ballein*] is in keeping with the continuation of imprisonment suggested by the ten-day length of the imprisonment." Thomas, *Rev 1–7*, 167 n.42; Beckwith, *Apocalypse*, 454.

[178] Zech 3:1–2; Luke 22:3; 23:2; John 13:2, 27; 19:12; Acts 17:5–8; 24:2.

[179] Osborne, *Revelation*, 133; Wilcock, *Heaven Opened*, 46.

[180] Hill, *NT Prophecy*, 78.

[181] Beale, *Revelation*, 242.

Whether the persecution is carried out, as Kiddle believes, by the "Imperial authorities,"[182] or as Bell proposes, by the Jewish element within Smyrna,[183] Satan is still at the root of both instruments. The procedure is described by Bell stating that the Jews "as private citizens, will bring charges against the Christians before the local magistrate and demand that he take action against them."[184] As indicated already, Satan is ascribed a significant role in the account of the martyrdom of Polycarp (see Figs. 50, 51; *Mart. Pol.* 2.4; 17.1) and was a common theme in the martyrdom accounts of the early church. This indicates a consciousness of satanic activity in the suffering of early Christian martyrs.[185] Here the Smyrnaean suffering and possible martyrdom is directly linked to the immediate treasonous activity of the devil, the antagonist of the Great King.

THE SUZERAIN'S TESTING—SUFFERING

The stipulations declared by the suzerain in the form of the imperatives "do not fear" (2:10a), and "be faithful" (2:10b) take on greater significance when the various elements are listed. The vassals may be expected to experience suffering, prison, testing, tribulation, and possibly death. God, the Great King, is conscious of the condition of his people, and, much like Job, brings them through a period of testing to purify them.

Prison: The partitive construction of ὑμῶν (*humōn*, "ten") with ἐξ (*ex*) indicates that the imprisonment and suffering was not universal. Several commentators recognize the idiomatic use of the partitive construction in the middle of verse ten (ὑμῶν, *humōn*, πειρασθῆτε, *peirasthēte* and ἕξετε, *exete*) and conclude that *only some* (see also Luke 11:49; Rev 3:9; 11:9)[186] from within the church would experience the suffering and imprisonment mentioned.[187] If John were speaking to the whole church collectively he would have used "*you* (singular) will be cast into prison." Since he wants to say "some of you," he is forced to use the plural form of *you* with the partitive construction.[188]

In support of the short-term theory of *ten days,* Krodel states that the Romans never used incarceration for an extended period as punishment.[189] An understanding of the purpose of

---

[182] Kiddle, *Revelation*, 28; Mounce, *Revelation*, 76. *contra* Bell, Jr., "Date of John's Apocalypse," 101.

[183] Bell, Jr., "Date of John's Apocalypse," 101.

[184] Ibid.

[185] *Mart. Asc. Isa.* 3.11; 5.1; *Mart. Ignat.* 7; Justin *Dial.* 5; *1 Apol.* 5; 30.78; 57.1; 63.10; 131.2; Origen *Cels.* 6:27; Cyprian *Laps.* 1, 2; Eusebius *Hist. eccl.* 5.1.16; Trench, *Commentary on Seven Churches*, 143; Lieu, "Accusations of Jewish Persecution," 279–95. For a detailed analysis of the role of the devil in martyrdom, see Lieu.

[186] Hemer shows that the grammatical construction also points to Johannine authorship. "The partitive with ἐκ [*ek*] expresses the object of a verb in 2.10 and the subject in 11.9 (cf. John 6.39; John 21.10, with ἀπό [*apo*]; 2 John 4, all in 'Johannine' writings." Hemer, *Letters to the Seven Churches*, 267 n.43; Thomas, *Rev 1–7*, 167 n.39; Beckwith, *Apocalypse*, 454; Robertson, *Word Pictures*, 6:302.

[187] Thomas, *Rev 1–7*, 167 n.43.

[188] Aune, *Rev 1–5*, 158.

[189] Krodel, *Revelation*, 112; Brian M. Rapske, *Book of Acts in Its First-Century Setting: Paul in Roman Custody*, BAFCS 3 (Grand Rapids, Mich.: Eerdmans, 2004), 19. Rapske corroborates Krodel's finding stating that "prisoners in this

ancient prison systems may be helpful here in determining the purpose of the imprisonment and testing. Were prisons used for punishment,[190] or for holding prisoners for trial and execution, or both? Rapske lists six different uses for prison in the Roman world, including protection, remand, awaiting sentence, execution, coercion (*coercitio*),[191] and punishment.[192] He comments, "whether temporary or lifelong, it [prison] is nowhere actually threatened in Republican legislation and no legal provisions for it seem to have been made."[193] In fact, Rapske states that in the Imperial period "confinement is explicitly prohibited as a punishment for citizens."[194] In support Rapske quotes Ulpian who states that imprisonment was explicitly forbidden as punishment: "prison indeed ought to be employed for confining men, not for punishing them" (*Dig.* 48.19.8.9). Further support comes from Callistratus who wrote the following in the third cent. AD:

> in the mandates given by the emperors to provincial governors, it is provided that no one is to be condemned to permanent imprisonment; and the deified Hadrian [AD 117–135] also wrote a rescript to this effect (Ulpian *Dig.* 48.19.35).

However, Ulpian's comments are undermined, as "Governors are in the habit of condemning men to be kept in prison or in chains" (*Dig.* 48.19.8.9; see Josephus *Ant.* 20.9.5).[195] Krodel demonstrates from the letter of Pliny how death could follow imprisonment "unless the Christians apostatized, 'cursed' Christ, and worshiped the emperor."[196] Therefore, the most likely understanding of prison in the context is as a method of confinement, with the expectation and real possibility of physical death (2:10).[197] The jurist Venuleius Saturninus (second cent. AD) confirms this: "Should the accused confess, he shall be thrown into a public prison until sentence is passed on him" (Philostratus *Vit. Apoll.* 7:21 [Conybeare, LCL]). Where

---

situation [imprisonment] were simply awaiting death; practically speaking, they were suffering punishment."

[190] Worth views Smyrna's punishment as "imprisonment alone" (*Greco-Asian Culture*, 77). Hemer, following Ramsay, suggests that prison was never used as a punishment in ancient times (*Letters*, 68; Ramsay, *Letters: Updated*, 199). Berger and Lintott assert that "Roman criminal law did not recognize the imprisonment of free persons as a form of punishment" ("Prison," *OCD* 1248). However, Mounce cautions that while most commentators observe that prison, in the first century, was more a place to await execution, several NT passages (Acts 16:23; 2 Cor 11:23) suggest that prison "also served as a place of temporary confinement and punishment" (*Revelation*, 76); cf. Morris, *Revelation*, 64. The cost to the city for mere confinement would be an unnecessary burden, and, according to Pliny, some cities used the unreliable service of slaves (Pliny *Ep.* 10.19, 20). See Jones, *Greek City*, 213.

[191] Ferdinand H. Hitzig, "Carcer," *PW* 3:1578; Gottfried Schiermann, "Carcer," in *BrillPauly*, vol. 3 (Leiden: Brill, 2007), op. cit.

[192] Rapske, *Paul in Roman Custody*, 10–20; Krodel, *Revelation*, 112; Hemer, *Letters to the Seven Churches*, 68; Osborne, *Revelation*, 133. Berger and Lintott only list three possibilities for imprisonment: (1) to enforce obedience to the magistrate's decisions (*coercitio*); (2) to detain until trial (*custodia reorum*); or (3) to detain after trial until execution (*OCD* 1248).

[193] Rapske, Paul in Roman Custody, 17.

[194] Rapske, *Paul in Roman Custody*, 17.

[195] See Rapske for more examples of prison as punishment (*Paul in Roman Custody*, 16–20).

[196] Krodel, *Revelation*, 112.

[197] Osborne, *Revelation*, 133; Thomas, *Rev 1–7*, 168; Johnson, "Revelation," 438.

Roman citizens were involved, sometimes the governors had to delay execution to confirm the sentence or refer the case to a higher court (Ulpian *Dig.* 28.3.7; 48.22.6); in fact, the phrase "being cast into prison" was used synonymously with execution.

Testing: The purpose for the imprisonment is "in order (ἵνα, *hina*) that you may be tried (πειρασθῆτε, *peirasthēte*)."[198] Debate exists over identification of the passive agent responsible for the testing. Is it the King or the adversary who is behind this testing? Πειράζω (*peirazō*) can be translated either *test* from God[199] or *tempt* from the Devil as in the temptation of Christ.[200]

Alford suggests that if testing were intended, then δοκιμασθῆτε (*dokimasthēte*, "may be approved") would have been used rather than πειράζω (*peirazō*).[201] However, the fact remains that πειράζω (*peirazō*) is used in the context of testing in other passages (see above). Therefore, πειράζω (*peirazō*) could have the meaning of testing in Revelation 2:10.

Osborne has provided a case for both meanings, which seems more appropriate given the use of the devil in the context (2:9), and of "μέλλει [*mellei*] which carries overtones of divine destiny each time it is used."[202] Tested (πειράζω, *peirazō*) is used with the Ephesian church (2:2) to determine the authenticity of the false apostles, so πειράζω (*peirazō*) in 2:9 could bear a similar meaning, referring to a test of their faith. The Great King employs the tempting of Satan for the *purpose* (ἵνα, *hina*) of strengthening his vassal's loyalty and faith by these tests.[203]

Completeness of Testing: Christ appears to provide a duration for the afflictions (tribulation 2:9) of *ten days*. A debate plays out on several levels over the meaning and significance of these ten days.[204] The majority of commentators take the *ten days* as symbolical/figurative.[205] What do *days* represent? Are they 24 hour periods,[206] years[207] or

---

[198] Robertson, *Word Pictures*, 6:302; Thompson, *Revelation*, 69.

[199] 1 Pet 1:7, 4:12; Luke 4:12; Jas 1:2–3; Heb 11:17. Lenski, *Revelation*, 1963, 99.

[200] See, also Matt 4:1; Mark 1:13; Luke 4:13; Gal 6:1; 1 Thess 3:5; 1 Cor 10:13; Heb 2:18; Jas 1:13; ὁ πειράζων [*ho peirazōn*] is a title for *the Devil*. Matt 4:3; "πειράζω," L&N 27.46, 332; 88.308, 775–6; Trench, *Commentary on Seven Churches*, 143–44; Swete, *Apocalypse*, 32; Simcox, *Revelation*, 14.

[201] Alford, *Revelation*, 4:4:566; Thomas, *Rev 1–7*, 168.

[202] Osborne, *Revelation*, 133; Thomas, *Rev 1–7*, 168; Swete, *Apocalypse*, 32; Beckwith, *Apocalypse*, 454.

[203] Job 1:8–12; 22:25; 23:10; 32:10; Beale, *Revelation*, 242.

[204] Hemer makes an unlikely local reference connection, based on inscriptions, with "gladiatorial contests" but acknowledged that the "possibility should not be pressed too far," while Barr connects them to the ten days of mourning in the "Rites of Niobe"; *contra* Osborne, *Revelation*, 134. Hemer, *Letters to the Seven Churches*, 69–70; Barr, "The Apocalypse of John as Oral Enactment," 245 n.9.

[205] Hoeksema points out that "it may safely be adopted as a general rule that the indications of time and space in the *Book of Revelation* are to be taken in the symbolical sense of the word." Hoeksema, *Behold, He Cometh!*, 71; Ramsay, *Letters: Updated*, 200; Martin, *Seven Letters*, 61; Beale, *Rev*, 243; Bauckham, *Climax of Prophecy*, 263 n.35.

[206] Thomas, *Rev 1–7*, 170–71; Beale, *Revelation*, 243 n.62. Beale disagrees with Thomas's argument because of his failure to recognize "a literary allusion to Daniel" (2:10; see also Dan 1:12–15).

[207] If a day is taken as equal to one calendar year (Num 14:34; Ezek 4:6; Dan 9:24–26; 12:11; Rev 11:2, 3; 12:6), ten days of persecution would be equal to ten years, the duration of the Diocletian persecution (AD 303–313). Tait, *Messages to the Seven Churches*, 204; Walter Scott, *Exposition of the Revelation of Jesus Christ* (Westwood, N.J.: Revell, 1968), 72. *contra* Thomas, *Rev 1–7*, 169 n. 47.

extended periods of time?[208] Is there an allusion to the local history, and literature?[209] Is this extended period, represented by the number ten, a short,[210] long,[211] prolonged (full),[212] or indefinite period[213] such as symbolical years? Because so many able scholars have proposed such a variety of theories,[214] caution must be exercised in the interpretation of this verse. The meaning may well be a combination of several views, as argued by some commentators.[215]

Several commentators identify ἡμερῶν, (hēmerōn) in Rev 2:10 as a genitive of time.[216] The significance of the genitive of time, according to Dana and Mantey, is "distinction of time rather than point of time (locative) or duration of time (accusative)."[217] Robertson maintains that the genitive "is the case of genus (γένος, genos) or kind."[218] Thus, Osborne maintains that in Revelation "the genitive ἡμερῶν (hēmerōn) should be translated as 'for' or 'during' (genitive of time), indicating a period of 'time within which.'"[219] This understanding of the genitive leads

---

[208] Aune, *Rev 1–5*, 166; Edward M. Blaiklock, *Cities of the New Testament* (New York, N.Y.: Revell, 1965), 100; Hendriksen, *Conquerors*; Kistemaker, *Revelation*, 125; F. F. Bruce, *The Revelation of John*, ed. G. C. D. Howley, NTC (Grand Rapids, Mich.: Zondervan, 1969), 638; Lenski, *Revelation*, 1963, 100; Swete, *Apocalypse*, 32; Mounce, *Revelation*, 76; Ramsay, *Letters: Updated*, 200; Morris, *Revelation*, 64.

[209] Hemer acknowleged that the "possibility should not be pressed too far." Hemer, *Letters to the Seven Churches*, 69, 77.

[210] In support of this position, the number *ten* is said to be an acknowledged symbol for a very short period (cf. Gen 24:55; Num 11:19; 14:22; 1 Sam 1:8; 25:38; Job 19:3; Jer 42:7; Neh 5:18; Dan 1:12; Acts 25:6; etc.). Charles, *Revelation*, 58; Caird, *Revelation*; Düsterdieck, *Revelation*, 139; Hoeksema, *Behold, He Cometh!*, 72; Hughes, *Revelation*, 61; Kiddle, *Revelation*, 28; Mounce, *Revelation*, 76; Simcox, *Revelation*, 14; Smalley, *Revelation*, 66.

[211] Ernst W. Hengstenberg, *The Revelation of John: Expounded for Those Who Search the Scriptures*, trans. Patrick Fairbairn (Edinburgh, U.K.: T&T Clark, 1852), 1:140; Hoeksema, *Behold, He Cometh!*, 71; Lenski, *Revelation*, 1963, 100; Osborne, *Revelation*, 134.

[212] Moses Stuart, *A Commentary on the Apocalypse* (Andover, Mass.: Allen, Morrill & Wardwell, 1845), 2:70.

[213] For Beckwith ten days "denotes a period not long, but enough so to bring severe trial to the sufferers" (*Apocalypse*, 254; cf. 454). There is a limit to the suffering (ten days), but it is known to God. Swete, *Apocalypse*, 32.

[214] For a general survey, see Worth, Jr., *Greco-Asian Culture*, 76; Osborne, *Revelation*, 133–34.

[215] Beale argues for a figurative interpretation but acknowledges that a literal position is "possible." *Revelation*, 243. Osborne argues for a combination of small "round numbers" signifying a "brief period of time" and "prolonged enough to designate serious persecution." *Revelation*, 134.

[216] Thomas, *Rev 1–7*, 170; Osborne, *Revelation*, 134 n.8; Mounce, *Revelation*, 76 n.18; Robertson, *Word Pictures*, 6:302. Beckwith mentions that "the gen. with vbs. denotes not *duration* of time, but a period to some point in which an event belongs; . . . In this place ἡμερῶν [hēmerōn] may be a gen. of measure after θλῖψιν [thlipsin], *a tribulation of ten days*; cf. Lk. 2:44" (*Apocalypse*, 454).

[217] H. E. Dana and Julius Mantey, *A Manual Grammar of the Greek New Testament* (New York, N.Y.: MacMillan, 1969), 77; F. Blass and A. DeBrunner, *A Greek Grammar of the New Testament and Other Early Christian Literature*, trans. Robert W. Funk (Chicago, Ill.: University of Chicago Press, 1961), §186; James H. Moulton, *A Grammar of New Testament Greek, Volume 3: Syntax* (Edinburgh, U.K.: Clarke, 1963), 3:235; Robertson, *Grammar*, 495. Robertson maintains that it "implies nothing as to duration."

[218] Robertson, *Grammar*, 493.

[219] Osborne, *Revelation*, 134 n.8. Mounce and Robertson translate the genitive of time as *within* ten days. Mounce, *Revelation*, 76 n.18; Robertson, *Word Pictures*, 6:302.

Smalley and Lenski to translate ἡμερῶν δέκα (*hēmerōn deka*) as literally "during ten days,"[220] which indicates that the trial is limited by the scope of the ten days. This signifies the kind or class of trial as a *ten-day* trial. The use of the genitive in this context lends itself to the Smyrnaean church, which experienced a kind of trial within a period of time (the last days) in contrast with "the millennium and life of the world to come (20:4–6; 21:1–8)."[221]

In addition, what does the number *ten* signify for the testing? Several scholars see a figurative OT allusion in the Torah[222] or the prophets[223] as predilection for the use of round numbers,[224] which were used to indicate a complete or "thorough testing."[225] Some see the reference to *ten* days as a symbolical reference to the concept of completeness, which indicates limitations to the extent of the suffering rather than a time period.[226] This argument is strengthened by the conclusion that SMR were influenced by the Torah[227] and by the general use of ten in Revelation (ten horns 13:1, ten royal diadems 17:3, 7, 12, 16).

Beale identifies Daniel and his friends, who are tested for *ten days* (Dan 1:12–14), against the backdrop of the imperial cult and trade guilds as its source: "for both Judaism and early Christianity Daniel and his three friends became the model for those who would rather be persecuted for their faith than worship idols."[228] As Daniel and his friends "were tempted to compromise with pagan religion,"[229] so the Smyrnaean church was tempted to compromise with the imperial cult.[230] The Jews were angry that the Christians were claiming the Jew's exemption

---

[220] Smalley, *Revelation*, 66; Lenski, *Revelation*, 1963, 99; William Graham MacDonald, *Greek Enchiridion: A Concise Handbook of Grammar for Translation and Exegesis* (Peabody, Mass.: Hendrickson, 1986), 80. MacDonald also identifies an adverbial genitive of time as "a temporal occasion, telling when something occurred." "ἡμέρα," *GELNT* 2389; cf. Sophocles *Aj.* 131.623; Euripides *Ion* 720; ἡμαρα πάντα (*hēmata panta*), Homer *Il.* 8.539; 12.133; 13.826.

[221] Krodel, *Revelation*, 113.

[222] Gen 24:55; 31:7, 41; Exod 7:14–25; 20:1–17; Num 14:22; Deut 23:3 with Neh 13:1; Job 19:2–3.

[223] 1 Sam 25:38; Neh 4:12; Dan 1:12–14, 20; 3:12, 18.

[224] John J. Davis, *Biblical Numerology: A Basic Study of the Use of Numbers in the Bible* (Grand Rapids, Mich.: Baker, 1968), 122; Adela Yarbro Collins, "Numerical Symbolism in Jewish and Early Christian Apocalyptic Literature," *ANRW* II.21.2 (1984): 1243. Osborne indicates ten as a "small but round number. . . . signifying a complete yet brief period of time as in Gen 24:55; Num 11:19; Dan 1:12; *m. Pir. 'Abot* 5:3." *Revelation*, 134. See Thomas, *Rev 1–7*, 170; Beckwith, *Apocalypse*, 254, 454; Mounce, *Revelation*, 76.

[225] Smalley identifies this OT connection but explains, "It is more likely that the numeral is chosen because it represents a period which includes real suffering." Smalley, *Revelation*, 66; Beale, *Use of the OT*, 243 n.63; Krodel, *Revelation*, 113; Martin, *Seven Letters*, 61; Beasley-Murray, *Revelation*, NCB, 82. See *The Transcendent Suzerain–The First and the Last*; contra Düsterdieck, *Revelation*, 139.

[226] Blaiklock, *Cities of the NT*, 100; Aune, *Rev 1–5*, 166; Ramsay, *Letters: Updated*, 200; Swete, *Apocalypse*, 32; Hoeksema, *Behold, He Cometh!*, 72; Sutton, *That You May Prosper*, 257.

[227] Graves, *SMRVT*, 120.

[228] Beale, *Revelation*, 242–3; cf. Rev 13:7–8; 14–15, 18 with Dan 3:12, 18 in the LXX; cf. 4 Macc 18:11–18. Thompson, *Revelation*, 69; Osborne, *Revelation*, 134; Chilton, *Vengeance*, 103.

[229] Beale, *Revelation*, 243.

[230] See the account of Polycarp who was martyred for refusing to "swear by the genius of Caesar" (*Mart. Pol.* 9.2; 10.1) when challenged by the Roman governor. Cf. Rev 13:7–8, 14–15, 18 comp. Dan 3:12, 18. Beale points out that in the early church Nebuchadnezzar's image was viewed "as prototypical of the Roman emperor's image" (*Revelation*, 243

from participating in the worship of Roma, since the Jews viewed Christianity as a non-Jewish sect. The Jews were turning Christians over to the authorities to be tested by the Roman authorities; in some cases, Christians were imprisoned and put to death.[231] This message, if connected to Daniel, would have encouraged the Smyrnaean Christians to know that Daniel endured the test, and after ten days was successful. The *ten days* show parallels to both the Torah and the prophets, arguing for its figurative use in Revelation.

Given the genitive mood for ἡμερῶν (*hēmerōn*), it seems erroneous to look for a *duration* of time for the meaning of the ten days.[232] Kistemaker interprets the ten days as "the completeness of the period of suffering, which is neither long nor short but full, for its termination is sure."[233] Smalley states that the *ten* days indicates "a period which includes real suffering, but is itself restricted; and the limit is known to God (see also 2 Cor 4:17–18)."[234] The persecution will not be prolonged and the church will survive it. Lenski sums up the argument best when he states the following:

> In these letters the Lord himself uses symbolical expressions; the seven stars and the seven pedestal lamps in which also the number seven is symbolical. So we take "during ten days" to mean "during a complete period," one that is long enough for the complete trial according to the Lord's purpose. "Ten" is here not multiplied by itself, and for this reason this period is *not* one of great duration. The actual duration is not revealed by this "ten."[235]

Hoeksema believes that "a certain definite period is allotted to the devil during which he may persecute the church of Christ, a period which is determined not by himself, but by the will and council of the Lord."[236]

The purpose of such a statement was to bring encouragement, so whenever the Smyrnaean church experienced eschatological woes,[237] the church would know that the woes would be for a complete fulfilled time. The Smyrnaean Christians knew that whenever they experience suffering or tribulation, under God it is for a controlled and limited time 2:10; see also Dan 1:12–15). They knew that suffering would ultimately come to completion, a knowledge that

---

n.60).

[231] Frend, *Martyrdom and Persecution*, 67; Price, *Rituals and Power*, 199. See Graves, *SMRVT*, 248.

[232] Thomas argues that the duration must be short to "provide an encouragement for those in Smyrna" (*Rev 1–7*, 170). Tait, *Messages*, 204–5; Trench, *Commentary*, 146. Charles, *Revelation*, 1:58; Alford, *Hebrews–Revelation*, 4:567. These commentators cite Isa 36:20; 54:8; Ps 30:5; Matt 24:22; 2 Cor 4:17; 1 Pet 1:6; 5:30; Rev 1:9; 2:3 for the idea of a short period. God reminds his Church that suffering is short from his perspective (2 Pet 3:8; Ps 90:4; 2 Cor 4:17). Hengstenberg, *Revelation*, 1:174; Swete, *Apocalypse*, 32. Several commentators allow for a long period extending to the martyrdom of Polycarp in AD 155; cf. Simcox, *Revelation*, 14.

[233] Kistemaker, *Revelation*, 125; Hendriksen, *More than Conquerors*, 65; Beckwith, *Apocalypse*, 254, 454.

[234] Smalley, *Revelation*, 66.

[235] Lenski, *Revelation*, 100.

[236] Hoeksema, *Behold, He Cometh!*, 72.

[237] Carson points out that θλῖψιν (*thipsin*) may refer to *eschatological woes* (Mark 13:9; Rom 2:9) or *persecution* (John 15:18–16:4a; Acts 11:19; Eph 3:13), but in Revelation 2:10 and John 16:33 both of these ideas are combined (cf. Matt 24; Rev 7:14). Donald A. Carson, *The Gospel According to John: An Introduction and Commentary*, PNTC (Grand Rapids, Mich.: Eerdmans, 1991), 549–50.

would have been encouraging and meaningful for them. This would certainly be a comforting motivation for these Smyrnaean Christians not to fear their suffering, but to persevere through these eschatological woes. Thus, the imperative message of their King was to fear not.

This prophecy is partially fulfilled through two of Smyrna's martyred bishops; Polycarp (AD 155; see Figs. 50, 51; *Mart. Pol.* 1.13; 12.2; *FrgPol.* 64.23) and Pionius (AD 250; *Mart. Pionii* 14.1). The Jews, identified as the "synagogue of Satan" (Rev 2:9; 3:9), played an integral role in the arrest and martyrdom of both bishops,[238] as well as in the early church (Acts 13:50; 17:13).

SECOND IMPERATIVE: BE FAITHFUL TO DEATH—2:10B

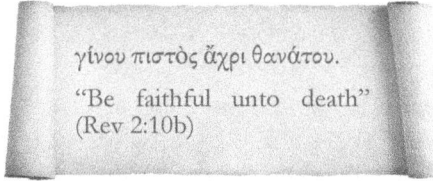

γίνου πιστὸς ἄχρι θανάτου.

"Be faithful unto death" (Rev 2:10b)

The stipulations are further emphasised with the declaration of the King's second imperative: to be faithful to death (γίνου πιστὸς ἄχρι θανάτου, *ginou pistos achri thanatou* 2:10). The Great King who states "I died, and behold I am alive forevermore" (1:18) is the one who will grant the crown of life to those who are *faithful unto death* (2:10).[239]

The statement "our most faithful and most ancient ally" (Cicero *Phil.* 11.2.5 [Yonge]) is often quoted to support this idea.[240] Regardless of whether Rome's enemies were Mithridates, Carthage, or the Seleucid kings, Smyrna was faithful to Rome.[241] The Great King now appeals to the Smyrnaean Christians to remain faithful[242] "as their community had been in the dangerous days before Rome's triumph was assured."[243]

---

[238] *Mart. Pol.* 12.2; 13:1; 17:2; 18:1; *Mart. Pionii* 2.1; 3.6; 4.2, 8; 13.1; 14.1.

[239] *Be faithful, even to the point of death* is understood as a proverbial statement on Smyrna's faithfulness, attested to by an inscription. Hemer, *Letters to the Seven Churches*, 69, 77. Cadoux believes this to be a fanciful connection. Cadoux, *Ancient Smyrna*, 320 n.1.

[240] Ramsay, Letters: Updated, 275–76; Ford, Revelation, 395; Meinardus, John of Patmos, 62; Charles C. Whiting, The Revelation of John: An Interpretation of the Book with an Introduction and a Translation (Boston, Mass.: Gorham, 1918), 73; Charles Brown, Heavenly Visions: An Exposition of the Book of Revelation (Boston, Mass.: Pilgrim, 1910), 63–64.

[241] Hemer and others trace Smyrna's boast of *faithfulness* to the early history of her loyalty to Seleucus II to the point of suffering under his rule (243 BC). Smyrna's allegiance was quickly transferred to Attalus I Soter (269–197 BC; see Fig. 57). Hemer, *Letters to the Seven Churches*, 70; *CIG* 2:3137; *OGIS* 1:229; McCabe, *Smyrna Inscriptions*, 9. Polybius (218 BC) testifies to Smyrna's loyal support of Attalus and the sympathetic reception of her ambassadors, "because the Smyrnaeans had most of all men kept faith with him" (*Hist.* 5.77.6). Cadoux, *Smyrna*, 128 n. 2; 113–5. Smyrna's faithfulness to the Romans is also supported in their application before Tiberius in AD 26 to build and become the keeper (*neōkoros*) for the second imperial cult temple in Asia (Tacitus *Ann.* 4:56). Unfortunately, to-date, no archaeological remains for this temple have been uncovered, although several coins depict the temple. Burrell, "Smyrna in Ionia: Koinon of Asia," in *Neokoroi*, 38–42; Friesen, *Imperial Cults*, 38.

[242] Can best be translated *keep on becoming faithful* (γίνου πιστὸς). Robertson translated it "'keep on proving faithful unto death' (Heb 12:4) as the martyrs have done" (*Word Pictures*, 6:301).

[243] Worth, *Greco-Asian Culture*, 78. Several scholars draw similarities between the Christians' faithful loyalty to Christ and Smyrna's allegiance to Rome. Hemer, *Letters*, 70; Cadoux, *Smyrna*, 113–5; Charles, *Revelation*, 1:55; Swete,

The Smyrnaeans' faithfulness is to extend even *to death* (ἄχρι θανάτου, *achri thanatou*); however, does ἄχρι, (*achri*) mean extent (*to the point of death*), or temporal (*when you die*)? As Osborne observes, "In the parallel 12:11 ('they did not love their lives to the point of death'), a reference to degree fits better in the context."[244] Trench agrees, pointing out that this phrase *until death* "is an intensive, not an extensive term. . . . 'to the sharpest and worst which the enemy can inflict upon thee, even to death itself.'"[245] To what extent does John expect death to be an inevitable outcome of following the Lamb (see also 14:1–5)? Smyrna is called to follow the Lamb "to the point of death", which sounds more like an exceptional possibility. The overcomer is called to follow the Lamb if necessary to death and "not live their lives so much as to shrink from death" (12:11). This statement may be partially fulfilled in the martyrdom of Polycarp (see Fig. 50, 51; *Mart. Pol.* 1.13; *FrgPol.* 64ver.23; See chapter 6, *Jewish Involvement in the Martyrdom of Polycarp* above.).[246]

There is a close similarity between the conditional promise, *Be faithful unto death, and I will give you the crown of life* (ver. 10; Cyprian *Test.* 490) and the *messenger formula* (ver. 8) which also "contains the same life/death contrast."[247] Ellul argues that the command to remain faithful is accompanied by a promise of eternal blessing:

> exhortation comes precisely from the one who gives the crown of life; it is he, and he alone, who *makes* us faithful. . . This church is under a threat of death; therefore, the one who speaks to her exhorts her, is the one who has passed through death (2:8) to live again. And it is the same for their destiny; these men are going to die in the persecution but will have nothing else to endure except physical death: they are assured of rising again (2:11).[248]

There appears to be a close relationship between πίστις (*Pistis*, 2:19; 14:12; 17:14) and πιστός (*pistos*, 2:10, 13; 13:10) in Revelation. The King requires that his people, if necessary, remain faithful even to the point of martyrdom. Believers persevere to the end by faith, by placing their trust in the sovereign King who will vindicate his people in time. It is to those who are faithful even unto death that the promise of ultimate victory is given (2:13). As Beale has reasoned, "it is by means of the churches 'perseverance' through such 'tribulation' that they reign in an invisible messianic 'kingdom' (see also 1:6, 9) which had previously been so long awaited."[249]

The fact that there were so many temples situated in Smyrna (see chapter 6, *A City of Temples*) would lend strength to the martyrdom prophecy given to the church (2:10). There would be a culture clash with the worshipers of these temples and, if their revenues were affected—as in the case of Demetrius the silversmith of Ephesus (Acts 19:23–29) and the owner

---

Apocalypse, lxi, 30; Blaiklock, *Cities*, 100; Ramsay, *Letters*, 201.

[244] Osborne, *Revelation*, 134–5.

[245] Trench, *Commentary on Seven Churches*, 146.

[246] Barclay, *Letters*, 31; Gregg, *Revelation: Four Views*, 66; Ramsay, *Letters: Updated*, 273; Clark, *The Message from Patmos*, 35.

[247] Krodel, *Revelation*, 113; Mulholland, *Revelation*, 99.

[248] Ellul, *Apocalypse*, 131.

[249] Beale, "Review of Colin J. Hemer, The Letters to the Seven Churches," 109.

of a fortune-telling slave girl in Philippi (Acts 16:16–24) — then it would not be unrealistic to see a similar persecution at Smyrna. After all, the news about the impact of Paul's preaching on the Artemis cult (or Diana, see Figs. 26, 27, 121, 124, 127) had extended throughout all Asia Minor (Acts 19:10, 27). It is also notable that the only two accounts of Christians being arrested in the book of Acts stem from the loss of revenue resulting from the life-changing effects of preaching the gospel. Since the persecution by the Jewish element in the early church was frequent,[250] and also present in Smyrna (2:10), it would not be unreasonable to expect a similar reaction to the impact of the gospel on cultic temple revenue.

SANCTIONS: BLESSINGS—2:10C, 11B

Although maledictions are present in five of the churches' messages, within the messages to Philadelphia[251] and Smyrna only the blessing is mentioned.[252] The ethical imperative of overcoming is accompanied with a divine benediction upon those faithfully enduring persecution. Within the Smyrnaean message the eschatological fulfilment of the covenant blessedness (*macarism*, 1:3) for those overcomers obedient to the stipulations is the King's gracious pledge of eternal preservation (eternal life), metaphorically conveyed by the crown of life. The King graciously grants the crown, which represents life in the fullest eternal sense, to the overcoming subjects.

The prophetic sanctions, where the vassal is cursed (maledictions) for disobedience (dishonors the treaty), and blessed (benedictions) for obedience to the stated stipulations (honors the treaty), is a central element of the ANEVT structure[253] and is also present within the SMR.[254] The fact that only the blessings are mentioned in two of the churches is not an argument against use of the ANEVT structure given the unique circumstances of these two exceptions; the early church would still be aware of the curses in the other five messages. The messages are crafted to address the individual circumstances of the churches and are similar to the various ANEVT constructions, but those models are not meant to impose a rigid structure to the text.

καὶ δώσω σοι τὸν στέφανον τῆς ζωῆς.
"I will give you the crown of life."
(Rev 2:10c)

THE BLESSING OF THE CROWN OF LIFE—2:10C

The blessing, from God the Great King, for the Smyrnaean overcomers who are "faithful, even

---

[250] Acts 6:9–15; 9:23, 29; 12:1–3; 13:45–50; 14:1–5, 19; 17:5, 13; 18:6, 12; 19:33; 20:3; 21:27; 22:30; 23:12; 24:9; 25:7–15; 26:7.

[251] This same blessing is implied in the covenant message to Philadelphia. "I am coming soon. Hold on to what you have, so that no-one will take your crown (τὸν στέφανόν)" (3:11).

[252] The curse is present in Ephesus 2:5b; Pergamum 2:16b; Thyatira 2:22–23; Sardis 3:3b; and Laodicea 3:16. Philadelphia, like Smyrna, is missing a curse; cf. Graves, *SMRVT*, 212; see chapter 4, *Inconsistent Pattern*.

[253] See chapter 3, *Sanctions*.

[254] Graves, *SMRVT*, 158–70.

to the point of death," is Christ's promise of "the crown of life" (τὸν στέφανον τῆς ζωῆς, *ton stephanon tes zōēs*, 2:10) and protection from the "second death" (2:11). The *macarism* for the Smyrnaean overcomers is metaphorically represented by the *crown of life* for the blessing of eternal life (see also Jas 1:12).[255]

THE PERVASIVE CROWN MOTIF

In the first century, Smyrna was culturally surrounded by crown or wreath (στέφανος, *stephanos*) imagery,[256] as well as popularized in early apocalyptic literature.[257] The *crown of life* has been associated with a crown of athletic victory,[258] a crown worn in cultic rites (Cybele or Tyche, Τύχη, see Figs. 52, 54, 98, 108, 160 or Bacchus),[259] and honorary crowns.[260] Beckwith summarizes the evidence:

> the crown occurs so often in antiquity as a mark of royalty, honor, a prize of victory, etc., that it is unnecessary to seek (so, some com[mentaries]) for a local origin of the metaphor, i.e., in the games celebrated at Smyrna.[261]

Hemer observes:

> the concept of a crown or wreath is in fact extraordinarily prominent in materials relating to Smyrna. Variations of the motif occur on every pre-Imperial coin listed in BMC (Nos. 1–119), and sometimes three times on the same coin (Nos. 35–46). Similar emblems are almost obsessively common throughout the abundant and otherwise more varied types of the Empire.[262]

In the ancient mind, the crown of life conjured up many types of images, including glory or honor.[263] The beauty in the structure of the imagery used in Smyrna was described as

---

[255] Royalty maintains that the "virtues that bring wealth to the Smyrnaeans are struggle and patient endurance" (*Ideology of Wealth*, 163). Royalty appears to strain the analogy to connect suffering and wealth in this context.

[256] For further details, see Grundmann, *TDNT* 7:615–36; Gregory M. Stevenson, "Conceptual Background to Golden Crown Imagery in the Apocalypse of John," *JBL* 114, no. 2 (1995): 257–72; Aune, *Rev 1–5*, 172–75; Hemer, *Letters to the Seven Churches*, 70–76; Stewart, "Greek Crowns and Christian Martyrs," 119–24; Erwin R. Goodenough, "The Crown of Victory in Judaism," *ABul* 28 (1946): 139–59.

[257] *T. Levi* 8.2, 9; also *crown of glory* used by *T. Benj.* 4.1; *Ascen. Isa.* 9.7, 24; 11.40; Hermas *Sim.* 8.2.1; 8.3.6.

[258] Cadoux, *Ancient Smyrna*, 195–96; Bruce M. Metzger, *Breaking the Code: Understanding the Book of Revelation* (Nashville, Tenn.: Abingdon, 1999), 33; Jean Pierre Prévost, *How to Read the Apocalypse*, trans. John Bowden and Margaret Lydamore, The Crossroad Adult Christian Formation (New York, N.Y.: Crossroad, 1993), 73; Sweet, *Revelation*, 86; Swete, *Apocalypse*, lxi; Reinhold Merkelbach, "Der Griechische Wortchatz Und Die Christen," *ZPE* 18 (1975): 108–36. For a comprehensive discussion of the athletic metaphor in early Christian writings, see Merkelbach.

[259] Ramsay, *Letters: Updated*, 258; R. K. Harrison, *Archaeology of the New Testament: The Stirring Times of Christ and the Early Church Come to Life in the Latest Findings of Science* (Grand Rapids, Mich.: Eerdmans, 1985), 53; Johnson, "Revelation," 618.

[260] Hemer, *Letters to the Seven Churches*, 73–74; 234 n. 58.

[261] Beckwith, *Apocalypse*, 455.

[262] Hemer, *Letters to the Seven Churches*, 59–60. Hemer, "στέφανος," *NIDNTT* 1:406.

[263] Isa 28:5; Jer 13:18; Aeschines *Ctes.* 45; Lucian *Luct.* 19, accomplishment, and victory (Aeschines *Ctes.* 179, Philo *Prob.* 26).

resembling a crown[264] by ancient writers.[265] Ramsay also compares Smyrna to a flower garland "crown."

> The crown or garland was usually a circlet of flowers; and the mention of a crown immediately aroused in the ancient mind the thought of a flower. Crowns were worn chiefly in the worship of the gods. The worshiper was expected to have on his head a garland of the flowers or foliage sacred to the god whose rites he was performing…Thus the ideas of the flower and of the crown suggest in their turn the idea of the god with whose worship they were connected, i.e., the statue of the god. The tutelary deity of Smyrna was the Mother-goddess, Cybele [Tyche, Τύχη, see Figs. 52, 54, 98, 108, 160]; and when Aristides pictured Smyrna as a statue sitting with her feet on the sea, and her head rising to heaven and crowned with a circlet of beautiful buildings, he had in mind the patroness and guardian of the city, who was represented enthroned and wearing a crown of battlements and towers.[266]

Ramsay argues that:

> "The crown of Smyrna" was the garland of splendid buildings with the street of gold, which encircled the rounded hill Pagus. Apollonius in a fully expressed comparison advised the citizens to prefer a crown of men to a crown of buildings. This author leaves one member of the figure to be understood: if we expressed his thought in full, it would be "instead of the crown of buildings which you boast of, or the crown of men that your philosophers recommend, *I will give you the crown of life*." [267]

CYBELE CROWNED ON COINS

Cybele (Tyche, Τύχη, see Fig. 54) was one of the most common images on the coins of Smyrna,[268] together with the harmony (Ὁμόνοια, *homonoia*) coins on where Smyrna's goddess proudly wore her crown. The priests of the imperial cult wore their crowns (Gr. *coronatus*) with the image of Caesar Augustus on them. The municipal officer or priests of this cult in Smyrna and other cities were called *stephanephoros* (*to wear a crown*, Wis 4:2) and wore their laurel crowns during their public ceremonies associated with "the temples of the emperors."[269] Ramsay

---

[264] Beasley-Murray view that the *crown of life* is related to a halo crown of light is unlikely. Beasley-Murray, *Revelation*, NCB, 83.

[265] Aristides *Orat.* 15, 20–22, 41; Philostratus *Vit. Apoll.* 1.4.7; 1.8.24.

[266] Ramsay, *Letters: Updated*, 187–88.

[267] Ibid., 147; Hemer, *Letters to the Seven Churches*, 60–75, 77; Cadoux, *Ancient Smyrna*, 320 n. 1; Johnson, "Revelation," 618. Cadoux believes Ramsay's connection of the garland and the city-buildings to be fanciful.

[268] "In Hellenistic time there is only four divinities and/or heroes, whose pictures appear on the Smyrnaean coins: Cybele, Apollon, Aphrodite Stratonikis and Homer…On the other hand the coinage is already taken up by coins with representation of the Cybele under Claudius and Nero again in large number; it is thus the only one, also in the Emperor era, which concerns the minting, their outstanding role could hold . . . Cybele is the only divinity, whose picture clearly appears equally frequent as in the Roman Emperor era on the coins. . . . on numerous *Homonoia* [Greek] coinage the sitting Cybele appears as representative of Smyrna." Klose, *Münzprägung*, 24–26; Head, *BMC Ionia*, 16:Nos. 1–11; Joseph Grafton Milne, *The Silver Coinage of Smyrna* (London, U.K.: Taylor & Walton, 1914), 275 2(b), xvi; Hans von Aulock and Gerhard Kleiner, *Sylloge Nummorum Graecorum, Vol. 1: Pontus, Paphlagonia, Bithynia, Mysia, Troas, Aiolis, Lesbos, Ionia* (Berlin: Gebr. Mann, 1957), no. 2162.

[269] Francis Vyvian J. Arundell, Discoveries in Asia Minor: Including a Description of the Ruins of Several Ancient

suggests that the terms *coronatus* and *stephanephoros* should be understood relating to the same role as cultic priest.[270]

REV 4 CROWN MOTIF

The crown motif is also picked up again in Revelation 4, where the elders are viewed by Hurtado as heavenly representatives of the faithful[271] wearing golden crowns (4:4). Their crowns are laid before the throne while they exalt the one on the throne (4:10–11; see also *1 En.* 61.11–12). Three elements from 4:4 are common to the SMR: The elect are promised (1) white garments (3:5), (2) crowns (2:10; 3:11), and (3) a throne to sit on (3:21; *Mart. Asc. Isa.* 8.26; 9.7–18). Hurtado believes that "the vision of the twenty-four elders [Rev 5] seems to be assurance of the heavenly reality of the promises."[272]

54. Silver Tetradrachm coin from Smyrna (*ca.* 155–145 BC). Obv.: The Anatolian goddess Tyche/Cybele wearing a turreted crown. Rev.: Displaying the magistrate's monogram ΙΜΥΡ ΝΑΙΩΝ (*izmur naiōn*) within a laurel wreath.

THE CROWN USED METAPHORICALLY

The perishable crown or wreath is used metaphorically for the eschatological reward of the righteous in the OT Pseudepigrapha and Apocrypha[273] and within the OT[274] and NT.[275] Στέφανος, (*stephanos*) is also used metaphorically by the authors of the *Martyrdom of Polycarp*: "*a crown of immortality*" (ἀφθαρσι, στέφανον", *aphtharsias stepahnon, Mart. Pol.* 17.1; 19.2 [Lightfoot and Harmer]; Eusebius, *Hist. eccl.* 5.1). Ignatius, who also wrote to Polycarp (see Figs. 50, 51) in his

---

Cities, and Especially Antioch of Pisidia (London, U.K.: Bentley & Son, 1834), 2:375.

[270] Ramsay, Cities and Bishoprics, 2:56–57.
[271] Larry W. Hurtado, "Revelation 4–5 in the Light of Jewish Apocalyptic Analogies," *JSNT* 25 (1985): 113–14.
[272] Ibid., 113.
[273] *T. Job* 40:3; *T. Ab.*10.9; *Gk. Apoc. Ezra* 6:17; *Apoc. El.* 1:8; *Ascen. Isa.* 7:22; 9:24; *Wis.* 5:16; Hermas *Sim.* 8.2.1–4; 8.3.6.
[274] 2 Sam 12:30; 1 Chr 20:2; Esth 8:15; 1 Macc 10:20; 13:37, 39; 2 Macc 14:4; Pss 20:4; 64:11f; Job 19:9; 31:36; 15:6; 32:2; 40:4; 45:12; Prov 1:9; 4:9; 12:4; 14:24; 16:31; 17:6; Sir 6:3; 11:11, 18; 25:6; 50:12; Zech 6:14; Isa 22:18, 21; 28:3, 5; 62:3; Jer 13:18; Lam 2:15; 5:16; Ezek 16:12; 21:31; 23:42; 28:12; LXX *a glorious crown a beautiful wreath for the remnant of his people* (ὁ στέφανος τῆς ἐλίδος, *o stephanos tēs elpisos*, Isa 28:5); *a crown of beauty* (στέφανος κάλλους, *stephanos callous*, Isa 62:3); *your glorious crowns* (στέφανος δόξης, *stephanos doxēs,* Jer 13:18; Lam 2:15); *a beautiful crown* (καὶ στέφανον καυχήσεως, *kai stephanon kauxēseōs*, Ezek 16:12); *beautiful crowns on their heads* (καὶ στέφανον στέ καυχήσεως, *kai stephanon kauxēseōs*, Ezek 23:42), etc.
[275] Acts 6:8; Phil 4:1; 1 Cor 9:25; 2 Tim 4:7–8; Jas 1:12; 1 Pet 5:4; 2 Tim 2:5; 1 Thess 2:19; Rev 6:2; 12:1; Hemer, Letters, 72. Στέφανος, (*stephanos*) occurs 19 times (Matt 27:29; Mark 15:17; John 19:2, 5; 1 Cor 9:25; Jas 1:12; 1 Pet 5:4; Phil 4:1; 1 Thess 2:19; 2 Tim 2:5; 4:8) in the NT (8 times in Rev 2:10; 3:11; 4:4, 10; 6:2; 9:7; 12:1; 14:14) while διάδημα (*diadēma, royal crown*) occurs 3 times (12:3; 13:1;19:12) all in Revelation. Other variations include *the crown of righteousness* (τῆς δικαιοσύνης στέφανος, *tēs dikaiosunēs stephanos,* 2 Tim 4:8); *crown of glory* (τῆς δόξης στέφανον, *tēs doxēs stephanon,*1 Pet 5:4); *the crown in which we will glory* (η‡ στέφανος, *hē stephanos* 1 Thess 2:19).

letter to the Magnesians, uses *crown* metaphorically to refer to the unity of church officers: "That beautifully woven spiritual crown which is your presbytery and the godly deacons" (πνευματικοῦ στεφάνου, *pneumasikou stephanou*, Ign. *Magn.* 13.1 [Lightfoot and Harmer]). It is clear that στέφανος (*stephanos*), used as a metaphor for eternal life, was familiar to the NT audience from its numerous occurrences demonstrated above. Goodenough makes this conclusion based on these occurrences:

> these instances are clearly an adaptation of the crown both as it appeared in Greek religious games and in the Greek mystery, where it symbolized deification and immortality. That is, we have Paul in two passages, and the authors of II Timothy, James and Revelation, all using the same pagan figure, but these are four authors who it is very hard to believe knew and drew upon each other. It is just as hard to believe that each of the four borrowed the figure for the Christian experience independently from paganism, even while Christians then and for a century and a half later were hating the pagan crowns and mysteries.[276]

In its leafy construction, the meaning or value of the crown conveyed the idea that "it brought to one who won it the divine power of the tree, a power which was basically that of life, as in the proverbial 'tree of life'"[277] (Plutarch *Cor.* 3.3; *Comp. Phil. Flam.* 3; *Quaest. conv.* 5.3). Clement of Alexandria argues against the adoption of the physical crown by Christians, but allows for the usage of a symbolical meaning (*2 Clem.* 7:3). Thus, the use of *crown* metaphorically is consistent with how many early authors have utilized it.

The "crown of life" used metaphorically for eternal life (Jas 1:12; *4 Macc.* 17:15)[278] is likely drawn from the prize given in athletic contests[279] or the crown buried with the deceased, symbolic of their victories in life.[280] While the athlete or deceased Smyrnaean only receives a crown of flowers, Christ promises the overcomers an authentic crown of eternal life.

AN EPEXEGETICAL GENITIVE

The genitive τῆς ζωῆς (*tēs zōēs*) has been interpreted either as possessive[281] (*the crown which belongs to eternal life*) or epexegetical[282] (appositional, *the crown which consists in life*). The majority of

---

[276] Goodenough, "Crown," 154.

[277] Goodenough, "Crown," 150.

[278] Beale, *Revelation*, 244; Smalley, *Revelation*, 67; Ladd, *Revelation*, 45.

[279] Aune, *Rev 1–5*, 175–76; Frend, *Martyrdom and Persecution*; Merkelbach, "Griechische Wortchatz," 108–36; Stewart, "Greek Crowns and Christian Martyrs," 119–24.

[280] Clement Alexandria *Paed.* 2.8; Cicero *Flac.* 31, 75; *Odes Sol.* 1:17, 20; Apuleius *Metam.* 11.24; *Mart. Pol.* 17.1; *Ascen. Isa.* 9.6–18, 7.22; Josephus *Ant.* 14.153; Demosthenes *Cor.* 54–55, 84, 116; Goodenough, "Crown," 139–59. For Lenski the crown imagery, "Need not insist on royalty, victory is enough. . . . This is the life of glory in heaven which is symbolized by a glorious crown." Lenski, Revelation, 101. Alford disagrees with the view later expressed by Lenski and states that "στέφανοι of ch. v. can only be royal crowns,—that the word is employed by all the Evangelists of the 'Crown of thorns,'—and that the imagery of this book is not anywhere drawn from Gentile antiquity, but is Jewish throughout" (*Revelation*, 4:567).

[281] Charles, *Revelation*, 1:59.

[282] Richard C. H. Lenski, *The Interpretation of The Epistle to the Hebrews and The Epistle of James* (Minneapolis, Minn.: Augsburg, 1966), 538; Alexander Ross, *The Epistles of James and John*, NICNT 13 (Grand Rapids, Mich.: Eerdmans,

commentators understand it to mean that the crown is symbolical of life, rather than that life possesses a crown.

There appears to be a connection to the *tree of life* [283] (τὸ ξύλον τῆς ζωῆ, *to xulon tēs zōēs*; Gen 2:9; 3:22, 24) applied to the overcomer of Revelation 2:7, which reads, "to him who overcomes, I will give the right to eat from the *tree of life,* which is in the paradise of God" (2:7). Beale summarizes the implications for the redemptive history of the tree of life and more correctly associates ξύλον (*xulon*) to the *effects* of the cross rather than to the cross itself:

> In genesis 2–3 the image of the "tree of life" together with the "paradise of God" symbolizes the life-giving presence of God, from which Adam and Eve are separated when they are cast out of the garden paradise (cf. 2:9; 3:22–24 [23–25] [LXX]; Ezek 28:13; 31:8–9). Revelation speaks of the consummated restoration of this divine presence among humanity in the future (22:1–4), which has already been inaugurated in the present. Therefore, the "tree" refers to the redemptive effects of the cross, which bring about the restoration of God's presence, and does not refer to the cross.[284]

Charles argues for an eschatological fulfilment for the *crown of life:* "as the tree of life (see also ii. 7 note, xxii. 2, 14) is a symbol of the blessed immortality in Christ, so the crown of life appears to symbolize its full consummation."[285]

The phrase *crown of life* appears to have OT Jewish wisdom roots (Prov 4:9; 3:18)[286] as an eschatological symbol referring to the "reward of eternal life for those who remain faithful even to death."[287] Beale describes the contrast in this way:

> yet their defeat in death by the authority of the Roman crown meant their victory of life and inheritance of a heavenly 'crown' (ver. 10). This crown connotes participation in Christ's heavenly, victorious rule (so στέφανος [*stephanos*, 'crown'] in 6:2; 14:14).[288]

According to the *Testament of Levi,* the reward of the blessed is eating the fruit of the tree of life (*T. Levi* 18.11). Roberts points out that the tree of life is placed in the Paradise of God (5:6;

1967), 32 n.14; Sophie Laws, *A Commentary on the Epistle of James*, BNTC 13 (London, U.K.: A & C Black, 1980), 68. Swete, *Apocalypse,* 33; Hemer, *Letters,* 72; Lenski, *Revelation,* 101; Hemer, "στέφανος," *NIDNTT* 1:406; Hemer points out that the possessive view "is connected by Charles with a supposed parallel in *2 Enoch* 14.2 and *3 Baruch* 6.1, referring to a nimbus of light surrounding the sun. It is much more natural to think of 'the crown (= prize) which consists in life'" (*Letters,* 72). Kistemaker considers the phrase "idiomatic . . . and can be translated 'the crown, that is, fullness of life'" (*Revelation,* 125). Mayor identifies the Greek as "genitive of definition" (*James,* 49). Beale uses the term "appositional to or explanatory of 'the crown,' explaining its nature" (*Revelation,* 244).

[283] Grundmann, *TDNT* 7:630. Hemer also finds a local setting for the tree of life in the sacred tree of Artemis in Ephesus (*Letters,* 44–50).

[284] Beale, *Revelation,* 235. Hemer, Kraft, and Roberts hold that the tree equals the cross (Hemer, *Letters,* 41–52, 55; Kraft, *Offenbarung,* 59). Richard Roberts maintains that in Ramsay "it is not impossible that here ξύλον (*xulon*) may contain an allusion to the cross." Roberts, "The Tree of Life (Rev 2:7)," 332.

[285] Charles, *Revelation,* 1:59.

[286] Mayor, *James,* 49.

[287] Wall, *Revelation,* 73.

[288] Beale, *Revelation,* 244.

13:8).[289] The ideas of paradise and heaven, the city of God, merge in *2 Bar.* 4 and *T. Dan* 5.12. Thus, they connect the imagery of the *tree of life* with the *crown of life* in an eschatological realization.[290]

The imminent return of Christ is explicitly stated in each of the SMR, except Smyrna's. The absence of the *Parousia* within this message may be explained by the presence of the pledge of the *Crown of Life* that would be given by the King at his return.[291] As Grundmann states, "The imperishable crown . . . is an eschatological gift of God which is granted to the victor in the contest."[292] Beale concludes that persevering faith "guarantees identification with Christ (see also 1:9) and hence participation in his eternal resurrection life (see also reference to death and resurrection in the introduction of Christ in 2:8ba)."[293] The eternal communion between God and his covenant people is represented by the imagery of the tree and crown in paradise.

CONCLUSION

The King will *bless* his subjects with the crown of life if they overcome (2:11 etc.) in *perseverance* (ὑπομονή, *hypomonē*, endurance Jas 1:3–4) under suffering (2:3, 2 Tim 3:11–15). This paraenetic *macarism* pattern has ancient roots and appears repeatedly in James 1:12, 25; 5:10–11a; 1 Peter 3:14; 4:14 and Rev 14:12–14.[294]

The similarities in the references to the *crown* motif within the biblical text (2:10; see also 4:4, Jas 1:12) suggest the use of an unwritten saying preserved in oral tradition, or borrowed from a written text.[295] Mayor suggests that "it is an instance of loose quotation"[296] that was borrowed from the various NT usages of στέφανος (*stephanos*). Hemer on the other hand states, "there is no ground for dogmatism here about possible literary relationship with James 1.12."[297] Grundmann believes that these many passages have "no literary dependence, so that they must go back to a common original."[298] The commonality between Revelation 2:10 and James 1:12 may be identified in the centrality of the blessing within the covenant relationship of God and His people.

---

[289] Roberts, "The Tree of Life (Rev 2:7)," 332.

[290] J. Schneider, "ξύλον," *TDNT* 5:40.

[291] Hemer, *Letters,* 74.

[292] Grundmann, *TDNT* 7:629.

[293] Beale, *Revelation,* 243.

[294] See, also Jas 1:2–4; 2 Tim 4:8; τῆς δόξης στέφανον, *tēs doxēs stephanon;* see 1 Pet 4:19–5:7. For Jewish references to the elect receiving crowns in the coming age; *cf.* 1QS 4:7; 1QH 9:25; *b. Bar.* 17; *T. Benj.* 4.1.

[295] Walter Grundmann believes that "the inner relation between the three sayings, which promise to those who suffer, and in some circumstances may even suffer martyrdom, the victor's crown from the Lord's hand, points to a common hortatory basis" ("στέφανος, στεφανόω," *TDNT* 7:630).

[296] Joseph B. Mayor, *The Epistle of Saint James*, 3rd ed. (Minneapolis, Minn.: Klock & Klock, 1977), 50.

[297] Hemer, *Letters,* 72.

[298] Grundmann, *TDNT* 7:630 n.76.

Ropes understands the *crown of life*, in James, as the gracious "mark of honour to be given by the Great King to his friends" (*Ep. Arist.* 280).[299] Tasker maintains that the crown motif in James "is not a sign of royalty, nor a prize as it is in 1 Cor ix. 25, but a gift showing the approval of the divine Giver."[300] The *macarism* for those who persevere under suffering is central to the NT covenantal blessing, but this idea of the blessing for the overcomers also finds support within the Rabbinical literature, *Nag Hammadi Codices*, and early Christians texts.[301] Likewise, in Revelation, following the overcomers' period of testing, the victor will receive the crown of life.[302]

Fensham brings out a similar parallel in the ANEVT where the suzerain promises to protect the vassal on the basis of his or her faithfulness and obedience.[303] In the vassal-treaty between *Muwattališ* and *Alakšanduš* we have a command for *Alakšanduš to protect* Muwattališ against his enemies.[304] Fensham comments that "one of the most humane stipulations in the Hittite treaties is the promise of protection of the vassal against enemies. . . . There was no enemy to fear."[305]

Likewise, Yahweh requires faithfulness because he is a jealous God (Exod 20:3–6) and promises protection in such passages as Exodus 23:22; 34:11–17; and Deuteronomy 3:8–24.[306] As Fensham points out, "The protection of Yahweh can only be attained by an obedient nation. Unfaithfulness of the vassal, in this case the people of the Lord, means punishment and

55. Bronze statue of a runner wearing the laurel wreath (crown) awarded to the winner. Found in the Aegean Sea off the coast of Cyme. Roman copy of a late Hellenistic statue dating to the second cent. AD.

---

[299] James Hard Ropes, *A Critical and Exegetical Commentary on the Epistle of James*, ICC (Edinburgh, U.K.: T&T Clark, 1954), 152.

[300] R. V. G. Tasker, *The General Epistle of James*, TNTC 16 (Grand Rapids, Mich.: Eerdmans, 1983), 45.

[301] *Shem. Rab.* 31; Hermas *Vis.* 2.2.7; *Gos. Thom.* 58.

[302] Simon J. Kistemaker, *Exposition of the Epistle of James and the Epistles of John*, NTC 10 (Grand Rapids, Mich.: Baker, 1986), 47.

[303] In the Akkadian *Sêfire* treaties we find *tšm'n* means obedience. There are no protection clauses in the *Sêfire* and Esarhaddon treaties. This is likely due to the fact that they are dated to the first millennium rather than the second millennium with the Hittite treaties. Fensham, "Clauses of Protection," 139 n. 1; Kitchen, *Reliability of the OT*, 285. The *Sêfire* and Esarhaddon treaties have more similarities with the prophets than the Pentateuch. Fensham, "Clauses of Protection," 142.

[304] Ibid., 139.

[305] Ibid., 140.

[306] Amos 1–2:3 also picks up on the judgment on foreign nations.

rejection."³⁰⁷ The covenant lawsuit against the seven churches is couched in this ancient legal language. For the overcomers there is the blessing of the King's divine protection. To put it another way, *perseverance in suffering* is to be consummated in the ultimate protection from all enemies in eternal life (21:4, 7–8, 27; 22:3). Kiddle states that the crown "bestowed alike for civil merit and military or athletic prowess, was for Christians the sign of immortality."³⁰⁸ The Great King grants the crown of eternal life to those who have finished the race in accordance with the King's stipulations.

The comfort for the Smyrnaean Christians focuses on the blessing given to those who overcome and persevere in suffering (also 21:7). The verb δίδωμι (*didōmi*) [καὶ δώσω σοι τὸν στέφανον, *kai dōsō soi ton stephanon*] has a basic meaning of *give*, but it varies greatly depending on the context. In this context the King graciously grants (*gives*) the covenant blessing of the crown of life because of their perseverance.³⁰⁹

OVERCOMERS

The overcomers (νικάω, *nikaō*) in Smyrna (2:11b) are strongly tied to the covenant formula in Revelation 21:7³¹⁰ as these are the ones who will be called sons and stand in covenant relationship with God to inherit the crown of life (2:10; Jas 1:12).³¹¹ The covenant formula is clearly present within Revelation 21:7 as God promises to stand in covenant relationship to the overcomers (νικάω, *nikaō*).

Hill examines the views of Käsemann, Hahn, and Müller³¹² who claim that the 'Overcoming-words' (*Überwinderspruch*) *to him who conquers* originated in the prophetic tradition. However, Hill links the "overcomers' words" to early Christian prophecy:

> the participial phrase does not describe an objective, generally valid, state of affairs leading to the expression of an automatic and inevitable judgment: it functions rather as a condition upon which certain promises or consequences depend. . . . the 'Overcoming-words', by reason of their

---

³⁰⁷ Fensham, "Clauses of Protection," 143.

³⁰⁸ Kiddle, *Revelation*, 28; Worth, *Greco-Asian Culture*, 79; Swete, *Apocalypse*, 33.

³⁰⁹ The idiomatic expression, "to give the right hand," is also coincidentally used in Deuteronomy 11:16 ("See, I am setting before you today a blessing and a curse–" [ἰδού ἐγώ δίδωμι ἐνώπιον, *idou egō didōmai enōpion*, LXX]) where δίδωμι (*didōmi*) is used in granting the covenant blessing; i.e., δεξιός δίδωμι (*dexias didōmi*); *to give right hands*, literally to shake hands, to establish a covenant. Gal 2:9; *make a covenant*, (δίδωμι αὐτῷ διαθήκην (*didōmi autō diathekēn*, LXX) Num 25:12; Deut 4:8; (διδοὺς νόμους, *didous nomous*) Heb 8:10; (ἐδόθη νόμος, *edothē nomos* Gal 3:15. "δίδωμι," *L&N* 34.42, 451.

³¹⁰ "I will be your God, and you will be my people" (21:7; Exod 6:7; Lev 26:12; Jer 7:23; 11:4; 30:22; Ezek 36:28; Joel 2:27). Revelation 21:7 appears to be a quote from 2 Sam 7:14 with modifications working to suit John's theological purpose. The promise given to King David by the prophet Nathan that Solomon would be his successor is a messianic prophecy pointing to the Son of God (Pss 89:26–29). Kistemaker, *Revelation*, 560. Qumran understood 2 Sam 7:14 to be fulfilled with God establishing forever the future temple and tabernacle (4Q174; *Midr. Rab.* 1:1–13). See "Antithetic Parallels to Chapters 21–22," in Graves, *SMRVT*, 203–8.

³¹¹ Rosscup persuasively argues that the 'overcomers' are all true believers for "every saved person overcomes." James E. Rosscup, "The Overcomer in the Apocalypse," *GTJ* 3, no. 2 (1982): 278–79.

³¹² Müller, *Prophetie*, 104ff.

eschatological character, may well have been a form used occasionally in early Christian prophecy.[313]

To *overcome* is legal language that the verdict must prevail in a legal suit (Rom 3:4). Thayer explains that, in keeping with the covenant lawsuit, νικάω (*nikaō*) used intransitively means, "when one is arraigned or goes to law, to win the case, maintain one's cause."[314] The overcomers (νικάω, *nikaō*) are those who refuse to compromise their faith despite the threat of persecution. Victory is theirs even when in the eyes of the world they look defeated. Carson states that the verb νικάω (*nikaō*) does not "merely refer to personal overcoming, the preservation of personal integrity in the fact of protracted opposition."[315] Rather, Christ has conquered (overcome) the world and is the prince of this world (John 17:33); those who are *in him* overcome. These are the true conquerors (2:26–29). Wilcock points out that "nowhere does the New Testament promise freedom from suffering in this life; indeed, without the cross there will be no crown."[316] To be an overcomer does not mean to be free from suffering but rather to experience suffering and persevere through it. For those who persevere, this persecution truly will be a victorious overcoming; in the prophetic sense, they will inherit the eternal blessing of God (Jas 1:12; 5:11).

John further explains the way in which one overcomes: "They overcame him by the blood of the Lamb and by the word of their testimony; they did not love their lives so much as to shrink from death" (12:11). As Homcy posits, the Lamb and his followers are both victorious: "Revelation is not only an apocalyptic portrait of the Lamb's triumph but also a prophetic exhortation for his followers to triumph in him... It is 'he who overcomes' that will inherit the blessings of the Lamb's victory (21:7)."[317]

Beale comments that "Polycarp's Martyrdom was probably interpreted against the background of this promise" for it is said that following his death he "was crowned with *the crown of immortality* (τὸν τῆς ἀφθαρσία στέφανον, *ton tēs aphtharsias stephanon*)."[318] The crown of life is the blessing for the overcomer, and one must persevere unto the end in order to wear it.

Müller regards the "overcoming words" as "paraenetical in character,"[319] and he argues that "The one overcoming by no means will be hurt" (Ὁ νικῶν οὐ μὴ ἀδικηθῇ, *ho nikōn ou mē adikēthē*, 2:11b). The use of the double negative (οὐ μὴ, *ou mē*) indicates an emphatic emphasis.[320] Krodel comments that not everyone will be an overcomer:

---

[313] Hill, *NT Prophecy*, 83.
[314] "νικάω," *GELNT* 3620.
[315] Carson, *Gospel According to John*, 550.
[316] Wilcock, *Message of Revelation*, 46.
[317] Stephen L. Homcy, "To Him Who Overcomes: A Fresh Look as What Victory Means for the Believer according to the Book of Revelation," *JETS* 38, no. 2 (n.d.): 193.
[318] Beale, *Revelation*, 244.
[319] Müller, *Prophetie*, 104.
[320] Dan Lioy, *The Book of Revelation in Christological Focus*, ed. Hemchand Gossai, StBL 58 (New York, N.Y.: Peter Lang, 2003), 127; Morris, *Revelation of St. John*, 65.

this is the only conqueror saying that is formulated negatively, probably in response to Jewish threats. It will not be the faithful Christians who will be subject to the second death after the final judgment. The expression second death has its origins in Judaism [cf. *Tg. Isa.* 22:14; 65.15; *Tg. Onq.* Deut 33:6; *Tg. Neof.* Deut 33:6; *Tg. Jer.* 51:39, 57; *Pirqe R. El.* 34], and in Revelation John uses it to point to the final fate of the wicked (20:14–15; 21:8).[321]

The Smyrnaean overcomers are emphatically promised that they *will not be hurt by the second death*. Overcomers are also made into a kingdom and transformed into priests according to Revelation 1:5b, 6 and 5:9–10, and many commentators have seen this as *already-and-not-yet* or *inaugurated eschatology*.[322] Bandstra best describes the relationship between overcomer and kingly function:

> John preserves the future sense of the saints reigning with Christ: …On one interpretation of this passage, this is a promise to martyrs (and perhaps to all Christians who die in the Lord) that even after death their priestly and royal functions will not cease—but continue in heaven. What Revelation 1:5b, 6 and 5:9, 10 therefore do is balance out the *"not yet"* of the future by affirming that *"already now"* Christians rule in Christ's name on the earth. To be sure, such reigning is not now apart from suffering—any more than was the case with Jesus himself. Jesus by being the Lamb that was slain and the One who conquered because He was slain, calls all of us to "conquer" in His name, thus "to conquer" or "to overcome" through the suffering of love that He demonstrated.[323]

Remarkably, the King dissolves the effects of martyrdom by raising the saints from the dead, eradicating all suffering, and making the subject a king and priest (1 Pet 2:9; Rev 1:6; 5:10; 20:6). The King has gone before his subjects and has experienced suffering and death as the ultimate martyr on their behalf. The Great King ultimately restored the breached covenant (21:3, 7) through the suffering servant (Isa 52:13; 53:11).

THE BLESSING OF NO SECOND DEATH—2:11B

Ὁ νικῶν οὐ μὴ ἀδικηθῇ ἐκ τοῦ θανάτου τοῦ δευτέρου.

"The one who conquers will not be hurt by the second death." (Rev 2:11b)

The King, as part of the covenant blessings, promises that the overcomers will definitely not experience the *second death* (ἐκ τοῦ θανάτου τοῦ δευτέρου, *ek tou thanatou tou deuterou*, 2:11b).[324] The promise of the second death is set against the overcomer's fulfilment within the New

---

[321] Krodel, *Revelation*, 113.

[322] Andrew J. Bandstra, "A Kingship and Priests: Inaugurated Eschatology in the Apocalypse," *CTJ* 27, no. 1 (1992): 22–23; Eugene M. Boring, "The Theology of Revelation: The Lord Our God the Almighty Reigns," *Int.* 40, no. 3 (1986): 108–11; Swete, *Apocalypse*, 82; Lohmeyer, *Offenbarung*, 57, 193, 197; Hendriksen, *Conquerors*, 112, 230–32; Caird, *Revelation*, 77, 297.

[323] Bandstra, "Kingship and Priests," 22–23.

[324] The Rabbinic phrase *second death* "perhaps answered a Jewish taunt in Smyrna." Hemer, *Letters to the Seven Churches*, 75–77.

Jerusalem in Revelation 20:6, 14; 21:8. The second death is the lake of fire, which is understood as eternal punishment, "the negation of eternal life."[325] The parallel passage is in Revelation 20:6: "Blessed and holy is the one who shares in the first resurrection! Over such the second death has no power, (ὁ δεύτερος θάνατος οὐκ ἔχει ἐξουσίαν, *ho deuterous thanatos ouk echei exousian*), but they will be priests of God and of Christ, and they will reign with him for a thousand years" (20:6).

If one sets aside the millennial controversy and focuses on the rest of the verse, it is striking and helpful to see the similarities between Revelation 20:6 and 2:11b. There is no doubt that for the overcomer the absence of the second death is a great blessing given by the king: "No true Christian, much less one who dies a martyr's death, need fear anything beyond the pang of the first death. The second death of condemnation in the lake of fire leaves the faithful scatheless, no matter how others may suffer from the terrors."[326]

Thompson draws significant conclusions from the OT relationship between Yahweh/Israel and the ANE suzerain/vassal, which have relevant principles that apply in the present context:

> The metaphor of the suzerain-vassal relationship gave expression to this relationship in a most vivid and concrete way. And yet, it was only a metaphor. The relationship between YHWH and Israel was something far deeper than could be defined as a legal compact. It was concerned with the solemn engagement and commitment of YHWH to Israel and of Israel to YHWH on the highest possible level. It involved a religious relationship of the highest order with reciprocal faithfulness of a kind that was unknown among the suzerains and vassals of the ancient Near East. In that relationship election and commitment were the fundamental elements. The suzerain-vassal metaphor only gave formal and concrete expression to the meaning of the relationship involved in that election and commitment.[327]

The message to Smyrna further develops the metaphor beyond election and commitment to yet a higher realm of *perseverance in suffering* consummated in the blessing of eternal life for overcomers. This was truly good news for those facing martyrdom.[328] Mulholland applies the significance of the message to the modern church by pointing out that "the church in Smyrna is but a microcosm of what the larger church is to be in the world; it is one example of what it means to be faithful citizens of New Jerusalem in the midst of Fallen Babylon."[329]

Remarkably, the King not only promises the overcomers deliverance from the second death, but he also promises a share in his kingdom. Here we see that the biblical idea of covenant is raised to an eschatological plane superior to the ANEVT. The covenant relationship is perfectly restored by the Great King (21:3, 7). The *first and the last* (2:8) delivers from the

---

[325] Morris, *Revelation*, 65; Thompson, *Revelation*, 70. Mulholland comments that "this was a common perception in rabbinic Judaism" *Revelation*, 103 n. 19; cf. *Tg. Neof.* on Deut 33:6, and the *Tg. Neof.* 51:39, 57; Isa 52:14; 65:6.

[326] Moffatt, *Revelation*, 355; Caird, *Revelation*, 36.

[327] Thompson, "Near Eastern Suzerain-Vassal," 16; George Ernest Wright, *The Old Testament Against Its Environment* (Chicago, Ill.: Allenson, 1951), 54–60.

[328] Morris, *Revelation*, 65.

[329] Mulholland, *Revelation*, 104.

second death and restores to full covenant fellowship those separated by its breach. The Smyrnaean readers would have seen in this statement an encouraging promise from the King to persevere in their suffering even to the point of the first death (martyrdom), knowing that the overcomers will definitely not experience the *second death*.

Summary

Hemer sums up by saying that "eternal life, untouched by the threat of spiritual death, shall be the prize of the faithful 'athlete' who endures persecution to the suffering of physical death."[330] This is not the attitude of heroism of just a few individuals, but it is "the self-evident consequence of faith; one who is a Christian must also be able to suffer."[331] Dibelius points out that "early Christianity was capable of arguing for the necessity of suffering by referring to eschatological"[332] ideals (Mark 13:7ff; Hermas *Vis.* 4.2.5; 4.3.4). The divine *macarism* upon the overcomers (those faithfully enduring persecution) is the eschatological fulfilment of the covenant blessing. Smyrna is blessed as she perseveres under trial, which is metaphorically consummated in the crown of life. The covenant blessing provided incentive for the suffering church to persevere.

Proclamation Witness Formula—2:11a

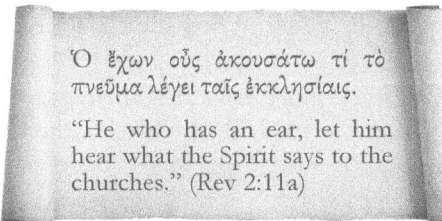

Ὁ ἔχων οὖς ἀκουσάτω τί τὸ πνεῦμα λέγει ταῖς ἐκκλησίαις.

"He who has an ear, let him hear what the Spirit says to the churches." (Rev 2:11a)

In the treaty between Smyrna and Magnesia in the third century BC, it was mutually agreed that representatives be appointed to ensure that none leave before the treaty had been heard by all present.[333]

Here in the oracle to Smyrna there is no need for a long list of witnesses, as the Spirit of Christ acts as his own witness (2:11) to the covenant lawsuit. The Smyrnaean congregation is called to hear what the Spirit-Judge has to say about the covenant breaking conduct of the churches. In the case of Smyrna (and Philadelphia) there is only commendation and not condemnation. The spirit testifies that there is no fault with her, and the call to persevere echoes forth from the courts.

The problem of theodicy within the church of Smyrna is addressed within the nature of God who knows their afflictions, exhorts the faithful not to be afraid, and grants the blessing of the crown of life to those who overcome. The Smyrnaean church is to be silenced by faith to witness "what the Spirit says to the churches" (2:11).

---

[330] Hemer, *NIDNTT* 1:406.

[331] Martin Dibelius, *James: A Commentary on the Epistle of James*, ed. Heinrich Greeven and Helmut Koster, trans. Michael A. Williams, Hermeneia (Philadelphia, Pa.: Fortress, 1976), 90.

[332] Ibid., 79.

[333] Hermann Bengtson and Hatto H. Schmitt, eds., *Die Staatsverträge Des Altertums*, vol. 3, Die Verträge Des Griechisch-Römischen Welt von 338 Bis 200 v. Chr. (Munich: Beck, 1969), 3.492:80–81.

Conclusion

Five unmistakable essential elements of the ANEVT, constituting a structure, are identified within the prophetic message to convey a covenant lawsuit message of encouragement to the overcomers within the church of Smyrna.

Firstly, the preamble, marked by the prophetic oracular formula τάδε λέγει Ω, (*tade legei omega*) calls attention to what the Great King, identified here as "the First and the Last," the eternal, transcendent, resurrected Christ, will say to Smyrna.

Secondly, the historical prologue is characterized by the omniscient King's intimate knowledge of Smyrna's suffering. This suffering results in physical poverty but also in spiritual wealth. The root of the suffering is identified with the activity of Satan through the Jewish synagogue in Smyrna. God is aware of this activity and sees it as treasonous against the Great King.

Thirdly, the Great King sets out Smyrna's stipulations in terms of two imperatives—*Do not fear* and *Be faithful*.

Fourthly, in response to these stipulations, God pledges to give the blessing of the crown of eternal life. The heart of the message to the Smyrnaean church is the covenant blessing expressed in obedience to the stated stipulations of faithfulness in the face of suffering. The eschatological *macarism* for the overcomers' obedience to the stipulations will be the King's gracious pledge of eternal preservation (eternal life) metaphorically conveyed by the crown of life.

Finally, acting as his own witness in the court case, the Spirit-Judge calls the Smyrnaean congregation to hear what he has to say to the covenant breaking conduct of the churches. There is no need to call upon external witnesses, as in the ANEVT, since God acts as his own witness in the court case.

8

Polytheistic Pergamum

The History of The City

*I*n order to understand the message to polytheistic Pergamum, with it many temples, it is helpful to examine both the cultural (Graeco-Roman) history of Pergamum, as well as the (Hebraic-Semitic) OT theological roots of the message. This chapter will examine the historical background to the city of Pergamum.

THE GEOGRAPHY OF PERGAMUM

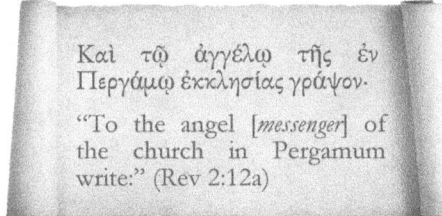

Καὶ τῷ ἀγγέλῳ τῆς ἐν Περγάμῳ ἐκκλησίας γράψον·

"To the angel [*messenger*] of the church in Pergamum write:" (Rev 2:12a)

Following the coastline north from Izmir for some 62 miles (100 km), turning inland into the Caicus valley of southern Mysia, one comes upon Pergamum (or Pergamon; Περγάμος, *Pergamos*; modern *Bergama*; coordinates: 39:07:57 N 27:11:03 E). The citadel is located on a precipice which rises 1100 ft. (335 meters) above the valley below (see Fig. 56).[1] The acropolis stands isolated, not easily accessible from any side, making it almost impregnable (see Fig. 44). The lower city is about 1.2 miles (2 km) away in the valley on the outskirts of the modern town of Bergama. The lower city is the site of the Asclepeion (see Figs. 60, 61), lower theater, Red hall, and stadium.

When Pergamum emerged as a community in the fourth cent. BC, the site was connected to the outside world with its own harbour at Elaia, 15 miles (24 km, now silted in) away on the Caicus River (modern-day *Bakırçay*),[2] and a good road system.[3] Water was supplied through

---

[1] Tevhit Kekec, *Pergamon* (Istanbul: Hitit Color, 1987), 3.

[2] Pausanias, *Guide to Greece, Vol. 1: Central Greece*, trans. Peter Levi (Harmondsworth: Penguin Classics, 1984), 321 n.36.

[3] Richard Evans, *A History of Pergamum: Beyond Hellenistic Kingship* (New York, N.Y.: Continuum International, 2012), 119–20.

56. Acropolis of Pergamum, with the Hellenistic theater (*ca.* 225–200 BC) carved vertically out of the side of the mountain with a capacity of *ca.* 10,000 citizens. Visible on the top are the pillars of the Temple of Trajan (second cent. AD).

seven aqueducts and to lift the water up to the acropolis the Attalids[4] developed (197–159 BC) the use of siphons, that were later adopted (second cent. BC) in other places by the Romans.[5]

The Roman author Pliny described it as *longe clarissimum Asiae,* celebrating it as "the most famous place of Asia" (Pliny *Nat.* 5.126 [Rackham]). W. M. Ramsay testified that:

> No city of the whole of Asia Minor—so far as I have seen, and there are few of any importance which I have not seen—possesses the same imposing and dominating aspect. It is the one city of the land which forced from me the exclamation "A royal city!"[6]

---

[4] The Attalids were the Hellenistic dynasty that ruled the city of Pergamum after the death of Lysimachus.
[5] Wilson, *Biblical Turkey*, 281.
[6] Ramsay, *Letters: Updated*, 216.

The History of Pergamum

According to Greek myth, depicted on the friezes of the Great Altar of Pergamum, the city was founded by Telephus, king of Asia Minor and the son of Hercules (grandson of Zeus).[7] In reality, it was originally settled by Aeolian Greeks in the 8th cent BC (Xenophon *Anab.* 7.8.8–22; *Hell.* 3.1.6).

Under Seleucid Control

Following the death of Alexander the Great, western Asia Minor was under the control of Lysimachus, one of Alexander's generals. However, another of Alexander's generals, Seleucus I Nicator (see Fig. 80), invaded Lysimachus' territory in 282 BC and Philetaerus, Lysimachus' treasurer, switched his allegiance to Seleucus. Lysimachus offered Seleucus his treasury for peace (Pausanias *Descr.* 1.10.3–4; Strabo *Geogr.* 13.4.1), but Seleucus eventually defeated and killed Lysimachus at the Battle of Corupedium in 281 BC (Pausanias *Descr.* 1.10.5).

Under Pergamene Control

The Pergamene dynasty of the Attalids was technically established in 283 BC by Lysimachus' treasurer, Philetaerus, who found himself the wealthy ruler in control of Lysimachus' great fortune of nine thousand talents of gold,[8] that he stored in Pergamum.[9] Through political marriages to the daughters of the Persian and Egyptian kings he established Pergamum as one of the great powers of western Asia Minor under Seleucid control. It prospered as the capital city of the Kingdom of Pergamum during the Hellenistic period, under the Attalid dynasty (281–133 BC).

Attalid Dynasty of Pergamene Kings		
King	Dates of Rule	Accomplishments
Philetaerus	283–263 BC	Defended Pergamum from the Galatians (278–276 BC) and established the dynasty.
Eumenes I	263–241 BC	Fought the Galatians and established Pergamum as a leading cultural center in art and science.

---

[7] Kevin Lee Osterloh, "Judea, Rome and the Hellenistic Oikoumene: Emulation and the Reinvention of Communal Identity," in *Heresy and Identity in Late Antiquity*, ed. Eduard Iricinschi and Holger M. Zellentin, Texts and Studies in Ancient Judaism 119 (Mohr Siebeck, 2008), 196–99.

[8] On the Coinage of the Attalids see Edward Theodore Newell, *The Pergamene Mint Under Philetaerus*, 76 (New York, N.Y.: American Numismatic Society, 1936); Christopher Howgego, *Ancient History from Coins*, Approaching the Ancient World (New York, N.Y.: Routledge, 2002), 54–56.

[9] Renée Dreyfus and Ellen Schraudolph, eds., *Pergamon: The Telephos Frieze from the Great Altar*, vol. 2 (San Francisco, Calif.: University of Texas Press, 1997), 24.

Attalus I	241–197 BC	Conquered the Galatians, began construction of the Great Altar of Zeus (see Figs. 65, 66), and established the library (see Fig. 59). An avid art collector with a significant private collection, the first in the western world (see Fig. 57).
Eumenes II	197–159 BC	Lavish building programme including the Altar of Zeus, in commemoration of Attalus I's victory over the Galatians, expanded the library and extending the sanctuary of *Athena Nikephoros*. A period of cultural expansion. This was the height of the Attalid Empire.
Attalus II	159–138 BC	Called Philadelphus. He was only twelve years old when he came to the throne but built and paid for the magnificent Stoa in Athens (see Fig. 112).
Attalus III	138–133 BC	With no male heirs, he left Pergamum to the Romans.

Table 2. Attalid Dynasty of Pergamene Kings

Under Roman control

The last ruler of the dynasty, Attalus III, bequeathed the kingdom to the Romans in 133 BC,[10] and Pergamum became the capital of the Roman province of Asia[11] until Augustus reorganized the province, around 30 BC,[12] and from then on, Ephesus functioned as the governmental center of the senatorial province,[13] where the Roman governor operated as the proconsul and where the procurators were headquartered. However, it is believed that the seat of government remained in Pergamum (*CAH* 11:581), where the center of a *conventus* or διοίκησις (*dioikēsis*) was located[14] but it was not the capital of the province in the first century.[15]

57. A Hellenistic portrait of the king of Pergamum, Attalus I.

[10] Strabo *Geogr.* 13.4.2; Pliny *Nat.* 33.53.148; *OGIS* 2.338.7.

[11] Ramsay maintains that Pergamum remained the capital city until ca. 130 AD, but is contested by Chapot who argues that it was Ephesus. Ramsay, "Pergamus or Pergamum," 3:750–51; Chapot Victor, *La Province Romaine Proconsulaire d'Asie* (Paris, France: Librairie Emile Bouillon, 1904), 138–39. Hemer suggests that Rome may have intentially left the situation ambiguous due to the intense civil rivarlry between Pergamum and Ephesus. Hemer, *Letters to the Seven Churches*, 82–84.

[12] Wolfgang Radt, *Pergamon: Geschichte Und Bauten Einer Antiken Metropole* (Darmstadt: Primus Verlag, 1999), 41–44.

[13] Alzinger and Knibbe, Ephesos Vom Beginn Der Römischen Herrschaft in Kleinasien Bis Zum Ende derPrincipatzeit, 759.

[14] Louis Robert, "Le Culte de Caligula À Milet et La Province d'Asie," *Hellenica* 7 (1949): 223–26.

[15] Steven J. Friesen, "Satan's Throne, Imperial Cults and the Social Settings of Revelation," *JSNT* 27, no. 3 (2005):

Unhappy about Attalus III's decision to give the Pergamene kingdom to Rome, riots broke out and rebellion followed with the Romans retaliating by force to suppress the revolt (*CAH* 9:102–105). In 131 BC, a Roman army under the command of Consul Licinius Crassus came to Anatolia, but was defeated by Aristorikos near Myrina. Aristorikos was eventually defeated by the Romans and killed in 130 BC. Many years of Roman oppression made the reception of Mithridates VI easy in 88 BC leading a savage revolt against the Romans (Appian *Mithrid.* 4.22; Paterculus *C. Rom. Hist.* 2.18) and garnering from the people the titles of both god (θεός, *theos*) and savior (σωτήρ, *sōtēr*; Diodorus *Hist. Lib.* 37.26).[16] Despite the resistance to the Roman occupation,[17] Pergamum remained a relatively free city.

By 27 BC Asia was a Roman senatorial province and in 29 BC Pergamum was granted the first imperial cult temple in Asia, in honor of Octavian and (perhaps) *Dea Roma* (see Fig. 173; Dio Cassius *Hist. Rom.* 51.20.6; Tacitus *Ann.* 4.37).[18] The temple is depicted on several Augustan coins[19] and was likely located at the base of the acropolis.

In AD 17 a severe earthquake, during the reign of Emperor Tiberius (AD 14–37; see Figs. 43, 97, 111), hit the Hermus Valley. Pliny (AD 77) states that it was "the greatest earthquake in human memory ... [with] twelve Asiatic cities being overthrown in one night" (Pliny *Nat.* 2.200; Tacitus *Ann.* 2.47).[20] Pergamum was one of the cities affected, but it was gradually rebuilt and granted the privilege of having a second imperial cult temple (see Trajaneium below), this time for Trajan (AD 98–117). According to Friesen "in the early years of Trajan's reign, the city of Pergamum stopped using the simple title '*ē boulē kai o dēmos*' in its inscriptions and replaced it with '*ē boulē kai o dēmos tōn neokorōn pergamenōn*' 'the boule and the *dēmos* of the *neokōrate* Pergamenes'" (*AvP* 8,2.461).[21] The rebuilding continued under Hadrian (r. AD 117–38; see Figs. 93, 109), who granted them the title of *mētropolis* (*AvP* 8,3.20; 23; 37; 38)[22] that stimulated an ambitious building programme including temples, an amphitheater, forum, the Red Hall, a

---

361.

[16] Adrienne Mayor, *The Poison King: The Life and Legend of Mithradates, Rome's Deadliest Enemy* (Princeton, N.J.: Princeton University Press, 2011); Adrian N. Sherwin-White, "Roman Involvement in Anatolia, 167–88 BC," *JRS* 67 (1977): 70–75.

[17] For Pergamum's involvement in the revolt and under Roman rule see Radt, *Pergamon*, 27–48; Helmut Halfmann, *Die Senatoren aus dem östlichen Teil des Imperium Romanum bis zum Ende des 2. Jahrhunderts n. Chr*, Hypomnemata 58 (Göttingen: Vandenhoeck und Ruprecht, 1979), 25–34.

[18] Aune, *Rev 1–5*, 180–81; Friesen, *Twice Neokoros*, 7–15.

[19] Behrendt Pick, "Die Neokorie-Tempel von Pergamon Und Der Asklepios Des Phyromachos," in *Festschrift. Walther Judeich, Zum 70. Geburtstag, Überreicht von Jenner Freunden* (Weimar: Hermann Boehlaus, 1929), 28–44; Carol Humphrey Vivian Sutherland, *The Cistophori of Augustus* (London, U.K.: Royal Numismatic Society, 1970), 36, 103.

[20] Elizabeth Keitel, "The Art of Losing: Tacitus and the Disaster Narrative," in *Ancient Historiography and Its Contexts: Studies in Honour of A. J. Woodman*, ed. Christina S. Kraus, John Marincola, and Christopher Pelling (Oxford, U.K.: Oxford University Press, 2010), 335.

[21] Friesen, *Twice Neokoros*, 58.

[22] Christian Habicht, *Die Inschriften Des Asklepieions*, vol. 3, Altertümer von Pergamon 8 (Berlin: De Gruyter, 1969), 160.

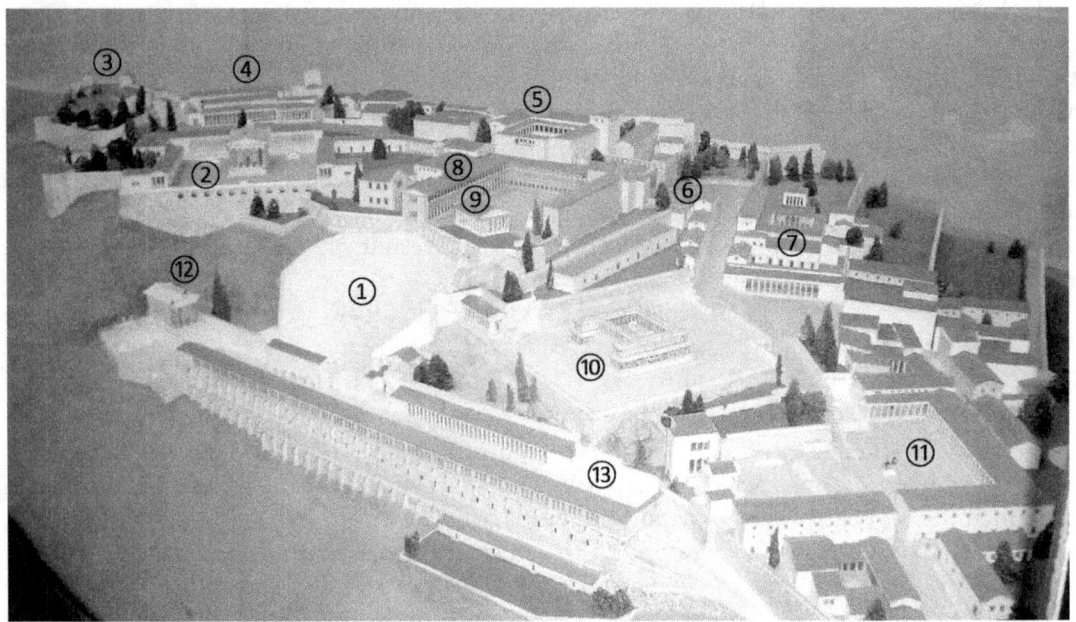

58. A model of the acropolis of the ancient Greek city of Pergamum, showing the situation in the second cent AD, by Hans Schleif (1902–1945). 1). Theater; 2). Trajaneium; 3). Arsenal Terrance; 4). Barraks; 5). Palace; 6). Citadel Gate; 7). Heroon; 8). Library; 9). Athena Temple; 10). Altar of Zeus; 11). Upper agora; 12). Dionysius Temple; 13). Stoa Terrace.

stadium, and the expansion of the Asclepeion.[23] During the second cent. AD many influential individuals were attracted to Pergamum, including the famous physician Galen (Claudius Galenus, AD 129–ca. 216; see Fig. 62), and the rhetorician Aelius Aristides.[24]

During the reign of Marcus Aurelius (AD 161–180) a small temple was built on the Acropolis for his wife Faustina (see Fig. 37). During his reign a plague inflicted Pergamum, attested to by an inscription that read in part: "Oh, Great Zeus, chase away the epidemic that is destroying the city of Asklepius."[25] In fact, the oracle to seek safety from the pestilence

---

[23] Mary Taliaferro Boatwright, *Hadrian and the Cities of the Roman Empire* (Princeton, N.J.: Princeton University Press, 2002), 90–91, 104, 188–89; Anthony R. Birley, *Hadrian: The Restless Emperor* (New York, N.Y.: Routledge, 2013), 166–68.

[24] Alexia Petsalis-Diomidis, *Truly Beyond Wonders: Aelius Aristides and the Cult of Asklepios* (Oxford, U.K.: Oxford University Press, 2010), 12; Ido Israelowich, *Society, Medicine and Religion in the Sacred Tales of Aelius Aristides* (Leiden: Brill, 2012), 123.

[25] Kekec, *Pergamon*, 19; R. J. Littman and M. L. Littman, "Galen and the Antonine Plague," *The American Journal of Philology* 94, no. 3 (1973): 243–55; Susan P. Mattern, *The Prince of Medicine: Galen in the Roman Empire* (Oxford, U.K.: Oxford University Press, 2013), 187–223.

mentions four of the patron deities of Pergamum including Zeus (see Figs. 95, 115, 126, 151, 154, 156), Athena (see Figs. 34, 124), Dionysus (see Fig. 35) and Asclepius (see Fig. 71).[26]

In AD 262, another earthquake badly damaged the city;[27] however the archaeology shows no evident damage to the houses of Pergamum.[28] The city never regained it glory and was destroyed by the Goths shortly thereafter.

The Population of Pergamum

Often the Roman population of Pergamum is estimated at ca. 200,000.[29] Galen, the Pergamum physician (see Fig. 62), perhaps gives a more accurate estimation. He places the population of Pergamum, including women and slaves, at 120,000 (Galen *Cogno.* 9; *Prop.* 5.49). Using Galen's numbers, Duncan-Jones calculates that the population of Pergamum in the second-century AD was ca. 180,000 total citizens, including slave and free.[30] But as Hanson points out, these numbers "would call for over 900 people per hectare within the city [of Pergamum] (a density only known in modern cities), or would require really quite substantial extramural habitation."[31] Hanson significantly lowers the population to between ca. 22,000 (based on 100/ha.) and ca. 88,000 (based on 400/ha.).[32] As Bagnall and Warden point out, Galen is concerned with other matters than accurate population figures, noting that Galen "gives the numbers while emphasizing how many Pergamenes (all but fewer than thirty) are less wealthy than his addressee and urging him not to wish to be richest of all, and he claims no great precision."[33] It may be safe to estimate the population at below 100,000 citizens in the second century AD.

The Important Buildings of Pergamum

Famous for her Library

The Pergamum library, identified by Conze in 1884 as located behind the north stoa on the acropolis (see Fig. 58 no. 8), was modelled on the famous Alexandrian library in Egypt and constructed during the rule of King Eumenes II (197–159 BC).[34] Another library is also located

---

[26] Ramsay, *Letters: Updated*, 207.

[27] Fant and Reddish note that this same earthquake also destroyed the interior of the Library of Celsus in Ephesus. Fant and Reddish, *Guide to Biblical Sites*, 194.

[28] Ulrike Wulf, Die Stadtgrabung: Die hellenistischen und römischen Wohnhäuser von Pergamon: unter besonderer Berücksichtigung der Anlagen zwischen der Mittel-und der Ostgasse (Berlin: de Gruyter, 1999), 212.

[29] Magie, *Roman Rule in Asia Minor*, 1:585; Tenney Frank, *An Economic Survey of Ancient Rome: Rome and Italy of the Empire* (Baltimore, Md.: John Hopkins University Press, 1975), 4:812–16.

[30] Duncan-Jones, *Economy*, 264 n.4.

[31] Hanson, "Urban System," 258.

[32] Ibid., 254.

[33] Warden and Bagnall, "Forty Thousand Citizens," 220 n.2.

[34] Lora Lee Johnson, "The Hellenistic and Roman Library: Studies Pertaining to Their Architectural Form" (Ph.D. diss., Brown University, 1989), 3.

59. The acropolis Library at Pergamum, Turkey. The holes used for the pins for the wooden shelves are still visible in the wall.

in the lower city in the Asclepium at the end of the North Stoa (see Fig. 58 no. 3).[35] After Alexandria, Pergamum contained the second largest library in the world, with over 200,000 hand-copied parchment scrolls at its peak (Plutarch *Ant.* 58.5),[36] attributed in part to the confiscation of private libraries (Strabo *Geogr.* 12.1.54f). However, it has been estimated that the main reading room of the library could only have held 12,000 scrolls, so the remaining works must have been stored elsewhere, no doubt in the library in the lower city.

The books were stored on the northern and western sides of the building with a 0.5 m. (20 in.) space between the wall and the book-shelves (Lat. *pegmata;* Cicero *Att.* 4.8.2) to protect them from the dampness on the opposite side of the wall.[37] Tradition holds that most of the works from Pergamum were sent to the Alexandrian library in 41 BC, as part of a wedding gift from Mark Anthony to Cleopatra, to help replace losses to the great library of the Ptolemies when it was destroyed by fire during the Roman war of 47 BC (Plutarch *Caes.* 49.3f; Dio Cassius *Hist. Rom.* 42.38.2).[38] However, the details are sketchy as even Plutarch, who reports the event, states that his source is unreliable (Plutarch *Ant.* 58.9–59.1).[39] There were marked differences between the collections of the two libraries in Pergamum and Alexandria. The scholars working at the Alexandrian library specialized in grammar (γραμματικό, *grammatikos*) and philology (φιλοςλόγοι, *philologoi*), while those working at the library of Pergamum specialized in the critical (κριτικόι, *kritikoi*) selection of works.[40]

The rivalry between the two libraries came to a head in the second cent. BC, as told by Marcus Varro and recounted by Pliny the Elder (*Nat.* 13.21). The librarian of the Alexandrian library was Aristophanes of Byzantium who was in high demand and desired by king Eumenes

---

[35] Akurgal, Ancient Civilizations, 106–7.

[36] Richard Billows, "Cities," in *A Companion to the Hellenistic World*, ed. Andrew Erskine, Blackwell Companions to the Ancient World (Oxford, U.K.: Blackwell, 2003), 202.

[37] Houston, Inside Roman Libraries, 183.

[38] Lionel Casson, *Libraries in the Ancient World* (New Haven, Conn.: Yale University Press, 2002), 46–53; Bernt Götze, *Antike Bibliotheken*, Jahrbuch Der Deutschen Archäologischen Instituts 52 (Berlin: de Greuyter, 1937), 230–37; Christian Callmer, "Antike Bibliotheken," *Opuscula Archaeologica* 3 (1944): 145–93.

[39] The Encylopaedia Britannica considers it a "doubtful tale." Hugh Chisholm, ed., *Encyclopædia Britannica*, 11th ed. (Cambridge, U.K.: Cambridge University Press, 1911), s.v. "Library," 13.1032.

[40] Gregory Nagy, "The Library of Pergamon as a Classical Model," in *Pergamon-Citadel of the Gods: Archaeological Record, Literary Description, and Religious Development*, ed. Helmut Koester, HTS 46 (Harrisburg, Pa.: Trinity Press International, 1998), 185.

60. Asclepeion complex and the north stoa viewed from the theater.

II of Pergamum for their own library. Ptolemy II of Alexandria was infuriated that another library had tried to lure such a great scholar away from his service; so he retaliated by putting Aristophanes in prison to keep him from taking employment in Pergamum (Vitruvius *Arch.* 7.4). But to reinforce his point, he restricted the export of papyrus to Asia Minor, which was an Egyptian government writing material monopoly. This ban made it necessary for Eumenes II to rediscover (Varro uses the Latin word *reperio*[41]) parchment, made from the skins of animals, as a substitute for papyrus. Parchment (also *vellum*) was commercialized by the sponsorship of king Eumenes II of Pergamum (Pliny *Nat.* 13.21) to replace the scarce supply of papyrus resulting from the Egyptian embargo.[42]

---

[41] The verb *reperio* used by Varro is defined by the *Latin Lexicon* as "supposes a previous concealment of the thing found and painstaking in the search for it." Frederick Percival Leverett, ed., *Latin Lexicon* (Philadelphia, Pa.: Peter Reilly Co., 1931), op cit. Rather than meaning "to invent" in the context it is more likely to mean "to rediscover".

[42] Esther Violet Hansen, *The Attalids of Pergamon* (Ithaca, NY: Cornell University Press, 1947), 274.

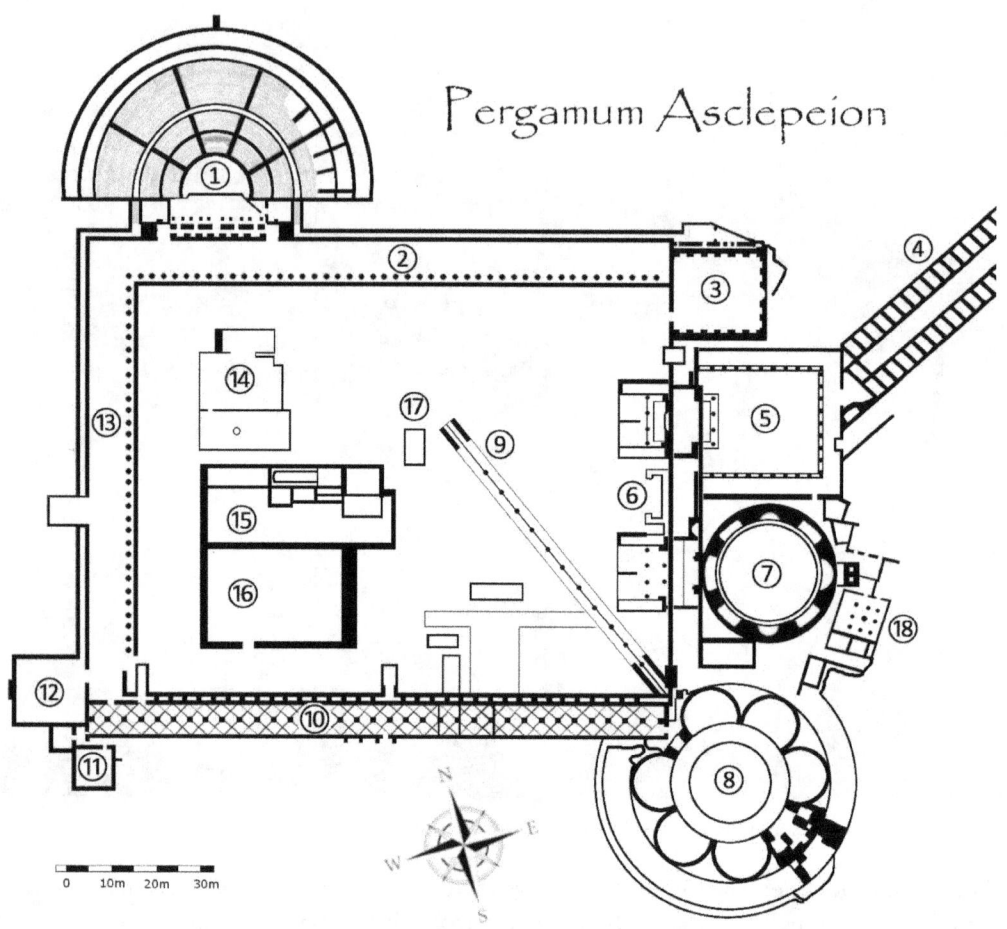

61. The Pergamum Asclepion, the sanctuary of *Asclepios Soter:* 1). Small theater; 2). North Stoa; 3). Small Library; 4). *Via Tecta,* Colonnaded Sacred Way leading to the Acropolis; 5). Propylaeum and Forecourt; 6). Cult niche; 7). Temple of Asclepius; 8). Treatment center; 9). Cryptopoticus, a vaulted underground tunnel; 10). South Stoa; 11). Latrines; 12). Southwest Hall; 13). West Stoa; 14). Hellenistic temple and Sacred Spring; 15 & 16). Incubation complex; 17). Pool; 18). Peristyle House.

It would be incorrect to draw from this that parchment was "invented" by Eumenes II. There are many parchment documents that predate this; one being a fine example of a parchment Parthian document, which dates from ca. 198 BC.[43] Johnson points out that:

---

[43] C. Bradford Welles, Robert O. Fink, and J. Frank Gilliam, *The Parchments and Papyri*, ed. Ann Perkins, Excavations at Dura-Europos, Final Report V, I (New Haven, Conn.: Yale University Press, 1959), 84ff; Richard R. Johnson, "Ancient and Medieval Accounts of the 'Invention' of Parchment," *CSCA* 3 (January 1, 1970): 117–18.

John Lydus [b. AD 490; Philadelphia] claims that Attalus was responsible for sending the first parchment to Rome. This is consistent with Varro's vague assertion that the utilization of parchment spread (to other regions) after its "discovery."[44]

Although parchment had a longer shelf-life it was much more expensive to manufacture than Papyrus. The common use of parchment would have brought down the cost of production. Thus more durable bound books began to replace the papyrus scrolls that had much shorter shelve-lives. The word *parchment* (περγαμηνή; *hē Pergamēnē charta*, "the Pergamene sheet"; Lat. *pergamentum*) is in fact derived from Pergamum (Hieronymus *Ep.* 7.2).

The library helped maintain Pergamum as a center of culture focusing on the arts, medicine, science, and education. Statues of important figures in Pergamum graced the walls of the library, including Athena Portenos, Hadrian (see Figs. 93, 109), and Sapho.[45]

FAMOUS FOR HER ASCLEPEION

Throughout the Graeco-Roman world numerous cities (i.e., Athens, Rome, Corinth, and Cos) had sanctuaries dedicated to the healing god, Asclepius (Ἀσκληπιός, *Asklēpiós* (see Fig. 71). The largest sanctuary was at Epidaurus,[46] Greece. This became the model for the sanctuary at Pergamum (Philostratus *Vit. Apoll.* 4.34), a major center for the cult of Asclepius.[47]

Pausanias states that the Asclepius Soter (savior) cult was introduced to Pergamum in ca. 350 BC from gratitude by Archias who was cured in the sanctuary of Epidaurus, following a hunting accident (*Descr.* 2.26.7; Aristides *Orat.* 39.5).[48] It reached the height of its popularity in the second cent. AD with a new temple of Zeus Asclepius built as part of the complex by L. Cuspius Pactumenius Rufinus in AD 142 (Aristides *Orat.* 42.6; Galen *Anat. Admin.* 1.2).[49]

The Asclepeion[50] (360 ft. by 425 ft.; see Figs. 60, 61),[51] modeled after the Roman Pantheon,[52] was more like an ancient religious spa with a healing center (hospital) that included

---

[44] Joannes Lydus, *Liber de Mensibus*, ed. Richard Wünsch (Leipzig: Teubneri, 1898), 14, lines 11–20; Johnson, "Ancient and Medieval Accounts of the 'Invention' of Parchment," 118, 120.

[45] Lee T. Pearcy, "Galen's Pergamum," *Archaeology* 38, no. 6 (1988): 33–39.

[46] Lynn R. LiDonnici, *The Epidaurian Miracle Inscriptions*, South Florida Studies in the History of Judaism 36 (Atlanta, Ga.: Scholars Press, 1995); Angeliki Charitonidou, "Epidaurus: The Sanctuary of Asclepius," in *Temples and Sanctuaries of Ancient Greece*, ed. Evi Melas (London: Thames & Hudson, 1973), 89–99.

[47] Lucian *Icar.* 24; Polybius *Hist.* 32.15.1; Galen *Anat. Admin.* 1.2; Aristides *Orat.* 42.4; Statius *Silv.* 3.4.21–25; Philostratus *Vit. Apoll.* 4.34.

[48] Emma Jeannette Levy Edelstein and Ludwig Edelstein, *Asclepius: A Collection and Interpretation of the Testimonies* (Baltimore, Md.: Johns Hopkins Press, 1998), 2:249.

[49] Akurgal, *Ancient Civilizations*, 105; Behr, *Aelius Aristides and the Sacred Tales*, 27–28.

[50] On the archaeology of the Asclepeion see John McRay, *Archaeology and the New Testament* (Grand Rapids, Mich.: Baker, 1991), 270–72; Pfeiffer, *Wycliffe Dictionary of Biblical Archaeology*, 438–40; Machteld J. Mellink, "Archaeology in Asia Minor," *AJA* 81, no. 3 (1977): 289–321; Oskar Ziegenaus and Gioia De Luca, *Altertümer von Pergamon* (Leiden: de Gruyter, 1968); Jörg Schäfer, "Pergamon Mysia, Turkey," in *The Princeton Encyclopedia of Classical Sites*, ed. Richard Stillwell, William L. MacDonald, and Marian Holland McAllister (Princeton, N.J.: Princeton University Press, 1976), 688–91.

[51] McRay, Archaeology and the New Testament, 271.

a large temple of Asclepius, three small temples (for Asclepius (see Figs. 71), Apollo (see Figs. 86, 90, 96), and Hygeia, three springs for drinking and bathing, a sacred pool, and an incubation or sleeping room to interpret dreams (Philostratus *Vit. Apoll.* 4.11).[53] They also often included a gymnasium (γυμνάσιον, *gumnasion*),[54] bath, library (see Fig. 59), and theater (see Figs. 56, 64) as this one did.[55] Visitors to the sanctuary would provide an offering to Asclepius when they were cured, commonly a replica of the body part that was healed.[56] Science and religion were not separated disciplines in the ancient world and they were inseparable in Pergamum.

One of the most famous ancient physicians was Galen (Claudius Galenus, AD 129–ca. 216; see Fig. 62), who was born in Pergamum and began his medical training there at the early age of sixteen, but after completing his studies in Smyrna, Alexandria and Corinth, returned to Pergamum when he was twenty-eight in order to care for sick and injured gladiators. He was also the court physician for emperors Marcus Aurelius, Commodus, and Septimius Severus, spending several years in Rome.[57] Much of his systematic medical work, derived from treating the wounds of gladiators and animals from the arena, formed the basis of western medicine.[58]

62. Statue of Galen of Pergamum.

---

[52] Petsalis-Diomidis, *Truly Beyond Wonders*, 194.

[53] Oskar Ziegenaus and Gioia De Luca, *Das Asklepieion*, vol. 1–4, Altertümer von Pergamon 11 (Berlin: Deutsches Archäologisches Institut, 1968); Adolf Hoffmann, "The Roman Remodeling of the Asklepieion," in *Pergamon-Citadel of the Gods: Archaeological Record, Literary Description, and Religious Development*, ed. Helmut Koester (Harrisburg, Pa.: Trinity Press International, 1998), 41–61.

[54] Three gymnasium were present in Pergamum on three levels, each dedicated to a different group: Young men (*neoi*), adolescents (*ephēboi*), and little boys (*paides*). Yegül, "Bath-Gymnasium Complex in Asia Minor"; Chambers, "Greek Athletics and the Jews."

[55] For other reconstructions of the Asclepeion, see Michael J. Vickers, *The Roman World*, 2nd ed., The Making of the Past (New York, N.Y.: Peter Bedrick Books, 1989), 124; Karl Kerényi, *Asklepios: Archetypal Image of the Physician's Existence* (Princeton, N.J.: Princeton University Press, 1959), 45.

[56] Examples of these replica body parts are on display in the Bergama and Corinth museums. Gerald David Hart, *Asclepius: The God of Medicine* (New York, N.Y.: Royal Society of Medicine, 2000); Kerényi, *Asklepios*; Edelstein and Edelstein, *Asclepius*.

[57] Vivian Nutton, "The Chronology of Galen's Early Career," *CQ* 23, no. 1 (1973): 158–71; Mattern, *The Prince of Medicine*, 7–35.

[58] John G. Simmons, Doctors and Discoveries: Lives That Created Today's Medicine from Hippocrates to the Present (New York, N.Y.: Houghton Mifflin, 2002), 34–38.

Aelius Aristides (AD 117/129–189), a hypochondriac, also spent two years in the Asclepeion for treatment of his ailments and described his experience in his *Sacred Tales*.[59] Patients were examined at the main gate and if there was no treatment for their illness they were refused entry, as the sign "For the exaltedness of all gods, entry of death to this sacred place is forbidden" was inscribed over the entrance of the healing center.[60] Patients who became sick inside the center were removed and pregnant women were not allowed to give birth inside.[61] The worshipers were of two categories: those like Aristides, who worshiped the old healing deity, and those who preferred to worship the imperial cult, as there was the statue of Hadrian (see Figs. 93, 109) in the cult niche on the western wall (given by Flavia Melitine).[62]

Treatments at the healing center ranged from incantations and magical potions to bloodletting, herbal medicine and ointments, but also included cold water and mud treatments, along with fasting, diet, and exercises one would expect to see at a typical modern-day spa.[63] Based on the presence of bronze and ivory surgical instruments in the Bergama Museum, it is believed that basic surgery was also performed there.[64]

The priest, Claudius Glycon, set up instructions (Lat. *lex sacra*) on the walls of the sanctuaries of the Asclepius outlining the procedures required for those inquiring through dreams about a remedy for their ailments.[65] It read in part:

63. Cistophoric Tetradrachm coin from Pergamum (*ca.* 160–150 BC). Obv.: A basket used for housing sacred snakes (Lat. *cista mystica*); all within an ivy wreath. Rev.: A bow-case with serpents; and stylis (*BMC* 88).

> Offer up a suckling pig on the altar to Asclepius, and lay on the table of sacrifices the right leg and entrails. Let him then contribute three obols to the treasury. In the evening, let him offer three nine-braided

---

[59] Israelowich, *Society, Medicine and Religion in the Sacred Tales of Aelius Aristides*; Christopher P. Jones, "Aelius Aristides and the Asklepieion," in *Pergamon-Citadel of the Gods: Archaeological Record, Literary Description, and Religious Development*, ed. Helmut Koester (Harrisburg, Pa.: Trinity Press International, 1998), 63–76.

[60] A. Atac, N. Aray, and R. V. Yildirim, "Asclepions in Turkey," *Balkan Military Medical Review* 9, no. 2 (2006): 83.

[61] Walter Addison Jayne, *Healing Gods of Ancient Civilizations* (New Haven, Conn.: Yale University Press, 1925), 176–85.

[62] Ido Israelowich, *Patients and Healers in the High Roman Empire* (Baltimore, Md.: Johns Hopkins University Press, 2015), 114; McDonagh, *Blue Guide: Turkey*, 163.

[63] Jayne, *Healing Gods*, 283–84.

[64] Atac, Aray, and Yildirim, "Asclepions in Turkey," 83; Howard C. Kee, "Self-Definition in the Asclepius Cult," in *Jewish and Christian Self-Definition: Self-Definition in the Graeco-Roman World*, ed. Ben F. Meyer and E. P. Sander, vol. 3 (Philadelphia, Pa.: Fortress, 1982), 129. Kee argues that only natural/miraculous healing took place at Pergamum due to the absence of surgical instruments, which have been found at other Asclepeion centres in Rhodes and Cyrene.

[65] Ramsay MacMullen and Eugene N. Lane, eds., *Paganism and Christianity 100–425 C. E.: A Sourcebook* (Minneapolis, Minn.: Augsburg Fortress, 1992), 31–32.

cakes. . . . Let him be ritually clean in the aforementioned respects, and from sexual intercourse, and goat's meat and cheese and . . . [come in after abstaining] on the third day. Let him who sleeps there take the wreath off and lay it on the bed. . . . They shall provide the god with good securities for the healing instructions [received by dreams during the nights in the sleeping-rooms] — whatever he may do to them—to render their accounts within a year . . . thank-victims for cure, not less than a year old. They shall contribute the thank-offerings for a cure to Asclepius' treasury, a sixth of a Phocacean stater to Apollo and a sixth of a Phocacean stater to Asclepius, when they are restored to health, and whatever else the god may require.[66]

Asclepius's symbol was two serpents entwined around a staff: the *caduceus* (or *kerykeion*) portrayed on the columns of the Asclepius (see Fig. 70) and the Cistophoric coins (see Fig. 63).[67] The snake and staff are still the symbol of modern medicine.[68] Live snakes were used in the healing process in the cult of Asclepius and permitted to roam freely in the healing center (Plutarch *Mor.* 755f; Homer *Il.* 2.299–332).[69]

A long (80 m./260 ft.) underground tunnel (see Fig. 58 no. 9) ran from the center of the courtyard to the southeast corner of the treatment center. On the southwest corner of the complex were two latrines for men (40 seats) and women (17 seats) finished in marble tiles with four Corinthian columns. At the northwest corner of the complex stood the small Roman theater (see Fig. 58 no. 1) that could seat about thirty-five hundred spectators.[70] It was used for small performances and to entertain the patients and visitors of the healing center with front row seats for dignitaries.

FAMOUS FOR HER THEATER

A larger, more dramatic theater (see Figs. 58 no. 1 and 56, 64) was built in the third cent. BC into the side of the acropolis with some of the steepest seats known in antiquity. It was divided into three parts by two *diazomas* with eighty rows of seats and an estimated capacity of 10,000 spectators. The seats were constructed of andesite, while the royal box of honor below was constructed of marble. The stage (σκηνή, *skēnē*) was some 37 metres (122 ft.) below the top row of seats and was made of wood so that it could be set up for performances and taken down

---

[66] Habicht, *Altertümer von Pergamon*, 3:168–69, no. 161.

[67] Ramsay, *Letters: Updated*, 208–11.

[68] Lura Nancy Pedrini and Duilio Thomas Pedrini, *Serpent Imagery and Symbolism: A Study of the Major English Romantic Poets* (New Haven, Conn.: College and University Press, 1966), 7.

[69] See "The Use of Live Snakes in the Worship of Asclepius" in James A. Kelhoffer, *Miracle and Mission: The Authentication of Missionaries and Their Message in the Longer Ending of Mark*, WUNT 112 (Tübingen: Mohr Siebeck, 2000), 369–71; Martin Persson Nilsson, *Geschichte Der Griechischen Religion*, 2nd ed., Handbuch Der Altertumswissenschaft, 5.2 (Munich: Beck, 1955), 2:216–17.

[70] Akurgal, *Ancient Civilizations*, 107; Finegan, *The Archeology of the New Testament*, 2014, 174; Ramsay MacMullen, *Paganism in the Roman Empire* (New Haven, Conn.: Yale University Press, 1983), 20; Yamauchi, *NT Cities*, 48; Wilson, *Biblical Turkey*, 290; McDonagh, *Blue Guide: Turkey*, 163; Cemil Toksöz, *Pergamum: Its History and Archaeology*, trans. Amhmet E. Uysal (Ankara, Turkey: Ayyildiz Matbassi, 1960), 13. Toksöz lists the seating capacity at 5,000.

64. The Hellenistic theater (*ca.* 225–200 BC) carved vertically out of the side of the mountain with a capacity of *ca.* 10,000 citizens.

when not in use so as not to obstruct the amazing view of the city below and the temple of Dionysus.[71]

FAMOUS FOR HER RELIGIOUS WORSHIP

Pergamum was famous as a religious center, prompting the apostle John to describe it as the place where "Satan's throne is" (Rev 2:13). There were many temples dedicated to such gods as Athena (see Figs. 34, 124),[72] Asclepius (see Fig. 71), Zeus (see Figs. 95, 115, 126, 151, 154, 156), Demeter (see Fig. 98),[73] Orpheus,[74] Persephone, Serapis, Isis, Harpocrates,[75] Dionysus (see Fig.

---

[71] Daria de Bernardi Ferrero, *Teatri classici in Asia Minore III: Città dalla Troade alla Pamfilia*, Studi Di Architettura Antica 4 (Rome: Di Bretschneider, 1974), 23–33.

[72] The temple to Athena Nikephoros ("Bearer of victory") was the divine protector of Pergamum and the most important temple in the city. Wilson, *Biblical Turkey*, 279; Voker Kästner, "Pergamon and the Attalids," in *Pergamon and the Hellenistic Kingdoms of the Ancient World*, ed. Carlos A. Picón and Seán Hemingway (Yale University Press, 2016), 32–39.

[73] Piok Zanon Cornelie, "The Sanctuary of Demeter at Pergamon: Architecture and Dynasty in the Early Attalid

35; *I.Perg.* 485–88), and Mithras (or Attis),[76] as well as the temples to the imperial cult and the worship of the emperor. The Asclepeion complex, mentioned above, had several temples dedicated to the goddess Hygieria, Apollo (see Figs. 86, 90, 96), and Telesphoros. Also, in AD 150 a new temple was erected to Asclepius and dedicated to Zeus.[77]

THE GREAT ALTAR OF ZEUS

Perhaps the most spectacular structure in Pergamum was to Zeus (see Figs. 95, 115, 126, 151, 154, 156) and Athena Nike (goddess of Victory; see Figs. 13, 87, 163; Ampelius *Lib. Mem.* 8.14). It has been called a temple and altar, but perhaps it is more accurate to describe it as a colonnaded court. Built around 170 BC by King Eumenes II of Greece, it became a prominent landmark in Asia Minor and the largest altar in antiquity. The base of the altar contained a frieze of the epic battle between the Giants and the Gigantomachy (Olympian gods).[78] Smoke from the altar would have continually marked the skyline, as Aune states, "sacrificial victims were burned twenty-four hours a day, seven days a week by a rotating group of priests,"[79] making this reminiscent of the smoke rising from the golden altar to the heavenly throne (Rev 8:3–4).

65. The Great Altar of Pergamum, on display in the Pergamum museum in Berlin, Germany. Some of the details, researched by Otto Puchstein based on coins, may not be accurate.

It was excavated between 1878 and 1886 by the German engineers, Carl Humann and Alexander Conze, who negotiated a deal with the Turkish officials to relocate the frieze fragments in 1910 to the Staatliche Museum in Berlin, where they remain today (see Fig. 65).[80] During the Second World War it was dismantled and housed in a bomb shelter that protected it

---

Capital" (Ph.D. diss., University of Pittsburgh, 2009).

[74] William Keith Guthrie, *Orpheus and Greek Religion: A Study of the Orphic Movement*, ed. L. Alderlink, 2nd ed. (Princeton, N.J.: Princeton University Press, 1993), 160–61.

[75] The Red Basilica, built by Trajan or Hadrian and still standing at Pergamum, was dedicated to Serapis, Isis, and Harpocrates. Akurgal, *Ancient Civilizations*, 103.

[76] Ibid.; Mellink, "Archaeology in Asia Minor," 310–13; Yamauchi, *NT Cities*, 43–45.

[77] Akurgal, *Ancient Civilizations*, 110; Lamar C. Berrett, *Discovering the World of the Bible* (Provo, Utah: Grandin, 1996), 615.

[78] Evamaria Schmidt, *The Great Altar of Pergamon* (Boston, Mass.: Boston Book and Art Shop, 1965); Max Kunze and Volker Kästner, *Der Altar von Pergamon: Hellenistische Und Römische Architektur*, 2nd ed., Antikensammlung II: Fuhrer Durch Die Ausstellung Des Pergamon Museums (Berlin: Henschelverlag Kunst und Gesellschaft, 1990), 30.

[79] Aune, *Rev 1–5*, 180; Metzger, *Breaking the Code*, 34.

[80] Aune, *Rev 1–5*, 194.

66. The remains of the Altar of Zeus. The structure around the altar is actually not a temple but an open air altar. The two trees mark the location of the altar, but the structure which surrounded it is now in the Staatliche (formerly Pergamum) Museum in Berlin.

from the allied bombing raids that heavily damaged the museum.[81] All that remains today at the site is the five-stepped base, with a large tree growing in the center (see Fig. 66). The remains were being looted by the local residents in Pergamos, who were using the stones as building materials and burning pieces of the marble for lime.

According to Kosmetatou, little is actually known about the Great Altar:

> We do not know to whom it was dedicated, when exactly it was built, its purpose or its impact on artistic developments of the period, while its reconstruction remains a matter of fierce debate among art and architectural historians. However, scholars agree that the popular Gigantomachy theme probably symbolized Attalid victories against the Galatians and functioned as a symbol of the struggle of good vs. evil and the forces of civilization vs. the "barbarians."[82]

However, the theory that it was a victory over the Gauls[83] is now rejected by most scholars,[84] and another frieze on the inside wall of the court depicted the account of Telephus, the son of Hercules who was hailed as the legendary founder of Pergamum.[85] Although one of the greatest works of Hellenistic art,[86] in antiquity it is only mentioned by Ampelius, who describes it as "a large marble altar, forty feet high with a great many sculptures, among which a Battle of the Giants" (*Lib. Mem.* 8.14).

---

[81] Yamauchi, *NT Cities*, 36.

[82] Elizabeth Kosmetatou, "The Attalids of Pergamon," in *A Companion to the Hellenistic World*, ed. Andrew Erskine, Blackwell Companions to the Ancient World (Oxford, U.K.: Blackwell, 2003), 165; Brunilde Sismondo Ridgway, *Hellenistic Sculpture II: The Styles of Ca. 200–100 B.C.*, Wisconsin Studies in Classics (Madison, Wisc.: University of Wisconsin Press, 2000), 19–102; Andrew Stewart, "Pergamo Ara Marmorea Magna: On the Date, Reconstruction, and Functions of the Great Altar of Pergamon," in *From Pergamon to Sperlonga: Sculpture and Context*, ed. Nancy T. de Grummond and Brunilde Sismondo Ridgway, Hellenistic Culture and Society (Berkeley, Calf.: University of California Press, 2001), 32–57.

[83] Akurgal, Ancient Civilizations, 71.

[84] Bernard Andreae, "Datierung Und Bedeutung Des Telephosfrieses Im Zusammenhang Mit Den Übrigen Stiftungen Der Ataliden von Pergamon," in *Der Pergamonaltar. Die Neue Präsentation Nach Restaurierung Des Telephosfrieses*, ed. Wolf-Dieter Heilmeyer (Tübingen: Wasmuth, 1997), 68.

[85] Wilson, *Biblical Turkey*, 285; Fant and Reddish, *Guide to Biblical Sites*, 294.

[86] Thomas Bertram Lonsdale Webster, *Hellenistic Poetry and Art* (London, U.K.: Methuen, 1964), 189–91.

Famous for the Imperial Cult

As the initial capital of Asia under the Romans, Pergamum had a long history of allegiance to the Romans and like Smyrna and Ephesus, it was famed for its worship of the emperor (imperial cult)[87] and was granted the title *neōkoros* (νεωκόρος), as the keeper of the temple (see *The Introduction: Imperial Cult*).[88] As Ramsay points out:

> Here was built the first Asian Temple of the divine Augustus [by the provincial council (κοινόν, *koinon*) of Asia in 29 BC], which for more than forty years was the one centre of the Imperial religion for the whole Province. A second Asian Temple had afterwards been built at Smyrna, and a third at Ephesus; but they were secondary to the original Augustan Temple at Pergamum.[89]

Three temples were dedicated to the imperial cult including Augustus, Trajan, and Severus,[90] granting Pergamum the distinction of three times *neōkoros* (τρίς νεωκόρος, "temple keeper").[91] While the temple of Augustus has yet to be identified in excavations,[92] is only known from numismatic records, the ruins of the Trajaneium, not to be confused with the temple of Augustus, can still be seen on the acropolis of the upper city (see Fig. 59). Coins with Augustus's image on one side and the temple front on the other were minted by Augustus and his successor in the first century. On some of the coins the temple was represented with six columns (hexastyle), while more commonly it had four columns (tetrastyle).[93] Hadrian (r. AD 117–38; see Figs. 93, 109) was later deified and worshiped in his own temple, which was also depicted on coins.[94]

---

[87] During the Hellenistic and Roman period, Attalus I (see Fig. 57) and Eumenes II were deified and worshipped in the Heroon as part of the Imperial cult (see Fig. 58 no. 7). Kekec, *Pergamon*, 30.

[88] For a comprehensive treatment of the Imperial Cult in Pergamum from numismatic and epigraphic remains, see chapter 1. Pergamon in Mysia (Augustus) in Burrell, *Neokoroi*, 17–37.

[89] Ramsay, *Letters: Updated*, 215.

[90] Hemer, *Letters to the Seven Churches*, 85, 87, 104; Franz, "Propaganda, Power and the Perversion," 80; Eugene M. Boring, *Revelation* (Louisville, Ky.: Westminster/Knox, 1989), 91; Ramsay, *Letters: Updated*, 215; Mounce, *Revelation*, 79; Charles, *Revelation*, 1:61; Kiddle, *Revelation*, 30; Swete, *Apocalypse*, 34; Osborne, *Revelation*, 141–43; Barclay, *Letters*, 44–45; Aune, *Rev 1–5*, 183–84; Friesen, "Satan's Throne," 366; Brent, *The Imperial Cult*, 178–90; Otto Pfleiderer, *Primitive Christianity: Its Writings and Teachings in Their Historical Connections*, trans. W. Montgomery (London, U.K.: Williams & Norgate, 1910), 415.

[91] Ramsay, *Letters: Updated*, 207.

[92] Wilson, *Biblical Turkey*, 284.

[93] Carol Humphrey Vivian Sutherland, *Coinage in Roman Imperial Policy, 31 B.C.–A.D. 68* (London, U.K.: Methuen & Company, 1951), 43 (see plate II, coin 4); Magie, *Roman Rule in Asia Minor*, 2:1293 n.15; Warwick Wroth, *A Catalogue of the Greek Coins in the British Museum: Mysia*, ed. Reginald Stuart Poole (London, U.K.: Quaritch, 1892), 137–38, nos. 236–37 and 252–53.

[94] Magie, *Roman Rule in Asia Minor*, 1:594; Akurgal, *Ancient Civilizations*, 82; Price and Trell, *Coins and Their Cities: Architecture on the Ancient Coins of Greece, Rome, and Palestine*, 16. Price and Trell provide a view of the temple from the coins of Pergamum.

THE TRAJANEIUM

The Trajaneium (Trajan temple, see Fig. 67) in Pergamum was built of white marble and was started under the Roman Emperor Trajan (AD 98–117) but enlarged and completed under Hadrian (AD 117–138). Colossal statues of both emperors have been discovered in the ruins along with a statue of Zeus (see Figs. 95, 115, 126, 151, 154, 156) who was also worshiped here. The temple extended 68 metres by 58 metres (223 by 190 ft.) with nine Corinthian columns on the two longer sides and six Corinthian columns on the two shorter sides.[95] According to Yamauchi, it was "the most splendid monument erected to Trajan anywhere in Asia."[96]

67. The partially restored Trajaneium in Pergamum.

This peristyle temple, for the worship of the emperor, may have been similar to the temple to Tiberius (see Figs. 43, 97, 111) which was built earlier in Smyrna. If one holds to a late date for the writing of Revelation, then this temple to the emperor Trajan was built shortly after the book was written. The temple was uncovered in the 1880's under the direction of the architect H. Stiller. It was abandoned, but received renewed interest in the 1960's from the Turkish Antiquities and German Archaeological Institute (DAI), who partially reconstructed it (see Fig. 67). Next to the entrance is an inscription from the *dēmos* and *boulē* of Thyatira congratulating Pergamum on the privilege of "becoming the *neokoros* for two imperial cult temples."[97]

---

[95] Fant and Reddish, *Guide to Biblical Sites*, 289.
[96] Yamauchi, *NT Cities*, 42.
[97] Wilson, *Biblical Turkey*, 285.

9

Praised Pergamum

Commentary on Revelation 2:12–17

*T*his chapter will examine the content of the message to Pergamum, who are praised for their faithfulness even to the point of death. Revelation 2:12–17 will be examined in the light of the proposed covenant background and structure. On the commission to write (γράψον, *graphon* 2:12) and the role of angels (ἄγγελος, *angelos*) as mediating messengers, see chapter 3, *The Messenger's Commission*.

MESSENGER PREAMBLE FORMULA—2:12A

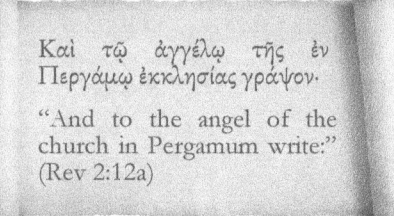

Καὶ τῷ ἀγγέλῳ τῆς ἐν Περγάμῳ ἐκκλησίας γράψον·

"And to the angel of the church in Pergamum write:" (Rev 2:12a)

John begins each message to the churches with τάδε λέγει Ω (*tade legei omega*, "These are the words" 2:1, 8,12,18; 3:1a, 7, 14), setting the context for the suzerain/King who will speak to the churches.[1] He proceeds to describe Christ in a way that echoes Revelation chapter 1 (vs. 13, 16), using a formula familiar to the Christian community. Within the OT prophetic structure[2] this prophetic *messenger preamble formula*[3] τάδε λέγει Ω, (*tade legei omega*, "These are the words") introduces the sovereign's message. On the prophetic *messenger preamble formula* see the discussion under "The Messenger's Commission" in chapter 1.

DESCRIPTION OF THE SUZERAIN WHO HAS A SWORD—2:12B

Here in the message to Pergamum, Christ the King is described as having a sharp two-edged sword and is reminiscent of the image of Christ who has a "sharp two–edged sword" (ῥομφαίαν τὴν δίστομον, *rhomphaian tēn distomon*) coming from his mouth in the first chapter of Revelation (1:16). The mention of the sword in verse 12, appearing from the mouth, is delayed until the

---

[1] Beale, *Revelation*, 229.
[2] Num 22:15–16; Judg 11:14–15; 1 Kgs 2:30; 2 Chr 36:23; Ezra 1:2.
[3] Graves, *SMRVT*, 141–47; Osborne, *Revelation*, 111.

> Τάδε λέγει ὁ ἔχων τὴν ῥομφαίαν τὴν δίστομον τὴν ὀξεῖαν·
>
> "*The words* of him who has the sharp two-edged sword." (Rev 2:12b)

68. Replica of the Pompeii *gladius* sword.

sixteenth verse (2:16), but indicates that this sword is not physically wielded by the hand in judgment, but projected in the word of God.[4]

The image of a sword issuing from the mouth is well established in the OT (Isa 11:4; 49:2) as well as in Revelation (19:15, 21). The two-edged sword is mentioned in Proverbs 5:4 and Psalm 146:6 as well as *Sir* 21:3, and *Ahiqar* 2.18. The Hebrew has only one word for sword, *ḥereb* (חרב), while in Greek there is a distinction made between two terms used for a sword; ῥομφαία (*rhomphaía*, long spear or javelin; Thracian broadsword 1:16; 2:16; 19:15, 21), and μάχαιρα (*machaira*, short sword or dagger; 6:4; 13:10, 14; Judg 3:16 LXX).[5] Whiting explains that the Greek word for sword here (ῥομφαία, *rhomphaía* 2:12, 16):

> is not the oriental scimitar or the ordinary cutting sword employed by many nations, especially the Greeks, but a two-edged, sharp-pointed weapon used by the Romans [see Fig. 68]. . . . In Roman estimation the sword was the symbol of highest official authority possessed by the proconsul of the province, and included the power of life and death.[6]

The Roman proconsul (senatorial governor) in Asia Minor was granted almost unlimited *imperium* power during his stay in office, subject to the emperor's *imperium maius*,[7] and the sword (μάχαιραν, *machairan*, see Figs. 68, 69; Rom 13:4) was the symbol of his power (Philostratus *Vit. Soph.* 1.25.2).[8] The emperor carried a sword around his neck as a symbol of imperial power.[9] However, during the first two centuries AD it was not strictly accurate to equate this power with the *ius gladii*, or "right of the sword (μάχαιρα, *macheira*)", which was the legal right to execute any Roman citizen who was an "enemy of the state" (Ulpian *Dig.* 1.18.6.8; dates to the

---

[4] Michaelis, *TDNT* 6:667.

[5] Anthony M. Snodgrass, *Arms and Armor of the Greeks* (Baltimore, Md.: The Johns Hopkins University Press, 1998), 97–98. See also O. Kaiser, *TDOT* 5:155.

[6] Whiting, Revelation of John, 78.

[7] Pliny *Ep.* 3.9.15; 10.96; Dio Cassius *Hist. Rom.* 53.13.6–8; Josephus *Ant.* 18.1.1; *J.W.* 2.8.1; Philippe Horovitz, "Essai Sur Les Pouvoirs Des Procurateurs-Gouverneurs," *RBPH* 17, no. 1 (1938): 54.

[8] James Leigh Strachan-Davidson, *Problems of the Roman Criminal Law* (Oxford, U.K.: Clarendon, 1912), 167–69; Adrian N. Sherwin-White, *Roman Society and Roman Law in the New Testament: The Sarum Lectures 1960–1961*, Oxford University Press Academic Monograph Reprints (Oxford, U.K.: Clarendon, 2004), 10–11.

[9] Tacitus *Ann.* 3.68; Suetonius *Galb.* 11; Dio Cassius *Hist. Rom.* 42.37.

third cent. AD) as the *ius gladii* was limited to soldiers.[10] However, the proconsul did have almost unlimited power[11] and as Garnsey argues

> while it is true that governors were not permitted to execute citizens *summarily*, they were certainly able to execute them *judicially*. That is to say, they could try, condemn and execute citizens, provided that an appeal did not reverse the sentence. . . Provincial governors may not have exercised criminal jurisdiction from the first, when their task was chiefly military and their subjects were predominantly foreign. But in time, probably by the late Republic [49–27 BC], they performed as civil and criminal judges [see *lex Rubria*]. For the exercise of both of these functions they were able to call upon powers which were part of their office.[12]

This is confirmed by Pilate, the governor of Judea (AD 26–36), who said to Jesus during his trial, "Do you not know that I have authority to release you and authority to crucify you?" (John 19:10), indicating he had the *ius gladii* over Jesus. Also, Antipas was mentioned as one of its victims in the next verse in Revelation (2:13, see also 6:9–11).

Although some think that the double-edged sword mentioned here is understood as an impending judgment threatened in verse 16,[13] it is more likely mentioned to contrast with Jesus, who also possessed the power of life and death.[14] John reminds his readers that they are

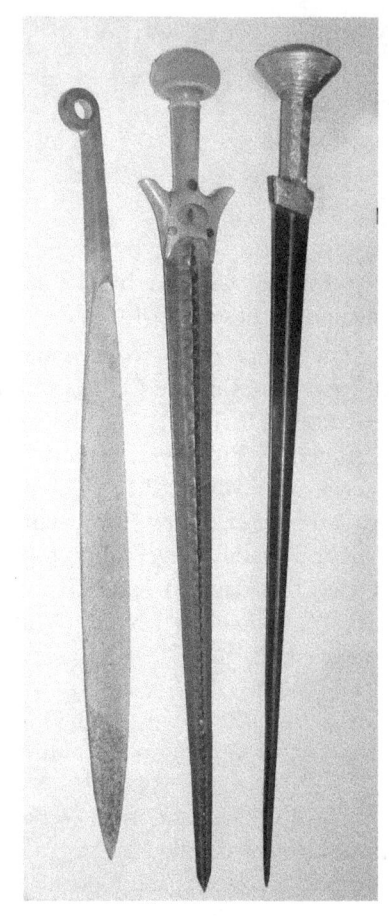

69. Reconstruction of Mycenaean replica swords, the left one being a *machaira*-type sword. From the museum in Mycenae.

---

[10] Polybius *Hist.* 6.37–38; *SEG* 39.851; 45.1133; Yann Le Bohec, "Military Penal Law," in *BrillPaulyA*, http://dx.doi.org/10.1163/1574-9347_bnp_e804570; Berger, *Encyclopedic Dictionary of Roman Law*, 529; Emil Schürer, *The History of the Jewish People in the Age of Jesus Christ (175 BC–AD 135)*, ed. G. Vermes, F. Miller, and M. Black, Rev (Edinburgh, U.K.: T&T Clark, 1979), 368 n.73; Sherwin-White, *Roman Society and Roman Law in the NT*, 8–10; Arnold Hugh Martin Jones, ed., *Studies in Roman Government and Law*, 2nd ed. (Oxford, U.K.: Blackwell, 1963), 60; Harry W. Tajra, *The Trial of St. Paul: A Juridical Exegesis of the Second Half of the Acts of the Apostles* (Eugene, Oreg.: Wipf & Stock, 2010), 113–14.

[11] Krodel, *Revelation*, 116.

[12] Peter Garnsey, "The Criminal Jurisdiction of Governors," *JRS* 58, no. 1 and 2 (1968): 54, 59.

[13] Witherington III, *Revelation*, 102; Beale, *Rev*, 245–46; Beasley-Murray, *Revelation*, NCB, 84.

[14] Ramsay, *The Letters to Seven Churches*, 291–2; Hemer, *Letters to the Seven Churches*, 82–84, 104; Osborne, *Revelation*, 140; Mulholland, *Revelation*, 105; Whiting, *Revelation of John*, 78; Mounce, *Revelation*, 79; *What Are We Waiting For?: A Commentary on Revelation*. (Eugene, Oreg.: Wipf & Stock, 2004), 9; James T. Draper, Jr., *The Unveiling: Inspirational Expositions of the Book of Revelation from a Premillennial Viewpoint* (Nashville, Tenn.: Broadman, 1984), 54; Ford, *Revelation*, 398.

citizens under a heavenly suzerain who needs no other sword than that of his mouth. As Caird explains:

> The Christians are reminded that, though they live under the authority of one who holds the sword of imperial justice, they are citizens also of the greater empire of him who needs no other weapon than the spoken word, *the sword* of his *mouth*, which is the word of God. If a Christian should be called to confess his faith before a Roman court of justice, he must remember that it is Christ, not the proconsul, who *has the sharp two-edged sword*.[15]

While the proconsul carried the right of the sword (*ius gladii*), Christ, the suzerain, wields the "sharp two-edged sword" (2:13) of authority, and would "fight against them with the sword" (2:16) of his mouth (1:16) if the vassals did not repent.

HISTORICAL PROLOGUE—2:13–15

The historical prologue acknowledges the historical intimacy and mutually binding recognition of the relationship between the suzerain and the vassal in a historical summary.[16] The omniscient suzerain intimately knew the Pergamum church. The suzerain knew where Satan had his throne, knew of Antipas' death, knew people who held to the teaching of Balaam, and knew of those who held to the teaching of the Nicolaitans.

THE SUZERAIN KNOWS WHERE SATAN HAS HIS THRONE—2:13A

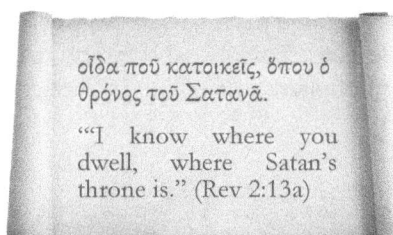

οἶδα ποῦ κατοικεῖς, ὅπου ὁ θρόνος τοῦ Σατανᾶ.

"'I know where you dwell, where Satan's throne is." (Rev 2:13a)

What could possibly have elicited John's objectionable statement that Satan's throne dwells in Pergamum? The suzerain certainly knew where the anti-God authority was located, although later commentators are less confident and have come to no unanimous consensus. The phrase ὁ θρόνος τοῦ Σατανᾶ (*ho thronos toū Satana*) is understood by most as a subjective genitive, meaning "where Satan is enthroned," rather than a possessive genitive meaning "Satan's throne."[17] But the question still remains: what was it about Pergamum that set it apart from other cities in Asia Minor as the seat of Satan, where he lived? Some maintain a very specific influence, while others are more general in their identification of a local reference.

MARTYRDOM IN A FUTURE TIME

Although only proposed by a few commentators and popularized by Bullinger, this view maintains that the messages to the seven churches are limited to the future day of the Lord and the throne of Satan is associated with Revelation 13:2 and the throne of the beast of the sea.[18]

---

[15] Caird, *Revelation*, 38.

[16] Berman, "Histories Twice Told," 232; Huffmon, "Treaty Background," 31–37; Mendenhall, "Covenant Forms," 59; Thompson, *ANE Treaties*, 16; Thompson, "Near Eastern Suzerain-Vassal," 4; Walton, *Ancient Israelite Literature*, 102.

[17] Thomas, *Rev 1–7*, 182; Osborne, *Revelation*, 141 n.4; Smalley, *Revelation*, 68.

[18] Ethelbert William Bullinger, *Commentary on Revelation* (New York, N.Y.: Revell, 1909), 92.

The throne of the beast will be at Pergamum (16:10). However, as Thomas points out, it is hermeneutically difficult, "unnatural and unjustified"[19] to attribute a future meaning to epistolary literature.

THE SHAPE OF THE ACROPOLIS

Wood and Charles have suggested that Satan's throne is likened to the shape of the acropolis[20] on which the upper-city was built, although Hemer believes the shape of the acropolis is only picturesque and the argument better suits Smyrna.[21] Beasley-Murray raises this as a possibility, but prefers the altar of Zeus as his primary connection.[22] Today, most scholars regard this theory about the shape of the acropolis as most unlikely.

THE GREAT ALTAR OF ZEUS

Prior to the archaeological work at Pergamum in the twentieth century, the common belief was that the shape of the altar of the temple of Zeus (see Fig. 66)[23] was identified with "Satan's throne" (2:13), since it was reconstructed and prominently on display in the Berlin museum (see Fig. 65).[24] Blaiklock combines the serpent allusions of Asclepius (see Figs. 63, 70, 71) and the "Savior" (Ζεύς σωτήρ, *Zeus sōtēr*) reference to conclude "perhaps," in reference to the physical appearance of the structure. While Blaiklock is tentative in his earlier work, he uses the stronger "must" to argue for the throne of Zeus in his *Archaeology of the NT*.[25] In 1990, Thompson supported the notion, though provided no grounds for this,[26] though more recently Adela Yarbro Collins has revived the idea and included not only the altar, but also the temple of Athena (see Figs. 34, 124) and the temple of Zeus, perhaps wrongly assuming that "Satan's throne" must refer to a physical monument.[27]

---

[19] Thomas, *Rev 1–7*, 184.

[20] Wood, "Local Knowledge," 264; Charles, *Revelation*, 1:61.

[21] Hemer, *Letters to the Seven Churches*, 84.

[22] Beasley-Murray, *Revelation*, NCB, 84.

[23] For the background of the Temple of Zeus see "Famous for the Great Altar of Zeus" above.

[24] Deissmann, *Light from the Ancient East*, 85, 280 nn.2, 281 3; Lohmeyer, *Offenbarung*, 25; Erwin Rohde, *Pergamon: Burgberg Und Altar* (Berlin: Henschelverlag, 1982), 60–62; Michael Avi-Yonah, ed., *Views of the Biblical World: The New Testament*, vol. 5 (Jerusalem: International, 1961), 271; Terence Kelshaw, *Send This Message to My Church: Christ's Words to the Seven Churches of Revelation* (Nashville, Tenn.: Nelson, 1984), 93–94; Ford, *Revelation*, 393; Beasley-Murray, *Revelation*, NCB, 84.

[25] Blaiklock, *Cities of the NT*, 105; Edward M. Blaiklock, *The Archaeology of the New Testament* (Grand Rapids, Mich.: Zondervan, 1970), 126–28.

[26] Thompson, *Apocalypse and Empire*, 173; Beasley-Murray, *Revelation*, NCB, 84; John E. Stambaugh and David L. Balch, *The New Testament in Its Social Environment*, LEC 2 (Philadelphia, Pa.: Westminster, 1986), 153.

[27] Adela Yarbro Collins, "Pergamon in Early Christian Literature," in *Pergamon-Citadel of the Gods*, ed. Helmut Koester, HTS 46 (Harrisburg, Pa.: Trinity Press International, 1998), 166–76.

However, this does not explain how local monuments in Pergamum would be the "adversarial mirror-image of the throne of God."[28] And while some commentators argue that the altar of Zeus resembles a throne, this is simply not the case, as ancient thrones looked very different from altars or the acropolis.[29] The Olympia in Greece also has open-air altars to Zeus,[30] so it seems unlikely that this one in Pergamum should be singled out as the throne of Satan.[31]

PERGAMUM WAS THE CAPITAL

This view is derived from the belief that Pergamum was the capital of the province of Asia and that Satan was essentially the god of the Romans, and that they were in some way doing Satan's work.[32] However, the premise that Pergamum was the capital of Asia in the first century can be challenged, as this honor more likely belonged to Ephesus.[33]

THE PROCONSUL'S BENCH OR TRIBUNAL

The judge's bench (βῆμα, *bēma*),[34] where the proconsul sat, has been suggested as perhaps being the throne of Satan. The word "throne" (θρόνος, *thronos*) has occasionally been identified with a judge's bench (Plutarch *Praec. ger. publ.* 807b), and in the NT it is always a seat of office or state for a judge (Matt 19:28), or a king (Luke 1:32, 52), or Christ, or God.[35] Understood as a subjective genitive, Pergamum was where "Satan was enthroned." As Aune explains:

> The Roman proconsul resided in Pergamon, and it was to Pergamon that Christians in the surrounding area were brought after being denounced by informers even at a later date (*Mart. Carp.* 1–23). The Province of Asia was divided into first nine, then eleven, regions; in the main city of each area (one of which was Pergamon), the *conventus juridicus*, "judicial assembly," was convened by the proconsul or the legates and a court of provincial judges called the *centumviri*. In a trial, the first state involved a hearing *in iure*, i.e., before the jurisdictional magistrate (the *praetor*), while the second stage of the trial was the *iudicium centumvirale*, i.e., an appearance before a court selected from the *centumviri* (Philostratus *Vit. Soph.* 1.22).[36]

---

[28] Ibid.

[29] Friesen, "Satan's Throne," 359 n.21.

[30] Frederick Norman Pryce et al., "Altar," ed. Simon Hornblower and Antony Spawforth, *OCD* (Oxford, U.K.: Clarendon, 2003), 66.

[31] Thomas, *Rev 1–7*, 183.

[32] Sherman E. Johnson, "Asia Minor and Early Christianity," in *Judaism and Christianity in the Age of Constantine*, ed. Jacob Neusner, vol. 2 (Leiden: Brill, 1975), 93; Farrer, *Revelation*, 73; George Aaron Barton, *Archaeology and the Bible* (Alexandria , Egypt: Library of Alexandria, 1933), 268; Bean, *Aegean Turkey*, 77. Bean contradicts himself by also claiming that "the most likely" explanation is the "temple of Rome and Augustus."

[33] Friesen, "Satan's Throne," 361.

[34] Matt 27:19; John 19:13; Acts 18:12; 25:10.

[35] Matt 5:34; 25:31; see also Rev 4:2–11; 7:9–12; 20:11–12; 21:3–5; Swete, *Apocalypse*, 34; Smalley, *Revelation*, 68; Mounce, *Revelation*, 79.

[36] Aune, Rev 1–5, 183; Berger, Encyclopedic Dictionary of Roman Law, 386, 521.

However, Pergamum was not the only region in Asia Minor with the responsibility of the *conventus juridicus* (see the trial of Polycarp in Smyrna; see Figs. 50, 51; *Mart. Pol.* 1.13; *FrgPol.* 64.23) and this does not explain what was so special about Pergamum to set it apart from other cities to deserve this title of Satan's throne.

The temple of Asclepius

The temple of Asclepius[37] offers two options: first, the Christian's aversion to calling the Greek god of healing, Asclepius, god-savior (θεός σωτήρ, *Theos sōtēr*, later called Zeus Asclepius, and second the Asclepeion emblem of the serpent (see Figs. 70, 71),[38] associated by Christians as Satan (12:9; 14, 15; 20:2; see also Gen 3:1–4; 1 Cor 11:3). Both have lead commentators to connect them with Satan's throne.[39] Pausanias speaks of Asclepius, "sitting on a seat [θρόνος, *thronos*, throne] grasping a staff; the other hand he is holding above the head of the serpent" (*Descr.* 2.27.2 [Jones]).

However, Barclay dismisses these connections, since Laodicea also had a similar connection with Asclepius and the phrase was not used for Laodicea.[40] Although Philostratus points out that Asclepius was pre-eminently the god of Pergamum (Philostratus *Vit. Apoll.* 4.34), Zeus was worshiped throughout Greece, Macedonia, and Asia Minor (Acts 14:12; (see Figs. 95, 115, 126,

70. Column in the courtyard of the entrance (*propylon*) of the Asclepion (hospital), from the lower site of Pergamum, decorated with three symbols of health: snakes, olive branches, and the wheel of life. Snakes were worshiped in the cult of Asclepius, the god of healing. The way serpents shed their skins to renew themselves became a symbol of new life. John stated that Satan lived in Pergamum, and some believe that this is one of the local references. The symbol of the intertwined snakes still decorates medical emblems today.

151, 154, 156), and the serpent appears in many other cults in the Roman period, including Dionysus (see Fig. 35), Demeter (see Fig. 98), Zeus and others.[41] The Asclepeion only became

---

[37] For the background of the temple of Asclepius see "Famous for her Asclepeion" above.

[38] Plutarch *Mor.* 755f; Homer *Il.* 2.299–332; See "The Use of Live Snakes in the Worship of Asclepius" in Kelhoffer, *Miracle and Mission*, 369–71; Nilsson, *Geschichte Der Griechischen Religion*, 2:216–17.

[39] Schmitz TDNT 3:166; Bousset, *Die Offenbarung Johannis*, 211; Swete, *Apocalypse*, 34; Theodor Zahn, *Die Offenbarung Des Johannes*, KZNT 17 (Leipzig: Deichert, 1924), 253–63; Tait, *Messages to the Seven Churches*, 228; Kraft, *Offenbarung*, 64; Ramsay, *Letters: Updated*, 285–86; Esther Onstad, *Courage for Today, Hope for Tomorrow: A Study of the Revelation* (Minneapolis, Minn.: Augsburg, 1993), 19; Barclay, *Letters*, 42–43.

[40] Barclay, *Letters*, 32; Beckwith, *Apocalypse*, 458. Beckwith points out the Asclepius cult at Epidauros.

[41] Steven J. Friesen, "Myth and Symbolic Resistance in Revelation 13," *JBL* 123 (2004): 218–313; "Satan's Throne," 361.

prominent in the second cent. AD. Friesen argues that in the late first cent. AD it was hardly the sort of institution where John would have located the throne of Satan. But although the Asclepeion was rebuilt several times and a new temple added in the second cent. AD, it was still a prominent feature from its founding in 350 BC (Pausanias *Descr.* 2.26.7; Aristides *Orat.* 39.5). Also, Barclay reasons that: "the Christians would regard the place where men went to be healed—and often were—with pity rather than with indignation."[42]

PERGAMUM AS A CENTER OF CHRISTIAN PERSECUTION

This view garners support from the context in which the martyrdom of Antipas (2:13b) is mentioned.[43] Eichhorn interprets Satan's throne as "the dominion of Satan," (Lat. *Satanae Imperium*) which led to the persecution of the Christians in Pergamum.[44] Friesen favours an adaptation of the old persecution theory put forth by Ramsay,[45] but limits "Satan's throne" only to "local hostility toward the Pergamene assembly"[46] and not to any physical structure.

AN IMPORTANT CENTER OF GRAECO-ROMAN RELIGION

71. Statue of Asclepius, exhibited in the Museum of Epidaurus Theater.

Andrew of Caesarea, one of the oldest Greek patristic commentators on that book of Revelation, describes the city as "full of idols"[47] (κατείδωλος, *kateidōlos*),[48] and the throne being

---

[42] Barclay, *Revelation*, 1:90; Donald D. Guthrie, *The Relevance of John's Apocalypse* (Exeter, U.K.: Paternoster, 1987), 76; Worth, Jr., *Greco-Asian Culture*, 135–36.

[43] Simcox, *Revelation*, 15–16.

[44] Johann G. Eichhorn, *Commentarius in Apocalypsin Joannis* (Göttingen: Dieterich, 1791), 1:93.

[45] For a summary of the persecution theory, see Ramsay, *Letters: Updated*, 67–81.

[46] Friesen, "Satan's Throne, Imperial Cults and the Social Settings of Revelation," 365.

[47] Eugenia Scarvelis Constantinou, "Andrew of Caesarea and the Apocalypse in the Ancient Church of the East: Studies and Translation" (Ph.D. diss., Université Laval, 2008), 36; Alan F. Johnson et al., *Hebrews - Revelation*, ed. Tremper Longman III and David E. Garland, Revised, EBC 13 (Grand Rapids, Mich.: Zondervan, 2006), 619–20. Johnson describes Pergamum as "a center for worship of the pagan gods" and "a center of idolatry."

[48] For the background of the gods worshipped in Pergamum see "Famous for Her Religious Worship" above and also Worth, Jr., *Greco-Asian Culture*, 112–16. See pages 136–37 for his treatment of this view.

representative of the immoral excesses displayed by Pergamum's citizens.[49] Some scholars suggest that Pergamum was somehow more pagan than other cities,[50] but this contradicts the common pagan and polytheistic culture of the first cent.[51] with a pervasive focus on the imperial cult throughout Asia Minor.[52] However, a case may be made for the combined concentration of pagan religious practices, considered satanic by Christians, that led to John's comments (see conclusion).

A MAJOR CENTER OF THE IMPERIAL CULT

With Pergamum hosting imperial cult temples to Augustus, Severus and Trajaneium, many scholars maintain this view,[53] with Hemer noting the "growth of a 'polemical parallelism' between Christ and Caesar."[54] The temple of Augustus,[55] built in 29 BC to the imperial cult,[56] was one of the first and most important temples built in the province of Asia,[57] with Tacitus stating that it was dedicated to "the divine Augustus and to the city of Rome" (*Ann.* 4.37; *Roma* [see Fig. 173] = whore, Rev 17). But as Hemer reminds us, there was "a prolonged and bitter rivalry between Ephesus, Smyrna and Pergamum"[58] for prominence (πρώτη, *prōtē*) among the province of Asia (Dio Chrysostom *Or.* 34.48). However, Pergamum responded to the challenges around it by achieving the status of *neōkoros* three times and being first (πρώτη, *prōtē*) in each

---

[49] Specific evidence is not provided by these authors. J. A Seiss, *The Apocalypse* (Colorado Springs, Colo.: Cook, 1906), 100–101; Tait, *Messages to the Seven Churches*, 229; John T. Hinds, *A Commentary on the Book of Revelation*, New Testament Commentaries (Gospel Advocate) (Nashville, Tenn.: Gospel Advocate, 1974), 34.

[50] Lenski, *Revelation*, 1963, 104; Homer Hailey, *Revelation: An Introduction and Commentary* (Grand Rapids, Mich.: Baker, 1979), 130; Roloff, *Revelation*, 50–51.

[51] Paul in Rome, Acts 17:16, 22; Dio Cassius *Hist. Rom.* 51.20.7.

[52] Karen Louise Jolly, *Tradition and Diversity: Christianity in a World Context to 1500* (New York, N.Y.: Routledge, 2015), 27; Steven Muir, "Religion on the Road in Ancient Greece and Rome," in *Travel and Religion in Antiquity*, ed. Philip A. Harland, ESCJ 21 (Waterloo, Ont.: Wilfrid Laurier University Press, 2011), 29–48; Harland, "Imperial Cults within Local Cultural Life: Associations in Roman Asia," 85–107; Naylor, "The Roman Imperial Cult and Revelation," 207–39; Duncan Fishwick, *The Imperial Cult in the Latin West*, Studies in the Ruler Cult of the Western Provinces of the Roman Empire, 2.1 (Leiden: Brill Academic, 2005).

[53] Zahn, *Die Offenbarung Des Johannes*, 1:249; Ramsay, *Letters: Updated*, 294–96; Hemer, *Letters to the Seven Churches*, 85, 87, 104; Franz, "Propaganda, Power and the Perversion," 80; Boring, *Revelation*, 91; Mounce, *Revelation*, 79; Charles, *Revelation*, 1:61; Kiddle, *Revelation*, 30; Swete, *Apocalypse*, 34; Osborne, *Revelation*, 141–43; Barclay, *Letters*, 44–45; Friesen, "Satan's Throne," 366; Brent, *The Imperial Cult*, 178–90; Pfleiderer, *Primitive Christianity: Its Writings and Teachings in Their Historical Connections*, 415; Heinrich Schlier, *Principalities and Powers in the New Testament* (New York, N.Y.: Herder & Herder, 1961), 29.

[54] Hemer, Letters to the Seven Churches, 87.

[55] Not to be confused with the Trajaneium on the acropolis as Ford and Kraft have done. Ford, *Revelation*, 398; Kraft, *Offenbarung*, 64.

[56] For the background of the Imperial Cult see "Famous for the Imperial Cult" above.

[57] Ramsay, *Letters: Updated*, 214–15; Mellor, *Thea Rhōmē*, 140–41.

[58] Hemer, Letters to the Seven Churches, 84.

case. It won this status without the addition of an Artemis-cult, as was the case with Ephesus.[59] As Hemer points out:

> there are many instructive indications on the coinage of the early years of Roman rule to suggest that Pergamum had a close, though perhaps not exclusive, connection with authority. . . [and] served as a precedent for the cult in other provinces (Tacitus *Ann.* 4.37)[60]

But while many scholars support this view, Aune points out that:

> While Pergamon did function as one among many important centers for the imperial cult, there is no explicit evidence in 2:12–17 (or in Rev 2–3) to suggest that the imperial cult was a major problem for the Christians of Asia or for the author of the final edition of Revelation.[61]

Also, as Friesen points out, the imperial cult was everywhere in first-century culture, as "Emperors were worshiped in their own temples, at temples of other gods, in theaters, in gymnasia, in stoas, in basilicas, in judicial settings, in private homes and elsewhere."[62] And while Aune is correct that the evidence in Revelation is not explicit, and Freisen's claim is correct that "Pergamum was not the center of imperial cults in Asia,"[63] others have demonstrated the threat of the imperial cult to the Christian community and the polemics which followed in Pergamum were implicit and real.[64]

CONCLUSION

These suggestions cannot individually be connected with "Satan's throne", but in combination[65] they provide support for the use of this statement, understanding Pergamum as the Roman "seat of special authority"[66] and the "*Roman opposition* to early Christianity."[67] Friesen prefers to represent Satan's throne as the "local hostility toward the Pergamene assembly."[68] Certainly, the Christian's aversion to calling Zeus (see Figs. 95, 115, 126, 151, 154, 156) and Asclepius θεός Σωτήρ (*theos sōtēr*, God Savior), along with the serpent–the Christian symbol for Satan–depicted on the structures and statues of the cult (see Figs. 63, 70, 71); combined with temples to Augustus, Severus, and Trajan,[69] and the seat of the proconsul's power being centerd in

---

[59] Ibid., 237–38 n.36.

[60] Ibid., 84–85.

[61] Aune, *Rev 1–5*, 183; Friesen, "Satan's Throne," 366.

[62] Friesen, "Satan's Throne," 363; *Imperial Cults*, 23–131.

[63] Friesen, "Satan's Throne," 362.

[64] Price, *Rituals and Power*, 155–65, 221–22; Harland, "Imperial Cults within Local Cultural Life: Associations in Roman Asia," 85–107; Friesen, *Imperial Cults*; "Satan's Throne," 351–73; Kraybill, *Imperial Cult and Commerce in John's Apocalypse*; *Apocalypse and Allegiance*; Naylor, "The Roman Imperial Cult and Revelation," 207–39; Beale, *Rev*, 246–47; Kistemaker, *Revelation*, 129 n.41.

[65] Pfleiderer, Primitive Christianity: Its Writings and Teachings in Their Historical Connections, 415; Johnson, Triumph of the Lamb, 75–76.

[66] Barclay, *Letters*, 35.

[67] Aune, *Rev 1–5*, 184.

[68] Friesen, "Satan's Throne," 365.

[69] Hemer, *Letters to the Seven Churches*, 85, 87, 104; Aune, *Rev 1–5*, 183–84; Barclay, *Letters*, 44–45; Charles, *Revelation*, 1:61; Mounce, *Revelation*, 79.

Pergamum; would altogether justify calling Pergamum the "throne of Satan." Pergamum was celebrated as the first (πρώτη, *prōtē*) *neōkoros* (temple keeper) on three separate occasions, setting it apart from other cities as an important center of the imperial cult and seat (βῆμα, *bēma*) of Roman rule.[70]

While some or all of these elements were present in other cities, it was the sheer scale and concentration of them here at Pergamum that justified John in identifying this place as Satan's throne, the very place where Satan lived.[71] The suzerain knew that, from a Christian perspective, Pergamum was a concentrated center of demonic activity, and it was this activity that elicited John's harsh comment.[72]

THE SUZERAIN KNOWS THEY HAVE REMAINED FAITHFUL—2:13B

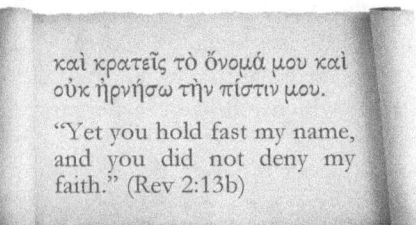

καὶ κρατεῖς τὸ ὄνομά μου καὶ οὐκ ἠρνήσω τὴν πίστιν μου.

"Yet you hold fast my name, and you did not deny my faith." (Rev 2:13b)

The combination of opposition from pagan polytheism outside and the false teachers from within the Pergamene church testified to the faithfulness of the real Christians to their King. They are acknowledged as having continued to "hold fast" (present tense κρατεῖς, *krateis*) or remain faithful to "my name" (objective genitive τὸ ὄνομά μου, *to onoma mou* 2:13b). The verb means to "hold securely".[73] While Jesus, the king seated on his throne, "firmly holds the seven stars" (1:16; 2:1) as he watches over his churches, here the vassals "hold firm" to his name. This rhetorical clause "yet you hold fast my name, and you did not deny my faith" (2:13), with both a positive and negative element, reinforces the faithfulness of the vassal to the suzerain. It is similar in construction to the historical prologue for the message to Sardis that states "yet you have kept my word and have not denied my name" (3:8).

THE SUZERAIN KNOWS OF ANTIPAS' DEATH—2:13C

The context and the aorist tense of the verb "deny" (ἠρνήσω, *ērnēsō*) indicate that the occasion in question was the martyrdom of Antipas (Ἀντιπᾶς)[74] as a single event, known to the suzerain from past history, rather than a continuing persecution. In the previous persecution Antipas

---

[70] Collins, *Crisis and Catharsis*, 101–2; Charles, *Revelation*, 1:60–61; Hemer, *Letters to the Seven Churches*, 82–84; Ramsay, *Letters: Updated*, 289; Tait, *Messages to the Seven Churches*, 225–26; Farrer, *Revelation*, 73; Ramsay, "Pergamus or Pergamum," 3:750.

[71] Thomas, *Rev 1–7*, 179–80.

[72] Caird, *Revelation*, 37; Martin, *Seven Letters*, 69; Wood, "Local Knowledge," 264; Johnson, *Triumph of the Lamb*, 440.

[73] Mark 7:3f, 8; Acts 2:24; Col 2:19.

[74] Walvoord and others suggest that Antipas means "against all," but there is no foundation for this or any identification with Athanasius or Timothy. Walvoord, *Revelation of Jesus Christ*, 67. Alford writes, "It is hardly possible to withold indignation at the many childish symbolic meanings which have been imagined for the name, in defiance of philology and sobriety alike" Alford, *Greek Testament*, 569.

> καὶ ἐν ταῖς ἡμέραις Ἀντιπᾶς ὁ μάρτυς μου ὁ πιστός μου, ὃς ἀπεκτάνθη παρ' ὑμῖν, ὅπου ὁ σατανᾶς κατοικεῖ.
>
> "even in the days of Antipas my faithful witness, who was killed among you, where Satan dwells." (Rev 2:13c)

alone had been martyred, but Eusebius mentions that Carpus, Papylus, and Agathonice were also later martyred in Pergamum (*Hist. eccl.* 4.15.48).[75]

Not a lot is known about this Antipas apart from the fact that he lived where Satan's seat of power dwelt and his name is Greek. His name is a contraction of *Antipatros* (Ἀντιπᾶτρος), a popular name in Greece and Macedonia during the Hellenistic and Roman period.[76]

Antipas was a "true witness" (μάρτυς, *martus*; used also of Christ: Rev 1:5; 3:14) to Christ's (objective genitive, μου, *mou*, my)[77] name and had been faithful to Christ, even to the point of being killed. The term μάρτυς (*martus*) only came to have the technical meaning of martyr/martyrdom during the third cent. AD.[78] The current understanding of martyr had not yet evolved in the first century, but Revelation paved the way by connecting "witness" with "put to death" (Acts 22:20; Rev 2:13).[79]

Nothing more is known of Antipas although Orthodox tradition, recounted by Simeon Metaphrastes (AD 900−984), claims that Antipas was martyred during the reign of Domitian (in ca. AD 92) and "was inclosed (sic.) in a brazen bull, over a fire, and scorched and suffocated to death therein"[80] (Menologia, April 11) for casting out demons worshiped by the local population (Martyrologia).[81]

Antipas was faithful to Christ (ὄνομά, *onoma*, name), not denying his faith (πίστιν, *pistin*) in his king, and refusing to submit to worship the Roman emperor (see the account of Polycarp; see Figs. 50, 51; *Mart. Pol.* 1.13; *FrgPol.* 64.23), but who nevertheless was killed in Pergamum, where Satan lived and ruled.[82] Like Antipas, the church's faithfulness is known to their suzerain, who testifies to their loyalty to Christ's rule and not to Rome.

---

[75] Eusebius does not mention Antipas, leading Swete to speculate that perhaps he was not from Pergamum and brought from another village to be persecuted as an example. Swete, *Apocalypse*, 35.

[76] Josephus *Ant.* 14.1.3–4, 10; 17.1.3; *CPJ* 1:29; *I.Smyr.* 2:102; 429.6; J. Reynolds and Robert F. Tannenbaum, *Jews and Godfearers at Aphrodisias*, Proceedings of the Cambridge Philological Society. Supplementary Volume (Cambridge Cambridgeshire: Cambridge Philological Society, 1987), 97–98.

[77] Donald S. Deer, "Whose Faith/Loyalty in Revelation 2.13 and 14.12?," *BT* 38, no. 3 (1987): 328–30; Swete, *Apocalypse*, 35; Hemer, *Letters to the Seven Churches*, 86; Osborne, *Revelation*, 142 n.5; Beale, *Rev*, 246.

[78] Charles claims this is the earliest use of the technical term "martyr" comparing this verse with Revelation 17:6. Charles, *Revelation*, 1:62.

[79] Morris, *Revelation*, 66; Thomas, *Rev 1–7*, 187; Smalley, *Revelation*, 69; Osborne, *Revelation*, 142; Aune, *Rev 1–5*, 185; Allison A. Trites, "Μάρτυς and Martyrdom in the Apocalypse: A Semantic Study," *NovT* 15, no. 1 (1973): 72–80.

[80] Sabine Baring-Gould, *The Lives of the Saints*, vol. 4 (London, U.K.: John Hodges, 1873), 4:136.

[81] For fanciful symbolic meanings for his name see Henry Alford, The Greek Testament: With a Critically Revised Text; a Digest of Various Readings; Marginal References to Verbal and Idiomatic Usage; Prolegomena; and a Critical and Exegetical Commentary (London, U.K.: Deighton, Bell, & Co., 1863), 4.2:569.

[82] Beckwith, *Apocalypse*, 458.

THE SUZERAIN KNOWS PEOPLE WHO HOLD TO THE TEACHING OF BALAAM—2:14

ἀλλ' ἔχω κατὰ σοῦ ὀλίγα ὅτι ἔχεις ἐκεῖ κρατοῦντας τὴν διδαχὴν Βαλαάμ, ὃς ἐδίδασκεν τῷ Βαλὰκ βαλεῖν σκάνδαλον ἐνώπιον τῶν υἱῶν Ἰσραὴλ φαγεῖν εἰδωλόθυτα καὶ πορνεῦσαι.

"But I have a few things against you: you have some there who hold the teaching of Balaam, who taught Balak to put a stumbling block before the sons of Israel, so that they might eat food sacrificed to idols and practice sexual immorality." (Rev 2:14)

For the exegesis of these verses, and more details on Balaam and the Nicolaitans, see the messages to Ephesus (2:6) and Thyatira (2:20–24).

The suzerain threatens the Pergamum church with the sword of justice (2:16b) for harbouring those who hold to the teachings (διδαχὴ, *didachē*, doctrine) of Balaam. Balaam is known from the Bible as a non-Israelite prophet/seer[83] who deceived Israel into worshiping idols and committing immorality (Philo *Mos*. 1.263–304; Josephus *Ant*. 4.126–30). The Suzerain knows well the past history of the account of the false prophet Balaam and the Israelites.[84]

The Pergamum church was unwilling to compromise with Roman authorities outside the church, but willing to compromise with those inside (ἔχεις ἐκεῖ, *echeis ekei*, you have there) the church to allow false teachers, nick named Balaamites (τὴν διδαχὴν Βαλαάμ, *tēn didachēn Balaam*, the teaching of Balaam), to peacefully co-exist within the church, allowing church members to "eat food sacrificed to idols and practice sexual immorality" (see also Thyatira 2:20). Witherington has demonstrated that all NT usages of εἰδωλόθυτος (*eidōlothutos*, "things sacrificed to idols" 1 Cor 10:1–22) refer to "meat sacrificed to and eaten in the presence of an idol, or in the temple precincts"[85] and is clearly a Christian polemical term.[86] Certainly the mention of Balaam,[87] clearly connected with idolatry, is in view here. This is not a matter of conscience as in 1 Corinthians 8,[88] but perhaps instead concerns the use of sacrifices associated with the imperial

---

[83] Num 22:5–25:3; 31:8, 16; Deut 23:4, 5; Josh 13:22; 24:9, 10; Neh 13:2; Mic 6:5; 2 Pet 2:15; Jude 11; and Rev 2:14.

[84] For a survey of the Jewish traditions of Balaam see K. G. Kuhn *TDNT* 1:524–25; Géza Vermès, *Scripture and Tradition in Judaism: Haggadic Studies* (Leiden: Brill, 1973), 127–77; John T. Greene, "Balaam: Prophet, Diviner, and Priest in Selected Ancient Israelite and Hellenistic Jewish Sources," *SBLSP* 28 (1989): 57–106; "The Balaam Figure and Type Before, During, and after the Period of the Pseudepigrapha," *JSP* 8 (1991): 67–110; Louis Ginzberg, *The Legends of the Jews*, trans. Paul Radin, Henrietta Szold, and Boaz Cohen (Philadelphia, Pa.: The Jewish Publication Society of America, 1909), 3:354–82.

[85] Witherington III, "Not So Idle Thoughts," 237.

[86] C. K. Barrett, "Things Sacrificed to Idols," *NTS* 11, no. 02 (1965): 138–53.

[87] See, also Jude 11; 2 Pet 2:15; Num 22–24.

[88] For a treatment of meat sold in the marketplace see Witherington III, "Not So Idle Thoughts," 237–54; E. P. Sanders, *Jewish Law From Jesus to the Mishnah: Five Studies* (Philadelphia, Pa.: Trinity Press International, 1990), 280; Wendell Lee Willis, *Idol Meat in Corinth: The Pauline Argument in 1 Corinthians 8 and 10*, SBLDS 68 (Chicago, Ill.: Scholars Press, 1985), 63; Gerd Theissen, *The Social Setting of Pauline Christianity* (Philadelphia, Pa.: Fortress, 1982), 124–27; Aune, *Rev 1–5*, 191–94. Friesen cautions that "whether the teachings associated with Balaam and Jezebel permitted full

cult[89] (to save one's life) or trade guild festivals[90] (to save one's livelihood), or perhaps both (*CIL* 3.550). The pressure to compromise was evident in early accounts (*Pliny* Ep. *10.96*) and parallel to the account of Balaam in the OT. Polycarp, who was martyred in Smyrna in ca. AD 155–160 (see Figs. 50, 51), was accused of being "the puller down of our gods, who teacheth numbers not to sacrifice nor worship" (*Mart. Pol.* 12.2 [Lightfoot]).

The problem in Pergamum was not so much a failure in *orthodoxy* (correct doctrine) in embracing some gnostic doctrine, as it was *heteropraxy* (deviant practice), and the discipleship to prohibit people from the desire to "eat food sacrificed to idols and practice sexual immorality." Hemer maintains that the

72. Drawing of the opening section of the Balaam text from Tell Deir 'Alla, *ca.* 700 BC. The writing appears to be laid out as a column of a scroll.

issues with the Balaam cult in Thyatira (2:20–24) were the same as here, but the order is reversed, focusing on immorality in Thyatira due to the strength of its guilds. In Pergamum, the focus was on idolatry because of the prominence of the imperial cult at Pergamum.[91]

These false teachers in the Pergamum church were also guiding their followers into sexual immorality (πορνεῦσαι, *porneusai*, to commit immorality). Some have suggested that this was metaphorically used for spiritual idolatry,[92] although it is more likely that the immorality mentioned here was literal promiscuity, since eating food sacrificed to idols is taken in the literal sense.[93] As Osborne points out: "there is no need for such redundancy as a statement on

---

participation in imperial cult rituals is unanswerable, given the state of our information." *Imperial Cults*, 193.

[89] John Wick Bowman, *The First Christian Drama: The Book of Revelation* (Philadelphia, Pa.: Westminster, 1968), 31; Keener, *Revelation*, 125.

[90] Jones, Greek City, 83; Magie, Roman Rule in Asia Minor, 1:48; 2:812 n. 78; Edwin Arthur Judge, The Social Pattern of the Christian Groups in the First Century: Some Prolegomena to the Study of New Testament Ideas of Social Obligation (Wheaton, Ill.: Tyndale, 1960), 40; Ramsay MacMullen, Roman Social Relations: 50 BC to AD 284 (New Haven, Conn.: Yale University Press, 1974), 77, 82; Hemer, "Unto the Angels of the Churches," 110.

[91] Hemer, Letters to the Seven Churches, 91.

[92] 2 Kgs 9:22; Jer 3:2, 9; 13:27; Ezek 16:15–58; 23:1–49; 43:7; Hos 5:4; 6:10; Nah 3:4; 4QpNah 3.4; Wis 14:12; Caird, *Revelation*, 39; Charles H. Talbert, *The Apocalypse: A Reading of the Revelation of John* (Louisville, Ky.: Westminster John Knox, 1994), 19–20; Beale, *Rev*, 250; Keener, *Revelation*, 124.

[93] Mounce, *Revelation*, 87; Krodel, *Revelation*, 117.

idolatry followed by an OT metaphor for the same thing."[94] Furthermore, sexual immorality was widely practiced in Greece and Asia Minor.[95]

In 1967 fragments of the book of Balaam were discovered during excavations at Deir 'Alla, Jordan (see Fig. 72).[96] There were 119 pieces of plaster recovered, dating to 840–760 BC,[97] and today they are displayed in the Amman Museum.[98] McCarter's translation reads in part: "[The sa]ying[s of Bala]am, [son of Be]or, the man who was a seer of the gods."[99] While some scholars do not believe that this Balaam is the same seer as the one mentioned in the Bible,[100] many scholars consider this "Balaam, son of Beor" to be the same person since the name is stated exactly as in the biblical texts.[101]

THE SUZERAIN KNOWS THOSE WHO HOLD TO THE TEACHING OF THE NICOLAITANS— 2:15

οὕτως ἔχεις καὶ σὺ κρατοῦντας τὴν διδαχὴν [τῶν] Νικολαϊτῶν ὁμοίως.

"So also you have some who hold the teaching of the Nicolaitans." (Rev 2:15)

The suzerain is also aware of the presence of Nicolaitans in the Pergamum church (2:15; also Ephesus 2:5). Little is known about them other than what is mentioned in the book of Revelation, but since the same teachings are attributed to the self-proclaimed prophetess, Jezebel, in the church in Thyatira (2:20–25), she was likely also a Nicolaitan prophetess.[102]

---

[94] Osborne, *Revelation*, 145; Mounce, *Revelation*, 81.

[95] See "Ephesus: A City of Immorality and Superstition" for more evidence.

[96] For the details of the story of its discovery see André LeMaire, "Fragments from the Book of Balaam Found at Deir Alla: Text Foretells Cosmic Disaster," *BAR* 11, no. 5 (1985): 26–39.

[97] Joseph Naveh, "The Date of the Deir 'Alla Inscription in Aramaic Script," *IEJ* 17 (1967): 236–38.

[98] David E. Graves, *Biblical Archaeology: Famous Discoveries That Support the Reliability of the Bible*, vol. 2 (Toronto, Can.: Electronic Christian Media, 2015), 117–19.

[99] P. Kyle McCarter Jr., "The Balaam Texts from Deir 'Alla: The First Combination," *BASOR* 239 (1980): 49–60; Jacob Hoftijzer and G. Van der Kooij, eds., *The Balaam Text from Deir 'Alla Re-Evaluated: Proceedings of the International Symposium Held at Leiden, 21–24 August 1989* (Leiden: Brill, 1991); Jacob Hoftijzer, "The Prophet Balaam in a 6th Century Aramaic Inscription," *BA* 39, no. 1 (1976): 11–17; Jacob Hoftijzer and G. Van der Kooij, *Aramaic Texts from Deir 'Alla* (Leiden: Brill, 1976). See also *COS* 2.27:140–45.

[100] Jo Ann Hackett, *The Balaam Text from Deir 'Allā*, Harvard Semitic Monographs 31 (Atlanta, Ga.: Scholars Press, 1980), 2:130; "Balaam (Person)," ed. David Noel Freedman et al., *ABD* (New York, N.Y.: Doubleday, 1996), 1:571–72.

[101] William H. Shea, "The Inscribed Tablets From Tell Deir 'Alla," *AUSS* 27 (1989): 21–37, 97–119; Bryant G. Wood, "Balaam Son of Beor," *BS* 8, no. 4 (1995): 114; Choon-Leong Seow, "Deir 'Alla Plaster Texts," in *Prophets and Prophecy in the Ancient Near East*, ed. Peter Machinist and Martti Nissinen (Atlanta, GA: Society of Biblical Literature, 2003), 207–12; Michael L Barré, "The Portrait of Balaam in Numbers 22–24," *Int.* 51, no. 3 (1997): 254–66.

[102] Panayotis Coutsoumpos, "The Social Implication of Idolatry in Revelation 2:14: Christ or Caesar?," *BTB* 27 (1997): 23.

Clement of Alexandria linked this group to Nicolas, proselyte of Antioch, one of the seven deacons of Acts 6:5,[103] although the historicity of his account is questioned (*Strom.* 3.25–26; see also Hippolytus *Haer.* 7.36).[104] Beasley-Murray based on Irenaeus claimed they were a gnostic group who taught immoral doctrines (*Haer.* 1.26.3; 3:11.1).[105] Some, following the Tübingen school, have proposed a Pseudo-Paulist's association (1 Cor 8–10; 16:9; 15:32).[106] Coutsoumpos concludes that "the Nicolaitans were probably a Christian libertine [antinomian] group within Ephesus, Pergamum and Thyatira."[107] But exactly who they were is difficult to ascertain from the lack of evidence.[108]

The other pressing question is how did they relate to the Balaam mentioned in the sentence? Scholars fall into three camps: those who maintain they are one group, those that argue they are two groups, and those that argue they are separate, but similar groups.[109] The debate over the relationship between Balaam and the Nicolaitans hinges, in part, on three sets of awkward Greek words: οὕτως (*houtōs*, similarly), καὶ σὺ (*kai su*, also you), and ὁμοίως (*homoiōs*, in like manner), with each word emphasising the comparison between Balaam and the Nicolaitans.

BALAAM AND NICOLAITANS ARE ONE GROUP

Based on the etymology (νικᾶν λαόν, *nikan laon* means "he overcomes the people" and *bl' 'm* means "he who consumes the people" [*b. Sanh.* 105a])[110] and orthopraxy (both practice eating idol meat and immorality) of the two groups, most scholars argue that the Nicolaitans and Balaamites should be identified as the same cult.[111] Charles believes that verse 15 is explaining verse 14 and referring to Ephesus. Balaam is just another term for the heresy of the Nicolaitans[112] and the two terms are used "as a comparison between a single movement."[113] This view maintains that the Greek word ὁμοίως (*homoiōs*, in like manner) refers back to those in Ephesus who also held their views. Smalley translates the sentence as "Similarly, you also

---

[103] Lightfoot, St. Paul's Epistle to the Galatians, 297; Swete, Apocalypse, 27–28.

[104] Friesen, Imperial Cults, 193; Hemer, Letters to the Seven Churches, 88–89.

[105] Beasley-Murray, *Revelation, NCB*, 86.

[106] Charles Kingsley Barrett, "What Minorities?," in Mighty Minorities?: Minorities in Early Christianity, Positions and Strategies : Essays in Honour of Jacob Jervell on His 70th Birthday, 21 May 1995, ed. David Hellholm et al. (Oslo: Scandinavian University Press North America, 1995), 9–10; Swete, Apocalypse, lxiii, 36–37; Boxall, "'For Paul' or 'For Cephas.'"

[107] Coutsoumpos, "Social Implication of Idolatry," 24; Mounce, *Revelation*, 81, 87.

[108] Barrett, "Things Sacrificed to Idols," 138–53; Coutsoumpos, "Social Implication of Idolatry," 25.

[109] For detailed arguments for each see W. M. MacKay, "Another Look at the Nicolaitans," *EQ* 45, no. 2 (1973): 111–15; Coutsoumpos, "Social Implication of Idolatry," 23–27.

[110] Krodel, *Revelation*, 118; Beale, *Rev*, 251.

[111] Charles, *Revelation*, 1:63–64; Krodel, *Revelation*, 115, 118; Hemer, *Letters to the Seven Churches*, 89–93; Caird, *Revelation*, 38–40; Aune, *Rev 1–5*, 188; Beale, *Rev*, 251; Smalley, *Revelation*, 69; Mounce, *Revelation*, 81; Kistemaker, *Revelation*, 132; Schüssler Fiorenza, *Book of Revelation*, 116.

[112] Tait, *Messages to the Seven Churches*, 159–60; Barclay, *Letters*, 23–24; Beale, *Rev*, 251; Watson, "Nicolaitans," 4:1107; Blaiklock, "Nicolaus, Nicolaitans," 823; Charles, *Revelation*, 1:63–64.

[113] Osborne, *Revelation*, 145.

(likewise, as well as the church in Ephesus, the members of which are pursued by false teachers) have some who are maintaining the teaching of the Nicolaitans."[114] However, Osborne argues that "a reference to Ephesus would be obscure in this context."[115]

BALAAM AND NICOLAITANS ARE SEPARATE GROUPS

Based on the fact that symbolism is used throughout the book of Revelation, Mackay maintains that three names are referring to three separate heresies. Balaam promoting a compromised worldliness, Jezebel promoting false doctrine and Nicolas promoting ritualism.[116] However, his arguments are based mostly on speculation. Friesen also speculates that "People with the teachings of Balaam and the Nicolaitans are probably two different orientations within the assembly."[117]

BALAAM AND NICOLAITANS ARE DIFFERENT BUT SIMILAR GROUPS

Thomas reaches this conclusion, translating the verse as: "You have also [in addition to those who hold the teachings of Balaam] those who hold in like manner [to the way the Balaamites hold their teachings] the teaching of the Nicolaitans."[118] Thomas limits the comparison (καὶ, *kai*, also) to within the local church and not with Ephesus. Those within the church had laid hold of the teachings of both Balaam and Nicholas.

ETHICAL STIPULATIONS—2:16A

The loyalty of the suzerain (church) is called for through obedience to stated stipulations. Here in Pergamum the stipulations involved correction of the deficiencies of the false teachings of Balaam and Nicholas. For Pergamum the imperative was that of repentance (μετανόησον, *metanoēson*).

IMPERATIVE: REPENT —2:16A

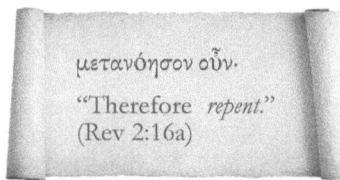

μετανόησον οὖν·
"Therefore *repent*."
(Rev 2:16a)

However, while only some in the church had been guilty of following the teachings of Balaam and Nicholas, the entire church[119] was called by the suzerain to repent (μετανόησον, *metanoēson*). The response was just the opposite of the Ephesians' response; they had purged the Nicolaitans from their church (2:6), but forgotten how to love (2:2, 4). The logical conclusion (οὖν, *sun*, therefore) of the suzerain's knowledge of their conduct was that the

---

[114] Smalley, *Revelation*, 69.
[115] Osborne, *Revelation*, 145.
[116] MacKay, "Another Look at the Nicolaitans," 111–15.
[117] Friesen, "Satan's Throne," 355; *Imperial Cults*, 192–93.
[118] Thomas, *Rev 1–7*, 194.
[119] The Greek imperative is singular and Lenski suggests that the messenger is addressed as a representative of the whole church. Lenski, *Revelation*, 1963, 108. The singular imperative may also refer to Balaam in the context.

vassals were to repent. If they did repent, they would receive blessing; if not, they would continue on their course and experience the malediction of the suzerain (2:16b), who would war against them with the sword of his mouth.

SANCTIONS: CURSES—2:16B–C

The prophetic sanctions, where the vassal is cursed (malediction) for disobedience (dishonors the treaty), and blessed (benedictions) for obedience to the stated stipulations (honors the treaty), is a central element of the ANEVT structure.[120] For Pergamum a malediction (2:16c) awaits those who do not repent, but a benediction for those who are overcomers.

THE CURSE OF THE SUZERAIN'S PRESENCE—2:16B

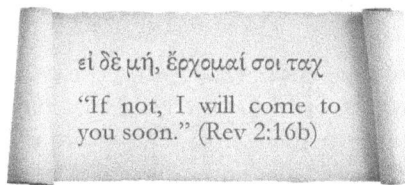
εἰ δὲ μή, ἔρχομαί σοι ταχ
"If not, I will come to you soon." (Rev 2:16b)

God, the Great King, will come to those in Pergamum who do not repent. This coming is a word of judgment by the sword of his mouth, but some see it not as a future judgment but as taking place in the first century when they will have access to the tree of life (2:7) and will receive the crown of life (2:10).[121] They argue that the bodily return of Christ cannot be dependent on the Nicolaitans repentance thus it must be an eminent coming in judgment.[122] For example, the Corinthians who were judged for their abuse of the Lord's Supper fell ill and death were visited by Christ in judgment in their congregation (1 Cor 10:14–22; 11:30).[123] Others see it as only future, fulfilled in the second coming of Christ.[124] Still others see the judgment as both present and future.[125] Osborne points out that ἔρχομαί σοι (*erchomai soi*, I am going to come to you) is a futuristic present and combined with ταχύ (*tachu*, soon) indicates that the coming "refers both to the present judgment upon the church and to the final judgment at the 'Parousia'"[126] Aune points out that ἔρχεσθαι (*erchesthai*, coming) has two meanings in Revelation, one in reference to the Parousia (22:7, 12, 20), and the other in reference to the messages (2:16; 3:11), where it "must be interpreted as 'comings' in judgment preceding the final and decisive coming of Jesus."[127]

---

[120] See chapter 3, *Sanctions*.
[121] Ladd, *Revelation*, 49; Caird, *Revelation*, 41; Witherington III, *Revelation*, 103; Beasley-Murray, "Revelation, NBC," 87; Morris, *Revelation*, 71–72; Keener, *Background Commentary: NT*, 734; Johnson, "Revelation," 621.
[122] Johnson, *Triumph of the Lamb*, 77.
[123] Lynn Harold Hough and Martin Rist, "The Revelation of St. John the Divine," in *The Interpreter's Bible*, ed. George A. Buttrick, vol. 12 (Nashville, Tenn.: Abingdon, 1957), 386.
[124] Thomas, *Rev 1–7*, 196; Mounce, *Revelation*, 82.
[125] Aune, *Rev 1–5*, 188; Beale, *Rev*, 251; Osborne, *Revelation*, 146; Smalley, *Revelation*, 70.
[126] Osborne, *Revelation*, 146.
[127] Aune, *Rev 1–5*, 188; George R. Beasley-Murray, "The Eschatology of the Fourth Gospel," *EvQ* 18 (1946): 97–108; "The Relation of the Fourth Gospel to the Apocalypse," *EvQ* 18 (1946): 181.

THE CURSE OF THE SUZERAIN'S WAR AGAINST THEM—2:16C

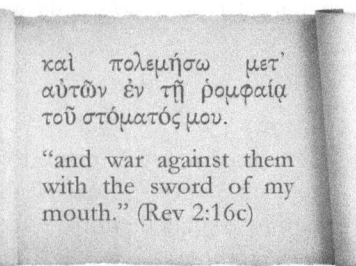

καὶ πολεμήσω μετ᾽ αὐτῶν ἐν τῇ ῥομφαίᾳ τοῦ στόματός μου.

"and war against them with the sword of my mouth." (Rev 2:16c)

The suzerain warns that if those in Pergamum who follow the teachings of Balaam do not repent then then they will know the malediction promised by the suzerain. He will come and war against them with the sword, though his sword would be words from his mouth. It is interesting to note that Balaam in the OT was also threatened with being "killed by the sword" by "the angle of the Lord" (Num 22:23, 31). In fact, Balaam did not repent and was "killed by the word," which prevented him from entering into the life of the "world to come" (*b. Sanh.* 90a). In Jewish tradition the disciples of the OT Balaam were reported to "inherit Gehenna (hell) and go down to the pit of destruction" (*m. Pir. ʾAbot* 5:22).[128]

Citizens of Asia Minor understood that the Roman governor of Asia (a suzerain) exercised the "right of the sword" (*ius gladii*) over his vassals. The appearance of Christ the great suzerain holding the "sharp, double-edged sword" (2:12) and warring against them with "the sword of his mouth" (2:16) asserts that Christ, as suzerain, maintains an even greater authority and power over his vassals than the Roman governor.

PROCLAMATION WITNESS FORMULA—2:17A

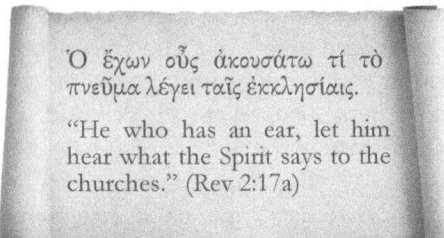

Ὁ ἔχων οὖς ἀκουσάτω τί τὸ πνεῦμα λέγει ταῖς ἐκκλησίαις.

"He who has an ear, let him hear what the Spirit says to the churches." (Rev 2:17a)

With the distribution of the stipulations, along with blessings and curses, it was customary for ancient treaty and oath documents to be sealed with a list of divine witnesses, traditionally the suzerain/vassal's pantheon of gods.[129] Since there is a change in the situation in the NT, because God is speaking as his own witness, there is a change of form from the polytheistic context of the ANE culture. The Spirit is the judge presiding over the covenant case. This proclamation witness or hearing formula,[130] repeated in each of the messages to the churches (2:7; 11, 17, 29, 3:13, 22), calls the churches to hear the proclamation of the divine witness[131] and to heed the message of the Spirit who spoke it.

---

[128] Hough and Rist, "Revelation of St. John," 386.

[129] See the *Introduction—Proclamation Witness Formula*.

[130] See parallels in Matt 11:15; 13:9, 43; Mark 4:9; Luke 8:8; 14:35; 1 Cor 14:37–38; *Odes Sol.* 3:10–11; The *hearing formula* is also found in the Gnostic texts. *Gos. Thom.* 8.21, 24, 63, 65, 96; *Gos. Mary* 7.10, 8, 16; *Pist. Soph.* 1.17, 19, 33, 42, 43; 2.68, 86, 87; 3.124, 125; *Soph. Jes. Chr.* 98, 105, 107.

[131] There are echoes of the OT phrase "hear the word of the Lord" (e.g. Isa 1:10; Jer 2:4; Hos 4:1; Amos 7:16).

Sanctions: Blessings—2:17b

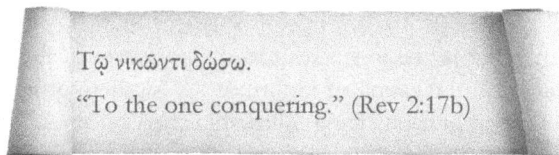

"To the one conquering." (Rev 2:17b)

The blessings (δώσω, *dōsō*, to give) to the Pergamum church are mentioned last, to those overcoming or conquering (τῷ νικῶντι, *tō nikōnti*). This is not an aorist participle, that would have indicated it was achieved at the end of life, but rather a present participle indicating that, throughout their life, they stood victorious because they keep overcoming the assaults of the enemy.

The Blessing of Hidden Manna—2:17c

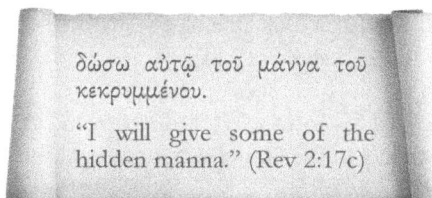

"I will give some of the hidden manna." (Rev 2:17c)

Those conquering the Balaam teaching are offered, not the food of idols, but hidden heavenly manna (μάννα, *manna*).[132] There is no doubt that the term "manna" refers back to the story of the Israelite wandering and their miraculous feeding in Exodus 16:4–36 (retold in Josephus *Ant.* 3.26–32).

The "hidden" (τοῦ κεκρυμμένου, *tou kekrymmenou*, having been hidden) manna has several interpretations.

1. The hidden manna refers back to the Jewish tradition[133] that Jeremiah hid the manna in the ark of the covenant prior to the temple's destruction (586 BC), but God would once again miraculously feed his people with manna to be revealed in the Messianic age.[134] The *Apocalypse of Baruch* states: "and it will happen at that time that the treasury of manna will come down

---

[132] Heb. מָן הוּא, *mān hû*, "what is it?"; Exod 16:15 τί τοῦτ' ἔστιν, *ti tout estin;* Josephus *Ant.* 3.32; sometimes called "bread from heaven"; Neh 9:15; Ps 105:40; John 6:31–33, 50–51; *Apos. Con.* 8.12.26, and the "food of angels"; LXX Ps 77:25 [MT 78:25]; Wis 16:20; 4 Ezra 1:19; *b. Yoma* 75b; Friedrich Simon Bodenheimer, "The Manna of Sinai," *BA* 10, no. 1 (1947): 2–6; Edwin M. Yamauchi, "The 'Daily Bread' Motif In Antiquity," *WTJ* 28, no. 2 (1966): 145–56; Kenneth A. Kitchen, "Manna," ed. I. Howard Marshall et al., *NBD* (Downers Grove, Ill.: InterVarsity, 1996), 725; Joel C. Slayton, "Manna," ed. David Noel Freedman et al., *ABD* (New York, N.Y.: Doubleday, 1996), 511; R. A. Donkin, *Manna: An Historical Geography*, Biogeographic 17 (New York, N.Y.: Springer, 2013), 2–7.

[133] For the Samaritan traditions, cf. Marilyn F. Collins, "The Hidden Vessels in Samaritan Traditions," *JSJ* 3 (1972): 97–116; Isaac Kalimi and James D. Purvis, "The Hiding of the Temple Vessels in Jewish and Samaritan Literature," *CBQ* 56, no. 4 (1994): 679–85.

[134] Exod 16:32; 2 Macc 2:4–7; *b. Ḥagigah* 12b; *Sib. Or.* 7.149; *Midr. Rab.* Eccl. 1.9; *Tg. Ps.-J.* Exod. 16:4, 15; *Tg. Noef.* Deut. 8:16; Eusebius *Praep. Ev.* 9.39.5 (Eupolemus frag. 4); Beckwith, *Apocalypse*, 460–61; Caird, *Revelation*, 42; Beasley-Murray, *Revelation*, NCB, 87–88; Beale, *Rev*, 252; Johnson, *Triumph of the Lamb*, 621; Osborne, *Revelation*, 148; Smalley, *Revelation*, 70; James L. Resseguie, *The Revelation of John: A Narrative Commentary* (Grand Rapids, Mich.: Baker Academic, 2009), 91; Ramsay, *Letters: Updated*, 308; Hemer, *Letters to the Seven Churches*, 96–102; Tait, *Messages to the Seven Churches*, 247–48.

again from on high, and they will eat of it in those years because these are they who have arrived at the consummation of time" (2 *Apoc. Bar.* 29:8 [Charlesworth, *OTP* 1:631]).[135]

2. Several scholars suggest that the mention of manna may be in contrast to the pressures of the imperial cult and "the things sacrificed to idols" and the eating of idol meats.[136] Witherington concludes that "the promise of a much more lasting and satisfying fellowship than one could get at a pagan feast drawing on Jewish messianic traditions about the repetition of the manna miracle in the messianic kingdom (*2 Bar.* 29:4–8)"[137] was being offered.

3. Some suggest that the manna is connected to the bread of the Lord's supper (Eucharist, 1 Cor 10:3ff.) in anticipation of the final messianic feast.[138]

4. A few suggest that the "overcomers will receive celestial food not available to the world."[139] The manna is restored in the great banquet of eternal life and in heaven (19:11).[140]

5. Some understand the hidden manna to be Christ ("bread of life" John 6:37), hidden from the unbeliever and revealed to believers.[141] But is Jesus who speaks to the churches hidden and the blessing?

6. Court explains that "'manna' in pagan Greek and Latin [Galen *Meth. Med.* 5.4.4; Pliny *Nat.* 12.3] indicated a crumb of incense [frankincense] used to prove loyalty to [the] Emperor."[142] Krodel also supports this view, but does not explain the connection between frankincense and manna. Krodel explains:

> in Greek the word *manna* could also refer to the granules of frankincense that were used in the emperor cult and a sign of loyalty to the emperor. . . . Those who resist worship before Satan's throne, refusing to offer granules of manna, frankincense, to him in the censer on his altar, to them Christ will *give some of the hidden*

---

[135] Jacoby, *Die Fragmente Der Griechischen Historiker*, 723, F 5; Ginzberg, *The Legends of the Jews*, 6:19 nn.111–12.

[136] Attilio Gangemi, "La Manna Nascosta E Il Nome Nuovo," *RivB* 25 (1977): 337–56; Charles, *Revelation*, 1:65–55; Beale, *Rev*, 252; Mounce, *Revelation*, 82; Keener, *Revelation*, 126; Hemer, *Letters to the Seven Churches*, 94–95, 105.

[137] Hough and Rist, "Revelation of St. John," 103; ibid., 387.

[138] Roloff, *Revelation*, 52; Krodel, *Revelation*, 120; Prigent, *Apocalypse*, 177; *L'Apocalypse*, 54; *Apocalypse et Liturgie*, Cahiers Théologiques 52 (Lausanne: Delachaux et Niestlé, 1964), 22; Barclay, *Revelation*, 1:105; Sweet, *Revelation*, 90; Hughes, *Revelation*, 46; Mulholland, *Revelation*, 109.

[139] Morris, *Revelation*, 72; Walvoord, *Revelation*, 70.

[140] Aune, *Rev 1–5*, 189; Mounce, *Revelation*, 82–83; Beasley-Murray, *Revelation*, NCB, 87–88; Wall, *Revelation*, 76; Beale, *Rev*, 252.

[141] Hendriksen, *Conquerors*, 67; Daniel K. K. Wong, "The Hidden Manna and the White Stone in Revelation 2:17," *BSac* 155, no. 619 (1998): 348–49; Wilson, *Revelation*, 26; Johnson, *Triumph of the Lamb*, 78; Hughes, *Revelation*, 46.

[142] Court, *Myth and History*, 33; Donkin, *Manna*, 7.

manna, heavenly frankincense, when they begin their reign with him as kings and priests unto God (1:6; 3:26; 5:10; 20:4–6; 22:5.[143]

Perhaps the most plausible explanations are the first and second, since they best explain the term *hidden* and the close association of eating idol meat with the imperial cult.

THE BLESSING OF A NEW NAME—2:17D

> καὶ δώσω αὐτῷ ψῆφον λευκήν, καὶ ἐπὶ τὴν ψῆφον ὄνομα καινὸν γεγραμμένον ὃ οὐδεὶς οἶδεν εἰ μὴ ὁ λαμβάνων.
>
> "and *I will give* him a *white stone*, with *a new name* written on the stone that *no one knows* except the one who receives it." (Rev 2:17d)

The second blessing granted by the suzerain, on those who repent, is of a secret new name written on a white stone or pebble (ψῆφον λευκήν, *psēphon leukēn*; see also Acts 26:10). However, the speculation of its meaning is as ambiguous as the hidden manna and hinges on identification of the "new name" (ὄνομά καινόν, *onoma kainon*) that is secret (ὃ οὐδεὶς οἶδεν, *ho oudeis oiden*, which no one has known).[144] Local references have been suggested from both Jewish and Graeco-Roman customs.

73. Artist's depiction of the high priest with the breastplate over the ephod and Aaron's rod that budded.

1. Jewish custom could suggest that the white stone mentioned here in Revelation was one of the gems (מאן, meaning, "diamond" Gr., σμῆρις, *smeris*; Pliny *Nat.* 36:54) in the breastplate (חֹשֶׁן, *ḥošen*) of the Jewish high priest (see Fig. 73), attached to the ephod (אֵפוֹד *'ēpōd*, cloth garment), with the names of the tribes of Israel written on them (Exod 28:15–21; *b. Yoma* 75a).[145] Hendrickson mentions that the secret name finds an OT parallel in Isaiah who states: "you shall be called by a new name that the mouth of the LORD will give" (Isa 62:2; see also 65:15; Rev 3:12).[146] This would also correspond with the giving of manna and the priestly office of believers (Alford 571–72), although there is no mention of priests in the context and the references in Isaiah are not associated with the high priest or

---

[143] Krodel, *Revelation*, 120–21; Court, *Myth and History*, 32–33.

[144] For an extensive survey of proposed solutions to the problem, cf. Hemer, *Letters to the Seven Churches*, 96–104.

[145] Proposed by Moses Stuart, "The White Stone of the Apocalypse," *BSac* 1 (1843): 472–77; *Apocalypse*, 2:78–79; Trench, *Commentary on Seven Churches*, 135–38; Bullinger, *Commentary on Rev*, 102; J. B. Smith, *A Revelation of Jesus Christ: A Commentary on the Book of Revelation*, ed. J. Otis Yoder (Eugene, OR: Wipf & Stock, 2004), 74; Beckwith, *Apocalypse*, 462–63; Hendriksen, *Conquerors*, 68–69; Kistemaker, *Revelation*, 134.

[146] Hendriksen, *Conquerors*, 69.

his garments. However, the message to Philadelphia does indicate that their "new name" belongs to Christ. (3:12) and that the name of Christ is written on the foreheads of the saints (3:12; 14:1; 22:4). As Hendrickson argues:

> Just as during the old dispensation the name of Jehovah was written on the forehead of the high-priest to indicate that he was specially consecrated servant of Jehovah; so believers—who are constantly called priests in the Apocalypse—shall have a new name written on their foreheads, namely, the name of Christ, His new name.[147]

That said, the gems in the breastplate were various colours (Exod 28:17–21) and twelve in number, while the stone described in Revelation was a single white stone.[148]

2. A second Jewish custom was that it is associated with the high priest's Urim and Thummim, worn under his ephod (see Fig. 73)[149] and known only to the priest; or with two onyx stones worn on the shoulders of the high priest's garment engraved with names of the sons of Israel, six on one and six on the other, [150] as jeweller-engraved signets.[151] However, the Urim is described as a precious stone (LXX, λίθος, *lithos*) in the NT[152] and not a stone or pebble (ψῆφον, *psēphon*).[153] While, onyx stones are usually black or red, sardonyx contains alternate white layers that include sard, and is mentioned in the Bible (Job 28:16; Rev 21:20). The *Gemma Augustea* is a famous first century sardonyx cameo engraving with a white relief on black. [154]

3. A white stone, attested in a first cent. inscription (*NewDocs* 4.202–209), was used in the Synagogue to cast a vote and select the honored member who received a wreath and a public declaration of his name before the congregation.[155]

---

[147] Ibid., 70.

[148] Edward Hayes Plumptre, *A Popular Exposition of the Epistles to the Seven Churches of Asia*, 2nd ed. (London, U.K.: Hodder & Stoughton, 1887), 126–27; Wong, "Hidden Manna and the White Stone," 351.

[149] Proposed by Stuart, *Apocalypse*, 2:78–79; Trench, *Commentary on Seven Churches*, 132–33; Chilton, *Days of Vengeance*, 110; Donald C. Guthrie, *The Apostles* (Grand Rapids, Mich.: Zondervan, 1992), 390; Marcus L Loane, *They Overcame: An Exposition of the First Three Chapters of Revelation* (Grand Rapids, Mich.: Baker, 1981), 63–64; Stott, *Christ Thinks*, 65–66; Smith, *Revelation*, 74.

[150] C. F. Keil and Franz Delitzsch, *The Pentateuch*, trans. James Martin, vol. 1, Commentary on the Old Testament (Grand Rapids, Mich.: Eerdmans, 1976), 1:198; Nahum M. Sarna, *Exodus*, JPS Torah Commentary 2 (Philadelphia, Pa.: The Jewish Publication Society, 2003), 2:181–82.

[151] Exod 28:9–12, 30; Num 27:21; Deut 33:8; 1 Sam 28:6; *b. Yoma* 73b; *T. Levi* 8.12–14.

[152] Luke 21:5; 1 Cor 3:12; Rev 4:3; 17:4.

[153] Refuted by Plumptre, Seven Churches of Asia, 126–30; Tait, Messages to the Seven Churches, 249–50; William Lee, "The Revelation of St. John," in The Holy Bible: With an Explanatory and Critical Commentary and a Revision of the Translation, by Bishops and Other Clergy of the Anglican Church, ed. Frederic Charles Cook, vol. 10 (London, U.K.: Murray, 1881), 525–26.

[154] Peter A. Clayton, *Treasures of Ancient Rome* (Wingdale, N.Y.: Crescent, 1995), 163–65.

[155] Lee I. Levine, *The Ancient Synagogue: The First Thousand Years*, 2nd ed. (New Haven, Conn.: Yale University Press, 2005), 101–2; Joyce Maire Reynolds, "Inscriptions," in *Excavations at Sidi Khrebish, Benghazi (Berenice): Buildings, Coins,*

4. The *white stone with an inscribed new name* has been understood against the Graeco-Roman background of Roman jurors using white stones (ψῆφον, *psēphon*, Acts 26:10; *SEG* 26.1817.80) to cast votes to convict or black stones to cast votes of guilty.[156] However, the text states that the overcomer will receive a stone and not cast a stone,[157] and voting was used in the context of a large jury, not by a single suzerain.[158] Also, no names were known to be written on these Roman trial pebbles, although ostraca were sometimes used in placing a vote, as in the ballots discovered at Masada with names perhaps identifying the order and role in the resulting suicide (see Fig. 74).[159] This allusion would fit with the judicial theme of the messages to the churches (2:13) and the book of Revelation in general, in where the judge will ultimately clear the persecuted Christians in Pergamum of all charges in the final judgment. Thomas has challenged this idea by questioning how an already redeemed person could be further acquitted,[160] but as Wong argues "having faith in Christ (1 John 5 4–5), is accepted by God now and will also be accepted in the final day."[161]

74. Ostracon found at Masada bearing the name "ben Yair" which could be short for Eleazar ben Ya'ir, the leader of the Zealots at Masada.

Inscriptions, Architectural Decoration, ed. John Alfred Lloyd (Libyan Arab Jamahiriya, 1977), 242–47.

[156] 2 *Bar.* 6:7; Ovid *Metam.* 15.41–42; Plutarch *Mor.* 186; Aelian *De nat. anim.* 13.38; Lucian *Dial. meretr.* 9; Theophrastus *Char.* 17.8; Aeschylus *Eum.* 741; Heliodorus *Aeth.* 3.3; *NewDocs* 1:84; The earliest view was proposed by Andrew of Caesarea (*Comm. Apoc.* 69) and Victorinus (*Comm. Apoc.* 2:17). Charles, *Revelation*, 1:67; Friedrich Bleek, *Vorlesungen über die Apokalypse* (Berlin: Georg Reimer, 2011), 178; Avi-Yonah, *Views of the Biblical World: NT*, 5:272; Barclay, *Letters*, 53–54; Ramsay, *Letters: Updated*, 302–6; Hemer, *Letters to the Seven Churches*, 242 n. 85; Keener, *Revelation*, 126–27; Witherington III, *Revelation*, 104; Brütsch, *Offenbarung*, 1:149–50; Beasley-Murray, *Revelation, NCB*, 88; Ford, *Revelation*, 399–400; Krodel, *Revelation*, 121. While for Ramsay the voting ballots analogy by itself is unsatisfactory, he accepts them as a useful visual connection for the custom innovation of the white stone. Osborne admits, "It is impossible to know for certain which of these is the best source for the imagery. . . . the best background would be a combination of the stone given victors at the games for entrance into a feast and possibly overtones of a vote of acquittal." Osborne, *Revelation*, 148–49. This view is refuted by Stuart, "White Stone," 461–77.

[157] Hengstenberg, *Revelation*, 189; Stuart, *Apocalypse*, 77; Hendriksen, *Conquerors*, 134.

[158] Worth, Jr., *Greco-Asian Culture*, 143.

[159] Yigael Yadin, Y. Hevrah, and Y. Meshorer, *Masada: The Aramaic and Hebrew Ostraca and Jar Inscriptions: The Coins of Masada* (Jerusalem: Israel Exploration Society, 1989); Ehud Netzer, "The Last Days and Hours at Masada," *BAR* 17, no. 6 (1991): 20–32; Allen R. Millard, *Reading and Writing in the Time of Jesus* (New York, N.Y.: Continuum International, 2004), 97.

[160] Thomas, *Rev 1–7*, 201.

[161] Wong, "Hidden Manna and the White Stone," 350.

5. The *white stone with an inscribed new name* is also understood from numerous usages of the *tessera* (Lat. pl. *tesserae*, Gr. κύβος, *kubos*, small mosaic tile, or σύμβολον, *sumbolon*, token) as tickets to tribunals or theater performances, as pawns in games, and as amulets. First, it was the custom of the *agōnothetēs* (ἀγωνοθέτης person in charge) of the athletic games to award the winner of the games with a white stone (rectangular tablet of bone)[162] with his name or the magistrate engraved on it, along with the day and year.[163] The token also granted the athlete admission to the victor's banquet of the great king (*tesserae conuiuiales*). The *tessera hospitalis* was also used with guild banquets[164] and was broken in two and given to the guest upon their departure to identify them if they ever returned.[165]

75. The left is a small white *tessera* (mosaic tile). To the right is a replica of an ivory or bone token (*tessara theatralis*) used as a theater ticket for entrance into special events. The token would have various images or writing depending on the performance

Another tessera *(theatralis)* granted admission to the theater for Roman citizens (see Fig. 75).[166] As Witherington suggests: "the new name implies a new identity and being someone special in the kingdom. Christians did not have to compromise on earth by socializing with pagans in temples when they had a much better engraved invitation to a much better banquet."[167] The use of tokens to enter the banquet (*tesserae conuiuiales*) can easily be applied to the idea of the supper of the Lamb.[168] Beasley-Murray concludes that in a similar way "the white stone would admit the recipient to the messianic feast, and the

---

[162] K. Welch, "The Roman Arena in Late-Republican Italy: A Re-Evaluation," in *Sport in the Greek and Roman Worlds: Greek Athletic Identities and Roman Sports and Spectacle*, ed. Thomas Francis Scanlon, vol. 2 (Oxford, U.K.: Oxford University Press, 2014), 214–15.

[163] *CIL* 1.717–76; Horace *Ep.* 1.1.1–3; Cicero *Phil.* 2.29.74; Ovid *Trist.* 4.8.34; Hanns Lilje, *The Last Book of the Bible: The Meaning of the Revelation of St. John*, trans. Olive Wyon (Philadelphia, Pa.: Muhlenberg, 1957), 82; Eichhorn, *Commentarius in Apocalypsin Joannis*, 1:105–6; Lee, "The Revelation of St. John," 256; Osborne, *Revelation*, 149; Smalley, "John's Revelation," 71; Witherington III, *Revelation*, 103–4; Barclay, *Letters*, 41–42; Alfred Wikenhauser, *Die Offenbarung des Johannes*, 3rd ed., RNT 9 (Regensburg: Pustet, 1959), 42; Krodel, *Revelation*, 121; Keener, *Revelation*, 126; Caird, *Revelation*, 42; Ford, *Revelation*, 399–400; Beasley-Murray, *Revelation*, NCB, 88; Hemer, *Letters to the Seven Churches*, 98–99, 103; Thomas, *Rev 1–7*, 201; Mounce, *Revelation*, 99–100.

[164] James Yates and William Wayte, "Tessera," in *DGRA*, ed. William Smith (London, U.K.: Murray, 1891), 1112–13; James M. Efird, *Revelation For Today: An Apocalyptic Approach* (Nashville, Tenn.: Abingdon, 1989), 57; Harrington, *Revelation*, 62; Mounce, *Revelation*, 83; Beale, *Rev*, 252–53; Johnson, "Revelation," 620; Hemer, *Letters to the Seven Churches*, 98; Giblin, *Revelation*, 57; Plumptre, *Seven Churches of Asia*, 127–28; Eichhorn, *Commentarius in Apocalypsin Joannis*, 1:105–6.

[165] Anthony Rich, *A Dictionary of Roman and Greek Antiquities*, 6th ed. (New York, N.Y.: Longman, 1884), 650; John Edwyn Sandys, ed., *A Companion to Latin Studies* (Cambridge, U.K.: Cambridge University Press, 1921), 753.

[166] Oskar Seyffert, *A Dictionary of Classical Antiquities: Mythology, Religion, Literature and Art*, ed. Henry Nettleship and John Edwin Sandys (New York, N.Y.: MacMillan & Co., 1895), 621.

[167] Witherington III, *Revelation*, 104.

[168] Charles, *Revelation*, 1:66–67; Swete, *Apocalypse*, 40–41.

symbolism would extend the idea of eating the hidden manna"¹⁶⁹ which will be the reward of the faithful (Matt 8:11; 22:10).¹⁷⁰

Second, tesserae were also awarded to discharged gladiators¹⁷¹ (*tesserae gladiatoriae*),¹⁷² with some containing the letters *SP*. It has been suggested that this stands either for the Latin *spectatus* (Lat. "proved" or "tested"),¹⁷³ or more likely *spectauit* or *spectat* (Lat. "spectator").¹⁷⁴ Sandys describes the inscriptions as:

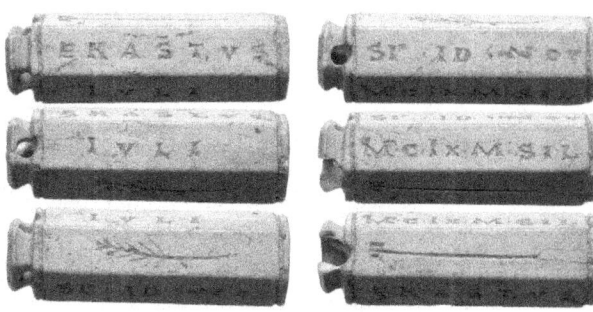

76. Bone or ivory tessera (*tesserae nummulariae*) seals which were attached to a coin bags (*folles*), certifying that the coins within were of the right number and genuine, by a mint official called a *nummularius*.

(1) the name of a person, whether slave or freedman, (2) that of his owner or trainer, (3) the word *spectauit* or the abbreviation *sp*. *spe*. or *spect*., (4) the month, with or without the day, and (5) the consuls of the year.¹⁷⁵

Third, it is a code word used as a token among soldiers (Lat. *tessera militarius*, Gr. σύνθημα, *sunthēma*) and handed out on a wooden tablet.¹⁷⁶ Before going into battle, the word was communicated to the troops so they might be able to distinguish between friend and foe (Polybius *Hist.* 6.34; Livy *Hist. Rome* 7.35; 27.46). At the battle of Cunaxa, the code word was "Zeus the Savior and Victory" (Xenophon *Anab.* 1.8.16; 6.3.25). In this context, it might refer to the secret name given to the vassal that would identify the bearer as belonging to the true suzerain. Some suggest that the name on the stone given to the overcomers was the *Tetragrammaton* יהוה – the extraordinary Hebrew name for God – YHWH (Yahweh). Although this was not a secret name, it was not spoken and in manuscripts like Dead Sea Scroll Testamonia (4Q175), it was written with four dots or with ancient Paleo-Hebrew letters. There could be parallels with the use of the god Zeus as a token code word.

---

¹⁶⁹ Beasley-Murray, *Revelation*, NCB, 88.

¹⁷⁰ Refuted by Stuart, "White Stone," 461–77.

¹⁷¹ Friedrich Wilhelm Ritschl, *Die Tesserae Gladiatoriae der Römer* (Munich: Akademie, 1864); Sandys, *A Companion to Latin Studies*, 753.

¹⁷² Ovid *Trist.* 4.8.23–24; Suetonius *Dom.* 4.5; Martial *Epig.* 8.7; Ramsay dismisses this analogy for failing to make the essential points of comparison, not written with a new name, and not drawing on the familiarity of the reader's experience. Ramsay, *The Letters to Seven Churches*, 303; Barclay, *Letters*, 54; Ford, *Revelation*, 400.

¹⁷³ Barclay, *Revelation*, 1:107.

¹⁷⁴ William M. Ramsay, "The White Stone and the 'Gladiatorial' Tessera," *ExpTim* 16, no. 12 (January 1, 1905): 558–61; M. Cary, "Tesserae Gladiatoriae Sive Nummulariae," *JRS* 13 (1923): 110–13; Laura M. Banducci, "A Tessera Lusoria from Gabii and the Afterlife of Roman Gaming," *Herom* 4, no. 2 (2015): 199–221.

¹⁷⁵ Sandys, A Companion to Latin Studies, 753.

¹⁷⁶ Yates and Wayte, "Tessera," 1113; Rich, Dictionary of Roman and Greek Antiquities, 650; Berger, Encyclopedic Dictionary of Roman Law, 732.

Fourth, magistrates also gave tokens (*tesserae*) to citizens so they could exchange them for money, food, corn, or grain (Lat. *tesserae frumentaria* and *nummularia;* Suetonius *Aug.* 40.2, 42.3; *Nero* 11; see Figs. 76, 77).[177] Real-Pauly define *nummularius* as:

> Validators of coins since the second half of the 2nd century BC. So-called *tesserae nummularia* [see Fig. 76] guaranteed that money was in a sealed container. Since the 1st century BC the four-sided *tesserae* had on side one the name of the *nummularius* (initially slaves, then released and free-born); on side 2 is the name of his owner, or the surname of a free *nummularius*; on side 3 the check note (*spectavit*) stating the day and month; and on side the consuls of the year.[178]

Generally, a tessera token was understood in first-century culture to represent a rite of passage for those given a tessera of any kind. An inscribed *tessera* easily fits the context in Revelation where overcomers are granted a stone with a secret name on it that would grant them access to the marriage feast of the suzerain or Lamb (19:9).[179]

6. *A new name* is connected to the historical event of Octavius being given the new name of Augustus, which was displayed in white stone in Pergamum (see Fig. 79).[180] While Pergamum was constructed using dark brown granite, the imperial edicts in the city were written on white marble.[181] Wilson documents that:

> One such relevant decree was issued in 9 BC by Paulus Fabius Maxiums, the governor of Asia. This edict, confirmed by the provincial league, decreed that Augustus's birthday should be made an official holiday in Asia as well as to mark the beginning of the municipal new year. It was inscribed in Latin and Greek on a white stone and set up in the imperial cult temple of Pergamum (*OGIS* 2.458).[182]

Numerous copies of this decree have been discovered in several other Asian cities. As a writing surface, stone was much more durable than Pergamum's famed parchment, but the suzerains stone was more durable than even an Imperial edict.

7. The *white stone with an inscribed new name* may be understood against the background of Anatolian religious superstition where a white magical gem or

77. Roman *tessera frumentaria* (left) compared to a Euro cent coin (right).

---

[177] Rich, *Dictionary of Roman and Greek Antiquities*, 640; William Smith, William Wayte, and George Elden Marindin, eds., *A Dictionary of Greek and Roman Antiquities*, 3rd ed. (London, U.K.: Murray, 1891), 1:879; 2:799.

[178] August Friedrich Pauly, *Realencyclopädie Der Classischen Altertumswissenschaft*, ed. Georg Wissowa and S. Kroll (Stuttgart: Metzler & Druckenmüller, 1894), 17:1415; Rudolf Herzog, *Aus der Geschichte des Bankwesens im Altertum: Tesserae nummulariae. Mit einer tafel* (Berlin: Töpelmann, 1919), 10.

[179] Tait, Messages to the Seven Churches, 253.

[180] Worth, Jr., *Greco-Asian Culture*, 152–53; Barclay, *Revelation*, 1:1:99; Ramsay, *Letters: Updated*, 306–11.

[181] Hemer, Letters to the Seven Churches, 101–2.

[182] Wilson, *Revelation*, 26; Paul Robinson Coleman-Norton, Allan Chester Johnson, and Frank Card Bourne, *Ancient Roman Statutes: A Translation with Introduction, Commentary, Glossary, and Index*, ed. Clyde Pharr (Austin, Tex.: University of Texas Press, 2009), 119 §142.

amulet (*PGM* 12.209, 280; see also 4.937, 1048, 1057)[183] was inscribed with a secret name of a god. It was more effective if the wearer alone knew what was written on it.[184] To know the name of a divine being or demon was to possess magical power over that supernatural being (i.e., Egyptian Scarab; see Fig. 78),[185] and therefore providing a spiritual bond between the owner of the *tessera* and the name on the stone.[186] Pritchard documents an Egyptian text that tells the story of the goddess Isis, who was plotting to acquire the secret name of the god Re using the venom of a snake in order to take over the unknown name of power for herself.[187] It is also interesting to note that the emblem of the Phrygian Mother Goddess, Cybele, was a black stone.[188] Cyranides describes Beryl as "a well-known white stone, very valuable" (*Cyr.* 1.2.6 [Waegeman]), and a favorite stone used as a magical amulet, called the "stone of Zeus" (*Cyr.* 1.2.20–26 [Waegeman]).[189] A papyri describes the procedure for making an amulet from a white stone and reads "You bring a ring of iron and you bring a white stone which is in the shape of a grape … Write this name on it [etc.]" (*PDM* 12.6–20).[190] They also mention the importance of inscribing the amulets with secret names "below the design on the stone is this name (conceal it!)" (*PGM* 1.146, "cannot be spoken" *PGM* 13.763–64, 845).

The practice of using God or Jesus's name for its magical efficacy is documented by the church fathers[191] and exorcism using various powerful names, including Jesus, is well

---

[183] Roy Kotansky, "Incantations and Prayers for Salvation on Inscribed Greek Amulets," in *Magika Hiera: Ancient Greek Magic and Religion*, ed. Christopher A. Faraone and Dirk Obbink (New York, N.Y.: Oxford University Press, 1997), 107–37; David E. Aune, "Magic in Early Christianity," in *ANRW*, ed. Hildegard Temporini and Wolfgang Haase, Part 2, Principat, 23.1 (Berlin: De Gruyter, 1980), 1556; "Amulets," in *OEANE*, ed. Eric M. Meyers, vol. 1 (Oxford, U.K.: Oxford University Press, 1997), 1:113–15.

[184] Livy *Hist. Rome* 39.30.4–5; Artemidorus *Oneir.* 5.26; "marked by the whitest of white stones" Pliny *Ep.* 6.11.3; Wilhelm H. F. Heitmüller, *"Im Namen Jesu": Eine Sprach- U. Religionsgeschichtliche Untersuchung Zum Neuen Testament, Speziell Zur Altchristlichen Taufe* (Göttingen: Vandenhoeck & Ruprecht, 1903), 174–75; 234–35; Bousset, *Die Offenbarung Johannis*, 215; Carl C. Clemen, *Religionsgeschichtliche Erklärung Des Neuen Testaments*, Die Abhängigkeit Des Ältesten Christentums von Nichtjüdischen Religionen Und Philosophischen Systemen (Gieben: Töpelmann, 1907), 373–74; Beckwith, *Apocalypse*, 461–63; Charles, *Revelation*, 1:66–67; Lohmeyer, *Offenbarung*, 27; Lohse, *Offenbarung*, 29; Metzger, *Breaking the Code*, 36.

[185] Barclay, *Letters*, 42.

[186] Moffatt, *Revelation*, 5:359; Charles, *Revelation*, 66; Beckwith, *Apocalypse*, 463; Swete, *Apocalypse*, 40; Barclay, *Letters*, 42; Bousset, *Die Offenbarung Johannis*, 215; Lohse, *Offenbarung*, 29; Müller, *Offenbarung*, 115; Roloff, *Revelation*, 52. Beale points out that believers all receive the same name and it is not a secret magical name just given to overcomers. However, he does entertain the possibility "that the magical background of secret, incantional divine names additionally enhanced the meaning of the concluding phrase in 2:17." Beale, *Rev*, 258.

[187] Pritchard, *ANETOT*, 12; Siegfried Morenz, *Egyptian Religion*, trans. Ann E. Keep (Ithaca, N.Y.: Cornell University Press, 1992), 21.

[188] Stambaugh and Balch, *NT in Its Social Environment*, 136.

[189] D. Kaimakis, *Die Kyraniden*, Beiträge Zur Klassichen Philologie 76 (Meisenheim am Glan: Sophie, 1976); Maryse Waegeman, *Amulet and Alphabet: Magical Amulets in the First Book of Cyranides* (Amsterdam: Gieben, 1987).

[190] Hans Dieter Betz, ed., *The Greek Magical Papyri in Translation, Including the Demotic Spells* (Chicago, Ill.: University of Chicago Press, 1996), 152.

[191] Origin *Cels.* 1.24; 4.33–34; 5.45; see also Justin *Dial.* 85, 135; Aune, "Magic in Early Christianity," 2:1545–49.

documented.¹⁹² Early Christian magical amulets have been recovered, although none as early as the second century.¹⁹³

Barclay concludes that the suzerain is saying that "you wear your amulets to keep you safe; you use your superstitious charms to protect you; you who are Christians have no need of that; for the man who has *my name* written on his heart is safe in life and in death."¹⁹⁴ Yet why would John condone these superstitions in the blessing for the overcomers at Pergamum?¹⁹⁵ Despite the attractiveness of Barclay's suggestion, it is highly unlikely that Jesus would derive this symbolism from superstitious pagan practices, especially when He had just warned against idolatrous pagan associations in verses 14–15.

8. The giving of a stone with a name inscribed on it was also used in conjunction with the cult of Asclepius during the initiation service (Aristides *Apol.* 10).

78. Egyptian scarab beetle with an inscription on the bottom and the figure of the goddess Taweret to be used as an amulet, to ward off evil spirits.

From the evidence presented here one can recognize that writing names on stones was a common practice in first century Asia Minor and would easily be recognized as an analogy to many parallels in common life. Probably Ramsay is correct in his assumption that "while none of these analogies is complete or satisfactory in itself, perhaps none is entirely wrong. . . . It had analogies with many things, though it was not an exact reproduction of any of them."¹⁹⁶

NEW NAME

The white stone is reported to have a "New Name" (ὄνομά καινόν, *onoma kainon*) written on it "that no one knows except the one who receives it."¹⁹⁷ Three possible explanations have been given for the new name, but it should also be understood against the background of the ancient

---

¹⁹² See Matt 12:27/Luke 11:19; Acts 3:6; 4:10; 9:34; 16:18; 19:11–20; Josephus *Ant.* 8.45–49; Justin *Dial.* 85; Irenaeus *Haer.* 2.6.2; Justin *2 Apol.* 6.6; *Dial.* 30.3; 76.6; 85.2; Irenaeus *Haer.* 2.32.4; 2.49.3; Origen *Cels.* 1.6, 25, 67; 3.24; *Acts John* 41; Arnobius *Adv. nat.* 1.46; Lactantius *Inst.* 2.16; 4.27.

¹⁹³ F. Eckstein and J. H. Waszink, "Amulett," *RAC* 1:407–10; H. Leclercq, "Amulettes," *DACL* 1:1795–1822; Campbell Bonner, *Studies in Magical Amulets: Chiefly Graeco-Egyptian* (London, U.K.: Oxford University Press, 1950), 208–28; A. Delatte and Ph. Derchain, *Les Intailles Magiques Gréco-Egyptiennes* (Paris: Bibliotheque Nationale, 1964), 238–87; Robert Walter Daniel and Franco Maltomini, *Supplementum Magicum* (Oplanden: Westdeutscher Verlag, 1990), 1: nos. 20–36.

¹⁹⁴ Barclay, *Letters*, 42.

¹⁹⁵ Thomas, *Rev 1–7*, 200; Smith, *Revelation*, 74.

¹⁹⁶ Ramsay, *Letters: Updated*, 222.

¹⁹⁷ On the New Name see Beale, *Rev*, 253–58; Hemer, *Letters to the Seven Churches*, 102–3; Worth, Jr., *Greco-Asian Culture*, 149–51.

Near Eastern belief that to give another their name was to possess (or have an intimate relationship with) that person (*Odes Sol.* 42:8, 9, 20; *1 En.* 69:14–19).[198] Pagan deities sometimes gave worshipers new names to provide them with a new identity.[199] Numerous biblical characters were given new names,[200] especially if something dramatic changed in their life.[201] The system worked by either assigning a new name for the suzerain (God) or a new name to the vassals (overcomers, individually or collectively).

1. First, the name might be an individual new name the suzerain will give to each vassal and only known to them.[202] Some have suggested that the late custom of taking a new name at baptism is read back into this reference to a new name.[203] However, while Simon's name was changed to Peter, it appears to be the only occurrence, and was not secret. Saul (a Jewish name) also had the Latin name Paul (Acts 16:37, 22:25–28), the custom of dual names being common in the Roman period, meaning that technically, his name was not changed. As Martin points out:

79. A white stone pillar at Pergamum with names inscribed on it (2:12, 17).

> The list of first generation Christians in Romans 16:3–16 shows that it was not then felt necessary to change names with heathen associations. Most of the names in a list of eighty-seven bishops in north Africa in AD 256 are ordinary pagan names, many of them incorporating names of gods. Clearly the practice of giving Christian names was not universal.[204]

---

[198] Walther Eichrodt, *Theology of the Old Testament*, Old Testament Library (Louisville, Ky.: Westminster/Knox, 1967), 2:40–45; 310–11; H. Bietenhard, "Ὄνομα," ed. Gerhard Kittel and Gerhard Friedrich, trans. Geoffrey W. Bromiley, *TDNT* (Grand Rapids, Mich.: Eerdmans, 1985), 5:253–8; Beale, *Rev*, 254; Johnson, "Revelation," 620; Talbert, *Apocalypse*, 19; Hemer, *Letters to the Seven Churches*, 99–100; Keener, *Revelation*, 127.

[199] Plutarch *Mor.* 288; Luke 1:59; Metaphorical see 1QpHab 8:9.

[200] Abram = Abraham, Gen 17:5; Sarai = Sarah, Gen 17:15; Jacob = Israel, Gen 35:10; Simon = Peter, Matt 16:18, John 1:41–42; etc.

[201] Otto Eissfeldt, "Renaming in the Old Testament," in *Words and Meanings*, ed. Peter R. Ackroyd and Barnabas Lindars (London, U.K.: Cambridge University Press, 1968), 69–80.

[202] Düsterdieck, *Revelation*, 148; Hengstenberg, *Revelation*, 153; Wikenhauser, *Die Offenbarung des Johannes*, 42; William R. Newell, *The Book of the Revelation* (Chicago, Ill.: Grace, 1941), 41; Hemer, *Letters to the Seven Churches*, 102–3; Thomas, *Rev 1–7*, 202.

[203] Ramsay, *Letters: Updated*, 223.

[204] Martin, *Seven Letters*, 77.

2. Second, the name might be one name given in common to all believers. It will be known to all overcomers or vassals. This view is supported by the fact that all things of God are known to his vassals (1 John 2:20, 27; 1 Cor 2:15–16), and by the promise in Isaiah that he will give his people a "new name" (Isa 62:2; see also 56:5; 65:15).

3. Third, the name might be that of the suzerain himself, either as God the Father[205] or Jesus Christ.[206] A hint of the nature of this name may already have been given in 3:12 where it states: "I will write on him the *name of my God*, and the name of the city of my God, the new Jerusalem, which comes down from my God out of heaven, and my own *new name*."[207] When taken in conjunction with the common magical practice of inscribing names of Gods on amulets for protection, then it may reflect the name of the suzerain who will protect his vassal from harm. Protection was one of the common events mentioned by the suzerain in the historical prologue of the ANEVT.[208] The suzerain would protect the overcomers from the evil of the false teachers and Nicolaitans at Pergamum.

SECRET

The secret name is difficult to ascertain, but Beckwith points out that the potency of an amulet with a divine name was more powerful if the name was kept secret.[209] The name of God and of Jesus is known openly unless the text is referring to a name of God like "I am what I am", which is still unknown until revealed to the overcomer by the suzerain. Beale explains that:

> "knowing" the "new name" does not connote mere cognitive knowledge but experiential access to the character and power that the name represents, so that those who know Christ's name share in his character and end-time power (*1 En.* 69:14–19; "hidden name").[210]

Smalley concludes: "It is therefore more reasonable to understand the new 'name' as that given to the Christian, symbolizing entrance to new life and new status".[211]

CONCLUSION

Six recognizable elements of the ANEVT, constituting a structure, are identified within the prophetic message to convey a covenant lawsuit message of encouragement to the overcomers within the church of Pergamum.

---

[205] Charles, *Revelation*, 1:67; Ellul, *Apocalypse*, 133; Lohse, *Offenbarung*, 29; Müller, *Offenbarung*, 115; Roloff, *Revelation*, 55; Smith, *Revelation*, 74; Ramsay, *Letters: Updated*, 224.
[206] Beckwith, *Apocalypse*, 461–62; Bruce, *Revelation*, 689; William John Limmer Sheppard, *The Revelation of St. John the Divine* (London, U.K.: Religious Tract Society, 1924), 41; Lilje, *The Last Book of the Bible*, 83; Krodel, *Revelation*, 121; Robertson, *Word Pictures*, 6:307; Heitmüller, *Im Namen Jesu*, 128–265; Smalley, *Revelation*, 71.
[207] See also Rev 14:1; 22:4, Isa 56:5; 62:2; 65:15; *Tg. Isa.* 65:15b.
[208] See chapter 1, *Historical Prologue*.
[209] Beckwith, *Apocalypse*, 461–62.
[210] Beale, *Rev*, 258.
[211] Smalley, *Revelation*, 71. See also Isa 62:2; 65:15; 2 Cor 5:17.

The suzerain commends his vassals at Pergamum for being faithful to his name even in spite of the martyrdom of Antipas, but reprimands them for entertaining false teachers who compromise with the local culture and the imperial cult. The curse of the suzerain will befall them in his warring visit if they do not repent. To the overcomer the suzerain promised both the blessing of the messianic kingdom and the assurance of a close relationship with the suzerain.

Firstly, the preamble, marked by the prophetic oracular formula τάδε λέγει Ω, calls attention to what the suzerain, identified here as the sovereign omnipotent one who weilds a "sharp two-edged sword" (2:12b), will say to the vassals in Pergamum.

Secondly, the historical prologue is characterized by the omniscient suzerain's intimate knowledge of Pergamum's faithfulness and knows where Satan has his throne. He knows they are being faithful to his name even in spite of the martyrdom of Antipas. He knows they are entertaining false teachers who compromise with the local culture and the imperial cult.

Thirdly, the Great King sets out an imperative for Pergamum church in the stipulation to repent.

Fourthly, the suzerain declared two curses against them if they do not repent. The curse of the suzerain's presence will befall them in his warring visit. If they are not faithful to the King, then the suzerain would come in judgment and make war against them. The curse will remind the churches of the omniscience of the suzerain and that he gives to each according to their works.

Fifthly, the eschatological *macarism* for the faithful overcomers' obedience to the stipulations will be the King's gracious pledge of the blessing of partaking in the hidden manna and possessing a new name on a white stone.

Finally, acting as his own witness in the court case, the Spirit-Judge calls the Pergamum congregation to hear what he has to say about the conduct of the churches.

10

Tireless Thyatira

The History of the City

In order to understand the message to Thyatira, who tirelessly worked in their trade guilds, it is helpful to examine both the cultural (Graeco-Roman) history of Thyatira, as well as the (Hebraic-Semitic) OT theological roots of the message. This chapter will examine the historical background to the city of Thyatira.

THE GEOGRAPHY OF THYATIRA

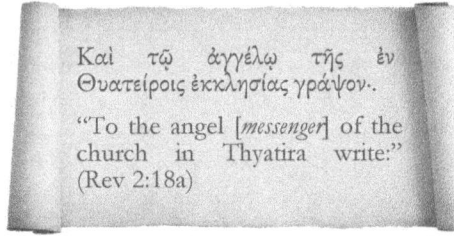

"To the angel [*messenger*] of the church in Thyatira write:" (Rev 2:18a)

Following the Hermus and Caicus river valleys 47 miles (75 km) inland southeast from Pergamum, one arrives at the small village of Thyatira (Θυάτειρα, *Thuateira*, "the town or citadel of Thya"[1]; modern *Akhiṣar*, "white castle"; coordinates: 38:55:15 N 27:50:30 E) in the Lycus valley (Pliny *Nat.* 5.126).[2] It is located between Pergamum and Sardis on the Hermus river in Lydia or Mysia (Strabo *Geogr.* 13.4).[3]

By contrast with Pergamum and Sardis, which were built on impressive defensive mountains, Thyatira is in a valley and exposed to enemy attack. Thus its importance was found in the protection it offered to Pergamum as Pergamum's first line of defense against an assault.[4] Due to its location as the "most important junction of roads between Lydia and Mysia"[5] it became a wealthy commercial center with a garrison headquarters.

---

[1] Stephanus of Byzantium, suggests the name is derived from θυγατέρα (*thugatēr, thugatera*), meaning "daughter" (*De Urb.* 869), although it is likely that it is an older, Lydian name.

[2] William M. Ramsay, "Thyatira," in *DBib*, ed. James Hastings, Frederick C. Grant, and Harold. H. Rowley, vol. 4 (New York, N.Y.: Scribner's Sons, 1909), 4:757.

[3] Strabo describes it as "a colony of the Macedonians, which some authors [Stephanus of Byzantium, *De Urbibus*] say is the last city belonging to the Mysians" (*Geogr.* 23.4.4).

[4] Worth, Jr., *Greco-Asian Culture*, 154.

[5] Aune, *Rev 1–5*, 213.

The history of Thyatira

Legend recounts how Thyatira was founded as *Pelopia* (Πελοπία) or *Euhippian Thyatira* (Pliny *Nat.* 5.31),[6] a sanctuary to the Lydian sun god Apollo Tyrimnos (see Figs. 82, 86; *I.Thyat.* 882–83; 946; 956; 960) and Artemis Boreitene (*I.Thyat.* 995–96), patron gods of the city.[7] Archaeological evidence indicates that there was a settlement here as early as 3000 BC.[8] Thyatira is identified early as a Seleucid colony that Strabo states was originally a Macedonian colony.[9] Diogenes called it "sacred Thyatira" (*Vit. Phil.* 4.31) in the Hellenistic period. The frontier garrison at Thyatira, established by Lysimachus,[10] was resettled by Seleucus I Nicator (ca. 301–281 BC; see Fig. 80)[11] following the defeat of Lysimachus (Stephanus *Byz. on Thyatira*) at the Battle of Corupedium (281 BC) in Lydia (Memnon *Hist. Her.* 12.7).[12] Jones points out that this is the earliest known colony to be settled with land-based forces by a Macedonian king and points out that it was a military settlement and not a city, as is made clear from inscriptions.[13] Thyatira struck Cistophoric coins in 196 BC and Jones suggests that the city was "probably therefore reorganized and enlarged at the same time."[14] It would continue to serve as an important military headquarters under Antiochus III (r. 222–187 BC; see Fig. 96) to protect Pergamum and the Caicus Valley from Seleucid kings invading from the south (Livy *Hist. Rome* 37.8.7; 37.44.4).[15] With the victory of the Romans over the Seleucids, at the battle of Magnesia (190 BC), Asia came under Roman rule (Livy *Hist. Rome* 37.8.8; 37.37.6, 9; 44.4) and Thyatira was added to the kingdom of Pergamum under the Attalid rules (189 BC; Livy *Hist. Rome* 37.44.4).

As an easy target, Thyatira was invaded by Prusias of Bithynia (Appian *Mith.* 1.3; 150 BC) following his defeat at Pergamum in 157/6 BC (Polybius *Hist.* 32.15.10). Thyatira was then

---

[6] Hemer does not accept these as older names for the city, but acknowledges them as *cognomina* of the city. Hemer, *Letters to the Seven Churches* 107.

[7] Ibid.

[8] Fant and Reddish, *Guide to Biblical Sites*, 328.

[9] *OGIS* 1.211; *BCH* 11 [1887], 466, no. 32; Strabo *Geogr.* 11.4.4; 13.4; *I.Thyat.* 973; 989.

[10] Schulten suggested that Seleucos I was the founder of the settlement at Thyatira, while Meyer proposed that the founder was Antiochos I Soter. A. Schulten, "Die Makedonischen Militärcolonien," *Hermes* 32, no. 3 (1897): 528; Eduard Meyer, "Die Makedonischen Militärcolonien," *Hermes* 33, no. 4 (1898): 647; Getzel M. Cohen, *The Hellenistic Settlements in Europe, the Islands, and Asia Minor* (Berkeley, Calf.: University of California Press, 1996), 240. See Cohen for more details on the debate.

[11] Hemer identified several inscriptions from Macedonia that date to this period, some dedicated to an unidentified Seleucus (*OGIS* 1.211; *BCH* 10 [1886], 398 no. 1 and 11 [1887], 466 no. 32). *Letters to the Seven Churches*, 245 n.2.

[12] John D. Grainger, *Seleukos Nikator: Constructing a Hellenistic Kingdom* (New York, N.Y.: Routledge, 1990), 55–56; "An Empire Builder—Seleukos Nikator," *History Today* 43, no. 5 (1993): 30.

[13] A. H. M. Jones, *The Cities of the Eastern Roman Provinces*, 2nd ed., Oxford University Press Academic Monograph (Eugene, Oreg.: Wipf & Stock, 2004), 44–45.

[14] Ibid., 54.

[15] Hemer, Letters to the Seven Churches, 107; Thomas, Rev 1–7, 206–7.

again invaded by Eumenes III (129 BC), who was defeated and captured by the Romans in the ensuing siege (Appian *Mith.* 13.61; Eutropius *Rom Hist.* 4.20).

Upon the death of Attalus III the Pergamene Kingdom was bequeathed to the Romans, who established the province of Asia in 133 BC, under which Thyatira belonged to the district or diocese (Lat. *conventus*) of Pergamum for the administration of justice,[16] but unrest continued and Thyatira was captured by Aristonicus, the son of Eumenes II the following year (Strabo *Geogr.* 14.38).[17]

Suetonius states that Tiberius (r. AD 14–37; see Figs. 43, 97, 111) "made a plea to the senate on behalf of the citizens of Laodicea, Thyatira and Chios, who had suffered loss from an earthquake [AD 17; Strabo *Geogr.* 12.8.18; Tacitus *Ann.* 2.47] and begged for help" (*Tib.* 8 [Rolfe]) to rebuild the city, and local residents built a colonnaded stoa dedicated to Augustus as the "son of god" (see 2:18).[18] Commemorative coins were

80. Bronze head of Seleucus I Nicator. Roman copy from a Greek original, from Herculaneum. (inv. no. 5590).

struck in AD 22–23 in Rome, showing Tiberius with the inscription "cities of Asia restored" (Lat. *Civitatibus Asiae Restitutis*)[19] to promote the generosity of the emperor in rebuilding the cities at Rome's expense (see Fig. 97).

Under Roman power Thyatira was known as "a city of no first-rate dignity" (Lat. *inhonora civitas;* Pliny *Nat.* 5.33 [Rackham]).[20] Unlike many of the other seven cities in Asia that received a message from the suzerain, Thyatira was not a beautiful cultural center with prominent

---

[16] Thyatira remained a *conventus* of Pergamum until the time of Caracalla (AD 211–17), when it was moved to a new *conventus* as the leading city. Jones, *Cities of the Eastern Roman Provinces*, 83. Stephen Mitchell, William M. Calder, and Eric William Gray, "Asia, Roman Province," ed. Simon Hornblower and Antony Spawforth, *OCD* (Oxford, U.K.: Clarendon, 2003), 182; Cohen, *Hellenistic Settlements*, 226. However, in the list of cities in the *conventus* of Pergamum provided by Pliny (*Nat.* 5.126) and the *Flavian Conventus,* neither list Thyatira.

[17] For the early history of Thyatira, see Magie, *Roman Rule in Asia Minor,* 2:977–78.

[18] Rüstem Duyuran, "Akhisar Tepe Mezarlığında Yapılan Arkeolojik Araştırmalar," *TAD* 17, no. 2 (1968): 73–76; "Akhisar Tepe Mezarlığında Yapılan Arkeolojik Araştırmalar II," *TAD* 20, no. 2 (1973): 17–27; Hasan Malay, *Researches in Lydia, Mysia and Aiolis*, Tituli Asiae Minoris, Supplement 23 (Vienna: Österreichischen Akademie der Wissenschaften, 1999), no. 24.

[19] *RIC* 1.48–50; *BMC Ionia* 70; Suetonius *Tib.* 48.2; Tacitus *Ann.* 2.47; Francis Hobler, *Records of Roman History: From Cnæus Pompeius to Tiberius Constantinus, as Exhibited on the Roman Coins* (New York, N.Y.: Nichols & sons, 1860), 69 nos. 126–127; Seth William Stevenson, *A Dictionary of Roman Coins: Republican and Imperial*, ed. Charles Roach Smith and Frederic William Madden (London, U.K.: George Bell & Sons, 1889), 207–9; Carol Humphrey Vivian Sutherland, *Roman History and Coinage, 44 BC–AD 69: Fifty Points of Relation from Julius Caesar to Vespasian* (Oxford: Clarendon Press, 1987), 47–49; Larry Joseph Kreitzer, *Striking New Images: Roman Imperial Coinage and the New Testament World*, JSNTSup 134 (Sheffield, U.K.: Sheffield Academic Press, 1996), 23.

[20] Trench, Commentary on Seven Churches, 182; Yamauchi, NT Cities, 51.

temples.²¹ However, it had military importance and was noted for its manufacturing, particularly of woolen goods, and for its thriving businesses, evidenced in the large number of trade guilds (*I.Thyat.* 974; 1002; see below). Thyatira prospered through trade since it was ideally positioned on the main road between Pergamum and Sardis. In fact, during the reign of Claudius (AD 41–54, see Fig. 2, 28) it was one of twelve cities granted the privilege of minting its own coins, a privilege lasting until the third century.²²

Emperor Hadrian (see Figs. 93, 109) visited the city in AD 124 and Caracalla (see Figs. 128, 162, 163) visited in 214 and established Thyatira as a judicial district.²³ The city responded by bestowing on the emperor the titles of "Founder and Savior of the City (Benefactor)."²⁴

THE POPULATION OF THYATIRA

The modern population of *Akhisar* grew from ca. 20,000 in 1915,²⁵ to 18,050 in 1927, to 73,944 in 1990,²⁶ to 81,572 in 1997,²⁷ to 73,944 in 1990,²⁸ to ca. 80,000 in 2003,²⁹ and to ca. 111,000 in 2014.³⁰ In one hundred years it has seen exponential growth, but what was the population in the second century AD? Its population in the Roman Period has been estimated—based on "analogies" with other parts of the Roman Empire—to be about 25,000. Mitchell reasons that this comparison:

> suggest[s] that few cities had more than about 25,000 urban inhabitants — Nicomedia, Cyzicus, Ancyra, Thyateira [sic.], and Sardis would certainly have come into this category—and the majority would have fallen in a range between 5,000 and 15,000. . . These figures are based on a comparison with those for North Africa, discussed by Duncan-Jones³¹

---

[21] While older commentaors (Ramsay, Swete, Barclay, Hemer, etc.) downplay the presence of the imperial cult in Thyatira, it was very much alive in the first and second cent. AD, although it did not entertain impressive temples such as at Ephesus and Pergamum. Koester, *Revelation,* 296.

[22] Hansen, *The Attalids of Pergamon,* 207; Jones, *Cities of the Eastern Roman Provinces,* 84; Edward M. Blaiklock, "Thyatira," ed. Merrill C. Tenney and Moises Silva, *ZEB* (Grand Rapids, Mich.: Zondervan, 2009), 5:854.

[23] Thompson, *Revelation,* 74.

[24] Fant and Reddish, *Guide to Biblical Sites,* 329.

[25] E. J. Banks, "Thyatira," ed. James Orr and Melvin Grove Kyle, *ISBE* (Grand Rapids, Mich.: Hendrickson, 1915), 2977.

[26] Bahriye Gulgun et al., "Determination of the Effects of Temporal Change in Urban and Agricultural Land Uses as Seen in the Example of the Town of Akhisar, Using Remote Sensing Techniques," *Environmental Monitoring and Assessment* 150, no. 1–4 (2009): 432, Table 3.

[27] Ibid., 430. Gulgun estimates that the modern city of *Alaşehir* has an area of 3.6879 km² or 368 ha.

[28] Ibid., 432, Table 3.

[29] Fant and Reddish, *Guide to Biblical Sites,* 328.

[30] http://www.citypopulation.de/php/turkey-manisa.php.

[31] Stephen Mitchell, *Anatolia: Land, Men, and Gods in Asia Minor* (Oxford, U.K.: Clarendon Press, 1995), 1:244 n.13; Duncan-Jones, *Economy,* 259–87.

City	Area (ha)	100/ha	150/ha	250/ha	400/ha
Sardis	356	35,600	53,400	89,000	142,400
Cyzicus	168	16,800	25,200	42,000	67,200

Table 3. The population of Sardis and Cyzicus based on their size

Of the sites that Mitchell groups in the 25,000 range, Hanson, based on the area (ha) of their site plans, only provides his population estimates for Sardis and Cyzicus.[32]

However, Sardis is almost twice the size of Cyzicus (see chart above),[33] which does not support Mitchell's claim that Nicomedia, Cyzicus, Ancyra, Thyatira, and Sardis should be estimated with the same population of 25,000. Hanson goes on to say that:

> The picture would almost certainly be reinforced by further study of sites such as Nicomedia, Ancyra, and Sinope, for which plans could not be accessed. Based on literary and secondary descriptions of the sites, it is most likely that these sites would have had large populations. The position and size of all of these sites as ports or major nodes on road networks, thus also indicates the importance of connectivity, both to sustain large sites and as potential reasons for their prosperity.[34]

Commentators regularly report that Thyatira was the smallest of the seven cities. However, Jones points out that "Thyatira appears to have owned a considerable territory: the city erected milestones six [Roman] miles away along the road to Pergamum and about ten [Roman] miles way along the road to Sardis." It may well have been larger than commentators report.[35] Hanson calculates four of the seven cities based on the site plans (Smyrna, Philadelphia and Thyatira have been overtaken and built on by their modern cities and no site plans are available).

City	Area (ha)	100/ha	150/ha	250/ha	400/ha
Sardis	356	35,600	53,400	89,000	142,400
Ephesus	224	22,400	33,600	56,000	89,600
Pergamum	219	21,900	32,850	54,750	87,600
Laodicea	89	8,900	13,350	22,250	35,600

Table 4. The population of Sardis compared with Revelation cities related to their size

If it is true that Thyatira was the smallest city,[36] it would place the population of the site around that of Laodicea at between 8,900 and 35,600. This would mean that Mitchell's estimate

---

[32] Hanson, "Urban System," 259.
[33] Ibid., 254.
[34] Ibid., 259.
[35] Jones, Cities of the Eastern Roman Provinces, 84.
[36] Perhaps the size of the city is also determined by the number of their gymnasia; Pergamum had seven; Ephesus had four, while Thyatira only had three. Sardis had one large gymnasium complex. P. J. J. Botha, "God, Emperor Worship and Society: Contemporary Experiences and the Book of Revelation," *Neot* 22, no. 1 (1988): 92.

81. The ancient ruins of Thyatira among the modern city.

of 25,000 would be reasonable. But interestingly as the smallest of the seven churches, Thyatira received the longest message, or perhaps Thyatira was not as small as first thought.

THE IMPORTANT BUILDINGS OF THYATIRA

Our knowledge of ancient Thyatira is limited due to the fact that many of the archaeological remains lie under the modern city of *Akhisar*. However, the city was confirmed by Paul Rycoult in 1670 as Thyatira from several inscriptions found there, bearing the Greek name *Thyateira*.[37] The hill on which the state hospital stands is likely the ancient acropolis of the city, since it is the highest point of the city and a Hellenistic sarcophagus is visible in the garden.[38] There are several archaeological remains near the center of the city (Lat. *Tepemezari*), including various arches, column bases, along with Ionic and Corinthian capitals, several with important inscriptions that were originally part of structures (see Fig. 81).[39] There was a triple gate, shops,

---

[37] Sonia P. Anderson, *An English Consul in Turkey: Paul Rycaut at Smyrna 1667–1678* (Oxford, U.K.: Clarendon Press, 1989), 220; Wilson, *Biblical Turkey*, 321.
[38] Fant and Reddish, *Guide to Biblical Sites*, 330.
[39] Wilson, *Biblical Turkey*, 321.

and stoas dedicated to Augustus as the *Sebastois* (Σεβαστοῖς, "son of god"; *I.Thyat.* 862 = *IGR* 4:1209; see 2:18), 100 colonnaded porticos where the *gerousia* (γερουσία, "council") met,[40] a theater,[41] and at least one Jewish synagogue.[42] Excavations conducted by Rüstem Duyuran between 1968 and 1971 have also uncovered the remains of a large administration building (sixth cent.) that at one time may have been used as a church, along with the remains of a second cent. Roman road.[43]

As a Hellenistic city, Thyatira had no less than three gymnasiums (*I.Thyat.* 978 = *IGR* 4:1239; 983)[44] and their importance is confirmed by the mention of a *gymnasiarch* at Hellenistic Thyatira (*BCH* 11 [1887], 465, no. 31).[45] Maggie describes the role of the gymnasium and the responsibilities of the *gymnasiarch*.

> While serving a special purpose in providing a place for bodily exercise, especially for the *ephebi* [ἔφηβη, *ephēbē*]—the youths engaged for a year or more in compulsory training, originally military and athletic but later also cultural—gymnasium was in most cities a place not merely for the physical but also the mental development of citizens. . . . The maintenance of this institution, so necessary to the general welfare, devolved upon the *gymnasiarch*. It was his duty to arrange for the training, both athletic and intellectual, which the gymnasium offered to the citizens. He had also to provide, often at his own expense, for the care of the building and its equipment, for the heating of the baths, and, at times for the lighting of the rooms after dark. . . . Among the responsibilities of the office was the organizing

82. *Homonoia* coin from Thyatira with Pergamum in Mysia. Obv.: *AVT KAI L CEP CEOVHPOC PER*. Bust of Moschios, magistrate laureate, draped, and cuirassed. Rev.: *EPI CTP MOCX OV B PERGAMHNWN QUATEIRHNWN OMONOIA*, Asclepius of Pergamum on the left, holding a serpent-entwined staff, and Apollo Tyrimnaeus of Thyatira standing to the right.

---

[40] John E. Stambaugh, "Thyatira (Place)," ed. David Noel Freedman et al., *ABD* (New York, N.Y.: Doubleday, 1996), 6:546.

[41] *I.Thyat.* 978 = *IGR* 4:1239; *I.Thyat.* 983.

[42] Menahem Stern, "The Jewish Diaspora," in The Jewish People in the First Century: Historical Geography, Political History, Social, Cultural and Religious Life and Institutions, ed. Menahem Stern and Shemuel Safrai, CRINT (Philadelphia, Pa.: Fortress, 1974), 1:143–53.

[43] Duyuran, "Akhisar Tepe," 73–76; "Akhisar Tepe II," 17–27; Malay, *Researches in Lydia, Mysia and Aiolis*, no. 24. In 1985 Hemer claimed that "it has not been excavated" but he is clearly mistaken evident from Duyuran's excavations from 1968 to 1971. Hemer, "Seven Cities," 242.

[44] Botha, "God, Emperor Worship and Society," 92.

[45] Louis Robert, Études Anatoliennes: Recherches Sur Les Inscriptionsgrecques de l'Asie Mineure (Paris: de Boccard, 1937), 175–76.

of contest and the giving of prizes. Sometimes, since the gymnasium served as the place of training for the athletes who took part in the games connected with the city-festivals, the *gymnasiarch* acted also as a *agonothete*, or president of the contests, a post which also was a liturgy, entailing no small expense on the holder.[46]

Although little archaeological work has been carried out, it is evident that Thyatira was a thriving and important city in Asia Minor.

THE COMMERCE OF THYATIRA

THE TRADE GUILDS

Trade guilds[47] flourished in Thyatira, especially from the textile industry, contributing to its economic growth as a manufacturing center. There were textile guild associations in such trades as dyers (βαφεῖς, *bapheis*; Lat. *lanarii carminatores*[48]), linen weavers (λινουργοί, *linourgoi*),[49] wool workers (λανάριοι; *lanarioi*; Lat. *lanarius*),[50] and clothes cleaners or fullers (γναφεῖς, *gnapheis*; Lat. *lanarii purgatories*, *SEG* 40.1045; *CIG* 3480).[51] Guilds involved in leather included, tanners (βυρσεῖς, *byrseis*),[52] leather cutters or shoemakers (σκυτοτόμοι, *skytotomoi*).[53] Other guild associations included coppersmiths ([χα]λκεῖς χαλκοτύποι, *chalkeis chalkotypoi*; *I.Thyat.* 936 = *IGR* 4.1259), blacksmiths (σιδηρουργός, *sidērourgos*),[54] potters (κεραμεῖς, *kerameis*),[55] and others.[56] While we may liken them to modern "trade unions," they were involved in both industry and religion. The city deity, Apollo Tyrimnaeus (see Figs. 82, 86), the patron of the guilds, was celebrated

---

[46] Magie, Roman Rule in Asia Minor, 62.

[47] For more details on trade guilds in Asia Minor see chapter 2, *External Problems*.

[48] *I.Thyat.* 935; 945; 972; 989; *CIG* 3422, 3496, 3497. For the meaning of *lanarii* see Suzanne Dixon, *Childhood, Class and Kin in the Roman World* (New York, N.Y.: Routledge, 2005), Dixon 216 n.12. and Perry, "Sub-Elites," 498–512.

[49] *I.Thyat.* 933 = *IGR* 4.1226 = PHI 264363.

[50] *IGR* 4:1252 = *AGRW* 141 = PHI 264450; *I.Thyat.* 933; 1019; *CIG* 3504.

[51] Jonathan S. Perry, "Sub-Elites," in *A Companion to Roman Italy*, ed. Alison E. Cooley, Blackwell Companions to the Ancient World (New York, N.Y.: John Wiley & Sons, 2016), see Working in Wool and Working for Status? 498–512.

[52] *I.Thyat.* 986 = *CIG* 3499 = *IGR* 4.1216 = PHI 264416.

[53] *SEG* 41.1033 = PHI 277547; *I.Thyat.* 1002 = *AGRW* 131 = *IGR* 4.1169 = PHI 264433. Jones, *Cities of the Eastern Roman Provinces*, 83–84; Philip A. Harland, *Associations, Synagogues, and Congregations: Claiming a Place in Ancient Mediterranean Society*, 2nd ed. (Kitchener, Ontario: Harland, 2011), 86 n.45.

[54] Jean Pierre Waltzing, Étude historique sur les corporations professionnelles chez les Romains depuis les origines jusqu'à la chute de l'Empire d'Occident, vol. 3 (Louvain: Louvain, C. Peeters, 1895), 3:59, no. 163.

[55] *I.Thyat.* 914 = *CIG* 3485 = *IGR* 4.1205 = PHI 264344), bakers (ἀρτοκόποι, *artokopoi*; *AGRW* 138 = *IGR* 4.1244 = *I.Thyat.* 966; *CIG* 3495.

[56] Hemer, "Unto the Angels of the Churches," 110; Aune, *Rev 1–5*, 201; Craig R. Koester, *Revelation: A New Translation with Introduction and Commentary*, ed. John J. Collins, AYBC 38A (New Haven, Conn.: Yale University Press, 2014), 295–96.

with feasts and religious activities.⁵⁷ Harland points out that some held important positions within the community:

> when individuals of particular occupations achieved local prestige and wealth that led to the assumption of other important civic positions, such as a slave-merchant (*sōmatemporos*) at Thyatira who assumed the relatively important position of market-overseer (*agoranomos*; cf. *TAM V* 2.932).⁵⁸

The purple dyers guilds were operated by an executive council (Lat. *proedria;* Hierapolis ἐργατηγοί, *ergatēgoi;* Thyatira ἐπιστάται, *epistatai; CIG* 3926),⁵⁹ who elected an annual president. Jones reports that "the dyers honoured Aurelius Artemagoras, who had been president of the guild of the dyers for the sixth time."⁶⁰ Broughton explains further what is known of the organization of the woollen industry in Lydia.

> In the guilds both of Hierapolis and elsewhere it is worth noting that, while there were wool washers, wool workers, fullers and dyers-that is, skilled workmen to prepare the wool for spinning and to treat the cloth afterward, — spinners do not appear at all and weavers only for fabrics of special difficulty such as tapestries or the one-piece garments (ἁπλουργοί, *aplourgoi*). It seems probable that, as in England before the industrial age, spinning and weaving were home activities, occupying the time of women and slaves of the various households. The prepared wool was brought in and the woven cloth taken to the skilled workmen for finishing. Finally, notice should be taken of the emporium at Laodicea, in which the fullers, dyers (?), and makers of one-piece garments were all concerned: could it have been a central market, a sort of Laodicean Cloth Hall (*IGR* 4.863)?⁶¹

Wilson reports on two inscriptions from Laodicea located on two marble bases (AD 218–22) and states:

> They honor a prominent citizen of Thyatira named C. Perlius Aurelius Alexander. The inscriptions still show the prominence of trade guilds in the city. The last line of each indicates that one was sponsored by the fullers (ΟΙ ΓΝΑΦΕΙΣ; *oi gnapheis*), the other by the wool workers (ΟΙ ΛΑΝΑΡΙΟΙ; *oi lanarioi*). In the fifth line of the fullers' inscription the name of the emperor Antoneinon, better known as Elagabulus, was erased. After Elagabulus was assassinated in AD 222, the Roman senate passed a decree damning his memory (*damnation memoriae* [see Fig. 111]). His name, like that of the emperors Domitian and Geta, was erased from the public monuments.⁶²

It must be noted that the proliferation of guilds in Thyatira was like that of many other cities of the time and this city should not be singled out as a community where the trade associations pressured Christians to join, as some commentators have done,⁶³ as though this

---

⁵⁷ Hemer, Letters to the Seven Churches, 109.
⁵⁸ Harland, Associations, Synagogues, and Congregations, 32.
⁵⁹ Ramsay, Cities and Bishoprics, 1:106.
⁶⁰ Jones, Cities of the Eastern Roman Provinces, 84.
⁶¹ Broughton, "Roman Asia Minor," 4:821.
⁶² Wilson, *Biblical Turkey*, 321.
⁶³ Ramsay, *Letters: Updated*, 238; Charles, *Revelation*, 1:68; Mounce, *Revelation*, 87; Osborne, *Revelation*, 156–57; Leslie N. Pollard, "The Function of Loipos in Contexts of Judgment and Salvation in the Book of Revelation" (Ph.D., Andrews University, 2007), 288–90; Pamela Thimmes, "Women Reading Women in the Apocalypse: Reading Scenario 1, the Letter to Thyatira (Rev. 2:18–29)," *CBR* 2, no. 1 (2003): 139.

was exceptional for Thyatira.⁶⁴ This was an issue that Christians faced in many first-century cities in Asia Minor, since guilds have been documented in many cities. Elaborate guild halls have been uncovered at Ostia and Ephesus.⁶⁵ There is also inscriptional evidence of the presence of guilds in Phrygian Hierapolis (dyers *CIJ* 2.36);⁶⁶ Pergamum (dyers? *IGR* 4.425); Smyrna (silversmiths and goldsmith *CIG* 3154; *IGR* 4.1427); Ephesus (money changers *SEG* 4.541; dyers⁶⁷); Philadelphia (wool workers, *IGR* 4. 1632); and Methylene (fullers *IG XII* 2.271; leather workers, *IG XII* 2.109).⁶⁸ However, for whatever reason, there does appear to be a large concentration of guilds in Thyatira. And as Keener points out "social pressures for Christians to accommodate the worship of Graeco-Roman deities would have come from various sources, not only from associations."⁶⁹

THE DYERS GUILD

The Roman province of Lydia and especially the city of Thyatira was famous for its clothing industry (Homer *Il.* 4.141–42)⁷⁰ and essential to this was the dyeing process and the prominent role that the dyers guild played in city associations.⁷¹ Calpino estimated that "of the 103 inscriptions that contain references to purple trade (πορφύρα, *porphura*), twenty-nine percent 29% are from Asia Minor,"⁷² and many of these were from Thyatira. Fifteen of the twenty-eight inscriptions from Thyatira are related to the trade of purple-dyers (πορφυροβαφεῖα, *porphurobapheia*),⁷³ although no inscriptions from Thyatira mention πορφυροβαφεῖα (*porphurobapheia*), "purple dyers," but only βαφεῖς (*bapheis*, "dyers").⁷⁴ More than half of the inscriptions (32/53) from Thyatira and the area of Saittai pertain to the textile industry.⁷⁵

---

⁶⁴ Broughton, "Roman Asia Minor," 4:841–44; cf. 819, 824–25, 830; Harland, *Associations, Synagogues, and Congregations*, 39–40; Koester, *Revelation*, 295–96.

⁶⁵ Russell Meiggs, *Roman Ostia* (Oxford, U.K.: Clarendon Press, 1973), 67–71.

⁶⁶ Philip A. Harland, "Acculturation and Identity in the Diaspora: A Jewish Family and 'Pagan' Guilds at Hierapolis," *JJS* 57, no. 2 (2006): 222–44.

⁶⁷ Elisabeth Trinkl, "Artifacts Related to Preparation of Wool and Textile Processing Found inside the Terrace Houses of Ephesus, Turkey," in *Ancient Textiles: Production, Craft and Society*, ed. Carole Gillis and Marie-Louise B. Nosch (Oxford, U.K.: Oxbow, 2007), 81–86.

⁶⁸ Hemer, "Unto the Angels of the Churches," 110; Broughton, "Roman Asia Minor," 2:841–44; Kraybill, *Imperial Cult and Commerce in John's Apocalypse*, 111 n.49; Magie, *Roman Rule in Asia Minor*, 1:48; 2:812 n. 78; Jones, *Cities of the Eastern Roman Provinces*, 83.

⁶⁹ Koester, *Revelation*, 295–96.

⁷⁰ Pliny the Elder claims it was invented in Sardis (*Nat.* 7.56.195).

⁷¹ Harland, *Associations, Synagogues, and Congregations*, 121–29; Magie, *Roman Rule in Asia Minor*, 1:48; 2:812 n. 80; Trinkl, "Washing and Dyeing," 81–86. There is also evidence of the dyers guild in Phrygian Hierapolis (*CIJ* 2.36) and Ephesus (see Trinkl).

⁷² Teresa J. Calpino, "Lydia of Thyatira's Call," in *Women, Work and Leadership in Acts* (Tübingen: Mohr Siebeck, 2014), 199 n.81.

⁷³ Tullia Ritti, "Associazioni di mestiere a Hierapolis di Frigia," in *Viaggi e commerci nell'antichità*, ed. Bianca Maria Giannattasio (Geneva: Università di Genova, Facoltà di Lettere, 1995), 71–72.

⁷⁴ Deborah Ruscillo, "Reconstructing Murex Royal Purple and Biblical Blue in the Aegean," in *Archaeomalacology:*

Members of the Dyers Guild (βαφεῖς) in Thyatira				
Name	Occupation	Association	Source	Date AD
Antiochos[76]		First dyer as a benefactor to the city	I.Philipp. 2:697/M580	?
Claudia Ammion[77]	Civic high-priestess and imperial cult priestess	Director of contests	I.Thyat. 972	ca. 50
T. Claudius Sokrates[78]	Provincial imperial cult high-priest Pergamum	—	I.Thyat. 978	ca. 100
T. Claudius Sokrates Sakerdotianos	Civic imperial high priest of Asia in the temple in Pergamum, *prytanis*, Crown bearer	—	I.Thyat. 978, 980; AGRW 132 = IGR 4.1239 = PHI 264408	ca. 106–114
Makedonos[79]	Civic Police chief	Market overseer	I.Thyat. 989	ca. 120
M. Julius Dionysios Akylianos	Civic Crown bearer	—	I.Thyat. 965	ca. 160–170
T. Antonius Claudius Alfenus Argnotus[80]	Equestrian military commander and procurator	Temple warden imperial cult and priest of Apollo	I.Thyat. 945	199–200
Aurelius Artemagoras	Member of the civic board of	—	I.Thyat. 945	Second to third cent.

Molluscs in Former Environments of Human Behaviour, ed. Daniella Bar-Yosef Mayer (Oxford, U.K.: Oxbow, 2005), 100.

[75] Ilias Arnaoutoglou, "Hierapolis and Its Professional Associations: A Comparative Analysis," in *Urban Craftsmen and Traders in the Roman World*, ed. Andrew Wilson and Miko Flohr (Oxford, U.K.: Oxford University Press, 2016), 282.

[76] Isabella Benda-Weber, "Textile Production Centres, Products and Merchants in the Roman Province of Asia," in *Making Textiles in Pre-Roman and Roman Times: People, Places, Identities*, ed. Margarita Gleba and Judit Pásztókai-Szeöke, Ancient Textile Series 13 (Oxford, U.K.: Oxbow Books, 2013), 185.

[77] Richard S. Ascough, Philip A. Harland, and John S. Kloppenborg, eds., *Associations in the Greco-Roman World: A Sourcebook* (Waco, Tex.: Baylor University Press, 2012), 129.

[78] Ibid., 132.

[79] Ibid., 133.

[80] Ibid., 136.

	ten			
Marcus, son of Menandros	Superintendent of the dyers	Market overseer and secretary of the people	*I.Thyat.* 991	Second to third cent.

Table 5. Members of the dyers guild (βαφεῖς) in Thyatira

MEMBERS OF THE DYERS GUILD IN THYATIRA

We get momentary glimpses of the ongoing links between dyers and guilds at several points in the group's history, which can be partially reconstructed from nine extant inscriptions,[81] five of which involve imperial cult connections. Table 5 provides a selection of the more important inscriptions mentioning the individuals involved in the dyers guild from Thyatira and their occupation, association and date.

Harland explains the details of the relationships between the guilds and the civil occupations of those from Thyatira. He explains:

> Around the year 50 CE the dyers set up an honorary monument for Claudia Ammion, a priestess of the Augusti (probably a civic-level cult) and high-priestess of the city who had also been director of contests "in a brilliant and extravagant manner with purity and modesty" (*TAM* V 1.972 = *AGRW* 129). Claudia Ammion belonged to an aristocratic family in Thyatira with kin in other cities of Asia (see the family tree in figure 37). Her brother, Andronikos, for instance, was a civic president (*prytanis*) and priest of the goddess Roma. Some of her other relatives were also benefactors of associations or gymnasium organizations. Claudia's kinsman, C. Julius Lepidus (probably a cousin once removed), was a high-priest in the provincial imperial cult like his father (see *I.Sard.* 8, line 99), and he had been a benefactor of an athletic club which met in the "third gymnasium" in Thyatira just decades earlier (*TAM* V 2.968 = *AGRW* 132; ca. 25 CE). Claudia's husband, T. Claudius Antyllos, was honored by a gymnastic association, the "partners" which met in this same gymnasium; he had supplied them with oil (*TAM* V 2.975; ca. 50 CE). Another kinsman of this Lepidus family, T. Julius Lepidus of Sardis, was secretary of the provincial council of Asia in the late-first or early-second century. This Lepidus was honored with marble plaques by both the organization of youths (*ephebes*) and "those engaged in business in the slave-market (*statariō*)" at Sardis (see *SEG* 46 [1996], no. 1524 = *AGRW* 124, revising *I.Sard.* 46). Around the turn of the century in Thyatira, dyers honored a member of another family, T. Claudius Sokrates. Sokrates was the founder of several civic building projects and director of contests. He had held a prestigious position as high-priest of Asia in the provincial imperial temple at Pergamon (*TAM* V 2.978 = *AGRW* 132; before 113 CE). The dyers were by no means the only occupational association at the time seeking the support of such imperial-affiliated citizens. At about the same time, the leather-cutters were honoring another man, T. Flavius Alexandros, the curator of the association (*conventus*) of Romans and Thyatira's ambassador to Rome (*TAM* V 2.1002 = *AGRW* 131). It seems that connections with local associations continued in the Sokrates family. A group, likely the guild of dyers, also honored his son Sakerdotianos, a high-priest of the Augusti (*Sebastoi*) who had displayed "love of honor since he was a boy" towards the city, conducting himself "in accordance with his ancestors' love of glory" (*TAM* V 2.980; ca. 120–30 CE). Yet the dyers'

---

[81] *I.Thyat.* 945, 965, 972, 978, 980, 989, 991, 1029, 1081.

allegiance was not limited to this particular family, for at about the same time the guild joined with civic institutions of Thyatira in honoring Makedonos, the police-chief (*eirēnarchos*) and market-overseer (*agoranomos*; *TAM* V 989 = *AGRW* 133). The dyers honored other persons in influential civic positions of Thyatira in the following decades, including two that were also members or leaders of the guild (e.g. *TAM* V 2.945, *TAM* V 2.965, *TAM* V 2.991). We get a final glimpse of imperial connections when about 213 CE the dyers honor T. Antonius Claudius Alfenus Arignotus, a military commander of the equestrian order who reached the office of procurator and had served in different parts of the Greek East (*TAM* V 2.935 = *AGRW* 136).3 Arignotus had also been priest of Thyatira's patron deity, Apollo Tyrimnos [see Figs. 82, 86], not to mention temple-warden in the imperial cult. The inscription also points out that his father and grandfather were high-priests of Asia in the provincial imperial cult. As with the contacts between members of the Julian family and associations, the content of the connections between the dyers and influential persons in imperial positions entails benefactor-beneficiary (or patron-client) relations, and it is reciprocal in directedness. As an ongoing group formed from occupational social network connections, the dyers were able to secure access to limited resources of financial assistance from the wealthy, furthering their own interests in competition with other associations, groups, and individuals within Thyatira.[82]

The intricate relationships between these city officials speak of the place that dyers carved out for themselves in the guild network and the political structures of the city and empire. Reimer rightly notes that Thyatira was known for more than purple goods (*purpurarii*), and likely produced a wide range of dyed products[83] in a variety of colours.[84]

LYDIA, THE SELLER OF PURPLE

The importance of the dyers guild is highlighted by the NT reference to Lydia,[85] one of Paul's first converts in Asia, who lived in Philippi as a πορφυρόπωλις (*porphuropōlis*), widely translated as a seller of purple (πορφύρα, *porphura*; Lat. *purpurarius/a*) cloth, but who probably learned her textile business (*IGR* 4.1252; *CIG* 3496–8 [λανάριοι, *lanarii carminatores*,[86] dyers]) in Thyatira.[87] The textile industry contributed greatly to Thyatira's prosperity. Menippus of Thyatira, was also of the *collegia* of purple-dyers (πορφυροβάφ, *porphuropobaph*), selling purple goods in

---

[82] Harland, *Associations, Synagogues, and Congregations*, 124–25.

[83] Ivoni Richter Reimer, *Women in the Acts of Apostles: A Feminist Liberation Perspective* (Minneapolis, Minn.: Fortress, 1995), 99–100.

[84] Reimer notes that *CIG* 3496 and 3497 do not specifically make mention of purple goods.

[85] Hemers suggested that her name is likely an ethnic cognomen, "The Lydian woman" (*TAM III* 661). Attested in the first century not only as a slave but also a women of high social prestige. i.e., Julia Lydia Laterane of Ephesus, high priestess and daughter of Asia (*SEG* 28) and Julia Lydia of Sardis. Louis Robert, "Documents d'Asie Mineure," *BCH* 101, no. 1 (1977): 43–132; Hemer, *The Book of Acts in the Setting of Hellenistic History*, 114 n.32.

[86] Inscriptional references to λανάριοι (*lanrioi*) include *AE* (1993): 1028a; (1909): 11a; (1946): 210; (1971) 49; (1987): 443; (1995): 146; (2001): 865; (2010): 326; *CIL* 5.4501; 5.4504; 5.4505; 6.9489; 6.9490; 6.9491; 6.9492; 6.9493; 6.9494; 6.9669; 6.31898; 6.33869; 6.38869; 9.826; 9.2226; 10.5678; 11.741; 11.862; 11.1031; 11.5835; 11.6367; 12.4480; 12.4481; *I.Eph.* 4.1387; 2.454; 3.727; *TAM V* 1.85; 2.1019.

[87] Magie, *Roman Rule in Asia Minor*, 1:47–48; 2:812 n.79; Keener, *Acts: 15:1–23:35*, 3:3:2399–2407.

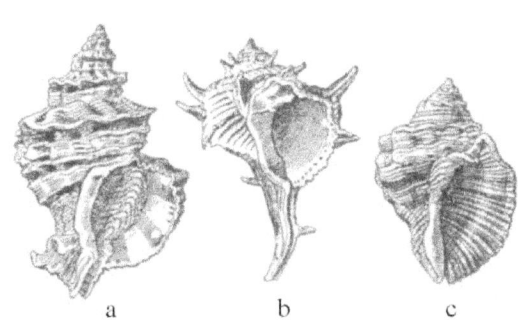

83. Principal Mediterranean molluscan species, yielding 6,6'-dibromoindigotin (DBI) and related indigoids: (a) *M. trunculus*; (b) *M. brandaris*; and (c) *P. haemastoma*.

Thessalonica[88] but originally came from Thyatira (Acts 16:14–15, 40). It is known that women were involved in the purple dye trade from an inscription where the term "purple dealers" is in the feminine form (*CIG* 2519).

Joshel suggests that most individuals both produced and sold purple goods from the same fullers' shop (*fullonica*[89]).[90] However, this is challenged by Hughes who provided new research, derived from inscriptional evidence, that the shops in Vicus (where Pubius Clodius Philonicus' wife Eurania was carrying out her business of *Purpuranii*) were not suitable for producing these goods.[91] She argued that the odor[92] and size of the location needed to carry out the dyeing process[93] making it impossible to have had the manufacturing shop located in Vicus. Also, Hughes demonstrated from an examination of the literary, epigraphic, and archaeological evidence of *purpurarii* in Rome, that "members of their *familia* could produce or sell a number of goods, other than textile, from their workshops,"[94] including foodstuffs, dye and pigments for paints (Pliny *Nat.* 36.26.45; Vitruvius *Arch.* 7.13.2–3).

Similarly, Lydia was probably selling a variety of purple goods in Philippi that were manufactured elsewhere. If she was producing the purple products in Philippi, then she would probably have owned a fairly large installation which was well ventilated,[95] although a small

---

[88] *IG* X 2.1 291 = PHI 137473; Istanbul Museum cat. no. 271. Hemer claims "that this term is not known otherwise from Thyatira," but this inscription would qualify as another. Hemer, *Letters to the Seven Churches*, 109.

[89] The Fullonica of Stephanus, or *Fullonica Stephani*, that is situated on the south side of the Via dell'Abbondanza is the only laundry (*fullonica*) in Pompeii. Only 103 Murex shell were discovered in Pompeii leading to a variety of opinions on the dyeing capabilities. See David S. Reese, "Marine Invertebrates, Freshwater Shells, and Land Snails: Evidence from Specimens Mosaics, Wall Paintings, Sculputure, Jewelry, and Roman Authors," in *The Natural History of Pompeii*, ed. Wilhelmina Feemster Jashemski and Frederick G. Meyer (Cambridge, U.K.: Cambridge University Press, 2002), 296–98.

[90] S. R. Joshel, *Work, Identity and Legal Status at Rome: A Study of the Occupational Inscriptions* (Norman, Okla.: University of Oklahoma Press, 1992), 71.

[91] Lisa Hughes, "Dyeing in Ancient Italy? Evidence for the Purpurarii," in *Ancient Textiles: Production, Craft and Society*, ed. Carole Gillis and Marie-Louise B. Nosch (Oxford, U.K.: Oxbow, 2007), 89.

[92] Robert J. Forbes, *Studies in Ancient Technology* (Leiden: Brill, 1993), 4:119; B. Bartosiewicz, "'There's Something Rotten in the State . . .': Bad Smells in Antiquity," *European Journal of Archaeology* 6 (2003): 175–95.

[93] J. P. Wild, *Textile Manufacture in the Northern Roman Provinces*, CCS (Cambridge, U.K.: Cambridge University Press, 1970), 82.

[94] Hughes, "Dyeing in Ancient Italy," 82.

[95] Ibid., 88; S. G. Schmid, "Decline or Prosperity at Roman Eretria? Industry, Purple Dye Works, Public Buildings,

number of sites have demonstrated that the production of purple dye was "carried out on a small-scale by households."[96] This suggests that Lydia likely did not dye her goods in Philippi unless at home, but rather her purple cloth was doubtless imported from a dyeing facility, perhaps from Thessalonica near Philippi.[97] However, Philippi was only 7.75 miles (12.5 km) from the coast and she could easily have transported the murex shells, used to collect purple dye, overland,[98] so the use of murex dye did not require that the facility be close to the coast.[99]

HISTORY OF PURPLE DYE

Porphyrology[100] has a long history, with much written[101] on the production of purple dye in ancient times.[102] It is not the intention to repeat it here. There is debate over the Minoan origin of Tyrian Purple[103] and whether it originated with the Phoenicians (Stabo *Geogr.* 16.2.23).[104] Koren claims the while the Minoans may have originated the process, Phoenicians perfected the craft.[105]

The archaeological indicators of the purple-dye industry include purple stained containers, crushed murex shells in large quantities or in occupational strata, burnt organic matter, and various equipment such as vats, cisterns, crushing and perforating tools.[106] There may also be

---

and Gravestones," *JRA* 12 (1999): 275–78.

[96] Cornelia Becker, "Did the People in Ayios Mamas Produce Purple Dye during the Middle Bronze Age? Considerations on the Prehistoric Production of Purple-Dye in the Mediterranean," in *Animals and Man in the Past: Essays in Honour of Dr. A.T. Clason Emeritus Professor of Archaeozoology*, ed. Hijlke Buitenhuis and Wietschke Prummel (Groningen: Rijksuniversiteit, 2001), 123. For example the small scale facility at the Middle Bronze Age tell Ayios Mamas in Greece.

[97] Keener, Background Commentary: NT, 370.

[98] This is confirmed by a vessel from the hill of "El Molinete" in Carthago Nova, Spain that contained an early Roman jar with 3 kg of crushed shells including *murex trunculus, murex thais,* and *murex brandaris.* David S. Reese, "The Industrial Exploitation of Murex Shells: Purple-Dye and Lime Production at Sidi Khrebish, Benghazi (Berenice)," *Libyan Studies* 11 (1980): 86.

[99] David E. Graves, "What Is the Madder with Lydia's Purple? A Re-Examination of the Purpurarii in Thyatira and Philippi," *NEASB* 62 (2017): 1–47.

[100] Rabbi Isaac Herzog coined the term Porphyrology (the study of purple) in his 1913 doctoral dissertation on the subject of Hebrew Porphyrology. Isaac Herzog, "Semitic Porphyrology (The Dyeing of Purple in Ancient Israel) I: Tekhelet" (D. Litt. diss., University of London, 1919)..

[101] Ehud Spanier, Nira Karmon, and Elisha Linder, "Bibliography Concerning Various Aspects of the Purple Dye," *Levantina* 37 (1982): 437–47.

[102] H. F. Heinisch, "Ancient Purple, an Historical Survey," *Fibre Engineering and Chemistry, Great Britain* 18, no. 6 (1957): 203–6; Lloyd B. Jensen, "Royal Purple of Tyre," *JNES* 22 (1963): 104–18.

[103] Robert R. Stieglitz, *Minoan and Canaanite Sea-Purple. First International Symposium on Harbours, Port Cities and Coastal Topography* (Haifa, 1986), 183–84; "The Minoan Origin of Tyrian Purple," *BA* 57, no. 1 (1994): 46–54.

[104] Michael C. Astour, "The Origin of the Terms Canaan, Phoenician and Purple," *JNES* 24 (1965): 346–50.

[105] Zvi C. Koren, "High-Performance Liquid Chromatographic Analysis of an Ancient Tyrian Purple Dyeing Vat from Israel," *IJC* 35 (1995): 118.

[106] Maria Emanuela Alberti, "Murex Shells as Raw Material: The Purple-Dye Industry and Its By-Products. Interpreting the Archaeological Record," *Kaskal* 5 (2008): 75–76.

weaving instruments such as loom weights and spinning apparatus nearby. The archaeological and literary evidence indicate that the most prestigious purple dye, "Tyrian Purple", was derived from the Mollusk shellfish (see Figs. 83, 85) which flourished along the Mediterranean coast (Pliny *Nat.* 35.26.45) [107] and was extracted in specialized workshops (Lat. *tinctoria*),[108] before being sold to local craftsmen. It is also worth noting that several of the sites are inland from the coast.

THE PROCESS OF PURPLE DYEING

Preparation for dyeing

Once the fleece (Lat. *lana sucida*) had been sheared from the sheep, it was submitted to a preliminary scouring (Lat. *putara*) to remove the impurities, grease, burrs, and lanolin (Varro *Rust.* 2.2.18; 2.11.6–9).[109] This was carried out at the *fullonica*[110] where the wool was cleaned (eleven *fullonicae* have been excavated in Pompeii and three in Ostia, where the guild was called *Corpus Fontanorum CIL* 14.4573).[111] The *fullonica* acted as both the finishers of loom-state (*de tela*) cloth and as the clothes' cleaners.[112] The occupation of the fuller was reserved for the wealthy with a large staff. As Wild points out:

> The plant and tools of the trade [of the fuller] were expensive to build, buy and maintain; and the series of special operations which took place in the fullery

84. Workers putting up clothes for drying. Roman fresco from the *fullonica* (dyer's shop) of Veranius Hypsaeus in Pompeii. Museo Archeologico Nazionale.

---

[107] For a general list of Mediterranean coastal purple dye centres see, Reese, "The Industrial Exploitation of Murex Shells: Purple-Dye and Lime Production at Sidi Khrebish, Benghazi (Berenice)," 82; "Palaikastro Shells and Bronze Age Purple-Dye Production in the Mediterranean Basin," *ABSA* 2 (1987): 201–5; Liza Cleland, Glenys Davies, and Karen Stears, eds., *Colour in the Ancient Mediterranean World*, BARI 1267 (Oxford, U.K.: John and Erica Hedges, 2004).

[108] Graves, "What Is The Madder With Lydia's Purple?," 6–7.

[109] Wild, Textile Manufacture in the Northern Roman Provinces, 23.

[110] *For the debate over the role of the fullonicae in textile production see* Andrew Wilson, "The Archaeology of the Roman Fullonica," *JRA* 16 (2003): 442–46; Miko Flohr, "Fullones and Roman Society: A Reconsideration," *JRA* 16 (2003): 447–50; M. Bradley, "'It All Comes out in the Wash': Looking Harder at the Roman Fullonica," *JRA* 15 (2008): 21–44; Miko Flohr, "The Textile Economy of Pompeii," *JRA* 26, no. 1 (2013): 53–78.

[111] Meiggs, *Roman Ostia*, 312.

[112] Wild, *Textile Manufacture in the Northern Roman Provinces*, 82; Flohr, "Fullones and Roman Society: A Reconsideration," 447; "The Textile Economy of Pompeii," 53–78; Claire Holleran, *Shopping in Ancient Rome: The Retail Trade in the Late Republic and the Principate* (Oxford, U.K.: Oxford University Press, 2012), 130 n.150; Andrew Wilson and Miko Flohr, *Urban Craftsmen and Traders in the Roman World* (Oxford, U.K.: Oxford University Press, 2016), 83, 87.

85. The two types of shellfish found in the western Mediterranean which produce small amounts of purple used for the dyeing of textiles (Pliny *Nat Hist.* 9.61). The *hexaplex trunculus* produces a red or violet purple (*left*), while the *haustellum brandaris* produces a blue purple (*right*).

could hardly have been carried out by one man [or woman]. Only the wealthy could afford to run a private *fullonica*, so that most of the cloth which was woven at home or bought had to pass through the professional fuller's establishment.[113]

The next process was to dye the wool at a *tinctoria* (dyeing or tinting) prior to spinning (i.e., "dyed in the wool"). *Fullonica* and *tinctoria* have been discovered across the street from each other and excavated at the *colonia* of Barcino (modern Barcelona), Spain.[114] Wool spun at home (*CIL* 1.2.1211, "she kept house, she made wool"; Cicero *Verr.* 4.59), as was performed in antiquity at Ephesus,[115] could not be dyed at home,[116] evident from individual colored yarns of a tartan pattern that logically had to be dyed before weaving and had to be brought to a *fullonica/tinctoria* to be processed.[117] Keener points out that: "most textiles were produced in homes, but more-precious ones could be produced in factories and exported."[118]

---

[113] Wild, Textile Manufacture in the Northern Roman Provinces, 82.

[114] Julia Beltrán de Heredia Bercero, "Los Restos Arqueológicos de Una Fullonica Y de Una Tinctoria En La Colonia Romana de Barcino (Barcelona)," *Complutum* 11 (2000): 253–59.

[115] Trinkl, "Washing and Dyeing," 81–86. The terrace houses at Ephesus showed evidence of sewing and weaving from spindle whirls, needles, loom-weights, and spindle hooks, and several decorated distaff were discovered; however no preserved textiles were recovered.

[116] Otto Lagercrantz, *Papyrus Graecus Holmiensis* (Uppsala, Sweden: Almquist and Wiksells, 1913); Earle Radcliffe Caley, "The Stockholm Papyrus: An English Translation with Brief Notes," *Journal of Chemical Education* 4, no. 8 (1927): 979–1002; Wild, *Textile Manufacture in the Northern Roman Provinces*, 23, 80.

[117] A. Luigi Pietrogrande and Giovanni Becatti, eds., *Le Fulloniche*, Scavi Ostia 8 (Rome: Istituto Poligrafico Dello Stato, Libreria Dello Stato, 1976).

[118] Acts: An Exegetical Commentary: 3:1–14:28, vol. 2 (Grand Rapids, Mich.: Baker Academic, 2013), 2396;

Dyes Used

There were various animal (shellfish and insects) and organic dyes (various plants) used to produce a rainbow of colours in antiquity. Among them were the murex shellfish species (see below), madder (ἐρυθρόδανον, *eputhrodanon*), cochineal (κόκκος, *kokkos*), seaweed (φύκος, *phukos*), woad (ἴσατις, *isatis*), saffron (κρόκος, *krokos*), black oak-apple (κηκίς, *kēkis*), and other organic dyes.[119]

The expensive Tyrian (Lat. *Purpura Tyria;* or Phoenician)[120] "true" or "pure" purple textile dye was first used by the ancient Phoenicians (1570 BC).[121] The ca. 3600–year-old ancient biochemical process[122] is described by Aristotle (*Hist. An.* 4.1–5, 8, 11; 5.15; fourth cent. BC), Pliny the Elder (*Nat.* 5.19; 6.201; 9.60–64; 14.12; 26.20; 35.44–45; first cent. AD) and the Talmud (*Menaÿ.* 42b; fourth cent. AD)[123] and has been scientifically replicated in the modern laboratory with various degrees of success, until Koren's triumph.[124] The relatively simple process was complicated due to various factors; including PH, illumination (Pollux *Onom.* 1.45–49), salinity, temperature (Aristotle *Col.* 32–33 [797a]), humidity, and washing.[125] The dye was

---

Introduction to the New Testament: History, Culture, And Religion Of The Hellenistic Age (Berlin: Gruyter, 1982), 1:77.

[119] Judith Lynn Sebesta, "Tunica Ralla, Tunica Spissa: The Colors and Textiles of Roman Costume," in *The World of Roman Costume*, ed. Judith Lynn Sebesta and Larissa Bonfante (Madison, Wisc.: University of Wisconsin Press, 2001), 69; Christopher J. Cooksey and R. S. Sinclair, "Colour Variations in Tyrian Purple Dyeing," *Dyes in History and Archaeology* 20 (2005): 127–35.

[120] Ovid *Metam.* 6.8–9; Vitruvius *Arch.* 7:13; Pliny *Nat.* 9.61.

[121] Patrick E. McGovern and R. H. Michel, "Royal Purple Dye: Tracing Chemical Origins of the Industry," *Analytical Chemistry* 57 (1985): 1514–22. Excavations at the Ugaritic site of Ras Shamra uncovered large quantities of shell fragments of the *Murex* (*Haxaplex*) *Trunculus* located in two rooms. While no dyeing workshop has been identified the presence of the murex shells led Matoïan to speculate that there was one there. Valérie Matoïan and Juan-Pablo Vita, "Wool Production and Economy at Ugarit," in *Wool Economy in the Ancient Near East*, ed. Catherine Breniquet and Cécile Michel (Oxford, U.K.: Oxbow Books, 2014), 323.

[122] Irving I. Ziderman, "3600 Years of Purple-Shell Dyeing: Characterization of Hyacinthine Purple (Tekhelet)," *Advances in Chemistry* 212 (1986): 187–98.

[123] Ehud Spanier and Nira Karmon, "Muricid Snails and the Ancient Dye Industries," in The Royal Purple and the Biblical Blue: Argaman and Tekhelet: The Study of Chief Rabbi Dr. Isaac Herzog on the Dye Industries in Ancient Israel and Recent Scientific Contributions, ed. Ehud Spanier (Jerusalem, Israel: Keter, 1987), 179–92; Nira Karmon and Ehud Spanier, "Archaeological Evidence of the Purple Dye Industry from Israel," in The Royal Purple and the Biblical Blue: Argaman and Tekhelet: The Study of Chief Rabbi Dr. Isaac Herzog on the Dye Industries in Ancient Israel and Recent Scientific Contributions, ed. Ehud Spanier (Jerusalem, Israel: Keter, 1987), 147–58; I. Irving Ziderman, "Seashells and Ancient Purple Dyeing," BA 53 (1990): 98–101; Nira Karmon, "The Purple Dye Industry in Antiquity," in Colors from Nature: Natural Colors in Ancient Times, ed. Ḥagit Sorek and Etan Ayalon (Eretz-Israel Museum, 1993), 35–37; Stieglitz, "The Minoan Origin of Tyrian Purple," 46–54.

[124] Zvi C. Koren, "The First Optimal All-Murex All-Natural Purple Dyeing in the Eastern Mediterranean in a Millennium and a Half," *Dyes in History and Archaeology* 20 (2005): 136–49.

[125] Patrick E. McGovern and R. H. Michel, "Royal Purple Dye: The Chemical Reconstruction of the Ancient Mediterranean Industry," *Accounts of Chemical Research* 23 (1990): 154; Koren, "High-Performance Liquid Chromatographic Analysis," 123; Jan Wouters, "A New Method for the Analysis of Blue and Purple Dyes in Textiles,"

produced from the very small hypobranchial gland[126] of sea snails of the family *Muricidae*, commonly called murex mollusks,[127] either secreted or extracted from the gland while it is alive, or when it is crushed in a vat (Pliny *Nat.* 9.61).[128] Only a small drop of fluid is produced by each snail, and it only turns purple when exposed to the air.[129] The most cost effective way to harvest large amounts of murex dye is by crushing, and thus large numbers of crushed shells act as archaeological clues pointing towards the presence of a dye facility, unless found at household level.[130] If found in a household, it may be indicative of a food preparation area, as the murex can also be eaten for food and used as fish bait.[131] The murex dye is identified as 6,6'-dibromoindigo[132] leading scientists to develop analytical methods to differentiate between murex shell fish, natural scale insects, madder root and indigoid dyes.[133]

Dyes in History and Archaeology 10 (1992): 19.

[126] Herzog, "Semitic Porphyrology (The Dyeing of Purple in Ancient Israel) I: Tekhelet"; Ehud Spanier, Elisha Linder, and Nira Karmon, *Purple Dye—Biology, Archaeology and History* (Haifa: University of Haifa, Center for Maritime Studies, 1980); Patrick E. McGovern, J. Lazar, and R. H. Michel, "The Chemical Composition of the Indigoid Dyes Derived from the Hypobranchial Glandular Secretions of Murex Mollusks," *Journal of the Society of Dyers and Colourists* 108, no. 3 (1992): 145–50; Christopher J. Cooksey, "Tyrian Purple: 6,6'-Dibromoindigo and Related Compounds," *Molecules* 6 (2001): 736–69.

[127] Koren, "First Optimal All-Murex," 136.

[128] Ajit Kumar Ngangbam et al., "Indole-Producing Bacteria from the Biosynthetic Organs of a Muricid Mollusc Could Contribute to Tyrian Purple Production," *Journal of Shellfish Research* 34, no. 2 (2015): 443–54.

[129] Joseph Doumet, A Study on the Ancient Purple Color and an Attempt to Reproduce the Dyeing Procedure of Tyre as Described by Pliny the Elder, trans. Robert Cook (Beirut: Imprimerie Catholique, 1980).

[130] Cornelia Becker, "Nourriture, Cuilléres, Ornament. Les Témoignages D'une Exploitation Variée Des Mollusques Marins À Ayios Mamas (Chalcidique, Grèce)," *Anthropozoologica* 24 (1996): 3–17.

[131] Canan Çakirlar and Ralf Becks, "Murex Dye Production at Troia: Assessment of Archaeomalacological Data from Old and New Excavations," *Studia Troica* 18 (2009): 89.

[132] McGovern, Lazar, and Michel, "The Chemical Composition of the Indigoid Dyes Derived from the Hypobranchial Glandular Secretions of Murex Mollusks," 145–50; Cooksey, "Tyrian Purple: 6,6'-Dibromoindigo and Related Compounds," 736–69. Differing from indigo only by the bromine E. J. W. Barber, *Prehistoric Textiles: The Development of Cloth in the Neolithic and Bronze Ages with Special Reference to the Aegean* (Princeton, N.J.: Princeton University Press, 1991), 235.

[133] Patrick E. McGovern, J. Lazar, and R. H. Michel, "Caveats on the Analysis of Indigoid Dyes by Mass Spectrometry," *Journal of the Society of Dyers and Colourists* 107 (1991): 2801; Jan Wouters and A. Verhecken, "High-Performance Liquid Chromatography of Blue and Purple Indigoid Natural Dyes," *Journal of the Society of Dyers and Colourists* 107 (1991): 266–69; McGovern, Lazar, and Michel, "The Chemical Composition of the Indigoid Dyes Derived from the Hypobranchial Glandular Secretions of Murex Mollusks," 145–50; Wouters, "A New Method for the Analysis of Blue and Purple Dyes in Textiles," 17–21; Zvi C. Koren, "Methods of Dye Analysis Used at the Shenkar College Edelstein Centre in Israel," *Dyes in History and Archaeology* 11 (1993): 25–33; "HPLC Analysis of the Natural Scale Insect, Madder and Indigoid Dyes," *Journal of the Society of Dyers and Colourists* 110 (1994): 273–77; G. Voss, "The Analysis of Indigoid Dyes as Leuco Forms by NMR Spectroscopy," *Journal of the Society of Dyers and Colourists* 116 (2000): 87–90; Zvi C. Koren, "The Purple Question Reinvestigated: Just What Is Really in That Purple Pigment?," in *20th Meeting of Dyes in History and Archaeology* (20th Meeting of Dyes in History and Archaeology, Instituut Collectie Nederland, Amsterdam, 2001).

Along the western Mediterranean Sea over 700 species of Mollusca have been identified, 16 of which are of the *Muricidae* species, though only three were used to produce purple dye.[134] These species include *Hexaplex trunculus* (also, *Murex trunculus, Phyllonotus trunculus, Truncalariopsis trunculus*); *Bolinus brandaris* (also, *Murex brandaris*) and *Stramonita haemastoma* (also, *Thais haemastoma, Purpura haemastoma*).[135]

The reddish liquid dye called ostrum,[136] frequently called *ostrinum, ostro, ostrum rubens, ostrum sanguineum,* or *ostrum puniceum*,[137] was produced from crushing the *Murex conchylium* (Marcellus *Comp. Doct.* 2.4.M549)[138] in a mortar and mixing it with honey to preserve it for export/transport (Vitruvius *Arch.* 7.13.1–3). Although Vitruvius is likely only talking about "pigments" for architecture, i.e., painting surfaces of buildings, walls, etc., and not textile dye, both pigment and dye were produced from the same murex species. It was used as a dye for clothes (Varro *Rust.* 133.9; see textiles below), bed covers (Propertius *Eleg.* 1.14.20), the *clavi* on napkins (*mappa;* Martial *Epig.* 4.46.17), and table cloths (*toralis*; Marcellinus *Hist.* 16.8.8).

Traditionally scholars have claimed that the textiles sold in Thyatira by *purpurarius,* such as Lydia, were made from the famous and expensive "Tyrian Purple" derived from several varieties of the *murex*[139] shellfish.[140] More recent commentators, led by William Ramsay and Colin Hemer, based on the research of French scholar Michel Clerc, have challenged this view,[141] as articulated by Ramsay's claim that

---

[134] Alexander Barash and Z. Zenziper, *Mediterranean Molluscs of Israel (Hebrew)* (Tel-Aviv: Society for the Protection of Nature in Israel, 1991), 8, 61.

[135] George E. Radwin and Anthony D'Attilio, Murex Shells of the World: An Illustrated Guide to the Muricidae (Stanford, Calif.: Stanford University Press, 1976), 93; Doumet, A Study on the Ancient Purple Color and an Attempt to Reproduce the Dyeing Procedure of Tyre as Described by Pliny the Elder; Koren, "First Optimal All-Murex," 137.

[136] The analysis of the *ostrum* was taken from a galley which sank in the time of Nero off of Ibiza, Spain Ted Falcon-Barker, *Roman Galley Beneath the Sea* (Philadelphia, Pa.: Clinton, 1964), 65..

[137] Lucretius *Re. Nat.* 2.35; Seneca *Med.* 99; Virgil *Aen.* 2.67; Flaccus *Argo*.2.342; Statius *Theb.* 4.265; Propertius *Eleg.* 2.29.26.

[138] Judith Lynn Sebesta and Larissa Bonfante, eds., *The World of Roman Costume* (Madison, Wisc.: University of Wisconsin Press, 2001), 75 n.48.

[139] The term "murex" is used here in a broad sense to indicate the molluscs that produce purple dye.

[140] Richard C. H. Lenski, *The Interpretation of the Acts of the Apostles*, CNT (Minneapolis, Minn.: Augsburg Fortress, 1961), 656–57; Keener, *Background Commentary: NT*, 370; F. F Bruce, *Paul, Apostle of the Heart Set Free* (Grand Rapids, Mich.: Eerdmans, 2000), 220. Horsley assumes that the government has a monopoly over the "royal" purple. However, this was only introduced late in the Roman Empire (Horsley, "The Purple Trade and the Status of Lydia of Thyatira," *NewDocs* 2:28). Keener states in the *IVP Bible Background Commentary* (1993) that the dye was "procured from the murex shellfish near Tyre, but in Macedonia it could have been procured from the mollusks near Thessalonica" (1993: Acts 16:15). However, in the newer edition (1994) Keener adds "Thyatiran purple often came from the madder plant, not the more expensive Tyrian shellfish" (*IVP Bible Background Commentary* 1994:370). Keener holds to this updated view in his *Acts Commentary* (2013, 2:2396).

[141] Michel Armand Edgar Anatole Clerc, *De rebus Thyatirenorum commentatio epigraphica* (Paris: Picard, 1893), 93; Ramsay, *Letters: Updated*, 238–39; Hemer, "Unto the Angels of the Churches," 114; *Letters to the Seven Churches*, 109; Mounce, *Revelation*, 85 n.4; Bradley B. Blue, "Acts and the House Church," in *Graeco-Roman Setting*, ed. David W. J. Gill and Conrad H. Gempf, BAFCS 2 (Eugene, Or.: Wipf & Stock, 2000), 186 n.258; Worth, Jr., *Greco-Asian Culture*, 289

the dyeing in Thyatira was performed in ancient times with madder-root, *[rubia peregrina L.* that also grew in the region of western Anatolia and used today in the region to dye carpets*]*. . . , [and that] the purple stuffs which the Thyatiran Lydia sold in Philippi (Acts 16:14) was dyed with what is, in modern times, called 'Turkey red'[142].[143]

Hemer also points to Strabo who testifies that "the water at Hierapolis is remarkably adapted also to the dyeing of wool, so that wool dyed with the roots [madder roots] rivals that dyed with the coccus [kermes] or with the marine purple [murex]. And the supply of water is so abundant that the city is full of natural baths" (*Geogr.* 13.4.14 [Jones]).[144]

The argument is also made that the "Tyrian Purple" dye could not have been used at Thyatira, because of the assumption that the dyeing facilities must be housed on the coast (Pliny *Nat.* 35.26.45) to take advantage of the marine supply of murex shellfish.[145] This old view is refuted by new research presented in an artilce by the author.[146]

LYDIA USED VARIOUS DYES

From the evidence presented in this article, Graves argues that various textiles were dyed using different methods and dye combinations, depending on the color, quality and value. More expensive dyes, such as purple, allowed for more expensive clothes, while more economical dyes provided for less expensive textiles. The diverse purple dyed product line formulated from the various shades of purple provided a wide range of priced textiles to meet the demand in the local and general economy.[147] While it is possible that madder alone was used to dye textiles purple in Laodicea or Philippi, it is more likely that both madder and murex, along with other ingredients, were used to provide a wide selection of variously priced textiles, as trade routes ensured murex shellfish did reach inland.[148]

Thus, it is fair to argue that Lydia likely did not deal in just one type of dye or method, but used a combination of dyes to participate in the competitive market of her day. Given the everyday use of togas and tunics, with purple *clavi*, in Roman society, along with the more specialty groups, such as the Jewish and military community in Philippi that used purple

---

n.44; Steven M. Baugh et al., *Zondervan Illustrated Bible Backgrounds Commentary Set*, ed. Clinton E. Arnold (Santa Rosa, CA: Zondervan, 2002), 27; Yamauchi, *NT Cities*, 54; Blaiklock, "Thyatira," 5:854; Eckhard J. Schnabel, *Acts*, ed. Clinton E. Arnold, ZECNT 5 (Grand Rapids, Mich.: Zondervan, 2012), 680; Keener, *Acts: 3:1–14:28*, 2:2:2396.

[142] Banks, "Thyatira," 2977–78.

[143] Ramsay, "Thyatira," 4:759. In his commentary on *CIG* 3496, Waltzing mentions Lydia's profession (Acts 16:14) and comments "La *teinture rouge* de Thyatire était renommée [the red dye of Thyatira was famous]" (emphasis added). Waltzing, *Étude historique*, 3:3:57.

[144] Hemer, *Letters to the Seven Churches*, 109. ἔστι δὲ καὶ πρὸς βαφὴν ἐρίων θαυμαστῶς σύμμετρον τὸ κατὰ τὴν Ἱερὰν πόλιν ὕδωρ, ὥστε τὰ ἐκ τῶν ῥιζῶν βαπτόμενα ἐνάμιλλα εἶναι τοῖς ἐκ τῆς κόκκου καὶ τοῖς ἁλουργέσιν· οὕτω δ᾽ ἐστὶν ἄφθονον τὸ πλῆθος τοῦ ὕδατος ὥστε ἡ πόλις μεστὴ τῶν αὐτομάτων βαλανείων ἐστί

[145] Barber, Prehistoric Textiles, 228–29.

[146] Graves, "What Is The Madder With Lydia's Purple?," 1–47.

[147] Meyer Reinhold, *History of Purple as a Status Symbol in Antiquity*, 116 (Brussels: Latomus, 1970).

[148] Graves, "What Is The Madder With Lydia's Purple?", 1–47.

garments, Lydia would have had a market for a wide price range of products to offer her customers. There seems little doubt that she would have either employed or purchased textiles, dyed from both madder as well as murex, to meet the demands of her clients. To insist that her products were only madder dyed seems to argue against the evidence.

It seems likely that Lydia was a wealthy woman who learned her trade in Thyatira, and moved to Philippi to carry on her business. She most likely not only dealt in purple textiles, made from madder root, but also from the murex shellfish, since there was a demand from many in Roman Society for a diverse quality purple cloth. The murex raw materials were available inland (Philippi is just 7.75 miles [12.5 km] from the coast) and less complicated to produce than madder dye.

THE SLAVE TRADE

Thyatira was also a major center for the Asian slave trade (στατάριον, *statarion*, slave market; σωματέμπορος, *sōmatemporos*, slave-merchant; *I.Thyat.* 932 = *IGR* 4.1257).[149] One of the inscriptions found reads:

> The workers [*ergastai*] in the slave market and those who broker in slaves [*proxenētai*] honored and set up (a dedication) for Alexander son of Alexander, a slave dealer [*sōmatemporos*], who oversaw the market with integrity for four months and gave generously from his own means to the city in the festival days of Augustan [*Sebastoi*] celebration (*I.Thyat.* 932 = *IGR* 4.1257 [Koester]).[150]

Alexander not only managed the public market, but also financially supported the imperial cult in Thyatira.

THE RELIGIOUS COMMUNITY OF THYATIRA

THE GODS OF THYATIRA

Thyatira adopted several Greek deities as their city gods, including Apollo Tyrimnos also Tyrimnaeus or Helius (see Figs. 82, 86; *I.Thyat.* 882–83; 946; 956; 960), Artemis Boreitene (*I.Thyat.* 995–96),[151] and Dionysus (see Fig. 35; *I.Thyat.* 931; 976; 995), each deity considered the protectors of the city. Although Thyatira did not possess many temples there was a shrine for divination, presided over by a female oracle called the *Sibyl Sambathe*, who some suggest was the prophetess Jezebel of Revelation 2:20.[152]

---

[149] Ascough, Harland, and Kloppenborg, *Associations in the Greco-Roman World*, 143.

[150] Craig R. Koester, "Roman Slave Trade and the Critique of Babylon in Revelation 18," *CBQ* 70, no. 4 (2008): 781.

[151] Barclay Vincent Head, *Catalogue of the Greek Coins of Lydia*, Catalogue of the Greek Coins in the British Museum 22 (London, U.K.: British Museum Press, 1901), 294–95.

[152] Banks, "Thyatira," 2:2977.

In addition, a pantheon of gods was worshiped, including Meter, the mother goddess (*I.Thyat.* 955; 962; 963), worshiped throughout Asia Minor, along with Tyche (Τύχη or Cybele see Figs. 52, 54, 98, 108, 160), the goddess of fortune (*I.Thyat.* 894–96). It is believed that some cults were imported from Pergamum, including Dionysus Kathegemon (the Leader); Zeus Keraunios (Thunderbolt); Asclepius the Savior (see Fig. 71), who was associated with Hygeia, or health; and Herakles.[153]

86. Coin from Thyatira, struck under Marcus Aurelius (AD 161–180). Obv.: *AY KAI M AYRHLIOC ANTWN*, Bust of Magistrate Titus Aurelius Barbaros, laureate, and draped. Rev.: *ΕΠΙ CTRA TITOY AYRH BARBARO ΘΥΑΤΕΙΡΗΝΩΝ*, Apollo Tyrimnaeus, the hero of Thyatira on horseback riding naked but for *chlamys* over his left shoulder, and holding a *bipennis* over his right shoulder (Mionnet Supp 7.606).

In addition, several Hellenistic deities were worshiped, including one referred to as God Most High (*Theos Hypsistos; I.Thyat.* 897–900).[154] The same language was used in the LXX for the God of Israel. While the book of Revelation argues for monotheism, the distinctions between religious traditions was not clear in the ancient world and in practice accommodation to multiple deities was common.[155]

THE IMPERIAL CULT

While there was no temple dedicate to the imperial cult in Thyatira,[156] there was an imperial altar with imperial priests.[157] The most popular emperor to receive imperial cult veneration in Thyatira was Augustus (*I.Thyat.* 902). Swete states that "there is no evidence that Thyatira was as yet a νεωκόρος of the Augusti,"[158] though several Thyatiran citizens became involved in the provincial cult of Augustus and Roma (see Fig. 173) at Pergamum (*I.Thyat.* 940; 970; 978); "Sokrates Sakerdotianos . . . high-priest of the Augusti (Sebastoi) for life" *I.Thyat.* 980

---

[153] María Paz de Hoz, *Die Lydischen Kulte Im Lichte Der Griechischen Inschriften*, AMStud. 36 (Bonn: Habelt, 1999), 34, 53, 60–70.

[154] Malay, *Researches in Lydia, Mysia and Aiolis*, no. 25.

[155] Stephen Mitchell, *Anatolia: Land, Men, and Gods in Asia Minor* (Oxford, U.K.: Clarendon Press, 1995), 2:49–51; Trebilco, *Jewish Communities*, 127–44.

[156] Thompson, *Apocalypse and Empire*, 159.

[157] Wes Howard-Brook and Anthony Gwyther, *Unveiling Empire: Reading Revelation Then and Now*, The Bible and Liberation (Maryknoll, N.Y.: Orbis Books, 1999), 104. See also Thompson, *Apocalypse and Empire*, 159.

[158] Swete, *Apocalypse*, lxi.

87. Coin from Thyatira. Obv.: *DOMITIANOC KAI CE GEPMANIKOC.* Bust of Domitian with laureate. Rev.: *QYATEIPHNWN.* The goddess Nike or Victory standing, holding a wreath and palm branch. (*BMC* 70 = *RPC* 2:942 = *SNG Tübingen* 3851 = Mionnet 4.895).

[Harland]), and Gaius Julius Xenon (*Xenoneion*), son of Apollonides from Thyatira, becoming provincial high-priest of Caesar Augustus and goddess *Roma* (see Fig. 173) in the first cent. BC. The temple was dedicated by Xenon,[159] while another citizen from Thyatira became provincial high priest and overseer of the imperial games (*I.Sard.* 8.99). Thyatira also had a municipal cult of the emperors in which a woman, Metrodoros Lepidas, served as priestess,[160] a practice not uncommon.[161] Domitian is also associated with the imperial cult, depicted on one side of coins from Thyatira, with a standing winged victory on the other side, a symbol of the imperial cult[162] (*RPC* 2:942; see Fig. 87). As Koester points out, "Domitian was called emperor, high priest, and son of the deified Vespasian, but as a living emperor he was not officially called 'god'" (*I.Thyat.* 870A).[163] Thus, throughout her history, Thyatira enthusiastically venerated Rome and the emperors.[164]

THE JEWISH COMMUNITY

The population of the city was predominantly Greek, and evidence for a Jewish community in Thyatira is ambiguous, a fact reflected in the absence of any reference to a Jewish element there in the message in the Book of Revelation. Lydia, "a God-fearer" from Thyatira, had come under the influence of a Jewish synagogue somewhere, as she is described in Acts 16:13 attending "a place of prayer [προσευχή, *proseuchē*], and we [Paul and Luke] sat down and spoke to the women who had come together [συνελθούσαις, *synelthousais*]" (Acts 16:13). Although there are no other NT instances of the use of the term "place of prayer" (προσευχή, *proseuchē*), extra biblical writers

---

[159] *I.Thyat.* 1098 = *TAM V* 2.1098 = *PHI* 264529.
[160] *AGRW* 129 = *I.Thyat.* 972 = *IGR* 4.1242.
[161] Koester, *Revelation*, 296.
[162] Ittai Gradel, *Emperor Worship and Roman Religion*, OCM (Oxford, U.K.: Oxford University Press, 2002), 78–98.
[163] Koester, *Revelation*, 297.
[164] Adela Yarbro Collins, "Insiders and Outsiders in the Book of Revelation and Its Social Context," in *"To See Ourselves As Others See Us": Christians, Jews, "Others" in Late Antiquity*, ed. Jacob Neusner and Ernest S. Frerichs, Scholars Press Studies in the Humanities (Chico, Ca.: Scholars Press, 1985), 215.

used the term to describe synagogues[165] (Josephus *Life* 277; Philo *Legat.* 155–58)[166] and a recent discovery of an inscription does reveal the existence of a synagogue in Philippi[167] in the third or fourth cent. AD.[168] Lydia may have originally been exposed to a synagogue in Thyatira, but this is not certain.[169] It is known that Jews were active in the dyeing and cloth industry of Thyatira.[170]

A second or third cent. AD inscription mentions a *sambatheion* at Thyatira.[171] It is possible that this was a Sabbath house (*sabbateion*, Josephus *Ant.* 16.164),[172] although given Thyatira's worship of Sambathe and the location of the inscription in the Chaldean quarter of the city, the term may have been connected to the Sibyl Sambathe (*IJO* 2:297–302).[173] If a synagogue did exist in Thyatira, there is no mention of hostility between the Jews and the Christian community there.

THE CHRISTIAN COMMUNITY

The origins of the Christian community in Thyatira are unknown, although they were long enough for John to look back on the churches former works (ca. mid 80's) and compare them with their present conduct (2:19). Epiphanius reports that according to the heterodox Christian works of the *Alogoi* (ἄλογοι), who oppose the prophetic work of the Montanists,[174] Thyatira did not have a Christian church when John wrote, which Epiphanius pointed out is refuted by their own words (Epiphanius *Pan.* 51.33.1–2). The Alogoi also claimed that by AD 200 the city in

---

[165] Based on the tradition of Lydia and the other women meeting at "a place of prayer" outside the city by the riverbank, some have inferred that the first century Jewish community in Philippi was not large enough (ten men or a *minyan*) to sustain a synagogue. Stambaugh and Balch, *NT in Its Social Environment*, 155–56. However, this stipulation of ten men was a later rabbinical regulation that postdates Lydia, with women being permitted to read the Torah in public and counted as members of the synagogue quorum. Brooten, *Women Leaders in the Ancient Synagogue*, 94. Also, it was Paul's practice to seek out the synagogue during his missionary activities, and Paul clearly expected to find a synagogue there.

[166] Reimer, *Women in Acts*, 87, 89, 90.

[167] Hartog, Polycarp and the NT, 55.

[168] Chaido Koukouli-Chrysanthaki, "Colonia Iulia Augusta Philippensis," in *Philippi at the Time of Paul and after His Death*, ed. Charalambos Bakirtzis and Helmut Koester (Eugene, Oreg.: Wipf & Stock, 2009), 26–29; "Philippi," in *Brill's Companion to Ancient Macedon: Studies in the Archaeology and History of Macedon, 650 BC - 300 AD*, ed. Robin J. Fox and Robin Lane Fox (Leiden: Brill, 2011), 451.

[169] Ramsay, *Letters: Updated*, 236; Thomas, *Rev 1–7*, 208 n.4.

[170] Karl Schneider, "Purpura," in *PW*, 46:1959.

[171] *CIJ* 752 = *IJO* 2.146 = PHI 264573. Ascough, Harland, and Kloppenborg, *Associations in the Greco-Roman World*, 134.

[172] Schürer, *History of the Jewish People*, 3:19.

[173] Koester, *Revelation*, 297.

[174] The Alogoi were a group of heterodox Chrisitians who flourished in Asia Minor around AD 170. They denied the continuation of spiritual gifts in the church in opposition to the Montanists who promoted them. Cross and Livingstone, *The Oxford Dictionary Of The Christian Church*, 45; Philip Schaff, "Alogi," in *A Dictionary of Christian Biography: And Literature to the End of the Sixth Century A.D. With an Account of the Principal Sects and Heresies*, ed. Henry Wace (Peabody, Mass.: Hendrickson, 1994), 34.

Thyatira was generally Christian, since the Montanist "converted the whole town to their sect, and at that time those who reject Revelation attacked this text [Revelation] in an effort to discredit it" (Epiphanius *Pan.* 51.33.3 [Williams]). While the Alogoi and Montanists in Thyatira may not have been Johannine Christians, since they were criticising John's writings, it is known that Christians were living in Thyatira. Carpus, the Bishop of Pergamum, was originally from Thyatira, and was martyred in Pergamum around this time (*Mart. Carp.* 27; Eusebius *Hist. eccl.* 4.15.48). Also, a bishop of Thyatira attended the First Council of Nicaea in 325 (Bishop Sarapas)[175] and the Council of Chalcedon in 451 (Bishop Phoscus).[176]

---

[175] Heinrich Gelzer, Heinrich Hilgenfeld, and Otto Cuntz, *Patrum Nicaenorum Nomina Latine, Graece, Coptice, Syriace, Arabice, Armeniace* (Lipsiae: Teubner, 1898), 13.

[176] Richard Price and Michael Gaddis, *The Acts of the Council of Chalcedon*, Translated Texts for Historians 45 (Liverpool, U.K.: Liverpool University Press, 2005), 336.

11

Threatened Thyatira

Commentary on Revelation 2:18–29

*A*gain John is commanded to write to the angel of the church in Thyatira. This chapter will examine the threatening tone of the message to Thyatira, for tolerating Jezebel. Revelation 2:18–29 will be examined in the light of the proposed covenant background and structure. On the commission to write (γράψον, *graphon* 3:7a) and the role of angels (ἄγγελος, *angelos*) as mediating messengers, see chapter 3, *The Messenger's Commission*.

MESSENGER PREAMBLE FORMULA—2:18

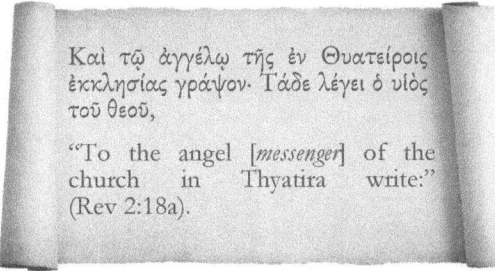

Καὶ τῷ ἀγγέλῳ τῆς ἐν Θυατείροις ἐκκλησίας γράψον· Τάδε λέγει ὁ υἱὸς τοῦ θεοῦ,

"To the angel [*messenger*] of the church in Thyatira write:" (Rev 2:18a).

John begins each message to the churches with τάδε λέγει Ω (*tade legei omega*, "These are the words" 2:1, 8,12,18; 3:1a, 7, 14), setting the context for the suzerain/king who will speak to the churches.[1] He proceeds to describe Christ in a way that echos Revelation chapter 1 (vs. 13, 16), in a format familiar to the Christian community. Within the OT prophetic structure[2] this prophetic *messenger preamble formula*[3] τάδε λέγει Ω, (*tade legei omega*, "These are the words") introduces the sovereign's message.

DESCRIPTION OF THE SUZERAIN

Here, in the message to Thyatira, Christ the King is identified, echoing chapter 1 (ver. 15; compare Dan 10:6), as "the Son of God" with "eyes like flaming fire" and "feet like fine brass." The message of the suzerain is identified as a word of the risen Lord and although John shares the views of the King, the maledictions and promises require divine action for their fulfillment.

---

[1] Beale, *Revelation*, 229.
[2] Num 22:15–16; Judg 11:14–15; 1 Kgs 2:30; 2 Chr 36:23; Ezra 1:2.
[3] Graves, *SMRVT*, 141–47; Osborne, *Revelation*, 111.

The suzerain's message is to be head through John's words but the identification of the king is what gives the message its authority.

THE TRANSCENDENT SUZERAIN: SON OF GOD—2:18B

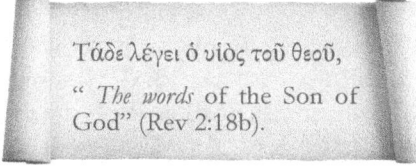

Τάδε λέγει ὁ υἱὸς τοῦ θεοῦ,
"*The words* of the Son of God" (Rev 2:18b).

This is the only place in Revelation where the phrase "the Son of God" (ὁ υἱὸς τοῦ θεοῦ, *ho uios tou theou*) is used, although it is found forty-six times in the NT. The parallel passage in chapter 1 of Revelation identified the suzerain as "the Son of Man" (ὅμοιον υἱὸν ἀνθρώπου, *homoion uion anthropou;* ver. 13, see also Rev 14:14 alluding to Dan 7:13 which has "a son of man"). In the Gospels the term was used by Jesus as a phrase of self-designation.[4] Daniel used the phrase to refer to somebody "like a man,"[5] who comes "with the clouds of heaven" and "was given dominion and glory and a kingdom that all peoples, nations, and languages should serve him; [and] his dominion is an everlasting dominion" (Dan 7:13–14). The Psalms also present the Son of God ruling the nations (Pss 2:7–8; 89:26–27). The two phrases, Son of God and Son of Man, appear together in early Christian writings.[6] The use of the Son of God in the message to the Thyatira church reminds the church of the dominion of the suzerain in several ways.

THE SUZERAIN'S MESSIANIC KINGSHIP

As Bauer points out, in Hebrew tradition "the divine sonship of the king has its basis in the covenant God made with David in 2 Samuel 7:4–17 (see also Pss 89:19–45) . . . infusing the notion of royal Son of God with the ideas of immutable divine promise, decree and covenant."[7] God's suzerain was understood as the begotten son, who would rule the nations with an iron rod (Ps 2:7–9), the Lion of Judah (Gen 49:9–10) and the Root of David (Isa 11:1; see also Rev 1:5; 5:5). The Dead Sea Scrolls spoke of the messianic hope suzerain (4Q174 1.10–19) who would usher in an eternal kingdom.[8] The early Christians believed Jesus to be the Son of God as

---

[4] Matt 9:6; 12:8; 16:13, 27–28; 17:9, 12, 22; 20:18, 28; 24:30; 26:2, 24, 45, 64; Mark 2:10, 28; 8:31, 38; 9:9, 12, 31; 10:33, 45; 13:26; 14:21, 41, 62; Luke 5:24; 6:5; 9:22, 26, 44; 17:22; 18:8, 31; 19:10; 21:27, 36; 22:22, 48, 69; 24:7. I. Howard Marshall, "Son of Man," ed. Joel B. Green, Scot McKnight, and I. Howard Marshall, *DJG* (Downers Grove, Ill.: InterVarsity, 1992), 781.

[5] Richard J. Bauckham, "The Son of Man: 'A Man in My Position' or 'Someone,'" *JSNT* 23 (1985): 23–33; Barnabas Lindars, "Response to Richard Bauckham: The Idiomatic Use of Bar Enasha," *JSNT* 23, no. 1 (February 1985): 35–41.

[6] Matt 26:63–64; Luke 22:69–70; John 5:25–27; see also 4 Ezra 13:3, 32.

[7] David R. Bauer, "Son of God," ed. Joel B. Green, Scot McKnight, and I. Howard Marshall, *DJG* (Downers Grove, Ill.: InterVarsity, 1992), 770.

[8] 4Q246 2.1–9; see also 4Q369 1.1–11; 4 Ezra 7:28–29; 13:32, 37, 52; 14:9; Joseph A. Fitzmyer, "The Contribution of Qumran Aramaic to the Study of the New Testament," *NTS* 20 (74 1973): 382–407; Bauer, "Son of God," 770; John Joseph Collins, *The Scepter and the Star: The Messiahs of the Dead Sea Scrolls and Other Ancient Literature*, ABRL (New York, N.Y.: Anchor Bible, 1995), 154–72.

the Messianic fulfillment (Matt 16:16; John 1:49; see also Rev 1:5; 5:5). The allusion to the "morning star" in Revelation 2:18 (see also 28; 22:16) promised to those who are faithful, is also a Messianic image for God's promised suzerain.[9]

THE SUZERAIN'S DIVINE CHARACTER

Within Judaism the king was God's son by adoption, while in Christianity the term "Son of God" conveyed the idea of deity, evident from the resurrection (Rom 1:4; Acts 13:33). Jesus is the Son of God in a unique sense (John 1:14, 18; 3:16).[10] The suzerain described as the "Son of God" shares the divine traits of the Alpha and Omega (1:8, 17; see also 21:6; 22:13).[11] The depiction of the suzerain with fiery eyes and feet that shine like bronze also conveys traits of divinity (2:18) along with the facility to search minds and hearts (2:23).

THE SUZERAIN'S EXCLUSIVE TITLE

Following the deification of Julius Caesar in the first cent. BC (*Divus Iulius* 42 BC; Cicero *Phil.* 2.110; see Fig. 88),[12] Augustus (or Octavian), his adopted son, was called "Emperor Caesar, son of the god Julius" (Αὐτοκράτωρ Καῖσαρ θεοῦ Ἰουλίου υἱός, *autokratōr kaisar theou Iouliou uois*, or *Divi Filius*).[13] This is attested by inscriptions at Thyatira (*I.Thyat.* 902–3), Pergamum (*IGR* 3.309–11, 3.314), Ephesus (*I.Eph.* 2.252–53),

88. Coin from Thyatira. Obv.: *CAESAR AVGVSTVS*, laureate head of Augustus Denarius. (r. *ca.* 19–18 BC). Rev.: *DIVVS IVLIV[S]*, (divus or deified Julius). Comet (44 BC) of eight rays representing the eight days it was visible with the tail pointing upward that was interpreted as the divine authentication of Caesar's deity. (*RIC* 1.37a = *BMC* 323).

Philadelphia (*SEG* 35.1169), Sardis (*I.Sard.* 8.22), and other cities. Tiberius (r. AD 14–37; see Figs. 43, 97, 111) became son of *divus* Augustus,[14] followed by Titus (r. AD 79–81; *I.Laod.* 9.6; 15.1–2). Domitian (r. AD 81–96) became "son of a god" (*I.Smyr.* 826),[15] since his father

---

[9] Num 24:17; *T. Levi* 18:3; *T. Jud.* 24:1; 4Q175 12.

[10] Richard J. Bauckham, "The Sonship of the Historical Jesus in Christology," *SJT* 31, no. 3 (1978): 245–60.

[11] James D. G. Dunn, *Christology in the Making: A New Testament Inquiry Into the Origins of the Doctrine of the Incarnation* (Grand Rapids, Mich.: Eerdmans, 1996), 12–64; Bauer, "Son of God," 769; Bauckham, *Theology of Revelation*, 54–69.

[12] Lily Ross Taylor, *The Divinity of the Roman Emperor*, ed. Joseph William Hewitt, American Philological Association 1 (New York, N.Y.: Scholars Press, 2011), 58–60.

[13] Ibid., 142–80; Reynolds and Erim, *Aphrodisias and Rome*, 101, document 12, line 1.

[14] Naphtali Lewis and Meyer Reinhold, eds., *Roman Civilization*, 3rd ed. (New York, N.Y.: Columbia University Press, 1991), 2:631; Helen Rhee, *Early Christian Literature: Christ and Culture in the Second and Third Centuries*, Routledge Early Church Monographs (New York, N.Y.: Routledge, 2005), 159–161.

[15] William Broad, *Alexander or Jesus?: The Origin of the Title "Son of God"* (Eugene, Oreg.: Wipf & Stock, 2015), 121–23.

Vespasian was *Divus Vespasianus* (ca. AD 80). Domitian's son was deified (*Divus Caesar* AD 73) and depicted seated on a globe as a throne surrounded by seven stars (Suetonius *Dom.* 3.1; see Fig. 39). Hadrian (r. AD 117–138; see Figs. 93, 109) was called the son of *divus* Trajan.[16]

The message to Thyatira that describes the suzerain as the "son of God," is contrasted with the imperial cult, in where the emperor was given the title of "son of a god," due to the ἀποθέωσις (*apotheōsis*) of his father. For the Christian in Thyatira, Jesus was the true "son of God" and grants his followers adoption as sons, with the inheritance of life in the new Jerusalem (21:7). Smith points out that Roman iconography represented the emperor exercising power over the nations,[17] in contrast with Revelation, where Jesus is identified as the Son of God who alone exercised sovereign power over the nations (Pss 2:7–8; 89:26–27).

THE TRANSCENDENT SUZERAIN: EYES LIKE A FLAME OF FIRE—2:18C

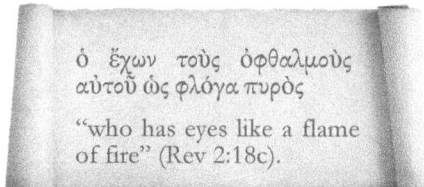

ὁ ἔχων τοὺς ὀφθαλμοὺς αὐτοῦ ὡς φλόγα πυρὸς

"who has eyes like a flame of fire" (Rev 2:18c).

This phrase is repeated in a slightly varied form from 1:14b, where it states "and his eyes were like a flame of fire" (καὶ οἱ ὀφθαλμοὶ αὐτοῦ ὡς φλὸξ πυρός, *kai oi ophthalmoi autou ōs phlox puros*). The phrase φλόγα πυρός (*phloga puros*) is a possible allusion to Psalm 103:4 in the Septuagint, quoted in Hebrews 1:7 where it states "and when God speaks about the angels, he says, 'I change my angels into wind and my servants into flaming fire'" (Heb 1:7; see also *1 Clem.* 36:3[18]). Duff proposes that Jezebel in the text (2:19–20) was a Hekáte sorceress (18:23; Lucian *Philop.* 22; *PGM* 4.1404) who practiced the magical evil eye[19] and whom John contrasts with the suzerain who was the more powerful all-seeing, fiery-eyed, "son of God".[20] In antiquity, eyes emitting flames were an indication of divine power (19:12; Plutarch *Quaest. conv.* 5.7.2), and Hercules is also described as having "flashed a gleam of fire from his eyes" (Apollodorus *Lib.* 2.4.9). However, the image here in 2:18b is likely drawn from Daniel,[21] where the angelic messenger or theophany is described with "eyes like flaming fires, his arms and legs like polished bronze" (Dan 10:6; see also *1 En.* 106:5–6).

---

[16] Rhee, *Early Christian Literature*, 159–61.

[17] R. R. R. Smith, "The Imperial Reliefs from the Sebasteion at Aphrodisias," *JRS* 77 (1987): 96.

[18] Donald Alfred Hagner, *The Use of the Old and New Testaments in Clement of Rome*, NovTSup 34 (Leiden: Brill, 1973), 46, 180.

[19] Frederick Thomas Elworthy, "The Evil Eye," in *Encylopaedia of Religion and Ethics*, ed. James Hastings, vol. 5, 12 vols. (New York, N.Y.: T&T Clark, 1908), 608–15; *The Evil Eye: An Account of This Ancient and Widespread Superstition* (London, U.K.: Murray, 1958), 5:608–15; Rivka Ulmer, *Evil Eye in the Bible and Rabbinic Literature* (Hoboken, N. J.: KTAV, 1994); Regina Dionisopoulous-Mass, "The Evil Eye and the Bewitchment in a Peasant Village," in *The Evil Eye*, ed. Clarence Maloney (New York, N.Y.: Columbia University Press, 1976), 44–45.

[20] Paul B. Duff, "I Will Give Each of You as Your Works Deserve": Witchcraft Accusations and the Fiery-Eyed Son of God in Rev 2.18–23," *NTS* 43, no. 1 (1997): 116–123; *Who Rides the Beast?: Prophetic Rivalry and the Rhetoric of Crisis in the Churches of the Apocalypse* (Oxford, U.K.: Oxford University Press, 2001), 116. However, it is worthy of note that sorcery is not mentioned in the text.

[21] Christopher Rowland, "The Vision of the Risen Christ in Rev. I. 13 Ff.: The Debt of an Early Christology to an

The Transcendent Suzerain: Feet Like Burnished Bronze—2:18d

καὶ οἱ πόδες αὐτοῦ ὅμοιοι χαλκολιβάνῳ·

"and whose feet are like burnished bronze" (Rev 2:18d).

The bronze imagery of the suzerain, identified as the Son of God with feet like burnished bronze (also described in chapter 1:15, "Son of man"; compare Dan 10:6), is contrasted with the cult statue of Apollo Tyrimnos (see Fig. 90), the Son of Zeus, or Helius, as depicted on the coins of Thyatira (see Figs. 82, 86).[22]

The brass metals workers were represented by the local bronze guild (χαλκεῖς, calkeis, coppersmiths or bronzesmiths)[23] which thrived in Thyatira (see Fig. 89),[24] attested to by a Greek inscription mentioning the Thyatira guild of bronze-workers (χαλκός, chalkos, copper or brass; Lat. aes, brass; IGR 4.1259). The term "like burnished bronze" (χαλκολιβάνῳ, chalkolibanō) for the feet is a unique term only found here and 1:15 in ancient writings, and identified as a copper-zinc metal[25] produced by a special distillation process.[26] Plumptre rejects this connection on the basis that "the imagery had already been used without reference to any local coloring."[27] However, as Hemer points out this misunderstands the nature of the unity of the structure (compare 1:15 and 2:18).[28]

89. Medallion coin minted under Commodus (AD 177–192) at Thyatira. Obv.: *AV K M AVRH KOMODOC*. It depicts the bust of magistrate T. Aurelius Barbarus laureate, draped, and cuirassed. Rev.: *EPI CTPA TIT-OV AVP-HLIOV BAPBAPO*. Hephaestus seated on wreathed *cippus*, putting finishing touches, with a hammer, on a Corinthian helmet set on a low column, while Athena, standing left, holding a spear and shield, touches the top of the column; (*BMC* 82). Ramsay describes it as "The Thyatiran bronze-smith." *Letters*, 325.

Aspect of Jewish Angelology," *JTS* 31, no. 1 (1980): 1–11.

[22] Mounce, *Revelation*, 85; Caird, *Revelation*, 43; Stambaugh, "Thyatira (Place)," 6:546.

[23] Joseph William Blakesley, "Thyatira," in *SDB*, ed. William Smith and H. B. Hackett, vol. 4 (Boston, Mass.: Houghton, Mifflin & Company, 1883), 4:3241; Banks, "Thyatira," 2977; Kiddle, *Revelation*, 37; Caird, *Revelation*, 43; Morris, *Revelation*, 73.

[24] Ramsay, *Letters: Updated*, 235; Franz, "Propaganda, Power and the Perversion," 84; Caird, *Revelation*, 43; Meinardus, *John of Patmos*, 94; Ford, *Revelation*, 405.

[25] Charles, *Revelation*, 1:29; Swete, *Apocalypse*, 17; Moffatt, *Revelation*, 5:244–45; Beckwith, *Apocalypse*, 438–39.

[26] Hemer argues primarily from a political, economic, and geographical position. Hemer, *Letters to the Seven Churches*, 111–17, 127; Kiddle, *Revelation*, 37; Kistemaker, *Revelation*, 136; Caird, *Revelation*, 43.

[27] Plumptre, Seven Churches of Asia, 135.

[28] Hemer, Letters to the Seven Churches, 111.

Keener suggests that it is a compound hybrid word (Cicero *De or.* 3.38.154),²⁹ originating from Dan 10:6 where the image is derived (see Theodotian's rendering of the Heb. of Dan. 10:6 as χαλκολιβάνω, *chalkolibanō*, "burnished brass"³⁰).³¹ Andrew of Caesarea (d. ca. 614 AD) suggested that because *libano* is the word for Frankincense, that the word should refer to metal and incense. Giesen suggests that χαλκολιβάνω (*chalkolibanō*) is so rare that it conveys the idea of transcendence, which would correspond with the suzerain's attributes of sovereign omniscience.³²

90. Coin from Thyatira (second cent. BC). Obv.: Laureate head of Apollo Rev.: ΘΥΑΤΕΙΡΗΝΩΝ, a *labrys* (double axe) with a bow on the left. (*SNG Cop.* 570).

HISTORICAL PROLOGUE—2:19–21

The historical prologue traces the history that exists between the suzerain and the vassals. In the messages to the seven churches in Revelation the relationship is expressed in terms of what the suzerain knows (οἶδα, *oida*, "I know") of the deeds (ἔργα, *erga*) of the vassals and indicates previous knowledge and a past relationship with the vassal. The king, who enters into covenant with his subjects, acknowledges his historical intimacy with their circumstances.

THE SUZERAIN KNOWS THEIR WORKS—2:19

οἶδά σου τὰ ἔργα καὶ τὴν ἀγάπην καὶ τὴν πίστιν καὶ τὴν διακονίαν καὶ τὴν ὑπομονήν σου, καὶ τὰ ἔργα σου τὰ ἔσχατα πλείονα τῶν πρώτων.

"*I know your works, your* love and faith and service and patient endurance, and that *your* latter works exceed the first" (Rev 2:19).

The suzerain has knowledge of the works (κόπος, *kopos*, "labor, toil") of this congregation, which are specified as a polysyndetic list of love (ἀγάπη, *agapē*), faith (πίστις, *pistis*), service (διακονία, *diakonia*) and patient endurance (ὑπομονή, *hypomonē*). The vassal's Christian behavioral qualities are praised by the suzerain, and also found repeated in the rest of the messages in Revelation (see below).

---

²⁹ Heinrich Lausberg, *Handbook of Literary Rhetoric: A Foundation for Literary Study*, ed. David E. Orton and R. Dean Anderson, trans. Matthew T. Bliss, Annemiek Jansen, and David E. Orton (Leiden: Brill, 1998), §§547–51.

³⁰ George Wesley Buchanan, *The Book of Revelation: Its Introduction and Prophecy* (Eugene, Oreg.: Wipf & Stock, 2005), 72.

³¹ Keener, *Revelation*, 246.

³² Heinz Giesen and Horst Eckert, *Die Offenbarung des Johannes*, RNT (Regensburg: Pustet, 1997), 2:18 op cit.

THE SUZERAIN KNOWS THEIR LOVE

The first to be mentioned is ἀγάπη (*agapē*) love, which Paul describes as the greatest quality (1 Cor 13:13), and includes both love for God and neighbor.[33] Love for others should be governed by God's love for us (1:5; 12:11; see also 2:4, 19). The suzerain notes that in contrast to the Ephesians who had lost their first love (ἀγάπη, *agapē*, 2:4), the love of the Thyatiran Christians was to be commended, even though it was exceeded by their patient endurance.

THE SUZERAIN KNOWS THEIR FAITH

The second quality mentioned is their faith (πίστις, *pistis* 2:13, 19; 13:10; 14:12). Πίστις (*pistis*) conveys the idea of faith in the suzerain and the faithfulness or dependability of his vassals.[34] In Greek mythology, *Pistis* (Πίστις) was the personified spirit (*daimona*) of trust, good faith, honesty and reliability. The personified concept of Pistis called *Fides* was significant in Roman culture. The Thyatiran Christians demonstrate their faithfulness to the suzerain through public loyalty and perseverance in the face of conflict (1:5; 2:13; see also 2:10; 13:10; 14:12).

THE SUZERAIN KNOWS THEIR SERVICE

Although the word "service" (διακονία, *diakonia*, ministry or service) is only found here in Revelation, it is used a total of thirty-three times in the NT, and is listed among the spiritual gifts in 1 Corinthians 12:4–6 and Romans 12:6–8. Service has been widely defined as "any 'discharge of service' in genuine love" (i.e., waiting on tables and providing for bodily sustenance),"[35] though Collins and others have broadened the definition to mean "the carrying out of a commissioned task."[36] However, the meaning is likely expanded to range "from witnessing to the gospel to providing for the needy."[37] As Aune points out "cognates of διακονία (*diakonia*) were used for servants, waiters, priests, statesmen, tradesmen, messengers, and so forth, i.e., a spectrum of roles from menial to privileged."[38]

THE SUZERAIN KNOWS THEIR PATIENT ENDURANCE

Thayer defines ὑπομονή (*hypomonē*) in the NT as "steadfastness, constancy, endurance. . . . the characteristic of a man who is unswerved from his deliberate purpose and his loyalty to faith

---

[33] Mark 12:30–31; Luke 10:27; 1 John 4:20.

[34] Karrer, *Johannesoffenbarung*, 1:204 n.283; Aune, *Rev 1–5*, 202; Keener, *Revelation*, 298.

[35] H. W. Beyer, "Diakonew, Diakonia, Diakonos," in *TDNT*, ed. Gerhard Kittel and Gerhard Friedrich, trans. Geoffrey W. Bromiley, Abridged, vol. 2 (Grand Rapids, Mich.: Eerdmans, 1985), 2:82–87; R. Eduard Schweizer, "Ministry in the Early Church," ed. David Noel Freedman et al., *ABD* (New York, N.Y.: Doubleday, 1996), 33–56.

[36] John Neil Collins, *Diakonia: Re-Interpreting the Ancient Sources* (Oxford, U.K.: Oxford University Press, 1990), 335–40; Paula Gooder, "Diakonia in the New Testament: A Dialogue with John N. Collins," *Ecclesiology* 3, no. 1 (2006): 33–56.

[37] Koester, *Revelation*, 298. Acts 6:1, 4; 11:29; 1 Cor 12:5; 2 Cor 4:1.

[38] Aune, *Rev 1–5*, 202.

and piety by even the greatest trials and sufferings"[39]. In late Jewish literature ὑπομονή (*hypomonē*) was "frequently applied to the virtue shewn by martyrs".[40] The suzerain is mindful of the patient endurance (ὑπομονή, *hypomonē*, 1:9; 2:2–3, 19; 3:10; 13:10; 14:12) of the Thyatirans in the face of hostile opposition (1:9; 13:10; 14:12) and false teaching (2:2–3).

The suzerain has history with this Christian community as he compares their present behavior with what it was in the past.[41] The phrase "Your later works are greater than your first" might be translated "your recent behavior is better than before" (καὶ τὰ ἔργα σου τὰ ἔσχατα πλείονα τῶν πρώτων, *kai ta erga sou ta eschata pleiona tōn protōn*).[42] A word of encouragement before the words of reproof that follow.

THE SUZERAIN KNOWS THAT YOU TOLERATE JEZEBEL—2:20

ἀλλὰ ἔχω κατὰ σοῦ ὅτι ἀφεῖς τὴν γυναῖκα Ἰεζάβελ, ἡ λέγουσα ἑαυτὴν προφῆτιν καὶ διδάσκει καὶ πλανᾷ τοὺς ἐμοὺς δούλους πορνεῦσαι καὶ φαγεῖν εἰδωλόθυτα·

"But *I have this against you*, that *you* tolerate that woman Jezebel, who calls herself a prophetess and is teaching and seducing my servants to practice sexual immorality and to eat food sacrificed to idols" (Rev 2:20).

Here in Thyatira the figure of Jezebel (1 Kgs 16:31; 21:25) is substituted for that of Balaam (Pergamum; 2:14) where the eating of εἰδωλόθυτος (*eidōlothutos*, "things sacrificed to idols") is connected with fornication, as in the OT.[43] As Krodel points out "she would no more call herself by that name then the Jews of Smyrna would identify themselves as the synagogue of Satan."[44] John calls this prophetess in the church Jezebel, to compare her to Queen Jezebel, the wife of King Ahab of Israel (869–850 BC; 1 Kgs 16:31). Her evil practices are legendary and include promoting 450 prophets of Asherah and Baal (1 Kgs 18:19; Josephus *Ant.* 8.330, 334), persecuting Elijah (1 Kgs 19:1–3; Josephus *Ant.* 8.347) and the murder of an innocent man to confiscate his vineyard (1 Kgs 21:1–16; Josephus *Ant.* 8.355–59). "Given the negative connotations of Queen Jezebel in Jewish tradition,"[45] it is likely that John called her Jezebel as a derogatory name.

Collins believes that Jezebel was an itinerant prophet,[46] while feminist writers believe that she belonged to the congregation of Thyatira and was opposing John's male authority.[47] It

---

[39] Thayer, *GELNT* §5480. See Luke 8:15; 21:19; Rom 5:3; 15:4; 2 Cor 6:4; 12:12; Col 1:11; 1 Thess 1:3; 2 Thess 1:4; 1 Tim 6:11; 2 Tim 3:10; Titus 2:2; Heb 10:36; Jas 1:3; 5:11; 2 Pet 1:6.
[40] MM 659; e.g. 4 Macc 1:11; 9:8, 30; 15:30; *Pss. Sol.* 2:40.
[41] Lausberg, *Handbook of Literary Rhetoric*, §404.
[42] Aune, *Rev 1–5*, 202–203.
[43] Num 22:5–25:3; 31:8, 16; Deut 23:4, 5; Josh 13:22; 24:9, 10; Neh 13:2; Mic 6:5.
[44] Krodel, *Revelation*, 118.
[45] Boxall, "'For Paul' or 'For Cephas,'" 211. 1 Kgs 18–21; 2 Kgs 9; 4Q382 1.3; Josephus *Ant.* 8.316–59; 9.47, 108, 122–23.
[46] Collins, "Insiders and Outsiders in the Book of Revelation and Its Social Context," 217.
[47] Schüssler Fiorenza, *Book of Revelation*, 116; Thimmes, "Women Reading Women," 132; Catherine Keller,

would appear that the feminist writers are reading more into the text than is there. John's issue with Jezebel was not that she was a woman but rather her teachings, which were unacceptable by Christian standards.

The suzerain reprimanded the church at Thyatira for tolerating "that woman Jezebel, who calls herself a prophetess and is teaching and seducing my servants to practice sexual immorality (πορνεύειν, *porneuein*) and to eat food sacrificed to idols (φαγεῖν εἰδωλόθυτα, *phagein eidōlothuta*)" (2:20). This is a striking reference to the practices of immorality and idolatry in the trade-guilds,[48] parallelling Jezebel's seduction of Israel – pulling Israel away from worship of Yahweh via syncretism with Baal, the Canaanite god, (1 Kgs 16:31; 21:25; 2 Kgs 9:22), and the first century potential for syncretism with the imperial cult, both of which practiced immorality and idolatry.[49] Joining a guild secured one's livelihood, but it also included immoral religious rituals and meals involving idol sacrifice. The pressure on Christians was enormous, for they were faced with financial ruin if they rejected the guilds. Perhaps "Jezebel" (2:20) suggested that an idol is nothing (see also 1 Cor 8:1–4), so that Christian tradesmen and women could freely participate in the guild. John thinks otherwise (2:22–23) and promises that the faithful will rule the nations with a rod of iron (2:27).

Some MSS (A 046; Andrew 2073, 2042; Byzantine Syriac MS; Westcott and Hort) read τὴν γυναῖκα σοῦ (*tēn gunaika sou*)[50] which translates as "your wife" and presupposes either that the angel (ἄγγελος, *angelos*) in 2:18 is the bishop of Thyatira,[51] and Jezebel is his wife; or maybe as Ramsay proposes, it is a metaphor for a prominent woman in the community[52] and the copyists likely dropped σοῦ (*sou*) to avoid calling Jezebel the wife of the bishop.[53] Others have identified Jezebel as the wife of an Asiarch (ruler of Asia)[54] or the woman, Lydia, now living in Philippi (Acts 16:14).[55] These theories are unlikely given there is no supporting evidence.

Based on an inscription (*CIG* 2:3509), Schürer identified Jezebel as Sibyl Sambathe (a local female prophetess and soothsayer), whose shrine was "before the city."[56] Ramsay remarks that

---

Apocalypse Now and Then: A Feminist Guide to the End of the World (Minneapolis, Minn.: Augsburg Fortress, 2009), 45.

[48] On trade guilds also see chapter 1, *Cultural Background of the Seven Messages: External Problems*. Hemer, *Letters to the Seven Churches*, 128; Charles, *Revelation of St John*, 1:70–71; Ramsay, *The Letters to Seven Churches*, 346–49; Kiddle, *The Revelation of St. John*, 17:39. Caird, *Revelation*, 44–45.

[49] Caird, *Revelation*, 44–45.

[50] Aune, *Rev 1–5*, 197.

[51] Zahn, Die Offenbarung Des Johannes, 1:286ff.

[52] Ramsay, Letters to Seven Churches, 341.

[53] Bernhard Weiss, *Die Johannes-Apokalypse: textkritische Untersuchungen und Textherstellung*, TU, 7.1 (Berlin: Hinrichs, 1904), 162; Bruce M. Metzger, *A Textual Commentary on the Greek New Testament*, 2nd ed. (Stuttgart, Germany: Deutsche Bibelgesellschaft, 2002), 664.

[54] Edward Carus Selwyn, *The Christian Prophets and the Prophetic Apocalypse* (New York, N.Y.: MacMillan, 2009), 123 n.1.

[55] Hemer, Letters to the Seven Churches, 250 n. 50.

[56] Emil Schürer, *Die Prophetin Isabel in Thyatira, Offen. Joh., II, 20, 11.*, ed. A. Von Harnack, Theologische Abhandlungen: Carl von Weizsäcker Zu Seinem Siebzigsten Geburtstage (Freiburg, Germany: Mohr Siebeck, 1892), 39–58.

this theory is "as yet a mere tantalising possibility,"[57] while Charles and Beckwith reject it, because the Sibylline priestess would not be a church member.[58] Hemer, on the other hand, argued that "this view deserves consideration."[59] The immoral practices of the trade-guilds are identified with some in the church of Thyatira who were committing adultery (2:22),[60] and as such were to experience death (spiritual and physical), like the Corinthian Christians who were also involved in immorality (1 Cor 11:30).

The presence of female prophets and women in religious leadership in Asia Minor in the first century is attested by several documented cases in the imperial cult, and in reports of women issuing oracles from the gods.[61] One inscription (*IJO* 2:187–92) testifies to a woman serving as "head of the synagogue," (ἀρχισυνάγωγος, *archisynagōgos*). Other Jewish women are described in inscriptions as "priestess" (ἱέρισσα, *herissa*), "mother of the synagogue" (μήτηρ συναγωγῆς, *metēr synagōgēs*), "elder" (πρεσβυτέρα, *presbutera*), and "leader" (προστάτης, *prostatēs* and ἀρχήγισσα, *archēgissa*).[62] Although there is little evidence of women prophesying in first century Judaism, the practice was present in the OT with Miriam (Exod 15:20), Deborah (Judg 4:4), Isaiah's wife (Isa 8:3), and Huldah[63] functioning as prophets. Female prophets are also documented in the NT period, such as Anna (Luke 2:36), Philip's daughters (Acts 21:9), certain women at Corinth (1 Cor 11:5), and Ammia of Philadelphia in Asia (Eusebius *Hist. eccl.* 5.17.3–4).[64] Aune suggests that Jezebel may have been a patroness[65] of one of the house churches in Thyatira, coming into conflict with other leaders over accommodation with the eating of meat offered to idols.[66] The suzerain's difficulty was not with women in religious leadership, but with the illegitimate content of her teaching.

On the charge of sexual immorality, Aune suggests that this should be taken figuratively as such groundless slander was customarily made by opponents (i.e., against the female followers of Dionysus).[67] This charge was shown to be groundless by eyewitnesses; Euripides *Bacch.* 686–87).[68] Koester suggests that "immoral (πορνεύω, *porneuō*) is a metaphor for religious infidelity."[69]

---

[57] Ramsay, *Letters: Updated*, 323.
[58] Charles, *Revelation*, 1:70; Beckwith, *Apocalypse*, 466.
[59] Hemer, Letters to the Seven Churches, 117.
[60] Barclay, *Letters*, 61; Hendriksen, *Conquerors*, 71.
[61] Aune, Prophecy in Early Christianity and the Ancient Mediterranean World, 28; Hoz, Die Lydischen, 90.
[62] Shaye J. D. Cohen, "Women in the Synagogues of Antiquity," *Conservative Judaism* 34 (1980): 25–26.
[63] 2 Kgs 22:14; 2 Chr 34:22; see also Noadiah in Neh 6:14.
[64] M. Eugene Boring, *The Continuing Voice of Jesus: Christian Prophecy and the Gospel Tradition* (Louisville, Ky.: Westminster/John Knox, 1991), 120–22.
[65] Ramsay MacMullen, "Women in Public in the Roman Empire," *Historia* 29 (1980): 211; E. Lyding Will, "Women's Roles in Antiquity: New Archeological Views," *Science Digest*, March 1980, 35–39.
[66] Aune, *Rev 1–5*, 191–94, 203.
[67] Euripides *Bacch.* 222–23, 237–38, 260–61, 353–54, 487, 957–58.
[68] Aune, *Rev 1–5*, 204; Luke Timothy Johnson, "The New Testament's AntiJewish Slander and the Conventions of Ancient Polemic," *JBL* 108 (1989): 419–41.
[69] Koester, *Revelation*, 299.

On the charge of eating meat offered to idols,[70] it is well documented in the first century that meat that had been offered to idols, and blood, had to be avoided by Christians at all costs.[71] The Didache instructed "keep strictly away from meat sacrificed to idols, for it involves the worship of dead gods" (*Did.* 6:3 [Lightfoot]). Paul had to deal with a similar problem in 1 Corinthians 8, although the Christians in Thyatira would have had more pressure from the trade guilds[72] to conform, which would involve attending the guild banquets,[73] where they would be required to eat meat that had been sacrificed to an idol, and stay for meetings which sometimes degenerated into sexual immorality. Refusal to participate in their respective trade guild may have led to poverty and financial ruin (2:9).[74] Apparently the prophetess Jezebel was counselling the Christians in the church that compromise was better than losing one's job.[75]

THE SUZERAIN KNOWS THAT JEZEBEL REFUSES TO REPENT—2:21

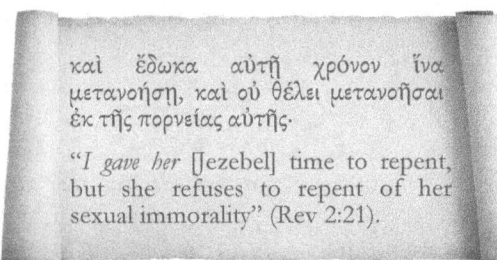

καὶ ἔδωκα αὐτῇ χρόνον ἵνα μετανοήσῃ, καὶ οὐ θέλει μετανοῆσαι ἐκ τῆς πορνείας αὐτῆς·

"I gave her [Jezebel] time to repent, but she refuses to repent of her sexual immorality" (Rev 2:21).

The suzerain has a past history with Jezebel and had called her to repentance for her behavior, possibly through the prophetic ministry of John or one of his associates. The suzerain also knows that Jezebel had refused to repent and calls her again to repentance.[76] The Dead Sea Scrolls have a relevant passage, based on Deut 18:18–19, that deals with calling prophets to account. It states: "and it will happen that the man who does not listen to my words, that the prophet will speak in my name, I shall require a reckoning from him" (4Q175.5–8 [Martínez]).[77]

The suzerain often withholds judgment in order that the vassal has time to repent,[78] but if no response is received, judgment follows. Like Jezebel, humanity in Revelation 9:21 also refuse

---

[70] On the parallel between prophecy in Deut 13:1–11 and eating sacrificed meat see Philo *Spec.* 1.315–17; 11Q19 44:18–20. Peder Borgen, *Paul Preaches Circumcision and Pleases Men* (Trondheim: TAPIR, 1983), 73; *Philo, John and Paul: New Perspectives on Judaism and Early Christianity* (Atlanta, Ga.: Scholars Press, 1987), 226; Torrey Seland, *Jewish Vigilantism in the First Centry C.E.: A Study of Selected Texts in Philo and Luke on Jewish Vigilante Reactions against Nonconformers to the Torah* (Trondheim: Doctor Artium Dissertation, 1990), 73–80, 98–107, 123–25, 136–37, 147–53.

[71] Arnold Ehrhardt, *The Framework of the New Testament Stories* (Harvard University Press, 1964), 276–90; Barrett, "Things Sacrificed to Idols," 138–53.

[72] Magie, *Roman Rule in Asia Minor*, 1:48; 2:812 n. 78; Jones, *Greek City*, 83; Hemer, "Unto the Angels of the Churches," 110.

[73] Aune, Revelation 6–16, 768.

[74] Aune, *Rev 1–5*, 161; Charles, *Revelation*, 1:56; Caird, *Revelation*, 35; Hemer, *Letters to the Seven Churches*, 68; Osborne, *Revelation*, 151–52.

[75] Morris, *Revelation*, 74–75.

[76] See also Jer 8:6; Acts 8:22; Heb 6:1; *1 Clem.* 8:3; Hermas *Man.* 3.3; *Sim.* 8.6.6; *Ep. Arist.* 188.

[77] Florentino García Martínez and W. G. E. Watson, *The Dead Sea Scrolls Translated: The Qumran Texts in English*, 2nd ed. (Leiden: Brill Academic, 1997), 137.

[78] Wis 12:10; Rom 2:4; 2 Pet 3:9; Plutarch *Mor.* 348–68.

to repent (μετανόησον, *metanoēson*) for their sins of murder, sorcery, sexual immorality (πορνεία, *porneia*) and theft. When sexual immorality is to be understood literally, it normally appears as part of a list of vices.[79] If not part of a vice list, it is probably being used metaphorically.[80]

Since both Jezebel and those participating with her were members of the church, they were guilty of adultery twice over: sexual and spiritual adultery. The piercing eyes and trampling feet of the suzerain come to her in the full strength of the shining sun (1:16), infinitely more terrible than the sun-god, Apollo, worshiped at Thyatira (see Figs. 82, 86).[81] The judgment to follow can also be understood in a physical and spiritual sense. It appears that Jezebel and others did not repent, as Thyatira became a center of the Montanist movement in which prophetesses had significant leadership and influence in the church (Epiphanius *Pan*. 51.33.1–3).

SANCTIONS—2:22-23

The prophetic sanctions, where the vassal is cursed (malediction) for disobedience (dishonors the treaty), and blessed (benedictions) for obedience to the stated stipulations (honors the treaty), is a central element of the ANEVT structure.[82] For the judgment against OT false prophets see Deuteronomy 13:5–11.[83] For Thyatira, several maledictions await those who do not repent,[84] but a blessing is promised for those who are overcomers.

THE CURSE OF THROWN ON A SICKBED—2:22A

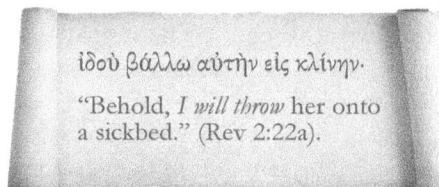
ἰδοὺ βάλλω αὐτὴν εἰς κλίνην·
"Behold, *I will throw* her onto a sickbed." (Rev 2:22a).

Jezebel would know the full force of the suzerain's judgment in the malediction of sickness. The bed (κλίνη, *klinē*, "couch", Eng. "recline"; see Fig. 91, 170) of suffering (2:22; Exod 21:18) she was to experience for her (ἔργων αὐτῆς, *ergōn autes*, not their) works of immorality is contrasted with the bed of adultery (Sir 23:18) and couch (κλίνη, *klinē*) of the banquet hall[85] (see Fig. 170). Farrer comments, that "the punishment fits the crime—she who profaned the bed of love is pinned to the bed of

---

[79] πορνεία, *porneia* in 9:21; πόρνος *pornos* in 21:8; 22:15.

[80] πορνεία, *porneia* in 14:8; 17:2, 4; 18:3; 19:2; πορνή, *pornē* in 17:1, 5, 15, 16; 19:2; πορνεύειν, *porneuein* in 17:2; 18:3, 9.

[81] Wilcock, *Heaven Opened*, 51.

[82] See chapter 3, *Sanctions*.

[83] See also 4Q375 1.4–5; 11Q19 54.10–15; 61:1–2; 4Q158 frag. 6, line 8; Philo *Spec*. 1.315–17.

[84] See also 18:6; 20:12, 13; 22:12; Pss 27:4; 61:1–3; 86:2; Prov 24:12; Sir 16:12, 14; *Pss. Sol*. 2:16, 34; 17:8; Jer 27:9; Lam 3:64; Rom 2:6; 2 Cor 11:15; 2 Tim 4:14; Ign. *Magn*. 11:3; *2 Clem*. 17:4. Thimmes describes them as "two violent threats." "Women Reading Women," 136.

[85] *NewDocs* 1:5; 2:28; P.Oxy. 3693; Ludwig Koenen, "Eine Einladung Zur Kline Des Sarapis," *ZPE* 1 (1967): 121–26 (pl. 2); David Gill, "Trapezomata: A Neglected Aspect of Greek Sacrifice," *HTR* 67, no. 2 (1974): 117–37; E. Will, "Banquets et salles de banquet dans le cultes de la Grece et de l'Empire romain," in *Mélanges d'histoire ancienne et d'archéologie offerts à Paul Collart*, ed. Pierre Ducrey (Lausanne, Switzerland: Bibliothèque historique vaudoise, 1976), 353–62; J. Frank Gilliam, "Invitations to the Kline of Sarapis," in *Collectanea Papyrologica: Texts published in honor of H. C. Youtie*, ed. A. E. Hanson, vol. 1, Papyrologische Texte und Abhandlungen (Bonn: Habelt, 1976), 1:315–24.

sickness."[86] Jezebel's couch of pleasures would be turned into a bed of suffering, if she did not repent. Ancient funerary monuments often depicted the deceased lying on a *klinē* as pictured at a banquet (see Fig. 91).[87] The phrase "put to bed" is a Hebrew idiom that means to punish someone with various types of sickness.[88] Koester suggests that Jezebel was teaching that "it is acceptable to recline on a bed or couch at meals honoring other deities, which is like going to bed in a kind of religious adultery, so the judgment is to be put to bed with illness."[89]

91. Votive relief showing a funerary banquet. The dead man is shown as a heroized man lying on a *klinē*, holding a *"kylix"* in his hand. *ca.* 470–460 AD. Istanbul Archaeological Museum (Inv. No. 1947).

However, the suzerain persistently holds out the olive branch of blessing if she would repent, a theme found throughout the book of Revelation (1:3; 1:13; 1:15; 1:9; 2:6; 2:7).

THE CURSE OF GREAT TRIBULATION—2:22B

καὶ τοὺς μοιχεύοντας μετ' αὐτῆς εἰς θλῖψιν μεγάλην, ἐὰν μὴ μετανοήσωσιν ἐκ τῶν ἔργων αὐτῆς·

"and those who commit adultery with her *I will throw* into great tribulation, unless they repent of her works." (Rev 2:22b)

Although Jezebel had been granted a season for repentance which had passed and now faced the curse of sickness (2:21), her followers were now given an opportunity to repent of her behavior or face the curse of great tribulation (θλῖψιν μεγάλην, *thlipsin megalēn;* see also 17:2; 18:3). Adultery in a sexual sense was a violation of a marriage covenant.[90] The sanction in the OT for adultery varied from death (Deut 22:22; Lev

---

[86] Farrer, *Revelation*, 77.

[87] Katherine M. D. Dunbabin, *The Roman Banquet: Images of Conviviality* (Cambridge, U.K.: Cambridge University Press, 2010), 103–40.

[88] See Exod 21:18; 1 Macc 1:5; Jdt 8:3; see also 2 Kgs 1:4; Ps 41:3; Matt 9:2. Charles, *Revelation*, 1:71–72; Lawrence H. Schiffman and M. D. Swartz, *Hebrew and Aramaic Incantation Texts from the Cairo Genizah: Selected Texts from Taylor-Schechter Box K1* (Sheffield, U.K.: Sheffield Academic Press, 1992), 85, 88.

[89] Koester, *Revelation*, 299; Greg Carey, *Elusive Apocalypse: Reading Authority in the Revelation to John*, StABH (Macon, Ga.: Mercer University Press, 1999), 158.

[90] Exod 20:14; Num 5:11–31; Deut 5:18; Josephus *Ag. Ap.* 2.215. Michael Fishbane, "Accusations of Adultery: A Study of Law and Scribal Practices in Num 5:11–31," *HUCA* 45 (1974): 25–45; H. McKeating, "Sanctions Against Adultery in Ancient Israelite Society, with Some Reflections on Methodology in the Study of Old Testament Ethics," *JSOT* 11 (1979): 57–72; J. T. Mueller, "Adultery," ed. Walter A. Elwell, *EDT*, Baker Reference Library (Grand Rapids, Mich.: Baker Academic, May 1, 2001), 26–27.

20:10), to being cut off from the people (Lev 18:29). Idolatry, covetousness, and apostasy are also spoken of as spiritual adultery.[91]

In the context of the message to Thyatira, "fornication" (μοιχεύοντας, *moicheuontas*) is used metaphorically to describe the violation of the covenant relationship with the suzerain through idolatry and apostasy.[92] Aune argues that the adultery here is metaphorical "for why should those who commit fornication with 'Jezebel' repent of her behavior?"[93]

THE CURSE OF DEAD CHILDREN—2:23A

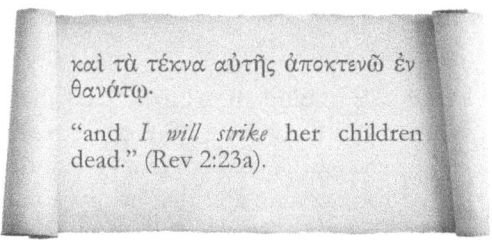

καὶ τὰ τέκνα αὐτῆς ἀποκτενῶ ἐν θανάτῳ·

"and *I will strike* her children dead." (Rev 2:23a).

There is some speculation as to who the children (τέκνα, *tekna*) of the adulteress Jezebel are. Several possibilities present themselves.

1. **Same group:** Some suggest that the adulterers and the children are the same group, with the adulterers participating in Jezebel's sin and the children accepting her teaching.[94]

2. **Literal children:** Hoeksema and Beckwith see a reference to her literal children.[95] This may be supported by a sixth cent. AD curse that calls upon God and angels to "strike down Philadelphia; and her children."[96] But while this cannot be ruled out, it seems less likely.

3. **Spiritual children:** The children are spiritual offspring of Jezebel.[97] In the first cent. Papylus, a Christian resident of Thyatira, was brought before the Roman proconsul who asked Papylus if he had children (τέκνα ἔχεις, *tekna echeis*). Papylus answered that he did, but upon further questioning confessed that they were spiritual children "in the Lord" (*Mart. Carp.* 34 [Musurillo]).

4. **Christian followers:** Identifying believers as "children" in the NT is well documented.[98] The Christians in the church who were following Jezebel, participating in her practices and flirting

---

[91] Jer 3:6, 8, 9; Ezek 16:32; Hos 1:2:3.
[92] Jer 3:9; Mark 8:38; Jas 4:4; Hermas *Man.* 4.1.9. Koester, *Revelation*, 299.
[93] Aune, *Rev 1–5*, 205.
[94] Beasley-Murray, *Revelation*, NCB, 91; Thomas, *Rev 1–7*, 222; Beale, *Rev*, 264; Johnson, *Triumph of the Lamb*, 81 n.23.
[95] Hoeksema, *Behold, He Cometh!*, op. cit.; Beckwith, *Apocalypse*, 467.
[96] Robert Walter Daniel and Franco Maltomini, *Supplementum Magicum*, Papyrologica Coloniensia 16 (Oppladen: Westdeutscher, 1990), 2:61, lines 1–3.
[97] Mounce, *Revelation*, 88; Kistemaker, *Revelation*, 139; Osborne, *Revelation*, 160; Smalley, *Revelation*, 75.
[98] 1 Cor 4:14, 17; Gal 4:19; Phlm 10; see also 1 Tim 1:2; 2 Tim 1:2; Titus 1:4; 2 John 1, 4; 3 John 4.

with her teachings.[99] However, Jezebel's followers seem to have been already dealt with in 22b, leaving her children as a third party.[100]

5. **Non-Christian disciples:** The heretical disciples of her intimate prophetic circle (see Isa 8:18; Amos 7:14) who were committed to her teachings.[101]

The curse of death (θάνατος, *thanatos*) or more likely pestilence, plague or sickness (θάνατος, translated 35 times in the LXX for pestilence) is threatened on the children of Jezebel (6:8; 18:8; Ezek 33:27).

THE CURSE OF RECEIVING ACCORDING TO THEIR WORKS—2:23B

καὶ γνώσονται πᾶσαι αἱ ἐκκλησίαι ὅτι ἐγώ εἰμι ὁ ἐραυνῶν νεφροὺς καὶ καρδίας, καὶ δώσω ὑμῖν ἑκάστῳ κατὰ τὰ ἔργα ὑμῶν.

"And all the churches *will know* that I am he who searches mind and heart, and *I will give* to each of you [pl.] according to your works." (Rev 2:23b)

The curse will remind the churches of the omniscience (lit. searcher of νεφροὺς καὶ καρδίας, *nephrous kai kardias*, "kidneys[102] and hearts") of the suzerain and that he gives to each according to their works.[103] This is a clear allusion to a verse in Jeremiah where it states: "I am the Lord who examines hearts and tests minds to give to each according to his ways and according to the fruits of his doings" (Jer 17:10 LXX). Originally in Jeremiah the speaker was Yahweh, but now the suzerain who speaks is Christ, who is attributed with the same attributes of omniscience as Yahweh.[104] Numerous passages in Jewish and Christian sources testify to the fact that God knows the mind and hearts of individuals.[105]

---

[99] Ian Boxall, *The Revelation of Saint John*, BNTC 19 (Peabody, Mass.: Hendrickson, 2006), 65.

[100] Koester, *Revelation*, 299–300.

[101] Sweet, *Revelation*, 91; Krodel, *Revelation*, 126; Barclay, *Letters*, 53; Caird, *Revelation*, 44; Aune, *Rev 1–5*, 206; Michaels, *Revelation*, 79; Keener, *Revelation*, 135; Fenton John Anthony Hort, *The Apocalypse of St. John I-III: The Greek Text with Introduction, Commentary, and Additional Notes* (London, U.K.: MacMillan & Co., 1908), 30; Johannes Lähnemann, "Die sieben Sendschreiben der Johannes-Apokalypse: Dokumente für die Konfrontation des frühen Christentums mit hellenistisch/römischer Kultur und Religion in Kleinasien," in *Studien Zur Religion Und Kultur Kleinasiens*, ed. S. Sahin, E. Schwertheim, and J. Wagner, Festschrift Fur Friedrich Karl Dorner Zum 65 (Leiden: Brill Academic Pub, 1997), 532 n. 30.

[102] The ancients believed that the kidney's (כליה *kilyah;* νεφρός, *nephros*) were the seat of the emotions.Carl Friedrich Keil and Franz Delitzsch, *The Pentateuch*, trans. James Martin (Edinburgh, U.K.: T&T Clark, 1835), 306 op cit. Lev 4:11–12.

[103] See also 20:13; 22:12; Ps 62:12 (LXX 61:13); Prov 24:12.

[104] See also Matt 9:4; John 2:25; 4:29, 39; 16:30; 18:4; 21:17.

[105] 1 Sam 16:7; 2 Sam 14:20; 1 Kgs 8:39; 1 Chr 28:9; 2 Chr 6:30; Pss 28:4; 62:12; 44:21; 139:1–6, 23; Prov 24:12; Wis 7:1; Sir 35:24; 42:18–19; Sus 42; Bar 3:32; 2 Macc 9:5; *2 Bar.* 83:2–3; *Pss. Sol.* 2:34–35; Matt 6:4, 6, 18; Acts 1:24; 15:8; Rom 2:16; 1 Cor 4:5; 14:25; 2 Tim 4:14; 1 Pet 1:17; Heb 4:12–13; Ign. *Phld.* 7:1; *Teach. Silv.* 116.3; Josephus *J.W.* 5.413; Philo *Opif.* 69; *Somn.* 1.87; *PGM* 4.3046–47.

"I will give to each according to his works" is a proverbial saying demonstrating the principle of *lex talionis* (i.e., "the law of retaliation"), which was ancient roots. *Lex talionis* is a major similarity between the code of Hammurabi and the Hebrew law code.[106] The Code of Hammurabi states: "If a man destroys the eye of another man, they shall destroy his eye" (*Hamm.* §196 [Harper]). Rather than encouraging revenge, this law safeguarded excessive inequity by maintaining that the punishment must fit the crime. An arm or leg could not be excised for the loss of an eye. Also, the death penalty was prescribed on those who committed adultery.[107]

Jesus demonstrated his ability to know the hearts and minds of those around him during his earthly ministry (Matt 9:4; John 2:25) and Revelation reveals that the exalted Christ will judge people before the final judgment (Rom 2:16) based on their works (2:18, 23). While all people will be judged according to their works and given the appropriate rewards, salvation will be by grace for those written in the book of life (20:11–15).

ETHICAL STIPULATIONS—2:24–25

ὑμῖν δὲ λέγω τοῖς λοιποῖς τοῖς ἐν Θυατείροις, ὅσοι οὐκ ἔχουσιν τὴν διδαχὴν ταύτην, οἵτινες οὐκ ἔγνωσαν τὰ βαθέα τοῦ σατανᾶ,

"But to the rest of you in Thyatira, who do not hold this teaching, who have not learned what some call the deep things of Satan," (Rev 2:24a)

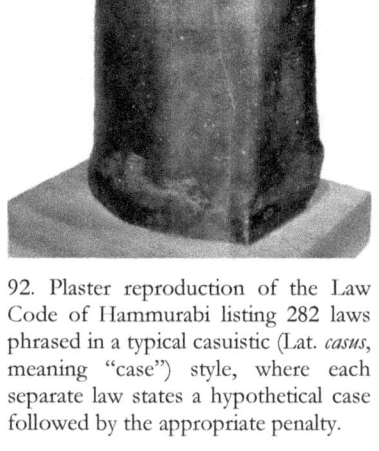

92. Plaster reproduction of the Law Code of Hammurabi listing 282 laws phrased in a typical casuistic (Lat. *casus*, meaning "case") style, where each separate law states a hypothetical case followed by the appropriate penalty.

Within the ANEVT context, ethical stipulations set forth the covenant "obligations[108] imposed upon and accepted by the vassal."[109] The dominant theme of the ANEVT stipulations was the vassal's loyalty and faithfulness, with all controversies to be settled by the suzerain.[110] Loyalty to the suzerain would

---

[106] Exod 21:22–25; Lev 20:10; 24:19–21; Deut 19:16–21; 22:22.

[107] Hammurabi's code §129–130; Lev 20:10; Deut 22:22.

[108] The vassal-treaties of Esarhaddon list thirty-three stipulations, which follow the divine witnesses, and are to be kept by the vassal. Parpola and Watanabe, *Neo-Assyrian Treaties*, nos. 1–6, 46–57; Wiseman, "Vassal-Treaties," 23–24.

[109] Mendenhall, "Covenant Forms," 59; "Covenant," 1:714; Shea, "Covenantal Form," 72; Bright, *Covenant and Promise*, 37; Thompson, "Near Eastern Suzerain-Vassal," 4; McCarthy, *Treaty and Covenant*, 51 n.3.

[110] Thompson, *ANE Treaties*, 16.

ensure protection and avoid punishment and possible attack.[111] The stipulations within the message to Thyatira are identified by the imperative verbs, and presented in terms of the commands "do not lay hold" and "hold fast."

The suzerain now turns his attention to those vassals who have not followed Jezebel's teaching (called by some the "deep things of Satan"). Aune suggests that the literary device used to speak to the angels of the churches is broken at this point to speak to the church at large.[112] Pollard argues that since this is the one time the church is addressed universally in the use of λοιπός (*loipos*, "rest", 2:24a), it supports the idea that Thyatira is the center of the chiastic (repetition) structure of the messages.[113] However, as Pollard admits, Homcy provides three arguments why the seven churches are representative of the entire historical church: "seven is the number of completeness; the refrain to each church is 'He who has an ear, let him hear'; and experience tells us that the kind of issues addressed are found in the church throughout all ages."[114] However, "the rest of you" (plural pronoun ὑμῖν, *hymin*, you) is referring to the remnant within the church of Thyatira who are not involved with Jezebel, with the vassals being called to hold fast their loyalty to the suzerain regardless of which church they attend.

Some in the congregation have referred to the teaching of Jezebel as "deep things" (βαθέα, *bathea*, 2:24a) and several possibilities are available for who these people might be. They might be the faithful followers within the church, or John himself, who are mockingly referring to the claims of the heretics as "deep things", though really these things belong to Satan (i.e., Synagogue of Satan, 2:9; 3:9).[115] Paul also used the phrase, claiming that the Spirit searches the "deep things of God" (1 Cor 2:10).[116] Paul dealt with the issue of eating meat offered to idols and spoke of a deep spiritual knowledge that could discern that idols were nothing (1 Cor 8:1–6).

Another possibility is that Jezebel and her disciples may be arguing that they have the special gnostic knowledge (mysteries)[117] of the "deep things" of Satan[118] and are able to eat meat offered to idols.[119] The reference to the "deep things" of Satan could be an early veiled

---

[111] Lucas argues for the gracious nature of the stipulations as "the vassal keeps the stipulations of the covenant not to earn favour but as a response of gratitude for the overlord's benefactions." Lucas, "Covenant, Treaty, and Prophecy," 23. However, Lucas misses the element of threat and obligation in his comments.

[112] Aune, *Rev 1–5*, 207.

[113] Pollard, "The Function of Loipos in Contexts of Judgment and Salvation in the Book of Revelation"; "The Function of Λοιπός in the Letter to Thyatira," *AUSS* 46, no. 1 (2008): 45–50.

[114] Pollard, "The Function of Λοιπός in the Letter to Thyatira," 48 n.15; Homcy, "To Him Who Overcomes," 194.

[115] Osborne, *Revelation*, 162; Roloff, *Revelation*, 55; Smalley, *Revelation*, 76; Giesen and Eckert, *Die Offenbarung des Johannes*, op. cit.

[116] See also Rom 11:33; see also *T. Job* 37:6; Dan 2:22; *2 Bar.* 14:8.

[117] Prigent, *Apocalypse*, 151 n.9; Aune, *Rev 1–5*, 207.

[118] *Acts Thom.* 143; Hippolytus *Haer.* 5.6.4; 6.30.7; *1 Clem.* 40:1; Irenaeus *Haer.* 2.22.1.

[119] Bousset, Die Offenbarung Johannis, op. cit.; Satake, Gemeindeordnung, op. cit.; Mounce, Revelation, 89; Morris, Revelation of St. John, 76.

reference to the secret knowledge of the gnostics, who believed in the liberty to sin in the body, holding that it would not affect their spiritual state (see also 1 Cor 6:12–18).[120] Koester disagrees, claiming that the "Gnostic sources come from the second and third centuries CE."[121] Krodel suggests that there may be a bit of irony here in that those who know the "deep things of Satan" are mocked for their gnostic claims of knowing the "deep things of God."[122]

FIRST IMPERATIVE: NO OTHER BURDENS—2:24B

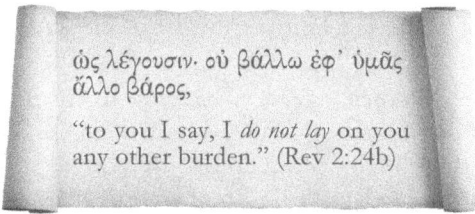

ὡς λέγουσιν· οὐ βάλλω ἐφ' ὑμᾶς ἄλλο βάρος,

"to you I say, I *do not lay* on you any other burden." (Rev 2:24b)

This phrase is reminiscent of the Apostolic Decree of the Jerusalem Council where Luke states: "For it has seemed good to the Holy Spirit and to us to lay on you no greater burden than these requirements: that you abstain from what has been sacrificed to idols, and from blood, and from what has been strangled, and from sexual immorality" (Acts 15:28–29; see also Lev 17–18). Alford states, "to my mind the allusion to the apostolic decree is too clear and prominent to allow of any other meaning coming into question."[123] While some commentators believe that John had the Apostolic Decree in mind,[124] others believe that they just shared similar concerns.[125]

The suzerain will not impose on them any other burden than to abstain from meat sacrifices to idols and from sexual immorality (2:22b). The use of "burden" indicates the cost to the vassal of abiding by the stipulation.

SECOND IMPERATIVE: HOLD FAST TO WHAT YOU HAVE—2:25

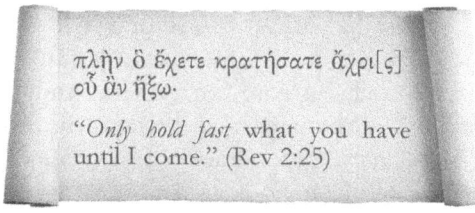

πλὴν ὃ ἔχετε κρατήσατε ἄχρι[ς] οὗ ἂν ἥξω.

"*Only hold fast* what you have until I come." (Rev 2:25)

The suzerain exhorts the vassals at Thyatira to hold fast (κρατήσατε, *kratēsate*, lit. "take a firm grip on") to what they have until his second coming. The theme of the Parousia (second coming) is also combined with holding fast to what you have (κράτει ὃ ἔχεις, *kratei ho echeis*) in the message to Philadelphia. The faithful remnant in the church at Thyatira are to keep a firm grip on resisting the idolatry of Jezebel and persevere in the works of love, faith, and service (2:19).[126] The coming that is mentioned here is not likely the immediate

---

[120] Wall, *Revelation*, 78–79; Barclay, *Letters*, 66.
[121] Koester, *Revelation*, 301.
[122] Krodel, *Revelation*, 118.
[123] Alford, *Revelation*, 4:577.
[124] Bousset, *Die Offenbarung Johannis*, 221; Zahn, *Die Offenbarung Des Johannes*, 1:292–93; Charles, *Revelation*, 1:74; Prigent, *Apocalypse*, 175; Beale, *Rev*, 265.
[125] Giesen and Eckert, *Die Offenbarung des Johannes*, op. cit.; Harrington, *Revelation*, 66; Aune, *Rev 1–5*, 208.
[126] Alford, *Revelation*, 4:577.

visit to judge Jezebel and others (2:5, 16; 3:3), but rather the second coming (i.e., the *Parousia* or end, 2:26).[127]

SANCTIONS: BLESSING—2:26–28

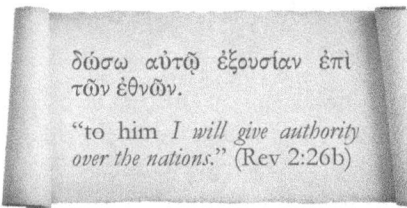

Καὶ ὁ νικῶν καὶ ὁ τηρῶν ἄχρι τέλους τὰ ἔργα μου

"The one who conquers and who keeps my works until the end," (Rev 2:26–28)

The structure moves from ethical stipulations and legal requirements to the sanctions set out for obedience or disobedience. A standard characteristic of the ANEVT is the regularity of the list of blessings and curses (see chapter 1, *Stipulations*).

All seven churches receive a blessing from the suzerain for faithfulness to the stipulations, and described as those who conquer or overcome (τῷ νικῶντι, *tō nikōnti*) and keep his works (i.e., love, faithfulness, and truth; 2:23b). Conquering is a common Johannine athletic and military metaphor[128] in a work that promises the victory of the suzerain and the vassal over their enemies (2:7, 17, 26; 3:5 3.5; 5:5; 12:11; 17:14; 21:7). The vassals are to keep the suzerain's works "until the end" (ἄχρι τέλους, *achri telous*) of their lives or Christ's second coming. The overcomers in Thyatira are promised authority to rule "over the nations" (see also Ps 2:9) with an iron rule, and given the "morning Star" (2:26–28).

THE BLESSING OF AUTHORITY OVER THE NATIONS—2:26B

δώσω αὐτῷ ἐξουσίαν ἐπὶ τῶν ἐθνῶν.

"to him *I will give authority over the nations.*" (Rev 2:26b)

The blessing for the overcomer in Thyatira (αὐτῷ, *autō*, lit. "him") is described as authority over the nations (ἐθνῶν, *ethnōn*, 23 times in Revelation[129]), which has a close similarity with the LXX of Psalm 2:8–9, understood in the early church as a Messianic Psalm.[130] The anointed suzerain tells his son: "Ask of me, and I will make the nations your heritage, and the ends of the earth your possession" (Ps 2:8) This is fulfilled in the Messianic enthronement in Revelation chapter 12: "She gave birth to a male child, one who is to rule all the nations with a rod of iron, but her child was caught up to God and to his throne" (ver. 9). Here the authority over the nations is granted to the vassals "even as I myself have received authority from my Father" (2:27; ὡς κἀγὼ εἴληφα παρὰ τοῦ πατρός μου, *hōs kagō eilēpha para tou Patros mou*).

The idea of Christians sharing authority with the Messianic suzerain is also found in the Odes of Solomon: "And He gave me the sceptre of His power, that I might subdue the devices of the Gentiles, and humble the power of the mighty" (*Odes Sol.* 29:8 [Charlesworth]). The

---

[127] Koester, *Revelation*, 301.
[128] John 16:33; 1 John 2:13–14; 4:4; 5:4–5.
[129] Rev 2:26; 11:2, 18; 12:5; 14:8; 15:3–4; 16:19; 18:3, 23; 19:15; 20:3, 8; 21:24, 26; 22:2.
[130] Acts 13:33; Heb 1:5; 5:5; Justin *Dial.* 61.6; 88.8; 122.6. Barnabas Lindars, *New Testament Apologetic: The Doctrinal Significance of the Old Testament Quotations* (London, U.K.: SCM, 1973), 139–44.

covenant promise and heir to David's throne expressed in "I will be his God and he will be my son" (2 Sam 7:14) is promised to those who conquer.[131] Witetschek suggests that the allusion is not Messianic, but only applies to the conquerors,[132] but is shown to be shared between the suzerain and the vassals.[133] The Messianic suzerain is also spoken of possessing authority (ἐξουσία, *exousia*, 12:10) in the conquest of Satan (12:10), but for a time the authority (ἐξουσία, *exousia*) over "every tribe and people and language and nation" is given to the Beast in Revelation 13:7.

THE BLESSING OF AN IRON RULE—2:27

> καὶ ποιμανεῖ αὐτοὺς ἐν ῥάβδῳ σιδηρᾷ ὡς τὰ σκεύη τὰ κεραμικὰ συντρίβεται, ὡς κἀγὼ εἴληφα παρὰ τοῦ πατρός μου.
>
> "and he will rule them with a rod of iron, as when earthen pots are broken in pieces, even as I myself have received authority from my Father." (Rev 2:27)

Christ, the suzerain, will share his Messianic rule with the conquering vassals.[134] This verse continues the allusions in the Messianic Psalm where it states "You shall break (LXX rule) them with a rod of iron and dash them in pieces like a potter's vessel" (2:9).[135] ποιμαίνειν (*poimainein*; Ps 2:9 = MT רעע, *rʿʿ*, "break in pieces"; LXX תרעם *trʿm*, "rule"; רעה *rʿh*, "to shepherd"; *Pss. Sol.* 17:23) translated here as "rule" (following the LXX) can literally mean "to feed, to tend a flock, keep sheep."[136] The shepherd imagery can also be identified with the "scepter" of iron that is closely related to a shepherd's "staff" or "crook" (Assy. *ḫaṭṭu* can mean both a ruler's scepter and a shepherd's staff; see Fig. 154 and Code of Hammurabi relief Fig. 92).[137]

However, Aune notes that a shepherding "meaning is problematic, since the context strongly suggests that it has a negative meaning"[138] and the shepherd imagery conveys something gentle and kind. While the image of God as shepherd who uses a staff is well attested

---

[131] Rev 21:7; cf. Ps 89:23; 2 Sam 7:11–14; Amos 9:11; 4Q174 1.1.1–13. Roloff, *Revelation*, 56; Aune, *Rev 1–5*, 210; Beale, *Rev*, 266; Osborne, *Revelation*, 166–67; Mounce, *What Are We Waiting For?*, 90; Smalley, *Revelation*, 77–78.

[132] Stephen Witetschek, "Der Lieblingspsalm Des Sehers: Die Verwendung von Ps 2 in Der Johannesapokalypse," in *The Septuagint and Messianism*, ed. Michael Anthony Knibb, BETL 195 (Leuven, Belgium: Leuven University Press, 2006), 487–502.

[133] Tze-Ming Quek, "'I Will Give Authority over the Nations': Psalm 2.8–9 in Revelation 2.26–27," in *Early Christian Literature and Intertextuality: Exegetical Studies*, ed. Craig A. Evans and H. Daniel Zacharias, vol. 2 (New York, N.Y.: T&T Clark, 2009), 175–87.

[134] Ibid., 187.

[135] See also Rev 12:5; 19:15; *Pss. Sol.* 17:23–24; 1QSa 2:11–12.

[136] Thayer, GELNT §4310.

[137] A. Leo Oppenheim et al., eds., *The Assyrian Dictionary of the Oriental Institute of the University of Chicago: H [Het]*, vol. 6 (Chicago, Ill.: University Of Chicago Press, 1956), 6:153–55.

[138] Aune, *Rev 1–5*, 210.

in the OT,[139] the scepter is usually associated with divine justice.[140] Morris points out that shepherds were actually autocrats. He observes that the shepherd's

> power over his flock was absolute, and it is this aspect of the shepherd's life that is in view. Shepherding with an iron rod might denote no more than strength or firmness were it not linked with breaking to pieces like clay vessels (cf. Ps 2:9; Jer 51:20).[141]

The comparative image of dashing pottery to pieces and ruling with an iron scepter or staff is again reminiscent of Psalm 2. Wells suggests that these two images should be understood against the background of the products of local industry.[142]

THE BLESSING OF THE MORNING STAR—2:28

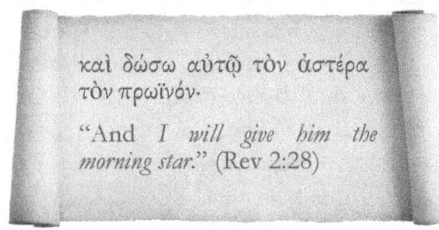

καὶ δώσω αὐτῷ τὸν ἀστέρα τὸν πρωϊνόν·

"And I will give him the morning star." (Rev 2:28)

The third blessing, offered to the overcomers, is the Messianic metaphor of the morning or rising star (ἀστέρα τὸν πρωϊνόν, *astera ton prōinon*),[143] who is David's heir, Jesus himself (2:18, 28; 22:16).[144] Later in Revelation the suzerain is referred to as "the bright Morning Star" (22:16). This recalls the Messianic metaphor of Balaam who said "I see him, but not now; I behold him, but not near: a star shall come out of Jacob, and a scepter (Heb. *shebet*) shall rise out of Israel; it shall crush the forehead of Moab and break down all the sons of Sheth" (Num 24:17; see also 2 Pet 1:19).

In the ancient mind the "morning star", the largest and brightest object in the sky after the sun and moon, carried regal connotations and was associated with the planet Venus,[145] the Greek Aphrodite, depicted on coins (see Figs. 93, 122, 123, 126). It was also symbolized as the bull in the zodiac and proudly displayed on the standards of the Roman legions.[146] However, Kistemaker points out that Christ's sovereignty would clash with this view.[147] It may also be an allusion to Lucifer's battle of the stars (Isa 14:12; *Sib. Or.* 5.516, 527).[148] There is a contrast

---

[139] Pss 23:1, 4; 80:2; Mic 5:5–6; 7:14; Jer 22:22.

[140] Isa 11:4; Ps 45:6–7; 110:2; Job 9:34; 21:9; Lam 3:1 Isa 10:5, 26; 30:31.

[141] Morris, *Revelation*, 78.

[142] Wall, *Revelation*, 77.

[143] See also φωσφόρος, *phōsphoros*, Num 24:17; *T. Livi* 18:3; *T. Jud.* 24:1; 4Q175 12; Num 24:17; Justin *Dial.* 106.4; Hippolytus *Comm. Dan.* 1.9; Origen *Cels.* 1.59–60; Cicero *Nat. d.* 2.53; Pliny *Nat.* 2.36–38; Manilius *Astron.* 1.177–78; *Jos. As.* 14:1; *PGM* 4.3045; 3068; 5.209–10.

[144] Hendriksen, *Conquerors*, 73; Kistemaker, *Revelation*, 142; Hughes, *Revelation*, 52–53; Sweet, *Revelation*, 97.

[145] Ausonius *App.* 2.15; Homer *Il.* 22.317; Dio Cassius *Hist. Rom.* 43.22.1–2; Isa 14:12; *Sib. Or.* 5.516, 527; Pliny *Nat.* 2.37. William M. Ramsay and A. S. Wilkins, "Planetae," in *DGRA*, ed. William Smith (London, U.K.: Murray, 1891), 2:432–33.

[146] Wilson, *Revelation*, 28; Gerald L. Stevens, *Revelation: The Past and Future of John's Apocalypse* (Eugene, Oreg.: Wipf & Stock, 2014), 330–31.

[147] Kistemaker, *Revelation*, 142 n.70.

[148] Lohmeyer, *Offenbarung*, 30; Lohse, *Offenbarung*, 28; Johann Lepsius, "Dr. Johann Lepsius on the Symbolic Language of the Apocalypse," ed. William M. Ramsay, trans. H. Ramsay, *The Expositor* 8, no. 1 (1911): 153–71; Wall,

93. Cistophoric Tetradrachm coin struck under Hadrian (AD 117–138). Aphrodisias mint, after 128 AD. Obv.: *HADRIANVS AVGVSTVS P P*. Bust of Hadrian Rev.: *COS III*, Cult statue of Venus (Aphrodite) *Aphrodisias* standing with outstretched hands, star and crescent on either side of *calathus*, lion-headed censer behind, Cupid seated left on low *cippus* before (*RIC* 516).

between the Roman idea of "morning star" and the Messianic Jewish belief of a coming king.[149] While the *morning star* is primarily referring to Christ (22:16),[150] there may be an allusion to Statius' comparing of Domitian with the morning star(*Silv.* 4.1.1–4). Hemer doubts that any one of these offers proof, but rather "each furnish materials for conjecture, but none which offers a secure background for the thought of the passage. . . . It is because it needed no amplification that we are given no context."[151]

A comet (44 BC) appeared after Julius Caesar's death, being called a "star" by contemporary witnesses, and lasting for eight days. Those seeing it claimed it signified his deification. A coin with eight rays representing the eight days it was visible, with tail upward (which was interpreted as the divine authentication of Caesar's deity), was minted under Augustus and Tiberius (see Fig. 88; *RIC* 1.37a = BMC 323).[152] In the book of Revelation, the suzerain is the rightful ruler, who shares his reign with his vassals. The suzerain is signified by the "morning star."

PROCLAMATION WITNESS FORMULA—2:29

Ὁ ἔχων οὖς ἀκουσάτω τί τὸ πνεῦμα λέγει ταῖς ἐκκλησίαις.

"He who has an ear, let him hear what the Spirit says to the churches." (Rev 2:29)

Acting as his own witness in the court case, the Spirit-Judge calls the Thyatiran congregation to hear what he has to say about the covenant-breaking conduct of the churches. There is no need to call upon external witnesses, as in the ANEVT, since God acts as his own witness in the court case. See the exposition under 2:7.

Revelation, 79.

[149] Attilio Gangemi, "La Stella Del Mattino (Apoc. 2,26–28)," *RivB* 26 (1978): 241–74; Collins, *The Scepter and the Star*, 61–80.

[150] Charles, *Revelation*, 1:77; Swete, *Apocalypse*, 47; Trench, *Commentary on Seven Churches*, 154–55; Plumptre, *Seven Churches of Asia*, 149–50; Tyconius, *The Turin Fragments of Tyconius' Commentary on Revelation*, ed. Francesco Lo Bue and Geoffrey Grimshaw Willis, TS: Contributions to Biblical and Patristic Literature 7 (Cambridge, U.K.: Cambridge University Press, 1963), 58; Hendriksen, *Conquerors*, 72–73.

[151] Hemer, The Letters to the Seven Churches, 126, 128, 253 n. 75.

[152] Horace *Od.* 1.12.47; see also the morning star in Statius *Silv.* 4.1.1–4.

Conclusion

Six unmistakable essential elements of the ANEVT, constituting a structure, are identified within the prophetic message to convey a covenant lawsuit message of encouragement to the overcomers within the church of Thyatira.

Firstly, the preamble, marked by the prophetic oracular formula τάδε λέγει Ω, calls attention to what the suzerain, identified here as the sovereign omnipotent and omniscient "son of God," will say to Thyatira.

Secondly, the historical prologue is characterized by the omniscient suzerain's intimate knowledge of Thyatira's works of love, faith service and patient endurance. But the suzerain also knows that they tolerate the works of Jezebel and have refused to repent of her teachings. They are charged with sexual immorality and eating meat offered to idols. God is aware of this activity and sees it as treasonous against the Great King.

Thirdly, the suzerain declared four curses against their actions. Jezebel would know the full force of the suzerain's judgment in the malediction of sickness. Likewise, her followers were also given an opportunity to repent of her behavior or face the curse of great tribulation. Then the curse of death or more likely pestilence, plague or sickness is threatened on the children of Jezebel. The curse will remind the churches of the omniscience of the suzerain and that he gives to each according to their works.

Fourthly, the Great King sets out two imperatives for Thyatira's stipulations: the suzerain will not impose on them any other burden than to *abstain from meat sacrifices to idols and from sexual immorality* (2:22b) and *hold fast to what you have*.

Fifthly, in response to these stipulations, God pledges to give the blessing of sharing his authority over all the nations to rule them with an iron scepter, and the Messianic promise of the "morning star" even Christ, the suzerain, himself. The eschatological *macarism* for the overcomers' obedience to the stipulations will be the King's gracious pledge of eternal preservation (eternal life), metaphorically conveyed by the morning star.

Finally, acting as his own witness in the court case, the Spirit-Judge calls the Thyatiran congregation to hear what he has to say about the covenant-breaking conduct of the churches.

12

Stalwart Sardis

The History of the City

*I*n order to understand the message to stalwart Sardis, who considered themselve invincible with their fortified acropolis, it is helpful to examine both the cultural (Graeco-Roman) history of Sardis, as well as the (Hebraic-Semitic) OT theological roots of the message. This chapter will examine the historical background to the city of Sardis.

THE GEOGRAPHY OF SARDIS

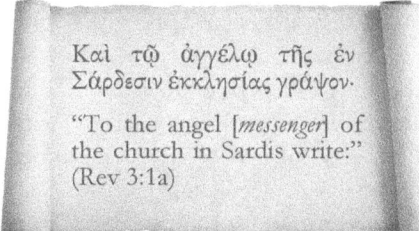

Καὶ τῷ ἀγγέλῳ τῆς ἐν Σάρδεσιν ἐκκλησίας γράψον·

"To the angel [*messenger*] of the church in Sardis write:" (Rev 3:1a)

Traveling south from Thyatira thirty-two miles (50 km), one will reach Sardis (Gr. Σάρδεις, *Sardeis*(Sappho *Frag*. 96, 98);[1] Lydian *Sfard*; Old Persian *Sparda*, modern *Sart*, or *Sartmahmut*; coordinates: 38:29:18 N, 28:02:25 E). It was situated about forty-five miles (72 km) east of Smyrna, and fifty miles (80 km) east of Ephesus, at the junction of five main roads,[2] so one could also easily travel to Sardis from Ephesus on the Royal Persian Road.[3] Strategically located on over 200 hectares (about 495 acres or 2,000 donum), with an acropolis rising 1,500 feet on top of Mount Tmolus (modern *Bozdag*), it overlooked the fertile Hermus plain.[4] Mitten points out that due to erosion, the acropolis is

---

[1] Sardis is the only city, of the seven cities of Revelation, possibly mentioned in the OT. According to an ancient bilingual Aramaic-Lydian inscription, discovered in 1916, *Sepharad* (Obad 20) is the Aramaic term for Sardis (*KAI* 1.260; 2.305–9). S. A. Cook, "A Lydian-Aramaic Bilingual," *JHS* 37 (1917): 77–87; Robert L. Wilken, "Melito, the Jewish Community at Sardis, and the Sacrifice of Isaac," *ThS* 37 (1976): 54; Bryan E. Beyer, *Obadiah, Jonah*, ed. Bryan E. Beyer and John H. Walton, BSCS (Grand Rapids, Mich.: Zondervan, 1988), 25; Worth, Jr., *Greco-Asian Culture*, 292–93 n.1.

[2] David H. French, *Roman Roads and Milestones of Asia Minor Vol. 3 Milestones Fasc. 3.5 Asia*, BAR International Series 5 (Ankara, Turkey: British Institute at Ankara, 2014), 33, 54–63, 81, 100–109, 130–48.

[3] Gill and Gempf, *The Book of Acts in Its Graeco-Roman Setting*, 2:308; Barbara Levick, *Roman Colonies in Southern Asia Minor* (Oxford, U.K.: Clarendon Press, 1967), 13.

[4] Crawford H. Greenewalt, Jr., "Sardis," *Sardis*, 2015, Introduction, http://www.sardisexpedition.org; Nicholas D.

about one-third its original size,[5] but of all the seven cities, Sardis' acropolis was the best protected, having a vertical rock face on three sides which formed a naturally defensible citadel making it almost an impregnable fortress.[6] On two separate occasions (546 and 213 BC) enemy troops scaled the cliff by night and discovered that the overconfident Sardians had left the walls unguarded. The lower and later city included, among other buildings, the impressive gymnasium, temple of Artemis (see Figs. 28, 29, 24) and large Beth Alpha Synagogue. About five miles (8 km) north of Sardis is the necropolis, as well as tumulus tombs north east at Bin Tepeler (Turk. *Bin Tepe*, "thousand hills"), consisting of over 200 tombs dating back to the seventh and sixth cent. BC. Three of the mounds house the tombs of Alyattes, Gyges and … Tos (Tmolus?; Hipponax of Ephesus *Frag.* 42; ca. 540 BC).[7] Due to the city's location, fertile soil, gold deposits and textile industry (Pliny *Nat.* 33.66; Philostratus *Vit. Apoll.* 6.37), Sardis became a wealthy and self-sufficient city.[8]

The History of Sardis

The city state of Sardis (modern *Sart*) was the capital of the kingdom of Lydia for most of the Archaic period (680–547 BC),[9] and exercised its power for over 1,500 years as an important city of the Persian and Seleucid Empires, as a seat for the proconsul under the Roman Empire, and as the metropolis of the province of Lydia in the Roman and Byzantine periods.[10]

Under Lydian control (1200–546 BC)

During the seventh cent. BC, Lydia was a major power in the Levant with friendly relations with the Egyptians (Psammetichus I, 664–610 BC) and Assyrians (Assurbanipal, 668–ca. 627 BC). It is believed that Sardis had regular diplomatic correspondence with Nineveh (636 BC, Rassam Cylinder BM 91026) and during this period it was the dominant power in western Anatolia, with Sardis as Lydia's capital.[11] Sardis was ruled by the Mermnad dynasty (687–546 BC), established by Gyges (r. ca. 680–652 BC; Strabo *Geogr.* 1.3.21; Herodotus *Hist.* 1.13–14).[12] Gyges was credited with the invention of coinage (Xenophanes *Pol.* 9.3; Herodotus *Hist.* 1.94; see below).

Cahill, "Mapping Sardis," in *Love for Lydia: A Sardis Anniversary Volume Presented to Crawford H. Greenewalt, Jr.*, ed. Nicholas D. Cahill, AESR 4 (Cambridge, Mass.: Harvard University Press, 2008), 116.

[5] David Gordon Mitten, "A New Look at Ancient Sardis," *BA* 29, no. 2 (1966): 55.

[6] Strabo *Geogr.* 13.4.5; Herodotus *Hist.* 1.84.3; Lucian *Merc. cond.* 13; *Char.* 9; Polyaenus *Strat.* 4.9.4; Arrian *Anab.* 1.17.4.

[7] Wilson, *Biblical Turkey*, 301–2.

[8] Colin J. Hemer, "The Sardis Letter and the Croesus Tradition," *NTS* 19, no. 1 (1972): 94–95.

[9] Peter John Rhodes, *A History of the Classical Greek World: 478–323 BC*, 2nd ed., Blackwell History of the Ancient World (Chichester, West Sussex, U.K.: Wiley-Blackwell, 2010), 6.

[10] John Griffiths Pedley, *Ancient Literary Sources on Sardis*, ASES (Cambridge, Mass.: Harvard University Press, 1972).

[11] Daniel David Luckenbill, *Ancient Records of Assyria and Babylon: Historical Records of Assyria from Sargon to the End*, vol. 2 (Chicago, Ill.: University Of Chicago Press, 1927), §§ 793–840, infra, n.3.

[12] Some biblical scholars believe that Gyges was Gog, ruler of Magog, mentioned in the Books of Ezekiel 38 and

94. Croesus prepared to burn on the pyre, perhaps a symbol of death and immortality or *apotheōsis*. There are various accounts of his escape (Herodotus *Hist.* 1.86–87; Bacchylides *Ep.* 3.23–62). Side A from an Attic red-figure amphora, *ca.* 500–490 BC. Louvre G 197.

Sardis began on the acropolis where the king of Lydia lived with the aristocrats in their royal buildings, but later expanded down onto the lower banks of the Pactolus river, where the ordinary citizens lived. Herodotus notes that the lower city was modest with no defensive wall (*Hist.* 1.7), although Polybius confirmed that the lower city was walled before 215 BC, as it was breached near the theater (Polybius *Hist.* 7.16.6).

Sardis was again mentioned by Aeschylus (472 BC) as being rich in gold (*Pers.* 45) and in Homer identified as *Hyde* (*Il.* 20.385), possibly the earliest name for Sardis or the district where Sardis was located (Strabo *Geogr.* 13.626). It had been the capital of the kingdom of Lydia[13] in the seventh and sixth cent. BC. With the discovery of gold in the Pactolus River which flowed through Sardis, the wealth of the city and her king, Croesus (r. 560–545 BC; see Fig. 94), became legendary[14] leading to the term "Golden Sardis".[15] In 1968, a gold refining facility was discovered at Sardis dating to the time of Croesus (see Fig. 99 no. 5), with three hundred crucibles used for refining gold, providing credibility to the legend of the ancient records.[16] Sardis was captured by the Cimmerians (Κιμμέριοι, *Kimmerioi*) twice,[17] once in 644 BC (Strabo *Geogr.* 14.1.40; Herodotus *Hist.* 1.15), under the leadership of Lygdamis

---

Revelation 20:8 as the figure of evil. Sverre Bøe, *Gog and Magog: Ezekiel 38–39 as Pre-Text for Revelation 19,17–21 and 20,7–10* (Tübingen: Mohr Siebeck, 2001), 98; Wilson, *Biblical Turkey*, 302.

[13] Μαιονία, *Maionia* or *Maeonia*; Homer *Il.* 2.865; 5.43, 11.431; Herodotus *Hist.* 1.7.

[14] Aeschylus *Pers.* 45; Dio Chrysostom *Or.* 77/78.31–32; Ovid *Metam.* 11.136–45. John Griffiths Pedley, *Sardis in the Age of Croesus*, 2nd ed., Centers of Civilization Series (Norman: University of Oklahoma Press, 2000), 71–73; George M. A. Hanfmann, "Recent Archaeological Research in Turkey: Sardis, 1975," *AS* 26, no. 1 (1976): 61; George M. A. Hanfmann, *Letters from Sardis* (Cambridge, Mass.: Harvard University Press, 1972), 228–29; William J. Young, "The Fabulous Gold of the Pactolus Valley," *Boston Museum Bulletin* 70, no. 359 (1972): 4–13.

[15] George M. A. Hanfmann, *From Croesus to Constantine: The Cities of Western Asia Minor and Their Arts in Greek and Roman Times* (Ann Arbor, Mich.: University of Michigan Press, 1974), 5.

[16] George M. A. Hanfmann and Jane C. Waldbaum, "New Excavations at Sardis and Some Problems of Western Anatolian Archaeology," in *Near Eastern Archaeolgoy in the Twentieth Century: Essays in Honor of Nelson Glueck*, ed. James A. Sanders (Garden City, N.Y.: Doubleday, 1970), 311–13.

[17] Sergei R. Tokhtas'ev, "Cimmerians," in *Encyclopædia Iranica*, ed. Ehsan Yarshater, vol. Facs. 6, 5 (London, U.K.: Eisenbrauns, 1991), 5:563–67.

who defeated Gyges,[18] and again in 637 BC, led by the Trereans and Lycians under their leader Kobos (Strabo *Geogr.* 13.4.8).[19]

Under Persian Control (547–334 BC)

On hearing of the advances of the Persians under Cyrus II (the Great), Croesus (r. 560–546 BC), the king of Sardis, inquired of the Oracle at Delphi, whether he should go to war against the Persian Empire. The Oracle replied "if he should send an army against the Persians he would destroy a great empire" (Herodotus *Hist.* 1.53 [Godley]). Pleased with the reply, Croesus prepared his army to engage the Persian army at the Halys River, but with events ending in a draw, he retreated to Sardis, where he sent home his allies to wait out the winter.

However, Cyrus would not wait the winter and attacked the lower city, defeating the Sardinian cavalry with dromedary camels in 547 BC (Herodotus *Hist.* 1.80–82), with Croesus protected behind the triple fortification walls of the upper city (Arrian *Anab.* 1.17.5).[20] The acropolis of Sardis was besieged for fourteen days (Herodotus *Hist.* 1.84–86), but Cyrus was unable to take the citadel until a Lydian soldier dropped his helmet over the wall and was observed climbing down to retrieve

> **Quotes from Antiquity**
>
> Now this is how Sardis was taken. When Croesus had been besieged for fourteen days, Cyrus sent horsemen about in his army to promise rewards to him who should first mount the wall. After this the army made an assault, but with no success. Then, all the rest being at a stand, a certain Mardian called Hyroeades essayed to mount by a part of the citadel where no guard had been set; for here the height on which the citadel stood was sheer and hardly to be assaulted, and none feared that it could be taken by an attack made here. This was the only place where Meles the former king of Sardis had not carried the lion which his concubine had borne him, the Telmessians having declared that if this lion were carried round the walls Sardis could never be taken. Meles then carried the lion round the rest of the wall of the acropolis where it could be assaulted, but neglected this place, because the height was sheer and defied attack. It is on the side of the city which faces towards Tmolus. So then it chanced that on the day before this Mardian, Hyroeades, had seen one of the Lydians descend by this part of the citadel after a helmet that had fallen down, and fetch it; he took note of this and considered it, and now he himself climbed up, and other Persians after him. Many ascended, and thus was Sardis taken and all the city like to be sacked. (Herodotus *Hist.* 1.84 [Godley])

---

[18] Mordechai Cogan and Hayim Tadmor, "Gyges and Assurbanipal; A Study in Literary Transmission," *Orientalia* 46 (1977): 78–79 nos. 25, 84.

[19] Anthony J. Spalinger, "The Date of the Death of Gyges and Its Historical Implications," *JAOS* 98, no. 4 (1978): 408.

[20] Max Mallowan, "Cyrus the Great," *Iran* 10 (1972): 1–17.

it. The Persians scaled the acropolis and penetrated an unguarded section of the citadel to conquer the upper city, and took Croesus captive in 546 BC.[21] Croesus was brought before Cyrus in chains and sentenced to burn to death, though legend says he was spared when he cried out to Apollo to save him and a sudden rainstorm broke over the fire and put it out. Croesus remained the captive of Cyrus (see Fig. 94).[22] Croesus was upset that he had been misled by the Oracle and that the great empire that was destroyed was his own.

Shortly after the fall of Sardis, the entire region of Ionia was incorporated into the Persian Empire with Croesus as the Persian advisor and Sardis as the Persian administration center. Although Sardis had to pay an annual tribute to the Persian suzerain, the city was left to manage its own affairs under the rule of a Persian appointed autocrat named *Artaphernes*, the brother of the Persian king, Darius I (Plutarch *De Herod.* 24). The Royal Persian Road from Susa was extended to Sardis, providing a 1,600-mile-long commercial highway that stimulated trade between the regions and was later extended to Ephesus.[23]

In 499 BC, following the burning and desecration of the shrine of Cybele, the Ionians revolted against their Persian tyrants. Aristagoras, the tyrant of Miletus, led a coalition against Artaphernes, the Persian governor of Sardis, and Aristagoras (Plutarch *Lacae.* 1). The Persians accidentally burned the city "when a soldier set one of these houses on fire, the flames spread rapidly from house to house until they engulfed the entire city" (498 BC; Herodotus *Hist.* 5.99–101 [Godley]). The Persians finally supressed the revolt in 494 BC and destroyed Miletus and other cities that supported the rebellion.[24] Sardis remained under Persian control for the next two centuries.

UNDER MACEDONIAN CONTROL (334–323 BC)

The Hellenistic period in Sardis extended from 334 BC to the earthquake of AD 17. In 334 BC, Sardis was ultimately liberated by Alexander the Great (r. 336–323 BC), who made several changes to the city (Diodorus *Hist. Lib.* 17.21.7). The old city was eventually abandoned to make way for the new lower city, located to the north of the acropolis, and there, Alexander erected the temple to Zeus (Arrian *Anab.* 1.17.3–6). The temple of Artemis (see Figs. 28, 29, 24) remained in the old city with a few people living around it, but the new lower city had access to the coast by a new road.

---

[21] Herodotus *Hist.* 1.91; Xenophon *Cyr.* 7.2.2–4; *Hell.* 3.4.11–24. J. K. Anderson, "The Battle of Sardis in 395 B.C.," *CSCA* 7 (1974): 27–53; Albert Kirk Grayson, *Assyrian and Babylonian Chronicles* (Winona Lake, Ind.: Eisenbrauns, 1975), 107.

[22] Herodotus *Hist.* 1.86–87; for another explanation for his escape, see Bacchylides *Ep.* 3.23–62. Donald John Wiseman, *Chronicles of Chaldaean Kings (626–556 B.C.)* (London, U.K.: Trustee of the British Museum, 1956), 42.

[23] Akurgal, Ancient Civilizations, 124.

[24] Koray Konuk, "Asia Minor to the Ionian Revolt," in *The Oxford Handbook of Greek and Roman Coinage*, ed. William E. Metcalf (Oxford, U.K.: Oxford University Press, 2012), 55; Elspeth R. M. Dusinberre, *Aspects of Empire in Achaemenid Sardis* (Cambridge, U.K.: Cambridge University Press, 2003), 43–44.

Under Seleucid Control (312–189 BC)

Following Alexander's death, at the battle of Ipsus in 301 BC, Achaeus managed to recover the Seleucid possessions that Attalus had lost, including Lydia, Phrygia and Mysia in Anatolia. Sardis became a Seleucid capital from 281 to 190 BC, following its capture by Seleucus (see Fig. 80) in 281 BC (Polyaenus *Strat.* 4.9.4). In ca. 225 BC Sardis became a *polis* and acquired the status of a Greek city-state.[25] A theater and a stadium were built in the new section of the city that was walled before 215 BC. This is confirmed in the account of the siege of Sardis, when Antiochus III breached the wall, near the theater (Polybius *Hist.* 7.16.6).

95. Drachma coin minted at Sardis under Alexander III "the Great", struck under Philip III, (ca. 323–319 BC). Obv.: Head of Heracles wearing a lion's skin. Rev.: *ALEXANDROU*, Zeus Aëtophoros seated holding an eagle; in left field, monogram above bee.

In 216 BC, under the treaty of alliance with Attalus I, king of Pergamum (269–197 BC; see Fig. 57), Antiochus III the Great (r. 222–187 BC; see Fig. 96) crossed the Taurus, attacked Achaeus, the son of Seleucus I Nicator (ca. 301–281 BC; see Fig. 80), and besieged Sardis. In 216–215 BC, the lower city of Sardis was captured by Antiochus following a year long siege (Polybius *Hist.* 7.15–17).[26] However, while the acropolis remained under Achaeus' control, Sardis was slack in their watch on the wall and left one section "which connects the citadel with the town" (Polybius *Hist.* 7.15 [Paton]), called the "Saw", unguarded. Antiochus' men noticed that the ravine, where the Sardinians threw dead animal carcasses, was frequented by vultures; but they noticed they also sat on the wall, indicating that it was unguarded, so Antiochus's men scaled the acropolis by night and took the city (Polybius *Hist.* 7.15). Achaeus was finally captured and put to death, causing the citadel to surrender.

By 213 BC, Antiochus III had regained control of all his Asiatic provinces (Polybius *Hist.* 5.107; 7.15–18; 8.17–23) and Sardis served as an administrative center during the Seleucid period, for the Anatolian region.[27]

Under Pergamese Control (189–133 BC)

With the victory of Rome over Antiochus III (r. 222–187 BC; see Fig. 96) at the battle of Magnesia (190 BC), Asia came under Roman control.[28] Sardis was given to the Pergamene king,

---

[25] Adrian N. Sherwin-White and Amélie Kuhrt, *From Samarkhand to Sardis: A New Approach to the Seleucid Empire*, Hellenistic Culture and Society 13 (Berkeley, Calf.: University of California Press, 1993), 180; Koester, *Revelation*, 309–10.

[26] Sherwin-White and Kuhrt, *From Samarkhand to Sardis*, 181.

[27] Hansen, *The Attalids of Pergamon*, 43; H. Heinen, "The Syrian–Egyptian Wars and the New Kingdoms of Asia Minor," in *CAH*, ed. Frank William Wallbank, vol. 7.1 (Cambridge, U.K.: Cambridge University Press, 1984), 440.

Eumenes II, in 188 BC and added to the kingdom of Pergamum to be ruled under the Attalid kings (189 BC; Livy *Hist. Rome* 37.44.4).

UNDER ROMAN CONTROL (133 BC–AD 660)

Sardis came under full Roman control after the death of Attalus III, who bequeathed the kingdom to the Romans in 133 BC.[29] During the Roman period Sardis became an important judicial center (seat of *conventus iuridcus*) for some 30 Lydian and Phrygian settlements (Pliny *Nat.* 5.111).[30] Once Lydia was re-established, Sardis became a provincial capital and important administrative center until it was devastated by a major earthquake in 17 AD, which Pliny called "the greatest earthquake in human memory" (Pliny *Nat.* 2.86.200 [Rackham]). Most of the city was destroyed,[31] but was rebuilt with financial aid from Tiberius (see Figs. 43, 97, 111) and Claudius (see Fig. 2, 28; Tacitus *Ann.* 2.47; Strabo *Geogr.* 13.4.8) although it never completely recovered.[32] Tacitus records that:

> In the same year, twelve important cities of Asia collapsed in an earthquake, the time being night, so that the havoc was the less foreseen and the more devastating. Even the usual resource in these catastrophes, a rush to open ground, was unavailing, as the fugitives were swallowed up in yawning chasms. Accounts are given of huge mountains sinking, of former plains seen heaved aloft, of fires flashing out amid the ruin. As the disaster fell heaviest on the Sardians, it brought them the largest measure of sympathy, the Caesar [Tiberius] promising ten million sesterces, and remitting for five years their payments to the national and imperial exchequers. (Tacitus *Ann.* 2.47 [Moore])

96. Gold *oktadrachm* coin minted in Seleukeia on the Tigris (*ca.* 211/210 BC). Obv.: Diademed head of Antiochus III "the Great" (223–187 BC), Seleucid king of Syria. Rev.: *BASILEWS ANTIOCOU*, Apollo Delphios is seated on an *omphalos* (ὀμφαλός), or *baetylus*. His right hand is holding an arrow and his left hand is on a bow.

97. A bronze Sestertius coin struck in Rome in AD 22–23. Obv.: *CIVITATIBVS ASIAE RESTITVTIS* "Cities of Asia restored." Depicts Tiberius (r. 14–37 AD) with laureate and toga, seated on a *curule* chair, his feet on a stool, holding a patera in his right hand and long scepter (*hasta pura*) in his left. (*RIC* 1.48).

---

[28] Livy *Hist. Rome* 37.8.8; 37.37.6, 9; 44.4.
[29] Strabo *Geogr.* 13.4.2; Pliny *Nat.* 33.53.148; *OGIS* 2.338.7.
[30] Habicht, "New Evidence," 67–71.
[31] Tacitus *Ann.* 2.47; Suetonius *Tib.* 48.2; Seneca *Nat. quaest.* 6.1.13.
[32] Keitel, "The Art of Losing: Tacitus and the Disaster Narrative," 335.

To honor the financial aid, twelve of the cities raised a colossal statue in honor of Tiberius in the Forum in Rome, with a representative from each city taking part. A copy of this statue with a frieze of the figures of six of the cities was erected in Puteoli, where it is now on display at the Museo Nazionale, Naples (*CIL* 10.1624).[33] A partial inscription found at Sardis contains eight of the signatories from the representative cities (*CIG* 3450; *IGR* 4.15.14).[34]

In AD 22–23, Roman commemorative coins were struck depicting Tiberius (see Figs. 43, 97, 111), with the Latin inscription

98. Coin from Sardis. Obv.: ΣΕΒΑΣΤΟΣ ΚΑΙΣΑΡΕΩΝ ΣΑΡΔΙΑΝΩΝ (*SEBASTOS KAISAREWN SARDIANWN*). Tiberius (AD 14–37) standing raising up a kneeling Tyche of Sardis. Rev.: ΣΕΒΑΣΤΗ ΙΟΥΛΙΟΣ ΚΛΕΩΝ ΚΑΙ ΜΕΜΝΩΝ Livia, the goddess Demeter, is seated holding a scepter and ears of grain. This coin marked the imperial relief efforts at Sardis after the devastating earthquake in AD 17 (*RPC* 1.2991; *BMC* Lydia 98; *SNG* Cop. 515).

"*Civitatibus Asiae Restitutis*" or "cities of Asia restored" (*RIC* 1.48; see Fig. 97). The city of Magnesia nearby minted a coin with the inscription "*ΤΙΒΕΡΙΟΝ ΣΕΒΑΣΤΟΝ ΚΤΙΣΤΗΝ*" or "Tiberius Augustus Founder".[35] In 43 AD a statue was erected in Sardis in Tiberius' honor, with the inscription the "founder of the city" (*I.Sard.* 54; 59–40).[36] A temple to Tiberius was built during the restoration and Sardis took the name Caesarea Sardis on her coins in his honor (*RPC* 1.2988, 2992).[37] Some believe that Sardis abandoned the Cybele cult (or Tyche, Τύχη, see Figs. 52, 54, 98, 108, 160) to embrace the imperial cult because of their veneration of Tiberius (see Figs. 43, 97, 111) for his restoration of the city. Additional earthquakes struck Sardis in AD 20,[38] AD 24,[39] and AD 29[40] (Strabo *Geogr.* 13.4.8), although they were not as severe.

---

[33] Ann L. Kuttner, *Dynasty and Empire in the Age of Augustus: The Case of the Boscoreale Cups* (Berkeley, Calf.: University of California Press, 1995), 75.

[34] William Hepburn Buckler and David M. Robinson, *Sardis: Greek and Latin Inscriptions*, vol. 1, ASES 7 (Leiden: Brill, 1932), 27–29.

[35] Larry J. Kreitzer, "Living in the Lycus Valley: Earthquake Imagery in Colossians, Philemon and Ephesians," in *Testimony and Interpretation: Early Christology in Its Judeo-Hellenistic Milieu. Studies in Honor of Petr Pokorný*, ed. Jiri Mrázek, Jan Roskovec, and Petr Pokorný, JSNTSup 272 (New York, N.Y.: Bloomsbury Academic, 2004), 83–84.

[36] George M. A. Hanfmann, William E. Mierse, and Clive Foss, eds., *Sardis from Prehistoric to Roman Times: Results of the Archaeological Exploration of Sardis, 1958–1975* (Cambridge, Mass.: Harvard University Press, 1983), 142 nn.28, 144; Fikret K. Yegül, *The Bath-Gymnasium Complex at Sardis*, ed. George M. A. Hanfmann and Jane Ayer Scott, AESR 3 (Cambridge, Mass.: Harvard University Press, 1986), 3.

[37] Prigent, *Apocalypse*, 192.

[38] Sutherland, Roman History and Coinage, 48.

[39] Edward T. Salmon, *A History of the Roman World: From 30 BC to AD 138*, 6th ed. (London, U.K.: Methuen & Company, 1959), 143.

In AD 23 Sardis competed against Smyrna for the privilege of being the newest metropolis to host the imperial cult, but narrowly lost out to Smyrna (Tacitus *Ann.* 4.55).

Emperor Hadrian (see Figs. 93, 109) visited the city in AD 123–124, and 128, confirmed by coins and inscriptions,[41] and in AD 297, Emperor Diocletian reorganized Asia into seven autonomous provinces[42] and made Sardis the capital of the revived district of Lydia. The western side of the city was expanded during the second and early third cent. AD with the construction of an aqueduct and colonnaded street; work also continued on the bath-gymnasium complex, theater and stadium.[43]

UNDER BYZANTINE CONTROL (AD 661–716)

After Constantine, designated Constantinople as the capital of the Roman Empire in AD 324, a new road system was constructed to connect the provinces with the capital which effectively cut off Sardis from main traffic and consequently lost it some of its status. It continued to be the seat of the metropolitan bishop of the province of Lydia and several representatives from Sardis attended the Councils of Nicaea in AD 325, and Ephesus in 431.[44] By the fifth cent AD a wall was built to enclose 156 hectares of the city.

The Persian's finally conquered eastern Anatolia, including Sardis, in AD 616 when it was destroyed by the Sassanian king Chosroes II. The city was so devastated that it never recovered, although the Sardians took back the citadel in AD 660 and established a military compound there, but the city was abandoned. In AD 716 Arabs sacked Sardis, although the city remained a part of the Byzantine Empire until the aftermath of the Battle of Manzikert with the Seljuk Turks in 1071. Eventually it was taken by the Ottoman Turks in 1306 and then was destroyed by the Mongol Turk Tamerlane (or Tamur) in 1402.[45]

THE POPULATION OF SARDIS

Greenewalt reports that "in the time of Croesus, Sardis was a large city of nearly 200 ha, including a fortified core of 108 ha, large extramural suburbs, and a fortified acropolis summit."[46] Pedley places the population in the days of Croesus at 50,000.[47]

---

[40] Ibid.

[41] Peter Weiss, "Hadrian in Lykien," *Chiron* 25 (1995): 213–14; Wilhelm Weber, *Untersuchungen zur Geschichte des Kaisers Hadrian* (Hildesheim: Olms, 2001), 217.

[42] Brian M. Fagan and Charlotte Beck, eds., *The Oxford Companion to Archaeology* (Oxford, U.K.: Oxford University Press, 1996), 616.

[43] Hanfmann, Mierse, and Foss, *Sardis from Prehistoric*, 141–44.

[44] Michel Le Quien, Oriens christianus in quatuor patriarchatus digestus, in quo exhibentur Ecclesiae patriarchae caeterique praesules totius Orientis, 3 vols. (Paris: Typographia Regia, 1740).

[45] Beatrice Forbes Manz, *The Rise and Rule of Tamerlane* (Cambridge, U.K.: Cambridge University Press, 1999), 90; Fant and Reddish, *Guide to Biblical Sites*, 305.

[46] Greenewalt, Jr., "Sardis," Introduction; Cahill, "Mapping Sardis," 116.

[47] Pedley, *Sardis in the Age of Croesus*, 122.

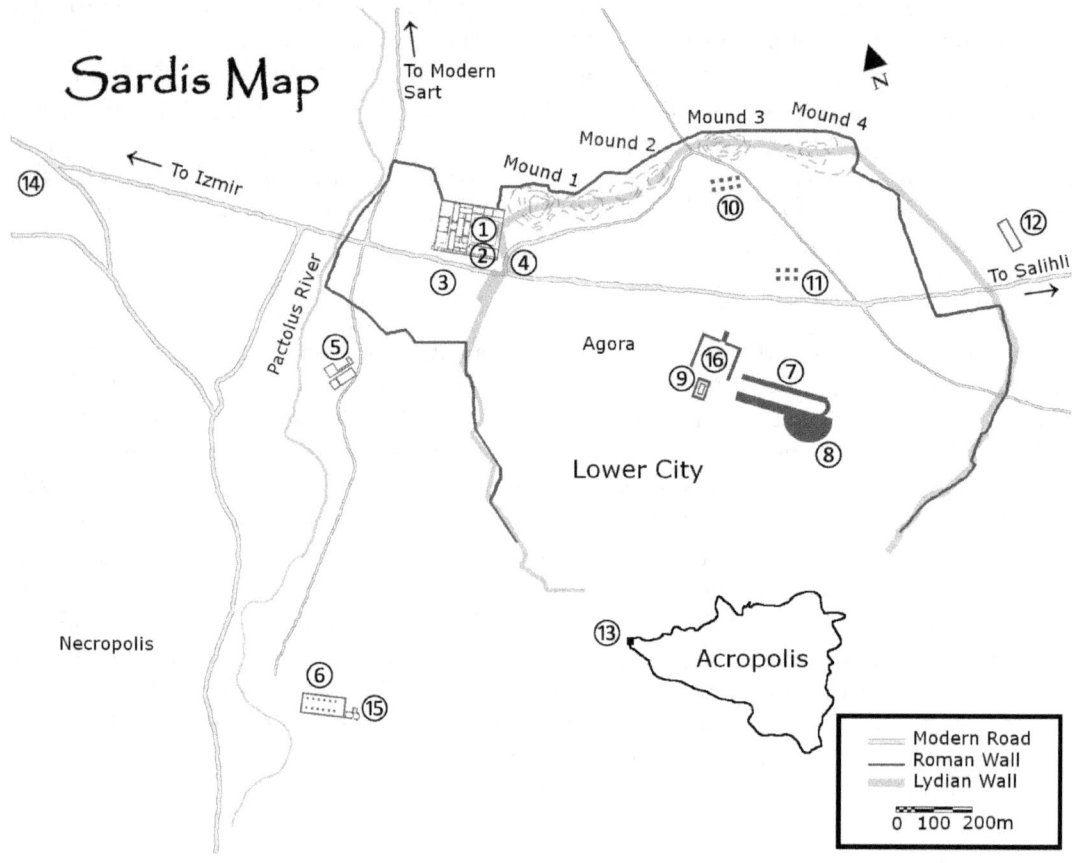

99. Urban plan of the city of Sardis. 1). Bath-Gymnasium; 2). Synagogue; 3). Byzantine Shops; 4). Lydian Gate; 5). Cybele Altar, Lydian Gold Refinery and Byzantine Churches; 6). Temple of Artemis; 7). Stadium; 8). Theater; 9). Temple of the Imperial Cult; 10). Temple?; 11). Temple?; 12). Bath; 13). Tower; 14). Sanctuary of Demeter; 15). Byzantine church; 16). Terrace.

Magie has estimated the population of Sardis in the Roman period at ca. 200,000.[48] Hanfmann suggests that the population of Sardis should be less, between 60,000 and 100,000,[49] which Mitchell says "seems generous"[50] based on the research of Duncan-Jones in comparison with other Roman cities of the period.[51] Mitchell notes that "analogies with other parts of the

---

[48] Magie, *Roman Rule in Asia Minor*, 1:585. Hanfmann suggests that the population in the second cent. AD reached 200,000. Hanfmann, *From Croesus to Constantine*, 49.

[49] Hanfmann, Mierse, and Foss, *Sardis from Prehistoric*, 146, 278 n.92; Aune, *Rev 1–5*, 218; Fant and Reddish, *Guide to Biblical Sites*, 305; Trebilco, *Jewish Communities*, 37.

[50] Mitchell, *Anatolia*, 244 n.13.

[51] Ibid.; Duncan-Jones, *Economy*, 259–87.

empire suggest that few cities had more than about 25,000 urban inhabitants-Nicomedia, Cyzicus, Ancyra, Thyateira, and Sardis would certainly have come into this category."[52] Hanson calculated the population of Sardis based on a significantly larger area of 356 ha. than Greenewalt, who argued for 200 ha. and actually excavated the site.[53]

Author	Area (ha.)	100/ha.	150/ha.	250/ha.	400/ha
Paul D. Hanson	356	35,600	53,400	89,000	142,400
Crawford Greenewalt	200	20,000	30,000	50,000	80,000

Table 6. The population of Sardis according to Hanson and Greenewalt for the size of the city.

Based on the calculations of population density and comparison with other Roman cities of the period, a population between 50,000 and 80,000 seems reasonable.

THE IMPORTANT BUILDINGS OF SARDIS

Several prominent buildings stand out in both the lower city and the acropolis in the discussion of Sardis (for the temples, see *the Gods of Sardis* below). A palace, built by Croesus, was well fortified and made of sun-dried bricks (Bacchylides *Ep.* 3.32; Herodotus *Hist.* 1.9; 1.34).[54] During the Roman period it housed the council of elders (γερουσία, *gerousia*).[55] While the palace has not been located, Hanfmann discusses the possibility of two palaces, one on the acropolis and the other in the lower city.[56]

100. Ruins of the Byzantine era shops at Sardis along the marble avenue. The synagogue is behind the stone wall and the Bath-gymnasium is visible in the distance.

---

[52] Mitchell, *Anatolia*, 244.
[53] Hanson, "Urban System," 254.
[54] Dusinberre, Aspects of Empire in Achaemenid Sardis, 73–75.
[55] Vitruvius *Arch.* 2.8.9–10; Pliny *Nat.* 35.172; Arrian *Anab.* 1.17.6.
[56] George M. A. Hanfmann, "On Lydian Sardis," in *From Athens to Gordion: The Papers of a Memorial Symposium for Rodney S. Young*, ed. Keith DeVries (Philadelphia, Pa.: University of Pennsylvania Museum of Archaeology and Anthropology, 1980), 104; Frank Brommer, Antje Krüg, and Ursula Hockmann, eds., *Festschrift für Frank Brommer* (Mainz: von Zabern, 1977), 145–54. On the various theories and proposed solutions for the location of the palace see Brommer.

101. The Bath-gymnasium complex at Sardis, late section dates to the early third cent. AD.

Based on similar Persian palaces at Pasargadae and Persepolis in Iran, it would have been a large royal complex with many rooms and halls.[57]

The size of the urban plan in Table 6 indicates that the lower city was a considerable size during the Persian period (ca. 108 ha),[58] with the city expanding to the North East in the Roman Period.

The Archaeological Exploration of Sardis began in 1958 under the direction of George M. A. Hanfmann, of Harvard University, and Henry Detweiler of Cornell University. Hanfmann excavated and partially restored the Roman bath-gymnasium complex, the Jewish synagogue, late Roman houses and shops, and a Lydian industrial area for processing *electrum* into pure gold and silver.[59]

---

[57] Hanfmann and Waldbaum, "New Excavations at Sardis," 17–19; Hanfmann, "On Lydian Sardis," 104.
[58] Cahill, "Mapping Sardis," 116. The complex measures 122.60 m. by 169.30 m.
[59] George M. A. Hanfmann and Jane C. Waldbaum, *A Survey of Sardis and the Major Monuments Outside the City Walls*, ed. George M. A. Hanfmann and Stephen W. Jacobs, AESR 1 (Cambridge, Mass.: Harvard University Press, 1975), 4.

Sardis Bath-Gymnasium Complex

102. Floor plan of the Bath-Gymnasium Complex at Sardis. 1). Palaestra; 2). Marble courtyard; 3). Frigidarium; 4). Tepidarium; 5). Caldarium; 6). Latrine; 7). Synagogue; 8). Forecourt; 9). Twenty-seven Byzantine shops; 10). Marble road.

THE BATH-GYMNASIUM COMPLEX

This partially restored (1964–1973) bath-gymnasium complex was mistakenly believed by early travellers to be the Palace of Croesus, given its size (measured 120 m. by 170 m.; 5.46 acres)[60] and grandeur. It was first identified as a Roman bath by Butler[61] and has become known as a *locus classicus* of Roman architecture.[62] It employed a common design for most bath-gymnasia throughout Asia Minor, four of which can be found in Ephesus alone.[63]

---

[60] Yegül, *Bath-Gymnasium Complex*, xiii.
[61] Howard Crosby Butler, *Sardis: Architecture: The Temple of Artemis, Part 1 Text*, ASES 1 (Leiden: American Society for the Excavation of Sardis, 1922), 31–33.
[62] Yegül, *Bath-Gymnasium Complex*, xii.
[63] Edmund Thomas, *Monumentality and the Roman Empire: Architecture in the Antonine Age* (Oxford, U.K.: Oxford University Press, 2007), 156–57.

In ancient Greece, the gymnasium (γυμνάσιον, *gymnasion*, "gymnastic school" derived from γυμνός, *gymnós*, "naked") functioned as a training facility, where athletes competed in the nude. It was the meeting place where organizations of boys (παιδες, *paides*), youths (έφηβη, *ephēbē*), young men (νέοι, *neoi*), and the elders (γεροντες, *gerontes*) engaged in social and intellectual pursuits (Pausanias *Descr.* 4.32.1).

The complex was complete by the middle of the second cent. AD with several alterations until it was abandoned in AD 616. The "marble court" was constructed in AD 211, identified by an inscription dedicating the space to the emperors Caracalla (see Figs. 128, 162, 163) and Geta (his name is erased) and their mother Julia Domna.[64]

The Sardis Complex was comprised of a *palaestra* (παλαίστρα, wrestling schools), long north hall, marble court, *frigidarium* (see Fig. 110), entrance halls, rooms, bath block, heated western halls and *caldarium* (see Figs. 99 no. 1, 101, 102).[65] The palaestra (64.6 m², ca. 220 Roman feet) was a large peristyle courtyard with 100 marble columns on pedestals.[66] The two story Marble Court (Ger. *Kaisersäle*) was dedicated to the imperial cult[67] and contained a surviving dedicatory inscription mentioning Septimus Severus and Caracalla (AD 211–212).[68] The *frigidarium* (cold pool; see Fig. 110) was designed as a long pool occupying the entire floor space, and the walls were decorated with niches for pools, basins and fountains.[69] Connected to the *frigidarium* were four changing rooms (Lat. *apodyteria*) and down an oblong hallway was the heated western halls, *caldarium* (Lat. *cella caldaria*, heated room) and *tepidarium* (Lat. *tepidus*, warm bathroom).[70] The water was heated by both a hypocaust (an underfloor heating system) and an elaborate wall heating system with *tubuli*.[71]

THE TEMPLE OF ARTEMIS

The temple of Artemis (erected in 334 BC; see Figs. 28, 29, 24), which by late Hellenistic times also shared the cult of Zeus Polieus (*I.Sard.* 7.1.9; 7.1.8.47–48) in the same precinct (*cella*),[72] was

---

[64] Yegül, *Bath-Gymnasium Complex*, xiii.

[65] Ibid., 5.

[66] Ibid., 5, 25–36.

[67] Fikret K. Yegül, "A Study in Architectural Iconography: Kaisersaal and the Imperial Cult," *ABul* 64, no. 1 (March 1, 1982): 7–31.

[68] Yegül, *Bath-Gymnasium Complex*, 5, 45–66; Clive Foss, "Inscriptions Related to the Complex," in *The Bath-Gymnasium Complex at Sardis*, ed. Fikret K. Yegül, George M. A. Hanfmann, and Jane Ayer Scott, AESR 3 (Cambridge, Mass.: Harvard University Press, 1986), 170 no.3.

[69] Yegül, *Bath-Gymnasium Complex*, 7–8, 67–76.

[70] Ibid., 112–16.

[71] Ibid., 8.

[72] This is also confirmed by the discovery of a large bust of Zeus in the temple area. Butler, *Temple of Artemis Part 1*; Buckler and Robinson, *Sardis*, vol. 1, no. 7; Hanfmann and Waldbaum, *Survey of Sardis*, 28–32; Peter Herrmann, "Mystenvereine in Sardeis," *Chiron* 26 (1996): 321–29; George M. A. Hanfmann, "On the Gods of Lydian Sardis," in *Beiträge Zur Altertumskunde Kleinasiens: Festschrift Für Kurt Bittel*, ed. Rainer M. Boehmer and Herald Hauptmann (Bücher: Mainz am Rhein, 1983), 229; George M. A. Hanfmann, L. Roberts, and William E. Mierse, "The Hellenistic Period," in

the fourth largest Ionic temple in the ancient world dedicated to Artemis (or Diana, see Figs. 26, 27, 121, 124, 127, sometimes called Artemis Coloene; Stabo *Geogr.* 13.4.5).[73] Although some originally believed the temple was dedicated to Cybele (or Tyche, Τύχη, see Figs. 52, 54, 98, 108, 160), Kore (see Fig. 109), or Zeus (see Figs. 95, 115, 126, 151, 154, 156),[74] it is now known, based on inscriptions, to be dedicated to Artemis (*I.Sard.* 7.1.8.50–55; 91–93),[75] the chief deity of Sardis.[76] It is known that other deities shared the sanctuary, such as Kore (see Fig. 109), as well as the imperial cult as early as Tiberius, then Antoninus Pius, and Faustina.[77]

The Romans renovated the temple in the 150 AD, serving also as a temple of the imperial cult. It was never completed (evident from unfluted columns) and has never been restored,[78] although two complete columns, 58 feet (18 m) high, of the original sixty-four, have

103. Marble column from the Temple of Artemis at Sardis.

Sardis from Prehistoric to Roman Times: Results of the Archaeological Exploration of Sardis, 1958–1975, ed. George M. A. Hanfmann, William E. Mierse, and Clive Foss (Cambridge, Mass.: Harvard University Press, 1983), 120, 265.

[73] Named after the shrine of Artemis located near Lake Coloe. Hemer, *Letters to the Seven Churches*, 138.

[74] Georges Radet, *Cybébé; Étude Sur Les Transformations Plastiques D'un Type Divin*, Bibliothèque Des Universités Du Midi 13 (Bordeaux, France: Feret & Fils, 1909); Ramsay, *Letters: Updated*, 266–67; *The Social Basis of Roman Power in Asia Minor* (Amsterdam: A. M. Hakkert, 1967), 113. Ramsay maintained that the Greek Artemis and the Anatolian Cybele were forms of the same goddess.

[75] William Hepburn Buckler and David M. Robinson, "Greek Inscriptions from Sardes I," *AJA* 16, no. 1 (1912): 26–28; Howard Crosby Butler, "First Preliminary Report on the American Excavations at Sardes in Asia Minor," *AJA* 14, no. 4 (1910): 408.

[76] Hanfmann, "On the Gods of Lydian Sardis," 221.

[77] William E. Mierse, "Artemis Sanctuary," in *Sardis from Prehistoric to Roman Times: Results of the Archaeological Exploration of Sardis, 1958–1975*, ed. George M. A. Hanfmann, William E. Mierse, and Clive Foss (Cambridge, Mass.: Harvard University Press, 1983), 120, 265 nn.20, 24; Vermeule, *Roman Imperial Art*, 18–19.

[78] After limited excavation in 1750, 1882, and 1904, the temple was fully exposed between 1910 and 1914 by the Howard Crosby Butler expedition. For the accounts of the excavation of the temple see: Butler, "First Preliminary Report," 401–13; "Second Preliminary Report on the American Excavations at Sardes in Asia Minor," *AJA* 15, no. 4 (1911): 445–58; "Third Preliminary Report on the American Excavations at Sardes in Asia Minor," *AJA* 16, no. 4 (1912): 465–79; "Fourth Preliminary Report on the American Excavations at Sardes in Asia Minor," *AJA* 17, no. 4 (1913): 471–78; "Fifth Preliminary Report on the American Excavations at Sardes in Asia Minor," *AJA* 18, no. 4 (1914): 425–37; *Temple of Artemis Part 1*, Chapters 3–7.

104. The Temple of Artemis in Sardis (330 BC). The scrolled (Ionic) capitals on the top of the columns add to the beauty of this temple. However, because these capitals were never fluted, it indicates the temple was never finished. The small red brick building in the foreground is a fourth cent. AD Byzantine church. The acropolis of the city is visible on the mountain in the distance. The only remains visible on the summit are Byzantine structures.

stood complete since antiquity.[79] Several of the large ionic capitals have survived, although the ornamentation of each is different.[80] On one of the columns is an inscription in Greek verse from the time of Trajan that states:

> My torus and my foundation block are carved from a single block of stone, furnished not by people but given by the "house" [of the temple] ...of all the columns ["stones"] I am the first to rise. (*I.Sard.* 7.1.181 [Buckler and Robinson])[81]

---

[79] Butler, *Temple of Artemis Part 1*, 17; Fikret K. Yegül, "A Victor's Message: The Talking Column of the Temple of Artemis at Sardis," *JSAH* 73, no. 2 (2014): 204–5.

[80] Butler, *Temple of Artemis Part 1*, 63–72.

[81] Yegül, "A Victor's Message," 204; "Roman Architecture in Sardis," in *Sardis: Twenty-Seven Years of Discovery*, ed. Eleanor Guralnick (Chicago, Ill.: Archaeological Institute of America, 1987), 50.

The temple began as just an altar (Xenophon *Anab.* 1.7), which dates from the late sixth-fifth cent. BC. The temple was likely built by King Croesus with a sandstone foundation and marble structure and then rebuilt after the burning of Sardis in 499 BC with the foundations of that temple still visible. Enlargements and repairs where carried out up until the first cent. AD when it was destroyed by the earthquake of AD 17 and covered by the accompanying landslide.[82] The temple faced west, like those at Magnesia and Ephesus, toward the steep side of the acropolis, but unlike Greek temples, which placed their entrance facing east.[83]

A Lydian inscription, also translated into Aramaic, was found in the temple, which proved to be a kind of Rosetta Stone, that led to the deciphering of the Lydian language.[84] The decline of the Artemis temple is likely due to the official status of Christianity in the fourth cent. AD that led to the closure of many pagan sanctuaries. A small church was built at the east end in the fifth cent. AD and Christian iconography was placed on the doorway of the temple. Much of the marble was burned for lime in the seventh cent. onward.[85] What remains visible today dates from the Roman reconstruction in the second cent. AD.

There is debate over the relationship of the appearance of the Ephesian Artemis (see Figs. 27, 121, 124, 127) and that of the Sardinians.[86] A rivalry between the two cities over Artemis is documented that may support an underlying tension between the two representations of Artemis as the hunter in Sardis (see Figs. 26) and the multibreasted goddess portrayed in Ephesus (see Figs. 27).[87]

THE JEWISH SYNAGOGUE

The synagogue (called Beth Alpha), discovered in 1961, was originally part of the north wing of the Palaestra, or Marble Hall, of the Bath Complex. However, in the late third cent. AD it was given to the Jewish community (*synodos;* Josephus *Ant.* 14.259–61), isolated from the Palaestra, and renovated as a large synagogue (see Figs. 99 no. 2, 105, 106).[88] Its importance is characterized by its large size (262 ft./80 m long), capable of holding a congregation of a

---

[82] Butler, *Temple of Artemis Part 1*, 101; Hanfmann, *Letters from Sardis*, 7; Akurgal, *Ancient Civilizations*, 124.

[83] Mierse, "Artemis Sanctuary," 120.

[84] Roberto Gusmani, Lydisches Wörterbuch, Mit Grammatischer Skizze Und Inschriftensammlung (Heidelberg: Winter, 1964), 25–27; Dusinberre, Aspects of Empire in Achaemenid Sardis, 114.

[85] Nicholas Cahill and Crawford H. Greenewalt, Jr., "The Sanctuary of Artemis at Sardis: Preliminary Report, 2002–2012," *AJA* 120, no. 3 (2016): 505; Yegül, "A Victor's Message," 214–15.

[86] Worth, Jr., *Greco-Asian Culture*, 297 n.68.

[87] F. Sokolowski, "A New Testimony to the Cult of Artemis in Ephesus," *HTR* 58, no. 4 (1965): 427–31; George M. A. Hanfmann and Jane C. Waldbaum, "Kybele and Artemis: Two Anatolian Goddesses at Sardis," *Archaeology* 22, no. 4 (1969): 265.

[88] Yegül, *Bath-Gymnasium Complex*, 5.

thousand people, and prominent location on the main street.[89] The building went through at least four stages of renovation.[90]

Stage 1: Originally after the AD 17 earthquake the structure served as a dressing room or lecture hall with three rooms extended from the Gymnasium complex.[91]

Stage 2: Between AD 150–250[92] it was transformed into a civic basilica[93] and perhaps turned over to the Jewish community during this time in gratitude for their assistance in rebuilding the city following the earthquake of AD 17.[94]

Stage 3: The first use of the building as a Jewish synagogue (AD ca. 170–250).[95]

Stage 4: Renovations carried out in the eastern end of the building provided a colonnaded entrance court (Forecourt, 20 m. long) and porch, separated from the long assembly hall (Main Hall, 60 m. long; AD 350–400).[96]

105. The *bēma* of the third cent. AD synagogue in Sardis (modern Turkey), which was used as the reading platform in the synagogue. Some believe that the lion statues and the eagles carved on both sides of the altar (table) are evidence of syncretism to appease the Roman authorities.

The large table or altar was decorated with two large Roman eagles on each of its stone legs (second cent. BC–first cent. AD; see Fig. 105),[97] leading some to speculate that the Jews were involved in a kind of syncretism to appease the Roman authorities.[98] Two lion statues (5–

---

[89] Lee I. Levine, "Synagogues," in *EDEJ*, ed. John J. Collins and Daniel C. Harlow (Grand Rapids, Mich.: Eerdmans, 2010), 1264.

[90] Andrew R. Seager, "The Building History of the Sardis Synagogue," *AJA* 76 (1972): 425–35.

[91] On the date of construction, see Ibid.; Marcus Rautman, "Sardis in Late Antiquity," in *Archaeology and the Cities of Late Antiquity in Asia Minor*, ed. Ortwin Dally and Christopher Ratté (Ann Arbor, Mich.: Kelsey Museum of Archaeology, 2012), 1–26; Jodi Magness, "The Date of the Sardis Synagogue in Light of the Numismatic Evidence," *AJA* 109 (2005): 443–75.

[92] Only the synagogues of Masada and Delos are older. Smallwood, *Jews Under Roman Rule*, 509 n.16.

[93] Fatih Cimok, *Guide To The Seven Churches* (Istanbul: Tuttle, 1999), 81.

[94] Shemuel Safrai, M. Stern, and David Flusser, The Jewish People in the First Century: Historical Geography, Political History, Social, Cultural and Religious Life and Institutions (Uitgeverij Van Gorcum, 1974), 479.

[95] Yegül, *Bath-Gymnasium Complex*, 5.

[96] Hanfmann, *Letters from Sardis*, 323; Andrew Ramage, Crawford H. Greenewalt, Jr., and Faruk Akca, "The Fourteenth Campaign at Sardis (1971)," *BASOR*, no. 206 (1972): 37–39; Kraabel, "Impact of the Discovery of the Sardis Synagogue," 168.

[97] The altar eagles at synagogue in Sardis have been replaced by replicas to protect them from vandalism. The originals now stand outside flanking the doorway of the permanently closed Manisa Archaeological Museum as mere decorations.

[98] Mitten, "A New Look at Ancient Sardis," 51–52; Hemer, *Letters to the Seven Churches*, 137.

fourth cent. BC), the symbol of the city and its goddess, were also located in the synagogue and may originally have been set beside a Cybele statue (or Tyche, Τύχη, see Figs. 52, 54, 98, 108, 160). Within the Jewish context, they would have symbolized the tribe of Judah (Gen 49:9). The central nave of the main hall was divided into two side aisles from two rows of pillars. On the western wall, there were two niches used as Torah shrines (*aediculae*) for the storage of the Torah scrolls.[99]

A Greek inscription refers to the Torah shrine as the *nomophulákion*, or "the place that protects the Torah."[100] The congregation stood or used wooden benches or sat on the floor. It was elaborately decorated with a beautiful mosaic floor[101] and marble panels (*skoutlōsis*) on the lower portion of the walls[102] and inlaid marble with geometric shapes on the upper portion, similar to the floor of the Herodian Second Temple complex in Jerusalem.[103] A menorah (*heptamyxion* "seven-branched lampstand") plaque, flanked by a *shofar* and *lulab* with a scrolled Torah, was carved into the main *aediculae* (see Fig. 106). The remains of some nineteen menorahs have been discovered etched on various materials.[104] Eighty-five Jewish dedicatory inscriptions in the mosaics and on the wall, two in Hebrew, have been recovered during excavations of the structure, indicating that the members of the Jewish community were wealthy. Eight men are identified as members of the city council.[105] A rare Hebrew inscription

106. The Torah shrine (*aediculae*) that would have housed the copy of the Torah used in worship in the synagogue.

---

[99] Levine, "Synagogues," 1265.

[100] Steven Fine, *Art and Judaism in the Greco-Roman World: Toward a New Jewish Archaeology*, Revised (Cambridge, U.K.: Cambridge University Press, 2010), 126.

[101] On the resetting of the mosaic floor of the Synagogue see the report from Greenewalt. Ramage, Greenewalt, Jr., and Akca, "The Fourteenth Campaign at Sardis (1971)," 20–23.

[102] Levine, "Synagogues," 1264–65.

[103] Daniel K. Eisenbud, "Archaeologists Restore Ancient Tiles from Second Temple in Jerusalem," *The Jerusalem Post*, September 6, 2016, 1, http://www.jpost.com/Israel-News/Archeologists-restore-tiles-from-Second-Temple-in-Jerusalem-467021. See also http://www.nrg.co.il/online/1/ART2/823/143.html.

[104] George M. A. Hanfmann, G. F. Swift, and Crawford H. Greenewalt, Jr., "The Ninth Campaign at Sardis (1966)," *BASOR*, no. 187 (1966): 27; Yigal Shiloh, "Torah Scrolls and the Menorah Plaque from Sardis," *IEJ* 18, no. 1 (1968): 54–57; Steven Fine and Leonard Victor Rutgers, "New Light on Judaism in Asia Minor During Late Antiquity: Two Recently Identified Inscribed Menorahs," *JSQ* 3, no. 1 (1996): 12, 15.

[105] Marianne Palmer Bonz, "The Jewish Community of Ancient Sardis," *HSCP* 93 (1990): 343–59; "Differing Approaches to Religious Benefaction: The Late Third-Cent. Acquisition of the Sardis Synagogue," *HTR* 86 (1993): 139–54; Hanfmann, *Letters from Sardis*, 119; Levine, "Synagogues," 1265.

mentions the word "shalom."[106] In the center of the mosaic is the inscription mentioning "Samoe, *hiereus* [priest] and *sophodidaskalos* [wise teacher or teacher of wisdom]."[107] Another Greek inscription found near the synagogue entrance directed the Jews to "Find, open, read, observe" the commands (*phylaxon*, observe) of God.[108]

The synagogue held a prominent place within the city of Sardis with twenty-seven Byzantine shops (AD 400) constructed along the south-eastern wall of the synagogue on the main avenue of the city, which were also used in earlier periods (see Fig. 100).[109] Six of the shops were occupied by Jews, identified by menorahs etched in their walls, and ten were used by Christians, identified by crosses. Even though the Jewish people were enmeshed in the daily activities of Sardis they managed to maintain their own customs and religion.

The main archaeological work at Sardis has been carried out by the American Society for the Excavation of Sardis, under the direction of Howard Crosby Butler of Princeton University, in 1910–1914 and 1922; and by the Archaeological Exploration of Sardis, directed by George M. A. Hanfmann of Harvard University and Cornell University, from 1958 to the present.[110]

THE COMMERCE OF SARDIS

Sardis, located on an important trade route at the end of the Royal Road from Susa, was a thriving commercial center supported by its natural resources of gold, silver, antimony, arsenic, marble and wool.[111] Trade guilds included textile workers (Athenaeus *Deipn.* 6.255; 12.514), goldsmiths (*IJO* 2.97–98), builders,[112] Italian businessmen (*SEG* 46.1521; ca. 88 BC),[113] slave-merchants (*SEG* 46.1524; AD 90's), and performers devoted to Dionysus (see Fig. 35) during the time of Hadrian (see Figs. 93, 109; *I.Sard.* 7.1.13–14).[114] Sardis was known for the manufacture and dyeing of delicate woolen products and carpets. In the late Roman period,

---

[106] Frank Moore Cross, "The Hebrew Inscriptions from Sardis," *HTR* 95, no. 1 (2002): 8–10.

[107] A. Thomas Kraabel, "The Diaspora Synagogue: Archaeological and Epigraphic Evidence since Sukenik," in *ANRW*, ed. Wolfgang Haase and Hildegard Temporini, 2.19 (Berlin: de Gruyter, 1979), 486; Louis H. Feldman, *Studies in Hellenistic Judaism* (Leiden: Brill, 1996), 588, 600; Levine, "Synagogues," 1265.

[108] Fine, Art and Judaism, 126.

[109] J. Stephens Crawford, *The Byzantine Shops at Sardis*, AESM 9 (Cambridge, Mass.: Harvard University Press, 1990).

[110] George M. A. Hanfmann, Nelson Glueck, and Jane C. Waldbaum, *New Excavations at Sardis and Some Problems of Western Anatolian Archaeology* (High Wycomb: University Microfilms, 1975); for a bibliography, see George M. A. Hanfmann, William E. Mierse, and Clive Foss, eds., *Sardis from Prehistoric to Roman Times: Results of the Archaeological Exploration of Sardis, 1958–1975* (Cambridge, Mass.: Harvard University Press, 1983), xvii–xxxv.

[111] Hanfmann and Waldbaum, *Survey of Sardis*, 21.

[112] Pedley, *Sardis*, 44–45; Hanfmann, Mierse, and Foss, *Sardis from Prehistoric*, 10–12; Philip A. Harland, *North Coast of the Black Sea, Asia Minor* (Berlin: De Gruyter, 2014), 248.

[113] Peter Herrmann, "Neues Vom Sklavenmarkt in Sardeis," *TAD* 4 (1996): 184–86.

[114] Philip A. Harland, "Spheres of Contention, Claims of Pre-Eminence Rivalries among Associations in Sardis and Smyrna," in *Religious Rivalries and the Struggle for Success in Sardis and Smyrna*, ed. Richard S. Ascough, SSEJC 14 (Waterloo, Ont.: Wilfrid Laurier University Press, 2006), 54.

Sardis was one of only three imperial weapon and shield factories in Asia Minor.[115] The Byzantine Shops with over one hundred objects recovered bear testimony to the bustling commerce and trading that took place in the Late Roman/Early Byzantine city.[116]

THE INVENTION OF COINS

In antiquity, gold dust was carried down the Pactolus river from Mount Tmolus through the city of Sardis to produce what was called "golden sands" (Strabo *Geogr.* 13.4).[117] The original form of nuggets, weighed ingots, and bags of "dust", called electrum (ἤλεκτρον, *elektron*), were comprised of gold and silver with small amounts of other elements such as copper, traces of tin, lead or iron.[118] Herodotus called it "white gold" (*Hist.* 1.50; χρυσὸς λευκός, *chrusus leukos*), as opposed to refined gold. Aristotle explains that initially the value of electrum (650–600 BC) was

107. A Lydian one-third stater ("standard") *electrum* coin from Sardis minted by King Alyattes (610–565 BC). Obv.: The head of a roaring lion with a rising sun with multiple rays on his forehead in the background. *Electrum* continued to be the only metal used in coinage until the process of refining gold and silver was perfected. Rev.: Double incuse punch (maximum dimension 13 mm. and 4.71 gm; *BMC Lydia* pg. 2, 6; *SNG Kayhan* 1013).

"defined merely by size and weight" of the metal (Aristotle *Pol.* 1.3.14 [Rackham]),[119] but it was difficult to use for commerce, since its intrinsic value had to be checked during every transaction using a "Lydian stone" or touchstone.[120] The natural Lydian electrum was composed of ca. 73% gold, 27% silver while the actual content of the coins was 54% gold and 44% silver, 1 or 2 % copper, resulting in a sizeable profit (ca. 20%) for the Lydian state.[121]

---

[115] Jane C. Waldbaum, "Metalwork and Metalworking in Sardis," in *Sardis: Twenty-Seven Years of Discovery*, ed. Eleanor Guralnick (Chicago, Ill.: Archaeological Institute of America, 1987), 42.

[116] George M. A. Hanfmann, Fikret K. Yegül, and Crawford H. Greenewalt, Jr., "The Roman and Late Antique Period," in *Sardis from Prehistoric to Roman Times: Results of the Archaeological Exploration of Sardis, 1958–1975*, ed. George M. A. Hanfmann, William E. Mierse, and Clive Foss (Cambridge, Mass.: Harvard University Press, 1983), 161–62.

[117] Theodore Leslie Shear, "The Golden Sands of the Pactolus," *The Classical Weekly* 17, no. 24 (1924): 186–88.

[118] Andrew Ramage, "Golden Sardis," in *King Croesus' Gold: Excavations at Sardis and the History of Gold Refining*, ed. Andrew Ramage and Paul T. Craddock, AESM 11 (Cambridge, Mass.: British Museum Press, 2000), 14–26; Konuk, "Asia Minor to the Ionian Revolt," 44.

[119] Later, Alyattes (610–561 BC), standardised the weight of coins to 1 Stater equal to 168 grains of wheat or equal to two *drachmae* (Xenophanes *Pol.* 4.173). Percy Garnder, "Stater," in *DGRA*, ed. William Smith (London, U.K.: Murray, 1891), 1056–58.

[120] Paul T. Craddock, "Assaying in Antiquity," in *King Croesus' Gold: Excavations at Sardis and the History of Gold Refining*, ed. Andrew Ramage and Paul T. Craddock, AESM 11 (Cambridge, Mass.: British Museum Press, 2000), 247.

[121] Nicholas D. Cahill and John H. Kroll, "New Archaic Coin Finds from Sardis," *AJA* 109 (2005): 612–13; William E. Metcalf, ed., *The Oxford Handbook of Greek and Roman Coinage* (Oxford, U.K.: Oxford University Press, 2012), 39.

During the reign of King Croesus (560–546 BC), the metallurgists of Sardis discovered the technique of separating gold from silver and refining both metals to a purity never known before.[122] Croesus is reported to be the first to mint pure gold and pure silver coins, known as "Croeseids,"[123] compelling ancient writers to declare that he invented (ἐξευρίσκειν, *exeuriskein*) coinage (Xenophanes *Pol.* 9.3; Herodotus *Hist.* 1.94). However, they likely meant that Sardis was the first "to produce gold and silver coins" and not that they invented coinage.[124] Nonetheless, gold industry made Sardis rich and Croesus' name synonymous with wealth (Ovid *Metam.* 11.142–45).

Later they stamped a design (lion sometimes with a bull) and Lydian name on the lump of metal (see Fig. 107),[125] in order "that this might relieve them of having to measure it; for the stamp was put on as a token of the amount" (Aristotle *Pol.* 1.3.15 [Rackham]). The symbol of Lydia was the royal lion that figured prominently as a head or paw on the coins from Sardis (see Fig. 107).[126] Some of these coins were also inscribed in Lydian with *walwet* or *kukalim* (meaning "I am of Kukaś" or "I belong to Kukaś").[127]

In 1968 a large industrial workshop was excavated at Sardis, exposing nine "furnaces for cementation, which is a method of separating gold and silver from alloy of the two,"[128] along with over 300 pieces of gold, that dated to ca. 560–550 BC.[129] While there was evidence of the manufacturing of jewelry at the site,[130] there is no doubt that coins were also minted here by Croesus as the analysis of the gold fragments and gold coins from the time of Croesus were similar.[131]

---

[122] Andrew Ramage and Paul T. Craddock, eds., *King Croesus' Gold: Excavations at Sardis and the History of Gold Refining*, AESM 11 (Cambridge, Mass.: British Museum Press, 2000), 14–26.

[123] Colin M. Kraay, *Archaic and Classical Greek Coins* (Berkeley, Calf.: University of California Press, 1976), 30–31; Cahill and Kroll, "New Archaic Coin Finds from Sardis," 589–617.

[124] Akurgal, *Ancient Civilizations*, 124; Robert A. Mundell, *The Birth of Coinage* (New York, N.Y.: Columbia University Press, 2002), 15; Kraay, *Archaic and Classical Greek Coins*, 34.

[125] Metcalf, *The Oxford Handbook of Greek and Roman Coinage*, 38; John H. Kroll, "The Monetary Use of Weighed Bullion in Archaic Greece," in *The Monetary Systems of the Greeks and Romans*, ed. W. V. Harris (Oxford, U.K.: Oxford University Press, 2010), 12–37.

[126] J. Spier, "Notes on Early Electrum Coinage and a Die-Linked Issue from Lydia," in *Studies in Greek Numismatics in Memory of Martin Jessop Price*, ed. Richard Ashton and S. Hurter (London: Spink & Son, 1998), 331.

[127] R. W. Wallace, "Kukalim, Walwet, and the Artemision Deposit: Problems in Early Anatolian Electrum Coinages," in *Agoranomia: Studies in Money and Exchange Presented to John H. Kroll*, ed. Peter G. Van Alfen (New York, N.Y.: American Numismatic Society, 2006), 37–49.

[128] Andrew Ramage, "The Excavations and Finds," in *King Croesus' Gold: Excavations at Sardis and the History of Gold Refining*, ed. Andrew Ramage and Paul T. Craddock, AESM 11 (Cambridge, Mass.: British Museum Press, 2000), 83.

[129] Ibid., 88.

[130] C. Densmore Curtis, *Sardis XIII: Jewelry and Gold Work, Part 1, 1910–1914*, ed. Andrew Ramage and Paul T. Craddock, AESM 13 (Rome: Sindacato Italiano Arti Grafiche, 1925).

[131] M. R. Cowell and K. Hyne, "Scientific Examination of the Lydian Precious Metal Coinages," in *King Croesus' Gold: Excavations at Sardis and the History of Gold Refining*, ed. Andrew Ramage and Paul T. Craddock, AESM 11 (Cambridge, Mass.: British Museum Press, 2000), 169–74.

Following the Persian invasion of Asia Minor, Cyrus continued the bimetallic system of coinage introduced by Croesus and continued to strike gold and silver coins at Sardis until ca. 520 BC.[132]

THE SLAVE TRADE

As the regional center for the Roman slave trade, Sardinian businessmen held high positions in Sardis and some were priests of the imperial cult (*I.Sard.* 7.1.45 = *IGR* 4.1509; ca. 80 AD). An inscription reads:

> The Sardinian people, by a decision taken in a general assembly, honored T. Julius Lepi[dus-]genianus, devoted to Caesar as [high priest] of Asia and the city, foremost person of the [city], for love of honor and incomparable goodwill toward the homeland [. . .], the dedication being set up, out of their own means, by those who do business in the slave market (*SEG* 46:1523, 1524 [Koester]).[133]

At Acmonia on the main road from Sardis to Phrygia, there was a slave market (*statarion*) built by C. Sornatius for slave-trading in the first cent. BC.[134] Koester suggests that there is a connection between the slave trade and Roman rule in Revelation 18:13, which mentions human slaves.[135]

TEXTILE INDUSTRY OF SARDIS

The Roman provinces of Lydia and Phrygia (i.e., Thyatira),[136] were famous for their clothing industry (i.e., dyeing, wool production,[137] and tapestry; [Homer *Il.* 4.141–42]). Essential to the textile trade was the purple dyeing process from the Bronze Age to the Byzantine period[138] and the prominent role that the first century AD dyers guild played in city associations.[139] Sardis played a key role in the textile industry of Lydia (Athenaeus *Deipn.* 6.255; 12.514).[140] Pliny the Elder claims that the purple dye industry was invented in Sardis (*Nat.* 7.56.195), although

---

[132] Ian A. Carradice, "The 'Regal' Coinage of the Persian Empire," in *Coinage and Administration in the Athenian and Persian Empires: The Ninth Oxford Symposium on Coinage and Monetary History*, ed. Ian A. Carradice, BARI 343 (Oxford, U.K.: British Archaeological Reports, 1987), 73–95; Mitten, "A New Look at Ancient Sardis," 56; E. S. G. Robinson, "Some Electrum and Gold Greek Coins," in *Centennial Publication of the American Numismatic Society*, ed. Harald Ingholt (New York, N.Y.: American Numismatic Society, 1958), 585–94.

[133] Herrmann, "Neues Vom Sklavenmarkt in Sardeis," 175–87; Koester, "Roman Slave Trade and the Critique of Babylon in Revelation 18," 783.

[134] *MAMA* 4.260; *SEG* 42.311; 45.1524. W. V. Harris, *Rome's Imperial Economy: Twelve Essays* (Oxford University Press, 2011), 79, 106.

[135] Koester, "Roman Slave Trade and the Critique of Babylon in Revelation 18," 766–86; *Revelation*, 310.

[136] *IGR* 4.1239, 1242, 1213, 1250, 1250, 1265; *IG* X 2.1 291 = PHI 137473.

[137] Sophocles *Phil.* 391–95; Dio Chrysostom *Or.* 78.31; Juvenal *Sat.* 14.298–300; Lucian *Phar.* 3.209–10; Philostratus *Vit. Apoll.* 6.37; Pliny *Nat.* 33.66.

[138] For the dyeing process see Thyatira. Graves, "What Is The Madder With Lydia's Purple?", 1–47.

[139] Magie, *Roman Rule in Asia Minor*, 1:48; 2:812 n.80; Trinkl, "Washing and Dyeing," 81–86; Harland, *Associations, Synagogues, and Congregations*, 121–29.

[140] Broughton, "Roman Asia Minor," 4:818 n.1, 819.

Broughton suggests that it "probably means the first use of madder root for that purpose".[141] The taxes that dyers had to pay were calculated at 24 drachmas a month, while traders of junk had to pay 8 to 12 drachmas, indicated that dyers were a significant economic trade in Roman society.[142]

THE RELIGIOUS COMMUNITY OF SARDIS

The religious life of Sardis was truly polytheistic, like every other city in the Roman Empire at that time. The city entertained Jews, Christians and Pagans, worshiping more than twenty deities in total. As Hemer points out "The public image largely represented on coinage identified the local deities with Hellenic counterparts, but the underlying Anatolian cult which had a much deeper influence upon the people, is almost hidden from us."[143] Many of the gods and goddesses celebrated at Sardis had a preoccupation with the theme of death and immortality, exemplified in death and the reunion with Mother Earth, the serpent shedding its skin, and being bathed in bull's blood (*taurobolium*, Strabo *Geogr.* 1.3.21; Pliny *Nat.* 25.5.14).[144]

THE GODS OF SARDIS

Following are a list of the gods of Sardis, and most have epigraphic or numismatic evidence attesting to a sanctuary or classical temple.

1. The temple of *Artemis* (*I.Sard.* 7.1.50–55; 91–93,[145] also called *Artemis Coloene*, Stabo *Geogr.* 13.4.5; see Figs. 28, 29, 24).[146] which by late Hellenistic times shared the cult of *Zeus Polieus*[147] in the same temple (*cella*) built in the second cent. BC (see *Temple of Artemis* above).[148] Artemis, along with the Anatolian counterpart *Cybele* (or Tyche, Τύχη; see Figs. 52, 54, 98, 108, 160), were the chief deities of Sardis.[149] Ramsay and Hemer maintained that the Greek Artemis and the Anatolian *Cybele* (see Figs. 26, 27) were forms of the same goddess,[150] but this theory has been overturned by evidence of separate features discovered on a relief reused in the

---

[141] Ibid., 4:818.

[142] Kerstin Drob-Krüpe, "Spatial Concentration and Dispersal of Roman Textile Crafts," in *Urban Craftsmen and Traders in the Roman World*, ed. Andrew Wilson and Miko Flohr (Oxford, U.K.: Oxford University Press, 2016), 335.

[143] Hemer, Letters to the Seven Churches, 138.

[144] Ibid., 138–39.

[145] Coins from the reigns of Marcus Aurelius, Commodus, and Elagabalus all depict the temple of Aretemis along with the cult image of Artemis. Price and Trell, *Coins and Their Cities: Architecture on the Ancient Coins of Greece, Rome, and Palestine*, 136.

[146] Named after the shrine of Artemis located near Lake Coloe. Hemer, *Letters to the Seven Churches*, 138.

[147] *I.Sard.* 7.1.9; 7.1.22; 7.1.47–48.

[148] Butler, *Temple of Artemis Part 1*; Buckler and Robinson, *Sardis*, vol. 1, no. 7; Hanfmann and Waldbaum, *Survey of Sardis*, 28–32; Herrmann, "Mystenvereine in Sardeis," 321–29; Hanfmann, "On the Gods of Lydian Sardis," 229.

[149] Hanfmann, "On the Gods of Lydian Sardis," 221.

[150] Ramsay maintains that the Greek Artemis and the Anatolian Cybele were forms of the same goddess. Ramsay, *Letters: Updated*, 266–67; *The Social Basis of Roman Power in Asia Minor*, 113; Hemer, *Letters to the Seven Churches*, 138.

synagogue. Artemis is represented holding a deer (see Fig. 30), while *Cybele* (Tyche) is depicted with a lion (see Figs. 108).[151] The priestess of Artemis (*I.Sard.* 7.1.50–55; 91–93) and priest of Zeus Polieus (*I.Sard.* 7.1.47–48) not only conducted religious rites, but also carried out the important civic role of underwriting the costs of festivals.

2. The sanctuary (*hieron*) of *Cybele* (or *Kybele*), the patron goddess of Lydia (Herodotus *Hist.* 5.102; Euripides *Bacch.* 55, 65 [462–3]), and Mother of the Mountains, who protected the metals in the mountains and the craftsmen who worked them.[152] *Zeus Sabazios* (Σεβαστὸν) is associated with Cybele or Artemis (or Diana, see Figs. 26, 27, 121, 124, 127) at Sardis *I.Sard.* 7.1.58 = *IGR* 4.1506).[153] Following a primitive frenzied ceremony, the male worshipers of Cybele would castrate themselves and become Galli, or eunuch-priests of the cult.[154]

3. The temple of *Demeter* (sees Fig. 99 no. 14), the goddess of fertility, is identified from the *Demeter Karpophoros* altar with a serpent coming out of a basket (see Fig. 63).[155] By AD 70–100, Sardis was

108. Marble statue of Cybele enthroned, with lion, cornucopia and mural crown in the shape of city walls (*ca.* AD 50).

---

[151] Hanfmann and Waldbaum, "Kybele and Artemis: Two Anatolian Goddesses at Sardis," 264–69; Mark Henderson Munn, *The Mother of the Gods, Athens, and the Tyranny of Asia: A Study of Sovereignty in Ancient Religion*, The Joan Palevsky Imprint in Classical Literature (Berkeley: University of California Press, 2006), 125–30.

[152] Burrell, *Neokoroi*, 110; George M. A. Hanfmann and Nancy H. Ramage, *Sculpture from Sardis: The Finds through 1975*, ed. George M. A. Hanfmann and S. W. Jacobs, AESR 2 (Cambridge, Mass.: Harvard University Press, 1978), 21.66, Figs. 105–117, nos. 27–29; J. H. Jongkees, "Gottesnamen in Lydischen Inschriften," *Mnemosyne* 3, no. 6 (1938): 355–67; Hanfmann, "On the Gods of Lydian Sardis," 223–25.

[153] Sherman Elbridge Johnson, "A Sabazios Inscription from Sardis," in *Religions in Antiquity: Essays in Memory of Erwin Ramsdell Goodenough*, ed. Jacob Neusner (Eugene, Or.: Wipf & Stock, 2004), 542–50; "Sabaoth/Sabazios: A Curiosity in Ancient Religion," *LTQ* 13, no. 4 (October 1978): 97–103; *The Present State of Sabazios Research* (Berlin: De Gruyter, 1984).

[154] See Nash for a good overview of Cybele. Ronald H. Nash, *Christianity and the Hellenistic World*, BSCS (Grand Rapids, Mich.: Zondervan, 1984), 138–39.

[155] Mükerrem Usman Anabolu, "Two Altars Dedicated to Demeter: The Goddess of Fertility," in Archaeology and Fertility Cult in the Ancient Mediterranean: Papers Presented at the First International Conference on Archaeology of the Ancient Mediterranean, University of Malta, 2–5 September 1985, ed. Anthony Bonanno (Amsterdam: John Benjamins, 1986), 268.

known as the city of Demeter.¹⁵⁶ Coins depict the sharing of honors between local deities and the imperial household, with Tiberius (AD 14–37; see Figs. 43, 97, 111) standing raising up a kneeling Tyche of Sardis, while on the other side, the goddess Demeter seated, holding a scepter and ears of grain (see Figs. 98). This coin marked the imperial relief efforts at Sardis after the devastating earthquake in AD 17.¹⁵⁷ Coins of Sardis depicting Demeter are more numerous than even Artemis.¹⁵⁸

4. A sanctuary on the top of Mount Tmolus is dedicated to the rain god, *Zeus Lydios*.¹⁵⁹ It is frequently depicted on coins from the reigns of Elagabalus and Philip with an eagle and scepter (Heracles; see Fig. 95 and Dionysus; see Fig. 35).¹⁶⁰ The appearance of Zeus (see Figs. 95, 115, 126, 151, 154, 156) changed in Sardis, having originally appeared in Lydian form.¹⁶¹ Zeus is called holy and righteous (*Theos Hosios kai Dikaios*) as a mediator between worlds.¹⁶² By contrast Revelation 15 and 16 speak of God exclusively as both "holy" and "righteous" (15:3–4; 16:5).

5. The temple of *Zeus Olympios* near the Palace of Croesus, built by Alexander the Great in 334 BC (Arrian *Anab*. 1.71.3–6).¹⁶³

6. The temple of *Zeus Asclepius*, described as "Protector of the city" (*Polieus*).¹⁶⁴

7. The mystery hall of *Attis*.¹⁶⁵ The Minotaur practice of being bathed in a bull's blood (*taurobolium*; see Strabo *Geogr*. 1.3.21) was associated with the cult of Attis, to represent the idea of death and rebirth.¹⁶⁶

---

[156] Peter Herrmann, "Demeter Karpophoros in Sardeis," *REA* 100 (1998): 495–508.

[157] *RPC* 1.2991; *BMC* Lydia 98; *SNG Cop*. 515. Michael Dräger, *Die Städte der Provinz Asia in der Flavierzeit: Studien zur kleinasiatischen Stadt- und Regionalgeschichte*, Europäische Hochschulschriften, III.576 (Frankfurt: Peter Lang, 1993), 435.

[158] Hemer, Letters to the Seven Churches, 259 n.43.

[159] Eumelus *Frag*. 18; *SEG* 46.1529; *AGRW* 126 = *SEG* 29.1205; *AGRW* 127 = *I.Sard*. 17. Louis Robert, "Une nouvelle inscription grecque de Sardes: Règlement de l'autorité perse relatif à un culte de Zeus," *CRAI* 119, no. 2 (1975): 306–30.

[160] Price and Trell, Coins and Their Cities: Architecture on the Ancient Coins of Greece, Rome, and Palestine, 49, 138.

[161] Hanfmann, "On the Gods of Lydian Sardis," 228–29.

[162] Hoz, *Die Lydischen*, no. 27.15.

[163] Hanfmann, Mierse, and Foss, *Sardis from Prehistoric*, 116.

[164] *CIG* 3159; *I.Sard*. 7.1.8; 7.1.221; Aristides *Orat*. 42.4; 47.45, 78; 49.7; 50.46. Cadoux, *Ancient Smyrna*, 203; Gregory Stevenson, *Beihefte Zur Zeitschrift Für Die Neutestamentliche Wissenschaft Und Die Kunde Der Älteren Kirche* (Berlin: de Gruyter, 2001), 100.

[165] *I.Sard*. 7.1.17; *IG II* 2.1315; Pausanias *Descr*. 7.17.9–12; Herodotus *Hist*. 5.102; Ovid *Fas*. 4.221–44. Clemens Bosch, *Die Kleinasiatischen Münzen Der Römischen Kaiserzeit* (Stuttgart, Germany: Kohlhammer, 1935), 245; Harland, *North Coast of the Black Sea, Asia Minor*, 209; Lynn E. Roller, *In Search of God the Mother: The Cult of Anatolian Cybele* (Berkeley,

8. The Hellenistic temple of *Metrōon*, the "Mother of the gods" (μητρῷον, *Metrōon*), state cult of Antiochus and a precinct of Laodicea, Antiochus's wife, known from the Antiochus inscription.¹⁶⁷

9. The sanctuary of *Aphrodite Paphia* is depicted on Hadrian coins.¹⁶⁸

109. Cistophoric Tetradrachm coin from Sardis. Struck after AD 128. Obv.: HADRIANVS AVGVSTVS P P. The image of Hadrian (AD 117–138) with a bare head. Rev.: COS III. The cult image of Kore wearing a high head-dress; on the left, a stalk of grain, on the right, a stalk of grain and a poppy. (RIC 2.510; RSC 279).

10. The temple of *Athena Nikephoros* (Νεικη[φό]-[ρου Ἀθην]ᾶς, "the bringer of victory"; see Figs. 13, 87, 163), a cult from Pergamum (*I.Sard.* 7.1.21; see also *SNG* Cop. 502).

11. The temple of *Baki-Dionysus*, the Lydian wine god (Rom. *Bacchus*) (ca. 150 BC; *I.Sard.* 7.1.4) celebrated with festivals.¹⁶⁹

12. The sanctuary (*hieron*) of *Qldans-Apollo*, the sun god and son of Zeus, was situated on the acropolis (ca. first cent. BC).¹⁷⁰ Prior to ca. 150 BC, a priest of Apollo, named Kadoas, was in the temple in Sardis (*SEG* 46.1519).

13. The temple of *Hera*, was dedicated by Sokrates Polemaiou Pardalas (ca. 100/50 BC).¹⁷¹

Calf.: University of California Press, 1999), 113–14; "Attis on Greek Votive Monuments; Greek God or Phrygian?," *Hesperia* 63, no. 2 (1994): 254; Hanfmann, "On the Gods of Lydian Sardis," 231. Roller notes that in the mid-second cent. BC, correspondence from the king of Pergamum to Cybele's shrine at Pessinos always addressed its chief priest as "Attis."

¹⁶⁶ George M. A. Hanfmann, "Lydiaka," *HSCP* 63 (1958): 66.

¹⁶⁷ Hanfmann, Mierse, and Foss, *Sardis from Prehistoric*, 111–12; Sherwin-White and Kuhrt, *From Samarkhand to Sardis*, 202–10.

¹⁶⁸ Price and Trell, Coins and Their Cities: Architecture on the Ancient Coins of Greece, Rome, and Palestine, 28.

¹⁶⁹ Hanfmann, "On the Gods of Lydian Sardis," 229. See also Cahill, "Sardis 2014," 156.

¹⁷⁰ Herodotus *Hist.* 5.102; Ctesias *Per.* Books 7–11, F9; Apollo Pleurenos; *SEG* 46.1520; 46.1528. T. V. Buttrey et al., *Greek, Roman, and Islamic Coins from Sardis*, AESM 7 (Cambridge, Mass.: Harvard University Press, 1981), 191–226; Hanfmann, Mierse, and Foss, *Sardis from Prehistoric*, 93–94, 118, 133, 155; Price and Trell, *Coins and Their Cities: Architecture on the Ancient Coins of Greece, Rome, and Palestine*, fig. 380; Burrell, *Neokoroi*, 109; Friedrich Wilhelm König, *Die Persika des Ktesias von Knidos* (Graz: Weidner, 1972), fr. 4; Andrew Nichols, "The Complete Fragments of Ctesias of Cnidus: Translation and Commentary with an Introduction" (Ph. D. diss., University of Florida, 2008), 89; Hoz, *Die Lydischen*, 54, 67, 102.

¹⁷¹ Louis Robert, "Documents d'Asie Mineure: V–XVII," *BCH* 102, no. 1 (1978): 405; *Documents d'Asia Mineure*, BEFAR 239 (Athens and Paris: École Française d'Athènes and De Boccard, 1987), 91–239; Hoz, *Die Lydischen*, nos.

14. A community dedicated to *Hekate*, the goddess of magic, patroness of witches, necromancy, and souls,[172] confirmed by a recent inscription (2014) that reads in part "the settlement of the Hekate-worshipers."[173]

15. The temple of *Kore* (Περσεφόνη, *Persephonē;* see Fig. 109), the grain goddess and daughter of Zeus (*I.Sard.* 7.1.77–79 = *IGR* 4.1519). During the time of Nero, following the earthquake of AD 17, focus seemed to shift from the worship of Artemis and Zeus to Kore.[174]

16. The sanctuary for *Meter* (Μητρί Θεών Λυδ[ίαι], *Mētri Theōn Lud[iai]*, mother of the gods).[175]

17. The temple of *Mên Askaenos* (Μήν, the moon god) was a recognized landmark at Sardis (*I.Sard.* 7.1.79 = *IGR* 4.1519).[176]

18. A *Hadrianeion* is mentioned along with the celebration of a Hadrianeia festival (*I.Sard.* 7.1.13, 14).[177]

19. *Tyche* (Τύχη, the goddess of fortune, or Cybele, see Figs. 52, 54, 98, 108, 160), and Heracles (see Fig. 95) were also worshiped at Sardis, although there is no mention of any sanctuaries for these gods.[178]

THE IMPERIAL CULT

Sardis has a cult of the goddess *Roma* (see Fig. 173) prior to the close of the second cent. BC. Inscriptions found identify the actual priest of Roma.[179] Before the end of the first cent. BC

21.1; 40.12.

[172] Ilmo Robert Von Rudloff and Robert Von Rudloff, *Hekate in Ancient Greek Religion* (Victoria, B.C: Horned Owl Publishing, 1999), 1–12.

[173] Nicholas D. Cahill, "Sardis 2014," *KST* 37, no. 3 (2015): 156.

[174] Head, *Catalogue of the Greek Coins of Lydia*, 110: 391; Fleischer, *Artemis von Ephesos*, 187–91; Buttrey et al., *Greek, Roman, and Islamic Coins from Sardis*, 7–10; Hanfmann, "On the Gods of Lydian Sardis," 226–28.

[175] Louis Robert, "Documents d'Asie Mineure," *BCH* 106, no. 3 (1982): 360–61; Peter Herrmann, "Sardeis Zur Zeit Der Iulisch-Claudischen Kaiser," in *Forschungen in Lydien*, ed. Elmar Schwertheim, AMStud. 17 (Bonn: Habelt, 1995), 30; Hoz, *Die Lydischen*, nos. 21.1; 40.12; Malay, *Researches in Lydia, Mysia and Aiolis*, no. 131; Roller, *In Search of God the Mother*, 196.

[176] Eugene N. Lane, *Corpvs Monvmentorvm Religionis Dei Menis: Interpretations and Testimonia*, vol. 3 (Leiden: Brill, 1976), 17, 43, 96; Hanfmann, "On the Gods of Lydian Sardis," 230 n.48.

[177] Burrell, *Neokoroi*, 110.

[178] James G. Frazer, *Adonis Attis Osiris: Studies In The History Of Oriental Religion* (London, U.K.: MacMillan & Co., 1906), 94–98; Koester, *Revelation*, 310. Frazer compares the annual burning of Heracles-Sandon of Tarsus with an attempt at *apotheōsis* in the account of the attempted burning on the pyre of Croesus. There are various accounts of his escape (Herodotus *Hist.* 1.86–87; Bacchylides *Ep.* 3.23–62).

[179] *I.Sard.* 7.1.8.75; 93; 112–15. For a comprehensive treatment of the Imperial Cult in Sardis from numismatic and epigraphic remains, see chapter 6, *Imperial Cult*. Sardis in Lydia (Antoninus Pius) in Burrell, *Neokoroi*, 100–115.

Sardis had a temple to Augustus (5 BC),[180] testified by some twenty-one inscriptions,[181] although there are no archaeological remains of this temple.[182] The Wadi B temple of the imperial cult has been partially excavated (see Fig. 99 no. 9).[183] The worship of the emperor no doubt was fueled in part by Sardis' gratitude for the relief supplied by the emperors Tiberius (see Figs. 43, 97, 111) and Claudius (see Figs. 2, 28) following the earthquake of AD 17. By the early second cent. AD, there was an early imperial pseudodipteral (style of Greek temple) provincial temple to Hadrian (ca. AD 117–138; in Ephesus see Fig. 33),[184] and not Vespasian (AD 69–79) as some have suggested. It has been partially excavated.[185]

Several times in the first century the city competed for the honor of being the *neōkoros* ("warden") of the provincial temple of the imperial cult (Tacitus *Ann.* 2.47), but on one occasion (AD 26) the honor went to Smyrna (Tacitus *Ann.* 4.55). However, despite the lack of a *neōkoros*, emperors such as Tiberius (r. AD 14–37, see Figs. 43, 97, 111), Caligula (r. AD 37–41) and Claudius (r. AD 41 to 54; see Fig. 2, 28) were honored as "god" at Sardis.[186] In ca. AD 80, T. Julius Lepidus, from Sardis, served as the provincial high priest in the imperial cult (*I.Sard.* 7.1.45 = *IGR* 4.1509).[187] Eventually Sardis was successful on three occasions in becoming *neōkoros*, first under Hadrian (r. AD 117–138; see Figs. 93, 109; *I.Sard.* 7.1.13, 14), second under Antoninus Pius (r. AD 138–161) using the renovated Artemis temple, and third under Elagabalus (Heliogabalus, r. AD 218–222). [188]

THE JEWISH COMMUNITY

If the term "Sepharad" in Obadiah 1:20 refers to Sardis,[189] then there may have been a Jewish community in Sardis as early as 586 BC, when Nebuchadnezzar destroyed Jerusalem. Regardless, evidence demonstrates that there was a large Jewish community at Sardis who were prosperous and influential.[190] Josephus reported that Antiochus III (r. 222–187 BC; see Fig. 96) transported 2,000 Jewish families from Mesopotamia and settled them in his newly acquired land of Phrygia and Lydia in 214 BC (Josephus *Ant.* 12.147–53).[191] It is very likely that many of

---

[180] *I.Sard.* 7.1.8.13–14; 7.8 = *IGR* 4.1756. Peter Thonemann, "A Copy of Augustus' Res Gestae at Sardis," *Historia* 61, no. 3 (2012): 288.

[181] Vermeule, *Roman Imperial Art*, 461.

[182] Yegül, *Bath-Gymnasium Complex*, 170; Hanfmann, *Letters from Sardis*, 33, figs. 17–18.

[183] Cahill, "Sardis 2014," 156.

[184] Burrell, *Neokoroi*, 100–103.

[185] Christopher Ratté, Thomas N. Howe, and Clive Foss, "An Early Imperial Pseudodipteral Temple at Sardis," *AJA* 90, no. 1 (1986): 45–68.

[186] Herrmann, "Sardeis Zur Zeit Der Iulisch," 31–36.

[187] Koester, "Roman Slave Trade and the Critique of Babylon in Revelation 18," 784.

[188] Burrell, *Neokoroi*, 100–110; Ratté, Howe, and Foss, "Early Imperial Pseudodipteral Temple," 45 n.1.

[189] Cook, "A Lydian-Aramaic Bilingual," 77–87; Beyer, *Obadiah, Jonah*, 25; Worth, Jr., *Greco-Asian Culture*, 292–93 n.1. For a list of authors who hold to Sephard being Sardis see Worth, although a more likely candidate for Sephard would be someplace in Mesopotamia. Worth, *Greco-Asian Culture*, 169.

[190] Kraabel, "Judaism in Western Asia Minor."

[191] Louis Robert, *Nouvelles Inscriptions de Sardes: Fasc. 1* (Paris, France: Librairie d'Amérique et d'Orient, 1964), 9–21.

the Jews settled in Sardis, given its central location and need for a large synagogue later in the third cent. AD. Jews are mentioned in the first cent. in the book of Revelation (1:11; 3:1–6) and mentioned in Josephus as an influential group (*politeuma*) with a place of worship (*Ant.* 14.235, 259–61; 16.171), and granted the right to send temple tax and ritually clean food (*Ant.* 14.261). The prominent location of the Jewish synagogue in Sardis, near the gymnasium, indicates the centrality of Jewish life and society of the city and the elaborate mosaics and richly decorated synagogue indicate the wealth and prominence of the Jewish citizens of Sardis (see *The Jewish Synagogue* above). The synagogue contained "more Jewish inscriptions than any other Diaspora centre except Rome."[192]

Around 49 BC, Lucius Antonius, the proconsul of the province of Asia, wrote to Sardis and stated:

> Jewish citizens of ours have come to me and pointed out that from the earliest times they have had an association of their own in accordance with their native laws and a place of their own [synagogue?], in which they decide their affairs and controversies with one another; and upon their request that it be permitted them to do these things, I decided that they might be maintained, and permitted them so to do (Josephus *Ant.* 14.235 [Marcus]).

Also, Gaius Norbanus Flaccus the proconsul, wrote to the council of Sardis and declared that the Jews in Sardis should not be prevented from sending the temple tax to Jerusalem "in accordance with their ancestral custom" (Josephus *Ant.* 16.171 [Marcus]; see also 14.232, 259–261).[193]

Sardis also passed a law by the council of Sardis confirming the privileges of the Jews who lived in the city. It stated:

> Whereas the Jewish citizens living in our city have continually received many great privileges from the people and have now come before the council and the people and have pleaded that as their laws and freedom have been restored to them by the Roman Senate and people, they may, in accordance with their accepted customs, come together and have a communal life and adjudicate suits among themselves, and that a place be given them in which they may gather together with their wives and children and offer their ancestral prayers and sacrifices to God, it has therefore been decreed by the council and people that permission shall be given them to come together on stated days to do those things which are in accordance with their laws, and also that a place shall be set apart by the magistrates for them to build and inhabit, such as they may consider suitable for this purpose, and that the market-officials of the city shall be charged with the duty of having suitable food for them brought in. (Josephus *Ant.* 16.259–261 [Marcus])

Several inscriptions document the role of Jews as goldsmiths (*IJO* 2.97–98), textile workers (Athenaeus *Deipn.* 6.255; 12.514), shopkeepers[194] and other profitable trades. No less than nine Jews are listed as members of the city's council (βουλευτής, *bouleutēs*).[195] While the Jewish text of

---

[192] Smallwood, *Jews Under Roman Rule*, 509; John H. Kroll, "Greek Inscriptions of the Sardis Synagogue," *HTR* 94 (2001): 5–55.

[193] This occurred until the destruction of the Jerusalem temple in AD 70.

[194] Waldbaum, "Metalwork and Metalworking in Sardis," 80.

[195] Hanfmann, *Letters from Sardis*, 100; Safrai, Stern, and Flusser, *The Jewish People in the First Century*, 479; Robert, *Nouvelles Inscriptions de Sardes: Fasc. 1*, 54–55; Andrew R. Seager, "The Architecture of the Dura and Sardis Synagogue,"

the Sibylline Oracles declares judgment against Sardis (5:289), the Jews were an integral part of Sardis society.[196] In the second cent. AD the Jews of Sardis are mentioned in the writing of Melito, the bishop of Sardis (died ca. AD 180).[197]

THE CHRISTIAN COMMUNITY

In contrast to the Jewish community, little is known about the Christian community at Sardis. The origins may be associated with Paul's missionary journeys to Asia Minor (Acts 18:18–23) and his extended stay for about three years at Ephesus (Acts 19). At the time of John's message to the church, the Christians in Sardis appeared to be successful and prospering, although in fact spiritually they were dead (3:1) but capable of being revived (3:3). Only "a few names in Sardis" (3:4) had remained faithful. The theme of death and resurrection would resonate in a city that celebrated in its many deities the idea of death followed by immortality and *apotheōsis*.

Melito, a Jew by birth, was a highly-praised leader in the early church (Jerome *Vir. ill.* 24)[198] and bishop of Sardis (ca. AD 160–177), who is called "the Eunuch" by Polycrates (Eusebius *Hist. eccl.* 5.24.5).[199] Melito is remembered for his work developing the first OT Canon (Eusebius *Hist. eccl.* 4.26.13–14) and his notable sermon titled "Concerning Passover" (*Peri pascha*), that dealt with the controversy at Laodicea over the observance of Easter.[200] Christians in Sardis followed the Jewish date for the Passover for their Easter observance,[201] earning Melito's strong criticism. He was very wary of the Jews in his work, as were other Christian writers of the period (see *Synagogue of Satan*).[202] He was martyred during the reign of Marcus Aurelius (ca. AD 177).[203]

---

in *The Synagogue: Studies in Origins, Archaeology and Architecture*, ed. Harry M. Orlinksy, South Florida Studies in the History of Judaism (New York, N.Y.: KTAV, 1975), 149–93.

[196] Trebilco, *Jewish Communities*, 37–54, 183–85.

[197] Eusebius *Hist. eccl.* 4.26.13; 5.24.5; Jerome *Vir. ill.* 24. A. Thomas Kraabel, "Melito the Bishop and the Synagogue at Sardis: Text and Context," in *Studies Presented to George M. A. Hanfmann*, ed. David Gordon Mitten, John Griffiths Pedley, and Jane Ayer Scott (Mainz: P. von Zabern, 1971), 77–85.

[198] A. Stewart-Sykes, *The Lamb's High Feast: Melito, Peri Pascha, and the Quartodeciman Paschal Liturgy at Sardis*, Supplements to Vigiliae Christianae (Leiden: Brill Academic, 1998), 1–4.

[199] Alexander Roberts et al., eds., *Nicene and Post-Nicene Fathers, Series I* (Peabody, Mass.: Hendrickson, 1994), 1:203.

[200] Lynn H. Cohick, *The Peri Pascha Attributed to Melito of Sardis: Setting, Purpose, and Sources*, Brown Judaic Studies (Atlanta, Ga.: Scholars Press, 2000), 6–7.

[201] Stewart-Sykes, *The Lamb's High Feast*, 11–25.

[202] Stephen G. Wilson and Stephen G. Wilson, eds., "Melito and Israel," in *Anti-Judaism in Early Christianity: Separation and Polemic*, vol. 2, ESCJ 2 (Waterloo, Ont.: Wilfrid Laurier University Press, 1986), 81–102.

[203] Lightfoot, *The Apostolic Fathers (APF)*, 2.1:462, 510.

13

Sedate Sardis

Commentary on Revelation 3:1–6

John is commanded to write to the angel of each church, and this chapter will examine the content of his message to sedate Sardis, who were lax in their watchfulness. Revelation 3:1–6 will be examined in light of the proposed covenant background and structure. A second or third cent. inscription from Saittai, some forty miles northeast of Sardis, refers to an ἄγγελος [*angelos*] or ἀγγελικος [*angelikos*], a divine messenger. It reads: ἄγγελος ὅσιος δίκαιος, [*aggelos osios dikaios*], "the holy and just intermediary" (or messenger).[1] On the commission to write (γράψον, *graphon* 3:7a) and the role of angels (ἄγγελος, *angelos*) as mediating messengers, see chapter 3, *The Messenger's Commission*.

MESSENGER PREAMBLE FORMULA—3:1B

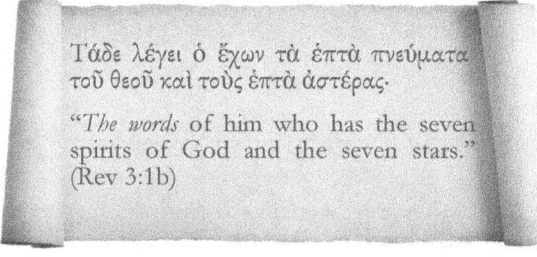

"The words of him who has the seven spirits of God and the seven stars."
(Rev 3:1b)

John begins each message to the churches with τάδε λέγει Ω (*tade legei omega*, "These are the words" 2:1, 8,12,18; 3:1a, 7, 14), setting the context for the suzerain/king who will speak to the churches.[2] He proceeds to describe Christ as an echo from Revelation chapter 1 (vs. 13, 16) in a format familiar to the Christian community. Within the OT prophetic structure[3] this prophetic *messenger preamble formula*[4] τάδε λέγει Ω, (*tade legei omega*, "These are the words") introduces the sovereign's message.

The messenger preamble to Sardis is almost identical to the message to Ephesus (2:1) and suggests a similar censure and purpose.[5] Sardis received the severest of all the censures to the

---

[1] Nilsson, *Geschichte Der Griechischen Religion*, 2.577; Louis Robert, "Reliefs Votifs et Cultes d'Anatolie," *Anatolia* 3 (1958): 120–23; F. Sokolowski, "Sur Le Culte d'Angelos Dans Ie Paganisme Grec et Romain," *HTR* 53 (1960): 225–29.

[2] Beale, *Revelation*, 229.

[3] Num 22:15–16; Judg 11:14–15; 1 Kgs 2:30; 2 Chr 36:23; Ezra 1:2.

[4] Graves, *SMRVT*, 141–47; Osborne, *Revelation*, 111.

churches, something which may be associated with its wealth and false sense of security. To prepare for these harsh words the sovereignty of the suzerain is portrayed in the imagery of one who "has the seven spirits of God and the seven stars" (3:1). The imagery here harkens back to Revelation chapter 1 where Christ appears in the vision to John holding seven stars in his right hand (ver. 16). Verse 20 of that chapter identifies the seven stars with the angels (ἄγγελος, *angelos*) of the churches under the control of the suzerain. The message begins with a reminder that it is the sovereign Christ who is the head of the church in Sardis, and it is he who speaks to his church, and these are his words.

Views differ on the identification of the seven spirits (τὰ ἑπτὰ πνεύματα, *ta epta pneumata*) and five main possibilities have been suggested:

1. **Planetary Deities:** which are identified with archangels.[6] However, this is unlikely since John is strongly against angel-worship (19:10),[7] and they have elsewhere been identified as angels (1:4).

2. **Seven-fold endowment of the Spirit of God:** "And the Spirit of the LORD shall rest upon him, the Spirit of wisdom and understanding, the Spirit of counsel and might, the Spirit of knowledge and the fear of the LORD" (Isa 11:2). These six spiritual endowments in Isaiah are given to the Messiah and transformed into the seven-fold operation of the Spirit of God.[8] It is unlikely that John was aware of this connection.[9]

3. **Symbolic depiction of Divine power:** Ramsay maintains that it "must certainly be taken as a symbol or allegorical way of expressing the full range of exercise of the Divine power in the seven churches."[10]

4. **Angelic beings:** are identified as the angelic entourage who serve as attendants of God (1:4; Tob 12:15) or "the archangels that stand before the countenance of God" (8:2).[11] Stars and spirits are used to symbolize angels[12] and as his eyes they are the servants of the Lamb. Spirits (πνεύματα, *pneumata*) are understood to be angelic beings.[13] The καί (*kai*) is epexegetic, indicating "even" or "namely", so it can be translated "the seven spirits of God, even the seven

---

[5] Beale, *Rev*, 272.
[6] Bousset, Die Offenbarung Johannis, 184–87.
[7] Charles, *Revelation*, 12.
[8] Justin *Dial.* 87; Irenaeus *Haer.* 3.18.2; Victorinus *Comm. Apoc.* 1.1. Swete, *Apocalypse*, 6; Charles, *Revelation*, 11; Alford, *Revelation*, 4:579. Also supported by the early writings of Victorinus, Primasius, Apringius and Beatus.
[9] K. Schlütz, Isaias 11:2 (Die Sieben Gaben Des Hl. Geistes) in Den Ersten Vier Jahrhunderten (Münster: Aschendorff, 1932).
[10] Ramsay, *Letters: Updated*, 272; Beckwith, *Apocalypse*, 425.
[11] Roloff, *Revelation*, 58; Mounce, *Revelation*, 93; Koester, *Revelation*, 311–12; Aune, *Rev 1–5*, 34–35.
[12] Heb 1:14; *Jub.* 15:31–32; *1 En.* 61:12; 86:1, 3; 1QM 3:22; 12:8–9; 4Q405 23:1.8–9; *TDNT* 6:375–76.
[13] Charles, *Revelation*, 13.

stars."[14] As Aune argues "since the seven spirits of God constitute a heavenly reality, while the seven stars are a symbol of a heavenly reality. Thus, the seven stars [ἀστέρας, *asteras*] are angels [*T. Levi* 18:2], just as the seven spirits are angels [1:20]"[15] (1.4 = 3:1; 4:5; 5:6; 8:2). Beckwith challenges this view by pointing out that throughout Revelation angels are clearly identified as angels, but the discovery of the DSS has challenged Beckwith's argument,[16] although Caird rightly reminds us that the spirits address the angels, so they cannot be the same.[17]

5. **The Holy Spirit:** The seven spirits (τὰ ἑπτὰ πνεύματα, *ta epta pneumata*) here (see 3:1; 4:5; 5:6) are based on the seven eyes of Zech 4:10, that symbolize the Spirit's omniscience, with eyes that canvas the earth (Zech 4:1–10). The seven churches are represented "by the third Person of the Trinity, who knows all and whose purpose is to testify through the seven lampstands established in these seven cities."[18] Swete argues that there are seven spirits because there are seven churches.[19] Aune believes this argument is artificial and based on later Trinitarian views of the church.[20]

It seems more probable that, given the strong OT imagery (Zech 4:1–10), this last option is closer to what John had in mind. The seven stars speak of the suzerain who has sovereign control over the seven churches. Thomas concludes that Christ's "constant control is not limited to the messengers, represented by the stars, but extends through them to the whole church."[21] The life-giving Spirit can correct the problems of the dead church in Sardis by imparting life.[22] The seven stars are in the hand of Christ the suzerain, where they are held securely but also subject to he who exercises judgment.

---

[14] Smalley, *Revelation*, 81; Aune, *Rev 1–5*, 219. Resseguie argues that "is unlikely since John lists two separate traits of the exalated Christ in other letters (e.g., 2:1, 19). Resseguie, *Revelation of John*, 94 n.43.

[15] Aune, *Rev 1–5*, 219, 33–37; Koester, *Revelation*, 312.

[16] Beckwith, *Apocalypse*, 424; John Strugnell, "The Angelic Liturgy at Qumran," in *Congress Volume, Oxford 1959*, ed. G. W. Anderson et al., VTSup 7 (Leiden: Brill, 1960), 318–45; Maxwell Davidson, *Angels at Qumran: A Comparative Study of 1 Enoch 1–36; 72–108 and Sectarian Writings from Qumran* (New York, N.Y.: A&C Black, 1992), 235–86.

[17] Caird, *Revelation*, 48.

[18] Thomas, *Rev 1–7*, 244; Beckwith, *Apocalypse*, 424–27; Krodel, *Revelation*, 130–31; Sweet, *Revelation*, 98; Hemer, *Letters to the Seven Churches*, 142; Osborne, *Revelation*, 173; Kistemaker, *Revelation*, 150; Frederick Fyvie Bruce, "The Spirit in the Apocalypse," in *Christ and Spirit in the New Testament: Studies in Honour of Charles Francis Digby Moule*, ed. Barnabas Lindars and Stephen S. Smalley (Cambridge, U.K.: Cambridge University Press, 2008), 336–37; Metzger, *Breaking the Code*, 23–24; Smalley, *Thunder and Love*, 130; Talbert, *Apocalypse*, 14; Bauckham, *Theology of Revelation*, 25, 110–15; Johnson, *Triumph of the Lamb*, 84.

[19] Henry Barclay Swete, *The Holy Spirit in the New Testament* (Eugene, Oreg.: Wipf & Stock, 1999), 274; *Apocalypse*, 6.

[20] Aune, *Rev 1–5*, 34.

[21] Thomas, *Rev 1–7*, 244–45.

[22] Rom 8:2; Acts 2:33; Eph 4:7–8. Moffatt, *Revelation*, 5:5:364; Beasley-Murray, *Revelation*, NCB, 94–95.

Historical prologue—3:1

The *historical prologue*[23] presents a synopsis of the suzerain's past relationship between the suzerain and the vassal. The mutually binding recognition of the relationship between the suzerain and the vassal is presented in a historical summary.[24] The omniscient suzerain intimately knew the Sardis church.

The first person οἶδα (*oida*, "I know") was a common feature in the historical prologues of ANEVT's,[25] as it is in the SMR. Christ has an intimate knowledge of Sardis, as well as their ongoing covenantal relationship.[26] Οἶδα conveys the idea of an intimate and intuitive knowledge,[27] and in Sardis' case he knows their works and their reputation of being alive, but in reality being dead.

The suzerain knows their works—3:1c

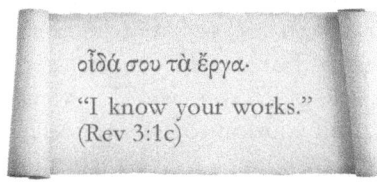

The suzerain has knowledge of the works (οἶδά σου τὰ ἔργα, *oida sou ta erga* "I know your works") of this congregation, although the actual works are not as clearly spelled out as in some of the other churches. Was it their reputation of being alive that was their remembered work, or was it their dead works? The conjunction ὅτι (*hoti*) introduces an object clause that infers that their works (τὰ ἔργα, *ta erga*) had a "living" nature.[28]

The suzerain knows their reputation—3:1d

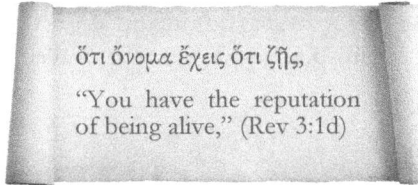

The suzerain knows that Sardis had the reputation (ὄνομα ἔχεις, *onoma echeis*, "you have a name"; see Herodotus *Hist.* 7.138) of being a lively church. Little positive is mentioned in the message to Sardis, other than their reputation of life (ζῇς, *zēs*). The word ὄνομα (*onoma*, "name") is used four times in this message (3:1, 4,

---

[23] For an extensive treatment of the "historical prologue" in the Hittite treaties, see Altman, *The Historical Prologue of the Hittite Vassal Treaties an Inquiry into the Concepts of Hittite Interstate Law.*

[24] Berman, "Histories Twice Told," 232; Huffmon, "Treaty Background," 31–37; Mendenhall, "Covenant Forms," 59; Thompson, *ANE Treaties*, 16; Thompson, "Near Eastern Suzerain-Vassal," 4; Walton, *Ancient Israelite Literature*, 102.

[25] Hartman, "The Book of Revelation," 143; Baltzer, *Covenant Formulary*, 20–24; Aune, *Rev 1–5*, 121. Aune identifies this as the *narratio* section.

[26] Allison, Sojourners and Strangers, 76–78.

[27] Robertson, *Word Pictures*, 6:297; James H. Moulton and George Milligan, *Vocabulary of the Greek Testament* (London, U.K.: Hodder & Stoughton, 1930), 439; Horst Balz and Gerhard Schneider, eds., *Exegetical Dictionary of the New Testament* (Grand Rapids, Mich.: Eerdmans, 1990), 2:494; Mounce, *Revelation*, 68.

[28] Alford, *Revelation*, 4:579.

5 twice) and the meaning varies from "reputation" here (3:1), to "an individual" in Revelation 3:4, 5.[29] While others may see the Christians at Sardis having a thriving reputation for life, the suzerain is aware of their deficiencies.

THE SUZERAIN KNOWS THEY ARE DEAD—3:1E

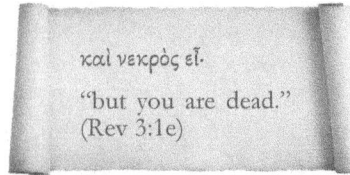
καὶ νεκρὸς εἶ.
"but you are dead."
(Rev 3:1e)

Although their outward reputation in the church and community is one of being a lively church, the suzerain knows otherwise. In fact, he knows they are dead, (νεκρὸς, *nekros*). There is an antithetical paradox described here in terms of "life" and "death." In Revelation 1:8 Jesus is presented as one who died and rose again, and now similar language is used to metaphorically describe the Sardians. There are several possible local references alluded to here.[30] First, the prominence of death and immortality within the polytheistic deities worshiped by Sardians (see *The Gods of Sardis* above), is paradoxically portrayed in the apparent life and death of the church there.[31] Second, understood against the background of the city's impressive nearby necropolis (city of death), is there a contrast with the declining acropolis? This view depicts the city as declining in the first century.[32] Wood suggests "an allusion to the opposing hills of Sardis, the acropolis and Necropolis, so that the Christians there appear lively like the acropolis but are actually dead like the city's almost equally visible necropolis."[33] However, the city was thriving during the first century.[34] Third, the allusion may be to the Synagogue in Sardis, that gave the appearance of having a positive reputation within the community but in reality was full of syncretism with the Roman authorities.

However, the exalted suzerain knows that the Christians in Sardis are not alive (ζῇς, *zēs*), but in reality spiritually dead (νεκρὸς, *nekros;* 3:1e; See also 2 Tim 3:5; Jas 2:17) with defiled clothes and in need of repentance and cleansing.[35]

ETHICAL STIPULATIONS—3:2–3A

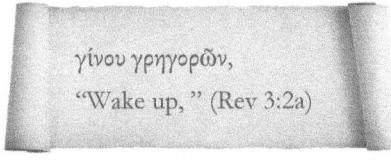
γίνου γρηγορῶν,
"Wake up, " (Rev 3:2a)

The loyalty of the churches (vassals) to the suzerain is demonstrated through obedience to stated ethical stipulations. While two of the churches, Smyrna and Philadelphia, are called to continued faithfulness, five churches are called to correct their deficiencies. The

---

[29] Swete, Revelation, 48; Beckwith, Apocalypse, 473; Hemer, Letters to the Seven Churches, 143.
[30] Johnson, "Revelation," 626; Wood, "Local Knowledge," 264; Thomas, *Rev 1–7*, 247.
[31] Keener, *Revelation*, 143; Osborne, *Revelation*, 174; Smalley, *Revelation*, 80.
[32] Ramsay, *Letters: Updated*, 272–75; Hemer, *Letters to the Seven Churches*, 143; Moffatt, *Revelation*, 5:364; Arthur S. Peake, *The Revelation of John* (London, U.K.: Johnson, 1919), 249; Charles, *Revelation*, 78; Thomas, *Rev 1–7*, 247.
[33] Wood, "Local Knowledge," 263–64.
[34] Koester, *Revelation*, 311.
[35] Col 2:13; Heb 6:1; Rev 3:3–4; 7:14; 22:14. Caird, *Revelation*, 48; Aune, *Rev 1–5*, 227.

stipulations surrounding the Sardis message are given in terms of five imperatives—wake up, strengthen, remember, keep, and repent.

FIRST IMPERATIVE: BE VIGILANT—3:2A

The suzerain prescribes the covenant obligation of constant vigilance in this first command to wake up (γρηγορῶν, grēgorōn).[36] The tense of the verb γίνου (ginou; present progressive) indicates a continuing state,[37] and can literally be translated as "become one who is watchful".[38] This must have resonated with the church in Sardis, where twice the city had been conquered due to a failure to be vigilant and watch their walls (see *Curses* below).[39]

SECOND IMPERATIVE: STRENGTHEN WHAT REMAINS—3:2B

> καὶ στήρισον τὰ λοιπὰ ἃ ἔμελλον ἀποθανεῖν, οὐ γὰρ εὕρηκά σου τὰ ἔργα πεπληρωμένα ἐνώπιον τοῦ θεοῦ μου.
>
> "and strengthen what remains and is about to die, for I have not found your works complete in the sight of my God." (Rev 3:2b)

The second imperative from the suzerain is to "strengthen what remains and is about to die" (καὶ στήρισον τὰ λοιπὰ ἃ ἔμελλον ἀποθανεῖν, *kai stērison ta loipa ha emellon apothanein*). The suzerain commands the Sardian Christians to strengthen (στήρισον, *stērison*; aorist imperative that conveys urgency) the remaining things (τὰ λοιπὰ, *ta loipa*). This is a rather unusual construction, though is also found in Revelation 8:13; 9:20; 11:13, and should be translated here as "that which survives".[40] The urgency indicates that the death is not absolute and there is hope remaining, although, as the aorist tense indicates, the precise moment of death (ἀποθανεῖν, *apothanein*; aorist) is in sight, perhaps an allusion to martyrdom.[41] As Thomas has described "the church was to erect once again the impressive spiritual fortress that had once stood in this pagan city."[42] While some commentators take the imperfect to be epistolary,[43] that is, viewing their dyeing from the perspective of the writer, it appears that they had been dyeing for some time.[44]

Further clarification of the "former things" (τὰ λοιπὰ, *ta loipa*) is now given in the rest of the verse by the suzerain who declares "for I have not found your works fulfilled before the

---

[36] See also Rev 3:3; 16:15; Matt 24:42 = Mark 13:25; Rom 13:11; 1 Cor 16:13.

[37] Morris, *Revelation*, 78.

[38] Stanley E. Porter, *Verbal Aspect in the Greek of the New Testament, with Reference to Tense and Mood*, 3rd ed., Studies in Biblical Greek (New York, N.Y.: Peter Lang, 2003), 491; Hort, *Apocalypse*, 32; Beckwith, *Apocalypse*, 473; Hemer, *Letters to the Seven Churches*, 143; Thomas, *Rev 1–7*, 248.

[39] Almost all commentators acknowelege the local allusion with the history of the city. Osborne, *Revelation*, 174; Smalley, *Revelation*, 81; Hemer, *Letters to the Seven Churches*, 144; Worth, Jr., *Greco-Asian Culture*, 184–88; Beale, *Rev*, 276.

[40] Hemer, Letters to the Seven Churches, 143–44; Thomas, Rev 1–7, 249.

[41] Trench, *Commentary on Seven Churches*, 209; Witherington III, *Revelation*, 105.

[42] Thomas, *Rev 1–7*, 249.

[43] Charles, *Revelation*, 1:79; Hemer, *Letters to the Seven Churches*, 144; Thomas, *Rev 1–7*, 249.

[44] Osborne, *Revelation*, 175.

eyes of My God[45] (οὐ γὰρ εὕρηκά σου τὰ ἔργα πεπληρωμένα ἐνώπιον τοῦ θεοῦ μου, *ou gar heurēka sou ta erga peplērōmena enōpion tou Theou mou*). The suzerain's evaluation of the vassal's performance indicated that the quality of the Sardian acts (τὰ ἔργα, *ta erga*) did not fulfill (πεπληρωμένα, *peplērōmena*, complete) God's[46] covenant requirements, although appeared to impress others (see 3:9). Aune sees here the judicial metaphor of a courtroom, with their works being presented, and a ruling of guilty or innocence being issued.[47] The suzerain on the throne has found their deeds "incomplete", both in quantity and quality. Koester points out that "early Christians could speak of completing their work, service,[48] and requirements of the law (Rom 13:8)."[49] Others have found a local comparison with the temple of Artemis (see Figs. 28, 29, 24).[50] Mounce states "like the unfinished temple of Artemis, the works of the church constantly fell short of completion."[51]

Some take the neuter plural form of "establish what is left" (στήρισον τὰ λοιπά, *stērison ta loipa*) to have a meaning that includes the past city of Sardis.[52] Building on this idea, Beale and Wilcock suggest that the problem was a spiritual lethargy that was symptomatic of "not *witnessing* to their faith before the unbelieving culture."[53] Koester also suggests that their failure was in not following through with the commitment to witness, love, and serve.[54] Whatever their failures were, the imperatives from the suzerain were to lead the vassal back from the brink of death to life through repentance, and land them back on their feet.[55]

THIRD IMPERATIVE: BEAR IN MIND WHAT YOU RECEIVED—3:3A

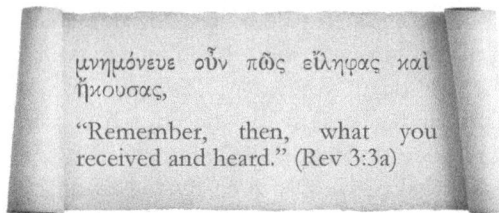

μνημόνευε οὖν πῶς εἴληφας καὶ ἤκουσας,

"Remember, then, what you received and heard." (Rev 3:3a)

The third ethical imperative, declared by the suzerain, continues in verse 3 with the imperative to "bear in mind" (μνημόνευε, *mnēmoneue*; present imperative).[56] Thomas and others have identified that μνημόνευε, (*mnēmoneue*) "is not a bid to the readers to recall [remember] something from the past, but a command to

---

[45] "My God" is only used here and in Revelation 3:12 where it occurs 4 times.

[46] "In the eyes or view of God" (ἐνώπιον τοῦ θεοῦ μου, *enōpion tou Theou mou*) is an OT formula used eight times in Revelation (3:2; 8:2, 4; 9:13; 11:4, 16; 12:10; 16:19). Smalley, *Revelation*, 82.

[47] 1QS 9:2; Sir 44:17, 20; Acts 5:39; 23:9; 1 Cor 15:15; 2 Cor 5:3; 1 Pet 1:7; 2 Pet 3:14; see also Rev 2:2; 5:4; 12:8; 14:5; 20:15. Pedersen, *EDNT* 2:84; Aune, *Rev 1–5*, 220; Osborne, *Revelation*, 175.

[48] Acts 12:25; 14:26; Rom 15:19.

[49] Koester, *Revelation*, 313.

[50] Mounce, *Revelation*, 94; Osborne, *Revelation*, 175–76.

[51] Mounce, *Revelation*, 94.

[52] Smalley, *Revelation*, 81; Swete, *Apocalypse*, 49.

[53] Beale, *Rev*, 273; Wilcock, *Heaven Opened*, 52.

[54] Koester, *Revelation*, 317.

[55] *TDNT* 7:653–57.

[56] Mounce, *Revelation*, 94.

keep in the forefront of their attention their rich spiritual heritage of the past as a motivating force in their restoration."⁵⁷ The remedy for spiritual death is to constantly bear in mind the gracious gift received (εἴληφας, *eilēthas;* perfect tense) and heard (καὶ ἤκουσας, *kai ēkousas;* aorist tense)⁵⁸ from the suzerain in the form of the gospel.⁵⁹ The word πῶς (*pōs*) usually means "what", signifying what they received, although here it is connected with τήρει (*tērei,* "pay attention to"), a word that demands an object, and changes the translation to "how"; i.e., how they received and heard the gospel message (1 Thess 1:5, 9).⁶⁰ They are to bear in mind that the gospel came to them through apostolic tradition ("received" 1 Cor 15:3) and the preaching of the gospel ("heard").⁶¹ A similar imperative "to remember . . . and repent" was issued to Ephesus (2:5).

FOURTH IMPERATIVE: KEEP IT OR PAY ATTENTION—3:3B

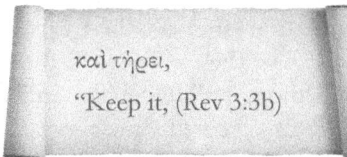
καὶ τήρει,
"Keep it, (Rev 3:3b)

The fourth ethical imperative, declared by the suzerain to Sardis, is keep τήρει, (*tērei,* present imperative; "pay attention to")⁶² your faith in the gospel.⁶³ Although some prefer "obey" for the meaning of τήρει, (*tērei*), it is better understood as "keep" (RSV, ESV), as in earnest attention,⁶⁴ or "keep on keeping."⁶⁵ Also debated is the object that is referred to here. Thomas argues for "the remaining things" in verse 2,⁶⁶ while others argue for the Gospel.⁶⁷

FIFTH IMPERATIVE: REPENT—3:3C

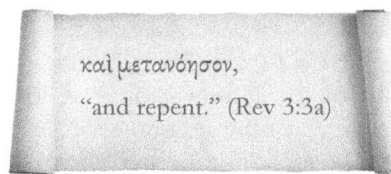
καὶ μετανόησον,
"and repent." (Rev 3:3a)

The fifth and final ethical imperative, declared by the suzerain to Sardis, is repent (μετανόησον, *metanoēson,* repent, aorist), intending to convey urgency. Aune points out that the two verbs τήρει καὶ μετανόησον, (*tērei kai metanoēson,* obey that and repent"):

are both in the imperative and are an example of the literary

---

⁵⁷ Thomas, *Rev 1–7*, 251; Robertson, *Word Pictures*, 6:314; Morris, *Revelation*, 76.
⁵⁸ On the change of tense see Swete, *Revelation*, 50; Mounce, *Revelation*, 94; Smalley, *Revelation*, 82.
⁵⁹ According to Vos, the object of the verbs "to receive" (εἴληφας, *eilēthas*) and "to hear" (καὶ ἤκουσας, *kai ēkousas*) is the gospel. Vos, *The Synoptic Traditions in the Apocalypse*, 211–14.
⁶⁰ Beckwith, *Apocalypse*, 474; Smalley, *Revelation*, 82; Koester, *Revelation*, 314.
⁶¹ Rev 2:7, 11, 17, 29; see also 1 Cor 11:23; 15:1; 1 Thess 2:13; John 17:8.
⁶² *TDNT* 8:142.
⁶³ Kistemaker, *Revelation*, 152.
⁶⁴ Sweet, *Revelation*, 99.
⁶⁵ Alford, *Revelation*, 4:4:580; Morris, *Revelation of St. John*, 76.
⁶⁶ Thomas, *Rev 1–7*, 251; Morris, *Revelation*, 79.
⁶⁷ Kistemaker, *Revelation*, 151; Vos, *The Synoptic Traditions in the Apocalypse*, 211–14; Eduard Schick, *Revelation of St. John*, trans. W. Kruppa, New Testament for Spiritual Reading (New York, N.Y.: Herder & Herder, 1971), 40; Mounce, *Revelation*, 94; Osborne, *Revelation*, 176; Adela Yarbro Collins, *The Apocalypse*, New Testament Message: A Biblical-Theological Commentary Series (Wilmington, Del.: Michael Glazier, Inc., 1979), 24; Johnson, "Revelation," 628.

device *hysteron-proteron*, "last-first" (i.e., placing two events in reverse order, a phenomenon that occurs frequently in Revelation: 3:17; 5:5; 6:4; 10:4, 9; 20:4–5, 12–13; 22:14), since one would normally expect the mention of "repentance" before "obey."[68]

In classical writings, "repent" (μετανόησον, *metanoēson;* Lat. *resipiscentia*, repentance) and its cognates express the idea of a "change of mind",[69] but in the NT it conveys the idea of "a complete change of attitude, spiritual and moral, towards God."[70] It differs from regret (μεταμέλομαι, *metamelomai*) as regret does not carry the idea of a complete change of heart in the same way that μετανόησον (*metanoēson*) does.[71]

SANCTIONS

The prophetic sanctions, where the vassal is cursed (malediction) for disobedience (dishonors the treaty), and blessed (benedictions) for obedience to the stated stipulations (honors the treaty, is a central element of the ANEVT structure.[72] Sanctions are found in all of the messages to the churches to Asia Minor and the curses are always mentioned first, although Philadelphia and Smyrna do not list a malediction in their message. The church at Sardis received the severest reprimand of the seven messages for accommodating its pagan surroundings,[73] prompting Caird to calls it "a perfect model of inoffensive Christianity"[74]. For Sardis, the malediction of a sudden visit in judgment of the suzerain awaits those who do not repent, but for those who overcome, white robes await as their benediction.

CURSES—3:3D-E

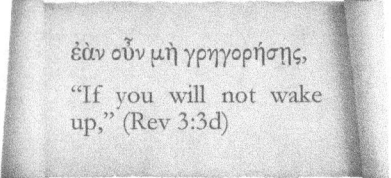

ἐὰν οὖν μὴ γρηγορήσῃς,

"If you will not wake up," (Rev 3:3d)

Maledictions, or what the ANEVTs identify as curses, were common in the treaties of the Hittite Empire, Old Babylonian, Assyrian, Egyptian, and other periods.[75] They were known in the OT (חרם *ḥērem*, "destruction"[76]) and also in the book of Revelation (22:3; κατάθεμα, *katanathema*, "accursed thing" see Zech 14:11; חרם *ḥērem*,

---

[68] Aune, *Rev 1–5*, 221.

[69] Thucydides *Hist.* 3.36.3; Polybius *Hist.* 4.66.7; Plutarch *Peric.* 100.10.

[70] MM 403. See Matt 3:8, 11; Luke 3:8; 15:7; 24:47; Acts 26:20.

[71] Richard C. Trench, *Synonyms of the New Testament* (New York, N.Y.: Cosimo Classics, 2007), 255. See also BDAG 512.

[72] See chapter 3, *Sanctions.*

[73] Peake, The Revelation of John, 249.

[74] Caird, *Revelation*, 48.

[75] For an analysis of the role of imprecation in the ANE as protectors of the law, see Assman, "When Justice Fails," 149–62.

[76] Lev 27:19, 28–29; Num 21:2; Deut 13:16–17; Josh 6:21; 10:28; See also Isa 11:15.

"destruction"; LXX ἀνάθεμα, *anathema*, "cursed" and Isa 34:1–2 (חרם; LXX ἀπόλλυμι, *apollumi*, "destroy" or "ruin"). The curse is removed by the redemptive work of the Lamb (5:6; 5:12; 7:14, 17; 12:11; 17:14; 22:3).[77]

The following malediction of the sudden appearance of the suzerain (3:3e) is awaiting those who "will not wake up" (μὴ γρηγορήσῃς, *mē grēgorēsēs;* 3:3d). Osborne argues that the ἐὰν οὖν μὴ (*ean oun mē*, "if you will not"), that introduces the challenge, should not be taken as an assumption of their response, but rather as a warning and not a condition, translated as "unless".[78] "Wake up" or "watch" (γρηγορήσῃς, *grēgorēsēs*) is tied to the first imperative (3:2a) and provides continuity between the ethical stipulations and the sanctions. The vassal must return to a state of covenant obedience to the suzerain if they are to know his blessings. For those who do not wake up, the suzerain will come unexpectedly as a thief.

Justin notes that the Jews cursed Christians in the Synagogue and spoke disparagingly about them after their prayers (*Dial.* 16, 93, 95, 96, 123, 133).[79] The Jewish "curse of the *Minim*" ("heretic"), found as an addition to *The Eighteen Benedictions*, prayed daily by Jews in the ancient world, is juxtaposed against the blessing of the Sardis congregation, overturning the curse of the *Minim* ("heretic"; 3:5b see below).[80]

CURSE OF COMING LIKE A THIEF—3:3E

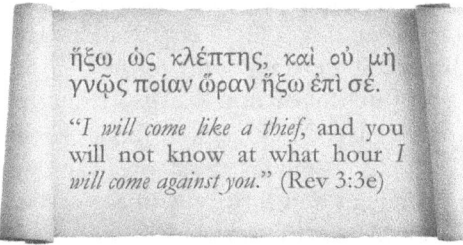

ἥξω ὡς κλέπτης, καὶ οὐ μὴ γνῷς ποίαν ὥραν ἥξω ἐπὶ σέ.

"*I will come like a thief,* and you will not know at what hour *I will come against you.*" (Rev 3:3e)

Bauckham (and others) hold that the sayings in Revelation 3:3, 20, 16:15 are influenced by the second coming parable of the watchful servants and the unexpected thief (κλέπτης, *kleptēs*).[81] Bauckham argued that these sayings are examples of "deparabolization", where the imagery in the parable is employed apart from its parabolic context (see *Quotes from Antiquity*).[82] Paul also exhorted believers to keep watch for Christ's return, as "the day of the Lord will come like a

---

[77] Beale, *Revelation*, 1112. D. Müller, "ἀνάθεμα," *NIDNTT* 1:414.

[78] Osborne, *Revelation*, 176. See also BDAG 211.

[79] William Horbury, "The Benediction of the 'Minim' and Early Jewish-Christian Controversy," *JTS* 33, no. 1 (1982): 19–61.

[80] David Instone-Brewer, "The Eighteen Benedictions and the Minim before 70 CE," *JTS* 54, no. 1 (April 1, 2003): 10; Yehezkel Luger, *The Weekday Amidah in the Cairo Genizah [Hebrew]* (Jerusalem, Israel: Orhot, 2002), 2:317; Wouter Jacques van Bekkum, "The Qedushta'ot of Yehudah according to Genizah Manuscripts" (Ph.D. diss., University of Groningen, 1988), 21–22; Moffatt, *Revelation*, 5:365; Hemer, *Letters to the Seven Churches*, 149; James M. Hamilton, *Revelation: The Spirit Speaks to the Churches*, ed. R. Kent Hughes, Preaching the Word (Wheaton, Ill.: Crossway, 2012), 106.

[81] Luke 12:35–40 = Matt 24:43–44; See *Quotes from Antiquity*. Jeremias *TDNT* 3:178; *Parables of Jesus*, 2 rev (Upper Saddle River, N.J.: Prentice Hall, 1972), 55; Vos, *The Synoptic Traditions in the Apocalypse*, 97–100; Kiddle, *Revelation*, 60; Bauckham, *Climax of Prophecy*, 106.

[82] Bauckham, "Synoptic Parousia Parables and the Apocalypse," 162–76; *Climax of Prophecy*, 104.

> **Quotes from Antiquity**
>
> Stay dressed for action [Gk. *Let your loins stay girded*; compare Exod 12:11] and keep your lamps burning, and be like men who are waiting for their master to come home from the wedding feast, so that they may open the door to him at once when he comes and knocks. Blessed are those servants whom the master finds awake when he comes. Truly, I say to you, he will dress himself for service and have them recline at table, and he will come and serve them. If he comes in the second watch, or in the third, and finds them awake, blessed are those servants! But know this, that if the master of the house had known at what hour the thief was coming, he [Some manuscripts add *would have stayed awake and*] would not have left his house to be broken into. You also must be ready, for the Son of Man is coming at an hour you do not expect. (Luke 12:35–40)

thief in the night" (1 Thess 5:2, 4). Three elements show parallels with the parables: the coming like a thief, the unknown time, and the suddenness of the coming. John identified the thief with Christ, the coming suzerain (3:5; 16:15).

Two types of coming are indicated in Revelation: a second advent of Christ that conveys positive implications (2:25; 3:11) and a coming in judgment which conveys negative implications (2:5, 16; 3:3). Some commentators suggest that the coming (ἥξω, *hēxō*) here (3:3a) is the coming of the second advent,[83] "that may come as either judgment or blessing,"[84] while others argue that it is a coming ἐπὶ σέ (*epi se*, "on you" or "against you") as an imminent judgment.[85] Support for this last view include some usages of the thief motif (*Gos. Thom.* 21; 103; 2 Pet 3:10) that lack reference to the second coming. Morris points out that this coming cannot apply to the second coming because it "will take place whether the Sardians are watchful or not."[86] Also, Ephesus (2:5 "I will come to you and remove your lampstand from its place"); Pergamum (2:16 "I will come to you soon and war against them") and Laodicea (3:19–20 "I stand at the door") likewise received a similar command to repent in the face of an imminent and historic coming of the suzerain. Beale's view, derived from his inaugurated eschatology, where Christ comes in personal judgment as a thief, an event that forms the final coming in judgment, is also shared by Smalley.[87]

While thieves could come at day[88] or night (Herodotus *Hist.* 2.121), John does not indicate the hour (ὥραν, *hōran*), implying that Christ could come at anytime, especially at a time they do not expect (οὐ μὴ γνῷς, *ou mē gnōs*, note the emphatic double negative).

---

[83] Bullinger, *Commentary on Rev*, 98–99; Bauckham, *Climax of Prophecy*, 104–9; Thomas, *Rev 1–7*, 253; Resseguie, *Revelation of John*, 96 n.47.

[84] Bauckham, *Climax of Prophecy*, 108.

[85] Alford, *Revelation*, 4:581; Lenski, *Revelation*, 1963, 130–31; Caird, *Revelation*, 48–49; Beasley-Murray, *Revelation, NCB*, 97; Mounce, *Revelation*, 111–12; Morris, *Revelation*, 76; Krodel, *Revelation*, 133; Beale, *Rev*, 275; Wilson, *Revelation*, 29; Witherington III, *Revelation*, 106; Smalley, *Revelation*, 83.

[86] Morris, *Revelation*, 79; Smalley, *Revelation*, 83. Contra Bauckham, *Climax of Prophecy*, 108.

[87] Beale, *Rev*, 275–76; Smalley, *Revelation*, 83; *Thunder and Love*, 62–63.

[88] Job 24:14; Philo *Spec.* 4.10; Apuleius *Metam.* 3.5, 28; 4.18; Dio Chrysostom *Or.* 69.8.

The suddenness of the suzerain's promised visit to the unrepentant vassals is treated by many scholars as prompts that would have reminded the Sardians of two possible local references. The imperatives "wake up" (3:2) and "*I will come like a thief*" (3:3). Sardis' history could have been in the back of the Sardian's minds as they listened to the message in Revelation.

1. The first reference could have been to the events of the sudden earthquakes which struck Sardis in AD 17 (Tacitus *Ann.* 2.47; Pliny *Nat.* 2.86.200), AD 20,[89] AD 24,[90] and AD 29[91] (Strabo *Geogr.* 13.4.8). During the 1st and second cent. the earthquakes were upon the minds of the architects and engineers as they reinforced the foundation walls of the Synagogue and gymnasium.[92] In AD 22–23 a coin was struck by Tiberius in Rome to celebrate reconstruction of the city (*CIVITATIBVS ASIAE RESTITVTIS*; *RIC* 1.48; see Fig. 97).[93]

2. The second event could be the historical background of the acropolis twice falling to the enemies of Sardis[94] due to a lack of vigilance among the city's defenders.[95] In both cases, the wall to the city was breached while the city slept.[96] It became proverbial in the literature of the day to speak of Sardis' overconfidence, pride and arrogance (Lucian *Merc. cond.* 13).[97]

   Ramsey Michaels refutes this connection, listing three arguments:
   > This is unlikely because 1). These incidents were centuries earlier; 2) the message is to the Christian congregation, not the city of Sardis; 3) the image of the thief in connection with a command to "watch" or "stay awake" was common in early Christianity, based on well-known sayings of Jesus (see Matt 24:43–44 par. Luke 12:39–40; 1 Thess 5:1).[98]

But Keener responds: "cities had enduring reputations, and local inhabitants grew up aware of such reputations."[99] Koester argues that a reference to the city is "improbable... The

---

[89] Sutherland, Roman History and Coinage, 48.
[90] Salmon, A History of the Roman World, 143.
[91] Ibid.
[92] Mitten, "A New Look at Ancient Sardis," 61–62.
[93] See chapter 14, *Under Roman Control*. Also see Sutherland, *Roman History and Coinage*, 48–49; Worth, Jr., *Greco-Asian Culture*, 183–84.
[94] Cyrus in 549 BC (Herodotus *Hist.* 1.84; Xenophon *Cyr.* 7.2.2–4) and Antiochus III in 195 BC (Polybius *Hist.* 7.15–18)
[95] Charles, *Revelation*, 1:79; Ramsay, *Letters: Updated*, 276–77; Mounce, *Revelation*, 93; Caird, *Revelation*, 47; Krodel, *Revelation*, 133; Worth, Jr., *Greco-Asian Culture*, 184–88; Wood, "Local Knowledge," 264; Morris, *Revelation*, 74–75; Hemer, *Letters to the Seven Churches*, 131–33; "Sardis Letter," 94–97; Aune, *Rev 1–5*, 219–20; Wilson, *Revelation*, 29; Court, *Myth and History*, 36; Beale, *Rev*, 276; Harrington, *Revelation*, 68; Keener, *Revelation*, 143–44; Osborne, *Revelation*, 177; Fant and Reddish, *Guide to Biblical Sites*, 306; Witherington III, *Revelation*, 106.
[96] See chapter 14, *The History of Sardis, Under Persian, Macedonian, and Seleucid Control*.
[97] Mounce, Revelation, 94; T. Scott Daniels, Seven Deadly Spirits: The Message of Revelation's Letters for Today's Church (Grand Rapids, Mich.: Baker Academic, 2009), 92.
[98] Michaels, *Revelation*, 82.
[99] Keener, *Revelation*, 144.

saying about the thief is used for Sardis not because it fits the city's history, but because it was a typical way to warn Christians of the need for vigilance."[100] There is little doubt that this warning of Christ's sudden coming to the Sardians in judgment, contrasted with the second coming in 1 Thessalonians 5:2 and 2 Peter 3:10, would have more relevance to Sardis in light of its history, than to another city.

The consequences of the curse appear to be deliberately vague, creating a kind of "crisis of discernment."[101] The same vagueness is found in the curses to the other churches. It is unclear how the "lampstand" would be removed at Ephesus (2:5), how the suzerain would make war with the "sword" of his mouth at Pergamum (2:16), or how he would spew the Laodiceans from his mouth (3:16).

BLESSINGS—3:4–5

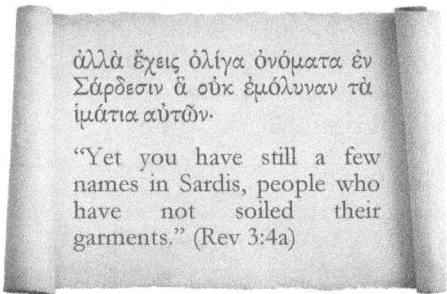

ἀλλὰ ἔχεις ὀλίγα ὀνόματα ἐν Σάρδεσιν ἃ οὐκ ἐμόλυναν τὰ ἱμάτια αὐτῶν·

"Yet you have still a few names in Sardis, people who have not soiled their garments." (Rev 3:4a)

There were a few names (ὀνόματα, honomata, "people" or "individuals"[102] See also 11:13; Acts 1:15) in Sardis who had "*not soiled their garments*" (οὐκ ἐμόλυναν τὰ ἱμάτια αὐτῶν, ouk emolunan ta himatia autōn, 3:4a). It appears that Sardis had a reputation for immorality (Herodotus *Hist.* 1.93; Aeschylus *Pers.* 40–45; Apollonius *Let.* 38–41; 56; 75; 76)[103] and commentators point to "soiled garments" (ἐμόλυναν ἱμάτια, emolunan himatia) as an allusion to their accommodation with the surrounding decadent culture.[104] Beale argues that μολύνω *(molunō,* stain) is a clear identification with the "pollution of idolatry" (cf. 14:4 with 14:6–9).[105]

The language of soiled garments recalls similar language with 1st to 3rd AD votive inscriptions, discovered near Dionysopolis (*MAMA* 4.279–90; *SEG* 6.252),[106] where physically

---

[100] Koester, *Revelation*, 314.

[101] Ibid., 318.

[102] Earlier, "name" meant reputation, but here it identifies a "person" (cf. 11:13 Acts 1:15; *NewDocs* 2:201–2; MM 451).

[103] Blaiklock suggests the cult of Cybele as "one of the co-called 'enthusiastic' religions, whose votaries worshipped by wild dancing, revel, and self-mutilation." Edward M. Blaiklock, *The Seven Churches: An Exposition of Revelation Chapters Two and Three* (London, U.K.: Marshall, Morgan & Scott, 1951), 60; Nash, *Christianity and the Hellenistic World*, 138–39. See chapter 14, *The Gods of Sardis*.

[104] See also Jude 23; Rev 7:13–14; 14:4; 22:14; Zech 3:1–5. Swete, *Revelation*, 50; Charles, *Revelation*, 78; Beckwith, *Apocalypse*, 475; Osborne, *Revelation*, 178; Smalley, *Revelation*, 83–84; Keener, *Revelation*, 144; Beasley-Murray, *Revelation, NCB*, 96; Mounce, *Revelation*, 95; Blaiklock, *The Seven Churches: An Exposition of Revelation Chapters Two and Three*, 60; Krodel, *Revelation*, 131; Tenney, *Revelation*, 64; Kistemaker, *Revelation*, 152; Beale, *Rev*, 276.

[105] Beale, *Rev*, 276.

[106] William Mitchell Ramsay, "Artemis-Leto and Apollo-Lairbenos," *JHS* 10 (1889): 216–30; Robert, *Nouvelles Inscriptions de Sardes: Fasc. 1*, no. 2, p. 23; Josef Keil, Anton von Premerstein, and Paul Wilhelm Kretschmer, eds., *Bericht*

or morally impure individuals were unfit for worship.[107] One example from the Lairmenos sanctuary states: "I, Sosandros of Hierapolis, perjured myself and entered the joint sanctuary in an unclean state. I was punished. I proclaim that none must despise Lairmenos, for he will have my stele before his eyes as a (cautionary) example" (*I.Smyr.* 120 [Huttner]).[108] The customary dress for approaching the gods in temples was white garments.[109]

For a city preoccupied with the dyeing of cloth in their textile industry (Pliny *Nat.* 29.3.47; Aristophanes *Ach.* 115),[110] and the woollen trade, as was Laodicea (3:18),[111] the obvious focus on clothing in verses 4 and 5 is curious.[112] Beasley-Murray poetically describes it this way: "the dye of their wool has coloured their souls as well as their hands."[113] Hemer suggested that the reference to the textile industry is less clear here than in the Laodicea passage.[114] In contrast, Aune believes that it is "a metaphor of ritual, moral, and spiritual purity."[115]

To the overcomers (νικῶν, *nikōn*) from Sardis, "who have not soiled their garments," three blessings were promised, including: 1) the privilege of walking with the suzerain dressed in white; 2) having their names not blotted from the book of life; and 3) acknowledged before God by Christ the suzerain.

BLESSING OF WALKING WITH THE SUZERAIN DRESSED IN WHITE—3:4B-5A

The first blessing granted by the suzerain to the overcoming vassals continues with the garment motif and is the future blessing of being able to walk with the suzerain dressed in white (See

---

über eine Reise in Lydien und der südlichen Aiolis, ausgeführt 1906 im Auftrage der Kaiserlichen Akademie der Wissenschaften, vol. 2, Kaiserliche [Österreichische] Akademie der Wissenschaften, Philosophisch-historische Klasse, Denkschriften 53 (Vienna: Hölder, 1908), no. 25, p. 16.

[107] Moffatt, *Revelation*, 5:365; Charles, *Revelation*, 81; Krodel, *Revelation*, 132; Hemer, *Letters to the Seven Churches*, 146, 261 n.65; Barclay, *Letters*, 77; Witherington III, *Revelation*, 106; Keener, *Background Commentary: NT*, 735. In *1 Apoc. Jas.* 28.16–17, James says to Jesus, regarding his resiliant clothing: "You walked in mud, and your garments were not soiled" (Robinson, *Nag Hammadi*, 263).

[108] Ulrich R. Huttner, *Early Christianity in the Lycus Valley*, trans. David Green, AJEC: ECAM, 85.1 (Leiden: Brill, 2013), 51; Ramsay, "Artemis-Leto," 218.

[109] Josephus *Ant.* 11.327; *J.W.* 2.1; Philo *Contempl.* 66; Euripides *Bacch.* 112; Pausanias *Descr.* 2.35.5; Diogenes *Vit. Phil.* 8.1.33; see 3:4b-5a below.

[110] Crawford, *The Byzantine Shops at Sardis*, 15–17. Two Byzantine shops associate with dye have been identified at Sardis.

[111] Crawford H. Greenewalt, Jr. and L. J. Majewski, "Lydian Textiles," in *From Athens to Gordion: The Papers of a Memorial Symposium for Rodney S. Young*, ed. Keith DeVries (Philadelphia, Pa.: University of Pennsylvania Museum of Archaeology and Anthropology, 1980), 133–48. See also chapter 8, *The Dyers Guild*.

[112] Moffatt, *Revelation*, 5:365; Ford, *Revelation*, 410; Johnson, *Triumph of the Lamb*, 54; Smalley, *Revelation*, 84; Thomas, *Rev 1–7*, 256; Witherington III, *Revelation*, 106; Johnson, "Revelation," 628. Mounce claims this is unlikely, and "nothing more than a general reference to the danger of contaminating the Christian witnesses by accommodation to the prevailing standards of a pagan city" Mounce, *Revelation*, 95.

[113] Beasley-Murray, *Revelation*, NCB, 96.

[114] Hemer, *Letters to the Seven Churches*, 146–47.

[115] Aune, *Rev 1–5*, 227.

> καὶ περιπατήσουσιν μετ' ἐμοῦ ἐν λευκοῖς, ὅτι ἄξιοί εἰσιν, Ὁ νικῶν οὕτως περιβαλεῖται ἐν ἱματίοις λευκοῖς
>
> "and they will walk with me in white, for they are worthy. The one who conquers will be clothed thus in white garments." (Rev 3:4b-5a)

also 6:11; 7:9, 13–14). This intimate relationship is depicted as walking (περιπατεῖν, *peripatein*) and in the NT depicts the idea of behavior[116] and discipleship (ἀκολουθῶν, *akolouthōn*, "following").[117] Although in Revelation ἄξιος (*axios, worthy*) is usually only attributed to God or Christ (4:11; 5:2, 4, 9, 12; 16:6), in early Christian writings it is more often used of Christians (e.g., Ign. *Eph.* 4:1; *Magn.* 2:1; 12:1). The vassal who has not soiled his garments and has conquered, is worthy (ὅτι ἄξιοί εἰσιν, *hoti axioi eisin*) to walk with the suzerain in white garments.

White garments were used throughout antiquity for a variety of purposes and John may have had in mind several of the following:

1. White robes were worn by the members of the Essene community (Josephus *J.W.* 2.123, 138; Hippolytus *Haer.* 9.19),[118] although it is unlikely that Jews and Christians in Asia Minor would be aware of this distant sect at Qumran.

2. Some commentators see a specific reference to the practice of wearing a white (Lat. *albatae vestes*)[119] baptismal robe.[120] Collins mentions that the candidates were baptised by immersion in the nude and then covered in a white garment, symbolizing purity, following the ceremony.[121] However, the practice does not date from the first century, but likely comes from the fourth or fifth century.[122] Koester affirms that "it is clear that the garment [in Revelation] signifies Christian identity, but whether it connotes baptism is uncertain."[123]

3. Following time in the *frigidarium* (cold pool) of the gymnasium (see chapter 14, *The Bath-Gymnasium Complex* above), naked members were given a white robe to cover themselves (see Fig. 110).[124] Soiled garments had been removed prior to entering the *caldarium* (Lat. *cella caldaria*,

---

[116] 1 Thess 2:12: see also Col 1:10; Eph 4:1; Pol. *Phil.* 5:1.

[117] John 8:12; 12:35; 1 John 1:6–7; 2:6, 11; see also Gen 5:22; 6:9; 17:1.

[118] Metzger, *Breaking the Code*, 39–40.

[119] Bryan D. Spinks, Early and Medieval Rituals and Theologies of Baptism: From the New Testament to the Council of Trent (Farnham, U.K.: Ashgate, 2006), 12, 36, 40.

[120] Victorinus of Petovium et al., *Latin Commentaries on Revelation*, trans. William C. Weinrich (Downers Grove, Ill.: IVP Academic, 2011), 122; Kistemaker, *Revelation*, 153; Hengstenberg, *Revelation*, 172; Guthrie, *Apocalypse*, 80; Collins, *The Apocalypse*, 25; Martin, *Seven Letters*, 90–91, cf. 93, 96. Krodel mentions baptism 4 times, but does not mention white (*Revelation*, 132).

[121] Collins, *The Apocalypse*, 25.

[122] Worth, Jr., *Greco-Asian Culture*, 188; Hughes Oliphant Old, *The Shaping of the Reformed Baptismal Rite in the Sixteenth-Century* (Grand Rapids, Mich.: Eerdmans, 2001), 2–3.

[123] Koester, *Revelation*, 314.

[124] Kelshaw, *Send This Message*, 133–34.

110. Painting titled "The Frigidarium" (1890) by Lawrence Alma-Tadema. Notice the bathers wrapped in white robes after exiting the water.

heated room). Such robes are depicted on a mosaic from the Piazza Armerina, a Late Roman Villa.[125] Worth observes that "just as one received the white garment of the gymnasium after cleansing oneself of dirt and grime, one received the heavenly white garment after cleansing oneself of the weaknesses and sins of the present life."[126]

4. John may have had in mind the new innovation of dying wool, which has been attributed to Sardis[127] (Pliny *Nat.* 29.3.47; Aristophanes *Ach.* 115).[128] However, white garments were not dyed, although the use of garment language would certainly have resonated with the

---

[125] R. Ross Holloway, *The Archaeology of Ancient Sicily* (New York, N.Y.: Routledge, 2002), fig. 216.15, 171.

[126] Worth, Jr., *Greco-Asian Culture*, 190.

[127] Crawford, *The Byzantine Shops at Sardis*, 15–17. Two Byzantine shops associated with dye have been identified at Sardis. See also chapter 8, *The Dyers Guild*.

[128] Moffatt, *Revelation*, 5:365; Ford, *Revelation*, 410; Johnson, *Triumph of the Lamb*, 54; Smalley, *Revelation*, 84; Thomas, *Rev 1–7*, 256; Witherington III, *Revelation*, 106; Johnson, "Revelation," 628. Mounce claims this is unlikely, and "nothing more than a general reference to the danger of contaminating the Christian witnesses by accommodation to the prevailing standards of a pagan city" Mounce, *Revelation*, 95.

congregation in Sardis, who would probably have had many direct connections with the textile industry. Also, the normal toga of a Roman citizen was made of white wool (*toga pura* or *libera*).[129]

5. White robes were worn for feasts or holiday occasions (Eccl 9:8; Juvenal *Sat.* 3.171–80),[130] resulting in the city being called *candida urbs* or "the city in white."[131]

6. White robes were worn for worship for example by angels;[132] priests;[133] kings (e.g., Josephus *J.W.* 8.186); and martyrs,[134] as well as worn for cultic acts, such as sacrifice.[135]

7. In the Roman world, as well as in Judaism (Pseudo-Philo *L.A.B.* 64.6), in the first cent. AD, the dead were wrapped and buried in a white cloth (Plutarch *Quaest. rom.* 26.270D–F).[136]

8. Understood against the practice of a victorious Roman general wearing a white toga (Lat. *trabea*)[137] during triumph celebrations in Rome (*toga praetexta*),[138] or those walking behind the triumphal procession wearing white togas (*toga praetexta;* Suetonius *Cl.* 17.3; 24.3; Juvenal *Sat.* 10.45).[139] Juvenal describes the scene as "the imposing procession of white-robed citizens marching" (*Sat.* 10.45). While often the *trabea* (Tacitus *Ann.* 3.2; Suetonius *Dom.* 8.14.4) was solid purple embroidered with gold (*Toga picta*, "Painted toga"),[140] occasionally it was white

---

[129] Berger, *Encyclopedic Dictionary of Roman Law*, 738; W. C. F. Anderson, "Toga," in *DGRA*, ed. William Smith, vol. 2 (London, U.K.: Murray, 1891), 2:849.

[130] Blaiklock, *Cities of the NT*, 117; Meinardus, *John of Patmos*, 106; Ramsay, *Letters: Updated*, 386.

[131] Ramsay, *Letters: Updated*, 282.

[132] Ibid., 386; Ford, *Revelation*, 409; Metzger, *Breaking the Code*, 39; Blaiklock, *Cities of the NT*, 117; Johnson, "Revelation," 626. e.g., Dan 10:5; 2 Macc 11:8; Mark 16:5 = John 20:12 = Matt 28:3; Acts 1:10; John 20:12; Acts 1:10; Rev 4:4; 19:14; *T. Levi* 8:2; Hermas *Vis.* 4.2.1; Lucian *Philop.* 25.

[133] e.g., Exod 28:4; Lev 16:4; Josephus *J.W.* 4.331; 5.229; *Pesiq. Rab.* 33:10; Appian *Bell. civ.* 4.6.47; Plutarch *Mor.* 352C; Apuleius *Metam.* 11.10, 23.

[134] Rev 6:11; Dan 7:9; c.f. Ps 104:2.

[135] Josephus *Ant.* 11.327; *J.W.* 2.1; Philo *Contempl.* 66; Plato *Leg.* 956A; Aristides *Orat.* 48.30; Plutarch *Mor.* 771D; Euripides *Bacch.* 112; Pausanias *Descr.* 2.35.5; Diogenes *Vit. Phil.* 8.1.33; *4 Ezra* 2:38–40; P.Oxy. 471.101.

[136] Samuel Krauss, *Talmudische Archäologie* (Leipzig: Fock, 1910), 1:550 n.212; Aune, *Rev 1–5*, 223.

[137] Fanny Dolansky, "Togam Virilem Sumere: Coming of Age in the Roman World," in *Roman Dress and the Fabrics of Roman Culture*, ed. Jonathan C. Edmondson and Alison Keith, Phoenix Supplementary Volumes (Toronto, Can.: University of Toronto Press, 2009), 26; Jonathan C. Edmondson, ed., *Two Industries in Roman Lusitania: Mining and Garum Production* (Oxford, U.K.: British Archaeological Reports, 1987), 55–60.

[138] Col 2:15; 2 Cor 2:14; 2 Macc 11:8; Tertullian *Scorp.* 12; c.f. Rev 7:14. For the debate over which toga was officially used by the emperor in procession, see Mary Beard, *The Roman Triumph* (Cambridge, Mass.: Harvard University Press, 2009), 70, 350 n.57.

[139] Ramsay, Letters: Updated, 282–84; Hemer, Letters to the Seven Churches, 146–47; Smalley, Revelation, 84.

[140] Pliny *Nat.* 9.63.136; *AE* (1972): 174; (1982): 268. Jonathan C. Edmondson, "Public Dress and Social Control in Late Republican and Early Imperial Rome," in *Roman Dress and the Fabrics of Roman Culture*, ed. Jonathan C. Edmondson and Alison Keith, Phoenix Supplementary Volumes (Toronto, Can.: University of Toronto Press, 2009), 26, 29;

with purple stripes (*angusti clavi*).[141] While some have pointed out that the victory parades took place in Rome, well away from Sardis, Wilson documents that there were celebrations in Asia Minor close to Sardis of which the Sardian may have known.[142]

9. White in the text signifies purity and holiness (4:4; 7:9).[143] There is no doubt that white garments are used to depict moral purity (robe of righteousness washed in the blood of the lamb, 7:9–10, 14; 19:11),[144] while soiled garments represent defilement (Zech 3:1–3). In the apocryphal story "The Shepherd of Hermas," the faithful are also rewarded with white clothing.[145]

While several of these local references may have been in the back of John's mind when he wrote, what is clear is that white garments surrounded the Roman citizen, from everyday apparel at the market or the gymnasium, to special celebrations and feasts, along with participating in worship and funerals. As Koester summarizes "by fusing all these aspects of meaning, the image of white garments enables readers to picture the resurrection hope in terms of worship, triumph, and a wedding celebration."[146]

BLESSING OF NOT HAVING THEIR NAME ERASED—3:5B

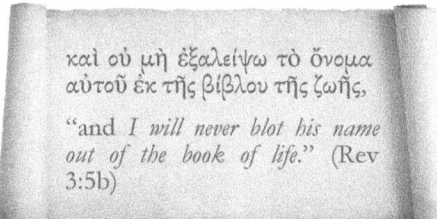

καὶ οὐ μὴ ἐξαλείψω τὸ ὄνομα αὐτοῦ ἐκ τῆς βίβλου τῆς ζωῆς,

"and *I will never blot his name out of the book of life.*" (Rev 3:5b)

The second blessing granted by the suzerain to the overcoming vassals was a judicial judgment that their names will not be blotted from the "book of life".[147] The metaphor had its origins in the ANE royal court where the king used official records to adjudicate cases (Ezra 4:15; Esth 6:1).[148] The practice goes back to the literature of the Sumerian and Akkadian

---

Michael Dewar, "Spinning the Trabea: Consular Robes and Propaganda in the Panegyrics of Claudian," in *Roman Dress and the Fabrics of Roman Culture*, ed. Jonathan C. Edmondson and Alison Keith, Phoenix Supplementary Volumes (Toronto, Can.: University of Toronto Press, 2009), 225–27; Michael Koortbojian, "The Double Identity of Roman Portrait Statues: Costumes and Their Symoblism at Rome," in *Roman Dress and the Fabrics of Roman Culture*, ed. Jonathan C. Edmondson and Alison Keith, Phoenix Supplementary Volumes (Toronto, Can.: University of Toronto Press, 2009), 80–83.

[141] Servius *ad Aem.* 7.612; Virgil *Aen.* 7.187, 612; 11.334; Ovid *Fas.* 2.504; Claudian *Rufin.* 1.249. "Toga," 2:845–50; W. Ehler, "Triumphus," *RE* 2. VIIA.1 (1939): 493–511; Dewar, "Spinning the Trabea," 219–34; Edmondson, "Public Dress and Social Control," 27.

[142] Mark Wilson, *The Victor Sayings in the Book of Revelation* (Eugene, Oreg.: Wipf & Stock, 2007), 92.

[143] Michaelis "λευκός," *TDNT* 4:249–50; Farrer, *Revelation*, 20:79–80; Swete, *Revelation*, 51–52; Kistemaker, *Revelation*, 153; Smalley, *Revelation*, 84–85; Hendriksen, *Conquerors*, 74; Beasley-Murray, "Revelation, NBC," 97; Johnson, *Triumph of the Lamb*, 83 n.29; Aune, *Rev 1–5*, 227; Koester, *Revelation*, 314.

[144] See also Isa 61:10; Dan 7:9; 10:5; Matt 17:2.

[145] Hermas *Vis.* 4.2:1; 4.3.5; *Sim.* 8.2:3; symbolising purification, Aristides *Orat.* 48.31.

[146] Koester, *Revelation*, 319.

[147] Rev 20:12–15; 21:27; Exod 32:33; Dan 7:9–10; Phil 4:3; *1 En.* 47:3; 90:20.

[148] Aune, *Rev 1–5*, 225.

cultures where the Sumerian ruler Ur-Nungal, possessed a "tablet of life" (*in-nam-ti-la*), although it began as a dynasty of the kings.[149]

Ancient Israel kept a list of citizens (Ps 69:28; Isa 4:3); a list that could be erased.[150] Extrabiblical texts suggest that individuals were listed on the scroll of life for the heavenly city as a reward (Hermas *Sim.* 2.9; *Apoc. Zeph.* 3:6–9), but the NT clearly states that people will be included on the scroll of life only through divine grace (Luke 10:20; Phil 3:20–4:3).[151] Citizens in Greek cities had their names written in the public registry (καταλόγου, *katalogou*),[152] while convicted criminals had their names erased (ἐξαλείφεται, *exaleiphetai*) from the registry (Dio Chrysostom *Or.* 31.84).[153] For disgraced Emperors or officials, *damnatio memoriae* was practiced,[154] where "statues could be defaced and toppled, images banned from public display, [and] names chiselled out of inscriptions [*fasti, lists*]" (see Fig. 111)[155] Roman citizens were given birth certificates (Lat. *testatio*) that were also registered (Lat. *professio liberi*)[156] in their place of birth within thirty days of birth (Cicero *Caecin.* 20.57).[157] Thus, one's name written in the "Book of Life" (see 13:8; 17:8; 20:15; 21:7) suggests heavenly citizenship with the suzerain,[158] while being blotted out conveys death,[159] and condemnation.[160]

The Jewish "curse of the *minîm*" ([מנים] "heretic"), found as a later addition to *The Eighteen Benedictions*, prayed daily by Jews in the ancient world, is juxtaposed to the blessing of the Sardis congregation, overturning the curse of the *Minîm* ("heretic"; 3:5b see below). The Jewish curse translates as "and may Naẓarim[161] and *Minîm* instantly perish; may they be blotted from the

---

[149] Shalom M. Paul, "Heavenly Tablets and the Book of Life," *JANES* 5 (1973): 345–53; Angel Manuel Rodríguez, "The Heavenly Books of Life and of Human Deeds," *JATS* 13, no. 1 (2002): 10–26.

[150] Exod 32:32–33; Jub. 30:20–22; *Jos. As.* 15:3.

[151] Koester, *Revelation*, 314–15.

[152] Xenophon *Hell.* 2.3.20, 51; Aristophanes *Eq.* 1369; Tacitus *Ann.* 3.17–18; *IGR* 3.63, 179; 4.860; *OGIS* 1.229.52. J. B. Moyle, "Civitas," in *DGRA*, ed. William Smith (London, U.K.: Murray, 1890), 1:445–46, 449; Jones, *Greek City*, 239, 357.

[153] Israel Smith Clare, *Ancient Greece and Rome*, vol. 2, The Unrivaled History of the World (Chicago, Ill.: Werner, 1893), 884; Kraabel, "Judaism in Western Asia Minor," 52; Barclay, *Revelation*, 1:47; Kiddle, *Revelation*, 47; Hemer, *Letters to the Seven Churches*, 148–49.

[154] Eric R. Varner, Monumenta Graeca et Romana: Mutilation and Transformation: Damnatio Memoriae and Roman Imperial Portraiture (Leiden: Brill, 2004), 1–2.

[155] Valerie Hope, *Death in Ancient Rome: A Sourcebook* (New York, N.Y.: Routledge, 2007), 80.

[156] Beryl Rawson, "Marriages, Familes, Households," in *The Cambridge Companion to Ancient Rome*, ed. Paul Erdkamp (Cambridge, Mass.: Cambridge University Press, 2013), 103.

[157] Fritz Schulz, "Roman Registers of Births and Birth Certificates Part 1," *JRS* 32, no. 1–2 (1942): 85; Bruce, *Paul, Apostle of the Heart Set Free*, 39–40. In error Koester claims it is forty days. Koester, *Revelation*, 315.

[158] Heb 12:23; 1 Pet 1:17; 4Q504 1–2 6.14.

[159] Exod 32:32–33; Pss 69:27–28; Isa 4:3; 4Q381 31.8.

[160] *Jub.* 30:22; 36:10; *1 En.* 108:3.

[161] Perhaps the name Nazarim was used to describe Christians. The early Chritians knew that "the Jews call us Nazareni" (Tertullian *Marc.* 4.8.1).

book of the living, and not be written with the righteous" (*Palestina* 12 [Geniza]).[162] The *Odes of Solomon* contain a similar formulation, only this time in favour of the Christians, stating: "put on the crown in the true covenant of the Lord, and all those who have conquered will be inscribed in His book" (*Odes Sol.* 9:11 [Charlesworth, *OTP*]).

The statement that conquering vassals will never have their names "erased from the book of life" raises the theological question of eternal security and whether the suzerain will blot out the names of those who are disobedient (i.e., loss of salvation)[163] or what Caird described as

111. Coin issued in Bilbilis (Calatayud), Hispania (Spain), under Tiberius. Lucius Aelius Sejanus was the praetorian prefect under Tiberius from AD 15–31 but following a failed conspiracy to overthrow emperor Tiberius in AD 31 his name was removed (*damnatio memoriae*). Obv: (TI CAESAR D)IVI AVGVSTI F AVGVSTVS. Laureate head of Tiberius. Rev: MV (ligate) AV(ligate)GVSTA BILBILIS [TI CÆSARE V L ÆLIO SEIANO] (Lucius Aelius Sejanus). The words *Caesar L. Aelio Seiano* are obliterated. Laurel wreath around COS. (*SNG* Cop. 620; *RPC* 1.398).

"conditional predestination."[164] Revelation indicates that the names were written in the Lamb's book of the living as citizens of heaven (21:27), by divine initiative, before the creation of the world (13:8; 17:8). Smalley maintains that the "right to appear in this roll cannot be earned; but it may be forfeited" through rejection of the gift.[165] However, several commentators point out that ἐξαλείψω (*exaleiphō*, "blot out" or "wipe away") is an example of a figure of speech called litotes,[166] where the statement "of an affirmative by the negative of its contrary" is an "ironical underestimation".[167] It is an understatement that emphatically states the assurance that the vassals who overcome will retain their name in the book of life. In countering this argument, Thomas points out that this is an empty promise if there is the possibility of their names being blotted out.[168] Beale argues that "unbelievers are never at any point associated positively with

---

[162] Instone-Brewer, "Eighteen Benedictions," 10; Luger, *The Weekday Amidah in the Cairo Genizah [Hebrew]*, 2:317; van Bekkum, "Qedushta'ot of Yehudah," 21–22; Moffatt, *Revelation*, 5:365; Hemer, *Letters to the Seven Churches*, 149; Hamilton, *Revelation*, 106.

[163] Roloff, *Revelation*, 59; Thomas, *Rev 1–7*, 263–64; Robert M. Royalty Jr., "Etched or Sketched? Inscriptions and Erasures in the Messages to Sardis and Philadelphia (Rev. 3.1–13)," *JSNT* 27, no. 4 (June 2005): 457–58.

[164] Caird, *Revelation*, 49–50.

[165] Smalley, *Revelation*, 86; Harrington, *Revelation*, 68; Caird, *Revelation*, 49–50; Osborne, *Revelation*, 180; Witherington III, *Revelation*, 106.

[166] Swete, *Apocalypse*, 51; Alford, *Revelation*, 4:4:582; Morris, *Revelation*, 77; Lenski, *Revelation*, 1963, 134.

[167] Christine A. Lindberg, Katherine M. Isaacs, and Ruth Handlin Manley, eds., *Oxford American Dictionary & Thesaurus*, 2nd ed. (New York, N.Y.: Oxford University Press, USA, 2009), 877.

[168] Thomas, *Rev 1–7*, 261.

the book of life. . . since their names were never written there in the first place (as 13:8 and 17:8 clearly show."[169]

However, the tension left to the reader is evident between human responsibility and divine sovereignty. Koester wisely states:

> There is no suggestion that God determined to exclude some people from his scroll at the dawn of time, thereby consigning them to the beast. At the last judgment, people are judged according to their works, but salvation ultimately depends on divine favor, as shown by their names being inscribed in the scroll of life (20:12–15; 21:27). Logically, the tension is awkward, but it shapes the readers' perspectives in a twofold way: On the one hand, people are accountable for what they do, so they are to resist sin and evil. On the other hand, if the world seems so dominated by evil that resistance appears futile (13:4), the scroll of life gives assurance that salvation is ultimately God's doing. The tension encourages people to resist compromise with evil without making them despair of the future.[170]

The positive statement given to the overcomers at Sardis, and elsewhere, is that the suzerain will never erase their names from the book of life.[171]

BLESSING OF BEING ACKNOWLEDGED BY THE SUZERAIN—3:5C

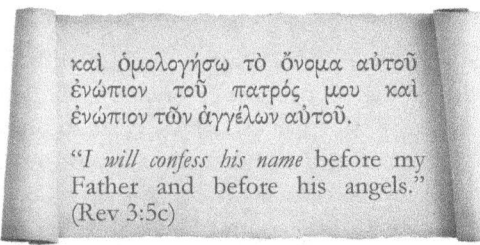

καὶ ὁμολογήσω τὸ ὄνομα αὐτοῦ ἐνώπιον τοῦ πατρός μου καὶ ἐνώπιον τῶν ἀγγέλων αὐτοῦ.

"*I will confess his name* before my Father and before his angels." (Rev 3:5c)

The third blessing granted by the suzerain to the overcoming vassals is they would be acknowledged by Christ, the suzerain and judge, before God and the angels.[172] The ὁμολογέω (*homologeō*, confess or acknowledge) is only found here in Revelation.[173] Those who acknowledge Jesus' name before earthly judges will receive the promise of having their name announced before the heavenly suzerain.

In addition, the honor of receiving a white stone and laurel wreath (2:10, 17) is accompanied in Graeco-Roman culture with the announcement in a public gathering of those who will be rewarded with a crown.[174] Also, the practice of honoring members of the Synagogue is attested in a first cent. inscription, where a white stone (see Pergamum, 2:19d) is cast to select the honored member, who would then receive a wreath and a public declaration of his name before the congregation (*NewDocs* 4.202–209).[175] In like manor the faithful vassals will

---

[169] Beale, *Rev*, 280. See also Johnson, *Triumph of the Lamb*, 85.

[170] Koester, *Revelation*, 319–20.

[171] Smalley, *Revelation*, 86; Hendriksen, *Conquerors*, 74.

[172] See also Matt 10:32; Luke 12:8; *2 Clem.* 3:2.

[173] BDF 220.2.

[174] Demosthenes *Cor.* 54–5, 118; *I.Eph.* 1a.27.8–14; *SIG* 3.709; 32.1243;. Lewis and Reinhold, *Roman Civilization*, 1:624–25; J. R. Harrison, "The Fading Crown: Divine Honour and the Early Christians," *JTS* 54, no. 2 (October 2003): 500–502.

[175] Levine, *The Ancient Synagogue*, 101–2; Reynolds, "Inscriptions," 242–47.

be honored in the most important congregation of the righteous, before the suzerain and his angels.[176]

PROCLAMATION WITNESS FORMULA—3:6

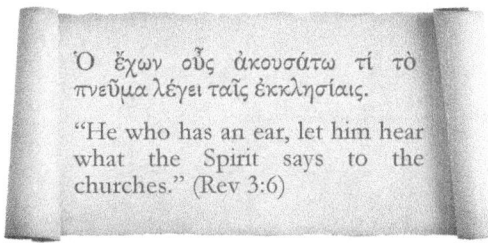

Ὁ ἔχων οὖς ἀκουσάτω τί τὸ πνεῦμα λέγει ταῖς ἐκκλησίαις.

"He who has an ear, let him hear what the Spirit says to the churches." (Rev 3:6)

For the overcomer, citizenship in the heavenly city is secured and the final sentence in the heavenly courtroom will reflect our relationship with Christ (3:5). With the distribution of the stipulations, along with blessings and curses, it was customary for ancient treaty and oath documents to be sealed with a list of divine witnesses, traditionally the suzerain/vassal's pantheon of gods.[177] Since there is a change in the situation in the NT, because God is speaking as his own witness, there is a change of form from the polytheistic context of the ANE culture. The Spirit is the judge presiding over the covenant case. This proclamation witness or hearing formula,[178] repeated in each of the messages to the churches (2:7; 11, 17, 29, 3:13, 22), calls the churches to hear the proclamation of the divine witness[179] and to heed the message of the Spirit who spoke it.

CONCLUSION

Six recognizable elements of the ANEVT, constituting a structure, are identified within the prophetic message to convey a covenant lawsuit message of encouragement to the overcomers within the church of Sardis.

Firstly, the preamble, marked by the prophetic oracular formula τάδε λέγει Ω, calls attention to what the suzerain, identified here as the sovereign omnipotent one who "has the seven spirits of God and the seven stars" (3:1), will say to the vassals in Sardis.

Secondly, the historical prologue is characterized by the omniscient suzerain's intimate knowledge of Sardis's works. He knows their reputation of appearing to be alive, but in reality being dead.

Thirdly, the Great King sets out five imperatives for Sardis's stipulations: the suzerain exhorts the vassals to be vigilant, strengthen what remains, bear in mind what they have received, pay attention to it and repent of their disobedient ways.

Fourthly, the suzerain declared one curse against their actions. If they were not faithful to the King, then the suzerain would come in judgment unexpectantly like a thief. The curse

---

[176] Koester, *Revelation*, 320.

[177] See the *Introduction—Proclamation Witness Formula*.

[178] See parallels in Matt 11:15; 13:9, 43; Mark 4:9; Luke 8:8; 14:35; 1 Cor 14:37–38; *Odes Sol.* 3:10–11. The *hearing formula* is also found in the Gnostic texts. *Gos. Thom.* 8.21, 24, 63, 65, 96; *Gos. Mary* 7.10, 8, 16; *Pist. Soph.* 1.17, 19, 33, 42, 43; 2.68, 86, 87; 3.124, 125; *Soph. Jes. Chr.* 98, 105, 107.

[179] There are echos of the OT phrase "hear the word of the Lord" (e.g. Isa 1:10; Jer 2:4; Hos 4:1; Amos 7:16).

reminds the churches of the omniscience of the suzerain and that he gives to each according to their works.

Fifthly, the eschatological *macarism* for the faithful overcomers' obedience to the stipulations will be the King's gracious pledge of the blessing of walking with the suzerain dressed in the white garments of righteousness, not having their names erased from the book of life, and being acknowledged by the suzerain.

Finally, acting as his own witness in the court case, the Spirit-Judge calls the Sardis congregation to hear what he has to say about the conduct of their church.

14

Prosperous Philadelphia

The History of the City

I n order to understand the message to Philadelphia, a city standing at the gateway to opportunity and prosperity, it is helpful to examine both the cultural (Graeco-Roman) history of Philadelphia, as well as the (Hebraic-Semitic) OT theological roots of the message. This chapter will examine the historical background to the city of Philadelphia.

THE GEOGRAPHY OF PHILADELPHIA

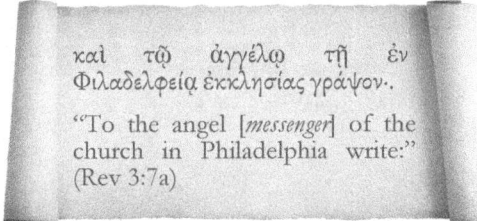

καὶ τῷ ἀγγέλῳ τῇ ἐν Φιλαδελφείᾳ ἐκκλησίας γράψον·.

"To the angel [*messenger*] of the church in Philadelphia write:" (Rev 3:7a)

Philadelphia (Φιλαδέλφεια, "brotherly love"; modern *Alaşehir*, "the red city"[1]; coordinates: 38:55:00 N 27:50:00 E) is about 30 miles (48 km) south-east of Sardis on the eastern end of the fertile valley in the province of Manisa. *Alaşehir* is 305 ft. (93 m.) above sea level and 37 miles (60 km) from the Aegean Sea.[2] Ancient Philadelphia is situated at the foot of the Tmolus mountains (*Boz dağlari*, Pliny *Nat.* 5.30; 14.9) and on the left bank of the Cogamus River (*Koca Çayi*), a tributary of the Hermus.[3] It was a strategic site on the border of three countries – Mysia, Lydia and Phrygia, and was called the "gateway to the east"[4], all of which helps explain why the city prospered. It was also one of the main junctures of the

---

[1] Ramsay, *HDB* 3.832; Irène Beldiceanu-Steinherr, "Notes pour l'histoire d'Alaşehir (Philadelphie) au XIVe siècle," in *Philadelphie et autres études*, ed. Héléna Ahrweiler, Byzantina Sorbonensia 4 (Paris, France: Publications de la Sorbonne, 1984), 33; Gerhard Doerfer, *Türkische und mongolische Elemente im Neupersischen: unter besonderer Berücksichtigung älterer neupersischer Geschichtsquellen, vor allem der Mongolen- und Timuridenzeit* (Wiesbaden: Steiner, 1965), §518, 95. In error Swete calls it "the white city" (*Apocalypse*, 52), likely confusing *Ala Shehr* with *Akhişar* (Thyatira) meaning "white castle."

[2] Gulgun et al., "Determination of the Effects of Temporal Change," 430.

[3] Sophron Pétridès, "Philadelphia," ed. Thomas Carson, *CE* (Detroit, Mich.: Gale, 1913), 11:793; Wilson, *Biblical Turkey*, 293.

[4] Mounce, *Revelation*, 98.

Imperial route for communication.[5] Philadelphia was located in the volcanic region of Phrygia called Κατακαυμένη (*katakekaumenē*, "the burnt land"), and susceptible to seismic activity both from volcanic and earthquake activity, which had a devastating impact on the buildings of the city (Strabo *Geogr.* 12.8.18; 13.4.10).[6] Given the agricultural productivity,[7] and strategic location, the city prospered,[8] although the impact of earthquakes kept the population small.[9] Since the ancient site is covered by the modern city of *Alaşehir*, few excavations have been completed, except by Recep Meriç from 1985–1991,[10] and few ancient artifacts have been recovered.[11]

THE HISTORY OF PHILADELPHIA

ANCIENT PHILADELPHIA

Philadelphia was the most recent of the seven cities, founded sometime between 189–138 BC as a missionary outpost for the spread of Hellenism throughout the province of Lydia.[12] The pottery during the excavation of Gavurtepe, on the eastern side of modern *Alaşehir* in the Hermus Valley, indicated "a Late Bronze Age level [1550–1200 BC] and a Hellenistic level [332–63 BC], and resulted in no intermediate cultural levels in between."[13] The Hellenistic site of Philadelphia probably absorbed the nearby Lydian population of ancient Callatebus (518–465 BC Herodotus *Hist.* 7.31).[14] It was either founded by Eumenes II (197–159 BC; *OGIS* 2.308.15)[15] or his younger

112. Stone relief of Attalus II (second cent. BC).

---

[5] Ramsay, *Letters: Updated*, 137–38; Beasley-Murray, "Revelation, NBC," 1426.

[6] Hemer, "Unto the Angels of the Churches," 172. A modern earthquake damaged the city in 1969.

[7] See *An Industrius City* below.

[8] Mounce, *Revelation*, 98.

[9] See *The Population of Philadelphia* below.

[10] Recep Meriç, "1985 Yılı Alaşehir Kazı Çalışmaları," *KST* 8, no. 2 (1986): 259–71; "1987 Yılı Alaşehir Kazısı," *KST* 10, no. 1 (1989): 157–70; "1988 Yılı Alaşehir Kazısı," *KST* 11, no. 1 (1990): 179–90; "1990 Yılı Alaşehir Kazısı," *KST* 13, no. 1 (1992): 227–35; "1991 Yılı Alaşehir Kazısı," *KST* 14, no. 2 (1993): 335–63. However, what is known about ancient Philadelphia is mostly based on surviving inscriptions and coins.

[11] Aune, *Rev 1–5*, 234. In error, Aune claims that Philadelphia has never been excavated.

[12] Ramsay, *Letters: Updated*, 286–87; Caird, *Revelation*, 51; Morris, *Revelation of St. John*, 80; Witherington III, *Revelation*, 106; Wall, *Revelation*, 82; Thomas, *Rev 1–7*, 271; Osborne, *Revelation*, 184.

[13] R. Gül Gürtekin-Demir, "A Small Group of Pottery with Lydian Character from Gavurtepe, Alaşehir," *Arkeoloji Dergisi* 15 (2010): 41.

[14] Lightfoot, The Apostolic Fathers (APF), 2:238 n.1; Ramsay, Cities and Bishoprics, 199–200; Jones, Cities of the Eastern Roman Provinces, 54; Mary Boyce and Frantz Grenet, A History of Zoroastrianism: Vol. 1 Zoroastrianism under Macedonian and Roman Rule, HO: Der Nahe Und Der Mittlere Osten 8 (Leiden: Brill, 1991), 215, 241.

[15] Magie, Roman Rule in Asia Minor, 982n.

brother, Attalus II Philadelphus of Pergamum (159–138 BC; see Fig. 112 and Table 2: *Attalid Dynasty of Pergamene Kings*).[16] The name of the city means "brotherly love," likely derived from the love between Attalus II, who was called *Philadelphus* (Gr. *philios* + *delphos*, "love of brother"), and his brother Eumenes II.

Hemer recounts two instances of brotherly love between Eumenes II and Attalus.[17] 1). In 172 BC, a false rumour emerged that Eumenes II had been assassinated. Attalus accepted the crown, thinking his brother dead; but when Eumenes returned alive, Attalus willingly relinquished the crown and power back to him.[18] 2). In 168–167 BC, Attalus was representing his brother in Rome as Eumenes II was under suspicion of corresponding with Perseus, an enemy. Attalus was offered a deal to take the throne from his brother with Roman help, but he resisted this and remained faithful to his brother.[19]

113. Coin from Neocaesarea. Obv.: AY KAI PO LIK ΓΑΛΛΙΗΝΟC. Laureated head of Gallienus (AD 262–263). Rev.: MHT NEOKAICARIAC around, ET PYΘ below. Prize urn containing two palm branches awarded at the games, set upon a low, three-legged table on the other (*SNG BnF* 1314; *SNG Righetti* 582).

Attalus III Philometer bequeathed his kingdom, including Philadelphia, to Rome upon his death in 133 BC.[20] By the third cent. AD public games called *Philadelphus* were celebrated in commemoration of the fraternal love between these brothers.[21] The province of Asia was established by the Romans in 129 BC by combining Ionia and the former Kingdom of

---

[16] Michaels, *Revelation*, 83; Caird, *Revelation*, 51; Beasley-Murray, *Revelation*, NCB, 99; Morris, *Revelation*, 80; Kistemaker, *Revelation*, 156; Wilson, *Biblical Turkey*, 293; Fant, *Guide to Biblical Sites*, 300; Koester, *Revelation*, 321. Some question Attalus II (see Fig. 112), given that it is based exclusively on a statement of Stephanus of Byzantium (s.v. Φιλαδέλφεια, [*Philadelphia*] where he states that Philadelphia was the Ἀττάλου κτίσμα τοῦ Φιλαδέλφου, [*Attalou ktisma tou Philadelphou*] "a foundation of Attalus Philadelphus." Lightfoot, *The Apostolic Fathers (APF)*, 1.1.237; Hemer, *Letters to the Seven Churches*, 153–54. This statement is contradicted by Joannes Lydus who claims that the Egyptians founded Philadelphia (Lydus *Mens.* 3.32), suggesting that Ptolemy Philadelphus (308–246 BC) laid the foundation of Philadelphia (Jones, *Greek City*, 17, 162; *Cities of the Eastern Roman Provinces*, 54, 70, 73, 83–84).

[17] Hemer, Letters to the Seven Churches, 155.

[18] Livy *Hist. Rome* 42.16.7–9; Diodorus *Hist. Lib.* 29.34.2.

[19] Livy *Hist. Rome* 45.19–20; Polybius *Hist.* 30:1–3; 31:1; 32:1; Diodorus *Hist. Lib.* 31.7.2.

[20] Strabo *Geogr.* 13.4.2; Pliny *Nat.* 33.53.148; *OGIS* 2.338.7.

[21] *CIG* 3427; *IGR* 4.1761. Lafaye commenting on *IGR* 4.1761 suggests that this was done to honour the friendship between Caracalla and his brother Geta, however Hemer believes it may also have had a memory of the loyalty between Eumenes and Attalus (Hemer, *Letters to the Seven Churches*, 263 n.10; Ramsay, *Cities and Bishoprics*, 2.366). Coins from *Neocaesarea* (Philadelphia) minted by Gallienus depict prize urns (See Fig. 113); *SNGvA* 1.116cf; *SNG BnF* 1314; *SNG Righetti* 582; *SNG Cop.* 220; Mionnet Supp. 4.201.

Pergamum. Little remains from this period, as the modern city of *Alaşehir* covers the ancient ruins.

ROMAN PHILADELPHIA

During the Roman period, Philadelphia was located in the administrative district (*conventus* or διοίκησις, *dioikēsis*) of Sardis (Pliny *Nat.* 5.111) and maintained good relations with Rome, dating their calendar from the victory of Augustus at Actium (31 BC; *I.Phil.* 1434; 1435; 1439). The devastating earthquake of AD 17 affected twelve cities, including Philadelphia, which

114. Coin from Philadelphia. Obv.: *OUESPASIANOS KAISAR*. Laureated head of Vespasian (AD 69–79). Rev.: *EPI MELHQ PLEMAIUO KAI HRWDOU FILADEL FLABI*, [Flavi] and Zeus standing holding an eagle and scepter, with an altar to the left (*RPC* 1.1329; *BMC* 61).

was levelled.[22] Due to the frequent aftershocks, many of the residents were forced to live outside the city or in other cities (Strabo *Geogr.* 12.8.18; 13.4.10). With five years of tax relief from Emperor Tiberius (r. AD 14–37; see Figs. 43, 97, 111), the city was rebuilt (Strabo *Geogr.* 12.8.18; Tacitus *Ann.* 2.47); and in gratitude the city added *Neocaesarea* (see Fig. 113) to its name during the reign of Tiberius and Claudius (see Figs. 2, 28), also erecting a monument in Rome (*CIL* 10.1624). Later the city became "Philadelphia Flavia" after Flavia Domitilla, the wife of Vespasian, (AD 69–79), as is attested on its coins (*RPC* 1.1329; *BMC* 60, 61, 62; see Fig. 114).[23] Apart from the coins, the only things to survive are one statue of Pompey and one of Hadrian, along with a stele of Caracalla (see Figs. 128, 162, 163).[24] Since 1985, some excavations have been conducted on the Roman stadium, theater and the Byzantine basilica of St. John.[25]

BYZANTINE PHILADELPHIA

From 325 AD, Philadelphia was the titular See of a bishop under the jurisdiction of the Metropolitanate of Sardis.[26] The bishopric of Philadelphia was promoted to metropolis in 1369 by Sardis[27] and all its area was annexed to the Metropolitanate of Philadelphia.[28] Le Quien mentions a number of the prominent bishops and metropolitans: Hetimasius, present at the Council of Nicaea (AD 325); Cyriacus, at the Council of Philippopolis (AD 344); Theodosius,

---

[22] Tacitus *Ann.* 2.47. 3–4; Pliny *Nat.* 2.86.200; Lydus *Mens.* 4.115.

[23] Mounce, *Revelation*, 99.

[24] Vermeule, *Roman Imperial Art*, 461.

[25] Meriç, "1985 Yılı Alaşehir Kazı Çalışmaları"; "1987 Yılı Alaşehir Kazısı"; "1988 Yılı Alaşehir Kazısı"; "1990 Yılı Alaşehir Kazısı"; "1991 Yılı Alaşehir Kazısı."

[26] Pétridès, "Philadelphia," 11:793.

[27] Siméon Vailhé, "Sardes," in *CE*, ed. Charles George Herbermann, Condé Bénoist Pallen, and Edward Aloysius Pace, vol. 13 (New York, N.Y.: Appleton & Company, 1913), 13:472.

[28] Demetrius Kiminas, *The Ecumenical Patriarchate: A History of Its Metropolitans with Annotated Hierarch Catalogs*, Orthodox Christianity 1 (San Bernadino, Calif.: Wildside, 2009), 89, 93.

115. Basilica of St. John in Alaşehir (ancient Philadelphia).

deposed at the Council of Seleucia (AD 359); Theophanes, present at the Council of Ephesus (AD 431); Asianus (AD 458); Eustathius (AD 518); John, present at the Council of Constantinople (AD 680); and Stephanus at Nicaea (AD 787).[29]

In the sixth cent. AD Philadelphia was a prosperous Byzantine city given the title "little Athens" (Lydus *Mens.* 4.58) due to its flourishing temples and festivals, indicating that it had not completely converted to Christianity (see *The Christian Community* below). During this time the domed basilica of St. John the Theologian was constructed in the *Beş Eylül* district which today is the dominant archaeological attraction of the city (see Fig. 115) reaching to 15 m. with walls 0.96 m. thick.[30] Given the date, this was not one of the seven churches to which John addressed his letter. The Byzantine walls of the ancient city have been incorporated into many of the modern buildings scattered throughout the northeast part of the city.[31]

From the eleventh cent. onward Philadelphia was repeatedly conquered by the Seljuk Turks, until it was finally subjugated by the Ottoman Turks in 1390, with its name being changed to *Alaşehir*. However, while several bishoprics and metropolises became inactive, the metropolitan rank and jurisdiction continued among the Greeks at Philadelphia and endured even when many of the neighboring sees were obliterated by the Turkish conquest (see Fig. 116).[32]

Kiminas documents how "in July 1577 the See of the Metropolitanate of Philadelphia was transferred to the city of Venice in order to care for the Orthodox of Italy and Western Europe. The See remained there officially until June 1712."[33]

MODERN PERIOD

Alaşehir was occupied by the Greek army during the Graeco-Turkish War (1919–1922). In the final stages of the war, many cities were set on fire, including Alaşehir resulting in the loss of life and property.[34] Mango reports that in the burning of Alaşehir "4,300 out of 4,500 houses were

---

[29] Le Quien, *Oriens christianus*, 1.867; Pétridès, "Philadelphia," 11:793.
[30] Meriç, "1990 Yılı Alaşehir Kazısı," 229.
[31] Wilson, *Biblical Turkey*, 295–96.
[32] Pétridès, "Philadelphia," 11:793.
[33] Kiminas, The Ecumenical Patriarchate, 18.
[34] Norman M. Naimark, *Fires of Hatred: Ethnic Cleansing in Twentieth-Century Europe* (Cambridge, Mass.: Harvard

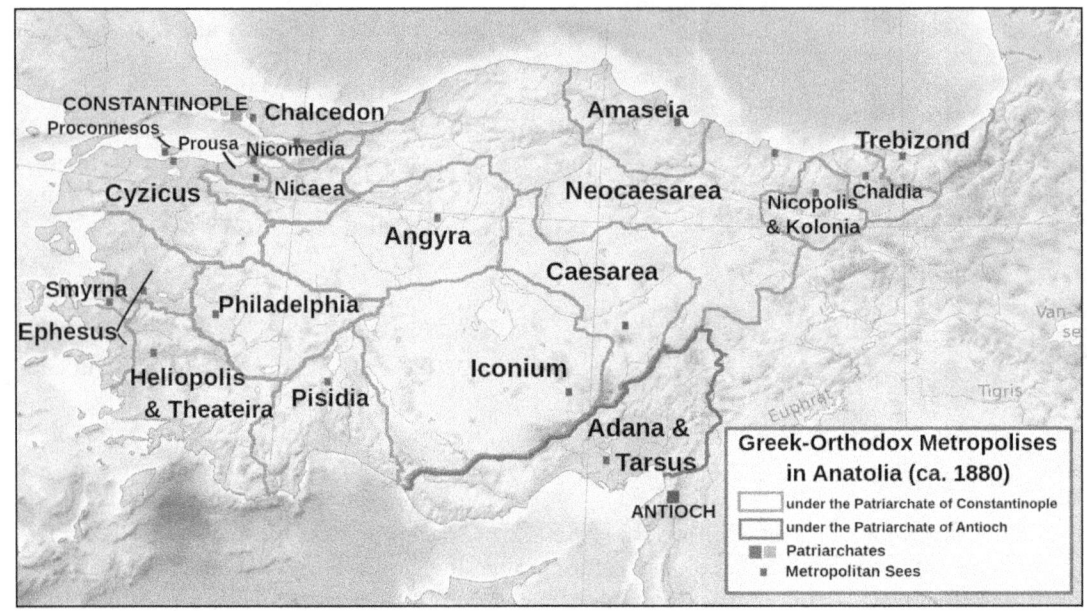

116. Map of the Greek Orthodox Metropolises in Asia Minor (Anatolia) *ca.* 1880.

destroyed with the loss of 3000 lives."[35] Today a suburb of Athens is called *Nea Filadelfia* ("New Philadelphia"), so named because of the Greek refugees annexed from Alaşehir in Turkey following the war in 1923.

THE POPULATION OF PHILADELPHIA

The modern population of *Alaşehir* grew from ca. 15,000 in 1913[36] before the Graeco-Turkish War, to 99,962 in 2014.[37] In the one hundred years following the Graeco-Turkish War, Philadelphia has seen exponential growth, but what was the population in the second cent. AD? During that time Philadelphia's population has been estimated—based on "analogies" with other parts of the Roman Empire—to be about 10,000[38] or a bit higher.[39] It is impossible to use

---

University Press, 2002), 17–56; William Ochsenwald and Sydney Nettleton Fisher, *The Middle East: A History*, 7th ed. (Boston, Mass.: McGraw-Hill, 2010), 386.

[35] Andrew Mango, *Ataturk: The Biography of the Founder of Modern Turkey* (Woodstock, N.Y.: The Overlook Press, 2002), 411.

[36] Pétridès, "Philadelphia," 11:793. Pétridès documents that in "the seventeenth century it had 8,000 inhabitants, of whom 2000 were Christians."

[37] http://www.citypopulation.de/php/turkey-manisa.php.

[38] J. C. Russell, *Late Ancient and Medieval Population*, APSP (Philadelphia, Pa.: American Philosophical Society, 1958), 80.

[39] Worth, Jr., *Greco-Asian Culture*, 194, 302 n.2.

Hanson comparisons based on the area, since the ancient city of Philadelphia has been encroached by the modern city of *Alaşehir*.⁴⁰

Due to the frequent earthquakes and tremors, the population always remained small, as many chose to live outside the city on agricultural farms (Strabo *Geogr.* 12.8.18; 13.4.10). The population was a mixture of Lydian and Mysian citizens along with Roman and Macedonian business people (*I.Phil.* 1423; 1455).

An Industrious City

Fertile Land

The volcanic plain (Κατακαυμένη, *katakekaumenē*, "the burnt land") on which Philadelphia was built provided a rich soil conducive to agriculture (Strabo *Geogr.* 13.4.11; Pliny *Nat.* 14.9.74). Viticulture (Lat. *vitis*, "vine") was highly developed in the provinces of Lydia and Phrygia,⁴¹ with the rich volcanic soil making the wines of Tmolus some of the most celebrated vintages of antiquity (Virgil *Georg.* 2.98; Pliny *Nat.* 5.30; 14.9). An inscription from the modern village of Hayallı, about 20 km north of Philadelphia, that dates to AD 161/162, describes "an association of lovers of vine" (νέοι φιλάυπελοι, *neoi philanpeloi* ID# 6423).⁴² Viticulture is abundantly attested to in Philadelphia's coinage,⁴³ imprinted (for example) with depictions of cornucopiae;⁴⁴ ears of corn (*BMC* 56, of Claudius; *BMC* 88); Demeter, goddess of the harvest and agriculture (*BMC* 71, of Marcus Aurelius; see Fig. 98); Dionysus, goddess of the vine and grape harvest (see Fig. 35);⁴⁵ and bunches of grapes⁴⁶ (see Fig. 117). The volcanic activity also developed hot mineral springs in Philadelphia. In AD 92 Domitian published an Edict that ordered half of the vineyards in Lydia to be cut down with no new ones to replace them (Suetonius *Dom.* 7.2; 14.2; Philostratus *Vit. Apoll.* 6.42). The reason was either

117. Coin from Philadelphia. Struck under Domitian. Obv.: Bust of Augusta (AD 82–96). Rev.: A bunch of grapes. (*RPC* 2.1336; *SNG Cop.* 379).

---

⁴⁰ Hanson, "Urban System."

⁴¹ On the extension of viticulture in Phrygia see, Marc Waelkens, "Phrygian Votive and Tombstones as Sources of the Social and Economic Life in Roman Antiquity," *Ancient Society* 8 (1977): 278–83; Louis Robert, "Documents d'Asie Mineure," *BCH* 107, no. 1 (1983): 541–42; *Documents d'Asia Mineure*, 385 ff.

⁴² Hasan Malay, "Φιλάνπελοι in Phrygia and Lydia," *EA* 38 (2005): 42–44.

⁴³ Lightfoot, *The Apostolic Fathers (APF)*, 2:238 n.1; Aune, *Rev 1–5*, 234.

⁴⁴ *BMC* 54, 55; *SNG BnF* 934, 940, 959, 1028; Waddington 5130 = Mionnet 4.542 = *RPC* 3.2380; *SNGvA* 2.3072; *RPC* 1.3029, 1.3030; *SNG Cop.* 370, 372, of Caligula, others.

⁴⁵ Rom. Bacchus; *BMC* 16, 17, 33, 35, 97; Mionnet 4.536; *SNG BnF* 918A, various see *The Gods of Philadelphia* below.

⁴⁶ *BMC* 64; *RPC* 2.1336, 3036; *SNG Cop.* 379, of Domitia.

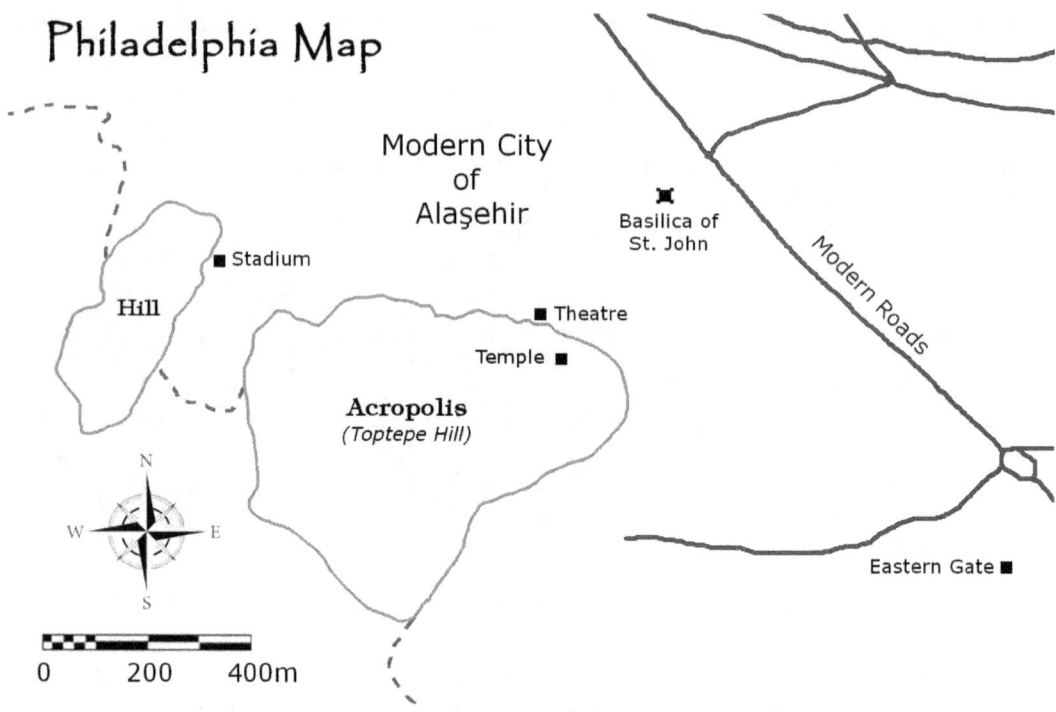

118. Urban plan of the city of Philadelphia (modern *Alaşehir*).

to protect Italian wine producers or to encourage the production of grain.[47] The edict was widely unpopular.

Textile and Leather

In the second to third cent. AD, Philadelphia was known for its wool ("the sacred tribe [φυλή, *phylē*] of wool-workers" [ἐριουργοί, *eriourgoi*][48]) and leather production ("the sacred tribe [φυλή, *phylē*] of leather-tanners" [σκυτέις, *skyteis*]; guild of leather-workers, *skytotomoi*; *IGLAM* 656) represented by guild associations (*I.Phil.* 1490–92; *IGR* 4.1644).[49] In the thirteenth and fourteenth cent. AD it was an important producer of leather goods and red-dyed (murex) silk.[50]

---

[47] W. Ward Gasque, "Philadelphia (Place)," ed. David Noel Freedman et al., *ABD* (New York, N.Y.: Doubleday, 1996), 5:305; Waelkens, "Phrygian Votive and Tombstones as Sources of the Social and Economic Life in Roman Antiquity," 283, 305 n.91. On grain production in Anatolia see Waelkens.

[48] *CIG* 3422 = *IGLAM* 648 = *IGR* 4.1632.

[49] Magie, Roman Rule in Asia Minor, 2:48–49; Koester, Revelation, 321–23; Harland, Associations, Synagogues, and Congregations, 26, 84.

[50] Beldiceanu-Steinherr, "Notes pour l'histoire d'Alaşehir," 33; Graves, "What Is The Madder With Lydia's Purple?", 1–47.

A CULTURED CITY

Philadelphia was considered an important cultural center and significant enough to be considered worthy of official honors with the likes of Ephesus (*I.Phil.* 1452–53). An architectural theme is prominent in the Revelation message to Philadelphia, with references to keys (3:7), doors (3:8), synagogue (3:9), pillars (3:12); and temples (3:12). From the constant preoccupation with their buildings susceptibility to earthquake damage (See *Roman Philadelphia* above), these structural references would immediately resonate with the Philadelphian Christians.

119. Coin from Philadelphia. Obv.: the Lauriate head of Trajan (AD 98–117). Rev.: An eagle standing within a distyle temple and an eagle with open wings on the pediment (*RPC* 3.3212).

THE AQUEDUCT

As is evident from any city in ancient times, aqueducts were built to supply water to the local population. An inscription (*I.Phil.* 1430; 1439) is all that tells us Philadelphia had an aqueduct, as so far, it has not been identified archaeologically.

THE THEATER

After AD 212, an inscription records that "Aurelius Hermippos, leader of the athletes (*xystarchēs*), priest of Artemis. . . [had] given 10,000 denarii towards the restoration of the awning of the theatre" (*CIG* 3422, ID# 12836 [Harland]; Also, *IGLAM* 648 = *IGR* 4.1632). The repairs were likely necessary due to earthquake damage. In 1985–1990, R. Meriç excavated the ruins of a small second cent. AD theater, along the northern edge of the acropolis (Toptepe Hill; see

120. The overgrown remains of the theater in Philadelphia.

Fig. 118).[51] The top of an arch from the theater is visible in the bottom center of Fig. 120).

THE STADIUM

The stadium is barely visible cut into the hillside with an exposed eastern end (see Fig. 118). All of the marble seats have been removed to be repurposed for constructing other buildings.[52] An inscription after AD 212 speaks of a gladiatorial match paid for by Aurelius Hermippos, the high priest of Artemis, which likely took place in the stadium. It reads:

> Aurelius Hermippos, leader of the athletes (ξυστάρχην, *xustarchēn*), priest of Artemis . . . With god–like beneficence, he has paid for a gladiatorial beast–hunt to the death in single pairs (i.e., a gladiator matched with a beast; *CIG* 3422 = *IGLAM* 648 = *IGR* 4.1632 [Harland]; see also Pompeii inscription *CIL* 4.9980).

Several other inscriptions speak of a victor (crown 3:11) from three separate games held there (*CIG* 3416 = 3427 = 3428; 3424). Hemer suggests that these games were "publicity for a small city."[53]

THE TEMPLES

The title "little Athens" was given to the city due to many temples situated there (Lydus *Mens.* 4.58). These temples and monumental structures were attested to by inscriptions (*I.Phil.* 1514; *TAM V* 2.1497)[54] and numismatic representations of numerous temples, including temples to Artemis Ephesia (see 121), Artemis Anaitis (the Persian Anahita), Zeus

121. Coin from Philadelphia. Obv.: *DOMITIANOC KAICAR.* Head of Domitian (AD 81–96). Rev.: *EPI LAGETA FILADELFEWN.* The cult statue of goddess Artemis Ephesia on the other (*RPC* 1.1334; *SNG München* 419).

(see Figs. 95, 115, 126, 151, 154, 156), Helios, Dionysus (see Fig. 35), and Aphrodite (see Figs. 93, 122, 123, 126).[55] In 1985–1986 R. Meriç excavated a temple on the acropolis (see map Fig. 118), which dates to the Roman period (late first cent. AD).[56] It was constructed with

---

[51] Meriç, "1985 Yılı Alaşehir Kazı Çalışmaları," 260; "1987 Yılı Alaşehir Kazısı," 170; Wilson, *Biblical Turkey*, 296; Fant and Reddish, *Guide to Biblical Sites*, 302; Meriç, "1990 Yılı Alaşehir Kazısı," 170; Stephen Mitchell, "Archaeology in Asia Minor, 1985–1989," *Archaeological Reports*, no. 36 (1990): 97.

[52] Wilson, *Biblical Turkey*, 296. See the photo of the remains of the stadium on page 294.

[53] Hemer, *Letters to the Seven Churches*, 268 n.51.

[54] Mitchell, "Archaeology in Asia Minor, 1985–1989," 97; Koester, *Revelation*, 323.

[55] Price and Trell, Coins and Their Cities: Architecture on the Ancient Coins of Greece, Rome, and Palestine, 267.

[56] Meriç, "1985 Yılı Alaşehir Kazı Çalışmaları," 260; Mitchell, "Archaeology in Asia Minor, 1985–1989," 97; Fant and Reddish, *Guide to Biblical Sites*, 302. Aune claims, in error, that Philadelphia has never been excavated. Aune, *Rev 1–5*, 243.

Corinthian columns and a fine monumental gateway of the second cent. AD with three arches and heart-shaped columns.[57]

A POLITICAL CITY

During the first cent. AD, Philadelphia was the administrative center (*conventus* or διοίκησις, *dioikēsis*) for the surrounding towns, with the region's judicial center being located in Sardis (Pliny *Nat.* 5.29–31, 111).[58] Philadelphia also engaged in a "political concord" or alliance (ὁμόνοια, *homonoia*)[59] with both Smyrna and Ephesus and produced a version of its *homonoia* coin for each alliance. For Smyrna, Philadelphia struck coins in the reigns of Antoninus (AD 134–138),[60] Commodus (AD 177–192; Imhoof *KM* 7A), Septimius Severus (AD 193–211),[61] Julia Domna (AD 193–217), and Gordian (AD 238–244; *BMC* 120 = *SNG BnF* 1021), each with an image of Tyche (Τύχη or Cybele, see Figs. 52, 54, 98, 108, 160), standing with a wool basket (κάλαθος, *kalathos*)[62] on her head and holding a rudder and cornucopia (the horn of Amalthea), the symbols of "guiding and conducting the affairs of the world."[63] The image conveyed all of the hope and good fortune invested in the relationship between Philadelphia and Smyrna. Coins of AD 198–260 feature *Dēmos* (see Figs. 122, 124, 156) and *Cybele* with the inscription *NEWKORWN OMONOIA (neōkorōn homonoia)*, celebrating the alliance (*homonoia*) with Smyrna and their shared honour of being awarded Temple-Warden (*neōkoros*) status.[64]

Philadelphia struck coins in the reigns of Domitian (AD 81–96; *RPC* 1.1332 = *SNG BnF* 97) and Trajan Decius (AD 249–251; *SNG Righetti* 1065) to celebrate its alliance with Ephesus. Both coins depict Tyche (Τύχη or Cybele, see Figs. 52, 54, 98, 108, 160) standing, one holding a scepter, clasping the hand of Tyche of Ephesus who is holding a statuette of Artemis Anaitis, while the coin of Trajan also has Tyche holding a statuette of Artemis Anaitis, but looking back at the *Dioskuri* (twin brothers, Castor and Pollux), with a distyle temple in perspective on the left side (see Fig. 124).

---

[57] See reconstruction of the arches in Recep Meriç, "1986 Yılı Alaşehir Kazıs Raporu," *KST* 9, no. 2 (1987): 247 fig.3.

[58] William M. Ramsay, "The Province of Asia," *The Classical Review* 3 (1889): 176; Georg Petzl, *Tituli Lydiae Linguis Graeca et Latina Conscripti: Fasciculus III, Philadelpheia et Ager Philadelphenus*, TAM, 5/3 (Vienna: Östereichishen Akademie der Wissenschaften, 2007), x; Koester, *Revelation*, 323.

[59] Lotz, "The Homonoia Coins of Asia Minor and Ephesians 1:21," 173–88; Kampmann, "Homonoia Politics," 385. Also, see chapter 4, *Homonoia Coins*.

[60] Mionnet 4.569 = *SNG BnF* 984 = *RPC* 3.2386.

[61] *BMC* 76 = Waddington 5147 = Mionnet Supp. 7.397.

[62] Elisabeth Trinkl, "The Wool Basket: Function, Depiction and Meaning of the Kalathos," in *Greek and Roman Textiles and Dress: An Interdisciplinary Anthology*, ed. Mary Harlow and Marie-Louise Nosch (Oxford, U.K.: Oxbow Books, 2014), 190–206.

[63] Leonhard Schmitz, "Tyche," in *Dictionary of Greek and Roman Biography and Mythology*, ed. William Smith, vol. 3 (Boston, Mass.: Little, Brown & Co., 1870), 3:1194.

[64] *SNG BnF* 1972.820; Mionnet Supp. 7.383 = *SNG BnF* 943; *SNG Cop.* 392; *SNGvA* 2.3067; *SNG Tübingen* 3754 = *SNGvA* 2.3068.

A RELIGIOUS CITY

There is no doubt that Philadelphia was a religious city. Numerous festivals were celebrated in Philadelphia, including the *Jovialia Solaria* (*CIG* 3427, 3428, 3416), the *Communia Asiae* (*CIG* 1068, 3428), and the *Agustalia Anaitea* (*CIG* 3424), each associated with their own gods.

THE GODS OF PHILADELPHIA

Some of the names of the local deities were similar to names used for Yahweh, such as "God Most High" (*Theos Hypsistos, I.Phil.* 1634–35) and "God Holy and Righteous" (*Theos Hosios kai Dikaios; I.Phil.* 1637; *ILydiaHoz,* 59–60). John's similar language in Revelation (15:3–4; 16:5) would have resonated with the local citizens of Philadelphia.[65] Following is a list of some of the gods of Philadelphia, and most have epigraphic or numismatic evidence attesting to their presence in the city.

1. The main deity of Philadelphia was a Persian goddess named *Anaitis*, who combined the Anatolian mother goddess Meter, and the Greek goddess Artemis,[66] and was worshiped by cultic prostitutes of both sexes.[67] She is attested to in both inscriptions (*I.Phil.* 1548; 1549; 1551) and numismatics, where she is portrayed either alone (30 BC–AD 276; see Fig. 124)[68] or held in the hand of Athena (Roma, see Figs. 34, 124),[69] or Tyche (Τύχη, or Cybele, see Figs. 52, 54, 98, 108, 160).[70] During the reign of Marcus Aurelius (r. AD 161–180), *Artemis Anaitis* is pictured in the center of either a distyle (See Fig. 125)[71] or tetrastyle temple (*SNGvA* 2.3077).

2. The temple of Artemis (see Figs. 28, 29, 24). *Artemis* was worshiped in Philadelphia[72] as both *Artemis Ephesia* (see Figs. 27, 121)[73] and *Artemis Anaitis* (see Fig. 125).[74] *Agdistis* (Ἀγδιστις, also

---

[65] Koester, *Revelation,* 323.

[66] Pausanias *Descr.* 3.16.6; *I.Phil.* 1550; *ILydiaHoz* 74–75.

[67] Willlam Alexander Greenhill, "Anaitis," in *Dictionary of Greek and Roman Biography and Mythology,* ed. William Smith, vol. 1 (Boston, Mass.: Little, Brown & Co., 1870), 1:158.

[68] Julia Domna, AD 193–217; Gordian, AD 238–244; *SNG Cop.* 365; 381; Mionnet 4.531; 4.563; 4.593; *SNG BnF* 985; 1024; *RPC* 3.2381; *BMC* 84.

[69] Caracalla, AD 198–268 (see Figs. 128, 162, 163); Gordian, AD 238–244; *BMC* 103; *SNG Cop.* 387; Mionnet 4.592; 4.545; *SNG BnF* 946; 1021B; *RPC* 1.1332.

[70] Domitian, AD 81–96; Trajan, AD 98–117; Faustina AD 161–169; Philip I, AD 244–249; *homōnoia* coins with Ephesus; *RPC* 1332; 3.2366; *SNG BnF* 952; 977; 1028; Mionnet 4.574; *SNG München* 424.

[71] Lanz 97.647; *SNG Righetti* 1065; Mionnet 4.597. Price and Trell, *Coins and Their Cities: Architecture on the Ancient Coins of Greece, Rome, and Palestine,* 476.

[72] *BMC* 8–9 = Mionnet Supp. 7.373; *BMC* 10 = *SNG Cop.* 337 = *SNGvA* 2.3058; *BMC* 13, 48; *SNG München* 400; Mionnet 4.529 = *SNG BnF* 923; Mionnet 4.545 = *SNG BnF* 913; 923A; 936; M5742; *BMC* 46–47 = *SNG Cop.* 356 = *SNGvA* 2.3070; *SNG Cop.* 357; 365 = Mionnet 4.531; *SNGvA* 2.3064; *SNG BnF* 938; 946; 952; *BMC* 10–12 = Mionnet Supp. 7.372 = Mionnet 4.534; Trajan, *RPC* 3.2381.

[73] Domitian, *SNG München* 419 = Mionnet 4.561 = *RPC* 1.1334.

[74] Domitian, *RPC* 1.1332; Trajan, *RPC* 3.2366; 3.2381; Marcus Aurelius, *SNGvA* 2.3077. Mary Boyce, "Anāhīd,"

spelled *Angdissis*[75] in Anatolia) was a wild androgynous deity in Anatolia that reportedly possessed both male and female sexual organs, and was associated with the worship of Attis and Cybele in Phrygia.[76] Households in Philadelphia worshiped Agdistis, who was identified, like Cybele, as mother of the gods (*AGRW* 52; 121 = *SIG* 3.985 = *ILydiaHoz* 1.2).[77] Aurelius Hermippos of Philadelphia (AD 212), was the high–priest of Artemis (*CIG* 3422 = *IGR* 4.1632; see also *I.Phil.* 1447).

122. Coin from Philadelphia. Obv.: ΔΗΜΟC ΦΙΛΑΔΕΛΦΕΩΝ. Laureated head of Demos, son of Aphrodite (AD 198–268). Rev.: *EPI P KAIKI KLEWNOC ARX A*. Aphrodite standing right in a long *chiton*, holding an apple in her outstretched left hand and draping herself with a chiton which she draws over her right shoulder (Lindgren 1:774).

3. Philadelphia was a major center for the worship of the wine god *Dionysus* (or *Dionysos*, see Fig. 35), who was likely worshiped in a temple or theater, and who was depicted on coins walking with a panther,[78] a common symbol of Dionysus.[79] The cult of *Dionysos Kathegemon* (Διόνυσον Καθηγεμόνα, *Dionuson Kathēgemona*, "Dionysos the Leader") was established in Pergamum by Attalus I and promoted by Attalus II.[80] Given that the city of Philadelphia was founded by Attalid rulers, who had their center at Pergamum, it is not surprising to discover that *Dionysos Kathegemon* was worshiped here as at Pergamum, where he was a guardian of sacred objects (ἱεροφάντης, *hierophantēs*). Numerous second and third cent. AD inscriptions pertaining to *Dionysos Kathegemon* associations attest to its popularity in Philadelphia.[81]

4. *Aphrodite*, the goddess of love (see Figs. 93, 122, 123, 126), is depicted on coins standing, holding an apple[82] in her outstretched left hand, her right hand, and with her right hand raised

---

in *Encyclopædia Iranica*, ed. Ehsan Yarshater, vol. 1 (London, U.K.: Eisenbrauns, 1991), 1006.

[75] Roller, In Search of God the Mother, 245–46 n.26.

[76] Leonhard Schmitz, "Agdistis," in *Dictionary of Greek and Roman Biography and Mythology*, ed. William Smith, vol. 1 (Boston, Mass.: Little, Brown & Co., 1870), 1:67–68; Roller, *In Search of God the Mother*, 240.

[77] Harland, Associations, Synagogues, and Congregations, 24–25, 50.

[78] *I.Phil.* 1632; *BMC* 16 = *SNGvA* 2.3057 = *SNG Cop.* 340 = *SNG BnF* 919; *BMC* 17–18 = *SNG Cop.* 341; *BMC* 33.

[79] Otto, Dionysus, 112–13.

[80] Helmut Müller, "Ein Neues Hellenistisches Weihepigramm Aus Pergamon," *Chiron* 19 (1989): 499–553; Beate Dignas and R. R. R. Smith, *Historical and Religious Memory in the Ancient World* (Oxford, U.K.: Oxford University Press, 2012), 134.

[81] *I.Phil.* 1462 = *ILydiaKP* 1.42; 1.42; 2.9; *I.Phil.* 1497; *TAM V* 2.1497.

[82] The apple figured prominently in the myth called the Judgment of Paris where Aphrodite promised Paris that he

up, drawing up the edge of her *chiton* (Greek clothing item; AD 193–268).[83] Aphrodite is also depicted standing in a tetrastyle and distyle temple with a dolphin at her feet (see Fig. 123).[84]

5. *Hekate* (or *Hecatē*) was the goddess of magic, patroness of witches, necromancy, and souls.[85] She is depicted on the coins of Philadelphia holding a torch and reclining with lions.[86] With a confirmed temple to Hecate in the western Anatolian city of Caria, Berg argues that Hecate was an Anatolian god worshiped as savior (*sōteira*), great (*magistē*), and most manifest (*epiphanestatē*).[87]

6. *Deimos* (or *Dēmos*, Δεῖμος) was the Greek god of terror or fear and son of Aphrodite (Pausanias *Descr.* 2.3.6; see Figs. 122, 124, 156).[88] He is depicted on the coins of Philadelphia with various goddesses.[89]

123. Coin from Philadelphia. (Struck under Septimius Severus). Obv.: *IOYLIA CEBACTH*. Portrait of Julia Domna (AD 170–217). Rev.: *EPI DOKIMOY ARXONTOC FILADELFEWN*, tetrastyle temple with statue of Aphrodite standing looking left, and dolphin at her foot (Apparently unpublished).

Several *homonoia* (alliance) coins, dating to ca. AD 198–268, were struck with Smyrna that also celebrate the status of *neōkoros* and depict the goddess Cybele.[90] Other *neōkoros* coins depict a lion walking (*BMC* 42; 43), while yet others portray Romulus and

---

could have the most beautiful woman in the world for his wife, if he would give Aphrodite the golden apple from the Garden of the Hesperides, inscribed "to the fairest (Gr. *kallistei*)" (Homer *Il.* 24.30; Sophocles *Frag.* 199; Ovid *Her.* 16.71ff, 149–152 and 5.35f; Lucian *Dial. d.* 20; Hyginus *Fab.* 92). Rachel Meredith Kousser, *Hellenistic and Roman Ideal Sculpture: The Allure of the Classical* (Cambridge, U.K.: Cambridge University Press, 2008), 31; Karl Kerényi, *The Heroes of the Greeks* (London, U.K.: Thames and Hudson, 1959), 163, 203, 252.

[83] Head of Zeus (see Figs. 95, 115, 126, 151, 154, 156); *BMC* 24 = *SNG Tübingen* 3749 = *RPC* 3.2385; Head of Dēmos (see Figs. 122, 124, 156); Lindgren 1:774; *SNG Righetti* 1054; *SNG Cop.* 360; *SNG Lewis* 1.1532; Mionnet 4.543.

[84] Mionnet 4.591 = *SNG BnF* 1020 = *SNG Cop.* 386; Waddington 5160.

[85] Rudloff and Rudloff, Hekate in Ancient Greek Religion, 1–12.

[86] Nero AD 54–68; *RPC* 2.3041; Titus AD 69–79; *RPC* 1.1330; Dēmos AD 193–211; *BMC* 30 = Mionnet 4.553 = Waddington 5128 = *SNG BnF* 955.

[87] William Berg, "Hecate: Greek or 'Anatolian'?," *Numen* 21, no. 2 (1974): 128–40.

[88] Leonhard Schmitz, "Deima," in *Dictionary of Greek and Roman Biography and Mythology*, ed. William Smith, vol. 1 (Boston, Mass.: Little, Brown & Co., 1870), 1:950.

[89] Hekate, AD 193–211 (*BMC* 30 = Mionnet 4.553); Artemis, AD 198–268 (*CNG* 22, 53); Aphrodite, AD 198–268 (Lindgren 774).

[90] *SNG Cop.* 392; Mionnet Supp. 7.383; *SNG BnF* 820, 943, 947; *BMC* 113, 118.

Remus, the founders of Rome,[91] Still more coins depict Athena (Mionnet 4.545; see Figs. 34, 124), Artemis,[92] Aphrodite (see Figs. 93, 122, 123, 126),[93] and Kybele.[94]

7. *Tyche* (Τύχη, the goddess of fortune, or Cybele, see Figs. 52, 54, 98, 108, 160), is portrayed on the coins of Philadelphia from AD 193–211,[95] together with Zeus, who is sometimes holding Nike (see Figs. 13, 87, 163).[96] Apollo, standing naked with his left hand on a lyre(*BMC* 32 = *SNG BnF* 925; see Fig. 86). Tyche is also portrayed on coins with other gods such as Dionysus (*BMC* 33), Asclepius (inscribed *neōkoros*),[97] Artemis;[98] Artemis Ephesia (see Fig. 121),[99] and Tyche holding a statuette of *Artemis Anaitis* (see Fig. 124, 125).[100]

124. Coin from Philadelphia. Obv.: *DHMOC.* laureated head of Demos (AD 198–268). Rev.: *FL FILADEL-FEWN !NEWKOR-WN*, Athena standing with *kalathos* on head, holding the cult figure of Artemis Anaitis on outstretched right hand, with a spear and shield in her left hand (Mionnet 4.545).

8. *Nikē* (νίκη), the goddess of victory (see Fig. 13), is portrayed on the coins of Philadelphia with Tyche, with the inscription *NEΩKOPΩN* or *NEWKOPOC* (*neōkoros*) either walking holding a *taenia* with both hands[101] or forming a wreath from an olive branch (*SNG Tübingen* 3752 = *SNG BnF* 951A). In one coin Zeus is seated on a stool, holding Nike (see Figs. 13, 87, 163) and a scepter (*BMC* 31 = Mionnet 4.530 = *SNG BnF* 924; see Fig. 114).

---

[91] *BMC* 49 = *SNG Cop.* 361; *SNG BnF* 941.
[92] AD 210–276, *BMC* 46–47 = *SNG Cop.* 356 = *SNGvA* 2.3070; *SNG Cop.* 357; *BMC* 46–47 = *SNG Cop.* 356–357; *BMC* 48; Waddington 5129 = *SNG BnF* 946.
[93] *SNG Righetti* 1054 = *SNG Cop.* 360; *SNG Lewis* 1:1532; Mionnet 4.543.
[94] *SNG Tübingen* 3754 = *SNGvA* 2.3068; Mionnet, 4.594; *BMC* 30 = Mionnet 4.553 = Waddington 5128 = *SNG BnF* 955.
[95] *SNG BnF* 940; Waddington 5130 = Mionnet 4.542 = *SNG BnF* 934 = *RPC* 3.2380; *RPC* 2.3036.
[96] *BMC* 31 = Mionnet 4.530 = *SNG BnF* 924; *SNG Righetti* 1056 = Lindgren 1.776 = *SNG Cop.* 364 = Mionnet Supp. 7.377; *BMC* 31 = Mionnet 4.530 = *SNG BnF* 924.
[97] *BMC* 50; *SNG Tübingen* 3753 = Mionnet 4.550 = *SNG BnF* 950.
[98] *SNG BnF* 923A; *SNG Righetti* 1065 = Mionnet 4.597.
[99] *SNGvA* 2.3064; *SNG München* 424 = Mionnet 4.574.
[100] *SNG Cop.* 365 = Mionnet 4.531; Waddington 5127 = *SNG BnF* 952; *RPC* 1.1332 = *SNG BnF* 977; Mionnet 4.574 = *SNG München* 424; *SNG BnF* 1001; *SNG BnF* 1028.
[101] *SNG Cop.* 366–367 = Mionnet 4.551 = *SNG BnF* 922 = *SNG München* 408.

9. *Cybele* (*Kybele* or Τύχη, *Tyche*, the goddess of fortune; or Cybele, see Figs. 52, 54, 98, 108, 160), the Anatolian mother goddess, is portrayed on coins of AD 198–260 featured with Deimos (see Figs. 122, 124, 156) along with the inscription *ΝΕΩΚΟΡΩΝ ΟΜΟΝΟΙΑ* (*neōkorōn homonoia*), in honor of the alliance (*homonoia*) with Smyrna and the shared honor of temple warden (*neōkoros*).[102] The coins of Domitian (AD 81–96; *RPC* 1.1338; cf. *BMC* 376), Trajan (AD 98–117; *BMC* 67; *RPC* 3.2376) and Antoninus Pius (AD 138–161; Unpublished) depict Cybele seated with one or two lions at her feet, while the Domitian coins have her resting on the back of a stag.

125. Coin from Philadelphia. Obv.: AYT K G M KY TRAIANOC DEKIOC. Laureate head of Trajan Decius (AD 249–251). Rev.: *EPI AYR ROYFEINOY ARX OMONOIA FILADELFEWN NEWK EFECIWN*. Alliance issue with Ephesus depicting a distyle temple seen in perspective on the left; in the center Tyche is standing, holding a statue of Artemis Anaitis, and looking back at the Dioskuri standing beside her (*SNG Righetti* 1065 = Mionnet 4.597).

10. The cult of *Apollo* was also attested by inscriptions (*I.Phil.* 1545–46) and coins. On coins from the second and first cent. BC, Apollo is seated holding a lyre and plectrum, appearing with the head of Artemis with a quiver with arrows over her shoulder (See Fig. 86).[103] On coins from AD 193–211, Apollo is standing naked with his hand on a lyre and the head of Tyche appearing alongside Apollo.[104]

126. Coin from Philadelphia (AD 193–211). Obv.: ZEYC KORYFAIOC. Head of *Zeus Koryphaeos* with his hair bound by a *taenia*. Rev.: ΦΙΛΑΔΕΛΦΕΩΝ. Aphrodite is standing holding an apple in her outstretched left hand, while her right hand is raised drawing up the edge of her *chiton* (*BMC* 24; *SNG Tübingen* 3749; *RPC* 3.2385).

---

[102] *SNG BnF* 1972.820; Mionnet Supp. 7.383 = *SNG BnF* 943; *SNG Cop.* 392; *SNGvA* 2.3067; *SNG Tübingen* 3754 = *SNGvA* 2.3068.
[103] *RPC* 1.1331; *BMC* 8–9, 62; *BMC* 10 = *SNG Cop.* 337 = *SNGvA* 2.3058.
[104] Waddington 5124 = *SNG BnF* 925 = *BMC* 32; *SNG BnF* 925.

11. The cult of *Zeus* (see Figs. 95, 115, 126, 151, 154, 156)is also mentioned on inscriptions (*I.Phil.* 1506; 1539–44) and coins. Households in Philadelphia worshiped Zeus Eumenes ("Kindly", or perhaps a reference identifying Zeus with King Eumenes II). Zeus had high more requirements for residents, prohibiting drugs, magic, abortion, contraceptive drugs, adultery, homosexuality, and slavery.[105] This type of conduct would render a member of this society unworthy to worship Zeus. Aurelius Artemon, son of Artemon, was the "secretary of the great, sacred contests in honor of Zeus" performed in Philadelphia (*TAM* V 2.1497 [Harland]). Zeus is usually accompanied on the coins of Philadelphia with Tyche, the goddess of fortune (AD 193–211; Τύχη, or Cybele, see Figs. 52, 54, 98, 108, 160). Zeus is either seated holding Nike and a scepter[106] or standing holding an eagle and scepter.[107] One coin features *Zeus Koryphaeos* with Aphrodite standing holding an apple (AD 193–211; see Fig. 126).[108]

127. Coin from Philadelphia. Obv.: Draped bust of Artemis, wearing a crown (*stephane*), with quiver and arrows behind her back on one side. Rev.: ERMIPPOS ERMOGENOUS ARCIEREUS. Apollo enthroned holding a lyre and plectrum, with an owl in left field (first cent. BC; *BMC* 10 = *SNG* Cop. 337 = *SNGvA* 2.3058).

12. Several lesser known deities were worshiped in Philadelphia, including *Mên Askaenos* (Μήν, the moon god; *I.Phil.* 1630–31), and *Meter Phileis* (Μητρί, the mother of the gods; *I.Phil.* 1625–26; *SEG* 35.1174–231) with a sanctuary 11 km (7 m) from the city.[109] A late first cent. BC-early first cent. AD inscription mentions the god *Sabathikos*, said to have answered the prayer for Roman citizenship of a man from Kastollos (Castollos) located just northeast of Philadelphia (*TAM* V 1.225 = *IlydiaKP* 2.224). Also mentioned in inscriptions are the Hellenistic deities of *Hestia* (Ἑστία, goddess of the hearth and state); *Aretē* (ἀρετή, personification of virtue); *Hygieia* (Ὑγιεία, goddess of health); *Agathos Daimōn* (ἀγαθοδαίμων, spirit of the vineyard); and *Mnēmē* (Μνήμη, the muse of memory; *I.Phil.* 1539).

---

[105] *AGRW* 52; 121 = *SIG* 3.985 = *ILydiaHoz* 1.2.
[106] *BMC* 31; Mionnet 4.530; *SNG BnF* 924.
[107] *SNG Righetti* 1056 = Lindgren 1.776 = *SNG Cop.* 364 = Mionnet Supp. 7.377.
[108] *BMC* 24; SNG *Tübingen* 3749; *RPC* 3.2385.
[109] Hasan Malay, "The Sanctuary of Meter Phileis near Philadelphia," *EA* 6 (1985): 111–26.

The Imperial Cult

While the cult of the emperor was not as prolific as in Ephesus or Smyrna,[110] it was present in Philadelphia by 27–26 BC,[111] with its own cult of Augustus and Rome (*I.Phil.* 1428).[112] In AD 40, Augustus' birthday was celebrated with sacrifices to the god Augustus (*I.Phil.* 1434), with the cultic priesthood being occupied by both men and women (*I.Phil.* 1472; 1484). The local games in the stadium were dedicated to Domitian and the goddess *Anaitis* (*I.Phil.* 1480; cf. 1460; 1505), both of which are depicted on their coins (*RPC* 1.1332 = *SNG BnF* 977). The benefits provided by the emperor are seen also as coming from Anaitis, the city's patron deity. Later in the first cent. AD the city adopted the name "Philadelphia Flavia" (see Fig. 114) in honor of the Flavian emperors and took the Flavian name during the reigns of Vespasian (r. AD 69–79) to Domitian (r. AD 81–96).[113]

Neōkoros

In AD 214, during the reign of Caracalla (r. AD 198–217; see Figs. 128, 162, 163), Philadelphia was granted the privilege of being "overseer of a temple" or "temple-warden" (νεωκόρος, *neōkoros*),[114] possibly confirmed by an inscription (*TAM V* 2.1497; AD 250) and celebrated with a coin of Caracalla depicting a tetrastyle temple and the inscription *NEWKORWN* (*neōkorōn*; *BMC* 86; *SNGvA* 2.3081; see Fig. 128). The term νεωκόρος (*neōkoros*) was a common term on the coins of Philadelphia. It is found on coins (AD 30 BC–AD 276) featuring Tyche with Artemis Anaitis (see Fig. 125) and others featuring Ephesia.[115] Other *NEWKOROC* (*neōkoros*) coins, from AD 198–268, depict Tyche with

128. Coin from Philadelphia Obv.: Showing the laureate head of Caracalla (AD 198–217) with inscription *AYT K M AYR CE ANTWNEINOC*, *Magistrate Kl. Kapitonos*. Rev.: *EPI KL KAPITWNOC ARX A FL FILADELFEWN NEWKORWN*, (*neōkorōn*). Depiction of a tetrastyle temple with curved architrave with Helios walking wearing short *chiton* and *chlamys*, and holding scepter over his shoulder (*BMC* 86 = *SNGvA* 2.3081).

---

[110] See chapter 2, *External Problems: Imperial Cult*.

[111] For a comprehensive treatment of the Imperial Cult in Philadelphia from numismatic and epigraphic remains, see chapter 9. Philadelphia in Lydia (Caracalla) in Burrell, *Neokoroi*, 126–29.

[112] This challenges Thompson's reports that Philadelphia did not have an imperial altar or priests. Thompson, *Apocalypse and Empire*, 159.

[113] *I.Phil.* 1453; 1456a; 1515. Eckart Olshausen, Kurt Tomaschitz, and Karl Jansen-Winkeln, "Philadelphia," *PW* 19/2, 209; Aune, *Rev 1–5*, 234; Koester, *Revelation*, 321–23.

[114] See chapter 2, *External Problems: Imperial Cult*, and chapter 4, *Keeper of the Temples (neōkoros)*.

[115] *SNG BnF* 1028; *BMC* 120 = *SNG BnF* 1021; *SNG Cop.* 365 = Mionnet 4.531; Waddington 5127 = *SNG BnF* 952.

Asclepius leaning on a serpent-entwined staff (see Fig. 71).[116] Coins of *Dēimos* (AD 198–268; see Figs. 122, 124, 156), represented with the term NEWKORW (*neōkorō*), are depicted with a walking lion[117] or a she-wolf standing suckling Romulus and Remus, the founders of Rome (see Fig. 3).[118] Several NEWKORWN (*neōkorōn*) coins from AD 198–268 are depicted showing *Dēimos* with Aphrodite;[119] *Dēimos* with Hekate (AD 193–211);[120] and *Dēimos* with Cybele (AD 200–276; *SNG Tübingen* 3754 = *SNGvA* 2.3068). Several of these NEWKORWN (*neōkorōn*) with Cybele are OMONOIA (*homonoia*) coins commemorating their alliance with Smyrna.[121] Another coin from AD 198–268 depicts Athena with a *kalathos* on her head and a double *chiton*, holding the cult figure of Artemis Anaitis (Mionnet 4.545; see Figs. 34, 124). Artemis is also depicted on coins with the term NEWKORWN (*neōkorōn*), with Artemis in a short chiton, with a strung bow in her left hand and drawing an arrow from a quiver in her right hand.[122] These coins depict the prominence with which the Philadelphian citizens held the honor of being guardians of the temple (*neōkoros*); an honour ranking alongside their worship of the various gods.

THE JEWISH COMMUNITY

There is evidence of a Jewish community in Philadelphia from Revelation 3:9 (synagogue of Satan) and the letter of Ignatius (*Phld.* 6:1; 8:2). As in many other Asian cities, Jewish communities had established their presence, evidenced at Philadelphia by an inscription from the third cent. AD mentioning a synagogue ten miles (16 km) east of Philadelphia at Deliler, and a "god fearer" who was also likely Jewish (*CIJ* 2.754; see also *IJO* 2.202–8).[123] Hemer speculated that there must have been a Jewish presence in Philadelphia due to its close proximity to Sardis.[124] However, no archaeological evidence, thus far, of a Jewish synagogue, has been found in Philadelphia.[125]

THE CHRISTIAN COMMUNITY

The Christian community was introduced in apostolic times and cited in a first cent. AD letter to Philadelphia (1:11; 3:7–13). In AD 110, Ignatius, the bishop of Antioch, briefly stayed here while being escorted under Roman guard on his way to his martyrdom in Rome. Ignatius later wrote to the church in Philadelphia, referring to the church leadership and confronting the

---

[116] *BMC* 50; *SNG Tübingen* 3753 = Mionnet 4.550 = *SNG BnF* 950.
[117] *BMC* 42 = Mionnet 4.547; *BMC* 43.
[118] *BMC* 49; *SNG Cop.* 361; *SNG BnF* 941.
[119] *SNG Righetti* 1054 = *SNG Cop.* 360; *SNG Lewis* 1:1532; Mionnet 4.543.
[120] *BMC* 30 = Mionnet 4.553 = Waddington 5128 = *SNG BnF* 955.
[121] *SNG Cop.* 392; Mionnet 7.383 = *SNG BnF* 943; *SNG BnF* 1972.820; *BMC* 118 = Mionnet 7.385; *BMC* 113 = Mionnet Supp. VII, 386–387 = *SNG BnF* 947.
[122] *BMC* 46–47 = *SNG Cop.* 356 = *SNGvA* 2.3070; *SNG Cop.* 357; *BMC* 46–47 = *SNG Cop.* 356–357; *BMC* 48; Waddington 5129 = *SNG BnF* 946.
[123] Trebilco, *Jewish Communities*, 162.
[124] Hemer, Letters to the Seven Churches, 160.
[125] Thomas, *Rev 1–7*, 272.

influence of Judaizers (Ign. *Phld.* 6.1–3). Ignatius indicated that the Philadelphian church was organized with elders (presbyters) and deacons subordinate to a ruling bishop, like a monarchical episcopate (Ign. *Phld.* 6:1).[126] The Montanists had their origins just up the Hermus Valley at Ardabav[127] and Philadelphia was influenced by the prophets and prophetesses of the Montanist sect,[128] even influencing Tertullian in his later years.[129] The apologist Pope, Miltiades (r. AD 311–314), mentioned the Montanist prophets, Ammia and Quadratus (AD 150), who taught that the *Paraclete* (Holy Spirit) would come just before the second coming of Christ. These false prophets likely belonged to the church of Philadelphia during the reign of Antoninus Pius (AD 138–161; Eusebius *Hist. eccl.* 5.17).[130] In AD 155, eleven Philadelphian Christians were martyred along with Polycarp, the bishop of Smyrna (see Fig. 50, 51; *Mart. Pol.* 19.1). According to the "Apostolic Constitutions" (*Apos. Con.* 8.46), the first bishop of Philadelphia was Demetrius, likely appointed by John.[131]

---

[126] William Schoedel, *Ignatius of Antioch: A Commentary on the Letters of Ignatius of Antioch*, ed. Helmut Koester, Hermeneia (Philadelphia, Pa.: Fortress, 1985), 195–215.

[127] William M. Calder, "Philadelphia and Montanism," *BJRL* 7, no. 3 (1923): 309–54.

[128] David F. Wright, "Why Were the Montanists Condemned?," *Themelios* 2, no. 8 (1976): 15–21.

[129] Timothy David Barnes, *Tertullian: A Historical and Literary Study*, 1985 edition (Oxford, U.K.: Oxford University Press, 1985).

[130] William Tabbernee, Prophets and Gravestones: An Imaginative History of Montanists and Other Early Christians (Grand Rapids, Mich.: Baker Academic, 2009), xv.

[131] Pétridès, "Philadelphia," 11:793.

15

Faithful Philadelphia

Commentary on Revelation 3:7–13

*J*ohn was commanded to write to the angel (ἄγγελος, *angelos*) of each church, and here at Philadelphia he continues to obey his instructions. This chapter will examine the content of the message to Philadelphia, a church faithful in keeping the faith. Revelation 3:7–13 will be examined in light of the proposed covenant background and structure. On the commission to write (γράψον, *graphon* 3:7a) and the role of angels (ἄγγελος, *angelos*) as mediating messengers, see chapter 3, *The Messenger's Commission*.

MESSENGER PREAMBLE FORMULA—3:7

Within the OT prophetic structure[1] this prophetic *messenger preamble formula*[2] τάδε λέγει Ω, (*tade legei omega*, "These are the words") introduces the sovereign's message. John also begins each message to the churches with τάδε λέγει Ω (*tade legei omega*, "These are the words" 2:1, 8,12,18; 3:1a, 7, 14), setting the context for the suzerain/King who will speak to the churches.[3]

DESCRIPTION OF THE SUZERAIN—3:7

Christ, the suzerain, is identified here using two self-designations, when compared with the other messages to the churches, are not as clearly echoes from Revelation chapter 1. It appears that John had Isaiah 22:20–22 in mind, even though Holy and True are

Τάδε λέγει ὁ ἅγιος, ὁ ἀληθινός, ὁ ἔχων τὴν κλεῖν Δαυίδ, ὁ ἀνοίγων καὶ οὐδεὶς κλείσει καὶ κλείων καὶ οὐδεὶς ἀνοίγει·

"Thus says the Holy One, the True One, the One with the key of David, who opens so that no one can shut and shuts so that no one can open" (Rev 3:7).

---

[1] Num 22:15–16; Judg 11:14–15; 1 Kgs 2:30; 2 Chr 36:23; Ezra 1:2.
[2] Graves, *SMRVT*, 141–47; Osborne, *Revelation*, 111.
[3] Beale, *Rev*, 229.

overarching characteristics found in chapter 1 (vs. 12–17).⁴ The messenger preamble to Philadelphia introduces the suzerain as both Holy (ὁ ἅγιος, *ho hagios*) and True (ὁ ἀληθινός, *ho alēthinos*) as the descendant of David who has his key (κλεῖν Δαυίδ, *klein David*), and as "the One who opens and shuts doors" (καὶ οὐδεὶς κλείσει καὶ κλείων καὶ οὐδεὶς ἀνοίγει., *kai oudeis kleisei kai kleiōn kai oudais anoigei*).

THE TRANSCENDENT SUZERAIN IS THE HOLY ONE—3:7B

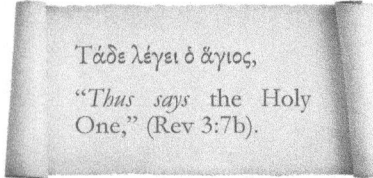

"Thus says the Holy One," (Rev 3:7b).

To the church in Philadelphia, the suzerain who speaks (Τάδε λέγει, *tade legei*) is first identified as "the Holy One" (ὁ ἅγιος, *ho hagios*). Jesus is not called holy in Revelation other than here, although Christians are often called "Holy Ones" (pl. ἅγιοι, *hagioi*) or saints (e.g. 5:8; 13:7), and God is called "the Holy One" in Revelation 6:10.⁵ In the rest of the NT, the adjective "Holy One" (ὁ ἅγιος, *ho hagios*) is occasionally used of Jesus as the Messiah,⁶ and connotes the idea of deity (cf. Isa 40:25; Hab 3:3). The term "holy" was also used by the imperial cult.⁷ The suzerain is understood here not so much as the one who is sinless, although he is,⁸ but conveys the notion of one set apart, belonging wholly to God.⁹

THE TRANSCENDENT SUZERAIN IS THE TRUE ONE—3:7C

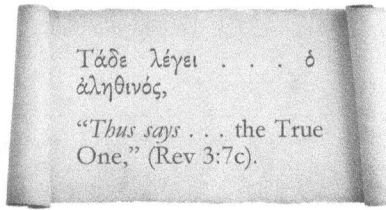

"Thus says . . . the True One," (Rev 3:7c).

Occasionally the adjective "true" (ἀληθινός, *alēthinos* or ἀληθής, *alēthēs*) is attributed to God,¹⁰ along with Christ,¹¹ to convey the suzerain's deity. There have been two different interpretations for the term "True One" (ἀληθινός, *alēthinos*). Some suggest that it means "genuine," in opposition to the false claims of the Jews who believed that Jesus was a false messiah (God is often described as "true" in contrast with other false gods),¹² while others understand it as meaning "faithfulness," in contrast to the unfaithful emperor.¹³ But, as Beal points out, the suzerain is both the real

---

⁴ Koester, *Revelation*, 328; Beale, *Rev*, 283.
⁵ See also Ps 16:10; Hab 3:3; Isa 40:25; 60:14; *1 En.* 1:3; *m. Pir. 'Abot* 3:1.
⁶ Mark 1:24 = Luke 4:34; John 6:69; Acts 3:14; 4:27, 30; *1 Clem.* 23:5; *Diogn.* 9.2; Justin *Dial.* 116.1; Clement *Paed.* 1.7; cf. Luke 1:35; 1 John 2:20.
⁷ Franz Sauter, *Der römische Kaiserkult bei Martial und Statius* (Berlin: Kohlhammer, 1934), 105–16.
⁸ 2 Cor 5:21; 1 Pet 2:22; 1 John 3:5; Heb 4:15; 7:26; 9:14.
⁹ Beckwith, *Apocalypse*, 478.
¹⁰ Rev 6:10; Exod 34:6; Isa 65:16; Ps 86:15; Jer 10:10; John 17:3; 1 Thess 1:9.
¹¹ Rev 3:14; 19:11; Mark 12:14 = Matt 22:16; John 7:18.
¹² Exod 34:6; 2 Chr 15:3; Neh 9:6; Isa 65:19; Jer 10:10; John 7:13; 17:3; 1 John 5:20; *1 Clem.* 43:14; *Diogn.* 8:9; Josephus *Ant.* 8.335, 337, 338, 343, 402; 9.256; 10.263. Beckwith, *Apocalypse*, 477; Kiddle, *Revelation*, 48; Alford, *Revelation*, 4:583; Chilton, *Days of Vengeance*, 126; Thomas, *Rev 1–7*, 273.
¹³ Rev 3:14; 19:11; 21:5; 22:6; Josephus *Ant.* 11.55. Charles, *Revelation*, 1:85–86; Hort, *Apocalypse*, 34; Hemer, *Letters*

FAITHFULL PHILADELPHIA – COMMENTARY

Messiah and the faithful king.[14] The one sitting on the white horse in Revelation 19 is "called Faithful and True" (ἀληθινός, *alēthinos*, 19:11). The phrase "holy and true" (ὁ ἅγιος, ὁ ἀληθινός, *ho hagios, ho alēthinos*; see also 6:10) is not otherwise used in early Jewish or early Christian literature for God or Christ.[15]

THE TRANSCENDENT SUZERAIN HAS THE KEY OF DAVID—3:7D

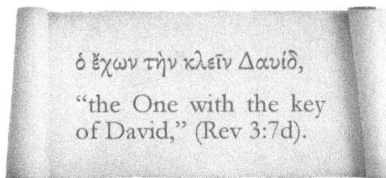

ὁ ἔχων τὴν κλεῖν Δαυίδ,
"the One with the key of David," (Rev 3:7d).

The reference to the suzerain holding the key of David is clearly drawn from Isaiah 22:22[16] that states: "and I will place on his shoulder the key of the house of David. He shall open, and none shall shut; and he shall shut, and none shall open" (Isa 22:22). God, the suzerain, states that he will replace the king's servant, Shebna, with Eliakim[17] as the royal steward (*'asher 'al habbayit*) of Hezekiah's house.[18] To validate the servant's authority, the suzerain gives Eliakim the key (see Fig. 130)[19] to the

129. Drawing of a reproduction of the locking mechanism found at a palace in Khorsabad (Nineveh; Bonomi, *Nineveh and its Palaces*, 170–71). The key was made with various pin combinations to provide security. It was made of wood, and it should be noted that the key would easily fit on a shoulder as stated in Isaiah 22:22.

---

to the Seven Churches, 161.

[14] Beale, *Rev*, 283.

[15] Aune, Revelation 6–16, 407.

[16] John Adney Emerton, "Binding and Loosing—Forgiving and Retaining," *JTS* 13 (1962): 325–31; Beale, *Rev*, 284–85; Thomas, *Rev 1–7*, 275; Osborne, *Revelation*, 187.

[17] Several seal impressions from jar handles excavated at Tell Beit Mirsim, Beth Shemesh, and Ramat Rahel mention Eliakim and date to the reign of Hezekiah (701 BC, IA stratum from Lachish). See Albright and others for the ongoing controversy surrounding the Eliakim seals. Nahman Avigad and Benjamin Sass, *Corpus of West Semitic Stamp Seals*, 2nd ed. (Jerusalem: Israel Academy of Sciences & Humanities, 1997); David Winston Thomas, *Documents from Old Testament Times*, Society for Old Testament Study (New York, N.Y.: Harper, 1961), 224; John H. Walton, Victor H. Matthews, and Mark W. Chavalas, *The IVP Bible Background Commentary: Old Testament* (Downers Grove, Ill.: InterVarsity, 2000), 614; William F. Albright, "The Seal of Eliakim and the Latest Preëxilic History of Judah, with Some Observations on Ezekiel," *JBL* 51, no. 2 (1932): 77–106; Yosef Garfinkel, "Commentary: The Eliakim Nacar Yokan Seal Impressions: Sixty Years of Confusion in Biblical Archaeological Research," *BA* 53, no. 2 (1990): 74–79; Anson F. Rainey, "A Rejoinder to the Eliakim Nacar Yokan Seal Impressions," *BA* 54, no. 1 (1991): 61; Lawrence J. Mykytiuk, *Identifying Biblical Persons in Northwest Semitic Inscriptions of 1200–539 B.C.E.*, SBL Academia Biblica 12 (Atlanta, Ga.: SBL, 2004), 23–25.

[18] Isa 22:15–25; see 2 Kgs 18:18 = Isa 36:3.

[19] This type of lock mechanism was found in the "ruins of Nineveh, and was apparently used to secure the door of a room in the Palace of King Sargon in Khorsabad" (see Fig. 129). F. Le Guet Tully, "Science and the Design of

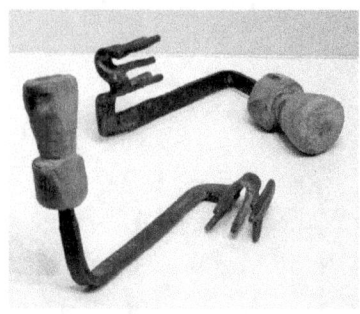

130. House keys. Cave of the Letters, Nahal Hever (AD 132–135).

house of David, granting him full access to the king, his palace, and the royal treasury (Isa 22:20–22; *Tg. Isa.* 22:22; see *The Transcendent Suzerain Opens and Shuts Doors–3:7d*).[20]

While some have understood this mention of David's house messianically,[21] most see this as a typological comparison with Christ who holds the keys of the kingdom (cf. Matt 16:18–19), symbols of power and authority.[22] Jesus claims to "have the keys" to "death and Hades" in chapter 1 (ver. 18b).[23] The suzerain is omnipotent and transcendent, exercising authority over death, judgment and the Davidic kingdom (heaven).

THE TRANSCENDENT SUZERAIN OPENS AND SHUTS DOORS—3:7D

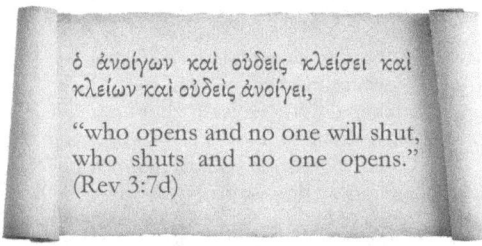

ὁ ἀνοίγων καὶ οὐδεὶς κλείσει καὶ κλείων καὶ οὐδεὶς ἀνοίγει,

"who opens and no one will shut, who shuts and no one opens."
(Rev 3:7d)

One of the benefits of the "Key of the house of David", significant in light of the Jewish population[24] and "synagogue" (3:9) in Philadelphia, is that the suzerain has the authority to "open" and "shut" (3:7d; see also Isa 22:22). The text here does not specify what can be opened and shut, but the mention of a key assumes the door (θύρας, *thuras*) mentioned in 3:8, although it may refer more generally to the suzerain's kingdom.

A fifth century AD Coptic magical exorcism text[25] is almost certainly dependant on this passage in Revelation. It translates: "Davithe [*sic* David] with the golden hair, whose eyes are

---

Mechanical and Optical Devices: A Few Case Studies," in *Design Methodology and Relationships with Science*, ed. Marc J. de Vries, Nigel Cross, and D. P. Grant, Behavioral and Social Sciences 71 (Dordrecht: Kluwer Academic, 1993), 32.

[20] Bruce D. Chilton, "Shebna, Eliakim, and the Promise to Peter," in *The Social World of Formative Christianity and Judaism: Essays in Tribute to Howard Clarke Kee*, ed. Jacob Neusner et al. (Philadelphia, Pa.: Fortress, 1988), 322–24.

[21] Johannes Horst, Proskynein: Zur Anbetung Im Urchristentum Nach Ihrer Religionsgeschichtlichen Eigenart (Gütersloh: Bertelsmann, 1932), 254; Jan Fekkes, Isaiah and Prophetic Traditions in the Book of Revelation: Visionary Antecedents and Their Development, LNTS 93 (New York, N.Y.: Bloomsbury, 1994), 131; Swete, Revelation, 54; Beckwith, Apocalypse, 479; Osborne, Revelation, 187 n.4; Smalley, Revelation, 88.

[22] Bousset, *Die Offenbarung Johannis*, 226; Wilhelm Hadorn, *Die Offenbarung Des Johannes*, THKNT 18 (Leipzig: Verlagsbuchhandlung, 1928), 60; Beale, *Rev*, 284–85; Thomas, *Rev 1–7*, 275; Osborne, *Revelation*, 187. Contra Aune, *Rev 1–5*, 235.

[23] The text was understood in textual tradition to be connected to 1:18b as some mss. replaced David (Δαυίδ) with Hades (αδου). Beale, *Rev*, 283 n.191.

[24] See chapter 16, *A Religious City: The Jewish Community*.

[25] Viktor Stegemann, *Die Gestalt Christi in Den Koptischen Zaubertexten* (Heidelberg: Bilabel, 1934), 19–20.

lightning, you are the one in whose hand is the key of deity; when you shut, no one can open again, and when you open, no man can shut again" (*AKZ* 2:151–52 [Aune]). Jesus tells Peter in Matt 16:19, "I will give you the keys of the kingdom of heaven, and whatever you bind on earth shall be bound in heaven, and whatever you loose on earth shall be loosed in heaven." While Jesus gives the keys to Peter, Revelation speaks of a unique authority of Jesus, the suzerain himself. The suzerain is the genuine Messiah and faithful king, totally set apart from any other suzerain. The authority to open and shut the Davidic kingdom, the heavenly Jerusalem, to anyone is his prerogative alone.

HISTORICAL PROLOGUE—3:8–9

The next section in vassal treaties, described as "a historical prologue,"[26] sets forth an acknowledgment of the historical intimacy of the relationship between the suzerain and vassals[27] as a historical summary.[28] It lists the mutual legal relationship between the parties,[29] particularly of the vassal's past relationship to the Great King.[30] The 'I–Thou' first person perspective, characteristic of the ANEVT, is also identifiable in the message to Philadelphia. As the author of the covenant, Christ the suzerain speaks in the first person to the vassals.[31]

THE SUZERAIN KNOWS THEIR WORKS—3:8A

οἶδά σου τὰ ἔργα, ἰδοὺ δέδωκα ἐνώπιόν σου θύραν ἠνεῳγμένην, ἣν οὐδεὶς δύναται κλεῖσαι αὐτήν,

"I know your works. Behold, I have set before you an open door, which no one is able to shut." (Rev 3:8a)

Following the *messenger preamble formula* of τάδε λέγει Ω (*tade legei*, "these are the words"), the message to Philadelphia continues with the classic prophetic lawsuit[32] phrase, οἶδά σου τὰ ἔργα (*oida sou ta erga*, "I am aware of the deeds").[33] Jesus conveys his knowledge (οἶδα, *oida*, "I know"; also ידע, *yds*) of the deeds (ἔργα, *erga*) of the Philadelphian vassals and proceeds to reveal that he knows they have little strength (3:8b), but have kept his word (3:8c), and remained faithful to his name (3:8d). He knows that those known as the "synagogue of Satan" are liars (3:9a) and will grovel at the feet of the Philadelphians (3:9b). The suzerain pledges his love to the church in Philadelphia (3:9c).

---

[26] Baltzer uses *antecedent history*, while Aune identifies this as the *narratio* section. Baltzer, *Covenant Formulary*, 20–24; Aune, *Rev 1–5*, 121.
[27] Berman, "Histories Twice Told," 232.
[28] Huffmon, "Treaty Background," 31–37.
[29] de Lassus, "Le Septénaire," 41; Bandy, *Prophetic Lawsuit*, 217.
[30] Mendenhall, "Covenant Forms," 59; Thompson, *ANE Treaties*, 16; Thompson, "Near Eastern Suzerain-Vassal," 4; Walton, *Ancient Israelite Literature*, 102.
[31] Mendenhall, "Covenant Forms," 59.
[32] Hillers, *Covenant*, 120.
[33] Hartman, "The Book of Revelation," 143.

The reference to the metaphor of the "open door" (θύρας, *thuras*, 3:8)³⁴ may be a veiled reference to the closed door represented by the excommunication of Christians from Jewish synagogues (see also John 9:22; 12:42; 16:2), formalized in the Jewish Council of Jamnia³⁵ in AD 90.³⁶ Rather than being an open door to evangelism for the spread of Greek culture³⁷ or Christianity,³⁸ the reference in this context is more likely to be understood eschatologically to contrast the Christians being kicked out of synagogues with the welcome they will receive into heaven (the new Jerusalem),³⁹ the door of which "no one is able to shut" (3:8; see Isa 26:2) and only the suzerain has the sovereign authority to open.⁴⁰

For the vassals in Philadelphia, this was encouraging news. The "synagogue of Satan" no longer held the authority of salvation and judgment, as now the door to the true synagogue of the suzerain was open to them (though it remained closed to those who opposed the suzerain). The suzerain is not only the keeper of the keys to release citizens from death and Hades (1:13, 18), he is also guardian of the key of David, having the authority to admit vassals into the company of the king and his kingdom, the new Jerusalem.⁴¹ Ramsay points out that θύρα (*thura*, "door") was engraved on several sepulchral monuments in Galatia, which represented "the passage of communication between the world of life and the world of death."⁴²

---

³⁴ Cf. Acts 14:27; *Barn.* 16:9; *Midr. Rab.* Cant. 5:2. See Lampe for the metaphorical use of θύρα (*thura*) in early Christian literature. G. W. H. Lampe, ed., *A Patristic Greek Lexicon*, 1 edition (Oxford, U.K.: Oxford University Press, 1961), 658; Deissmann, *Light from the Ancient East*, 303. Deissmann argues that because the term does not have any parallels outside the NT in early Jewish literature in the first cent. AD or earlier, the metaphor must have Hellenistic origins.

³⁵ Jack P. Lewis, "What Do We Mean by Jabneh?," *JBR* 32 (1964): 125–32; "Jamnia (Jabneh), Councel of," ed. David Noel Freedman et al., *ABD* (New York, N.Y.: Doubleday, 1996), 3:634–37.

³⁶ Horbury, "The Benediction of the 'Minim' and Early Jewish-Christian Controversy," 19–61; Wilson, *Revelation*, 32.

³⁷ Ramsay, *Letters: Updated*, 297; Brown, *Heavenly Visions*, 105–6; Ford, *Revelation*, 415; Meinardus, *John of Patmos*, 115; Worth, Jr., *Greco-Asian Culture*, 199–200; Wilson, *Biblical Turkey*, 293.

³⁸ 1 Cor 16:9; 2 Cor 2:12; Col 4:3. Trench, *Commentary on Seven Churches*, 180–81; Hort, *Apocalypse*, 35; Charles, *Revelation*, 1:87; Caird, *Revelation*, 51; Swete, *Apocalypse*, 54; Walvoord, *Revelation*, 85; Robertson, *Word Pictures*, 6:317; Barclay, *Letters*, 68.

³⁹ Moffatt and Sweet suggest that the door is Christ (Ign. *Phld.* 9.1; *1 Clem.* 48.2, 3) but unlikely since he opens the door (Moffatt, *Revelation*, 366; Sweet, *Revelation*, 103). Kiddle argues that the door is prayer and immediate access into God's presence through Martyrdom. (Kiddle, *Revelation*, 50). Barnabas 16:9 suggests that repentance opens the door (see John 10:7–9; *Midr. Rab.* Cant. 5:2).

⁴⁰ Beckwith, *Apocalypse*, 480; Bousset, *Die Offenbarung Johannis*, 227; Lohmeyer, *Offenbarung*, 35; Kraft, *Offenbarung*, 81; Lohse, *Offenbarung*, 33; Roloff, *Revelation*, 61; Beasley-Murray, *Revelation*, NCB, 100; Hemer, *Letters to the Seven Churches*, 162; Harrington, *Revelation*, 70; Aune, *Rev 1–5*, 236; Osborne, *Revelation*, 187–88; Kistemaker, *Revelation*, 158; Beale, *Rev*, 285; Smalley, *Revelation*, 89; Keener, *Background Commentary: NT*, 149–50; Mounce, *Revelation*, 101; Koester, *Revelation*, 324; Morris, *Revelation of St. John*, 81; Lenski, *Revelation*, 1963, 140; Thomas, *Rev 1–7*, 277–78.

⁴¹ Rev 3:12; 4:1; 5:9–10; 21:2.

⁴² Ramsay, *Cities and Bishoprics*, 2:395, No. 210, 227, 242, 247, 251; "Sepulchral Customs in Ancient Phrygia," *JHS* 5 (1884): 251.

Several scholars suggest that the "open door" phrase (3:8a) is a parenthesis and that the main thought is found in "I know that you have but little power" (ὅτι μικρὰν ἔχεις δύναμιν, *hoti mikran echeis dunamin*, 3:8b).[43] This would support the ANEVT structure of the historical prologue where the main emphasis is on what the suzerain knows of their historical relationship.

THE SUZERAIN KNOWS THEY HAVE LITTLE STRENGTH—3:8B

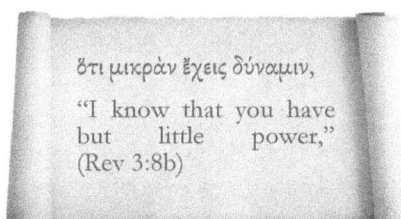

The suzerain acknowledges three of their characteristics, the first of which is that they have little power (μικρὰν ἔχεις δύναμιν, *mikran echais dunamin*). Some believe this points to the small number of believers in the church resulting in a limited spiritual power and influence in the church.[44] Others suggest that it was the size of the city (Strabo *Geogr.* 13.4.10; 12.8.18)[45] and stature in the civil community (Acts 17:5–7; Suetonius *Nero* 16.2) that prompted the suzerain to acknowledge their limited power and strength,[46] since the members must have come from the lower classes (cf. 1 Cor 1:26–27), contrasted with their wealthy Jewish adversaries (who were designated "the Synagogue of Satan"–3:9).[47] See Hemer for a discussion of "placing the church's confession of Christ's name in a Jewish setting at so late a date."[48] Torrey argues that Revelation was written at an early Neronian date, thus accounting for the Christians being in the synagogue, as many had yet to be formally excommunicated from Judaism.[49]

While Ramsay and Hemer see the problem of little power resulting from a general Jewish persecution, although Hemer suggests that the persecution came as a result of Christians seeking asylum in the synagogues and faceing rejection from the Jews.[50] He points out that there appears to be hints of this kind of persecution later in the correspondence of Ignatius (Ign. *Phld.* 1).

THE SUZERAIN KNOWS THEY HAVE KEPT HIS WORD—3:8C

The conjunction καί (*kai, and*) in this verse is important for determining the meaning of their "little power" (μικρὰ δύναμις, *mikra dunamis*). If καί (*kai, and*) is translated as "but or yet"

---

[43] Alford, *Revelation*, 4:584; Hort, *Apocalypse*, 35; Charles, *Revelation*, 1:87; Swete, *Revelation*, 54; Beckwith, *Apocalypse*, 479–80; Thomas, *Rev 1–7*, 276; Morris, *Revelation*, 81; Osborne, *Revelation*, 188; Beale, *Rev*, 286; Smalley, *Revelation*, 89.

[44] *L&N*, §12.44; Walvoord, Revelation of Jesus Christ, 85.

[45] See chapter 16, *The Population of Philadelphia*.

[46] Trebilco, *Jewish Communities*, 167–85; Harland, *Associations, Synagogues, and Congregations*, 200–210; Koester, *Revelation*, 329; Osborne, *Revelation*, 189; Thomas, *Rev 1–7*, 279; Beale, *Rev*, 286.

[47] Hort, *Apocalypse*, 35; Beckwith, *Apocalypse*, 479; Alford, *Revelation*, 4:4:584; Robertson, *Word Pictures*, 6:317.

[48] Hemer, *Letters to the Seven Churches*, 163.

[49] Charles C. Torrey, "The Aramaic Period of the Nascent Christian Church," ZNW, 53 1952, 205–33; *The Apocalypse of John* (New Haven, Conn.: Yale University Press, 1958), 80–81.

[50] Hemer, *Letters to the Seven Churches*, 163.

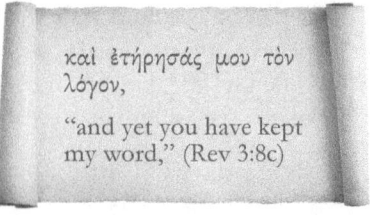

καὶ ἐτήρησάς μου τὸν λόγον,

"and yet you have kept my word," (Rev 3:8c)

(adversative sense)[51] it would mean that in spite of their spiritually weak power, they had nevertheless obeyed the suzerain's word. However, καί (*kai, and*) is rarely used in the adversative sense in the NT. Alternatively, Lövestam argues that δύναμις means "limited strength" and καί (*kai*) means "also" or "even."[52] This would mean that despite the Philadelphian Christian's weakness, they still proved faithful to Christ in the face of opposition. The phrase "to keep the word" (τηρεῖν τὸν λόγον, *tērein ton logon*), is repeated again in 3:10, and used with a plural object in 22:7, 9 (τηρεῖν τοὺς λόγους, *tērein tous logous* [53]).

In 1 John 2:3–5, the phrases "keep his commandments" (τηρεῖν τὰς ἐντολάς, *tērein tas entolas*, i.e., the law of God contained in the Decalogue or "the ten words"; cf. Exod 20:2–17) and "keep his word" (τηρεῖν τὸν λόγον, *tērein ton logon*, דבר *dābār;* 1QS 1:13) are synonymous[54] and characteristically Johannine.[55] The suzerain is mindful of the vassal's obedience to his orders.

THE SUZERAIN KNOWS THEY HAVE NOT DENIED HIS NAME—3:8D

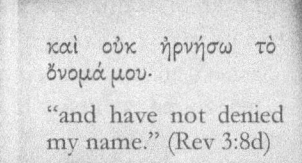

καὶ οὐκ ἠρνήσω τὸ ὄνομά μου.

"and have not denied my name." (Rev 3:8d)

Conversely obedience to the suzerain's orders and commands is not denying his name. Repudiating the name of the suzerain is the same as a rejection of the Christian faith.[56]

Verse 8 assumes that the Philadelphian church had been pressured to deny their faith by the Jews associated with the synagogue (3:9). Jews were known to turn over Christians to the Roman magistrates, who would make them pledge their loyalty to Rome or suffer punishment (Pliny *Ep.* 10.96.3, 5; *Mart. Perp.* 3). However, Koester reasons that since "the Philadelphians refused to deny Christ's name and yet were not punished, it is unlikely that the Romans were involved."[57]

The means used by the Jewish community to pressure the Christians to deny their faith are not mentioned, but there were several options available. In some cases, the leaders of the synagogue were involved[58] and in other cases verbal pressure from some [Nicolaitans][59] within

---

[51] Charles, Revelation, 1:87; Hemer, Letters to the Seven Churches, 163; Osborne, Revelation, 189.

[52] Evald Lövestam, "Apokalypsen 3:8b," *SEÅ* 30 (1965): 91–101.

[53] John 8:51, 52, 55; 14:23, 24; 15:20; 17:6; 1 John 2:5.

[54] See, *Excursus 12B: The Commandments of God and the Torah.* Aune, Revelation 6–16, 710–12; Smalley, Revelation, 90.

[55] 1 John 2:4, 7, 8; 3:22–24; 4:21; 5:2–3. The phrase τηρεῖν τὰς ἐντολάς is only found elsewhere in the NT in Matt 19:17; 1 Tim 6:14 (cf. 1 Cor 7:19). Stephen S. Smalley, *1, 2, 3 John*, WBC 51 (Dallas, Tex.: Word Books, 1989), 45–46. See further H.-H. Esser, *NIDNTT* 1 (1975) 337–39.

[56] Luke 12:9–10 = Matt 10:33; 2 Tim 2:12; *Mart. Pol.* 9:2–3; Justin *1 Apol.* 31.6; *1 Clem.* 3:4.

[57] Koester, *Revelation*, 324; Friesen, "Satan's Throne," 354.

[58] Matt 10:17; Mark 13:9; Luke 21:12; John 9:22; 12:42; 16:2; Acts 26:11.

[59] Harland, Associations, Synagogues, and Congregations, 229 n.36.

the synagogue (3:9; Acts 13:50; 17:13) warned the followers of Jesus that there was a societal cost for following Christ.[60]

The aorist tense of the verbs "you kept" (ἐτήρησάς, *etēresas*) and "you did not deny" (οὐκ ἠρνήσω, *ouk ērnēsō*, 3:8d) indicate a specific historical crisis the church had faced and overcome.[61] The suzerain recounts their historical relationship in the classic sense of the ANEVT Historical Prologue.

THE SUZERAIN KNOWS THE ENEMY—3:9A

ἰδοὺ διδῶ ἐκ τῆς συναγωγῆς τοῦ σατανᾶ τῶν λεγόντων ἑαυτοὺς Ἰουδαίους εἶναι, καὶ οὐκ εἰσὶν ἀλλὰ ψεύδονται·

"Behold, I will make those of the synagogue of Satan who say that they are Jews and are not, but lie." (Rev 3:9a)

Not only are the vassals known to the King, but the conduct of their enemies is also laid bare before his omniscient gaze. This gaze recognizes *"the synagogue of Satan who say that they are Jews and are not, but lie"* (3:9). As in the case of Smyrna (2:9), there was a conflict between the church in Philadelphia and the Jewish community. Some suggest that there had been converts from Judaism to Christianity.[62] Jesus is "holy" and "true" (3:7; 6:10) like his Father and thus can be worshiped (5:13–14; 22:3),[63] and this led to Jewish opposition. Those of Jewish decent claimed to be the true Israel, both by "national identity and religious heritage,"[64] while the Christian congregation, who believed in Jesus as the Messiah, were the Israel of God.[65] Only Jesus completely fulfilled all of the Father's righteous laws for Israel and was the true Son of God (Matt 2:13–14). Thus, the Jews in Philadelphia who claimed to be Jews by their attachment to the synagogue had proven themselves to be "liars".[66]

---

[60] See Acts 13:50; 17:13; 1 Pet 4:14, 16. Bruce J. Malina and Jerome H. Neyrey, "Honor and Shame in Luke-Acts: Pivotal Values of the Mediterranean World," in *The Social World of Luke-Acts: Models for Interpretation*, ed. Jerome H. Neyrey (Grand Rapids, Mich.: Baker Academic, 1999), 29–32; Mayo, *Those Who Call Themselves Jews*, 67–73.

[61] Thomas, *Rev 1–7*, 279; Smalley, *Revelation*, 89.

[62] Edmundo F. Lupieri, *A Commentary on the Apocalypse of John*, trans. Maria Poggi Johnson and Adam Kamesar, Italian Texts and Studies on Religion and Society (Grand Rapids, Mich.: Eerdmans, 1999), 126.

[63] Bauckham, *Theology of Revelation*, 54–65.

[64] Mounce, *Revelation*, 101; John M. G. Barclay, *Jews in the Mediterranean Diaspora: From Alexander to Trajan (323 BCE-117 CE)* (Berkeley, Calif.: University of California Press, 1999), 399–444; Steve Mason, "Jews, Judeans, Judaizing, Judaism: Problems of Categorization in Ancient History," *JSJ* 38 (2007): 457–512.

[65] Rom 2:29; Gal 6:16; cf. Deut 30:6. Lohse, "Synagogue of Satan," 105–23; Borgen, "Polemic in the Book of Revelation," 199–211; Jan Willem van Henten, "Anti-Judaism in Revelation? A Response to Peter Tomson," in *Anti-Judaism and the Fourth Gospel*, ed. Reimund Bieringer, Didier Pollefeyt, and Frederique Vandecasteele-Vanneuville, Jewish and Christian Heritage 1 (Assen: Royal van Gorcum, 2001), 111–25; Jan Lambrecht, "'Synagogues of Satan' (Rev. 2:9 and 3:9): Anti-Judaism in the Book of Revelation," in *Anti-Judaism and the Fourth Gospel*, ed. Reimund Bieringer, Didier Pollefeyt, and Frederique Vandecasteele-Vanneuville (Louisville, Ky.: Westminster/Knox, 2001), 279–92; Duff, "Synagogues of Satan," 147–68.

[66] For Satan's deception see 12:9; Job 1:6–12; 2:1–6; Zech 3:1–5; John 8:44; 2 Cor 11:14; 2 Thess 2:9–10. For the

The true Israel will acknowledge Yahweh as the true suzerain.[67] The Christian community will comprise both Jews and Gentiles through conversion. Wall calls this "a stunning example of the apocalyptic reversal motif,"[68] in which the arguments against the church are turned upside down and make the Jews of the synagogue to be liars and the Christians the "true Israel" (Gal 6:16). However, Kraybill suggests that "John implies that certain Jews in those cities [Smyrna and Philadelphia] are in the same category as Rome—that is, in league with Satan."[69] While all the cities mentioned in Revelation 2–3 had a Jewish community, only Smyrna and Philadelphia were singled out for having a conflict with the synagogue, indicating that John is not using polemical language indiscriminately and cannot be charged with anti-Semitism.[70]

FORCED TO COME AND GROVEL AT YOUR FEET—3:9B

ἰδοὺ ποιήσω αὐτοὺς ἵνα ἥξουσιν καὶ προσκυνήσουσιν ἐνώπιον τῶν ποδῶν σου,

"behold, I will make them come and bow down before your feet," (Rev 3:9b)

In contrast with the Jews in the synagogue, Jesus is portrayed as bearer of the key of David (recalling Isaiah 22:22), promising that those from the synagogue will bow before the feet of the real suzerain's followers.

In the Graeco-Roman world, being cast before someone's feet in prostration (προσκυνήσουσιν, *proskyēsousin*) indicated an abandoned appeal and submission of homage (see Fig. 131).[71] It was not necessarily as an act of religious worship (i.e., before God).[72] Again this is likely taken from a reference in Isaiah where the Gentile nations are made to submit to Israel: "The sons of those who afflicted you shall come bending low to you, and all who despised you shall bow down at your feet; they shall call you the City of the Lord [also 3:12], the Zion of the Holy One [also 3:7b] of Israel" (60:14). Prostration is also mentioned in Isaiah 49:23: "With their [kings'] faces to the ground they shall bow down to you, and lick the dust of your feet. Then you will know that I am the LORD; those who wait for me shall not be put to shame" (see Fig. 131). While Isaiah portrays the Gentiles giving homage to Israel,[73] in Revelation the meaning is reversed as some of the Jews in

---

details of the "synagogue of Satan" in Smyrna see chapter 9, *The Suzerain Knows the Enemy* (2:9; cf. 2 Cor 11:14–15; Rev 12:10; Ign. *Phld.* 6:1–2).

[67] Isa 45:14; cf. 49:23; Zech 8:20–23.
[68] Wall, *Revelation*, 84.
[69] Kraybill, Imperial Cult and Commerce in John's Apocalypse, 170.
[70] Lohse, "Synagogue of Satan," 105–23; Borgen, "Polemic in the Book of Revelation," 199–211; van Henten, "Anti-Judaism in Revelation? A Response to Peter Tomson," 111–25; Lambrecht, "'Synagogues of Satan' (Rev. 2:9 and 3:9): Anti-Judaism in the Book of Revelation," 279–92; Duff, "Synagogues of Satan," 147–68; Collins, "Vilification," 320; Friesen, "Sarcasm in Revelation," 127–46.
[71] 2 Kgs 4:37; Jdt 14:7; Acts 10:25; Caesar *Bell. gall.* 1.27, 31; Tacitus *Ann.* 12.18; Polybius *Hist.* 1.66; 10.18; 15.1.
[72] Rev 4:10; 5:14; 15:4; 19:20; 20:4; 22:3; before the Beast 13:4, 8; 14:9. Horst, *Proskynein*, 253–91; Aune, *Rev 1–5*, 238; Osborne, *Revelation*, 191.
[73] Cf. Isa 45:14; Zech 8:20–23; 1QM 12:14–15; 19:6–7; *1 En.* 10:21; 90:30; *Sib. Or.* 3.716–20, 725–31. Kekkes sees

131. One of the panels of the Black Obelisk depicting the Israelite King Jehu prostrate, bringing tribute to King Shalmaneser III in around 841 BC.

Philadelphia will be made to render homage to the Christians and acknowledge that the church is the object of Christ's love. The vassal's faith in the suzerain will be vindicated (Rom 10:19–11:32). Jesus the suzerain, here also described as the Holy One, undertakes God's covenant role of lover and protector of his people.

There is a debate over the nature of the Jews who bow, as some suggest that it refers to the eschatological salvation of the Jews,[74] while other argue that it does not imply the Jew's salvation (Phil 2:10–11), but rather the vindication of Christians,[75] which may also occur at the end of the age.[76] In either case the fulfillment of this vindication must be treated as a metaphor as is John's practice when writing to the other churches (2:5, 16, 22; 3:16).

THE SUZERAIN KNOWS THEY ARE LOVED—3:9C

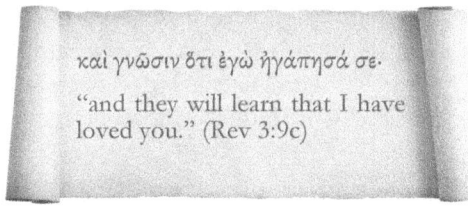

καὶ γνῶσιν ὅτι ἐγὼ ἠγάπησά σε.
"and they will learn that I have loved you." (Rev 3:9c)

The suzerain continues to know (γνῶσιν, gnōsin) more about the vassals and appears to continue echoing Isaiah: "Because you are precious in my eyes, and honored, and I love you" (43:4).[77] Most commentators acknowledge that this love (ἠγάπησά, ēgapēsa) is not referring to affection, but rather election (choosing and redeeming).[78] It is

---

no thought of conversion here. Fekkes, *Isaiah*, 134–35.

[74] Rev 21:25–26; 1 Cor 14:25; Rom 11:26. Hort, *Apocalypse*, 35; Trench, *Commentary on Seven Churches*, 235–36; Beckwith, *Apocalypse*, 480–82; Caird, *Revelation*, 52; Ladd, *Revelation*, 60–61; Thomas, *Rev 1–7*, 282; Beale, *Rev*, 288.

[75] Sweet, *Revelation*, 102; Charles, *Revelation*, 89; Krodel, *Revelation*, 138; Beasley-Murray, "Revelation, NBC," 101; Mounce, *Revelation*, 102; Frederick J. Murphy, *Fallen Is Babylon: The Revelation to John*, NTCC (Harrisburg, Pa.: Trinity, 1998), 152–54; Koester, *Revelation*, 330; Johnson, *Triumph of the Lamb*, 88; Aune, *Rev 1–5*, 237–38; Osborne, *Revelation*, 190–91; ibid., 191.

[76] Giesen and Eckert, *Die Offenbarung des Johannes*; Müller, *Offenbarung*; Hadorn, *Die Offenbarung Des Johannes*, 60; Anthony A. Hoekema, *The Bible and the Future* (Grand Rapids, Mich.: Eerdmans, 1994), 139–47. For discussion of an "already-and-not-yet" debate see Hoekema.

[77] Hemer, Letters to the Seven Churches, 164.

[78] Rev 1:5; 3:9; cf. John 13:1; Gal 2:20; Eph 5:2. Aune, *Rev 1–5*, 238; Fekkes, *Isaiah*, 136–37; Koester, *Revelation*, 325.

saying that the Jews in Philadelphia will eventually know that I (ἐγώ, *egō*, emphatic), the true messianic suzerain, have loved those who believe in the true Messiah (cf. John 13:1; Rom 8:35–39).

THE SUZERAIN KNOWS THEY HAVE KEPT HIS WORD—3:10A

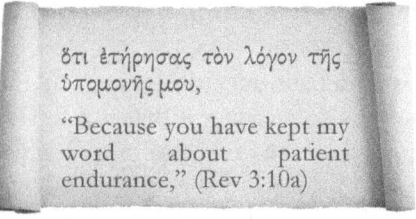

ὅτι ἐτήρησας τὸν λόγον τῆς ὑπομονῆς μου,

"Because you have kept my word about patient endurance." (Rev 3:10a)

The "because" (ὅτι, *hoti*, vausal clause) at the beginning of 3:10 modifies what follows in this verse, not 3:9. Their perseverance is the basis of God's protection for them. The verb τηρεῖν (*terein*, "to keep") occurs twice in this verse, but with two different meanings representing an example of paronomasia (παρονομασία, *paronomasia*, "one name" or pun).[79] The first occurance means "obey" (3:10a, ἐτήρησάς, *etērēsas*),[80] while the second occurance means "keep, preserve, cause to continue" (3:10b, τηρήσω, *tērēsō*; *Odes Sol.* 9.6).[81]

This expression, "kept my word," can be understood in two ways. (1). First, some understand it to mean "keep my command (12:17; 14:12) to endure patiently" (NIV, NRSV).[82] The "word", is Christ's "word" to persevere[83] and the Philadelphian church have kept (ἐτήρησάς, *etērēsas*, "obeyed") it.[84] The term ὁ λόγος is used eighteen times in Revelation, and sometimes it means "the gospel" (e.g. 12:11).[85]

(2). The second way it can be understood can be translated as: "the word of *[teachings about]* my endurance",[86] where the patient endurance in view is demonstrated by Christ in persevering through his ministry and death.[87] In this view μου (*mou*, "of me") governs ὑπομονῆς (*hupomeonēs*, "endurance"; objective genitive), rather than the entire phrase.[88] Christ the suzerian calls for Christians to persevere, even as Christ has persevered.

The suzerain knows of the Philadelphians' past relationship to the Great King. The suzerain knows of their works (3:8a), that they have little strength (3:8b), they have kept his

---

[79] *BDF* §488.1; Aune, *Rev 1–5*, 238–239; Smalley, *Revelation*, 91.

[80] *L&N*, § 36.19.

[81] *L&N*, § 13.32.

[82] Krodel, *Revelation*, 139; Satake, *Gemeindeordnung*; Mounce, *Revelation*, 102–3; Bruce, *Revelation*, 650; Smalley, *Revelation*, 91; Koester, *Revelation*, 325; Resseguie, *Revelation of John*, 98.

[83] Mark 13:13; Matt 10:22; 24:13; 2 Tim 2:12; Jas 1:12; Rev 13:10; 14:12.

[84] Theodore Mueller, "The Word of My Patience in Revelation 3:10," *CTQ* 46, no. 2–3 (1982): 233. Mueller translates it as: "You have kept the word with the result of perserverence in Me." Although Thomas argues that this meaning is unwarranted in the context (Thomas, *Rev 1–7*, 283 n.39).

[85] BDAG, 478 (1.b.β); Thompson, "Sociological Analysis," 150–53; Ladd, *Revelation*, 61.

[86] Cf. KJV, NAB, NASB; e.g., 2 Thess 3:5; Heb 12:2–3.

[87] Charles, *Revelation*, 89; Prigent, *Apocalypse*, 205; Beckwith, *Apocalypse*, 483; Hemer, *Letters to the Seven Churches*, 165; Thomas, *Rev 1–7*, 283; Beale, *Rev*, 289; Osborne, *Revelation*, 192 n.18.

[88] Kiddle, *Revelation*, 367; Bruce, *Revelation*, 640; Mounce, *Revelation*, 102. Aune argues that the pronoun "my" modifies both "word" and "endurance" (Aune, *Rev 1–5*, 239).

word (3:8c), and that they have not denied his name (3:8d). In addition he knows their enemy (3:9a) and that some of the Jews from the synagogue will come to bow at their feet (3:9b). The suzerain knows they are loved and have kept (ἐτήρησάς, *etērēsas*, 3:8c, 3:10a) his word [to endure], and so he will keep (τηρήσω, *tērēsō*) them in the hour of trial that is coming on the whole world (3:10a).

SANCTIONS: BLESSINGS—3:10A

The prophetic sanctions, where the vassal is cursed (malediction) for disobedience (dishonors the treaty), and blessed (benedictions) for obedience to the stated stipulations (honors the treaty), is a central element of the ANEVT structure.[89] Of the seven churches, only Philadelphia and Smyrna are missing a curse associated with the sanctions. However, curses were known in Philadelphia, attested to by an inscription with both blessing and curses. It reads in part:

> For in this house altars… have been set up for Zeus Eumenes and Hestia … his consort, for the other Saviour gods. . . Zeus has given instructions to this man for the performance of the purifications, the cleansings, … and the mysteries … in accordance with ancestral custom and in accordance with what has now … been written here. When entering… this house let men … and women, free people and household slaves, … swear by all… the gods that they do not know about any deceptive action against a man or … a woman… or about any drug harmful to people, and that they neither know nor … use… harmful spells, a love charm, an abortive drug, or a contraceptive. . . Beyond his own wife, … a man… is not to seduce someone else's wife, whether … free or … slave, … nor a boy, nor a virgin girl. Nor shall he advise someone else to do so. . . For the god… does not want these things to happen at all, … nor does he wish it. Rather, he wants obedience. The gods will be merciful to those … who obey and will always give… them all good things, whatever things gods give to people whom they love. But if any transgress, the gods… will hate… such people and inflict upon them great punishments (*TAM V* 2.1539 [Harland]).[90]

BLESSING OF BEING KEPT FROM THE HOUR OF TRIAL—3:10B

The Philadelphian church receives a promise that it will be kept (τηρήσω, *tērēsō*) from the hour[91] of trial (ὥρας τοῦ πειρασμοῦ, *ōras tou peirasmou*; impending trials and suffering). A similar idea can be found in John 17:15, where the same expression (τηρήσω ἐκ, *tērēsō ek*, "you shall keep from")[92] is used: "I do not ask that you take them out of the world, but that you keep them from the evil one."[93] Those living in the center of evil in Philadelphia will be protected from

---

[89] See chapter 3, *Sanctions*.

[90] *AGRW* 121 = *TAM V* 2.1539 = *SIG* 3.985 = *ILydiaHoz* 1.2. G. H. R. Horsley and S. C. Barton, "A Hellenistic Cult Group and the New Testament," *JAC* 24 (1981): 8–10; Harland, *Associations, Synagogues, and Congregations*, 24–25.

[91] The term "hour" (ὥρας, *ōras*) conveys the notion of a short period similar to Smyrna's "ten days" (2:10).

[92] The Greek can mean either "keep you from undergoing the trial" or "keep you right through the trial". Morris, *Revelation of St. John*, 82.

[93] Thomas objects that John is speaking of a form of evil, while Revelation speaks of a judgment from God; in addtion, the saints in the tribulation are not exempt from suffering: many are martyred (6:9–11; 7:9–14, etc.). Thomas, *Rev. 1–7*, 284–85. However, those in Philadelphia were also not exempt from martyrdom (*Mart. Pol.* 19.1).

> κἀγώ σε τηρήσω ἐκ τῆς ὥρας τοῦ πειρασμοῦ τῆς μελλούσης ἔρχεσθαι ἐπὶ τῆς οἰκουμένης ὅλης πειράσαι τοὺς κατοικοῦντας ἐπὶ τῆς γῆς·
>
> "I will keep you from the hour of trial that is coming on the whole world, to try those who dwell on the earth." (Rev 3:10b)

that evil.[94] Some argue that John 17 has a different context, referring to a present context for the conflict in the Gospel of John.[95]

The main issue this verse raises is whether the "hour of trial" is a local persecution[96] or an eschatological event.[97] This verse is often debated between those who hold to a pre-tribulation rapture,[98] and those who maintain a post-tribulation view.[99] However, as Ladd puts it, "this verse neither asserts that the rapture is to occur before the tribulation, nor does its interpretation require us to think that such a removal [rapture] is intended."[100] Keener argues that "in the final analysis, it is possible that Revelation may not refer to the specific three-and-a-half or seven-year tribulation [Dan 12:2; Mark 13:19; 2 Thess 2:1–12; Rev 9:3–21; 13:5–10] emphasized in modern prophecy teaching anyway; if it does not, it might not even comment directly on such a question as we have addressed here."[101]

But as Hemer points out: "if the church then believed it was living in the last times it made no distinction between immediate and eschatological fulfilment."[102] Aune adds that "the promise made here pertains to Philadelphian Christians only and cannot be generalized to include Christians in the other churches of Asia, much less all Christians in all places and times."[103] The Philadelphian Christians will not be touched by what affects others ("ten-day tribulation" in Smyrna; 2:10, 22). Reddish states "to keep them from the coming trials does not mean the church will be exempt from the difficulties. Rather, this is a promise of Christ's

---

[94] Moffatt, *Revelation*, 5:368; Mounce, *Revelation*, 103; Robert Horton Gundry, *The Church and the Tribulation: A Biblical Examination of Posttribulationism* (Grand Rapids, Mich.: Zondervan, 1973), 55–60; Beasley-Murray, *Revelation*, NCB, 101; Schuyler Brown, "The Hour of Trial, Rev 3:10," *JBL* 85, no. 3 (1966): 308–14; Hemer, *Letters to the Seven Churches*, 164–65; Beale, *Rev*, 289–92; Aune, *Rev 1–5*, 239–40; Osborne, *Revelation*, 193.

[95] Walvoord, *Revelation of Jesus Christ*, 87; Allen R. Kerkeslager, ""The Day of the Lord, the 'Hour' in the Book of Revelation and Rev. 3:10," in *Annual National Meeting of the Society of Biblical Literature* (Annual National Meeting of the Society of Biblical Literature, Kansas City, MO, 1991); Johnson, "Revelation," 633; Jeffrey L. Townsend, "The Rapture in Revelation 3:10," *BSac* 137, no. 547 (July 1980): 252–66; David G. Winfrey, "The Great Tribulation: Kept 'Out Of' Or 'Through'?," *GTJ* 3, no. 1 (1982): 3–18; Thomas, *Rev 1–7*, 285.

[96] J. Barton Payne, *The Imminent Appearing Of Christ* (Grand Rapids, Mich.: Eerdmans, 1962), 78–79.

[97] For this and other issues see, Brown, "The Hour of Trial," 308–14.

[98] Townsend, "Rapture in Revelation 3," 252–66; Winfrey, "The Great Tribulation: Kept 'Out Of' Or 'Through'?," 3–18; Thomas R. Edgar, "Robert H. Gundry and Revelation 3:10," *GTJ* 3, no. 1 (1982): 19–49; Walvoord, *Revelation of Jesus Christ*, 87; Thomas, *Rev 1–7*, 286–88; Edward E. Hindson, *The Book of Revelation: Unlocking the Future*, ed. Mal Couch, Twenty-First Century Biblical Commentary Series (Chattanoooga, TN: AMG, 2002), 47.

[99] Gundry, The Church and the Tribulation: A Biblical Examination of Posttribulationism.

[100] George Eldon Ladd, *The Blessed Hope* (Grand Rapids, Mich.: Eerdmans, 1954), 86.

[101] Keener, *Revelation*, 154.

[102] Hemer, Letters to the Seven Churches, 165.

[103] Aune, *Rev 1–5*, 240. See also Caird, *Revelation*, 53–54.

abiding presence with the church that will strengthen and sustain it regardless of the trials ahead."[104]

The strongest argument against a local persecution is the phrase "those who dwell on the earth" (οἱ κατοικοῦντες ἐπὶ τῆς γῆς, *oi katokountes epi tēs gēs* "earth-dwellers"). There is a great tradition in prophetic, apocalyptic and Christian writings that mentions a time of great suffering ("messianic woes" i.e., earthquakes, floods, war, famine, false teachers, persecution, etc.) accompanying the Day of the Lord and prior to the future victory of God.[105] This "hour of trial" is described in more detail in the rest of the chapters in Revelation. The phrase, "dwell on the earth," occurs several other times in Revelation[106] and in each case refers to the enemies of the church, and is used as a technical term for unbelieving idolaters ("beast-worshipers").[107] Similarly, here in 3:10b, the trials (πειρασμος, *peirasmos*, "testing", i.e., false worship, persecution, economic hardship, war, and violence) may also be instigated by the enemies of the Christian community (i.e., emperor worshipers; Jews in the synagogue); trials that will be felt across the world.[108] But as Beale points out "the period may just as well refer to a trial to come imminently on all in Asia Minor or in the limited known world of that time"[109], and and thus perhaps does not refer to the Great Tribulation (7:14, τῆς θλίψεως τῆς μεγάλης, *tēs thlipheōs tēs megalēs*).

While there still is much that is not clear in this verse, this is a wonderful blessing of the suzerain's protection (τηρήω, *tēreō*, "keep") for those who have protected (τηρήω, *tēreō*, "keep") his word by being loyal and obedient to the king.[110]

BLESSING OF THE SUZERAIN'S SOON COMING—3:11A

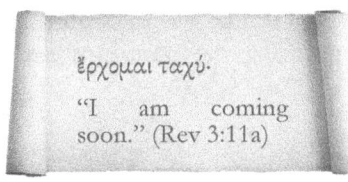

"I am coming soon." (Rev 3:11a)

The suzerain next provides an encouraging promise to bless his faithful vassals—those who will face the coming tribulation. The emphasis of ταχύ (*tachu*) is on the imminent coming of the suzerain and not on his swiftness (KJV).[111] He will come very soon, "without delay".[112] While most scholars see this as either an imminent coming to the church in

---

[104] Mitchell G. Reddish, *Revelation*, Smyth & Helwys Bible Commentary (Macon, Ga.: Smyth & Helwys Publishing, 2001), 76; Witherington III, *Revelation*, 107; Resseguie, *Revelation of John*, 99; Collins, *The Apocalypse*, 28; Beale, *Rev*, 293.

[105] Jer 30:7; Amos 5:18–20; Joel 2:1–32; Zeph 1:14–18; Dan 12:1; *T. Mos.* 8:1; *2 Bar.* 26:1–27:15; Matt 24:15–31; Mark 13:7–20; 2 Thess 2:1–12; Rev 7:14.

[106] Rev 6:10; 8:13; 11:10; 12:12; 13:8, 14; 14:6; 17:2, 8; cf. Isa 24; Jer 13:12–14; 1QH 16.19–36.

[107] Beale, *Rev*, 290.

[108] Brown, "The Hour of Trial," 309–10.

[109] Beale, *Rev*, 290.

[110] It is equally possible for "testing" to hold both a positive sense of faith and a negative sense of unbelief. Bauckham, *Climax of Prophecy*, 238–42; *Theology of Revelation*, 98–104.

[111] For the treatment of an imminent coming from a pretribulation perspective, see Robert L. Thomas, "The 'Comings' of Christ in Revelation 2–3," *MSJ* 7, no. 2 (1996): 153–81.

[112] See BDAG, ταχύ §6339.

Philadelphia[113] or reference to the second coming, Osborne[114] believes that this "coming" has "an inaugurated thrust, that it is first Jesus' 'coming' to them in comfort and protection, and second, is his final 'coming' to vindicate them for their suffering."[115] The phrase "I am coming soon" (present tense) is mentioned in several places in Revelation,[116] along with similar references to Christ's coming.[117] The early Christian tradition indicated both a coming to gather and bless (reward) the righteous (elect)[118] and to bring judgment on God's enemies.[119]

Of the messages to the churches, this is the only positive association with his coming. To Ephesus (2:5) his coming would mean the removal of its lampstand, to Pergamum (2:16) it meant judgment by the sword of his mouth, and to Sardis (3:3) it would bring sudden and unexpected judgment, like a thief in the night. In scripture, his coming heralds both blessing for believers (1 Thess 4:13–18) and judgment for unbelievers (1 Thess 5:1–10). Aune suggests that here the coming should be understood as the Parousia, to rescue and deliver his people (22:7, 20), and not as a coming in judgment as in Revelation 2:5, 16; and 3:3.[120]

Aune draws our attention to some ritual magical texts that display an impatience at the end of their spells. A number of spells end with variations of the formula ἤδη, ταχὺ ταχύ, "now, now! quick quick!" (*PGM* 3.123–24; 4.1245, 1593, 1924, 2037, 2098). Occasionally they are accompanied by invocations to a god or demon to "come quickly" (*PGM* 1.89–90; 4.236–37; 6.14; 7.248–49), to assist the magician in their requested tasks. Aune rightly notes that it is not John here who is impatient in requesting the suzerain's presence, but rather the exalted Christ who uses a similar formula, typical of the magicians, to announce his own coming.[121]

The imminence of his coming is not specified. Some scriptures suggested that it would take place in the generation of the apostles,[122] while others suggest that only God knows the hour.[123] Because of the delay, some declared that John was mistaken concerning the timing of the

---

[113] Alford, *Revelation*, 4:586; Moffatt, *Revelation*, 5:368; Walvoord, *Revelation*, 87; Thomas, *Rev 1–7*; "The 'Comings' of Christ," 156–59; Caird, *Revelation*, 54; Beale, *Rev*, 293.

[114] Mounce, *Revelation*, 104; Krodel, *Revelation*, 139; Witherington III, *Revelation*, 107; Johnson, *Triumph of the Lamb*, 89.

[115] Osborne, *Revelation*, 194. See also Smalley, *Revelation*, 92; Beale, *Rev*, 293 n.255.

[116] Rev 2:16; 3:11; 22:7, 12, 20.

[117] Rev 1:7; 2:5; 3:3; 16:15.

[118] Rev 14:14–17; 22:12; cf. Matt 24:29–31; 26:64; Mark 13:24–27; 14:62; Luke 21:25–28; John 14:1–3; Acts 1:11; 1 Thess 1:10; 2 Thess 1:7–10; 2:8; 1 Cor 15:24; 1 John 2:28–3:2.

[119] Rev 19:11–21; cf. Matt 16:27; 25:31–32.

[120] Aune, *Rev 1–5*, 245; *Revelation 17–22*, WBC 52C (Dallas, Tex.: Word Books, 1998), 1184–85.

[121] Aune, *Revelation 17–22*, 1184–85.

[122] Matt 24:34; Mark 13:30; 1 Thess 4:17; cf. Jas 5:7–9; Heb 9:28; 10:37.

[123] Matt 24:36; Mark 13:32; Acts 1:7; cf. 1 Tim 6:14–15; 2 Tim 4:8; Titus 2:13. Edward Adams, "The 'Coming of God' Tradition and Its Influence on New Testament Parousia Texts," in *Biblical Traditions in Transmission: Essays in Honour of Michael A. Knibb*, ed. Michael Anthony Knibb, Charlotte Hempel, and Judith Lieu, JSJSup 3 (Brill, 2006), 1–19; Christopher Rowland, "Parousia," ed. David Noel Freedman et al., *ABD* (New York, N.Y.: Doubleday, 1992), 5:166–70.

Parousia.¹²⁴ Others suggest that John's visions have transported him to the end of the age, a perspective from which Christ's second advent appears to be "soon,"¹²⁵ while others stress imminence from the divine perspective of the concept of the covenant relationship.¹²⁶ As Travis concludes "passages suggesting imminence indicate a *theological* rather than chronological relationship between present and future."¹²⁷

ETHICAL STIPULATIONS—3:11B

Within the ANEVT context, this section sets forth the covenant "obligations¹²⁸ imposed upon and accepted by the vassal."¹²⁹ The dominant theme of the ANEVT stipulations was the vassal's loyalty and faithfulness, with all controversies to be settled by the suzerain.¹³⁰ Within the SMR, the transition to ethical stipulations is indicated by the imperative verbs, and presented in terms of commands.¹³¹ All of the churches are exhorted to repent,¹³² except Smyrna and Philadelphia; these churches are exhorted to continue in faithfulness. These exhortations to the churches convey the new covenant obligation of faithfulness to their king.¹³³

IMPERATIVE: HOLD FAST WHAT YOU HAVE—3:11B

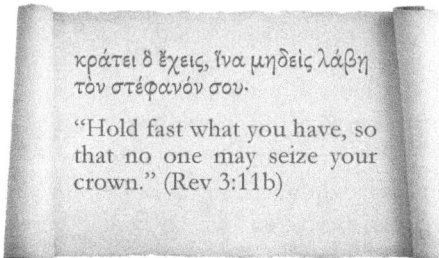

κράτει ὃ ἔχεις, ἵνα μηδεὶς λάβῃ τὸν στέφανόν σου.

"Hold fast what you have, so that no one may seize your crown." (Rev 3:11b)

The Philadelphian Christians are here exhorted to hold fast to what they have (κράτει ὃ ἔχεις, *kratei ho echeis*, i.e., and an open door). This present imperative verb was also used in 2:13–15 to contrast faithful supporters of the name of Christ (2:13) with those holding heretical views (2:14–15), and in 2:25 to commend those who persevere in the faith. It conveys the idea of "keep a firm grip on".

There is a warning or curse attached to this

---

¹²⁴ Boring, *Revelation*, 73.

¹²⁵ Beale, *Rev*, 293; Osborne, *Revelation*, 194–95.

¹²⁶ Smalley, *Revelation*, 92–93; Wall, *Revelation*, 85.

¹²⁷ S. H. Travis, "Eschatology," in *New Dictionary of Theology*, ed. Sinclair B. Ferguson, David F. Wright, and James I. Packer (Downers Grove, Ill.: InterVarsity, 1988), 230.

¹²⁸ The vassal-treaties of Esarhaddon list thirty-three stipulations, which follow the divine witnesses, and are to be kept by the vassal. Parpola and Watanabe, *Neo-Assyrian Treaties*, nos. 1–6, 46–57; Wiseman, "Vassal-Treaties," 23–24.

¹²⁹ Mendenhall, "Covenant Forms," 59; "Covenant," 1:714; Shea, "Covenantal Form," 72; Bright, *Covenant and Promise*, 37; Thompson, "Near Eastern Suzerain-Vassal," 4; McCarthy, *Treaty and Covenant*, 51 n.3.

¹³⁰ Thompson, *ANE Treaties*, 16.

¹³¹ Aune identifies the central sections of each proclamation as *dispositio*, which means "arrangement," not marked by any characteristic phrase but imperative verbs. Aune, *Rev 1–5*, 122.

¹³² Thyatira is to change its ways.

¹³³ Shea, "Covenantal Form," 75.

stipulation, where their holding fast will prevent the seizure of their crown (στέφανός, *stephanos*, wreath).[134] Here, the metaphor of a crown is considered by most commentators to represent the victor's wreath, awarded as the prize in an athletic competition (1 Cor 9:25; 2 Tim 4:8).[135] Several inscriptions from Philadelphia speak of a victor (crown 3:11) from three separate games[136] held at the stadium in Philadelphia (see Fig. 113).

However, Beale points out that the crown metaphor may be a further development of the Isa 22:22 passage, already relied upon by John. In Isaiah, God promises to remove evil Shebna's crown and give it to faithful Eliakim (Isa 22:17, 21).[137] The Philadelphian Christians would have been very familiar with the athletic imagery of the crown from their games, and instantly understood the allusion when John used it.

Aune points out that the metaphor "to take away someone's wreath," (λαμβάνειν τὸν στέφανον τινός, *lambanein ton stephanon tinos*) would mean to be "disqualified in a contest."[138] Krodel suggests that it is a metaphor for "the redemption already received (cf. 1:5–6)"[139] and not the future reward (2:10). Keener understands the metaphor of the lost or stolen crown as "exclusion from the kingdom"[140] while Koester suggests that not losing the crown "signifies resurrection to life in new Jerusalem."[141]

SANCTIONS: BLESSINGS—3:12

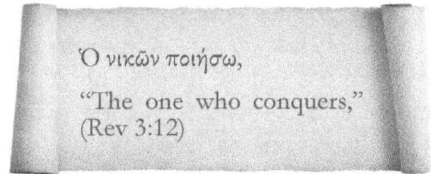

Ὁ νικῶν ποιήσω,
"The one who conquers,"
(Rev 3:12)

Together with Smyrna, Philadelphia was not reprimanded for their conduct, but instead praised and warned of coming suffering from the "synagogue of Satan." Because the Philadelphian church has endured patiently (3:10), they can be called overcomers. There are seven blessings mentioned to the church of Philadelphia: two have already been considered under 3:10b and 3:11a. Now five more blessings will be laid out for the vassals by the suzerain (For the meaning of the blessings, see 3:10a and chapter 3, *Sanctions*).

These blessings are promised to the ones who conquer or overcome (νικῶν, *nikōn*). This is a common Johannine athletic and military metaphor, used to promise victory to the suzerain and

---

[134] See chapter 9, *The Blessing of the Crown of Life—2:10c* for a detailed treatment of the usages of crown.
[135] Hemer, *Letters to the Seven Churches*, 165; Osborne, *Revelation*, 195; Koester, *Revelation*, 326; Morris, *Revelation of St. John*, 82; Aune, *Rev 1–5*, 241; Mounce, *Revelation*, 104; Smalley, *Revelation*, 92; Keener, *Revelation*, 151.
[136] *CIG* 3416 = 3427 = 3428; 3424; 3428. Hemer suggests that these games were "publicity for a small city." Hemer, *Letters to the Seven Churches*, 268 n.51.
[137] Beale, *Rev*, 293.
[138] Aune, *Rev 1–5*, 241.
[139] Krodel, *Revelation*, 139.
[140] Keener, *Revelation*, 151.
[141] Koester, *Revelation*, 326; Thomas, *Rev 1–7*, 291.

vassal over their enemies.¹⁴² For the Philadelphians, victory is identified as "'holding fast' to their present faith and spiritual inheritance."¹⁴³ Each message contains a blessing to the overcomers that uses a different synonym for eternal life. For Philadelphia, John uses building metaphors to refer to eternal life.

BLESSING OF BECOMING A TEMPLE PILLAR—3:12A

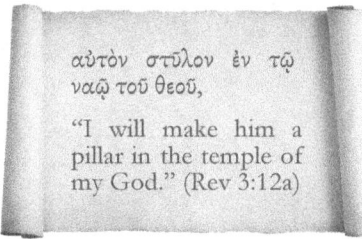

αὐτὸν στῦλον ἐν τῷ ναῷ τοῦ θεοῦ,

"I will make him a pillar in the temple of my God." (Rev 3:12a)

The overcomers in Philadelphia are promised the reward of becoming "a pillar in the temple of God" (3:12a), with 3:12c indicating that they will wear "the name of God". This metaphor is based on the image of a temple supported by pillars (στῦλοι, *styloi*), common in the ancient world. There are various potential references being made when looking at the imagery of the pillar (cf. Jer. 1:18) with a name.

1. Some columns in antiquity were shaped to look like human figures (Καρυάτιδες, *Karuatides*, "maidens of Karyai"), the most famous being the six maidens supporting the Caryatid Porch of the Erechtheion temple in Athens (421–407 BC; see Fig. 132).¹⁴⁴ Apart from their beauty, they represented the notion of perpetual service to a deity.¹⁴⁵ Commentators, based on Bousset who misinterpreted Hirschfeld,¹⁴⁶ often recount a speculative custom of erecting a statue in the temple precinct of the imperial cult with the engraved names of the retired provincial priest and his father etched on the statue.¹⁴⁷ Although plausible, it appears that these commentators perpetuate this tradition without primary evidence, and Hemer found no evidence of the practice in parallel sources.¹⁴⁸ In addition, Hemer points out there was no provincial temple of the imperial cult in Philadelphia until it received its *neocorate* in ca. AD 213.¹⁴⁹

---

¹⁴² Rev 2:7, 17, 26; 3:5; 5:5; 12:11; 17:14; 21:7; John 16:33; 1 John 2:13–14; 4:4; 5:4–5. Osborne, *Revelation*, 122.

¹⁴³ Smalley, *Revelation*, 92.

¹⁴⁴ James Morton Paton, *The Erechtheum: Measured, Drawn, and Restored* (Cambridge, Mass.: Harvard University Press, 1927), 290.

¹⁴⁵ Stevenson, *Power and Place*, 63–67.

¹⁴⁶ Bousset, *Die Offenbarung Johannis*, 230; Von Otto Hirschfeld, "Zur Geschichte Des Römischen Kaiserkultus," *SPAW* 2 (1888): 859–60. Hirschfeld was referencing a practice documented in the *Lex Narbonensis* (*CIL* 12.6038) for the instruction of the imperial cult at Gallia Narbonensis (Spain) founded in honor of the Numen Augusti in AD 11.

¹⁴⁷ Lohmeyer, *Offenbarung*, 37; Charles, *Revelation*, 1:91–92; Moffatt, *Revelation*, 5:369; Kiddle, *Revelation*, 53–54; L. van Hartingsveld, *Revelation: A Practical Commentary*, trans. John Vriend (Grand Rapids, Mich.: Eerdmans, 1985), 23–24; Barclay, *Letters*, 134–35; Ford, *Revelation*, 417.

¹⁴⁸ Hemer, *Letters to the Seven Churches*, 166; Prigent, *Apocalypse*, 207. Prigent is skeptical of this view.

¹⁴⁹ Hemer, Letters to the Seven Churches, 166.

2. The Jewish Midrash records that Abraham was viewed as a pillar on which the weight of the world is supported (*Shem. Rab.* 2),[150] but this does not suit the imagery used in Revelation. Closer parallels exist in *Joseph and Asenath* (*Jos. As.* 17:6); the Hermas *Vision* (*Vis.* 3.8.2).

132. The Caryatid Porch of the Erechtheion, Athens, 421–407 BC.

3. Some suggest that the pillar is another allusion to Isaiah 22, where Eliakim is told he would become "like a peg in a secure place . . . a throne of honor to his father's house" (22–23).[151] However, in Isaiah the prediction is that the peg will give way and the house will fall (Isa 22:25), whereas here the house will endure and the pillar will be sturdy in God's temple.[152] This contrast may have been intentional in John's mind.[153]

4. The LXX called the columns supporting the tabernacle freestanding "pillars" (Exod 26:15–25), and the two bronze pillars that stood in front of Solomon's temple were named Jachin ("he establishes") and Boaz ("in him is strength,"[154]).[155] Wilkinson calls attention to the pillars in Solomon's temple where kings were crowned or the covenant was renewed (1 Kgs 11:14; 23:3).[156] However, these are all excluded by the phrase "in the temple" (ἐν τῷ ναῷ, *en tō naō*) and these references have little to do with the pillar in the new Jerusalem.[157]

---

[150] Lohmeyer, *Offenbarung*; Moffatt, *Revelation*, 5:369.

[151] Kraft, *Offenbarung*; Mounce, *Revelation*, 104–5; Beale, *Rev*, 293; Smalley, *Revelation*, 94; Robert A. Briggs, *Jewish Temple Imagery in the Book of Revelation*, SBL 10 (New York, N.Y.: Lang, 1999), 71–74; Fekkes, *Isaiah*, 133; Michaels, *Revelation*, 85–86.

[152] Beasley-Murray, *Revelation*, NCB, 101–2.

[153] Morris, *Revelation*, 83.

[154] 1 Kgs 7:15–21; 2 Chr 3:15–16; Josephus *Ant.* 8.77–78. Robert B. Y. Scott, "The Pillars of Jachin and Boaz," *JBL* 58, no. 1 (1939): 143–49; S. Yeivin, "Jachin and Boaz," *PEQ* 91 (1959): 1–15; Carol L. Meyers, "Jachin and Boaz in Religious and Political Perspective," *CBQ* 45 (1983): 167–78.

[155] Campegius Vitringa, *Anakrisis Apocalypsios Joannis Apostoli* (Amsterdam: Henricus Strickius, 1719), 141; Farrer, *Revelation*, 81; Swete, *Apocalypse*, 57.

[156] See also Richard H. Wilkinson, "The ΣΤΥΛΟΣ of Revelation 3:12 and Ancient Coronation Rites," *JBL* 107, no. 3 (1988): 498–501.

[157] Trench, *Commentary on Seven Churches*, 242; Swete, *Apocalypse*, 57; Kistemaker, *Revelation*, 164.

5. Beasley-Murray sees a parallel with commemorative bronze tablets set up on Mt Zion for Simon Maccabeus (1 Macc 14.26–48).[158] However as Royalty points out "no Christian writer refers to the Maccabees before Clement of Alexandria."[159]

6. The fact that most Graeco-Roman temples were built with rows of columns supporting their roofs (Herodotus *Hist.* 2.44),[160] providing strength and stability, would have been familiar to Philadelphian citizens (see Figs. 24, 65, 67, 103, 104, 128, 146).[161] Many columns have dedicatory inscriptions on them,[162] and examples include two inscriptions on pillars (στήλη) from the Capernaum synagogue, in Israel. One inscription is in Greek and reads: "Herod (the son) of Monimos and his son Justus together with their children erected this column" (*CIJ* 2.983; see Fig. 133). The other inscription is in Aramaic and translates: "Alphaeus, the son of Zebedee, the son of John, made this column. May it be for him a blessing (*CIJ* 2.982)."[163] Also, closer to Philadelphia, columns in the temples of Artemis at Ephesus (*I.Eph.* 4.1518–19) and Sardis (*I.Sard.* 7.1.38),[164] as well as the imperial temple at Ephesus (*I.Eph.* 2.239, 240), were all inscribed with the names of their donors.[165] In Laodicea, eight inscriptions were found on

133. Greek inscription on a pillar in the Capernaum synagogue. It translates: "Herod (the son) of Monimos and his son Justus together with their children erected this column" (*CIJ* 2.983).

---

[158] Beasley-Murray, *Revelation*, *NCB*, 102 n.3.

[159] For a list of additional column inscriptions from other surrounding cities, see Royalty Jr., "Etched or Sketched?," 452.

[160] John W. Marshall, "Columna," in *DGRA*, ed. William Smith (London, U.K.: Murray, 1890), 1:489–96; Janet Delaine, "Architecture," ed. Simon Hornblower and Antony Spawforth, *OCD* (Oxford, U.K.: Clarendon, 2003), 141–44.

[161] Mounce, *Revelation*, 104; Osborne, *Revelation*, 196; Smalley, *Revelation*, 93; Barclay, *Letters*, 70–71; Johnson, "Revelation," 634.

[162] Strabo *Geogr.* 1.3.4; 3.5.5–6; Pausanias *Descr.* 5.20.6–7; 10.11.6; *PGM* 8.40–41.

[163] Mounce, *ISBE*, 1:610; Gonzalo Báez-Camargo, *Archaeological Commentary on the Bible: From Genesis to Revelation* (Garden City, N.Y.: Doubleday, 1984), 264; Jonathan L. Reed, "Capernaum," in *EDB*, ed. David Noel Freedman, Allen C. Myers, and Astrid B. Beck (Grand Rapids, Mich.: Eerdmans, 2000), 220.

[164] Yegül, "A Victor's Message," 204–25; Friedrich Ragette, *Baalbek* (Park Ridge, N.J.: Noyes, 1981), 37–38; Howard Crosby Butler, *Publications of the American Society for the Excavation of Sardis. II/1. Sardis: Architecture. The Temple of Artemis* (Leiden: Brill, 1925), 42, 57–72.

[165] Royalty Jr., "Etched or Sketched?," 452–53; Stevenson, *Power and Place*, 249.

two columns from Temple A with four names on each column under a wreath. The names Laodicea, Apollo and Artemis are mentioned (see Figs. 160)

7. Koester points out that inscriptions on steles were even more common than on pillars.[166] Several inscriptions are documented from first-century Philadelphia. One lists the names of the donar along with his god: "Plution son of Plutioin, from Maionia, dedicated to Zeus Koryphaeos" (*I.Phil.* 1540; see Fig. 126), while another lists the god, Zeus of Targyenos (*I.Phil.* 1542; cf. *I.Sard.* 100).

8. It may be an allusion to the temple pillars that provided strength and stability to the temples within the city of Philadelphia. Some early writers mentioned the pillars of Herod's temple in Jerusalem (κιονες, *kiones,* Josephus *J.W.* 5.190–91, 200, 203) or the pillars of the Artemision (Aristides *Orat.* 23.25) in Ephesus (see chapter 6, *The Temple of Artemis*).

9. The imagery of a pillar in the temple of a city plagued by earthquakes, no doubt invites the reader to draw comparisons with the stability that is found in God's temple.[167] Wilson describes the construction methods used for temples to fortify them against earthquakes, making temples the most secure buildings (Pliny *Nat.* 36.95). He describes that:

> their foundations were laid on beds of charcoal covered with fleeces, which caused the structure to 'float' on the soil like a raft. Each block was joined to another by metal cramps, so the platform was a unity.[168]

10. Some suggest that it is an allusion to the heavenly eschatological temple[169] with the gathering of all the elect, and metaphorical of future salvation.[170] The mention of God's temple here is surely metaphorical (God's people as the temple),[171] since there is no temple in heaven "as its temple is the Lord God the Almighty and the Lamb" (21:22), and elsewhere in the NT Christians are described as pillars in the church.[172] Influential community leaders were also called "pillars".[173] John's emphasis here is on the stable permanency of the overcomers in the presence of God[174] who is the temple (21:22; *1 En.* 90.28–29).[175] The imagery of a pillar with a name in verse 12 likely has both Hellenistic and Jewish elements to it.[176]

---

[166] Koester, *Revelation*, 327.
[167] Kiddle, *Revelation*, 53; Smalley, *Revelation*, 94; Michaels, *Revelation*, 85.
[168] Wilson, *Revelation*, 33.
[169] Rev 7:15; 11:1–2, 19; 14:15, 17; 15:5–8; 16:1, 17.
[170] Aune, *Rev 1–5*, 241; Georg Klinzing, *Die Umdeutung des Kultus in der Qumrangemeinde und im Neuen Testament* (Göttingen: Vandenhoeck & Ruprecht, 1997), 201; Osborne, *Revelation*, 197.
[171] 1 Cor 3:16–17; 2 Cor 6:16; Eph 2:19–22; 1 Pet 2:4–10.
[172] Gal 2:9; 1 Tim 3:15; cf. *1 Clem.* 5:2.
[173] Philo *QE* 1.21; *Abr.* 124; Aeschylus *Ag.* 897; Euripides *Iph. taur.* 57; Pindar *Ol.* 2.81–82; Lycophron *Alex.* 281.
[174] John M. Court, *Revelation*, NTG (Sheffield: Sheffield Academic Press, 1994), 68.
[175] Charles, *Revelation*, 1:91; Krodel, *Revelation*, 139; Morris, *Revelation*, 82–83; Aune, *Rev 1–5*, 241; Osborne,

The phrase "my God" (τοῦ θεοῦ, *tou theou*) is rarely used in Revelation (3:12; 1:6 "his God"), but it is used four times in this verse. It stresses the close relationship and oneness of the Father and the Son.[177] Revelation adapts the practice of inscription on pillars and stelae by inscribing the name of God, Christ, and God's city on the pillars of faith to identify their allegiance. The Philadelphian Christians would recognize this imagery from their own cultural practices. The temple of God is a metaphor for eternal salvation, where the vassal is secure and protected in the presence of God, the suzerain king, and contrasts with the false synagogue used by the Jews.[178]

BLESSING OF NEVER LEAVING THE TEMPLE OF GOD—3:12B

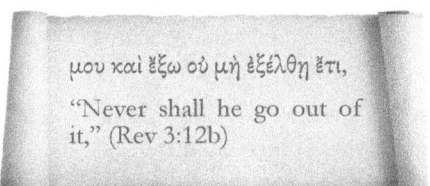

μου καὶ ἔξω οὐ μὴ ἐξέλθῃ ἔτι,

"Never shall he go out of it," (Rev 3:12b)

In close connection with the previous comments about the pillars in the temple, John says "and you will never again[179] go outside." (καὶ ἔξω οὐ μὴ ἐξέλθῃ ἔτι *kai ecō ou mē exelthē eti*). Several commentators understand this phrase against the background of the city's evacuation following the earthquakes in AD 17 and 23,[180] when many of the residents moved out to the countryside to live on farms due to the aftershocks and instability in damaged buildings (Strabo *Geogr.* 12.8.18; 13.4.10).[181] As pillars in the heavenly temple, the Philadelphian Christians would no longer need to run from the city in fear of their lives; they would now never need to leave God's presence (the temple, 21:22). Eternal security is certainly a comfort for believers living under constant fear of seismic destruction.

BLESSING OF WEARING THE NAME OF GOD—3:12C

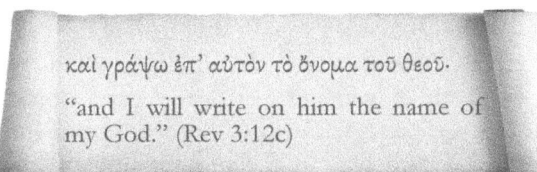

καὶ γράψω ἐπ' αὐτὸν τὸ ὄνομα τοῦ θεοῦ·

"and I will write on him the name of my God." (Rev 3:12c)

The suzerain's promise to write his name on the overcomer, making them permanent residents of the new Jerusalem,[182] would have registered with everyone familiar with the practice of writing names on pillars. The

---

Revelation, 196; Smalley, *Revelation*, 93; Kistemaker, *Revelation*, 164.

[176] Osborne, *Revelation*, 197.

[177] Smalley, *Thunder and Love*, 60–62, 129–31–152; *Revelation*, 93; Osborne, *Revelation*, 197.

[178] Michaels, *Revelation*, 86; Reddish, *Revelation*, 78; Witherington III, *Revelation*, 107; Beale, *Rev*, 294.

[179] On the double negative see BDAG 315. See also Heb 8:12; 10:17; Rev 18:21–23.

[180] Tacitus *Ann.* 2.47. 3–4; Pliny *Nat.* 2.86.200; Lydus *Mens.* 4.115. Otto F. A. Meinardus, *St. Paul in Ephesus and the Cities of Galatia and Cyprus*, In the Footsteps of the Saints (New Rochelle, N.Y.: Caratzas, 1979), 76.

[181] Charles W. Budden and Edward Hastings, *The Local Colour of the Bible* (Edinburgh, U.K.: T&T Clark, 1925), 3:329–30; Fred H. Wight, *Highlights of Archaeology in Bible Lands* (Chicago, Ill.: Moody, 1955), 188; Hemer, "Unto the Angels of the Churches," 171–73; Franz, "Propaganda, Power and the Perversion," 84; Caird, *Revelation*, 55; Krodel, *Revelation*, 135; Harrington, *Revelation*, 71; Budden and Hastings, *The Local Colour of the Bible*, 3:329–30; Harrington, *Revelation*, 71; Osborne, *Revelation*, 197; Worth, Jr., *Greco-Asian Culture*, 201.

[182] See also Gal 4:26; Phil 3:20; Rev 21:2, 10.

writing of names for commemorative purposes and to express ownership would have been easily recognized. For example, during the reign of Domitian, a pillar at Ephesus (first cent. AD) was inscribed with the names of the city of Teos and the emperor to commemorate building of the imperial temple (*I.Eph.* 2.239, 240, See *Blessing of Becoming a Temple Pillar* above no. 6).[183]

In Exodus 28:36–38 a plate with "Holy to the Lord" (ἁγίασμα κυρίῳ, *hagiasma kuriō*) was placed on Aaron's high priestly headdress, on his forehead,[184] so the idea could also refer to placing God's name on the conquered vassal's forehead (14:1; 22:4). John also elaborates on the idea of wearing the names of the Lamb and of the Father written on the foreheads of the saints (14:1; 22:4; unbelievers receive the name and number of the beast; 13:17–18). This metaphor represents both ownership by the suzerain and their dedication to the suzerain, who inscribed them with his name.

BLESSING OF WEARING THE NAME OF THE NEW JERUSALEM—3:12D

καὶ τὸ ὄνομα τῆς πόλεως τοῦ θεοῦ μου, τῆς καινῆς Ἰερουσαλὴμ ἡ καταβαίνουσα ἐκ τοῦ οὐρανοῦ ἀπὸ τοῦ θεοῦ μου,

"and the name of the city of my God, the new Jerusalem, which comes down from my God out of heaven," (Rev 3:12d)

This blessing speaks of citizenship. The Philadelphian overcomers are now vassals of the new Jerusalem with full citizenship rights.[185] The changing of their name would have been appreciated by Philadelphians, who had experienced their city name being changed twice to Neocaesarea (see Fig. 113) and Flavia (see Fig. 114) in honor of the imperial cult.[186] However, Koester is doubtful of this, arguing that the same could be said of Sardis (Caesarea) or Laodicea (Rhoas, Diospolis); cities that also had their names changed (Pliny *Nat.* 5.29.105).[187]

The popular heresy of Montanism had its prophetic origins near Philadelphia. Montanists anticipated that the new Jerusalem would come down from heaven and rest near Pepuza, some 113 km (70 m.) east of Philadelpia.[188] Several scholars see the reference to the new Jerusalem not as a large city coming down from heaven, but rather as a figurative representation of the

---

[183] Friesen, *Twice Neokoros*, 31–32, n.8.

[184] See Num 6:27; Philo *Abr.* 103, see also Josephus *J.W.* 5.235; *Ant.* 3.178; *Ep. Arist.* 98; Origen *Fr. Ps.* 2.2. Barclay, *Revelation*, 1:135.

[185] See also Gal 4:26; Heb 11:10; 12:22; 13:14. Charles, *Revelation*, 1:92; Thomas, *Rev 1–7*, 293; Aune, *Rev 1–5*, 244; Kistemaker, *Revelation*, 164.

[186] Ramsay, Letters: Updated, 397–98; Franz, "Propaganda, Power and the Perversion," 84; Hemer, Letters to the Seven Churches, 176; Giesen and Eckert, Die Offenbarung des Johannes; Blaiklock, The Seven Churches: An Exposition of Revelation Chapters Two and Three, 64; Osborne, Revelation, 198; Morris, Revelation, 82–83; Smalley, Revelation, 95; Mounce, Revelation, 105; Koester, Revelation, 327.

[187] Koester, *Revelation*, 327.

[188] Epiphanius *Pan.* 48, 14; 49.1; Augustine *Ep.* 41.2; *Haer.* 27–28. Calder, "Philadelphia and Montanism," 309–54; "The New Jerusalem of the Montanists," *Byzantion* 6 (1931): 421–25.

Christian community.[189] The word "city" (πόλις, *polis*) is used here for the first time, though many commentators see this as anticipating the descent of the new Jerusalem in Revelation 21:2, 10, where the term new (καινῆς, *kainēs*) is again used for Jerusalem and the city is called holy (see also Ezek 48:35b).[190]

BLESSING OF WEARING GOD'S NEW NAME—3:12E

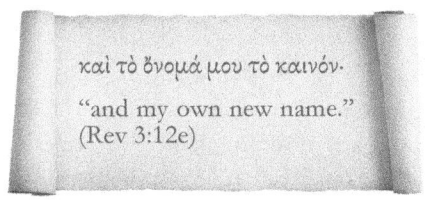

καὶ τὸ ὄνομά μου τὸ καινόν·
"and my own new name."
(Rev 3:12e)

One further name (ὄνομα, *onoma*) is mentioned, bringing the total to three, not unlike the Trinity. However, here the names are the Father, the Son and the new Jerusalem. Having lived in a city that had already undergone two name changes (Neocaesarea; see Fig. 113, and Flavia; see Fig. 114), notification that a third permanent name change would take place (3:12) would certainly have grasped the attention of the Christians resident in Philadelphia.[191] Change of a city's name indicated a change of function or status for that city.[192] Although Philadelphia briefly took the name "new city of Caesar", the Christian church in Philadelphia will forever take the name "new city of God."[193]

Throughout the Bible, an individual's name is a revelation of their character, so when a person's character changed, their name also changed.[194] Keener also reports that "when a suzerain put a vassal on the throne, he sometimes gave him a new name, demonstrating his power over that vassal."[195] This is demonstrated in God changing the name of Eliakim to Jehoiakim (2 Kgs 24:17).

The new (καινός, *kainos*) name is not identified, but its designation as "new" sets it apart from other known names for Christ, such as Yahweh (Τετραγράμματον, *Tetragrammaton* "having four letters", *YHWH* (יהוה), Lord (κύριος, *kurios*), Son of God (υἱὲ τοῦ θεοῦ, *uie tou theou* Matt 4:3, 6; 8:29; 9:6), Word (Λόγος, *Logos*, John 1:1), "King of Kings and Lord of Lords"[196] (Βασιλευσ Βασιλεων καὶ Κύριος Κυριων, *basileus basileōn kai kurios kuriōn*, 19:12, 16). The restored Israel would "be called by a new name [LXX τὸ ὄνομα σου τὰ καινόν, *to honoma sou ta kainon*] that the mouth of the Lord will give" Isa 62:2), while Isaiah 65:15 speaks that the righteous will be called "by another name [LXX ὄνομα καινόν, *honoma kainon*]." This new name was thought by early

---

[189] Roloff, *Revelation*, 62; Resseguie, *Revelation of John*, 99–100; Aune, *Rev 1–5*, 245; Robert H. Gundry, *Commentary on Revelation*, CNT 19 (Grand Rapids, Mich.: Baker Academic, 2011), op. cit.; Kistemaker, *Revelation*, 164.

[190] Aune, *Rev 1–5*, 244–45; Kistemaker, *Revelation*, 165; Smalley, *Revelation*, 94.

[191] Aune, *Rev 1–5*, 244.

[192] Isa 1:26; 60:14; 65:15; Jer 3:17; 23:6; 33:16; Ezek 48:35; Zech 8:3.

[193] Johnson, Triumph of the Lamb, 89.

[194] Gen 32:27–28; 41:45; 2 Kgs 23:34; 24:17; 1 Sam 25:25; Dan 1:7; Mark 3:17; John 1:42; Abram – Abraham, Gen 17:5, 17; Jacob – Israel, Gen 35:10; Saul – Paul, Acts 13:9; etc.

[195] Walton, Matthews, and Chavalas, *IVP Bible Background Commentary: OT*, 65.

[196] Koester, *Revelation*, 327.

Christians to be the name "Christian".[197] Paul records that Christ will have "bestowed on him the name that is above every name" (Phil 2:9), and John states in Revelation that "he [Christ] has a name written that no one knows but himself" (19:12). Several commentators believe that the new name is a unique name associated with the redemptive work of Christ,[198] and concealed until the *eschaton*.[199] Smalley suggests that the redemptive blessings are immediate and "need not apply simply to the distant future"[200] as proposed by Charles.[201]

PROCLAMATION WITNESS FORMULA—3:13

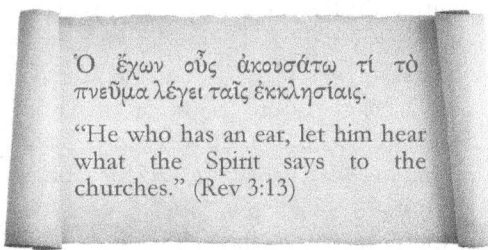

Ὁ ἔχων οὖς ἀκουσάτω τί τὸ πνεῦμα λέγει ταῖς ἐκκλησίαις.

"He who has an ear, let him hear what the Spirit says to the churches." (Rev 3:13)

With the distribution of the stipulations, along with blessings and curses, it was customary for ancient treaty and oath documents to be sealed with a list of divine witnesses, traditionally the suzerain/vassal's pantheon of gods.[202] Since there is a change in the situation in the NT, because God is speaking as his own witness, there is a change of form from the polytheistic context of ANE culture. The Spirit is the judge presiding over the covenant case. This proclamation witness or hearing formula,[203] repeated in each of the messages to the churches (2:7; 11, 17, 29, 3:13, 22), calls the churches to hear the proclamation of the divine witness[204] and to heed the message of the Spirit who speaks it.

CONCLUSION

Six recognizable elements of the ANEVT, constituting a structure, can be identified within the prophetic message, conveying a covenant lawsuit message of encouragement to the overcomers within the church of Philadelphia.

Firstly, the preamble, marked by the prophetic oracular formula τάδε λέγει Ω, calls attention to what the suzerain, identified here as the sovereign omnipotent and omniscient "holy and true one," will say to Philadelphia. The suzerain possesses the keys of David and can open and shut the doors of his kingdom, exercising authority over death, judgment and the Davidic kingdom (heaven).

---

[197] Cyprian *Test.* 1.22; Eusebius *Dem. ev.* 2.3.80; *Hist. eccl.* 1.4.3–4; Ign. *Magn.* 10:1; Clement *Paed.* 1.5; *Apos. Con.* 3.15.
[198] Col 3:4; 1 John 3:2; Ign. *Phld.* 5. Swete, *Revelation*, 58; Smalley, *Revelation*, 95; Thomas, *Rev 1–7*, 293.
[199] Charles, *Revelation*, 92; Thomas, *Rev 1–7*, 293; Osborne, *Revelation*, 199.
[200] Smalley, *Revelation*, 95; *Thunder and Love*, 150–52, 174–76; Caird, *Revelation*, 55.
[201] Charles, *Revelation*, 92.
[202] See the *Introduction—Proclamation Witness Formula*.
[203] See parallels in Matt 11:15; 13:9, 43; Mark 4:9; Luke 8:8; 14:35; 1 Cor 14:37–38; *Odes Sol.* 3:10–11.
[204] There are echos of the OT phrase "hear the word of the Lord" (e.g. Isa 1:10; Jer 2:4; Hos 4:1; Amos 7:16).

Secondly, the historical prologue is characterized by the omniscient suzerain's intimate knowledge of Philadelphia's works of faithfulness in not denying the name of the suzerain, in spite of the fact that they have little strength. The enemy is known to the king and will come and fall prostrate before the overcoming vassals, who are loved by the suzerain.

Thirdly, the suzerain declared two blessings upon the faithful vassals. They will be kept by the suzerain from the hour of trial, and reassured that the Great King is coming soon.

Fourthly, the Great King stipulates one imperative: for Philadelphia's stipulation: the vassals are exhorted to hold fast to what they have, and in so doing, no one will seize their crown.

Fifthly, in response to these stipulations, God pledges to give five additional blessings. These are blessings of security and stability, metaphorically conveyed as a pillar in the temple of God possessing the names of God, the suzerain, the new Jerusalem and an unknown name. The vassals will know the eternal blessings of the presence of the suzerain himself, ruling forever in his kingdom.

Finally, acting as his own witness in the court case, the Spirit-Judge calls the Philadelphian congregation to hear what he has to say to the faithful and disobedient churches.

16

Luxurious Laodicea

The History of the City

*I*n order to understand the message to Laodicea it is helpful to examine both the cultural (Graeco-Roman) history of Laodicea (Λαοδίκεια or Λαοδικία, "justice of the people", modern *Laodikeia*), as well as the (Hebraic-Semitic) OT theological roots of the message. This chapter will examine the historical background to the city of Laodicea, a place prosperous due to its textile industry and medical school. The name of the city is derived from Laodice, the wife of Seleucid Antiochus II (261–246 BC).[1] Antiochus II founded the city in the third cent. BC (Stephanus *Byz. on Laodicea;* Eustathius *Dion. Perieg.* 915),[2] though later divorced his wife in 253 BC.

THE GEOGRAPHY OF LAODICEA

Laodicea (Turk. *Laodikeia*) is situated 53 miles (85 km) south-east of Philadelphia in the fertile Lycus (Turk. *Çürüksu*) River valley, six miles (9.7 km.) south of Hierapolis (Col 4:13), and ten miles (16 km.) west of Colossae (Col 2:1; 4:13–16) in the

> Καὶ τῷ ἀγγέλῳ τῆς ἐν Λαοδικείᾳ ἐκκλησίας γράψον·.
>
> "To the angel [*messenger*] of the church in Laodicea write:" (Rev 3:14a)

---

[1] Radet maintains that Laodicea was founded by Antiochus I, but likely from a misreading of Stephanus and Eustathius. Georges Radet, "Sur Quelques Points de L'histoire Des Séleucides," in *Revue de Philologie, de Littérature et D'histoire Anciennes*, ed. E. Chatelain, L. Ouvau, and B. Haussoullier, vol. 17 (Paris, France: Klincksieck, 1893), 59.

[2] Ramsay, Cities and Bishoprics, 1:32; Trench, Commentary on Seven Churches, 200; Magie, Roman Rule in Asia Minor, 986; John Anthony Cramer, A Geographical and Historical Description of Asia Minor (Oxford, U.K.: Oxford University Press, 1832), 2:38; Jones, Cities of the Eastern Roman Provinces, 42; Hemer, Letters to the Seven Churches, 180; Yamauchi, NT Cities, 137; Wilson, Biblical Turkey, 245.

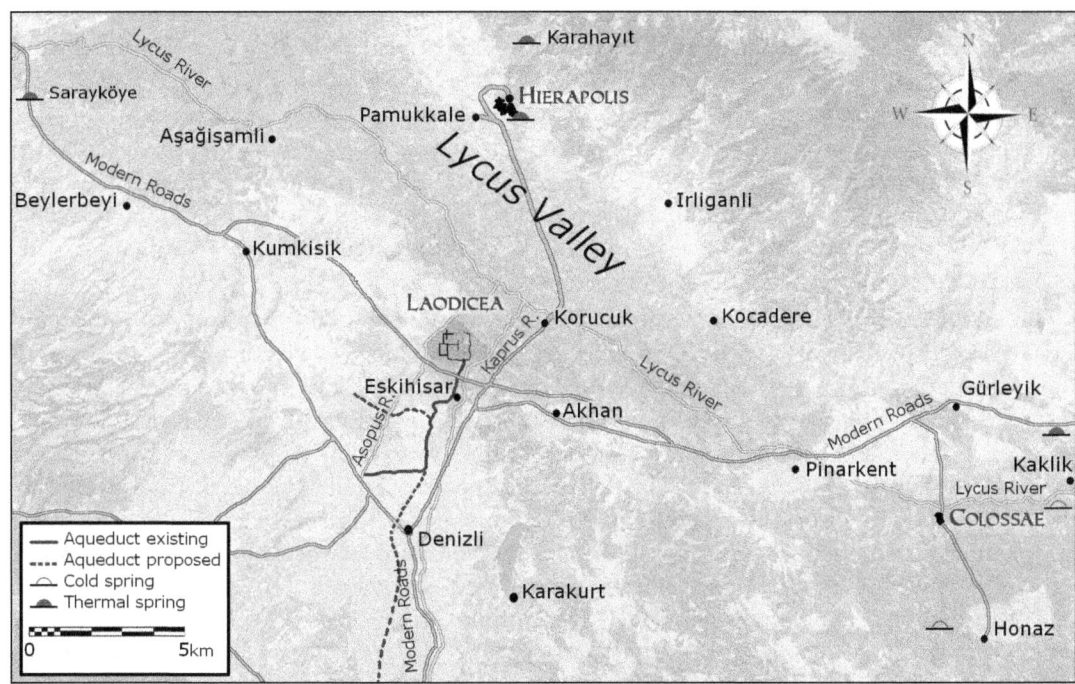

134. Map of the modern area around Laodicea indicating the location of ancient sites, the location of the existing and proposed aqueduct, and the thermal and cold springs.

south-west region of ancient Phrygia (Coordinates: 37°50'9"N 29°6'27"E)³ near the boundary with Caria. It was in the region of Caria during the Roman period (Philostratus *Vit. Soph.* 1.25).⁴

It is just one mile (1.6 km) north of the modern village of Eskihisar ("old fortress"; see Fig. 134), and just 3.7 miles (6 km) north of the modern city of Denizli ("Full of Waters"), situated on the SW bank of the Lycus river, a tributary of the Maeander (Turk. *Büyük Menderes)* and personified on its coins as a wolf.⁵ It is called "Laodicea on the Lycos" (Λαοδίκεια ἡ πρός τω Λύκω, *Laodikeia hē pros tō Lykō;* Lat. *Laodicea ad Lycum*) to distinguish it from other cities of the same name and identify it with the Lycus River.⁶

---

³ Xenophon *Anab.* 1.2.6; Diodorus *Hist. Lib.* 16.80.8; Polyaenus *Strat.* 7.16.1; Polybius *Hist.* 2.5.5; Strabo *Geogr.* 12.8.16. It is strange that Strabo locates Hierapolis in Lydia (*Geogr.* 13.4).

⁴ Trent C. Butler et al., eds., *Holman Illustrated Bible Dictionary* (Nashville, Tenn.: Broadman & Holman, 2003), 1011–12; Wilson, *Biblical Turkey*, 245; W. White, Jr., "Laodicea," ed. Merrill C. Tenney and Moises Silva, ZEB (Grand Rapids, Mich.: Zondervan, September 19, 2009), 3:987.

⁵ *BMC Phrygia* 287.52–53; 296.111–112; 299.127; 313.215; 319.235. Head, *Historia Numorum*, 678.

⁶ Frederick Fyvie Bruce, "Laodicea (Place)," ed. David Noel Freedman et al., *ABD* (New York, N.Y.: Doubleday, 1996), 4:229; M. J. S. Rudwick and Colin J. Hemer, "Laodicea," in *NBD*, ed. J. D. Douglas (Grand Rapids, Mich.: Eerdmans, 1962), 672; Beasley-Murray, "Revelation, NBC," 1432; White, Jr., "Laodicea," 3:987.

The site of Laodicea is a kilometer square with each corner representing one point on the compass, and the streets arranged at right angels in a grid pattern, according to a Hippodamian[7] plan (see Fig. 137).[8] It is situated on a raised plateau overlooking the Lycus Valley and surrounded by two streams: the Asopus (Ασοπος; Turk. *Gümüşçay-Goncalı-Deresi*) on the northwest,[9] and the Kaprus[10] (Κάπρος; or Capros, Turk. *Başlıçay*)[11] on the east. The Kaprus is fed by the "copious springs at Denizli, but diverted for irrigation and insignificant."[12] Both rivers feed into the Lycus River (Strabo *Geogr.* 12.8.16), north of the town of Korucuk.[13] The main river that runs north of Laodicea is the Lycus (Λύκω; Turk. *Çürüksu*), a tributary of the larger Maeander river (Turk. *Büyük Menderes*) in the west.[14]

The importance of Laodicea was driven by its location at the crossroad of two important imperial routes, facilitating the development of the city into a wealthy commercial and administrative center. These routes intersect at Laodicea with the east-west road leading from Ephesus to Syria in the east (Ephesus and Syrian gates) through the Meander River Valley and on to the Euphrates; and the north-south road across the Lycus valley coming from the north in Pergamum and Sardis to Perga, until it reached the port of Attalia (modern Antalya) in the south (Hierapolis gate; Strabo *Geogr.* 14.4.1; Xenophon *Anab.* 1.2; see Fig. 137).[15] The Lycus Valley was the easiest route to transport goods to the coastal ports of Miletus and Ephesus.[16] Due to its strategic location, Laodicea thrived at the expense of both Tripolis (Τρίπολις)[17] and Colossae (Κολοσσαί; Col. 1:2; founded 480 BC; Herodotus *Hist.* 7.30).[18]

The snow-capped mountains of Salbascus (Turk. *Baba Dağ*) and Cadmus (Turk. *Honaz Dağı*) can be enjoyed year-round to the south, rising to a height of ca. 8000 ft. (2438 m.), while

---

[7] Grid-planned cities were created by Hippodamus of Miletus (498–408 BC), the father of rational city planning.

[8] Paolo Verzone, "L'urbanistica Di Hierapolis Di Frigia: Tracciato Viario E Monumenti Rimessi Alla Luce Dal 1957 Al 1972," in *Atti Del XVI Congresso Di Storia dell'Architettura* (Rome: Atene, 1977), 4.

[9] Saturnino Ximénez, *Asia Minor in Ruins*, trans. Arthors Chambers (London, U.K.: Hutchinson & Co., 1925), 160.

[10] The stream is personified on its coins as a boar (*BMC Phrygia* 287.52–53; 296.111; 299.127; 313.215; 319.235; Head, *Historia Numorum*, 678.).

[11] Ramsay identified this stream in Turk. as *Gök Pinar Su*. *Letters: Updated*, 304; Celal Şimşek, M. Bilgin, and M. Okunak, "Laodikeia Nekropolleri ve Mezar Tipleri," *TAD* 20 (2015): 133, pl. 4; Celal Şimşek and M. Ayşem Sezgın, "The West and North Theatres in Laodicea," in *Restoration and Management of Ancient Theatres in Turkey, Methods, Research, Results*, ed. Filippo Masino, Paolo Mighetto, and Giorgio Sobrà, Archeologia E Storia 11 (Turkey: Lecce, 2012), 103.

[12] Hemer, Letters to the Seven Churches, 277 n.45.

[13] G. Weber, "Die Flüsse von Laodicea: Lykos, Kadmos, Kapros, Elnos Und Asopos," *MDAI* 23 (1898): 178–95; Ramsay, *Cities and Bishoprics*, 1:35–36; Celal Şimşek, "A Menorah with a Cross Carved on a Column of Nymphaeum A at Laodicea Ad Lycum," *JRA* 19 (2006): 343.

[14] For the description of the rivers of Laodicea, see J. G. C. Anderson, "A Summer in Phrygia: I," *JHS* 17 (1897): 404–8; Weber, "Die Flüsse von Laodicea: Lykos, Kadmos, Kapros, Elnos Und Asopos," 178–95.

[15] On the maintenance of the Roman road see *OGIS* 2.483.24ff. and Magie, *Roman Rule in Asia Minor*, 40–41. 157; Hemer, *Letters to the Seven Churches*, 180.

[16] Hemer, Letters to the Seven Churches, 178.

[17] Tripolis is 20 km to the northwest of Hierapolis.

[18] Hemer, Letters to the Seven Churches, 180; Huttner, Early Christianity in the Lycus Valley, 25.

Laodicea is only ca. 900 ft. (280 m.) above sea level (Strabo *Geogr.* 12.8.16).[19] The travertine terraces of carbonate minerals from the hot springs of Hierapolis ("The city of the *hieron*"), just to the north of Laodicea, are also visible across the Lycus valley from Laodicea, identified as a white imprint in the distance on the slopes of the modern site of Pamukkale (see Fig. 165).[20] These are symptomatic of the mineral laden hot springs and ground water in the region, which also affected the drinking water of Laodicea (see *Water System* below).

The History of Laodicea

The origins of the ancient site prior to being called Laodicea are not well known. White speculates that during the Neolithic period it must have been "a station on the caravan route from Ephesus to northern Syria."[21] Pliny states that it was established on the older settlements of *Diospolis* ("the city of Zeus")[22] and Rhoas (*Nat.* 5.105; Strabo *Geogr.* 12.8, 16).[23] The fourth cent. BC dates are confirmed by black-painted pottery and coins from that period excavated in the western part of the city.[24]

Under Seleucid control

Following Alexander the Great's death (301 BC), Seleucus I Soter (r. 281–261 BC; see Fig. 80) invaded Asia Minor and killed Alexander's former bodyguard. The Pergamene dynasty of the Attalids was technically established in 283 BC by Lysimachus' treasurer, Philetaerus, who found himself the wealthy ruler in control of Lysimachus' great fortune of nine thousand talents of gold,[25] that he stored in Pergamum.[26] At the battle of Corpupedium, Lydia (281 BC), Lysimachus took control of Asia Minor (Memnon *Hist. Her.* 12.7). With the ascension of Antiochus I to the throne later that year, he proceeded to establish a series of military colonies along the Lycus Valley to the west coast to protect against the Galatians, among others. Some of the colonies included Thyatira (Acts 16:14; Rev 2:18–29), Pisidian Antioch (Acts 13:14; 14:21), Hierapolis (Col 4:13), and Rhoas (Laodicea; Col 4:13; Rev 3:14–22).[27]

---

[19] Sherman E. Johnson, "Laodicea and Its Neighbors," *BA* 13, no. 1 (1950): 12; Hemer, *Letters to the Seven Churches*, 178; Morris, *Revelation*, 83; William M. Ramsay, "Laodicea," in *DBib*, ed. James Hastings, Frederick C. Grant, and Harold. H. Rowley, vol. 3 (New York, N.Y.: Scribner's Sons, 1909), 3:44; Huttner, *Early Christianity in the Lycus Valley*, 24.

[20] Paul W. Wallace, "Journey by Lamplight: A Visit to the Seven Churches of Asia — Part 4," *BS* 5, no. 4 (1976): 101–13.

[21] White, Jr., "Laodicea," 3:987.

[22] Zeus was also the chief god of Laodicea (see *The Gods of Laodicea* below).

[23] George E. Bean, *Turkey Beyond the Maeander*, 2nd ed. (London, U.K.: Murray, 1989), 249.

[24] Şimşek and Sezgın, "West and North Theatres," 103 n.3.

[25] On the Coinage of the Attalids see Newell, *The Pergamene Mint Under Philetaerus*; Howgego, *Ancient History from Coins*, 54–56.

[26] Dreyfus and Schraudolph, *Pergamon*, 2:24.

[27] David W. J. Gill, "Seleucids and Antiochids," in *DNTB*, ed. Craig A. Evans and Stanley E. Porter (Downers Grove, Ill.: InterVarsity, 2000), 1092; Mitchell, *Anatolia*, 1:20.

Antiochus II Theus (r. 261–246 BC) rebuilt the earlier settlement of Rhoas and continued to fortify the city, changing its name to Laodicea, after his first wife, Laodice. This took place sometime between his coming to the throne in 261 BC and divorcing of Laodice in 253 BC.[28]

With the death of Antiochus II (246 BC), Seleucus II Callinicus came to power and ruled over Anatolia,[29] but his brother, Antiochus Hierax, took up arms against him to take Anatolia for himself. Antiochus defeated Seleucus at the Battle of Ancyra in 235 BC, but was himself defeated by Attalus, king of Pergamon, at the battle of Harpasus (229 BC).[30] The Seleucids under Antiochus III (r. 223–187 BC; Polybius *Hist.* 5.57.5; see Fig. 96) managed to take back much of Anatolia from the control of the Attalids of Pergamum, but this expansion was short lived as the Roman forces intervened. These were commanded by Publius Cornelius Scipio Africanus (ca. 235–183 BC),[31] with the help of Eumenes II of Pergamum (r. 197–159 BC), who had defeated Antiochus the Great (III) at the battle of *Magnesia ad Sipylum* (Μαγνησία ἡ ἐπὶ Σιπύλου, *Magnēsia hē epi Sipylou*), in 190 BC (Livy *Hist. Rome* 37.37–45; 38.58.9).[32]

UNDER PERGAMENE CONTROL

With the defeat of Antiochus III (see Fig. 96), the Treaty of Apamea (188 BC; Polybius *Hist.* 21.43; see Table 2: "Attalid Dynasty of Pergamene Kings" under *The History of Pergamum: Under Pergamene Control*) placed Lydia and Laodicea under Pergamum control.[33] With the death of Attalus III (133 BC), the last king of Pergamum, Lydia and Laodicea were bequeathed to the Romans (Livy *Per.* 58.4).

UNDER ROMAN CONTROL (133 BC–AD 660)

During the Roman period, Laodicea continued to be important on the Palestine-Syria highway, as a wealthy trading center and a strategic military settlement controlled by a Roman garrison.[34] Laodicea was one of the few Asia Minor cities to hold out against the siege of Mithridates VI, king of Pontus, when he invaded and ravaged the region in 88 BC (Livy *Per.* 78). It did this by offering the Roman proconsul, Quintus Oppius,[35] over to Mithridates in return for amnesty for the citizens of Laodicea.[36] Only four years later it was back under Roman control.

---

[28] Aune, *Rev 1–5*, 249; Wallace, "Journey by Lamplight," 101–13.

[29] Josephus *Ag. Ap.* 1.206–207; Justinus *Epit.* 27.1–3; Appian *Hist. rom.* 11.66.

[30] William Smith, ed., *Dictionary of Greek and Roman Biography and Mythology* (Boston, Mass.: Little, Brown & Co., 1870), 1:194.

[31] The elder son of Publius Cornelius Scipio who became consul in 218 BC.

[32] Hans Kaletsch, "Magnesia," *BrillPauly* 7:696; Akurgal, *Ancient Civilizations*, 177–78.

[33] The Seleucids gave up their empire in Asia Minor north of the Taurus mountains; although they retained Pamphylia and Cilicia. Gill, "Seleucids and Antiochids," 1092; John D. Grainger, *The Roman War of Antiochos the Great*, Mnemosyne Supplements 239 (Leiden: Brill, 2002), 307–25.

[34] White, Jr., "Laodicea," 3:987.

[35] *CIL* 9.5831 = *ILS* 6572 = *AE* (2003): 19; *CIL* 9.5832 = *ILS* 6573.

[36] Athenaeus *Deipn.* 5:213; Strabo *Geogr.* 12.8.16; Appian *Mith.* 11–14; Plutarch *Sull.* 14.1–7; 15.1–3; *SIG* 3.741; *CAH* 9:146. Federico Santangelo, *Sulla, the Elites and the Empire: A Study of Roman Policies in Italy and the Greek East*

In 56 BC Laodicea, Apamea and Synnada were detached from Asia and joined to Cilicia, where Cicero was the reluctant proconsul. Laodicea served as the capital and judicial (Lat. *iuridcus*) center of Cibyratic, a region (Lat. *conventus; haec mea Asia;* Cicero *Att.* 5.15.2–9) comprising twenty-five districts, that included the cities of Hierapolis and Colossae.[37] While Marcus Tullius Cicero was proconsul of Cilicia (May, 51 BC to November, 50 BC),[38] he spent two and a half months at Laodicea hearing cases and stayed as the guest of his good friend Andro of Laodicea, the son of Artemo (Cicero *Fam.* 13.67; 9.7). On 3rd of August, 51 BC, he wrote that, although he had received a warm welcome from the citizens of Laodicea, he was bored and jealous of Aulus Plotius who was sitting in Rome (Cicero *Att.* 5.15). Laodicea has a long and close tie with Rome.

Laodicea also resisted the Parthian army, led by Quintus Labienus, when they invaded the region in 40 BC and remained faithful to Rome.[39] To reward their loyalty, Mark Anthony (83–30 BC) conferred Roman citizenship on several of the leading citizens of Laodicea, including Marcus Antonius Zeno and his son Polemon (Strabo *Geogr.* 12.8.16).[40]

Polman's father, Zenon, an orator and a prominent aristocrat from Laodicea, remained loyal to his Roman friend Mark Antony. This allowed him to play a leading role during the Parthian invasion in 40 BC. In gratitude, the Romans granted his son, Polemon I of Pontus (Πολέμων, see Fig. 135), a citizen of Laodicea, the title of Roman client King of Cilicia Tracheia in 39 BC,[41] of Pontus in 37 BC, and of Lesser Armenia around 33 BC.[42] This was highly celebrated by the Laodiceans, who now considered themselves a "royal city" and depicted the Zenoid family on their coinage (see Fig. 135; Strabo *Geogr.* 11.493, 495).[43]

(Leiden: Brill, 2007), 53; Ronald Mellor, "The Dedications on the Capitoline Hill," *Chiron* 8 (1978): 323–24; Brian C. McGing, *The Foreign Policy of Mithridates VI Eupator, King of Pontus* (Leiden: Brill, 1986).

[37] Cicero *Fam.* 3.8.5; Strabo *Geogr.* 13.4.17; Pliny *Nat.* 5.105. William Moir Calder and Ronald Syme, eds., "Observations on the Province of Cilicia," in *Anatolian Studies Presented to William Hepburn Buckler* (Manchester: Manchester University Press, 1939), 301–2; Habicht, "New Evidence," 67–71; Wayne A. Meeks, *The First Urban Christians: The Social World of the Apostle Paul*, 2nd ed. (New Haven, Conn.: Yale University Press, 2003), 44.

[38] Anthony Everitt, *Cicero: The Life and Times of Rome's Greatest Politician* (New York, N.Y.: Random House, 2003), xiv, 186–88.

[39] Charles A. Hersh, "The Coinage of Quintus Labienus Parthicus," *SNR* 59 (1980): 42; John Curran, "The Ambitions of Quintus Labienus 'Parthicus,'" *Antichthon* 41 (2007): 33–53.

[40] Bruce, "Laodicea (Place)," 4:229.

[41] Appian *Bell. civ.* 5.75; Plutarch *Ant.* 38.61.2; Strabo *Geogr.* 11.578.

[42] Schürer, *History of the Jewish People*, 1:449; Sviatoslav Dmitriev, "Claudius' Grant of Cilicia to Polemo," *CIQ* 53, no. 1 (2003): 286–91.

[43] V. A. Anokhin, *Monetnoe Delo Bospora* (Kiev: Naukova dumka, 1986), 81–82; Magie, *Roman Rule in Asia Minor*, 1407, n. 26; R. D. Sullivan, "Dynasts in Pontus," *ANRW* 7, no. 2 (1980): 925–30; Henri Seyrig, "Monnaies hellénistiques," *RevNum* 6, no. 11 (1969): 36–52; Wilson, *The Victor Sayings in the Book of Revelation*, 163.

135. Coin from *Laodicea ad Lycum* (AD 41–55), struck by Nero Obv.: head of Polemon, the son of Zenon. Rev.: *Tripod lebes* (cauldron) surmounted by a serpent. (*RPC* 2915 = *SNG* Cop. 560 = *BMC* 163).

In AD 26, the provincial council (Lat. *Commune Asiae*) decreed that a second temple to the goddess of Rome be built (Lat. *dea Roma*; Tacitus *Ann.* 4.56).[44] Representatives from 11 Asia Minor cities, including Laodicea, aggressively competed for the privilege of becoming keeper (νεωκόρος, *neōkoros*) of the second imperial cult temple in Asia (Tacitus *Ann.* 4:56). Emperor Tiberius (see Figs. 43, 97, 111) heard the arguments (see Smyrna: *Quotes from Antiquity*) and narrowed the decision down to Sardis and Smyrna (Tacitus *Ann.* 4.55–56),[45] eliminating Laodicea based on their lack of resources required to maintain a provincial cult. Following the arguments, Tiberius granted Smyrna the right to construct a temple to the goddess of Roma, deified Tiberius and the genius of the Senate (Tacitus *Ann.* 4:56).[46]

The economic hardship of Laodicea is evident from the events which followed the severe earthquake of AD 17 (6.74–6.81 magnitude),[47] which Pliny called "the greatest earthquake in human memory" (Pliny *Nat.* 2.86.200 [Rackham]) that affected twelve Asiatic cities (Tacitus *Ann.* 2.47).[48] Laodicea, severely damaged by the quake, sought financial aid from Rome (Strabo *Geogr.* 12.8.18; Suetonius *Tib.* 8). An inscription mentioned cities all around Laodicea that had received economic assistance to restore their cities (*CIL* 10.1624). Suetonius states that Tiberius (r. AD 14–37; see see Figs. 43, 97, 111) "made a plea to the senate on behalf of the citizens of Laodicea, Thyatira and Chios, who had suffered loss from an earthquake [AD 17; Strabo *Geogr.* 12.8.18; Tacitus *Ann.* 2.47] and begged for help" (*Tib.* 8 [Rolfe]). A commemorative inscription reads:

> To Tiberius Caesar Augustus, son of the emperor Augustus, nephew of the emperor Julius, pontifex maximus, consul for the fourth time, emperor for the eighth time, granted tribunician power for the thirty-second time, the Augustales. The city authority restored [...] Sardis [...],

---

[44] Cadoux, *Ancient Smyrna*, 239.

[45] Mellor, *Thea Rhōmē*, 14; Friesen, *Twice Neokoros*, 15–16; Aune, *Rev 1–5*, 160; Cadoux, *Ancient Smyrna*, 239.

[46] Gradel, *Emperor Worship*, 15. The collective genius of the Senate was usually personified as a bearded, elderly man. See the image at http://www.livius.org/pictures/spain/merida/merida-civic-forum/senatus.

[47] Halil Kumsar et al., "Historical Earthquakes That Damaged Hierapolis and Laodikeia Antique Cities and Their Implications for Earthquake Potential of Denizli Basin in Western Turkey," *Bulletin of Engineering Geology and the Environment*, September 10, 2015, 15.

[48] Keitel, "The Art of Losing: Tacitus and the Disaster Narrative," 335. Tacitus *Ann.* 2.47

[Magnes]ia, Philadelphia, Tmolus, Cyme, Temnus, Cibyra, Myrina, Ephesus, Apollonidea, Hyrca[nia], Mostene [Aeg]ae and [Hieroc]aesarea. (*CIL* 10.1624 [Guidoboni]).⁴⁹

Although Laodicea is not mentioned in the inscription, it was the *conventus* of Cibyra that, according to the inscription, also received financial aid to rebuild their city. Suetonius also testifies to Laodicea requesting aid (*Tib.* 8). Commemorative coins were struck in AD 22–23 in Rome, showing Tiberius with the inscription "cities of Asia restored" (Lat. *Civitatibus Asiae Restitutis; RIC* 1.48–50; *BMC Ionia* 70)⁵⁰ to promote the generosity of the emperor in rebuilding the cities at Rome's expense (see Fig. 97).⁵¹

The economic situation for the city seems to have improved by the middle of the century. Following the AD 60 earthquake, that severely devastated the city (7.0–7.1 magnitude)⁵² – and also Hierapolis and Colossae⁵³ – it was among the only Asian cities that did not require help from Nero to rebuild, as it had prospered and could fund its own repairs. Tacitus records that, "in the same year, [AD 60] Laodicea, one of the famous Asiatic cities, was laid in ruins by an earthquake, but recovered by its own resources, without assistance from ourselves [i.e., the Romans]" (*Ann.* 14.27.1 [Jackson]). Koester points out however, that "Tacitus says nothing about the Romans offering help or about the Laodiceans refusing it; he simply observes that the city had sufficient means to

136. Coin from *Laodikeia ad Lycum*, Phrygia. Tiberius *AE* 19 of AD 43–37. Obv.: Magistrate Dioskourides with inscription ΣΕΒΑΣΤΟΣ. Rev.: Inscription ΔΙΟΣΚΟΥΡΙΔΗΣ ΤΟ ΔΕΥΤΕΡΟΝ ΛΑΟΔΙΚΕΩΝ, Zeus standing holding an eagle and scepter (*RPC* 1.2911 = *BMC* 143–144 = *IGLAM* 6263 = *SNG* Cop. 549 = Imhoof *KM* 118).

---

⁴⁹ For the addition of Ephesus and Cibyra to the list of cities in Tacitus, see Guidoboni et al., *Catalogue*, 184. Guidoboni, Comastri, and Traina, *Catalogue of Ancient Earthquakes*, 184; Christopher M. Higgins, "Popular and Imperial Response to Earthquakes in the Roman Empire" (M.A. diss., College of Arts and Sciences of Ohio University, 2009), 41.

⁵⁰ Hobler, *Records of Roman History*, 69 nos. 126–127; Stevenson, *A Dictionary of Roman Coins*, 207–9; Sutherland, *Roman History and Coinage*, 47–49; Kreitzer, *Striking New Images*, 23; Guidoboni, Comastri, and Traina, *Catalogue of Ancient Earthquakes*, 185.

⁵¹ Robert Hoge and David L. Vagi, *Coinage and History of the Roman Empire, Ca. 82 BC–AD 480* (New York, N.Y.: Routledge, 2001), 2:243, no. 442.

⁵² Kumsar et al., "Historical Earthquakes That Damaged Hierapolis and Laodikeia," 6. Strabo described Laodicea as a city that was suceptable to earthquakes (*Geogr.* 12.8.16).

⁵³ Luigi Piccardi, "The AD 60 Denizli Basin Earthquake and the Apparition of Archangel Michael at Colossae (Aegean Turkey)," in *Myth and Geology*, ed. W. Bruce Masse and Luigi Piccardi, Special Publications 273 (London: Geological Society, 2007), 95–105.

rebuild."⁵⁴ In AD 129, the Roman emperor Hadrian (see Figs. 93, 109) visited the city, and the prominent orator and aristocrat Polemon I of Pontus (Πολέμων, see Fig. 135), was likely there to greet him.⁵⁵

The Council of Laodicea,⁵⁶ in the newly established Phrygia Pacatiana, was convened in ca. AD 341–381,⁵⁷ with approximately thirty bishops attending from Asia Minor. It was assembled shortly after the war between the Romans and Persians, waged by Emperor Julian (d. AD June 26, 363). The city council responded to the heretical teachings of the Montanists and the Quartodeciman Christians. The synod reviewed the canon of the NT and confirmed twenty-six books with the only book not on the list being the book of Revelation (Cyril of Jerusalem *Cat.* 4.36; AD 350; Eusebius *Hist. eccl.* 6.25).⁵⁸ Although several of the canons were directed at the proper order of bishops and laymen,⁵⁹ they also dealt with specific issues such as relations with heretics,⁶⁰ Jews⁶¹ and pagans.⁶² They also outlawed the keeping of the Sabbath (Saturday) and encouraged rest on Sunday.⁶³

In AD 494 Syria and Asia Minor were hit once again by a severe earthquake (6.4–6.5 magnitude)⁶⁴ that heavily damaged and collapsed the cities of Laodicea, Hierapolis,⁶⁵ Tripolis, and Agathicum, from which Laodicea never fully recovered.⁶⁶ In the early seventh cent. AD (AD 602–610), during the reign of Emperor Focus, another earthquake (6.4–6.5 magnitude) delivered the final blow to the city. It's citizens permanently relocated to Denizli,⁶⁷ which was then also called Laodicea.⁶⁸

---

⁵⁴ Craig R. Koester, "The Message to Laodicea and the Problem of Its Local Context: A Study in the Imagery in Rev 3.14–22," *NTS* 49, no. 3 (2003): 417; Magie, *Roman Rule in Asia Minor*, 1:564; Prigent, *Apocalypse*, 210–11.

⁵⁵ Birley, *Hadrian*, 223.

⁵⁶ For a detailed discussion of The Synod of Laodicea, see Huttner, *Early Christianity in the Lycus Valley*, 291–316.

⁵⁷ Philip Schaff, "The Canons of the Councils of Ancyra, Gangra, Neocæsarea, Antioch and Laodicea, Which Canons Were Accepted and Received by the Ecumenical Synods," in *Nicene and Post-Nicene Fathers: Series: The Seven Ecumenical Councils*, ed. Alexander Roberts et al., vol. 2.14 (Grand Rapids, Mich.: T&T Clark, 2005), 2.14:124; Huttner, *Early Christianity in the Lycus Valley*, 294–95.

⁵⁸ Karl Joseph von Hefele, *Histoire Des Conciles D'après Les Documents Originaux* (Paris, France: Letouzey et Ané, 1907), 1026–27; Schaff, "The Canons of the Councils of Laodicea," 2.14:229, Canon 60.

⁵⁹ Schaff, "The Canons of the Councils of Laodicea," 2.14:181–227, Canons 3–5, 11–13, 21–27, 40–44, 56–57.

⁶⁰ Ibid., 2.14:183–86, 213–14, 216, Canons 6–10, 31–34, 37.

⁶¹ Ibid., 2.14:193, 216–17, Canons 16, 37–38.

⁶² Ibid., 2.14:217, Canon 39.

⁶³ Ibid., 2.14:212, Canons 29.

⁶⁴ Kumsar et al., "Historical Earthquakes That Damaged Hierapolis and Laodikeia," 6.

⁶⁵ Daria de Bernardi Ferrero, "Excavations and Restorations in Hierapolis During 1995," *KST* 18 (1996): 87.

⁶⁶ Marcellinus, *Comes: Chronicon*, ed. Jacques Paul Migne, Patrologia Latina 51 (Paris, France: 1861), 934; E. Hull, "Earthquake," in *DBib*, ed. James Hastings, Frederick C. Grant, and Harold. H. Rowley, vol. 1 (New York, N.Y.: Scribner's Sons, 1909), 1:634; Bruce, "Laodicea (Place)," 4:231; Robert Mallet and John William Mallet, *The Earthquake Catalogue of the British Association: With the Discussion, Curves, and Maps, Etc.*, British Association for the Advancement of Science (London, U.K.: Taylor & Francis, 1858), 8; Ramsay, *Cities and Bishoprics*, 262; Kumsar et al., "Historical Earthquakes That Damaged Hierapolis and Laodikeia," 1–18.

⁶⁷ Kumsar et al., "Historical Earthquakes That Damaged Hierapolis and Laodikeia," 6; Celal Şimşek, *The Ancient*

Under Byzantine control

Laodicea was also a strategic city in the Byzantine period. In 1119, Emperor John II Komnenos or Comnenus ("John the Beautiful"; r. 1118–1143), together with his lead military aid John Axuch, captured Laodicea from the Seljuk Turks.[69] It was then fortified by the emperor Manuel I Comnenus (r. 1143–1180) who "built a wall around Laodikeia, after taking the city, and routed Alp-qara, who had been entrusted with her defense."[70] The sultan Mascud:

> with select troops . . . laid siege to Laodikeia in Phrygia, which was not as thickly peopled at that time as it is now, nor was it fortified by secure walls, but spilled out to the villages along the slopes of the mountains. He carried off large numbers of men and countless animals; furthermore, he slew no small number of men, among whom was the bishop Solomon, a eunuch who otherwise was gracious and elegant in manner and godlike in virtue.[71]

Korobeinikov maintains that "the decline of the Greek community in Laodikeia occurred at the end of the reign of Andronikos II Palaiologos."[72] The city was devastated by the rebel Michael Doukas Komnenos Angelos, while the city itself was burnt by Sljukid troops in 1200.[73] The city was conquered by Sultan Kay-Khusraw I in 1207 and then, until 1230, the city was ruled by Manuel Komnenos Maurozomes, a Seljuk vassal.[74] The city was eventually completely destroyed by the invading Turks and Mongols.

City of Laodicea (Introduction Guide-English) (Denizli, Turkey: Denizli Municipality, 2010), 3; "West and North Theatres," 104.

[68] Korobeinikov points out that, according to the inscriptional evidence, the city of Denizli, "continued to be called Laodikeia/Lādīq, along side the new name of Tonguzlu'/Denizli, until the end of the thirteenth century." Dimitri Korobeinikov, *Byzantium and the Turks in the Thirteenth Century*, Oxford Studies in Byzantium (Oxford, U.K.: Oxford University Press, 2014), 222 n.38.

[69] P. M. Holt, Ann K. S. Lambton, and Bernard Lewis, eds., *The Cambridge History of Islam: Volume 1A, The Central Islamic Lands from Pre-Islamic Times to the First World War* (Cambridge, U.K.: Cambridge University Press, 1995), 240.

[70] Niketas Choniates, *O City of Byzantium: Annals of Niketas Choniates*, trans. Harry J. Magoulias, Byzantine Texts in Translation (Detroit, Mich.: Wayne State University Press, 1984), 9.

[71] Ibid., 70.

[72] Korobeinikov, *Byzantium and the Turks*, 220.

[73] Ibid.

[74] Choniates, *Annals of Niketas Choniates*, 350; Alexander P. Kazhdan, "Maurozomes," in *The Oxford Dictionary of Byzantium*, ed. Alexander P. Kazhdan (Oxford, U.K.: Oxford University Press, 1991), 1320; Korobeinikov, *Byzantium and the Turks*, 219–22.

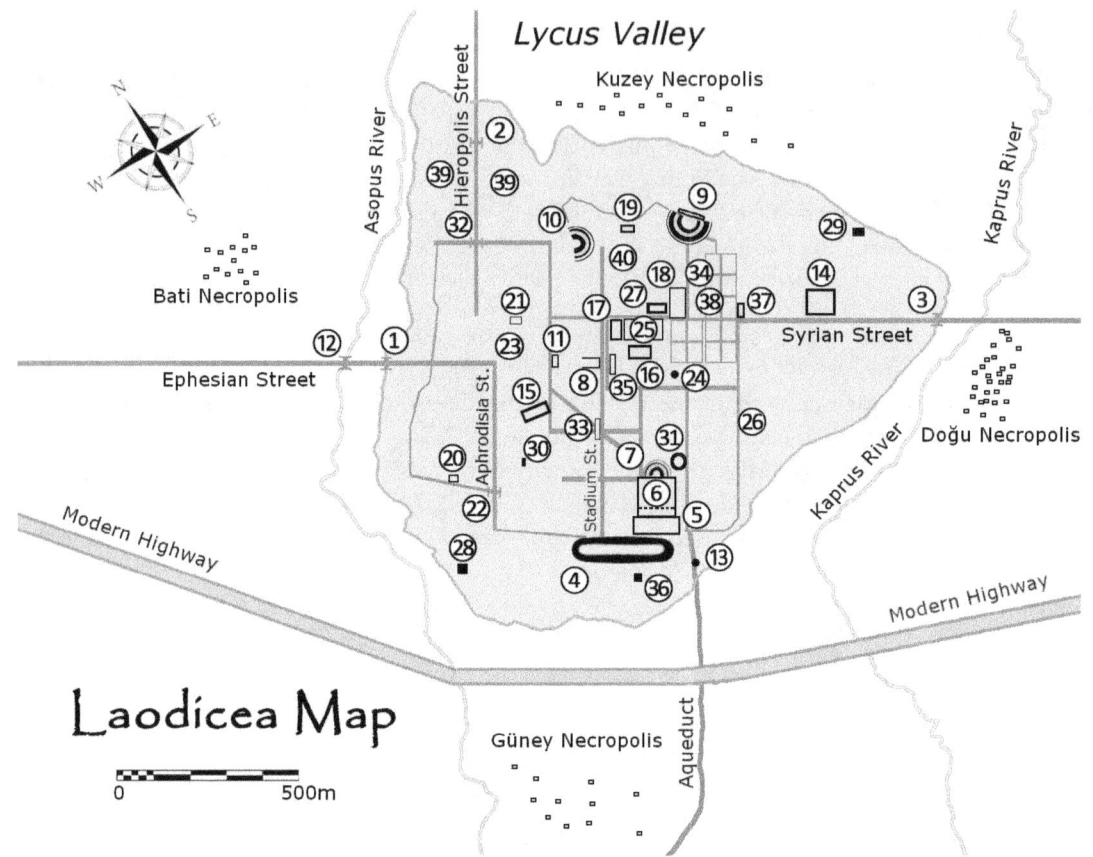

137. Urban plan of the city of Laodicea according to the latest discoveries by Pamukkale University, University of Venice and Denizli University. 1). Ephesus Gate; 2). Hierapolis Gate; 3). Syrian Gate and Byzantine Nymphaeum; 4). Stadium; 5). Gymnasium/Bath complex; 6). Civic agora; 7). Bouleuterion; 8). Ephesus Porticos; 9). N. Theater; 10). W. Theater; 11). Monumental passage; 12). Roman Bridge on Ephesian Street; 13). Water Tower I; 14). East Baths; 15). West Baths; 16). Central Baths; 17). Caracalla Nymphaeum; 18). Temple A; 19). North Church; 20). SW Church; 21). NW Church; 22). Aphrodisian Gate; 23). W agora, Temple and W. Nymphaeum; 24). Water Tower II; 25). Central agora; 26). Byzantine walls; 27). Nymphaeum A; 28). Roman villa; 29). N. Workshop; 30). SW Temple; 31). Round Pytaneion; 32). NW Byzantine Gate; 33). S. Nymphaeum; 34). Laodicea Church; 35). Nymphaeum B, latrine and water storage; 36). Stadium Church; 37). E. Byzantine Nymphaeum; 38). House A and street water distribution center; 39). Asopos I–II; 40). North state agora.

THE POPULATION OF LAODICEA

Although the population of Laodicea (89 acres) in the first cent. is not known, it was certainly larger than nearby Colossae (only 23 acres).[75] As a Seleucid garrison, the population was

---

[75] Wendy J. Cotter, "Women's Authority Roles in Paul's Churches: Countercultural or Conventional?," *NovT* 36 (1994): 356.

originally specially selected to be loyal to the Seleucid king, and was largely Syrian,[76] with a significant number of Jewish citizens (see Jewish Community below).[77] Among the population of Laodicea, several tribes have been identified, including Laodicis, Aollonis, Athenais, Sebaste, Attalis, and Ias tribes.[78] Representatives from each of the tribes formed a part of the governing body, which likely may have also included local Jewish representatives (Josephus *Ant.* 12.3.4), at least until the Jewish revolt in AD 70.[79]

Strabo indicated that it underwent a major population surge after 88 BC, "Laodicea, though formerly small, grew large in our time and in that of our fathers, even though it had been damaged by siege in the time of Mithridates Eupator [88 BC]" [Strabo *Geogr.* 12.8.16 [Jones]). During this same period the city's economy began to flourish due to the textile industry, also increasing the population of the city.

Hanson states that Laodicea had an area of 89 ha. (220 acres),[80] the same area as Thyatira.[81] Based on the likely population of 250 people per hectare (ha.), the population of both cities could be about 22,250, although Barclay, based on the Jewish population in 62 BC, puts it as high as 50,000.[82] The stadium is estimated to hold a capacity of 20–25,000 people.[83]

City	Area (ha.)	100/ha.	150/ha.	250/ha.	400/ha.
Sardis	356	35,600	53,400	89,000	142,400
Colossae	23	2,300	3,450	5,750	9,200
Thyatira	89	8,900	13,350	22,250	35,600
Laodicea	89	8,900	13,350	22,250	35,600

Table 7: Population distribution for Sardis, Colossae, Thyatira and Laodicea according to Hanson.[84]

THE IMPORTANT BUILDINGS OF LAODICEA

Besides what can be gleaned about Laodicea from the excavations, coins and inscriptions discovered there, what is known can be compared with Hierapolis across the valley, as both both cities were important—and competing—trading centers. In many respects, they share

---

[76] Ramsay, Cities and Bishoprics, 1:33.
[77] Hemer, Letters to the Seven Churches, 180.
[78] Jones, *Cities of the Eastern Roman Provinces*, 74; Ramsay, *Cities and Bishoprics*, 60. Only the first three were known to Ramsay in his earlier work.
[79] Ramsay, Cities and Bishoprics, 71, 114.
[80] Hanson, "Urban System," 254.
[81] Mitchell, *Anatolia*, 1:244 n.13.
[82] William Barclay, *The Letters to the Philippians, Colossians, and Thessalonians*, NDSB (Louisville, Ky.: Westminster/Knox, 2003), 93.
[83] Şimşek, *Ancient City of Laodicea*, 19.
[84] Hanson, "Urban System," 254.

similar histories, and to understand one is to know the other. While the ruins of Laodicea have only recently been excavated,[85] the remains of Hierapolis are remarkably well preserved and aid in understanding Laodicea.[86] It held the reputation of being the wealthiest city in Phrygia in the Roman period, primarily due to its textile (black wool), and banking industries (Cicero *Fam.* 3.5.4). There is evidence of several important structures worthy of note. The site of Laodicea did not have an acropolis, but was surrounded by a circular wall with access through three city gates.

THE CITY GATES (NO. 1, 2, 3, 32)

The western Ephesian Gate (Fig. 137 no. 1) led to Ephesus and was dedicated to Domitian (AD 81–96). It consisted of three arches flanked by towers. The tops of the three arches are still visible above ground but some idea of its construction can be seen in the triple Domitian Gate at Hierapolis that resembles it (Fig. 138). The road crossed the Asopus River by a Roman bridge that is still evident from the remaining piers.

138. The Frontinus Gate at Hierapolis built during the time of Domitian that is contemporaneous with the triple arched Ephesian Gate at Laodicea.

On the east side of the city lies the remains of the Syrian Gate (Fig. 137 no. 3), built in AD 84–85 in the Doric style by Emperor Domitian. The gate was built out of travertine blocks with three archways and resembles the contemporaneous Frontinus Gate in Hierapolis (Fig. 138).[87]

The eastern Byzantine Gate (Fig. 137 no. 32) is closer to the city, as the Byzantine site was smaller. It resembles the Byzantine gate at Hierapolis and was constructed in the late fourth cent. AD by emperors Theodosius (r. AD 378–395) and Arcadius (r. AD 395–408).[88] This gate is the best preserved, leading out to Syria in the east. It has been restored to a height of 20 ft. (6 m).[89] Little remains of the Hierapolitan Gate (Fig. 137 no. 2) on the north side of the site and the Aphrodisian Gate (Fig. 137 no. 22) that is situated on the south side.

---

[85] The site was partly excavated in 1961–1963 by an archaeological team from Laval University in Quebec, Canada, under the direction of Jean des Gagniers. From 1999–present, Celal Şimşek, has been the director of the Laodikeia excavation, working out of nearby Pamukkale University.

[86] Yamauchi, *NT Cities*, 147–54.

[87] Şimşek, *Ancient City of Laodicea*, 2.

[88] Wilson, *Biblical Turkey*, 251.

[89] Şimşek, *Ancient City of Laodicea*, 3.

THE NORTH STATE AGORA

The northern state agora (see Fig. 139) with a covered portico has been described as the largest "sacred field in Anatolia."[90] However, while the agora is large and across from a temple (see Fig. 137 no. 18) it is more likely to be a state agora and not a sacred agora given is location between the two theaters (see Fig. 137 no. 40). Even the director of the excavation, Celal Şimşek, admits that "the northern sacred agora is the only one in the world,"[91] suggesting that it is a unique creation for Turkish tourism, rather than a new type of agora. It covers an area of 41,860 square yards (35,000 sq. m) with a covered portico that presently has 34 restored columns. The back wall measures 328 ft. (100 m) long by 36 ft. (11 m) high and was originally covered with paintings. It was destroyed during the 494 AD earthquake.

139. The north state agora uncovered in 2016 under 7 meters of debris.

THE WATER SYSTEM

Laodicea was founded based on its trade routes and central roadways. However, it had a serious disadvantage: the city lacked an adequate fresh water supply,[92] with the Lycus river drying up in the summer.[93] The drinkable water at Laodicea came from the Karcı mountains, supplied through five miles (8 km) of aqueducts from the *Başpınar*[94] (Turkish "the head or main") spring,[95] at Denizli in the south,[96] that was the source of the Kaprus river.[97] However, even this

---

[90] Doğan News Agency, "Sacred Agora Unearthed in Laodicea," *Hurriot Daily News*, January 3, 2017, n.p., http://www.hurriyetdailynews.com/sacred-agora-unearthed-in-laodicea.aspx?pageID=238&nID=108030&NewsCatID=375; "Sacred Agora Excavated at Laodicea," *Artifax* 32, no. 2 (2017): 20.

[91] Doğan News Agency, "Sacred Agora Unearthed in Laodicea," n.p.

[92] Chandler records the testimony of a local landowner of Eçirli (Denizli see Hemer, *Letters to the Seven Churches*, 189–90, 277 n.49) who "expressed his regret, that no waters fit to drink could be discovered there." Chandler, *Travels in Asia Minor*, 270. Aqueducts were considered a real asset for cities in the ancient world and people believed the water they provided was safe to drink (Athenaeus *Deipn.* 2.42).

[93] M. J. S. Rudwick and E. M. B. Green, "The Laodicean Lukewarmness," *ExpTim* 69, no. 6 (1958): 177.

[94] William John Hamilton, *Researches in Asia Minor, Pontus and Armenia: With Some Account of Their Antiquities and Geology* (London, U.K.: Murray, 1842), 1:510; "Extracts from Notes Made on a Journey in Asia Minor in 1836 by W. I. [= J.] Hamilton," *JRGS* 7 (1837): 59–61. Hamilton described the location of the pure spring as a mile and a half on the road from Chonos (Honaz) to Denizli and confirmed that one of the three streams (*Ak Su*, white water) that merged in Khonas (Chonos) was highly petrified (Pliny *Nat.* 31.20.29; cf. Herodotus *Hist.* 7.30) and left travertine deposits similar to those at Hierapolis. Ramsay identified it with the sacred spring (*ayasma*) of mediaval legend (Ramsay, *The Church of the Roman Empire*, 469–71).

[95] Şimşek, "A Menorah with a Cross," 343; *Ancient City of Laodicea*, 18; Celal Şimşek and Mustafa Büyükkolancı, "Die Aquädukte Und Das Wasserverteilungssystem von Laodikeia Ad Lycum," in *Cura Aquarum In Ephesus: Proceedings of the Twelfth International Congress on the History of Water Management and Hydraulic Engineering in the Mediterranean Region (Ephesus-Selçuk, October 2–10, 2004), Part 1*, ed. Gilbert Wiplinger, BABesch Suppl. 12 (Leuven, Belgium: Peeters, 2006),

water contained a high percentage of minerals, as is evident from the thick calcified buildup inside the clay pipes (see Figs. 140, 142). An inscription on a structure near the water tower possibly highlights the quality of the drinking water. The inscription stated "Hedychrous built me and named me 'Hedychrous'" (*I.Laod.* 13.1–4). According to Corsten the name "Hedychrous" means "sweet complexioned", and was related to the pleasant drinking water provided in the first cent. AD.[98] The quality of the drinking water at Laodicea is also attested by an inscription from the fourth or fifth cent. AD, from one of the pumping stations that states: "To good fortune! We, the nymphs of the spring, have the sweet, clear water of the Aidiskos", likely the name of the supplying stream (*I.Laod.* 11.1–2 [Koester]).[99]

140. Water distribution tower (*castellum aquae*), terminal 1 at Laodicea.

Porter argued that the water supply at Laodicea was from the hot springs in Hierapolis because of the calcification from the hard water evident in the *terra-cotta* water pipes.[100] But Strabo reported:

> The changing of water into stone [cake] is said also to be the case with the rivers in Laodicea, although their water is potable [ποτίμων, *potimōn;* i.e., drinkable, fresh, or sweet]. The water at Hierapolis is remarkably adapted also to the dyeing of wool, so that wool dyed with the roots [madder] rivals that dyed with the coccus [kermes oak] or with the marine purple [murex]. And the

---

137. Porter suggested that the cold water supplied to Laodicea came from the spring (Turk. *Bounar Bashi*) at Colossae, however the fresh water was known to be from the spring south at Denizli. Porter, "Why the Laodiceans Received Lukewarm Water (Rev 3:15–18)," 147; Blaiklock, *Cities of the NT*, 124; Finegan, *The Archeology of the New Testament*, 2014, 182.

[96] Bean, Turkey Beyond the Maeander, 255–56; Jack Finegan, The Archeology of the New Testament: The Mediterranean World of the Early Christian Apostles, Routledge Library Editions: Archaeology (New York, N.Y.: Routledge, 2015), 179; Hemer, Letters to the Seven Churches, 188; Fant and Reddish, Guide to Biblical Sites, 236–37.

[97] Ulrich R. Huttner, "Wolf Und Eber: Die Flüsse von Laodikeia in Phrygien," in Internationales Kolloquium Zur Kaiserzeitlichen Münzprägung Kleinasiens, 27.-30. April 1994 in Der Staatlichen Münzsammlung, München, Mailand, ed. Johannes Nollé, Bernhard Overbeck, and Peter Weiss, Nomismata 1 (Milano: Ennerre, 1997), 100–109; Early Christianity in the Lycus Valley, 156, 157 n.65. According to Ramsay "the water [for Laodicea] was brought from the upper springs of a branch of the Kadmos [Cadmus] which rises in Mount Salbakos near Denizli." (*Cities and Bishoprics,* 1:48).

[98] Thomas Corsten, Die Inschriften von Laodikeia Am Lykos (Bonn: Habelt, 1997), 48–49.

[99] Koester, "Message to Laodicea," 410 n.6.

[100] Porter, "Why the Laodiceans Received Lukewarm Water (Rev 3:15–18)," 147; Blaiklock, *Cities of the NT*, 124; Finegan, *The Archeology of the New Testament*, 2014, 182; Ford, *Revelation*, 418–19.

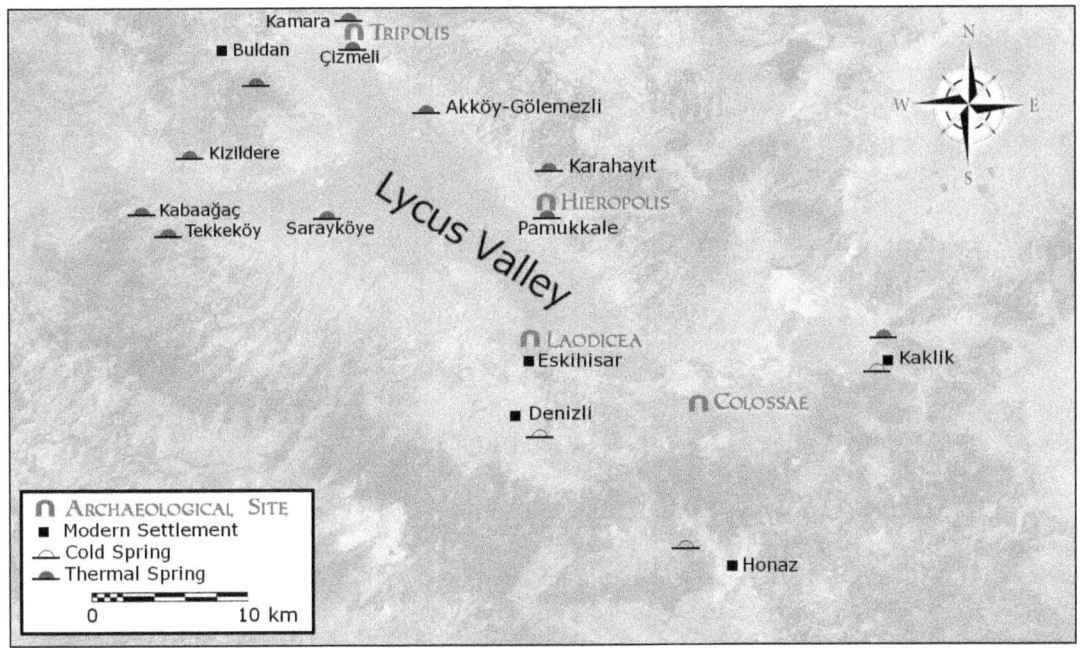

141. Map of the modern area around Laodicea, indicating the location of the archaeological sites, and the thermal and cold springs.

supply of water is so abundant that the city is full of natural baths. (*Geogr*. 13.4.14 [Jones]; see also Vitruvius *Arch*. 8.3.1)[101]

A section of the aqueduct, which supplied the water, has been identified (see map Fig. 137 no. 13, 143), and dated to the time of Hiero (Strabo *Geogr*. 12.8.16)[102] in the first cent. BC.[103] The aqueduct was created by hewed stones, about 36 inches (91 cm) by 18 inches (46 cm) square, with a 12–inch (30 cm) hole carved out of the middle, each stacked together to form the aqueduct pipe. The stream flowed at a rate of 80–150 liters per second.[104] There is also an all-season stream known as *Baş Pınar Çay* at Eskihisar, a Turkish village just south of Laodicea. Hemer, based on discussions with a local Turkish water-engineer, claimed it was a "constant

---

[101] E. J. Davis, Anatolia: Or The Journal of a Visit to Some of the Ancient Ruined Cities of Caria, Phrygia, Lycia and Pisidia (London, U.K.: Grant & Co., 1874), 101.

[102] Ramsay, Cities and Bishoprics, 1:48; Hemer, Letters to the Seven Churches, 190.

[103] G. Weber, "Die Hochdruck Wasserleitung von Laodicea Ad Lycum," *JDAI* 13 (1898): 1–13, pl. 3; Şimşek and Büyükkolancı, "Die Aqueduct Und Das Wasserverteilungssystem," 137–46; Hamilton, *Researches in Asia Minor, Pontus and Armenia*, 1:515–16.

[104] Y. Ersel Tanriöver and N. Orhan Baykan, "The Water Supply Systems of Caria," in Cura Aquarum In Ephesus: Proceedings of the Twelfth International Congress on the History of Water Management and Hydraulic Engineering in the Mediterranean Region (Ephesus-Selçuck, October 2–10, 2004), Part 1, ed. Gilbert Wiplinger, BABesch Suppl. 12 (Leuven, Belgium: Peeters, 2006), 128.

tepid temperature,"[105] but goes on to state that the "actual temperature cannot be deduced from the uncertain data."[106] Koester points out that "If Laodicea's water was lukewarm, the same would have been true at Ephesus, Smyrna, Pergamum, and Sardis"[107] since they also had several aqueducts.

The clay pipes supplied water by force of gravity to a clearing pool (*castellum aquae*) on the south side of Laodicea,[108] and from there it was distributed in four directions under pressure, to a central water station using a triple staining and inverted siphon system,[109] that supplied a fountain dedicated to Emperor Trajan.[110] The water of the fountain was closely managed, as evident from a recent discovery in 2011 of a Greek inscription uncovered by Celal Şimşek, director of the Laodicea excavations.[111] The inscription was prepared by Aulus Vicirius Martialis,[112] the proconsul of Asia (AD 113/114), who also intervened in a water dispute over provisions in Ephesus.[113] The Laodicean inscription, dating to between AD 113 and 120, reads in part:

142. Closeup of the water distribution tower (*castellum aquae*), terminal 1 at Laodicea. Calcification is visible inside the terra-cotta water pipes, formed by the mineral laden ground water from the springs.

> Those who divide the water for his personal use, should pay 5,000 denarius to the empire treasury; it is forbidden to use the city water for free or grant it to private individuals; those who buy the water cannot violate the Vespasian Edict; those who damage water pipes should pay 5,000 denarius; protective roofs should be established for the water depots and water pipes in the city; the governor's office [will] appoint two citizens as curators every year to ensure the safety of the water

---

[105] Hemer, Letters to the Seven Churches, 277 n. 47.

[106] Ibid., 277 n. 48.

[107] Koester, "Message to Laodicea," 411.

[108] See map 34 no. 13. Water Tower I; map 34 no. 24. Water Tower II.

[109] Bruce, "Laodicea (Place)," 4:230; Weber, "Die Hochdruck Wasserleitung von Laodicea Ad Lycum," 1898, 1–13; "Die Hochdruck Wasserleitung von Laodicea Ad Lycum," *JDAI* 19 (1904): 95–96. See the map pl. 3.

[110] See Laodicea map. 13. Water Tower I; 17. Caracalla's Nymphaeum; 24. Water Tower II; 27. Nymphaeum and Fountain of S. Severus.

[111] Şimşek and Büyükkolancı, "Die Aqueduct Und Das Wasserverteilungssystem," 137–46.

[112] John D. Grainger, *Nerva and the Roman Succession Crisis of AD 96–99*, Roman Imperial Biographies (New York, N.Y.: Routledge, 2003), xiii, 101. Not Matrialis as initially reported.

[113] Tilborg, *Reading John*, 108; Werner Eck, "Jahres- Und Provinzialfasten Der Senatorischen Statthalter von 69/70 Bis 138/139, 1. Teil," *Chiron* 12 (1982): 355; "Jahres- Und Provinzialfasten Der Senatorischen Statthalter von 69/70 Bis 138/139. 2. Teil," *Chiron* 13 (1983): 154, 210..

resource; nobody who has farms close to the water channels can use this water for agriculture (*I.Eph.* 3217 a + b = *SEG* 31.953; 55.2001; [Şimşek].[114]

To help understand the severity of this penalty, the Gospel of Matthew (last quarter of the first cent. AD) reported that a denarius was equivalent to an average day's wage for an agricultural worker (Matt 20:2–13), thus 5,000 denarii were equal to about 13.7 years of work for a farmer. With inflation, in AD 301, the Diocletian Edict of Maximum Prices listed the daily wage for most experienced tradesmen, such as carpenter, baker, blacksmith, stone mason, wagon wright, tailor of silk and teacher as 50 denarii.[115] One pound of gold was 50,000 denarii.[116] During the republic (509–527 BC), professional legionary soldiers were paid 112.5 denarii per year (0.3/day), which was later doubled by Julius Caesar (early second cent. AD) to 225 denarii (0.6/day), although soldiers had to pay for their own food and arms (Tacitus *Ann.* 1.17; Suetonius *Jul.* 26.3).[117] During this period, based on a legionary's wage, 5,000 denarii were equal to about 22 years of work. Thus any Laodicean found tampering with the water system would be hit with severe penalties, indicating the extreme value of ancient water systems.

143. Ground level aqueduct at Laodicea. Calcification is visible inside the terra-cotta water pipes, formed by the mineral laden ground water that flowed from the spring at Denizli.

The thermal springs in the region are located on the opposite side of the Lycus valley at *Pamukkale* (at Hierapolis, 82°–138° F. [28–59°C.][118] with 17 spring discharges; Ca-Mg-HCO$_3$-SO$_4$ type), Buldan (36–57°C.), *Kabaağaç*, *Kamara* (32–57°C.; Na-HCO$_3$ type), *Çizmeli* (Yenice at Tripolis), *Akköy-Gölemezli* (4 springs), *Tekkeköy* (Roman baths), *Karahayıt* (42–54.4°C.; Ca-Mg-HCO$_3$-SO$_4$ type), *Kaklik*, and *Kizildere* (55–100°C, Na-SO$_4$-HCO$_3$ type),[119] but no thermal springs

---

[114] Celal Şimşek, "Ancient 'water Law' Unearthed in Laodicea," *Hürriyet Daily News*, September 13, 2011, n.p., http://www.hurriyetdailynews.com/ancient-water-law-unearthed-in-laodicea-.aspx?pageID = 238&nid = 87259.

[115] Elsa R. Graser, "A Text and Translation of the Edict of Diocletian," in *An Economic Survey of Ancient Rome: Rome and Italy of the Empire*, ed. Tenney Frank, vol. 5 (Baltimore, Md.: John Hopkins University Press, 1975), 5:338–45, § 7.1–14, 49, 64–66, 69.

[116] Ibid., 5:412, § 30.1.

[117] Pat Southern, *The Roman Army: A Social and Institutional History* (Oxford, U.K.: Oxford University Press, 2007), 106–8.

[118] Ali Gökgöz, "Geochemistry of the Kizildere-Tekkehamambuldan-Pamukkale Geothermal Fields, Turkey," *Geothermal Training Programme The United Nations University Reports* 5 (1998): 119. Davies described the water in Hierapolis as "not wholesome, and good drinking water must be brought from a considerable distance; but after the water of the source has been thoroughly exposed to the air it loses its injurious properties, and though not palatable, may be drunk." Davis, *Anatolia*, 101.

[119] A. Ten Dam and C. Erentöz, "Kizildere Geothermal Field — Western Anatolia," *Geothermics* 2 (January 1,

are identified to the south of Laodicea near Denizli.[120] The closest thermal spring on the southern side of the Lycus valley is *Sarayköy*, 12 miles (19 km) north-east of Laodicea. Akşit, a Turkish archaeologist born in Denizli, indicated that there are aqueducts at Hierapolis[121] that carried water to Laodicea,[122] however the archaeological reports from Hierapolis only identified two aqueducts, both drawing drinking water from the northern region above Hierapolis, and leading to a large settling tank (*castellum aquae*) in the east.[123]

The water from Hierapolis emerged with a heavy concentration of carbon dioxide ($CaCO_3$), that when mixed with water, formed a weak carbonic acid (H_2CO_3). When these elements are mixed together, they form calcium bicarbonate ($Ca(HCO_3)_2$) sometimes called "hard water", which, when some of the Carbon dioxide evaporated, left the white insoluble calcium carbonate limestone deposit that formed a formation 300 ft. (91 m) high, extending for almost a mile (1.6 km). They are visible on the slopes of Pamukkale from Laodicea and in the water pipes of the region.[124] Fresh water for Hierapolis had to be provided by an aqueduct to the north of the city. However, the ground water in the region still had mineral deposits that over time calcified. The subterranean network of springs extended some fifty miles under the mountains and surfaced at Hierapolis and other locations with a temperature range of 82°–138° F. (28°–59°C.) and a flow rate of ca. 5,547 gallons per minute (350 lit./sec.).[125]

THE NYMPHAEUMS

Closely connected with the water system is the location of some six water fountains (nymphaeum; νυμφαῖον, *numphaion*) predominantly in the center of the city,[126] with the East Byzantine fountain located near the eastern Syrian Gate. While most Roman cities had fountains, Laodicea had an abundance of water features.[127]

1970): 124–29.

[120] Kumsar et al., "Historical Earthquakes That Damaged Hierapolis and Laodikeia," 4, Fig. 2; Tanriöver and Baykan, "Die Aqueduct Und Das Wasserverteilungssystem," 127–32; Francesco D'Andria, Mustafa Büyükkolancı, and Lorenzo Campagna, "The Castellum Aquae of Hierapolis of Phrygia," in *Cura Aquarum In Ephesus: Proceedings of the Twelfth International Congress on the History of Water Management and Hydraulic Engineering in the Mediterranean Region (Ephesus-Selçuck, October 2–10, 2004), Part 1*, ed. Gilbert Wiplinger, BABesch Suppl. 12 (Leuven, Belgium: Peeters, 2006), 359–61; Gökgöz, "Geochemistry," 115–56.

[121] The source of the water is from Müştak, Kocapinar, Çaltıh, Karahayıt along an 18 km aqueduct. Tanriöver and Baykan, "Die Aqueduct Und Das Wasserverteilungssystem," 128.

[122] İlhan Akşit, *Pamukkale Hierapolis* (Istanbul: Akşit, 2003), 65.

[123] D'Andria, Büyükkolancı, and Campagna, "Die Aqueduct Und Das Wasserverteilungssystem," 359–60.

[124] Hemer, *Letters to the Seven Churches*, 277 n.48; Tarhan Toker, *Pamukkale (Hierapolis)* (Denizli, Turkey: Haber Gazetecilik, 1976), 6.

[125] Gökgöz, "Geochemistry," 127.

[126] On the individual by the name of Nympha (a rare name) of Laodicea, see Huttner, *Early Christianity in the Lycus Valley*, 95–97.

[127] Celal Şimşek, *Laodikeia (Laodicea Ad Lycum) 2013*, Laodikeia Çalışmaları (Studies) 2 (Istanbul: Ege Yayinlari, 2013), 146–78.

NYMPHAEUM A (FOUNTAIN OF SEPTIMIUS SEVERUS, NO. 27)

On the north side of the Syrian Street is the two storey "Nymphaeum A" with a rectangular pool (136.5 ft. [41.6 m] by 47 ft. [14.3 m]), with four taps to supply water, excavated in 2003 (see map no. 27).[128] An inscription on the Nymphaeum indicated that it was dedicated to emperor Septimus Severus (r. 193–211),[129] with repairs carried out during the time of Diocletian. It was finally destroyed in the earthquake of AD 494.[130] See the menorah and cross engraving on a column found here under *The Jewish Community at Laodicea* below.

144. The nymphaeum (AD 130–150) of Perga, located 113 miles (182 km) southeast of Laodicea. Water from a stream once flowed over the fountain and then on down the colonnaded street in a raised channel. A statue of the river god Kestros is located in the center of the fountain.

NYMPHAEUM B (NO. 35)

The Nymphaeum B structure was rectangular, 21 ft. (6.3 m) by 59 ft. (18 m). It is located at the east side of Stadium Street and southwest of the central bath (map no. 35). It supplied water to the 80–person latrine (third cent. AD) next door and water storage basins close by. The fountain was built in the first cent. AD, but needed constant repair due to calcification, until it was finally abandoned in the seventh cent. AD.[131]

CARACALLA NYMPHAEUM (NO. 17)

The Caracalla Nymphaeum is located on the north side of the central agora (see map no. 25) at the junction of Syrian Street and Stadium Street leading south (see map no. 17).[132] It was first excavated in 1961–1963 by Laval University in Quebec, under the direction of Jean des Gagniers.[133] It was built in honor of the visit of Emperor Caracalla (AD 215–216; see Figs. 128, 162, 163)[134] and dedicated to him (*I.Laod.* 16). The water for the fountain was supplied through

---

[128] Şimşek, *Ancient City of Laodicea*, 9.
[129] Celal Şimşek, "2003 Yılı Laodikeia Antik Kenti Kazıları," *KST* 26 (2005): 308–18, figs. 9–13.
[130] Ibid., 308–10, 312–13.
[131] Şimşek, *Ancient City of Laodicea*, 22.
[132] Celal Şimşek, "Laodicea, A Long-Lived City," *World Archaeology Magazine* 41, no. 4.5 (July 2010): 35.
[133] Jean des Gagniers et al., *Laodicée du Lycos: le nymphée; campagnes 1961–1963* (Québec: l'Université Laval, 1969), 123–24.
[134] Peter Thonemann, *The Maeander Valley: A Historical Geography from Antiquity to Byzantium* (Cambridge, U.K.:

clay pipes that ran under the agora. Renovated at least four times before the fifth cent. AD, it revealed two semicircular fountains, a square water basin, and storage chambers that date to the early third cent AD.¹³⁵ A life-size statue of Isis or her priestess was uncovered, along with building material with carved crosses, indicating that it had been used as a meeting place for Christians in later periods.¹³⁶

EAST BYZANTINE NYMPHAEUM (NO. 3)

The rectangular Byzantine Nymphaeum (70.5 ft. [21.5 m] by 32.3 ft. [9.85 m]) is adjoined to the north tower of the east Byzantine Gate. It dates to the early fifth cent. AD and provided water to those living outside the city wall and for travelers arriving to the city.¹³⁷

THE STADIUM (NO. 4)

The stadium (στάδιον ἀμφιθέατρον, *stadion amphitheatron; CIG* 3936 = *IGR* 4.861)¹³⁸ was built entirely of marble and runs east-west into the hillside at the southwestern end of the city, and measures 935 ft. (285 m) by 230 ft. (70 m) with both ends rounded (*sphenodones*).¹³⁹ The seats were built around the entire circumference of the stadium in 34 sections of 22 rows. It was estimated that the stadium seated from 20,000 to 25,000 people, which supports the estimated population of the city (see *The Population of Laodicea*).¹⁴⁰

145. The overgrown Ladoicean stadium.

Based on a Greek inscription found on the largest gate of the stadium, it was dedicated to Titus (r. 79–81), Vespasian's son, and built by Nicostratus (Νεικοστράτος, *Neikostratos;* cf. *IGR* 4.846),¹⁴¹ a wealthy citizen of the city, though completed in AD 79 by his heir following Nicostratus' death.¹⁴² The inscription translates:

Cambridge University Press, 2011), 214.

¹³⁵ Meinardus, "The Christian Remains of the Seven Churches of the Apocalypse," 82; Fant and Reddish, *Guide to Biblical Sites*, 237.

¹³⁶ Yamauchi, *NT Cities*, 141–42; Bruce, "Laodicea (Place)," 5:230.

¹³⁷ Şimşek, Ancient City of Laodicea, 4.

¹³⁸ Ramsay, *Cities and Bishoprics*, 1:72 no.3.

¹³⁹ Şimşek, *Ancient City of Laodicea*, 19. Wilson provides measurements of the arena of 631.9 by 112 ft (192.3 by 34 m), perhaps referring to the inside of the arena. *Biblical Turkey*, 252.

¹⁴⁰ Ramsay, Cities and Bishoprics, 1:47; Şimşek, Ancient City of Laodicea, 19; Hemer, Letters to the Seven Churches, 194; Wilson, Biblical Turkey, 252.

¹⁴¹ He is known to have also heated the covered walkways and provided the oil for the pipes at the baths. Hemer,

> To the Emperor Titus Caesar Augustus Vespasian[us], seven times consul, son of the emperor the god Vespasian; and to the people. Nicostratus the younger son of Lycius, son of Nicostratus, dedicated . . . at his own expense; Nicostratus, . . . his heir having completed what remained of the work, and Marcus Ulpius Trajanus the proconsul having consecrated it. (*CIG* 3935 = *IGR* 4.845 [Chandler])[143]

Trajan's father, Marcus Ulpius Trajanus, was the proconsul of Asia in AD 79–80 under Titus and Domitian.[144] The stadium would had entertained the people with gladiators[145] and athletic contests with wild beasts, attested to by inscriptions (*CIG* 3942).[146]

THE TEMPLES

Şimşek reported in 2011 that "As far as we have learned from Laodicea, there are three temples in this 250–by-100 meter divine area. One was dedicated to Zeus and [a second to] Athena. There is a bust of Athena on a column in the temple. We are still searching for the god of the third temple."[147]

TEMPLE A, AD 26–60 (NO. 18)

On the north side of Syria Street is an impressive prostyle Temple (A) measuring 91 ft. (27.75 m) by 45 ft. (13.6 m), with fluted columns with Corinthian capitals, situated within a rectangular courtyard that measures 190 ft. (58 m) by 139 ft. (42.3 m) with marble floors, and surrounded by a 54–columned portico (see Fig. 146). Two columns were discovered, each with three registers in wreaths. Column A (broken in two) was inscribed with the image and inscription of Artemis, two deer and Laodicea (see Fig. 155),

146. The restored Temple A with 19 columns restored and raised. It was originally dedicated to Apollo.

while Column B had Apollo, two griffins and Fortuna (see Fig. 160). The structure must have

---

Letters to the Seven Churches, 195.

[142] For a detailed description of the inscription, see Ramsay, *Cities and Bishoprics*, 1:79; Hemer, *Letters to the Seven Churches*, 279 n.70.

[143] Chandler, *Travels in Asia Minor*, 1:260; Vermeule, *Roman Imperial Art*, 238–39.

[144] Werner Eck, "Traianus," in *BrillPaulyA*, ed. Hubert Cancik and Helmuth Schneider, trans. Christine F. Salazar and Francis G. Gentry (Leiden: Brill, 2006), n.p., http://dx.doi.org/10.1163/1574–9347_bnp_e1218650.

[145] Gladiatorial performances were conducted in Laodicea as early as 50 BC, (Cicero *Att.* 6.3.9), but Cicero was not referring to this stadium as it was not completed until AD 79. Fant and Reddish are incorrect associating Cicero's reference with this stadium. *Guide to Biblical Sites*, 237.

[146] Ramsay, *Cities and Bishoprics*, 1:75–77; Louis Robert, *Les Gladiateurs dans l'Orient grec* (Paris: Champion, 1941), 151–52.

[147] Celal Şimşek, "Temple of Athena Found in Laodicea," *Hurriot Daily News*, September 12, 2011, n.p.

been magnificent in its day as it was constructed with travertine blocks all faced with marble. The temple was restored during the 2010 excavation season.[148]

In AD 26 several Asia Minor cities, including Laodicea, petitioned Rome for the right to build a temple to Emperor Tiberius (see Figs. 43, 97, 111; Tacitus *Ann.* 4.56). Although Rome's reply was that the city's resources were considered insufficient for this project, it appears that by the middle of the first cent. AD, Laodicea had recovered sufficiently to build this temple. It was originally dedicated to Apollo, and not Zeus, as some have speculated.[149] In addition, Apollo's sister Artemis was also worshiped here. The temple was repaired under Emperor Severus (AD 193–211), with significant renovations under Emperor Diocletian (AD 284–305), when it was used for the worship of the imperial cult.[150] During the fourth cent. AD, the temple was used as a Christian archive and church, until it was finally destroyed in the earthquake of AD 494.[151]

The Theaters

There are two theaters, something unique when compared to many Roman cities. They were located at the north-eastern side of the city.[152]

West Theater (No. 10)

The west theater (see Fig. 147) is the smallest of the two and was the first theater built in Laodicea in the Hellenistic period.[153] In classic Hellenistic style it was built into the hillside, likely to catch the westerly breeze. The stage building (Lat. *scaenae frons*), stood 20–23 ft. (6–7 m) high, with two stories. The first floor has completely survived, while the second floor partially survived. The *cavea* (Lat. "enclosure" for seating) contained nine sections (κερκίδες, *kerkides*) accessed by seven stairways. The lower sections, containing 23 rows of seats, were built of marble,[154] while the upper sections of 19 rows, made of travertine, indicate that the expansion used less expensive building materials.[155] The diameter of the highest row is 279 ft. (85 m), with

---

[148] Şimşek, "Laodicea," 34–35.

[149] Wilson compared the "vaulted substructure" of Temple A with "the Zeus temple in Aizanoi," implying that Temple A was the temple of Zeus. Wilson, *Biblical Turkey*, 251.

[150] Carl G. Rasmussen, "Temple A at Laodicea (Turned into a 'library'?) — Part 1 of 2 Parts," August 27, 2014, n.p., https://holylandphotos.wordpress.com/2014/08/27/temple-a-at-laodicea-turned-into-a-library-part-1-of-2-parts/.

[151] Şimşek, Ancient City of Laodicea, 11.

[152] Luigi Sperti, "Ricognizione Archeologica a Laodicea Di Frigia: 1993–1998," in *Laodicea Ricognizione Archeologica a Laodicea Di Frigia*, ed. Gustavo Traversari et al., Rivista Di Archeologia, Supp. 24 (Roma: Bretschneider, 2000), 81–91; Şimşek and Sezgın, "West and North Theatres," 106; *Laodikeia 2013*, 207–20.

[153] Fant and Reddish suggest that it was built in the middle of the second cent. AD. Fant and Reddish, *Guide to Biblical Sites*, 239–40. Şimşek and Wilson maintain that it was built in the Hellenistic period. Şimşek, *Ancient City of Laodicea*, 12; Wilson, *Biblical Turkey*, 251.

[154] Much of the marble has been removed up until the 1990's for the production of line.

[155] Şimşek and Sezgın, "West and North Theatres," 108.

147. West theater looking toward the Lycus Valley. The white travertine cliffs of Hierapolis (Pammukale) are visible just over the top of the theater.

the retaining wall (Lat. *analemma*) measuring 323 ft. (98.5 m).[156] It is estimated that the theater could seat about 8,000 people, similar to the capacity of the theater in Aphrodisias.[157]

The seats were numbered using the Greek alphabet, to assign seating to the tribes, governing groups and associations.[158] Also, holes were found around the upper seats (Lat. *summa cavea*) in both theaters to secure the supports for the protective wall or pillars (Lat. *parapet*) of the *diazoma*,[159] that supported the canopy or sail (Lat. *velarium*) to protect the audience from the elements.[160] The main stage structure was also used as a city wall in the 5th cent. when the size of the city was reduced. The structure went through various stages of repair until it was abandoned in the seventh century.[161]

NORTH THEATER (NO. 9)

The north theater is the largest of the two and was the second theater built in Laodicea in the second cent. AD,[162] when the west theater was outgrown. It was built in the Greek style into the hillside and faced the Lycus Valley.[163] The diameter of the spectator's area, including the retaining wall (Lat. *analemma*), is 367 ft. (112 m) by 399 ft. (121.5 m), but like the theater in Hierapolis, it is larger than a semicircle.[164] There were a total of 23 rows of seats (8 rows

---

[156] There appears to be some unproportionate measurements perhaps due to earthquake damage. Ibid.; Frank Sear, *Roman Theatres: An Architectural Study* (Oxford, U.K.: Oxford University Press, 2006), 340. Sear documents that the theaters diameter was 328 ft. (100 m) with only 9 *cunei* (κερκίδες, *kerkides*) and 16 rows of seats of the *summa cavea* visible.

[157] Kenan T. Erim, *Aphrodisias: City of Venus Aphrodite* (New York, N.Y: Facts on File, 1986), 79.

[158] Şimşek and Sezgın, "West and North Theatres," 108.

[159] The *diazoma* was the passageway of an ancient Greek theater dividing the lower from the upper rows of seats aiding in access to the area. Ibid., 108, 110 Fig. 7.

[160] Ibid., 115–16; Frank Sear, *Roman Architecture* (Abingdon, Oxfordshire: Routledge, 1998), 144. The holes for the *velarium* have also been discovered in the Roman Colosseum (Suetonius *Cal.* 26; Juvenal *Sat.* 4.121), and at Aspendos, Limyra, Pompeii and Segobriga, Spain. See De Bernardi Ferrero, *Bati Anadolu'nun*, 142–43.

[161] Şimşek notes the Corinthian capitals from the theater date to the fifth and sixth cent. AD. Şimşek and Sezgın, "West and North Theatres," 110; *Ancient City of Laodicea*, 12; Wilson, *Biblical Turkey*, 251; Fant and Reddish, *Guide to Biblical Sites*, 239–40.

[162] An inscription dedicated to Aelius Caesar and Hadrian was uncovered in the theater that dates to 136–37 AD. Vermeule, *Roman Imperial Art*, 474.

[163] Sear, *Roman Theatres*, 340.

[164] Şimşek and Sezgın, "West and North Theatres," 115.

conserved) in the lower section (*ima cavea*) and 26 rows of seats (15 rows conserved) in the upper section (Lat. *summa cavea*).[165] It is estimated that the theater could seat between 10,000 and 12,000 people.[166]

Şimşek notes that "the remains of the layer of reddish impermeable mortar and calcareous deposits [in the orchestra] show that the theater was used for aquatic spectacles by transforming the orchestra into a *kolymbēthra* [κολυμβήθρα, theater pool]."[167] Although texts mention entertainment featuring gladiators in Laodicea from Thyatira and other cities (*I.Laod.* 73; 75; 81A; Cicero *Att.* 6.3.9), no evidence of gladiatorial games has been identified in the north theater.[168]

148. This drawing by Leon de Laborde depicts the north theater in 1838, when the stage building still indicated three rows of cut stone visible and the seats appeared to be in excellent condition. de Laborde, *Voyage de l'Asie Mineure* 1838, 86–87, Pl. xxxix-83. PD-Old.

Numerous inscriptions on the seats indicate that some of the seats were assigned the tribes, associations and citizens of other communities (*Trapezopolitans*) such as Hierapolis.[169] Crosses and Christograms etched into the seats indicate that it was later used into the seventh cent. AD.[170] With the rest of the city, it was abandoned in the seventh century.[171]

THE BOULEUTERION (NO. 7)

Facing southwest is the *bouleutērion* (βουλευτήριον), city hall or council chamber) situated north of the central agora. It may have also served as a small *ōdeum*. The cavea (small enclosure) measured ca. 230 ft. (70 m)[172] and held ca. 500–600 people, and dates from the time of Hadrian

---

[165] Ibid., Page 114 Fig. 10.

[166] Sear and Şimşek suggest 10,000. Sear, *Roman Theatres*, 340; Şimşek and Sezgın, "West and North Theatres," 112. For the various calculations by previous scholars, see Şimşek and Sezgın, "West and North Theatres," 112–14. Şimşek suggests that the capacity was approximately 12,000 people (*Ancient City of Laodicea*, 13), as does Wilson (*Biblical Turkey*, 251).

[167] Şimşek and Sezgın, "West and North Theatres," 117; Daria de Bernardi Ferrero, *Bati Anadolu'nun Eskiçağ Tiyatrolari*, trans. Erendiz Özbayoğlu (Ankara, Turkey: İtalyan Kültür Heyeti Ark. Ar. Böl., 1990), 72, 162–63.

[168] de Bernardi Ferrero, *Bati Anadolu'nun*, 72, 155–61; Bean, *Turkey Beyond the Maeander*, 247–57.

[169] Şimşek and Sezgın, "West and North Theatres," 122.

[170] Ibid., 123.

[171] Dated by de Bernardi Ferrero from the pattern of one of the stylized plant motifs found on a marble slab in the theater. de Bernardi Ferrero, *Teatri classici in Asia Minore III*, 151, fig. 227; *Bati Anadolu'nun*, 164, Fig. 227.

[172] Ramsay, Cities and Bishoprics, 1:49; Jean Ch Balty, Curia ordinis: Recherches d'architecture et d'urbanisme antiques sur les curies provinciales du monde romain (Bruxelles: Academie royale de Belgique, 1991), 531–32; Sear,

(r. AD 117–138; see Figs. 93, 109).[173] An inscription, with the name ΖΗΝΩΝΟΣ (*zēnōnos*) in large letters, perhaps mentioned the orator (*CIG* 3944).

THE SOUTH BATH-GYMNASIUM COMPLEX (NO. 5)

Just north of the stadium and south of the agora is the Bath-Gymnasium complex. This is the best preserved monument in Laodicea. The complex measures 436 ft (133 m) by 246 ft. (75 m) and features the "cascaded twin baths" style typical of the region. The facility serviced those athletes performing in the stadium.[174]

An inscription (*IGR* 4.848)[175] on the building was dedicated to Hadrian (see Figs. 93, 109) and his wife Sabina. Some scholars[176] associate this with their visit to Laodicea in AD 129.[177] However, the inscription also mentions the proconsul Gargilius Antiquus, who was the proconsul of Asia in ca. AD 134–135.[178] The inscription was likely erected during the Proconsulship of Antiquus, but commemorated an earlier visit of Hadrian and his wife.

149. The south Bath-Gymnasium complex arches at Laodicea, that is sometimes confused with an aqueduct.

Roman Theatres, 340.

[173] Şimşek, Ancient City of Laodicea, 20.

[174] Bruce, "Laodicea (Place)," 4:230; Wilson, *Biblical Turkey*, 254.

[175] Werner Eck, "Hadrian als pater patriae und die Verleihung des Augustatitels an Sabina," in Romanitas - Christianitas: Untersuchungen zur Geschichte und Literatur der römischen Kaiserzeit. Johannes Straub zum 70. Geburtstag am 18. Oktober 1982 gewidmet, ed. Gerhard Wirth (Berlin: De Gruyter, 1982), 223.

[176] Yamauchi, *NT Cities*, 140.

[177] Birley, *Hadrian*, 223; Thomas Witulski, "Die Aufenthalte Des Kaisers Hadrian in Der Römischen Provinz Asia," in *Paulus Und Die Antike Welt. Beiträge Zur Zeit- Und Religionsgeschichtlichen Erforschung Des Paulinischen Christentums*, ed. David C. Bienert, Joachim Jeska, and Thomas Witulski, 1st ed., Festgabe Für Dietrich-Alex Koch Zum 65. Geburtstag, FRLANT (Göttingen: Vandenhoeck & Ruprecht, 2008), 158–63; Huttner, *Early Christianity in the Lycus Valley*, 215 n.13.

[178] Eck, "Jahres- Und Provinzialfasten 1. Teil," 361; "Jahres- Und Provinzialfasten 2. Teil," 148–76; David E. Graves, "Governors of Judaea and New Discoveries," *BS* 30, no. 1 (Spring 2017): 1–17. Wilson dates the visit to AD 135 (*Biblical Turkey*, 254) although it is likely that their visit was commemorative and happened earlier since in 134 Hadrian returned to Rome suffering illness and lived at his villa near Tivoli. Ramsay places Gargilius porconsulship in AD 123–124, but indicates some debate on this period in his footnotes and it is now universally accepted in 134–35. Ramsay, *Cities and Bishoprics*, 1:47–48

CENTAL BATHS (NO. 16)

Located to the south of the central agora, the central bath complex covered a large area of 294 ft (89.6 m) by 189 ft (57.6 m) and contained a *caldarium* (hot bath), *tepidarium* (lukewarm bath), *frigidarium* (cold bath (see Fig. 110) and *apodyterium* (change room), while on the north side of the building, peculiar to Laodicea, there was a second *apodyterium* and *frigidarium*. A triple arched entrance was situated on the weatern side. It dates to the Roman period and was destroyed in the AD 494 earthquake, but was then used for various purposes until it was finally abandoned in the early seventh cent. AD.[179]

150. The Central Bath complex looking across the Lycus Valley to Hierapolis.

THE NECROPOLIS

The necropolis area of Laodicea had on all four of its sides the graves of wealthy citizens. They were buried closest to the city's four gates. The middle and lower class were located outside the main streets and in insignificant places. Şimşek identified the underground and above ground tombs (*Tumuli*) as follows: "The above-ground tomb types are: House-type Flat Roof, Temple, Podium Sarcophagus, and Sarcophagus placed at the door. The underground grave types are: Tumuli, Domed-Arcosolium, Hypogeium with Dromos, Chest Tomb (bond trough) and tile."[180] Among the items uncovered during excavations were burial gifts, and coins.[181]

THE COMMERCE OF LAODICEA

The city of Laodicea was a thriving commercial center known for its wine, worked marble production,[182] wool, textiles and eye medication. Facilitating these industries were the banking institutions, all of which made Laodicea a wealthy city in the Roman period.

MEDICAL CENTER AND OPHTHALMOLOGY

The Lycus Valley had a long history of healing associated with the gods Asclepios[183] and Apollo.[184] There were also associations of physicians at Ephesus[185] and Thyatira (*IGR* 4.1278),[186]

---

[179] Şimşek, *Ancient City of Laodicea*, 10.
[180] Şimşek, Bilgin, and Okunak, "Laodikeia Nekropolleri ve Mezar Tipleri," 111.
[181] Huttner, Early Christianity in the Lycus Valley, 24–25; Şimşek, Laodikeia 2013, 400–434.
[182] Şimşek and Sezgın, "West and North Theatres," 104 n.6.
[183] Adolf Hoffmann, "The Roman Remodeling of the Asklepieion," in *Pergamon-Citadel of the Gods: Archaeological Record, Literary Description, and Religious Development*, ed. Helmut Koester, HTS 46 (Harrisburg, Pa.: Trinity Press

along with several medical schools, including one at Smyrna (*I.Smyr.* 536–37)[187] and one near Laodicea.

The temple of *Mên Karou* in Gereli near Saraykӧye, 13 miles (21 km) northwest of Laodicea, is connected with the later establishment of a famous medical school that specialized in ophthalmology[188] which was established by Zeuxis (see Fig. 153). It became associated with Laodicea, and was celebrated on Laodicea coins (see Fig. 151).[189] Barclay believes that the medical school was *established* at the temple and then was *transferred* to Laodicea,[190] while Rudwick and Green assume it was always at the temple.[191] Strabo reports that:

151. Coin from *Laodikeia ad Lycum*. Struck under Augustus in 15 BC. Obv.: ΣΕΒΑΣΤΟΣ, (Sebastos) Augustus laureate head. Rev.: ZEUXIS FILALHQHS ΛΑΟΔΙΚΕΩΝ, (Zeuxis Philalethes of Laodicea). Zeus standing left, holding eagle and scepter (*RPC* 2894; *SNG* Cop. 555).

> Between Laodiceia and Carura is a temple of Mên Carus, as it is called, which is held in remarkable veneration. In my own time a great Herophileian school of medicine has been established by Zeuxis, and afterwards carried on by Alexander Philalethes, just as in the time of our fathers the Erasistrateian school[192] was established by Hicesius, although at the present time the case is not at all the same as it used to be.[193] (*Geogr.* 12.8.20 [Jones])

International, 1998), 41–61.

[184] Robert Ginouvès in Gagniers has collected twenty-five inscriptions from the Apollo shrine at Claros near Ephesus that attests to Laodicea consulting the orable of Apollo in Claros for healing and that list "prophets" of Apollo from Laodicea. Gagniers et al., *Laodicée du Lycos*, 298–303; Robert Flacelière, *Greek Oracles* (New York, N.Y: Beekman, 1980), 44–47.

[185] Broughton, "Roman Asia Minor," 851; Vivian Nutton, "The Medical Profession in the Roman Empire from Augustus to Justinian" (Ph.D. diss., University of Cambridge, 1970), 169–70; "Healers in the Medical Market Place: Towards a Social History of Graeco-Roman Medicine," in *Medicine in Society: Historical Essays*, ed. Andrew Wear (Cambridge, U.K.: Cambridge University Press, 1992), 42–43.

[186] Three generation of the Moschianos' family in Thyatira were civic doctors in Thyatira. Nutton, "The Medical Profession in the Roman Empire from Augustus to Justinian," 71, 76.

[187] Cadoux, *Ancient Smyrna*, 150–51.

[188] See Ralph P. J. Jackson, "Eye Medicine in the Roman Empire," in *ANRW II*, ed. Wolfgang Haase and Hildegard Temporini, vol. 37.3 (Berlin: De Gruyter, 1996), 2226–51.

[189] Vivian Nutton, "Theodas," in *BrillPaulyA*, ed. Hubert Cancik and Helmuth Schneider, trans. Christine F. Salazar and Francis G. Gentry (Leiden: Brill, 2006), op. cit., http://dx.doi.org/10.1163/1574-9347_bnp_e1207730.

[190] Barclay, *Revelation*, 1:151.

[191] Rudwick and Green, "The Laodicean Lukewarmness," 176; Sweet, *Revelation*, 118; Harrington, *Revelation*, 75.

[192] Jones' critical note states: "Erasistratus, the celebrated physician and anatomist, was born in the island of Ceos and flourished 300–260 BC."

[193] Jones' critical note states: "The Greek for this last clause is obscure and probably corrupt. Strabo means either that schools like the two mentioned 'no longer arise' or that one of the two schools mentioned (more probably the latter) 'no longer flourishes the same as before.' To ensure the latter thought, Meineke (from conj. of Corais) amends

Herophilus, one of the greatest Alexandrian physicians, practiced medicine near Laodicea, studying the optic nerve. His investigations were published in his important work entitled *On Eyes* (Strabo *Geogr.* 12.8.20). He was born at Chalcedon in Bithynia, and lived at Alexandria under Ptolemy I (r. 323–285 BC).[194] His work was carried on in the first cent. AD by Alexander Philalethes and his ophthalmologist student, Demosthenes Philalethes.[195] Demosthenes was known for his studies of the pulse, in addition to his significant work entitled *Ophthalmikós*, a lost work which was used by specialists in ophthalmology until the late Middle Ages (Aëtius of Amida *Medi.* 7.81).

In the early first cent. BC, Themison (Θεμίσων) of Laodicea was a physician[196] who founded the Methodic school of medicine (Celsus *Med.* 3.6; Galen *Meth. Med.* 10.1.4, 7).[197] Other physicians of influence from Laodicea include one of Zeuxis' students, Antiochus (Ἀντίοχος Λαοδικεύς, Diogenes *Vit. Phil.* 9.11.106; 9.12.116) and his student Theodas (Θεοδᾶς) or Theiodas Θειωδᾶς Λαοδικεύς, Galen *Meth. Med.* 2.142; Diogenes *Vit. Phil.* 9.12.116), who followed the Empirical school.[198] This is also documented by coins from the region that contain the names of the schools' leading physicians, Zeuxis and Philalethes (Ζευξισ Φιλαλήθους; see Figs. 136, 153 RPC 2893, 2894; 2898, = *SNG* Cop. 555), and depicting either the gods Asclepius (RPC 2893–2895) or Zeus.[199]

Galen, the famous physician of Pergamon (see Fig. 62), mentions a medical treatment of eye ailments (Aristides *Orat.* 39.15) consisting of a *dry collyrium* [κολλύριον] made from a Phrygian stone (Galen *San. Tu.* 6.12), and the use of a Laodicean nard (νάρδινον, *nardinon*) to treat ear ailments. He describes the treatment as:

> the eyes you will strengthen by using the *dry collyrium* [κολλύριον] made of Phrygian[200] stone,[201] applying the mixture to the eyelids without touching the membrane of the eye inside. For this is what women do every day, when they make their eyes glamorous. But for strengthening the ears,

the Greek text (see critical note)."

[194] Heinrich Von Staden, *Herophilus: The Art of Medicine in Early Alexandria: Edition, Translation and Essays* (Cambridge, U.K.: Cambridge University Press, 1989), 397–426.

[195] Ibid., 532–39. Vivian Nutton, "Demosthenes Philalethes Physician," in *BrillPaulyA*, ed. Hubert Cancik and Helmuth Schneider, trans. Christine F. Salazar and Francis G. Gentry (Leiden: Brill, 2006), 4:297–98, http://dx.doi.org/10.1163/1574-9347_bnp_e315480.

[196] Juvenal *Sat.* 10.221; *IGR* 4.1278; Pseudo-Galen *Introd.* 100.4.

[197] Willlam Alexander Greenhill, "Themison," in *Dictionary of Greek and Roman Biography and Mythology*, ed. William Smith, vol. 3 (Boston, Mass.: Little, Brown & Co., 1870), 1023–24.

[198] William Smith, "Theudas," in *Dictionary of Greek and Roman Biography and Mythology*, ed. William Smith, vol. 3 (Boston, Mass.: Little, Brown & Co., 1870), 1103; Nutton, "Theodas," op. cit.

[199] William Martin Leake, *A Supplement to Numismata Hellenica: A Catalogue of Greek Coins* (London, U.K.: John Murray, 1859), 63; Ramsay, *Letters: Updated*, 307–308, 317; Hemer, *Letters to the Seven Churches*, 179; Hemer, "Unto the Angels of the Churches," 189 n.34; Fant and Reddish, *Guide to Biblical Sites*, 233.

[200] Ramsay argued that "Phrygian" sometimes stood for "Laodicean" and was equivalent to it. Ramsay *Letters: Updated*, 309.

[201] The stone was ground into a powder or ash (Aristotle *Mir.* 58), mixed with water, and then applied to the eyes as a paste (Celsus *Med.* 6.6.2–8). Ramsay, *Cities and Bishoprics*, 1:52.

celandine alone is needed, pulverized on a stone with vinegar and then infused very gently through a tube, or through that familiar instrument called by all an ear-syringe. And when it seems to you that they are strengthened, so that nothing more runs from them, continue to instill the best *ripe nard* (μύρον νάρδινον *muron nardinon*), formerly made best only in *Laodicea* in Asia, but now also in other cities. (*San. Tu.* 6.12 [Green] emphasis added)

Ramsay argued that "Phrygian" sometimes stood for "Laodicean" and was equivalent to it.[202] While the Phrygian region was known for the production of a mineral that was used for eye treatments and a nard (νάρδινον, *nardinon*), associated with Laodicea, for the treatment of ear, liver or stomach inflammations (Galen *Comp. Med.* 13.119; *Meth. Med.* 10.791), Koester stresses that the "salves were not tied to specific medical schools" (Pliny *Nat.* 34.108; Arrian *Diatr.* 3.21.20–21) or to Laodicea.[203] However, Hemer points out that the direct connection between eye-salve and Laodicea is circumstantial,[204] though states "there are independent grounds for locating an advanced and specialized ophthalmology at Laodicea".[205] A number of the active ingredients mentioned by ancient writers, including copper, zinc, alum, metallic salts and several herbal drugs (Pliny *Nat.* 35.52.186), are known to be elements in the hotsprings of Hierapolis and surrounding region,[206] and used in various modern eye ointments.[207]

John used the same Greek term κολλύριον (*kollurion*; cf. Rev 3:18) for the Phrygian eye-salve as did Galen (*San. Tu.* 6.12),[208] Celsus (*Med.* 6.6.2–8) and Horace (*Sat.* 1.5.30–31). According to Arrian, Epictetus of Hierapolis also used the term twice in his writings (Arrian *Diatr.* 2.21.20; 3.21.20–22). Collyrium was formed into an ointment stick that was designed to be rubbed on the eyes. As Nielsen, an expert on ancient eye medications points out:

> As time went on, the term "collyrium" came to designate all eye disease remedies, prescritions being given [by physicians] also for the production of liquid collyria and collyria resembling fish scales, but the prescriptions for ointment sticks were still predominant.[209]

Oculist stamps were used by eye doctors and producers of eye-salve to identify their goods and some 300 are known from the Roman period,[210] many of which bore the name κολλύριον (*kollurion*).

---

[202] Ramsay *Letters: Updated*, 309.

[203] Koester, "Message to Laodicea," 419; *Revelation*, 339.

[204] Hemer, Letters to the Seven Churches, 197.

[205] Hemer, "Unto the Angels of the Churches," 189 n.43.

[206] Ramsay, Cities and Bishoprics, 1:106; Hemer, Letters to the Seven Churches, 198–99.

[207] Henry Beasley, *The Druggist's General Receipt Book, Etc.* (London, U.K.: Churchill, 1850), 92; Julius Hirschberg, *The History of Ophthalmology*, trans. Frederick C. Blodi and D. L. Blanchard (Amsterdam: Wayenborgh, 1982), 1: § 11.

[208] Richard J. Durling, *A Dictionary of Medical Terms in Galen*, Studies in Ancient Medicine, Monumenta Graeca Et Romana 5 (Leiden: Brill, 1993), 207.

[209] Harald Nielsen, Ancient Ophthalmological Agents: A Pharmaco-Historical Study of the Collyria and Seals for Collyria Used during Roman Antiquity, as Well as of the Most Frequent Components of the Collyria, trans. Lars McBride, Acta Historica Scientiarum Naturalium et Medicinalium 31 (Odense, Denmark: Odense University Press, 1974), 100.

[210] Jacques Voinot, *Les cachets à collyres dans le monde romain*, Monographies instrumentum 7 (Montagnac: Mergoil, 1999).

According to the Acts of Philip (ca. AD 400), the apostle Philip and his companions Mariamme and Bartholomew arrived in Ophioryme (Hierapolis) to set up a "medical practice" (ἰατρεῖον, *hiatreiron*) to treat the sick in the city (*Acts Phil.* 13.4). Blind Stachys, a high priest of the serpents (which were venerated in Laodicea), and a former enemy of Christians, approached the apostle Philip for healing. The poultice of fluid from serpent eggs – a common remedy for eye ailments (Celsus *Med.* 6.6.12), and one that he had already tried – only inflamed his problem. Following the death of his wife, who had been treating him, he became totally blind. After seeking the apostle Philip's help, he was cured of his blindness.

TEXTILE INDUSTRY AND WOOL

Laodicea was famous for its textile industry, consisting of professional *collegia* of linenweavers (*CIG* 3504); dyers (*CIG* 3422, 3496, 3497), tailors (*CIG* 3480), and leatherworkers and shoemakers (*BCH* 10 [1866], 422). The city also specialised in purple and black textiles.[211] The purple textiles were made from dyed purple cloths for which the region was famous, as mentioned in Acts with reference to Lydia the seller of purple (πορφυρόπωλις, *porphuropōlis*; Acts 16:14;[212] Homer *Il.* 4.141–42),[213] and the black cloth was produced from a specific Laodicean black wool characteristic in the Lycus Valley (Strabo *Geogr.* 3.2.6).[214] Strabo reports that:

152. Reconstruction of a vertical loom with genuine loom weights and string heddles, National museum of textile industry, Sliven, Bulgaria. Similar loom weights have been excavated at Laodicea (Şimşek, "Textile," 139).

> Laodicea, though formerly small, grew large in our time and in that of our fathers, even though it had been damaged by siege in the time of Mithridates Eupator. However, it was the fertility of its territory and the prosperity of certain of its citizens that made it

---

[211] Strabo *Geogr.* 12.8.16; Vitruvius *Arch.* 8.3.14; Pliny *Nat.* 8.73.190.

[212] Lydia from Thyatira (Acts 16:14), lived in Philippi as a πορφυρόπωλις, (*porphuropōlis*) widely translated as a seller of purple (πορφύρα, Lat. *purpurarius/a*) cloth, but probably learned her textile business (*IGR* 4.1252; *CIG* 3496–8; λανάριοι, *lanarioi*, Lat. *lanarii carminatores,* dyers]) in Thyatira. Magie, *Roman Rule in Asia Minor*, 1:47–48; 2:812 n.79; Keener, *Acts: 15:1–23:35*, 3:3:2399–2407; Calpino, "Lydia of Thyatira's Call," 199–203. Inscriptional references to λανάριοι (*lanrioi*) include *CIL* 5.4501; 4504; 4505; 6.9489; 9490; 9491; 9492; 9493; 9494; 9669; 31898; 33869; 38869; 9.826; 2226; 10.5678; 11.741; 862; 1031; 5835; 6367; 12.4480; 4481; *I.Eph.* 1.1387; 2.454; 3.727; *TAM V* 1.85; 2.1019.

[213] Graves, "What Is The Madder With Lydia's Purple?," 1–47.

[214] Ramsay, *Cities and Bishoprics*, 1:40–42; Ramsay, *Letters: Updated*, 307; Hemer, *Letters to the Seven Churches*, 199–201; Hatice Erdemir, "Woollen Textiles: An International Trade Good in the Lycus Valley in Antiquity," in *Colossae in Space and Time: Linking to an Ancient City*, ed. Alan H. Cadwallader and Michael Trainor, NTOA SUNT (Göttingen: Vandenhoeck & Ruprecht, 2011), 104–29; Celal Şimşek, "Textile and Production Ateliers in Laodikeia," *Home Textile* 86 (2015): 138–41.

great... The country round Laodicea produces sheep that are excellent, not only for the softness of their wool, in which they surpass even the Milesian wool, but also for its raven-black colour (cf. Strabo *Geogr.* 3.2.6), so that the Laodiceians derive splendid revenue from it, as do also the neighbouring Colosseni from the colour which bears the same name [i.e., the "Colossian" wool, dyed purple or madder-red (see Pliny *Nat.* 25.9.67; 21.9.27)]." (Strabo *Geogr.* 12.8.16 [Jones]).

The textile guild in Laodicea of weavers or garment makers (ἀπλουργοί, *aplourgoi*) is mentioned in an undated inscription (*CIG* 3938).[215] One of the associations was called "The Most August Guild of the Wool Washers" (*IJO* 2.40).[216] The export of textiles and wool from Laodicea and the Lycus Valley[217] is attested in Diocletian's *Edict of Maximum Prices* (AD 301 AD; *CIL* 3, Suppl. 1910–53), where Laodicea is named as one of the chief textile centers,[218] and in the *Expositio totius mundi*, where it is stated "its [Phrygia's] chief city [Lat. *maxima civitas*] is called Laodicia [*sic.* Laodicea], and it exports the only fur [i.e., wool] which is named thus: Laodician [*Laodicina*]."[219] The *Edict* set out the wages in Laodicea for embroiderers (gold brocade and embroidery),[220] silk workers (*Edict. Diocl.* § 20:1–12) and wool weavers, who made repairs to warm clothing and soft-finished cloth (ranged from 40–750 denarii, *Edict. Diocl.* § 21.1–12).

Laodicea's association with textiles involves not only trade, but also specific garments were made there. Various quality linen garments were produced in Laodicea (*Edict. Diocl.* § 26.16, 21, 26, 37, 42, 47), where there was a *collegia* of linenweavers (*CIG* 3504), along with various woollen garments of first, second and third quality (see chart below). An inscription from Laodicea mentioned a seller of garments (εἱματιοπώλης, *eimatiopōlēs*; *BCH* 11 [1887], 352), the artisans were noted for their production of *phainoula* (φαίνουλα, *Edict. Diocl.* § 19.51), a woollen outer rain garment embroidered with silk and gold, imitated from garments from Modena (Mutina) in Italy, and likely similar to *paenulae*, a woollen hooded cloak or cape (φαινόλη, *phainole* in Arrian *Diatr.* 4.8.34; Pliny *Nat.* 8.73.190; and φελόνη, *phelone* in 2 Tim 4:13).[221]

The following chart describes the textiles, listed in Diocletian's *Edict of Maximum Prices*, that were made in Laodicea or from their products.

---

[215] On the meaning of ἀπλουργοί (*aplourgoi*), cf. Kai Ruffing, "Städtische Wirtschaftspolitik Im Hellenistisch-Römischen Kleinasien? Zur Funktion Der Emporia," in *Staatlichkeit Und Politisches Handeln in Der Römischen Kaiserzeit*, Millennium Studien 10 (Berlin: De Gruyter, 2006), 133; Ulrich R. Huttner, "Die Färber von Laodikeia Und Hierapolis. Eine Nachricht Aus Dem Corpus Der Alchemisten," *MBAH* 26 (2008): 141–43.

[216] Ramsay, Cities and Bishoprics, 1.118 no.26; Jones, Cities of the Eastern Roman Provinces, 73; Jeffers, Greco-Roman World of the NT Era, 269; Erdemir, "Woollen Textiles," 114.

[217] On the importance of textile production in the Lycus valley, cf. Erdemir, "Woollen Textiles," 104–29.

[218] *I.Laod.* 50 = *CIG* 3.3938 = *IGR* 4.863.

[219] Jesse Earle Woodman, "The Expositio Totius Mundi et Gentium: Its Geography and Its Language" (M.A. diss., The Ohio State University, 1964), 36; Tibor Grüll, "Expositio totius mundi et gentium. A peculiar work on the commerce of Roman Empire from the mid-fourth century – compiled by a Syrian textile dealer?," in *Studies in Economic and Scoail History of the Ancient Near East in Memory of Péter Vargyas*, ed. Zoltán Csabai, Ancient Near Eastern and Mediterranean Studies 2 (Budapest: Department of Ancient History, University of Pécs & L'Harmattan, 2014), 636.

[220] Phrygia was believed by the ancients to have invented embroidery (Pliny *Nat.* 8.84.195–96).

[221] Ramsay, Cities and Bishoprics, 1:41.

Textile	Greek name	Price in denarii	Edict. Diocl. §
Birros: woollen hooded cloak or cape	βίρρος, *birros* or *birrus*[222]	4,500	7.42; 19.26; 22.21 = CIL 3.831; HA Carin. 20.4
Birros: an imitation after the French region of Nervii	βίρρος, *birros* or *birrus*	10,000	19.27
Dalmatic: large sleeved tunic (*trimitia*) with wide stripes (clavi)	δελματικῶν, *delmatikōn*[223] τρίμιτος, *trimitos*	2,000	19.28; IG V,1 1115. 15, 24; IG IX,1 118 (AD 301)
Dalmatic: women's unmarked	δελματικῶν, *delmatikōn*	8,000	26.37
Dalmatic: men's unmarked	δελματικῶν, *delmatikōn*	7,500	26.42
Laodikeian fibulatoria: a woollen cloak either with or without purple bands and with a clasp	φιβουλατώριον, *fiboulalōrion*	4,000	19.16
Paenulae: hooded cape	φαινόλη, *phainole*	5,000	19.51
Stichai: shirts, unmarked	στίχαι, *stichai*	4,500	19.16
Paragauda: purple bordered tunic	παραγαῦδιν, *paragaudin*	value of the purple	19.29
Colobia: short-sleeved tunic for men and women	κολοβίων, *colobiōn*	5,000–7,500	26.39, 49, 62

---

[222] William Smith and J. F. Flather, "Birrus," in *DGRA*, ed. William Smith (London, U.K.: Murray, 1890), 1:299; Alfred Holder, *Alt-Celtischer Sprachschatz* (Leipzig: Teubner, 1896), 1:425; Ramsay, *Cities and Bishoprics*, 1:40–41.

[223] J. F. Flather, "Dalmatica," in *DGRA*, ed. William Smith (London, U.K.: Murray, 1890), 1:594.

Embroidered silk work on a *chlanis* a light cloak, resembling one from Mutina, Italy	χλανίς, *chlanis*	1 ounce = 25	20.4
Anabolaia: linen wraps	αναβόλαις, *anabolais*	3,000–5,500	26.78, 81, 86, 91
Phakialia: linen face cloths	φακιαλίων, *phakialiōn*	1,500–2,250	26.99, 102, 107, 112; P.Oxy. 7.1026.4
Caracallae: linen hoods	καρακάλλων, *karakallōn*	1,750–2,250	26.120, 123, 128, 133; IG V,1 1115.157 (AD 301)
Linen pocket handkerchiefs	σκυτοπολιτάνων, *skutopolitanōn*	400–600	27.8, 11, 16, 21
Phaskias: linen bands	φασκίνια, *phaskinia*	1,400–1,700	28.37
Bed linens	σινδόνων κοιταρίων, *sindonōn koitariōn*	?–5,250	28.16, 19, 24, 29, 37

Table 8. Textiles produced in Laodicea according to Diocletian's *Edict of Maximum Prices*.

Laodicea also produced small and cheap upper garments, called *himatia* (ἱμάτιον; diminutive of ἱειμα, *heima* meaning dress)[224] that were sometimes worn as an outer garment.[225] A fragmentary inscription from Laodicea mentions Fullers (clothes cleaners, Lat. *fullones* or *haplourgoi*), who made one-piece garments (*chlamvdes simplices* equivalent to *haplous; Expositio totius mundi* § 142) and a clothes market or hall (*emporion*).[226]

Vitruvius recounts that the reason for the softness and black color (*coracino colore*) of the wool was due to the water from the hot springs (*Arch.* 8.3.14). The production system of the dying and wool facility at Laodicea, based on archaeology, is depicted in a drawing by Şimşek in the magazine *Home Textile*.[227] The soft jet-black, glossy wool[228] produced in the region[229] was woven into various garments used in Laodicea and valued for export. Laodicean textiles were

---

[224] Cf. Matt 9:20; 17:2; 21:7–8; 26:65; 27:31, 35; Mark 9:3; 11:7–8; 15:20, 24; Luke 19:35–36; 23:34; John 13:4, 12; 19:23–24; Acts 7:58; 9:39; 14:14; 16:22; 18:6; 22:20, 23; Jas 5:2; Rev 3:4; 3:18; 16:15.

[225] H. Weigelt, "Clothe, Naked, Dress, Garment, Cloth," ed. Colin Brown, *NIDNTT* (Grand Rapids, Mich.: Zondervan, 1976), 1:316–17.

[226] Harry W. Pleket, "Models and Inscriptions: Export of Textiles in the Roman Empire," *EA* 30 (1998): 125.

[227] Şimşek, "Textile," 144.

[228] Hemer recounts several nineteenth and twentieth cent. travelers who testify to the black sheep and wool, but admits that he could not confirm the black color of the product (Hemer, *Letters to the Seven Churches*, 200, 281 n. 92).

[229] Strabo *Geogr.* 12.8.16; Vitruvius *Arch.* 8.3.14; Pliny *Nat.* 8.73.190.

exported as far away as Gaul and Africa.[230] A first-cent. AD inscription on a mausoleum mentions a merchant named Titus Flavius Zeuxis from Hireopolis who took 72 trips around Kap Malea to Italy, apparently to sell garments (*CIG* 3.3920; see Fig. 153).

The *trimitia* (τρίμιτια, τρίμιτος; *Edict. Diocl.* § 19.28, cf. *IGR* 3.228), a tunic, was reportedly so famous, that it replaced Laodicea as the name of Laodicea with *Trimitaria* as the name of the city, being listed in the Council of Chalcedon (§ 209; AD 451),[231] and in later documents.[232] Laodicea gave its name to the blankets or rugs called *lodices*,[233] which were apparently first made there and then exported or imitated throughout the world.[234]

153. The tomb of Flavius Zeuxis at Hierapolis.

It is known that Laodicea had a strong trade relationship with Ephesus, Pergamum, Smyrna, Sardis, Aphrodisias, etc. from their common pressed *homonoia* coins and their strategic location on the major trade routes. Access to the port of Ephesus allowed for Laodicea to export by ship to the whole ancient world, especially to the island of Samos (Sisam), Athens and Italy without involving a intermediary.

THE FINANCIAL WORLD AT LAODICEA

Laodicea's wealth was acquired via its textile industry and from its position acting as a medical center. This helped the city become a leading banking center, where Roman officials and tax collectors kept funds. This is attested to by Cicero in his correspondence with his friends, when he refers to the city's significant banking assets.[235] On the 27 or 28th of July 51 BC, Cicero wrote to his friend Appius Claudius Pulcher, proconsul in Cilicia, (a man depicted on Laodicean coins),[236] remarking that perhaps he could cash his letters of credit in the city. He stated, "I expect to reach Laodicea on 31 July. I shall stay only a very few days, to collect the sum due on my Treasury draft." (*Fam.* 68.3.5.4 [Shackleton-Bailey]; see also *Att.* 5.15, 21; 6.2). Then in a letter to Gnaeus Sallustius Proquaestor of Syria dated 18 July 50 BC, Cicero reported:

---

[230] J. Rougé, "Un Negotiator Laudecenarius À Lyon," *Zeitschrift Für Papyrologie Und Epigraphik* 27 (1977): 263–69.
[231] Price and Gaddis, *The Acts of the Council of Chalcedon*, 145, 167, 230, 278, 348.
[232] Ramsay, Cities and Bishoprics, 1:41; Letters: Updated, 307.
[233] Martial *Epig.* 14.128; Pliny *Nat.* 8.191, 193; *P.Ryl.* 2.189; P.Oxy. 19.2230. Jennifer A. Sheridan, *Columbia Papyri IX: The Vestis Militaris Codex*, SFSHJ (Atlanta, Ga: Scholars Press, 1998), 83; Jinyu Liu, *Collegia Centonariorum: The Guilds of Textile Dealers in the Roman West*, Columbia Studies in the Classical Tradition 34 (Brill, 2009), 113 n.68.
[234] Grüll, "Expositio totius mundi et gentium," 636.
[235] Morris, *Revelation*, 83–84.
[236] Head, Historia Numorum, 678.

> It would not have been correct for me to send you my Quaestor's accounts, and in any case they are not ready. I intend to deposit them at Apamea. Not a penny of my booty has been or will be touched by any person except the City Quaestors, which is to say the Roman People. I propose to take *sureties [vasarium] at Laodicea for all public moneys*, so that both the state and I myself may be insured against transport risks. (Cicero *Fam.* 117.4 [Shackleton-Bailey] emphasis added)

In 62 BC, Flaccus, the governor of Asia, confiscated 20 Roman pounds of gold (7,500 to 9,000 half-shekels)[237] from the Jewish population living in Laodicea to be sent to Jerusalem as the temple tax (Cicero *Flac.* 68),[238] though later, following the destruction and plundering of the temple in Jerusalem in AD 70, this would no longer be necessary. Collection of these funds demonstrates that a large population of wealthy Jews lived in Laodicea. Strabo also testified to Laodicea's economic prosperity at the beginning of the first cent. AD:

154. Votive stele of *Zeus Ktesios Patrios* from Laodicea holding a shepherd's staff in his left hand and an eagle in his right hand.

> Laodiceia, though formerly small, grew large in our time and in that of our fathers, even though it had been damaged by siege in the time of Mithridates Eupator. However, it was the fertility of its territory and the prosperity of certain of its citizens that made it great: at first Hieron, who left to the people an inheritance of more than two thousand talents and adorned the city with many dedicated offerings. . . . The country round Laodiceia produces sheep that are excellent, not only for the softness of their wool, in which they surpass even the Milesian wool, but also for its raven-black colour, so that the Laodiceians derive splendid revenue from it, as do also the neighbouring Colosseni from the colour which bears the same name. (*Geogr.* 12.8.16)

Tacitus records that, following the earthquake of AD 60, t in which the city was ruined, Laodicea "recovered by its own resources, without assistance from ourselves [ie. from the Romans]" (*Ann.* 14.27.1 [Jackson]). Inscriptions found in Laodicea from the late first cent. testify that the rebuilding was supported in large part by local benefactors who funded a new gate, stadium and public water works at their own expense (ἐκ τῶν ἰδίων; *ek tōn idiōn*),[239] although – as Koester points out – this was not a practice unique to Laodicea, as demonstrated by the abundant demonstrated inscriptions uncovered throughout the Roman Empire, including Asia Minor.[240]

The wealth of Laodicea is attested by the common use of the griffin motif. The mythical griffin was "a fabulous, bird-like species of animal, dwelling in the Rhipaean mountains,

---

[237] Fant and Reddish, *Guide to Biblical Sites*, 233.

[238] Mitchell, *Anatolia*, 2:33.

[239] *I.Laod.* 9.9; 12; 15.3; 13; 24; *CIG* 3935 = *IGR* 4.845.

[240] Cf. *I.Eph.* 1a.20.10; 2.422; 7.3008; *I.Smyr.* 599.7; 643.6–7; 22.4–5; *I.Perg.* 2.402.2; 3.47.7; etc. Koester, "Message to Laodicea," 417.

between the Hyperboreans and the one-eyed Arimaspians, and guarding the gold of the north"[241] and the gold of India (Philostratus *Vit. Apoll.* 3.48). The griffin is found on coins[242] from Laodicea, and some more have been found inside a wreath on one of the columns of the temple of Apollo (A) with the Latin inscription under it, reading *VOTIS XX* (the vows or prayers for twenty years of rule, *Votis Vicennalibus;* see Fig. 160).[243] The griffin imagery and inscriptions of the column conveyed the message of long life for the emperor, and protection for the wealth of Laodicea.

However, while it was a banking center in the first cent. BC and continued to be a judicial center in the first cent. AD (Pliny *Nat.* 5.105), Koester, citing Magie, points out that "the city's importance for finance in the first century CE is unclear, since methods of tax collection changed, and communities began sending funds directly to the quaestor of the province."[244]

The Religious Community of Laodicea

The Gods of Laodicea

As with all Roman cities there were many deities venerated in Laodicea. This is attested to by many coins and inscriptions. Here follows a list of the Laodicea's gods.

1. Within the Phrygian region the early nomadic tribes worshiped the mother goddess *Cybele* (or *Kybele*), the patron goddess of Lydia (Herodotus *Hist.* 5.102; Euripides *Bacch.* 55, 65 [462–3]), and Mother of the Mountains. She is portrayed on coins between two lions (*BMC Phrygia* 319.236; 319.236). They gathered in open-air sanctuaries situated in the rocky countryside.[245]

2. Not only was Rome personified and worshiped in the imperial cult at Laodicea (see *Imperial Cult* below), but they also personified and worshiped the city itself as *Ladicia Sacrum*, portrayed on coins with a turreted headress.[246] The city appointed a "Priest of the City" (ἱεράτευσέν [τε] τες πόλεως, *hierateusen [te] tes poleōs*)[247] to encourage and facilitate her worship among Laodicean

---

[241] Leonhard Schmitz, "Gryps or Gryphus," in *Dictionary of Greek and Roman Biography and Mythology*, ed. William Smith, vol. 2 (Boston, Mass.: Little, Brown & Co., 1870), 315.

[242] Ramsay, Cities and Bishoprics, 1:51.

[243] Huttner, *Early Christianity in the Lycus Valley*, 54–55; Celal Şimşek, *Laodikeia (Laodicea Ad Lycum) 2007* (Istanbul: Ege Yayinlari, 2007), 232; *Laodikeia 2013*, 464. For a photo of the column, see http://holylandphotos.org/browse.asp?s = 1,3,7,23,598&img = TWSCLDRS11. The Latin *VOTIS XX* is also depicted inside a wreath on coins from Constantine I (AD 306–337). Stevenson, *A Dictionary of Roman Coins*, 908.

[244] Koester, *Revelation*, 338; Magie, *Roman Rule in Asia Minor*, 1:165, 407.

[245] Celal Şimşek, "Regional Cults In The Lycos Valley And Its Neighbourhood," in *Altan Çilingiroğlu'na Armağan Yukarı Denizin Kıyısında Urartu Krallığı'na Adanmış Bir Hayat*, ed. Haluk Sağlamtimur et al. (Istanbul: Arkeoloji ve Senat Yayinlari, 2009), 673.

[246] *BMC Phrygia* 291.82–84; 292.92–93; 317.228–229; 285.40–47.

[247] *CIG* 3936; *I.Laod.* 4b.9; 8.1; 53.3; 83.13–14; 85.14; 132.

citizens.[248] This is also attested by the recent discovery of a bas relief on column A of *Laodikeia* or *Forturna* (Gr. *Tyche*, Τύχη; see below) wearing a turreted crown within a wreath, and having a Latin inscription underneath that reads *LADICIA SACRUM* (*Laodikeia sacred;* see Fig. 155).[249]

3. *Zeus* (Ζεύς; see Figs. 95, 115, 126, 151, 154, 156) was the patron god of the city, worshiped under the name of *Zeus Aseis* (BMC Phrygia 311.201) and *Zeus Laodikeus*, sometimes portrayed on coins with an eagle and cornucopia (Lat. *cornucopiae;* BMC Phrygia 286.48), while most of the time with an eagle and scepter.[250] The city was originally named *Diospolis* meaning "the city of Zeus" (Pliny *Nat.* 5.105). As the greatest of the Olympian Greek gods, Zeus was normally called "the father of gods and men" (Homer *Od.* 1.22), however, in the Lycus valley he was worshiped as "the defender father of the shepherds"*(MAMA* 6.87), sometimes under the name of *Zeus Ktesios Patrios* (see Fig. 154, 157).[251] The title is documented on an altar from Herakleia Salbace exhibited in the

155. The middle wreath on column A with the relief of Laodicea (Fortuna/Tyche) with a turreted crown representing the city wall of Laodicea. The Latin inscription reads *LADICIA SACRUM* translated as "Laodicea Scared".

156. Coin from *Laodikeia ad Lycum*. Struck under Antoninus Pius (AD 138–161). Obv.: ΔΗΜΟC ΛΑΟΔΙΚΕΩΝ, laureate and draped bust of Demos. Rev.: Inscription ΠΟ (ligate)-[Α]Λ ΑΙΟC-ΔΙΟΝΥCΙΟC CABINIA-NOC. transliteration P. Aelius Dionysius Sabinianus, magistrate. *Zeus Laodiceus* standing, holding an eagle in his outstretched right hand and cradling a scepter in his left arm (Imhoof KM 28 = SNGvA 2.3820).

---

[248] Bean, Turkey Beyond the Maeander, 215; Koester, Revelation, 330.
[249] Huttner, *Early Christianity in the Lycus Valley*, 54–55; Şimşek, *Laodikeia 2007*, 232; *Laodikeia 2013*, 464. For a photo of the column, see http://holylandphotos.org/browse.asp?s = 1,3,7,23,598&img = TWSCLDRS25.
[250] BMC Phrygia 289.70 318.231; 293.94–95; 294.101; 296.109; 297.114; 300.138; 302.147; 303.159; 311.209. Bean, *Turkey Beyond the Maeander*, 215; Ramsay, *Cities and Bishoprics*, 1:34, 52; Yamauchi, *NT Cities*, 143.
[251] Şimşek reports that "The only difference between *Zeus Laodikeus* and *Zeus Ktesios Patrios* is the lack of the thin, curled wool clothing as underwear." (see Fig.) Şimşek, "Regional Cults," 680; Robert Fleischer, "Ein Heiligtum Für Apollon, Artemis Und Leto Bei Heracleia Salbace in Karien," *Archäologischer Anzeiger*, 2000, 421; "Ein Unbekanntes Heiligtum Für Apollon, Artemis Und Leto in Der Südwestlichen Turkei," *Antike Welt* 33 (2002): 330.

Hierapolis Archaeological Museum (see Fig. 157).²⁵² Zeus is depicted in the region dressed as a shepherd holding a staff, wearing the local thick woollen garments with his right shoulder bare (see Figs. 95, 151). Although, some suggest that Temple A is the temple of Zeus, Şimşek has identified Temple A with Apollo (see *Apollo* below).²⁵³ However, a sculpture of Zeus was discovered during his excavations between 2002–2011.²⁵⁴ While in passing Şimşek mentioned that the temple of Zeus has been recognized, he does not indicate its location,²⁵⁵ although an inscription states that there was a white pavement in front of the temple paid for by Q. Pomponius Flaccus.²⁵⁶

157. Marble altar to *Zeus Ktesios Patrios* from Herakleia Salbace.

4. Veneration of *Apollo*, son of Zeus, is attested on the coins of the city (*BMC Phrygia* 288.61). The temple of *Apollo* was prominent in the city, attested to by both the size of the temple (see *Temple A* above) and a column (B) with the figure of Apollo and Latin inscription reading *APOLLINI SACRUM* (*Apollo sacred*; see Fig. 160 top inscription),²⁵⁷ along with twenty-five inscriptions at the Apollo temple at Claros,²⁵⁸ north of Ephesus, referring to "prophets" of Apollo from Laodicea who consulted the oracle of Apollo at Claros.²⁵⁹

5. *Mên* (Μήν) was the regional moon god, also called *Mên Karou* or *Mên-of-the-Carians*.

158. Coin from *Laodicea ad Lycum*. Obv.: Domitian, with Domitia (AD 81–96). Cornelius Dioscurides, magistrate. Bust of Domitian, laureate, draped, and cuirassed, and Domitia, draped. Rev.: Hera standing, holding a scepter and pomegranate, facing *Zeus Laodiceus*, holding eagle and scepter, and Athena, holding olive branch, spear, and shield, both standing. (*RPC* 2.1283; BMC 186).

---

²⁵² Louis Robert and Jeanne Robert, *La Carie: histoire et géographie historique avec le recueil des inscriptions antiques* (Paris, France: Adrien-Maisonneuve, 1954), 165 no. 42; Celal Şimşek, "Hierapolis Güney Nekropolü, Konya" (Ph.D. diss., Konya, Selçuk University, Institute of Social Sciences, 1997), 64 no. 177; "Regional Cults," 680, 689 n.17.

²⁵³ Şimşek, "Temple of Athena Found in Laodicea," n.p.

²⁵⁴ Celal Şimşek, "Laodicea Becoming New Ephesus," *Hurriot Daily News*, December 7, 2011, n.p.

²⁵⁵ As of the writing of this commentary the author has been unable to locate the exact location of the Temple of Zeus. However, with the ongoing work at Laodicea by Şimşek it will likely be identified in the future.

²⁵⁶ Ramsay, *Cities and Bishoprics*, 1:50; Gagniers et al., *Laodicée du Lycos*, 275.

²⁵⁷ Huttner, Early Christianity in the Lycus Valley, 54–55; Şimşek, Laodikeia 2007, 232; Laodikeia 2013, 464.

²⁵⁸ Flacelière, *Greek Oracles*, 44–47.

²⁵⁹ Gagniers et al., *Laodicée du Lycos*, 298–303; Bruce, "Laodicea (Place)," 4:230; Yamauchi, *NT Cities*, 145.

The temple was situated in Gereli[260] near Sarayköye, 13 miles (21 km) northwest of Laodicea, and connected to a medical school either there or in Laodicea (See *Medical Center and Ophthalmology* above). His standard symbol was the cresent moon, something often depicted on coins.[261] *Mên* was frequently depicted wearing traditional regional attire, including a "Phrygian cap, trousers, boots, and cloak, and with a crescent moon at his shoulders."[262] He is commonly depicted standing with either a cock or bull.[263] Ramsay argued that Apollo, Asklepios, and Zeus Laodiceus were local Hellenistic manifestations of the local *Mên Karou*.[264] However each of these deities are represented on coins with their own unique attributes and do not indicate any kind of assimilation.[265] *Mên* was also worshiped at three of the other seven cities, including Sardis, Smyrna, and Pergamum.[266]

159. The third cent. AD votive stele of Zeus Laodiceus from İcikli in Baklan, Denizli, in which he is portrayed as a shepherd.

6. *Artemis* (Gr. *Diana;* see Figs. 26, 27, 121, 124, 127)[267] was also worshiped in Temple A (*I.Laod.* 5.36), where recently a statue of the goddess was discovered. Also, a broken column (A) from the temple was excavated with the bas relief bust of Artemis, wearing a turreted headdress, with a partial Latin inscription underneath that reads, *???E SACRUM* (not shown).[268] A

---

[260] Since the bust of Mên has the legend *MHN KAPOV* on coins from Attouda (*SNG München* 185), the sanctuary is assumed to have been associated with this city 16 miles (26 km) west of Laodicea. Huttner, *Early Christianity in the Lycus Valley*, 171.

[261] G. H. R Horsley, "Expiation and the Cult of Men," in *New Documents Illustrating Early Christianity*, ed. G. H. R. Horsley and Stephen R. Llewelyn, vol. 3, NewDocs (Grand Rapids, Mich.: Eerdmans, 1983), 21.

[262] Eugene N. Lane, "Men: A Neglected Cult of Roman Asia Minor," in *ANRW*, II.18.3 (Berlin: De Gruyter, 1990), 2161. *BMC Phrygia* 288.64; 289.68; 293.97.

[263] Ibid.

[264] Ramsay, *Cities and Bishoprics*, 1:52–53.

[265] Gagniers et al., *Laodicée du Lycos*, 290–91; Yamauchi, *NT Cities*, 145.

[266] Lane, "Men," 2161–62.

[267] The reference to Laodicea in *Historia Augusta* that is sometimes quoted for "the emblem of Diana, from its holy place at Laodicea, where it had been dedicated by Orestes" (*HA Elag.* 17.8.4–5) is for the Laodicea (now *Latakiyeh*) on the Syrian coast. See critical footnote in David Magie, trans., *Historia Augusta: Elagabalus,* vol. 2, 3 vols., LCL 140 (Cambridge, Mass.: Harvard University Press, 1924), 121 n.1.

[268] The name of the deity has been defaced and one wonders if it may have been removed when the temple was used as a Christian church (see *Temple A* above). For a photo of the column, see

second wreath below it contained two stags, the emblem of Artemis, with the Latin inscription *VOTIS XX* (*Votis Vicennalibus;* "the vows or prayers for twenty years of rule" not shown).²⁶⁹ The middle register on column B also bears the inscription *VOTIS XX* below two griffins (see Fig. 160, middle inscription). Some of the coins display Artemis in her Ephesian style flanked by two stags,²⁷⁰ while other coins portray her as the typical huntress with turreted headress and bow and arrow (*BMC Phrygia* 278.1).

7. *Tyche* (Τύχη, also called Cybele, Lat. *Fortūna*, see Figs. 52, 54, 98, 108, 160) is the goddess of good fortune often represented on Laodicean coinage standing holding a rudder, with ears of corn and cornucopiae.²⁷¹ A bas relief of Tyche in a wreath was recently discovered on column B during excavations of Temple A. Below the relief was a Latin inscription that reads *FORTUNAE SACRUM* meaning "Fortuna sacred" (see Fig. 160, bottom inscription).²⁷² Above it was another wreath with the relief of two griffins and the Latin inscription *VOTIS XX* ("the vows or prayers for twenty years of rule," *Votis Vicennalibus;* see Fig. 160, middle inscription).²⁷³ Ramsay states "The goddess of Laodiceia is not actually named in any of our authorities; but she is represented on a coin, wearing a double *chiton*, standing towards the left; the *kalathos* is on her head, the crescent of the moon-goddess on her shoulders; with her right

160. Column B from Temple A. Displays three registers (with figures inside of wreaths) with Latin inscriptions. In the upper wreath is a relief of the god Apollo, (*APOLLINIS SACRUM*); the middle relief of two griffins (*VOTIS XX*), and the last of Fortuna (Gr. Tyche, *FORTUNAE SACRUM*).

---

http://holylandphotos.org/browse.asp?s = 1,3,7,23,598&img = TWSCLDRS23.

²⁶⁹ Huttner, *Early Christianity in the Lycus Valley*, 54–55; Şimşek, *Laodikeia 2007*, 232 fig. 79c; *Laodikeia 2013*, 464. For a photo of the column, see http://holylandphotos.org/browse.asp?s = 1,3,7,23,598&img = TWSCLDRS24.

²⁷⁰ *BMC Phrygia* 295.106; Imhoof *KM* 39, *RPC* 9792.

²⁷¹ *BMC Phrygia* 205.222; 295.107; 296.108; 298.126; 310.199; 311.205; 315.222; 318.233; 320.243; 311.205; 314.217; 323.256.

²⁷² Huttner, Early Christianity in the Lycus Valley, 54–55; Şimşek, Laodikeia 2007, 232; Laodikeia 2013, 464.

²⁷³ Huttner, *Early Christianity in the Lycus Valley*, 54–55; Şimşek, *Laodikeia 2007*, 232; *Laodikeia 2013*, 464. The Latin *VOTIS XX* is also depicted inside a wreath on coins from Constantine I (AD 306–337). Stevenson, *A Dictionary of Roman Coins*, 908.

161. Coin from *Laodicea ad Lycum*. Minted under Caracalla (AD 198–217). Obv.: Ailios Pisoneinos, asiarch. ...ΑΙΛΩΣ ΠΙΣΟΝΕΙΝΚ ΑΡCΙΕΡ. Rev.: CONEWHC ΛΑΟΔΙΚΕΩΝ ΝΕΩΚΟΡΩΝ (*Laodikeon Neōkoron*). Tyche of Laodicea or winged Nemesis, standing holding a patera and scepter, and at her feet a small statue of Minerva. She is facing the *neocorate*, an octostyle temple of Laodicea, the temple of Laodicea, seen in three-quarters perspective, with a statue standing inside. (Mionnet 4.769).

162. Medallion from *Laodicea ad Lycum*. Struck under Caracalla (AD 198–217). Obv.: ΑΥΤ Κ Μ ΑΥΡ ΑΝΤΩΝΕΙΝΟC. Caracalla bust laureate, draped and cuirassed bust of Caracalla (Year 88, AD 211–212). Rev.: ΛΑΟΔΙΚΕΩΝ ΝΕΩΚΟΡΩΝ ΤΟ ΠΗ three tetrastyle temples on a high podia; side-to-side 4 columns, left containing a statue of Caracalla (?), in the middle a four-column temple with the statue of Zeus with a scepter, and on the right a statue of Asclepius (*SNGvA* 2.3858).

hand she presents a *patera* to a serpent which is twined round her left arm, and in her left hand she has a cornucopiae. A griffin stands before her."[274] The cornucopia (Lat. *cornucopiae*) was a symbols of Tyche, while the griffin was the guardian of gold and treasures (Philostratus *Vit. Apoll.* 3.48).[275] The imagery and inscriptions of the column conveyed the message of long life for the emperor, good luck and protection for the wealth of Laodicea.

8. A late second cent. AD sanctuary to *Isis* has been discovered by archaeologists.[276] In addition, a cohort of *Sarpis* was also worshiped there.[277] A life-size statue of Isis or her priestess was uncovered in the Caracalla Nymphaeum (no. 17) at Laodicea.[278]

9. *Asclepius*, the healing god (see Fig. 71), was highly revered in Laodicea, especially given his and the city's association with the medical school. He is portrayed on Laodiean coins with the traditional serpent staff (*BMC Phrygia* 297.115–116).

10. *Dionysus* (see Fig. 35) is documented on Laodicean coins (*BMC Phrygia* 286.50–51), with Şimşek reporting the discovery of the head sculpture of *Dionysus* during his excavations between 2002–2011.[279]

---

[274] Ramsay, Cities and Bishoprics, 1:51.
[275] Schmitz, "Gryps or Gryphus," 315.
[276] Johnson, "Asia Minor and Early Christianity," 84; Şimşek, "Regional Cults," 674; Şimşek, *Laodikeia 2013*, 349–355. Res . 149.
[277] Yamauchi, *NT Cities*, 143.
[278] Ibid., 141–42; Bruce, "Laodicea (Place)," 5:230.

11. Other female deities venerated in Laodicea were a veiled *Hera* portrayed in long chiton and peplos, holding a scepter and pomegranate (*BMC Phrygia* 309.193; 311.209); a nude or draped *Aphrodite* (see Figs. 93, 122, 123, 126) holding a dove,[280] and a helmeted *Athena* holding a shield and spear.[281] Şimşek reported the discovery of the sculptured heads of *Hera* and *Aphrodite* during his excavations between 2002–2011.[282]

163. Medallion of *Laodicea ad Lycum*. Minted under Caracalla (AD 198–217). Obv.: AVTKAI MAVP ANT ONEINOCCEB, Bust of Caracalla, bearded laureate, draped and cuirassed. Rev.: EPIAILPIGR HTOC ACIAP LAODIKEWN NEWKORWN, Caracalla standing in a chariot driving four lions with heads turned back towards the Emperor, holding an eagle-tipped scepter in his left hand and Nike on a globe with a wreath and palm in his right hand. (*BMC Phrygia* 225).

12. Other male deities portrayed on coins include a naked *Hermes* (*BMC Phrygia* 297.117–123), winged *Nemesis* (*BMC Phrygia* 295.107; 314.220), naked *Eros* with bow and arrow (*BMC Phrygia* 299.130–132), veiled *Demeter* with a scepter (*BMC Phrygia* 313.210; 314.219), advancing *Nike* with wreath and palm (see Figs. 13, 87, 163; *BMC Phrygia* 290.77–81; 315.225), and enthroned *Hades-Sarapis* holding a scepter (*BMC Phrygia* 295.104; 311.204).

THE IMPERIAL CULT

In AD 26, eleven cities including Laodicea competeted for the priviledge of hosting the second *koinon* temple in Asia, this time in honor of *Tiberius Divus* (see Figs. 43, 97, 111). Laodicea was eliminated in favour of the more impressive Smyrna (Tacitus *Ann.* 4.55–56; see chapter 8, *Smyrna: A City of the Imperial Cult*).

During the reign of Domitian (r. AD 81–96) coins were pressed with the image of a temple with three steps depicting 4 or 6 columns (*BMC Phrygia* 307.181; 185; 308.187–188). This image was likely the four columns that were in front of Temple A (see Fig. 160) prior to the introduction of the imperial cult.[283] In about AD 130–150 the festival of *Zeus Laodikeus* (Δεῖα Λαοδίκεια, *Deia Laodikeia*) was modified to join the worship of Zeus (see Figs. 95, 115, 126, 151, 154, 156) with worship of the emperor, and introduce the imperial cult to the temple of Zeus.[284]

---

[279] Şimşek, "Laodicea Becoming New Ephesus," n.p.

[280] *BMC Phrygia* 278.3; 283.25–30; 287.57; 292.92–93; 312.206. Ramsay, *Cities and Bishoprics*, 1:50.

[281] *BMC Phrygia* 300.133; 308.186; 309.194; 311.209. Gagniers et al., *Laodicée du Lycos*, 257; Yamauchi, *NT Cities*, 143; Keener, *Background Commentary: NT*, 736.

[282] Şimşek, "Laodicea Becoming New Ephesus," n.p.

[283] For a comprehensive treatment of the Imperial Cult in Laodicea from numismatic and epigraphic remains, see chapter 8. Laodikeia in Phrygia (Commodus) in Burrell, *Neokoroi*, 119–25.

[284] Δεῖα Σεβαστὰ Οἰκουμενικὰ ἐν Λαοδικείᾳ ἀγενείων πυγμ[ήν], *Deia Sebasta Oikoumenika en Laodikeia pugm[en]*. (*GIBM* 3.605.5). Ramsay, *Cities and Bishoprics*, 1:53–54.

Thompson reports that Laodicea had an imperial temple, but no imperial priest or altar,[285] perhaps because the city had its own priest, representing the deified city of Laodicea (See no. 2 above).

Inscriptions and coins confirm the presence of the imperial cult and Laodicea's *neōkoria*, but only appear on coins beginning under Commodus (AD 180–192),[286] while Hierapolis received its first and only *neōkoria* under Caracalla (r. AD 211–218; see Figs. 128, 162, 163).[287] There also appeared to be a rivalry between Hierapolis and Laodicea for the right to the title *neōkoros*, "temple warden". This was short lived however, as Commodus was assassinated on December 31, AD 192 and thereafter his name was erased from public record (*damnatio memoriae* [see Fig. 111]; Dio Cassius *Hist. Rom.* 74.2.1–3; *HA Comm.* 18–20) and from its association with the *Deia Kommodeia* festival celebrated with that of Zeus (*BMC Phrygia* 316.230), that was later changed to *Deia Severeia*. The *neōkoria* would not return to Laodicea until the reign of Severus's son, Caracalla (r. AD 198–217; *IG XIV* 1063; *IGR* 1.130) under the title of "Neōkoros of Commodus and Caracalla."[288] Later, Laodicea celebrated the renewal of its *neokoria* with a medallion[289] depicting Caracalla, the year eighty-eight,[290] and three tetrastyle temples in Laodicea (*SNGvA* 2.3858, see Fig. 162).[291]

The *neōkoria* appears on the following coins of Laodicea, sometimes as a tetrastyle (four column) temple:

1. Caracalla (r. AD 211–218; see Figs. 128, 162, 163).[292]
2. Julia Domna (ca. AD 185).[293]
3. Elagabalus (r. AD 218–222).[294]
4. Annia Faustina (Married to Elagabalus AD 221–222).[295]

---

[285] Thompson, Apocalypse and Empire, 159.

[286] *I.Laod.* 45; *BMC Phrygia* 314.217, 221; 315.225; 316.226–227. Tullia Ritti, "Iura sepulcrorum a Hierapolis di Frigia nel quadro dell'epigrafia sepolcrale microasiatica. Iscrizione edite e inedite," in *Libitina e Dintorni. Libitina e i Luci Sepolcrali, le Leges Libitinariae Campane Iura Sepulcrorum: Vecchie e Nuove Iscrizioni*, ed. S. Panciera (Roma: Quasar, 2004), 298 n.6; Burrell, *Neokoroi*, 135–38. For a comprehensive treatment of the Imperial Cult in Laodicea from numismatic and epigraphic remains, see chapter 8. Laodikeia in Phrygia (Commodus) in Ibid., 119–25.

[287] Ritti, "Iura sepulcrorum a Hierapolis di Frigia nel quadro dell'epigrafia sepolcrale microasiatica. Iscrizione edite e inedite," 298 n.6; Burrell, *Neokoroi*, 135–38. Burrell, apparently unfamiliar with Titti's work, and relying on numismatic evidence, states that Hierapolis did not receive their *neokoria* until much later in the reign of Heliogabalus (Elagabalus r. AD 218–222).

[288] *CIG* 3938 = *IGR* 4:863 (Caracalla); *I.Laod.* 135 = *IGR* 4:859 (after Caracalla). William Hepburn Buckler, "CIG 3938, 3952, and 3953 F," *JHS* 56, no. 1 (1936): 78–80.

[289] J. M. C. Toynbee, "Roman Medallions: Their Scope and Purpose," *The Numismatic Chronicle and Journal of the Royal Numismatic Society* 4, no. 1/4 (1944): 27.

[290] On the destination of eighty-eight on the coins, see Burrell, *Neokoroi*, 121.

[291] Ibid., 120–21.

[292] *BMC Phrygia* 225–236; *SNG Cop.* 589–591; *SNGvA* 2.3856–3862, 2.8418, 2.8419.

[293] *BMC Phrygia* 214–218, 221; *SNG Cop.* 583–586; *SNGvA* 2.3851–3854, 8417. Imhoof Nymphen 411 var; SNG München 391.

[294] *BMC Phrygia* 228–45; *SNG Cop.* 595–97; *SNGvA* 2.8414.

5. Julia Maesa (deified AD 224).²⁹⁶
6. Severus Alexander Caesar (r. AD 222–235; *BMC Phrygia* 251–253; *SNG* Cop. 600–601).

Huttner point out that:

> Unlike the conventional cults, the emperor cult often lacked continuity. The Zeus of Laodicea always remained the same; his rigid attitude, visible on innumerable coins, was a guarantee of reliablility. His was a primordial cult, observed in Laodicea generation after generation. In the emperor cult, however, the gods constantly acquired new faces, and it was particularly fatal when a *damnatio memoriae* [see Fig. 111] even meant that the images had to be destroyed.²⁹⁷

While the imperial cult was present in the east, it was seen as one of many avenues of worship in the first cent. for local citizens.

THE JEWISH COMMUNITY

It is known that around 213 BC, Antiochus III (see Fig. 96), resettled 2,000 Jewish families from Babylonia to Lydia and Phrygia (Josephus *Ant*. 12.147–49),²⁹⁸ and it is reasonably speculated that many of them made Laodicea their home. In 62 BC, the Jews of Asia Minor took their proconsul, L. Valerius Flaccus, to court for prohibiting the transfer of the temple tax to Jerusalem. Twenty pounds (9 kg) of gold (9,000 half-shekels), collected from the Jews in Laodicea, was confiscated by Lucius Peducaeus, one of the judges, who refused to let the gold leave the country (Cicero *Flac*. 68).²⁹⁹ Its value has been calculated at 9,000 half-shekels or 15,000 silver drachmae with the tax consisting of two drachma's per person.³⁰⁰ Based on the amount collected, one could estimate the Jewish population at about 7,000 adults.

In ca. 45 BC, the city magistrates corresponded with Caius Rubilius, proconsul of Asia, to grant freedom of worship to the Jewish residents in accordance with the proconsul's wishes, and allowing them to keep the Sabbath (Josephus *Ant*. 14.240–243). In AD 2/3, Augustus published a statement of Jewish rights in Lycia and Galatia, which was posted in Ancyra, the capital of Galatia (Josephus *Ant*. 16.162–65).³⁰¹ The Jewish population lived in a highly

164. Column from Laodicea with an inscribed menorah with flames, a *lulav* to the left of the *menorah*, a *shophar* to the right, and above the *menorah* a cross.

---

²⁹⁵ *BMC Phrygia* 246; *SNG Cop*. 598; *SNGvA* 2.3863.
²⁹⁶ *BMC Phrygia* 247–250; *SNG Cop*. 599; *SNGvA* 2.8420.
²⁹⁷ Huttner, *Early Christianity in the Lycus Valley*, 66.
²⁹⁸ F. F. Bruce, "Colossian Problems, Part 1: Jews and Christians in the Lycus Valley," *BSac* 141 (1984): 4–8.
²⁹⁹ Dirk Erkelenz, "Cicero, pro Flacco 55–59: Zur Finanzierung von Statthalterfesten in Der Friihphase Des Koinon von Asia," *Chiron* 29 (1999): 43–57; Eckhard J. Schnabel, "Jewish Opposition to Christians in Asia Minor in the First Century," *BBR* 18, no. 2 (2008): 253–54.
³⁰⁰ Ramsay, *Letters: Updated*, 309–10; Bruce, "Laodicea (Place)," 230.
³⁰¹ Smallwood, *Jews Under Roman Rule*, 120–43.

polytheistic community, and following the destruction of Jerusalem in AD 70, the Jewish dispersion continued, founding a generally hospitable community in Asia Minor (Josephus *Ant.* 12.121; *J.W.* 7.100–111),[302] in spite of having to pay the half-shekel tax to the temple of Jupiter Capitolinus in Rome (Josephus *J.W.* 7. 218; Dio Cassius *Hist. Rom.* 65.7).

An inscription from the Nymphaeum A, dedicated to Septimus Severus (r. 193–211 AD), was discovered in 2003. It displays a Christian cross above the Jewish symbols of a menorah (seven-branched lamp or *heptamyxion*) with flames, flanked by a shofar (ram's horn), and *lulav* (palm branch), on a column, believed to be from the lower colonnade of the two-storied nymphaeum.[303] Şimşek, who discovered the column fragment, noted that "it is the first known example of such a combination from Asia Minor."[304] There is a similar styled Latin cross with a globe carved on a capital dating to the Early Byzantine period (fourth to fifth cent.) in the cathedral at Hierapolis, but with no menorah.[305] Fine argues that the placing of the cross above the menorah was a "manner of Christianization" where "at some point, a Christian took control of the column, haphazardly inscribing a large and deep cross over the menorah."[306] Fairchild suggests "that these symbols suggest that the Christian church in Laodicea emerged from the synagogue—which is consistent with the apostle Paul's mission strategy that prioritized cities and towns with a Jewish population (see Romans 1:16; Acts 13:46)."[307] The fact that neither image was defaced shows that the Jewish and Christian communities in Laodicea coexisted in harmony. Although no Jewish synagogue has been discovered in Laodicea, they have been excavated at Priena, Miletus and Sardis.

Schnabel points out that there is no apparent evidence of Jewish opposition in Laodicea, in contrast to other Asia Minor cities in the first cent. AD,[308] although, following the death of Julian the Apostate, in AD 363, there was an anti-Jewish Council held at Laodicea, indicating a later Christian opposition to the Jewish presence in Laodicea.[309]

THE CHRISTIAN COMMUNITY

Very little is known about the history of Christianity in Laodicea outside of the Bible, which mentions it in Paul's letter to the Colossians (4:12–13) and the Book of Revelation (3:14–22). It

---

[302] Tullia Ritti, "The Jewish Community in Hierapolis," in *Hierapolis Di Figia 1957–1987*, ed. A. Peres (Rome: Fabbri, 1987), 116–17; Harland, "Acculturation and Identity in the Diaspora: A Jewish Family and 'Pagan' Guilds at Hierapolis," 222–44.

[303] Şimşek, "A Menorah with a Cross," 343–46.

[304] Ibid., 343.

[305] G. Ciotta and L. Palmucci Quaglino, "La Cattedrale Di Hierapolis," in *Saggi in Onore Di Paolo Verzone*, ed. Daria de Bernardi Ferrero, Hierapolis: Scavi E Ricerche 4 (Rome: Bretschneider, 2002), 185–94.

[306] Steven Fine, *The Menorah: From the Bible to Modern Israel* (Cambridge, Mass.: Harvard University Press, 2016), 55.

[307] Mark R. Fairchild, "The 'Lukewarm' Legacy of Laodicea: Conflicts of Prosperity in an Ancient Christian City," *BAR* 43, no. 2 (March 2017): 33.

[308] Schnabel, "Jewish Opposition to Christians in Asia Minor in the First Century," 239.

[309] Schaff, "The Canons of the Councils of Laodicea," 2.14:124; Huttner, *Early Christianity in the Lycus Valley*, 294–95.

is not believed that the apostle Paul ever visited the Lycos valley,[310] although he spent two years in Ephesus. While there he established a school for training disciples, called "the School of Tyrannus"[311] that likely spread the gospel throughout the Lycos valley, "so that all who lived in Asia heard the word of the Lord, both Jews and Greeks" (Acts 19:10). Although the Laodiceans never saw Paul, he had a pastoral concern for them as he wrote: "For I want you to know how great a struggle I have for you and for those at Laodicea and for all who have not seen me face to face" (Col 2:1). The leader and possible founder of the Colossian church was a man by the name of Epaphras (Col 1:7) who had also "worked hard for you and for those in Laodicea and in Hierapolis" (Col 4:12–13). It is reasonable to believe that Epaphras, a likely convert under the apostle Paul, was responsible for establishing the Christian church in Laodicea. The Laodicean church met in the home of Nympha (Col 4:15), who is otherwise unknown to us, but evidently a leader in the church. Fairchild reports that "about 20 churches and chapels have been found in Laodicea. Some of these structures used to be private houses, . . . with a peristyle courtyard that was converted into a chapel."[312]

Paul instructs the churches of Colossia and Laodicea to exchange the letters that were sent to them (Col 4:16). The "letter from Laodicea"[313] (Col 4:16) has not survived,[314] or as some suggest, it may be one of the existing Epistles of Paul, such as Hebrews,[315] Philemon[316] or the

---

[310] During Paul's Second Journey (Acts 16:6–9), Paul arrived at Apamea traveling westward. Uggeri has the apostolic party traveling westward through Laodicea and onward to Philadelphia, Sardis, Thyatira, and Pergamum. However, his map on page 154 contradicts the route described in his text. Based on the archaeological and hodological research, Thompson and Wilson, following Robert Jewett, argue that Paul traveled north from Apamea in to provinces of Phrygia and Asia bypassing the Lycos valley. Giovanni Uggeri, "Sulle Strade di San Paolo in Anatolia: Il secondo e il terzo viaggio," in *Seminario di studi Paolo di Tarso: il messaggio, l'immagine, i viaggi: studi in memoria di Luigi Padovese*, ed. Stella Uggeri Patitucci and Luigi Padovese, Quaderni di archeologia medievale 12 (Palermo: Officina di Studi Medievali, 2011), 134; Robert Jewett, "Mapping the Route of Paul's 'Second Missionary Journey' from Dorylaeum to Troas.," *TynBul* 48, no. 1 (1997): 1–22; Glen L. Thompson and Mark Wilson, "The Route of Paul's Second Journey in Asia Minor: In the Steps of Robert Jewett and Beyond," *TynBul* 67, no. 2 (2016): 228–32.

[311] A Tyrannus is mentioned in inscriptions from Ephesus (*I.Eph.* 4.1001.5 [AD 14–37]; *I.Eph.* 1.20B [AD 54–59]; *I.Eph.* 4.1012.4 [AD 92–93]). Hemer, *The Book of Acts in the Setting of Hellenistic History*, 234; Peter Lampe, "Acta 19 Im Spiegel Der Ephesischen Inschriften," *BZ* 36 (1992): 59–76; Graves, *Biblical Archaeology Vol 2: Famous Discoveries*, 2:190–91.

[312] Fairchild, "The 'Lukewarm' Legacy of Laodicea," 67.

[313] If the author was not an apostle, then this overcomes the difficulty of how an apostolic epistle could become lost. Anderson suggests that it was Epaphras, the leader of the Laodicean church. C. P. Anderson, "Who Wrote 'The Epistle from Laodicea'?," *JBL* 85 (1966): 436–40.

[314] Ralph P. Martin, *Ephesians, Colossians, and Philemon*, Interpretation (Atlanta, Ga.: Westminster John Knox Press, 1991), 131; Peter T. O'Brien, *Colossians, Philemon*, WBC 44 (Waco, Tex.: Thomas Nelson, 1982), 258; Murray J. Harris, *Colossians and Philemon*, EGGNT (Nashville, Tenn.: B&H Academic, 2010), 182. O'Brien suggests that is may have been destroyed "accidentally" in the earthquake of AD 60.

[315] C. P. Anderson, "Hebrews among the Letters of Paul," *SR* 5, no. 3 (December 1, 1975): 258–66; Contra. Joseph Barber Lightfoot, Saint Paul's Epistles to the Colossians and to Philemon, Classic Commentary Library (Grand Rapids, Mich.: Zondervan, 1880), 280.

[316] William Barclay, *The Letters to Timothy, Titus, and Philemon*, NDSB (Louisville, Ky.: Westminster/Knox, 2003),

more popular Ephesians.[317] It is also believed that Philemon either lived at Colossae or Laodicea.[318] Certainly the Pseudo-Laodicean epistle (*Epistola ad Laodicenses*), compiled from a variety of Pauline texts (second to third cent. AD), is not a viable option due to its late date.[319]

Although Paul is perhaps only partly responsible for the spread of the Gospel in the Lycos Valley, it is significant that Epaphras, Nymphas, Mark, Timothy, Philip the Apostle and John were involved in the spread of Christianity there. As Ramsay documents

> Archippus, Nymphas (Col 4:15), and Diotrephes (3 Jn 9), are named by untrustworthy tradition as the first bishops of Laodicea. Sagaris, a bishop of Laodicea, died a martyr about AD 166. Sisinnius, a bishop, and Artemon a presbyter, under Diocletian, are mentioned in the *Acta S. Artermonis* (Oct. 8), a late and poor production.[320]

The remains of numerous Christian churches in the city of Laodicea – churches that survived Domitian's rule – and the fact that the Laodicean church had become a bishopric and held a Christian council between AD 344–363, speaks of the strength of the Christian witness in the city. Laodicea was represented at the Council of Nicaea (AD 325); by bishop Nounechios.[321]

273–75.

[317] The strength of this argument is based on the fact that the city name "in Ephesus" is missing from several early manuscripts ($\mathfrak{p}^{46}$ ℵ B) and added based on the prominence of Ephesus in the region. George Bradford Caird, *Paul's Letters from Prison: Ephesians, Philippians, Colossians, Philemon*, New Clarendon Bible Commentary Series 6 (Oxford, U.K.: Oxford University Press, 1976), 212; Michael D. Goulder, "The Visionaries of Laodicea," *JSNT* 14, no. 43 (July 1, 1991): 39; W. H. Griffith Thomas, *Studies in Colossians and Philemon* (Grand Rapids, Mich.: Kregel, 1986), 134. Contra. Bruce, "Laodicea (Place)," 230.

[318] Paul Robinson Coleman-Norton, "The Apostle Paul and the Roman Law of Slavery," in *Studies in Roman Economic and Social History: In Honor of Allan Chester Johnson*, ed. Paul Robinson Coleman-Norton (Princeton, N.J.: Princeton University Press, 1951), 166.

[319] Wilhelm Schneemelcher and Edgar Henneche, eds., *New Testament Apocrypha: Writings Relating to the Apostles Apocalypses and Related Subjects*, trans. R. M. Wilson, Rev. (Louisville, Ky.: Westminster/Knox, 1992), 2:42–46; Philip Sellew, "Laodiceans and the Philippians Fragments Hypothesis," *HTR* 87, no. 1 (1994): 17–28; Paul A. Holloway, "The Apocryphal 'Epistle to the Laodiceans' and the Partitioning of Philippians," *HTR* 91, no. 3 (1998): 321–25.

[320] Ramsay, "Laodicea," 44–45.

[321] G. L. Borchert, "Laodicea," in *ISBE*, ed. Geoffrey W. Bromiley, Revised (Grand Rapids, Mich.: Eerdmans, 1995), 73.

17

Lukewarm Laodicea

Commentary on Revelation 3:14–22

John was commanded to write to the angel (ἄγγελος, *angelos*) of each church, and here at Laodicea he repeated the same instructions. In the light of the proposed covenant background and structure, this chapter will examine the content of the message to lukewarm Laodicea (Rev 3:14–22), whom the angel had nothing good to say. On the commission to write (γράψον, *graphon* 3:7a) and the role of angels (ἄγγελος, *angelos*) as mediating messengers, see chapter 3, *The Messenger's Commission*. Smalley suggests that since this is the last message that the καί (lit. "and") can mean "finally".[1]

MESSENGER PREAMBLE FORMULA— 3:14B

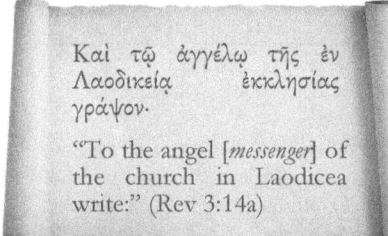

Καὶ τῷ ἀγγέλῳ τῆς ἐν Λαοδικείᾳ ἐκκλησίας γράψον.

"To the angel [*messenger*] of the church in Laodicea write:" (Rev 3:14a)

John begins each message to the churches with τάδε λέγει Ω (*tade legei omega*, "These are the words" 2:1, 8,12,18; 3:1a, 7, 14), setting the context for the suzerain/King who will speak to the churches.[2] Within the OT prophetic structure[3] this prophetic *messenger preamble formula*[4] τάδε λέγει Ω, (*tade legei omega*, "These are the words") introduces the sovereign's message. In most of the messages John proceeds to describe Christ as a resonance from Revelation chapter one (1:13, 16), but most commentators agree that this message does not refer back to chapter one.[5] Here, in the message to Laodicea, the king is described as *the amen, the faithful and true,* and *the beginning of God's creation*. Although there is no

---

[1] Smalley, *Revelation*, 96.
[2] Beale, *Rev*, 229.
[3] Num 22:15–16; Judg 11:14–15; 1 Kgs 2:30; 2 Chr 36:23; Ezra 1:2.
[4] Graves, *SMRVT*, 141–47; Osborne, *Revelation*, 111.
[5] Morris, *Revelation*, 84; Aune, *Rev 1–5*, 263–64; Osborne, *Revelation*, 203 n.3; Smalley, *Revelation*, 96.

doubt these descriptions refer back to the OT in Isaiah 65:16–18,[6] they may also be alluded to in chapter one (see *Amen* and *Faithful* below).

DESCRIPTION OF THE SUZERAIN

While the imagery, as in the previous messages, ralates back to chapter 1 (vs. 6–7; see *The Amen*), where Christ appears in the vision to John, here John appears to be familiar with the letter to the church at Colossae which was also read at Laodicea.[7] Colossians' opening chapter, presents a similar description of the preexistent Christ, described as "the image of the invisible God, the firstborn of all creation. For by him all things were created, in heaven and on earth, visible and invisible, whether thrones or dominions or rulers or authorities—all things were created through him and for him" (Col 1:16).[8] The message begins with a reminder that it is the pre-existent Christ who is the head of the church in Laodicea, and it is he who speaks to his church, and these are his words.

THE PREEXISTENT SUZERAIN: THE AMEN—14B

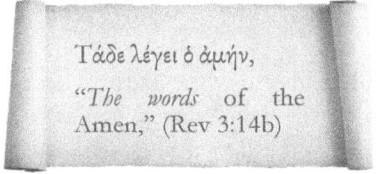

Τάδε λέγει ὁ ἀμήν,
"The words of the Amen," (Rev 3:14b)

The description of Christ here as "the Amen" (ἀμήν) hearkens back to chapter 1 where the doxology ends with "Amen" (ver. 6) and "all the tribes of the earth will wail" at Christ's coming, which also concludes with "Amen" (ver. 7). Now the suzerain identifies himself as "the Amen." Koester points out that here "the Amen" represents "the affirmation of the promises and reproofs given in the message to Laodicea."[9]

The titular use of *Amen* (ἀμήν) only occurs here in the NT (see also LXX Isa 65:16) and is uniquely included with the article, ὁ (*ho*, "the") to make it a descriptive title[10] for the suzerain. Smalley argues that "it is most unlikely, therefore, that the term has been drawn in at this point to serve as an appropriate liturgical conclusion to the seven letters."[11] The different Hebrew vocalizations of the consonants אמן (*'mn*) can mean "Amen" (אֱמֻן, *'ēmûn*), "Faithful" (אָמֵן, *'āmēn;* or אֱמוּן, *'ēmûn*, "faithfulness"), or "Truth" (אֹמֶן, *'ōmen*). In Judaism, אָמֵן means that which is "sure and valid"[12] indicating something which has a binding validity (lit. "the God of Amen", Isa 65:16; LXX τὸν θεὸν τὸν ἀληθινός which implies אֹמֶן, *'ōmen*). Jesus often used *Amen* in a unique

---

[6] Gregory K. Beale, "The Old Testament Background of Rev 3.14," *NTS* 42, no. 1 (1996): 133–52.
[7] Mounce, *Revelation*, 108.
[8] Charles, *Revelation*, 1:94–95; Witherington III, *Revelation*, 107. The connection with Colossians would rule out any association with the Arian notion that Jesus was "the first thing created" and therefore not God. For a discussion on the Arian view, see Swete, *Apocalypse*, 59; Beckwith, *Apocalypse*, 488–89.
[9] Koester, *Revelation*, 343.
[10] Thomas, *Rev 1–7*, 300.
[11] Smalley, *Revelation*, 96.
[12] Heinrich Schlier, "Ἀμήν," ed. Gerhard Kittel and Gerhard Friedrich, trans. Geoffrey W. Bromiley, *TDNT* (Grand Rapids, Mich.: Eerdmans, 1985), 336.

way as well.¹³ As Hawthorne point out, Jesus used the expression "not so much to direct attention to his divinity as to his authority to speak for God as *the* messenger of God."¹⁴ In this context *Amen* indicates that the suzerain is guaranteeing the veracity of his message¹⁵ and supports a strong Christology, since it credits the suzerain with an attribute only associated with God.¹⁶ The reliability of the suzerain stands in sharp contrast to the unfaithful and lukewarm Laodiceans.¹⁷

While Silberman had earlier proposed, that "the Amen" here in Revelation, was a mistranslation of the Hebrew אָמוֹן (*'āmôn;* see *Cant.* 7:2, אָמָן *'ammān*, "master workman"), used to describe Wisdom in Proverbs 8:30,¹⁸ Beale has convincingly argued that "the Amen" along with "The Faithful and True" were derived from Isaiah 65:16.¹⁹ Here the name of God is mentioned in connection with the use of both blessings and oath in the phrases "he shall bless by the God of Amen," (יִתְבָּרֵךְ בֵּאלֹהֵי אָמֵן *yitbārēk bē'lōhê'āmēn*), and "he shall swear by the God of Amen" (יִשָּׁבַע בֵּאלֹהֵי אָמֵן *yiššaba' bē'lōhê'āmēn*). Aune suggests that "God, who is sometimes depicted in the OT as swearing oaths, need not swear by another since he is his own witness (Heb 6:13–17), alluding to Gen 22:1b"²⁰ (Philo *Sacr.* 91–92; see chapter 3, *Proclamation Witnesses Formula*).

THE PREEXISTENT SUZERAIN: FAITHFUL AND TRUE—14C

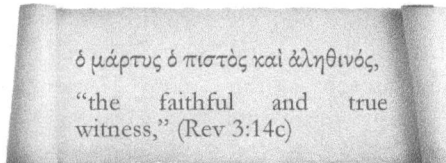
ὁ μάρτυς ὁ πιστὸς καὶ ἀληθινός,
"the faithful and true witness," (Rev 3:14c)

The suzerain is further identified as "the faithful and true witness" (ὁ μάρτυς ὁ πιστὸς καὶ ἀληθινός, *ho martus ho pistos kai alēthinos*). Again, depending on the vocalization of אמן (*'mn*) in Isaiah 65:16, it can mean both "Faithful" (אָמֵן, *'āmēn*), and "True" (אֹמֶן, *'ōmen*). Ford suggests that the phrase "faithful and true witness" was added to help clarify the meaning of "the Amen" for a non-Jewish audience.²¹ This phrase also refers to chapter 1 (ver. 5) where Christ is referred to as ὁ μάρτυς ὁ πιστὸς (*ho martys ho pistos*, "the faithful witness"), the only two places in the NT where Jesus is called a

---

¹³ Matt 31 times; Mark 13 times; Luke 6 times; John 25 times.

¹⁴ Gerald F. Hawthorne, "Amen," in *Dictionary of Jesus and the Gospels*, ed. Joel B. Green, Scot McKnight, and I. Howard Marshall (Downers Grove, Ill.: InterVarsity, 1992), 8.

¹⁵ Smalley, *Revelation*, 96; Beasley-Murray, *Revelation*, NCB; Beckwith, *Apocalypse*, 488.

¹⁶ Mathias Rissi, *Future of the World: An Exegetical Study of Revelation 19.11–22.15*, SBT 23 (London, U.K.: Scm-Canterbury, 1972), 92 n.17; Smalley, *Revelation*, 96.

¹⁷ Mounce, *Revelation*, 108.

¹⁸ Lou H. Silberman, "Farewell to OAMHN," *JBL* 82, no. 2 (1963): 213–15; Charles F. Burney, "Christ as the APXH of Creation," *JBL* 27, no. 1/2 (1926): 160–77; Paul Trudinger, "Ho Amen (Rev III:14), and the Case for a Semitic Original of the Apocalypse," *NovT* 14, no. 4 (1972): 277–79.

¹⁹ Beale, "The OT Background of Rev 3.14," 133–52; Fekkes, *Isaiah*, 137–38.

²⁰ Aune, *Rev 1–5*, 255; Harold W. Attridge, *Hebrews: A Commentary on the Epistle to the Hebrews*, Hermeneia (Philadelphia, Pa.: Fortress, 1989), 178–82.

²¹ Ford, *Revelation*, 418; Koester, *Revelation*, 343; Klaus Berger, *Die Amen-Worte Jesus: Eine Untersuchung zum Problem der Legitimation in apokalyptischer Rede*, ZNW 39 (Berlin: de Gruyter, 1970), 109.

witness (possible exceptions are Rom 1:9 and Rev 22:20). Aune sees an allusion to Psalm 89:37 (LXX 88:37) where the moon is described as "a faithful witness in the skies" (cf. Job 16:19).²² "Faithful and true" are also used of the Messiah on the white horse (19:11); of John's prophetic message (21:5; 22:6); and of God (*3 Macc.* 2:11). See also the faithful witness of Antipas (2:13). While some have designated Christ's witness as only referring to the historical Jesus²³ or the exalted Jesus,²⁴ it would be fair to say that both the active and passive obedience of Christ including his exaltation, fulfilled the role of the witness.²⁵ The suzerain is trustworthy (πιστός, *pistos*) and makes for an ideal witness confirming the veracity (ἀληθινός, *alēthinos*) of his message in John's book.²⁶ The suzerain witnesses to the veracity of John's message in the closing words of Revelation. John states: "He who testifies to these things says, "Surely I am coming soon." Amen. Come, Lord Jesus!"

THE PREEXISTENT SUZERAIN: THE BEGINNING OF GOD'S CREATION—14D

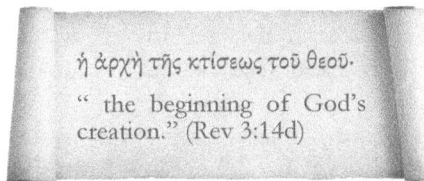

The suzerain is further described as pre-existent based on the phrase "the beginning of God's Creation" (ἡ ἀρχὴ τῆς κτίσεως τοῦ θεοῦ· *hē archē tēs ktiseōs tou theou*, lit. "the beginning of the Creation of God" cf., John 1:2–3).²⁷ Again this phrase harkens back to chapter 1 where the suzerain calls himself "the ruler (ἄρχων, *archōn*) of the kings of the earth" (ver. 5). The Greek ἀρχή (*archē*) literally means "ruler" "origin" or "beginning" and combines the thoughts of Christ's supreme authority over creation (5:8–13; 11:18) and the originator and renewer of created beings.²⁸ In early Christian documents Christ was given the title of ἀρχή (*archē*).²⁹

The parallels with Colossians seems to indicate that John was aware of the existence of the letter which Paul directed to be read in Laodicea (Col 4:16)³⁰ that suggests a theological connection between John and Paul.³¹ The suzerain calls the wealthy Laodiceans to repentance and "renewed commitment to creation's rightful sovereign."³²

---

²² Aune, *Rev 1–5*, 255–56.
²³ Holtz, *Christologie*, 143.
²⁴ Aune, *Rev 1–5*, 255–56.
²⁵ Koester, *Revelation*, 343.
²⁶ Beckwith, *Apocalypse*, 488.
²⁷ "He was in the beginning [ἐν ἀρχῇ, *en archē*] with God. All things were made through him" (John 1:2–3).
²⁸ Cf. John 1:3; Col 1:15–18; Rev 21:1–22:5; D. Müller, L. Coenen, and H. Bietenhard, "Beginning, Origin, Rule, Ruler, Originator," ed. Colin Brown, *NIDNTT* (Grand Rapids, Mich.: Zondervan, 1976), 164–69.
²⁹ Justin *Dial.* 61.1; 62.4; Theophilus *Autol.* 2.10; 2.13; Tatian *Or. Graec.* 5.1; Clement of Alexandria *Ecl.* 4.1; *Strom.* 6.58.1; 7.1; Origen *Comm. Gen.* 1.1; *Comm. Job.* 1.19; Irenaeus *Haer.* 1.18.1; Hippolytus *Haer.* 6.38.4; Burney, "Christ as the APXH of Creation," 160–77.
³⁰ Lightfoot, Saint Paul's Epistles to the Colossians and to Philemon, 41–44.
³¹ Stephen S. Smalley, "The Christ-Christian Relationship in Paul and John," in *Pauline Studies: Essays Presented to F. F. Bruce on His 70th Birthday*, ed. Donald A. Hagner and Murray J. Harris (Exeter, U.K.: Paternoster, 1980), 95–105;

HISTORICAL PROLOGUE—3:15–16A

The *historical prologue*[33] sets forth the historical intimacy of the relationship between the vassal and the Great King.[34] The suzerain "knows" (οἶδά, *oida*) the "works" (ἔργα, *erga*) of the Laodiceans. Thomas points out that "in each case the works are more than the deeds done. They reflect life and conduct in general, including outward and inward spiritual activities. They are evidence of the inward spiritual condition the Lord alone sees and knows directly."[35]

THE SUZERAIN KNOWS THEIR WORKS—3:15A

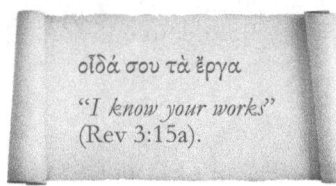

οἶδά σου τὰ ἔργα
"I know your works"
(Rev 3:15a).

The Laodiceans were neither cold (ψυχρός, *physchros*) nor hot (ζεστός, *zestos*) and the suzerain preferred that they were either one or the other, rather than lukewarm (χλιαρός, *chliaros*). There seems little doubt that the imagery is derived, in part, from the unique characteristics of the Laodicean water supply from the surrounding region,[36] although Koester has recently suggested that the reference is to hot and cold beverages at a banquet meal (see below).[37] Due to Laodicea's location being determined by the trade routes it suffered from an adequate fresh water supply. Water had to be transported through a five mile (8 km) aqueduct system from the hot spring in Denizli (Turk. "full of waters").[38] The drinkable water at Laodicea came from the Karcı mountains supplied through five miles (8 km) of aqueducts from the *Başpınar*[39] (Turkish

---

Morris, *Revelation of St. John*, 84.

[32] Aune, *Rev 1–5*, 257.

[33] See Chapter Three: *Historical Prologue*. For an extensive treatment of the "historical prologue" in the Hittite treaties, see Altman, *The Historical Prologue of the Hittite Vassal Treaties an Inquiry into the Concepts of Hittite Interstate Law*.

[34] Mendenhall, "Covenant Forms," 59; Thompson, *ANE Treaties*, 16; Huffmon, "Treaty Background," 31–37; Thompson, "Near Eastern Suzerain-Vassal," 4; Walton, *Ancient Israelite Literature*, 102; Berman, "Histories Twice Told," 232.

[35] Thomas, *Rev 1–7*, 304; Alford, *Revelation*, 4:588; Beckwith, *Apocalypse*, 449.

[36] Rudwick and Green, "The Laodicean Lukewarmness," 176–78; Bruce, "Colossian Problems, Part 1: Jews and Christians in the Lycus Valley," 3–15; Sweet, *Revelation*, 107; Yamauchi, *NT Cities*, 141; Court, *Myth and History*, 40; Mounce, *Revelation*, 123; Johnson, "Laodicea and Its Neighbors," 1–18; Hemer, *Letters to the Seven Churches*, 186–91; Harrington, *Revelation*, 74; Chilton, *Days of Vengeance*, 134; Porter, "Why the Laodiceans Received Lukewarm Water (Rev 3:15–18)," 143–49; Beasley-Murray, *Revelation, NCB*, 105; Giblin, *Revelation*, 65; Swete, *Apocalypse*, 60; Kelshaw, *Send This Message*, 165; Huttner, *Early Christianity in the Lycus Valley*, 154–58.

[37] Koester, "Message to Laodicea," 409–11.

[38] Porter, "Why the Laodiceans Received Lukewarm Water (Rev 3:15–18)," 147. Porter erroneously argues that the water came from Hierapolis evident from the calcification in the terra cotta water pipes found by archaeologists and hardness mentioned by Strabo (*Geogr*. 13.4.14), however all the water in the area were identified with mineral contents.

[39] Hamilton, *Researches in Asia Minor, Pontus and Armenia*, 1:510; "Extracts from Notes Made on a Journey in Asia Minor in 1836 by W. I. [=J.] Hamilton," 59–61. Hamilton described the location of the pure spring as a mile and a half on the road from Chonos (Honaz) to Denizli and confirmed that one of the three streams (*Ak Su*, white water) that merged in Khonas (Chonos) was highly petrified (Pliny *Nat*. 31.20.29; cf. Herodotus *Hist*. 7.30) and left travertine deposits similar to those at Hierapolis. Ramsay identified it with the sacred spring (*ayasma*) of Medieval legend (Ramsay,

"the head or main") spring,⁴⁰ at Denizli in the south,⁴¹ that was the source of the Kaprus river⁴² (See chapter 16, *Water System*).

THE SUZERAIN KNOWS THEY ARE NEITHER COLD NOR HOT—15B

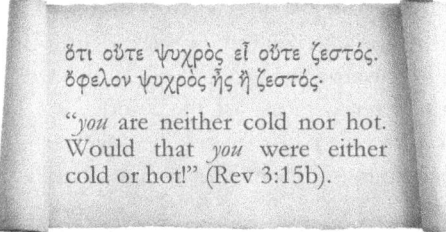

ὅτι οὔτε ψυχρὸς εἶ οὔτε ζεστός. ὄφελον ψυχρὸς ἦς ἢ ζεστός·

"*you* are neither cold nor hot. Would that *you* were either cold or hot!" (Rev 3:15b).

The all-important question here is: why the suzerain prefers either hot or cold to lukewarm? While it is certainly understandable that the suzerain would want his subjects to be hot (ζεστός, *zestos*; i.e., spiritual fervour) toward him, it is not suitable that he should want them cold (ψυχρός, *psychros*). Aune points out that: "in OT wisdom literature, the images of the 'hot' (negative) and 'cold' (positive) person relate to the motif of self-control, for 'hot' is a pejorative metaphor for a lack of control (Prov 15:18), while "cold" is a positive metaphor for restraint (Prov 17:27; *m. Pir. 'Abot* 1:17)."⁴³ However, in the context of this message both hot and cold are positive images, while lukewarm is negative. Several explanations have been proposed for the meaning of "cold" in this context.

1. An unlikely view is that ψυχρός (*psychros*) pertains to a cold backslidden Christian.⁴⁴ However, this is similar to the lukewarm condition and not a possitive image.

2. A second view maintains that "cold" refers to an unbeliever who has never heard the gospel.⁴⁵ Lenski held that "cold=never converted, never touched by the gospel fire."⁴⁶ Tait maintains that while "numbered amongst the Lord's people, their hearts have never yet been

---

The Church of the Roman Empire, 469–71).

⁴⁰ Şimşek, "A Menorah with a Cross," 343; *Ancient City of Laodicea*, 18; Şimşek and Büyükkolancı, "Die Aqueduct Und Das Wasserverteilungssystem," 137. Porter and Finegan suggest that the cold water supplied to Laodicea came from the spring (Turk. *Bounar Bashi*) at Colossae, however the fresh water was known to be from the spring south at Denizli. Porter, "Why the Laodiceans Received Lukewarm Water (Rev 3:15–18)," 147; Blaiklock, *Cities of the NT*, 124; Finegan, *The Archeology of the New Testament*, 2014, 182.

⁴¹ Bean, Turkey Beyond the Maeander, 255–56; Finegan, The Archeology of the New Testament, 2015, 179; Hemer, Letters to the Seven Churches, 188; Fant and Reddish, Guide to Biblical Sites, 236–37.

⁴² Huttner, "Wolf Und Eber: Die Flüsse von Laodikeia in Phrygien," 100–109; *Early Christianity in the Lycus Valley*, 156, 157 n.65. According to Ramsay "the water [for Laodicea] was brought from the upper springs of a branch of the Kadmos [Cadmus] which rises in Mount Salbakos near Denizli." (*Cities and Bishoprics*, 1:48).

⁴³ Jay G. Williams, Those Who Ponder Proverbs: Aphoristic Thinking and Biblical Literature (Sheffield, U.K.: Almond, 1981), 29–30.

⁴⁴ Scott, *Revelation*, Rev. 3:15 op. cit.

⁴⁵ Trench, Commentary on Seven Churches, 258–63.

⁴⁶ Lenski, *Revelation*, 1963, 154.

touched by grace."⁴⁷ However, Christ is speaking to those in the church who would have heard the gospel, unless he preferred they had never heard which seems unlikely.

3. The traditional interpretation moralizes the term ψυχρός (*psychros*) representing an unbeliever who has rejected⁴⁸ or is "unwilling to listen to the gospel"⁴⁹ and demonstrating an "antagonism towards religious matters."⁵⁰ Aune suggests that "'cold' and 'hot' are figures of speech meaning 'against me' and 'for me' or 'hostile towards me' and 'friendly towards me'."⁵¹ It conveys the notion of the degree of spiritual temperature of the Laodiceans,⁵² however, this does not explain why the suzerain prefers either hot or cold to lukewarm, although it is possible to have some of these type of people in a church. Alford states that it:

> keeps its meaning of fervent, warm, and earnest in the life of faith and love, ψυχρός [*psychros*] cannot here mean "dead and cold," as we say of the listless and careless professor of religion: for this is just what these Laodiceans were, and what is expressed by χλιαρός [*chliaros*] below. So that we must, so to speak, go farther into coldness for χλιαρός [*chliaros*] and take it as meaning, not only entirely without the spark of spiritual life, but also and chiefly, by consequence, openly belonging to the world without, and having no part nor lot in Christ's church, and actively opposed to it.⁵³

4. Recently, some have understood the adjectives "hot," "cold" (ψυχρός (*psychros*) and "lukewarm" as metaphors associated with the Laodicean water supply,⁵⁴ which they contrast to the positive medicinal properties of the hot springs from Hierapolis (see Fig. 165) and the cool, refreshing spring waters from Colossae (see chapter 16, *Water System*). This view does not see any moral connection to any religious state (i.e., backslidden, unbeliever,

165. Hierapolis' (modern Pamukkale, Turkey) travertine terrace pools formed by the mineral laden hot springs. The water not only provided a medical eye-salve, but also water for the city of Laodicea across the valley.

---

⁴⁷ Tait, Messages to the Seven Churches, 406.
⁴⁸ Beasley-Murray, *Revelation*, NCB, 105; Charles, *Revelation*, 1:96; Swete, *Apocalypse*, 60; Kiddle, *Revelation*, 58; Thomas, *Rev 1–7*, 306–7.
⁴⁹ Krodel, *Revelation*, 142.
⁵⁰ Caird, *Revelation*, 57; Plumptre, *Seven Churches of Asia*, 198–202.
⁵¹ Aune, *Rev 1–5*, 257.
⁵² Swete, *Apocalypse*, 60–61; Aune, *Rev 1–5*, 257–58.
⁵³ Alford, *Revelation*, 4:588.
⁵⁴ Bruce, "Colossian Problems, Part 1: Jews and Christians in the Lycus Valley," 3–15; Yamauchi, *NT Cities*, 141; Mounce, *Revelation*, 123; Johnson, "Laodicea and Its Neighbors," 1–18; Chilton, *Days of Vengeance*, 134; Beasley-Murray, *Revelation*, NCB, 105.

hypocrisy, etc.). Thus, the church in Laodicea "was providing neither refreshment for the spiritually weary nor healing for the spiritually sick. It was totally ineffective, and thus distasteful to its Lord."[55] According to this view, Laodicea is not rebuked for its lack of spiritual temperature but rather their ineffective[56] service.[57] This exegesis solves the problem of why the suzerain would prefer a *cold* church to one that was *lukewarm*.[58] As Smalley points out:

> this congregation is being chastised for the barrenness of its works, rather than the nature of its commitment: although it has to be said that the two (praxis [works] and faith) are inextricably related. . . . Despite the threatened judgment (vomiting), repentance is still possible (verses 18–20). As ever, condemnation can lead to commendation (Rev 3:21).[59]

166. A bronze cylindrical device (*authepsa*) for heating water to mix with wine (first cent. AD from Pompeii).

However, while the water that supplied Laodicea by aqueduct, shared many of the same qualities as Hierapolis, it is known that the water for Laodicea came from springs near Denizli to the south (see Fig. 137), rather than the hot springs of Hierapolis to the north (see chapter 16, *Water System*).

This view proposes that passion for Christ ought to lead to a healing for the spiritually sick (hot) and refreshment for the spiritually weary (cold). Christian service should flow with fresh water of service and not a lukewarm apathy for the needs of others.

5. In addition the city of Laodicea had several bath complexes (see chapter 16, *The Important Buildings of Laodicea*), including the gymnasium/bath complex (see Fig. 137 no. 5) and the central baths (see Fig. 137 no. 16;). The central baths contained a *caldarium* (hot bath), *tepidarium* (lukewarm bath), *frigidarium* (cold bath; see Fig. 110). The notion of hot, cold,

---

[55] Rudwick and Green, "The Laodicean Lukewarmness," 178.

[56] Tyconius (*ca.* AD 370–390) suggested that the phrase "neither cold nor hot" means that "it is useless." Tyconius, *Turin Fragments of Tyconius*, 74–75.

[57] Beckwith, *Apocalypse*, 489; Rudwick and Green, "The Laodicean Lukewarmness," 176–78; Wood, "Local Knowledge," 263–64; Mounce, *Revelation*, 125–26; Sweet, *Revelation*, 107; Hemer, *Letters to the Seven Churches*, 187–91; Osborne, *Revelation*, 205.

[58] Contra. Thomas, *Rev 1–7*, 306–7. However, Koester takes exception to this idea and believes that "the imagery is clear without special knowledge of Laodicean topography" (*Revelation*, 415) and that John used "common expressions to address local issues." *Revelation*, 420.

[59] Smalley, *Revelation*, 98.

and lukewarm were well known bathing concept in the ancient world, although in this context the warm or lukewarm room did not have a negative connotation.

6. Koester has recently reintroduced an earlier view proposed by Jeremy Taylor in the 1800's. Taylor wrote: "In feasts or sacrifices the ancients did use *"apponere frigidain"* [Lat. "add cold"] or *"calidam"* [Lat. "hot"]; sometimes they drank hot drink, sometimes they poured cold upon their gravies or in their wines, but no services of tables or altars were ever with lukewarm."[60] Koester envisions a banquet scene where guests are offered hot and cold drinks (Plato *Resp.* 2.437D) but not lukewarm. This preserves the positive sense of hot and cold metaphor, and negative sense of lukewarm. Refreshing drinks were made either from water heated in a *authepsa* (αὐθέψης, *authephēs* "self-boiler,"[61] or μιλιάριον, *miliarion*[62]), to an enjoyable temperature or chilled with snow or placing underground in a jar to cool (Athenaeus *Deipn.* 3.123a–d). The Romans also preferred a

168. Roman bronze wine-strainer found near Nijmegen in the River Waal. First cent. AD, made possibly in Campania (Inv. No. APM 3422).

167. *Thermopolium* in Herculaneum.

drink of heated wine and water (*caldum*),[63] as only barbarians drank their wine unmixed.[64] Koester goes on to describe that "even more desirable was wine that had been heated or chilled. Both Greeks and Romans chilled wine by placing it in a well or mixing it with snow and ice. A common

---

[60] Jeremy Taylor and Reginald Heber, The Whole Works of the Right Rev. Jeremy Taylor: With a Life of the Author and a Critical Examination of His Writings (London, U.K.: Rivington, 1828), 186–87.
[61] William Smith and William Wayte, "Authepsa," in *DGRA*, ed. William Smith (London, U.K.: Murray, 1891), 1:263. Cicero *Rosc. Amer.* 133; Seneca *Nat. quaest.* 3.24.2; Lucian *Lex.* 8; Heron of Alexandria *Pneum.* 2.34–5.
[62] Henry George Liddell and Robert Scott, *An Intermediate Greek-English Lexicon*, 9th ed. (Oxford, U.K.: Clarendon, 1889), 28451 op. cit.
[63] Plautus *Curc.* 292–93; *Rud.* 1013–14; Petronius *Sat.* 65; Lucian *Lex.* 8.
[64] Dunbabin, *Roman Banquet*, 20.

method was to cool wine by pouring it through a strainer [*colum nivarium*, see Fig. 168] filled with snow".[65] A first cent. AD Bronze *authepsa* was discovered at Pompeii used for heating water (*calda*) to mix with wine (*caldum*, see Fig. 166). Coals were put inside a chamber in the bottom of the cylinder to heat the water, then the host could offer their guest either hot or cold water to mix with their wine (Martial *Epig.* 14.105).[66] Most cities in Asia would have had a *thermopolium* where hot drinks could be purchased at stands along the street, such as were discovered at Herculaneum (see Fig. 167) and Pompeii.

The imagery of the banquet is further alluded to later in the message where the suzerain says "Behold, I stand at the door and knock. If anyone hears my voice and opens the door, I will come in to him and eat with him, and he with me." (3:20). The suzerain prefers either hot or cold service, but lukewarm (χλιαρός, *chliaros*) behavior makes him want to vomit (ἐμέσαι, *emesai*).

THE SUZERAIN KNOWS THEY ARE LUKEWARM—3:16A

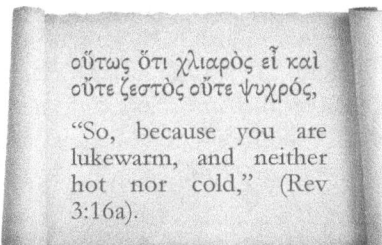

οὕτως ὅτι χλιαρὸς εἶ καὶ οὔτε ζεστὸς οὔτε ψυχρός,

"So, because you are lukewarm, and neither hot nor cold," (Rev 3:16a).

The suzerain wishes (ὄφελον, *ophelon*)[67] that they were either hot or cold, but alas, they were lukewarm (χλιαρόν, *chliaron*, "warm, or tepid"). Porter argued that Laodicea's water supply was from the hot springs in Hierapolis (see Fig. 165) based on the calcification in the terra-cotta water pipes found by archaeologists[68] and speculated that the water carried along the aqueduct likely arrived lukewarm.[69] But Koester points out that there is

no evidence that the water from Laodicea's aqueduct was regarded as lukewarm and objectionable. Laodicea was flanked by two rivers, the Asopus and the Carpus, which supplied some of the city's water needs, but in Roman times the Laodiceans were also served by an aqueduct that was fed by a spring about 5 miles south of the city.[70]

However, Strabo does acknowledge that the water of Laodicea was like Hierapolis in that it did calcify, but was drinkable unlike the water at Hierapolis (*Geogr.* 13.4.14). To make his case Porter draws upon Herodotus, who testified to the sharp change in temperature of the hot springs at the Oasis of Siwah in Libya, which he reports being cold during the day, but hot at night (see Herodotus *Quotes from Antiquity*).

---

[65] Koester, *Revelation*, 343. Xenophon *Mem.* 2.1.30; Athenaeus *Deipn.* 3.124cd; Seneca *Ep. Mor.* 78.23; Martial *Epig.* 5.64.1–2; 14.103–4.

[66] Katherine M. D. Dunbabin, "Wine and Water at the Roman Convivium," *JRA* 6 (1993): 116–41; *Roman Banquet*, 178; Koester, "Message to Laodicea," 413–15.

[67] See BDF 359.1

[68] Porter, "Why the Laodiceans Received Lukewarm Water (Rev 3:15–18)," 147.

[69] Rudwick and Green, "The Laodicean Lukewarmness," 177; Hemer, *Letters to the Seven Churches*, 187; Aune, *Rev 1–5*, 257–58; Court, *Myth and History*, 20–28; Porter, "Why the Laodiceans Received Lukewarm Water (Rev 3:15–18)," 143–49; Osborne, *Revelation*, 216–17. Contra Thomas, *Rev 1–7*, 305–7; Michaels, *Revelation*, 88.

[70] "Message to Laodicea," 410.

> **Quotes from Antiquity**
>
> Herodotus states:
>
> They have another spring of water besides, which is warm [χλιαρόν, *chliaron*] at dawn, and colder [ψυχρότερον, *phuchroteron*] at market-time, and very cold [ψυχρόν, *phuchron*] at noon; and it is then that they water their gardens; as the day declines the coldness [ψυχροῦ, *phuchrou*] abates, till at sunset the water grows warm [χλιαρόν, *chliaron*]. It becomes ever hotter and hotter till midnight, and then it boils [ζέει; *zeei* the verbal cognate of ζεστός, *zestos*] and bubbles; after midnight it becomes ever cooler till dawn. (*Hist.* 4.181.3–4 [Godley]; cf. Arrian *Anab.* 3.4.2; Lucretius *Re. Nat.* 6.848–78; Xenophon *Mem.* 3.13.3)

SANCTIONS: CURSES—3:16B–17

The prophetic sanctions, where the vassal is cursed (malediction) for disobedience (dishonours the treaty), and blessed (benedictions) for obedience to the stated stipulations (honour the treaty), is a central element of the ANEVT structure.[71] For Laodicea a malediction awaits those who do not repent, but a benediction for those who are overcomers. Here the word μέλλω (*meleō*), translated "I am about to," conveys the imminence (2:10; 3:2, 10) of the suzerain's judgment (eschatological wrath),[72] if they do not repent. The οὕτως (*houtōs*, "therefore") that begins this verse ties verse 16 to the previous verse as a natural result of their lukewarm condition.

THE CURSE OF BEING SPIT OUT OF HIS MOUTH—3:16B

> μέλλω σε ἐμέσαι ἐκ τοῦ στόματός μου.
>
> "I will spit you out of my mouth." (Rev 3:16b).

The graphic image of Christ vomiting (ἐμέσαι, *emesai*, "emetic, spit") the lukewarm (χλιαρόν, *chliaron*, "warm, tepid" i.e., neither hot nor cold) Christians out of his mouth is meant to draw the attention of the readers and move them to repentance. Hope for repentance and deliverance from the curse is still held out to the lukewarm Laodiceans by the ever gracious suzerain.

The imagery would have been familiar to the Laodiceans from ordering wine at a banquet or *thermopolium*. One of the stock phrases used at such functions was, "mix it hot for me, not boiling and not lukewarm."[73] Lukewarm was objectionable to the guests and they would also have been familiar with someone spitting out bad wine (Athenaeus *Deipn.* 3.123a) or vomiting from eating and drinking too much (Cicero *Phil.* 2.104.41). Aesop recounts the story of slaves being induced to vomit by using lukewarm water (*Vit. Aes.* 2–3). The imagery of vomiting in the biblical context clearly indicated the idea of rejection (Lev 18:5, 28). Just as a banqueter would prefer hot and cold drinks over lukewarm, so the suzerain prefered the Laodiceans to be either

---

[71] See chapter 1, *Sanctions*.
[72] Charles, *Revelation*, 1:96; Thomas, *Rev 1–7*, 309.
[73] From the fourth-cent. work *Corpus Glossariorum Latinorum*, quoted in Dunbabin, "Wine and Water," 129.

hot or cold, but are found to be lukewarm and "devoid of works and useless to the Lord."[74] Like lukewarm drinks at a banquet that are undesirable, the Laodicean church are indistinguishable (the same temperature) from their surrounding environment.[75] Medically lukewarm water with salt was sometimes used as an emetic by ancient doctors.[76] Celsus prescribed such an emetic for a fever, stating: "he should be given to drink tepid water with a little salt in it, and so made to vomit" (*Med.* 3.12.3 [Spencer]).[77]

Hemer testified that the bad quality of water at Laodicea "was primarily due to its impurity rather than its warmth"[78] evident from the crusty deposits around the terra cotta pipes. The waters likely caused an emetic tendency irrespective of its temperature, but Hemer's friend, Dr. G. W. Blanchard, calculated that the temperature in the pipes would not change significantly from the source, thus cold water would remain cold and hot water would remain hot.[79] Strabo testified that although the waters of Laodicea were petrifying they were still drinkable (*Geogr.* 13.4.14), which cannot be said of the waters of the Lycus river that are described as "nauseous and undrinkable"[80] since they are "turbid with white mud."[81]

THE CURSE OF PROSPERITY—17A

ὅτι λέγεις ὅτι πλούσιός εἰμι καὶ πεπλούτηκα καὶ οὐδὲν χρείαν ἔχω,

"For you say, I am rich, I have prospered, and I need nothing." (Rev 3:17a).

The true spiritual condition of the Laodiceans is stated using irony[82] in the following words "For you say, I am rich, I have prospered,[83] and I need nothing" (3:17). This is clearly connected to the affluence of the city which was well known (see chapter 16, *The Financial World at Laodicea*) and possibly interpreted as a blessing from God.[84] The most striking example of its wealth is a statement by Tacitus, who wrote: "Laodicea, one of the famous Asiatic cities, was laid in ruins by an earthquake [AD 60], but recovered by its own resources [unlike Philadelphia], without assistance

---

[74] Osborne, *Revelation*, 206.

[75] Koester, "Message to Laodicea," 415; *Revelation*, 344.

[76] Huttner, Early Christianity in the Lycus Valley, 157.

[77] Cf. Celsus *Med.* 1.3.22; Vitruvius *Arch.* 8.3.1; Galen *San. Tu.* 6.3.7.

[78] Hemer, Letters to the Seven Churches, 189.

[79] Ibid., 189, 277 n.48.

[80] Ramsay, *Cities and Bishoprics*, 1:215 n.2.

[81] Davis, *Anatolia*, 77.

[82] Blaiklock, The Seven Churches: An Exposition of Revelation Chapters Two and Three, 77; Mounce, Revelation, 111.

[83] Several have noted that "I am rich and I have prospered" is a rhetorical device called a *hysteron-proteron* (ὕστερον πρότερον, "later before") where the more important idea is put first to help make a point and used several times in Revelation (cf. 3:9; 5:2, 5; 10:4, 9; 12:10; 19:13). Logically, obtaining riches comes before one attains to a status of wealthy. Beckwith, *Apocalypse*, 243–44; Thomas, *Rev 1–7*, 311; Aune, *Rev 1–5*, 258–59.

[84] Johnson, "Revelation," 637.

from ourselves [Rome]" (*Ann.* 14.27.1 [Jackson]). Cicero cashed his treasury bill here, as it was a major banking center (Cicero *Fam.* 3.5.4; *Att.* 5.15.2). But the suzerain was aware that this community was also claiming spiritual prosperity and self-sufficiency as a result (cf. 18:7[85]). Their arrogance is reinforced by the use of the first person pronoun "I" (εἰμι, *eimi;* ἔχω, *echō*).[86] There is a striking parallel[87] in Hosea that states "Ephraim has said, 'Ah, but I am rich; I have found wealth for myself; in all my labors they cannot find in me iniquity or sin'" (12:8). Like Ephraim of old the Laodicean's monetary riches and self sufficiency are contrasted with their spiritual poverty.

THE CURSE OF NOT REALIZING THAT THEY ARE A PITITFUL WRETCH—17B

καὶ οὐκ οἶδας ὅτι σὺ εἶ ὁ ταλαίπωρος καὶ ἐλεεινὸς καὶ πτωχὸς καὶ τυφλὸς καὶ γυμνός.

"not realizing that *you* are wretched, pitiable, poor, blind, and naked." (Rev 3:17b).

The Laodicean church is oblivious (οὐκ οἶδας, *ouk oidas,* "do not know") to their spiritual condition, contrasted with the suzerain who knows their condition perfectly (3:15a). The Greek uses the conjunction "and" (καί, *kai*) with each adjective for the purpose of emphasis (*polysyndeton*).[88] According to the "Granville Sharp's Rule" of Greek grammar:

When the copulative καί connects two nouns of the same case, if the article ὁ or any of its cases precedes the first of the said nouns or participles, and is not repeated before the second noun or participle, the latter always relates to the same person that is expressed or described by the first noun or participle; i.e., it denotes a further description of the first-named person.[89]

Following Sharp's rule the article applies to the five characteristics listed in the verse and treats them as a single whole describing the spiritual condition of the Laodiceans.[90] Thus, as a collective community the adjectives ταλαίπωρος (*telaipōros*, "wretched", i.e., miserable, cf. Rom 7:24; Jam 4:9) and ἐλεεινὸς (*eleeinos*, "pitiful," i.e., in need of mercy[91]) can be translated as "pitiful wretch", who are also figuratively poor, blind and naked.

---

[85] Mark D. Mathews, "The Function of Imputed Speech in the Apocalypse of John," *CBQ* 74, no. 2 (2012): 320.

[86] Cf. Zech 11:5; *1 En.* 97:8–10; Luke 12:16–21; Arrian *Diatr.* 3.7.29; Robert M. Royalty Jr., "The Streets of Heaven: The Imagery and Ideology of Wealth in the Apocalypse of John" (Ph.D. diss., Yale University, 1995), 209; *Ideology of Wealth.*

[87] Beale suggests that this is "more than a mere coincidental parallel" and "that John is intentionally alluding to Hosea." Beale, *Rev,* 304; Charles, *Revelation,* 1:96.

[88] This literary device is the repetition of the conjunctions "and", "or" or "but" for the purpose of emphasis. Aune, *Rev 1–5,* 259.

[89] Dana and Mantey, *Manual Grammar,* 147; Daniel B. Wallace, "The Article with Multiple Substantives Connected by Kai in the New Testament: Semantics and Significance" (Ph.D. diss., Dallas Theological Seminary, 1995), 134–35.

[90] Osborne, *Revelation,* 207 n.15.

[91] Cf. 1 Cor 15:19; LXX Dan 9:23; 10:11.

THE CURSE OF NOT REALIZING THAT THEY ARE POOR—17B

Despite the cities financial prosperity (see chapter 16, *The Financial World at Laodicea*), the Laodicean Christians are spiritually "poor" (πτωχὸς, *ptōchos*)[92] and impoverished in their commitment to the suzerain.

THE CURSE OF NOT REALIZING THAT THEY ARE BLIND—17B

Despite the cities medical school and the regions famous eye-salve (see chapter 16, *Medical Center and Ophthalmology*), the Laodicean Christians are spiritually blind (τυφλὸς, *tuphlos*) and unable to see their true condition. The metaphorical use of blindness[93] is almost universally accepted as a local reference to the eye-salve (cf. 18)[94] produced from the Phrygian powder from Hierapolis, likely developed at the medical school (Strabo *Geogr.* 12.8.20) founded by Zeuxis at Laodicea.[95] There was a living memory of eye treatment in the Lycus Valley, which John drew upon in writing his letter to Laodicea.[96] Blindness is often the plight of the poorest of society.[97] While the Laodiceans have access to the salve to treat blindness, the suzerain declares that they do not realize they are blind.

THE CURSE OF NOT REALIZING THAT THEY ARE NAKED—17B

Despite the cities flourishing textile industry (see chapter 16, *Textile Industry and Wool*), the Laodicean Christians are spiritually "naked" (γυμνός, *gymnos*).[98] In antiquity nakedness was another sign of poverty,[99] shame[100] and humiliation within Judaism (contra the Greeks).[101] While the Sardian Christian's clothes were defiled, the Laodicean Christians had none, further exposing them to shame in a message meant to be read publicly in the other churches.[102] Indeed, before the all-seeing eye of the suzerain they are really naked and open to the gaze of the omniscient one.[103] As Osborne put it "it is possible to wear Armani suits and Dior dresses

---

[92] Cf. 17:3–4; 18:11–19; Philo *Prob.* 9.

[93] For the metaphorical use of blindness see Exod 23:8; Deut 16:19; Isa 42:19–20; 56:10; Matt 23:16–17; John 9:40–41; Epictetus *Diatr.* 3.22.26–27; cf. 3.26.3. F. Graber, "Blind," ed. and trans. Colin Brown, *NIDNTT* (Grand Rapids, Mich.: Zondervan, 1976), 1:218–20.

[94] Ramsay, *Letters*, 316–17; Hemer, *Letters*, 196–201.

[95] Colin J. Hemer, "Seven Cities of Asia Minor," in *Major Cities of the Biblical World*, ed. R.K. Harrison (Nashville, Tenn.: Nelson, 1985), 196–99; Ramsay, *Cities and Bishoprics*, 2:52; Rudwick and Green, "The Laodicean Lukewarmness," 176; Wilcock, *Heaven Opened*, 56–57; Yamauchi, *NT Cities*, 145–46; Blaiklock, *Cities of the NT*, 125.

[96] Huttner, Early Christianity in the Lycus Valley, 170–77.

[97] Cf. 2 Sam 5:6–10; 1QM 7:4f.; 1Qsa 2:5ff.

[98] Later in Revelation, Babylon/Rome are stripped naked (17:16).

[99] Job 31:19; Tob 1:17; Matt 25:36; Jas 2:15.

[100] Cf. Gen 2:25; 3:7; Isa 20:4–5; Rev 16:15.

[101] Cf. 2 Sam 10:4; Isa 20:4; Ezek 16:37–39; Nah 3:5; etc.

[102] David Arthur DeSilva, *Seeing Things John's Way: The Rhetoric of the Book of Revelation* (Louisville, Ky.: Westminster/John Knox, 2009), 190.

[103] Cf. *1 En.* 9:5; Philo *Cher.* 17; Heb 4:13.

but to be 'naked' in the eyes of God."[104] White garments of righteousness[105] are available to the overcomers (3:18).

ETHICAL STIPULATIONS—3:18-19

The ethical stipulations and obligations[106] in the ANEVT that were set forth by the suzerain and accepted vassal[107] are mentioned next in the structure of the messages. Within the SMR, the transition to ethical stipulations is indicated by the imperative verbs, and presented in terms of commands.[108] Five imperatives are given by the suzerain for the Laodicean's obedience; buy gold, buy wool, buy medicine, be zealous and repent. These exhortations to the churches convey the new covenant obligation of faithfulness to their king.[109]

FIRST IMPERATIVE: BUY FROM THE SUZERAIN—3:18A

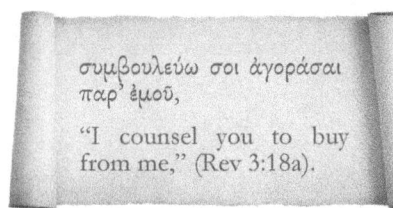

συμβουλεύω σοι ἀγοράσαι παρ' ἐμοῦ,

"I counsel you to buy from me," (Rev 3:18a).

Now the suzerain speaks in tones of counsel and advice (συμβουλεύω σοι, *symbouleuō soi;* cf. John 18:14). Osborne translates the term as "Let me give you some advice. You should...."[110] The Laodiceans are counseled to buy three things from the suzerain (ἀγοράσαι παρ' ἐμοῦ, *agorasai par'emou,* "buy from me" 3:18a); gold, wool and eye-salve. The first three ethical stipulations were introduced in 3:17, but here the order of the second and third adjective, applied as a stipulation, are reversed, likely for rhetorical purposes.[111] Only the suzerain can provide the needed remedies of gold, garments and eye-salve, to correct the deficiencies of the lukewarm Laodiceans.

SECOND IMPERATIVE: BUY GOLD TO BECOME RICH—18B

Since the Laodiceans are poor spiritually (17b), they need to purchase (ἀγοράσαι, *agorasai*) from the suzerain, gold refined by fire[112] to become spiritually rich. However, how is it possible for the poor to purchase something as expensive as gold? In monetary terms the Laodiceans were likely wealthy, but spiritually poor. Isaiah could also put a similar paradox before his readers

---

[104] Osborne, *Revelation*, 209.

[105] Rev 3:3, 5; 4:4; 6:11; 7:9; 13–14; 19:14.

[106] The vassal-treaties of Esarhaddon list thirty-three stipulations, which follow the divine witnesses, and are to be kept by the vassal. Parpola and Watanabe, *Neo-Assyrian Treaties*, nos. 1–6, 46–57; Wiseman, "Vassal-Treaties," 23–24.

[107] Mendenhall, "Covenant Forms," 59; "Covenant," 1:714; Shea, "Covenantal Form," 72; Bright, *Covenant and Promise*, 37; Thompson, "Near Eastern Suzerain-Vassal," 4; McCarthy, *Treaty and Covenant*, 51 n.3.

[108] Aune identifies the central sections of each proclamation as *dispositio*, which means "arrangement," not marked by any characteristic phrase but imperative verbs. Aune, *Rev 1–5*, 122.

[109] Shea, "Covenantal Form," 75.

[110] Osborne, *Revelation*, 208.

[111] Ibid.

[112] Mal 3:2–3; Job 23:10; Zech 13:9; 1 Pet 1:6–9.

> χρυσίον πεπυρωμένον ἐκ πυρὸς
> ἵνα πλουτήσῃς,
>
> "gold refined by fire, so that you may be rich," (Rev 3:18b).

when he exhorted: "he who has no money, come, buy and eat" (55:1–2). It is no doubt to be understood metaphorically as the suzerains' riches cannot be bought with gold, since it has already been purchased (Isa 55:1; Gal 3:13) and must be accepted as a gracious gift by faith (Eph 2:8–9).

Gold refined in fire is a well known metaphor for being purified through suffering.[113] Thomas sees gold as corresponding to their lack of genuine faith.[114] Koester points out that the kind of commitment the suzerain is calling for from the Laodiceans "will set them at odds with others in their social context and require perseverance."[115]

This reference to gold would be understood by the Laodiceans who had boasted of their wealth and were known for their banking[116] and commerce (see chapter 16, *The Financial World at Laodicea*).[117] However, it is worth noting that Ephesus was Asia's main banking center (Dio Chrysostom *Or.* 31.54–55; Aristides *Orat.* 23.24), and there was an important financial center at Pergamum (*IGR* 352)[118] and Sardis was legendary for its gold wealth.[119] Smyrna also had goldsmiths and street named in honor of gold (*I.Smyr.* 721; Aristides *Orat.* 18.6). What was so special about Laodicea for John to focus on gold with this city? It is not so much this reference to gold alone that would draw their attention, but when included alongside wool and eye-salve, the three together describe Laodicea's unique local setting.[120]

THIRD IMPERATIVE: BUY WHITE GARMENTS TO HIDE YOUR NAKEDNESS—18C

> καὶ ἱμάτια λευκὰ ἵνα περιβάλῃ καὶ μὴ φανερωθῇ ἡ αἰσχύνη τῆς γυμνότητός σου,
>
> "and *white garments* so that you may clothe yourself and the shame of your nakedness may not be seen, " (Rev 3:18c).

Their "nakedness" (3:17b) is contrasted with the "white garments so that you may clothe yourself and the shame of your nakedness may not be seen" (3:18). Osborne suggests that this is an epexegetical genitive and could be translated "shameful nakedness."[121] This is further contrasted against Laodicea's

---

[113] 1 Pet 1:7; Ps 66:10; cf. Zech 13:9; Isa 1:25.

[114] Thomas, *Rev 1–7*, 316.

[115] Koester, *Revelation*, 347.

[116] Worth, Jr., *Greco-Asian Culture*, 218–19; Hemer, *Letters to the Seven Churches*, 191–96, 208; Charles, *Revelation of St John*, 1:93. Merrill F. Unger, *Archaeology and the New Testament* (Grand Rapids, Mich.: Zondervan, 1975), 267. Unger connects their wealth with their proximity to several major trade routes.

[117] Hemer, *Letters*, 195; cf. Ford, *Revelation*, 419; Caird, *Commentary*, 56; Sweet, *Revelation*, 107. Contra Koester, *Revelation*, 338.

[118] Broughton, "Roman Asia Minor," 888–97; Magie, *Roman Rule in Asia Minor*, 1.624.

[119] Ovid *Metam.* 11.136–45; Lucian *Phar.* 3.209–10; Philostratus *Vit. Apoll.* 6.37.

[120] Koester, "Message to Laodicea," 416–20.

[121] Osborne, *Revelation*, 209 n.20.

dependence on their thriving textile industry (*I.Laod.* 51b.2), which was centered around the black wool from Laodicea (Strabo *Geogr.* 12.8.16; see chapter 16, *Textile Industry and Wool*).[122] In spite of the fact they have access to excellent wool, they are in fact naked, but for the overcomer the suzerain promises white garments[123] of righteousness to hide their shame and they will receive honour.[124]

In ancient society white garments were reserved for lawyers, the wealthy, and if worn by the master their slaves were also permitted to wear the same (Artemidorus *Oneir.* 2.3; 4.2). White robes were also worn by those attending festival gathering (Aelius Aristides *Orat.* 48.30; Plutarch *Mor.* 771d). Revelation uses the color white for garments suitable for the suzerain (God and Christ)[125] and his vassals around his throne.[126] The redeemed have garments washed white in the blood of the Lamb (7:14; cf. 1:5; 5:9) and have a place in the New Jerusalem.[127] Only the suzerain can provide the white garments of righteousness.

FOURTH IMPERATIVE: BUY SALVE TO ANOINT YOUR EYES—18D

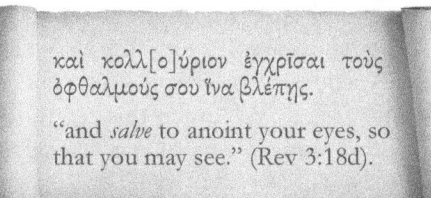

καὶ κολλ[ο]ύριον ἐγχρῖσαι τοὺς ὀφθαλμούς σου ἵνα βλέπῃς.

"and *salve* to anoint your eyes, so that you may see." (Rev 3:18d)

Although Koester suggests that eye-salve "was not uniquely tied to Laodicea"[128] the region of Phrygia, in which Laodicea was part, produced a *dry collyrium* [κολλύριον, *kollurion*] made of Phrygian stone (Galen *San. Tu.* 6.12) used for medical treatment of eye ailments (see chapter 16, *Medical Center and Ophthalmology*). In spite of the medical treatment available for blindness, the Laodiceans were still spiritually blind[129] and could not see their own condition. They were advised to purchase eye-salve (κολλ[ο]ύριον, *koll[o]urion*)[130] from the suzerain. The Greek word (Lat. *collyrium*) is derived from κολλούρα (*kalloura*) which means "a loaf of bread"[131] and is believed that the medicine was applied to the eyes as a "doughy paste".[132] Such medications were produced by grinding up plants and minerals into a power and

---

[122] Hemer, *Letters to the Seven Churches*, 247; Ramsay, *Letters: Updated*, 234; Ford, *Revelation*, 419; Sweet, *Revelation*, 108; Worth, Jr., *Greco-Asian Culture*, 217–18. Contra Mounce, *Revelation*, 111; Koester, "Message to Laodicea," 420.

[123] Cf. Rev 3:4–5; 4:4; 6:11; 7:9–14; 19:8, 14.

[124] Cf. Gen 41:42; Esth 6:6–11; Dan 5:29.

[125] Rev 1:14; 20:11; cf. Aelius Aristides *Orat.* 48.30–31; Plato *Leg.* 956A; Plutarch *Mor.* 771d; Josephus *Ant.* 11.327, 331).

[126] Rev 4:4; 7:9–14; cf. Dan 7:9; Matt 17:2; John 20:12; Acts 1:10; *1 En.* 14:20.

[127] Rev 22:14; cf. *1 En.* 62:15–16; 2 Esd 2:39, 45; 1 Cor 15:53–54; 2 Cor 5:1–4; *Mart. Asc. Isa.* 4:16; 9:9, 17; Hermas *Sim.* 8.2.3.

[128] Koester, *Revelation*, 339.

[129] Spiritual blindness was a typical Johannine motif. John 9:39; 20:29; 1 John 3:2.

[130] On the ancient background to κολλύριον *(kollurion)*, see Hemer, *Letters to the Seven Churches*, 196–99; Paul R Berger, "Kollyrium Für Die Blinden Augen, Apk 3:18," *NovT* 27, no. 2 (April 1985): 174–95; Durling, *A Dictionary of Medical Terms in Galen*, 207.

[131] Smalley, *Revelation*, 100.

[132] Mounce, *Revelation*, 111 n.33.

then mixing them into an ointment or paste with water or other liquids (e.g., Pliny *Nat.* 29.38.117–32; 33.27.114) to be applied topically to the eyes.[133] Horace applied black ointment (*collyrium*) on his "sore eyes" (*Sat.* 1.5.30–31).

Some have attempted to allegorize the eye-salve to represent: a new heart,[134] the grace and forgiveness of God,[135] the Word of God,[136] fellowship with God,[137] or the work of the Holy Spirit.[138] Any one of these suggestions falls short, when the eye-salve represents all of these and more.[139] Only the suzerain can provide the salve to correct their spiritual blindness and lack of discernment of their spiritual condition.

FIFTH IMPERATIVE: BE ZEALOUS—19A

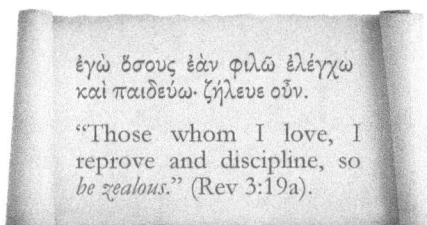

ἐγὼ ὅσους ἐὰν φιλῶ ἐλέγχω καὶ παιδεύω· ζήλευε οὖν.

"Those whom I love, I reprove and discipline, so be zealous." (Rev 3:19a).

Ramsay has suggested that because there is no conjunction between verse 18 and 19, that the remaining verses should be taken as an epilogue for all the messages and not part of the message to Laodicea.[140] However, this would leave Laodicea without the promise of blessings, and without the proclamation witness formula that is similar to the other six messages.[141] Hemer demonstrates that there are local references to Laodicea in verses 20 and 21[142] and thus should be considered part of the message to Laodicea.

The use of φιλῶ (*philō*) here instead of ἀγαπάω (*agapaō*) is debated by scholars, since ἀγαπάω (*agapaō*) is used in the LXX of Proverbs 3:12, which many believe is behind this verse. Several scholars accept φιλῶ (*philō*) as a warm personal affection, instead of ἀγαπάω (*agapaō*), the deep intimate love that was used for the Philadelphians (3:9).[143] However, as Carson points out they are used synonymously by John.[144]

The sentence begins with ἐγὼ (*egō*, "I") stressing that it is the suzerain who is the subject carrying out the discipline. Mounce paraphrases it as "Now my practice is that all those I love, I also correct and discipline."[145] The reproof (ἐλέγχω, *elegchō*, "to punish" or "convict"[146]) and

---

[133] *NewDocs* 3:56–57; Jackson, "Eye Medicine in the Roman Empire," 2228–51; Vivian Nutton, "The Drug Trade in Antiquity," *Journal of the Royal Society of Medicine* 78 (1985): 143.

[134] Charles, *Revelation*, 1:99.

[135] Swete, *Apocalypse*, 63; Hughes, *Revelation*, 67.

[136] Lenski, *Revelation*, 1963, 160; Kistemaker, *Revelation*, 173.

[137] Beasley-Murray, *Revelation, NCB*, 106.

[138] Alford, *Revelation*, 4:591; Thomas, *Rev 1–7*, 316.

[139] Beckwith, *Apocalypse*, 291; Osborne, *Revelation*, 210; Smalley, *Revelation*, 100.

[140] Ramsay, *Letters: Updated*, 317.

[141] Thomas, *Rev 1–7*, 317; Mounce, *Revelation*, 112.

[142] Hemer, Letters to the Seven Churches, 465–73, 480.

[143] Barclay, *Revelation*, 1:1:183; Mounce, *Revelation*, 112; Thomas, *Rev 1–7*, 318.

[144] Carson, *Gospel According to John*, 676–77; Alford, *Revelation*, 4:4:591; Smalley, *Revelation*, 100.

[145] Mounce, *Revelation*, 112.

discipline (παιδεύω, *paideuō*, "bring up, instruct, train, educate"[147]) of the suzerain is out of love and not hostility. It is often noted that this verse is loosely based on Proverbs 3:11–12: "My son, do not despise the Lord's discipline or be weary of his reproof, for the Lord reproves him whom he loves, as a father the son in whom he delights."[148] Fürst states that "God is the Father; he chastens because he loves, in order to keep men in the status of being children of God, and to cause his children to turn round and come home."[149] It contains the idea of "rousing" or "stirring."[150]

Osborne draws the attention to the order of ζήλευε (*zēleue*, "zealous", present imperative), preceding μετανόησον (*metanoēson*, "repent", aorist), challenging many commentators[151] who reverse the order for a decisive act of repentance followed by a continual zeal set against the lukewarm condition of the Laodiceans.[152] Alford argues that "change of purpose must precede *zeal*, which is the effectual working in a man's life of that change of purpose."[153] Thomas considers this another case of *hysteron proteron* (cf. 3:17).[154]

The word ζήλευε (*zēleue*, "zealous") is related to the Greek word ζεστός (*zestos*, "hot") used earlier in 3:15, 16. The imperative for the Laodiceans is to be in a continuing state of zeal and earnestness (ζήλευε, *zēleue*, present imperative). The lukewarm, self-sufficient, and blind Laodiceans must replace their complacency with genuine enthusiasm for their suzerain.

SIX IMPERATIVE: REPENT—19B

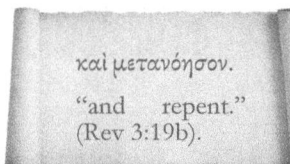
καὶ μετανόησον.
"and repent."
(Rev 3:19b).

The classic meaning of μετανόησον (*metanoēson*, "to repent"; c. 2:5; 3:3) is a change of mind and here it is in the aorist tense, meaning it is a once-for-all repentance. The judgment and discipline of the suzerain are inseparable from his love for his vassals. Only the suzerain can provide, by his grace, what is needed in salvation. Only Christ can make the poor rich,[155] cover the naked person's shame (Gen 3:7; 21; Rev 16:15), and correct the spiritual sight of blind vassals.

---

[146] It means to convict of sin that summons to repentance. F. Büchsel, "ἐλέγχω," *TDNT* 2: 473–47; Hans-Georg Link, "Ἐλέγχω," ed. and trans. Colin Brown, *NIDNTT* (Grand Rapids, Mich.: Zondervan, 1986), 2.140–42. Cf. John 3:20; 8:46; 16:8; Eph 5:13; 2 Tim 4:2.

[147] Dieter Fürst, "Παιδεύω," ed. and trans. Colin Brown, *NIDNTT* (Grand Rapids, Mich.: Zondervan, 1986), 3.775–80. See also G. Bertram "παιδεύω, κτλ," *TDNT* 5:596–625.

[148] Proverbs is quoted verbatim from the LXX in Heb 12:6, *1 Clem.* 56:4, and Philo *Congr.* 177. See also 2 Tim 2:25; Heb 12:6, 7, 10.

[149] Fürst, "Παιδεύω," 3:778.

[150] Bertram "παιδεύω, κτλ," *TDNT* 5:623.

[151] Moffatt, *Revelation*, 5:372; Mounce, *Revelation*, 112; Thomas, *Rev 1–7*, 319–20.

[152] Osborne, *Revelation*, 211.

[153] Alford, *Revelation*, 4:591; Stott, *Christ Thinks*, 123.

[154] Thomas, *Rev 1–7*, 320.

[155] Matt 5:3; Luke 1:52–53; Jas 2:5.

SANCTIONS: BLESSING—3:20–21

Blessings are promised to the those who conquer or overcome (τῷ νικῶντι, *tō nikōnti*). Each message contains a blessing to the overcomers that uses a different synonym for eternal life. Here we have a prophetic oracle declared by a Christian prophet in the name of Christ, that contains three blessings.[156] Here the imagery recalls a communal banquet with the suzerain. However, here John reverses the roles, as the Laodiceans who are described as poor, blind, naked, and pitiful, the typical image of outsiders to a banquet hall, are depicted inside the hall giving audience to the suzerain who is outside the door knocking to gain entrance to participate in a meal with his vassals. All three blessings must be seen as part of the same picture.[157]

THE BLESSING OF THE SUZERAIN WHO KNOCKS—20A

> Ἰδοὺ ἕστηκα ἐπὶ τὴν θύραν καὶ κρούω·
>
> "Behold, I stand at the door and knock." (Rev 3:20a)

There have been several possible identifications for the door in this saying. The most common include:

169. Oil on Canvas painting of *The Light of the World* (Manchester version) by William Holman Hunt (1851–1856).

1. The doors of the city gate. Hemer argues that the doors are derived from the local reference of the doors in the four city gates that were an important aspects of the city being on a trade route.[158]

2. Phoebus at the door. Aune suggests that this metaphorical reference to a door and knocking has a parallel in the *Hymn to Apollo* that states: "Now surely Phoebus knocketh at the door with his beautiful foot." (Callimachus *Hymn. Apoll.* 3 [Mair]).[159]

3. The lover at the door. Some consider it an allusion to the metaphorical use in the Song of Song that states: "I slept, but my heart was awake. A sound! My beloved is knocking" (Song

---

[156] Rudolf Bultmann, *The History of the Synoptic Tradition*, trans. John Marsh, Revised (Grand Rapids, Mich.: Hendrickson, 1994), 134–35; Müller, *Prophetie*, 75.

[157] Tim Wiarda, "Revelation 3:20: Imagery And Literary Context," *JETS* 38, no. 2 (1995): 205.

[158] Ramsay, *Letters: Updated*, 236; Hemer, *Letters to the Seven Churches*, 204; Rudwick and Green, "The Laodicean Lukewarmness," 178–79.

[159] Aune, *Rev 1–5*, 260.

5:2).[160] Several Jewish commentators see Song 5:2 as "a call for Israel's repentance within the purported context of a covenant relationship with God"[161] (*Midr. Rab.* Exod 33:3; *Midr. Rab. Cant.* 5:2).

4. The door to the human heart. Allegorized to mean an evangelistic call made to unbelievers to open the door to Christ.[162] This has been popularized by Homan Hunt's famous oil painting called "The Light of the World" (see Fig. 169). Morris and others see the phrase "if anyone" as an appeal to individuals. Morris argues: "even if the church as a whole does not heed the warning, some individuals may".[163] However, the verse is addressed to the church and those who are weak professing Christians in need of repentance.

5. The eschatological door. James 5:9 portrays the image of a judge standing at the door (cf. Mark 13:29; Matt 24:33). This eschatological door is one through which the suzerain (Christ) will pass at the *parousia*. As an eschatological image the words "I stand at the door and knock" conveys a warning of imminent eschatological judgment.[164] The theme of an eschatological door is again picked up at the start of the next chapter where the suzerain passes through a heavenly door to return to earth (4:1). Wirada contends that because the three images must be treated as one, that the middle scene involves an individual response that is missing in James 5:9 and Mark 13:29 and "certainly do not portray Jesus waiting for anyone on earth to open the door for his return".[165] Beal argues that given the present tense of the verbs ἕστηκα (*estēka*, "stands") and κρούω (*krouō*, "knocks") that the coming of the suzerain is imminent and not referring to the *parousia*. However, Bauckham makes a persuasive argument based on 1) a reference to the *parousia* is to be expected; 2) the sequence of 3:20–21; and 3) Christ is not the guest,[166] but the "master whose servants are expected to be ready to open to him at his return. . . . [that] the parousia may come either as judgment or as blessing."[167]

---

[160] André Feuillet, "Le Cantique Des Cantiques et l'Apocalypse: Etude Des Deux Reminiscences Du Cantique Dans l'Apocalypse Johannique (Apc 3,20 et Cant 5.1–2; Apc 12 et Cant 6,10)," *RSR* 49 (1961): 321–53; Kraft, *Offenbarung*, 86; E. Cortes, "Una Interpretación Judía Del Cant 5, 2 En Apocalipsis 3, 19b-20," *RCT* 4, no. 2 (1979): 239–58; Sweet, *Revelation*, 109; Beale, *Rev*, 308; Osborne, *Revelation*, 212.

[161] Beale, *Rev*, 308.

[162] Johnson, "Revelation," 638.

[163] Morris, *Revelation*, 86; Wiarda, "Revelation 3:20," 213.

[164] Bousset, Die Offenbarung Johannis, 233; Swete, Revelation, 63; Lohmeyer, Offenbarung, 39; Lohse, Offenbarung, 32; Vos, The Synoptic Traditions in the Apocalypse, 95; Thomas, Rev 1–7, 321; Sweet, Revelation, 109.

[165] Wiarda, "Revelation 3:20," 205.

[166] Karrer and Aune argue that Jesus is the guest rather than the host. Karrer, *Johannesoffenbarung*, 1:215 n.331; Aune, *Rev 1–5*, 261.

[167] Bauckham, *Climax of Prophecy*, 106–9.

6. The parabolic door of the returning master. The most common proposal is an adaptation by John, of the parable of the doorkeeper in the gospels (Mark 13:33–37; Luke 12:35–38).[168] Bauckham argued that Revelation 3:20 has "deparabolized" Luke 12:35–38.[169] Aune disagrees appealing to the dissimilarity between this verse and the parable.[170]

Hospitality in the ancient world was highly valued and an honor to provide. It is known that under Roman law people could be forced to provide food and lodging for Roman officials (Philostratus *Vit. Soph.* 1.2; *MAMA* 6.15, lines 8-10).[171] By contrast Jesus knocks to request access, rather than rely on Roman law for entry. Abraham and Lot were known for their hospitality, with Abraham entertaining three strangers who were the messengers of God (Gen 18:1–15).[172] The tradition of hospitality in the ANE is expressed by presenting visitors with bread and salt to be eaten together in a meal of covenant friendship.[173] The Greeks maintained that the gods could appear at any moment disguised to test one's hospitality (Homer *Od.* 6.207–8; Ovid *Metam.* 8.626–78).[174] Here in Revelation the suzerain appears at the door as a visitor, although it is his meal.

THE BLESSINGS OF A COMMUNION MEAL—20B

ἐάν τις ἀκούσῃ τῆς φωνῆς μου καὶ ἀνοίξῃ τὴν θύραν [καὶ] εἰσελεύσομαι πρὸς αὐτὸν καὶ δειπνήσω μετ᾽ αὐτοῦ καὶ αὐτὸς μετ᾽ ἐμοῦ.

"If anyone hears my voice and opens the door, I will come in to him and eat with him, and he with me." (Rev 3:20b).

This communal fellowship meal, where the suzerain first "will come in to him" and then "will eat with him δειπνήσω (*deipnēsō*), and he with me" (3:20b), is reminiscent of the covenant formula[175] mentioned later in Revelation: "I will be

---

[168] Smalley, *Revelation*, 102; Beale, *Rev*, 308.

[169] Jeremias, *Parables of Jesus*, 54–55; Bauckham, "Synoptic Parousia Parables and the Apocalypse," 162–76; "Synoptic Parousia Parables Again," *NTS* 29, no. 1 (1983): 129–34; *Climax of Prophecy*, 109.

[170] Aune, *Rev 1–5*, 251.

[171] Hemer, Letters to the Seven Churches, 204; Worth, Jr., Greco-Asian Culture, 219.

[172] Cf. Philo *Abr.* 107–18; *T. Ab.* 1:2, 5; Heb 13:2; Josephus *Ant.* 1.200; *Gen. Rab.* 41:8; 50:4; Samuel Rapaport, *Tales and Maxims from the Midrash* (London, U.K.: Routledge & Sons, 1907); H. Freedman and Maurice Simon, eds., *Midrash Rabbah* (London, U.K.: Soncino, 1992), 1:437.

[173] Num 18:19; 2 Chr 13:5: the covenant of salt; Aristotle *Eth. eud.* 7.1239b; *Eth. nic.* 8.3.8; Aeschines *Fals. leg.* 2.22; Cicero *Amic.* 19.67; Dio Chrysostom *Or.* 7.65; Plutarch *Mor.* 612d; Matt 9:10; Mark 2:16; Luke 15:2.

[174] Amy G. Oden, ed., And You Welcomed Me: A Sourcebook on Hospitality in Early Christianity (Nashville, Tenn.: Abingdon, 2002); Andrew Arterbury, Entertaining Angels: Early Christian Hospitality in Its Mediterranean Setting, New Testament Monographs 8 (Sheffield, U.K.: Sheffield Phoenix, 2005), 15–93.

[175] Baltzer, Covenant Formulary; Paul Kalluveettil, Paul, Declaration and Covenant: A Comprehensive Review of Covenant Formulae from the Old Testament and the Ancient Near East, AnBib 88 (Rome: Biblical Institute, 1982), 15; Rolf Rendtorff, The Covenant Formula: An Exegetical and Theological Investigation (Edinburgh, U.K.: Bloomsbury, 2000).

your God and you will be my people" (21:7). As Beale states, the covenant formula[176] in Revelation 21:3, 7 indicates "that the new creation, towards which history is moving, will bring to fulfilment the new covenant promised in the book of Jeremiah and inaugurated by Jesus Christ."[177]

δειπνήσω (*deipnēsō*) is derived from δειπνέω (*deipneō*) "to make a meal,"[178] without indicating what kind of food or time of day it was served.[179] However, the related noun δεῖπνον (*deipnon*), can refer to "a main meal, dinner, supper, banquet"[180] and used in conjunction with the Passover meal in Judaism (Josephus *Ant*. 2.312) and the Christian celebration of the Lord's Supper (κυριακόν δεῖπνον, *kuriakon deipnon*, Luke 22:20; 1 Cor 11:20). In Hellenistic religion, it refered to the cultic meal where the participants sat at God's table and entered into fellowship with the deity.[181]

The motif of a common meal is understood by scholars in several ways:

1. An individual call to repentance and intimate fellowship (3:19) for "self-deluded members of the church"[182] that is present and not future.[183] Wirada believes that 3:19–20 is a general exhortation that applies to everyone, both unbeliever and believer.[184]

2. An eschatological messianic banquet, either imminent[185] or in the future (3:21).[186] Neither view necessarily excludes the other.[187] The NT mentions the "messianic banquet" where in the coming kingdom believers will eat together with their Lord (Matt 8:11; 26:29; Luke 14:15; 22:30; Rev 19:9). Those who hold to this view appeal to the similarities to the common meal found in Luke 12:35–37 (cf. Mark 13:33–37) but unlike common practice the returning

---

[176] The covenant formula "I will be your God, and you will be my people" is found throughout the OT. See Exod 6:7; Lev 26:12; Jer 7:23; 11:4; 24:7; 30:22; 31:1, 33; 32:28; Ezek 11:20; 14:11; 36:28; 37:23, 27; Hos 1:10; Joel 2:27; Zech 2:11; 8:8.

[177] Gregory K. Beale, "Revelation (Book)," in *NDBT*, ed. T. Desmond Alexander et al. (Downers Grove, Ill.: InterVarsity, 2000), 359; Smalley, *Revelation*, 528.

[178] LSJ 9628.

[179] Aune, *Rev 1–5*, 261.

[180] Bertold Klappert, "Lord's Supper," ed. Colin Brown, *NIDNTT* (Grand Rapids, Mich.: Zondervan, 1976), 520.

[181] P.Oxy. 1.110; 3.523; 13.1755; 52.3693; *NewDocs* 1:5; 2:28; Homer *Od.* 14.3; Aristophanes *Pax* 1084; *Eccl.* 1133; Xenophon *Cyr.* 5.3.35; Diodorus *Hist. Lib.* 11.9.

[182] Mounce, *Revelation*, 113.

[183] Beasley-Murray, *Revelation*, NCB, 107; Mounce, *Revelation*, 113–14; Beale, *Rev*, 308–9.

[184] Wiarda, "Revelation 3:20," 211–12.

[185] Charles, *Revelation*, 1:100–101; Beasley-Murray, *Revelation*, NCB, 107.

[186] Bousset, Die Offenbarung Johannis, 233; Swete, Revelation, 63–64; Lohmeyer, Offenbarung, 39; Lohse, Offenbarung, 35; Müller, Prophetie, 75; Sweet, Revelation, 109; Beckwith, Apocalypse, 491; Kiddle, Revelation, 60; Vos, The Synoptic Traditions in the Apocalypse, 95; Thomas, Rev 1–7, 321; Bauckham, "Synoptic Parousia Parables and the Apocalypse," 172.

[187] Lohmeyer, *Offenbarung*, 39.

170. Reproduction of a *triclinium* (dining room, Lat. *lectus triclinaris*) with two couches (κλίνη, *klinē*) for reclining at meals (first cent. AD; see Fig. 91).

suzerain (κύριος, *kurios*) is not served by his servants,[188] but rather presents the meal to them, similar to the festival of Saturnalia.[189] As Keener points out "Such an image would offend the well-to-do but would be a powerful symbol of how Jesus would treat those who remained faithful to the end."[190]

3. The common meal is a reference to the Lord's Supper (δεῖπνον, *deipnon*) or Eucharist (see Luke 24:30–31).[191]

---

[188] Contra. Aune, *Revelation 1–5*, 261.

[189] John F. Miller, "Roman Festivals," in *OEAGR*, ed. Michael Gagarin, vol. 3 (New York, N.Y.: Oxford University Press, 2010), 172.

[190] Keener, Background Commentary: NT, 214.

[191] Beasley-Murray, *Revelation, NCB*, 107; Johnson, "Revelation," 638; Smalley, *Revelation*, 102; *Thunder and Love*, 58–60; Caird, *Revelation*, 58; Aune, *Rev 1–5*, 251; Beale, *Rev*, 309.

4. Aune has identified it with the Graeco-Roman background as a meal with a god, understood as a τραπεζώματα (*trapezomata*) where "the god and his worshipers both partook of the food [i.e., meal] offer[ed]"[192] on a sacrificial table.[193] Some thirteen papyrus invitations to the couch (κλίνη, *klinē*, banquet couch; Eng. "recline"; see Fig. 91, 170) of Sarapis in a banquet hall[194] have been discovered.[195] In Graeco-Roman culture, the πάρεδρος δαίμων (*paredros daimōn*, "divine being") was also known as an ἄγγελος (*angelos*) and served in the role of a prophetic medium and assistant. The Greeks used the terms θεός (*theos*), δαίμων (*daimōn*), and ἄγγελος (*angelos*) interchangeably in their magical incantations (see *Quotes from Antiquity*).[196]

> **Quotes from Antiquity**
> Magical incantation
>
> Then question him by the same oaths. If he tells you his name, take him by the hand, descend and have him recline as I have said above, setting before him part of the / foods and drinks which you partake of. And when you release him, sacrifice to him after his departure what is prescribed and pour a wine offering, and in this way you will be a friend of the mighty angel [ἄγγελος]. When you go abroad, he will go abroad with you; when you are destitute, he will give you money. He will tell you what things will happen both when and at what time of the night or day. And if / anyone asks you "What do I have in mind?" or "What has happened to me?" or even "What is going to happen?," question the angel [ἄγγελος], and he will tell you in silence. But you speak to the one who questions you as if from yourself (*PGM* 1.167–77 [Betz]).

A sacrificial meal is also found in the cult of Zeus Panamaros (second cent. BC to fourth cent. AD), where the god was the host of the meal (*SEG* 4.247–61; cf., *SEG* 4.247.2; 4.250.2).[197] A funerary meal called the *lectisternium* (Lat. *lectum sternere*, "to prepare [or "drape"] a couch") was also eaten in the presence of the deified dead (Servius *ad Aen.* 10.76; Livy *Hist. Rome* 5.13.6; Cicero *Dom.* 13.6; see Fig. 91).[198] The Greek origin in the θεοξένια (*theoxenia*) is a similar feast, except that the gods played the part of the host. In the Imperial era, chairs (Lat. *sellae*) were

---

[192] Gill, "Trapezomata," 117.

[193] Aune, *Rev 1–5*, 251–52.

[194] Koenen, "Eine Einladung Zur Kline Des Sarapis," 121–26 (pl. 2); Gill, "Trapezomata," 117–37; Will, "Banquets et salles de banquet dans le cultes de la Grece et de l'Empire romain," 353–62; Gilliam, "Invitations to the Kline of Sarapis," 1:315–24.

[195] At the time Horsley wrote there were only eleven invitations known. P.Oxy. 1.110; 3.523; 13.1755; 52.3693; *NewDocs* 1:5; 2:28.

[196] Abt, *Die Apologie Des Apuleius von Madaura Und Die Antike Zauberei*, 253–57. See *PGM* 1, which contains spells for acquiring a πάρεδρος δαίμων (*paredros daimōn*, in which they equate the term θεός (*theos*, "god" lines 40, 77, 86, 88, 89, 90, 92, 93), with ἄγγελος (*aggelos*, "angel" lines 76, 78, 87, 172, 176).

[197] J. Hatzfeld, "Inscriptions de Panamara," *BCH* 51 (1927): 57–122.

[198] Anne Viola Siebert, "Lectisternium," in *BrillPaulyA*, ed. Hubert Cancik and Helmuth Schneider, trans. Christine F. Salazar and Francis G. Gentry, vol. 12 (Leiden: Brill, 2006), op. cit., http://dx.doi.org/10.1163/1574-9347_bnp_e633370.

substituted for couches in the case of goddesses, and the *lectisternium* in their case became a *sellisternium* (Tacitus *Ann.* 15.44; *CIL* 6.32323).[199] During the Christian era, *lectisternium* was used for a feast in memory of a deceased person (Sidonius *Ep.* 4.15; AD 430).

A magical incantation for a love potion has similar features to Rev 3:20 with the use of the πάρεδρος δαίμων (*paredros daimōn*. See *Quotes from Antiquity*).

> **Quotes from Antiquity**
>
> Magical incantation
>
> Go late at night to the house [of the woman] you want, knock on her door with the Eros [his πάρεδρος δαίμων, *paredros daimōn*] and say: "Lo, she NN resides here; wherefore stand beside her and, after assuming the likeness of the god or *daimōn* whom she worships, say what I propose." And go to your home, set the table, spread a pure linen cloth, and seasonal flowers, and set the figure upon it. Then make a burnt offering to it and continuously say the spell of invocation. And send him, and he will act without fail. And whenever you bend her to your will with the stone, on that night it sends dreams, for on a different night it is busy with different matters. (PGM 4.1851–67 [Betz]).

171. The marble Lansdowne throne of Apollo (Roman late first cent.). William Randolph Hearst Collection (no. 50.33.14).

The similarity with knocking on the door and preparing a meal, demonstrates that such a motif was generally understood in the ancient world. And while John was not producing a magical incantation, it must be noted that these various interpretations are not to be "considered mutually exclusive[200]. . . . The metaphorical character of the saying exhibits a polyvalent ambiguity produced by the author's combination of imagery from Jewish, Christian, and Graeco-Roman traditions."[201]

---

[199] Jerzy Linderski, "Sellisternium," ed. Simon Hornblower and Anthony J. S. Spawforth, *OCD* (Oxford, U.K.: Clarendon, 2003), 1382.

[200] Hemer, *Letters to the Seven Churches*, 207.

[201] David E. Aune, "The Polyvalent Imagery of Rev 3:20 in the Light of Greco-Egyptian Divination Texts," in *Greco-Roman Culture and the New Testament: Studies Commemorating the Centennial of the Pontifical Biblical Institute*, ed. David E. Aune and Frederick E. Brenk, NovTSup 143 (Leiden: Brill, 2012), 173, 183.

THE BLESSINGS OF SITTING WITH CHRIST ON HIS THRONE—21

> Ὁ νικῶν δώσω αὐτῷ καθίσαι μετ' ἐμοῦ ἐν τῷ θρόνῳ μου, ὡς κἀγὼ ἐνίκησα καὶ ἐκάθισα μετὰ τοῦ πατρός μου ἐν τῷ θρόνῳ αὐτοῦ.
>
> "The one who conquers, *I will grant him to sit with me on my throne*, as I also conquered and sat down with my Father on his throne." (Rev 3:21)

The final blessing is the promise to the overcomers of covenant fellowship through participation with the suzerain in reigning with him on his throne like his father. The timing of this rule is somewhat ambiguous, and could mean upon their death or at the final *parousia*,[202] or perhaps a combination of the two. Jesus in the context of the Lord's Supper makes a similar promise, but it is equally ambitious: "You are those who have stayed with me in my trials, and I assign to you, as my Father assigned to me, a kingdom, that you may eat and drink at my table in my kingdom and sit on thrones judging the twelve tribes of Israel." (Luke 22:28–30; cf. Matt 19:28; Mark 8:38–9:1; 4Q521 2.2.7). This event could transpire either at the *parousia*, transfiguration or Pentecost (cf. Mark 9:2–8). There is a sense in which overcomers (νικῶν, *nikōn*) in the church may presently be participating in this reign in the kingdom of God (1:5-6, 9; 2:26-28). In the consummation of all things the throne of God, and the Lamb are one and shared with his people (20:4; 22:5).

172. Special armchair of honor (*poedria*) at ground level in the theater of Priene, with profile in the form of lion's paws.

Thrones (θρόνος, *thronos*, Lat. *solium*, "seat, chair, throne, chair of state")[203] were understood in ancient culture to represent the rule of monarchs or gods. The word throne is used 55 times in the NT of which 41 are in the book of Revelation (cf. chap. 4–5). The throne of Laodicea was awarded to the orator Zeno, and the Zenoid family who defended the city and defeated Labienus Parthicus in 40 BC.[204] Also, magical incantations to invoke a medium, sometimes included a shared ritual meal with the god or daimon (*PDM* 14.55, 550) along with the use of a ritual throne to summon an epiphany.[205] The temple of Apollo (Temple A; see Fig. 146) likely contained a throne (τρίπoδος, *tripod*; Euripides *Iph. taur.* 976), similar to the Throne of Apollo in Amyclae (see

---

[202] Bauckham, "Synoptic Parousia Parables and the Apocalypse," 173.
[203] Homer *Od.* 1.145; Herodotus *Hist.* 1.14; Xenophon *Hell.* 1.5.3.
[204] Hemer, Letters to the Seven Churches, 205–6, 209.
[205] *PGM* 1.1–195; 4.1840–70; 11a.1–40; 12.14–95.

173. Roman cameo of *Gemma Augustea* (AD 9–12). A depiction of Emperor Augustus and *Dea Roma* seated on a *bisellium* surrounded by goddesses and allegories (no. IX A 79).

Fig. 171).[206] Theaters also had a seat of honor *(poedria)* that was used for special dignitaries (see Fig. 172).

The notion of sharing a throne, called a *bisellium* (double-throne), was well known in the ancient world as the seat of honour in the *municipia* (Varro *Ling.* 5.128).[207] One of the most famous examples of the *bisellium* is the *Gemma Augustea* cameo depicting Augustus and *Dea Roma* seated beside one another on a single throne (see Fig. 173). Another example of the *bisellium* can be found with Despoina and Demeter (Pausanias *Descr.* 8.37.4), Demeter and Kore,[208] Zeus (see

---

[206] Adolf Michaelis, *Ancient Marbles in Great Britain*, trans. Charles Augustus Maude Fennell (Cambridge, U.K.: Cambridge University Press, 1882), 441–42; Angelos Delivorrias, "The Throne of Apollo at the Amyklaion: Old Proposals, New Perspectives," *British School at Athens Studies* 16 (2009): 133–35.

[207] Rolf Hurschmann, "Seat," in *BrillPaulyA*, ed. Hubert Cancik and Helmuth Schneider, trans. Christine F. Salazar and Francis G. Gentry, 22 vols. (Leiden: Brill, 2006), http://dx.doi.org/10.1163/1574-9347_bnp_e1124640.

[208] *LIMC* 4.1.866–67; 4.2.578; 4.1.865; 4.2.581.

Figs. 95, 115, 126, 151, 154, 156) and Hera,²⁰⁹ and Hades and Persephone.²¹⁰ The close association of the gods on the *bisellium* carries the same theological idea of equality between those sharing the throne in Revelation 3:21.²¹¹

Central to Roman imperial ideology was the notion of conquest (νικῶν, *nikōn*) and enthronement (θρόνος, *thronos*) with Domitian being celebrated in Laodicea as a military conqueror who occupied the throne in Rome from AD 81–96. As Koester points out by contrast "Revelation identifies such conquest and enthronement with the beast, which oppresses people of every nation and shares the throne of Satan (2:13; 13:2, 7)." ²¹²

CONCLUSION

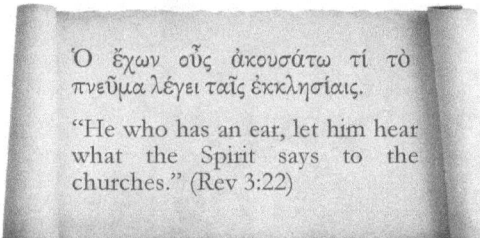

Ὁ ἔχων οὖς ἀκουσάτω τί τὸ πνεῦμα λέγει ταῖς ἐκκλησίαις.

"He who has an ear, let him hear what the Spirit says to the churches." (Rev 3:22)

The final message to the churches ends the seven messages with the promise of an ultimate victory and rule of authority for the overcomers (νικῶν, *nikōn*). The love of the suzerain is such that the overcomers are granted the privilege of sharing in the authority on a throne (θρόνος, *thronos*) with the suzerain himself. The nature of the divine victory will be further described in the rest of the book of Revelation. The victory is won by the death of the suzerain on the cross and subsequent resurrection with his ultimate consummation and enthronement. The conquering suzerain is proclaimed as the faithful witness to the world.²¹³ The faithful overcomers, who resist other earthly allegiances, are also promised a place on the throne of the suzerain and bear witness to the rule and reign of their suzerains (God and Christ, the Lamb) sharing a single throne (7:17; 22:1, 3).²¹⁴ They will also share in the iron scepter of the suzerain (2:26–27).

PROCLAMATION WITNESS FORMULA—3:22

With the distribution of the stipulations, along with blessings and curses, it was customary for ancient treaty and oath documents to be sealed with a list of divine witnesses, traditionally the suzerain/vassal's pantheon of gods (see chapter 3, *Proclamation Witnesses Formula* and chapter 5,

---

[209] *LIMC* 4.1.684; 4.2.415, 416.

[210] *LIMC* 4.1.378 = 4.2.213; 4.2.220; Christoph Markschies, "'Sessio Ad Dexteram': Bemerkungen Zu Einem Altchristlichen Bekenntnismotiv in Der Christologischen Diskussion Der Altkirchlichen Theologen," in *Le Trône de Dieu*, ed. M. Philonenko (Tübingen: Mohr-Siebeck, 1993), 260–65.

[211] Aune, *Rev 1–5*, 262.

[212] Koester, *Revelation*, 349.

[213] Caird, *Revelation*, 58.

[214] The idea of a shared throne does not imply that overcomers will share the same unity with the God and Christ found in the Godhead. In fact, Revelation 20:4 describes the faithful, who are raised, reigning on multiple thrones. The overcomers share in the blessings of the suzerain while remaining distict from him. Bauckham *Theology of Revelation*, 54–65; Koester, *Revelation*, 349.

Hearing Formula–2:7a).²¹⁵ Once again, the suzerain speaks to the seventh historic church. The Spirit is the judge presiding over the covenant case in the NT context and calls for a different witness than the polytheistic witnesses of the ANE culture. For the seventh and last time the exhortation is made to listen to "what the Spirit says to the churches." While the Spirit speaks to these seven historical churches it is still a word of encouragement (blessing) and challenge (cursing) for the church universal for all times.

Conclusion

Six recognizable elements of the ANEVT, constituting a structure, are identified within the prophetic message to convey a covenant lawsuit message of encouragement to the overcomers within the church of Laodicea.

Firstly, the preamble, marked by the prophetic oracular formula τάδε λέγει Ω, calls attention to what the suzerain, identified here as the pre-existent Amen, who is "faithful and true," will say to Laodicea. The suzerain is "the beginning of the Creation of God" a further reference to his pre-existence.

Secondly, the historical prologue is characterized by the omniscient suzerain's intimate knowledge of Philadelphia's works of being neither hot nor cold, but Lukewarm (vs. 15–16a). The metaphor may be drawn from the area's water supply.

Thirdly, the suzerain declared several maledictions upon the unfaithful vassals. They will be spit out of his mouth (ver. 16b) for being spiritually arrogant and self-sufficient with riches and lacking nothing when they were, wretched, pitiable, poor, blind, and naked (ver. 17).

Fourthly, the Great King sets out six imperatives for the Laodicean ethical stipulations: the Laodicean vassals are exhorted to buy from the suzerain, gold refined in the fires of testing, white garments of purity and eye-salve to restore their sight (ver. 18). Furthermore, they are exhorted to be zealous and repent (ver. 19).

Fifthly, in response to these stipulations, the suzerain pledges to give three blessings of the visiting suzerain who knocks, participation in the banquet meal and the privilege of ruling with him on his throne (vs. 20–21). The vassal will know the eternal blessing of ruling with the suzerain himself forever in his kingdom.

Finally, acting as his own witness in the court case, the Spirit-Judge calls the Laodicean congregation to hear what he must say to all the faithful and disobedient churches.

---

²¹⁵ See the *Introduction—Proclamation Witness Formula*.

18

Conclusion

The evidence of the ANEVT structure is characterized by the presence of their classic elements: *messenger preamble formula, historical prologue,* ethical *stipulations, sanctions (blessing and cursing), proclamation witness formula,* and *deposit/public reading* within the SMR. It appears that John did not randomly arrange the sequence of the elements in the seven messages, but that he rather purposefully chose these particular elements and arranged them in this closely structured order. Of all the possible elements and orders that John could have chosen, he followed this one, the ANEVT structure from Deuteronomy. There is enough of a definable ANEVT pattern and functional equivalence, with breadth of treaty material in each of the messages, that the original readers would have read them as *treatyesque* prophetic oracles that call the churches to repentance.

THE SOCIAL SETTING

The social setting described in each of these messages reveal several revealing points about the nature of these early churches. First, the churches each had a different social makeup which likely reflected the makeup of most congregations of the first century. While some were economically poor, others had a congregation of wealth with some members holding positions of prominence in the community. Second, they had both external and internal issues to deal with. Internally, with John's exile, prophets took control of some of the churches. Externally they faced conflict from the Jewish synagogues, not to mention the imperial cult. Third, the early church faced growing social issues in how to relate to the pagan culture around them and religiously how to interact with the emperor cult. The Christians were facing persecution for their faith and pressure to compromise. John addresses issues in each of the churches that all had difficulties although some were in worse shape than others.[1]

But as Witherington has so eloquently state:

---

[1] Witherington III, *Revelation*, 108.

Isolation from the socio-historical context in which this material was written has led to misuse of this book. It is also true that this book was not intended to be read by those with mere idle curiosity about the future. It was meant to be read in the context of the Christian faith, and it was meant to be obeyed, not merely studied.[2]

BLESSINGS FOR OVERCOMERS

Each church is called to repentance because they have broken the covenant relationship and violated God's stipulations (7 of the 10 commandments are mentioned). If they return to the Lord, they will know his blessing; but if they do not, then they will know his malediction (curse). John calls the churches to repentance before they must experience the consequences with a similar covenantal framework to the OT prophets.

The suzerain (Christ) promises a uniquely worded blessing through various images to the overcomers in each of the churches. However, they are all synonyms for the promise of heaven and blessing of eternal life.

- Ephesus: To eat of the tree of life in the paradise of God (2:7).
- Smyrna: To not be hurt by the second death (2:11).
- Pergamum: To be given some of the hidden manna and a new name (2:17).
- Thyatira: To have authority over the nations and given the Morning Star (2:26–28).
- Sardis: To be dressed in white and their name never blotted from the book of life (3:5).
- Philadelphia: To be made a pillar in the temple of God with the name of God, city of God, and Jerusalem on it (3:12).
- Laodicea: To sit with God on His throne like Christ (3:21).

Each message ends with the refrain, "he who has an ear, let him hear what the Spirit says to the churches" (2:7; 11, 17, 29; 3: 6, 13, 22. cf. Mark 4:11, 12; Isa 6:9, 10), issuing a call to hear the voice of the Spirit. Throughout history there are churches like these seven churches. The call extends to the church today to hear the voice of the Spirit in a culture that summons the church to compromise. The church still struggles with formalism, idolatry, materialism, apathy, lack of love, persecution, and false teachers. As the church awaits the Lord's return, it must watch (Matt 24:52; Mark 13:35) and pray to be faithful to the Savior, their suzerain. King Jesus still deals with his church in terms of covenant blessing which includes the promises of the kingdom and eternal life for those who overcome and resist the compromise of cultural pressures and obey the suzerain.

---

[2] Ibid., 111.

Appendix A – The Graeco-Roman Literary Context

There are local references mentioned in the seven oracles to the churches in Revelation. If two or three of these examples strike a chord of credibility, then a case for references to local and cultural settings has been made. The messages proclaimed to each church have relevance for today, but it must also be remembered that they were first given to the churches living in the first century and they likely understood them better than we do.

METHODOLOGY

In the following chart, listing various options for local references, certain criteria were established for their consideration. *Unlikely* means there is very little possibility of a connection between the cultural context and the text, since it is unlikely that the first century readers would have recognized the connection.[1] There would be a limited numbers of commentators taking this position and generally, strong reasons argue against it.

Possible means there is a good possibility that there is a connection, but for some reason it has been prevented from becoming a mainstream consideration. This would be due to the weight of the scholars opposed to it and the strength of their arguments.

The *likely* indicates a strong likelihood of a connection due to the strength of the social-historical parallels with the text and likelihood of the first century readers' recognition of the connection. In addition, based on the strength of scholarly support, the allusions are identified as Likely.

Certainly, one does not settle the issue of local reference by counting scholars; however, while this methodology is somewhat subjective, it does give a comparative analysis between the various weaknesses/strengths of the local references. This demonstrates that the approach to local reference is not an all-or-nothing proposition. It requires the examination of each allusion on its own merits. Although at times there can be a good deal of speculation (*unlikely*) there are also some solid (*likely*) connections with the local socio-historical setting.

---

[1] There is a significant difference between what the first century readers actually understood and what the modern reader believes the first century readers understood. Ramsey makes much of the difference between the twenth-century (European) and first-century (Asiatic) readers. Ramsay, *The Letters to the Seven Churches*, v–ix.

CHART-Possible Local Reference Connections

Ephesus	Unlikely	Possible	Likely
	2:1 *Holds the seven stars in his right hand* represents Ephesus as the leading city in Asia.[1] 2:6 The practice of the *Nicolaitans* is identified with the prostitution cult of the priestesses of Artemis.[2] 2:7 The church was a *paradise of God* and haven for repentant sinners, while the Artemis temple was an asylum for criminals.[3] 2:7 The *tree of life* is associated with the cross of Christ.[4]	2:1 Receives the first message as *Ephesus* is the most important city in Asia.[5] 2:2 *Deeds, hard work and perseverance* are pictured in "manifesting similar virtues in keeping the harbour" from silting up.[6] 2:4 *Giving up loving one another as they did at first* is recognized as a fault of the ordinary citizens (trade guild and commerce workers) of Ephesus according to Apollonius of Tyana.[7] 2:5 *Repent and do the things you did at first*. In a secular sense, this may have been a call to act now on the problem of the River Cayster silting as it had done in the past.[8] 2:5 *Remove your lampstand from its place* is understood to mean that the primacy of the	2:3 *You have persevered and have endured hardships* is exemplified by the persecution of Alexander the coppersmith (led by Jews; 2 Tim 4:14) and Demetrius the silversmith (led by Gentile; Acts 19:32–38).[13] 2:7 The *tree of life* is reminiscent of the sacred palm tree on Ephesian coins.[14] 2:7 *Tree of life* and *paradise of God* (Gen 3:23–24) had an analogue with the sacred groves of the temple of Artemis (see Figs. 28, 29, 24) and the new Jerusalem (21:16–18).[15]

---

[1] Ramsay, *Letters: Updated*, 237–39.

[2] Johnson, "Revelation," 614.

[3] Hemer, *Letters to the Seven Churches*, 50–52.

[4] Ibid., 42; Schneider, "TDNT," 5:40; Roberts, "The Tree of Life (Rev 2:7)," 332; Kraft, *Offenbarung*, 59; Osborne, *Revelation*, 124; Beale, *Revelation*, 235.

[5] Mounce, *Revelation*, 66.

[6] Worth, Jr., *Greco-Asian Culture*, 63; Chilton, *Days of Vengeance*, 96–97.

[7] Kiddle, *Revelation*, 23.

[8] Worth, Jr., *Greco-Asian Culture*, 63; Chilton, *Days of Vengeance*, 96–97. Richard E. Oster, "Ephesus," ed. David Noel Freedman et al., *ABD* (New York, N.Y.: Doubleday, 1996), 2:543. Oster indicates that documents from the second and fifth centuries AD indicate that the dredging was successful, revealing that the harbour was not silted up and at risk during the first century.

	Ephesus ecclesiastical Holy See will be moved. It is now at the city of Magnesia ad Sipylum (modern Manisa, Turkey) only surpassed by Smyrna. Also, over time the citizens of Ephesus have relocated to Kirkindje.[9]	
	2:5 The danger for both city and church was it "would be moved back under the deadening power of the temple" of Artemis.[10]	
	2:6 The practice of the *Nicolaitans* is connected to the second cent. gnostic sect of the same name (Irenaeus *Haer.* 1.26.3; 3.9.1).[11]	
	2:6 The practice of the *Nicolaitans* is identified with the Balaamites (Num 22–23) based on a	

---

[13] Tait, Messages to the Seven Churches, 136.

[14] While the obvious source of the tree of life imagery is the OT (Gen 2:9; 3:23–24; Ezek 31:2–9) and clearly a Jewish eschatological concept (*1 En.* 25:5; *3 En.* 23:18; *T. Levi* 18:11; *Apoc. Mos.* 28:4; *Apoc. El.* 5:6), Ramsay identified it with their Graeco-Asian roots. See Aune for a full development of the OT background. Aune, *Revelation 1–5*, 152–4. The *tree of life* motif was also known in other cultural contexts. Darice E. Birge, "Sacred Groves in the Ancient Greek World" (Ph.D. diss., University of California-Berkely, 1982), 27; Osborne, *Revelation*, 124; Ramsay, *The Letters to Seven Churches*, 246–9; Hemer, *The Letters to the Seven Churches*, 41–47; Gordon Franz, "Propaganda, Power and the Perversion of Biblical Truths: Coins Illustrating the Book of Revelation," *BS* 19, no. 3 (2006): 80; Ford, *Revelation*, 388; Earl F Palmer, *1, 2, 3 John; Revelation* (Atlantia, Ga.: Nelson, 1982), 130; Worth, Jr., *Greco-Asian*, 68.

[15] Colin J. Hemer, "Seven Cities of Asia Minor," in *Major Cities of the Biblical World*, ed. R.K. Harrison (Nashville, Tenn.: Nelson, 1985), 238; Hemer, *Letters to the Seven Churches*, 42, 44–45, 51; Franz, "Propaganda, Power and the Perversion," 80; Gerhard A. Krodel, *Revelation* (Minneapolis, Minn.: Augsburg Fortress, 1989), 109–110. Certainly, the Smyrnaean citizens would have known the Artemision royal gardens but the primary OT allusion in Genesis 2:9 is predominant.

[9] Ramsay, *Letters to the Seven Churches*, 243–44. Hemer comments that where the city moved to is debatable and the this interpretation "may be open to some doubt." Hemer, *Letters to the Seven Churches*, 53, 37.

[10] Hemer, Letters to the Seven Churches, 53.

[11] For a survey of the interpretations of the Nicolaitans see, Henry Alford, *Hebrews-Revelation*, ed. Everett F. Harrison, GTCEC 4 (Chicago, Ill.: Moody, 1968), 4:563–4; Tait, *Messages to the Seven Churches*, 157–8.

| | similar etymology (2:14; Acts 15:20).[12] | |

---

[12] Tait, Messages to the Seven Churches, 159–60; Barclay, Letters, 23–24; Beale, Revelation, 251.

Smyrna	Unlikely	Possible	Likely
	2:8 The name *Smyrna* (myrrh) has coincidental connection to suffering from the NT use of myrrh in weeping, burial, and resurrection.[16]	2:9 *Synagogue of Satan* is understood against the parallel in the assembly of Belial (1QH 2:22) and the syncretistic worship of Zeus in the Jewish synagogues in Mysia and Delos.[22]	2:8 *The first and the last* is contrasted with Smyrna being the leading city of Asia, as prominently displayed on her coins.[26]
	2:8 *Who died and came to life* is compared to the resurrection of the Phoenix.[17]	2:9 *Synagogue of Satan* is referring to a "hybrid Jewish-pagan cult."[23]	2:8 *Who died and came to life* is understood against the background of Smyrna's own destruction and restoration in 290 BC.[27]
	2:9 *Synagogue of Satan* is partially justified by a reference to the reference to Rufina the Jewess, head of the synagogue, indicating that women were holding improper roles in the Synagogue.[18]	2:9 *Synagogue of Satan* is referring to a Christian gnostic group within the church.[24]	2:9 *Synagogue of Satan* is understood against the backdrop of antagonism shown by local Jews, jealousy of Christian's exemption from participation in the imperial cult, to the church.[28]
	2:10 *Be faithful, even to the point of death* is understood as a proverbial statement on Smyrna's faithfulness, attested to by an inscription.[19]	2:11 The Rabbinic phrase *second death* "perhaps answered a Jewish taunt in Smyrna."[25]	2:10 *Be faithful, even to the point of death* is understood against the background of Smyrna's faithfulness to Rome (Cicero *Phil.* 11.2.5),[29] and partially fulfilled in the martyrdom of Polycarp (*Mart. Pol.* 1.13; *FrgPol.* 64ver.23).[30]
	2:10 *Ten Days* of tribulation alluded to in local history, literature and an inscription.[20]		
	2:10 The *crown of life* is related to a halo crown of light.[21]		2:10 The *crown of life* is related to several allusions in coins, inscriptions, writings, victor's

---

[16] Hemer, Letters to the Seven Churches, 58–59, 76; Thomas, Rev 1–7, 158; Criswell, Expository Sermons on Revelation, 92.

[17] Hemer, *Letters to the Seven Churches*, 63–64; 231 n.28; Beale, "Review of Colin J. Hemer," 110. Beale agrees that this view is possible but argues that it is not necessary as the connection with death and resurrection is made in the context.

[18] Bernadette J. Brooten, *Women Leaders in the Ancient Synagogue: Inscriptional Evidence and Background Issues*, BJS (Atlanta, Ga.: Scholars Press, 1982), 5; Trebilco, *Jewish Communities in Asia Minor*, 104–13; Worth, Jr., *Greco-Asian Culture*, 82–84. The inscription is from the second century and may not be reflective of conditions in the first century.

[19] Hemer, *Letters to the Seven Churches*, 69, 77. Cecil J. Cadoux, *Ancient Smyrna: A History of the City from the Earliest Times to 224 A.D.* (Oxford, U.K.: Basil Blackwell, 1938), 320 n. 1. Cadoux believes this to be a fanciful connection.

[20] Hemer acknowledged that the "possibility should not be pressed too far." Hemer, *Letters to the Seven Churches*, 69, 77.

[21] Beasley-Murray, *Revelation*, NCB, 83.

		wreaths, and Mount Pagus.[31]
		2:10 The *crown of life* is related to a crown of athletic victory,[32] crown worn in cultic rites (Cybele or Bacchus),[33] honorary crowns[34] and a laurel crown depicted on coins.[35]

---

[22] Ford, *Revelation*, 393; Oesterley and Robinson, *A History of Israel*, 424.

[23] Cuthbert H. Turner, *Studies in Early Church History: Collected Papers* (Oxford, U.K.: Oxford University Press, 1912), 202, 225. Worth, Jr., *Greco-Asian Culture*, 84; Martin Hengel, *Judaism and Hellenism: Studies in Their Encounter in Palestine During the Early Hellenistic Period*, trans. John Bowde (Eugene, Oreg.: Wipf & Stock, 2003), 308; W. W. Tarn, *Hellenistic Civilization*, 3d ed. (London, U.K.: Arnold & Co., 1952), 225. Turner describes them as "some Judaeo-Gnostic sect."

[24] Kraabel, "Impact of the Discovery of the Sardis Synagogue," 180; Pilch, "Lying and Deceit in the Letters to the Seven Churches: Perspectives from Cultural Anthropology," 131.

[25] Hemer, Letters to the Seven Churches, 75–77.

[26] Krodel, *Revelation*, 110; Worth, Jr., *Greco-Asian Culture*, 75. Both Ramsay and Hemer overlook this allusion.

[27] While Hemer questions the details of Ramsay's evidence for Smyrna's desolation, he still supports the basic thesis on more recent evidence. Ramsay, *The Letters to Seven Churches*, 251–2, 269–70. Hemer, *Letters to the Seven Churches*, 60–4, 76; Franz, "Propaganda, Power and the Perversion," 80; John Philip McMurdo Sweet, *Revelation*, T P I New Testament Commentaries (Valley Forge, Pa.: Trinity Press International, 1990), 651; Johnson, "Revelation," 617; Steve Gregg, *Revelation: Four Views: A Parallel Commentary* (Nashville, Tenn.: Nelson, 1997), 66; David L. Barr, "The Apocalypse of John as Oral Enactment," *Int* 40, no. 3 (1986): 245 n. 9; M. Robert Mulholland, *Revelation: Holy Living in an Unholy World* (Grand Rapids, Mich.: Asbury, 1990), 97–99. Steve Moyise, "Does the Author of Revelation Misappropriate the Scriptures?," *AUSS* 40, no. 1 (2002): 3–21. Moyise believes that this allusion is "extremely unlikely" but based on insufficient historical evidence.

[28] Hemer, *Letters to the Seven Churches*, 65–68, 76; Osborne, *Revelation*, 131; Collins, "Vilification," 313; Kiddle, *Revelation*, 27; Grant, "Smyrna," 927; Mulholland, *Revelation*, 360.

[29] Ramsay, *Letters: Updated*, 275–76; Ford, *Revelation*, 395; Meinardus, *John of Patmos*, 62; Whiting, *Revelation of John*, 73; Brown, *Heavenly Visions*, 63–64.

[30] Barclay, *Letters*, 31; Gregg, *Revelation: Four Views*, 66; Ramsay, *Letters: Updated*, 273; Clark, *The Message from Patmos*, 35.

[31] Ramsay, *The Letters to Seven Churches*, 256–9; Hemer, *The Letters to the Seven Churches of Asia*, 60–75, 77. Cadoux, *Ancient Smyrna*, 320 n. 1; Johnson, "Revelation," 618. Cadoux believes Ramsay's connection of the garland and the city-buildings to be fanciful.

[32] Cadoux, *Ancient Smyrna*, 195–96; Metzger, *Breaking the Code*, 33; Prévost, *How to Read the Apocalypse*, 73; Sweet, *Revelation*, 86; Swete, *Apocalypse*, lxi.

[33] Ramsay, Letters: Updated, 258; Harrison, Archaeology of the New Testament: The Stirring Times of Christ and the Early Church Come to Life in the Latest Findings of Science, 53; Johnson, "Revelation," 618.

[34] Hemer, Letters to the Seven Churches, 73–74; 234 n. 58.

[35] Barclay, *Letters*, 38–39.

Pergamum	Unlikely	Possible	Likely
	2:13 *In the days of Antipas, my faithful witness, who was put to death in your city* according to the document *Acta Sanctorum*, Antipas was roasted to death in a bronze bull.[36]	2:13 *where Satan has his throne* supports several possibilities in the cult of the Asclepeion (healing temple),[45] shape of the altar of Zeus,[46] and as Asia Minor's center of Roman rule.[47]	2:12, 16 *Sharp two-edged sword* is contrasted with the right and power of the sword of the Roman proconsul in the city where Antipas was one of its victims (as an *ius gladii* Lat. for "enemies of the state").[55]
	2:13 *Satan's throne* is likened to the shape of the acropolis.[37]	2:13 *where Satan has his throne* represents outside sentiments and the "local hostility toward the Pergamene assembly [church]."[48]	2:13 *where Satan has his throne* is understood against the background of Pergamum being Asia Minor's center of the imperial cult at the temple of Augustus, Severus and Trajaneium.[56]
	2:13 *where Satan has his throne* represented by the immoral excesses displayed by Pergamum's citizens.[38]	2:17b The *white stone with a new name written on it* is understood against the background of a *tessera* which "served as a token for admission to the banquet"[49] and thus connected to the supper of the Lamb.[50]	2:13 *where Satan has his throne* represented as the collective polytheistic groups.[57]
	2:17b The *hidden manna* may also have its background in the pressures of the imperial cult.[39]		2:14 *The teaching of Balaam. . .eating food sacrificed to idols and by committing sexual immorality* refers literally to the pagan feasts.[58]
	2:17b The *hidden manna* is understood as part of the Eucharist,[40] or granules of frankincense placed on temple altars.[41]	2:17b The *white stone with a new name written on it* is understood against the background of jurors using white stones to cast votes of acquittal (Plutarch *Mor.* 186; *NewDocs* 1:84).[51]	2:17b The *hidden manna* is used in conjunction with Jewish tradition where the manna (Exod 16:1–36; Num 11:1–9) would be hidden
	2:17b The *white stone with a new name written on it* is understood against the background of rewards for athletic victors,[42] discharged		

---

[36] Eusebius, who mentions other martyrs of Pergamum, does not mention Antipas (Eusebius *Hist. eccl.* 2.4.15). Tait, *Messages to the Seven Churches*, 232.

[37] Hemer believes this to be only picturesque and the argument better suites Smyrna. Beasley-Murray raises this as a possibility but prefers the altar of Zeus as his primary connection. Peter Wood, "Local Knowledge of the Letters of the Apocalypse," *ExpTim* 73 (1962 1961): 264; Charles, *Revelation of St John*, 1:61. Hemer, *Letters to the Seven Churches*, 84. Beasley-Murray, *Book of Revelation*, 84.

[38] Specific evidence is not provided by these authors. J. A Seiss, *The Apocalypse* (Colorado Springs, Colo.: Cook, 1906), 100–101; Tait, *Messages to the Seven Churches*, 229; John T. Hinds, *A Commentary on the Book of Revelation*, New Testament Commentaries (Gospel Advocate) (Nashville, Tenn.: Gospel Advocate, 1974), 34.

[39] Hemer, Letters to the Seven Churches, 94–95, 105.

[40] Prigent, *Apocalypse et Liturgie*, 22; *L'Apocalypse*, 54; Hughes, *Revelation*, 46; Mulholland, *Revelation*, 109.

[41] Krodel, *Revelation*, 120–21; Court, *Myth and History*, 32–33.

[42] Lilje, The Last Book of the Bible, 82.

⁴⁵ Here there are two possibilities. First, the Christian's aversion to calling the Greek god of healing, Asclepius, God-savior (Gr. *theos soter*), and the Asclepion emblem of the serpent, associated by Christians as Satan (12:9), both would justify calling Pergamum the seat of Satan. However, Barclay dismisses these connections, since Laodicea also had a similar connection but the phrase was not used for Laodicea. Tait, *Messages to the Seven Churches*, 228; Ramsay, *The Letters to Seven Churches*, 285–86; Esther Onstad, *Courage for Today, Hope for Tomorrow: A Study of the Revelation* (Minneapolis, Minn.: Augsburg, 1993), 19. Barclay, *Letters*, 42–43.

⁴⁶ Blaiklock combines the serpent allusions and the Savior (Gr. *soter*) reference to conclude "perhaps," in reference to the physical appearance of the structure. While Blaiklock is tentative in his earlier work he uses the stronger "must" to argue for the throne of Zeus in his *Archaeology of the NT*. Deissmann, *Light from the Ancient East*, 85, 281 n. 3; Ford, *Revelation*, 393. Edward M. Blaiklock, *Cities of the New Testament* (New York, N.Y.: Revell, 1965), 105. Edward M. Blaiklock, *The Archaeology of the New Testament* (Grand Rapids, Mich.: Zondervan, 1970), 126–8; Michael Avi-Yonah, ed., *Views of the Biblical World: The New Testament*, vol. 5 (Jerusalem: International, 1961), 271; Terence Kelshaw, *Send This Message to My Church: Christ's Words to the Seven Churches of Revelation* (Nashville, Tenn.: Nelson, 1984), 93–94.

⁴⁷ Adela Yarbro Collins, *Crisis and Catharsis: The Power of the Apocalypse* (Louisville, Ky.: Westminster/Knox, 1984), 101–102; Charles, *A Critical and Exegetical Commentary on the Revelation of St John*, 1:60–61. Hemer legitimately challenges Ramsay's defence of Pergamum as the official capital of Asia Minor in favour of its rival Ephesus. Hemer, *Letters to the Seven Churches*, 82–84; Ramsay, *The Letters to Seven Churches*, 289; "Pergamum," ed. James Hastings, Frederick C. Grant, and Harold. H. Rowley, *DBib* (New York, N.Y.: Scribner's Sons, 1963), 3:750; Tait, *Messages to the Seven Churches*, 225–6; Austin M. Farrer, *The Revelation of St. John the Divine: Commentary on the English Text* (Oxford, U.K.: Clarendon, 1964), 73.

⁴⁸ Friesen, "Satan's Throne," 365.

⁴⁹ James M Efird, *Revelation For Today: An Apocalyptic Approach* (Nashville, Tenn.: Abingdon, 1989), 57; Wilfrid J Harrington, *Revelation*, ed. Daniel J Harrington, Sacra Pagina Series 16 (Collegeville, Minn.: Liturgical, 2008), 62; Mounce, *The Book of Revelation*, 83. "That the banquet meal is in mind is supported by the reference to 'manna'" Beale, *The Book of Revelation*, 252–3; Johnson, "Revelation," 620; Hemer, *The Letters to the Seven Churches*, 98; Charles Homer Giblin, *The Book of Revelation: The Open Book of Prophecy*, Good News Studies 34 (Collegeville, Minn.: Liturgical, 1991), 57.

⁵⁰ Charles, *Revelation*, 1:66–67; Swete, *Apocalypse*, 40–41.

⁵¹ Avi-Yonah, *Views of the Biblical World: NT*, 5:272; Barclay, *Letters*, 53–54; Ramsay, *Letters: Updated*, 302–6; Hemer, *Letters to the Seven Churches*, 242 n. 85. While, for Ramsay, the voting ballots analogy by itself is unsatisfactory, he accepts them as a useful visual connection for the custom innovation of the white stone. See Hemer for further allusions. Osborne admits, "It is impossible to know for certain which of these is the best source for the imagery. . . . the best background would be a combination of the stone given victors at the games for entrance into a feast and possibly overtones of a vote of acquittal". Osborne, Revelation, 148–49.

⁵⁵ In contrast, Jesus possessed the power of life and death. Ramsay, *The Letters to Seven Churches*, 291–2; Hemer, *Letters to the Seven Churches*, 82–84, 104; Osborne, *Revelation*, 140; Mulholland, *Revelation*, 105; Whiting, *Revelation of John*, 78; Mounce, *Revelation*, 79; *What Are We Waiting For?: A Commentary on Revelation*. (Eugene, Oreg.: Wipf & Stock, 2004), 9; James T. Draper, Jr., *The Unveiling: Inspirational Expositions of the Book of Revelation from a Premillennial Viewpoint* (Nashville, Tenn.: Broadman, 1984), 54; Ford, *Revelation*, 398.

⁵⁶ Ramsay, *The Letters to Seven Churches*, 294–6; Hemer, *Letters to the Seven Churches*, 85, 87, 104; Franz, "Propaganda, Power and the Perversion," 80; Boring, *Revelation*, 91; Mounce, *Revelation*, 79; Charles, *Revelation of St John*, 1:61; Kiddle, *The Revelation of St. John*, 17:30; Swete, *The Apocalypse of St. John*, 34; Osborne, *Revelation*, 141–3; Barclay, *Letters*, 44–45; Aune, *Revelation 1–5*, 183–4. Friesen, "Satan's Throne, Imperial Cults and the Social Settings of Revelation," 366. Allen Brent, *The Imperial Cult and the Development of Church Order: Concepts and Images of Authority in Paganism and Early Christianity Before the Age of Cyprian* (Leiden: Brill, 1999), 178–90; Otto Pfleiderer, *Primitive Christianity: Its Writings and Teachings in Their Historical Connections*, trans. W. Montgomery (London, U.K.: Williams & Norgate, 1910), 415. Certainly, the allusion within the other temples of Zeus and Asclepius may also be relevant. Friesen contends, "that there are no

gladiators,[43] initiation to the service of Asclepius, the Greek god of healing, and permanent writings in contrast to impermanence of parchment.[44]	2:17b The *white stone with a new name written on it* is understood against the background of Anatolian religious superstition where to know the name of a divine being or demon was to possess magical power over that supernatural being (i.e., Egyptian Scarab)[52] therefore, a spiritual union of the name of the victorious Christian with the name of God written on the white *tessera*.[53] 2:17b *A new name written on it* is understood against the background of the ancient near eastern belief that to give another their name was to possess (intimate relationship) that person (*Odes Sol.* 42:8, 9, 20; *1 En.* 69:14–19).[54]	under Mount Sinai, in the ark of the covenant, only to be revealed at the return of the Messiah (2 Macc 2:4–7; *2 Bar.* 6.7–8; 29.8; *Sib. Or.* 7.149).[59] 2:17b The *white stone with a new name written on it* is associated with the OT High Priest's Urim and Thummim[60] or two onyx stones with names written on them worn on his ephod (Exod 28:9–12; *T. Levi* 8.12–14).[61] 2:17b *A new name* is connected to the historical setting of the new name given to Octavius of Augustus.[62]

references to imperial cults anywhere in Rev. 2–3." Brent finds allusions to the imperial cult throughout the seven messages.

[57] Martin, *The Seven Letters*, 69; Lilje, *The Last Book of the Bible*, 79–80; Wood, "Local Knowledge of the Letters of the Apocalypse," 264; Caird, *Revelation*, 37; Tait, *Messages to the Seven Churches*, 225; Metzger, *Breaking the Code*, 35; Swete, *The Apocalypse of St. John*, 34–35; Johnson, "Revelation," 619–20. Johnson defends this view by arguing that there was a concentration of polytheism in Pergamum compared with other polytheistic centres.

[58] Mounce places the emphasis on the literal understanding of the phrases while Caird argues that they could both be metaphorical and literal. The Balaam practice was similar to the beliefs of the Nicolaitans. Mounce, *Revelation*, 81; Caird, *Revelation*, 39; Barclay, *Letters*; Beale, *The Book of Revelation*, 251; Tait, *Messages to the Seven Churches*, 236–40, 243.

[43] Ramsay dismisses this analogy for failing to make the essential points of comparison and not drawing on the familiarity of the reader's experience. Ramsay, *The Letters to Seven Churches*, 303; Barclay, *Letters*, 54; Ford, *Revelation*, 400.

[44] Ramsay, Letters: Updated, 302–6; Hemer, Letters to the Seven Churches, 96–103, 105.

[52] Barclay prefers the protection of the amulet as the best association. Barclay, *Letters to the Seven Churches*, 54.

[53] Ramsay, *The Letters to Seven Churches*, 306–308. Beale, *The Book of Revelation*, 258. Beale points out that believers all receive the same name and it is not a secret magical name just given to overcomers. However, he does entertain the possibility "that the magical background of secret, incantional divine names additionally enhanced the meaning of the concluding phrase in 2:17."

[54] Eichrodt, *Theology of the Old Testament*, 2:40–45; 310–11; Bietenhard, "TDNT," 5:253–8; Beale, *Rev*, 254; Johnson, "Revelation," 620.

[59] Ramsay, Letters: Updated, 308; Charles, Revelation, 1:65; Hemer, Letters to the Seven Churches, 96–102; Barclay, Letters, 53; Bruce J. Malina, The Palestinian Manna Tradition: The Manna Tradition in the Palestinian

Thyatira	Unlikely	Possible	Likely
	2:20 *Jezebel* is identified as the wife of an Asiarch (ruler of Asia)[63] or the woman, Lydia (Acts 16:14).[64] 2:28 The *morning star* refers to the planet Venus as the symbol of Roman authority or Lucifer's battle of the stars (Isa 14:12; *Sib. Or.* 5.516, 527).[65]	2:18 *The Son of God who has eyes like flaming fire* and *feet like fine brass* is contrasted with Apollo, the Son of Zeus, as seen on coins grasping the hand of the emperor[66] and the fact that the brass guild thrived in Thyatira.[67] 2:20 *Jezebel* is identified as Sibyl Sambathe, a local female soothsayer, whose shrine was "before the city."[68] 2:28 While the *morning star* is primarily referring to Christ (22:16)[69] there may be an	2:18 *feet are like burnished bronze* is identified as a metal[72] familiar to the local bronze guild[73] and identified as a copper-zinc produced by a special distillation process.[74] 2:20 *tolerate that woman Jezebel, who calls herself a prophetess. . . promoting sexual immorality and the eating of food sacrificed to idols* is identified with the trade-guilds immorality practices and idolatry.[75] 2:22 *Those who commit adultery* are identified with the trade

Targums and its Relationship to the New Testament Writings, AGSU 7 (Leiden: Brill, 1968); Mounce, Revelation, 82; Osborne, Revelation, 148; Caird, Revelation, 42; Beale, Rev, 252; Tait, Messages to the Seven Churches, 247–48.

[60] Tait dismisses Trench's application of the Urim and Thummim. Tait, *The Messages to the Seven Churches of Asia Minor*, 249–50.

[61] Beale, *Rev*, 253, 258; Stuart, *Apocalypse*, 2:78–79; Chilton, *Days of Vengeance*, 110; Guthrie, *The Apostles*, 390; Loane, *They Overcame*, 63–64.

[62] Worth, Jr., *Greco-Asian Culture*, 152–53; Barclay, *Revelation*, 1:1:99; Ramsay, *Letters: Updated*, 306–11.

[63] Selwyn, The Christian Prophets and the Prophetic Apocalypse, 123 n. 1.

[64] Hemer, Letters to the Seven Churches, 250 n. 50.

[65] Kistemaker points out that Christ's sovereignty would clash with this view. Ernst Lohmeyer, *Die Offenbarung Des Johannes*, HNT 16 (Tübingen: Siebeck, 1926), 30; Eduard Lohse, *Die Offenbarung Des Johannes*, Das Neue Testament Deutsch 11 (Göttingen: Vandenhoeck & Ruprecht, 1960), 28. Kistemaker, *Book of Revelation*, 142 n. 70; Johann Lepsius, "Dr. Johann Lepsius on the Symbolic Language of the Apocalypse," ed. William M. Ramsay, trans. H. Ramsay, *The Expositor* 8, no. 1 (1911): 153–71; Robert W. Wall, *Revelation*, ed. W. Ward Gasque, New International Biblical Commentary (Peabody, Mass.: Hendrickson, 2002), 79.

[66] Mounce, *Revelation*, 85.

[67] Ramsay, *Letters: Updated*, 235; Franz, "Propaganda, Power and the Perversion," 84; Caird, *Revelation*, 43; Meinardus, *John of Patmos*, 94; Ford, *Revelation*, 405.

[68] Charles and Beckwith rejected it because the sibylline priestess would not be a church member. Hemer on the other hand, argues, "This view deserves consideration." Ramsay remarks that this theory is "as yet a mere tantalising possibility." CIG 2:3509; August Boeckh et al., *Corpus Inscriptionum Graecarum* (Berolini, Italy: ex Officina academica, 1877), 2:3509; Emil Schürer, *Die Prophetin Isabel in Thyatira, Offen. Joh., II, 20 , 11.*, ed. A. V. Harnack, Theologische Abhandlungen: Carl von Weizsäcker Zu Seinem Siebzigsten Geburtstage (Freiburg, Germany: Mohr Siebeck, 1892), 39–58; Arthur S. Peake, *The Revelation of John* (London, U.K.: Johnson, 1919), 246–47 n. 1; Swete, *The Apocalypse of St. John*, 42–43. Ramsay, *The Letters to Seven Churches*, 323. Charles, *Revelation of St John*, 1:70; Isbon T. Beckwith, *The Apocalypse of John* (New York, N.Y.: MacMillan, 1919), 466. Hemer, *Letters to the Seven Churches*, 117.

[69] Charles, Revelation, 1:77; Swete, Apocalypse, 47; Trench, Commentary on Seven Churches, 154–55; Plumptre,

		allusion to Statius' comparing of Domitian with the morning star (Statius *Silv.* 4.1.1–4).[70] 2:28 The *morning star* alludes to Balaam's words in Numbers 24:17 as both a scepter and a star.[71]	guilds practice of immorality.[76] 2:24 *Satan's so-called deep secrets* is an allusion to the proto-gnostics identified with Jezebel and their deep secrets (mysteries).[77] 2:27 *Iron scepter and dash them to pieces like pottery* (Ps 2:9) are understood against the background of the products of local industry.[78]

Seven Churches of Asia, 149–50; Tyconius, Turin Fragments of Tyconius, 58; Hendriksen, Conquerors, 72–73.

[72] Charles, *Revelation*, 1:29; Swete, *Apocalypse*, 17; Moffatt, *Revelation*, 5:244–45; Beckwith, *Apocalypse*, 438–39.

[73] Plumptre rejects this connection on the basis that "the imagery had already been used without reference to any local coloring." However, as Hemer points out this misunderstands the nature of the unity of the structure (compare 1:15 and 2:18). Kiddle, *The Revelation of St. John*, 17:37; Caird, *Revelation*, 43. Plumptre, *The Seven Churches of Asia*, 135. Hemer, *Letters to the Seven Churches*, 111.

[74] Hemer argues primarily from a political, economic, and geographical position. Hemer, *Letters to the Seven Churches*, 111–17, 127. A Greek inscription mentions the Thyatiran guild of *Chalkos* (Lat. *aes*, brass). Lafaye, Cagnat, and Toutain, *IGR* , 4:1259; Kistemaker, *Revelation*, 136.

[75] While there is no direct identification of Jezebel with an individual, the practices correlate to the trade-guilds. The parallel between Jezebel's seduction of Israel from her worship of Yahweh through syncretism with Baal (2 Kgs 9:22) and the first century potential for syncretism with the imperial cult is striking. Hemer, *Letters to the Seven Churches*, 128; Charles, *Revelation of St John*, 1:70–71; Ramsay, *The Letters to Seven Churches*, 346–49; Kiddle, *The Revelation of St. John*, 17:39. Caird, *Revelation*, 44–45.

[70] Hemer doubts that any one of these offers proof but rather "each furnish materials for conjecture, but none which offers a secure background for the thought of the passage. . . . It is because it needed no amplification that we are given no context." Hemer, *The Letters to the Seven Churches*, 126, 128, 253 n. 75.

[71] Hendriksen, *Conquerors*, 73; Kistemaker, *Revelation*, 142; Hughes, *Revelation*, 52–53; Sweet, *Revelation*, 97.

[76] Hendriksen, *Conquerors*, 71; Barclay, *Letters*, 61.

[77] Wall, *Revelation*, 78–79; Barclay, *Letters*, 66.

[78] Wall, *Revelation*, 77.

Appendix A – Graeco-Roman Literary Content

Sardis	Unlikely	Possible	Likely
	3:1c–2 *but you are dead* is understood against the background of the impressive necropolis (city of death) and temple of Artemis (see Figs. 28, 29, 24).[79] 3:5 *Be dressed in white* is understood based upon the practice of wearing white for baptism candidates or members of the Essene community.[80]	3:5 *Be dressed in white*. White garments were proper attire for worship,[81] festal occasions,[82] and the Gymnasium.[83] 3:5 *Be dressed in white* is understood against the invention of dyeing wool attributed to Sardis.[84] 3:5 *I will not erase his name from the book of life* is explained against the practice of blotting out the names of criminal offenders from the list of citizens.[85]	3:2 *Be watchful,* (KJV) and 3:3 *I will come like a thief* are understood against the historical background of the acropolis twice falling to the enemies of Sardis (Cyrus and Antiochus III, see Fig. 96) due to a lack of vigilance among the city's defenders.[86] 3:3b *I will come like a thief, and you will not know at what time I will come to you.* Understood against the history of four sudden earthquakes in twelve years (AD 17–29).[87]

---

[79] Worthy dismisses this connection since it would require a "limiting of the description to *one apparently specific location.*" Johnson, "Revelation," 626; Wood, "Local Knowledge," 264. Worth, Jr., *Greco-Asian Culture*, 192.

[80] Martin, *Seven Letters*, 90–91; Collins, *The Apocalypse*, 25; Guthrie, *Apocalypse*, 80.

[81] Ramsay, *Letters: Updated*, 386; Ford, *Revelation*, 409; Metzger, *Breaking the Code*, 39; Blaiklock, *Cities of the NT*, 117; Johnson, "Revelation," 626.

[82] Blaiklock, *Cities of the NT*, 117; Meinardus, *John of Patmos*, 106; Ramsay, *Letters: Updated*, 386.

[83] Kelshaw, *Send This Message*, 133–34.

[84] Ford, *Revelation*, 410; Johnson, "Revelation," 627–28; Mounce, *Revelation*, 112.

[85] Barclay, *Revelation*, 1:47; Kiddle, *Revelation*, 47; Hemer, *Letters to the Seven Churches*, 148–49.

[86] Mounce, *Revelation*, 93; Caird, *Revelation*, 47; Krodel, *Revelation*, 133; Worth, Jr., *Greco-Asian Culture*, 184–88; Wood, "Local Knowledge," 264.

[87] Mitten, "A New Look at Ancient Sardis," 61.

Philadelphia	Unlikely	Possible	Likely
	3:12 *I will make him a pillar in the temple of My God ... and I will write upon him the name of My God.* Understood against the background of the imperial cult where the high priest carved his name into a bust which was placed in the temple.[88]	3:12 *Pillar in the temple of my God* connected with the temple pillars and the stability necessary for a city plagues by earthquakes.[89] 3:12 *I will make him a pillar in the temple of My God ... and I will write upon him the name of My God.* Understood against the background of cutting inscriptions into pillars.[90]	3:8 *I have placed before you an open door that no-one can shut.* Understood against Philadelphia's cultural position as the door to the east in the spread of Greek culture.[91] 3:12 *Never again will he leave it* is understood against the background of the city being evacuated following the earthquake in AD 17 and 23.[92] 3:12 *I will write on him the name of my God and the name of the city of my God, the New Jerusalem* is understood in light of the city adopting two new names: Neocaesarea (see Fig. 113) and Flavia see Fig. 114.[93]

---

[88] L. van Hartingsveld, *Revelation: A Practical Commentary*, trans. John Vriend (Grand Rapids, Mich.: Eerdmans, 1985), 23–24; Barclay, *Revelation of John*, 1:134–35; Ford, *Revelation*, 417. Hemer, *Letters to the Seven Churches*, 268. However, Hemer points out that there is no evidence of this custom and the imperial cult rank of *neocorate* was not given to Philadelphia until AD 213.

[89] Kiddle, *Revelation*, 53.

[90] Hemer, Letters to the Seven Churches, 268.

[91] Ford, *Revelation*, 415; Meinardus, *John of Patmos*, 115; Brown, *Heavenly Visions*, 105–6.

[92] Strabo *Geogr.* 12.8.18; 13.4.10; Hemer, "Unto the Angels of the Churches," 171–73; Franz, "Propaganda, Power and the Perversion," 84; Caird, *Revelation*, 55; Krodel, *Revelation*, 135; Harrington, *Revelation*, 71; Budden and Hastings, *The Local Colour of the Bible*, 3:329–30.

[93] Ramsay, *Letters: Updated*, 397–98; Franz, "Propaganda, Power and the Perversion," 84; Blaiklock, *The Seven Churches: An Exposition of Revelation Chapters Two and Three*, 64.

Appendix A – Graeco-Roman Literary Content

Laodicea	Unlikely	Possible	Likely
		3:18 *I counsel you to buy from me gold refined in the fire, so that you can become rich.* The wealth of Laodicea (a banking center), was well known, as they refused funds from the Romans to rebuild following the earthquake of AD 17.[94]	3:15–16 *neither cold nor hot…because you are lukewarm–neither hot nor cold–I am about to spit you out of my mouth.* This is well accepted to be an allusion to the local water supply[98] from the surrounding region.[99]
		3:18 *white garments, that you may clothe yourself, and that the shame of your nakedness may not be revealed.* Contrasted with Laodicea's dependence on the black wool clothing trade.[95]	3:17 *You say "I am rich," have become wealthy and have need of nothing* is connected to the affluence and self sufficiency of the city. It declined aid from the government following the earthquake of AD 60.[100]
		3:20 *I stand at the door and knock.* The door of the four city gates, important aspects of the city being on a trade route.[96]	3:17 *you are blind… buy…eye salve to anoint your eyes, that you may see.* Connected to the Phrygian eye powder or salve produced in Hierapolis.[101]
		3:21 *I will give the right to sit with me on my throne.* The throne of Laodicea awarded to the orator Zeno, and the Zenonid family who defended the city and defeated Labienus Parthicus in 40 BC.[97]	

---

[94] Worth, Jr., *Greco-Asian Culture*, 218–19; Hemer, *Letters to the Seven Churches*, 191–96, 208; Charles, *Revelation of St John*, 1:93. Merrill F. Unger, *Archaeology and the New Testament* (Grand Rapids, Mich.: Zondervan, 1975), 267. Unger connects their wealth with their proximity to several major trade routes.

[95] Hemer, Letters to the Seven Churches, 247; Ramsay, Letters: Updated, 234; Ford, Revelation, 419; Sweet, Revelation, 108; Worth, Jr., Greco-Asian Culture, 217–18.

[96] Ramsay does not believe that verse 20 is part of the message to Laodicea, but identified it as an added epilogue; however Hemer disagrees, arguing that it must have a conclusion like all the other messages. Ramsay, *Letters: Updated*, 236; Hemer, *Letters to the Seven Churches*, 204; Rudwick and Green, "The Laodicean Lukewarmness," 178–79.

[97] Hemer, Letters to the Seven Churches, 205–6, 209.

[98] Porter argues that the water supply was from the hot springs in Hierapolis based on the calcification in the terra-cotta water pipes found by archaeologists. Porter, "Why the Laodiceans Received Lukewarm Water (Rev 3:15–18)," 147.

[99] Rudwick and Green, "The Laodicean Lukewarmness," 176–78; Bruce, "Colossian Problems, Part 1: Jews and Christians in the Lycus Valley," 3–15; Sweet, *Revelation*, 107; Yamauchi, *NT Cities*, 141; Court, *Myth and History*, 40;

Mounce, *Revelation*, 123; Johnson, "Laodicea and Its Neighbors," 1–18; Hemer, *Letters to the Seven Churches*, 277; Harrington, *Revelation*, 74; Chilton, *Days of Vengeance*, 134; Beasley-Murray, *Revelation, NCB*, 105; Giblin, *Revelation*, 65; Swete, *Apocalypse*, 60; Kelshaw, *Send This Message*, 165.

[100] Franz, "Propaganda, Power and the Perversion," 84.

[101] Hemer, *Letters to the Seven Churches*, 196–99; Ramsay, *Cities and Bishoprics*, 2:52; Harrington, *Revelation*, 75; Rudwick and Green, "The Laodicean Lukewarmness," 176; Sweet, *Revelation*, 118; Wilcock, *Heaven Opened*, 56–57; Yamauchi, *NT Cities*, 145–46; Blaiklock, *Cities of the NT*, 125.

Glossary

Acropolis: Although technically this has referred to the citadel in Athens which houses the Parthenon it can refer to any high elevation of a city which is easily fortified. This is usually where cities placed their temples, palaces and civic buildings.

Aedicula: (Lat. *aedes;* pl. *aediculae* "Temple building"). A small decorative pavilion, niche or shrine in a home, public building or temple used to ornament a façade, that typically held statues of gods and goddesses (See Ephesus Fig. 23 and Sardis synagogue Fig. 106).

Aegis: (αἰγίς, *aigis*), the shield of Zeus made of goat-skin and worn as a garment across the right shoulder to left waist. Herodotus states "Athene's garments and *aegis* were borrowed by the Greeks from the Libyan women, who are dressed in exactly the same way, except that their leather garments are fringed with thongs, not serpents" (*Hist.* 4.189 [Godley]).

Agora: (Ἀγορά; Lat. *forum*). The central market place of a city where commerce, administration and even sacrifices were performed.

Amphitheater: (ἀμφιθέατρον, *amphitheatron*; from ἀμφί, *amphi* "on both sides" or "around" and θέατρον, *theatron*, "place for viewing"). An oval theater round on both ends used for open-air venues such as special performances, entertainment, and spectacle sports such as gladiatorial games.

Apocalypse: (ἀποκάλυψις, *apokalypsis*; ἀπεκάλυψέν, *apokalyptein* "to unveil, reveal, or disclose" from *apo*, "from" + *kalyptein*, "to cover"). The Greek name for the Book of Revelation. It means an unveiling or a revelation of Jesus Christ (Rev 1:1).

Apocrypha: (ἀπόκρυφος, *apókruphos* "hidden", "obscure", or "spurious"). Non-canonical books which bear resemblance to the NT books and containing figures from Scripture. Some found a place in the Septuagint (LXX) and the Latin Vulgate version of the OT but not the Jewish or Protestant Bible.

Apotheosis: (ἀποθέωσις from ἀποθεοῦν, *apotheoun* "to deify"; Latin *deificatio,* "making divine"). The glorification of a man or woman to divine level among the gods.

Aqueduct: Water channel usually associated with high arches to traverse a ravine, though they can also run along the ground, as at Laodicea.

Ark of the Covenant: (also ark of the testimony). The central piece of furniture in the OT tabernacle and only piece of furniture in the Holy of holies. The cloud of God's glory, the manifestation of God's presence, rested over the Ark of the Covenant between two heavenly creatures called cherubim. It was believed that this was where God dwelt. The box contained the copy of the Ten Commandments, manna and Aaron's rod which budded. The lid of the box called the *kapporeth* or mercy seat was sprinkled with the blood of the sacrifice (propitiation) indicating that God's grace would intervene between the holiness of God's presence in the cloud and the witness of man's sin in the law underneath the mercy seat.

Asiarchs: (Ἀσιάρχης, *Asiarchēs*). A male official in the province of Asia Minor. Most scholars believe that this is the title equivalent to the bishop or priest (ἀρχιερεύς, *archiereus*) of Asia that described an office applied to the head of the imperial cult in the Roman province of Asia, in the second cent. AD (Acts 19:31). Others believe that it was a type of ἀγωνοθέτης (*agōnothetēs*) who presided over the provincial festivals and sacred games, while others maintain that it was a life-long office.

Assize: (Lat. *assidēre* "to sit beside, assist in the office of a judge" or *conventus*). A regional center within a Roman province annually visited by the proconsul for judicial and other state business.

Authepsa: A device used for heating water (*calda*) to mix with wine (*caldum*, see Fig. 166).

Basilica: A rectangular building or hall with a central nave, two side aisles and one or two apses (semi-circle vault or recess). The Romans used them for administrative buildings, while the Christians converted them for Churches.

Bema: (βῆμα, *bēma* "a step"). A raised platform around the altar of a church or synagogue for the clergy and choir that is associated with a place of judgment (2 Cor 5:10).

Bipennis: (Lat. "two-winged"; λάβρυς, *labrys*). A double bladed axe that originated in Crete and a symbol of the Greek civilization (see Fig. 86, 90).

Bar-Kochba: (בר כוכבא) The Jewish revolt (AD 132–135) againts the Roman Empire led by the Jewish leader Simon bar Kokhba, that established an independent Jewish state, but was later conquered by the Romans (AD 135).

Bisellium: (Lat. *bis-sella* "two chair"). An ancient Roman double-throne or seat of honor that could occupy two persons and was richly decorated (see Fig. 173).

Boule: (βουλή, *boulē*; pl. βουλαί, *boulai*). A council of 400–500 citizens who served as the ruling body of a Greek city and carried out the wishes of the *dēmos*.

Bouleuterion: (βουλευτήριον, *bouleutērion*). The council house or assembly where the *boulē* met. It was either square in shape or semi-circular, similar to a theater with ample seating for large groups. Occasionally it functioned as an *Odeion*, entertaining theatrical and musical performances.

Calathus: (κάλαθος, *kalathos*, also τάλαρος, *talaros*). A reed woven basket for carrying fruits, corn, flowers, etc., but especially women placed their material for spinning in it.

Calda: Hot water to be mixed with wine (see Fig. 166).

Caldarium: (Lat.). The hot steam chamber (also the boiler) with a hot plunge bath of a Roman bath complex that was heated using the underfloor hypocaust heating system.

Caldum: *Wine* and hot water mixed together.

Canon: (κανών, *kanōn* 'rule, measuring stick, or pattern". Heb. *qaneh*, reed). It conveys the idea of meeting a standard or being complete. The authoritative list of books accepted by the church and regarded as Scripture; generally understood as the OT and NT.

Capital: The top decorative section or member of a classical column or pilaster. In classical architecture, there are three main types: Doric, Ionic, and Corinthian.

Cavea: (Lat.). The seating in the auditorium of a Greek theater.

Chiton: (χιτών, *khitōn*) A Greek garment worn by both men and women that was sewn and draped over the shoulder and fastened with a pins (*fibulae*) or buttons.

Chlamys: (χλαμύς). An ancient Greek short cloak that appeared in the Byzantine era as the state costume of the emperor and high officials.

Cippus: A small, low column containing an inscription that indicated the distance to a location, landmark or funerary inscriptions (see Fig. 93).

Cista mystica: (Lat.) A basket used for housing sacred snakes in association with the initiation ceremony into the cult of Bacchus (Dionysus) and the healing cult of Asclepius (See Fig. 60).

Codex: (Lat. *caudex;* pl. *codices* "tree trunk", "book", or "notebook"). A ancient bound manuscript (distinguished from a scroll) comprising a collection of single pages stitched together with a binding to form a book.

Colonnade: A long row of columns either part of a building or free-standing. When the door to a building is closed in it is called a portico and when enclosing an open court, it is called a peristyle (see *peristyle*).

Coptic: The religious writing of the Egyptian Coptic Church which replaced demotic and uses the Greek alphabet.

Cornucpopiae: (Lat. *cornu copiae*) The horn of plenty, depicted by a large horn-shaped container filled with flowers and nuts as a symbol of harvest, prosperity, or spiritual abundance. It became the symbol of the goddess Tyche or Cybele in Asia Minor (see Figs. 52, 54, 98, 108, 160).

Covenant: A covenant is an agreement between two parties. In the OT it means to fetter, bondage, to bind, an intensified oath, making an oath part of a covenant, or a contract. In the NT the term signifies an agreement, testament, or will.

Curule: (Lat. *sella curulis* from *currus* "chariot") A small seat or chair that became a Roman symbol of political or military power where magistrates holding imperium were entitled to sit. It had X shaped legs and a small seat.

Damnatio memoriae: (Lat. "condemnation of memory"). Judgment by the Roman Senate, as a form of dishonor upon a person or emperor, who had discredited the Roman State. Their names were often chiselled out of monuments and removed from official documents. The term was not used by the Romans and is a modern designation (see Fig. 111.

Decalogue: (δεκάλογος, *dekálogos* "ten words"). The Ten Commandments or ten words given to Moses on Mount Sinai and written by the finger of God on two tablets of stone (Exod 20; 31:18; 32:15; Deut 5:22). The tablets were stored in the Ark of the Covenant (Exod 40:20; Deut 10:5).

Demos: (δῆμος, *dēmos* "the people"). The representative assembly of citizens in a Greek city. The English word democracy (δημοκρατία, *dēmokratía*, "rule of the commoners" κρατος, *kratos* "to "rule" + δῆμος, *dēmos*, "of the people") is derived from it (see Figs. 122, 124, 156).

Demotic: (δημοτική, *dēmotikē* "people of the town"). An abbreviated and simplified form of the Egyptian Hieratic character invented to more quickly write hieroglyphics. It was generally used for literary and commercial purposes. It was one of the translations found on the Rosetta Stone.

Denarius: (Lat. *dēnārius* pl. *dēnāriī*). The word is derived form the Lat. *dēnī* "containing ten". It was a small silver coin first minted about 211 BC, worth 10 *assēs*, although in the middle of the second cent. BC it was recalibrated so that it was now worth sixteen *assēs* or four *sēstertiī*.

Diaspora: (διασπορά, "a scattering" Heb. *galut* "forced exile"). The dispersion of the Jewish people outside the boarders of the Holy Land, e.g., after the Babylonian Exile and following the Jewish and Roman persecution of Christians in the first century.

Didache: or *The Teaching of the Twelve Apostles* (διδαχή, *didachē* "teaching"). It is a short early (late first/second cent.) Christian document discovered in 1873, which contains three sections: including Christian ethics, ordinances (baptism and Eucharist) and church structure. Parts of the document are formulated as a catechism. Protestants do not consider it to be part of the NT, but it is included in the writings of the Apostolic Fathers.

Diazoma: The passageway of an ancient Greek theater dividing the lower from the upper rows of seats aiding in access to the area

Dioskuri: (*Dioscuri* or *Dioskouroi*; Lat. *Gemini* or *Castores*). In Greek and Roman mythology, the twin brothers Castor (Kastor, the mortal son of Tyndareus) and Pollux (Polydeuces, divine son of Zeus).

Divus: (from Lat. *deus* "god"; Fem. *diva*). A divinized or deified emperor. There was no equivalent term in Greek.

Doric: Developed by the Dorian Greeks and often referred to a Doric column with no ornamental base and a simple circular capital at the top. In classical architecture, there was also the Ionic, and Corinthian.

Electrum: (ἤλεκτρον, *ēlektron*). An alloy comprised of gold and silver with small amounts of other elements such as copper, traces of tin, lead or iron (See Fig. 107).

Ephebe: (ἔφηβος, ; pl. ἐφηβη, *ephēbē*). A young male adolescent usually from an aristocratic family who is being trained *ephēbē* for civic leadership.

Epigraphy: (ἐπιγραφή, *epigraphē*; from ἐπι, *epi* "on" + γράφειν, *graphein* "to write"). The study of ancient languages and writing.

Eschaton: (ἔσχατον "last things"). The last or final events as in "future things". It forms the root of "eschatology" which is "the study of last things" and the consummation of world history.

Essenes: (Ἐσσαῖου, *essaiou* the "silent" or "reticent" ones, Pliny *Nat.* 5.17). A Jewish sect identified by Josephus and Pliny residing around the Dead Sea and who are generally identified by scholars as the residents of Qumran and the custodians of the Dead Sea Scrolls.

Exedra: (ἐξέδρα "a seat out of doors"). A semicicular seat or bench, made from stone or marble.

First Temple Period: (ca. 965–586 BC). The period from the building of Solomon's temple until its destruction.

Fresco: (It. "in fresh," with a sense of "painted on fresh mortar or plaster"). A color painted on mortar or plastered walls.

Frigidarium: (Lat.). The room of a Roman bath complex that contained a pool of cold water sometimes cooled with snow (see Fig. 110).

Gematria: (Heb. *gimatria*; Aramaic *gīmatrĕyā*; γεωμετρία *geōmetria*). A traditional Jewish numerical system used to assign values to words or phrases in the Hebrew language. Many commentators believe that 666 represents Emperor Nero's name.

Genizah: (גניזה, *geniza* "storage"). A temporary repository or archive storage area in a Jewish synagogue or cemetery designated for the storage of worn-out or copies of Hebrew texts with mistakes.

Gnostic: (γνωστικός, *gnōstikos* "having knowledge"). A sect in the early church that believed that the cosmos emanated from a transcendent god and salvation is achieved through acquiring secret knowledge (γνῶσις, *gnōsis*). Gnostics also believe in a dualism between good and evil where there is not a salvation from sin, but rather a deliverance from the ignorance of which caused sin.

Graffito(i): (γράφω, *graphō* "to write", It. *graffiare* "to scratch"), any writing, slogan, figure or inscription scratched into a surface, often on a wall or public building. Examples found in Pompeii among other sites.

Grammateus: (γραμματεύς) The town-clerk or the secretary of the city.

Gymnasium: (γυμνάσιον, *gymnasion* "gymnastic school" derived from γυμνός, *gymnos* "naked"; pl. *gymnasia*) functioned as a training facility, where athletes competed in the nude. It was the meeting place where organizations of boys (παιδες, *paides*), youths (ἐφηβη, *ephēbē*), young men (νέοι, *neoi*), and the elders (γεροντες, *gerontes*) engaged in social and intellectual pursuits (Pausanias *Descr.* 4.32.1).

Hellenism: The spread of ancient Greek culture and ideas that included language, art, architecture, and literature.

Heresy: (αἵρεσις, *airesis* "a strong, distinctive opinion"), a teaching or belief condemned by the Church as unorthodox and corrupting the dogma.

Hermeneutic: (ἑρμηνεύω, *hermēneuō* "translate, interpret"). The science of interpreting the Bible. It uses scientific rules and principles to help understand the meaning of the scriptural text.

Herodian: The time period or architectural structures connected with Herod the Great or his family.

Heroon: (ἡρῷον, pl. ἡρῷα, *heroa* "hero"; sometimes called *heroum*). A shrine dedicated to an ancient Greek or Roman hero to commemorate the hero often erected over their tomb or cenotaph.

Hieron: (ἱερόν "holy place"). A sacred or holy shrine, temple or precinct used as a sanctuary.

Hippodamian: The grid plan based on right-angles of an ancient city (i.e, Priene) developed by Hippodamus of Miletus the father of rational city planning.

Hypocaust: (Lat. *hypocaustum*). A system of central heating in a building produced through circulating hot air through a small chamber under the floor and through pipes in the wall.

in situ: (Lat. "in position" or "on site."). The precise location of an artifact and indicates that it has not been moved from its original location. This is critical for the dating and interpretation of the strata.

Kerkides: (κερκίδες, Lat. *cuneus*) A vertical or wedge-shaped seating section in a theater.

Khirbet: (Arabic خربة conjunctive form meaning "ruin of" or "ruin on a hill."). Their archaeological ruins are usually exposed aboveground.

Klinē: (κλίνη, banquet couch; Eng. "recline") A couch used to recline on and eat a meal (see Fig. 91, 170).

Koine: (ἡ κοινὴ διάλεκτος, *he koinē dialektos* "the common dialect"). The common Greek language of the NT period used in the Septuagint, The NT, and other commercial documents.

Koinon: (Κοινόν, pl. Κοινά, *Koina* "common"; Lat. *res publica* "public"). The provincial council or assembly of Greek cities that met in the provincial capital of a Roman province and had oversight of the imperial cults.

Kore: (κόρη "maiden"; pl. *korai*) 1). A free-standing votive Greek statue of a sculpted young girl. 2). In Greek mythology another name for Persephone (Περσεφόνη), the queen of the underworld, who was the daughter of Zeus and the harvest goddess Demeter.

Labrys: See *Bipennis*.

Laureate: (Lat. *Laurus*) In ancient Greece, the laurel plant was used for laurel wreaths and was sacred to Apollo. The leaves were fashioned into a crown or wreath of honor for poets and heroes. It is often worn by emperors on coins (see ex. Fig. 29, 31, 55, 96, 113, 122, 124).

Lectisternium: (Lat. *lectum sternere* "to prepare or drape a couch"). A funerary meal in honour of the gods where the images of the gods, lying on pillows, was placed in the streets. (Servius *ad Aen.* 10.76; Livy *Hist. Rome* 5.13.6; Cicero *Dom.* 13.6; see Fig. 91).

Levant: The eastern Mediterranean countries of Israel, Jordan, Palestine, Syria, Lebanon, Turkey, Cyprus, Egypt and Greece.

Libation: Liquid offering (i.e., milk, wine or olive oil) to the gods.

Lulav: (Heb. לולב). It is closed frond of the date palm tree and one of the four spices used during the Jewish festival of Sukkot. It is also bound together with the four spices to form what is called "the Lulav" (see also Fig. 164).

Martyrium: (Lat.; μαρτύριον, *Martyrion*, pl. *martyria*). A circular or octagonal shrine for a Christian martyr.

Medallion: A Roman memorial coin struck to commemorate a special event or idea.

Messiah: (מָשִׁיחַ *Mashiah*, LXX *Christos* "anointed"). Within Judaism the promised deliverer, who will bring a kingdom of peace and justice (Dan 9:25, 26). For Christians the term refers to Jesus who is regarded as the fulfillment of the Jewish prophecy of a deliverer (John 1:41; 4:25) and thus called the Christ (Matt 26:54; Mark 9:12; Luke 18:31; 22:37; John 5:39; Acts 2; 16:31; 26:22, 23).

Metropolitanate: The see or office of a metropolitan bishop.

Mishnah: (מִשְׁנָה *mishna* "(oral) instruction" from *shanah* "to study by repetition"; pl. *Mishnayot*). The oral interpretations and sayings of Rabbi Judah the Patriarch (third cent. AD) which are collected as part of the Jewish writing called the Talmud.

Montanism: An early Christian sect (late second cent. AD) names after its founder, Montanus from Phrygia, Asia Minor (sometimes called Cataphrygian). They held to the New Prophecy, similar to the beliefs of the modern day charismatic movement.

Nave: (Lat. *navem*). The central aisle of a church.

Necropolis: (νεκρόπολις "city of the dead"). Cemetery usually outside the city along the main arteries with elaborate tomb monuments.

Neokōros: (νεωκόρος, from νεώς, *neōs* "temple" + κορέω, *koreō* "to sweep", literally a "temple-sweeper" or "temple warden or keeper"), originally a temple official; from the late 1st cent. AD formalized as a title for a city which held a provincial temple to the Roman Emperor. Today this term is used for a custodian in the Greek Orthodox church.

Neolithic: (νεῖος, *neios* "new" + λίθος, *lithos* "stone"). The new Stone Age period (ca. 10,200-4,500/2,000 BC).

Numismatic: (νόμισμα, *nomisma* "current coin, money, usage"; Lat. *numismatis*). The science and study of coins.

Numphaeum: A monumental foundation that in Roman times displayed sumptuous architectural decoration, statues, reliefs and often a water feature.

Obelisk: (ὀβελίσκος, *obeliskos*; derived from ὀβελός, *obelos* "spit, nail, pointed pillar"). A four-sided stone pillar with a tapered pyramidal point at the top that looks like a nail.

Obverse: (Lat. *obversus* "turned toward" or "against"). The front side of a coin or medal that is first placed into an engraved template before being struck on the other side (i.e., on the reverse) and often bearing the head of the imperial family or image of a deity, commonly called heads.

Odeum: (Ὠδεῖον, *ōideion*; Lat. *odeum* "singing place"). A Greek or Roman building that was usually roofed, often used for musical competitions or as a school of music (see bouleuterion).

Omphalos: (ὀμφαλός "navel"). A religious stone artifact that was regarded as a symbol of power (see Fig. 93).

Onomasticon: (ὀνομαστικόν, *onomastikon* "belonging to names"). An alphabetical list of geographical places most often identified with the one written by Eusebius and translated by Jerome mentioning places in the Bible.

Oracle: (Lat. *ōrāre* "to speak"). During the ancient Greek and Roman period an oracle could have several meanings. It usually referred to the medium or priest who prophesied although it could also refer to their prophetic revelation (χρησμοί, *khrēsmoi*) from the deity (divination). Sometimes it could refer to the place where a medium consulted the deity. The most famous oracle in Greek culture was the Pythia, priestess to Apollos at Delphi. There were temples to Apollo in Didyma, Corinth, Bassae and Delos. A famous collection of prophetic oracles uttered by the Sibyl prophetesses is called the *Sibylline Oracles*. These oracles were usually exercises in the art of studied ambiguity, with multiple fulfillments to protect the Oracle from failure.

Ostracon: (ὄστρακον, *ostracon*; pl. ὄστρακα, *ostraka* "a shard of pottery"). A piece of pottery or other substance with an inscription on it.

Palaestra: (παλαίστρα). A training facility normally located close to the bath complex or gymnasia. It consisted of various sized small rooms, around a colonaded courtyard, used to entertain such sports as boxing and wrestling that did not require significant space.

Pantokrator: (Παντοκράτωρ "the Almighty One"). Used for Christ by Paul (2 Cor 6:18) and John (1:8, 4:8, 11:17, 15:3, 16:7, 16:14, 19:6, 19:15, and 21:22).

Papyrus: (πάπυρος, *papyrus;* Lat. pl. *papyri*). A kind of writing paper made from the Egyptian papyrus reed which grows along the Nile River.

Paraenesis: (παραινέω, *paraineō* "to exhort" or "admonish"). A series of encouraging persuasive exhortations or admonitions, which do not necessarily refer to concrete situations (for example, Col 3–4, Eph 4–6, and various sections of James).

Parchment: (Περγαμηνός, *Pergamenos* "of Pergamon"). Writing paper made from animal skins (vellum) that originated at Pergamum, Asia Minor.

Parousia: (παρουσία, *parousia* "presence", "arrival", or "official visit"). It is generally understood in the NT to mean the second coming or second advent of Jesus Christ.

Paleo: (παλαιός, *palaios*). Old or ancient.

Pentecost: (Πεντηκοστή [ἡμέρα], *Pentēkostē [hēmera]* "the fiftieth [day]"). The term is derived from "fiftieth" because it was seven weeks after Passover that the "Feast of Weeks" (Exod 34:22; Deut 16:10) or the "Feast of Harvest" (Exod 23:15–22) was observed. It marked the end of the barley harvest and the beginning of the wheat harvest. It was one of the three occasions in the year in which male Israelites were to appear before the Lord but it was much less observed as an occasion of pilgrimage than the feasts of Passover and tabernacle (Num 28:26–31).

Peristyle: (περίστυλος, *peristylos*). A Hellenistic and Roman row of columns surrounding the perimeter of a building or inside courtyard with a colonnade (see *colonnade*).

Pistis: (Πίστις) In Greek mythology, *Pistis* was the personified spirit (*daimona*) of trust, good faith, honesty and reliability (Ovid *Metam.* 5.43). *Fides* was her Roman equivalent significant in Roman culture as a personified concept. Her counterparts were *Apate* (Deception) and *Pseudologoi* (Lies).

Portico: (Lat. *porticus* "porch"). A colonnaded porch to a building, with a roof over the walkway and supported on at least one side by columns or enclosed walls.

Plectrum: (Lat. *plectrum*, πλῆκτρον, *plēktron*, or πλήσσειν, *plēssein* "to strike"). A pick used to strike an instrument such as a lyre or harp.

Prefect: (Lat. *praefectus*). The governor of a Roman province with low rank.

Proconsul: (Lat. *pro consule*) A Roman official who acted on behalf of a consul. They became one of the three types of Roman provincial governors (i.e., *praetor* and the *propraetor*).

Procurator: (Lat. "manager, overseer, agent, deputy"). The governor of a Roman province with high rank.

Pseudepigrapha: (ψευδής, *pseudēs* "false" + επιγραφή, *epigraphē* "to inscribe or write"). It commonly refers to numerous works of Jewish religious literature dealing with people and events from the OT. They were written between 200 BC and AD 200. Many are mentioned by other writers but lost and not included in the canon of the OT (e.g., *1 En., 2 Bar., 3–4 Macc., As. Mos.,* and *Sib. Or.*).

Qumran: An archaeological site about one mile inland on a plateau northwest of the Dead Sea. It is the location of the Jewish sect called the Essenes and near the caves where the Dead Sea Scrolls were discovered in 1947.

Rabbah: (Abbr. *Rab.*). A Jewish collection of ancient rabbinical interpretations usually on one of the Books of the Pentateuch (i.e., Genesis Rabbah; *Rab.* Gen 3:15).

Rapture: (Lat. *raptura* "seizure, kidnapping"; ἁρπαγησόμεθα, *harpagisometha* "we shall be caught up" or "taken away" or ἁρπάζω, *harpazō*). A sudden event often associated with the coming of Christ where Christians or non-Christians will be taken (cf. 1 Thess 4:17; Acts 8:39; 2 Cor 12:2–4 and Rev 12:5). Some dispensationalist premillennialists hold the return of Christ to be two distinct events, or one second coming in two stages.

Reverse: (Lat. *reversus* "revert"). The back side of a coin or medal that does not bear the principal design, commonly called tails. A wide range of designs can be found on the reverse, including temples, gods, animals, deities, commemorative, etc.

Sanhedrin: (סַנְהֶדְרִין *sanhedrín* "[great] council"; Συνέδριον, *synedrion*, "assembly" from *syn*, "together" + *hedra,* "seat" thus "sitting together"). Aramaic term designating the Jewish political assembly at Jerusalem that represented the highest magistracy of the country (Josephus *Ant.* 14.5.4). It was also an assembly of twenty to twenty-three men (*m. Sanh.* 1:1) appointed in every city in the biblical land of Israel.

Sarcophagus: (σαρκοφάγος, *sarkophagos* "flesh-eating" from σάρξ, *sarx* "flesh" + φαγεῖν, *phagein* "to eat"; pl. *sarcophagi*). A stone (λίθος, *lithos*) coffin for a corpse made of limestone which was believed to decompose the flesh. They were usually beautifully carved and displayed above ground sometimes with an inscription.

Scepter: (Lat. *sceptrum* "royal staff"). An ornamental staff or wand usually held by monarchs as an royal insignia to symbolize their imperial authority.

Scarab: (κάραβος, *karabos* "beetle"). An Egyptian seal made in the shape of a scarab beetle.

Sebastos: (Σεβαστός, *Sebastos* "venerable one", from σέβας, *sebas* "awe, reverence, dread"; pl. *Sebastoi;*Lat. *Sebastianus* "from Sebastia"). Sebastos was an ancient Greek honorific term for Roman emperors used in the first cent. onward in place of Augustus. Temples of the *Sebastoi* only venerated the family of the Emperor (the family of Vespasian, Titus and Domitian). The term also used to honor the Roman emperors by naming certain cities, such as Sebaste, Sebasteia and Sebastopolis.

Second Temple Period: 536 BC–AD 70. The period from the return of the Babylonian exiles to the destruction of Jerusalem and the temple.

Septuagint: (Lat. *septuāgintā* "The Seventy"; abbr. LXX). The Greek translation of the Hebrew OT made in Alexandria by seventy-two translators between 280–150 BC.

Shofar: (שׁוֹפָר). A ram's horn cut to turn into a horn blown in ancient times as a trumpet to call the people to prayer or warn of the enemy. It is still blown in synagogues on Rosh Hashana and at the end of Yom Kippur.

Spolia: (Lat. "spoils"), the repurposing of building materials for new construction elsewhere.

Stadium: (Lat. pl. *stadia;* στάδιον, *stadion*). A measure of length equivalent to 600 human feet (125 Roman *passūs*= 607 ft [185 m]), or a running track of the same length.

Stēlē or stela: (στήλη, "pillar, upright rock; or column"; pl. στῆλαι *stēlai* or *stēlae*). An upright stone pillar often containing an inscription to commemorate a military victory, boundary or tombstone.

Stoa: (στοά "base stand"; pl. *stoae*). A long covered hallway, usually in front of shops, supported with a colonnade of pillars, often with a portico (Lat. *Porticus*, "porch") to protect the public from the elements.

Stratēgos: (στρατηγός, pl. στρατηγοί, *strategoi* "army leader"). Originally a term for a Greek general or commander, but by NT times it had developed into a political office of praetor (Acts 16:20), a high level municipal magistrate in western Asia Minor.

Stratum: (Lat. pl. *strata* "a spread for a bed, quilt, or blanket"). In archaeology it refers to a horizontal layer of soil containing artifacts and debris representing a particular time period and dated by using pottery and coins.

Synagogue: (συναγωγή, *synagōgē*, from συν, *syn* "together" + αγωγή, *agoge* "learning or training"; בית כנסת, *Bet Kenesset* "house of assembly" or בית תפילה, *beyt t'fila* "house of prayer"). A Jewish house of prayer and worship. Their exact date of origin is uncertain, although they appear after the Babylonian Exile.

Synoptic: (Lat. *synopticus;* συνοπτικός, *sunoptikós* "seeing the whole together at a glance", from σύνοψις, *súnopsis* "a general view, synopsis" from σύν, *sún* "the same" + ὄψις, *ópsis* "to see or view"). In biblical studies the word "synoptic" is used with the Gospels to mean the eyewitnesses saw things the same way. Thus, the gospel writers saw Jesus with a similar view of his life, particularly in the area of his Deity.

Tainia: (ταινία; pl. ταινίες, *tainies;* Lat. *taenia;* pl. *taeniae*). A "band", "ribbon", or "fillet" used as a headband to hold hair and worn at Greek festivals. In the Roman Empire worn as a symbol of kings.

Talmud: (תַּלְמוּד, *talmūd* "instruction, learning"). The authoritative body of Jewish tradition comprising Jewish civil and ceremonial law comprising the Mishnah (abbr. *m.*) and the Gemarah. There are two versions of the Talmud: The Babylonian Talmud (which dates from the fifth cent. AD but includes earlier material) and the earlier Palestinian or Jerusalem Talmud. There is the Babylonian Talmudic tractate (ca. AD 550; abbr. *b.*) and the Palestinian Talmudic tractate from Jerusalem (ca. AD 450; abbr. *y.*).

Tepidarium: (Lat. *tepidus* "warm room"). In the Roman bath this was the room with the lukewarm bath (see Sardis Fig. 102 no. 4). In this room bathers would coat their bodies with oil while slaves would scrape the oil off their skin to remove dirt and impurities using a curved metal tool (Lat. *strigil*).

Targum: (תרגום "translation, or interpretation"). Aramaic translation of the Hebrew Bible (*Tanakh*). Collected over a five-hundred-year period, it is difficult to date individual passages. Fragments were found at Qumran among the Dead Sea Scrolls.

Terracotta: (also terra-cotta or terra cotta; It. from *terra* "earth" + *cotta* "baked" i.e., "baked earth"). Reddish clay or unglazed ceramic pottery or earthenware.

Tessera: (τέσσερα, pl. *tesserae,* "four"). Small individual squares (four sides) of wood, ivory, or stone used to create a mosaic picture or as a ticket, or token.

Tetragrammaton: (Τετραγράμματον "having four letters"). It has become a technical term for the name YHWH (יהוה) in the Bible. Ancient Hebrew words did not contain vowels. Because Jews would not say Yahweh occasionally this special name for God was represented by the old Paleo-Hebrew letters or four dots.

Tetrarch: (τετραρχία, *tetrarchia* "leadership of four [people]"; Lat. *tetrarches*). A governor of the fourth part of a province in Ancient Rome, first instituted by Diocletan (AD 292).

Theater: (θέατρον, *theatron;* pl. θέατρα, *theatra;* Lat. *theatrum* "play-house; stage; spectators in a theater"). A Greek or Roman semi-circular structure where civic assemblies and theatrical performances were conducted having impressive acoustics. Greek theaters were usually built into the side of a hill and later modified by the Romans unless the turrain did not allow in which case they were free standing and completely enclosed on all sides.

Sometimes an awning (*vela*) was used to protect the audience from the elements. Actors performed in front of the *skene* (Gr.) or stage (Rom.). Gladitorial games were later introduced to modified theaters.

Tosefta: (Heb. "supplement") is another large collection of writings, written in Mishnaic Hebrew, that are similar to the Mishnah but not as authoritative for Jews.

Vassal: A subordinate ruler who paid tribute to a dominant king.

Vellum: (Fr. *vélin* from *vel* "veal"). A fine parchment prepared from the skin of the young skin of a calf or lamb used by scribes to write documents such as biblical manuscripts.

Votive: (Lat. *vōtīvus* from *vōtum* "vow"). An object dedicated in fulfillment of a vow for a religious purpose.

Vulgate: (Lat. *versio vulgate* "edition in vernacular language"). The Latin translation of the Bible by St. Jerome (fourth cent. AD) and the official Bible used by the Roman Catholic Church.

Zealots: (ζηλωτής, *zelōtēs* "one who is a zealous follower," from ζῆλος *zelos* "zeal"; Lat. *zelotes*). A rebellious Jewish sect who opposed the Roman domination during the intertestamental period and Jewish revolt of the first century. The sect of the Zealots ('fourth philosophy' Josephus *J.W.* 2.117; *Ant.* 18.1.2–6), was founded by Judas the Galilean, who led the Jewish revolt against Rome in AD 6. Other notable Zealots include the Maccabean leaders, Mattathias and his sons and followers (1 Macc 2:24–27), Menahem, who attempted to seize the leadership of the anti-Roman revolt in AD 66 (Josephus *J.W.* 2.433) and Eleazar ben Yar, leader of the Jewish revolt at Masada (AD 66–73; Josephus *J.W.* 7.8.6). Simon, one of the twelve apostles, was also a Zealot (Luke 6:15; Acts 1:13), along with the apostle Paul (Acts 22:3; Gal 1:14).

Bibliography

PRIMARY SOURCES

Abegg, Jr., Martin G., Michael O. Wise, and Edward M. Cook. *The Dead Sea Scrolls: A New Translation*. San Francisco, Calf.: HarperCollins, 2005.

Ackermann, Hans Christoph, and Jean-Robert Gisler. *Lexicon iconographicum mythologiae classicae*. 8 vols. Zurich: Artemis, 1997.

Aelian, Claudius. *On Animals: Books 12–17*. Translated by A. F. Scholfield. Vol. 3. 3 vols. LCL 449. Cambridge, Mass.: Harvard University Press, 1959.

———. *Historical Miscellany*. Translated by N. G. Wilson. LCL 486. Cambridge, Mass.: Harvard University Press, 1997.

Aeschines. *Speeches*. Translated by C. D. Adams. LCL 106. Cambridge, Mass.: Harvard University Press, 1919

———. *Oresteia: Agamemnon. Libation-Bearers. Eumenides*. Edited and translated by Alan H. Sommerstein. Vol. 2. 3 vols. LCL 146. Cambridge, Mass.: Harvard University Press, 2009.

Aeschylus. *Persians. Seven against Thebes. Suppliants. Prometheus Bound*. Edited and translated by Alan H. Sommerstein. Vol. 1. 3 vols. LCL 145. Cambridge, Mass.: Harvard University Press, 2009.

Allegro, John M., and A. A. Anderson. *Qumrân Cave 4: I (4Q 158–4Q 186)*. DJD 5. Oxford, U.K.: Clarendon, 1968.

Amidenus, Aëtius. *Aetii medici graeci contractae ex veteribus medicinae sermones 16*. Edited by Janus Cornarius and Hugo Solerius. Venetiis: Gryphius, 1553.

Ampelius, Lucius. *Lucii Ampelii Liber Memorialis*. Translated by Edidit Erwin Assmann. Leipzig: Teubner, 1935.

Andrew of Caesarea. *Commentary on the Apocalypse*. Translated by Eugenia Scarvelis Constantinou. Washington, D.C: The Catholic University of America Press, 2011.

Apollodorus. *The Library: Books 1–3.9*. Translated by James George Frazer. Vol. 1. 2 vols. LCL 121. Cambridge, Mass.: Harvard University Press, 1921.

Apollonius of Tyana. *Letters of Apollonius. Ancient Testimonia. Eusebius's Reply to Hierocles Philostratus*. Edited and translated by Christopher P. Jones. Vol. 3. 3 vols. LCL 458. Cambridge, Mass.: Harvard University Press, 2006.

Appian. *Roman History: The Civil Wars, Books 1–3.26*. Translated by Horace White. Vol. 3. 4 vols. LCL 4. Cambridge, Mass.: Harvard University Press, 1913.

———. *Roman History: The Civil Wars, Books 3.27–5*. Translated by Horace White. Vol. 4. 4 vols. LCL 5. Cambridge, Mass.: Harvard University Press, 1913.

———. *Roman History: Books 8.2–12*. Translated by Horace White. Vol. 2. 4 vols. LCL 3. Cambridge, Mass.: Harvard University Press, 1912.

———. *The Foreign Wars*. Translated by Horace White. New York, N.Y.: MacMillan & Co., 1899.

BIBLIOGRAPHY—PRIMARY SOURCES

Apuleius. *Metamorphoses (The Golden Ass): Books 1–6*. Edited and translated by J. Arthur Hanson. Vol. 1. 2 vols. LCL 44. Cambridge, Mass.: Harvard University Press, 1996.

———.*Metamorphoses (The Golden Ass): Books 7–11*. Edited and translated by J. Arthur Hanson. Vol. 2. 2 vols. LCL 453. Cambridge, Mass.: Harvard University Press, 1989.

Aristides, Publius Aelius. *Orations*. Edited and translated by Michael Trapp. Vol. 1. LCL 533. Cambridge, Mass.: Harvard University Press, 2017.

———.*The Complete Works: Orations 1–16*. Translated by Charles A. Behr. Vol. 1. 2 vols. Leiden: Brill, 1986.

———.*The Complete Works: Orations 17–53*. Translated by Charles A. Behr. Vol. 2. 2 vols. Leiden: Brill, 1981.

Aristophanes. *Acharnians. Knights*. Edited and translated by Jeffrey Henderson. Vol. 1. 5 vols. LCL 178. Cambridge, Mass.: Harvard University Press, 1998.

———. *Clouds. Wasps. Peace*. Edited and translated by Jeffrey Henderson. Vol. 2. 5 vols. LCL 488. Cambridge, Mass.: Harvard University Press, 1998.

———. *Frogs. Assemblywomen. Wealth*. Edited and translated by Jeffrey Henderson. Vol. 4. 5 vols. LCL 180. Cambridge, Mass.: Harvard University Press, 2002.

Aristotle. *Athenian Constitution. Eudemian Ethics. Virtues and Vices*. Translated by H. Rackham. Vol. 20. 23 vols. LCL 285. Cambridge, Mass.: Harvard University Press, 1935.

———. *Minor Works: On Colours. On Things Heard. Physiognomics. On Plants. On Marvellous Things Heard. Mechanical Problems. On Indivisible Lines. The Situations and Names of Winds. On Melissus, Xenophanes, Gorgias*. Translated by W. S. Hett. Vol. 14. 23 vols. LCL 307. Cambridge, Mass.: Harvard University Press, 1936.

———. *Nicomachean Ethics*. Translated by H. Rackham. Vol. 19. 23 vols. LCL 73. Cambridge, Mass.: Harvard University Press, 1926.

———. *Politics*. Translated by H. Rackham. Vol. 21. 23 vols. LCL 264. Cambridge, Mass.: Harvard University Press, 1932.

———. *The History of Animals: Volume II: Books 4–6*. Translated by A. L. Peck. Vol. 10. 23 vols. LCL 438. Cambridge, Mass.: Harvard University Press, 1970.

Arrian. *Anabasis of Alexander: Books 1–4*. Translated by P. A. Brunt. Vol. 1. 2 vols. LCL 236. Cambridge, Mass.: Harvard University Press, 1976.

———. *Epictetus Discourses, Books 1–2*. Translated by W. A. Oldfather. Vol. 1. LCL 131. Cambridge, Mass.: Harvard University Press, 1925.

———. *Epictetus Discourses, Books 3–4. Fragments. The Encheiridion*. Translated by W. A. Oldfather. Vol. 2. LCL 218. Cambridge, Mass.: Harvard University Press, 1928.

Artemidorus. *Interpretation of Dreams: Oneirocritica*. Translated by Robert J. White. 2nd ed. Park Ridge, N. J.: Original Books, 1990.

Athenaeus. *The Learned Banqueters: Books 1–3.106e*. Edited and translated by S. Douglas Olson. Vol. 1. 7 vols. LCL 204. Cambridge, Mass.: Harvard University Press, 2007.

———. *The Learned Banqueters: Books 3.106e–5*. Edited and translated by S. Douglas Olson. Vol. 2. 7 vols. LCL 208. Cambridge, Mass.: Harvard University Press, 2007.

———. *The Learned Banqueters: Books 6–7*. Edited and translated by S. Douglas Olson. Vol. 3. 7 vols. LCL 224. Cambridge, Mass.: Harvard University Press, 2008.

———. *The Learned Banqueters: Books 12–13.594b*. Edited and translated by S. Douglas Olson. Vol. 6. 7 vols. LCL 327. Cambridge, Mass.: Harvard University Press, 2010.

Attridge, Harold, Torleif Elgvin, Jozef Milik, Saul Olyan, John Strugnell, Emanuel Tov, James Vanderkam, and Sidnie White. *Qumran Cave 4: VIII: Parabiblical Texts, Part I*. DJD 13. Oxford, U.K.: Clarendon, 1995.

Ausonius. *Books 18–20. Paulinus Pellaeus: Eucharisticus*. Translated by Hugh G. Evelyn-White. Vol. 2. 2 vols. LCL 115. Cambridge, Mass.: Harvard University Press, 1921.

Avot, Pirke. *Sayings of the Jewish Fathers*. Whitefish, Mont.: Kessinger, 2004.

Bacchylides, and Corinna. *Greek Lyric: Bacchylides, Corinna, and Others*. Edited and translated by David A. Campbell. Vol. 4. LCL 461. Cambridge, Mass.: Harvard University Press, 1992.

Baillet, M., ed. *Qumrân Grotte 4.III (4Q482–4Q520)*. DJD 7. Oxford, U.K.: Clarendon, 1982.

Baillet, M., Józef Tadeusz Milik, and Roland de Vaux, eds. *Les "petites grottes" de Qumrân*. DJD 3. Oxford, U.K.: Clarendon, 1962.

Balz, Horst, and Gerhard Schneider, eds. *Exegetical Dictionary of the New Testament*. 3 vols. Grand Rapids, Mich.: Eerdmans, 1990.

Bauer, Walter, Frederick W. Danker, William F. Arndt, and F. Wilbur Gingrich, eds. *A Greek-English Lexicon of the New Testament, and Other Early Christian Literature*. 3rd ed. Chicago, Ill.: University of Chicago Press, 1999.

Betz, Hans Dieter, ed. *The Greek Magical Papyri in Translation, Including the Demotic Spells*. Chicago, Ill.: University of Chicago Press, 1996.

Blass, F., and A. DeBrunner. *A Greek Grammar of the New Testament and Other Early Christian Literature*. Translated by Robert W. Funk. Chicago, Ill.: University of Chicago Press, 1961.

Blümel, Wolfgang. *Die Inschriften von Iasos*. 2 vols. IGSK 28.1–2. Bonn: Habelt, 1985.

Böeckh, August, Johannes Franz, Ernst Curtius, and Adolf Kirchhoff. *Corpus Inscriptionum Graecarum*. 4 vols. Berolini, Italy: Officina academica, 1877.

Bovon, François, and Christopher R. Matthews, trans. *The Acts of Philip: A New Translation*. Waco, Tex.: Baylor University Press, 2012.

Breitenstein, Niels, and Willy Schwabacher, eds. *Sylloge Nummorum Graecorum, Denmark, The Royal Collection of Coins and Medals, Danish National Museum*. 7 vols. Copenhagen, Denmark: Publié sous le Patronage de l'Union Académique Internationale, 1942.

Brenton, Lancelot C. L. *The Septuagint Version of the Old Testament with Apocrypha: Greek and English*. London, U.K.: Bagster & Sons, 1851.

Briggs, Charles A., Samuel R. Driver, and Francis Brown. *Hebrew-Aramaic and English Lexicon of the Old Testament. Complete and Unabridged*. Peabody, Mass.: Hendrickson, 1996.

Brooke, George, John Collins, Torleif Elgvin, Peter Flint, and Jonas Greenfield. *Discoveries in the Judaean Desert: Qumran Cave 4: XVII: Parabiblical Texts, Part 3*. DJD 22. Oxford, U.K.: Clarendon, 1996.

Buckler, William Hepburn, and David M. Robinson. *Sardis: Greek and Latin Inscriptions*. Vol. 7. Leiden: Brill, 1932.

Buckler, William Hepburn, William M. Calder, and William Keith C. Guthrie, eds. *Monumenta Asiae Minoris Antiqua IV: Monuments and Documents from Eastern Asia and Western Galatia.* Vol. 4. 11 vols. JRSM. Manchester: Society for the Promotion of Roman Studies, 1933.

———. eds. *Monumenta Asiae Minoris Antiqua VI: Monuments and Documents from Phrygia and Caria.* Vol. 6. 11 vols. JRSM. Manchester: Society for the Promotion of Roman Studies, 1939.

Burnett, Andrew, Michel Amandry, and Pere Pau Ripollés Alegre, eds. *Roman Provincial Coinage.* 9 vols. London, U.K.: British Museum Press, 2003.

Cabrol, Fernand, and Henri Leclercq, eds. *Dictionnaire d'archéologie chrétienne et de liturgie.* 15 vols. Letouzey et Ané, 1907–1953.

Caesar, Julius. *Civil War.* Edited and translated by Cynthia Damon. LCL 39. Cambridge, Mass.: Harvard University Press, 2016.

Callimachus, Aratus, and Lycophron. *Hymns and Epigrams. Lycophron: Alexandra. Aratus: Phaenomena.* Translated by A. W. Mair and G. R. Mair. LCL 129. Cambridge, Mass.: Harvard University Press, 1955.

Carradice, Ian A. *Sylloge Nummorum Graecorum, Great Britain VI, Corpus Christi College Cambridge, The Lewis Collection Part I: The Greek and Hellenistic Coins (with Britain and Parthia).* Oxford, U.K.: British Archaeological Reports, 1972.

Cassius Dio. *Roman History: Books 1–11.* Translated by Ernest Cary and Herbert B. Foster. Vol. 1. 9 vols. LCL 32. Cambridge, Mass.: Harvard University Press, 1914.

———. *Roman History: Books 51–55.* Translated by Ernest Cary and Herbert B. Foster. Vol. 6. 9 vols. LCL 83. Cambridge, Mass.: Harvard University Press, 1917.

———. *Roman History: Books 56–60.* Translated by Ernest Cary and Herbert B. Foster. Vol. 7. 9 vols. LCL 175. Cambridge, Mass.: Harvard University Press, 1924.

———. *Roman History: Books 61–70.* Translated by Ernest Cary and Herbert B. Foster. Vol. 8. 9 vols. LCL 176. Cambridge, Mass.: Harvard University Press, 1924.

Celsus. *On Medicine: Books 1–4.* Translated by W. G. Spencer. Vol. 1. 3 vols. LCL 292. Cambridge, Mass.: Harvard University Press, 1935.

Chaniotis, Angelos, Thomas Corsten, Nikolaos Papazarkadas, and Rolf Tybout, eds. *Supplementum Epigraphicum Graecum.* Leiden: Brill, 1923–2015.

Charles, Robert H., ed. *The Apocrypha and Pseudepigrapha of the Old Testament.* 2 vols. Oxford: Clarendon, 1913.

Charlesworth, James H., ed. *The Old Testament Pseudepigrapha.* 2 vols. ABRL. Peabody, Mass.: Hendrickson, 1983.

Chilton, Bruce D. *The Isaiah Targum: Introduction, Translation, Apparatus and Notes.* Aramaic Bible 11. Wilmington, Del.: Glazier, 1987.

Chrysostom, Dio. *Discourses 1–11.* Translated by J. W. Cohoon. Vol. 1. 5 vols. LCL 257. Cambridge, Mass.: Harvard University Press, 1939.

———. *Discourses 12–30.* Translated by J. W. Cohoon and H. Lamar Crosby. Vol. 2. 5 vols. LCL 339. Cambridge, Mass.: Harvard University Press, 1939.

———. *Discourses 31–36.* Translated by J. W. Cohoon and H. Lamar Crosby. Vol. 3. 5 vols. LCL 358. Cambridge, Mass.: Harvard University Press, 1940.

———. *Discourses 37–60.* Translated by H. Lamar Crosby. Vol. 4. 5 vols. LCL 376. Cambridge, Mass.: Harvard University Press, 1946.

———. *Discourses 61–80.* Fragments. Letters. Translated by H. Lamar Crosby. Vol. 5. 5 vols. LCL 385. Cambridge, Mass.: Harvard University Press, 1951.

Cicero, Marcus Tullius. *De Oratore Books 1–2.* Translated by E. W. Sutton and H Rackham. Vol. 3. 29 vols. LCL 348. Cambridge, Mass.: Harvard University Press, 1996.

———. *In Catilinam 1–4. Pro Murena. Pro Sulla. Pro Flacco.* Translated by C. Macdonald. Vol. 10. 29 vols. LCL 324. Cambridge, Mass.: Harvard University Press, 1976.

———. *Letters to Atticus.* Translated by D. R. Shackleton-Bailey. Vol. 22. 29 vols. LCL 7. Cambridge, Mass.: Harvard University Press, 1999.

———. *Letters to Friends: Vol. 1: Letters 1–113.* Translated by D. R. Shackleton-Bailey. Vol. 25. 29 vols. LCL 205. Cambridge, Mass.: Harvard University Press, 2001.

———. *Letters to Friends: Vol. 2: Letters 114–280.* Translated by D. R. Shackleton-Bailey. Vol. 26. 29 vols. LCL 216. Cambridge, Mass.: Harvard University Press, 2001.

———. *On Old Age. On Friendship. On Divination.* Translated by W. A. Falconer. Vol. 20. LCL 154. Cambridge, Mass.: Harvard University Press, 1923.

———. *On the Nature of the Gods (De natura deorum), Academica.* Translated by H Rackham. LCL 268. Cambridge, Mass.: Harvard University Press, 1980.

———. *On the Orator: Books 1–2.* Translated by E. W. Sutton and H Rackham. Vol. 3. 29 vols. LCL 348. Cambridge, Mass.: Harvard University Press, 1942.

———. *On the Republic. On the Laws.* Translated by Clinton W. Keyes. Vol. 16. 29 vols. LCL 213. Cambridge, Mass.: Harvard University Press, 1928.

———. *Orations: Pro Caelio. De Provinciis Consularibus. Pro Balbo.* Translated by R. Gardner. Vol. 13. 29 vols. LCL 447. Cambridge, Mass.: Harvard University Press, 1958.

———. *Orations: Pro Lege Manilia. Pro Caecina. Pro Cluentio. Pro Rabirio. Perduellionis Reo.* Translated by H. Grose Hodge. Vol. 9. 29 vols. LCL 198. Cambridge, Mass.: Harvard University Press, 1990.

———. *Philippics 1–6.* Edited by John T. Ramsey and Gesine Manuwald. Translated by D. R. Shackleton Bailey. Vol. 15a. 29 vols. LCL 189. Cambridge, Mass.: Harvard University Press, 2010.

———. *Philippics 7–14.* Edited by John T. Ramsey and Gesine Manuwald. Translated by D. R. Shackleton. Vol. 15b. 29 vols. LCL 507. Cambridge, Mass.: Harvard University Press, 2010.

———. *Pro Archia. Post Reditum in Senatu. Post Reditum Ad Quirites. De Domo Sua. De Haruspicum Responsis. Pro Plancio.* Translated by N. H. Watts. Vol. 11. 29 vols. LCL 158. Cambridge, Mass.: Harvard University Press, 1923.

———. *Pro Quinctio. Pro Roscio Amerino. Pro Roscio Comoedo. On the Agrarian Law.* Translated by J. H. Freese. Vol. 6. 29 vols. LCL 240. Cambridge, Mass.: Harvard University Press, 1930.

———. *The Orations of Marcus Tullius Cicero.* Edited and translated by Charles D. Yonge. 4 vols. London, U.K.: Bell & Sons, 1913.

———. *The Verrine Orations I: Against Caecilius. Against Verres, Part 1; Part 2, Books 1–2.* Translated by L. H. G. Greenwood. Vol. 7. 29 vols. LCL 221. Cambridge, Mass.: Harvard University Press, 1928.

———. *The Verrine Orations II: Against Verres, Part 2, Books 3-5.* Translated by L. H. G. Greenwood. Vol. 8. 29 vols. LCL 293. Cambridge, Mass.: Harvard University Press, 1935.

Claudian. *On Stilicho's Consulship 2–3. Panegyric on the Sixth Consulship of Honorius. The Gothic War. Shorter Poems. Rape of Proserpina.* Translated by M. Platnauer. Vol. 2. 2 vols. LCL 136. Cambridge, Mass.: Harvard University Press, 1922.

———. *Panegyric on Probinus and Olybrius. Against Rufinus 1 and 2. War against Gildo. Against Eutropius 1 and 2. Fescennine Verses on the Marriage of Honorius. Epithalamium of Honorius and Maria. Panegyrics on the Third and Fourth Consulships of Honorius. Pane.* Translated by M. Platnauer. Vol. 1. 2 vols. LCL 135. Cambridge, Mass.: Harvard University Press, 1922.

Collins, John, Peter W. Flint, James C. VanderKam, George Brooke, Torleif Elgvin, Jonas C. Greenfield, Erik Larson, Carol A. Newsom, Émile Puech, and Lawrence H. Schiffman. *Qumran Cave 4: XVII, Parabiblical Texts, Part 3.* DJD 22. Oxford, U.K.: Clarendon, 1997.

Comfort, Philip Wesley, and David P. Barrett, eds. *The Text of the Earliest New Testament Greek Manuscripts.* Corrected and Enlarged ed. Wheaton, Ill.: Tyndale, 2001.

———. *The Complete Text of the Earliest New Testament Manuscripts.* Grand Rapids, Mich.: Baker, 1999.

Comfort, Philip Wesley. *Early Manuscripts and Modern Translations of the New Testament.* Eugene, Oreg.: Wipf & Stock, 2001.

———. *Encountering the Manuscripts: An Introduction to New Testament Paleography & Textual Criticism.* Nashville, Tenn.: Broadman & Holman Academic, 2005.

Commodianus, Gazaeus. "The Instructions of Commodianus in Favour of Christian Discipline, Against the Gods of the Heathens." In *Ante-Nicene Fathers: Fathers of the Third Century: Tertullian, Part Fourth: Minucius Felix; Commodian; Origen, Parts First and Second*, edited by Alexander Roberts, James Donaldson, Philip Schaff, and Henry Wace, translated by Robert Ernest Wallis, New Ed., 4:199–402. Peabody, Mass.: Hendrickson, 1994.

Corsten, Thomas. *Die Inschriften von Laodikeia Am Lykos.* IGSK 49. Bonn: Habelt, 1997.

Demosthenes. *Orations 18-19: De Corona, De Falsa Legatione.* Translated by C. A. Vince and J. H. Vince. Vol. 2. 7 vols. LCL 155. Cambridge, Mass.: Harvard University Press, 1926.

Dessau, Hermann. *Inscriptiones Latinae Selectae.* In 5 parts. 3 vols. Berlin: De Gruyter, 1892.

Dio Cassius. *Roman History: Books 41–45.* Translated by Ernest Cary and Herbert B. Foster. Vol. 4. 9 vols. LCL 66. Cambridge, Mass.: Harvard University Press, 1916.

———. *Roman History: Books 51–55.* Translated by Ernest Cary and Herbert B. Foster. Vol. 6. 9 vols. LCL 83. Cambridge, Mass.: Harvard University Press, 1917.

———. *Roman History: Books 56–60.* Translated by Ernest Cary and Herbert B. Foster. Vol. 7. 9 vols. LCL 175. Cambridge, Mass.: Harvard University Press, 1924.

———. *Roman History: Books 61–70.* Translated by Ernest Cary and Herbert B. Foster. Vol. 8. 9 vols. LCL 176. Cambridge, Mass.: Harvard University Press, 1924.

———. *Roman History: Books 71–80.* Translated by Ernest Cary and Herbert B. Foster. Vol. 9. 9 vols. LCL 177. Cambridge, Mass.: Harvard University Press, 1927.

Diodorus Siculus. *Library of History: Books 9–12.40.* Translated by C. H. Oldfather. Vol. 4. 12 vols. LCL 375. Cambridge, Mass.: Harvard University Press, 1946.

———. *Library of History: Books 15.20–16.65*. Translated by Charles L. Sherman. Vol. 7. 12 vols. LCL 389. Cambridge, Mass.: Harvard University Press, 1952.

———. *Library of History: Books 16.66–17*. Translated by C. Bradford Welles. Vol. 8. 12 vols. LCL 422. Cambridge, Mass.: Harvard University Press, 1963.

———. *Library of History: Fragments of Books 21–32*. Translated by Francis R. Walton. Vol. 11. 12 vols. LCL 409. Cambridge, Mass.: Harvard University Press, 1957.

———. *Library of History: Fragments of Books 33–40*. Translated by Francis R. Walton. Vol. 12. 12 vols. LCL 423. Cambridge, Mass.: Harvard University Press, 1967.

Diogenes Laertius. *Lives of Eminent Philosophers: Books 1–5*. Translated by Robert Drew Hicks. Vol. 1. 2 vols. LCL 184. Cambridge, Mass.: Harvard University Press, 1925.

———. *Lives of Eminent Philosophers: Books 6–10*. Translated by Robert Drew Hicks. Vol. 2. 2 vols. LCL 185. Cambridge, Mass.: Harvard University Press, 1925.

Dittenberger, Carl Friedrich Wilhelm, ed. *Inscriptiones graecae IX.1: Inscriptiones Phocidis, Locridis, Aetoliae, Acarnaniae, insularum maris Ionii*. Vol. 1. Berlin: De Gruyter, 1897.

Dittenberger, Carl Friedrich Wilhelm, Johann Gaertringen, Johannes E. Kirchner, Joannes Pomtow, Georg Wissowa, and Erich Ziebarth, eds. *Sylloges insciptionum graecarum. Orientis graeci inscriptiones selectae: Supplementum*. 3rd ed. 4 vols. Leipzig: Nachdruck der Ausgabe, 1915–1924.

Donner, Herbert, and Wolfgang Röllig. *Kanaanäische und aramäische Inschriften*. 5th ed. Wiesbaden: Harrassowitz, 2002.

Edson, Charles F., ed. *Inscriptiones graecae, X: Inscriptiones Epiri, Macedoniae, Thraciae, Scythiae. Pars II, Fasc. 1: Inscriptiones Thessalonicae et Viciniae*. Berlin: De Gruyter, 1972.

Elliott, J. K., ed. *The Apocryphal New Testament: A Collection of Apocryphal Christian Literature in an English Translation Based on M. R. James*. Oxford, U.K.: Oxford University Press, 2005.

Epiphanius of Salamis. *Panarion: Book II and III (Sects 47-80, De Fide)*. Translated by Frank Williams. Leiden: Brill, 1993.

Etheridge, J. W., ed. *Targum Pseudo Jonathan on the Pentateuch*. London, U.K.: Longman, Green, Longman, & Roberts, 1862-1865.

Euripides. *Bacchae. Iphigenia at Aulis. Rhesus Euripides*. Edited and translated by David Kovacs. Vol. 6. 8 vols. LCL 495. Cambridge, Mass.: Harvard University Press, 2003.

———. *Trojan Women. Iphigenia among the Taurians. Ion*. Translated by David Kovacs. Vol. 4. 8 vols. LCL 10. Cambridge, Mass.: Harvard University Press, 1999.

Eusebius, Pamphilus, and Jerome. *The Bodleian Manuscript of Jerome's Version of the Chronicles of Eusebius*. Edited by John Knight Fotheringham. Oxford, U.K.: Clarendon, 2012.

Eusebius, Pamphilus. *De Praeparatio Evangelica*. Translated by Edward Hamilton Gifford. Grand Rapids, Mich.: Baker, 1981.

———. *Ecclesiastical History: Books 1–5*. Translated by Kirsopp Lake. Vol. 1. 2 vols. LCL 153. Cambridge, Mass.: Harvard University Press, 1926.

———. *The Onomasticon of Eusebius Pamphili: Compared with the Version of Jerome and Annotated*. Edited by Noel C. Wolf. Translated by C. Umhau Wolf. Washington, D.C.: Catholic University of America Press, 1971.

———. *The Proof of the Gospel-2 Vol in One*. Translated by W. J. Ferrar. Eugene, Oreg.: Wipf & Stock, 2001.

Eustathius. *Commentarii Ad Homeri Iliadem et Odysseam*. Edited by Gottfried Stallbaum. Reprint of 1825–30 edition. 4 vols. Hildesheim: Olms, 1970.

Eutropius. *Justin, Cornelius Nepos, and Eutropius*. Translated by John Selby Watson. London: George Bell & Sons, 1886.

Felix, Marcus Minucius, and Tertullian. *Apology. De Spectaculis. Minucius Felix: Octavius*. Translated by T. R. Glover and Gerald H. Randall. LCL 250. Cambridge, Mass.: Harvard University Press, 1931.

Fiorelli, Giuseppe. *Descrizione di Pompeii*. Napoli: Tipografia italiana, 1875.

Flaccus, Gaius Valerius. *Argonautica*. Translated by John Henry Mozley. LCL 286. Cambridge, Mass.: Harvard University Press, 1934.

Franke, Peter Robert, and Harald Küthmann. *Sylloge Nummorum Graecorum, Deutschland: Staatliche Münzsammlung München*. Berlin: Mann, 1968.

Fränkel, Max, Ernst Fabricius, and Carl Schuchhardt. *Die Inschriften von Pergamon*. 2 vols. Sonderausgabe Aus Den Altertümern von Pergamon 8. Berlin: Spemann, 1890.

Freedman, H., and Maurice Simon, eds. *Midrash Rabbah*. 10 vols. London, U.K.: Soncino, 1992.

Freeman-Grenville, G. S. P., and Joan E. Taylor, eds. *The Onomasticon by Eusebius of Caesarea and the Liber Locorum of Jerome: Palestine in the Fourth Century AD*. Translated by G. S. P. Freedman-Grenville. Jerusalem: Carta, 2003.

Frey, P. Jean-Baptiste. *Corpus Inscriptionum Iudaicarum: Recueil Des Inscriptions Juives Qui Vont Du IIIe Siècle de Notre Ère*. Vol. 3. Rome: Pontifico Istituto di Archeologa Cristiana, 1936.

Friedlander, Gerald, trans. *Pirke De Rabbi Eliezer (The Chapters of Rabbi Eliezer The Great): According to the Text of the Manuscript Belonging to Abraham Epstein of Vienna Translated and Annotated with Introduction and Indices*. London, U.K.: Kegan Paul, Trench, Trubner & Co., 1916.

Galen, and Hippocrates. *The Writings of Hippocrates and Galen*. Translated by John Redman Coxe. Philadelphia, Pa.: Philadelphia : Lindsay and Blakiston, 1846.

Galen. *A Translation Of Galen's Hygiene: De Sanitate Tuenda*. Translated by Robert Montraville Green. Springfield, IL.: Thomas, 1951.

———. *Galen on Anatomical Procedures: De Anatomicis Administrationibus*. Translated by Charles Singer. London, U.K.: Oxford University Press, 1956.

———. *Galen on the Passions and Errors of the Soul*. Translated by Walther Riese. Ohio State University Press, 1963.

———. *Method of Medicine: Books 1–4*. Edited and translated by G. H. R. Horsley and Ian Johnston. Vol. 1. 3 vols. LCL 516. Cambridge, Mass.: Harvard University Press, 2011.

———. *Method of Medicine: Books 5–9*. Edited and translated by G. H. R. Horsley and Ian Johnston. Vol. 2. 3 vols. LCL 517. Cambridge, Mass.: Harvard University Press, 2011.

———. *Method of Medicine: Books 10–14*. Edited and translated by G. H. R. Horsley and Ian Johnston. Vol. 3. 3 vols. LCL 518. Cambridge, Mass.: Harvard University Press, 2011.

George, Andrew R. *The Babylonian Gilgamesh Epic: Introduction, Critical Edition and Cuneiform Texts HELP*. Vol. 1. 2 vols. Oxford, U.K.: Oxford University Press, 2003.

Gesenius, Friedrich Wilhelm, Samuel Prideaux Tregelles, and Joseph Henry Thayer. *A Greek-English Lexicon of the New Testament & Gesenius' Hebrew And Chaldee Lexicon To The Old Testament Scriptures*. Grand Rapids, Mich.: Baker, 1987.

Goldwurm, Hersh, and Nosson Scherman, eds. *The Talmud*. Schottenstein Edition. 73 vols. Brooklyn, N.Y.: Mesorah, 1990.

Graser, Elsa R. "A Text and Translation of the Edict of Diocletian." In *An Economic Survey of Ancient Rome: Rome and Italy of the Empire,* edited by Tenney Frank, 5:307–421. Baltimore, Md.: John Hopkins University Press, 1975.

Grenfell, Bernard Pyne, and Arthur Surridge Hunt. *The Oxyrhynchus Papyri*. 75 vols. London, U.K.: Egypt Exploration Society, 2009.

Haase, Wolfgang, and Hildegard Temporini, eds. *Aufstieg und Niedergang der römischen Welt: Geschichte und Kultur Roms im Spiegel der neueren Forschung. Principat. Religion. 2. 26.* Berlin: de Gruyter, 1995.

———. *Geschichte und Kultur Roms im Spiegel der neueren Forschung.* Principat. Religion. ANRW, 2.26. Berlin: de Gruyter, 1995.

Hallo, William W., and K. Lawson Younger, eds. *The Context of Scripture: Archival Documents from the Biblical World.* 3 vols. Leiden: Brill Academic, 2002.

Harper, Robert Francis, trans. *The Code of Hammurabi King of Babylon about 2250 BC*. Chicago, Ill.: The University of Chicago Press, 1904.

Harris, Keith N. "The 'De Ave Phoenice' of Lactantius: A Commentary and Introduction." M.A. diss., University of British Columbia, 1978.

Head, Barclay Vincent. *A Catalogue of the Greek Coins in the British Museum: Lydia* . Vol. 22. London, U.K.: Oxford University Press, 1902.

———. *Catalogue of the Greek Coins of Ionia in the British Museum*. Edited by Reginald Stuart Poole. Oxford, U.K.: Oxford University Press, 1892.

Heberdey, Rudolf, ed. *Tituli Pisidiae Linguis Graeca et Latina Conscripti, 1. Tituli Termessi et Agri Termessensis*. TAM III, 1. Vienna: ÖAW, 1941.

Heliodorus of Emesa. *Heliodorus: An Ethiopian Romance*. Translated by Moses Hadas. Philadelphia, Pa.: University of Pennsylvania Press, 1999.

Heraclitus of Ephesus. *The Fragments of the Work of Heraclitus of Ephesus on Nature*. Translated by Ingram Bywater and G. T. W. Patrick. London, U.K.: Murray, 1889.

Herodian. *History of the Empire: Books 1–4*. Translated by C. R. Whittaker. Vol. 1. 2 vols. LCL 454. Cambridge, Mass.: Harvard University Press, 1969.

———. *History of the Empire: Books 5–8*. Translated by C. R. Whittaker. Vol. 2. 2 vols. LCL 455. Cambridge, Mass.: Harvard University Press, 1970.

Herodotus . *Historia: The Persian Wars: Books 1–2*. Translated by Alfred Denis Godley. Vol. 1. 4 vols. LCL 117. Cambridge, Mass.: Harvard University Press, 1920.

———. *Historia: The Persian Wars: Books 3–4*. Translated by Alfred Denis Godley. Vol. 2. 4 vols. LCL 118. Cambridge, Mass.: Harvard University Press, 1921.

———. *Historia: The Persian Wars: Books 5–7*. Translated by Alfred Denis Godley. Vol. 3. 4 vols. LCL 119. Cambridge, Mass.: Harvard University Press, 1922.

Bibliography—Primary Sources

Heron of Alexandria. *Druckwerke Und Automatentheater: Pneumatica Et Automata.* Translated by Wilhelm Schmidt. Griechisch und Deutsch. 5 vols. Stuttgart, Germany: Teubner, 1976.

Herrmann, Peter, ed. *Tituli Lydiae Linguis.* TAM V, 2. Vienna: ÖAW, 1989.

Hesiod. *Theogony. Works and Days. Testimonia.* Translated by Glenn W. Most. Vol. 1. 3 vols. LCL 57. Cambridge, Mass.: Harvard University Press, 2007.

Hipponax of Ephesus, Archiochus, and Semonides. *Greek Iambic Poetry From the Seventh to the Fifth Centuries BC.* Edited and translated by Douglas E. Gerber. LCL 259. Cambridge, Mass.: Harvard University Press, 1999.

Homer. *Iliad: Books 1–12.* Edited by George E. Dimock. Translated by A. T. Murray. Vol. 1. 2 vols. LCL 170. Cambridge, Mass.: Harvard University Press, 1924.

———. *Iliad: Books 13–24.* Edited by William F. Wyatt. Translated by A. T. Murray. Vol. 2. 2 vols. LCL 171. Cambridge, Mass.: Harvard University Press, 1925.

———. *Odyssey: Books 1–12.* Edited by George E. Dimock. Translated by A. T. Murray. Vol. 1. 2 vols. LCL 104. Cambridge, Mass.: Harvard University Press, 1919.

———. *Odyssey: Books 13–24.* Edited by George E. Dimock. Translated by A. T. Murray. Vol. 2. 2 vols. LCL 105. Cambridge, Mass.: Harvard University Press, 1919.

———. *Odes and Epodes.* Translated by Niall Rudd. LCL 33. Cambridge, Mass.: Harvard University Press, 2004.

Horace. *Satires. Epistles. The Art of Poetry.* Translated by H. Rushton Fairclough. LCL 194. Cambridge, Mass.: Harvard University Press, 1926.

Horsley, G. H. R., and Stephen R. Llewelyn, eds. *New Documents Illustrating Early Christianity.* 10 vols. NewDocs. Grand Rapids, Mich.: Eerdmans, 1981.

Hoz, María Paz de. *Die lydischen Kulte im lichte der griechischen inschriften.* AMStud. 36. Bonn: Habelt, 1999.

Hunt, A.S., trans. *Select Papyri: Public Documents.* Vol. 2. 5 vols. LCL 282. Cambridge, Mass.: Harvard University Press, 1934.

Hyginus, Caius Julius. *The Myths of Hyginus.* Edited and translated by Mary Amelia Grant. University of Kansas Publications in Humanistic Studies 34. Lawrence, Kans.: University of Kansas Press, 1960.

Imhoof-Blumer, Friedrich. *Kleinasiatische Münzen.* 2 vols. Sonderschriften Des Österreichischen Archäologischen Institutes. Vienna: Hölder, 1901.

Josephus, Flavius. *Jewish Antiquities: Volume II, Books 4–6.* Translated by H. St. J. Thackeray and Joel Marcus. Vol. 6. 13 vols. LCL 490. Cambridge, Mass.: Harvard University Press, 1930.

———. *Jewish Antiquities: Volume III, Books 7-8.* Translated by Ralph Marcus. Vol. 7. 13 vols. LCL 281. Cambridge, Mass.: Harvard University Press, 1934.

———. *Jewish Antiquities: Volume IV, Books 9–11.* Translated by Ralph Marcus. Vol. 8. 13 vols. LCL 326. Cambridge, Mass.: Harvard University Press, 1937.

———. *Jewish Antiquities: Volume V, Books 12–13.* Translated by Ralph Marcus. Vol. 9. 13 vols. LCL 365. Cambridge, Mass.: Harvard University Press, 1943.

———. *Jewish Antiquities: Volume VI, Books 14–15.* Translated by Ralph Marcus and Allen Wikgren. Vol. 10. 13 vols. LCL 489. Cambridge, Mass.: Harvard University Press, 1943.

———. *Jewish Antiquities: Volume VII, Books 16–17*. Translated by Ralph Marcus and Allen Wikgren. Vol. 11. 13 vols. LCL 410. Cambridge, Mass.: Harvard University Press, 1963.

———. *Jewish Antiquities: Volume VIII, Books 18–19*. Translated by Louis H. Feldman. Vol. 12. 13 vols. LCL 433. Cambridge, Mass.: Harvard University Press, 1965.

———. *Jewish Antiquities: Volume IX, Book 20*. Translated by Louis H. Feldman. Vol. 13. 13 vols. LCL 456. Cambridge, Mass.: Harvard University Press, 1965.

———. *The Jewish War: Volume I, Books 1–2*. Translated by H. St. J. Thackeray. Vol. 2. 13 vols. LCL 203. Cambridge, Mass.: Harvard University Press, 1927.

———. *The Jewish War: Volume II, Books 3–4*. Translated by H. St. J. Thackeray. Vol. 3. 13 vols. LCL 487. Cambridge, Mass.: Harvard University Press, 1927.

———. *The Jewish War: Volume III, Books 5–7*. Translated by H. St. J. Thackeray. Vol. 4. 13 vols. LCL 210. Cambridge, Mass.: Harvard University Press, 1928.

———. *The Life. Against Apion*. Translated by H. St. J. Thackeray. Vol. 1. 13 vols. LCL 186. Cambridge, Mass.: Harvard University Press, 1926.

———. *The Works of Josephus: Complete and Unabridged*. Translated by William Whiston. New Updated. Peabody, Mass.: Hendrickson, 1980.

Justinus, Marcus Junianus. *Epitome of the Philippic, History of Pompeius Trogus*. Edited by James J. Clauss. Translated by J. C. Yardley. APAACS 3. Atlanta, Ga.: Scholars Press, 1994.

Juvenal, and Persius. *Juvenal and Persius*. Edited and translated by Susanna Morton Braund. LCL 91. Cambridge, Mass.: Harvard University Press, 2004.

Kaibel, Georg, ed. *Inscriptiones graecae, XIV. Inscriptiones Siciliae et Italiae, Additis Galliae, Hispaniae, Britanniae, Germaniae Inscriptionibus*. Berlin: De Gruyter, 1890.

Kapossy, Balázs. *Sylloge nummorum graecorum Schweiz II. Katalog der Sammlung Jean-Pierre Righetti im Bernischen Historischen Museum II*. Bern: Haupt, 1993.

Keil, Josef, and Anton von Premerstein, eds. *Bericht über eine Reise in Lydien und der südlichen Aiolis*. Denkschriften der Kaiserlichen Akademie der Wissenschaften in Wien, Philosophisch-Historische Klasse 53, 54, 57. Vienna: Hölder, 1910–1914.

Kent, John Harvey. *The Inscriptions, 1926 to 1950: Corinth*. Vol. 8, Part 3. Athens: American School of Classical Studies at Athens, 1966.

Kirchner, Johannes E., De Gaertingen, and F. Hiller, eds. *Inscriptiones graecae, Inscriptiones Atticae: Editio Minor*. 2nd ed. 8 vols. Berlin: De Gruyter, 1923.

Kitchen, Kenneth A. *Ramesside Inscriptions—Translated and Annotated, Translations, Vol. IV: Merenptah and the Late Nineteenth Dynasty*. Vol. 4. Oxford, U.K.: Wiley-Blackwell, 2003.

Knibb, Michael Anthony. "Martyrdom and Ascension of Isaiah: A New Translation and Introduction." In *The Old Testament Pseudepigrapha: Apocalyptic Literature and Testaments*, edited by James H. Charlesworth, 1:143–76. Peabody, Mass.: Hendrickson, 1983.

Koehler, Lidwig, Walter Baumgartner, B. Hartmann, and Johann J. Stamm, eds. *The Hebrew and Aramaic Lexicon of the Old Testament*. Translated by M. E. J. Richardson. 3rd ed. 5 vols. Leiden: Brill, 1994.

Kolbe, Walther, ed. *Inscriptiones graecae, V.1: Inscriptiones Laconiae et Messeniae*. Vol. 1. Berlin: De Gruyter, 1967.

Kropp, Angelicus M., ed. *Ausgewählte koptische zaubertexte*. 3 vols. Bruxelles: Égyptologique Reine Élisabeth, 1930–1931.

Kühn, Karl Gottlob, ed. *Claudii Galeni Opera Omnia*. 22 vols. Hildesheim: Georg Olms, 1964.

Kutscher, Edward Yechezkel. *The Language and Linguistic Background of the Isaiah Scroll: 1QIsaᵃ*. Studies on the Texts of the Desert of Judah 6. Leiden: Brill, 1974.

Lactantius. *Lactanti De Ave Phoenice: With Introduction, Text, Translation, and Commentary*. Edited by Mary Cletus Fitzpatrick. Philadelphia, Pa.: University of Pennsylvania, 1933.

Lafaye, Georges, René Cagnat, J. Toutain, and Victor Henry, eds. *Inscriptiones graecae ad res romanas pertinentes*. 4 vols. Paris: Leroux, 1901–1927.

Lanz, Hubert. *Numismatik Lanz München, Auction Catlogues*. Munchin: Numismatik Lanz, 2016.

Le Bas, Philippe, William Henry Waddington, Eugène Landron, and Paul François Foucart. *Voyage archéologique en Grèce et en Asie Mineure, Tome III: Inscriptions grecques et latines recueillies en Asie Mineure*. Paris, France: Chez Firmin Didot Frères, 1870.

LeMaire, André. *Inscriptions Hébraïques. I. Les Ostraca*. Vol. 1. Littératures Anciennes Du Proche-Orient 9. Paris: Les Éditions du Cerf, 1977.

Liddell, H. G., Robert Scott, and Stuart Jones. *A Greek-English Lexicon*. 10th ed. Oxford, U.K.: Oxford University Press, 1940.

Lightfoot, Joseph B. *The Apostolic Fathers: Greek Texts and English Translations*. Edited by Michael William Holmes. 3rd ed. Grand Rapids, Mich.: Baker Academic, 2007.

Lindgren, Henry Clay, and Frank L. Kovacs. *Ancient Bronze Coins of Asia Minor and the Levant from the Lindgren Collection*. Vol. 1. 3 vols. San Mateo: Chrysopylon, 1985.

Lipman, Eugene J., ed. *The Mishnah; Oral Teachings of Judaism*. Berlin: Schocken, 1974.

Livy. *History of Rome: Books 3–4*. Translated by B. O. Foster. Vol. 2. 14 vols. LCL 133. Cambridge, Mass.: Harvard University Press, 1922.

———. *History of Rome: Books 5–7*. Translated by B. O. Foster. Vol. 3. 14 vols. LCL 172. Cambridge, Mass.: Harvard University Press, 1924.

———. *History of Rome: Books 8–10*. Translated by B. O. Foster. Vol. 4. 14 vols. LCL 191. Cambridge, Mass.: Harvard University Press, 1926.

———. *History of Rome: Books 26–27*. Translated by Frank Gardner Moore. Vol. 7. 14 vols. LCL 367. Cambridge, Mass.: Harvard University Press, 1943.

———. *History of Rome: Books 31–34*. Translated by Evan T. Sage. Vol. 9. 14 vols. LCL 295. Cambridge, Mass.: Harvard University Press, 1935.

———. *History of Rome: Books 35–37*. Translated by Evan T. Sage. Vol. 10. 14 vols. LCL 301. Cambridge, Mass.: Harvard University Press, 1935.

———. *History of Rome: Books 38–39*. Translated by Evan T. Sage. Vol. 11. 14 vols. LCL 313. Cambridge, Mass.: Harvard University Press, 1936.

———. *History of Rome: Books 40–42*. Translated by Evan T. Sage and Alfred Cary Schlesinger. Vol. 12. 14 vols. LCL 332. Cambridge, Mass.: Harvard University Press, 1938.

———. *Periochae Livianae: Abrégés Des Livres de L'histore Romaine de Tite-Live*. Edited and translated by P. Jal. Budé 34. Paris: Les Belles Lettres, 1984.

Llewelyn, Stephen R., and J. R. Harrison. *New Documents Illustrating Early Christianity: A Review of the Greek and Other Inscriptions and Papyri Published Between 1988 and 1992*. Edited by E. J. Bridge. Vol. 10. Grand Rapids, Mich.: Eerdmans, 2012.

Louw, Johannes E., and Eugene A. Nida. *Greek-English Lexicon of the New Testament: Based on Semantic Domains*. 2nd ed. 2 vols. New York, N.Y.: United Bible Societies, 1989.

Lubetski, Meir, and Edith Lubetski, eds. *New Inscriptions and Seals Relating to the Biblical World*. Atlanta, Ga.: SBL, 2012.

Lucian of Samosata. *The Civil War (Pharsalia)*. Translated by J. D. Duff. LCL 220. Cambridge, Mass.: Harvard University Press, 1928.

———. *Anacharsis or Athletics. Menippus or The Descent into Hades. On Funerals. A Professor of Public Speaking. Alexander the False Prophet. Essays in Portraiture. Essays in Portraiture Defended. The Goddesse of Surrye*. Translated by A. M. Harmon. Vol. 4. 8 vols. LCL 162. Cambridge, Mass.: Harvard University Press, 1925.

———. *Dialogues of the Dead. Dialogues of the Sea-Gods. Dialogues of the Gods. Dialogues of the Courtesans*. Translated by M. D. Macleod. Vol. 8. LCL 431. Cambridge, Mass.: Harvard University Press, 1961.

———. *The Dead Come to Life or The Fisherman. The Double Indictment or Trials by Jury. On Sacrifices. The Ignorant Book Collector. The Dream or Lucian's Career. The Parasite. The Lover of Lies. The Judgement of the Goddesses. On Salaried Posts in Great Houses*. Translated by A. M. Harmon. Vol. 3. 8 vols. LCL 130. Cambridge, Mass.: Harvard University Press, 1921.

———. *The Downward Journey or The Tyrant. Zeus Catechized. Zeus Rants. The Dream or The Cock. Prometheus. Icaromenippus or The Sky-Man. Timon or The Misanthrope. Charon or The Inspectors. Philosophies for Sale*. Translated by A. M. Harmon. Vol. 2. LCL 54. Cambridge, Mass.: Harvard University Press, 1915.

———. *The Passing of Peregrinus. The Runaways. Toxaris or Friendship. The Dance. Lexiphanes. The Eunuch. Astrology. The Mistaken Critic. The Parliament of the Gods. The Tyrannicide. Disowned*. Translated by A. M. Harmon. Vol. 5. 8 vols. LCL 302. Cambridge, Mass.: Harvard University Press, 1936.

Lucretius. *On the Nature of Things*. Edited by Martin F. Smith. Translated by W. H. D. Rouse. LCL 181. Cambridge, Mass.: Harvard University Press, 1924.

Lycophron, Callimachus, and Aratus. *Hymns and Epigrams. Lycophron: Alexandra. Aratus: Phaenomena*. Translated by A. W. Mair and G. R. Mair. LCL 129. Cambridge, Mass.: Harvard University Press, 1955.

Lydus, Ioannes. *On the Months (De Mensibus)*. Edited by Anastasius C. Bandy, Craig J. N. De Paulo, and Demetrios J. Constantelos. Lewiston, N.Y.: Edwin Mellen, 2013.

Macrobius. *Saturnalia: Books 1–2*. Translated by Robert A. Kaster. Vol. 1. 3 vols. LCL 510. Cambridge, Mass.: Harvard University Press, 2011

Magie, David, trans. *Historia Augusta: Caracalla. Geta. Opellius Macrinus. Diadumenianus. Elagabalus. Severus Alexander. The Two Maximini. The Three Gordians. Maximus and Balbinus*. Vol. 2. 3 vols. LCL 140. Cambridge, Mass.: Harvard University Press, 1924.

———. *Historia Augusta: The Two Valerians. The Two Gallieni. The Thirty Pretenders. The Deified Claudius. The Deified Aurelian. Tacitus. Probus. Firmus, Saturninus, Proculus and Bonosus. Carus, Carinus and Numerian*. Vol. 3. 3 vols. LCL 263. Cambridge, Mass.: Harvard University Press, 1932.

Manilius. *Astronomica*. Translated by G. P. Goold. LCL 469. Cambridge, Mass.: Harvard University Press, 1977.

Mannsperger, D., ed. *Sylloge Nummorum Graecorum, Deutschland: Münzsammlung Der Universität Tübingen*. 6 vols. Munchin: Universität Tübingen, 1981.

Marcellinus, Ammianus. *History: Books 14–19*. Translated by John C. Rolfe. Vol. 1. 3 vols. LCL 300. Cambridge, Mass.: Harvard University Press, 1950.

Marcellus, Nonius. *De compendiosa doctrina libros 20*. Edited by Wallace Martin Lindsay. 3 vols. Lipsiae: Teubner, 1903.

Martial, Marcus Valerius. *Epigrams: Spectacles, Books 1–5*. Edited and translated by D. R. Shackleton Bailey. Vol. 1. 3 vols. LCL 94. Cambridge, Mass.: Harvard University Press, 1999.

———. *Epigrams: Books 6–10*. Edited and translated by D. R. Shackleton-Bailey. Vol. 2. 3 vols. LCL 95. Cambridge, Mass.: Harvard University Press, 1993.

———. *Epigrams: Books 11–14*. Edited and translated by D. R. Shackleton-Bailey. Vol. 3. 3 vols. LCL 480. Cambridge, Mass.: Harvard University Press, 1993.

Martínez, Florentino García, and W. G. E. Watson. *The Dead Sea Scrolls Translated: The Qumran Texts in English*. 2nd ed. Leiden: Brill Academic, 1997.

Mattingly, Harold B., Edward Allen Sydenham, and Carol Humphrey Vivian Sutherland, eds. *The Roman Imperial Coinage*. 13 vols. London, U.K.: Spink & Son, 1923–1994.

Mead, G. R. S. trans. *Pistis Sophia: A Gnostic Gospel*. San Diego: Book Tree, 2006.

Memnon. *Die Fragmente Der Griechischen Historiker: History of Heracleia. No. 434*. Translated by Felix Jacoby. Leiden: Brill, 1955.

Merlin, Alfred, ed. *L'Année épigraphique*. Villejuif: Collège de France, 1963.

Meyer, Marvin, and James M. Robinson, eds. *The Nag Hammadi Scriptures: The Revised and Updated Translation of Sacred Gnostic Texts Complete in One Volume*. New York, N.Y.: HarperCollins, 2009.

Mionnet, Théodore Edme. *Description de médailles antiques, grecques et romaines, avec leur degré de rareté et leur estimation*. Vol. 5. 16 vols. Paris: chez l'auteur, 1835.

Mommsen, Theodor, and Herbert Nesselhauf, eds. *Corpus Inscriptionum latinarum: Diplomata militaria*. Vol. 16. 20 vols. Berlin: De Gruyter, 1974.

Moulton, James H., and George Milligan. *Vocabulary of the Greek Testament*. London, U.K.: Hodder & Stoughton, 1930.

Musée du Louvre. *Textes cunéiformes*. Département des Antiquités Orientales. Paris, France: Geuthner, 1910.

Musurillo, Hebert, ed. *The Acts of the Christian Martyrs*. Translated by Hebert Musurillo. Oxford, U.K.: Clarendon, 1972.

Newton, Charles Thomas. *The Collection of Ancient Greek Inscriptions in the British Museum*. Edited by E. L. Hicks. 5 vols. Oxford, U.K.: Clarendon, 1874.

Nicolet, Helene, Jean Delepierre, Marie Delepierre, and Georges Le Rider. *Sylloge Nummorum Graecorum. France, Bibliothéque Nationale, Cabinet Des Médailles. Collection Jean et Marie Delepirre*. Paris, France: Bibliothéque Nationale, 1983–2001.

Noy, David, and Hanswulf Bloedhorn, eds. *Inscriptiones judaicae orientis*. 3 vols. TSAJ 99, 101, 102. Tübingen: Mohr Siebeck, 2004.

Oppenheim, A. Leo. *Assyrian Dictionary of the Oriental Institute of the University of Chicago*. 21 vols. Chicago, Ill.: University Of Chicago Press, 1977.

Origen. *Homilies on Luke: Fragments on Luke*. Translated by Joseph T. Lienhard. Washington, D.C.: Catholic University of America Press, 1996.

———. *Homilies on Numbers*. Edited by Christopher A. Hall. Translated by Thomas P. Scheck. Downers Grove, Ill.: InterVarsity Press, 2009.

Ovid. *Fasti*. Edited by G. P. Goold. Translated by James G. Frazer. Vol. 5. 6 vols. LCL 253. Cambridge, Mass.: Harvard University Press, 1931.

———. *Heroides. Amores*. Edited by G. P. Goold. Translated by Grant Showerman. Vol. 1. 6 vols. LCL 41. Cambridge, Mass.: Harvard University Press, 1914.

———. *Metamorphoses: Books 1–8*. Edited by G. P. Goold. Translated by Frank Justus Miller. Vol. 1. 6 vols. LCL 42. Cambridge, Mass.: Harvard University Press, 1916.

———. *Metamorphoses: Books 9–15*. Edited by G. P. Goold. Translated by Frank Justus Miller. Vol. 2. 6 vols. LCL 43. Cambridge, Mass.: Harvard University Press, 1916.

———. *Tristia, Ex Ponto*. Edited by G. P. Goold. Translated by A. L. Wheeler. Vol. 6. 6 vols. LCL 151. Cambridge, Mass.: Harvard University Press, 1924.

Paterculus, Velleius. *Compendium of Roman History. Res Gestae Divi Augusti*. Translated by Frederick W. Shipley. LCL 152. Cambridge, Mass.: Harvard University Press, 1924.

Paton, William R., ed. *Inscriptiones graecae, XII. Inscriptiones Insularum Maris Aegaei Praeter Delum: 2. Inscriptiones Lesbi, Nesi, Tenedi*. Vol. 12. Berlin: De Gruyter, 1899.

———. trans. *The Greek Anthology: Book 13: Epigrams in Various Metres. Book 14: Arithmetical Problems, Riddles, Oracles. Book 15: Miscellanea. Book 16: Epigrams of the Planudean Anthology Not in the Palatine Manuscript*. Vol. 5. Loeb Classical Library 86. Cambridge, Mass.: Harvard University Press, 1918.

Pauly, August Friedrich. *Realencyclopädie Der Classischen Altertumswissenschaft*. Edited by Georg Wissowa and S. Kroll. 50 vols in 84 parts. Stuttgart: Metzler & Druckenmüller, 1894–1980.

Pausanias . *Description of Greece, Books 1–2: Attica and Corinth*. Translated by Henry A Ormerod and W. H. S. Jones. Vol. 1. 5 vols. LCL 93. Cambridge, Mass.: Harvard University Press, 1918.

———. *Description of Greece, Books 3–5: Laconia, Messenia, Elis 1*. Translated by W. H. S. Jones and Henry A Ormerod. Vol. 2. 5 vols. LCL 188. Cambridge, Mass.: Harvard University Press, 1926.

———. *Description of Greece, Books 6–8.21: Elis 2, Achaia, Arcadia*. Translated by W. H. S. Jones. Vol. 3. 5 vols. LCL 272. Cambridge, Mass.: Harvard University Press, 1933.

———. *Description of Greece, Books 8.22–10: Arcadia, Boeotia, Phocis and Ozolian Locri*. Translated by W. H. S. Jones. Vol. 4. 5 vols. LCL 297. Cambridge, Mass.: Harvard University Press, 1935.

Perry, Ben Edwin. *Aesopica: Studies in Text History of Life and Fables of Aesop: Greek and Latin Texts*. 2 vols. Urbana, Ill.: University of Illinois Press, 1952.

Petronius, Seneca. *Satyricon. Apocolocyntosis*. Edited by E. H. Warmington. Translated by Michael Heseltine and W. H. D. Rouse. LCL 15. Cambridge, Mass.: Harvard University Press, 1913.

Pettinato, Giovanni, and A. Alberti. *Catalogo Dei Testi Cuneiformi Di Tell Mardikh-Ebla*. Materiali Epigrafici Di Ebla 1. Naples: Istituto Universitario Orientale di Napoli, 1979.

Petzl, Georg. *Die Inschriften von Smyrna*. 2 vols. IGSK 23–24. Bonn: Habelt, 1982–1990.

———. *Tituli Lydiae Linguis Graeca et Latina Conscripti: Fasciculus III, Philadelpheia et Ager Philadelphenus*. TAM V, 3. Vienna: ÖAW, 2007.

Pfann, Stephen, and Philip Alexander, eds. *Qumran Cave 4: Cryptic Texts and Miscellanea, Part 1: Miscellaneous Texts from Qumran*. DJD 36. Oxford, U.K.: Clarendon, 2000.

Pharr, Clyde. *The Theodosian Code and Novels, and the Sirmondian Constitutions*. Union, NJ: The Lawbook Exchange, 2001.

Philo. *Every Good Man Is Free. On the Contemplative Life. On the Eternity of the World. Against Flaccus. Apology for the Jews. On Providence.* Translated by F. H. Colson. Vol. 9. 10 vols. LCL 363. Cambridge, Mass.: Harvard University Press, 1941.

———. *On Abraham. On Joseph. On Moses.* Translated by F. H. Colson. Vol. 6. 10 vols. LCL 289. Cambridge, Mass.: Harvard University Press, 1935.

———. *On Flight and Finding. On the Change of Names. On Dreams.* Translated by F. H. Colson and G. H. Whitaker. Vol. 5. 10 vols. LCL 275. Cambridge, Mass.: Harvard University Press, 1934.

———. *On the Cherubim. The Sacrifices of Abel and Cain. The Worse Attacks the Better. On the Posterity and Exile of Cain. On the Giants.* Translated by F. H. Colson and G. H. Whitaker. Vol. 2. 10 vols. LCL 227. Cambridge, Mass.: Harvard University Press, 1929.

———. *On the Confusion of Tongues. On the Migration of Abraham. Who Is the Heir of Divine Things? On Mating with the Preliminary Studies.* Translated by F. H. Colson and G. H. Whitaker. Vol. 4. 10 vols. LCL 261. Cambridge, Mass.: Harvard University Press, 1932.

———. *On the Creation. Allegorical Interpretation of Genesis 2 and 3.* Translated by F. H. Colson and G. H. Whitaker. Vol. 1. 10 vols. LCL 226. Cambridge, Mass.: Harvard University Press, 1929.

———. *On the Decalogue. On the Special Laws, Books 1–3.* Translated by F. H. Colson. Vol. 7. 10 vols. LCL 320. Cambridge, Mass.: Harvard University Press, 1937.

———. *On the Embassy to Gaius. General Indexes.* Edited by J. W. Earp. Translated by F. H. Colson. Vol. 10. 10 vols. LCL 379. Cambridge, Mass.: Harvard University Press, 1962.

———. *On the Unchangeableness of God. On Husbandry. Concerning Noah's Work As a Planter. On Drunkenness. On Sobriety.* Translated by F. H. Colson and G. H. Whitaker. Vol. 3. 10 vols. LCL 247. Cambridge, Mass.: Harvard University Press, 1930.

———. *Supplement II: Questions on Exodus.* Translated by Ralph Marcus. LCL 401. Cambridge, Mass.: Harvard University Press, 1953.

Philostratus, and Eunapius. *Lives of the Sophists. Eunapius: Lives of the Philosophers and Sophists.* Translated by Wilmer C. Wright. Vol. 4. 4 vols. LCL 134. Cambridge, Mass.: Harvard University Press, 1921.

Philostratus, Flavius. *Life of Apollonius of Tyana: Books 1–4.* Translated by Christopher P. Jones. Vol. 1. 4 vols. LCL 16. Cambridge, Mass.: Harvard University Press, 2005.

———. *Life of Apollonius of Tyana: Books 5–8.* Edited and translated by Christopher P. Jones. Vol. 2. 4 vols. LCL 17. Cambridge, Mass.: Harvard University Press, 2005.

———. *The Life of Apollonius of Tyana, The Epistles of Apollonius, and the Treatise of Eusebius*. Translated by Frederick C Conybeare. 2 vols. LCL 16. Cambridge, Mass.: Harvard University Press, 1989.

Pilhofer, Peter. *Philippi. Band II. Katalog der Inschriften von Philippi*. 2nd ed. 2 vols. WUNT 119. Tübingen: Mohr Siebeck, 2009.

Pindar. *Olympian Odes. Pythian Odes*. Edited and translated by William H. Race. Vol. 1. 2 vols. LCL 56. Cambridge, Mass.: Harvard University Press, 1997.

Plato. *Laws: Volume II, Books 7–12*. Translated by R. G. Bury. Vol. 11. 12 vols. LCL 192. Cambridge, Mass.: Harvard University Press, 1926.

———. *Republic: Volume I, Books 1–5*. Edited and translated by William Preddy and Chris Emlyn-Jones. Vol. 5. LCL 237. Cambridge, Mass.: Harvard University Press, 2013.

Plautus, Titus Maccius. *Amphitryon. The Comedy of Asses. The Pot of Gold. The Two Bacchises. The Captives*. Translated by Wolfgang David Cirilo de Melo. Vol. 1. 5 vols. Loeb Classical Library 60. Cambridge, Mass.: Harvard University Press, 2011.

———. *Casina. The Casket Comedy. Curculio. Epidicus. The Two Menaechmuses Plautus*. Edited and translated by Wolfgang David Cirilo de Melo. Vol. 2. 5 vols. LCL 61. Cambridge, Mass.: Harvard University Press, 2011.

———. *The Little Carthaginian. Pseudolus. The Rope*. Edited and translated by Wolfgang David Cirilo de Melo. Vol. 4. 5 vols. Loeb Classical Library 260. Cambridge, Mass.: Harvard University Press, 2012.

Pliny the Elder. *Natural History: Books 1–2*. Translated by H. Rackham. Vol. 1. 10 vols. LCL 330. Cambridge, Mass.: Harvard University Press, 1938.

———. *Natural History: Books 3–7*. Translated by H. Rackham. Vol. 2. 10 vols. LCL 352. Cambridge, Mass.: Harvard University Press, 1942.

———. *Natural History: Books 8–11*. Translated by H. Rackham. Vol. 3. 10 vols. LCL 353. Cambridge, Mass.: Harvard University Press, 1940.

———. *Natural History: Books 12–16*. Translated by H. Rackham. Vol. 4. 10 vols. LCL 370. Cambridge, Mass.: Harvard University Press, 1945.

———. *Natural History: Books 20–23*. Translated by William H. S. Jones. Vol. 6. 10 vols. LCL 392. Cambridge, Mass.: Harvard University Press, 1951.

———. *Natural History: Books 24–27*. Translated by William H. S. Jones and A. C. Andrews. Vol. 7. 10 vols. LCL 393. Cambridge, Mass.: Harvard University Press, 1956.

———. *Natural History: Books 28–32*. Translated by William H. S. Jones. Vol. 8. 10 vols. LCL 418. Cambridge, Mass.: Harvard University Press, 1963.

———. *Natural History: Books 33–35*. Translated by William H. S. Jones. Vol. 9. 10 vols. LCL 394. Cambridge, Mass.: Harvard University Press, 1952.

———. *Natural History: Books 36–37*. Translated by D. E. Eichholz. Vol. 10. 10 vols. LCL 419. Cambridge, Mass.: Harvard University Press, 1962.

Pliny the Younger. *Letters, Books 1–7*. Translated by Betty Radice. Vol. 1. 2 vols. LCL 55. Cambridge, Mass.: Harvard University Press, 1969.

———. *Letters, Books 8–10: Panegyricus*. Translated by Betty Radice. Vol. 2. 2 vols. LCL 59. Cambridge, Mass.: Harvard University Press, 1969.

Bibliography—Primary Sources

Plutarch. *Lives: Agis and Cleomenes. Tiberius and Gaius Gracchus. Philopoemen and Flamininus*. Translated by Bernadotte Perrin. Vol. 10. 11 vols. Loeb Classical Library 102. Cambridge, Mass.: Harvard University Press, 1921.

———. *Lives: Alcibiades and Coriolanus. Lysander and Sulla*. Translated by Bernadotte Perrin. Vol. 4. 11 vols. LCL 80. Cambridge, Mass.: Harvard University Press, 1916.

———. *Lives: Demetrius and Antony. Pyrrhus and Gaius Marius*. Translated by Bernadotte Perrin. Vol. 9. 11 vols. LCL 101. Cambridge, Mass.: Harvard University Press, 1920.

———. *Lives: Demosthenes and Cicero. Alexander and Caesar*. Translated by Bernadotte Perrin. Vol. 7. 11 vols. LCL 99. Cambridge, Mass.: Harvard University Press, 1919.

———. *Lives: Pericles and Fabius Maximus. Nicias and Crassus*. Translated by Bernadotte Perrin. Vol. 3. 11 vols. LCL 65. Cambridge, Mass.: Harvard University Press, 1916.

———. *Lives: Sertorius and Eumenes. Phocion and Cato the Younger*. Translated by Bernadotte Perrin. Vol. 8. 11 vols. LCL 100. Cambridge, Mass.: Harvard University Press, 1919.

———. *Moralia: Isis and Osiris. The E at Delphi. The Oracles at Delphi No Longer Given in Verse. The Obsolescence of Oracles*. Translated by Frank Cole Babbitt. Vol. 5. 15 vols. LCL 306. Cambridge, Mass.: Harvard University Press, 1936.

———. *Moralia: Love Stories. That a Philosopher Ought to Converse Especially With Men in Power. To an Uneducated Ruler. Whether an Old Man Should Engage in Public Affairs. Precepts of Statecraft. On Monarchy, Democracy, and Oligarchy. That We Ought Not to Borrow. Lives*. Translated by Harold North Fowler. Vol. 10. 16 vols. LCL 321. Cambridge, Mass.: Harvard University Press, 1936.

———. *Moralia: On the Malice of Herodotus. Causes of Natural Phenomena*. Translated by Lionel Pearson and F. H. Sandbach. Vol. 11. 16 vols. LCL 426. Cambridge, Mass.: Harvard University Press, 1965.

———. *Moralia: Roman Questions. Greek Questions. Greek and Roman Parallel Stories. On the Fortune of the Romans. On the Fortune or the Virtue of Alexander. Were the Athenians More Famous in War or in Wisdom?* Translated by Frank Cole Babbitt. Vol. 4. 16 vols. Loeb Classical Library 305. Cambridge, Mass.: Harvard University Press, 1936.

———. *Moralia: Sayings of Kings and Commanders. Sayings of Romans. Sayings of Spartans. The Ancient Customs of the Spartans. Sayings of Spartan Women. Bravery of Women*. Translated by Frank Cole Babbitt. Vol. 3. 15 vols. LCL 245. Cambridge, Mass.: Harvard University Press, 1931.

———. *Moralia: Table-Talk, Books 1–6*. Translated by P. A. Clement and H. B. Hoffleit. Vol. 8. 16 vols. LCL 424. Cambridge, Mass.: Harvard University Press, 1969.

———. *Moralia: Table-Talk, Books 7–9, Dialogue on Love*. Translated by Edwin L. Minar, Jr., F. H. Sandbach, and W. C. Helmbold. Vol. 9. 15 vols. LCL 425. Cambridge, Mass.: Harvard University Press, 1961.

Pollux, Julius. *Onomasticon (Greek Edition)*. Edited by Karl Wilhelm Dindorf. Charleston, S.C.: Nabu, 1824, reprint 2012.

Polyaenus. *Stratagems of War*. Translated by Richard Shepherd. London, U.K.: Nichol, 1793.

Polybius. *The Histories: Books 1–2*. Edited by F. W. Walbank and Christian Habicht. Translated by William R. Paton. Vol. 1. 6 vols. LCL 128. Cambridge, Mass.: Harvard University Press, 2010.

———. *The Histories: Books 5–8*. Edited by F. W. Walbank and Christian Habicht. Translated by William R. Paton. Vol. 3. 6 vols. LCL 138. Cambridge, Mass.: Harvard University Press, 2011.

———. *The Histories: Books 9–15*. Edited by F. W. Walbank and Christian Habicht. Translated by William R. Paton. Vol. 4. 6 vols. LCL 159. Cambridge, Mass.: Harvard University Press, 2011.

———. *The Histories: Books 16–27*. Edited by F. W. Walbank and Christian Habicht. Translated by William R. Paton. Vol. 5. 6 vols. LCL 160. Cambridge, Mass.: Harvard University Press, 2012.

———. *The Histories: Books 28–39*. Fragments. Edited by F. W. Walbank, Christian Habicht, and S. Douglas Olson. Translated by William R. Paton and S. Douglas Olson. Vol. 6. 6 vols. LCL 161. Cambridge, Mass.: Harvard University Press, 2012.

Preisigke, Friedrich, ed. *Sammelbuch Griechischer Urkunden aus Ägypten*. 5 vols. Strassburg: Trübner, 1915.

Pritchard, James Bennett. *Ancient Near Eastern Texts Relating to the Old Testament with Supplement*. 3rd ed. Princeton, N.J.: Princeton University Press, 1969.

Procopius of Caesarea. *History of the Wars: Books 3–4. (Vandalic War)*. Translated by H. B. Dewing. Vol. 2. 7 vols. LCL 81. Cambridge, Mass.: Harvard University Press, 1916.

———. *On Buildings. General Index*. Translated by H. B. Dewing and Glanville Downey. Vol. 7. 7 vols. LCL 343. Cambridge, Mass.: Harvard University Press, 1940.

———. *The Anecdota or Secret History*. Translated by H. B. Dewing. Vol. 6. 7 vols. LCL 290. Cambridge, Mass.: Harvard University Press, 1935.

Propertius, Sextus. *Elegies*. Translated by G. P. Goold. LCL 18. Cambridge, Mass.: Harvard University Press, 1990.

Pseudo-Galen. *Oeuvres, III. Le Médecin. Introduction*. Edited by Caroline Petit. Paris, France: Belles Lettres, 2009.

Puech, Émile. *Qumran Cave 4.XVIII: Textes Hébreux (4Q521–4Q528, 4Q576–4Q579)*. DJD 25. Oxford, U.K.: Clarendon, 1998.

Quasten, Johannes. *Patrology*. 4 vols. Westminster: Christian Classics, 1986.

Rawlinson, Henry C. *The Persian Cuneiform Inscription at Behistun, Decyphered and Translated; With a Memoir on Persian Cuneiform Inscriptions in General, and on That of Behistun in Particular*. Journal of the Royal Asiatic Society of Great Britain and Ireland, 1848.

Roberts, Alexander, James Donaldson, Philip Schaff, and Henry Wace, eds. *Nicene and Post-Nicene Fathers, Series 1*. 14 vols. Peabody, Mass.: Hendrickson, 1994.

———. eds. *Nicene and Post-Nicene Fathers, Series 2*. 14 vols. Peabody, Mass.: Hendrickson, 1994.

———. eds. *Ante-Nicene Fathers*. New Ed. 10 vols. Peabody, Mass.: Hendrickson, 1994.

Robinson, James M., ed. *The Nag Hammadi Library: A Translation of the Gnostic Scriptures*. London, U.K.: HarperCollins, 1990.

Rodkinson, Michael L. *New Edition of the Babylonian Talmud: Original Text, Edited, Corrected, Formulated and Translated into English*. 20 vols. Boston, Mass.: The Talmud Society, 1918.

Sallust, Gaius. *The War with Catiline. The War with Jugurtha*. Translated by John C. Rolfe and John T. Ramsey. Vol. 1. 2 vols. LCL 116. Cambridge, Mass.: Harvard University Press, 2013.

Sanders, J. A. *The Psalms Scroll of Qumran Cave 11*. DJD 4. Oxford, U.K.: Oxford University Press, 1965.

Sappho, and Alcaeus. *Greek Lyric, Volume 1: Sappho and Alcaeus*. Edited and translated by David A. Campbell. LCL 142. Cambridge, Mass.: Harvard University Press, 1982.

Bibliography—Primary Sources

Schuller, Eileen, Esther Eshel, Hanan Eshel, Carol A. Newsom, Bilhah Nitzan, and Ada Yardeni. *Qumran Cave 4. VI: Poetical and Liturgical Texts, Part 1*. DJD 11 Oxford, U.K.: Clarendon, 1998.

Seneca, Lucius Annaeus. *Epistles, Volume I: Epistles 1–65*. Translated by Richard M. Gummere. Vol. 4. 10 vols. LCL 75. Cambridge, Mass.: Harvard University Press, 1917.

———. *Epistles: Volume II, Epistles 66–92*. Translated by Richard M. Gummere. Vol. 5. 10 vols. LCL 76. Cambridge, Mass.: Harvard University Press, 1920.

———. *Epistles: Volume III, Epistles 93–124*. Translated by Richard M. Gummere. Vol. 6. 10 vols. LCL 77. Cambridge, Mass.: Harvard University Press, 1925.

———. *Moral Essays, Volume I De Providentia. De Constantia. De Ira. De Clementia*. Translated by John W. Basore. Vol. 1. 10 vols. LCL 214. Cambridge, Mass.: Harvard University Press, 1928.

———. *Natural Questions: Books 1–3*. Translated by Thomas H. Corcoran. Vol. 7. 10 vols. LCL 450. Cambridge, Mass.: Harvard University Press, 1971.

———. *Tragedies, Volume I Hercules. Trojan Women. Phoenician Women. Medea. Phaedra*. Translated by John G. Fitch. Vol. 8. 10 vols. LCL 62. Cambridge, Mass.: Harvard University Press, 2002.

Servius, Maurus Honoratus. *Servii Grammatici Qui Feruntur in Vergilii Carmina Commentarii: Vol 2. Aeneid Books 6–12*. Translated by Georgius Thilo and Herman Hagen. Vol. 2. 4 vols. Cambridge Library Collection – Classics. New York, N.Y.: Cambridge University Press, 2011.

Sidonius Apollinaris. *Letters Books 3–9*. Translated by W. B. Anderson. Vol. 2. 2 vols. LCL 420. Cambridge, Mass.: Harvard University Press, 1965.

Sophocles, Oedipus Tyrannus. *Ajax. Electra*. Translated by Hugh Lloyd-Jones. Vol. 1. 3 vols. LCL 20. Cambridge, Mass.: Harvard University Press, 1994.

———. *Antigone. The Women of Trachis. Philoctetes. Oedipus at Colonus*. Translated by Hugh Lloyd-Jones. Vol. 2. 3 vols. LCL 21. Cambridge, Mass.: Harvard University Press, 1994.

———. *Fragments*. Translated by Hugh Lloyd-Jones. Vol. 3. 3 vols. LCL 483. Cambridge, Mass.: Harvard University Press, 1996.

Sparks, H. F. D., ed. *The Apocryphal Old Testament*. Oxford, U.K.: Oxford University Press, 1984.

Statius. *Silvae*. Translated by D. R. Shackleton Bailey. Vol. 1. 3 vols. LCL 206. Cambridge, Mass.: Harvard University Press, 2003.

———. *Thebaid, Volume I: Books 1–7*. Translated by D. R. Shackleton-Bailey. Vol. 2. 3 vols. LCL 207. Cambridge, Mass.: Harvard University Press, 2004.

Stephanus of Byzantium. *De Urbanus*. Edited by Thomas de Pinedo. Typis Jacobi de Jonge, 1678.

Strabo. *Geography: Books 1–2*. Translated by Horace Leonard Jones. Vol. 1. 8 vols. LCL 49. Cambridge, Mass.: Harvard University Press, 1917.

———. *Geography: Books 3–5*. Translated by Horace Leonard Jones. Vol. 2. 8 vols. LCL 50. Cambridge, Mass.: Harvard University Press, 1923.

———. *Geography: Books 6–7*. Translated by Horace Leonard Jones. Vol. 3. 8 vols. LCL 182. Cambridge, Mass.: Harvard University Press, 1924.

———. *Geography: Books 8–9*. Translated by Horace Leonard Jones. Vol. 4. 8 vols. LCL 196. Cambridge, Mass.: Harvard University Press, 1927.

———. *Geography: Books 10–12*. Translated by Horace Leonard Jones. Vol. 5. 8 vols. LCL 211. Cambridge, Mass.: Harvard University Press, 1928.

———. *Geography: Books 13–14*. Translated by Horace Leonard Jones. Vol. 6. 8 vols. LCL 223. Cambridge, Mass.: Harvard University Press, 1929.

———. *Geography: Books 15–16*. Translated by Horace Leonard Jones. Vol. 7. 8 vols. LCL 241. Cambridge, Mass.: Harvard University Press, 1930.

Stronk, Jan P., trans. *Ctesias' Persian History: Introduction, Text and Translation Pt. 1*. Düsseldorf: Wellem Verlag, 2010.

Strugnell, John, Daniel J Harrington, and Torleif Elgvin, eds. *Qumran Cave 4.XXIV: Sapiential Texts, Part 2, 4QInstruction (Musar Le Mevin): 4Q415ff*. DJD 34. Oxford, U.K.: Clarendon, 1999.

Strugnell, John, Magen Broshi, Esther Eshel, Joseph Fitzmyer, Erik Larson, Carol Newsom, Lawrence Schiffman, Mark Smith, Michael Stone, and James Vanderkam. *Qumran Cave 4: XIV: Parabiblical Texts, Part 2*. DJD 19. Oxford, U.K.: Clarendon, 1996.

Suetonius Tranquillus, Gaius. *Lives of the Caesars: Claudius. Nero. Galba, Otho, and Vitellius. Vespasian. Titus, Domitian. Lives of Illustrious Men: Grammarians and Rhetoricians. Poets (Terence. Virgil. Horace. Tibullus. Persius. Lucan). Lives of Pliny the Elder and Passienus Crispus*. Translated by J. C. Rolfe. Vol. 2. 2 vols. LCL 38. Cambridge, Mass.: Harvard University Press, 1914.

———. *Lives of the Caesars: Julius. Augustus. Tiberius. Gaius. Caligula*. Translated by J. C. Rolfe. Vol. 1. 2 vols. LCL 31. Cambridge, Mass.: Harvard University Press, 1914.

———. *The Twelve Caesars*. Edited by Michael Grant. Translated by Robert Graves. Rev. Penguin Classics. Harmondsworth, U.K.: Penguin, 1987.

Sukenik, Eleazar Lipa. *The Dead Sea Scrolls of the Hebrew University*. Jerusalem: Hebrew University Press Magnes, 1955.

Sussman, Lewis A. *The Declamations of Calpurnius Flaccus: Text, Translation, and Commentary*. Leiden: Brill, 1994.

Tacitus, Cornelius. *Annals: Books 1–3*. Translated by Clifford H. Moore. Vol. 3. 5 vols. LCL 249. Cambridge, Mass.: Harvard University Press, 1931.

———. *Annals: Books 4–6, 11–12*. Translated by John Jackson. Vol. 4. 5 vols. LCL 312. Cambridge, Mass.: Harvard University Press, 1937.

———. *Annals: Books 13–16*. Translated by John Jackson. Vol. 5. 5 vols. LCL 322. Cambridge, Mass.: Harvard University Press, 1937.

———. *Histories: Books 1–3*. Translated by Clifford H. Moore. Vol. 2. 5 vols. LCL 111. Cambridge, Mass.: Harvard University Press, 1925.

———. *Histories: Books 4–5. Annals: Books 1–3*. Translated by Clifford H. Moore and John E. Jackson. Vol. 3. 5 vols. LCL 249. Cambridge, Mass.: Harvard University Press, 1931.

Talmon, Shemaryahu, and Yigael Yadin, eds. *Masada VI:The Yigael Yadin Excavations 1963–1965: Hebrew Fragments from Masada*. The Masada Reports 6. Jerusalem, Israel: Israel Exploration Society and The Hebrew University of Jerusalem, 1999.

Tatius, Achilles. *Leucippe and Clitophon*. Translated by S. Gaselee. LCL 45. Cambridge, Mass.: Harvard University Press, 1969.

BIBLIOGRAPHY—PRIMARY SOURCES

Tekin, Oguz, Aliye Erol Ozdizbay, and Konuk Koray. *Sylloge Nummorum Graecorum: Turkey 1, The Muharrem Kayhan Collection Part 2*. 2 vols. Istanbul: Ege Yayinlari, 2015.

Theophrastus, Herodas, and Sophron. *Characters. Herodas: Mimes. Sophron and Other Mime Fragments*. Edited and translated by Jeffrey Ruston and I. C. Cunnigham. LCL 225. Cambridge, Mass.: Harvard University Press, 2003.

Thucydides. *History of the Peloponnesian War: Books 3–4*. Translated by C. F. Smith. Vol. 2. 2 vols. LCL 109. Cambridge, Mass.: Harvard University Press, 1920.

Trever, John C. *Scrolls from Qumran Cave I: The Great Isaiah Scroll the Order of the Community, the Pesher to Habakkuk*. Sheffield, U.K.: Sheffield Academic, 1974.

Tyrtaeus, Salon, and Theognis. *Greek Elegiac Poetry From the Seventh to the Fifth Centuries BC*. Edited and translated by Douglas E. Gerber. LCL 258. Cambridge, Mass.: Harvard University Press, 1999.

Ulmer, Rivka, ed. *A Synoptic Edition of Pesiqta Rabbati Based upon All Extant. Manuscripts and the Editio Princeps*. 3 vols. South Florida Studies in the History of Judaism 155. Lanham, Md.: University Press of America, 2002.

———. ed. *Pesiqta Rabbati: A Synoptic Edition of Pesiqta Rabbati Based Upon All Extant Manuscripts and the Editio Princeps*. 3 vols. Atlanta, Ga.: Scholars Press, 2002.

Ulpian. *The Digest of Justinian*. Edited and translated by Alan Watson. Philadelphia, Pa.: University of Pennsylvania Press, 1998.

Ulrich, Eugene, Frank Moore Cross, and Sidnie White Crawford, eds. *Qumran Cave 4: IX. Deuteronomy, Joshua, Judges, Kings*. DJD 14. Oxford, U.K.: Clarendon, 1999.

Varro, Marcus Terentius, and M. Porcius Cato. *On Agriculture*. Translated by W. D. Hooper and Harrison Boyd Ash. LCL 283. Cambridge, Mass.: Harvard University Press, 1934.

Varro, Marcus Terentius. *On the Latin Language: Books 5–7*. Translated by Roland G. Kent. Vol. 1. 3 vols. LCL 233. Cambridge, Mass.: Harvard University Press, 1938

Victorinus, Apringius of Beja, Caesarius of Arles, and The Venerable Bede. *Latin Commentaries on Revelation: Victorinus of Petovium, Apringius of Beja, Caesarius of Arles and Bede the Venerable*. Edited and translated by William C. Weinrich. ACT. Downers Grove, Ill.: IVP Academic, 2012.

Virgil. *Aeneid: Books 7–12. Appendix Vergiliana*. Edited by G. P. Goold. Translated by H. Rushton Fairclough. Vol. 2. 2 vols. LCL 64. Cambridge, Mass.: Harvard University Press, 2011.

———. *Eclogues. Georgics. Aeneid: Books 1–6*. Edited by G. P. Goold. Translated by H. Rushton Fairclough. Vol. 1. 2 vols. LCL 63. Cambridge, Mass.: Harvard University Press, 1999.

Vitruvius. *On Architecture: Books 1–5*. Translated by Frank Granger. Vol. 1. 2 vols. LCL 251. Cambridge, Mass.: Harvard University Press, 1931.

———. *On Architecture: Books 6–10*. Translated by Ernest Granger. Vol. 2. 2 vols. LCL 280. Cambridge, Mass.: Harvard University Press, 1934.

Von Aulock, Sammlung Hans. *Sylloge Nummorum Graecorum: Collection of Greek Coins from Asia Minor*. Edited by Gerhard Kleiner. 4 vols. Seattle, Wash.: Sunrise, 1987.

Waltzing, Jean Pierre. *L'épigraphie Latine et Les Corporations Professionnelles de L'empire Romain*. Gand: Siffer, 1892.

Wankel, Hermann, ed. *Die Inschriften von Ephesos*. 8 vols. IGSK 11.1–17.4. Bonn: Habelt, 1979.

Weidmann, Frederick W. *Polycarp and John: The Harris Fragments and Their Challenge to the Literary Traditions.* Christianity and Judaism in Antiquity 12. Notre Dame, Ind.: University of Notre Dame Press, 2010.

Wessner, Paul, ed. *Scholia in Juvenalem Uetustiora.* Leipzig: Teubner, 1931.

West, Martin L., ed. *Greek Epic Fragments From the Seventh to the Fifth Centuries BC.* Translated by Martin L. West. LCL 497. Cambridge, Mass.: Harvard University Press, 2003.

Wiegend, Theodor, Georg Kawerau, Albert Rehm, and Peter Herrmann. *Milet: Ergebnisse Der Ausgrabungen Und Untersuchungen Seit Dem Jahre 1899.* Berlin: De Gruyter, 1889.

Xenophon of Ephesus, and Longus. *Daphnis and Chloe. Anthia and Habrocomes.* Edited and translated by Jeffrey Henderson. LCL 69. Cambridge, Mass.: Harvard University Press, 2009.

Xenophon of Ephesus. "An Ephesian Tale." In *Collected Ancient Greek Novels,* edited by Bryan P. Reardon, translated by Graham Anderson, 2nd ed., 125–69. Oakland, Calf.: University of California Press, 2008.

———. *Anabasis.* Edited by Jeffrey Henderson. Translated by Carleton L. Brownson and John Dillery. Vol. 3. 7 vols. LCL 90. Cambridge, Mass.: Harvard University Press, 1998.

———. *Cyropaedia: Volume 2: Books 5–8.* Translated by Walter Miller. Vol. 6. 7 vols. LCL 52. Cambridge, Mass.: Harvard University Press, 1914.

———. *Hellenica: Books 1–4.* Translated by Carleton L. Brownson. Vol. 1. 7 vols. LCL 88. Cambridge, Mass.: Harvard University Press, 1918.

———. *Memorabilia. Oeconomicus. Symposium. Apology.* Edited by Jeffrey Henderson. Translated by E. C. Marchant and O. J. Todd. Vol. 4. 7 vols. LCL 168. Cambridge, Mass.: Harvard University Press, 2013.

Yadin, Yigael. *The Temple Scroll: The Hidden Law of the Dead Sea Sect.* New York, N.Y.: Random House, 1985.

SECONDARY SOURCES

Abt, A. *Die Apologie Des Apuleius von Madaura Und Die Antike Zauberei*. Giessen: Töpelmann, 1908.

Adams, Edward. "The 'Coming of God' Tradition and Its Influence on New Testament Parousia Texts." In *Biblical Traditions in Transmission: Essays in Honour of Michael A. Knibb*, edited by Michael Anthony Knibb, Charlotte Hempel, and Judith Lieu, 1–19. JSJSup 3. Brill, 2006.

Akşit, İlhan. *Pamukkale Hierapolis*. Istanbul: Akşit, 2003.

Aktüre, Zynep. "Reading into the Mysteries of Artemis Ephesia." In *Curating Architecture and the City*, edited by Sarah Chaplin and Alexandra Stara, 145–63. New York, N.Y.: Routledge, 2009.

Akurgal, Ekrem. *Ancient Civilizations and Ruins of Turkey from Prehistoric Times until the End of the Roman Empire*. Translated by John Whybrow and Mollie Emre. 2nd ed. Istanbul: Mobil Oil Turk A. S., 1985.

———. "Smyrna." Edited by Richard Stillwell, William L. MacDonald, and Marian Holland. *PECS*. Princeton, N.J.: Princeton University Press, 1976.

Alberti, Maria Emanuela. "Murex Shells as Raw Material: The Purple-Dye Industry and Its By-Products. Interpreting the Archaeological Record." *Kaskal* 5 (2008): 73–90.

Albright, William F. *From the Stone Age to Christianity: Monotheism and the Historical Process*. La Vergne, Tenn.: Lightning Source, 2008.

———. "The Seal of Eliakim and the Latest Preëxilic History of Judah, with Some Observations on Ezekiel." *JBL* 51, no. 2 (1932): 77–106.

Alford, Henry. *Hebrews-Revelation*. Edited by Everett F. Harrison. Vol. 4. GTCEC. Chicago, Ill.: Moody, 1968.

———. *The Greek Testament: With a Critically Revised Text; a Digest of Various Readings; Marginal References to Verbal and Idiomatic Usage; Prolegomena; and a Critical and Exegetical Commentary*. 8 vols. London, U.K.: Deighton, Bell, & Co., 1863.

Allison, Gregg R. *Sojourners and Strangers: The Doctrine of the Church*. Wheaton, Ill.: Crossway, 2012.

Altman, Amnon. "Rethinking the Hittite System of Subordinate Countries from the Legal Point of View." *Journal of the American Oriental Society* 123, no. 4 (2003): 741–56.

———. *The Historical Prologue of the Hittite Vassal Treaties an Inquiry into the Concepts of Hittite Interstate Law*. Bar-Ilan Studies in Near Eastern Languages and Culture. Ramat-Gan: Bar-Ilan University Press, 2004.

———. "Who Took an Oath on a Vassal Treaty: Only the Vassal King or Also the Suzerain?—the Hittite Evidence." *Zeitschrift Für Altorientalische Und Biblische Rechtgeschichte* 9 (2003): 178–84.

Alzinger, Wilhelm, and Dieter Knibbe. *Ephesos Vom Beginn Der Römischen Herrschaft in Kleinasien Bis Zum Ende derPrincipatzeit*. Edited by Hildegard Temporini. ANRW, II 7.2. Berlin: De Gruyter, 1980.

Anabolu, Mükerrem Usman. "Two Altars Dedicated to Demeter: The Goddess of Fertility." In *Archaeology and Fertility Cult in the Ancient Mediterranean: Papers Presented at the First International Conference on Archaeology of the Ancient Mediterranean, University of Malta, 2-5 September 1985*, edited by Anthony Bonanno, 267–72. Amsterdam: John Benjamins, 1986.

Anderson, C. P. "Hebrews among the Letters of Paul." *SR* 5, no. 3 (December 1, 1975): 258–66.

———. "Who Wrote 'The Epistle from Laodicea'?" *JBL* 85 (1966): 436–40.

Anderson, J. G. C. "A Summer in Phrygia: I." *JHS* 17 (1897): 396–424.

Anderson, J. K. "The Battle of Sardis in 395 B.C." *CSCA* 7 (1974): 27–53.

Anderson, Sonia P. *An English Consul in Turkey: Paul Rycaut at Smyrna 1667-1678*. Oxford, U.K.: Clarendon Press, 1989.

Anderson, W. C. F. "Toga." In *DGRA*, edited by William Smith, 2:2:845-50. London, U.K.: Murray, 1891.

Andreae, Bernard. "Datierung Und Bedeutung Des Telephosfrieses Im Zusammenhang Mit Den Übrigen Stiftungen Der Ataliden von Pergamon." In *Der Pergamonaltar. Die Neue Präsentation Nach Restaurierung Des Telephosfrieses*, edited by Wolf-Dieter Heilmeyer, 60–78. Tübingen: Wasmuth, 1997.

Anokhin, V. A. *Monetnoe Delo Bospora*. Kiev: Naukova dumka, 1986.

Applebaum, Shimon. "The Legal Status of the Jewish Communities of the Diaspora." In *The Jewish People in the First Century*, edited by Shemuel Safrai and Y. Aschkenasy, 2:420–63. CRINT. Assen: Van Gorcum, 1987.

Arnaoutoglou, Ilias. "Hierapolis and Its Professional Associations: A Comparative Analysis." In *Urban Craftsmen and Traders in the Roman World*, edited by Andrew Wilson and Miko Flohr, 278–98. Oxford, U.K.: Oxford University Press, 2016.

Arnold, Clinton E. *Ephesians: Power and Magic: The Concept of Power in Ephesians in Light of Its Historical Setting*. SNTS 63. Cambridge, Mass.: Cambridge University Press, 1989.

———. *Ephesians: Power and Magic : The Concept of Power in Ephesians in Light of Its Historical Setting*. SNTS 63. Cambridge, Mass.: Cambridge University Press, 1989.

Arterbury, Andrew. *Entertaining Angels: Early Christian Hospitality in Its Mediterranean Setting*. New Testament Monographs 8. Sheffield, U.K.: Sheffield Phoenix, 2005.

Arundell, Francis Vyvian J. *A Visit to the Seven Churches of Asia with an Excursion into Pisidia*. London, U.K.: Rodwell, 1828.

———. *Discoveries in Asia Minor: Including a Description of the Ruins of Several Ancient Cities, and Especially Antioch of Pisidia*. 2 vols. London, U.K.: Bentley & Son, 1834.

Ascough, Richard S., Philip A. Harland, and John S. Kloppenborg, eds. *Associations in the Greco-Roman World: A Sourcebook*. Waco, Tex.: Baylor University Press, 2012.

Assman, Jan. "When Justice Fails: Jurisdiction and Imprecation in Ancient Egypt and the Near East." *JEA* 78 (1992): 149–62.

Astour, Michael C. "The Origin of the Terms Canaan, Phoenician and Purple." *JNES* 24 (1965): 346–50.

Atac, A., N. Aray, and R. V. Yildirim. "Asclepions in Turkey." *Balkan Military Medical Review* 9, no. 2 (2006): 82–84.

Atalay, Erol. "Die Kurudağ-Höhle [Bei Ephesos] Mit Archäologischen Funden." *JÖAI* 52 (1980 1978): 33–44.

Attridge, Harold W. *Hebrews: A Commentary on the Epistle to the Hebrews*. Hermeneia. Philadelphia, Pa.: Fortress, 1989.

Aulock, Hans von, and Gerhard Kleiner. *Sylloge Nummorum Graecorum, Vol. 1: Pontus, Paphlagonia, Bithynia, Mysia, Troas, Aiolis, Lesbos, Ionia*. Berlin: Gebr. Mann, 1957.

Aune, David E. "Amulets." In *OEANE*, edited by Eric M. Meyers, 1:113–15. Oxford, U.K.: Oxford University Press, 1997.

———. "Magic in Early Christianity." In *ANRW*, edited by Hildegard Temporini and Wolfgang Haase, 1507–57. Part 2, Principat, 23.1. Berlin: De Gruyter, 1980.

———. *Prophecy in Early Christianity and the Ancient Mediterranean World*. Grand Rapids, Mich.: Eerdmans, 2002.

———. *Revelation 1-5*. WBC 52A. Dallas, Tex.: Word Books, 1997.

———. *Revelation 6-16*. WBC 52B. Dallas, Tex.: Word Books, 1998.

———. *Revelation 17-22*. WBC 52C. Dallas, Tex.: Word Books, 1998.

———. "The Apocalypse of John and the Problem of Genre." In *Early Christian Apocalypticism: Genre and Social Setting*, 65–69. Semeia 36. Atlanta, Ga.: Scholars Press, 1986.

———. "The Form and Function of the Proclamations to the Seven Churches." *NTS* 36 (1990): 182–204.

———. *The New Testament in Its Literary Environment*. LEC 8. Cambridge, U.K.: Clarke & Co., 1988.

———. "The Polyvalent Imagery of Rev 3:20 in the Light of Greco-Egyptian Divination Texts." In *Greco-Roman Culture and the New Testament: Studies Commemorating the Centennial of the Pontifical Biblical Institute*, edited by David E. Aune and Frederick E. Brenk, 167–84. NovTSup 143. Leiden: Brill, 2012.

Aune, David E. "The Prophetic Circle of John of Patmos and the Exegesis of Revelation 22:16." *JSNT* 37 (1989): 103–16.

Aune, David E. "The Social Matrix of the Apocalypse of John." *Biblical Research* 26 (1981): 16–32.

Avigad, Nahman, and Benjamin Sass. *Corpus of West Semitic Stamp Seals*. 2nd ed. Jerusalem: Israel Academy of Sciences & Humanities, 1997.

Avi-Yonah, Michael, ed. *Views of the Biblical World: The New Testament*. Vol. 5. Jerusalem: International, 1961.

Báez-Camargo, Gonzalo. *Archaeological Commentary on the Bible: From Genesis to Revelation*. Garden City, N.Y.: Doubleday, 1984.

Bagnall, Roger S. "Christianity." In *Graffiti from the Basilica in the Agora of Smyrna*, edited by Roger S. Bagnall, Roberta Casagrande-Kim, Akin Ersoy, and Cumhur Tanriver, 45–46. Institute for the Study of the Ancient World. New York, N.Y.: New York University Press, 2016.

———. "Isopsephisms of Desire." In *Graffiti from the Basilica in the Agora of Smyrna*, edited by Roger S. Bagnall, Roberta Casagrande-Kim, Akin Ersoy, and Cumhur Tanriver, 48–51. Institute for the Study of the Ancient World. New York, N.Y.: New York University Press, 2016.

Bailey, Colin. "The Gerousia of Ephesus." Ph.D. diss., The University of British Columbia, 2006.

Balty, Jean Ch. *Curia ordinis: Recherches d'architecture et d'urbanisme antiques sur les curies provinciales du monde romain*. Bruxelles: Academie royale de Belgique, 1991.

Baltzer, Klaus. *The Covenant Formulary in Old Testament, Jewish, and Early Christian Writings*. Translated by David E. Green. Oxford, U.K.: Basil Blackwell, 1971.

Balz, Horst, and Gerhard Schneider, eds. *Exegetical Dictionary of the New Testament*. 3 vols. Grand Rapids, Mich.: Eerdmans, 1990.

Bandstra, Andrew J. "A Kingship and Priests: Inaugurated Eschatology in the Apocalypse." *CTJ* 27, no. 1 (1992): 1–25.

Banducci, Laura M. "A Tessera Lusoria from Gabii and the Afterlife of Roman Gaming." *Herom* 4, no. 2 (2015): 199–221.

Bandy, Alan S. "Patterns of Prophetic Lawsuits in the Oracles to the Seven Churches." *Neot* 45, no. 2 (2011): 178–205.

———. *The Prophetic Lawsuit in the Book of Revelation*. NT Monograph 29. Sheffield, U.K.: Sheffield Phoenix, 2010.

———. "Word and Witness: An Analysis of the Lawsuit Motif in Revelation Based on the Witness Terminology." In *Unpublished Paper Presented at the Evangelical Theological Society*. Valley Forge, Penn. November 17, 2005.

Banks, E. J. "Ephesus." Edited by James Orr and Melvin Grove Kyle. *ISBE*. Grand Rapids, Mich.: Hendrickson, 1915.

———. "Smyrna." Edited by Geoffrey W. Bromiley. *ISBE*. Grand Rapids, Mich.: Eerdmans, 1995.

———. "Thyatira." Edited by James Orr and Melvin Grove Kyle. *ISBE*. Grand Rapids, Mich.: Hendrickson, 1915.

Barash, Alexander, and Z. Zenziper. *Mediterranean Molluscs of Israel (Hebrew)*. Tel-Aviv: Society for the Protection of Nature in Israel, 1991.

Barber, E. J. W. *Prehistoric Textiles: The Development of Cloth in the Neolithic and Bronze Ages with Special Reference to the Aegean*. Princeton, N.J.: Princeton University Press, 1991.

Barclay, John M. G. *Jews in the Mediterranean Diaspora: From Alexander to Trajan (323 BCE-117 CE)*. Berkeley, Calf.: University of California Press, 1999.

Barclay, William. *Letters to the Seven Churches*. Louisville, Ky.: Westminster John Knox, 2001.

———. *The Letters to the Philippians, Colossians, and Thessalonians*. NDSB. Louisville, Ky.: Westminster/Knox, 2003.

———. *The Letters to Timothy, Titus, and Philemon*. NDSB. Louisville, Ky.: Westminster/Knox, 2003.

———. *The Revelation of John: Chapters 1 to 5*. Vol. 1. NDSB. Louisville, Ky.: Westminster/Knox, 2004.

Baring-Gould, Sabine. *The Lives of the Saints*. Vol. 4. 12 vols. London, U.K.: John Hodges, 1873.

Barnard, Leslie W. "In Defense of Pseudo-Pionius' Account of Polycarp's Martyrdom." In *Kyriakon Festschrift Johannes Quasten*, edited by Josef A. Jungman and Patrick Granfield, 1:192–204. Münster: Aschendorff, 1970.

Barnes, Timothy David. *Tertullian: A Historical and Literary Study*. 1985 edition. Oxford, U.K.: Oxford University Press, 1985.

Barr, David L. "The Apocalypse of John as Oral Enactment." *Interpretation* 40, no. 3 (1986): 243–56.

Barré, Michael L. "The Portrait of Balaam in Numbers 22-24." *Int.* 51, no. 3 (1997): 254–66.

Barrett, C. K. "Paul's Address to the Ephesian Elders." In *God's Christ and His Peopl E, Studies in Honour of Nils Alstrup Dahl*, edited by J. Jervell and W. A. Meeks, 107–21. Oslo: Univer sitetsforlaget, 1977.

———. "Things Sacrificed to Idols." *NTS* 11, no. 02 (1965): 138–53.

Barrett, Charles Kingsley. *A Critical and Exegetical Commentary on the Acts of the Apostles: Introduction and Commentary on Acts XV-XXVIII*. Vol. 2. 2 vols. Edinburgh, U.K.: T&T Clark, 1998.

———. "What Minorities?" In *Mighty Minorities?: Minorities in Early Christianity, Positions and Strategies : Essays in Honour of Jacob Jervell on His 70th Birthday, 21 May 1995*, edited by David Hellholm, Jacob Jervell, Turid Karlsen Seim, and Halvor Moxnes, 1–10. Oslo: Scandinavian University Press North America, 1995.

Barton, George Aaron. *Archaeology and the Bible*. Alexandria , Egypt: Library of Alexandria, 1933.

Bartosiewicz, B. "'There's Something Rotten in the State . . .': Bad Smells in Antiquity." *European Journal of Archaeology* 6 (2003): 175–95.

Bauckham, Richard J. "Apocalyptic." Edited by Sinclair B. Ferguson, David F. Wright, and James I. Packer. *NDT*. Downers Grove, Ill.: InterVarsity, 1988.

———. "Synoptic Parousia Parables Again." *NTS* 29, no. 1 (1983): 129–34.

———. "Synoptic Parousia Parables and the Apocalypse." *NTS* 23, no. 2 (1977): 162–76.

———. *The Climax of Prophecy: Studies on the Book of Revelation*. New Ed. Edinburgh, U.K.: T&T Clark, 1999.

———. "The Son of Man: 'A Man in My Position' or 'Someone.'" *JSNT* 23 (1985): 23–33.

———. "The Sonship of the Historical Jesus in Christology." *SJT* 31, no. 3 (1978): 245–60.

———. *The Theology of the Book of Revelation*. New Testament Theology. Cambridge, U.K.: Cambridge University Press, 1993.

Bauer, David R. "Son of God." Edited by Joel B. Green, Scot McKnight, and I. Howard Marshall. *DJG*. Downers Grove, Ill.: InterVarsity, 1992.

Baugh, Steven M. "Cult Prostitution in New Testament Ephesus: A Reappraisal." *JETS* 42, no. 3 (1999): 443–60.

———. "Paul and Ephesus: The Apostle among His Contemporaries." Ph.D. diss., University of California-Irvine, 1990.

Baugh, Steven M., Peter H. Davids, David E. Garland, David W. J. Gill, George H. Guthrie, Moyer V. Hubbard, Andreas J. Köstenberger, et al. *Zondervan Illustrated Bible Backgrounds Commentary Set*. Edited by Clinton E. Arnold. 4 vols. Santa Rosa, CA: Zondervan, 2002.

Beagley, Alan James. *The "Sitz Im Leben" of the Apocalypse With Particular Reference to the Role of the Church's Enemies*. Berlin: De Gruyter, 1987.

Beale, Gregory K. *John's Use of the Old Testament in Revelation*. LNTS. New York, N.Y.: Bloomsbury, 2014.

———. "Revelation (Book)." In *NDBT*, edited by T. Desmond Alexander, Graeme Goldsworthy, D. A. Carson, and Brian S. Rosner, 356–63. Downers Grove, Ill.: InterVarsity, 2000.

———. "Review of Colin J. Hemer, The Letters to the Seven Churches of Asia in Their Local Setting." *Trinity Journal* 7, no. 2 (1986): 110.

———. *The Book of Revelation: A Commentary on the Greek Text*. NIGTC 12. Grand Rapids, Mich.: Eerdmans, 1998.

———. "The Hearing Formula and the Visions of John in Revelation." In *Vision for the Church*, edited by Markus N. A. Bockmuehl and Michael B. Thompson, 167–80. Studies in Early Christian Ecclesiology. Edinburgh, U.K.: T&T Clark, 1997.

———. "The Old Testament Background of Rev 3.14." *NTS* 42, no. 1 (1996): 133–52.

Bean, George E. *Aegean Turkey: An Archaeological Guide*. New York, N.Y.: Praeger, 1966.

———. *Turkey Beyond the Maeander*. 2nd ed. London, U.K.: Murray, 1989.

Beard, Mary. *The Roman Triumph*. Cambridge, Mass.: Harvard University Press, 2009.

Beasley, Henry. *The Druggist's General Receipt Book, Etc.* London, U.K.: Churchill, 1850.

Beasley-Murray, George R. "Revelation." In *NBC*, edited by D. A. Carson, R. T. France, and J. A. Motyer, 4th ed., 1421–55. Downers Grove, Ill.: InterVarsity, 1992.

———. *Revelation: Three Viewpoints*. Nashville: Baptist Sunday School Board, 1981.

———. *The Book of Revelation*. NCB 23. Grand Rapids, Mich.: Eerdmans, 1992.

———. "The Eschatology of the Fourth Gospel." *EvQ* 18 (1946): 97–108.

———. "The Relation of the Fourth Gospel to the Apocalypse." *EvQ* 18 (1946): 173–86.

Becker, Cornelia. "Did the People in Ayios Mamas Produce Purple Dye during the Middle Bronze Age? Considerations on the Prehistoric Production of Purple-Dye in the Mediterranean." In *Animals and Man in the Past: Essays in Honour of Dr. A.T. Clason Emeritus Professor of Archaeozoology*, edited by Hijlke Buitenhuis and Wietschke Prummel, 122–134. Groningen: Rijksuniversiteit, 2001.

———. "Nourriture, Cuilléres, Ornament. Les Témoignages D'une Exploitation Variée Des Mollusques Marins À Ayios Mamas (Chalcidique, Grèce)." *Anthropozoologica* 24 (1996): 3–17.

Beckman, Gary M. *Hittite Diplomatic Texts*. Edited by Harry A Hoffner. 2nd ed. SBLWAW 7. Atlanta, Ga.: Scholars Press, 1999.

Beckman, Gary M. "Hittite Treaties and the Development of Cuneiform Treaty Tradition." In *Beihefte Zur Zeitschrift Für Die Alttestamentliche Wissenschaft Die Deuteronomistischen Geschichtswerke: Redaktions– Und Religionsgeschichtliche Perspektiven Zur "Deuteronomismus"–Diskussion in Tora Und Vorderen Propheten*, edited by Marku Witte, Konrad Schmid, Doris Prechel, and Jan Christian Gertz, 279–301. BZAW 365. Berlin: de Gruyter, 2006.

Beckwith, Isbon T. *The Apocalypse of John*. New York, N.Y.: MacMillan, 1919.

Bederman, David J. *International Law in Antiquity*. Cambridge Studies in International and Comparative Law. Cambridge, U.K.: Cambridge University Press, 2001.

Beek, Gus W. van. "Frankincense and Myrrh in Ancient South Arabia." *JAOS* 78, no. 3 (1958): 141–52.

———. "Frankincense and Myrrh in Ancient South Arabia." *BA* 23 (1960): 70–95.

Behr, Charles A. *Aelius Aristides and the Sacred Tales*. Amsterdam: Hakkert, 1968.

Bekkum, Wouter Jacques van. "The Qedushta'ot of Yehudah according to Genizah Manuscripts." Ph.D. diss., University of Groningen, 1988.

Beldiceanu-Steinherr, Irène. "Notes pour l'histoire d'Alaşehir (Philadelphie) au XIVe siècle." In *Philadelphie et autres études*, edited by Hélèna Ahrweiler. Byzantina Sorbonensia 4. Paris, France: Publications de la Sorbonne, 1984.

Bell, Jr., Albert A. "The Date of John's Apocalypse: The Evidence of Some Roman Historians Reconsidered." *NTS* 10, no. 1 (1978): 93–102.

Bellamare, Pierre M. "Meteorite Sparks a Cult." *JRASC* 90 (1996): 287–91.

Beloch, Julius. *Die bevölkerung der griechisch-römischen welt*. Historische Beiträge Zur Bevölkerungslehre 1. Duncker & Humblot, 1886.

Beltrán de Heredia Bercero, Julia. "Los Restos Arqueológicos de Una Fullonica Y de Una Tinctoria En La Colonia Romana de Barcino (Barcelona)." *Complutum* 11 (2000): 253–59.

Benda-Weber, Isabella. "Textile Production Centres, Products and Merchants in the Roman Province of Asia." In *Making Textiles in Pre-Roman and Roman Times: People, Places, Identities*, edited by Margarita Gleba and Judit Pásztókai-Szeöke, 171–91. Ancient Textile Series 13. Oxford, U.K.: Oxbow Books, 2013.

Bengel, Johann Albrecht. *New Testament Word Studies*. Translated by John H Vincent and Charlton T. Lewis. 2 vols. Kregel Reprint Library. Grand Rapids, Mich.: Kregel, 1971.

Bengtson, Hermann, and Hatto H. Schmitt, eds. *Die Staatsverträge Des Altertums*. Vol. 3. Die Verträge Des Griechisch-Römischen Welt von 338 Bis 200 v. Chr. Munich: Beck, 1969.

Berding, Kenneth. "Historical Connections to John but Literary Connections to Paul: Can We Resolve a Dilemma in Our Understanding of Polycarp of Smyrna?" In *Paper Presented at the First International Symposium on Ancient Smyrna*. Izmir, Turkey, 2003.

———. *Polycarp and Paul: An Analysis of Their Literary and Theological Relationship in Light of Polycarp's Use of Biblical and Extra-Biblical Literature*. Leiden: Brill, 2002.

Berg, William. "Hecate: Greek or 'Anatolian'?" *Numen* 21, no. 2 (1974): 128–40.

Berger, Adolf. *Encyclopedic Dictionary of Roman Law*. TAPS 43. Philadelphia, Pa.: American Philological Society, 1953.

Berger, Klaus. "Apostelbrief Und Apostolische Rede: Zum Formular Frühchristlicher Briefe." *Zeitschrift Für Die Neutestamentliche Wissenschaft Und Die Kunde Der Älteren Kirche* 65 (1974): 212–19.

———. *Die Amen-Worte Jesus: Eine Untersuchung zum Problem der Legitimation in apokalyptischer Rede*. ZNW 39. Berlin: de Gruyter, 1970.

Berger, Paul R. "Kollyrium Für Die Blinden Augen, Apk 3:18." *NovT* 27, no. 2 (April 1985): 174–95.

Berenbaum, Michael, and Fred Skolnik, eds. *Encyclopedia Judaica*. 2nd ed. 22 vols. New York, N.Y.: MacMillan, 2006.

Berman, Joshua A. "Histories Twice Told: Deuteronomy 1-3 and the Hittite Treaty Prologue Tradition." *JBL* 132, no. 2 (2013): 229–50.

Bernabé, Alberto. "The Ephesia Grammata: Genesis of a Magical Formula." In *The Getty Hexameters: Poetry, Magic, and Mystery in Ancient Selinous*, edited by Christopher A. Faraone and Dirk Obbink, 71–96. Oxford, U.K.: Oxford University Press, 2013.

Bernardi Ferrero, Daria de. *Bati Anadolu'nun Eskiçağ Tiyatrolari*. Translated by Erendiz Özbayoğlu. Ankara, Turkey: İtalyan Kültür Heyeti Ark. Ar. Böl., 1990.

———. "Excavations and Restorations in Hierapolis During 1995." *KST* 18 (1996): 85–100.

———. *Teatri classici in Asia Minore III: Città dalla Troade alla Pamfilia*. Studi Di Architettura Antica 4. Rome: Di Bretschneider, 1974.

Berrett, Lamar C. *Discovering the World of the Bible*. Provo, Utah: Grandin, 1996.

Betz, Hans Dieter, ed. *The Greek Magical Papyri in Translation, Including the Demotic Spells*. Chicago, Ill.: University of Chicago Press, 1996.

Beyer, Bryan E. *Obadiah, Jonah*. Edited by Bryan E. Beyer and John H. Walton. BSCS. Grand Rapids, Mich.: Zondervan, 1988.

Beyer, H. W. "Diakonew, Diakonia, Diakonos." In *TDNT*, edited by Gerhard Kittel and Gerhard Friedrich, translated by Geoffrey W. Bromiley, Abridged., 2:81. Grand Rapids, Mich.: Eerdmans, 1985.

Bickerman, Elias. "Couper Une Alliance." *Archives D'histoire Du Droit Oriental* 5 (1951 1950): 133–56.

Bieber, Margarete. *The History of the Greek and Roman Theater*. Princeton, N.J.: Princeton University Press, 1961.

Bierstadt, Edward Hale. *The Great Betrayal: A Survey of the Near East Problem*. Pontian Greek Society of Chicago, 2008.

Bietenhard, H. "Ὄνομα." Edited by Gerhard Kittel and Gerhard Friedrich. Translated by Geoffrey W. Bromiley. *TDNT*. Grand Rapids, Mich.: Eerdmans, 1985.

Billerbeck, Paul, and Hermann L. Strack. *Kommentar Zum Neuen Testament Aus Talmud Und Midrasch*. 6 vols. Munich: C. H. Beck, 1922.

Billows, Richard. "Cities." In *A Companion to the Hellenistic World*, edited by Andrew Erskine, 196–216. Blackwell Companions to the Ancient World. Oxford, U.K.: Blackwell, 2003.

Birge, Darice E. "Sacred Groves in the Ancient Greek World." Ph.D. diss., University of California-Berkely, 1982.

Birley, Anthony R. *Hadrian: The Restless Emperor*. New York, N.Y.: Routledge, 2013.

Blaiklock, Edward M. *Cities of the New Testament*. New York, N.Y.: Revell, 1965.

———. "Nicolaus, Nicolaitans." In *NBD*, edited by I. Howard Marshall, Alan R. Millard, James I. Packer, and D. J. Wiseman, 3rd ed., 823. Downers Grove, Ill.: InterVarsity, 1996.

———. *The Archaeology of the New Testament*. Grand Rapids, Mich.: Zondervan, 1970.

———. *The Seven Churches: An Exposition of Revelation Chapters Two and Three*. London, U.K.: Marshall, Morgan & Scott, 1951.

———. "Thyatira ." Edited by Merrill C. Tenney and Moises Silva. *ZEB*. Grand Rapids, Mich.: Zondervan, 2009.

Blakesley, Joseph William. "Thyatira." In *SDB*, edited by William Smith and H. B. Hackett, 4:3241–42. Boston, Mass.: Houghton, Mifflin & Company, 1883.

Blass, F., and A. DeBrunner. *A Greek Grammar of the New Testament and Other Early Christian Literature*. Translated by Robert W. Funk. Chicago, Ill.: University of Chicago Press, 1961.

Bleek, Friedrich. *Vorlesungen über die Apokalypse*. Berlin: Georg Reimer, 2011.

Blevins, James L. "The Genre of Revelation." *RevExp* 77, no. 3 (1980): 393–408.

Blue, Bradley B. "Acts and the House Church." In *Graeco-Roman Setting*, edited by David W. J. Gill and Conrad H. Gempf, 119–222. BAFCS 2. Eugene, Or.: Wipf & Stock, 2000.

Blumell, Lincoln H. *Lettered Christians: Christians, Letters, and Late Antique Oxyrhynchus*. NTTS 39. Leiden: Brill Academic, 2012.

Boatwright, Mary T. "Theaters in the Roman Empire." *BA* 53, no. 4 (1990): 184–92.

Boatwright, Mary Taliaferro. *Hadrian and the Cities of the Roman Empire*. Princeton, N.J.: Princeton University Press, 2002.

Bodenheimer, Friedrich Simon. "The Manna of Sinai." *BA* 10, no. 1 (1947): 2–6.

Bøe, Sverre. *Gog and Magog: Ezekiel 38-39 as Pre-Text for Revelation 19,17-21 and 20,7-10*. Tübingen: Mohr Siebeck, 2001.

Böeckh, August, Johannes Franz, Ernst Curtius, and Adolf Kirchhoff. *Corpus Inscriptionum Graecarum*. 4 vols. Berolini, Italy: Officina academica, 1877.

Bonner, Campbell. *Studies in Magical Amulets: Chiefly Graeco-Egyptian*. London, U.K.: Oxford University Press, 1950.

Bonomi, Joseph. *Nineveh and Its Palaces: The Discoveries of Botta and Layard, Applied to the Elucidation of Holy Writ*. London, U.K.: Bohn, 1857.

Bonz, Marianne Palmer. "Differing Approaches to Religious Benefaction: The Late Third-Cent. Acquisition of the Sardis Synagogue." *HTR* 86 (1993): 139–54.

———. "The Jewish Community of Ancient Sardis." *HSCP* 93 (1990): 343–59.

Borchert, G. L. "Laodicea." In *ISBE*, edited by Geoffrey W. Bromiley, Revised., 72–74. Grand Rapids, Mich.: Eerdmans, 1995.

Borgen, Peder. *Paul Preaches Circumcision and Pleases Men*. Trondheim: TAPIR, 1983.

———. *Philo, John and Paul: New Perspectives on Judaism and Early Christianity*. Atlanta, Ga.: Scholars Press, 1987.

———. "Polemic in the Book of Revelation." In *Anti-Semitism and Early Christianity: Issues of Polemic and Faith*, edited by Craig A. Evans and Donald A. Hagner, 199–211. Minneapolis, Minn.: Fortress, 1993.

Boring, Eugene M. *Revelation*. Louisville, Ky.: Westminster/Knox, 1989.

———. "The Theology of Revelation: The Lord Our God the Almighty Reigns." *Int.* 40, no. 3 (1986): 257–69.

Boring, M. Eugene. *The Continuing Voice of Jesus: Christian Prophecy and the Gospel Tradition*. Louisville, Ky.: Westminster/John Knox, 1991.

Bosch, Clemens. *Die Kleinasiatischen Münzen Der Römischen Kaiserzeit*. 2.1 vols. Stuttgart, Germany: Kohlhammer, 1935.

Botha, P. J. J. "God, Emperor Worship and Society: Contemporary Experiences and the Book of Revelation." *Neot* 22, no. 1 (1988): 87–102.

Botterweck, G. Johannes, Helmer Ringgren, and Heinz-Josef Fabry, eds. *Theological Dictionary of the Old Testament*. Translated by Douglas W. Stott. 15 vols. Grand Rapids, Mich.: Eerdmans, 2003.

Bousset, Wilhelm. *Die Offenbarung Johannis*. Göttingen: Vandenhoeck & Ruprecht, 1906.

Bowman, John Wick. *The First Christian Drama: The Book of Revelation*. Philadelphia, Pa.: Westminster, 1968.

Boxall, Ian. "'For Paul' or 'For Cephas.'" In *Understanding, Studying and Reading: New Testament Essays in Honour of John Ashton*, edited by Christopher Rowland and Crispin H. Fletcher-Louis, 198–218. New York, N.Y.: A&C Black, 1998.

———. *The Revelation of Saint John*. BNTC 19. Peabody, Mass.: Hendrickson, 2006.

Boyce, Mary. "Anāhīd." In *Encyclopædia Iranica*, edited by Ehsan Yarshater, 1:1003–1009. London, U.K.: Eisenbrauns, 1991.

Boyce, Mary, and Frantz Grenet. *A History of Zoroastrianism: Vol. 1 Zoroastrianism under Macedonian and Roman Rule*. HO: Der Nahe Und Der Mittlere Osten 8. Leiden: Brill, 1991.

Boyle, Marjorie O'Rourke. "The Covenant Lawsuit in the Prophet Amos: III 1-IV 13." *VT* 21, no. 3 (1971): 338–62.

Bradley, M. "'It All Comes out in the Wash': Looking Harder at the Roman Fullonica." *JRA* 15 (2008): 21–44.

Bremmer, Jan N. "Paradise: From Persia, via Greece, into the Septuagint." In *Paradise Interpreted: Representations of Biblical Paradise in Judaism and Christianity*, edited by Gerard P. Luttikhuizen, 1–19. Themes in Biblical Narrative 2. Leiden: Brill, 1999.

Brenk, Frederick E. "Artemis of Ephesos: An Avant Garde Goddess." *Kernos* 11 (1998): 157–71.

Brent, Allen. *The Imperial Cult and the Development of Church Order: Concepts and Images of Authority in Paganism and Early Christianity Before the Age of Cyprian*. Leiden: Brill, 1999.

Briese, Christoph. "Ostrich Eggs." In *BrillPauly*, 10:290–91. Leiden: Brill, 2007.

Briggs, Charles A., Samuel R. Driver, and Francis Brown, eds. *A Hebrew and English Lexicon of the Old Testament with an Appendix Containing the Biblical Aramaic*. Based on the Lexicon of William Gessenius as Translated by Edward Robinson. Boston, Mass.: Houghton Milfflin, 1907.

Briggs, Robert A. *Jewish Temple Imagery in the Book of Revelation*. SBL 10. New York, N.Y.: Lang, 1999.

Bright, John. *Covenant and Promise: The Prophetic Understanding of the Future in Pre-Exilic Israel*. Philadelphia, Pa.: Westminster/Knox, 1976.

Brinks, C. L. "'Great Is Artemis of the Ephesians': Acts 19:23-41 in Light of Goddess Worship in Ephesus." *CBQ* 71, no. 4 (2009): 776–94.

Broad, William. *Alexander or Jesus?: The Origin of the Title "Son of God."* Eugene, Oreg.: Wipf & Stock, 2015.

Brodersen, Kai. "Seven Wonders." In *OEAGR*, edited by Michael Gagarin, 6:289. New York, N.Y.: Oxford University Press, 2010.

Broek, Roelof Van den. *The Myth of the Phoenix: According to Classical and Early Christian Traditions*. Translated by I. Seeger. Leiden: Brill, 1972.

Brommer, Frank, Antje Krüg, and Ursula Hockmann, eds. *Festschrift für Frank Brommer*. Mainz: von Zabern, 1977.

Bromiley, Geoffrey W., ed. *The International Standard Bible Encyclopedia*. Revised. 4 vols. Grand Rapids, Mich.: Eerdmans, 1995.

Brooten, Bernadette J. *Women Leaders in the Ancient Synagogue: Inscriptional Evidence and Background Issues*. Brown Judaic Studies 36. Atlanta, Ga.: Scholars Press, 1982.

Broughton, T. R. S. "Roman Asia Minor." In *An Economic Survey of Ancient Rome: Africa, Syria, Greece, Asia Minor*, edited by Tenney Frank, 4:499–916. Baltimore, Md.: John Hopkins University Press, 1975.

Brown, Charles. *Heavenly Visions: An Exposition of the Book of Revelation*. Boston, Mass.: Pilgram, 1910.

Brown, Colin, ed. *New International Dictionary of New Testament Theology*. Translated by Colin Brown. 4 vols. Grand Rapids, Mich.: Zondervan, 1986.

Brown, John Pairman. *Ancient Israel and Ancient Greece Religion, Politics, and Culture*. Minneapolis, Minn.: Augsburg Fortress, 2003.

Brown, Schuyler. "The Hour of Trial, Rev 3:10." *JBL* 85, no. 3 (1966): 308–14.

Brownlee, William H. "The Priestly Character of the Church in the Apocalypse." *NTS* 5, no. 3 (1959): 224–25.

Bruce, F. F. "Colossian Problems, Part 1: Jews and Christians in the Lycus Valley." *BSac* 141 (1984): 3–15.

Bruce, F. F. *Paul, Apostle of the Heart Set Free*. Grand Rapids, Mich.: Eerdmans, 2000.

Bruce, F. F. *The Book of Acts*. New International Commentary on the New Testament. Grand Rapids, Mich.: Eerdmans, 1988.

———. *The Epistles to the Colossians, to Philemon, and to the Ephesians*. 2nd ed. NICNT. Grand Rapids, Mich.: Eerdmans, 1984.

———. *The Revelation of John*. Edited by G. C. D. Howley. NTC. Grand Rapids, Mich.: Zondervan, 1969.

Bruce, Frederick Fyvie. "Laodicea (Place)." Edited by David Noel Freedman, Gary A. Herion, David F. Graf, and John David Pleins. *ABD*. New York, N.Y.: Doubleday, 1996.

———. "The Spirit in the Apocalypse." In *Christ and Spirit in the New Testament: Studies in Honour of Charles Francis Digby Moule*, edited by Barnabas Lindars and Stephen S. Smalley, 333–344. Cambridge, U.K.: Cambridge University Press, 2008.

Brütsch, Charles. *Die Offenbarung Jesu Christi*. 3 vols. ZBK 18. Zürich: Zwingh, 1970.

Buchanan, George Wesley. *The Book of Revelation: Its Introduction and Prophecy*. Eugene, Oreg.: Wipf & Stock, 2005.

Buckler, William Hepburn. "CIG 3938, 3952, and 3953 F." *JHS* 56, no. 1 (1936): 78–80.

Buckler, William Hepburn, and David M. Robinson. "Greek Inscriptions from Sardes I." *AJA* 16, no. 1 (1912): 11–82.

———. *Sardis: Greek and Latin Inscriptions*. Vol. 1. ASES 7. Leiden: Brill, 1932.

Budden, Charles W., and Edward Hastings. *The Local Colour of the Bible*. 3 vols. Edinburgh, U.K.: T&T Clark, 1925.

Bullinger, Ethelbert William. *Commentary on Revelation*. New York, N.Y.: Revell, 1909.

Bultmann, Rudolf. *The History of the Synoptic Tradition*. Translated by John Marsh. Revised. Grand Rapids, Mich.: Hendrickson, 1994.

Bürchner, Ludwig. "Ephesos." In *Paulys Realencyclopädie Der Classischen Altertumswissenschaft*, edited by August Friedrich Pauly, Georg Wissowa, and S. Kroll, 5th ed., 2:2773–2822. Stuttgart, Germany: Metzler, 1905.

Burkert, Walter. *Greek Religion*. Cambridge, Mass.: Harvard University Press, 1985.

Burkill, T. Alec. "The Hidden Son of Man in St. Mark's Gospel." *ZNW* 52, no. 3–4 (1961): 189–213.

Burnett, Andrew, Michel Amandry, and Pere Pau Ripollés Alegre, eds. *Roman Provincial Coinage*. 9 vols. London, U.K.: British Museum Press, 2003.

Burney, Charles F. "Christ as the ΑΡΧΗ of Creation." *JBL* 27, no. 1/2 (1926): 160–77.

Burrell, Barbara. *Neokoroi: Greek Cities and Roman Emperors*. CCS 9. Leiden: Brill, 2004.

Burton, G. P. "Proconsuls, Assizes and the Administration of Justice under the Empire." *JRS* 65 (1975): 92–106.

Butler, Howard Crosby. "Fifth Preliminary Report on the American Excavations at Sardes in Asia Minor." *AJA* 18, no. 4 (1914): 425–37.

———. "First Preliminary Report on the American Excavations at Sardes in Asia Minor." *AJA* 14, no. 4 (1910): 401–13.

———. "Fourth Preliminary Report on the American Excavations at Sardes in Asia Minor." *AJA* 17, no. 4 (1913): 471–78.

———. *Publications of the American Society for the Excavation of Sardis. II/1. Sardis: Architecture. The Temple of Artemis*. Leiden: Brill, 1925.

———. *Sardis: Architecture: The Temple of Artemis, Part 1 Text*. 2 vols. ASES 1. Leiden: American Society for the Excavation of Sardis, 1922.

———. "Second Preliminary Report on the American Excavations at Sardes in Asia Minor." *AJA* 15, no. 4 (1911): 445–58.

———. "Third Preliminary Report on the American Excavations at Sardes in Asia Minor." *AJA* 16, no. 4 (1912): 465–79.

Butler, Trent C., Chad Brand, Charles Draper, and Archie England, eds. *Holman Illustrated Bible Dictionary*. Nashville, Tenn.: Broadman & Holman, 2003.

Buttrey, T. V., Ann E. M. Johnston, Kenneth M. Mackenzie, and Michael L. Bates. *Greek, Roman, and Islamic Coins from Sardis*. AESM 7. Cambridge, Mass.: Harvard University Press, 1981.

Buttrick, George A., and Keith R. Crim, eds. *The Interpreter's Dictionary of the Bible*. 5 vols. Nashville, Tenn.: Abingdon, 1976.

Buttrick, George A., ed. *The Interpreter's Dictionary of the Bible*. 4 vols. Nashville, Tenn.: Abingdon, 1984.

Cadoux, Cecil J. *Ancient Smyrna: A History of the City from the Earliest Times to 224 A.D.* Oxford, U.K.: Basil Blackwell, 1938.

Cahill, Nicholas D. "Mapping Sardis." In *Love for Lydia: A Sardis Anniversary Volume Presented to Crawford H. Greenewalt, Jr.*, edited by Nicholas D. Cahill, 111–24. AESR 4. Cambridge, Mass.: Harvard University Press, 2008.

———. "Sardis 2014." *KST* 37, no. 3 (2015): 147–64.

Cahill, Nicholas D., and John H. Kroll. "New Archaic Coin Finds from Sardis." *AJA* 109 (2005): 589–617.

Cahill, Nicholas, and Crawford H. Greenewalt, Jr. "The Sanctuary of Artemis at Sardis: Preliminary Report, 2002–2012." *AJA* 120, no. 3 (2016): 473–509.

Caird, George B. *The Language and Imagery of the Bible*. London, U.K.: Duckworth, 1980.

———. *The Revelation of St. John the Divine*. HNTC. Peabody, Mass.: Hendrickson, 1987.

Caird, George Bradford. *Paul's Letters from Prison: Ephesians, Philippians, Colossians, Philemon*. New Clarendon Bible Commentary Series 6. Oxford, U.K.: Oxford University Press, 1976.

Çakirlar, Canan, and Ralf Becks. "Murex Dye Production at Troia: Assessment of Archaeomalacological Data from Old and New Excavations." *Studia Troica* 18 (2009): 87–103.

Calder, William M. "Philadelphia and Montanism." *BJRL* 7, no. 3 (1923): 309–54.

———. "Smyrna as Described by the Orator Aelius Aristides." In *Studies in the History and Art of the Eastern Provinces of the Roman Empire*, edited by William Mitchell Ramsay, 95–116. Aberdeen, Scotland: Aberdeen University, 1906.

———. "The New Jerusalem of the Montanists." *Byzantion* 6 (1931): 421–25.

Calder, William Moir, and Ronald Syme, eds. "Observations on the Province of Cilicia." In *Anatolian Studies Presented to William Hepburn Buckler*, 299–32. Manchester: Manchester University Press, 1939.

Caley, Earle Radcliffe. "The Stockholm Papyrus: An English Translation with Brief Notes." *Journal of Chemical Education* 4, no. 8 (1927): 979–1002.

Callmer, Christian. "Antike Bibliotheken." *Opuscula Archaeologica* 3 (1944): 145–93.

Calpino, Teresa J. "Lydia of Thyatira's Call." In *Women, Work and Leadership in Acts*, 181–226. Tübingen: Mohr Siebeck, 2014.

Calvin, John. *Commentaries on The Twelve Minor Prophets*. 13-15 vols. Grand Rapids, Mich.: Baker, 1979.

Campbell, Gordon. "Findings, Seals, Trumpets, and Bowls: Variations upon the Theme of Covenant Rupture and Restoration in the Book of Revelation." *WTJ* 66 (2004): 71–96.

Campbell, J. L. *The Patmos Letters*. London, U.K.: Morgan & Scott, 1898.

Cancik, Hubert, and Helmuth Schneider, eds. *Brill's New Pauly, Antiquity Volumes Online*. Translated by Christine F. Salazar and Francis G. Gentry. 22 vols. Leiden: Brill, 2006.

Carey, Greg. *Elusive Apocalypse: Reading Authority in the Revelation to John*. StABH. Macon, Ga.: Mercer University Press, 1999.

Carradice, Ian A. "The 'Regal' Coinage of the Persian Empire." In *Coinage and Administration in the Athenian and Persian Empires: The Ninth Oxford Symposium on Coinage and Monetary History*, edited by Ian A. Carradice, 73–95. BARI 343. Oxford, U.K.: British Archaeological Reports, 1987.

Carroll, Howard. "Polycarp of Smyrna: With Special Reference to Early Christian Martyrdom." Ph.D. diss., Duke University, 1946.

Carson, Donald A. *The Gospel According to John: An Introduction and Commentary*. PNTC. Grand Rapids, Mich.: Eerdmans, 1991.

Carson, Donald A., and Douglas J. Moo. *An Introduction to the New Testament*. Grand Rapids, Mich.: Zondervan, 2009.

Carson, Donald A., R. T. France, and J. A. Motyer. *New Bible Commentary: 21st Century Edition*. 4th ed. Downers Grove, Ill.: InterVarsity, 1994.

Cary, M. "Tesserae Gladiatoriae Sive Nummulariae." *JRS* 13 (1923): 110–13.

Casson, Lionel. *Libraries in the Ancient World*. New Haven, Conn.: Yale University Press, 2002.

Chambers, Roger. "Greek Athletics and the Jews: 165 BC-AD 70." Ph.D. diss., Miami University, 1980.

Chandler, Richard. *Travels in Asia Minor, and Greece: Or An Account of a Tour Made at the Expense of the Society of Dilettanti*. 2 vols. London, U.K.: Booker & Priestley, 1817.

Charitonidou, Angeliki. "Epidaurus: The Sanctuary of Asclepius." In *Temples and Sanctuaries of Ancient Greece*, edited by Evi Melas, 89–99. London: Thames & Hudson, 1973.

Charles, Robert H. *A Critical and Exegetical Commentary on the Revelation of St John*. 2 vols. ICC. Edinburgh, U.K.: T&T Clark, 1963.

Charlesworth, M. P. *Trade-Routes and Commerce of the Roman Empire*. 2nd ed. New York, N.Y.: Cooper Square, 1970.

Chilton, Bruce D. "Shebna, Eliakim, and the Promise to Peter." In *The Social World of Formative Christianity and Judaism: Essays in Tribute to Howard Clarke Kee*, edited by Jacob Neusner, Peder Borgen, Ernest S. Frerichs, and Richard A. Horsley, 311–26. Philadelphia, Pa.: Fortress, 1988.

Chilton, David. *The Days of Vengeance: An Exposition of the Book of Revelation*. Fort Worth: Dominion, 1987.

Chisholm, Hugh, ed. *Encyclopædia Britannica*. 11th ed. 32 vols. Cambridge, U.K.: Cambridge University Press, 1911.

Choniates, Niketas. *O City of Byzantium: Annals of Niketas Choniates*. Translated by Harry J. Magoulias. Byzantine Texts in Translation. Detroit, Mich.: Wayne State University Press, 1984.

Cimok, Fatih. *Guide To The Seven Churches*. Istanbul: Tuttle, 1999.

Ciotta, G., and L. Palmucci Quaglino. "La Cattedrale Di Hierapolis." In *Saggi in Onore Di Paolo Verzone*, edited by Daria de Bernardi Ferrero, 185–94. Hierapolis: Scavi E Ricerche 4. Rome: Bretschneider, 2002.

Clare, Israel Smith. *Ancient Greece and Rome*. Vol. 2. 5 vols. The Unrivaled History of the World. Chicago, Ill.: Werner, 1893.

Clark, David S. *The Message from Patmos: A Postmillennial Commentary on the Book of Revelation*. Grand Rapids, Mich.: Baker, 1989.

Clarke, Graeme Wilber. "The Persecution of Decius." In *The Letters of St. Cyprian*, edited by Graeme Wilber Clarke, 1:103–14. Ancient Christian Writers 43. New York, N.Y.: Newman, 1984.

Clayton, Peter A. *Treasures of Ancient Rome*. Wingdale, N.Y.: Crescent, 1995.

Cleland, Liza, Glenys Davies, and Karen Stears, eds. *Colour in the Ancient Mediterranean World*. BARI 1267. Oxford, U.K.: John and Erica Hedges, 2004.

Clemen, Carl C. *Religionsgeschichtliche Erklärung Des Neuen Testaments*. Die Abhängigkeit Des Ältesten Christentums von Nichtjüdischen Religionen Und Philosophischen Systemen. Gieben: Töpelmann, 1907.

Clerc, Michel Armand Edgar Anatole. *De rebus Thyatirenorum commentatio epigraphica*. Paris: Picard, 1893.

Clogg, Richard. "Little Known Orthodox Neo-Martyr, Athanasios of Smyrna (1819)." *ECR* 5 (1973): 28–36.

Cogan, Mordechai, and Hayim Tadmor. "Gyges and Assurbanipal; A Study in Literary Transmission." *Orientalia* 46 (1977): 65–85.

Cohen, Getzel M. *The Hellenistic Settlements in Europe, the Islands, and Asia Minor*. Berkeley, Calf.: University of California Press, 1996.

Cohen, Shaye J. D. "Women in the Synagogues of Antiquity." *Conservative Judaism* 34 (1980): 25–26.

Cohick, Lynn H. *The Peri Pascha Attributed to Melito of Sardis: Setting, Purpose, and Sources*. Brown Judaic Studies. Atlanta, Ga.: Scholars Press, 2000.

Coleman-Norton, Paul Robinson. "The Apostle Paul and the Roman Law of Slavery." In *Studies in Roman Economic and Social History: In Honor of Allan Chester Johnson*, edited by Paul Robinson Coleman-Norton, 155–77. Princeton, N.J.: Princeton University Press, 1951.

Coleman-Norton, Paul Robinson, Allan Chester Johnson, and Frank Card Bourne. *Ancient Roman Statutes: A Translation with Introduction, Commentary, Glossary, and Index*. Edited by Clyde Pharr. Austin, Tex.: University of Texas Press, 2009.

Collins, Adela Yarbro. *Crisis and Catharsis: The Power of the Apocalypse*. Louisville, Ky.: Westminster/Knox, 1984.

———. "Dating the Apocalypse of John." *BR* 26, no. 1 (1981): 33–45.

———. "Insiders and Outsiders in the Book of Revelation and Its Social Context." In *"To See Ourselves As Others See Us": Christians, Jews, "Others" in Late Antiquity*, edited by Jacob Neusner and Ernest S. Frerichs, 187–218. Scholars Press Studies in the Humanities. Chico, Ca.: Scholars Press, 1985.

———. "Numerical Symbolism in Jewish and Early Christian Apocalyptic Literature." *ANRW* II.21.2 (1984): 1221–87.

———. "Pergamon in Early Christian Literature." In *Pergamon-Citadel of the Gods*, edited by Helmut Koester, 163—84. HTS 46. Harrisburg, Pa.: Trinity Press International, 1998.

———. "Persecution and Vengeance in the Book of Revelation." In *Apocalypticism in the Mediterranean World and the Near East: Proceedings of the International Colloquium on Apocalypticism, Uppsala, August 12-17, 1979*, edited by David Hellholm, 729–49. Tübingen: Mohr Siebeck, 1983.

———. *The Apocalypse*. New Testament Message: A Biblical-Theological Commentary Series. Wilmington, Del.: Michael Glazier, Inc., 1979.

———. "The Book of Revelation." In *The Encyclopedia of Apocalypticism*, edited by John Joseph Collins, Bernard McGinn, and Stephen J. Stein, 384–414. New York, N.Y.: T&T Clark, 2000.

———. *The Combat Myth in the Book of Revelation*. HDR 9. Atlanta, Ga.: Scholars Press, 1976.

———. "Vilification and Self-Definition in the Book of Revelation." *HTR* 79 (1986): 308–20.

Collins, John Joseph, and Daniel C. Harlow, eds. *The Eerdmans Dictionary of Early Judaism*. Grand Rapids, Mich.: Eerdmans, 2010.

Collins, John Joseph. "Introduction: Towards the Morphology of a Genre." In *Apocalypse: The Morphology of a Genre*, edited by John Joseph Collins, 14:1–20. Semeia 294. Atlanta, Ga.: SBL, 1979.

———. *The Scepter and the Star: The Messiahs of the Dead Sea Scrolls and Other Ancient Literature*. ABRL. New York, N.Y.: Anchor Bible, 1995.

Collins, John Neil. *Diakonia: Re-Interpreting the Ancient Sources*. Oxford, U.K.: Oxford University Press, 1990.

Collins, Marilyn F. "The Hidden Vessels in Samaritan Traditions." *JSJ* 3 (1972): 97–116.

Constantinou, Eugenia Scarvelis. "Andrew of Caesarea and the Apocalypse in the Ancient Church of the East: Studies and Translation." Ph.D. diss., Université Laval, 2008.

Conzelmann, Hans. *Acts of the Apostles: A Commentary on the Acts of the Apostles*. Hermeneia. Philadelphia, Pa.: Fortress, 1987.

Cook, J. M. *The Greeks: In Ionia and the East*. Edited by Glyn Daniel. Ancient Peoples and Places 31. New York, N.Y.: Praeger, 1963.

Cook, S. A. "A Lydian-Aramaic Bilingual." *JHS* 37 (1917): 77–87.

Cooksey, Christopher J. "Tyrian Purple: 6,6'-Dibromoindigo and Related Compounds." *Molecules* 6 (2001): 736–69.

Cooksey, Christopher J., and R. S. Sinclair. "Colour Variations in Tyrian Purple Dyeing." *Dyes in History and Archaeology* 20 (2005): 127–35.

Cornelie, Piok Zanon. "The Sanctuary of Demeter at Pergamon: Architecture and Dynasty in the Early Attalid Capital." Ph.D. diss., University of Pittsburgh, 2009.

Corsten, Thomas. *Die Inschriften von Laodikeia Am Lykos*. Bonn: Habelt, 1997.

Cortes, E. "Una Interpretación Judía Del Cant 5, 2 En Apocalipsis 3, 19b-20." *RCT* 4, no. 2 (1979): 239–58.

Cothenet, Édouard. *Le Prophétisme Dans Le Nouveau Testament*. Edited by Louis Pirot, André Robert, Jacque Briend, and Édouard Cothenet. 14 vols. DBSup 8. Paris: Letouzey et Ané, 1972.

Cotter, Wendy J. "Women's Authority Roles in Paul's Churches: Countercultural or Conventional?" *NovT* 36 (1994): 350–72.

Court, John M. *Myth and History in the Book of Revelation*. Louisville, Ky.: Westminster/Knox, 1979.

Court, John M. *Revelation*. NTG. Sheffield: Sheffield Academic Press, 1994.

———. *The Book of Revelation and the Johannine Apocalyptic Tradition*. Sheffield, U.K.: Sheffield Academic, 2000.

Coutsoumpos, Panayotis. "The Social Implication of Idolatry in Revelation 2:14: Christ or Caesar?" *BTB* 27 (1997): 23–27.

Cowell, M. R., and K. Hyne. "Scientific Examination of the Lydian Precious Metal Coinages." In *King Croesus' Gold: Excavations at Sardis and the History of Gold Refining*, edited by Andrew Ramage and Paul T. Craddock, 169–74. AESM 11. Cambridge, Mass.: British Museum Press, 2000.

Craddock, Paul T. "Assaying in Antiquity." In *King Croesus' Gold: Excavations at Sardis and the History of Gold Refining*, edited by Andrew Ramage and Paul T. Craddock, 245–50. AESM 11. Cambridge, Mass.: British Museum Press, 2000.

Craigie, Peter C. *The Book of Deuteronomy*. Edited by R. K. Harrison. NICOT 5. Grand Rapids, Mich.: Eerdmans, 1976.

Cramer, John Anthony. *A Geographical and Historical Description of Asia Minor*. Oxford, U.K.: Oxford University Press, 1832.

Crawford, J. Stephens. *The Byzantine Shops at Sardis*. AESM 9. Cambridge, Mass.: Harvard University Press, 1990.

Criswell, W. A. *Expository Sermons on Revelation*. Grand Rapids, Mich.: Zondervan, 1975.

Cross, Frank Leslie, and Elizabeth A. Livingstone, eds. "Pionius, St." In *The Oxford Dictionary Of The Christian Church*, Revised., 1298. Oxford, U.K.: Oxford University Press, 2005.

———, eds. *The Oxford Dictionary Of The Christian Church*. Oxford, U.K.: Oxford University Press, 2005.

Cross, Frank Moore. "The Hebrew Inscriptions from Sardis." *HTR* 95, no. 1 (2002): 3–19.

Curran, John. "The Ambitions of Quintus Labienus 'Parthicus.'" *Antichthon* 41 (2007): 33–53.

Curtis, C. Densmore. *Sardis XIII: Jewelry and Gold Work, Part 1, 1910-1914*. Edited by Andrew Ramage and Paul T. Craddock. AESM 13. Rome: Sindacato Italiano Arti Grafiche, 1925.

Daltrop, Georg, Ulrich Hausmann, and Max Wegner. *Die Flavier: Vespasian, Titus, Domitian, Nerva, Julia Titi, Domitilla, Domitia*. Berlin: Mann, 1966.

Dana, H. E., and Julius Mantey. *A Manual Grammar of the Greek New Testament*. New York, N.Y.: MacMillan, 1969.

D'Andria, Francesco, Mustafa Büyükkolancı, and Lorenzo Campagna. "The Castellum Aquae of Hierapolis of Phrygia ." In *Cura Aquarum In Ephesus: Proceedings of the Twelfth International Congress on the History of Water Management and Hydraulic Engineering in the Mediterranean Region (Ephesus-Selçuck, October 2-10,*

2004), Part 1, edited by Gilbert Wiplinger, 359–61. BABesch Suppl. 12. Leuven, Belgium: Peeters, 2006.

Daniel, Robert Walter, and Franco Maltomini. *Supplementum Magicum*. Opladen: Westdeutscher Verlag, 1990.

———. *Supplementum Magicum*. 2 vols. Papyrologica Coloniensia 16. Oppladen: Westdeutscher, 1990.

Daniels, T. Scott. *Seven Deadly Spirits: The Message of Revelation's Letters for Today's Church*. Grand Rapids, Mich.: Baker Academic, 2009.

Davidson, Maxwell. *Angels at Qumran: A Comparative Study of 1 Enoch 1-36; 72-108 and Sectarian Writings from Qumran*. New York, N.Y.: A&C Black, 1992.

Davies, W. D. "A Note on Josephus, Antiquities 15:136." *HTR* 47, no. 3 (1954): 135–40.

Davis, Dean R. *The Heavenly Court Judgment of Revelation 4-5*. Lanham, Md.: University Press of America, 1992.

Davis, E. J. *Anatolia: Or The Journal of a Visit to Some of the Ancient Ruined Cities of Caria, Phrygia, Lycia and Pisidia*. London, U.K.: Grant & Co., 1874.

Davis, John J. *Biblical Numerology: A Basic Study of the Use of Numbers in the Bible*. Grand Rapids, Mich.: Baker, 1968.

Davis, R. Dean. "The Heavenly Court Scene of Revelation 4–5." Ph.D. diss., Andrews University, 1986.

Day, N. John. "The Imprecatory Psalms and Christian Ethics." Ph.D. diss., Dallas Theological Seminary, 2001.

De Roche, Michael. "Yahweh's Rîb against Israel: A Reassessment of the So-Called 'Prophetic Lawsuit' in the Pre-Exilic Prophets." *JBL* 102, no. 4 (1983): 563–74.

Deer, Donald S. "Whose Faith/Loyalty in Revelation 2.13 and 14.12?" *BT* 38, no. 3 (1987): 328–30.

Dehandschütter, Boudewijn. "The Martyrium Polycarpi: A Century of Research." Edited by Wolfgang Haase and Hildegard Temporini. *Aufstieg Und Niedergang Der Römischen Welt: Geschichte Und Kultur Roms Im Spiegel Der Neueren Forschung* 27, no. 2 (1993): 485–522.

———. "The Meaning of Witness in the Apocalypse." In *L'Apocalypse Johannique et L' Apocalyptique Dans Le Nouveau Testament*, edited by Jan Lambrecht, 283–88. Gembloux, Belgium: Louvain University Press, 1980.

Deissmann, Gustav Adolf. *Light from the Ancient East*. Translated by Lionel R. M. Strachan. New York, N.Y.: Harper & Brothers, 1927.

Delaine, Janet. "Architecture." Edited by Simon Hornblower and Antony Spawforth. *OCD*. Oxford, U.K.: Clarendon, 2003.

Delatte, A., and Ph. Derchain. *Les Intailles Magiques Gréco-Egyptiennes*. Paris: Bibliotheque Nationale, 1964.

Delitzsch, Franz. *Isaiah*. 10 vols. COT 7. Grand Rapids, Mich.: Eerdmans, 1977.

Delivorrias, Angelos. "The Throne of Apollo at the Amyklaion: Old Proposals, New Perspectives." *British School at Athens Studies* 16 (2009): 133–35.

Dempster, Stephen G. "The Prophetic Invocation of the Ban as Covenant Curse: A Historical Analysis of a Prophetic Theme." Th.M. diss., Westminster Theological Seminary, 1978.

Derin, Zafer. "Yeşilova Höyük." *Actual Archaeology Magazine* 2 (2012): 108–20.

———. "Yeşilova Höyük Excavations." *Ege University*, December 12, 2015. http://www.yesilova.ege.edu.tr/eng/.

Derin, Zafer, and T. Caymaz. "İzmir'in Prehistorik Yerleşimi, Yeşilova Höyüğü 2012 Yılı Kazı Çalışmaları." *Kazi Sonuçlari Toplantisi* 35, no. 1 (2014): 419–33.

Derwbear, Thomas. "Secret of Ancient Graffiti." *Turks.US Daily EU News*, July 22, 2003. www.turks.us/article.php?story=20030722090305725.

deSilva, David A. "The Revelation to John: A Case Study in Apocalyptic Propaganda and the Maintenance of Sectarian Identity." *Sociological Analysis* 53, no. 4 (1992): 375–95.

DeSilva, David A. "The Social Setting of the Revelation to John: Conflicts Within, Fears Without." *WTJ* 54, no. 2 (1992): 273–302.

DeSilva, David Arthur. *Seeing Things John's Way: The Rhetoric of the Book of Revelation*. Louisville, Ky.: Westminster/John Knox, 2009.

Desnier, Jean-Lu. "Divus Caesar Imp. Domitiani F." *REA* 81 (1979): 54–64.

Destrée, Pierre, and Penelope Murray. *A Companion to Ancient Aesthetics*. Hoboken, N.J.: Wiley & Sons, 2015.

Dewar, Michael. "Spinning the Trabea: Consular Robes and Propaganda in the Panegyrics of Claudian." In *Roman Dress and the Fabrics of Roman Culture*, edited by Jonathan C. Edmondson and Alison Keith, 217–37. Phoenix Supplementary Volumes. Toronto, Can.: University of Toronto Press, 2009.

Dibelius, Martin. *James: A Commentary on the Epistle of James*. Edited by Heinrich Greeven and Helmut Koster. Translated by Michael A. Williams. Hermeneia. Philadelphia, Pa.: Fortress, 1976.

———. "Wer Ohren Hat Zu Hören, Der Höre." *TSK* 83 (1910): 461–71.

Dignas, Beate, and R. R. R. Smith. *Historical and Religious Memory in the Ancient World*. Oxford, U.K.: Oxford University Press, 2012.

Dijkstra, Meindert. "Prophecy by Letter (Jeremiah 29:24–32)." *Vetus Testamentum* 33 (1983): 319–22.

Dillon, John M. "Dionysus (Deity)." Edited by David Noel Freedman, Gary A. Herion, David F. Graf, and John David Pleins. *ABD*. New York, N.Y.: Doubleday, 1996.

Dionisopoulous-Mass, Regina. "The Evil Eye and the Bewitchment in a Peasant Village." In *The Evil Eye*, edited by Clarence Maloney, 42–62. New York, N.Y.: Columbia University Press, 1976.

Dixon, Suzanne. *Childhood, Class and Kin in the Roman World*. New York, N.Y.: Routledge, 2005.

Dmitriev, Sviatoslav. "Claudius' Grant of Cilicia to Polemo." *ClQ* 53, no. 1 (2003): 286–91.

Dobkin, Marjorie H. *Smyrna 1922: The Destruction of a City*. New York, N.Y.: Newmark, 1988.

Doerfer, Gerhard. *Türkische und mongolische Elemente im Neupersischen: unter besonderer Berücksichtigung älterer neupersischer Geschichtsquellen, vor allem der Mongolen- und Timuridenzeit*. Wiesbaden: Steiner, 1965.

Doğan News Agency. "Sacred Agora Excavated at Laodicea." *Artifax* 32, no. 2 (2017): 20.

———. "Sacred Agora Unearthed in Laodicea." *Hurriot Daily News*, January 3, 2017. http://www.hurriyetdailynews.com/sacred-agora-unearthed-in-laodicea.aspx?pageID=238&nID=108030&NewsCatID=375.

Dolansky, Fanny. "Togam Virilem Sumere: Coming of Age in the Roman World." In *Roman Dress and the Fabrics of Roman Culture*, edited by Jonathan C. Edmondson and Alison Keith, 47–70. Phoenix Supplementary Volumes. Toronto, Can.: University of Toronto Press, 2009.

Donkin, R. A. *Manna: An Historical Geography*. Biogeographic 17. New York, N.Y.: Springer, 2013.

Doughty, Darrell J. "Persecution and Martyrdom in Early Christianity," 2003. http://courses.drew.edu/FA2001/bibst-720s-001.

Doumet, Joseph. *A Study on the Ancient Purple Color and an Attempt to Reproduce the Dyeing Procedure of Tyre as Described by Pliny the Elder*. Translated by Robert Cook. Beirut: Imprimerie Catholique, 1980.

Downing, F. Gerald. "Pliny's Prosecutions of Christians." *Journal for the Study of the New Testament* 34 (1988): 105–23.

Dräger, Michael. *Die Städte der Provinz Asia in der Flavierzeit: Studien zur kleinasiatischen Stadt- und Regionalgeschichte*. Europäische Hochschulschriften, III.576. Frankfurt: Peter Lang, 1993.

Draper, Jr., James T. *The Unveiling: Inspirational Expositions of the Book of Revelation from a Premillennial Viewpoint*. Nashville, Tenn.: Broadman, 1984.

Dreyfus, Renée, and Ellen Schraudolph, eds. *Pergamon: The Telephos Frieze from the Great Altar*. Vol. 2. San Francisco, Calif.: University of Texas Press, 1997.

Drob-Krüpe, Kerstin. "Spatial Concentration and Dispersal of Roman Textile Crafts." In *Urban Craftsmen and Traders in the Roman World*, edited by Andrew Wilson and Miko Flohr, 334–51. Oxford, U.K.: Oxford University Press, 2016.

Du Preez, James. "Ancient Near Eastern Vassal Treaties and the Book of Revelation: Possible Links." *RSA* 2, no. 2 (1981): 33–43.

———. "Mission Perspective in the Book of Revelation." *EvQ* 42 (1970): 152–67.

Duff, Paul B. "I Will Give Each of You as Your Works Deserve": Witchcraft Accusations and the Fiery-Eyed Son of God in Rev 2.18–23." *NTS* 43, no. 1 (1997): 116–23.

———. "The 'Synagogues of Satan': Crisis Mongering and the Apocalypse of John." In *The Reality of Apocalypse: Rhetoric and Politics in the Book of Revelation*, edited by L. Barr David, 147–68. SBLSS 39. Atlanta, Ga.: Scholars Press, 2006.

———. *Who Rides the Beast?: Prophetic Rivalry and the Rhetoric of Crisis in the Churches of the Apocalypse*. Oxford, U.K.: Oxford University Press, 2001.

Dunbabin, Katherine M. D. *The Roman Banquet: Images of Conviviality*. Cambridge, U.K.: Cambridge University Press, 2010.

———. "Wine and Water at the Roman Convivium." *JRA* 6 (1993): 116–41.

Duncan-Jones, Richard P. *The Economy of the Roman Empire: Quantitative Studies*. Cambridge, Mass.: Cambridge University Press, 1974.

Dunn, James D. G. *Christology in the Making: A New Testament Inquiry Into the Origins of the Doctrine of the Incarnation*. Grand Rapids, Mich.: Eerdmans, 1996.

Durant, Will. *The Story of Civilization, Part II: The Life of Greece*. 11 vols. New York, N.Y.: Simon & Schuster, 1966.

Durham, John I. *Exodus*. 32 vols. WBC 3. Dallas, Tex.: Word Books, 1987.

Durling, Richard J. *A Dictionary of Medical Terms in Galen*. Studies in Ancient Medicine, Monumenta Graeca Et Romana 5. Leiden: Brill, 1993.

Dusinberre, Elspeth R. M. *Aspects of Empire in Achaemenid Sardis*. Cambridge, U.K.: Cambridge University Press, 2003.

Düsterdieck, Friedrich. *Critical and Exegetical Handbook to the Revelation of John*. Translated by Henry E. Jacobs. 3rd ed. New York, N.Y.: Funk & Wagnalls, 1887.

Duyuran, Rüstem. "Akhisar Tepe Mezarliğinda Yapilan Arkeolojik Araştirmalar." *TAD* 17, no. 2 (1968): 73–76.

———. "Akhisar Tepe Mezarliğinda Yapilan Arkeolojik Araştirmalar II." *TAD* 20, no. 2 (1973): 17–27.

Ebert, J. "Zur Stiftungsurkunde Der Leukophryena in Magnesia Am Mäander." *Philologus* 126 (1982): 198–216.

Eck, Werner. "Hadrian als pater patriae und die Verleihung des Augustatitels an Sabina." In *Romanitas - Christianitas: Untersuchungen zur Geschichte und Literatur der römischen Kaiserzeit. Johannes Straub zum 70. Geburtstag am 18. Oktober 1982 gewidmet*, edited by Gerhard Wirth, 217–29. Berlin: De Gruyter, 1982.

———. "Jahres- Und Provinzialfasten Der Senatorischen Statthalter von 69/70 Bis 138/139, 1. Teil." *Chiron* 12 (1982): 281–362.

———. "Jahres- Und Provinzialfasten Der Senatorischen Statthalter von 69/70 Bis 138/139. 2. Teil." *Chiron* 13 (1983): 147–237.

———. "Traianus." In *BrillPaulyA*, edited by Hubert Cancik and Helmuth Schneider, translated by Christine F. Salazar and Francis G. Gentry. Leiden: Brill, 2006. http://dx.doi.org/10.1163/1574-9347_bnp_e1218650.

Edelstein, Emma Jeannette Levy, and Ludwig Edelstein. *Asclepius: A Collection and Interpretation of the Testimonies*. 2 vols. Baltimore, Md.: Johns Hopkins Press, 1998.

Edgar, Thomas R. "Robert H. Gundry and Revelation 3:10." *GTJ* 3, no. 1 (1982): 19–49.

Edmondson, Jonathan C. "Public Dress and Social Control in Late Republican and Early Imperial Rome ." In *Roman Dress and the Fabrics of Roman Culture*, edited by Jonathan C. Edmondson and Alison Keith, 21–46. Phoenix Supplementary Volumes. Toronto, Can.: University of Toronto Press, 2009.

———, ed. *Two Industries in Roman Lusitania: Mining and Garum Production*. Oxford, U.K.: British Archaeological Reports, 1987.

Edwards, Catharine. *The Politics of Immorality in Ancient Rome*. Cambridge, U.K.: Cambridge University Press, 1993.

Efird, James M. *Revelation For Today: An Apocalyptic Approach*. Nashville, Tenn.: Abingdon, 1989.

Ehler, W. "Triumphus." *RE* 2. VIIA.1 (1939): 493–511.

Ehrhardt, Arnold. *The Framework of the New Testament Stories*. Harvard University Press, 1964.

Eichhorn, Johann G. *Commentarius in Apocalypsin Joannis*. 2 vols. Göttingen: Dieterich, 1791.

Eichrodt, Walther. "Prophet and Covenant: Observations on the Exegesis of Isaiah." In *Proclamation and Presence: Old Testament Essays in Honour of Gwynne Henton Davies*, edited by John I. Durham and J. Roy Porter, 167–88. Louisville, Ky.: Westminster/Knox, 1970.

———. *Theology of the Old Testament*. 2 vols. Old Testament Library. Louisville, Ky.: Westminster/Knox, 1967.

Eisenbud, Daniel K. "Archaeologists Restore Ancient Tiles from Second Temple in Jerusalem." *The Jerusalem Post*, September 6, 2016. http://www.jpost.com/Israel-News/Archeologists-restore-tiles-from-Second-Temple-in-Jerusalem-467021.

Eissfeldt, Otto. "Renaming in the Old Testament." In *Words and Meanings*, edited by Peter R. Ackroyd and Barnabas Lindars, 69–80. London, U.K.: Cambridge University Press, 1968.

Ellul, Jacques. *Apocalypse: The Book of Revelation*. Translated by George W. Schreiner. New York, N.Y.: Seabury, 1977.

Elwell, Walter A., ed. *Evangelical Dictionary of Theology*. 2nd ed. Baker Reference Library. Grand Rapids, Mich.: Baker Academic, 2001.

Elworthy, Frederick Thomas. "The Evil Eye." In *Encylopaedia of Religion and Ethics*, edited by James Hastings, 5:608–15. New York, N.Y.: T&T Clark, 1908.

———. *The Evil Eye: An Account of This Ancient and Widespread Superstition*. London, U.K.: Murray, 1958.

Emerton, John Adney. "Binding and Loosing—Forgiving and Retaining." *JTS* 13 (1962): 325–31.

Enroth, Anne-Mart. "The Hearing Formula in the Book of Revelation." *NTS* 36, no. 4 (1990): 598–608.

Erdemir, Hatice. "Woollen Textiles: An International Trade Good in the Lycus Valley in Antiquity." In *Colossae in Space and Time: Linking to an Ancient City*, edited by Alan H. Cadwallader and Michael Trainor, 104–29. NTOA SUNT. Göttingen: Vandenhoeck & Ruprecht, 2011.

Erim, Kenan T. *Aphrodisias: City of Venus Aphrodite*. New York, N.Y: Facts on File, 1986.

Erkelenz, Dirk. "Cicero, pro Flacco 55-59: Zur Finanzierung von Statthalterfesten in Der Friihphase Des Koinon von Asia." *Chiron* 29 (1999): 43–57.

Eusebius. *Eusebius: The Church History*. Translated by Paul L. Maier. Grand Rapids, Mich.: Kregel Academic & Professional, 2007.

Evans, Craig A., and Stanley E. Porter, eds. *Dictionary of New Testament Background: A Compendium of Contemporary Biblical Scholarship*. Downers Grove, Ill.: InterVarsity, 2000.

Evans, Richard. *A History of Pergamum: Beyond Hellenistic Kingship*. New York, N.Y.: Continuum International, 2012.

Everitt, Anthony. *Cicero : The Life and Times of Rome's Greatest Politician*. New York, N.Y.: Random House, 2003.

Exell, Joseph S. *Revelation*. BI 23. Grand Rapids, Mich.: Baker, 1978.

Fagan, Brian M., and Charlotte Beck, eds. *The Oxford Companion to Archaeology*. Oxford, U.K.: Oxford University Press, 1996.

Fagan, Garrett G. *Bathing in Public in the Roman World*. Ann Arbor, Mich.: University of Michigan Press, 2002.

Fairchild, Mark R. "The 'Lukewarm' Legacy of Laodicea: Conflicts of Prosperity in an Ancient Christian City." *BAR* 43, no. 2 (March 2017): 30–39, 67–68.

Falcon-Barker, Ted. *Roman Galley Beneath the Sea*. Philadelphia, Pa.: Clinton, 1964.

Falkener, Edward. *Ephesus, and the Temple of Diana*. London, U.K.: Day & Son, 1862.

Fanning, Buist M. *Verbal Aspect in New Testament Greek*. Edited by J. Barton. Oxford Theology and Religion Monographs. Oxford, U.K.: Oxford University, 1990.

Fant, Clyde E., and Mitchell G. Reddish. *A Guide to Biblical Sites in Greece and Turkey*. Oxford, U.K.: Oxford University Press, 2003.

Farmer, David Hugh. *The Oxford Dictionary of Saints*. 5th ed. Oxford, U.K.: Oxford University Press, 2011.

Farnell, Lewis Richard. *The Cults of the Greek States*. Cambridge Library Collection - Classics. Cambridge, U.K.: Cambridge University Press, 2010.

Farrer, Austin M. *The Revelation of St. John the Divine: Commentary on the English Text*. Oxford, U.K.: Clarendon, 1964.

Fekkes, Jan. *Isaiah and Prophetic Traditions in the Book of Revelation: Visionary Antecedents and Their Development*. LNTS 93. New York, N.Y.: Bloomsbury, 1994.

Feldman, Louis H. *Studies in Hellenistic Judaism*. Leiden: Brill, 1996.

Fensham, F. Charles. "Clauses of Protection in Hittite Vassal-Treaties and the Old Testament." *VT* 13 (1963): 133–43.

———. "Common Trends in Curses of the Near East: Treaties and Kudurru Inscriptions Compared with Maledictions of Amos and Isaiah." *ZAW* 75 (1963): 155–75.

———. "Maledictions and Benedictions in Ancient Near Eastern Vassal–Treaties and the Old Testament." *ZAW* 74 (1962): 1–9.

Ferguson, Everett. *Demonology of the Early Christian World*. Symposium 12. New York, N.Y.: Mellen, 1984.

Ferguson, Sinclair B., David F. Wright, and James I. Packer, eds. *New Dictionary of Theology*. Downers Grove, Ill.: InterVarsity, 1988.

Ferreiro, Alberto. "Priscillian and Nicolaitism." *VC* 52, no. 4 (1998): 382–92.

Feuillet, André. "Le Cantique Des Cantiques et l'Apocalypse: Etude Des Deux Reminiscences Du Cantique Dans l'Apocalypse Johannique (Apc 3,20 et Cant 5.1-2; Apc 12 et Cant 6,10." *RSR* 49 (1961): 321–53.

———. *The Apocalypse*. Translated by T. E. Crane. New York, N.Y.: Alba, 1965.

Fine, Steven. *Art and Judaism in the Greco-Roman World: Toward a New Jewish Archaeology*. Revised. Cambridge, U.K.: Cambridge University Press, 2010.

———. *The Menorah: From the Bible to Modern Israel*. Cambridge, Mass.: Harvard University Press, 2016.

Fine, Steven, and Leonard Victor Rutgers. "New Light on Judaism in Asia Minor During Late Antiquity: Two Recently Identified Inscribed Menorahs." *JSQ* 3, no. 1 (1996): 1–23.

Finegan, Jack. *The Archeology of the New Testament: The Life of Jesus and the Beginning of the Early Church*. Revised. Princeton, N.J.: Princeton University Press, 2014.

———. *The Archeology of the New Testament: The Mediterranean World of the Early Christian Apostles*. Routledge Library Editions: Archaeology. New York, N.Y.: Routledge, 2015.

Finet, André. "Les Dieux Voyageurs En Mésopotamie." *Akkadica* 21 (1981): 1–13.

Fink, Amir Sumaka'i. "The Historical Prologue in a Letter from Šuppiluliuma II to 'Ammurapi', King of Ugarit (RS 18.038)." In *"I Will Speak the Riddles of Ancient Times:" Archaeological and Historical Studies in Honor of Amihai Mazar on the Occasion of His Sixtieth Birthday*, edited by Aren M. Maeir and Pierre de Miroschedji, 2:673–88. Winona Lake, Ind.: Eisenbrauns, 2006.

Fiorenza, Elisabeth Schüssler. "Apocalyptic and Gnosis in the Book of Revelation and Paul." *JBL* 92 (1973): 565–81.

Fishbane, Michael. "Accusations of Adultery: A Study of Law and Scribal Practices in Num 5:11–31." *HUCA* 45 (1974): 25–45.

Fishwick, Duncan. *The Imperial Cult in the Latin West*. Studies in the Ruler Cult of the Western Provinces of the Roman Empire, 2.1. Leiden: Brill Academic, 2005.

Fitzmyer, Joseph A. "The Contribution of Qumran Aramaic to the Study of the New Testament." *NTS* 20 (74 1973): 382–407.

Flacelière, Robert. *Greek Oracles*. New York, N.Y: Beekman, 1980.

Flather, J. F. "Dalmatica." In *DGRA*, edited by William Smith, 1:594. London, U.K.: Murray, 1890.

Fleischer, Robert. *Artemis von Ephesos: und verwandte Kultstatuen aus Anatolien und Syrien*. ÉPRO 35. Leiden: Brill, 1973.

———. "Ein Heiligtum Für Apollon, Artemis Und Leto Bei Heracleia Salbace in Karien." *Archäologischer Anzeiger*, 2000, 405–53.

———. "Ein Unbekanntes Heiligtum Für Apollon, Artemis Und Leto in Der Südwestlichen Turkei." *Antike Welt* 33 (2002): 325–37.

———. "Neues Zu Kleinasiastischen Kultstatuen." *AA* 98 (1983): 81–93.

Flohr, Miko. "Fullones and Roman Society: A Reconsideration." *JRA* 16 (2003): 447–50.

———. "The Textile Economy of Pompeii." *JRA* 26, no. 1 (2013): 53–78.

Forbes, Robert J. *Studies in Ancient Technology*. Leiden: Brill, 1993.

Ford, J. Massyngberde. *Revelation: Introduction, Translation and Commentary*. AYBC 38. New York, N.Y.: Doubleday, 1985.

Foss, Clive. "Appendix III: The Silting of the Harbor of Ephesus." In *Ephesus After Antiquity: A Late Antique, Byzantine and Turkish City*, 185–87. Cambridge, Mass.: Cambridge University Press, 2010.

———. *Ephesus After Antiquity: A Late Antique, Byzantine and Turkish City*. Cambridge, Mass.: Cambridge University Press, 2010.

———. "Inscriptions Related to the Complex." In *The Bath-Gymnasium Complex at Sardis*, edited by Fikret K. Yegül, George M. A. Hanfmann, and Jane Ayer Scott, 169–72. AESR 3. Cambridge, Mass.: Harvard University Press, 1986.

Foster, John. "Note on St. Polycarp." *ExpTim* 77 (1966): 319.

Fox, Kenneth A. "The Nicolaitans, Nicolaus and the Early Church." *SR* 23, no. 4 (1994): 485–96.

Frank, Tenney. *An Economic Survey of Ancient Rome: Rome and Italy of the Empire*. 5 vols. Baltimore, Md.: John Hopkins University Press, 1975.

Frankfurter, David. "Jews or Not? Reconstructing The 'other' in Rev 2:9 and 3:9." *HTR* 94, no. 4 (2001): 403–25.

Franz, Gordon. "Propaganda, Power and the Perversion of Biblical Truths: Coins Illustrating the Book of Revelation." *Bible and Spade* 19, no. 3 (2006): 73–87.

Frazer, James G. *Adonis Attis Osiris: Studies In The History Of Oriental Religion*. London, U.K.: MacMillan & Co., 1906.

Freedman, David Noel, Allen C. Myers, and Astrid B. Beck, eds. *Eerdmans Dictionary of the Bible*. Grand Rapids, Mich.: Eerdmans, 2000.

Freedman, David Noel, Gary A. Herion, David F. Graf, and John David Pleins, eds. *The Anchor Yale Bible Dictionary*. 6 vols. New York, N.Y.: Doubleday, 1996.

Freedman, H., and Maurice Simon, eds. *Midrash Rabbah*. 10 vols. London, U.K.: Soncino, 1992.

French, David H. *Roman Roads and Milestones of Asia Minor Vol. 3 Milestones Fasc. 3.5 Asia*. BAR International Series 5. Ankara, Turkey: British Institute at Ankara, 2014.

Frend, William H. C. *Martyrdom and Persecution in the Early Church: A Study of a Conflict from the Maccabees to Donatus*. Oxford, U.K.: Blackwell, 1965.

———. "The Persecutions: Some Links between Judaism and the Early Church." *JEH* 9 (1958): 141–58.

Friesen, Steven J. "Asiarchs." *ZPE* 126 (1999): 275–90.

———. "Ephesus: Key to a Vision in Revelation." *BAR* 19, no. 3 (1993): 24–37.

———. *Imperial Cults and the Apocalypse of John: Reading Revelation in the Ruins*. Oxford, U.K.: Oxford University Press, 2001.

———. "Myth and Symbolic Resistance in Revelation 13." *JBL* 123 (2004): 281–313.

———. "Revelation, Realia, and Religion: Archaeology in the Interpretations of the Apocalypse." *HTR* 88, no. 3 (1995): 291–314.

———. "Sarcasm in Revelation 2–3: Churches, Christians, True Jews, and Satanic Synagogues." In *The Reality of Apocalypse: Rhetoric and Politics in the Book of Revelation*, edited by L. Barr David, 127–46. SBLSS 39. Atlanta, Ga.: Scholars Press, 2006.

———. "Satan's Throne, Imperial Cults and the Social Settings of Revelation." *JSNT* 27, no. 3 (2005): 351–73.

———. "The Cult of the Roman Emperors in Ephesos: Temple Wardens, City Titles, and the Interpretation of the Revelation of John." In *Ephesos Metropolis of Asia: An Interdisciplinary Approach to Its Archaeology, Religion, and Culture*, edited by Helmut Koester, 229–50. HTR 41. Valley Forge, PA: Trinity, 1995.

———. *Twice Neokoros: Ephesus, Asia and the Cult of the Flavian Imperial Family*. Leiden: Brill Academic, 1993.

Fürst, Dieter. "Παιδεύω." Edited and translated by Colin Brown. *NIDNTT*. Grand Rapids, Mich.: Zondervan, 1986.

Gaffney, Jr., Edward McGlynn. "Of Covenants Ancient and New: The Influence of Secular Law on Biblical Religion." *Journal of Law and Religion* 2, no. 1 (1984): 117–44.

Gagarin, Michael, ed. *The Oxford Encyclopedia of Ancient Greece and Rome*. 7 vols. New York, N.Y.: Oxford University Press, 2010.

Gager, John C. *The Origins of Anti-Semitism*. Oxford, U.K.: Oxford University Press, 1983.

Gagniers, Jean des, Robert Ginouvès, P. Devambez, and L. Kahil. *Laodicée du Lycos: le nymphée; campagnes 1961–1963*. Québec: l'Université Laval, 1969.

Gallusz, Laszlo. *The Throne Motif in the Book of Revelation*. LNTS. New York, N.Y.: Bloomsbury, 2013.

Gamber, Klaus. *Das Geheimnis Der Sieben Sterne*. Regensburg: Pustet, 1987.

Gangemi, Attilio. "La Manna Nascosta E Il Nome Nuovo." *RivB* 25 (1977): 337–56.

———. "La Stella Del Mattino (Apoc. 2,26–28)." *RivB* 26 (1978): 241–74.

Gardner, Paul. "Review of Colin J. Hemer, The Letters to the Seven Churches of Asia in Their Local Setting." *Churchman* 101, no. 3 (1987): 279–80.

Garfinkel, Yosef. "Commentary: The Eliakim Nacar Yokan Seal Impressions: Sixty Years of Confusion in Biblical Archaeological Research." *BA* 53, no. 2 (1990): 74–79.

Garnder, Percy. "Stater." In *DGRA*, edited by William Smith, 2:695-96. London, U.K.: Murray, 1891.

Garnsey, Peter. "The Criminal Jurisdiction of Governors." *JRS* 58, no. 1 and 2 (1968): 51–59.

Garstang, John, and Oliver Robert Gurney. *The Geography of the Hittite Empire*. OPBIAA 5. London, U.K.: British Institute of Archaeology at Ankara, 1959.

Garthwaite, John. "Martial, Book 6, on Domitian's Moral Censorship." *Prudentia* 22 (1990): 12–22.

Gasparro, Giulia Sfameni. *Soteriology and Mystic Aspects in the Cult of Cybele and Attis*. ÉPRO 103. Leiden: Brill Academic, 1985.

Gasque, W. Ward. "Philadelphia (Place)." Edited by David Noel Freedman, Gary A. Herion, David F. Graf, and John David Pleins. *ABD*. New York, N.Y.: Doubleday, 1996.

Gelzer, Heinrich, Heinrich Hilgenfeld, and Otto Cuntz. *Patrum Nicaenorum Nomina Latine, Graece, Coptice, Syriace, Arabice, Armeniace*. Lipsiae: Teubner, 1898.

Gemser, Berend. "The Rîb-or Controversy-Pattern in Hebrew Mentality." In *Wisdom in Israel and in the Ancient Near East*, edited by Martin Noth and David Winton Thomas, 120–37. VTSup 3. Leiden: Brill, 1955.

Gentry, Kenneth L., Jr. *Before Jerusalem Fell: Dating the Book of Revelation*. Powder Springs, GA: American Vision, 1998.

Giblin, Charles Homer. *The Book of Revelation: The Open Book of Prophecy*. GNS 34. Collegeville, Minn.: Liturgical, 1991.

Gibson, Elizabeth Leigh. "Jews in the Inscriptions of Smyrna." *JJS* 56, no. 1 (2005): 66–79.

Giesen, Heinz, and Horst Eckert. *Die Offenbarung des Johannes*. RNT. Regensburg: Pustet, 1997.

Gill, David. "Trapezomata: A Neglected Aspect of Greek Sacrifice." *HTR* 67, no. 2 (1974): 117–37.

Gill, David W., and Conrad H. Gempf, eds. *The Book of Acts in Its Graeco-Roman Setting*. Vol. 2. Book of Acts in Its First Century Setting 2. Grand Rapids, Mich.: Eerdmans, 1994.

Gill, David W. J. "Seleucids and Antiochids." In *DNTB*, edited by Craig A. Evans and Stanley E. Porter, 1092–93. Downers Grove, Ill.: InterVarsity, 2000.

Gill, John. *Exposition of the New Testament: Galatians to Revelation*. Vol. 3. Philadelphia, Pa.: Woodward, 1811.

Gilliam, J. Frank. "Invitations to the Kline of Sarapis." In *Collectanea Papyrologica: Texts published in honor of H. C. Youtie*, edited by A. E. Hanson, 1:315–24. Papyrologische Texte und Abhandlungen. Bonn: Habelt, 1976.

Gilman, Sander L., Steven T. Katz, and Moshe Lozer, eds. "The Lamb and the Scapegoat: The Dehumanization of the Jews in Medieval Propaganda Imagery." In *Anti-Semitism in Times of Crisis*, 38–80. New York, N.Y.: New York University Press, 1993.

Ginzberg, Louis. *The Legends of the Jews*. Translated by Paul Radin, Henrietta Szold, and Boaz Cohen. 7 vols. Philadelphia, Pa.: The Jewish Publication Society of America, 1909.

Glazebrook, Allison, and Madeleine M. Henry, eds. *Greek Prostitutes in the Ancient Mediterranean, 800 BCE–200 CE*. Madison, Wisc.: University of Wisconsin Press, 2011.

Gökgöz, Ali. "Geochemistry of the Kizildere-Tekkehamambuldan-Pamukkale Geothermal Fields, Turkey." *Geothermal Training Programme The United Nations University Reports* 5 (1998): 115–56.

Goodenough, Erwin R. "The Crown of Victory in Judaism." *ABul* 28 (1946): 139–59.

Gooder, Paula. "Diakonia in the New Testament: A Dialogue with John N. Collins." *Ecclesiology* 3, no. 1 (2006): 33–56.

Götze, Bernt. *Antike Bibliotheken*. Jahrbuch Der Deutschen Archäologischen Instituts 52. Berlin: de Greuyter, 1937.

Goulder, Michael D. "The Visionaries of Laodicea." *JSNT* 14, no. 43 (July 1, 1991): 15–39.

Gow, Mary. *Measuring the Earth: Eratosthenes and His Celestial Geometry*. Berkeley Heights, N.J.: Enslow, 2009.

Graber, F. "Blind." Edited and translated by Colin Brown. *NIDNTT*. Grand Rapids, Mich.: Zondervan, 1976.

Gradel, Ittai. *Emperor Worship and Roman Religion*. OCM. Oxford, U.K.: Oxford University Press, 2002.

Grainger, John D. "An Empire Builder—Seleukos Nikator." *History Today* 43, no. 5 (1993): 25–30.

———. *Nerva and the Roman Succession Crisis of AD 96-99*. Roman Imperial Biographies. New York, N.Y.: Routledge, 2003.

———. *Seleukos Nikator: Constructing a Hellenistic Kingdom*. New York, N.Y.: Routledge, 1990.

———. *The Roman War of Antiochos the Great*. Mnemosyne Supplements 239. Leiden: Brill, 2002.

Grant, Frederick C. "Smyrna." In *DBib*, edited by James Hastings, Frederick C. Grant, and Harold. H. Rowley, 4:927. New York, N.Y.: Scribner's Sons, 1909.

Graser, Elsa R. "A Text and Translation of the Edict of Diocletian." In *An Economic Survey of Ancient Rome : Rome and Italy of the Empire*, edited by Tenney Frank, 5:307–421. Baltimore, Md.: John Hopkins University Press, 1975.

Graves, David E. *Biblical Archaeology: An Introduction with Recent Discoveries That Support the Reliability of the Bible*. Vol. 1. Toronto, Ont.: Electronic Christian Media, 2017.

———. *Biblical Archaeology: Famous Discoveries That Support the Reliability of the Bible*. Vol. 2. Toronto, Can.: Electronic Christian Media, 2015.

———. "Governors of Judaea and New Discoveries." *BS* 30, no. 1 (Spring 2017): ??

———. "Influence of the Ancient Near Eastern Vassal Treaties on the Hippocratic Oath." *NEASB* 57 (2012): 27–45.

———. "Jesus Speaks to Seven of His Churches, Part 1." *Bible and Spade* 23, no. 2 (Spring 2010): 46–56.

———. "Jesus Speaks to Seven of His Churches, Part 2." *Bible and Spade* 23, no. 3 (Summer 2010): 66–74.

———. "Local References in the Letter to Smyrna (Rev 2:8–11), Part 1: Archaeological Background." *BS* 18, no. 4 (2005): 114–23.

———. "Local References in the Letter to Smyrna (Rev 2:8–11), Part 2: Historical Background." *BS* 19, no. 1 (2006): 23–31.

———. "Local References in the Letter to Smyrna (Rev 2:8–11), Part 3: Jewish Background." *BS* 19, no. 2 (2006): 41–47.

———. "Local References in the Letter to Smyrna (Rev 2:8–11), Part 4: Religious Background." *BS* 19, no. 3 (2006): 88–96.

———. *The Seven Messages of Revelation and Vassal Treaties: Literary Genre, Structure, and Function*. GDBS 41. Piscataway, N.J.: Gorgias, 2009.

———. "What Is the Madder with Lydia's Purple? A Re-Examination of the Purpurarii in Thyatira and Philippi." *NEASB* 62 (2017): 1–47.

Grayson, Albert Kirk. *Assyrian and Babylonian Chronicles*. Winona Lake, Ind.: Eisenbrauns, 1975.

Green, Joel B., Scot McKnight, and I. Howard Marshall, eds. *Dictionary of Jesus and the Gospels*. Downers Grove, Ill.: InterVarsity, 1992.

Greene, John T. "Balaam: Prophet, Diviner, and Priest in Selected Ancient Israelite and Hellenistic Jewish Sources." *SBLSP* 28 (1989): 57–106.

———. "The Balaam Figure and Type Before, During, and after the Period of the Pseudepigrapha." *JSP* 8 (1991): 67–110.

Greenewalt, Jr., Crawford H. "Ekrem Akurgal, 1911–2002." *AJA* 109, no. 3 (2005): 561–63.

———. "Sardis." *Sardis*, 2015. http://www.sardisexpedition.org.

Greenewalt, Jr., Crawford H., and L. J. Majewski. "Lydian Textiles." In *From Athens to Gordion: The Papers of a Memorial Symposium for Rodney S. Young*, edited by Keith DeVries, 133–48. Philadelphia, Pa.: University of Pennsylvania Museum of Archaeology and Anthropology, 1980.

Greenhill, Willlam Alexander. "Anaitis." In *Dictionary of Greek and Roman Biography and Mythology*, edited by William Smith, 1:158. Boston, Mass.: Little, Brown & Co., 1870.

———. "Themison." In *Dictionary of Greek and Roman Biography and Mythology*, edited by William Smith, 3:1023–24. Boston, Mass.: Little, Brown & Co., 1870.

Gregg, Steve. *Revelation: Four Views: A Parallel Commentary*. Nashville, Tenn.: Nelson, 1997.

Gresseth, Gerald K. "The 'Gilgamesh Epic and Homer." *CJ* 70 (1975): 1–18.

Gritz, Sharon Hodgin. *Paul, Women Teachers, and the Mother Goddess at Ephesus: A Study of 1 Timothy 2:9-15 in Light of the Religious and Cultural Milieu of the First Century*. Washington, D.C.: University Press of America, 1991.

Groom, Nigel. *Frankincense & Myrrh: A Study of the Arabian Incense Trade*. London, U.K.: Longman, 1981.

Grüll, Tibor. "Expositio totius mundi et gentium. A peculiar work on the commerce of Roman Empire from the mid-fourth century – compiled by a Syrian textile dealer?" In *Studies in Economic and Scoail History of the Ancient Near East in Memory of Péter Vargyas*, edited by Zoltán Csabai, 629–43. Ancient Near Eastern and Mediterranean Studies 2. Budapest: Department of Ancient History, University of Pécs & L'Harmattan, 2014.

Guidoboni, Emanuela, Alberto Comastri, and Giusto Traina. *Catalogue of Ancient Earthquakes in the Mediterranean Area Up to the 10th Century*. Rome: Istituto nazionale di geofisica, 1994.

Gulgun, Bahriye, İsmail Yörük, Bahar Turkyilmaz, Mustafa Bolca, and Aslı Güneş. "Determination of the Effects of Temporal Change in Urban and Agricultural Land Uses as Seen in the Example of the Town of Akhisar, Using Remote Sensing Techniques." *Environmental Monitoring and Assessment* 150, no. 1–4 (2009): 427–36.

Gundry, Robert H. *Commentary on Revelation*. CNT 19. Grand Rapids, Mich.: Baker Academic, 2011.

Gundry, Robert Horton. *The Church and the Tribulation: A Biblical Examination of Posttribulationism*. Grand Rapids, Mich.: Zondervan, 1973.

Gürtekin-Demir, R. Gül. "A Small Group of Pottery with Lydian Character from Gavurtepe, Alaşehir." *Arkeoloji Dergisi* 15 (2010): 41–48.

Gusmani, Roberto. *Lydisches Wörterbuch, Mit Grammatischer Skizze Und Inschriftensammlung*. Heidelberg: Winter, 1964.

Guthrie, Donald D. *The Apostles*. Grand Rapids, Mich.: Zondervan, 1992.

———. *The Relevance of John's Apocalypse*. Exeter, U.K.: Paternoster, 1987.

Guthrie, William K. C. *The Greeks and Their Gods*. Ariadne Series. Boston, Mass.: Beacon, 1950.

Guthrie, William Keith. *Orpheus and Greek Religion: A Study of the Orphic Movement*. Edited by L. Alderlink. 2nd ed. Princeton, N.J.: Princeton University Press, 1993.

Habicht, Christian. *Die Inschriften Des Asklepieions*. Vol. 3. Altertümer von Pergamon 8. Berlin: De Gruyter, 1969.

———. "New Evidence on the Province of Asia." *JRS* 65 (1975): 64–91.

Hackett, Jo Ann. "Balaam (Person)." Edited by David Noel Freedman, Gary A. Herion, David F. Graf, and John David Pleins. *ABD*. New York, N.Y.: Doubleday, 1996.

———. *The Balaam Text from Deir ʿAllā*. Harvard Semitic Monographs 31. Atlanta, Ga.: Scholars Press, 1980.

Hadorn, Wilhelm. *Die Offenbarung Des Johannes*. THKNT 18. Leipzig: Verlagsbuchhandlung, 1928.

Haenchen, Ernst. *The Acts of the Apostles: A Commentary*. Hoboken, N.J.: Wiley & Sons, 1971.

Hagner, Donald Alfred. *The Use of the Old and New Testaments in Clement of Rome*. NovTSup 34. Leiden: Brill, 1973.

Hahn, Ferdinand. "Die Sendschreiben Der Johannesapokalypse: Ein Beitrag Zur Bestimmung Prophetischer Redeformen." In *Tradition Und Glauben: Das Frühe Christentum in Seiner Umwelt*, edited by Karl Georg Kuhn, Gert Jermias, Heinz-Wolfgang Kuhn, and Hartmut Stegemann, 257–94. Göttingen: Vandenhoeck & Ruprecht, 1971.

Hahn, Scott W. "Canon, Cult and Covenant: The Promise of Liturgical Hermeneutics." In *Canon And Biblical Interpretation*, edited by Scott W. Hahn, Craig Bartholomew, Robin Parry, Christopher Seitz, and Al Wolters, 201–35. Scripture and Hermeneutics Series 7. Grand Rapids, Mich.: Zondervan, 2006.

———. "Covenant in the Old and New Testaments: Some Current Research (1994–2004)." *CBR* 3, no. 2 (2005): 263–92.

Hailey, Homer. *Revelation: An Introduction and Commentary*. Grand Rapids, Mich.: Baker, 1979.

Halfmann, Helmut. *Die Senatoren aus dem östlichen Teil des Imperium Romanum bis zum Ende des 2. Jahrhunderts n. Chr.* Hypomnemata 58. Göttingen: Vandenhoeck und Ruprecht, 1979.

Halsberghe, Gaston H. *The Cult of Sol Invictus.* Leiden: Brill Archive, 1972.

Hamel, Gildas H. *Poverty and Charity in Roman Palestine, First Three Centuries C.E.* NES 23. Berkeley, Calf.: University of California Press, 1990.

Hamilton, James M. *Revelation: The Spirit Speaks to the Churches.* Edited by R. Kent Hughes. Preaching the Word. Wheaton, Ill.: Crossway, 2012.

Hamilton, William John. "Extracts from Notes Made on a Journey in Asia Minor in 1836 by W. I. [=J.] Hamilton." *JRGS* 7 (1837): 34–61.

———. *Researches in Asia Minor, Pontus and Armenia: With Some Account of Their Antiquities and Geology.* 2 vols. London, U.K.: Murray, 1842.

Hanfmann, George M. A. *From Croesus to Constantine: The Cities of Western Asia Minor and Their Arts in Greek and Roman Times.* Ann Arbor, Mich.: University of Michigan Press, 1974.

———. *Letters from Sardis.* Cambridge, Mass.: Harvard University Press, 1972.

———. "Lydiaka." *HSCP* 63 (1958): 65–88.

———. "On Lydian Sardis." In *From Athens to Gordion: The Papers of a Memorial Symposium for Rodney S. Young*, edited by Keith DeVries, 99–132. Philadelphia, Pa.: University of Pennsylvania Museum of Archaeology and Anthropology, 1980.

———. "On the Gods of Lydian Sardis." In *Beiträge Zur Altertumskunde Kleinasiens: Festschrift Für Kurt Bittel*, edited by Rainer M. Boehmer and Herald Hauptmann, 219–31. Bücher: Mainz am Rhein, 1983.

———. "Recent Archaeological Research in Turkey: Sardis, 1975." *AS* 26, no. 1 (1976): 58–62.

Hanfmann, George M. A., William E. Mierse, and Clive Foss, eds. *Sardis from Prehistoric to Roman Times: Results of the Archaeological Exploration of Sardis, 1958-1975.* Cambridge, Mass.: Harvard University Press, 1983.

Hanfmann, George M. A., and Nancy H. Ramage. *Sculpture from Sardis : The Finds through 1975.* Edited by George M. A. Hanfmann and S. W. Jacobs. AESR 2. Cambridge, Mass.: Harvard University Press, 1978.

Hanfmann, George M. A., L. Roberts, and William E. Mierse. "The Hellenistic Period." In *Sardis from Prehistoric to Roman Times: Results of the Archaeological Exploration of Sardis, 1958-1975*, edited by George M. A. Hanfmann, William E. Mierse, and Clive Foss, 109–39. Cambridge, Mass.: Harvard University Press, 1983.

Hanfmann, George M. A., G. F. Swift, and Crawford H. Greenewalt, Jr. "The Ninth Campaign at Sardis (1966)." *BASOR*, no. 187 (1966): Hanfmann, "The Ninth Campaign at Sardis (1966)."

Hanfmann, George M. A., and Jane C. Waldbaum. *A Survey of Sardis and the Major Monuments Outside the City Walls.* Edited by George M. A. Hanfmann and Stephen W. Jacobs. AESR 1. Cambridge, Mass.: Harvard University Press, 1975.

———. "Kybele and Artemis: Two Anatolian Goddesses at Sardis." *Archaeology* 22, no. 4 (1969): 264–69.

———. "New Excavations at Sardis and Some Problems of Western Anatolian Archaeology." In *Near Eastern Archaeolgoy in the Twentieth Century: Essays in Honor of Nelson Glueck*, edited by James A. Sanders, 307–26. Garden City, N.Y.: Doubleday, 1970.

Hanfmann, George M. A., Fikret K. Yegül, and Crawford H. Greenewalt, Jr. "The Roman and Late Antique Period." In *Sardis from Prehistoric to Roman Times: Results of the Archaeological Exploration of Sardis, 1958-*

1975, edited by George M. A. Hanfmann, William E. Mierse, and Clive Foss, 139–67. Cambridge, Mass.: Harvard University Press, 1983.

Hansen, Esther Violet. *The Attalids of Pergamon*. Ithaca, NY: Cornell University Press, 1947.

Hansen, Ryan Leif. *Silence and Praise: Rhetorical Cosmology and Political Theology in the Book of Revelation*. Emerging Scholars. Minneapolis, Minn.: Fortress, 2014.

Hanson, J. W. "The Urban System of Roman Asia Minor and Wider Urban Connectivity." In *Settlement, Urbanization, and Population*, edited by Alan Bowman and Andrew Wilson, 229–75. OSRE. Oxford, U.K.: Oxford University Press, 2011.

Hare, Douglas R. A. *The Theme of Jewish Persecution of Christians in the Gospel According to St. Matthew*. SNTS 6. Cambridge, U.K.: Cambridge University Press, 2005.

Harland, Philip A. "Acculturation and Identity in the Diaspora: A Jewish Family and 'Pagan' Guilds at Hierapolis." *JJS* 57, no. 2 (2006): 222–44.

———. *Associations, Synagogues, and Congregations: Claiming a Place in Ancient Mediterranean Society*. 2nd ed. Kitchener, Ontario: Harland, 2011.

———. "Imperial Cults within Local Cultural Life: Associations in Roman Asia." *Ancient History Bulletin* 17, no. 1–2 (2003): 85–107.

———. *North Coast of the Black Sea, Asia Minor*. Berlin: De Gruyter, 2014.

———. "Spheres of Contention, Claims of Pre-Eminence Rivalries among Associations in Sardis and Smyrna." In *Religious Rivalries and the Struggle for Success in Sardis and Smyrna*, edited by Richard S. Ascough, 53–63. SSEJC 14. Waterloo, Ont.: Wilfrid Laurier University Press, 2006.

Harnack, A. Von. "The Sect of the Nicolaitans and Nicolaus, the Deacon of Jerusalem." *JR* 3 (1923): 413–22.

Harrelson, Walter J. *Interpreting the Old Testament*. New York, N.Y.: Holt, Rinehart & Winston, 1964.

Harrington, Wilfrid J. *Revelation*. Edited by Daniel J Harrington. SPS 16. Collegeville, Minn.: Liturgical, 2008.

Harris, J. Rendel. "The Early Colonists of the Mediterranean." *BJRL* 10, no. 2 (1926): 303–61.

Harris, Murray J. *Colossians and Philemon*. EGGNT. Nashville, Tenn.: B&H Academic, 2010.

Harris, W. V. *Rome's Imperial Economy: Twelve Essays*. Oxford University Press, 2011.

Harrison, J. R. "The Fading Crown: Divine Honour and the Early Christians." *JTS* 54, no. 2 (October 2003): 493–529.

Harrison, R. K. *Archaeology of the New Testament: The Stirring Times of Christ and the Early Church Come to Life in the Latest Findings of Science*. Grand Rapids, Mich.: Eerdmans, 1985.

Hart, Gerald David. *Asclepius : The God of Medicine*. New York, N.Y.: Royal Society of Medicine, 2000.

Hartingsveld, L. van. *Revelation: A Practical Commentary*. Translated by John Vriend. Grand Rapids, Mich.: Eerdmans, 1985.

Hartman, Lars. "Form and Message: A Preliminary Discussion of 'Partial Texts' in Rev 1–3 and 22, 6ff." In *L'Apocalypse Johannique et L'Apocalyptique Dans Le NouveauTestament*, edited by Jan Lambrecht, 129–49. Leuven: Leuven University Press, 1980.

Hartog, Paul. *Polycarp and the New Testament: The Occasion, Rhetoric, Theme, and Unity of the Epistle to the Philippians and Its Allusions to New Testament Literature*. WUNT, 2.134. Tübingen: Siebeck, 2002.

Harvey, Julien. *Le Plaidoyer Prophétique, Contre Israël Après La Rupture de L'alliance: Étude D'une Formule Littéraire de l'Ancien Testament*. Paris: Bruges, 1967.

———. "Le 'RIB-Pattern', Réquisitoire Prophétique Sur La Rupture de L'alliance." *Biblica* 43, no. 2 (1962): 172–96.

Hastings, James, and John A. Selbie, eds. *A Dictionary of the Bible: Dealing with Its Language, Literature and Contents Including the Biblical Theology*. 5 vols. New York, N.Y.: Scribner's Sons, 1911.

Hatzfeld, J. "Inscriptions de Panamara." *BCH* 51 (1927): 57–155.

Hawkins, J. David. "The Arzawa Letters in Recent Perspective." *British Museum Studies in Ancient Egypt and Sudan* 14 (2009): 78–83.

Hawthorne, Gerald F. "Amen ." In *Dictionary of Jesus and the Gospels*, edited by Joel B. Green, Scot McKnight, and I. Howard Marshall, 7–8. Downers Grove, Ill.: InterVarsity, 1992.

Head, Barclay Vincent. *Catalogue of the Greek Coins of Ionia in the British Museum*. Edited by Reginald Stuart Poole. Oxford, U.K.: Oxford University Press, 1892.

———. *Catalogue of the Greek Coins of Lydia*. Catalogue of the Greek Coins in the British Museum 22. London, U.K.: British Museum Press, 1901.

———. *Historia Numorum: A Manual of Greek Numismatics*. 2nd ed. Oxford, U.K.: Clarendon, 1911.

Hefele, Karl Joseph von. *Histoire Des Conciles D'après Les Documents Originaux*. 2 vols. Paris, France: Letouzey et Ané, 1907.

Heiken, Grant, Renato Funiciello, and Donatella de Rita. *The Seven Hills of Rome: A Geological Tour of the Eternal City*. Princeton University Press, 2013.

Heinen, H. "The Syrian–Egyptian Wars and the New Kingdoms of Asia Minor." In *CAH*, edited by Frank William Wallbank, 7.1:412–45. Cambridge, U.K.: Cambridge University Press, 1984.

Heinisch, H. F. "Ancient Purple, an Historical Survey." *Fibre Engineering and Chemistry, Great Britain* 18, no. 6 (1957): 203–6.

Heitmüller, Wilhelm H. F. *"Im Namen Jesu": Eine Sprach- U. Religionsgeschichtliche Untersuchung Zum Neuen Testament, Speziell Zur Altchristlichen Taufe*. Göttingen: Vandenhoeck & Ruprecht, 1903.

Hekster, Olivier. *Emperors and Ancestors: Roman Rulers and the Constraints of Tradition*. OSACR. Oxford, U.K.: Oxford University Press, 2015.

Hekster, Olivier Joram, and Nicholas Zair. *Rome and Its Empire: Ad 193-284*. Edinburgh, U.K.: Edinburgh University Press, 2008.

Heller, Anna. *Les bêtises des Grecs: Conflits et rivalités entre cités d'Asie et de Bithynie à l'époque romaine (129 AD.-235 AD)*. SA 17. Bordeaux, France: Ausonius, 2006.

Hellholm, David, and Kungl Vitterhets. *Apocalypticism in the Mediterranean World and the Near East: Proceedings of the International Colloquium on Apocalypticism, Uppsala, August 12-17, 1979*. Tübingen: Siebeck, 1989.

Hellig, Jocelyn. *The Holocaust and Antisemitism: A Short History*. Oxford, U.K.: One World, 2003.

Hemer, Colin J. "Nicolaitan." Edited by Colin Brown. *NIDNTT*. Grand Rapids, Mich.: Zondervan, 1976.

———. "Seven Cities of Asia Minor." In *Major Cities of the Biblical World*, edited by R.K. Harrison, 234–48. Nashville, Tenn.: Nelson, 1985.

———. *The Book of Acts in the Setting of Hellenistic History.* Edited by Conrad H. Gempf. WUNT 49. Winona Lake, Ind.: Eisenbrauns, 1990.

———. *The Letters to the Seven Churches of Asia in Their Local Setting.* The Biblical Resource Series. Grand Rapids, Mich.: Eerdmans, 2001.

———. "The Sardis Letter and the Croesus Tradition." *NTS* 19, no. 1 (1972): 94–97.

———. "The Speeches of Acts: I. The Ephesian Elders at Miletus." *TynBul* 40, no. 1 (1989): 77–85.

———. "Unto the Angels of the Churches." *Buried History* 11 (1975): 4–27, 56–83, 110–35, 164–90.

Hendriksen, William. *More than Conquerors.* Grand Rapids, Mich.: Baker, 1982.

Hengel, Martin. *Judaism and Hellenism: Studies in Their Encounter in Palestine During the Early Hellenistic Period.* Translated by John Bowde. Eugene, Oreg.: Wipf & Stock, 2003.

———. *The Johannine Question.* Translated by John Bowden. Philadelphia, Pa.: Trinity, 1989.

Hengstenberg, Ernst W. *The Revelation of John: Expounded for Those Who Search the Scriptures.* Translated by Patrick Fairbairn. 2 vols. Edinburgh, U.K.: T&T Clark, 1852.

Henten, Jan Willem van. "Anti-Judaism in Revelation? A Response to Peter Tomson." In *Anti-Judaism and the Fourth Gospel*, edited by Reimund Bieringer, Didier Pollefeyt, and Frederique Vandecasteele-Vanneuville, 111–25. Jewish and Christian Heritage 1. Assen: Royal van Gorcum, 2001.

Herbermann, Charles George, Condé Bénoist Pallen, and Edward Aloysius Pace, eds. *The Catholic Encyclopedia; An International Work of Reference on the Constitution, Doctrine, Discipline, and History of the Catholic Church.* 16 vols. New York, N.Y.: Appleton & Company, 1913.

Herrmann, Peter. "Demeter Karpophoros in Sardeis." *REA* 100 (1998): 495–508.

———. "Mystenvereine in Sardeis." *Chiron* 26 (1996): 315–48.

———. "Neues Vom Sklavenmarkt in Sardeis." *TAD* 4 (1996): 175–87.

———. "Sardeis Zur Zeit Der Iulisch-Claudischen Kaiser." In *Forschungen in Lydien*, edited by Elmar Schwertheim, 21–36. AMStud. 17. Bonn: Habelt, 1995.

Hersh, Charles A. "The Coinage of Quintus Labienus Parthicus." *SNR* 59 (1980): 41–51.

Herzog, Isaac. "Semitic Porphyrology (The Dyeing of Purple in Ancient Israel) I: Tekhelet." D. Litt. diss., University of London, 1919.

Herzog, Rudolf. *Aus der Geschichte des Bankwesens im Altertum: Tesserae nummulariae. Mit einer tafel.* Berlin: Töpelmann, 1919.

Hester, James D. *Paul's Concept of Inheritance: A Contribution to the Understanding of Heilsgeschichte.* SJTOP 19. Edinburgh, U.K.: Oliver & Boyd, 1968.

Heyman, George. "Review of Loren L. John's The Lamb Christology of the Apocalypse of John: An Investigation into Its Origins and Rehetorical Force." *RBL* 2 (2005): 1–4.

Higgins, Christopher M. "Popular and Imperial Response to Earthquakes in the Roman Empire." M.A. diss., College of Arts and Sciences of Ohio University, 2009.

Hill, Andrew E. "Ancient Art and Artemis: Toward Explaining the Polymastic Nature of the Figurine." *JANES* 21 (1992): 91–94.

Hill, David. *New Testament Prophecy*. Marshall's Theological Library. London, U.K.: Marshall, Morgan & Scott, 1979.

Hillers, Delbert R. *Covenant: The History of a Biblical Idea*. Baltimore: Johns Hopkins University Press, 1969.

———. *Treaty-Curses and the Old Testament Prophets*. Biblica et Orientalia 16. Rome: Pontifical Biblical Institute, 1964.

Hinds, John T. *A Commentary on the Book of Revelation*. New Testament Commentaries (Gospel Advocate). Nashville, Tenn.: Gospel Advocate, 1974. Commentary on Revelation.

Hindson, Edward E. *The Book of Revelation: Unlocking the Future*. Edited by Mal Couch. Twenty-First Century Biblical Commentary Series. Chattanoooga, TN: AMG, 2002.

Hirschberg, Julius. *The History of Ophthalmology*. Translated by Frederick C. Blodi and D. L. Blanchard. 11 vols. Amsterdam: Wayenborgh, 1982.

Hirschfeld, Von Otto. "Zur Geschichte Des Römischen Kaiserkultus." *SPAW* 2 (1888): 833–62.

Hobler, Francis. *Records of Roman History: From Cnæus Pompeius to Tiberius Constantinus, as Exhibited on the Roman Coins*. New York, N.Y.: Nichols & sons, 1860.

Hoekema, Anthony A. *The Bible and the Future*. Grand Rapids, Mich.: Eerdmans, 1994.

Hoeksema, Herman. *Behold, He Cometh! An Exposition of the Book of Revelation*. 2nd ed. Grand Rapids, Mich.: Reformed Free Publishing Association, 1974.

Hoffmann, Adolf. "The Roman Remodeling of the Asklepieion." In *Pergamon-Citadel of the Gods: Archaeological Record, Literary Description, and Religious Development*, edited by Helmut Koester, 41–61. Harrisburg, Pa.: Trinity Press International, 1998.

———. "The Roman Remodeling of the Asklepieion." In *Pergamon-Citadel of the Gods: Archaeological Record, Literary Description, and Religious Development*, edited by Helmut Koester, 41–61. HTS 46. Harrisburg, Pa.: Trinity Press International, 1998.

Hoffmann, Matthias Reinhard. *The Destroyer and the Lamb : The Relationship Between Angelomorphic and Lamb Christology in the Book of Revelation*. WUNT 203. Tübingen: Siebeck, 2005.

Hoftijzer, Jacob. "The Prophet Balaam in a 6th Century Aramaic Inscription." *BA* 39, no. 1 (1976): 11–17.

Hoftijzer, Jacob, and G. Van der Kooij. *Aramaic Texts from Deir 'Alla*. Leiden: Brill, 1976.

———, eds. *The Balaam Text from Deir 'Alla Re-Evaluated: Proceedings of the International Symposium Held at Leiden, 21–24 August 1989*. Leiden: Brill, 1991.

Hogarth, David George. *Excavations at Ephesus: The Archaic Artemisia*. London, U.K.: Longmans & Co., 1908.

Hoge, Robert, and David L. Vagi. *Coinage and History of the Roman Empire, Ca. 82 BC–AD 480*. 2 vols. New York, N.Y.: Routledge, 2001.

Holder, Alfred. *Alt-Celtischer Sprachschatz*. 3 vols. Leipzig: Teubner, 1896.

Holladay, John S. "Assyrian Statecraft and the Prophets of Israel." *HTR* 63, no. 1 (1970): 29–51.

Holleran, Claire. *Shopping in Ancient Rome: The Retail Trade in the Late Republic and the Principate*. Oxford, U.K.: Oxford University Press, 2012.

Holloway, Paul A. "The Apocryphal 'Epistle to the Laodiceans' and the Partitioning of Philippians." *HTR* 91, no. 3 (1998): 321–25.

Holloway, R. Ross. *The Archaeology of Ancient Sicily*. New York, N.Y.: Routledge, 2002.

Holt, P. M., Ann K. S. Lambton, and Bernard Lewis, eds. *The Cambridge History of Islam: Volume 1A, The Central Islamic Lands from Pre-Islamic Times to the First World War*. Cambridge, U.K.: Cambridge University Press, 1995.

Holtz, Traugott. *Die Christologie Der Apokalypse Des Johannes*. 2nd ed. TU 85. Berlin: Akademie-Verlag, 1971.

Holtzmann, Heinrich Julius. *Evangelium, Briefe und Offenbarung des Johannes*. Edited by R. A. Lipsius. 2nd ed. Hand-Commentar Zum Neuen Testament. Halle: Gebauer & Schwetschke, 1906.

Holwerda, David E. *Jesus and Israel: One Covenant or Two?* Grand Rapids, Mich.: Eerdmans, 1995.

Homcy, Stephen L. "To Him Who Overcomes: A Fresh Look as What Victory Means for the Believer according to the Book of Revelation." *JETS* 38, no. 2 (n.d.): 193–201.

Hooker, Morna D. "Artemis of Ephesus." *JTS* 64, no. 1 (2013): 37–46.

Hope, Valerie. *Death in Ancient Rome: A Sourcebook*. New York, N.Y.: Routledge, 2007.

Horbury, William. "The Benediction of the 'Minim' and Early Jewish-Christian Controversy." *JTS* 33, no. 1 (1982): 19–61.

Horn, Friedrich W. "Zwischen Der Synagoge Des Satans Und Dem Neuen Jerusalem: Die Christlich-Jüdische Standortbestimmung in Der Apokalypse Des Johannes." *ZRGG* 46, no. 2 (1994): 143–62.

Hornblower, Simon, and Anthony J. S. Spawforth, eds. *The Oxford Classical Dictionary*. 3rd ed. Oxford, U.K.: Clarendon, 2003.

Horovitz, Philippe. "Essai Sur Les Pouvoirs Des Procurateurs-Gouverneurs." *RBPH* 17, no. 1 (1938): 53–62.

Horsley, G. H. R. "Expiation and the Cult of Men." In *New Documents Illustrating Early Christianity*, edited by G. H. R. Horsley and Stephen R. Llewelyn, 3:20–31. NewDocs. Grand Rapids, Mich.: Eerdmans, 1983.

Horsley, G. H. R. "The Inscriptions of Ephesos and the New Testament." *NovT* 34, no. 2 (1992): 105–68.

Horsley, G. H. R., and S. C. Barton. "A Hellenistic Cult Group and the New Testament." *JAC* 24 (1981): 7–41.

Horst, Johannes. *Proskynein: Zur Anbetung Im Urchristentum Nach Ihrer Religionsgeschichtlichen Eigenart*. Gütersloh: Bertelsmann, 1932.

Horst, Pieter Willem van der. "Jews and Christians in Aphrodisias in the Light of Their Relations in Other Cities of Asia Minor." *NedTT* 43 (1989): 106–7.

Hort, Fenton John Anthony. *The Apocalypse of St. John I-III: The Greek Text with Introduction, Commentary, and Additional Notes*. London, U.K.: MacMillan & Co., 1908.

Horton, George. *The Blight of Asia: An Account of the Systematic Extermination of Christian Populations by Mohammedans and of the Culpability of Certain Great Power; with the True Story of the Burning of Smyrna*. Indianapolis, Ind.: Bobbs-Merrill, 1953.

Hough, Lynn Harold, and Martin Rist. "The Revelation of St. John the Divine." In *The Interpreter's Bible*, edited by George A. Buttrick, 12:345–613. Nashville, Tenn.: Abingdon, 1957.

Houston, George W. *Inside Roman Libraries: Book Collections and Their Management in Antiquity*. Raleigh, NC: University of North Carolina Press, 2014.

How, Walter W., and Joseph Wells, eds. *A Commentary on Herodotus: With Introduction and Appendices*. Vol. 2. 2 vols. Oxford, U.K.: Oxford University Press, 1990.

Howard-Brook, Wes, and Anthony Gwyther. *Unveiling Empire: Reading Revelation Then and Now*. The Bible and Liberation. Maryknoll, N.Y.: Orbis Books, 1999.

Howgego, Christopher. *Ancient History from Coins*. Approaching the Ancient World. New York, N.Y.: Routledge, 2002.

Hoz, María Paz de. *Die Lydischen Kulte Im Lichte Der Griechischen Inschriften*. AMStud. 36. Bonn: Habelt, 1999.

Hubbard, Moyer V. *Christianity in the Greco-Roman World: A Narrative Introduction*. Peabody, Mass.: Hendrickson, 2010.

Huffmon, Herbert B. "Prophecy in the Mari Letters." *BA* 31 (1968): 101–24.

———. "The Covenant Lawsuit in the Prophets." *JBL* 68, no. 4 (1959): 285–95.

———. "The Treaty Background of Hebrew Yāda'." *BASOR* 181 (1966): 31–37.

Huffmon, Herbert B., and Simon B. Parker. "A Further Note on the Treaty Background of Hebrew Yāda'." *BASOR* 184 (1966): 36–38.

Hughes, Lisa. "Dyeing in Ancient Italy? Evidence for the Purpurarii." In *Ancient Textiles: Production, Craft and Society*, edited by Carole Gillis and Marie-Louise B. Nosch, 87–92. Oxford, U.K.: Oxbow, 2007.

Hughes, Philip Edgcumbe. *The Book of the Revelation: A Commentary*. PNTC 16. Grand Rapids, Mich.: Eerdmans, 1990.

Hull, E. "Earthquake." In *DBib*, edited by James Hastings, Frederick C. Grant, and Harold. H. Rowley, 1:634–35. New York, N.Y.: Scribner's Sons, 1909.

Hurschmann, Rolf. "Seat." In *BrillPaulyA*, edited by Hubert Cancik and Helmuth Schneider, translated by Christine F. Salazar and Francis G. Gentry. Leiden: Brill, 2006. http://dx.doi.org/10.1163/1574-9347_bnp_e1124640.

Hurtado, Larry W. "Revelation 4–5 in the Light of Jewish Apocalyptic Analogies." *JSNT* 25 (1985): 105–24.

Huttner, Ulrich R. "Die Färber von Laodikeia Und Hierapolis . Eine Nachricht Aus Dem Corpus Der Alchemisten." *MBAH* 26 (2008): 139–57.

———. *Early Christianity in the Lycus Valley*. Translated by David Green. AJEC: ECAM, 85.1. Leiden: Brill, 2013.

———. "Wolf Und Eber: Die Flüsse von Laodikeia in Phrygien." In *Internationales Kolloquium Zur Kaiserzeitlichen Münzprägung Kleinasiens, 27.-30. April 1994 in Der Staatlichen Münzsammlung, München, Mailand*, edited by Johannes Nollé, Bernhard Overbeck, and Peter Weiss, 93–109. Nomismata 1. Milano: Ennerre, 1997.

Inan, Jale, and Elisabeth Rosenbaum. *Roman and Early Byzantine Portrait Sculpture in Asia Minor*. Oxford, U.K.: Oxford University Press, 1966.

Instone-Brewer, David. "The Eighteen Benedictions and the Minim before 70 CE." *JTS* 54, no. 1 (April 1, 2003): 25–44.

Israelowich, Ido. *Patients and Healers in the High Roman Empire*. Baltimore, Md.: Johns Hopkins University Press, 2015.

———. *Society, Medicine and Religion in the Sacred Tales of Aelius Aristides*. Leiden: Brill, 2012.

Jackson, Ralph P. J. "Eye Medicine in the Roman Empire." In *ANRW II*, edited by Wolfgang Haase and Hildegard Temporini, 37.3:2226–51. Berlin: De Gruyter, 1996.

Jacoby, Felix , ed. *Die Fragmente Der Griechischen Historiker*. Translated by Felix Jacoby. Part 2 Zeitgeschichte: A: Universalgeschichte Und Hellenika. Leiden: Brill Academic, 2004.

Jahreshefte des Österreichischen Archäologischen Institutes in Wien. Vol. 26. Wien: ÖAI, 1930.

Jayne, Walter Addison. *Healing Gods of Ancient Civilizations*. New Haven, Conn.: Yale University Press, 1925.

Jeffers, James S. *The Greco-Roman World of the New Testament Era: Exploring the Background of Early Christianity*. Downers Grove, Ill.: InterVarsity, 1999.

Jenkins, Ferrell. *The Old Testament in the Book of Revelation*. Grand Rapids, Mich.: Baker, 1976.

Jensen, Lloyd B. "Royal Purple of Tyre." *JNES* 22 (1963): 104–18.

Jeremias, Joachim. *Parables of Jesus*. 2 rev. Upper Saddle River, N.J.: Prentice Hall, 1972.

Jewett, Robert. "Mapping the Route of Paul's 'Second Missionary Journey' from Dorylaeum to Troas." *TynBul* 48, no. 1 (1997): 1–22.

Jobst, Werner. "Das 'Öffentliche Freudenhaus' in Ephesos." *JÖAI* 51 (1976): 61–84.

Johns, Loren L. *The Lamb Christology of the Apocalypse of John: An Investigation into Its Origins and Rhetorical Force*. WUNT 167. Tübingen: Siebeck, 2003.

Johnson, Alan F. "Revelation." In *Hebrews-Revelation*, edited by Tremper Longman and David E Garland, Revised., 573–789. EBC 13. Grand Rapids, Mich.: Zondervan, 2006.

Johnson, Alan F., Dick T. France, George H. Guthrie, Daryl Charles, and Tom Thatcher. *Hebrews - Revelation*. Edited by Tremper Longman III and David E. Garland. Revised. EBC 13. Grand Rapids, Mich.: Zondervan, 2006.

———. *Hebrews - Revelation*. Edited by Tremper Longman III and David E. Garland. Revised. EBC 13. Grand Rapids, Mich.: Zondervan, 2006.

Johnson, Dennis E. *Triumph of the Lamb : A Commentary on Revelation*. Phillipsburg, N.J.: P&R, 2001.

Johnson, Gary J. "De Conspiratione Delatorum: Pliny and the Christians Revisited." *Latomus* 47, no. 2 (1988): 417–22.

Johnson, Lora Lee. "The Hellenistic and Roman Library: Studies Pertaining to Their Architectural Form." Ph.D. diss., Brown University, 1989.

Johnson, Luke Timothy. *The Acts of the Apostles*. Edited by Daniel J. Harrington. SPS 5. Collegeville, Minn.: Liturgical, 1992.

———. "The New Testament's AntiJewish Slander and the Conventions of Ancient Polemic." *JBL* 108 (1989): 419–41.

Johnson, Richard R. "Ancient and Medieval Accounts of the 'Invention' of Parchment." *CSCA* 3 (January 1, 1970): 115–22.

Johnson, Sherman E. "Asia Minor and Early Christianity." In *Judaism and Christianity in the Age of Constantine* , edited by Jacob Neusner, 2:77–145. Leiden: Brill, 1975.

———. "Laodicea and Its Neighbors." *BA* 13, no. 1 (1950): 1–18.

———. "The Apostle Paul and the Riot in Ephesus ." *LTQ* 14 (1979): 79–88.

Johnson, Sherman Elbridge. "A Sabazios Inscription from Sardis ." In *Religions in Antiquity: Essays in Memory of Erwin Ramsdell Goodenough*, edited by Jacob Neusner, 542–50. Eugene, Or.: Wipf & Stock, 2004.

———. "Sabaoth/Sabazios : A Curiosity in Ancient Religion." *LTQ* 13, no. 4 (October 1978): 97–103.

———. *The Present State of Sabazios Research*. Berlin: De Gruyter, 1984.

Johnson, William A., and Holt N. Parker, eds. *Ancient Literacies: The Culture of Reading in Greece and Rome : The Culture of Reading in Greece and Rome*. Oxford, U.K.: Oxford University Press, 2009.

Johnston, Ann. "The Provinces After Commodus." In *The Oxford Handbook of Greek and Roman Coinage*, edited by William E. Metcalf, 453–67. Oxford, U.K.: Oxford University Press, 2012.

Jolly, Karen Louise. *Tradition and Diversity: Christianity in a World Context to 1500*. New York, N.Y.: Routledge, 2015.

Jones, A. H. M. *The Cities of the Eastern Roman Provinces*. 2nd ed. Oxford University Press Academic Monograph. Eugene, Oreg.: Wipf & Stock, 2004.

———. *The Greek City: From Alexander to Justinian*. Oxford, U.K.: Clarendon, 1940.

Jones, Arnold Hugh Martin, ed. *Studies in Roman Government and Law*. 2nd ed. Oxford, U.K.: Blackwell, 1963.

Jones, Christopher P. "Aelius Aristides and the Asklepieion." In *Pergamon-Citadel of the Gods: Archaeological Record, Literary Description, and Religious Development*, edited by Helmut Koester, 63–76. Harrisburg, Pa.: Trinity Press International, 1998.

———. *The Roman World of Dio Chrysostom*. Cambridge, Mass.: Harvard University Press, 1978.

Jongkees, J. H. "Gottesnamen in Lydischen Inschriften." *Mnemosyne* 3, no. 6 (1938): 355–57.

Joshel, S. R. *Work, Identity and Legal Status at Rome : A Study of the Occupational Inscriptions*. Norman, Okla.: University of Oklahoma Press, 1992.

Judge, Edwin Arthur. "The Social Pattern of Christian Groups in the First Century: Some Prolegomena to the Study of New Testament Ideas of Social Obligation." In *Social Distinctives of the Christians in the First Century: Pivotal Essays by E. A. Judge*, edited by David M. Scholer, 1–56. Grand Rapids, Mich.: Baker Academic, 2007.

———. *The Social Pattern of the Christian Groups in the First Century: Some Prolegomena to the Study of New Testament Ideas of Social Obligation*. Wheaton, Ill.: Tyndale, 1960.

Kaimakis, D. *Die Kyraniden*. Beiträge Zur Klassichen Philologie 76. Meisenheim am Glan: Sophie, 1976.

Kalimi, Isaac, and James D. Purvis. "The Hiding of the Temple Vessels in Jewish and Samaritan Literature." *CBQ* 56, no. 4 (1994): 679–85.

Kalluveettil, Paul. *Paul , Declaration and Covenant: A Comprehensive Review of Covenant Formulae from the Old Testament and the Ancient Near East*. AnBib 88. Rome : Biblical Institute, 1982.

Kampmann, Ursula. "Homonoia Politics in Asia Minor." In *Pergamon-Citadel of the Gods: Archaeological Record, Literary Description, and Religious Development*, edited by Helmut Koester, 373–93. Harrisburg, Pa.: Morehouse, 2002.

Karavites, Peter. *Promise-Giving and Treaty-Making Homer and the Near East*. Leiden: Brill, 1992.

Karmon, Nira. "The Purple Dye Industry in Antiquity." In *Colors from Nature: Natural Colors in Ancient Times*, edited by Ḥagit Sorek and Etan Ayalon, 35–37. Eretz-Israel Museum, 1993.

Karmon, Nira, and Ehud Spanier. "Archaeological Evidence of the Purple Dye Industry from Israel ." In *The Royal Purple and the Biblical Blue: Argaman and Tekhelet: The Study of Chief Rabbi Dr. Isaac Herzog on the Dye Industries in Ancient Israel and Recent Scientific Contributions*, edited by Ehud Spanier, 147–58. Jerusalem , Israel: Keter, 1987.

Karrer, Martin. *Die Johannesoffenbarung Als Brief: Studien Zu Ihrem Literarischen, Historischen Und Theologischen Ort*. Vol. 1. FRLANT 140. Göttingen: Vandenhoeck & Ruprecht, 1986.

Karweise, Stefan. "Ephesos." *RE Supp* 12 (1970): 323–26.

Kästner, Voker. "Pergamon and the Attalids ." In *Pergamon and the Hellenistic Kingdoms of the Ancient World*, edited by Carlos A. Picón and Seán Hemingway, 32–39. Yale University Press, 2016.

Kazhdan, Alexander P. "Maurozomes." In *The Oxford Dictionary of Byzantium* , edited by Alexander P. Kazhdan, 1319–20. Oxford, U.K.: Oxford University Press, 1991.

Kearsley, Rosalinde A. "Asiarchs ." In *The Book of Acts in Its Graeco-Roman Setting*, edited by David W. Gill and Conrad H. Gempf, 2:362–76. Book of Acts in Its First Century Setting 2. Grand Rapids, Mich.: Eerdmans, 1994.

———. "Asiarchs ." Edited by David Noel Freedman, Gary A. Herion, David F. Graf, and John David Pleins. *ABD*. New York, N.Y.: Doubleday, 1996.

Kee, Howard C. "Self-Definition in the Asclepius Cult." In *Jewish and Christian Self-Definition: Self-Definition in the Graeco-Roman World*, edited by Ben F. Meyer and E. P. Sander, 3:118–36. Philadelphia , Pa.: Fortress, 1982.

Keener, Craig S. *Acts: An Exegetical Commentary: 3:1-14:28*. Vol. 2. 3 vols. Grand Rapids, Mich.: Baker Academic, 2013.

———. *Acts: An Exegetical Commentary: 15:1-23:35*. Vol. 3. 3 vols. Grand Rapids, Mich.: Baker Academic, 2014.

———. *Revelation*. Edited by Terry C. Muck. NIVAC 20. Grand Rapids, Mich.: Zondervan, 2000.

———. *The IVP Bible Background Commentary: New Testament*. 2nd ed. Downers Grove, Ill.: InterVarsity, 2004.

Keil, C. F., and Franz Delitzsch. *The Pentateuch*. Translated by James Martin. Vol. 1. 10 vols. Commentary on the Old Testament. Grand Rapids, Mich.: Eerdmans, 1976.

Keil, Carl F. *The Twelve Minor Prophets*. Edited by Carl F. Keil and Franz Delitzsch. Translated by James Martin. 10 vols. Commentary on the OT. Grand Rapids, Mich.: Eerdmans, 1977.

Keil, Carl Friedrich, and Franz Delitzsch. *The Pentateuch*. Translated by James Martin. Edinburgh, U.K.: T&T Clark, 1835.

Keil, Josef. "Die Erste Neokorie von Ephesos." *NZ* 48 (1919): 125–30.

———. *Zur Topographie Und Geschichte von Ephesos*. JÖAI 21–22. Vienna: ÖAI, 1922.

Keil, Josef, Anton von Premerstein, and Paul Wilhelm Kretschmer, eds. *Bericht über eine Reise in Lydien und der südlichen Aiolis, ausgeführt 1906 im Auftrage der Kaiserlichen Akademie der Wissenschaften*. Vol. 2. Kaiserliche [Österreichische] Akademie der Wissenschaften, Philosophisch-historische Klasse, Denkschriften 53. Vienna: Hölder, 1908.

Keil, Josef, E. Reisch, and F. Knoll. *Die Marienkirche in Ephesos*. FiE, 4.1. Wien: ÖAI, 1932.

Keitel, Elizabeth. "The Art of Losing: Tacitus and the Disaster Narrative." In *Ancient Historiography and Its Contexts: Studies in Honour of A. J. Woodman*, edited by Christina S. Kraus, John Marincola, and Christopher Pelling, 331–53. Oxford, U.K.: Oxford University Press, 2010.

Kekec, Tevhit. *Pergamon*. Istanbul: Hitit Color, 1987.

Kelhoffer, James A. *Miracle and Mission: The Authentication of Missionaries and Their Message in the Longer Ending of Mark*. WUNT 112. Tübingen: Mohr Siebeck, 2000.

Keller, Catherine. *Apocalypse Now and Then: A Feminist Guide to the End of the World*. Minneapolis, Minn.: Augsburg Fortress, 2009.

Kelshaw, Terence. *Send This Message to My Church: Christ's Words to the Seven Churches of Revelation*. Nashville, Tenn.: Nelson, 1984.

Kerényi, Karl. *Asklepios: Archetypal Image of the Physician's Existence*. Princeton, N.J.: Princeton University Press, 1959.

———. *The Heroes of the Greeks*. London, U.K.: Thames and Hudson, 1959.

Keresztes, Paul. "The Decian Libelli and Contemporary Literature." *Latomus* 34, no. 3 (1975): 761–81.

Kerkeslager, Allen R. ""The Day of the Lord, the 'Hour' in the Book of Revelation and Rev. 3:10." In *Annual National Meeting of the Society of Biblical Literature*. Kansas City, MO, 1991.

Kiddle, Martin. *The Revelation of St. John*. Edited by James Moffatt. 17 vols. MNTC 17. London, U.K.: Hodder & Stoughton, 1952.

Kiminas, Demetrius. *The Ecumenical Patriarchate: A History of Its Metropolitans with Annotated Hierarch Catalogs*. Orthodox Christianity 1. San Bernadino, Calif.: Wildside, 2009.

King, Philip J., and Lawrence E. Stager. *Life in Biblical Israel*. Louisville, Ky.: Westminster/Knox, 2001.

Kirby, John T. "The Rhetorical Situation of Revelation 1–3." *NTS* 34, no. 2 (1988): 197–207.

Kistemaker, Simon J. *Exposition of the Book of Revelation*. NTC 12. Grand Rapids, Mich.: Baker Academic, 2001.

———. *Exposition of the Epistle of James and the Epistles of John*. NTC 10. Grand Rapids, Mich.: Baker, 1986.

Kitchen, Kenneth A. *Ancient Orient and Old Testament*. Wheaton, Ill.: Tyndale, 1966.

———. "Manna." Edited by I. Howard Marshall, A. R. Millard, J. I. Packer, and D. J. Wiseman. *NBD*. Downers Grove, Ill.: InterVarsity, 1996.

———. *On the Reliability of the Old Testament*. Grand Rapids, Mich.: Eerdmans, 2003.

———. "The Fall and Rise of Covenant, Law and Treaty." *TB* 40 (1989): 118–35.

Kittel, Gerhard, and Gerhard Friedrich, eds. *Theological Dictionary of the New Testament*. Translated by Geoffrey W. Bromiley. Abridged. 10 vols. Grand Rapids, Mich.: Eerdmans, 1985.

Kittel, Gerhard, and Gerhard Friedrich, eds. *Theologisches Wörterbuch zum Neuen Testament*. 10 vols. Stuttgart, Germany, 1932–1979.

Klappert, Bertold. "Lord's Supper." Edited by Colin Brown. *NIDNTT*. Grand Rapids, Mich.: Zondervan, 1976.

Klauser, T., ed. *Reallexikon für Antike und Christentum*. 10 vols. Stuttgart, Germany: Hiersemann, 1950.

Kline, Meredith G. *Structure of Biblical Authority*. Grand Rapids, Mich.: Eerdmans, 1972.

———. *Treaty of the Great King : The Covenant Structure of Deuteronomy: Studies and Commentary*. Grand Rapids, Mich.: Eerdmans, 1963.

Klinzing, Georg. *Die Umdeutung des Kultus in der Qumrangemeinde und im Neuen Testament*. Göttingen: Vandenhoeck & Ruprecht, 1997.

Klose, Dietrich O. A. *Die Münzprägung Von Smyrna in Der Römischen Kaiserzeit*. Berlin: de Gruyter, 1987.

Knibbe, Dieter, and Helmut Engelmann. "Aus Ephesischen Skizzenbuchern." *JÖAI* 52 (1980): 19–61.

Knipfing, John R. "The Libelli of the Decian Persecution." *HTR* 16, no. 4 (1923): 345–90.

Knoppers, Gary N. "Ancient Near Eastern Royal Grants and the Davidic Covenant: A Parallel?" *JAOS* 116, no. 4 (1996): 670.

Knox, John. *Philemon among the Letters of Paul*. Chicago, Ill.: University of Chicago Press, 1960.

Koenen, Ludwig. "Eine Einladung Zur Kline Des Sarapis." *ZPE* 1 (1967): 121–26.

Koester, Craig R. *Revelation: A New Translation with Introduction and Commentary*. Edited by John J. Collins. AYBC 38A. New Haven, Conn.: Yale University Press, 2014.

———. "Roman Slave Trade and the Critique of Babylon in Revelation 18." *CBQ* 70, no. 4 (2008): 766–86.

———. "The Message to Laodicea and the Problem of Its Local Context: A Study in the Imagery in Rev 3.14–22." *NTS* 49, no. 3 (2003): 407–24.

Koester, Helmut. "Ephesos in Early Christian Literature." In *Ephesos Metropolis of Asia: An Interdisciplinary Approach to Its Archaeology, Religion, and Culture*, edited by Helmut Koester, 119–40. Harvard Theological Studies 41. Cambridge, Mass.: Harvard Divinity School, 1995.

———, ed. *Ephesos Metropolis of Asia: An Interdisciplinary Approach to Its Archaeology, Religion, and Culture*. HTS 41. Cambridge, Mass.: Harvard Divinity School, 1995.

———. "GNOMAI DIAPHORAI: The Origin and Nature of Diversification in the History of Early Christianity." In *Trajectories through Early Christianity*, edited by James McConkey Robinson and Helmut Koester, 114–57. Philadelphia : Fortress Press, 1971.

———. *Introduction to the New Testament: History, Culture, And Religion Of The Hellenistic Age*. Berlin: Gruyter, 1982.

Kohler, Kaufmann. *The Origins of the Synagogue and the Church*. New York, N.Y.: MacMillan, 1929.

König, Friedrich Wilhelm. *Die Persika des Ktesias von Knidos*. Graz: Weidner, 1972.

Konuk, Koray. "Asia Minor to the Ionian Revolt." In *The Oxford Handbook of Greek and Roman Coinage*, edited by William E. Metcalf, 43–60. Oxford, U.K.: Oxford University Press, 2012.

Koortbojian, Michael. "The Double Identity of Roman Portrait Statues: Costumes and Their Symoblism at Rome ." In *Roman Dress and the Fabrics of Roman Culture*, edited by Jonathan C. Edmondson and Alison Keith, 71–93. Phoenix Supplementary Volumes. Toronto, Can.: University of Toronto Press, 2009.

Koren, Zvi C. "High-Performance Liquid Chromatographic Analysis of an Ancient Tyrian Purple Dyeing Vat from Israel ." *IJC* 35 (1995): 117–24.

———. "HPLC Analysis of the Natural Scale Insect, Madder and Indigoid Dyes." *Journal of the Society of Dyers and Colourists* 110 (1994): 273–77.

———. "Methods of Dye Analysis Used at the Shenkar College Edelstein Centre in Israel." *Dyes in History and Archaeology* 11 (1993): 25–33.

———. "The First Optimal All-Murex All-Natural Purple Dyeing in the Eastern Mediterranean in a Millennium and a Half." *Dyes in History and Archaeology* 20 (2005): 136–49.

———. "The Purple Question Reinvestigated: Just What Is Really in That Purple Pigment?" In *20th Meeting of Dyes in History and Archaeology*. Instituut Collectie Nederland, Amsterdam, 2001.

Korobeinikov, Dimitri. *Byzantium and the Turks in the Thirteenth Century*. Oxford Studies in Byzantium. Oxford, U.K.: Oxford University Press, 2014.

Korošec, Viktor. *Hethitische Staatsverträge: Ein Beitrag Zu Ihrer Juristischen Wertung*. Leipzig: Weicher, 1931.

Kosmetatou, Elizabeth. "The Attalids of Pergamon." In *A Companion to the Hellenistic World*, edited by Andrew Erskine, 159–174. Blackwell Companions to the Ancient World. Oxford, U.K.: Blackwell, 2003.

Kotansky, Roy. "Incantations and Prayers for Salvation on Inscribed Greek Amulets." In *Magika Hiera: Ancient Greek Magic and Religion*, edited by Christopher A. Faraone and Dirk Obbink, 107–37. New York, N.Y.: Oxford University Press, 1997.

Koukouli-Chrysanthaki, Chaido. "Colonia Iulia Augusta Philippensis." In *Philippi at the Time of Paul and after His Death*, edited by Charalambos Bakirtzis and Helmut Koester, 5–36. Eugene, Oreg.: Wipf & Stock, 2009.

———. "Philippi." In *Brill's Companion to Ancient Macedon: Studies in the Archaeology and History of Macedon, 650 BC - 300 AD*, edited by Robin J. Fox and Robin Lane Fox, 437–52. Leiden: Brill, 2011.

Kousser, Rachel Meredith. *Hellenistic and Roman Ideal Sculpture: The Allure of the Classical*. Cambridge, U.K.: Cambridge University Press, 2008.

Kraabel, A. Thomas. "Impact of the Discovery of the Sardis Synagogue." In *Sardis from Prehistoric to Roman Times: Results of the Archaeological Exploration of Sardis, 1958-1975*, edited by George M. A. Hanfmann, William E. Mierse, and Clive Foss, 178–90. Cambridge, Mass.: Harvard University Press, 1983.

———. "Judaism in Western Asia Minor under the Roman Empire, with a Preliminary Study of the Jewish Community in Sardis, Lydia." Ph.D. diss., Harvard University, 1968.

———. "Melito the Bishop and the Synagogue at Sardis: Text and Context." In *Studies Presented to George M. A. Hanfmann*, edited by David Gordon Mitten, John Griffiths Pedley, and Jane Ayer Scott, 77–85. Mainz: P. von Zabern, 1971.

———. "The Diaspora Synagogue: Archaeological and Epigraphic Evidence since Sukenik." In *ANRW*, edited by Wolfgang Haase and Hildegard Temporini, 477–510. 2.19. Berlin: de Gruyter, 1979.

———. "The Roman Diaspora: Six Questionable Assumptions." *JJS* 33 (1982): 455–64.

Kraabel, A. Thomas, J. Andrew Overman, and Robert S. MacLennan, eds. *Diaspora Jews and Judaism: Essays in Honor Of, and in Dialogue With, A. Thomas Kraabel*. Atlanta, Ga.: Scholars Press, 1992.

Kraay, Colin M. *Archaic and Classical Greek Coins*. Berkeley, Calf.: University of California Press, 1976.

Kraft, Heinrich. *Die Offenbarung Des Johannes*. HNT 16a. Tübingen: Siebeck, 1974.

Krauss, Samuel. *Talmudische Archäologie*. 3 vols. Leipzig: Fock, 1910.

Kraybill, J. Nelson. *Apocalypse and Allegiance: Worship, Politics, and Devotion in the Book of Revelation*. Grand Rapids, Mich.: Brazos Press, 2010.

———. *Imperial Cult and Commerce in John's Apocalypse.* JSNTSup 132. Sheffield, U.K.: Sheffield Academic, 1999.

Kreitzer, Larry J. "Living in the Lycus Valley: Earthquake Imagery in Colossians, Philemon and Ephesians." In *Testimony and Interpretation: Early Christology in Its Judeo-Hellenistic Milieu. Studies in Honor of Petr Pokorný*, edited by Jiri Mrázek, Jan Roskovec, and Petr Pokorný, 81–94. JSNTSup 272. New York, N.Y.: Bloomsbury Academic, 2004.

Kreitzer, Larry Joseph. *Striking New Images: Roman Imperial Coinage and the New Testament World.* JSNTSup 134. Sheffield, U.K.: Sheffield Academic Press, 1996.

Krinzinger, Friedrich. *Ephesos: Architecture, Monuments and Sculpture.* Edited by Ahmet Ertuğ and Sabine Ladstätter. Istanbul: Ertuğ & Kocabıyık, 2007.

Krodel, Gerhard A. *Revelation.* ACNT. Minneapolis, Minn.: Augsburg Fortress, 1989.

Kroll, John H. "Greek Inscriptions of the Sardis Synagogue." *HTR* 94 (2001): 5–55.

———. "The Monetary Use of Weighed Bullion in Archaic Greece ." In *The Monetary Systems of the Greeks and Romans*, edited by W. V. Harris, 12–37. Oxford, U.K.: Oxford University Press, 2010.

Kumsar, Halil, Ömer Aydan, Celal Şimşek, and Francesco D'Andria. "Historical Earthquakes That Damaged Hierapolis and Laodikeia Antique Cities and Their Implications for Earthquake Potential of Denizli Basin in Western Turkey." *Bulletin of Engineering Geology and the Environment*, September 10, 2015, 1–18.

Kunze, Max, and Volker Kästner. *Der Altar von Pergamon: Hellenistische Und Römische Architektur.* 2nd ed. Antikensammlung II: Fuhrer Durch Die Ausstellung Des Pergamon Museums. Berlin: Henschelverlag Kunst und Gesellschaft, 1990.

Kupper, J. R. "Zimri-Lim et Ses Vassaux." In *Marchands, Diplomates et Empereurs: Études Sur La Civilisation Mésopotamienne Offertes À Paul Garelli*, edited by Dominique Charpin and Francis Joannès, 179–84. Paris, France: Recherche sur les civilisations, 1991.

Kuttner, Ann L. *Dynasty and Empire in the Age of Augustus : The Case of the Boscoreale Cups.* Berkeley, Calf.: University of California Press, 1995.

Laale, Hans Willer. *Ephesus (Ephesos): An Abbreviated History from Androclus to Constantine XI.* Bloomington, Ind.: WestBow, 2011.

Laborde, Leon de. *Voyage de l'Asie Mineure Par Mrs Alexandre de Laborde, Becker, Hall, et Leon de Laborde.* Paris, France: Firmin Didot, 1838.

Ladd, George Eldon. *A Commentary on the Revelation of John.* Grand Rapids, Mich.: Eerdmans, 1972.

———. *The Blessed Hope.* Grand Rapids, Mich.: Eerdmans, 1954.

Lafaye, Georges, René Cagnat, J. Toutain, and Victor Henry, eds. *Inscriptiones Graecae Ad Res Romanas Pertinentes.* 4 vols. Paris: Leroux, 1901.

Lagercrantz, Otto. *Papyrus Graecus Holmiensis.* Uppsala, Sweden: Almquist and Wiksells, 1913.

Lähnemann, Johannes. "Die sieben Sendschreiben der Johannes-Apokalypse: Dokumente für die Konfrontation des frühen Christentums mit hellenistisch/römischer Kultur und Religion in Kleinasien." In *Studien Zur Religion Und Kultur Kleinasiens*, edited by S. Sahin, E. Schwertheim, and J. Wagner, 516–39. Festschrift Fur Friedrich Karl Dorner Zum 65. Leiden: Brill Academic Pub, 1997.

Lambrecht, Jan. "Jewish Slander: A Note on Revelation 2:9–10." *ETL* 75, no. 4 (1999): 421–29.

———. "Paul's Farewell-Address at Miletus, Acts 20, 17-38." In *Les Actes Des Apôtres: Traditions, Rédaction, Théologie*, edited by Jacob Kremer, 307–37. BETL 48. Gembloux: Duculot, 1979.

———. "'Synagogues of Satan' (Rev. 2:9 and 3:9): Anti-Judaism in the Book of Revelation." In *Anti-Judaism and the Fourth Gospel*, edited by Reimund Bieringer, Didier Pollefeyt, and Frederique Vandecasteele-Vanneuville, 279–92. Louisville, Ky.: Westminster/Knox, 2001.

———. "The Book of Revelation and Apocalyptic in the New Testament." In *L'Apocalypse Johannique et L' Apocalyptique Dans Le NouveauTestament*, edited by Jan lambrecht, 1–18. Leuven: Leuven University Press, 1980.

Lampe, G. W. H., ed. *A Patristic Greek Lexicon*. 1 edition. Oxford, U.K.: Oxford University Press, 1961.

Lampe, Peter. "Acta 19 Im Spiegel Der Ephesischen Inschriften." *BZ* 36 (1992): 59–76.

Landfester, Manfred, and Francis G. Gentry, eds. *Brill's Encyclopaedia of the Ancient World New Pauly*. Translated by Christine F. Salazar and Francis G. Gentry. 28 vols. Leiden: Brill, 2007.

Lane, Eugene N. *Corpvs Monvmentorvm Religionis Dei Menis: Interpretations and Testimonia*. Vol. 3. Leiden: Brill, 1976.

———. "Men: A Neglected Cult of Roman Asia Minor." In *ANRW*, 2161–74. II.18.3. Berlin: De Gruyter, 1990.

Lane Fox, Robin. *Pagans and Christians*. New York, N.Y.: HarperCollins, 1988.

Lanfer, Peter T. "Allusion to and Expansion of the Tree of Life and Garden of Eden in Biblical and Pseudepigraphal Literature." In *Early Christian Literature and Intertextuality: Thematic Studies*, edited by Craig A. Evans and H. Danny Zacharias, 1:96–108. LNTS. London, U.K.: T&T Clark, 2009.

Langlands, Rebecca. *Sexual Morality in Ancient Rome*. Cambridge, U.K.: Cambridge University Press, 2009.

Lassus, Alain-Marie de. "Le Septénaire Des Lettres de L'apocalypse de Jean: De La Correction Au Témoignage Militant." Ph.D. diss., University of Strasbourg, 2005.

Laurence, Ray. *The Roads of Roman Italy: Mobility and Cultural Change*. New York, N.Y.: Routledge, 1999.

Laurence, Ray, and Gareth Sears. *The City in the Roman West, C. 250 BC-C. AD 250*. Cambridge, Mass.: Cambridge University Press, 2011.

Lausberg, Heinrich. *Handbook of Literary Rhetoric: A Foundation for Literary Study*. Edited by David E. Orton and R. Dean Anderson. Translated by Matthew T. Bliss, Annemiek Jansen, and David E. Orton. Leiden: Brill, 1998.

Laws, Sophie. *A Commentary on the Epistle of James*. BNTC 13. London, U.K.: A & C Black, 1980.

Le Grys, Alan. "Conflict and Vengeance in the Book of Revelation." *ExpTim* 104, no. 3 (1992): 76–80.

Le Quien, Michel. *Oriens christianus in quatuor patriarchatus digestus, in quo exhibentur Ecclesiae patriarchae caeterique praesules totius Orientis*. 3 vols. Paris: Typographia Regia, 1740.

Leadbetter, W. L. "Libellus of the Decian Persecution." In *NewDocs*, edited by G. H. R. Horsley, 2:180–85. Liverpool, U.K.: Liverpool University Press, 1982.

Leake, William Martin. *A Supplement to Numismata Hellenica: A Catalogue of Greek Coins*. London, U.K.: John Murray, 1859.

Lee, William. "The Revelation of St. John." In *The Holy Bible: With an Explanatory and Critical Commentary and a Revision of the Translation, by Bishops and Other Clergy of the Anglican Church*, edited by Frederic Charles Cook, 10:496–844. London, U.K.: Murray, 1881.

LeMaire, André. "Fragments from the Book of Balaam Found at Deir Alla: Text Foretells Cosmic Disaster." *BAR* 11, no. 5 (1985): 26–39.

Lenormant, Françoise. "Sol Elagablus." *RHR* 3 (1881): 310.

Lenski, Richard C. H. *The Interpretation of St. John's Revelation*. CNT. Minneapolis, Minn.: Augsburg Fortress, 1963.

———. *The Interpretation of the Acts of the Apostles*. CNT. Minneapolis, Minn.: Augsburg Fortress, 1961.

———. *The Interpretation of The Epistle to the Hebrews and The Epistle of James*. Minneapolis, Minn.: Augsburg, 1966.

Lepsius, Johann. "Dr. Johann Lepsius on the Symbolic Language of the Apocalypse." Edited by William M. Ramsay. Translated by H. Ramsay. *The Expositor* 8, no. 1 (1911): 160–80.

Lethaby, W. R. *The Sculptures of the Later Temple of Artemis at Ephesus*. London, U.K.: The Society for the Promotion of Hellenic Studies, 1913.

———. "The Earlier Temple of Artemis at Ephesus." *JHS* 37 (1917): 1–16.

Levenson, Jon D. *Sinai and Zion*. New York, N.Y.: HarperOne, 1987.

Leverett, Frederick Percival, ed. *Latin Lexicon*. Philadelphia, Pa.: Peter Reilly Co., 1931.

Levick, Barbara. *Roman Colonies in Southern Asia Minor*. Oxford, U.K.: Clarendon Press, 1967.

Levine, Lee I. "Synagogues." In *EDEJ*, edited by John J. Collins and Daniel C. Harlow, 1260–71. Grand Rapids, Mich.: Eerdmans, 2010.

———. *The Ancient Synagogue: The First Thousand Years*. 2nd ed. New Haven, Conn.: Yale University Press, 2005.

Lewis, Jack P. "Jamnia (Jabneh), Councel of." Edited by David Noel Freedman, Gary A. Herion, David F. Graf, and John David Pleins. *ABD*. New York, N.Y.: Doubleday, 1996.

———. "What Do We Mean by Jabneh?" *JBR* 32 (1964): 125–32.

Lewis, Naphtali, and Meyer Reinhold, eds. *Roman Civilization*. 3rd ed. 2 vols. New York, N.Y.: Columbia University Press, 1991.

Ley, Anne. "Artemis." In *BrillPauly*, 2:145–46. Leiden: Brill, 2007.

Liddell, Henry George, and Robert Scott. *An Intermediate Greek-English Lexicon*. 9th ed. Oxford, U.K.: Clarendon, 1889.

LiDonnici, Lynn R. *The Epidaurian Miracle Inscriptions*. South Florida Studies in the History of Judaism 36. Atlanta, Ga.: Scholars Press, 1995.

———. "The Images of Artemis Ephesia and Greco-Roman Worship: A Reconsideration." *HTR* 85, no. 4 (October 1992): 389–415.

Lieu, Judith M. "Accusations of Jewish Persecution in Early Christian Sources, with Particular Reference to Justin Martyr and the Martyrdom of Polycarp." In *Tolerance and Intolerance in Early Judaism and Christianity*, edited by Graham N. Stanton and Gedaliahu A. G Stroumsa, 279–95. Cambridge, U.K.: Cambridge University Press, 1998.

Lightfoot, J. B. *The Apostolic Fathers (APF)*. Edited by J. R. Harmer. 2nd ed. London, U.K.: Macmillan, 1898.

Lightfoot, John. *Horæ Hebraicæ et Talmudicæ*. Translated by Robert Gandell. 4 vols. Oxford, U.K.: Oxford University Press, 1859.

Lightfoot, Joseph B. *St. Paul's Epistle to the Galatians*. 6th ed. London, U.K.: MacMillan, 1880.

———. *The Apostolic Fathers: Greek Texts and English Translations*. Edited by Michael W. Holmes. Translated by J. R. Harmer. 2nd ed. Grand Rapids, Mich.: Baker Academic, 1989.

Lightfoot, Joseph Barber. *Saint Paul's Epistles to the Colossians and to Philemon*. Classic Commentary Library. Grand Rapids, Mich.: Zondervan, 1880.

Lilje, Hanns. *The Last Book of the Bible: The Meaning of the Revelation of St. John*. Translated by Olive Wyon. Philadelphia, Pa.: Muhlenberg, 1957.

Lincoln, Andrew T. *Truth on Trial: The Lawsuit Motif in the Fourth Gospel*. Peabody, Mass.: Hendrickson, 2000.

Lindars, Barnabas. *New Testament Apologetic: The Doctrinal Significance of the Old Testament Quotations*. London, U.K.: SCM, 1973.

———. "Response to Richard Bauckham: The Idiomatic Use of Bar Enasha." *JSNT* 23, no. 1 (February 1985): 35–41.

Lindberg, Christine A., Katherine M. Isaacs, and Ruth Handlin Manley, eds. *Oxford American Dictionary & Thesaurus*. 2nd ed. New York, N.Y.: Oxford University Press, USA, 2009.

Linderski, Jerzy. "Sellisternium." Edited by Simon Hornblower and Anthony J. S. Spawforth. *OCD*. Oxford, U.K.: Clarendon, 2003.

Link, Hans-Georg. "Ἐλέγχω." Edited and translated by Colin Brown. *NIDNTT*. Grand Rapids, Mich.: Zondervan, 1986.

Lioy, Dan. *The Book of Revelation in Christological Focus*. Edited by Hemchand Gossai. StBL 58. New York, N.Y.: Peter Lang, 2003.

Littman, R. J., and M. L. Littman. "Galen and the Antonine Plague." *The American Journal of Philology* 94, no. 3 (1973): 243–55.

Liu, Jinyu. *Collegia Centonariorum: The Guilds of Textile Dealers in the Roman West*. Columbia Studies in the Classical Tradition 34. Brill, 2009.

Loane, Marcus L. *They Overcame: An Exposition of the First Three Chapters of Revelation*. Grand Rapids, Mich.: Baker, 1981.

Lohmeyer, Ernst. *Die Offenbarung Des Johannes*. HNT 16. Tübingen: Siebeck, 1926.

Lohse, Eduard. *Die Offenbarung Des Johannes*. Das Neue Testament Deutsch 11. Göttingen: Vandenhoeck & Ruprecht, 1993.

———. "Synagogue of Satan and Church of God." *SEÅ* 58 (1993): 105–23.

Long, George. "Ephesus." In *Dictionary of Greek and Roman Geography*, edited by William Smith, 833–39. London, U.K.: Murray, 1878.

López, René A. "Israelite Covenants in the Light of Ancient Near Eastern Covenants: Part 1." *CTSJ* 9, no. 4 (2003): 92–111.

———. "Israelite Covenants in the Light of Ancient Near Eastern Covenants: Part 2." *CTSJ* 10, no. 4 (2004): 72–106.

Lotz, John Paul. "The Homonoia Coins of Asia Minor and Ephesians 1:21." *TynBul* 50, no. 2 (1999): 173–88.

Lövestam, Evald. "Apokalypsen 3:8b." *SEÅ* 30 (1965): 91–101.

Lowry, Rich. *Admonition and Curse*. London, U.K.: T&T Clark, 2004.

Lucas, E. C. "Covenant, Treaty, and Prophecy." *Themelios* 8, no. 1 (1982): 19–23.

Luckenbill, Daniel David. *Ancient Records of Assyria and Babylon: Historical Records of Assyria from Sargon to the End*. Vol. 2. 2 vols. Chicago, Ill.: University Of Chicago Press, 1927.

Luger, Yehezkel. *The Weekday Amidah in the Cairo Genizah [Hebrew]*. Jerusalem, Israel: Orhot, 2002.

Luijendijk, AnneMarie. *Greetings in the Lord: Early Christians and the Oxyrhynchus Papyri*. Cambridge, Mass.: Harvard University Press, 2009.

Lunde, Jonathan M. "Repentance." Edited by Joel B. Green, I. Howard Marshall, and Scot McKnight. *DJG*. Downers Grove, Ill.: InterVarsity, 1992.

Lupieri, Edmundo F. *A Commentary on the Apocalypse of John*. Translated by Maria Poggi Johnson and Adam Kamesar. Italian Texts and Studies on Religion and Society. Grand Rapids, Mich.: Eerdmans, 1999.

Lydus, Joannes. *Liber de Mensibus*. Edited by Richard Wünsch. Leipzig: Teubneri, 1898.

MacDonald, William Graham. *Greek Enchiridion: A Concise Handbook of Grammar for Translation and Exegesis*. Peabody, Mass.: Hendrickson, 1986.

Mach, Michael. *Entwicklungsstadien Des Jüdischen Engelglaubens in Vorrabbinischer Zeit*. TSAJ 34. Tübingen: Mohr Siebeck, 1992.

MacKay, W. M. "Another Look at the Nicolaitans." *EQ* 45, no. 2 (1973): 111–15.

MacKendrick. *The Greek Stones Speak: The Story of Archaeology in Greek Lands*. 2nd ed. New York, N.Y.: Norton & Company, 1983.

MacLeod, David J. "The Lion Who Is a Lamb: An Exposition of Revelation 5:1-7." *BSac* 164, no. 655 (2007): 323–40.

MacLeod, Donald. "The Lion and the Lamb." *PSB* 44, no. 3 (1950): 61–62.

MacMullen, Ramsay. *Paganism in the Roman Empire*. New Haven, Conn.: Yale University Press, 1983.

———. *Roman Social Relations: 50 BC to AD 284*. New Haven, Conn.: Yale University Press, 1974.

———. "Women in Public in the Roman Empire." *Historia* 29 (1980): 208–18.

MacMullen, Ramsay, and Eugene N. Lane, eds. *Paganism and Christianity 100-425 C. E.: A Sourcebook*. Minneapolis, Minn.: Augsburg Fortress, 1992.

Magie, David. *Roman Rule in Asia Minor to the End of the Third Century After Christ*. Edited by T. James Luce. 2 vols. Roman History. New York, N.Y.: Arno, 1975.

Magness, Jodi. "The Date of the Sardis Synagogue in Light of the Numismatic Evidence." *AJA* 109 (2005): 443–75.

Malay, Hasan. *Researches in Lydia, Mysia and Aiolis*. Tituli Asiae Minoris, Supplement 23. Vienna: Österreichischen Akademie der Wissenschaften, 1999.

———. "The Sanctuary of Meter Phileis near Philadelphia." *EA* 6 (1985): 111–26.

———. "Φιλάνπελοι in Phrygia and Lydia." *EA* 38 (2005): 42–44.

Malina, Bruce J. *On the Genre and Message of Revelation: Star Visions and Sky Journeys*. Peabody, Mass.: Hendrickson, 1995.

———. *The Palestinian Manna Tradition: The Manna Tradition in the Palestinian Targums and its Relationship to the New Testament Writings*. AGSU 7. Leiden: Brill, 1968.

———. "Wealth and Poverty in the New Testament and Its World." *Interpretation* 41 (1987): 356–67.

Malina, Bruce J., and Jerome H. Neyrey. "Honor and Shame in Luke-Acts: Pivotal Values of the Mediterranean World." In *The Social World of Luke-Acts: Models for Interpretation*, edited by Jerome H. Neyrey, 25–66. Grand Rapids, Mich.: Baker Academic, 1999.

Malina, Bruce J., and John J. Pilch, eds. *Handbook of Biblical Social Values*. Grand Rapids, Mich.: Baker Academic, 2009.

Mallet, Robert, and John William Mallet. *The Earthquake Catalogue of the British Association: With the Discussion, Curves, and Maps, Etc*. British Association for the Advancement of Science. London, U.K.: Taylor & Francis, 1858.

Mallowan, Max. "Cyrus the Great." *Iran* 10 (1972): 1–17.

Mango, Andrew. *Ataturk: The Biography of the Founder of Modern Turkey*. Woodstock, N.Y.: The Overlook Press, 2002.

Manz, Beatrice Forbes. *The Rise and Rule of Tamerlane*. Cambridge, U.K.: Cambridge University Press, 1999.

Marcellinus. *Comes: Chronicon*. Edited by Jacques Paul Migne. Patrologia Latina 51. Paris, France, 1861.

Markschies, Christoph. "'Sessio Ad Dexteram': Bemerkungen Zu Einem Altchristlichen Bekenntnismotiv in Der Christologischen Diskussion Der Altkirchlichen Theologen." In *Le Trône de Dieu*, edited by M. Philonenko, 252–317. Tübingen: Mohr-Siebeck, 1993.

Marshall, I. Howard, Alan R. Millard, James I. Packer, and Donald J. Wiseman, eds. *New Bible Dictionary*. 3rd ed. Downers Grove, Ill.: InterVarsity, 1996.

Marshall, I. Howard. "Son of Man." Edited by Joel B. Green, Scot McKnight, and I. Howard Marshall. *DJG*. Downers Grove, Ill.: InterVarsity, 1992.

Marshall, John W. "Columna." In *DGRA*, edited by William Smith, 1:489-96. London, U.K.: Murray, 1890.

———. *Parables of War: Reading John's Jewish Apocalypse*. Edited by Peter Richardson. SCJS 10. Waterloo, Ont.: Wilfrid Laurier University Press, 2001.

Martin, Hugh. *The Seven Letters: Christ's Message to His Church*. Philadelphia, Pa.: Westminster, 1956.

Martin, Ralph P. *Ephesians, Colossians, and Philemon*. Interpretation. Atlanta, Ga.: Westminster John Knox Press, 1991.

Martin, Ralph P., and Peter H. Davids, eds. *Dictionary of the Later New Testament and Its Developments*. IVPBD. Downers Grove, Ill.: InterVarsity, 1997.

Martínez, Florentino García, and W. G. E. Watson. *The Dead Sea Scrolls Translated: The Qumran Texts in English*. 2nd ed. Leiden: Brill Academic, 1997.

Mason, Steve. "Jews, Judeans, Judaizing, Judaism: Problems of Categorization in Ancient History." *JSJ* 38 (2007): 457–512.

Mathews, Mark D. "The Function of Imputed Speech in the Apocalypse of John." *CBQ* 74, no. 2 (2012): 319–38.

Mathewson, David. "Revelation in Recent Genre Criticism: Some Implications for Interpretation." *TJ* 13 (1992): 193–213.

Matoïan, Valérie, and Juan-Pablo Vita. "Wool Production and Economy at Ugarit." In *Wool Economy in the Ancient Near East*, edited by Catherine Breniquet and Cécile Michel, 310–39. Oxford, U.K.: Oxbow Books, 2014.

Mattern, Susan P. *The Prince of Medicine: Galen in the Roman Empire*. Oxford, U.K.: Oxford University Press, 2013.

Mattingly, Harold B., and Edward Allen Sydenham, eds. *The Roman Imperial Coinage: Vespasian to Hadrian (69–138)*. Vol. 2. 13 vols. London, U.K.: Spink & Son, 1926.

Mayo, Philip L. *Those Who Call Themselves Jews: The Church and Judaism in the Apocalypse of John*. PTMS 60. Eugene, Oreg.: Pickwick, 2006.

Mayor, Adrienne. *The Amazons : Lives and Legends of Warrior Women across the Ancient World*. Princeton, N.J.: Princeton University Press, 2014.

———. *The Poison King: The Life and Legend of Mithradates, Rome's Deadliest Enemy*. Princeton, N.J.: Princeton University Press, 2011.

Mayor, Joseph B. *The Epistle of Saint James*. 3rd ed. Minneapolis, Minn.: Klock & Klock, 1977.

Mazzaferri, Frederick David. *The Genre of the Book of Revelation from a Source Critical Perspective*. Berlin: de Gruyter, 1989.

———. "Martyria Iesou Revisited." *BT* 39, no. 1 (1988): 114–22.

McCabe, Donald F. *Smyrna Inscriptions: Texts and List*. Edited by Tad Brennan and R. Neil Elliott. Princeton, N.J.: Princeton Institute for Advanced Study, 1988.

McCarter Jr., P. Kyle. "The Balaam Texts from Deir 'Alla: The First Combination." *BASOR* 239 (1980): 49–60.

McCarthy, Dennis J. *Treaty and Covenant: A Study in the Ancient Oriental Documents and in the Old Testament*. AnBib 21. Rome : Biblical Institute, 1981.

McDonagh, Bernard. *Blue Guide: Turkey*. 3rd ed. London, U.K.: A & C Black, 2001.

McGing, Brian C. *The Foreign Policy of Mithridates VI Eupator, King of Pontus*. Leiden: Brill, 1986.

McGinn, Thomas A. J. *Prostitution, Sexuality, and the Law in Ancient Rome* . Oxford, U.K.: Oxford University Press, 2003.

———. *The Economy of Prostitution in the Roman World: A Study of Social History and the Brothel*. Ann Arbor, Mich.: University of Michigan Press, 2004.

McGovern, Patrick E., J. Lazar, and R. H. Michel. "Caveats on the Analysis of Indigoid Dyes by Mass Spectrometry." *Journal of the Society of Dyers and Colourists* 107 (1991): 2801.

———. "The Chemical Composition of the Indigoid Dyes Derived from the Hypobranchial Glandular Secretions of Murex Mollusks." *Journal of the Society of Dyers and Colourists* 108, no. 3 (1992): 145–50.

McGovern, Patrick E., and R. H. Michel. "Royal Purple Dye: The Chemical Reconstruction of the Ancient Mediterranean Industry." *Accounts of Chemical Research* 23 (1990): 152–58.

———. "Royal Purple Dye: Tracing Chemical Origins of the Industry." *Analytical Chemistry* 57 (1985): 1514–22.

McKeating, H. "Sanctions Against Adultery in Ancient Israelite Society, with Some Reflections on Methodology in the Study of Old Testament Ethics." *JSOT* 11 (1979): 57–72.

McKechnie, Paul. "Roman Law and the Laws of the Medes and Persians : Decius' and Valerian's Persecutions of Christianity." In *Thinking Like a Lawyer: Essays on Legal History and General History for John Crook on His Eightieth Birthday*, edited by J. A. Crook and Paul McKechnie, 253–69. Mnemosyne, Bibliotheca Classica Batava Supplementum 231. Leiden: Brill Academic, 2002.

McMahon, Gregory , and Sharon R. Steadman, eds. *The Oxford Handbook of Ancient Anatolia*. Oxford, U.K.: Oxford University Press, 2011.

McRay, John. *Archaeology and the New Testament*. Grand Rapids, Mich.: Baker, 1991.

Meeks, Wayne A. *The First Urban Christians: The Social World of the Apostle Paul.* 2nd ed. New Haven, Conn.: Yale University Press, 2003.

Meiggs, Russell. *Roman Ostia*. Oxford, U.K.: Clarendon Press, 1973.

Meinardus, Otto F. A. *St. John of Patmos and the Seven Churches of the Apocalypse*. In the Footsteps of the Saints. New York, N.Y.: Caratzas, 1979.

———. *St. Paul in Ephesus and the Cities of Galatia and Cyprus*. In the Footsteps of the Saints. New Rochelle, N.Y.: Caratzas, 1979.

———. "The Christian Remains of the Seven Churches of the Apocalypse." *BA* 37, no. 3 (September 1, 1974): 69–82.

Mellink, Machteld J. "Archaeology in Asia Minor." *AJA* 81, no. 3 (1977): 289–321.

Mellor, Ronald. "The Dedications on the Capitoline Hill." *Chiron* 8 (1978): 319–30.

———. *Thea Rhōmē: The Worship of the Goddess Roma in the Greek World*. Hypomnemata 42. Göttingen: Vandenhoeck & Ruprecht, 1975.

Mendenhall, George E. "Covenant." Edited by G. A. Buttrick and Keith R. Crim. *IDB*. Nashville, Tenn.: Abingdon, 1962, 1:1179–1202.

———. "Covenant Forms in Israelite Tradition." *BA* 17 (1954): 50–76.

Mendenhall, George E. *Law and Covenant in Israel and the Ancient Near East*. Pittsburgh: Biblical Colloquium, 1955.

Mendenhall, George E., and Gary A. Herion. "Covenant." Edited by David Noel Freedman, Gary A. Herion, David F. Graf, and John David Pleins. *ABD*. New York, N.Y.: Doubleday, 1996.

Meriç, Recep. "1985 Yılı Alaşehir Kazı Çalışmaları." *KST* 8, no. 2 (1986): 259–71.

———. "1986 Yılı Alaşehir Kazıs Raporu." *KST* 9, no. 2 (1987): 243–52.

———. "1987 Yılı Alaşehir Kazısı." *KST* 10, no. 1 (1989): 157–70.

———. "1988 Yılı Alaşehir Kazısı." *KST* 11, no. 1 (1990): 179–90.

———. "1990 Yılı Alaşehir Kazısı." *KST* 13, no. 1 (1992): 227–35.

———. "1991 Yılı Alaşehir Kazısı." *KST* 14, no. 2 (1993): 335–63.

Merkelbach, Reinhold. "Der Griechische Wortchatz Und Die Christen." *ZPE* 18 (1975): 108–36.

Meshorer, Ya 'akov. *Jewish Coins of the Second Temple Period.* Tel Aviv, Israel : Am Hassefer and Masada , 1967.

Metcalf, William E., ed. *The Oxford Handbook of Greek and Roman Coinage.* Oxford, U.K.: Oxford University Press, 2012.

Metzger, Bruce M. *A Textual Commentary on the Greek New Testament.* 2nd ed. Stuttgart, Germany: Deutsche Bibelgesellschaft, 2002.

———. *Breaking the Code: Understanding the Book of Revelation.* Nashville, Tenn.: Abingdon, 1999.

Meyer, Eduard. "Die Makedonischen Militärcolonien." *Hermes* 33, no. 4 (1898): 643–47.

Meyers, Carol L. "Jachin and Boaz in Religious and Political Perspective." *CBQ* 45 (1983): 167–78.

Meyers, Eric M., ed. *The Oxford Encyclopedia of Archaeology in the Near East.* 5 vols. Oxford, U.K.: Oxford University Press, 1997.

Michaelis, Adolf. *Ancient Marbles in Great Britain.* Translated by Charles Augustus Maude Fennell. Cambridge, U.K.: Cambridge University Press, 1882.

Michaelis, Wilhelm. "Σμύρνα." Edited by Gerhard Kittel and Gerhard Friedrich. Translated by Geoffrey W. Bromiley. *TDNT.* Grand Rapids, Mich.: Eerdmans, 1985.

Michaels, J. Ramsey. *Interpreting the Book of Revelation.* Guides to New Testament Exegesis. Grand Rapids, Mich.: Baker, 1992.

———. *Revelation.* Downers Grove, Ill.: InterVarsity, 1997.

Michl, Johann. "Engel I–IX." *RAC* 5 (1962): 53–258.

Mierse, William E. "Artemis Sanctuary." In *Sardis from Prehistoric to Roman Times: Results of the Archaeological Exploration of Sardis, 1958-1975*, edited by George M. A. Hanfmann, William E. Mierse, and Clive Foss, 119–21. Cambridge, Mass.: Harvard University Press, 1983.

Millard, Allen R. *Reading and Writing in the Time of Jesus.* New York, N.Y.: Continuum International, 2004.

———. "The Tablets in the Ark." In *Reading the Law: Studies in Honour of Gordon J. Wenham*, edited by J. Gordon McConville and Karl Möller, 254–66. LHSOT 461. New York, N.Y.: T&T Clark, 2007.

Miller, John F. "Roman Festivals." In *OEAGR*, edited by Michael Gagarin, 3:172. New York, N.Y.: Oxford University Press, 2010.

Milne, Joseph Grafton. *The Silver Coinage of Smyrna* . London, U.K.: Taylor & Walton, 1914.

Minear, Paul S. *I Saw a New Earth: An Introduction to the Visions of the Apocalypse.* Washington, D.C.: Corpus Books, 1968.

Mitchell, Stephen. *Anatolia: Land, Men, and Gods in Asia Minor.* 2 vols. Oxford, U.K.: Clarendon Press, 1995.

———. "Archaeology in Asia Minor, 1985–1989." *Archaeological Reports*, no. 36 (1990): 83–131.

Mitchell, Stephen, William M. Calder, and Eric William Gray. "Asia, Roman Province." Edited by Simon Hornblower and Antony Spawforth. *OCD.* Oxford, U.K.: Clarendon, 2003.

Mitchell, T. C. *Biblical Archaeology: Documents from the British Museum* . Cambridge, U.K.: Cambridge University Press, 1988.

Mitsopoulos-Leon, Veronika. *Die Basilika Am Staatsmarkt in Ephesos – Kleinfunde. 1. Teil: Keramik Hellenistischer Und Römischer Zeit*. FiE, 9.2.2. Wien: Schindler, 1991.

Mitten, David Gordon. "A New Look at Ancient Sardis ." *BA* 29, no. 2 (1966): 38–68.

Modeste, Rakoto E. "Unity of the Letters and Visions in the Revelation of John." Ph.D. diss., Lutheran School of Theology, 1991.

Moffatt, James. *The Revelation of St. John the Divine*. Edited by W. Robertson Nicoll. Vol. 5. 5 vols. EGT. London, U.K.: Hodder & Stoughton, 1910.

Montague, George T. *The Apocalypse: Understanding the Book of Revelation and the End of the World*. Ann Arbor, Mich.: Servant, 1992.

Morenz, Siegfried. *Egyptian Religion*. Translated by Ann E. Keep. Ithaca, N.Y.: Cornell University Press, 1992.

Moretti, Luigi. *Iscrizioni agonistiche greche*. SPDI 12. Rome : Angelo Signorelli, 1953.

Morris, Leon L. *Revelation*. Downers Grove, Ill.: Intervarsity, 2007.

———. *The Revelation of St. John*. TNTC 20. Grand Rapids, Mich.: Eerdmans, 1975.

Moule, C. F. D. "The Judgment Them in the Sacraments." In *The Background of the New Testament and Its Eschatology*, edited by William David Davies and D. Daube, 464–81. Cambridge, U.K.: Cambridge University Press, 2009.

Moulton, James H. *A Grammar of New Testament Greek, Volume 3: Syntax*. Edinburgh, U.K.: Clarke, 1963.

———. "It Is His Angel." *JTS* 3, no. 12 (1902): 514–22.

Moulton, James H., and George Milligan. *Vocabulary of the Greek Testament*. London, U.K.: Hodder & Stoughton, 1930.

Mounce, Robert H. *The Book of Revelation*. Revised. NICNT 17. Grand Rapids, Mich.: Eerdmans, 1997.

Mounce, Robert H. *What Are We Waiting For?: A Commentary on Revelation*. Eugene, Oreg.: Wipf & Stock, 2004.

Moyise, Steve. "Does the Author of Revelation Misappropriate the Scriptures?" *AUSS* 40, no. 1 (2002): 3–21.

———. "The Language of the Old Testament in the Apocalypse." *JSNT* 22, no. 76 (2000): 97–113.

———. *The Old Testament in the Book of Revelation*. JSNTSup 115. Sheffield, U.K.: Sheffield Academic, 1995.

Moyle, J. B. "Civitas." In *DGRA*, edited by William Smith, 1:441-50. London, U.K.: Murray, 1890.

Mueller, J. T. "Adultery." Edited by Walter A. Elwell. *EDT*. Baker Reference Library. Grand Rapids, Mich.: Baker Academic, May 1, 2001.

Mueller, Theodore. "The Word of My Patience in Revelation 3:10." *CTQ* 46, no. 2–3 (1982): 231–34.

Muir, Steven. "Religion on the Road in Ancient Greece and Rome ." In *Travel and Religion in Antiquity*, edited by Philip A. Harland, 29–48. ESCJ 21. Waterloo, Ont.: Wilfrid Laurier University Press, 2011.

Mulholland, M. Robert. *Revelation: Holy Living in an Unholy World*. Grand Rapids, Mich.: Asbury, 1990.

Müller, D., L. Coenen, and H. Bietenhard. "Beginning, Origin, Rule, Ruler, Originator." Edited by Colin Brown. *NIDNTT*. Grand Rapids, Mich.: Zondervan, 1976.

Müller, Helmut. "Ein Neues Hellenistisches Weihepigramm Aus Pergamon." *Chiron* 19 (1989): 499–553.

Müller, Karl, Theodor Müller, and Victor Langlois. *Fragmenta historicorum graecorum*. Paris, France: Ambrosio Firmin Didot, 1841.

Müller, Ulrich B. *Die Offenbarung Des Johannes*. ÖTKNT 19. Gütersloh: Mohn, 1984.

———. *Prophetie Und Predigt Im Neuen Testament: Formgeschichtliche Untersuchungen Zur Urchristlichen Prophetie*. SNT 10. Gütersloh: Mohn, 1975.

———. *Zur Frühchristlichen Theologiegeschichte. Judenchristentum Und Paulinismus in Kleinasien an Der Wende Vom Ersten Zum Zweiten Jahrhundert Nach Christus*. Gütersloh: Mohn, 1976.

Mullin, Redmond. *The Wealth of Christians*. Maryknoll, N.Y.: Orbis Books, 1984.

Mundell, Robert A. *The Birth of Coinage*. New York, N.Y.: Columbia University Press, 2002.

Munn, Mark Henderson. *The Mother of the Gods, Athens, and the Tyranny of Asia: A Study of Sovereignty in Ancient Religion*. The Joan Palevsky Imprint in Classical Literature. Berkeley: University of California Press, 2006.

Murphy, Frederick J. *Fallen Is Babylon: The Revelation to John*. NTCC. Harrisburg, Pa.: Trinity, 1998.

Murphy-O'Connor, Jerome. *St. Paul's Ephesus : Texts and Archaeology*. Minneapolis, Minn.: Liturgical, 2008.

Muse, Robert L. "Revelation 2–3: A Critical Analysis of Seven Prophetic Messages." *JETS* 29, no. 2 (1986): 147–61.

Muss, Ulrike. "The Artemision at Ephesos: From Paganism to Christianity." In *Mustafa Büyükkolancı'ya Armağan: Essays in Honour of Mustafa Büyükkolancı*, edited by Celal Şimşek, Bahadır Duman, and Erim Konakçi, 413–22. Istanbul: Yayinlari, 2015.

Mussies, Gerard. "Artemis." In *Dictionary of Deities and Demons in the Bible*, edited by Karel van der Toorn, Bob Becking, and Pieter Willem van der Horst, 2nd ed., 91–97. Grand Rapids, Mich.: Eerdmans, 1999.

———. "Pagans, Jews, and Christians at Ephesus." In *Studies on the Hellenistic Background of the New Testament*, edited by Pieter Wilhelm van der Horst and Gerard Mussies, 177–94. Utrechtse Theologische Reeks 10. Utrecht: Theological Faculty Utrecht University, 1990.

———. *The Morphology of Koine Greek, As Used in the Apocalypse of St. John: A Study in Bilingualism*. NovTSup 27. Leiden: Brill, 1971.

Musurillo, Hebert, ed. *The Acts of the Christian Martyrs*. Translated by Hebert Musurillo. Oxford, U.K.: Clarendon, 1972.

Mykytiuk, Lawrence J. *Identifying Biblical Persons in Northwest Semitic Inscriptions of 1200-539 B.C.E.* SBL Academia Biblica 12. Atlanta, Ga.: SBL, 2004.

Nagy, Gregory. "The Library of Pergamon as a Classical Model." In *Pergamon-Citadel of the Gods: Archaeological Record, Literary Description, and Religious Development*, edited by Helmut Koester, 185–232. HTS 46. Harrisburg, Pa.: Trinity Press International, 1998.

Naimark, Norman M. *Fires of Hatred: Ethnic Cleansing in Twentieth-Century Europe*. Cambridge, Mass.: Harvard University Press, 2002.

Nash, Ronald H. *Christianity and the Hellenistic World*. BSCS. Grand Rapids, Mich.: Zondervan, 1984.

Naveh, Joseph. "The Date of the Deir 'Alla Inscription in Aramaic Script." *IEJ* 17 (1967): 236–38.

Naylor, Michael. "The Roman Imperial Cult and Revelation." *CBR* 8, no. 2 (2010): 207–39.

Netzer, Ehud. "The Last Days and Hours at Masada." *BAR* 17, no. 6 (1991): 20–32.

Newell, Edward Theodore. *The Pergamene Mint Under Philetaerus*. 76. New York, N.Y.: American Numismatic Society, 1936.

Newell, William R. *The Book of the Revelation*. Chicago, Ill.: Grace, 1941.

Newman, Barclay Moon. *Rediscovering the Book of Revelation*. Valley Forge, Penn.: Judson, 1968.

Newton, Charles Thomas. *The Collection of Ancient Greek Inscriptions in the British Museum*. Edited by E. L. Hicks. 5 vols. Oxford, U.K.: Clarendon, 1874.

Ngangbam, Ajit Kumar, Daniel L.E. Waters, Steve Whalan, Abdul Baten, and Kirsten Benkendorff. "Indole-Producing Bacteria from the Biosynthetic Organs of a Muricid Mollusc Could Contribute to Tyrian Purple Production." *Journal of Shellfish Research* 34, no. 2 (2015): 443–54.

Nichols, Andrew. "The Complete Fragments of Ctesias of Cnidus: Translation and Commentary with an Introduction." Ph. D. diss., University of Florida, 2008.

Nicholson, Ernest W. *God and His People: Covenant and Theology in the Old Testament*. Oxford, U.K.: Clarendon, 1988.

Nielsen, Harald. *Ancient Ophthalmological Agents: A Pharmaco-Historical Study of the Collyria and Seals for Collyria Used during Roman Antiquity, as Well as of the Most Frequent Components of the Collyria*. Translated by Lars McBride. Acta Historica Scientiarum Naturalium et Medicinalium 31. Odense, Denmark: Odense University Press, 1974.

Nielsen, Kirsten. *Yahweh as Prosecutor and Judge: An Investigation of the Prophetic Lawsuit (Rîb-Pattern)*. Sheffield, U.K.: University of Sheffield, 1978.

Nielsen, Marjatta. "Diana Efesia Multimammmia: The Metamorphoses of a Pagan Goddess from the Renaissance to the Age of Neo-Classicism." In *From Artemis to Diana: The Goddess of Man and Beast*, edited by Tobias Fischer-Hansen and Birte Poulsen, 455–96. AH 12. Copenhagen: Museum Tusculanum, 2009.

Nilsson, Martin Persson. *Geschichte Der Griechischen Religion*. 2nd ed. 2 vols. Handbuch Der Altertumswissenschaft, 5.2. Munich: Beck, 1955.

Nobbs, Alanna M. "Christians in a Pluralistic Society: Papyrus Evidence from the Roman Empire." *International Journal of New Perspectives in Christianity* 1, no. 1.7 (2009): 51–55.

Nogueira, Paulo Augusto de Souza. "Celestial Worship and Ecstatic-Visionary Experience." Translated by Leslie Milton. *JSNT* 25, no. 2 (2002): 165–84.

Nutton, Vivian. "Demosthenes Philalethes Physician." In *BrillPaulyA*, edited by Hubert Cancik and Helmuth Schneider, translated by Christine F. Salazar and Francis G. Gentry, 4:297–98. Leiden: Brill, 2006. http://dx.doi.org/10.1163/1574-9347_bnp_e315480.

———. "Healers in the Medical Market Place: Towards a Social History of Graeco-Roman Medicine." In *Medicine in Society: Historical Essays*, edited by Andrew Wear, 15–58. Cambridge, U.K.: Cambridge University Press, 1992.

———. "The Chronology of Galen's Early Career." *CQ* 23, no. 1 (1973): 158–71.

———. "The Drug Trade in Antiquity." *Journal of the Royal Society of Medicine* 78 (1985): 138–45.

———. "The Medical Profession in the Roman Empire from Augustus to Justinian." Ph.D. diss., University of Cambridge, 1970.

———. "Theodas." In *BrillPaulyA*, edited by Hubert Cancik and Helmuth Schneider, translated by Christine F. Salazar and Francis G. Gentry. Leiden: Brill, 2006. http://dx.doi.org/10.1163/1574-9347_bnp_e1207730.

O'Brien, Peter T. *Colossians, Philemon*. WBC 44. Waco, Tex.: Thomas Nelson, 1982.

Ochsenwald, William, and Sydney Nettleton Fisher. *The Middle East: A History*. 7th ed. Boston, Mass.: McGraw-Hill, 2010.

Oden, Amy G., ed. *And You Welcomed Me: A Sourcebook on Hospitality in Early Christianity*. Nashville, Tenn.: Abingdon, 2002.

Oesterley, W. O. E., and T. H. Robinson. *A History of Israel*. Oxford, U.K.: Oxford University Press, 1932.

Old, Hughes Oliphant. *The Shaping of the Reformed Baptismal Rite in the Sixteenth-Century*. Grand Rapids, Mich.: Eerdmans, 2001.

O'Neal, William J. "Delation in the Early Empire." *CB* 55 (1978): 24–28.

Onstad, Esther. *Courage for Today, Hope for Tomorrow: A Study of the Revelation*. Minneapolis, Minn.: Augsburg, 1993.

Oppenheim, A. Leo. *Assyrian Dictionary of the Oriental Institute of the University of Chicago*. 21 vols. Chicago, Ill.: University Of Chicago Press, 1977.

Oppenheim, A. Leo, Ignace J. Gelb, Thorkild Jacobsen, and Benno Landsberger, eds. *The Assyrian Dictionary of the Oriental Institute of the University of Chicago: H [Het]*. Vol. 6. 21 vols. Chicago, Ill.: University Of Chicago Press, 1956.

O'Rourke, John J. "Roman Law and the Early Church." In *The Catacombs and the Colosseum: The Roman Empire as the Setting of Primitive Christianity*, edited by Stephen Benko and John J. O'Rourke, 165–86. Valley Forge, Penn.: Judson, 1971.

Osborne, Grant R. *Revelation*. BECNT. Grand Rapids, Mich.: Baker Academic, 2002.

Oster, Richard. *A Bibliography of Ancient Ephesus*. Dorst: Scarecrow, 1987.

Oster, Richard E. "Ephesus as a Religious Center Under the Principate, I: Paganism Before Constantine." *ANRW* 18, no. 3 (1990): 1661–1728.

———. "Ephesus (Place)." Edited by David Noel Freedman, Gary A. Herion, David F. Graf, and John David Pleins. *ABD*. New York, N.Y.: Doubleday, 1996.

———. "The Ephesian Artemis as an Opponent of Early Christianity." *JAC* 19 (1976): 24–44.

Osterloh, Kevin Lee. "Judea, Rome and the Hellenistic Oikoumene: Emulation and the Reinvention of Communal Identity." In *Heresy and Identity in Late Antiquity*, edited by Eduard Iricinschi and Holger M. Zellentin, 168–206. Texts and Studies in Ancient Judaism 119. Mohr Siebeck, 2008.

Otto, Walter Friedrich. *Dionysus: Myth and Cult*. Translated by Robert B. Palmer. Bloomington, Ind.: Indiana University Press, 1965.

Otzen, Benedikt. "The Paradise Trees in Jewish Apocalyptic." In *Apocryphon Severini: Presented to Søren Giversen*, edited by Pia Guldager Bilde, H. K. Nielsen, and J. Podemann Sørensen, 140–54. Aarhus, Denmark: Aarhus University Press, 1993.

Palmer, Earl F. *1, 2, 3 John; Revelation*. Atlanta, Ga.: Nelson, 1982.

Pardee, Dennis. *Handbook of Ancient Hebrew Letters*. SBLSBS 15. Atlanta, Ga.: Scholars Press, 1982.

Parez, C. H. "The Seven Letters and the Rest of the Apocalypse." *JTS* 12, no. 46 (1911): 284–86.

Park, Hyung Dae. *Finding Herem?: A Study of Luke-Acts in the Light of Herem*. Edited by Mark Goodacre. 1st ed. LNTS 357. London, U.K.: T&T Clark, 2007.

Parkes, James William. *The Conflict of the Church and the Synagogue: A Study in the Origins of Antisemitism*. New York, N.Y.: Meridian, 1964.

Parpola, Simo, and Kazuko Watanabe. *Neo-Assyrian Treaties and Loyalty Oaths*. State Archives of Assyria 2. Helsinki, Finland: Helsinki University Press, 1988.

Paton, James Morton. *The Erechtheum: Measured, Drawn, and Restored*. Cambridge, Mass.: Harvard University Press, 1927.

Paul, Shalom M. "Heavenly Tablets and the Book of Life." *JANES* 5 (1973): 345–53.

Pauly, August Friedrich. *Realencyclopädie Der Classischen Altertumswissenschaft*. Edited by Georg Wissowa and S. Kroll. 50 in 84 parts vols. Stuttgart: Metzler & Druckenmüller, 1894.

Pausanias. *Guide to Greece, Vol. 1: Central Greece*. Translated by Peter Levi. Harmondsworth: Penguin Classics, 1984.

Payne, J. Barton. *The Imminent Appearing Of Christ*. Grand Rapids, Mich.: Eerdmans, 1962.

Peake, Arthur S. *The Revelation of John*. London, U.K.: Johnson, 1919.

Pearcy, Lee T. "Galen's Pergamum." *Archaeology* 38, no. 6 (1988): 33–39.

Peck, Harry Thurston. *Harper's Dictionary of Classical Literature and Antiquities*. New York, N.Y.: Harper & Brothers, 1898.

Pedley, John Griffiths. *Ancient Literary Sources on Sardis*. ASES. Cambridge, Mass.: Harvard University Press, 1972.

———. *Sardis in the Age of Croesus*. 2nd ed. Centers of Civilization Series. Norman: University of Oklahoma Press, 2000.

Pedrini, Lura Nancy, and Duilio Thomas Pedrini. *Serpent Imagery and Symbolism: A Study of the Major English Romantic Poets*. New Haven, Conn.: College and University Press, 1966.

Peek, Werner. "Die Hydrophore Vera von Patmos." *Rheinisches Museum Für Philologie*, 1964, 315–25.

Perry, Jonathan S. "Sub-Elites." In *A Companion to Roman Italy*, edited by Alison E. Cooley, 498–512. Blackwell Companions to the Ancient World. New York, N.Y.: John Wiley & Sons, 2016.

Peters, Francis E. *The Harvest of Hellenism: A History of the Near East from Alexander the Great to the Triumph of Christianity*. New York, N.Y.: Barnes & Noble, 1996.

Petovium, Victorinus of, Apringius of Beja, Caesarius of Arles, Bede the Venerable, Thomas C. Oden, and Gerald L. Bray. *Latin Commentaries on Revelation*. Translated by William C. Weinrich. Downers Grove, Ill.: IVP Academic, 2011.

Pétridès, Sophron. "Philadelphia." Edited by Thomas Carson. *CE*. Detroit, Mich.: Gale, 1913.

Petsalis-Diomidis, Alexia. *Truly Beyond Wonders: Aelius Aristides and the Cult of Asklepios*. Oxford, U.K.: Oxford University Press, 2010.

Petzl, Georg. *Die Inschriften von Smyrna*. Vol. 1. 2 vols. AÖAW 23–24. Bonn: Habelt, 1982.

———. *Tituli Lydiae Linguis Graeca et Latina Conscripti: Fasciculus III, Philadelpheia et Ager Philadelphenus*. TAM, 5/3. Vienna: Östereichishen Akademie der Wissenschaften, 2007.

Pfeiffer, Charles F., ed. *The Biblical World: A Dictionary of Biblical Archaeology*. Nashville, Tenn.: Broadman, 1976.

———, ed. *Wycliffe Dictionary of Biblical Archaeology*. Peabody, Mass.: Hendrickson, 2000.

Pfleiderer, Otto. *Primitive Christianity: Its Writings and Teachings in Their Historical Connections*. Translated by W. Montgomery. 3 vols. London, U.K.: Williams & Norgate, 1910.

Pharr, Clyde. *The Theodosian Code and Novels, and the Sirmondian Constitutions*. Union, N.J.: The Lawbook Exchange, 2001.

Piccardi, Luigi. "The AD 60 Denizli Basin Earthquake and the Apparition of Archangel Michael at Colossae (Aegean Turkey)." In *Myth and Geology*, edited by W. Bruce Masse and Luigi Piccardi, 95–105. Special Publications 273. London: Geological Society, 2007.

Pick, Behrendt. "Die Neokorie-Tempel von Pergamon Und Der Asklepios Des Phyromachos." In *Festschrift. Walther Judeich, Zum 70. Geburtstag, Überreicht von Jenner Freunden*. Weimar: Hermann Boehlaus, 1929.

Pietrogrande, A. Luigi, and Giovanni Becatti, eds. *Le Fulloniche*. Scavi Ostia 8. Rome : Istituto Poligrafico Dello Stato, Libreria Dello Stato, 1976.

Pilch, John J. "Lying and Deceit in the Letters to the Seven Churches: Perspectives from Cultural Anthropology." *Biblical Theology Bulletin* 22, no. 3 (1992): 126–35.

Pilhofer, Peter. "The Early Christian Community of Smyrna —Smyrna in the New Testament and Beyond." In *Paper Presented at the First International Symposium on Ancient Smyrna*. Izmir , Turkey, 2003.

Pirot, Louis, André Robert, Jacques Briend, and Édouard Cothenet, eds. *Dictionnaire de la Bible: Supplément*. Paris: Létouzey et Ané éditeurs, 1928.

Pleket, Harry W. "Models and Inscriptions: Export of Textiles in the Roman Empire." *EA* 30 (1998): 117–28.

Plumptre, Edward Hayes. *A Popular Exposition of the Epistles to the Seven Churches of Asia*. 2nd ed. London, U.K.: Hodder & Stoughton, 1887.

Pollard, Leslie N. "The Function of Loipos in Contexts of Judgment and Salvation in the Book of Revelation." Ph.D., Andrews University, 2007.

———. "The Function of Λοιπός in the Letter to Thyatira ." *AUSS* 46, no. 1 (2008): 45–63.

Portefaix, Lilian. "The Image of Artemis Ephesia - A Symbolic Configuration Related to Her Mysteries?" In *100 Jahre Österreichische Forschunge in Ephesos*, edited by Herwig Friesinger and Friedrich Krinzinger, 611–17. Archäologische Forschungen 1. Wien: VÖAW, 1999.

Porter, H. "Money." Edited by Geoffrey W. Bromiley. *ISBE*. Grand Rapids, Mich.: Eerdmans, 1995.

Porter, Stanley E. *Verbal Aspect in the Greek of the New Testament, with Reference to Tense and Mood*. 3rd ed. Studies in Biblical Greek. New York, N.Y.: Peter Lang, 2003.

———. "Why the Laodiceans Received Lukewarm Water (Rev 3:15–18)." *TynBul* 38 (1987): 143–49.

Potter, David S. "Persecution of the Early Church." Edited by David Noel Freedman, Gary A. Herion, David F. Graf, and John David Pleins. *ABD*. New York, N.Y.: Doubleday, 1996.

———. "Smyrna ." Edited by David Noel Freedman. *ABD*. New York, N.Y.: Doubleday, 1996.

Praschniker, E., F. Miltner, and H. Gerstinger. *Das Coemeterium Der Sieben Schläfer*. FiE, 4.2. Baden: Rohrer, 1937.

Prévost, Jean Pierre. *How to Read the Apocalypse*. Translated by John Bowden and Margaret Lydamore. The Crossroad Adult Christian Formation. New York, N.Y.: Crossroad, 1993.

Price, Martin J., and Bluma L. Trell. *Coins and Their Cities: Architecture on the Ancient Coins of Greece , Rome , and Palestine*. Detroit, Mich.: Wayne State University Press, 1977.

Price, Richard, and Michael Gaddis. *The Acts of the Council of Chalcedon* . Translated Texts for Historians 45. Liverpool, U.K.: Liverpool University Press, 2005.

Price, S. R. F. *Rituals and Power: The Roman Imperial Cult in Asia Minor*. Reprint. Cambridge, U.K.: Cambridge University Press, 1985.

Prigent, Pierre. *Apocalypse et Liturgie*. Cahiers Théologiques 52. Lausanne: Delachaux et Niestlé, 1964.

———. *Commentary on the Apocalypse of St. John*. Translated by Wendy Pradels. Tübingen: Siebeck, 2004.

———. *L'Apocalypse de saint Jean*. Commentaire du Nouveau Testament. Lausanne: Delachaux et Niestlé, 1981.

Pritchard, James Bennett. *Ancient Near Eastern Texts Relating to the Old Testament with Supplement*. 3rd ed. Princeton, N.J.: Princeton University Press, 1969.

Pryce, Frederick Norman, Pierre Briant, Anthony J. S. Spawforth, and J. Linderski. "Altar." Edited by Simon Hornblower and Antony Spawforth. *OCD*. Oxford, U.K.: Clarendon, 2003.

Quek, Tze-Ming. "'I Will Give Authority over the Nations': Psalm 2.8–9 in Revelation 2.26–27." In *Early Christian Literature and Intertextuality: Exegetical Studies*, edited by Craig A. Evans and H. Daniel Zacharias, 2:175–87. New York, N.Y.: T&T Clark, 2009.

Rad, Gerhard von. *Old Testament Theology*. 2 vols. New York, N.Y.: Harper & Row, 1962.

———. *Theologie Des Alten Testaments*. 6th ed. 2 vols. Munich: Auflage, 1975.

Radet, Georges. *Cybébé; Étude Sur Les Transformations Plastiques D'un Type Divin*. Bibliothèque Des Universités Du Midi 13. Bordeaux, France: Feret & Fils, 1909.

———. "Sur Quelques Points de L'histoire Des Séleucides." In *Revue de Philologie, de Littérature et D'histoire Anciennes*, edited by E. Chatelain, L. Ouvau, and B. Haussoullier, 17:56–62. Paris, France: Klincksieck, 1893.

Radt, Wolfgang. *Pergamon: Geschichte Und Bauten Einer Antiken Metropole*. Darmstadt: Primus Verlag, 1999.

Radwin, George E., and Anthony D'Attilio. *Murex Shells of the World: An Illustrated Guide to the Muricidae* . Stanford, Calif.: Stanford University Press, 1976.

Ragette, Friedrich. *Baalbek*. Park Ridge, N.J.: Noyes, 1981.

Rainey, Anson F. "A Rejoinder to the Eliakim Nacar Yokan Seal Impressions." *BA* 54, no. 1 (1991): 61.

Räisänen, Heikki. "The Nicolaitans : Apoc. 2; Acts 6." *ANRW* II, 26.2 (1996): 1602–44.

Rakicic, Mark. "The Bees of Ephesos." *The Celator* 8, no. 12 (1994): 6–12.

Ramage, Andrew. "Golden Sardis ." In *King Croesus' Gold: Excavations at Sardis and the History of Gold Refining*, edited by Andrew Ramage and Paul T. Craddock, 14–26. AESM 11. Cambridge, Mass.: British Museum Press, 2000.

———. "The Excavations and Finds." In *King Croesus' Gold: Excavations at Sardis and the History of Gold Refining*, edited by Andrew Ramage and Paul T. Craddock, 14–26. AESM 11. Cambridge, Mass.: British Museum Press, 2000.

Ramage, Andrew, and Paul T. Craddock, eds. *King Croesus' Gold: Excavations at Sardis and the History of Gold Refining*. AESM 11. Cambridge, Mass.: British Museum Press, 2000.

Ramage, Andrew, Crawford H. Greenewalt, Jr., and Faruk Akca. "The Fourteenth Campaign at Sardis (1971)." *BASOR*, no. 206 (1972): 9–39.

Ramsay, William M. *Cities and Bishoprics of Phrygia*. 2 vols. Oxford, U.K.: Clarendon, 1895.

———. "Exploration of Asia Minor: As Bearing on the Historical Trustworthiness of the New Testament." *JTVI*, 1907, 200–217.

———. "Laodicea." In *DBib*, edited by James Hastings, Frederick C. Grant, and Harold. H. Rowley, 3:44–45. New York, N.Y.: Scribner's Sons, 1909.

———. "Pergamus or Pergamum." In *DBib*, edited by James Hastings, Frederick C. Grant, and Harold. H. Rowley, 3:749–52. New York, N.Y.: Scribner's Sons, 1909.

———. "Roads and Travel (in NT)." In *DBib*, edited by James Hastings, Frederick C. Grant, and Harold. H. Rowley, 5:375–402. New York, N.Y.: Scribner's Sons, 1909.

———. "Sepulchral Customs in Ancient Phrygia." *JHS* 5 (1884): 241–62.

———. *St. Paul the Traveler and Roman Citizen: Updated*. Edited by Mark W. Wilson. Reprinted of 1897. Grand Rapids, Mich.: Baker, 2001.

———. *The Bearing of Recent Discovery on the Trustworthiness of the New Testament*. London, U.K.: Hodder & Stoughton, 1915.

———. "The Date of St. Polycarp's Martyrdom." *JÖAI* 27 (1932): 245–58.

———. *The Letters to Seven Churches of Asia and Their Place in the Plan of the Apocalypse*. London, U.K.: Hodder & Stoughton, 1904.

———. *The Letters to Seven Churches: Updated*. Edited by Mark W. Wilson. Peabody, Mass.: Hendrickson, 1994.

———. "The Province of Asia." *The Classical Review* 3 (1889): 174–79.

———. "The White Stone and the 'Gladiatorial' Tessera." *ExpTim* 16, no. 12 (January 1, 1905): 558–61.

———. "Thyatira." In *DBib*, edited by James Hastings, Frederick C. Grant, and Harold. H. Rowley, 4:757–59. New York, N.Y.: Scribner's Sons, 1909.

Ramsay, William M., and A. S. Wilkins. "Planetae." In *DGRA*, edited by William Smith, 2:432-33. London, U.K.: Murray, 1891.

Ramsay, William Mitchell. "Artemis -Leto and Apollo -Lairbenos." *JHS* 10 (1889): 216–30.

———. *The Social Basis of Roman Power in Asia Minor*. Amsterdam: A. M. Hakkert, 1967.

Rapaport, Samuel. *Tales and Maxims from the Midrash*. London, U.K.: Routledge & Sons, 1907.

Rapske, Brian M. *Book of Acts in Its First-Century Setting: Paul in Roman Custody*. BAFCS 3. Grand Rapids, Mich.: Eerdmans, 2004.

———. "Exiles, Islands, and the Identity and Perspective of John in Revelation." In *Christian Origins and Greco-Roman Culture: Social and Literary Contexts for the New Testament*, edited by Stanley E. Porter and

Andrew W. Pitts, 311–46. Texts and Editions for New Testament Study: Early Christianity in Its Hellenistic Context 1. Leiden: Brill, 2012.

Rasmussen, Carl G. "Temple A at Laodicea (Turned into a 'library'?) — Part 1 of 2 Parts," August 27, 2014. https://holylandphotos.wordpress.com/2014/08/27/temple-a-at-laodicea-turned-into-a-library-part-1-of-2-parts/.

Ratté, Christopher, Thomas N. Howe, and Clive Foss. "An Early Imperial Pseudodipteral Temple at Sardis." *AJA* 90, no. 1 (1986): 45–68.

Rautman, Marcus. "Sardis in Late Antiquity." In *Archaeology and the Cities of Late Antiquity in Asia Minor*, edited by Ortwin Dally and Christopher Ratté, 1–26. Ann Arbor, Mich.: Kelsey Museum of Archaeology, 2012.

Rawson, Beryl. "Marriages, Familes, Households." In *The Cambridge Companion to Ancient Rome*, edited by Paul Erdkamp, 93–109. Cambridge, Mass.: Cambridge University Press, 2013.

Reddish, Mitchell G. *Revelation*. Smyth & Helwys Bible Commentary. Macon, Ga.: Smyth & Helwys Publishing, 2001.

Reed, Jonathan L. "Capernaum." In *EDB*, edited by David Noel Freedman, Allen C. Myers, and Astrid B. Beck, 220–21. Grand Rapids, Mich.: Eerdmans, 2000.

Reese, David S. "Marine Invertebrates, Freshwater Shells, and Land Snails: Evidence from Specimens Mosaics, Wall Paintings, Sculputure, Jewelry, and Roman Authors." In *The Natural History of Pompeii*, edited by Wilhelmina Feemster Jashemski and Frederick G. Meyer, 292–314. Cambridge, U.K.: Cambridge University Press, 2002.

———. "Palaikastro Shells and Bronze Age Purple-Dye Production in the Mediterranean Basin." *ABSA* 2 (1987): 201–5.

———. "The Industrial Exploitation of Murex Shells: Purple-Dye and Lime Production at Sidi Khrebish, Benghazi (Berenice)." *Libyan Studies* 11 (1980): 79–93.

Reichelt, Hansgünter. *Angelus Interpres - Texte in Der Johannes-Apokalypse*. Frankfurt: Peter Lang, 1994.

Reimer, Ivoni Richter. *Women in the Acts of Apostles: A Feminist Liberation Perspective*. Minneapolis, Minn.: Fortress, 1995.

Reinhold, Meyer. *History of Purple as a Status Symbol in Antiquity*. 116. Brussels: Latomus, 1970.

Rendtorff, Rolf. *The Covenant Formula: An Exegetical and Theological Investigation*. Edinburgh, U.K.: Bloomsbury, 2000.

Resseguie, James L. *The Revelation of John: A Narrative Commentary*. Grand Rapids, Mich.: Baker Academic, 2009.

Reynolds, Joyce Maire, and Kenan T. Erim. *Aphrodisias and Rome*. JRSM. London, U.K.: Society for the Promotion of Roman Studies, 1982.

Reynolds, Joyce Maire, and Robert F. Tannenbaum. *Jews and Godfearers at Aphrodisias*. Proceedings of the Cambridge Philological Society. Supplementary Volume. Cambridge Cambridgeshire: Cambridge Philological Society, 1987.

Reynolds, Joyce Maire. "Further Information on the Imperial Cult at Aphrodisias." *Studii Clasice* 24 (1986): 109–17.

———. "New Evidence for the Imperial Cult in Julio-Claudian Aphrodisias." *ZPE* 43 (1981): 317–27.

———. "Inscriptions." In *Excavations at Sidi Khrebish, Benghazi (Berenice): Buildings, Coins, Inscriptions, Architectural Decoration*, edited by John Alfred Lloyd, 233–48. Libyan Arab Jamahiriya, 1977.

Rhee, Helen. *Early Christian Literature: Christ and Culture in the Second and Third Centuries*. Routledge Early Church Monographs. New York, N.Y.: Routledge, 2005.

Rhodes, Peter John. *A History of the Classical Greek World: 478-323 BC*. 2nd ed. Blackwell History of the Ancient World. Chichester, West Sussex, U.K.: Wiley-Blackwell, 2010.

Rich, Anthony. *A Dictionary of Roman and Greek Antiquities*. 6th ed. New York, N.Y.: Longman, 1884.

Ridgway, Brunilde Sismondo. *Hellenistic Sculpture II: The Styles of Ca. 200-100 B.C.* Wisconsin Studies in Classics. Madison, Wisc.: University of Wisconsin Press, 2000.

Rigsby, Kent J. *Asylia: Territorial Inviolability in the Hellenistic World*. Oakland, Calf.: University of California Press, 1997.

Rissi, Mathias. *Future of the World: An Exegetical Study of Revelation 19.11-22.15*. SBT 23. London, U.K.: Scm-Canterbury, 1972.

Ritschl, Friedrich Wilhelm. *Die Tesserae Gladiatoriae der Römer*. Munich: Akademie, 1864.

Ritti, Tullia. "Associazioni di mestiere a Hierapolis di Frigia." In *Viaggi e commerci nell'antichità*, edited by Bianca Maria Giannattasio, 65–84. Geneva: Università di Genova, Facoltà di Lettere, 1995.

———. "Iura sepulcrorum a Hierapolis di Frigia nel quadro dell'epigrafia sepolcrale microasiatica. Iscrizione edite e inedite." In *Libitina e Dintorni. Libitina e i Luci Sepolcrali, le Leges Libitinariae Campane Iura Sepulcrorum: Vecchie e Nuove Iscrizioni*, edited by S. Panciera, 455–634. Roma : Quasar, 2004.

———. "The Jewish Community in Hierapolis ." In *Hierapolis Di Figia 1957-1987*, edited by A. Peres, 116–17. Rome : Fabbri, 1987.

Rives, J. B. "The Decree of Decius and the Religion of Empire." *JRS* 89 (1999): 135–54.

Robbins, Vernon K. *The Invention of Christian Discourse: From Wisdom to Apocalyptic*. Rhetoric of Religious Antiquity 1. Dorset: Deo, 2008.

Robert, Louis. *Documents d'Asia Mineure*. BEFAR 239. Athens and Paris: École Française d'Athènes and De Boccard, 1987.

———. "Documents d'Asie Mineure." *BCH* 101, no. 1 (1977): 43–132.

———. "Documents d'Asie Mineure." *BCH* 106, no. 3 (1982): 309–78.

———. "Documents d'Asie Mineure." *BCH* 107, no. 1 (1983): 497–599.

———. "Documents d'Asie Mineure: V–XVII." *BCH* 102, no. 1 (1978): 395–543.

———. *Études Anatoliennes: Recherches Sur Les Inscriptionsgrecques de l'Asie Mineure*. Paris: de Boccard, 1937.

———. "Le Culte de Caligula À Milet et La Province d'Asie." *Hellenica* 7 (1949): 206–38.

———, ed. *Le Martyre de Pionios Pretre de Smyrne*. Washington, D.C.: Dumbarton Oaks Research Library and Collection, 1994.

———. *Les Gladiateurs dans l'Orient grec*. Paris: Champion, 1941.

———. *Nouvelles Inscriptions de Sardes: Fasc. 1*. Paris, France: Librairie d'Amérique et d'Orient, 1964.

———. "Reliefs Votifs et Cultes d'Anatolie." *Anatolia* 3 (1958): 112–23.

———. "Une nouvelle inscription grecque de Sardes: Règlement de l'autorité perse relatif à un culte de Zeus ." *CRAI* 119, no. 2 (1975): 306–30.

Robert, Louis, and Jeanne Robert. *La Carie: histoire et géographie historique avec le recueil des inscriptions antiques*. Paris, France: Adrien-Maisonneuve, 1954.

Roberts, Alexander, James Donaldson, Philip Schaff, and Henry Wace, eds. *Nicene and Post-Nicene Fathers, Series I*. 14 vols. Peabody, Mass.: Hendrickson, 1994.

Roberts, J. H. "A Letter to Seven Churches in the Roman Province of Asia." In *Reading Revelation*, edited by J. E. Botha, P. G. R. Villiers, and J. Engelbrecht, 17–35. Pretoria: Van Schaik Uitgewers, 2004.

Roberts, Richard. "The Tree of Life (Rev 2 :7)." *ExpTim* 25, no. 7 (1914): 332.

Robertson, A. T. *A Grammar of the Greek New Testament in the Light of Historical Research*. Nashville, Tenn.: Broadman, 1934.

———. *Word Pictures in the New Testament*. 6 vols. Nashville, Tenn.: B&H, 1998.

Robertson, O. Palmer. *The Final Word: A Biblical Response to the Case for Tongues and Prophecy Today*. Carlisle, Pa.: Banner of Truth, 1993.

Robinson, E. S. G. "Some Electrum and Gold Greek Coins ." In *Centennial Publication of the American Numismatic Society*, edited by Harald Ingholt, 585–94. New York, N.Y.: American Numismatic Society, 1958.

Rodríguez, Angel Manuel. "The Heavenly Books of Life and of Human Deeds." *JATS* 13, no. 1 (2002): 10–26.

Rogers, Guy MacLean. *The Mysteries of Artemis of Ephesos: Cult, Polis, and Change in the Greaeco-Roman World*. New Haven, Conn.: Yale University Press, 2012.

Rogers, Guy Maclean. *The Sacred Identity of Ephesos: Foundation Myths of a Roman City*. Routledge Revivals. New York, N.Y.: Routledge, 2014.

Rohde, Erwin. *Pergamon: Burgberg Und Altar*. Berlin: Henschelverlag, 1982.

Roller, Lynn E. *In Search of God the Mother: The Cult of Anatolian Cybele* . Berkeley, Calf.: University of California Press, 1999.

Roller, Lynn Emrich. "Attis on Greek Votive Monuments; Greek God or Phrygian?" *Hesperia* 63, no. 2 (1994): 245–62.

Roloff, Jürgen. *The Revelation of John*. Translated by John E. Alsup. CC. Minneapolis, Minn.: Fortress, 1993.

Ropes, James Hard. *A Critical and Exegetical Commentary on the Epistle of James*. ICC. Edinburgh, U.K.: T&T Clark, 1954.

Ross, Alexander. *The Epistles of James and John*. NICNT 13. Grand Rapids, Mich.: Eerdmans, 1967.

Rosscup, James E. "The Overcomer in the Apocalypse." *GTJ* 3, no. 2 (1982): 261–86.

Rougé, J. "Un Negotiator Laudecenarius À Lyon." *Zeitschrift Für Papyrologie Und Epigraphik* 27 (1977): 263–69.

Rowland, Christopher. "Parousia ." Edited by David Noel Freedman, Gary A. Herion, David F. Graf, and John David Pleins. *ABD*. New York, N.Y.: Doubleday, 1992.

———. "The Vision of the Risen Christ in Rev. I. 13 Ff.: The Debt of an Early Christology to an Aspect of Jewish Angelology." *JTS* 31, no. 1 (1980): 1–11.

Royalty Jr., Robert M. "Etched or Sketched? Inscriptions and Erasures in the Messages to Sardis and Philadelphia (Rev. 3.1-13)." *JSNT* 27, no. 4 (June 2005): 447–63.

———. "Review of Loren L. Johns The Lamb Christology of the Apocalypse of John: An Investigation into Its Origins and Rehetorical Force." *RBL* 8 (2006): 1–6.

———. *The Ideology of Wealth in the Apocalypse of John*. Macon, Ga.: Mercer University Press, 1998.

———. "The Streets of Heaven: The Imagery and Ideology of Wealth in the Apocalypse of John." Ph.D. diss., Yale University, 1995.

Rudloff, Ilmo Robert Von, and Robert Von Rudloff. *Hekate in Ancient Greek Religion*. Victoria, B.C: Horned Owl Publishing, 1999.

Rudwick, M. J. S., and E. M. B. Green. "The Laodicean Lukewarmness." *ExpTim* 69, no. 6 (1958): 176–78.

Rudwick, M. J. S., and Colin J. Hemer. "Laodicea ." In *NBD*, edited by J. D. Douglas, 671–72. Grand Rapids, Mich.: Eerdmans, 1962.

Ruffing, Kai. "Städtische Wirtschaftspolitik Im Hellenistisch-Römischen Kleinasien? Zur Funktion Der Emporia." In *Staatlichkeit Und Politisches Handeln in Der Römischen Kaiserzeit*, 123–50. Millennium Studien 10. Berlin: De Gruyter, 2006.

Ruiz, Jean-Pierre. "Betwixt and Between on the Lord's Day: Liturgy and the Apocalypse." In *The Reality of Apocalypse: Rhetoric and Politics in the Book of Revelation*, edited by L. Barr David, 221–41. SBLSS 39. Atlanta, Ga.: Scholars Press, 2006.

Ruscillo, Deborah. "Reconstructing Murex Royal Purple and Biblical Blue in the Aegean." In *Archaeomalacology: Molluscs in Former Environments of Human Behaviour*, edited by Daniella Bar-Yosef Mayer, 99–106. Oxford, U.K.: Oxbow, 2005.

Rushdoony, Rousas John. *Thy Kingdom Come: Studies in Daniel and Revelation*. Vallecito, Calif.: Ross House, 2001.

Russell, J. C. *Late Ancient and Medieval Population*. APSP. Philadelphia , Pa.: American Philosophical Society, 1958.

Saffrey, H. D. "Relire l'Apocalypse À Patmos ." *RB* 82 (1975): 385–417.

Safrai, Shemuel, M. Stern, and David Flusser. *The Jewish People in the First Century: Historical Geography, Political History, Social, Cultural and Religious Life and Institutions*. Uitgeverij Van Gorcum, 1974.

Safrai, Shemuel, and Menahem Stern. "The Synagogue." In *The Jewish People in the First Century: Historical Geography, Political History, Social, Cultural and Religious Life and Institutions*, edited by Shemuel Safrai, Vol. 2. Assen: Van Gorcum, 1987.

Saftner, Bernard. *Punctuated Equilibrium Featuring The Proepistrephomeniad*. Bloomington, Ind.: Xlibris, 2008.

Salmon, Edward T. *A History of the Roman World: From 30 BC to AD 138*. 6th ed. London, U.K.: Methuen & Company, 1959.

Sanders, E. P. *Jewish Law From Jesus to the Mishnah: Five Studies*. Philadelphia , Pa.: Trinity Press International, 1990.

Sandmel, Samuel. "Parallelomania." *JBL* 81, no. 1 (1962): 1–13.

Sandys, John Edwyn, ed. *A Companion to Latin Studies*. Cambridge, U.K.: Cambridge University Press, 1921.

Santangelo, Federico. *Sulla, the Elites and the Empire: A Study of Roman Policies in Italy and the Greek East*. Leiden: Brill, 2007.

Sarna, Nahum M. *Exodus*. JPS Torah Commentary 2. Philadelphia, Pa.: The Jewish Publication Society, 2003.

Satake, Akira. *Die Gemeindeordnung in Der Johannesapokalypse*. WMANT 21. Neukirchener: Neukirchen-Vluyn, 1966.

Saunders, Stanley P. "Between Blessing and Curse: Reading, Hearing and Performing the Apocalypse in a World of Terror." In *Shaking Heaven and Earth: Essays in Honor of Walter Brueggemann and Charles B. Cousar*, edited by Christine Roy Yoder, Kathleen M. O'connor, E. Elizabeth Johnson, and Stanley P. Saunders, 141–55. Louisville, Ky.: Westminster John Knox, 2005.

———. "Revelation and Resistance: Narrative and Worship in John's Apocalypse." In *Narrative Reading, Narrative Preaching: Reuniting New Testament Interpretation and Proclamation*, edited by Joel Green and Michael Pasquarello III, 117–50. Grand Rapids, Mich.: Baker, 2009.

Sauter, Franz. *Der römische Kaiserkult bei Martial und Statius*. Berlin: Kohlhammer, 1934.

Schäfer, Jörg. "Pergamon Mysia, Turkey." In *The Princeton Encyclopedia of Classical Sites*, edited by Richard Stillwell, William L. MacDonald, and Marian Holland McAllister, 688–91. Princeton, N.J.: Princeton University Press, 1976.

Schaff, Philip. "Alogi." In *A Dictionary of Christian Biography: And Literature to the End of the Sixth Century A.D. With an Account of the Principal Sects and Heresies*, edited by Henry Wace, 34. Peabody, Mass.: Hendrickson, 1994.

———. "The Canons of the Councils of Ancyra, Gangra, Neocæsarea, Antioch and Laodicea, Which Canons Were Accepted and Received by the Ecumenical Synods." In *Nicene and Post-Nicene Fathers: Series: The Seven Ecumenical Councils*, edited by Alexander Roberts, James Donaldson, Philip Schaff, and Henry Wace, 2.14:123–30. Grand Rapids, Mich.: T&T Clark, 2005.

Scherrer, Peter, ed. *Ephesus: The New Guide*. Turkey: Ege Yayinin, 2000.

Schick, Eduard. *Revelation of St. John*. Translated by W. Kruppa. 2 vols. New Testament for Spiritual Reading. New York, N.Y.: Herder & Herder, 1971.

Schiermann, Gottfried. "Carcer." In *BrillPauly*, Vol. 3. Leiden: Brill, 2007.

Schiffman, Lawrence H., and M. D. Swartz. *Hebrew and Aramaic Incantation Texts from the Cairo Genizah: Selected Texts from Taylor-Schechter Box K1*. Sheffield, U.K.: Sheffield Academic Press, 1992.

Schlatter, Adolf. *The History of the Christ: The Foundation of New Testament Theology*. Translated by Andreas J. Köstenberger. Grand Rapids, Mich.: Baker Academic, 1997.

Schlier, Heinrich. *Principalities and Powers in the New Testament*. New York, N.Y.: Herder & Herder, 1961.

———. "Ἀμήν." Edited by Gerhard Kittel and Gerhard Friedrich. Translated by Geoffrey W. Bromiley. TDNT. Grand Rapids, Mich.: Eerdmans, 1985.

Schlütz, K. *Isaias 11:2 (Die Sieben Gaben Des Hl. Geistes) in Den Ersten Vier Jahrhunderten*. Münster: Aschendorff, 1932.

Schmid, S. G. "Decline or Prosperity at Roman Eretria? Industry, Purple Dye Works, Public Buildings, and Gravestones." *JRA* 12 (1999): 273–93.

Schmidt, Evamaria. *The Great Altar of Pergamon*. Boston, Mass.: Boston Book and Art Shop, 1965.

Schmitz, Leonhard. "Agdistis." In *Dictionary of Greek and Roman Biography and Mythology*, edited by William Smith, 1:67–68. Boston, Mass.: Little, Brown & Co., 1870.

———. "Deima." In *Dictionary of Greek and Roman Biography and Mythology*, edited by William Smith, 1:1:950. Boston, Mass.: Little, Brown & Co., 1870.

———. "Gryps or Gryphus." In *Dictionary of Greek and Roman Biography and Mythology*, edited by William Smith, 2:315. Boston, Mass.: Little, Brown & Co., 1870.

———. "Tyche ." In *Dictionary of Greek and Roman Biography and Mythology*, edited by William Smith, 3:1194. Boston, Mass.: Little, Brown & Co., 1870.

Schmiz, Leonhard, and George Elden Marindin. "Panionia ." In *DGRA*, edited by William Smith, 2:334. London, U.K.: Murray, 1891.

Schnabel, Eckhard J. *Acts*. Edited by Clinton E. Arnold. ZECNT 5. Grand Rapids, Mich.: Zondervan, 2012.

———. "Jewish Opposition to Christians in Asia Minor in the First Century." *BBR* 18, no. 2 (2008): 233–70.

Schneemelcher, Wilhelm, and Edgar Henneche, eds. *New Testament Apocrypha: Writings Relating to the Apostles Apocalypses and Related Subjects*. Translated by R. M. Wilson. Rev. 2 vols. Louisville, Ky.: Westminster/Knox, 1992.

Schneider, J. "Ξύλον." Edited by Gerhard Kittel and Gerhard Friedrich. Translated by Geoffrey W. Bromiley. *Theological Dictionary of the New Testament*. Grand Rapids, Mich.: Eerdmans, 1985.

Schoedel, William. *Ignatius of Antioch : A Commentary on the Letters of Ignatius of Antioch*. Edited by Helmut Koester. Hermeneia. Philadelphia , Pa.: Fortress, 1985.

Schuler, E. Von. "Sonderformen Hethitischer Staatsverträge." *Jahrbuch Für Kleinasiatische Forschung* 2 (1965): 445–64.

Schulten, A. "Die Makedonischen Militärcolonien." *Hermes* 32, no. 3 (1897): 523–37.

Schulz, Fritz. "Roman Registers of Births and Birth Certificates Part 1." *JRS* 32, no. 1–2 (1942): 78–91.

Schürer, Emil. *Die Prophetin Isabel in Thyatira , Offen. Joh., II, 20, 11*. Edited by A. Von Harnack. Theologische Abhandlungen: Carl von Weizsäcker Zu Seinem Siebzigsten Geburtstage. Freiburg, Germany: Mohr Siebeck, 1892.

———. *The History of the Jewish People in the Age of Jesus Christ (175 BC–AD 135)*. Edited by G. Vermes, F. Miller, and M. Black. Rev. 4 vols. Edinburgh, U.K.: T&T Clark, 1979.

Schüssler Fiorenza, Elisabeth. "Apokalypsis and Propheteia: The Book of Revelation in the Context of Early Christian Prophecy." In *The Book of Revelation: Justice and Judgment*, edited by Gerhard A. Krodel, 2nd ed., 133–56. PC. Minneapolis, Minn.: Fortress, 1999.

———. *Revelation: Vision of a Just World*. Edited by Gerhard A. Krodel. PC. Minneapolis, Minn.: Fortress, 1991.

———. *The Book of Revelation: Justice and Judgment*. Edited by Gerhard A. Krodel. PC. Minneapolis, Minn.: Fortress, 1998.

Schweizer, R. Eduard. "Ministry in the Early Church." Edited by David Noel Freedman, Gary A. Herion, David F. Graf, and John David Pleins. *ABD*. New York, N.Y.: Doubleday, 1996.

Scobie, Charles H. "Local References in the Letters to the Seven Churches." *NTS* 39, no. 4 (1993): 606–24.

Scott, R. B. Y. "The Literary Structure of Isaiah's Oracles." In *Studies in Old Testament Prophecy*, edited by Harold. H. Rowley, 179–86. Edinburgh, U.K.: T&T Clark, 1950.

Scott, Robert B. Y. "The Pillars of Jachin and Boaz." *JBL* 58, no. 1 (1939): 143–49.

Scott, Walter. *Exposition of the Revelation of Jesus Christ.* Westwood, N.J.: Revell, 1968.

Scroggs, Robin. "The Sociological Interpretation of the New Testament: The Present State of Research." *NTS*, Sociological Interpretation of the NT, 26, no. 2 (1980): 164–79.

Seager, Andrew R. "The Architecture of the Dura and Sardis Synagogue." In *The Synagogue: Studies in Origins, Archaeology and Architecture*, edited by Harry M. Orlinksy, 149–93. South Florida Studies in the History of Judaism. New York, N.Y.: KTAV, 1975.

———. "The Building History of the Sardis Synagogue." *AJA* 76 (1972): 425–35.

Sear, Frank. *Roman Architecture.* Abingdon, Oxfordshire: Routledge, 1998.

———. *Roman Theatres: An Architectural Study.* Oxford, U.K.: Oxford University Press, 2006.

Sebesta, Judith Lynn. "Tunica Ralla, Tunica Spissa: The Colors and Textiles of Roman Costume." In *The World of Roman Costume*, edited by Judith Lynn Sebesta and Larissa Bonfante, 65–100. Madison, Wisc.: University of Wisconsin Press, 2001.

Sebesta, Judith Lynn, and Larissa Bonfante, eds. *The World of Roman Costume.* Madison, Wisc.: University of Wisconsin Press, 2001.

Seiss, J. A. *The Apocalypse.* 3 vols. Colorado Springs, Colo.: Cook, 1906.

Seiterle, Gérard. "Artemis - Die Grosse Göttin von Ephesus." *Antike Welt* 10, no. 3 (1979): 3–16.

Seland, Torrey. *Jewish Vigilantism in the First Centry C.E.: A Study of Selected Texts in Philo and Luke on Jewish Vigilante Reactions against Nonconformers to the Torah.* Trondheim: Doctor Artium Dissertation, 1990.

Selles, Lubbertus. *The Book of Revelation: A Series of Outlines for Societies and Bible Study Clubs.* Vol. 1. London, Ont.: Interleague Publication Board of Canadian Reformed Societies, 1972.

Sellew, Philip. "Laodiceans and the Philippians Fragments Hypothesis." *HTR* 87, no. 1 (1994): 17–28.

Selwyn, Edward Carus. *The Christian Prophets and the Prophetic Apocalypse.* New York, N.Y.: MacMillan, 2009.

Seow, Choon-Leong. "Deir 'Alla Plaster Texts." In *Prophets and Prophecy in the Ancient Near East*, edited by Peter Machinist and Martti Nissinen. Atlanta, GA: Society of Biblical Literature, 2003.

Setzer, Claudia J. *Jewish Responses To Early Christians.* Minneapolis, Minn.: Fortress, 1994.

Seyffert, Oskar. *A Dictionary of Classical Antiquities: Mythology, Religion, Literature and Art.* Edited by Henry Nettleship and John Edwin Sandys. New York, N.Y.: MacMillan & Co., 1895.

Seyrig, Henri. "Monnaies hellénistiques." *RevNum* 6, no. 11 (1969): 36–52.

Shanks, Monte A. *Papias and the New Testament.* Eugene, Oreg.: Wipf & Stock, 2013.

Shea, William H. "A Further Note on the Covenantal Form in the Book of Revelation." *AUSS* 21 (1983): 251–64.

———. "The Covenantal Form of the Letters to the Seven Churches." *AUSS* 21 (1983): 71–84.

———. "The Inscribed Tablets From Tell Deir 'Alla." *AUSS* 27 (1989): 21–37; 97–119.

Shear, Theodore Leslie. "The Golden Sands of the Pactolus." *The Classical Weekly* 17, no. 24 (1924): 186–88.

Shepherd, Jr., Massey H. "Smyrna in the Ignatius Letters." *JR* 20 (1940): 141–59.

Sheppard, William John Limmer. *The Revelation of St. John the Divine.* London, U.K.: Religious Tract Society, 1924.

Sheridan, Jennifer A. *Columbia Papyri IX: The Vestis Militaris Codex*. SFSHJ. Atlanta, Ga: Scholars Press, 1998.

Sherwin-White, Adrian N. "Roman Involvement in Anatolia, 167-88 BC." *JRS* 67 (1977): 62–75.

———. *Roman Society and Roman Law in the New Testament: The Sarum Lectures 1960-1961*. Oxford University Press Academic Monograph Reprints. Oxford, U.K.: Clarendon, 2004.

Sherwin-White, Adrian N., and Amélie Kuhrt. *From Samarkhand to Sardis : A New Approach to the Seleucid Empire*. Hellenistic Culture and Society 13. Berkeley, Calf.: University of California Press, 1993.

Shiloh, Yigal. "Torah Scrolls and the Menorah Plaque from Sardis ." *IEJ* 18, no. 1 (1968): 54–57.

Siebert, Anne Viola. "Lectisternium ." In *BrillPaulyA*, edited by Hubert Cancik and Helmuth Schneider, translated by Christine F. Salazar and Francis G. Gentry, Vol. 12. Leiden: Brill, 2006. http://dx.doi.org/10.1163/1574-9347_bnp_e633370.

Silberman, Lou H. "Farewell to OAMHN." *JBL* 82, no. 2 (1963): 213–15.

Silberschlag, Eisig. "The Earliest Record of Jews in Asia Minor." *JBL* 52, no. 1 (1933): 66–77.

Simcox, William H. *The Revelation of St. John the Divine*. CBSC. Cambridge, U.K.: Cambridge University Press, 1890.

Simmons, John G. *Doctors and Discoveries: Lives That Created Today's Medicine from Hippocrates to the Present*. New York, N.Y.: Houghton Mifflin, 2002.

Şimşek, Celal. "2003 Yılı Laodikeia Antik Kenti Kazıları." *KST* 26 (2005): 305–20.

———. "A Menorah with a Cross Carved on a Column of Nymphaeum A at Laodicea Ad Lycum." *JRA* 19 (2006): 343–46.

———. "Ancient 'water Law' Unearthed in Laodicea ." *Hürriyet Daily News*, September 13, 2011. http://www.hurriyetdailynews.com/ancient-water-law-unearthed-in-laodicea-.aspx?pageID=238&nid=87259.

———. "Hierapolis Güney Nekropolü, Konya." Ph.D. diss., Konya, Selçuk University, Institute of Social Sciences, 1997.

———. "Laodicea , A Long-Lived City." *World Archaeology Magazine* 41, no. 4.5 (July 2010): 34–35.

———. "Laodicea Becoming New Ephesus ." *Hurriot Daily News*, December 7, 2011.

———. *Laodikeia (Laodicea Ad Lycum) 2007*. Istanbul: Ege Yayinlari, 2007.

———. *Laodikeia (Laodicea Ad Lycum) 2013*. Laodikeia Çalışmaları (Studies) 2. Istanbul: Ege Yayinlari, 2013.

———. "Regional Cults In The Lycos Valley And Its Neighbourhood." In *Altan Çilingiroğlu'na Armağan Yukarı Denizin Kıyısında Urartu Krallığı'na Adanmış Bir Hayat*, edited by Haluk Sağlamtimur, Eşref Abay, Safer Derin, Aylin Ü. Erdem, Atilla Batmaz, Fulya Dedeoğlu, Mücella Erdalkiran, Mahmut Bilge Baştürk, and Erim Konakçi, 673–90. Istanbul: Arkeoloji ve Senat Yayinlari, 2009.

———. "Temple of Athena Found in Laodicea ." *Hurriot Daily News*, September 12, 2011.

———. "Textile and Production Ateliers in Laodikeia ." *Home Textile* 86 (2015): 138–44.

———. *The Ancient City of Laodicea (Introduction Guide-English)*. Denizli , Turkey: Denizli Municipality, 2010.

Şimşek, Celal, M. Bilgin, and M. Okunak. "Laodikeia Nekropolleri ve Mezar Tipleri." *TAD* 20 (2015): 111–57.

Şimşek, Celal, and Mustafa Büyükkolancı. "Die Aquäducte Und Das Wasserverteilungssystem von Laodikeia Ad Lycum." In *Cura Aquarum In Ephesus : Proceedings of the Twelfth International Congress on the History of Water Management and Hydraulic Engineering in the Mediterranean Region (Ephesus-Selçuck, October 2-10, 2004), Part 1*, edited by Gilbert Wiplinger, 137–46. BABesch Suppl. 12. Leuven, Belgium: Peeters, 2006.

Şimşek, Celal, and M. Ayşem Sezgın. "The West and North Theatres in Laodicea ." In *Restoration and Management of Ancient Theatres in Turkey, Methods, Research, Results*, edited by Filippo Masino, Paolo Mighetto, and Giorgio Sobrà, 103–28. Archeologia E Storia 11. Turkey: Lecce, 2012.

Singer, Isidore, Cyrus Adler, Gotthard Deutsch, Kaufmann Kohler, and Emil G. Hirsch, eds. *The Jewish Encyclopedia*. 12 vols. New York, N.Y.: Funk & Wagnalls, 1906.

Skeat, T. C., and E. G. Turner. "An Oracle of Hermes Trismegistos at Saqqara." *Journal of Egyptian Archaeology* 54 (1968): 199–208.

Slayton, Joel C. "Manna." Edited by David Noel Freedman, Gary A. Herion, David F. Graf, and John David Pleins. *ABD*. New York, N.Y.: Doubleday, 1996.

Smalley, Stephen S. *1, 2, 3 John*. WBC 51. Dallas, Tex.: Word Books, 1989.

———. "John's Revelation and John's Community." *BJRL* 69 (1987): 564–65.

———. "The Christ-Christian Relationship in Paul and John." In *Pauline Studies: Essays Presented to F. F. Bruce on His 70th Birthday*, edited by Donald A. Hagner and Murray J. Harris, 95–105. Exeter, U.K.: Paternoster, 1980.

———. "The Paraclete: Pneumatology in the Johannine Gospel and Apocalypse." In *Exploring the Gospel of John: In Honor of D. Moody Smith*, edited by R. Alan Culpepper and C. Clifton Black, 289–300. Louisville, Ky.: Westminster/Knox, 1996.

———. *The Revelation to John: A Commentary on the Greek Text of the Apocalypse*. Downers Grove, Ill.: InterVarsity, 2005.

———. *Thunder and Love: John's Revelation and John's Community*. Milton Keynes, England: Wood, 1994.

Smallwood, E. Mary. *The Jews Under Roman Rule: From Pompey to Diocletian : A Study in Political Relations*. SJLA 20. Leiden: Brill, 1981.

Smith, J. B. *A Revelation of Jesus Christ: A Commentary on the Book of Revelation*. Edited by J. Otis Yoder. Eugene, OR: Wipf & Stock, 2004.

Smith, R. R. R. "The Imperial Reliefs from the Sebasteion at Aphrodisias ." *JRS* 77 (1987): 88–138.

Smith, Thomas. *Remarks upon the Manners, Religion and Government of the Turks: A Survey of the Seven Churches of Asia, as They Now Lye in Their Ruines*. Early History of Travel and Geography. London, U.K.: Pitt, 1678.

Smith, William. *Dictionary of the Bible*. Edited by H. B. Hackett. 4 vols. Boston, Mass.: Houghton, Mifflin & Company, 1883.

Smith, William, ed. *Dictionary of Greek and Roman Biography and Mythology*. 3 vols. Boston, Mass.: Little, Brown & Co., 1870.

———. "Theudas." In *Dictionary of Greek and Roman Biography and Mythology*, edited by William Smith, 3:1103. Boston, Mass.: Little, Brown & Co., 1870.

Smith, William, and J. F. Flather. "Birrus." In *DGRA*, edited by William Smith, 1:299. London, U.K.: Murray, 1890.

Smith, William, and William Wayte. "Authepsa ." In *DGRA*, edited by William Smith, 1:263. London, U.K.: Murray, 1891.

Smith, William, William Wayte, and George Elden Marindin, eds. *A Dictionary of Greek and Roman Antiquities*. 3rd ed. 2 vols. London, U.K.: Murray, 1891.

Snodgrass, Anthony M. *Arms and Armor of the Greeks* . Baltimore, Md.: The Johns Hopkins University Press, 1998.

Sokolowski, F. "A New Testimony to the Cult of Artemis in Ephesus ." *HTR* 58, no. 4 (1965): 427–31.

———. "Sur Le Culte d'Angelos Dans Ie Paganisme Grec et Romain." *HTR* 53 (1960): 225–29.

Sourvinou-Inwood, Christine. "Artemis ." Edited by Simon Hornblower and Anthony J. S. Spawforth. *OCD*. Oxford, U.K.: Clarendon, 2003.

Southern, Pat. *The Roman Army: A Social and Institutional History*. Oxford, U.K.: Oxford University Press, 2007.

Spalinger, Anthony J. "The Date of the Death of Gyges and Its Historical Implications." *JAOS* 98, no. 4 (1978): 400–409.

Spanier, Ehud, and Nira Karmon. "Muricid Snails and the Ancient Dye Industries." In *The Royal Purple and the Biblical Blue: Argaman and Tekhelet: The Study of Chief Rabbi Dr. Isaac Herzog on the Dye Industries in Ancient Israel and Recent Scientific Contributions*, edited by Ehud Spanier, 179–92. Jerusalem , Israel: Keter, 1987.

Spanier, Ehud, Nira Karmon, and Elisha Linder. "Bibliography Concerning Various Aspects of the Purple Dye." *Levantina* 37 (1982): 437–47.

Spanier, Ehud, Elisha Linder, and Nira Karmon. *Purple Dye—Biology, Archaeology and History*. Haifa: University of Haifa, Center for Maritime Studies, 1980.

Sperti, Luigi. "Ricognizione Archeologica a Laodicea Di Frigia: 1993–1998." In *Laodicea Ricognizione Archeologica a Laodicea Di Frigia*, edited by Gustavo Traversari, Giorgio Bejor, Manuela Fano Santi, Luigi Sperti, Jacopo Bonetto, Claudio Negrelli, and Sauro Gelichi, 29–103. Rivista Di Archeologia, Supp. 24. Roma : Bretschneider, 2000.

Spier, J. "Notes on Early Electrum Coinage and a Die-Linked Issue from Lydia ." In *Studies in Greek Numismatics in Memory of Martin Jessop Price*, edited by Richard Ashton and S. Hurter, 321–26. London: Spink & Son, 1998.

Spinks, Bryan D. *Early and Medieval Rituals and Theologies of Baptism: From the New Testament to the Council of Trent*. Farnham, U.K.: Ashgate, 2006.

Spitta, Friedrich. *Die Offenbarung des Johannes*. Halle: Waisenhaus, 1889.

Stambaugh, John E. "Thyatira (Place)." Edited by David Noel Freedman, Gary A. Herion, David F. Graf, and John David Pleins. *ABD*. New York, N.Y.: Doubleday, 1996.

Stambaugh, John E., and David L. Balch. *The New Testament in Its Social Environment*. LEC 2. Philadelphia , Pa.: Westminster, 1986.

Starke, Robert. "The Tree of Life: Protological to Eschatological." *Kerux* 11, no. 2 (2010): 1–12.

Ste. Croix, G. E. M. de. "Aspects of the 'Great' Persecution." *HTR* 47, no. 2 (1954): 73–113.

———. "Christianity's Encounter with the Roman Imperial Government." In *The Crucible of Christianity: Judaism, Hellenism and The Historical Background to the Christian Faith*, edited by Arnold Toynbee, 345–46. New York, N.Y.: Thames & Hudson, 1969.

———. "Why Were the Early Christians Persecuted?" *Past and Present* 26 (1963): 1–38.

Stegemann, Viktor. *Die Gestalt Christi in Den Koptischen Zaubertexten*. Heidelberg: Bilabel, 1934.

Stern, David H. *Jewish New Testament Commentary*. Chandler, Ariz.: Messianic Jewish Resources International, 1992.

Stern, Ephraim, Ayelet Levinson-Gilboa, and Joseph Aviram, eds. *The New Encyclopedia of Archaeological Excavations in the Holy Land*. 4 vols. New York, N.Y.: MacMillan, 1993.

Stern, Menahem. "The Jewish Diaspora." In *The Jewish People in the First Century: Historical Geography, Political History, Social, Cultural and Religious Life and Institutions*, edited by Menahem Stern and Shemuel Safrai, 143–53. CRINT. Philadelphia, Pa.: Fortress, 1974.

Stern, Philip D. *The Biblical Hêrem a Window on Israel's Religious Experience*. Brown Judaic Studies 211. Atlanta, Ga.: Scholars Press, 1991.

Stevens, Gerald L. *Revelation: The Past and Future of John's Apocalypse*. Eugene, Oreg.: Wipf & Stock, 2014.

Stevenson, Gregory. *Beihefte Zur Zeitschrift Für Die Neutestamentliche Wissenschaft Und Die Kunde Der Älteren Kirche*. Berlin: de Gruyter, 2001.

———. *Power and Place: Temple and Identity in the Book of Revelation*. Berlin: de Gruyter, 2001.

Stevenson, Gregory M. "Conceptual Background to Golden Crown Imagery in the Apocalypse of John." *JBL* 114, no. 2 (1995): 257–72.

Stevenson, Seth William. *A Dictionary of Roman Coins : Republican and Imperial*. Edited by Charles Roach Smith and Frederic William Madden. London, U.K.: George Bell & Sons, 1889.

Stewart, Andrew. "Pergamo Ara Marmorea Magna: On the Date, Reconstruction, and Functions of the Great Altar of Pergamon." In *From Pergamon to Sperlonga: Sculpture and Context*, edited by Nancy T. de Grummond and Brunilde Sismondo Ridgway, 32–57. Hellenistic Culture and Society. Berkeley, Calf.: University of California Press, 2001.

Stewart, Zeph. "Greek Crowns and Christian Martyrs." In *Mémorial André-Jean Festugière: Antiquité Païenne et Chrétienne*, edited by E. Lucchesi and H. D. Saffrey, 119–24. Geneva: Cramer, 1984.

Stewart-Sykes, A. *The Lamb's High Feast: Melito, Peri Pascha, and the Quartodeciman Paschal Liturgy at Sardis*. Supplements to Vigiliae Christianae. Leiden: Brill Academic, 1998.

Stieglitz, Robert R. *Minoan and Canaanite Sea-Purple. First International Symposium on Harbours, Port Cities and Coastal Topography*. Haifa, 1986.

———. "The Minoan Origin of Tyrian Purple." *BA* 57, no. 1 (1994): 46–54.

Storey, Glenn R. "The Population of Ancient Rome." *Antiquity* 71, no. 274 (1997): 966–78.

Stott, John. *What Christ Thinks of the Church: An Exposition of Revelation 1-3*. Grand Rapids, Mich.: Baker, 2003.

Strachan-Davidson, James Leigh. *Problems of the Roman Criminal Law*. 2 vols. Oxford, U.K.: Clarendon, 1912.

Strand, Kenneth A. "A Further Note on the Covenantal Form in the Book of Revelation." *AUSS* 21 (1983): 251–64.

Strelan, Rick. *Paul, Artemis, and the Jews in Ephesus*. Berlin: de Gruyter, 1996.

Strugnell, John, Daniel J Harrington, and Torleif Elgvin, eds. *Qumran Cave 4. XXIV: Sapiential Texts, Part 2, 4QInstruction (Musar Le Mevin): 4Q415ff.* DJD 34. Oxford, U.K.: Clarendon, 1999.

Strugnell, John. "The Angelic Liturgy at Qumran." In *Congress Volume, Oxford 1959*, edited by G. W. Anderson, P. A. H. De Boer, Henri Castellio, E. Hammershaimb, Herbert G. May, and Walther Zimmerli, 318–345. VTSup 7. Leiden: Brill, 1960.

Stuart, Moses. *A Commentary on the Apocalypse*. 2 vols. Andover, Mass.: Allen, Morrill & Wardwell, 1845.

———. "The White Stone of the Apocalypse." *BSac* 1 (1843): 461–77.

Stuckenbruck, Loren T. *Angel Veneration and Christology: A Study in Early Judaism and the Christology of the Apocalypse of John*. WUNT, 2/70. Tübingen: Mohr Siebeck, 1995.

———. "Revelation." In *Eerdmans Commentary on the Bible*, edited by James D. G. Dunn and John W. Rogerson, 1535–1629. Grand Rapids, Mich.: Eerdmans, 2003.

Sullivan, R. D. "Dynasts in Pontus." *ANRW* 7, no. 2 (1980): 925–30.

Sutherland, Carol Humphrey Vivian. *Coinage in Roman Imperial Policy, 31 B.C.–A.D. 68*. London, U.K.: Methuen & Company, 1951.

———. *Roman History and Coinage, 44 BC-AD 69: Fifty Points of Relation from Julius Caesar to Vespasian*. Oxford: Clarendon Press, 1987.

———. *The Cistophori of Augustus*. London, U.K.: Royal Numismatic Society, 1970.

Sutton, Ray R. *That You May Prosper: Dominion by Covenant*. Tyler, Tex.: Institute for Christian Economics, 1987.

Sweet, John P. M. *Revelation*. TPINTC. Valley Forge, PA: Trinity Press International, 1990.

Swete, Henry Barclay. *Commentary on Revelation*. Reprint 1906. Eugene, Oreg.: Wipf & Stock, 1999.

———. *The Apocalypse of St. John*. 3rd ed. London, U.K.: MacMillan & Co., 1917.

———. *The Holy Spirit in the New Testament*. Eugene, Oreg.: Wipf & Stock, 1999.

Tabbernee, William. *Prophets and Gravestones: An Imaginative History of Montanists and Other Early Christians*. Grand Rapids, Mich.: Baker Academic, 2009.

Tait, Andrew. *The Messages to the Seven Churches of Asia Minor: An Exposition of the First Three Chapters of the Book of the Revelation*. London, U.K.: Hodder & Stoughton, 1884.

Tajra, Harry W. *The Trial of St. Paul: A Juridical Exegesis of the Second Half of the Acts of the Apostles*. Eugene, Oreg.: Wipf & Stock, 2010.

Talbert, Charles H. *The Apocalypse: A Reading of the Revelation of John*. Louisville, Ky.: Westminster John Knox, 1994.

Tanriöver, Y. Ersel, and N. Orhan Baykan. "The Water Supply Systems of Caria." In *Cura Aquarum In Ephesus: Proceedings of the Twelfth International Congress on the History of Water Management and Hydraulic Engineering in the Mediterranean Region (Ephesus-Selçuck, October 2-10, 2004), Part 1*, edited by Gilbert Wiplinger, 127–32. BABesch Suppl. 12. Leuven, Belgium: Peeters, 2006.

Tarn, W. W. *Hellenistic Civilization*. 3rd ed. London, U.K.: Arnold & Co., 1952.

Tasker, R. V. G. *The General Epistle of James*. TNTC 16. Grand Rapids, Mich.: Eerdmans, 1983.

Taslialan, Mehmet. "New Excavations and Restorations in the Agora of Smyrna ." In *Paper Presented at Institut Für Archäologie, Abt. Archäologie Des Mittelmeerraumes*. University of Berne, Institute of Archaeology, June 24, 2004.

Taylor, Jeremy, and Reginald Heber. *The Whole Works of the Right Rev. Jeremy Taylor: With a Life of the Author and a Critical Examination of His Writings*. London, U.K.: Rivington, 1828.

Taylor, Justin. *Les Actes Des Deux Apôtres VI: Commentaire Historique (Act. 18,23-28,31)*. Etudes Bibliques 30. Paris, France: Gabalda, 1996.

Taylor, Lily Ross. *The Divinity of the Roman Emperor*. Edited by Joseph William Hewitt. American Philological Association 1. New York, N.Y.: Scholars Press, 2011.

Ten Dam, A., and C. Erentöz. "Kizildere Geothermal Field — Western Anatolia." *Geothermics* 2 (January 1, 1970): 124–29.

Tengbom, Luverne C. "Studies in the Interpretation of Revelation Two and Three." Ph.D. diss., Hartford Seminary, 1976.

Tenney, Merrill C., and Moises Silva, eds. *The Zondervan Encyclopedia of the Bible: Revised Full-Color Edition*. Revised. 5 vols. Grand Rapids, Mich.: Zondervan, 2009.

Tenney, Merrill C. *Interpreting Revelation*. Grand Rapids, Mich.: Eerdmans, 1988.

Thayer, Joseph Henry. *Thayer's Greek-English Lexicon of the New Testament. Complete and Unabridged*. Grand Rapids, Mich.: Baker, 1889.

Theissen, Gerd. *The Social Setting of Pauline Christianity*. Philadelphia , Pa.: Fortress, 1982.

Thimmes, Pamela. "Women Reading Women in the Apocalypse: Reading Scenario 1, the Letter to Thyatira (Rev. 2:18–29)." *CBR* 2, no. 1 (2003): 128–44.

Thiselton, Anthony C. "The Supposed Power of Words in the Biblical Writings." *JTS* 25, no. 2 (1974): 283–99.

Thomas, David Winston. *Documents from Old Testament Times*. Society for Old Testament Study. New York, N.Y.: Harper, 1961.

Thomas, Edmund. *Monumentality and the Roman Empire: Architecture in the Antonine Age*. Oxford, U.K.: Oxford University Press, 2007.

Thomas, J. David. "Strategos and Exactor in the Fourth Century: One Office or Two?" *ChrEg* 70 (1995): 230–39.

Thomas, Robert L. *Revelation 1–7 Commentary*. Chicago, Ill.: Moody, 1992.

———. "The 'Comings' of Christ in Revelation 2-3." *MSJ* 7, no. 2 (1996): 153–81.

Thomas, W. H. Griffith. *Studies in Colossians and Philemon*. Grand Rapids, Mich.: Kregel, 1986.

Thommen, Geraldine. "The Sebasteion at Aphrodisias : An Imperial Cult to Honor Augustus and the Julio-Claudian Emperors." *Chronika* 2 (2012): 82–91.

Thompson, Glen L., and Mark Wilson. "The Route of Paul's Second Journey in Asia Minor: In the Steps of Robert Jewett and Beyond." *TynBul* 67, no. 2 (2016): 217–46.

Thompson, John A. *The Ancient Near Eastern Treaties and the Old Testament*. Wheaton, Ill.: Tyndale, 1964.

———. "The Near Eastern Suzerain-Vassal Concept in the Religion of Israel ." *JRH* 3 (1964): 1–19.

Thompson, Leonard L. "A Sociological Analysis of Tribulation in the Apocalypse of John." In *Early Christian Apocalypticism: Genre and Social Setting*, edited by Adela Yarbro Collins, 147–74. Semeia 36. Decatur, Ga.: SBL, 1986.

———. *Revelation*. Nashville, Tenn.: Abingdon, 1998.

———. *The Book of Revelation: Apocalypse and Empire*. New York, N.Y.: Oxford University Press, USA, 1997.

Thonemann, Peter. "A Copy of Augustus' Res Gestae at Sardis ." *Historia* 61, no. 3 (2012): 282–88.

———. *The Maeander Valley: A Historical Geography from Antiquity to Byzantium* . Cambridge, U.K.: Cambridge University Press, 2011.

Tigay, Jeffrey H. "On Evaluating Claims of Literary Borrowing." In *The Tablet and the Scroll: Near Eastern Studies in Honor of William W. Hallo*, edited by Mark E. Cohen, Daniel C. Snell, and David B. Weisberg, 250–55. Bethesda, Md.: Capital Decisions Ltd, 1993.

Tigchelaar, Eibert J. C. "Eden and Paradise: The Garden Motif in Some Early Jewish Texts (1 Enoch and Other Texts Found at Qumran)." In *Paradise Interpreted: Representations of Biblical Paradise in Judaism and Christianity*, edited by Gerard P. Luttikhuizen, 37–62. Themes in Biblical Narrative 2. Leiden: Brill, 1999.

Tilborg, Sjef Van. *Reading John in Ephesus* . NovTSup 83. Leiden: Brill Academic, 1997.

Toker, Tarhan. *Pamukkale (Hierapolis)*. Denizli , Turkey: Haber Gazetecilik, 1976.

Tokhtas'ev, Sergei R. "Cimmerians." In *Encyclopædia Iranica*, edited by Ehsan Yarshater, Facs. 6, 5:563–67. London, U.K.: Eisenbrauns, 1991.

Toksöz, Cemil. *Pergamum : Its History and Archaeology*. Translated by Amhmet E. Uysal. Ankara, Turkey: Ayyildiz Matbassi, 1960.

Toorn, Karel van der. "Cultic Prostitution." In *ABD*, edited by David Noel Freedman, Gary A. Herion, David F. Graf, and John David Pleins, 5:510–13. New York, N.Y.: Doubleday, 1996.

Torrey, Charles C. *The Apocalypse of John*. New Haven, Conn.: Yale University Press, 1958.

———. "The Aramaic Period of the Nascent Christian Church." *ZNW*, 53 1952, 205–33.

Townsend, Jeffrey L. "The Rapture in Revelation 3:10." *BSac* 137, no. 547 (July 1980): 252–66.

Toynbee, J. M. C. "Roman Medallions: Their Scope and Purpose." *The Numismatic Chronicle and Journal of the Royal Numismatic Society* 4, no. 1/4 (1944): 27–44.

Travis, S. H. "Eschatology." In *New Dictionary of Theology*, edited by Sinclair B. Ferguson, David F. Wright, and James I. Packer, 228–31. Downers Grove, Ill.: InterVarsity, 1988.

Trebilco, Paul. *The Early Christians in Ephesus from Paul to Ignatius* . Grand Rapids, Mich.: Eerdmans, 2007.

Trebilco, Paul R. "Asia." In *The Book of Acts in Its Graeco-Roman Setting*, edited by David W. Gill and Conrad H. Gempf, 2:291–362. Book of Acts in Its First Century Setting 2. Grand Rapids, Mich.: Eerdmans, 1994.

Trebilco, Paul R. *Jewish Communities in Asia Minor*. SNTS 69. Cambridge, U.K.: Cambridge University Press, 2006.

Trell, Bluma L. "The Temple of Artemis at Ephesos." In *The Seven Wonders of the Ancient World*, edited by Peter A. Clayton and Martin Price, 78–99. New York, N.Y.: Routledge, 2013.

Trench, Richard C. *Commentary on the Epistles to the Seven Churches in Asia: Revelation 2, 3*. 2nd ed. London, U.K.: Parker, Son & Bourn, 1862.

———. *Synonyms of the New Testament*. New York, N.Y.: Cosimo Classics, 2007.

Trinkl, Elisabeth. "Artifacts Related to Preparation of Wool and Textile Processing Found inside the Terrace Houses of Ephesus, Turkey." In *Ancient Textiles: Production, Craft and Society*, edited by Carole Gillis and Marie-Louise B. Nosch, 81–86. Oxford, U.K.: Oxbow, 2007.

———. "The Wool Basket: Function, Depiction and Meaning of the Kalathos." In *Greek and Roman Textiles and Dress: An Interdisciplinary Anthology*, edited by Mary Harlow and Marie-Louise Nosch, 190–206. Oxford, U.K.: Oxbow Books, 2014.

Trites, Allison A. "Μάρτυς and Martyrdom in the Apocalypse: A Semantic Study." *NovT* 15, no. 1 (1973): 72–80.

Trudinger, Paul. "Ho Amen (Rev III:14), and the Case for a Semitic Original of the Apocalypse." *NovT* 14, no. 4 (1972): 277–79.

Tsevat, Matitiahu. "The Neo-Assyrian and Neo-Babylonian Vassal Oaths and the Prophet Ezekiel." *JBL* 78, no. 3 (1959): 199–204.

Tully, F. Le Guet. "Science and the Design of Mechanical and Optical Devices: A Few Case Studies." In *Design Methodology and Relationships with Science*, edited by Marc J. de Vries, Nigel Cross, and D. P. Grant, 29–61. Behavioral and Social Sciences 71. Dordrecht: Kluwer Academic, 1993.

Tupper, E. Frank. "The Revival of Apocalyptic in Biblical and Theological Studies." *Review and Expositor* 72, no. 3 (1975): 279–303.

Turcan, Robert. *Héliogabale et le sacre du soleil*. Paris: Michel, 1986.

Turner, Cuthbert H. *Studies in Early Church History: Collected Papers*. Oxford, U.K.: Oxford University Press, 1912.

Tyconius. *The Turin Fragments of Tyconius' Commentary on Revelation*. Edited by Francesco Lo Bue and Geoffrey Grimshaw Willis. TS: Contributions to Biblical and Patristic Literature 7. Cambridge, U.K.: Cambridge University Press, 1963.

Uggeri, Giovanni. "Sulle Strade di San Paolo in Anatolia: Il secondo e il terzo viaggio." In *Seminario di studi Paolo di Tarso: il messaggio, l'immagine, i viaggi: studi in memoria di Luigi Padovese*, edited by Stella Uggeri Patitucci and Luigi Padovese, 125–73. Quaderni di archeologia medievale 12. Palermo: Officina di Studi Medievali, 2011.

Ulmer, Rivka. *Evil Eye in the Bible and Rabbinic Literature*. Hoboken, N. J.: KTAV, 1994.

Unger, Merrill F. *Archaeology and the New Testament*. Grand Rapids, Mich.: Zondervan, 1975.

Ustinova, Yulia. *The Supreme Gods of the Bosporan Kingdom: Celestial Aphrodite and the Most High God*. Leiden: Brill, 1999.

Vailhé, Siméon. "Sardes." In *CE*, edited by Charles George Herbermann, Condé Bénoist Pallen, and Edward Aloysius Pace, 13:472. New York, N.Y.: Appleton & Company, 1913.

———. "Smyrna." In *CE*, edited by Charles George Herbermann, translated by Mario Anello, 14:60. New York, N.Y.: Appleton & Company, 1913.

Vanhoye, Albert. *Old Testament Priests and the New Priest*. Revised. Herefordshire England: Gracewing, 2009.

Vanni, Ugo. "Liturgical Dialogue as a Literary Form in the Book of Revelation." *NTS* 37, no. 3 (1991): 348–72.

Varner, Eric R. "Domitia Longina and the Politics of Portraiture." *AJA* 99, no. 2 (1995): 187–206.

———. *Monumenta Graeca et Romana: Mutilation and Transformation: Damnatio Memoriae and Roman Imperial Portraiture*. Leiden: Brill, 2004.

Varone, Antonio. *Erotica Pompeiana: Love Inscriptions on the Walls of Pompeii*. Translated by Ria P. Berg. Rome : Di Bretschneider, 2003.

Vawter, Bruce. *The Conscience of Israel ; Pre-Exilic Prophets and Prophecy*. New York, N.Y.: Sheed & Ward, 1961.

Vermès, Géza. *Scripture and Tradition in Judaism: Haggadic Studies*. Leiden: Brill, 1973.

Vermeule, Cornelius C. *Roman Imperial Art in Greece and Asia Minor*. Cambridge, U.K.: Harvard University Press, 1968.

Verzone, Paolo. "L'urbanistica Di Hierapolis Di Frigia: Tracciato Viario E Monumenti Rimessi Alla Luce Dal 1957 Al 1972." In *Atti Del XVI Congresso Di Storia dell'Architettura*, 401–13. Rome : Atene, 1977.

Vickers, Michael J. *The Roman World*. 2nd ed. The Making of the Past. New York, N.Y.: Peter Bedrick Books, 1989.

Victor, Chapot. *La Province Romaine Proconsulaire d'Asie*. Paris, France: Librairie Emile Bouillon, 1904.

Vitringa, Campegius. *Anakrisis Apocalypsios Joannis Apostoli*. Amsterdam: Henricus Strickius, 1719.

Vogel, Lise. *The Column of Antoninus Pius*. Cambridge, Mass.: Harvard University Press, 1973.

Voinot, Jacques. *Les cachets à collyres dans le monde romain*. Monographies instrumentum 7. Montagnac: Mergoil, 1999.

Von Staden, Heinrich. *Herophilus: The Art of Medicine in Early Alexandria: Edition, Translation and Essays*. Cambridge, U.K.: Cambridge University Press, 1989.

Vos, Louis A. *The Synoptic Traditions in the Apocalypse*. Kampen, Netherlands: Kok, 1965.

Voss, G. "The Analysis of Indigoid Dyes as Leuco Forms by NMR Spectroscopy." *Journal of the Society of Dyers and Colourists* 116 (2000): 87–90.

Waal, Cornelis van der. *The Covenantal Gospel*. Edited by H. DeJong. Translated by G. L. Bertram. Alberta: Inheritance, 1990.

Waddington, William Henry. *Inventaire Sommaire de La Collection Waddington Acquise Par L'état En 1897 Pour Le Département Des Médailles et Antiques de La Bibliothèque Nationale, Rédigé Par Ernest Babelon*. Paris, France: Rollin et Feuardent, 1898

Waegeman, Maryse. *Amulet and Alphabet: Magical Amulets in the First Book of Cyranides*. Amsterdam: Gieben, 1987.

Waelkens, Marc. "Phrygian Votive and Tombstones as Sources of the Social and Economic Life in Roman Antiquity." *Ancient Society* 8 (1977): 277–315.

Waldbaum, Jane C. "Metalwork and Metalworking in Sardis ." In *Sardis: Twenty-Seven Years of Discovery*, edited by Eleanor Guralnick, 36–45. Chicago, Ill.: Archaeological Institute of America, 1987.

Walker, Larry L. "Deuteronomy." Edited by Merrill C. Tenney and Moises Silva. *ZEB*. Grand Rapids, Mich.: Zondervan, 2009.

Wall, Robert W. *Revelation*. Edited by W. Ward Gasque. NIBC 18. Peabody, Mass.: Hendrickson, 2002.

Wallace, Daniel B. "The Article with Multiple Substantives Connected by Kai in the New Testament: Semantics and Significance." Ph.D. diss., Dallas Theological Seminary, 1995.

Wallace, Paul W. "Journey by Lamplight: A Visit to the Seven Churches of Asia — Part 4." *BS* 5, no. 4 (1976): 101–13.

Wallace, R. W. "Kukalim, Walwet, and the Artemision Deposit: Problems in Early Anatolian Electrum Coinages." In *Agoranomia: Studies in Money and Exchange Presented to John H. Kroll*, edited by Peter G. Van Alfen, 37–49. New York, N.Y.: American Numismatic Society, 2006.

Walton, John H. *Ancient Israelite Literature in Its Cultural Context: A Survey of Parallels between Biblical and Ancient Near Eastern Texts*. 2nd ed. Library of Biblical Interpretation. Grand Rapids, Mich.: Zondervan, 1990.

Walton, John H., Victor H. Matthews, and Mark W. Chavalas. *The IVP Bible Background Commentary: Old Testament*. Downers Grove, Ill.: InterVarsity, 2000.

Waltzing, Jean Pierre. *Étude historique sur les corporations professionnelles chez les Romains depuis les origines jusqu'à la chute de l'Empire d'Occident*. Vol. 3. 4 vols. Louvain: Louvain, C. Peeters, 1895.

Walvoord, John F. *Revelation*. Edited by Roy B. Zuck. Wheaton, Ill.: Victor, 1983.

———. *The Revelation of Jesus Christ*. Chicago, Ill.: Moody, 1989.

Warden, Duane. "Imperial Persecution and the Dating of First Peter and Revelation." *NTS* 34, no. 2 (1991): 203–12.

Warden, Preston Duane, and Roger S. Bagnall. "The Forty Thousand Citizens of Ephesus." *CP* 83, no. 3 (1988): 220–23.

Watson, Duane F. "Nicolaitans." Edited by David Noel Freedman, Gary A. Herion, David F. Graf, and John David Pleins. *ABD*. New York, N.Y.: Doubleday, 1996.

Watson, Richard. *A Biblical and Theological Dictionary*. New York, N.Y.: Waugh & Mason, 1833.

Weber, G. "Die Flüsse von Laodicea: Lykos, Kadmos, Kapros, Elnos Und Asopos." *MDAI* 23 (1898): 178–95.

———. "Die Hochdruck Wasserleitung von Laodicea Ad Lycum." *JDAI* 13 (1898): 1–13.

———. "Die Hochdruck Wasserleitung von Laodicea Ad Lycum." *JDAI* 19 (1904): 95–96.

Weber, Wilhelm. *Untersuchungen zur Geschichte des Kaisers Hadrian*. Hildesheim: Olms, 2001.

Webster, Thomas Bertram Lonsdale. *Hellenistic Poetry and Art*. London, U.K.: Methuen, 1964.

Weeks, Noel. *Admonition and Curse the Ancient Near Eastern Treaty/Covenant Form as a Problem in Inter-Cultural Relationships*. JSOTSup 407. Edinburgh, U.K.: T&T Clark, 2004.

———. *Admonition and Curse: The Ancient Near Eastern Treaty/Covenant Form as a Problem in Inter-Cultural Relationships*. New York, N.Y.: T&T Clark, 2004.

Weigelt, H. "Clothe, Naked, Dress, Garment, Cloth." Edited by Colin Brown. *NIDNTT*. Grand Rapids, Mich.: Zondervan, 1976.

Weinfeld, Moshe. "Ancient Near Eastern Patterns in Prophetic Literature." *VT* 27 (1977): 178–95.

———. "Covenant Making in Anatolia and Mesopotamia." *The Ancient Near Eastern Society of Columbia University* 22 (1992): 135–39.

———. "Covenant Terminology in the Ancient Near East and Its Influence on the West." *JAOS* 93, no. 2 (1973): 190–99.

———. *Deuteronomy and the Deuteronomic School*. Oxford, U.K.: Clarendon, 1983.

———. "The Common Heritage of Covenantal Traditions in the Ancient World." In *I Trattati Nel Mondo Antico-Forma, Ideologia, Funzione (Saggi Di Storia Antica)*, edited by Luciano Canfora, Mario Liverani, and Carlo Zaccagnini, 2:175–91. Roma : L'Erma, 1990.

———. "The Loyalty Oath in the Ancient Near East." *UF* 8 (1976): 379–414.

Weiss, Bernhard. *Die Johannes-Apokalypse: textkritische Untersuchungen und Textherstellung*. TU, 7.1. Berlin: Hinrichs, 1904.

Weiss, Peter. "Hadrian in Lykien." *Chiron* 25 (1995): 213–14.

Welch, K. "The Roman Arena in Late-Republican Italy: A Re-Evaluation." In *Sport in the Greek and Roman Worlds: Greek Athletic Identities and Roman Sports and Spectacle*, edited by Thomas Francis Scanlon, Vol. 2. Oxford, U.K.: Oxford University Press, 2014.

Welles, C. Bradford, Robert O. Fink, and J. Frank Gilliam. *The Parchments and Papyri*. Edited by Ann Perkins. Excavations at Dura-Europos, Final Report V, I. New Haven, Conn.: Yale University Press, 1959.

Wendel, Clarence A. "Land Tilting or Silting? Which Ruined Ancient Aegean Harbors?" *Archaeology* 22, no. 4 (1969): 322–24.

Wernicke, H. "Artemis ." In *PW*, edited by A. F. Pauly and Georg Wissowa, New., 2:1336–1440. Munich: Buchhandlung, 1895.

Westermann, Claus. *Basic Forms of Prophetic Speech*. Translated by Hugh Clayton White. Louisville, Ky.: Westminster/Knox, 1991.

White, Jr., W. "Laodicea ." Edited by Merrill C. Tenney and Moises Silva. *ZEB*. Grand Rapids, Mich.: Zondervan, September 19, 2009.

White, L. Michael. "Urban Development and Social Change in Imperial Ephesos." In *Ephesos Metropolis of Asia: An Interdisciplinary Approach to Its Archaeology, Religion, and Culture*, edited by Helmut Koester, 27–80. HTS 41. Cambridge, Mass.: Harvard Divinity School, 1995.

Whitehorne, J. E. G. "P. Oxy. XLIII 3119: A Document of Valerian's Persecution?" *ZPE* 24, no. 1 (1977): 187–96.

Whiting, Charles C. *The Revelation of John: An Interpretation of the Book with an Introduction and a Translation*. Boston, Mass.: Gorham, 1918.

Wiarda, Tim. "Revelation 3:20: Imagery And Literary Context." *JETS* 38, no. 2 (1995): 203–12.

Wight, Fred H. *Highlights of Archaeology in Bible Lands*. Chicago, Ill.: Moody, 1955.

Wijngaards, J. *Vazal van Jahweh*. Baarn: Bosch & Keuning, 1965.

Wikenhauser, Alfred. *Die Offenbarung des Johannes*. 3rd ed. RNT 9. Regensburg: Pustet, 1959.

Wilcock, Michael. *The Message of Revelation: I Saw Heaven Opened*. BST. Downers Grove, Ill.: InterVarsity, 1975.

Wild, J. P. *Textile Manufacture in the Northern Roman Provinces*. CCS. Cambridge, U.K.: Cambridge University Press, 1970.

Wilken, Robert L. "Melito, the Jewish Community at Sardis, and the Sacrifice of Isaac." *ThS* 37 (1976): 53–69.

Wilkinson, Richard H. "The ΣΤΥΛΟΣ of Revelation 3:12 and Ancient Coronation Rites." *JBL* 107, no. 3 (1988): 498–501.

Will, E. "Banquets et salles de banquet dans le cultes de la Grece et de l'Empire romain." In *Mélanges d'histoire ancienne et d'archéologie offerts à Paul Collart*, edited by Pierre Ducrey, 353–62. Lausanne, Switzerland: Bibliothèque historique vaudoise, 1976.

Will, E. Lyding. "Women's Roles in Antiquity: New Archeological Views." *Science Digest*, March 1980, 35–39.

Williams, Jay G. *Those Who Ponder Proverbs: Aphoristic Thinking and Biblical Literature*. Sheffield, U.K.: Almond, 1981.

Willis, Wendell Lee. *Idol Meat in Corinth: The Pauline Argument in 1 Corinthians 8 and 10*. SBLDS 68. Chicago, Ill.: Scholars Press, 1985.

Wilson, Andrew. "The Archaeology of the Roman Fullonica." *JRA* 16 (2003): 442–46.

Wilson, Andrew, and Miko Flohr. *Urban Craftsmen and Traders in the Roman World*. Oxford, U.K.: Oxford University Press, 2016.

Wilson, J. Christian. "The Problem of the Domitianic Date of Revelation." *NTS* 39, no. 4 (1993): 587–605.

Wilson, Mark. *The Victor Sayings in the Book of Revelation*. Eugene, Oreg.: Wipf & Stock, 2007.

Wilson, Mark W. "A Pie in a Very Bleak Sky? Analysis and Appropriation of the Promise Sayings in the Seven Letters to the Churches in Revelation 2-3." D.Litt., University of South Africa, 1997.

———. *Biblical Turkey: A Guide to Jewish and Christian Sites of Asia Minor*. Istanbul: Ege Yayinlari, 2010.

———. *Revelation*. ZIBBC. Grand Rapids, Mich.: Zondervan, 2007.

Wilson, Stephen G. "Gentile Judaizers." *NTS* 38, no. 4 (1992): 605–16.

Wilson, Stephen G., and Stephen G. Wilson, eds. "Melito and Israel." In *Anti-Judaism in Early Christianity: Separation and Polemic*, 2:81–102. ESCJ 2. Waterloo, Ont.: Wilfrid Laurier University Press, 1986.

Winfrey, David G. "The Great Tribulation: Kept 'Out Of' Or 'Through'?" *GTJ* 3, no. 1 (1982): 3–18.

Wiseman, Donald J. "The Vassal-Treaties of Esarhaddon." *Iraq* 20 (1958): 1–99.

Wiseman, Donald John. *Chronicles of Chaldaean Kings (626-556 B.C.)*. London, U.K.: Trustee of the British Museum, 1956.

Witetschek, Stephen. "Der Lieblingspsalm Des Sehers: Die Verwendung von Ps 2 in Der Johannesapokalypse." In *The Septuagint and Messianism*, edited by Michael Anthony Knibb, 487–502. BETL 195. Leuven, Belgium: Leuven University Press, 2006.

Witherington III, Ben. *New Testament History: A Narrative Account*. Grand Rapids, Mich.: Baker, 2003.

———. "Not So Idle Thoughts About Eidolothuton." *TynBul* 44, no. 2 (1993): 237–54.

———. *Revelation*. Cambridge, U.K.: Cambridge University Press, 2003.

Witt, Peter Daniel MacDearmon. "The Judicial Function of the Strategos in the Roman Period." Ph.D. diss., Duke University, 1977.

Witulski, Thomas. "Die Aufenthalte Des Kaisers Hadrian in Der Römischen Provinz Asia." In *Paulus Und Die Antike Welt. Beiträge Zur Zeit- Und Religionsgeschichtlichen Erforschung Des Paulinischen Christentums*, edited by David C. Bienert, Joachim Jeska, and Thomas Witulski, 1st ed., 150–66. Festgabe Für Dietrich-Alex Koch Zum 65. Geburtstag, FRLANT. Göttingen: Vandenhoeck & Ruprecht, 2008.

Wojciechowski, Michael. "Seven Churches and Seven Celestial Bodies (Rev 1,16; Rev 2 -3)." *BN* 45 (1988): 48–50.

Wong, Daniel K. K. "The Hidden Manna and the White Stone in Revelation 2:17." *BSac* 155, no. 619 (1998): 346–54.

———. "The Tree of Life in Revelation 2:7." *BSac* 155, no. 618 (1998): 211–26.

Wood, Bryant G. "Balaam Son of Beor." *BS* 8, no. 4 (1995): 115–17.

Wood, John Turtle. *Discoveries at Ephesus : Including the Sites and Remains of the Great Temple of Diana*. London, U.K.: Longmans, Green & Company, 1877.

Wood, Peter. "Local Knowledge of the Letters of the Apocalypse." *ExpTim* 73, no. 9 (1962): 263–64.

Woodman, Jesse Earle. "The Expositio Totius Mundi et Gentium: Its Geography and Its Language." M.A. diss., The Ohio State University, 1964.

Worth, Jr., Roland H. *The Seven Cities of the Apocalypse and Greco-Asian Culture*. New York, N.Y.: Paulist, 2002.

———. *The Seven Cities of the Apocalypse and Roman Culture*. New York, N.Y.: Paulist, 2002.

Wotschitzky, Alfons. "Ephesus : Past, Present and Future of an Ancient Metropolis." *Archaeology* 14, no. 3 (1961): 205–12.

Wouters, Jan. "A New Method for the Analysis of Blue and Purple Dyes in Textiles." *Dyes in History and Archaeology* 10 (1992): 17–21.

Wouters, Jan, and A. Verhecken. "High-Performance Liquid Chromatography of Blue and Purple Indigoid Natural Dyes." *Journal of the Society of Dyers and Colourists* 107 (1991): 266–69.

Wright, David F., Sinclair B. Ferguson, and James I. Packer, eds. *New Dictionary of Theology*. Downers Grove, Ill.: InterVarsity, 1988.

Wright, David F. "Why Were the Montanists Condemned?" *Themelios* 2, no. 8 (1976): 15–21.

Wright, George Ernest. "The Lawsuit of God: A Form-Critical Study of Deuteronomy 32." In *Israel's Prophetic Heritage: Essays in Honor of James Muilenberg*, edited by Bernhard W. Anderson and Walter Harrelson, 26–67. New York, N.Y.: Harper & Row, 1962.

———. *The Old Testament Against Its Environment*. Chicago, Ill.: Allenson, 1951.

Wright III, Benjamin G. "The Categories of Rich and Poor in the Qumran Sapiential Literature." In *Sapiential Perspectives: Wisdom Literature in Light of the Dead Sea Scrolls : Proceedings of the Sixth International Symposium of the Orion Center for the Study of the Dead Sea Scrolls and Associated Literature, 20-22 May, 2001*, edited by John Joseph Collins, Gregory E. Sterling, and Ruth A. Clements, 101–23. STTJ 51. Leiden: Brill Academic, 2004.

Wright, N. T. *The New Testament and the People of God: Christian Origins and the Question of God*. Minneapolis: Fortress Press, 1992.

Wright, William. *Apocryphal Acts of the Apostles*. 2 vols. London, U.K.: Williams & Norgate, 1871.

Wroth, Warwick. *A Catalogue of the Greek Coins in the British Museum : Mysia*. Edited by Reginald Stuart Poole. London, U.K.: Quaritch, 1892.

Wulf, Ulrike. *Die Stadtgrabung: Die hellenistischen und römischen Wohnhäuser von Pergamon: unter besonderer Berücksichtigung der Anlagen zwischen der Mittel-und der Ostgasse*. Berlin: de Gruyter, 1999.

Ximénez, Saturnino. *Asia Minor in Ruins*. Translated by Arthors Chambers. London, U.K.: Hutchinson & Co., 1925.

Yadin, Yigael, Y. Hevrah, and Y. Meshorer. *Masada : The Aramaic and Hebrew Ostraca and Jar Inscriptions: The Coins of Masada*. Jerusalem : Israel Exploration Society, 1989.

Yamauchi, Edwin M. *New Testament Cities in Western Asia Minor: Light from Archaeology on Cities of Paul and the Seven Churches of Revelation*. Eugene, Oreg.: Wipf & Stock, 2003.

———. "Ramsay's View on Archaeology in Asia Minor Reviewed." In *The New Testament Student and His Field*, edited by John Skilton, 27–40. Phillipsburg, N.J: P & R Press, 1982.

———. "Synagogues." Edited by Joel B. Green, Scot McKnight, and I. Howard Marshall. *DJG*. Downers Grove, Ill.: InterVarsity, 1992.

———. "The 'Daily Bread' Motif In Antiquity." *WTJ* 28, no. 2 (1966): 145–56.

Yates, James, and William Wayte. "Tessera." In *DGRA*, edited by William Smith, 2:799. London, U.K.: Murray, 1891.

Yavuz, Mehmet Fatih. "Ephesus ." In *OEAGR*, edited by Michael Gagarin, 3:78–81. New York, N.Y.: Oxford University Press, 2010.

Yeatts, John R. *Revelation*. Believers Church Bible Commentary. Harrisonburg, VA: Herald, 2003.

Yegül, Fikret K. "A Study in Architectural Iconography: Kaisersaal and the Imperial Cult." *ABul* 64, no. 1 (March 1, 1982): 7–31.

———. "A Victor's Message: The Talking Column of the Temple of Artemis at Sardis ." *JSAH* 73, no. 2 (2014): 204–25.

———. "Roman Architecture in Sardis ." In *Sardis: Twenty-Seven Years of Discovery*, edited by Eleanor Guralnick, 46–61. Chicago, Ill.: Archaeological Institute of America, 1987.

———. *The Bath-Gymnasium Complex at Sardis*. Edited by George M. A. Hanfmann and Jane Ayer Scott. AESR 3. Cambridge, Mass.: Harvard University Press, 1986.

———. "The Bath-Gymnasium Complex in Asia Minor During the Imperial Roman Age." Ph.D. diss., Harvard University, 1975.

Yeivin, S. "Jachin and Boaz." *PEQ* 91 (1959): 1–15.

Young, William J. "The Fabulous Gold of the Pactolus Valley." *Boston Museum Bulletin* 70, no. 359 (1972): 4–13.

Younger, John. *Sex in the Ancient World from A to Z*. New York, N.Y.: Routledge, 2005.

Zahn, Theodor. *Die Offenbarung Des Johannes*. 2 vols. KZNT 17. Leipzig: Deichert, 1924.

Ziderman, I. Irving. "Seashells and Ancient Purple Dyeing." *BA* 53 (1990): 98–101.

Ziderman, Irving I. "3600 Years of Purple-Shell Dyeing: Characterization of Hyacinthine Purple (Tekhelet)." *Advances in Chemistry* 212 (1986): 187–98.

Ziegenaus, Oskar, and Gioia De Luca. *Altertümer von Pergamon*. Leiden: de Gruyter, 1968.

———. *Das Asklepieion*. Vol. 1–4. Altertümer von Pergamon 11. Berlin: Deutsches Archäologisches Institut, 1968.

Zincone, Sergio. "Smyrna ." In *Encyclopedia of the Early Church*, edited by Angelo Di Berardino, translated by Adran Walford, 2:688–89. Oxford, U.K.: Oxford University Press, 1992.

Zuiderhoek, Arjan. "Cities, Roman Empire (East)." In *The Encyclopedia of Ancient History*, edited by Roger S. Bagnall, Kai Brodersen, Craige B. Champion, Andrew Erskine, and Sabine R. Huebner, 1:1516–20. Malden, Mass.: Wiley-Blackwell, 2012.

Credits and Permissions

The following photographic credits indicate ownership of the original color prints and use with permission to publish the black and white photographs. Numbers refer to the photograph number in the text. Appreciation to the sources named for permission to publish the following photographs.

Historical Chapter Headings – Detail from the mosaic floor in the Gallery Vittorio Emanuele II in Milan, Italy: the coat of arms of Rome. (Photograph by Giovanni Dall'Orto, June 22, 2007, PD).

Exegetical Chapter Headings – Monogramme of Christ (the Chi Rho) on a plaque of a sarcophagus, fourth cent. AD, marble, Musei Vaticani, on display in a temporary exhibition at the Colosseum in Rome, Italy. (Photogrph courtesy of Jebulon, PD).

PHOTOGRAPHS

Allard Pierson Museum (Courtesy of Near EMPTiness)
Figure 168

Antalya Müzesi, Antalya, Turkey (Photograph by the author)
Figure 11

Archaeological Museum of Epidaurus, Greece (Photograph by Michael F. Mehnert, PD)
Figure 71

Archaeological Museum of Zaragoza, Spain (Photograph by Ecelan, PD)
Figure 170

Ashmolean Museum, Oxford, U.K. (Photograph by Jonund, PD)
Figure 9

Beit Guvrin-Maresha National Park, Israel (Photograph by the author)
Figure 53

© Bertolami Fine Arts (Photographs courtesy of Andrea Pancotti)
Figure 76

Besnier, Maurice "Purpura," *Dictionnaire des antiquites gracques et romaines*; 1873–1919: 4.1:770, Fig. 5887. PD-Old
Figure 83

© Bolen, Todd (Photographs courtesy of www.BiblePlaces.com)
Figures 1, 16

© Copyright the Trustees of the British Museum, London, England (all photographs by the author)
Figures 45, 131

Capitoline Museum, Rome (Photograph by Matthias Kabel, PD)
Figure 4

© Classical Numismatic Group, Inc. (CNG). (Photographs courtesy of www.cngcoins.com)
Figures 8, 28, 29, 30, 34, 39, 42, 54, 63, 86, 87, 88, 89, 90, 93, 95, 96, 97, 98, 107, 109, 111, 113, 114, 117, 119, 121, 122, 123, 124, 125, 126, 127, 128, 135, 136, 151, 156, 158, 161, 162, 163

Creative Commons. CC-BY-SA 3.0. Public Domain (PD)
   Photograph by Iocanus – Figure 12
   Photograph by Magnus Manske – Figure 24
   Photograph by Adam Carr – Figure 25
   Photograph by Saiko – Figure 31
   Photograph by Marie-Lan Nguyen – Figure 35
   Photograph by Wladyslaw Sojka with overlay by David E. Graves – Figure 58
   Photography by Bernard Gagnon (cropped) – Figures 62, 64
   Photography by Raimond Spekking – Figure 65
   Photography by Rama – Figure 68
   Photography by Elke Wetzig – Figure 77
   Photography by Akkinvet – Figure 81
   Photography by Dezidor [left] and M. Violante [right] – Figure 85
   Photography by Simon Jenkins – Figure 115
   Photography by Thermos – 132
   Photography by Rjdeadly – 146, 147, 150
   Photography by Edal Anton Lefterov – 152
   Photography by Aldo Ardetti – 167
   Photography by Dmitry Rozhkov – 169

© eweb93 (Photograph courtesy of)
   Figure 133

Ephesus Archaeological Museum (Turk. *Efes Müzesi*), Selçuk, Turkey (all photographs by the author)
   Figure 27, 32, 41, 43

J. Paul Getty Museum, Los Angeles, California (Photograph by Marshall Astor, PD)
   Figure 108

© Graves, David E.
   Figures 3, 7, 13, 19, 20, 21, 22, 23, 33, 36, 37, 38, 40, 44, 46, 47, 50, 51, 56, 59, 60, 66, 67, 70, 74, 75, 79, 100, 101, 104 (Cover), 105, 106, 120, 138, 140, 142, 144, 145, 172

Hierapolis Archeology Museum, Turkey
   Photograph by Cobija, PD – Figure 112
   Photograph courtesy of © Mark Wilson – Figures 154, 157, 159

Istanbul Archaeology Museum, Istanbul, Turkey
   Photographs by the author – Figures 2, 26, 48, 52, 91
   Photograph by Iocanus, PD – Figure 12

İzmir Archaeological Museum (Turk. *İzmir Arkeoloji Müzesi*), İzmir, Turkey (all Photographs by the author)
   Figures 6, 49, 55

Israel Museum, Jerusalem (Photograph by Chamberi, PD)
   Figure 130

© Jenkins, Ferrell (Photograph courtesy of)
   Figure 153

Kunsthistorisches Museum (Photograph by James Steakley, PD)

Credits and Permissions

Figure 173

Laborde, Leon de, *Voyage de l'Asie Mineure* 1838, 86–87, Pl. xxxix-83. PD–Art
Figure 148

© Museum Associates/ LACMA Los Angeles County Museum of Art (Photograph courtesy of)
Figure 171

© Manske, Magnus (Photograph by, PD).
Figure 30

© Martens, John W. (Photograph courtesy of)
Figure 164

Metropolitan Museum of Art, New York City, New York (Photograph by Matthew Bisanz, PD)
Figure 103

Musée du Louvre, Paris, France
Figure 94 (Photograph by Bibi Saint-Pol, PD)
Figure 31 (Photograph by Saiko, PD)

Museo Archeologico Nazionale, Naples, Italy
Photograph by Herkulaneischer Meister, PD – Figure 17
Photograph by Massimo Finizio, PD – Figure 80
Photograph by Wolfgang Rieger, PD–Art – Figure 84

Museum of Anatolian Civilizations (Turk. *Anadolu Medeniyetleri Müzesi*), Boğazköy, Turkey (Photograph by the author)
Figure 14

Mycenae Museum, Greece (Photograph by Janmad, PD)
Figure 69

Oil on Canvas "The Frigidarium" (1890) by Lawrence Alma-Tadema (PD-Art)
Figure 110

© Oriental Institute Museum, University of Chicago, Chicago, Ill. (Photograph by the author)
Figures 92

Pergamon Museum, Berlin Germany (Photograph by Nicolás Pérez, PD)
Figure 57

© The British Museum Exhibition (Photograph courtesy of Mary Beard)
Figure 166

Proceedings of the Society of Biblical Archæology, Volume 25 (January-December 1903), 56. (Nash Papyrus PD-Old)
Figure 15

Side Müze Müdürlüğü, Side, Turkey (Photograph by the author)
Figure 5

Vatican Museum, Cortile delle Corazze (Photograph courtesy of Author Lalupa)
Figure 10

Walters Art Museum, Baltimore, Maryland (PD)
Figure 78

© Wilson, Mark (Photographs courtesy of)
Figures 139, 143, 154, 155, 157, 159, 160,

DRAWINGS

Graves, David E.
Figures 18, 61, 72, 99, 102, 118, 129, 137

Steeves, David (Comissioned by the author)
Figure 73

MAPS AND CHARTS

Graves, David E.
Map of the Seven Churches
Figure 134, 141

Creative Commons CC-BY-SA 3.0. Public Domain (PD)
Map by Alexikoua – Figure 116

Index of Subjects

Aaron 81, 422
acropolis 225–26, 229–31, 238, 242, 248–49, 252, 281, 325, 327–28, 330, 333, 335, 351, 367, 387–88, 438, 512, 517, 521
Actium, battle of 105, 381
Acts of John 118
Acts of Philip 456
Acts, book of 60
Adramytteum 110
adultery 311, 314, 317, 515
aedicula 521
Aegean 44, 153
aegis 521
Aelian, Claudius 149, 267
Aeschines 212, 495
Aeschylus 267, 327, 368, 420
Aesop 484
Aëtius Amidenus 454
affliction 188–90, 192, 200, 205, 223
Agabus 82
agora 105, 107–11, 163–65, 445, 450–52, 521
agriculture 380, 384, 443
Aidiskos 440
Akkadian 78, 79, 83, 89, 189, 218
Alabanda 110
Alexander the coppersmith 135
Alexander the Great 102–3, 118, 154, 227, 329, 350, 429
Alexandria 62, 215, 454, 529
Alexandria Troas 103
Alpha and Omega 182–83, 188, 304
alphabet 523
Alphaeus 419
Altar of Zeus 248
altar(s) 58, 119, 162, 248–49, 411, 482, 512, 522
alum 455
Alyattes 154, 187, 326, 345, 346
Amazons 101–2, 122, 153
Amen 475–76, 503
Amman Museum 258
Amorgus 44
Amos 80, 86
amulet(s) 268, 271–72, 274
Amurru 200
Anaitis 388–90, 393, 396
analogy 67, 74, 76, 212
Anatolia(n) 52, 74, 116–17, 153, 270, 327, 330, 339, 341, 344, 346, 348–50, 390, 392, 394, 431, 512
ancient Near East 67, 79, 88, 93, 95, 144–45, 222, 262, 364, 377, 424
ancient Near Eastern vassal treaties
 ANEVT 65–68, 70, 78–81, 84–85, 87–91, 93–94, 97, 99, 144, 150, 188, 190, 200–1, 211, 218, 222, 224, 275, 317, 324, 377, 415, 424, 503–4
Ancyra 279–80, 335, 430, 434, 470
Andrew of Caesarea 251–52, 267, 307, 310

Andrew of Crete 128
Androclus 114, 122
Andronicus 133
angel(s) 71–77, 79, 94, 129, 131, 137, 180, 244, 263, 302, 305, 315, 318, 356–58, 372, 376–77, 399, 428, 474
Anthesteria 124
Anthony, Mark 232, 431
Antioch 103, 127–28, 134, 143, 161, 177, 214, 259, 397, 398, 429, 434
Antioch Syria 103
Antiochus II 430
Antiochus III 367, 430, 517
Antiochus IV 139
Antiochus the Great 102, 155, 170, 277, 330, 351, 353, 426, 429, 454, 470
Antipas 246–47, 251, 254–55, 275, 477, 512
Antiquus, Gargilius 451
Antoninus Pius 63, 122, 158–59, 339, 352–53, 389, 394, 398
Antony, Mark 105
Apamea 110, 430, 431, 460, 472
Apate 528
Aphrodisia festival 143
Aphrodisian Gate 438
Aphrodisias 58, 120, 170, 198, 255, 304, 305, 449, 460
Aphrodite 116, 123–24, 143, 169, 213, 322, 351, 388, 391–92, 395, 397, 449, 468
Apocalypse 42, 44, 46, 48, 54, 101, 202, 252, 511–15, 521
Apocalypse of Elijah 508
Apocalypse of Moses 508
apocalyptic 47, 70–71, 76–77, 212, 220
Apocrypha 94, 214, 521
Apocrypha, Syriac 47
apodyterium 452
Apollo 115, 122–23, 169, 236, 238, 240, 283, 286, 297, 313, 329, 351, 368, 393–94, 420, 447, 448, 452, 462, 464–65, 493, 500–1, 515, 526–27
Apollo Tyrimnos 277, 288, 306
Apollodorus 306
Apollonius of Tyana 103, 136, 213, 368, 507
Apollos 527
apostasy 190, 315
apostle(s) 44, 46–47, 133–35, 142, 205, 414, 531
apostle(s), false 134
Apostolic Decree 319
Appian of Alexandria 110, 118, 229, 277–78, 372, 430–31
Apuleius 78, 215, 366, 372, 498
aqueduct(s) 161, 333, 387, 441, 444, 478, 481, 483–84, 521
Aquila 108, 127
Aramaic 524, 529, 530
Aramean 66
Arcadian Way 108, 112
archaeology 53, 168, 344, 489, 513–14, 519
Archaic 119, 154, 326, 345, 346
archangel(s) 357
arche(s) 281, 389, 438, 521

Archias 235
Ardabav 398
Aristagoras 329
Aristides, Publius Aelius 74, 106, 117–18, 153–55, 160–61, 165, 172–73, 184, 186, 213, 230, 235, 237, 251, 272, 350, 372–73, 420, 454, 489–90
Aristonicus 278
Aristophanes 232–33, 369, 371, 374, 496
Aristotle 293, 345–46, 454, 495
Ark of the Covenant 96, 521, 523
army 109
Arnobius 272
Arrian 326, 328–29, 335, 350, 455, 457, 483, 486
arrow 115, 397, 466, 468
Artaphernes 329
Artemesion 111, 120
Artemidorus 490
Artemis 111, 115, 147
Artemis Boreitene 277
Artemis Colonene 348
Artemis Ephesia 390
Artemis, cult of 45–46, 60, 101–2, 108, 111–19, 121–24, 126, 132, 135, 141, 143, 147–50, 160, 167, 169, 194, 211, 216, 253, 297, 326, 329, 337–41, 348–50, 352–53, 362, 368–69, 387–94, 396–97, 419–20, 447–48, 463, 465–66, 507, 517
Artemis, Cyrene 127
Artemis, temple of 45–46, 110, 113–14, 116–19, 141, 147, 160, 319, 326, 329, 338, 348, 507
Artemision 112, 117–18, 147–48, 346, 420, 508
Artemon, Aurelius 395, 473
artifact(s) 525, 530
Asclepeion 225, 230, 235–37, 240, 250–51, 512
Asclepius 123, 166, 169, 231, 235–38, 240, 248, 250, 253, 272, 298, 350, 393, 397, 454, 467, 512–14, 523
Asherah 309
Asia 73–74, 145, 181–83, 198
Asia Minor 43, 48–49, 52, 55, 59, 98, 103, 198, 233, 508, 510, 512–15
Asopus River 428, 438, 484
Assurbanipal 326, 328
Assyrian 66, 76, 78, 80, 83–84, 87–88, 318, 322, 329, 364, 415, 488
Assyrian treaties 83, 87
Athena 122–23, 154, 228, 231, 235, 239–40, 249, 351, 390, 393, 397, 447, 464, 468
Athenaeus 344, 347, 354, 430, 439, 482–84
Athens 228, 235, 335, 349, 351, 369, 382–83, 388, 417, 460, 501, 521
athletic(s) 146, 173, 212, 215, 219, 268, 282, 287, 320, 416, 447, 511–12
Attalia 178, 428
Attalids 226–27, 234, 239, 241, 279, 330, 429–30
Attalus 209, 228–29, 235, 242, 278, 330–31, 381, 430
Attalus I 391
Attalus II 381, 391
Attalus III 430
Attis 166, 240, 350–52, 391
Augusteion temple 123
Augusti 159, 160, 287, 298, 417
Augustine 196, 422
Augustus 58–59, 62–63, 102, 105, 107, 109–10, 119–20, 123, 158, 162, 213, 228–29, 242, 249, 252, 270, 278, 282, 298, 304, 323, 332, 353, 381, 396, 432, 447, 453, 470, 501, 512, 514, 529
Ausonius 160, 322
authepsa 482, 522
Baal 309–10, 516
Babylon 523
Babylonia 78, 88, 91, 364
Babylonian Exile 523, 530
Babylonian(s) 139, 529–30
Bacchus 212, 351, 385, 511, 523
Bacchylides 326, 329, 335, 352
bakers 56, 283
Baki-Dionysus 351
Balaam 64, 134, 142, 148, 189, 247, 256, 257–58, 259–60, 262–63, 309, 322, 512, 514–15
Balaamite(s) 142, 144, 256, 259–60, 507
banking 438, 486, 519
banquet(s) 264, 268, 314, 478, 482–85, 493, 496, 498, 503, 512–14, 525
baptism 273, 370, 517, 524
Barcino 292
Bar-Kochba 126, 522
Barnabas 133, 273, 303, 320, 358, 404
Baruch 184, 216, 263, 514, 528
Basil the Great 73, 84, 510
basilica(s) 45, 46, 107, 123, 127, 158, 164, 253, 342, 382, 383, 522
Bassae 527
bath(s) 109, 125, 282, 296, 441, 443, 446, 451–52, 481
bathing 125, 236, 482
Bauckham, Richard J. 42, 49–50, 80, 97–98, 141, 199, 205, 303–4, 358, 365–66, 407, 413, 494–96, 500, 502
Beatitudes 87, 193
bed cover(s) 295
bed(s) 238, 295, 313–14, 530
bees 115–16, 147
bench(es) 249, 524
benediction(s) 66, 68, 86–89, 211, 261, 313, 364, 411, 484
Bergama 225, 236–37
Beryl 271, 374
Bible 514
Bible, Hebrew 530
Bin Tepeler 326
bisellium 501, 522
bishop(s) 46, 55, 62, 73–74, 128, 134, 172–73, 175, 177, 196, 209, 274, 301, 310, 333, 355, 382, 398, 434–35, 473, 521, 526
Bithynia 63, 213, 277, 454
Black Obelisk 409
black stone(s) 122, 267, 271
blacksmith(s) 283, 443
blanket(s) 460
blasphemy 193–94
blessing 49, 66, 68, 85, 87–88, 90–91, 93, 96, 99, 146, 211–12, 217–20, 222–24, 324, 504–5
blessing and curses 49, 87
blind 456, 519
blood 220
book of life 54, 369, 373–74, 505, 517
Book of Life 373
bouleuterion 450, 522, 527
bow 86, 115, 397, 408–9, 411, 466, 468

Index of Subjects

bread of life 264
breastplate 265–66
British Museum 61, 102, 111, 114, 119, 242, 297, 329, 345–46
bronze 107–8, 139, 167, 237, 304, 306, 418–19, 512, 515
bronzesmith(s) 306
brothel 125
bull(s) 115–16, 255, 323, 346, 348, 350, 465, 512
burial 128, 152, 186, 452, 510
Byzantine 105–6, 120, 127, 155, 310, 326, 333, 344–45, 347, 369, 371, 382, 435, 438, 444, 446, 471, 522
Byzantine Gate 446
Byzantium 232, 276, 381, 435, 446
Cabeiri 123
Cadmus 428, 440, 479
Caesar 207
Caesar, Julius 57
Caicus 276–77
Caicus River 225
Caicus valley 225
caldarium 522
caldum 522
Callimachus 101, 493
cameo 266, 501
Campus Martius 63, 122
Canaanite(s) 290, 310
candelabrum 138
canon, the 522, 528
Capernaum synagogue 419
capital 522
capital of Asia 159–60
Caracalla 113, 158–59, 167, 278–79, 338, 381–82, 390, 396, 442, 445, 467, 469
Caria 392, 427, 441
carpet(s) 296, 344
Carpus 249, 255, 301, 484
Carthage 61–62, 209
Carthage, Council of 62
Castor 389, 524
Cataphrygian 526
cave(s) 528
cavea 522
Cayster River 105, 137, 140, 507
Celsus, Aulus Cornelius 112, 454–56, 485
ceramic 530
Chalcedon 301, 454, 460
chariot(s) 523
cherubim 521
Chest Tomb 452
children 86, 189, 200, 315–16, 324, 354, 419, 492
Chios 278, 432
chiton 522
chlamys 522
Chosroes II 333
Christ 68, 73, 75, 77, 81, 90, 93–96, 98, 129, 146, 150, 180–84, 188, 190-91, 193–94, 198, 201, 204–5, 208, 216–17, 220–24, 275, 302, 324, 356, 377, 424, 474, 503, 526
Christian(s) 55, 57–58, 63–64, 73, 77, 98, 129, 180, 191, 197, 198, 201, 203, 215, 220, 222–23, 250, 302, 311, 356, 398, 404, 421, 474, 510, 513–14, 523, 526
Christianity 51, 63, 149, 513–14
Christograms 450

Chrysostom 112, 118, 137, 163, 179, 199, 253, 327, 347, 366, 374, 489, 495
church(es) 43, 46, 49–50, 55, 62, 64, 68, 70–76, 77, 79, 81, 84–85, 87–88, 94, 96–98, 129, 141, 144, 146, 150, 180, 188–90, 195–96, 200, 209–11, 223–24, 244, 262, 275, 302, 310, 324, 356, 377–78, 399, 415–16, 424–25, 474, 503–7, 510, 515, 524
Cibyra 105, 110, 433
Cicero 107, 131, 160–61, 167, 170, 196, 209, 215, 232, 268, 292, 304, 307, 322, 374, 431, 438, 447, 450, 460–61, 470, 482, 484, 486, 495, 498, 510, 526
Cicero, Marcus Tullius 112, 431
Cistophoric coin(s) 238, 277
citadel 225, 276, 326, 328, 330, 333, 521
citizen(s) 55, 57, 59, 63, 108–9, 136, 140, 148–49, 155, 160, 181–82, 187, 203–5, 213, 222, 231, 246–47, 252, 268, 270, 278, 282, 287, 298, 327, 354, 372, 374, 375, 385, 390, 397, 404, 419, 430–32, 435, 437, 442, 450, 452, 456, 461–62, 470, 507–8, 512, 517, 522–23
citizenship 377
Claudian 58, 373
Claudius 47, 111–12, 120, 162, 213, 236, 237, 279, 287, 331, 353, 382, 385, 431, 460
Clement of Alexandria 126, 130, 142, 156, 177, 185–86, 196, 215, 259, 305, 400, 419, 424, 477
cloak 116, 457, 458, 465, 522
cloth(es) 283, 291, 295, 296, 360, 459, 487
clothiers 56
Code of Hammurabi 317
Codex 46, 523
Codex Purpureus Petropolitanus 46
coercion 204
coin(s) 53, 102, 111, 113–15, 119, 122–23, 130–31, 139, 147, 152, 154, 158–60, 163, 166–67, 182, 209, 212–13, 227, 229, 238, 242, 266–67, 270, 277–79, 297, 299, 306, 322, 323, 332–33, 345–48, 350–52, 367, 380–82, 388–97, 427–29, 433, 437, 452, 453–54, 460, 462–70, 507–8, 510–11, 515, 523, 526–27, 529–30
coinage, invented 346
collyrium 454–55, 490
colonnade 107, 164, 165, 471, 528–29
Colossae 427
column(s) 118, 164, 238, 242–43, 338–40, 389, 417–20, 447, 462, 468, 523, 528
comet 323
commentary 246, 252, 511–15, 518
congregation(s) 50, 73, 77, 82, 150, 178, 191, 199, 223–24, 261, 266, 275, 307, 310, 318, 324, 341, 343, 359, 365, 367, 372, 374, 376–78, 407, 425, 481, 503–4
Constantine 102, 114, 249, 327, 333–34, 462, 466
Constantinople 333, 382
content 145, 199, 244, 399, 474
continuity 96
copper 56, 306, 345, 455, 515, 524
coppersmith(s) 56, 118, 132, 135, 283, 306, 507
Coptic 523
Corinth 123, 127, 235–36, 257, 311, 527
Corinthian captial 522
Corinthian(s) 128, 164, 238, 243, 281, 311, 389, 447, 449, 524
corn 162, 270, 385, 466, 522
cornucopiae 385, 389, 463, 466
cornucpopiae 523

Page | 641

Corupedium, Battle of 227, 277
couch 313, 498, 526
covenant 65–66, 68–71, 76–77, 79, 80–82, 84–85, 87–88, 90–93, 95–97, 99, 129, 132, 144–46, 150, 180–81, 183, 188–90, 193–94, 200–1, 211, 217, 219–24, 244, 262, 275, 302–3, 307, 314–15, 317–18, 321, 324, 356, 361–62, 365, 375, 377, 399, 403, 409, 415, 418, 424, 474, 494–96, 500, 503, 505, 514, 523
covenant formula 189
covenant renewal 70, 95–97
covenant, ark of the 263
covetousness 315
Croesus 102, 117, 126, 326–29, 333–35, 337, 341, 345–47, 352
Croesus, Palace of 350
cross(es) 90, 148–49, 194, 201, 216, 220, 344, 445–46, 471, 502, 507
crown 54, 211–15, 217, 510–11
crown of life 150, 188, 193, 200–1, 209–12, 216–20, 223–24
crown(s) 117, 154, 169, 173, 188, 193, 200–1, 209–20, 223–24, 261, 286, 375–76, 381, 388, 416, 425, 463, 526
crucify 246
Ctesias 351
culture 144, 191, 262, 377, 424
Cunaxa, battle of 269
curse(s) 66, 68, 85–91, 93, 138–40, 142, 145, 147, 150, 189, 194, 211, 219, 261–62, 275, 313–16, 320, 324, 364–65, 368, 374, 377, 411, 415, 424, 484–87, 502, 504–5
Cybele 99, 117, 122–23, 166, 169, 183, 212–13, 271, 298, 329, 332, 339, 343, 348–50, 352, 368, 389–95, 397, 462, 466, 511, 523
Cyprian 57, 60, 62, 171, 202–3, 210, 424, 513–14
Cyriacus 382
Cyrus 102, 183, 328, 347, 367, 517
Cyrus II 328
Cyzicus 279–80, 335
damnatio memoriae 523
Daniel 67, 99, 106, 109, 134, 148, 153, 183, 205, 207, 264, 272, 303, 306, 315, 321, 326, 342–43, 486, 513–14
Darius 329
dates 530
David's throne 321
deacon(s) 143, 215, 259, 398
Dead Sea 524, 528, 530
Dead Sea scrolls 190, 303, 312–13, 358, 524, 528, 530
death 47, 57, 61, 90, 98, 102, 117, 120, 122, 151–52, 156, 172, 175, 179, 181, 182–84, 187–88, 201–4, 208–10, 212, 216–17, 220–23, 226–27, 237, 244–47, 254–55, 261, 272, 278, 311, 314, 316–17, 323–24, 329–31, 348, 350, 355, 360–63, 374, 381, 388, 402, 404, 410, 424, 429, 430, 446, 456, 471, 500, 502, 505, 510, 512–14, 517
Decalogue 92, 96, 406, 523
Decian persecution 62
Decius 60
decrees 67, 79
deer 115, 117, 147, 349, 447
deification of emperor 58
deified 131
Dēimos 392, 394, 397
Deir ʿAlla 258
deity(ies) 59, 91, 110, 113, 116, 143, 165, 213, 231, 237, 273, 283, 285, 288, 297–98, 304, 314, 323, 339, 348, 350, 355, 357, 360, 390–91, 395–96, 400, 403, 417, 462, 465, 467–68, 496, 527, 529–30
Delian League 102
Delos 199, 342, 510, 527
Delphi 527
Demeter 123, 165, 240, 251, 349–50, 385, 468, 501, 526
Demeter Karpophoros 349, 350
Demetrius 108, 111, 118, 132, 210, 382, 398, 507
Demetrius the silversmith 118
dēmos 123, 389, 392
Demosthenes 215
Demosthenes Philalethes 376, 454
Demotic 523
denarius 130, 187, 387, 442–43, 457–58
Denizli 427–28, 432–33, 435, 439–40, 444, 478–79, 481
deposit 66, 95–97, 504
Despoina 501
destruction 86
Deuteronomy 81, 83, 91, 200
devil 202–3, 205, 208
Diana 111–12, 114–17, 119, 122–23, 169, 211, 339, 349, 465
Diaspora 523
dibromoindigo 294
Didache 312, 524
Didyma 527
Dio Cassius 105, 109, 184, 229, 232, 245, 252, 322, 469, 471
Diocletian 170, 205, 333, 443, 445, 448, 457, 459, 473
Diocletian Edict 443
Diodorus Siculus 110, 229, 329, 381, 427, 496
Dionysian festival 124
Dionysopolis 368
Dionysus 162, 240, 312, 391, 393
distaff 292
distyle 389–90, 392
divus 109, 131, 304–5, 468, 524
dog 115
dolphin(s) 392
Domed-Arcosolium 452
Domitia Longinas 130
Domitian 44, 46–47, 63, 109, 113–14, 119–20, 130–31, 163, 255, 284, 299, 304, 323, 385, 389–90, 394, 396, 422, 438, 447, 468, 473, 502, 515, 529
Domitian Gate 438
Domitilla, Flavia 120, 382
donum 325
Donusa 44
door(s) 387, 400, 402, 424, 493, 524
dophin 392
Doric 522
Doric capital 438, 524
double-throne 501, 522
doxology 475
drachma(s) 345, 348, 470
dyers 56, 283, 284–85, 287–88, 347, 456
eagle(s) 184, 350, 395, 463
earth 88, 93, 146, 183, 189, 193, 221
earthquake(s) 105, 115, 155, 162–63, 165, 184, 186, 229, 231, 278, 329, 331, 341–42, 350, 352, 353, 380–81, 387, 420–21, 432–34, 445, 448–49, 452, 461, 472, 485, 517–19
eating meat 143, 312, 318, 324
Eden, Garden of 147
Edict of Diocletian 443

Index of Subjects

edicts 48, 51, 55
egg(s) 116, 456
Egypt 49, 61, 67, 83, 89, 102, 189, 231–32, 249, 271, 326, 381, 512, 526
Egyptian 233–34
Egyptian Hieratic 523
Elagabalus 113, 114, 122, 348, 350, 353, 465, 469
elder(s) 73, 96, 105, 134, 173, 214, 335, 338, 398, 525
Eleazar ben Yar 531
electrum 345
Eliakim 401–2, 416, 418, 423
embalm 152
Emesa 122
Emperor 46, 57–58, 60, 63–64, 306, 382, 515, 529
emperor worship 55, 123, 168
endurance 45, 132, 134, 150, 210, 212, 217, 307–8, 324, 410
Enoch 508, 512, 528
Epaphras 73, 472, 473
Ephesian 182, 205
Ephesus 43, 47, 58, 60, 84, 88, 101–30, 134, 136, 138–51, 153, 157–63, 169, 177, 181, 184, 210–11, 216, 228, 231, 242, 249, 253, 256, 258–60, 279–80, 285, 288, 292, 304, 325, 329, 333, 337, 341, 353, 355–56, 363, 366, 368, 382, 387, 389–90, 396, 414, 419–22, 428–29, 433, 438–39, 441–42, 444, 452–53, 460, 464, 467–68, 472–73, 489, 505, 507, 513–14, 521
Ephesus, theater 111
Ephesus, tree-shrine 147
ephod 265, 266, 514
Ephraim 486
Epictetus of Hierapolis 455
Epidaurus 235
epigraphy 59, 106, 113, 123, 166, 242, 289, 348, 352, 390, 396, 468–69, 524
epilogue 50, 519
Epiphanius of Salamis 47, 128, 300, 301, 313, 422
Epistles 48
Erechtheion 417
Esarhaddon 84, 89, 91, 218, 317, 415, 488
eschatological 508
eschatology 221
Essene(s) 370, 517, 524
eternal security 421
Eucharist 138, 264, 497, 512, 524
Eumelus 350
Eumenes II 155, 227–28, 231, 233–34, 240, 242, 278, 331, 381, 395, 411, 430
eunuch(s) 117, 349, 435
Euphrates 428
Euripides 207, 312, 349, 369, 372, 420, 462, 500
Eusebius 43–47, 49, 128, 143, 171, 173, 175–76, 255, 263, 301, 311, 355, 398, 424, 434, 512, 527
Eustathius 117, 382, 426
Eutropius 278
execution 90–91, 176, 204–5
exhortations 69, 85, 415, 488, 527
Exodus 92
exorcism 272, 402
eye-salve 455, 487–91, 503
eyewitness 530
Ezekiel 80, 99
Fabian 62

faithfulness 68, 69, 85–88, 136, 180, 188, 200, 209–10, 218, 222, 224, 244, 254, 256, 275, 308, 318, 320, 360, 400, 415, 425, 475, 488, 510
Faustina 63, 165, 230, 339, 390, 469
Feast of Harvest 528
Feast of Weeks 528
Felix, Minucius 58, 62, 115
fertility 115–16, 124–25, 349, 456, 461
festival(s) 111–12, 124, 126, 162, 257, 283, 349, 351, 382, 390, 522, 530
Fides 308, 528
Field of Mars 63
fifth century 155, 341, 370, 402, 440, 446, 471, 530
first and the last 181–83, 202, 222, 224
first century 46, 53–55, 62, 76–77, 103, 105–6, 110, 123, 143, 155, 157, 160–61, 163, 170, 175, 182, 184–85, 198, 200, 204, 212, 228, 242, 249, 251, 252, 255, 261, 266, 272, 288, 293, 299–300, 304, 310–12, 315, 341, 342, 347, 352–54, 360, 370, 372, 376, 388–89, 394–97, 404, 422, 436, 440, 441, 443, 445, 454, 461–62, 470–71, 483, 504, 506–7, 510, 516, 523, 529, 531
first love 64, 135, 308
First Temple Period 524
Flaccus, C. Valerius 295, 354, 461, 464, 470
Flavia 382, 422–23, 518
Flavia Melitine 237
Flavian dynasty 113, 119–20, 278, 396
fleece 291
formula 66, 68, 79–81, 83, 93–94, 96–97, 129, 144–45, 150, 180–81, 210, 219, 224, 244, 262, 275, 302, 324, 356, 377, 399, 424, 474, 503–4
fornication 143, 309, 315
Fortuna 448, 466
fourth century 46, 225, 293, 300, 341, 343, 429, 438, 448, 498, 531
frankincense 108, 151, 264, 512
French 66
fresco 524
Friesen, Steven J. 251
fuller(s) 283–85, 289
functionally equivalent 94, 97
funeral(s) 63, 373
funerary banquet(s) 314
Gagniers, Jean des 438, 445, 452–53, 464–65, 468
Gaian heresy 143
Galatia 470
Galen 230–31, 235–36, 264, 454–55, 485, 490
Galli 349
games, athletic 110–12, 120, 162, 173, 175, 212, 215, 267, 268, 283, 299, 381, 388, 396, 416, 450, 513–14, 521–22, 531
garment(s) 130, 265–66, 369–70, 371, 457, 459, 489, 517, 519, 521, 522
gate(s) 107, 237, 281, 379, 389, 428, 438, 446, 461, 493
gem(s) 265–66
gematria 524
genizah 314, 365, 375, 524
genre 48–51, 91
genre, letter 50
Gentile 194, 198–99, 215, 507
geography 52
German 66, 86

German of Constantinople	128
gladiator(s)	205, 388, 450, 521
globe	130, 305, 471
gnostic(s)	142–44, 195, 257, 259, 319, 507, 510, 516, 525
Gnostics	195, 511
God Saviour, Theos Soter	254
goddess(es)	111–15, 117, 121, 123, 147–49, 155, 166–67, 213, 240, 271, 287, 298–99, 339, 341, 343, 348–50, 352, 385, 390–96, 432, 462, 465, 466, 499, 521, 523, 526
gods	85–86, 92, 96, 144, 182, 262, 377, 424, 503
God's throne	423
gold	108, 213, 227, 326–27, 336, 344–47, 372, 429, 443, 457, 461, 466, 470, 488–89, 503, 519, 524
Gospel(s)	530
Gospels	530
Goths	118, 231
governor(s)	63, 110, 207, 228, 245–46, 262, 270, 329, 442, 461, 528, 530
grace	91, 201, 492, 521
Graeco-Roman	54, 71, 76, 78, 99, 101–2, 106, 109, 112, 137, 147, 151, 225, 237, 276, 295, 325, 379, 426, 453
Graeco-Turkish War	383, 384
graffiti	525
grain	270, 350, 352, 386
granite	270
grape(s)	385
Great King	66, 78–79, 81, 83, 150, 194, 199–200, 202–3, 205, 209, 211, 218–19, 221–22, 224, 261, 275, 324, 377, 403, 410, 424–25, 478, 503
Greece	44–45, 65, 103, 107, 143, 149, 153, 161, 163, 166, 225, 235, 240, 242, 249–50, 252, 255, 258, 290, 338, 346, 348, 350–51, 374, 388, 390, 526
Greek language	525
Greek(s)	60, 62, 78, 82, 94, 114–15, 127, 132, 147, 153, 156–57, 160–61, 167, 176, 191, 193, 197, 215–16, 227, 245, 248, 254, 346, 374, 383, 392, 432, 472, 482, 495, 498, 508, 513–16, 518, 521, 523–24, 527, 529
Gregory of Nazianzus	42, 54, 72, 97, 102, 114, 128, 145, 190, 212, 232, 350, 475, 496
Gregory of Tours	128
griffin(s)	448, 461–62, 466
guild(s)	56, 57, 136, 192, 257, 268, 283–85, 287–88, 291, 306, 310–12, 347, 386, 457, 507, 515–16
Gyarus	44
Gyges	326, 328
gymnasium(s)	127, 161, 236, 253, 280, 282, 287, 326, 332, 333, 336–38, 341–42, 353–54, 367, 370, 373, 451, 481, 517, 525, 527
Hades	201–2, 404, 468, 502
Hadrian	102, 113, 120–22, 131, 158, 161–62, 204, 229–30, 235, 237, 240, 242–43, 279, 305, 333, 344, 351, 353, 382, 434, 449–51
Hadrianeion	352
Halys River	328
Hammurabi	317, 322
harbour	45, 105–8, 112, 127, 132, 137, 225, 507
headdress	116–17, 422, 465
hearing formula	76
heart	78, 146, 189, 224
heaven	88, 93, 192, 215, 217, 221, 505
heaven and earth	94
Hebraic-Semitic	71, 99, 101, 151, 225, 276, 325, 379, 426
Hebrew	54, 67, 76, 80, 83, 93, 189, 529, 530
Hebrews	508
Hecate	123, 392
Hedychrous	440
Hekate	352, 392, 397
Hellenism	45, 49, 60, 103, 195, 380, 511, 525
Hellenistic	115
helmet	127
Hephaestus	123
Hera	351, 467, 502
Heracles	350, 352
Heraclitus	123
Herakles	122, 298
Hercules	123, 227, 241, 305
heresy	64
heretic(s)	365, 374
Hermas, Shepherd of	96, 212, 214, 218, 223, 312, 315, 372, 373–74, 418, 490
Hermippos, Aurelius	387–88, 391
Hermus Valley	229
Herod the Great	525
Herodian	122, 343, 525
Herodotus	102, 110, 149, 154, 184–85, 187, 326–29, 335, 345, 346, 349–52, 359, 366–68, 380, 419, 428, 439, 462, 478, 484, 500, 521
Heron of Alexandria	482
heroon	242, 525
Herophilus	454
Herostratus	117
heroum	525
Hesiod	115
heteropraxy	257
Hierapolis	284–86, 296, 369, 426–29, 431–35, 437–38, 440, 443–44, 449–50, 457, 463, 469, 471–72, 480–81, 483–84, 487, 519
Hierapolitan Gate	438
hieroglyph(s)	523
hieron	461, 525
high priest	266, 514, 518
Hippocratic Oath	65
Hippodamian	428, 525
Hippodamus of Miletus	525
Hippolytus	73, 142, 171, 195, 259, 319, 322, 370, 477
Hipponax of Ephesus	326
historical prologue	66, 82–84, 91, 150, 188, 200, 224, 275, 324, 377, 403, 425, 478, 503–4
Hittite	65–78, 82–89, 91, 93, 95, 101, 145, 153, 189, 200, 218, 359, 364, 478
Holy Land	523
holy of holies	96, 521
Holy One	400
Homer	65, 115, 148, 161, 207, 213, 238, 250, 252, 285, 322, 327, 347, 392, 456, 463, 495, 496, 500, 513–14
Horace	268, 323, 455, 491
hot spring(s)	429, 440, 459, 480–81, 483–84, 519
hot water	485, 522
humiliation	152, 186–87
hybrid	91
Hygeia	236, 298
Hyginus, Gaius Julius	392
hypobranchial gland	294
hypocaust	338, 522, 525

INDEX OF SUBJECTS

Hypogeium 452
iconography 305, 341
idol(s) 64, 118, 143, 207, 251, 256–57, 263–64, 309–12, 318–19, 324, 512, 515
idolatry 123, 126, 143, 252, 256–59, 310, 315, 320, 368, 505, 515
Ignatius 105, 128, 133–34, 141, 161, 177–78, 194–96, 214–15, 313, 317, 370, 397–98, 404–5, 408, 424
immersion 370
immorality 64, 123–26, 142–44, 252, 256–57, 259, 309–13, 319, 324, 368, 512, 515–16
imperial cult 47, 55–60, 64, 111, 113–14, 120–23, 143–44, 155, 166–68, 191, 196, 198, 207, 209, 213, 229, 237, 240, 242–43, 252–54, 257, 264–65, 270, 275, 279, 286–87, 297–98, 305, 310–11, 332–33, 339, 347, 352–53, 396, 400, 417, 422, 432, 462, 468, 470, 504, 510, 512–14, 516, 518, 521
imperial edict 79
imperial edict(s) 49, 79, 99, 112, 270
imprecation 88, 364
imprison 208
imprisonment 194, 202–5
in situ 525
incantation(s) 78, 117, 126, 237, 498, 500
incense 108, 143, 264, 307
indigoid 294
inscription(s) 45–46, 53, 103, 107, 111–12, 123, 125, 131, 147, 158, 162, 164, 187, 198, 209, 230, 243, 266, 278, 284, 288–89, 300, 306, 311, 325, 332, 338, 340–41, 343–44, 347, 350–52, 356, 376, 385, 387–89, 393–97, 411, 419, 421, 432–33, 440, 442, 445–47, 449, 451, 457, 459–60, 462–66, 471, 510, 516, 518, 522, 525, 527, 529
intercourse 124, 238
Ionia 102–3, 113–14, 153, 159–60, 166, 209, 213, 278, 329, 381
Ionian league 101, 154
Ionic captial 522, 524
Irenaeus 44, 46–47, 126–28, 142, 148, 161, 171–72, 177, 194, 195, 259, 272, 319, 357, 477, 507
Isaiah 80, 182, 183
Isidore of Seville 128
Isis 109, 240, 271, 446, 467
Israel 65–66, 69, 76, 79–80, 88–89, 96, 139–42, 145–46, 152, 183, 189–90, 197, 199, 222, 256, 265–67, 273, 290, 293, 294–95, 298, 309–10, 322, 343, 355, 365, 374, 401, 407–8, 419, 423, 471, 494, 500, 511, 516, 526, 529
Israelite(s) 67, 142, 256, 528
Izmir 153, 156–57, 161–62, 164–65, 172–73, 197, 225
James 246, 513–14
Jamnia, Council of 404
javelin 120, 245
Jeremiah 49, 80, 99, 189
Jerome 46, 73, 111, 115, 355, 407, 527, 531
Jerusalem 46, 62, 90, 106, 128, 134, 139, 143, 177, 197, 222, 248, 267, 274, 293, 305, 343, 353–54, 365, 401, 403–4, 416, 418, 420–23, 425, 434, 461, 470, 490, 505, 507, 513–14, 518, 529–30
Jerusalem Council 143, 319
Jerusalem, destruction of 529
Jerusalem, new 150
Jesus 42, 45, 75, 81, 84, 94, 97, 99, 146, 182, 194, 201, 221, 246, 403, 513–14, 521, 526, 530
Jewish 43, 47–49, 54–56, 70, 73, 76–77, 82, 84, 107, 126–27, 130, 139–40, 147, 149, 156, 169, 170–80, 184, 187, 190–92, 194–200, 203, 207–8, 210–11, 214–17, 221, 224, 237, 246, 256–57, 262–66, 273, 282, 285, 296, 298–300, 306, 309, 311–12, 316, 323, 325, 334, 336, 341–44, 353–55, 365, 374, 397, 401–2, 404–8, 418, 420, 431, 437, 445, 461, 470–71, 476, 494, 499, 504, 508, 510, 512, 521–24, 526, 528–31
Jews 55, 70, 192–99, 209, 510, 530–31
Jezebel 64, 143, 148, 257–58, 260, 297, 302, 305, 309–20, 324, 515–16
Johannine 76, 203
John 42, 71, 73, 75, 77, 79–82, 91, 94, 96–98, 129, 146, 180, 183, 193, 197, 199, 202–3, 210, 219–21, 244, 302, 356, 399, 474, 504
John of Damascus 128
John the Baptist 77
John, Monastery of St. 46
John, the apostle 44–47, 50–52, 55, 74, 99, 147, 246, 310, 404, 489, 505, 508, 512–16, 518–19, 526
Josephus, Flavius 74, 76, 79, 110, 112, 130, 139, 149, 170, 196, 198, 204, 245, 255–56, 263, 272, 300, 309, 315, 317, 341, 353–54, 369–70, 372, 400, 418, 420, 422, 430, 437, 470–71, 490, 495, 496, 524, 529, 531
Joshua 81, 93
Judah 526
Judaism 63, 77–78, 197–99, 207, 221–22, 511, 526
Judaizer(s) 134, 195, 398
Judea 126, 139, 176, 227, 246
Judea captured 139
judge 145, 150, 223–24, 275, 324, 378, 425, 503
Julia 120, 167–68, 288, 292, 338, 389–90, 469
Julius, Divus 109
Junias 133
Justin Martyr 43, 55, 128, 171, 194, 199, 203, 272, 320, 357, 365, 400, 406, 477
Justin Martyr 322
Justinus, Marcus Junianus 430
Juvenal 347, 372, 449, 454
Kadoas 351
Kaprus River 428, 440, 479
Karcı mountains 439, 478
Key of the house of David 402
key(s) 201, 387, 402–4, 424
Khirbet 525
kingdom 45, 69, 88, 95, 99, 149, 155, 193, 210, 221–22, 228–29, 264, 268, 275, 277, 303, 326–27, 331, 381, 402–4, 416, 424–25, 496, 500, 503, 505, 526
Kingdom of God 193
Kobos 328
Koine Greek 525
Kore 339, 352, 501, 526
Korressos, Mt. 120
Lactantius 184–85, 272
Lairmenos sanctuary 369
lamb Christology 194, 201
lamb(s) 54, 81, 89–90, 194–95, 199, 201, 210, 220–21, 253–54, 261, 263–64, 268, 270, 315, 355, 357–58, 365, 369, 371, 373, 375–76, 409, 414, 420, 422, 490, 500, 502, 512, 531
lamp(s) 127, 130–31, 138–41, 208, 471

lampstand(s) 84, 88, 130–32, 138–41, 148, 150, 188, 190, 343, 358, 366, 368, 414, 507
language 94, 181, 194, 219, 220
lanolin 291
Laodicea 43, 53, 58, 64, 88, 106, 142, 193, 211, 250, 278, 280, 284, 296, 351, 355, 366, 369, 419, 422, 426–85, 487, 489–91, 500, 502, 505, 513–14, 519–21
Latin 48, 57, 62–63, 106, 108–9, 114, 117, 139, 278, 317, 332, 374, 433, 512, 516, 521, 530–31
latrine 125, 445
laureate 526
Laval University 438, 445
law, Roman 194, 204
lawcourt 220
lawsuit(s) 68–69, 75, 80, 84, 91, 93, 97, 145–46, 150, 182–83, 200, 219–20, 223–24, 275, 324, 377, 403, 424, 503
leather 283, 285, 287, 386, 521
leather cutter(s) 283
lectisternium 498, 526
legal 70, 83, 86, 89, 91, 94, 189, 198, 204, 219–20, 222
legion(s) 323
Lepidas, Metrodoros 299
let him hear 85, 94, 97–98
letter 43, 50, 63
libellus 58, 60–62, 64
library 107, 112, 127, 228, 231–32, 235–36, 448
library of Celsus 107, 112, 127, 231
library, Alexandria 231–32
linen weavers 283
Lion of Judah 303
lion(s) 90, 115, 164, 194, 342, 346, 349, 392, 394, 397, 462
liturgy 70, 96, 283
liver 455
Livy 166, 269, 271, 277, 331, 381, 430, 526
local reference 52–55, 99, 190, 360, 367, 373, 491, 506
loom-weights 292
Lord's Supper 97
love for God 308
Lucian of Samosata 212, 235, 267, 305, 326, 347, 367, 372, 392, 482, 489
Lucifer 323, 515
Lucretius 295, 483
Luke 52, 526
lukewarm 53, 64, 442, 452, 474, 476, 478–84, 488, 492, 519, 530
lulav 471, 526
Lycophron 420
Lydia 102–3, 117, 126, 130, 27–78, 282, 284–85, 288–89, 295–300, 310, 326–27, 330–31, 333, 346–47, 349, 352, 353, 379–80, 385, 396, 427, 429–30, 456, 462, 470, 515
Lydia, from Thyatira 290–91, 296, 347, 386, 456
Lydian 154, 276–77, 288, 325–26, 328, 331, 335–36, 338–39, 341, 345–46, 348–53, 369, 380, 385
Lydus, Ioannes 235, 381–82, 388, 421
Lysimachus 102, 154, 184, 226–27, 277, 429
macarism 150, 212, 217–18, 223–24, 275, 324, 378
Maccabees 170, 215, 419, 514
Maccabeus 419
Macedonia 251, 255, 277, 295, 329, 367, 380, 385
madder root(s) 293, 294–97, 348, 441, 457
Magi 152

magic 78, 90–91, 237, 271–72, 274, 305, 402, 414, 498–500, 512–14
magistrate(s) 109, 194, 199, 270, 354, 406, 470, 523
Magnesia 111, 140, 223, 330, 332, 341, 430, 507
Magnesia, battle of 277
malediction(s) 68, 87–90, 261–62, 313, 324, 364–65, 411, 484, 505
Manilius 322
manna 505, 512–14, 521
manuscript(s) 46, 523, 531
Manzikert, Battle of 333
Marcellinus 295, 434
Marcellus, Nonius 295
Marcus Aurelius 122, 155, 163, 165, 171, 175, 230, 236, 348, 355, 385, 390
Mari 80, 189
Martial, Marcus Valerius 125, 131, 269, 295, 400, 460, 483
martyr(s) 188, 190, 203, 209, 221–22
martyrdom 45, 55, 152, 162, 166, 169, 172–73, 175–76, 178, 181, 188, 196, 198, 203, 208–10, 217, 221–23, 251, 254–55, 275, 361, 397, 411, 510
Martyrdom of Polycarp 209–10, 250, 255, 510
Mary 46
Masada 139, 267, 342, 531
materialism 505
meal(s) 310, 314
Meander River 106, 428
medallion 469
mediator 76
medicine 236, 426, 453–56, 460, 465, 467, 487, 490
Mediterranean 51, 160
medium 78, 498, 500, 527
Meles River 154, 161
Melito 325, 355
Memnon 277, 429
Mên Karou 464
menorah(s) 127, 139–40, 343–45, 471
Mesopotamia 67
messenger formula 68, 80, 82, 210, 504
messenger(s) 71, 73–81, 95, 97, 101, 107, 129, 131, 146, 180–81, 210, 225, 244, 276, 302, 308, 325, 356, 358, 379, 399, 403, 426, 474, 495, 504
Messiah 55, 193, 357, 400–1, 403, 407, 410, 477, 514, 526
Messianic 195, 263, 303–4, 320–24
metaphor 69, 146–47, 192, 211–12, 215, 222, 258, 310, 312, 320, 322, 362, 369, 373, 404, 409, 416–17, 421–22, 479, 482, 489, 503
Meter 298, 352, 390, 395
Methylene 285
metropolis 158, 160–61, 187, 326, 333, 382
metropolitan 156, 333, 383, 526
Miletus 44–45, 105–6, 134, 329, 428, 471
military 54, 146, 179, 219, 246, 277, 279, 282, 286, 288, 296, 320, 333, 416, 429–30, 435, 502, 523, 529
millennium 67, 83, 207, 218
mineral(s) 385, 429, 440, 444, 455, 478, 490
Minoan(s) 290, 293
Minotaur 350
Mishnah 526, 530
Mishnaic 531
missionary 45
missionary journey, second 127

Index of Subjects

Mithridates 112, 155, 209, 229, 430–31, 437, 456, 461
Moab 322
Moabite 142
Mollusk 291
mollusk(s) 294, 295
money 107, 110, 118, 270, 489, 498, 527
money changer(s) 285
Mongol 333
Montanist(s) 300–1, 398, 422, 434, 526
Montanus 526
moon 73, 322, 352, 395, 464, 466, 477
Morning Star 320, 322, 505
mosaic tile 268
mosaic(s) 268, 343, 371, 530
Moses 81, 96, 99, 523
murex 290, 293–97, 386, 441
Mycale, Mt. 110
Myra 151
myrrh 108, 151–52, 185–86, 510
Mysia 199, 213, 225, 235, 242, 276, 278, 282, 298, 330, 352, 379, 510
myth 54
Nag Hammadi 218
nakedness 489, 519
napkin(s) 295
nard 454–55
Nash Papyrus 92
necklace 117
necropolis 326, 360, 452, 517, 526
Nemesis 166, 468
Neocaesarea 381–82, 422–23, 518
neōkoros 396
Nero 46–47, 107, 112–14, 120, 158, 213, 295, 352, 392, 433, 524
Nero, sestertius coin 56
Nerva 47
new covenant 69, 85, 87, 90, 189, 415, 488
New Testament 42, 48, 50–51, 252, 489, 511–14, 519, 524
Nicaea 382
Nicaea, Council of 155, 301, 333, 382, 473
Nicator 227, 277, 330
Nicolaitan(s) 64, 134, 141–43, 195, 247, 256, 258–61, 274, 406, 507–8, 514
Nicolas of Damascus 58
Nicolaus of Antioch 142–43, 259
Nicomedia 279, 280, 335
Nicostratus 446–47
Nile River 527
Nineveh 326, 401
Northern Sodom Theory (NST) 504
nude 63, 161, 338, 370, 467, 525
numismatic(s) 53, 113, 130, 166, 242, 348, 352, 388, 390, 396, 468, 469, 527
numphaeum 527
Nympha 472–73
nymphaeum 428, 442, 444–46, 467, 471
oath 85–87, 89, 91, 201, 523
obedience 86, 88, 90–91, 150, 200–1, 204, 211, 218, 224, 275, 324, 378
obelisk 527
Octavian 105, 229, 304
Octavius 270, 514, 539

Odeion 522
Odes of Solomon 512
oil lamp 127
ointment(s) 237, 455
Old Testament 48–49, 51, 54, 64, 68, 76, 80–82, 85, 87–89, 93, 96–97, 99, 101, 129, 145, 149–51, 180, 182–83, 189–90, 207, 214, 216, 222, 225, 244, 266, 276, 302, 325, 356, 379, 399, 426, 474, 508, 514, 521
olive branch 314, 393
Olympia 162, 249
Olympic games 111
Olympics 120
omniscient 150, 189, 193, 224, 247, 275, 324, 359, 377, 407, 424–25, 487, 503
Onesimus 128, 134
Onomasticon 527
onyx 266, 514
ophthalmology 452–55
oracle(s) 49, 50, 70, 76, 80, 84, 90–91, 94, 97, 145, 223, 328, 329, 506, 527
Origen 60, 72, 171, 203, 272, 322, 422, 477
Origen of Alexandria 44–45
orthodox 525
orthodoxy 135, 173, 257
ostracon(-ca) 267, 527
Ottoman 333, 383
overcome 88, 188, 216–17, 219–21, 223
overcomer 96, 150, 192, 210, 211–12, 216, 218–24, 275, 324, 377–78, 424, 503
Ovid 115, 184–85, 267–69, 293, 327, 346, 350, 373, 392, 489, 495
P.Oxy. 61–62, 459, 496
Pagus, Mt. 154, 162, 187, 213, 511
Palaestra 341, 526
Paleo-Hebrew 530
Palestine 511
Pamukkale 429, 438, 443–44
Panionia festival 110–11
Panionian 111
Panionium 110
Papylus 255, 315
papyrus(-ri) 61–62, 78, 233–35, 271, 292, 498, 527
parable(s) 94, 99
paradise 146, 149, 505, 507
paraenesis 70, 94, 145, 217, 220
parallelomania 67
parchment(s) 233, 528
Parousia 138, 141, 217, 261, 320, 365, 414–15, 495–96, 500, 528
Parthenon 521
Pasargadae 336
Passover 528
Paterculus, Marcus Velleius 229
Patmos 42, 44–47, 73, 127–28, 155–57, 175, 178, 199, 209–10, 306, 372, 404, 511, 515, 517–18
Paul 50, 111, 127, 157, 288
Pausanias 102, 110, 114, 117, 125, 154, 162, 166, 225, 227, 235, 250, 251, 338, 350, 369, 372, 390, 392, 419, 501, 525
Peducaeus, Lucius 470
Peloponnesian war 102
Pentateuch 218, 528
Pentecost 528

Pergamene Kingdom 278
Pergamum (Pergamos) 43, 58, 84, 88, 102, 110, 142–43, 157–60, 163, 181, 199, 211, 225–44, 247–63, 267, 270, 272, 274–80, 285–86, 298, 301, 304, 309, 330–31, 351, 366, 368, 376, 381, 391, 414, 428–30, 442, 460, 465, 472, 489, 505, 512–14, 528
peristyle 125, 243, 338, 472, 523
persecute 58, 134, 171, 190, 207, 255, 267
persecution 43, 44, 47, 55, 62–64, 90, 99, 135, 146, 166, 168–71, 173–74, 176, 181–92, 195–201, 203, 205–6, 208, 210–11, 220, 223, 251, 255, 405, 412–13, 504–5, 507, 523
Persephone 240, 502, 526
Persepolis 336
perseverance 132, 135, 209–10, 217–20, 222–23, 308, 410, 489, 507
Persian(s) 60, 73, 79, 102, 149, 154, 184, 227, 325–26, 328–29, 333, 336, 347, 367, 388, 390, 434
Persian, royal road 329
Peter 512
Petronius 482
Pharaoh 81
Philadelphia 43, 47, 55, 58, 66, 69, 74, 85, 88, 98, 106, 135–36, 172, 195–200, 211, 223, 233, 235, 237, 248, 256–57, 266, 268, 280, 282, 285, 295, 304, 311, 315, 320, 335, 360, 364, 369, 375, 379–411, 414–17, 419–20, 422–26, 433, 472, 476, 485, 505, 518
Philadelphia Flavia 382, 396
Philalethes 453–54
Philetaerus 227, 429
Philippi 151, 158, 177, 211, 288–90, 296–97, 300, 456
Philippopolis 382
Philo 92, 130, 142, 170, 193, 212, 256, 300, 312–13, 317, 366, 369, 372, 420, 422, 476, 487, 492, 495
Philomelium 110
Philostratus, Flavius 103, 114, 136, 154, 158, 160, 182, 184, 204, 213, 235–36, 245, 250, 326, 347, 385, 427, 462, 466, 489, 495
Phoenician(s) 290, 293
phoenix 184–86
Phoscus 301
Phrygia 158, 330, 347, 353, 379, 385, 391, 404, 427–28, 434–35, 438, 441, 444, 457, 463, 468, 470, 472, 490, 526
Phrygian eye salve 487
Piazza Armerina 371
Pilate 246
pillar(s) 164, 343, 387, 417–21, 449, 505, 518, 529
Pion, Mt. 112
Pionius 55, 160–62, 165–66, 168–69, 172, 175–78, 196, 198, 209
Pionius, Martyrdom of 172, 176, 209
pipe(s) 440, 442, 444, 446, 478, 483, 485, 519, 525
Pistis 210, 307–8, 528, 545
Plato 372, 482, 490
Plautus, Titus Maccius 118, 482
Pliny the Elder 45–47, 63–64, 102, 105, 110, 117–18, 152–53, 169, 184, 194, 204, 226, 228–29, 232, 234, 245, 257, 264, 265, 271, 276–78, 285, 289, 291, 293–96, 322, 326, 331, 335, 347–48, 367, 369, 371–72, 379, 381–82, 385, 389, 406, 420–22, 429, 431–32, 439, 455–57, 459–60, 462–63, 478, 491, 524
Pliny the Younger 55, 63–64, 107

Plutarch 107, 118, 126, 161, 163, 184, 215, 232, 238, 249–50, 267, 273, 305, 313, 329, 364, 372, 430–31, 490, 495, 512
Pluto 123, 420
Polemo 431
Polemon 158, 162, 165, 175, 431, 434
Pollux, Julius 293, 389, 524
Polyaenus 326, 330, 427
Polybius 166, 235, 246, 269, 277, 327, 330, 364, 367, 381, 408, 427, 430
Polycarp 46, 55, 154, 161, 172–75, 177–78, 187, 191, 194, 196, 198, 203, 207–10, 214, 220, 250, 255, 257, 300, 398, 510
Polycarp, martyrdom 56
Polydeuces 524
polytheism 55, 93, 126, 144, 225, 252, 262, 348, 360, 377, 424, 470, 503, 512, 514
pomegranate(s) 116
Pompeii 96, 123, 164, 289, 291, 388, 449, 483, 525
Porphyrology 290, 294
Poseidon 123, 165
pottery 527, 530
poverty 57, 86, 188, 190–93, 200, 224, 312, 486, 487
preamble 66, 68, 79–82, 129, 150, 180–81, 183, 188, 224, 244, 275, 302, 324, 356, 377, 399, 403, 424, 474, 503–4
prefect 528
Priapus 125
Priene 105, 525
priest(s) 58, 76, 107, 117, 157, 169, 196, 213, 221–22, 240, 265, 266, 288, 298, 308, 347, 349, 372, 396
priestess(es) 115, 147, 286–88, 299, 311, 349, 446, 467, 515, 527
priesthood 111, 396
priests 59
Priscilla 108, 127
prison(s) 47, 61, 73, 202–5, 233
proclamation formula 94
proclamations 76, 98
proconsul(s) 110, 173, 228, 245–47, 249, 254, 315, 326, 354, 430–31, 442, 447, 451, 460, 470, 512, 522
prodigal 137
prologue 50
Propertius, Sextus 295
prophecy 48, 76, 81, 87, 146, 219, 220
prophet(s) 48, 49, 51, 54, 68–70, 73–75, 76, 79–83, 91, 94, 96–97, 99, 133–34, 145–46, 182, 189–90, 207–8, 218–19, 256, 309–13, 398, 453, 464, 493, 504, 505
prophetic 48–51, 80, 86, 99, 527
prophetic letters 49
prophetic oracles 50, 70, 87, 91, 96, 99, 504
propitiation 521
prostitute(s) 390
prostitution 124–26, 143, 507
Prusias of Bithynia 277
Prytaneion 109, 115
Psammetichus 326
Pseudepigrapha 214, 528
pseudodipteral 353
Pseudologoi 528
Ptolemy II 232–33
public reading 66, 95, 97, 504
punishment 85, 89, 203–4, 218, 222, 314, 317–18, 406
purple dye 289–91, 295, 347

INDEX OF SUBJECTS

purple dye invented 347
purple-dyer(s) 285, 288
Puteoli 332
Qldans-Apollo 351
Quartodeciman 355, 434
Qumran 73, 197, 199, 219, 524, 528, 530
Rabbah 528
ram 115
rapture 412
Ras Shamra 189, 293
ratification 87, 94, 96
redemption 89
reincarnation 186
reliability 52, 56
remnant 190, 214
repent(ance) 69–70, 85, 88, 90–91, 99, 136–39, 145, 150, 247, 260–62, 265, 275, 312–15, 324, 360–64, 366, 377, 404, 415, 477, 481, 484, 488–96, 500, 503, 505, 527
resurrection 133, 140, 152, 181–82, 184–88, 201, 217, 222, 304, 355, 373, 416, 502, 510
revelation 49, 521, 527
Revelation 87
Revelation, book of 42
Revelation, genre 48
righteousness 490
robe(s) 364, 370–73, 490
Roma 55, 57, 89, 109, 120, 155, 166–68, 208, 229, 252, 287, 298, 352, 390, 432, 448, 469, 501
Roman 46, 55–59, 63, 99, 103, 108–9, 245, 254, 344, 438, 506, 512, 515, 523, 527–29
Roman cities 108
Roman citizen 60
Roman emperor(s) 59, 113, 131, 158, 207
Roman law 55
Roman(s) 60, 63, 192, 197, 199, 203, 522
Rome 43, 44, 57–58, 60–63, 65, 102–7, 109, 119–20, 122–24, 128, 131, 155, 163, 166–68, 174, 177, 191, 209, 227–29, 231, 235–36, 242, 249, 252, 256, 266, 271, 278, 287, 289, 291–92, 299, 304–5, 330, 332, 346–48, 350–51, 354, 367, 372, 374, 381, 388, 390, 393, 396–97, 406, 408, 428, 431–32, 433, 443, 448, 451, 462, 471, 486–87, 495, 502, 510, 526, 530–31
Romulus and Remus 63
roof 452
Rosetta Stone 341, 523
Rubilius, Caius 470
rug(s) 460
Sabbath 55, 173, 175, 198, 300, 434, 470
Sabina 166, 169, 175, 451
sacred groves 149, 507
sacrifice(s) 55–56, 58, 61–62, 64, 111–12, 120, 142, 175, 238, 256, 319, 324, 354, 396, 482, 521
Saittai 285, 356
Salbascus 428
salt(s) 455
salvation 51, 492
salve(s) 455
Samos 460
sanctions 68, 79, 86–90, 211, 320, 364, 368, 483, 493, 504
Sanhedrin 529
Sapho 235
Sappho 325
Sarapas 301
sarcophagus 281, 452, 529
sard 266
Sardis 43, 88, 103, 106, 110, 126, 130, 137, 149, 167, 195, 211, 254, 276, 279–80, 285, 287–88, 304, 325–69, 371, 373–82, 389, 397, 414, 419, 422, 428, 432, 437, 442, 460, 465, 471–72, 489, 505, 511, 517, 521, 530
Satan 143, 169–70, 175, 193, 195, 197, 199–200, 202–3, 205, 209, 224, 228, 242, 247, 249–56, 260, 264, 275, 309, 318, 319, 321, 355, 397, 403–8, 416, 512–16
Satan's throne 57, 239, 247–53, 502, 512–14
Saturnalia 497
Saturninus, Venuleius 204
scarab 529
scepter(s) 321–22, 324, 350, 389, 393, 395, 463, 467–68, 502, 515–16
schema 68, 99
Scripture 49
scroll 54, 96, 195, 374, 376, 523
sea 92–93, 103, 106, 165, 213, 248, 294, 379, 429
seal(s) 78, 92, 401
Sebaste 529
Sebasteia 529
Sebastoi 58, 113, 119–21, 123, 158, 287, 297–98, 529
Sebastopolis 529
Sebastos 58, 529
second century 55, 106, 113, 117, 119–20, 126–28, 142, 172, 187, 204, 226, 230, 232, 235, 251, 279, 282, 334, 338, 341–42, 348, 351–53, 355, 367, 384, 387, 389, 443, 448–49, 467, 498, 507, 521, 523–24, 526
second millennium 83, 218
Second Temple Period 529
Secundus 64
Sefire 89
Seleucid(s) 102, 155, 170, 209, 227, 277, 326, 330, 367, 426, 429, 430, 436–37
Seleucus I 209, 227, 277, 330, 429–30
Semitic 76, 199
Senate, Roman 57, 120, 159–60, 354, 432, 523
Seneca, Lucius Annaeus 137, 193, 295, 331, 482, 483
Septimus Severus 338, 445, 471
Septuagint (LXX) 76, 80, 89, 189–91, 202, 207, 214, 216, 219, 365, 521, 525, 529
Serapis 113, 240
serpent(s) 195, 248, 250–51, 254, 348–49, 397, 456, 466–67, 513–14
Servius Maurus Honoratus 373, 498, 526
Sestertius 139
seven churches 71, 73–74, 84, 86, 88, 96, 145, 219
seven hills 131
seven letters 73–74, 77, 93
seventh century 326, 341, 434, 445, 449–50, 452
Severus, Sulpicius 252, 254, 512
sexual behavior 64, 123–25, 142–43, 238, 256–58, 310–14, 319, 324, 391, 512, 515
sheep 108, 134, 291, 321, 457, 459, 461
shekel(s) 461, 470–71
Shepherd of Hermas 373
ship 124, 460
shoemakers 56, 283
shofar 127, 343, 471, 529
shop(s) 107, 112, 164, 281, 289, 336, 344, 369, 371, 529

Sibyl Sambathe 297, 311
Sibylline Oracle(s) 323, 355, 514–15, 527
Sidonius Apollinaris 499
SIG-Sylloges insciptionum graecarum, Dittenberger 112
Silas 133
silk 108, 386, 443, 457, 458
silver 108, 130, 336, 344–47, 470, 523–24
silversmith(s) 106, 108, 111, 118, 132, 210, 285, 507
Sinai 82
Sinai, Mt. 514, 523
Sirach 52
sixth century 46, 282, 315, 326–27, 382, 449
slander 188, 193–94, 196, 200
slave market 297, 347
slave traders 56, 347
slave(s) 85, 108, 117, 204, 231, 270, 284, 297, 347, 411, 484, 490, 530
SMR
   Seven Messages of Revelation 68, 70, 76, 81, 84, 87, 91, 93–94, 97–98, 183, 200, 207, 211, 214, 217, 504
Smyrna 43, 46, 55, 56, 58, 61, 69, 72, 74, 85, 88, 98, 102, 110, 120, 136, 140, 150–204, 208–13, 217, 219, 221–24, 236, 242–43, 248, 250, 253, 257, 275, 280–81, 285, 309, 324–25, 333, 344, 350, 353, 360, 364, 377, 389, 392, 394, 396–98, 407–8, 411–12, 415–16, 424–25, 432, 442, 453, 460, 465, 468, 474, 489, 503, 505, 507, 510–12
Smyrnaean 188, 190–93, 198, 200, 202–3, 207–12, 219, 221, 223–24
Snynnada 110
soil 530
Solomon, King 524
Son of God 219, 302–6, 407, 423, 515
Sophocles, Oedipus Tyrannus 207, 347, 392
Sophronius of Jerusalem 128
sovereign 129, 180–81, 190–91, 193, 202, 210, 244, 302, 356, 399, 474
Spain 61, 290, 292, 295, 417, 449
spindle whirls 292
Spirit 72, 94, 181, 223
spiritual gift(s) 300, 308
St. Anne, Chapel of 46
stadium 55, 111, 162, 225, 230, 330, 333, 382, 388, 396, 416, 437, 446–47, 451, 461
staff 238, 250, 291, 322, 397, 464, 467, 529
stag 115, 147, 394
star(s) 73, 84, 130–31, 148, 150, 208, 254, 304, 305, 322–24, 357–58, 377, 507, 515
Statius 172, 235, 295, 323, 400, 515
statue(s) 63, 112
statuette(s) 389, 393
stele (stela) 529
Stephanus of Byzantium 276–77, 289, 381, 382, 426
stipulations 66, 68, 83–86, 90–92, 150, 189, 200–1, 203, 209, 211, 218–19, 224, 317–18, 324, 415, 425, 488, 503–4
stoa(s) 107, 115, 164, 228, 231–32, 253, 278, 282, 529
stomach 455
Strabo 101–3, 105, 110, 117, 124, 147, 151, 153–54, 160–61, 164, 184, 187, 191, 227–28, 232, 276–78, 296, 326–27, 331–32, 345, 348, 350, 367, 380–82, 384–85, 405, 419, 421, 427–33, 437, 440–41, 453–54, 456–57, 459, 461, 478, 484–85, 487, 490, 518
Strabo, Geography 147, 421, 487, 518

strata 525, 530
Suetonius Tranquillus, Gaius 59, 63, 125, 131, 245, 269, 270, 278, 305, 331, 372, 385, 405, 432–33, 443, 449
Suetonius, Domitian 63
suffering 43–44, 99, 313, 510
Sukkot 526
Susa 329, 344
suzerainty 65–66, 95
sword(s) 57, 244–47, 256, 261–62, 275, 368, 414, 512
symbol 75, 90, 201, 205–8, 215–16
synagogue of Satan 55, 195, 197, 199, 209, 318, 416, 510
synagogue(s) 55, 77, 126–27, 156, 169–70, 175, 177, 193, 195, 197–200, 224, 282, 299, 300, 309, 311, 336, 341–44, 349, 354, 387, 397, 402–8, 411, 413, 421, 471, 510, 521–22, 524, 530
synagogue, Beth Alpha 326, 341
syncretism 111, 143, 199, 510
Synoptic Gospels 94, 530
Syria 91
Syria Street 447
Syrian Gate 438, 444
Syro-Palestinian 67
tabernacle 139, 219, 418, 521, 528
table cloth(s) 295
Tacitus 44–46, 58, 105–6, 112, 119, 125, 166–68, 184–85, 191, 209, 229, 245, 252–53, 278, 331, 333, 353, 367, 372, 374, 382, 408, 421, 432–33, 443, 448, 461, 468, 485, 499
Talmud(ic) 77, 293, 526, 530
Tamerlane 156, 333
tanners 56, 283, 386
Tantalus 154
tapestry 97, 347
Targum 530
Tatian 477
Tatius, Achilles 184
Taweret 271
tax(es) 382, 460, 462, 470–71
Telephus 227, 241
temperature 293, 442, 444, 480–82, 484–85
temple 199, 219, 417, 421, 505, 518
Temple A 447, 464
temple altars 512
Temple of Augustus 254, 512
Temple of Sebastoi 58
Temple of Zeus 248
temple tax 354, 461, 470
temple warden (neokoros) 59, 60, 114, 121
temple(s) 58, 102, 111, 113–14, 118, 120–23, 147, 166, 169, 183, 210, 213, 225, 229, 236, 239, 242–43, 252–54, 268, 279, 297, 335, 341, 369, 382, 387–88, 419–20, 447, 469, 513–14, 521, 527, 529
Ten Commandments 80, 83, 86, 521, 523
ten days 203, 205–8
terracotta 440, 485, 530
Tertullian 45, 142–43, 171–72, 184–85, 194, 197, 372, 374, 398
tessera(e) 268, 270–71, 512, 530
Testament of Levi 508, 514
Testamonia 269
testimony 75, 94, 146, 201, 220
Tetragrammaton 269, 423, 530
Tetrarch 530

Index of Subjects

tetrastyle 167, 242, 390, 392, 396, 469
textile industry 347
textile(s) 283, 285, 288–89, 291–97, 326, 344, 347, 354, 369, 372, 426, 437–38, 452, 456–57, 459–60, 487, 490
theater(s) 108, 109, 111–12, 121, 127, 162, 225, 236, 238, 268, 282, 327, 330, 333, 382, 387, 391, 448, 449–22, 524–25, 530
Themison 454
theocracy 194
Theodosius 92, 382, 438
Theophilus of Antioch 477
Theophrastus 267
Theopompus 117
thermopolium 483, 484
Thessalonica 289–90, 295
Thessalonica, Archbishop of 117
Thesus 154
thief 365, 517
third century 61, 112, 113, 154, 158, 167, 187, 204, 223, 238, 246, 255, 279, 286–87, 300, 333, 341, 354, 356, 381, 386, 391, 397, 426, 445, 473, 526
Throne of Apollo 500
throne of God 249, 362, 500
throne(s) 57, 194, 199, 214, 228, 239–40, 247–54, 264, 275, 305, 321, 381, 418, 429–30, 475, 490, 500–5, 512–14, 519
Thucydides 60, 111, 364
Thummim 266, 514–15
Thyatira 43, 56, 58, 85, 88, 98, 142–43, 211, 243, 256–58, 276–90, 295–13, 315, 318–20, 324–25, 347, 379, 415, 429, 432, 437, 450, 452–53, 456, 472, 505, 515
Tiberius 59, 119–21, 123, 155, 166–67, 209, 229, 243, 278, 304, 323, 331–32, 339, 350, 353, 367, 382, 432–33, 448, 468
Timothy 127
Titus 58, 63, 529
Titus, arch of 139
Titus, Emperor 63, 120, 139
Tmolus, Mt. 325–26, 345, 350, 379, 385, 433
toga(s) 296, 372
token(s) 268–70, 346, 512
Torah 77, 89, 91, 189, 193, 207, 208
Torah shrine 343
trade guild(s) 207, 276, 279, 283–84, 310, 312, 516
tradition 44, 47, 51, 99, 512
Trajan 46, 47, 63, 64, 112, 128, 161, 165, 175, 229, 240, 242–43, 254, 305, 340, 389–90, 394, 407, 442, 447
Trajan, Emperor 47, 64, 254
Trajan, temple 209
transcendent 81, 181–84, 188, 224, 303, 305–6, 400–2, 525
travertine 429, 438–39, 448, 478
treaty 65–68, 82–86, 88–96, 145, 189, 201, 211, 218, 223, 261–62, 313, 317, 330, 359, 364, 377, 411, 415, 424, 478, 484, 488, 502, 504
Treaty of Kadesh 67
tree of life 54, 146–50, 215–16, 261, 505, 507–8
tribulation 45, 189–90, 192, 198, 203, 205–6, 208, 210, 314, 324, 411–12, 413, 510
Tribulation, Great 413
Trinity 47, 54, 60, 136, 232, 236–37, 249, 257–58, 409, 423, 452, 511
Tripolis 428, 434, 443
Tryho 128

Tübingen school 52, 515
Tumuli 452
tunic(s) 296, 458, 460
Tuppi-Teshshup 200
Tyche 117, 122–23, 166, 169, 183, 212–13, 298, 332, 339, 343, 348, 350, 352, 389–90, 393–96, 463, 466, 523
Tyrannus 472
Tyrian Purple 290–96
Ulpian 110, 204, 245
unity 67, 70, 98, 215
Urim 266, 514–15
Varro, Marcus Terentius 232–33, 235, 291, 295, 501
vassal 66, 78–92, 144–45, 189, 193–94, 200–1, 205, 211, 218, 222, 262, 317–18, 377, 407, 415, 424, 488, 502
Vatican Museum 63
vellum 528, 531
Venice 383
Venus 322, 449, 515
Vespasian, Emperor 58, 63, 114, 119–20, 131, 139, 278, 299, 305, 353, 382, 396, 442, 446–47, 529
Victorinus of Pettau 44, 46, 267, 357, 370
vine 385
vineyard(s) 385
Virgil 131, 295, 373, 385
virgin(s) 117
Viticulture 385
Vitruvius 118, 233, 289, 293, 295, 335, 441, 456, 459, 485
volcanic 380, 385
vomit 483–84
vote(s) 267, 512
votive 531
vow(s) 462, 465–66
Vulgate 521
wax 90
wax tablet 96
wealth 191, 193, 212, 224
white stone 265–68, 270, 273, 275–76, 512–14
white stone(s) 271
wine 108, 124, 152, 160, 351, 386, 391, 452, 482, 484, 498, 522, 526
witness 45, 61, 66, 68, 84, 91–94, 97–98, 133, 135, 141, 144, 146, 150, 182, 223–24, 255, 262, 275, 317, 324, 362, 377, 378, 415, 424–25, 473, 476, 488, 491, 502–4, 512, 521
witness formula 94–95, 98
wolf 63, 397, 427
Wood, J. T. 147
wool 283–85, 291–92, 296, 344, 347, 369, 371, 386, 389, 438, 440, 452, 456–59, 461, 463–64, 488–90, 517, 519
wool workers 283–85
wool(en) 279, 344
worship 55, 57–59, 63, 149, 199, 510, 516–17, 530
Xenon, Gaius Julius 299
Xenophanes of Colophon 326, 345–46
Xenophon 112, 149, 227, 269, 329, 341, 367, 374, 427–28, 483, 496, 500
Yahweh, YHWH 69, 76, 80–81, 83, 89, 145–46, 182–83, 189–90, 200, 218, 222, 269, 310, 316, 390, 408, 423, 516, 530
Yom Kippur 529
Zealot 531
Zechariah 80, 89, 130, 140
Zeno, Marcus Antonius 431, 500, 519

Zenoid	431, 500	Zeus Laodikeus	463
Zenon	431	Zeus of Targyenos	420
Zeus	115, 120, 123, 165–66, 169, 183, 199, 227–28, 230, 235, 239, 240, 243, 248–50, 253, 269, 271, 298, 306, 329, 338, 350–52, 388, 392–93, 395, 411, 429, 447–48, 454, 463–65, 468–70, 498, 501, 510, 512–15, 521, 524, 526	Zeus Olympios	350
		Zeus Polieus	348–49
		Zeus Sabazios	349
		Zeuxis	487
Zeus Asclepius	350	Zeuxis Philathethes	453–54, 460
Zeus Koryphaeos	395, 420	zinc	306, 455, 515
Zeus Ktesios Patrios	463	zodiac	323

Index of Foreign Words

'asher 'al habbayit 401
'ēpōd 265
accusatio 194
adikēthē 220
Adramyttion 151
aedes 521
aediculae 343, 521
agapaō 491
agapē 307–8
agapēn 135
Agdistis 390, 391
agoge 530
agōnothetēs 268, 522
agoranomos 284, 288
Agrotera 115
Agustalia Anaitea 390
airesis 525
Akhişar 276, 279, 281, 379
Akköy-Gölemezli 443
akolouthōn 370
akousatō 87
Alakšanduš 218
Alaşehir 379–84, 386, 388–89
albatae vestes 370
alēthinos 400-1, 476–77
āliku 78
ālikum 78
ālikūtu 78
alla 142, 192, 199, 239
Alogoi 300
'āmēn 475–76
'āmmān 476
amphitheatron 446, 521
anabolais 459
analemma 449–50
Angdissis 391
angelikos 356
angelos 71–79, 129, 180, 244, 302, 310, 356–57, 399, 474, 498
angelus interpres 71, 76
Anthestēria 124
anthropou 303
Antipatros 255
aphēkas 135
aphtharsias 214, 220
aplourgoi 284, 457
apodyteria 338

apokalypsis 42, 48, 521
apokalyptein 521
apókruphos 521
apostolos 133
apothanein 361
apotheōsis 62–63, 305, 329, 352, 355
apotheoun 521
archē 477
archiereus 521
archisynagōgos 77, 311
argurokopos 111, 118
Artemisia 112
Asiarch(ēs) 110–11, 521
Asias 158–60, 182
assēs 523
assidēre 522
astera 322
Attalou 381
atuentores 109
authephēs 482
autō 320
autokratōr 304
autōn 189, 368
axios 370
ba'al'am 142
bapheis 283, 285
Baş Pınar Çay 441
basilicam 123
basilikē 123
Başpinar 439, 478
bastasai 134
bathea 318
Bayraklı 153–54
Bayraklı Höyük 153
bēma xiv, 249, 254, 522
Bin Tepe 326
Bipennis 522, 526
Birros 458
blasphēmia 193, 202
Bolinus brandaris 295
boulē 109–10, 229, 243, 522
bouleutērion 109
bouleutēs 354
Boz dağlari 379
Bozdag 325
Büyük Menderes 427–28
byrseis 283

calda 483, 522
caldaria 338, 370
caldarium 338, 370, 452, 481
caldum 482, 522
calidam 482
candida urbs 372
castellum aquae 442, 444
caudex 523
cella 338, 348, 370
centumvirale 250
centumviri 249
chalkeis 283
chalkolibanō 306–7
chalkos 306
chalkotypoi 283
chiton 392, 397, 466–67
chlanis 458
chliaros 478, 480, 483
Christos 526
chrusus 345
cippus 522
cista mystica 523
civitas 113, 278, 457
Civitatibus 278, 332–33
Çizmeli 443
clavi 295–96, 373, 458
coercitio 204
collegia 288, 456–57
collyrium 490–91
colobiōn 458
colonia 108, 292
colum nivarium 482
Commune 167, 432
conciliabula 108
conventus 110, 228, 249–50, 278, 287, 331, 381, 389, 431, 433, 522
copiae 523
coracino colore 459
cornu copiae 523
coronatus 213
cotta 440, 478, 483, 485, 519, 530
cuneus 525
curator 107, 287
currus 523
Çürüksu 426, 428
curulis 523
custodia reorum 204

dābār	406	
daimonion	126	
damnatio memoriae	119, 122, 284, 374, 468–69	
deificatio	521	
deipnēsō	495–96	
deka	207	
dekálogos	523	
delatores	194	
delmatikōn	458	
dēmokratía	523	
demos	121	
dēmos	523	
dēmotikē	523	
dēnārius	523	
deus	524	
Deus Sol Invictus	122	
deuterou	221	
deuterous	222	
diabolos	202	
diakonia	307, 308	
dialektos	525	
diaspora	354, 407, 470, 523	
diathēkēs	76	
diazoma	449, 524	
didachē	256, 524	
didōmi	219	
dikaios	356	
dioceseis	110	
dioikēsis	228, 381, 389	
Dionuson	391	
Dionysus	122–24, 231, 239–40, 251, 297–98, 344, 350, 385, 388, 391, 467, 523	
Dioscuri	524	
Dioskouroi	524	
Dioskuri	389, 524	
dispositio	85, 415, 488	
distomon	244	
dīva	524	
Divi Filius	304	
Divus Caesar	305	
Divus Vespasianus	305	
dominus et Deus	63	
dominus et dues noster	63	
dōsō	219, 263	
dunamin	405	
ebastasas	134	
echeis	222, 256, 315, 320, 359, 405, 415	
echōn	87, 130, 144	
ēgapēsa	200, 409	
egeneto	183	
eidōlaion	166	
eidōlothutos	256, 309–10	
eilēpha	321	
ēkein	138	
ekklēsia	109, 197	
electrum	336, 345	
ēlektron	345, 524	
emellon	361	
emesai	483–84	
emolunan	368	
emporion	103, 459	
'ēmûn	475	
enōpion	362	
entolas	406	
ephēbos	121, 282, 287, 338, 524–25	
epigraphē	524, 528	
epiphanestatē	392	
Epistola ad Laodicenses	473	
eputhrodanon	293	
erchesthai	261	
erchomai	138, 261	
erga	84, 132, 137, 307, 309, 359, 362, 403, 478	
ergastai	297	
ergatēgoi	284	
ergōn	313	
eriourgoi	386	
ērnēsō	254, 407	
eschaton	524	
eschatos	182, 184	
essaiou	524	
etērēsas	407, 410–11	
ethnōn	320	
exactor	109	
exaleiphetai	374	
exaleiphō	375	
exedra	524	
exelthē	421	
exete	203	
exeuriskein	346	
exousia	321	
exousian	222	
ezēsen	183	
Fiboulalōrion	458	
fora	108	
Forturna	463	
forum	229, 432, 521	
frigidarium	338, 370, 452, 481, 524	
fullonica	289, 291–92	
galut	523	
geniza	524	
geōmetria	524	
gerontes	338, 525	
gerousia	109, 282, 335	
gīmatrĕyā	524	
gimatria	524	
ginōskō	132, 189	
gnapheis	283–84	
gnōsin	409	
gnōsis	525	
gnōstikos	525	
graffiare	525	
grammata	117, 126	
grammateus	60, 110, 525	
grammatikos	232	
graphō	525	
graphon	48, 129, 180, 244, 302, 356, 399, 474	
grapson	71	
grēgorēsēs	365	
grēgorōn	361	
Gümüşçay-Goncalı-Deresi	428	
gymnasiarch	282	
gymnasion	338, 525	
gymnos	525	
hagiasma	422	
hagios	400–1	
haplourgoi	459	
harpagisometha	528	
harpazō	528	
haṭṭu	322	
Heliogabalus	122, 353, 468	
hēmerōn	206, 208	
heptamyxion	343, 470	
ḥērem	88–89, 145, 364	
hermēneuō	525	
heroa	525	
Hestia	109, 123, 126, 395, 411	
hetairai	125	
Hexaplex trunculus	295	
hēxō	366	
hierateusen	462	
hieron	162, 349, 351, 429	
hierophantēs	391	
himatia	368, 459	
hina	205	
homoiōs	259, 260, 303	
homologeō	376	
homonoia	102, 163, 213, 389, 392, 394, 397, 460	
honomata	368	

Index of Foreign Words

hopites	109	kerkides	448–49	luchniōn	131
hōran	366	khitōn	522	lulab	343
horologion	107	khrēsmoi	527	Lumen	110
ḥošen	265	Kimmerioi	327	macheira	245
humōn	202–3	kinēsō	138, 139	magistē	392
hymin	318	kiones	420	mappa	295
hypocaustum	525	Kizildere	444	marturia	94, 146
hypomonē	217, 307–9	klein	400	martus	94, 146, 255, 476
idû	83	kleptēs	365	Martyrion	526
Iēsou Christou	146	klinē	313, 498, 525	Mashiah	526
Imperium	251	Koca Çayi	379	megalē	314, 413
impudicitia	123	Koina	526	mellei	192, 202
in situ	49	koinē	525	Mên Askaenos	352, 395
incolae	109	koinon	58, 242, 467, 526	Mên Karou	453
in-nam-ti-la	374	kokkos	293	mēnōrâ	139
Ioudaious	195	kollurion	455, 490	menorat	140
Iouliou	304	kolymbethra	450	metamelomai	364
isatis	293	kopos	132, 307	metanoēson	136–37, 260, 313, 363–64, 492
iudicium	250	koreō	113, 526		
iuridcus	331, 431	kratei	320, 415	Metrōon	351
ius gladii	245–47, 262, 512	kratēsate	320	mikran	405
IVDAEA CAPTA	139	kratos	130, 523	miliarion	482
Jovialia Solaria	390	kritikoi	232	minîm	374
Kabaağaç	443	krokos	293	mishna	526
kagō	321	krouō	494	mlakyw	76
kai	158–59, 182–83, 219, 229, 259–60, 305, 309, 316, 350, 357, 361, 363, 390, 400, 405, 421, 423, 476, 486	kubos	268	mlan	76
		Küçük Menderes	105	mnēmoneue	136, 362
		kukalim	346	moicheuontas	315
kainēs	423	kurios	423, 497	mōr	151, 152
kainon	265, 273, 423	kuriou	76	mores	123
kainos	423	Ladicia Sacrum	462	municipia	108, 501
Kaisersäle	338	lambanein	416	Muricidae	294–95
Kaklik	444	lana sucida	291	Muwattališ	218
kakous	133	lanarii carminatores	283, 288, 456	nardinon	454–55
kalathos	389, 397, 466, 522	lanarii purgatories	283	narratio	84, 403
kanōn	522	lanarius	283–84, 456	navem	526
kapporeth	521	lanrioi	288	Naẕarim	374
karabos	529	Laodicea ad Lycum	427	Nea Filadelfia	383
Karahayıt	443–44	laon	259	Neikostratos	446
karakallōn	459	Laurus	526	neios	527
kardias	316	lectisternium	499	nekros	183, 360
katakekaumenē	380, 385	lectum sternere	498, 526	neoi	338, 385, 525
katalogou	374	leukos	265, 345	neōkorōn	114
katanathema	364	lex talionis	141, 317	neōkoros	59, 113, 122, 229, 353
katara	90	lithos	266, 527, 529	neōs	113, 526
katathema	90	locus classicus	337	nephrous	316
kateidōlos	251	lodices	460	ner	139
Kathēgemona	391	logos	406	Nikalaitai	142
kēkis	293	loipa	361, 362	nikan	259
kekrymmenou	263	loipos	318	nikaō	219–20
kerameis	283	luchnia	141	Nikolaıitai	142

nikōn	220, 369, 416, 500, 502	Pergamos	225, 241	proseuchē	299
nikōnti	146, 263, 320, 493	Peri pascha	355	proskyēsousin	408
nomisma	527	peripatein	370	prōtē	158, 182, 253–54
nomophulákion	343	peristylos	528	prōtos	135, 181
numismatis	527	Persephonē	352	proxenētai	297
nummularius	270	phagein	310, 529	prutanis	110
obeliskos	527	phainole	457–58	psēphon	265–67
obelos	527	phakialiōn	459	pseudeis	133, 528
obversus	527	phaskinia	459	pseudomain	196
ōdeum	450, 527	Philadelphus	228, 381	psychros	479–80
odunēn	189	philanpeloi	385	ptōcheia	191, 202
oida	84, 131, 188–89, 192, 307, 359, 403, 478	philō	491	ptōchos	191, 193, 487
		philologoi	232	publica	526
ōideion	109	phlox	305	puros	305
oiden	265	phobou	201, 202	Purpura haemastoma	295
Olympieion	121	phōsphoros	322	purpurarius	288–89
Olympios	120–21, 350	phukos	293	putara	291
omphalos	527	phulakēn	202	qaneh	522
onoma	254–55, 265, 273, 359, 423	phylē	386	qyma	76
		Phyllonotus trunculus	295	raison d'être	83
onomastikon	527	physchros	478	raptura	528
ophthalmoi	305	pistin	255	religio licita	198
ōrāre	527	pistos	146, 209–10, 476	reperio	233
ostrinum	295	plectrum	394, 528	Restitutis	278, 332, 433
oudeis	265, 400	plēktron	528	reversus	529
paides	338, 525	plēssein	528	r'h	321
paidikoin	125	plousios	192	rhomphaia	244–45
palaestra	338	pneumata	357–58	rîb	145
palaios	528	poiēson	136–37	'ry	189
panegyris	110	poimainein	321	Sabazios	349
Pantokrator	76, 201	Polieus	350	sabbateion	300
paradeisos	147, 149	polis	154, 187, 330, 423	šak	83
paraenesis	99	politeuma	354	sallarium	125
paraineō	527	polysyndeton	486	sambatheion	300
parainesis	70	porneia	313	sanhedrîn	529
parapet	449	porneuein	310, 313	Sappho	96, 327
paredros daimōn	78, 498–99	porneuō	143, 312	šapru	78
paronomasia	134, 410	porneusai	257	sarcophagi	529
parousia	494, 500, 528	porphurobapheia	285	Sardeis	325, 338, 344, 347–48, 350, 352–53
paschein	192, 201	porphuropobaph	288		
passūs	529	porphuropōlis	288, 456	Sartmahmut	325
Patros	321	porticus	528	Satana	199, 247, 251
pegmata	232	pōs	363	ṣbwr	77
peirasmos	411, 413	Potnia Therōn	115	scaenae frons	448
peirasthēte	203, 205	praefecturae	108	sceptrum	529
penēs	191	praefectus	528	Sebastoi	58–59, 113, 119–20, 282, 529
Pentēkostē	528	Praetorian Testament	92	Sĕfire	218
peplērōmena	362	presbutera	311	sellae	498
peptōkas	137	pro consule	528	sellarii	125
Pergamēnē	235	professio liberi	374	sellisternium	499
Pergamenos	528	prōinon	322	septuāgintā	529
pergamentum	235				

Index of Foreign Words

sēstertiī	523
Sfard	325
shanah	526
shebet	322
sidērourgos	283
sindonōn koitariōn	459
Sitz im Leben	199
skoutlōsis	343
skutopolitanōn	459
skyteis	386
skytotomoi	283, 386
slyḥ	77
smeris	265
smurna	151–52, 185
smurnidzō	152
sōmatemporos	284, 297
sōteira	392
sōtēr	229, 248, 250, 254
Sparda	325
spectatus	269
sphenodones	446
spolia	529
stadia	153, 529
stadion	446, 529
statarion	297, 347
stēlae	529
stephanephoros	213
stephanos	212
stērison	361–62
stichai	458
Stramonita haemastoma	295
strategoi	109, 529
sumbolon	268
summa cavea	449–50
súnopsis	530
sunoptikós	530
sunthēma	269
synagōgē	197, 199, 311, 530
synedrion	529
synelthousais	299
synodos	341
tachu	261, 413
tade legei	79–82, 84, 129, 180, 224, 244, 302, 356, 399, 400, 403, 474
taenia	530
tainies	530
talaros	522
talmūd	530
taurobolium	348, 350
Tekkeköy	443
tekna	315
telaipōros	486
temenos	109
Tepemezari	281
tepidarium	338, 452, 481
tepidus	338, 530
tērei	363
tērein	406, 410
tērēō	413
tērēsō	410–11
terra	440, 478, 483, 485, 519, 530
tessera(e)	268–70, 530
tesserae conuiuiales	268
tesserae frumentaria	270
tesserae gladiatoria	269
tesserae hospitalis	268
tesserae militarius	269
tesserae nummularia	270
tesserae theatralis	268
testatio	374
tetragōnos	107
tetrarches	530
tetrarchia	530
Thais haemastoma	295
thanatos	209, 222
theos	229, 254, 498, 513–14
thlibō	190
thlipheōs	413
thlipsin	189, 206, 314
thronos	247, 249–50, 500, 502
Thuateira	276
thura	402, 404
tinctoria	291–92
Toga picta	372
toga praetexta	372
toralis	295
trabea	372
trapezomata	498
Trapezopolitans	450
trimitia	458, 460
trʿm	321
tšmʿn	218
tubuli	338
Tumuli	452
vela	531
velarium	449
vélin	531
versio vulgate	531
viae	106
vitis	385
Votis Vicennalibus	462, 465–66
vōtīvus	531
vōtum	531
walwet	346
Weckformel	66, 145
Weckruf	66, 145
xulon	216
xustarchēn	388
xystarchēs	387
ydʿ	83
yiššābaʿ	476
yitbārēk	476
zelōtēs	531
zēnōnos	451
zēs	359–60
zestos	478–79, 483, 492
zōēs	212, 215

Index of Greek Words

ἀγαθοδαίμων	395	ἀποστόλος	133	γάρ	189, 362
ἀγαπάω	491	ἀργυροκόπος	118, 132	γεροντες	338, 525
ἀγάπη	307, 308	ἀργυροκόπων	111	γερουσία	109, 282, 335
ἀγάπην	135	ἀρετή	395	γῆς	413
ἄγγελοι	72, 73, 75, 76	ἀρνίον	81	γίνου	209, 361
ἀγγελικος	356	ἀρχή	477	γινώσκω	132, 189
ἄγγελος	72–79, 129, 180, 244, 302, 310, 356–57, 399, 474, 498	ἀρχήγισσα	311	γναφεισ	284
		ἀρχισυνάγωγος	77, 311	γναφεῖς	283
Ἄγδιστις	390	ἄρχων	198, 477	γνῷς	366
ἀγενείων	468	Ἀσίας	158–60, 182	γνῶσιν	409
ἀγίασμα	422	Ἀσκληπιός	235	Γράμματα	117, 126
ἅγιος	400–1	Ασοπος	428	γραμματεύς	60, 525
Ἀγορά	110, 521	ἀστέρα	322	γράψον	48, 71, 129, 180, 244, 302, 356, 399, 474
ἀγοράσαι	488	ἀστέρας	358		
ἀδικηθῇ	220	Ἀττάλου	381	γρηγορήσῃς	365
Ἀδραμύττιον	151	αὐθέψης	482	γρηγορῶν	361
Ἀθηνᾶς	351	αὐτῆς	313	γυμνάσιον	161, 236, 338, 525
αἰγίς	521	Αὐτοκράτωρ	304	γυμνός	161, 338, 487, 525
αἰῶνας	181	αὐτομάτων	296	γυναῖκα	310
αἰώνων	181	αὐτοῦ	305	δαίμων	78, 498–99
ἀκολουθῶν	370	αὐτῷ	320	Δεῖα	467–68
ἀκουσάτω	87	αὐτῶν	189, 368	Δεῖμος	392
ἀληθής	400	ἀφῆκας	135	δειπνέω	496
ἀληθινός	400–1, 475, 477	ἀφθαρσι	214	δειπνήσω	495–96
ἀλλά	142, 192, 199	ἀφθαρσία	220	δεῖπνον	496–97
ἄλογοι	300	ἄφθονον	296	δέκα	207
ἁλουργέσιν	296	ἄχρι	209–10, 320	δελματικῶν	458
ἀμήν	475	βαθέα	318	δεξιός	219
ἀμφιθέατρον	446, 521	Βαλαάμ	256	δεύτερος	222
ἀναβόλαις	459	βαλανείων	296	δευτέρου	221
ἀνάθεμα	89, 365	βάλλειν	202	διάβολος	202
Ἀνθεστήρια	124	βαπτόμενα	296	διαθήκην	219
ἀνθρώπου	303	Βασιλευσ	423	διαθήκης	76
ἀνοίγει	400	Βασιλεων	423	διακονία	307–8
Ἀντίοχος	454	βασιλικὴ	123	διδαχὴ	256
Ἀντιπᾶς	254	βαστάσαι	134	διδοὺς	219
Ἀντιπᾶτρος	255	βαφεῖς	283, 285–87	δίδωμι	219
ἄξιοί	370	βαφήν	296	δίκαιος	356
ἄξιος	370	βῆμα	249, 254	δικῶν	110
ἁπλουργοί	284, 457	βίρρος	458	διοίκησις	110, 228, 381, 389
ἀπό	203	βλασφημία	193, 202	Διόνυσον	391
ἀποθανεῖν	361	βουλευτήριον	109, 450, 522	δίστομον	244
ἀποθέωσις	62–63, 305, 521	βουλευτής	354	δοκιμασθῆτε	205
Ἀποκάλυψις	42, 48	βουλή	109, 522	δόξης	214, 217
ἀπόλλυμι	89, 365	βυρσεῖς	283	δύναμιν	405
				δύναμις	405

INDEX OF GREEK WORDS

δώσω	219, 263
ἐάν	365
ἐβάστασας	134
ἐγένετο	181, 183
ἐγενόμην	181
ἐγώ	410, 491
ἔζησεν	181, 183
ἐθνῶν	320
εἰδώλαιον	166
εἰδωλόθυτος	256, 310
εἴληφα	321
εἱματιοπώλης	457
εἰμι	486
εἰσιν	370
ἐκεῖ	256
ἐκκλησία	197
ἐκκλησίας	48
ἐλίδος	214
ἔμελλον	361
ἐμέσαι	483–84
ἐμόλυναν	368
ἐμοῦ	488
ἐμπόριον	103
ἐνάμιλλα	296
ἐνώπιον	362
ἐξαλείφεται	374
ἐξαλείψω	375
ἐξέλθῃ	421
ἔξετε	203
ἐξευρίσκειν	346
ἐξουσία	321
ἐξουσίαν	222
ἔξω	421
Ἐπιστάται	284
ἑπτά	131, 357–58
ἔργα	84, 132, 137, 307, 309, 359, 362, 403, 478
ἐργατηγοί	284
ἔργων	313
ἐριουργοί	386
ἐρυθρόδανον	293
ἔρχεσθαι	261
ἔρχομαί	138, 261
ἕστηκα	494
ἔστιν	263
ἔσχατα	309
ἔσχατος	181–83
ἐτήρησάς	407, 410–11
εὕρηκά	362
Ἐφέσια	117, 126
Ἐφεσίοις	159
Ἔφεσος	101
ἐφηβη	338, 525
ἔχει	222
ἔχεις	256, 315, 320, 359, 405, 415
ἔχω	486
ἔχων	87, 130, 144
ζέει	483
ζεστός	478–79, 483, 492
Ζεῦξισ	454
Ζεύς	248, 463
ζήλευε	492
ζηνωνοσ	451
ζῇς	359–60
ζωῇ	216
ζωῆς	212, 215
ζῶν εἰμι	181
ἠγάπησά	200, 409
ἤδη	414
ἥκειν	138
ἤκουσας	363
ἤλεκτρον	345, 524
ἡμερῶν	206–8
ἥξω	366
ἠρνήσω	254, 407
θάνατος	222, 316
θανάτου	209–10, 221
θαυμαστῶς	296
Θειωδᾶς	454
Θεμίσων	454
Θεοδᾶς	454
θεός	78, 229, 250, 253, 498
θεοῦ	303–4, 362, 421, 423, 477
Θεῶν	352
Θηρῶν	115
θλίβω	190
θλίψεως	413
θλῖψιν	189, 206, 208, 314
θρόνος	247, 249–50, 500, 502
Θυάτειρα	276
θύρα	404
θύρας	402, 404
ἰατρεῖον	456
ἰδίων	461
ἰδού	181, 202, 219
ἱειμα	459
Ἱερὰν	296
ἱεράτευσεν	462
ἱέρισσα	311
ἱεροφάντης	391
Ἰησοῦ	146
ἱμάτια	368
ἱμάτιον	459
Ἰουδαῖοι	198
Ἰουδαίους	195–96
Ἰουλίου	304
ἴσατις	293
κἀγώ	321
Καθηγεμόνα	391
καί	132, 158–59, 181–83, 219, 259–60, 305, 309, 316, 357, 361, 363, 400, 405, 421, 423, 476
καινῆς	423
καινόν	265, 273, 423
Καῖσαρ	304
κακούς	133
κάλαθος	389, 522
κάλλει	158–59
κάλλους	214
καλοῶσιν	198
Κάπρος	428
καρακάλλων	459
καρδίας	316
Καρυάτιδες	417
κατά	296
κατάθεμα	89–90, 364
Κατακαυμένη	380, 385
καταλόγου	374
κατάρα	90
κατείδωλος	251
κατοικοῦντες	413
καυχήσεως	214
κεκρυμμένου	263
κερκίδες	448, 525
κηκίς	293
Κιμμέριοι	327
κινήσω	138–39
κίονες	420
κλείσει	400
κλείων	400
κλέπτης	365
κλίνη	313–14, 498, 525
κοινόν	58
κοιταρίων	459
κόκκος	293

κόκκου	296	μάννα	263	ξύλον	148, 216–17
κολλούρα	490	μαρτυρέω	146	ξυστάρχην	388
κολλύριον	454–55, 490	μαρτυρία	94, 146	ὀδύνην	189
κολλύριον	490	μαρτυρίαν	45	οἶδα	84, 131–32, 188–90, 192, 307, 359, 403, 478, 486
κολοβίων	458	μάρτυς	94, 146, 255, 476		
Κολοσσαί	428	μάχαιραν	245	οἶδεν	265
κολυμβήθρα	450	μεγαθι	159	Οἰκουμενικὰ	468
κόπος	132	μεγάλης	314, 413	ὅμοιον	303
κόπος	307	μεγέθει	158	ὁμοίως	259–60
κράτει	320, 415	μέλεις	192	ὁμολογέω	376
κρατεῖς	254	μέλλει	201–2, 205	ὁμόνοια	102, 163, 213, 389
κρατήσατε	320	μέλλω	484	ὄνομα	254, 359
κρατῶν	130	μέσος	188	ὄνομά	255, 265, 273
κριτικοὶ	232	μεταμέλομαι	364	ὀνόματα	368
κρόκος	293	μετανόησον	313, 363–64	ὅτι	359, 370, 405, 410
κρούω	494	μετανόησον	136, 137, 260, 492	οὐδεὶς	265, 400
κτίσεως	477	μηδὲν	201–2	οὐκ	222, 368, 407, 486
κτίσμα	381	Μήν	352, 395, 464	οὕτως	259, 484
κτιστην	332	μήτηρ	311	ὄφελον	483
κύβος	268	Μητρί	352, 395	ὀφθαλμοὶ	305
κύριος	80, 423, 497	Μητρόπολις	158	παιδες	338, 525
κυρίου	76	μητρῷον	351	παιδεύω	492
κυρίῳ	422	μικρὰ	405	παιδικοιν	125
λαμβάνειν	416	μικρὰν	405	παλαίστρα	338, 527
λανάριοι	284	μιλιάριον	482	πανήγυρις	110
λανάριοι	283, 288	Μνήμη	395	παντοκράτορός	76
λανάριοι	288	μνημόνευε	362	παρὰ	321
λανάριοι	456	μοιχεύοντας	315	παραγαῦδιν	458
Λαοδικεία	454	μολύνω	368	παράδεισος	147, 149
Λαοδικεία	426, 454	μύρον	455	παραίνεσις	70, 99
Λαοδικεία	468	νάρδινον	454–55	πάρεδρος	78, 498–99
Λαοδικία	426	ναῷ	418	παρονομασία	134, 410
λαόν	259	Νεικηφόρου	351	πάσχειν	192, 201
λέγει	79	Νεικοστράτος	446	πατρός	321
λέγοντας	133	νεκρός	181, 183, 360	πειράζω	205
λευκός	345	νέοι	338, 525	πειρασθῆτε	203, 205
λευκήν	265	νεφροὺς	316	πειρασμος	411
λίθος	266, 527, 529	νεωκόρος	59–60, 113–14, 119, 123, 155, 159–60, 167–68, 242, 298, 396, 432, 526	πειρασμος	413
λινουργοί	283			Πελοπία	277
λόγος	410	νεωκορων	393–94	πένης	191
λόγους	406	νικᾶν	259	πεπληρωμένα	362
λοιπὰ	361–62	νικάω	219–20	πέπτωκας	137
λοιπός	318	Νικολαῖται	141–42	περγαμηνή	235
Λυδίαι	352	νικῶν	220, 369, 416, 500, 502	περιπατεῖν	370
Λύκω	427–28	νικῶντι	146, 263, 320, 493	πίστιν	255
λυχνία	139, 141	νόμος	219	πίστις	210, 307–8
λυχνιῶν	131	νόμους	219	πιστὸς	209–10, 476–77
μαγίστη	158	νυμφαῖον	444	πλείονα	309
Μαγνησία	430			πλῆθος	296

Index of Greek Words

πλούσιος	192–93	σεβαστον	332	Τύχη	117, 122–23, 166, 169, 183, 212–13, 298, 332, 339, 343, 348, 352, 389–90, 393–95, 463, 465	
Πλούτων	123	Σεβαστὸν	349			
πνεύματα	357–58	σινδόνων	459			
πνευματικοῦ	215	Σιπύλου	430	Ὑγιεία	395	
πόθεν	137	σκηνή	239	ὕδατος	296	
ποίησον	136–37	σκυτέις	386	ὕδωρ	296	
ποιμαίνειν	321	σκυτοπολιτάνων	459	υἱός	303	
Πολέμων	431	σκυτοτόμοι	283	ὑμῶν	202–3	
πόλεως	462	σμύρνα	151–53, 185	ὑπομονή	217, 307–8	
πόλις	154, 187, 296, 423	Σμυρναιων	159	ὑπομονῆς	410	
Πολύκαρπος	172	σμύρνης	152	φαγεῖν	310, 529	
πορνεία	313	στάδιον	446, 529	φαινόλη	457–58	
πορνεύειν	310, 313	σταταριον	297	φαίνουλα	457	
πορνεῦσαι	257	στέφανος	212, 214–15, 217, 219–20, 416	φακιαλίων	459	
πορνεύω	143, 312	στέφανος	212, 215–17	φασκίνια	459	
πορφύρα	285, 288, 456	στήλη	419	φελόνη	457	
πορφυροβάφ	288	στήρισον	361–62	φιβουλατώριον	458	
πορφυροβαφεῖα	285	στίχαι	458	Φιλαδέλφεια	379, 381, 454	
πορφυρόπωλις	288, 456	σύμβολον	268	φιλοσέβαστος	167	
ποτίμων	440	σύμμετρον	296	φιλολόγοι	232	
Πότνια	115	συναγωγάς	198	φιλῶ	491	
πρεσβυτέρα	311	συναγωγὴ	199	φλόγα	305	
πρός	427	συναγωγῆς	311	φλόξ	305	
προσευχὴ	299	συνελθούσαις	299	φοβοῦ	201–2	
προσκυνήσουσιν	408	σύνθημα	269	φοῖνιξ	185	
προστάτης	311	σωματεμπορος	297	φύκος	293	
προφητεία	48	σωτήρ	229, 248, 250	φυλακὴν	202	
προφήτης	76	τάδε λέγει Ὦ	79–82, 84, 129, 150, 180, 224, 244, 275, 302, 324, 356, 377, 403, 424, 503	φυλή	386	
πρύτανις	110			χαλκεῖς	283, 306	
πρωϊνὸν	322			χαλκολιβάνω	306–7	
πρῶτα	137	ταινία	530	χαλκοτύποι	283	
πρώτη	135, 158, 182, 253–54	ταλαίπωρος	486	χλανίς	458	
πρώτοις	158	ταχύ	261, 413–14	χλιαρόν	483–84	
πρῶτος	181–83	τέκνα	315	χλιαρός	478, 480, 483	
πρώτωη	159	τέμενος	109	Χριστοῦ	146	
πρώτων	309	Τετραγράμματον	423, 530	χρυσὸς	345	
πτωχεία	191, 202	τετράγωνος	107	ψευδεῖς	133	
πτωχός	191, 487	τήρει	363	ψεύδομαιν	196	
πυγμήν	468	τηρεῖν	406	ψῆφον	265–67	
Πυθόδωρος	431	τηρήσω	410–11	ψυχρόν	483	
πυρός	305	τηρῶ	413	ψυχρός	478–80	
ῥομφαία	245	τιβεριον	332	ψυχρότερον	483	
ῥομφαίαν	244	τραπεζώματα	498	ὥραν	366	
Σάρδεις	325	τρίμιτια	460	ὥρας	411	
σατανᾶ	199	τρίμιτος	458, 460	Ὡρολόγιον	107	
Σατανᾶ	247	τρίποδος	500			
Σεβαστά	468	Τρίπολις	428			
Σεβαστοῖς	282	τυφλὸς	487			

Index of Scripture and Ancient Writings

Reference	Page
1 Apoc. Jas. 28.16–17	369
1 Chr 20:2	214
1 Chr 28:9	316
1 Clem. 3:4	406
1 Clem. 5:2	420
1 Clem. 8:3	312
1 Clem. 23:5	400
1 Clem. 25	184–85
1 Clem. 25:1–5	185
1 Clem. 36:3	305
1 Clem. 40:1	318
1 Clem. 43:14	400
1 Clem. 53:1	136
1 Clem. 56:4	492
1 Cor 1:26	192
1 Cor 1:5	193
1 Cor 2:10	318
1 Cor 2:15–16	274
1 Cor 3:12	266
1 Cor 3:16–17	420
1 Cor 3:21–3	88
1 Cor 4:14, 17	315
1 Cor 4:5	316
1 Cor 5, 6	122
1 Cor 6:12–18	319
1 Cor 7:19	406
1 Cor 8:1–4	310
1 Cor 8:1–6	318
1 Cor 8–10	259
1 Cor 9:1	132
1 Cor 9:25	214, 218, 416
1 Cor 9:9	191
1 Cor 10:1–22	256
1 Cor 10:13	205
1 Cor 10:14–22	261
1 Cor 10:30	194, 199
1 Cor 10:3ff.	264
1 Cor 11:20	496
1 Cor 11:23	97, 363
1 Cor 11:23-26	97
1 Cor 11:28–32	138
1 Cor 11:3	250
1 Cor 11:30	261, 311
1 Cor 11:5	311
1 Cor 12:4–6	308
1 Cor 12:5	308
1 Cor 12:8–11	132
1 Cor 13:13	308
1 Cor 14:25	316, 409
1 Cor 14:37–38	94, 144, 262, 377, 424
1 Cor 15:1	363
1 Cor 15:15	362
1 Cor 15:19	486
1 Cor 15:24	414
1 Cor 15:3	363
1 Cor 15:32	126, 259
1 Cor 15:53–54	490
1 Cor 16:13	361
1 Cor 16:3	192
1 Cor 16:9	126, 259
1 Cor 20:7	132
1 En. 1:3	400
1 En. 2:44–25:7	148
1 En. 6–18	136
1 En. 9:5	487
1 En. 10:21	408
1 En. 14:20	490
1 En. 25:5	146
1 En. 61.11–12	214, 357
1 En. 62:15–16	490
1 En. 64–69	136
1 En. 69:14–19	273–74
1 En. 86:1, 3	357
1 En. 90.28–29	420
1 En. 90:30	408
1 En. 91–108	49
1 En. 97:8–10	486
1 En. 102:4–104:8	88
1 En. 106:5–6	305
1 Esd 2:2	80
1 John 1:6–7	370
1 John 2:13–14	145, 320, 417
1 John 2:20	274, 400
1 John 2:20, 27	274
1 John 2:28–3:2	414
1 John 2:5	406
1 John 2:6, 11	370
1 John 2:7, 8	406
1 John 2:8	130
1 John 3:2	424, 490
1 John 3:22–24	406
1 John 3:5	400
1 John 4:1	133
1 John 4:20	308
1 John 4:21	406
1 John 4:4	145, 320, 417
1 John 5 4–5	267
1 John 5:20	400
1 John 5:2–3	406
1 John 5:4	146
1 John 5:4–5	145, 320, 417
1 Kgs 2:30	80, 128, 180, 244, 302, 356, 399, 474
1 Kgs 7:15–21	418
1 Kgs 7:21	148
1 Kgs 8:39	316
1 Kgs 11:14	418
1 Kgs 16:31	148, 309, 310
1 Kgs 18:19	309
1 Kgs 18:4	148
1 Kgs 18–21	309
1 Kgs 19:1	148
1 Kgs 19:2	76
1 Kgs 20:2, 5	80
1 Kgs 21:1–16	309
1 Kgs 21:25	309–10
1 Kgs 23:3	418
1 Macc 10:20	214
1 Macc 13:37	214
1 Macc 13:39	214
1 Macc 14.26–48	419
1 Pet 1:1	49
1 Pet 1:17	316, 374
1 Pet 1:6	208
1 Pet 1:6–9	488
1 Pet 1:7	205, 362, 489
1 Pet 2:22	400
1 Pet 2:24	147, 148
1 Pet 2:4–10	420
1 Pet 3:14	217
1 Pet 4:14	217
1 Pet 4:14, 16	407

INDEX OF SCRIPTURE AND ANCIENT WRITINGS

Reference	Page
1 Pet 4:19–5:7	217
1 Pet 4:4	194, 199
1 Pet 5:30	208
1 Pet 5:4	214
1 Sam 1:8	206
1 Sam 15:32	152
1 Sam 16:7	316
1 Sam 22:2	152
1 Sam 25:25	423
1 Sam 25:38	206, 207
1 Sam 28:6	266
1 Thess 1:10	414
1 Thess 1:3	309
1 Thess 1:5	363
1 Thess 1:5–10	136
1 Thess 1:9	363, 400
1 Thess 2:12	370
1 Thess 2:13–14	136, 363
1 Thess 2:19	214
1 Thess 2:6	132
1 Thess 3:4	190
1 Thess 3:5	205
1 Thess 4:1–2	136
1 Thess 4:17	414, 528
1 Thess 5:1	367
1 Thess 5:2	368
1 Thess 5:2, 4	366
1 Tim 1:2	315
1 Tim 1:3	126–27
1 Tim 3:15	420
1 Tim 4:8	161
1 Tim 6:11	309
1 Tim 6:14	406
1 Tim 6:18	193
11Q19 44:18–20	312
11Q19 54.10–15	313
11Q19 61:1–2	313
1QH 2:22	197, 199
1QH 6:14–19	146
1QH 7:24	146
1QH 9:25	217
1QH 16.19–36	413
1QM 1:2	197
1QM 3:22	357
1QM 4:9	197
1QM 7:4f.	487
1QM 12:14–15	408
1QM 12:8–9	357
1QM 15:9	197
1QM 19:6–7	408
1QpHab 8:9	273
1QS 4:7	217
1QS 9:2	362
1Qsa 2:5ff	487
2 Apoc. Bar. 29:8	264
2 Bar. 4	217
2 Bar. 6:7	267
2 Bar. 14:8	318
2 Bar. 22:1–30:5	77
2 Bar. 26:1–27:15	413
2 Bar. 29:4–8	264
2 Bar. 39:1–43:3	77
2 Bar. 50:1–51:16	77
2 Bar. 77:17–19	49
2 Bar. 78–87	49
2 Bar. 83:2–3	316
2 Chr 3:15–16	418
2 Chr 6:30	316
2 Chr 13:5	495
2 Chr 15:3	400
2 Chr 21:12	80
2 Chr 21:12–15	49
2 Chr 34:22	311
2 Chr 36:7	138
2 Chr 36:15–16	76
2 Chr 36:23	128, 180, 244, 302, 356, 399, 474
2 Clem. 7:3	215
2 Clem. 17:4	313
2 Cor 4:1	308
2 Cor 4:17	208
2 Cor 4:17–18	208
2 Cor 5:1–4;	490
2 Cor 5:21	400
2 Cor 5:3	362
2 Cor 6:10	192–93
2 Cor 6:16	420
2 Cor 6:4	309
2 Cor 8:2	192
2 Cor 8:2–5	192
2 Cor 8:9	193
2 Cor 11:13–23	133
2 Cor 11:14	407
2 Cor 11:14–15	408
2 Cor 11:15	313
2 Cor 11:22	196
2 Cor 11:23	204
2 Cor 12:12	132, 309
2 En. 14.2	216
2 Esd 2:39, 45	490
2 John 1, 4	315
2 John 4	203
2 Kgs 1:11	80
2 Kgs 4:37	408
2 Kgs 5:10	76
2 Kgs 9	309, 310, 516
2 Kgs 9:22	257, 310, 516
2 Kgs 18:18	401
2 Kgs 18:19, 29	80
2 Kgs 22:14	311
2 Kgs 23:1–3	93, 95
2 Kgs 23:34	423
2 Kgs 24:17	423
2 Macc 2:4–7	263
2 Macc 9:5	316
2 Macc 14:4	214
2 Pet 1:19	322
2 Pet 1:6	309
2 Pet 2:15	256
2 Pet 2:4	72
2 Pet 3:10	366, 368
2 Pet 3:14	362
2 Pet 3:8	208
2 Pet 3:9	312
2 Sam 5:6-10	487
2 Sam 7	88
2 Sam 7:11–14	321
2 Sam 7:14	219, 321
2 Sam 7:4–17	303
2 Sam 10:4	487
2 Sam 12:30	214
2 Sam 14:20	316
2 Thess 1:4	309
2 Thess 1:7–10	414
2 Thess 2:1–12	412, 413
2 Thess 2:8	414
2 Thess 2:9	132, 407
2 Thess 3:5	410
2 Tim 1:2	315
2 Tim 2:12	406, 410
2 Tim 2:25	492
2 Tim 2:5	214
2 Tim 2:8	188
2 Tim 3:10	309
2 Tim 3:11–15	217
2 Tim 3:5	360
2 Tim 3:8	132
2 Tim 4:14	117, 134, 313, 316, 507
2 Tim 4:2	492
2 Tim 4:7–8	214
2 Tim 4:8	214, 217, 414, 416
3 Bar. 6.1	216
3 En. 23:18	146, 508

3 John 4	315	
3 John 9	473	
3 Macc. 2:11	477	
4 Esd 8:27	190	
4 Ezra 1:19	263	
4 Ezra 7:28–29	303	
4 Ezra 8:27–9:25	77	
4 Ezra 10:22	139	
4 Ezra 13:20–56	77	
4 Ezra 13:3, 32	303	
4 Ezra 13:32, 37, 52	303	
4 Ezra 14:9	303	
4 Macc 1:11	309	
4 Macc 9:30	309	
4 Macc 9:8	309	
4 Macc 15:30	309	
4 Macc 18:11–18	207	
4 P.Oxy. 3.3119	62	
4Q158 frag. 6, line 8	313	
4Q174 1.1.1–13	321	
4Q174 1.10–19	303	
4Q246 2.1–9	303	
4Q369 1.1–11	303	
4Q375 1.4–5	313	
4Q382 1.3	309	
4Q405 23:1.8–9	357	
4Q521 2.2.7	500	
4QFlor	219	
4QpNah 3.4	257	
Acts 1:11	414	
Acts 1:13	132	
Acts 1:15	368	
Acts 1:21, 22	132	
Acts 1:24	316	
Acts 1:7	414	
Acts 2:23	202	
Acts 2:24	254	
Acts 2:33	358	
Acts 2:36	202	
Acts 2:43	132	
Acts 2:45	192	
Acts 2:9	177	
Acts 3:6	272	
Acts 3:14	400	
Acts 4:10	202, 272	
Acts 4:27, 30	400	
Acts 5:30	147, 148	
Acts 5:39	362	
Acts 6:1, 4	308	
Acts 6:1–6	142	
Acts 6:5	259	
Acts 6:8	214	
Acts 6:9–15	170, 174, 196, 211	
Acts 7:38	197	
Acts 7:58	459	
Acts 8:22	312	
Acts 9:23	170, 174, 196	
Acts 9:29	196	
Acts 9:34	272	
Acts 9:39	459	
Acts 10:25	408	
Acts 10:39	147, 148	
Acts 11:19	208	
Acts 11:25–30	105	
Acts 11:29	308	
Acts 12:1–3	170, 174, 196	
Acts 12:15	72	
Acts 12:25	362	
Acts 13:14	429	
Acts 13:15	77	
Acts 13:29	147	
Acts 13:33	304, 320	
Acts 13:45	194	
Acts 13:45–50	170, 174	
Acts 13:50	209, 407	
Acts 13:5–12	194	
Acts 13:9	423	
Acts 14:1	132	
Acts 14:12	250	
Acts 14:14	459	
Acts 14:1–5	170, 174	
Acts 14:21	429	
Acts 14:26	362	
Acts 14:27	404	
Acts 15:20	142, 507	
Acts 15:28–29	319	
Acts 15:29	142	
Acts 15:8	316	
Acts 16:13	299	
Acts 16:14	289, 296, 310, 429, 456, 515	
Acts 16:14–15	289	
Acts 16:18	272	
Acts 16:20	108, 529	
Acts 16:22	459	
Acts 16:23	204	
Acts 16:6–9	471	
Acts 17:13	407	
Acts 17:16	252	
Acts 17:5, 13	170, 174	
Acts 17:5–7	405	
Acts 17:5–8	202	
Acts 18:1–17	77	
Acts 18:12	174, 249	
Acts 18:13–17	194	
Acts 18:17	77	
Acts 18:18–22	126	
Acts 18:2–3	107	
Acts 18:6	174, 459	
Acts 18:6; 12	170	
Acts 18:8	77	
Acts 19	56, 58, 60, 107–11, 113, 131, 194, 210, 355, 507, 521	
Acts 19:10	56, 126, 211, 472	
Acts 19:11–20	272	
Acts 19:23–41	107, 110, 113, 117	
Acts 19:23–42	117, 131	
Acts 19:31	110, 521	
Acts 19:32–34	111	
Acts 19:33	170, 174	
Acts 19:35	58, 60, 109, 112, 113	
Acts 19:35–38	60	
Acts 19:37	194	
Acts 19:39	108	
Acts 20:17	105	
Acts 20:23	190	
Acts 20:29	133	
Acts 20:29–30	126	
Acts 20:3	170, 174	
Acts 20:31	126	
Acts 20:34	107	
Acts 21:11	82	
Acts 21:27	170, 174, 211, 303, 375, 376	
Acts 21:9	311	
Acts 22:14, 15	132	
Acts 22:20	255	
Acts 22:20, 23	459	
Acts 22:30	170, 174, 194	
Acts 23:12	170, 174	
Acts 23:25–30	194	
Acts 23:9	362	
Acts 24:1–22	194	
Acts 24:2	202	
Acts 24:9	170, 174	
Acts 25:10	249	
Acts 25:1–27	194	
Acts 25:6	206	
Acts 25:7–15	170, 174	
Acts 26:10	265, 267	
Acts 26:11	194, 406	
Acts 26:1–7	194	
Acts 26:20	364	
Acts 26:7	170, 174	
Acts 27:5	151	

Index of Scripture and Ancient Writings

Reference	Page
Acts of John 41	272
Acts of John 42	117
Acts Phil. 13.4	455
Acts Thom. 143	318
AE (1909): 11a	288
AE (1971): 49	288
AE (1995): 146	288
AE (1946): 210	288
AE (2010): 326	288
AE (2001): 865	288
AE (1987): 443	288
AE (1993): 1028a	288
Aelian De nat. anim. 13.38	267
Aelian Var. hist. 2.14	148
Aeschines Fals. leg. 2.22	495
Aeschylus Eum. 741	267
Aeschylus Pers. 40–45	368
Aeschylus Pers. 45	327
Aesop Vit. Aes. 2–3	484
AGRW 121	391, 395, 411
AGRW 124	287
AGRW 126	350
AGRW 127	350
AGRW 129	287, 299
AGRW 131	283, 287
AGRW 132	286, 287
AGRW 136	288
AGRW 138	283
AGRW 141	283
AGRW 52	391, 395
AKZ 2:151–52	403
Amos 1:6	80
Amos 1–2	86
Amos 1–2:3	218
Amos 3:2	189
Amos 5:18–20	413
Amos 7:14	316
Amos 7:16	143, 262, 377, 424
Amos 8:10	152
Amos 9:11	321
Ampelius Lib. Mem. 8.14	240, 241
Andrew Comm. Apoc. 69	267
Antipater of Sidon Gr. Ant. 9.58	116
Ap. John II,1.35	87
Apoc. Ab. 20–31	77
Apoc. El. 1:8	214
Apoc. El. 5:6	146, 508
Apoc. Mos. 28:4	146, 508
Apoc. Zeph. 3:6–9	374
Apollodorus Lib. 2.4.9	305
Apollonius Let. 38–41	368
Apollonius Let. 56	368
Apollonius Let. 75; 76	368
Apos. Con. 3.15	424
Apos. Con. 8.12.26	263
Apos. Con. 8.46	398
Appian Bell. civ. 3.33	117
Appian Bell. civ. 5.75	431
Appian Mith. 1.3	277
Appian Mith. 11–14	430
Appian Mith. 13.61	278
Appian Mithrid. 4.22	229
Apuleius Metam. 11.24	215
Apuleius Metam. 3.5	366
Apuleius Metam. 4.18	366
Aristides Apol. 10	272
Aristides Orat. 18, 19	155
Aristides Orat. 18.6	489
Aristides Orat. 2.17.2	186
Aristides Orat. 2.18.9	186
Aristides Orat. 2.18–21	186
Aristides Orat. 2.20.19	186
Aristides Orat. 23.24	105, 489
Aristides Orat. 23.25	116, 420
Aristides Orat. 26	74
Aristides Orat. 39.15	454
Aristides Orat. 39.5	235, 251
Aristides Orat. 41.19	160
Aristides Orat. 42.4	235, 350
Aristides Orat. 42.522	117
Aristides Orat. 42.6	235
Aristides Orat. 42.770–76	160
Aristides Orat. 47.45	350
Aristides Orat. 49.7	350
Aristides Orat. 50.46	350
Aristides Panath. 328	161
Aristophanes Ach. 115	369, 371
Aristotle Col. 32–33	293
Aristotle Eth. eud. 7.1239b	495
Aristotle Eth. nic. 8.3.8	495
Aristotle Hist. An. 4.1–5, 8, 11	293
Aristotle Hist. An. 5.15	293
Aristotle Mir. 58	454
Aristotle Pol. 1.3.15	346
Arnobius Adv. nat. 1.46	272
Arrian Anab. 1.17.3–6	329
Arrian Anab. 1.17.4	326
Arrian Anab. 1.17.5	328
Arrian Anab. 1.17.6	335
Arrian Anab. 3.4.2	484
Arrian Diatr. 2.21.20	455
Arrian Diatr. 3.21.20–22	455
Arrian Diatr. 3.7.29	486
Artemidorus Oneir. 2.3	490
Artemidorus Oneir. 4.2	490
Ascen. Isa. 7.22	215
Ascen. Isa. 7.22	214
Ascen. Isa. 9.6–18	215
Ascen. Isa. 9.7, 24	212
Ascen. Isa. 9:24	214
Ascen. Isa. 11.40	212
Athenaeus Deipn. 3.123a	482, 484
Athenaeus Deipn. 3.123a–d	482
Athenaeus Deipn. 3.124cd	483
Athenaeus Deipn. 5:213	430
Athenaeus Deipn. 6.255	344, 347, 354
Athenaeus Deipn. 12.514	344
Augustine Civ. 6.11	196
Ausonius App. 2.15	322
AvP 8,3.20; 23; 37; 38	229
b. Bar. 17	217
b. Ḥagigah 12b	263
b. Sanh. 105a	259
b. Sanh. 90a	262
b. Yoma 73b	266
b. Yoma 75a	265
b. Yoma 75b	263
Bacchylides Ep. 3.23–62	329, 352
Bacchylides Ep. 3.32	335
Bar 3:32	316
Barn. 16:9	404
BCH 10 [1866], 422	456
BCH 10 [1886], 398 no. 1	277
BCH 11 [1887], 352	457
BCH 11 [1887], 465, no. 31	282
BCH 11 [1887], 466 no. 32	277
BCH 11 [1887], 466, no. 32	277
BCH 101, no. 1 [1977]: 43–132	288
BCH 102, no. 1 [1978]: 405	351
BCH 106, no. 3 [1982]: 360–61	352
BCH 107, no. 1 [1983]: 541–42	385
BMC 10	395
BMC 31	393, 395
BMC 32	393, 394
BMC 42	392, 397
BMC 42; 43	392
BMC 56	385
BMC 60–62	382
BMC 61	382
BMC 67	394
BMC 71	385
BMC 82	306
BMC 86	396

Entry	Pages
BMC 88	238, 385
BMC 120	389, 396
BMC 143–144	433
BMC 229	116
BMC 323	323
BMC 376	394
BMC Ionia 70	433
BMC Ionia 92, no. 307	112
BMC Ionia 268, nos. 263–65	167
BMC Ionia 268. nos. 266–68	167
BMC Ionia 286, no. 389	167
BMC Ionia 288, no. 403	167
BMC Ionia 289, no. 410	167
BMC Ionia 293, no. 434	167
BMC Ionia 299, no. 467	167
BMC Ionia nos. 405, 413–4	182
BMC Ionia, nos. 405, 423–24	158
BMC Lydia 98	332, 350
BMC Phrygia 205.222	466
BMC Phrygia 214–218	469
BMC Phrygia 221	469
BMC Phrygia 225	469
BMC Phrygia 225–236	469
BMC Phrygia 228–45	469
BMC Phrygia 234	118
BMC Phrygia 246	469
BMC Phrygia 247–250	469
BMC Phrygia 251–253	469
BMC Phrygia 278.1	465
BMC Phrygia 278.3	467
BMC Phrygia 283.25–30	467
BMC Phrygia 285.40–47	462
BMC Phrygia 286.48	463
BMC Phrygia 286.50–51	467
BMC Phrygia 287.52–53	427, 428
BMC Phrygia 287.57	467
BMC Phrygia 288.61	464
BMC Phrygia 288.64	465
BMC Phrygia 289.68	465
BMC Phrygia 289.70	463
BMC Phrygia 290.77–81	468
BMC Phrygia 291.82–84	462
BMC Phrygia 292.92–93	462, 467
BMC Phrygia 293.94–95	463
BMC Phrygia 293.97	465
BMC Phrygia 294.101	463
BMC Phrygia 295.104	468
BMC Phrygia 295.106	465
BMC Phrygia 295.107	468
BMC Phrygia 296.108	466
BMC Phrygia 296.109	463
BMC Phrygia 296.111	427, 428
BMC Phrygia 296.111–112	427
BMC Phrygia 297.114	463
BMC Phrygia 297.115–116	467
BMC Phrygia 297.117–123	468
BMC Phrygia 298.126	466
BMC Phrygia 299.127	427, 428
BMC Phrygia 299.130–132	468
BMC Phrygia 300.133	468
BMC Phrygia 300.138	463
BMC Phrygia 302.147	463
BMC Phrygia 307.181	58, 468
BMC Phrygia 307.185	58, 468
BMC Phrygia 308.186	468
BMC Phrygia 308.187–188	58, 468
BMC Phrygia 309.193	467
BMC Phrygia 309.194	468
BMC Phrygia 310.199	466
BMC Phrygia 311.204	468
BMC Phrygia 311.205	466
BMC Phrygia 311.209	463, 467, 468
BMC Phrygia 312.206	467
BMC Phrygia 313.210	468
BMC Phrygia 313.215	427, 428
BMC Phrygia 314.217	58, 466, 468
BMC Phrygia 314.219	468
BMC Phrygia 314.220	468
BMC Phrygia 314.221	58, 468
BMC Phrygia 315.222	466
BMC Phrygia 315.225	58, 468
BMC Phrygia 316.226–227	58, 468
BMC Phrygia 316.230	469
BMC Phrygia 317.228–229	462
BMC Phrygia 318.231	463
BMC Phrygia 318.233	466
BMC Phrygia 319.235	427, 428
BMC Phrygia 319.236	462
BMC Phrygia 320.243	466
BMC Phrygia 323.256	466
Caesar *Bell. gall.* 1.27, 31	408
CAH 9:102–105	229
CAH 9:146	430
Callimachus *Hymn. Apoll.* 3	493
Callimachus *Hymn. Dian.* 3.233	101
Cant. 4:14	152
Cant. 5:1–2	494
Cant. 7:2	476
Cassius *Hist. Rom.* 42.37	245
Cassius *Hist. Rom.* 42.38.2	232
Cassius *Hist. Rom.* 43.22.1–2	322
Cassius *Hist. Rom.* 51.20.6	104, 108, 229
Cassius *Hist. Rom.* 51.20.6–7	104, 108
Cassius *Hist. Rom.* 51.20.7	252
Cassius *Hist. Rom.* 53.13.6–8	245
Cassius *Hist. Rom.* 65.7	471
Cassius *Hist. Rom.* 67.13.4	63
Cassius *Hist. Rom.* 67.4.7	63
Cassius *Hist. Rom.* 74.2.1–3	469
Celsus *Med.* 1.3.22	485
Celsus *Med.* 3.12.3	485
Celsus *Med.* 3.6	454
Celsus *Med.* 6.6.12	456
Celsus *Med.* 6.6.2–8	454, 455
Chrysostom *Or.* 7.24	111
Chrysostom *Or.* 7.65	495
Chrysostom *Or.* 17.2	136
Chrysostom *Or.* 31.54–55	117, 489
Chrysostom *Or.* 31.84	374
Chrysostom *Or.* 34.48	252
Chrysostom *Or.* 40.6	111
Chrysostom *Or.* 69.8	366
Chrysostom *Or.* 77/78.31–32	327
Chrysostom *Or.* 78.31	347
Chrysostom *Or.* 78.39	136
Cicero *Arch.* 7.8.19	160
Cicero *Att.* 4.8.2	232
Cicero *Att.* 5.15	431
Cicero *Att.* 5.15, 21	460
Cicero *Att.* 5.15.2	431, 486
Cicero *Att.* 5.15.2–9	431
Cicero *Att.* 6.2	460
Cicero *Att.* 6.3.9	450
Cicero *Att.* 6.5	130
Cicero *Caecin.* 20.57	374
Cicero *De or.* 3.38.154	307
Cicero *Fam.* 3.5.4	438, 486
Cicero *Dom.* 13.6	498
Cicero *Fam.* 13.67	431
Cicero *Fam.* 68.3.5.4	460
Cicero *Fam.* 9.7	431
Cicero *Flac.* 16	111
Cicero *Flac.* 31	215
Cicero *Flac.* 68	170, 196, 461, 470
Cicero *Nat. d.* 2.53	322
Cicero *Phil.* 2.104.41	484
Cicero *Phil.* 2.110	304
Cicero *Phil.* 2.29.74	268
Cicero *Phil.* 11.2.5	167, 209, 510
Cicero *Verr.* 4.59	292
CIG 2:2953b	117
CIG 2:3148	170
CIG 2:3509	310, 515

CIG 1068 390
CIG 2519 289
CIG 2972 112–13
CIG 3114 162
CIG 3148.30 187
CIG 3154 285
CIG 3159 350
CIG 3179 158
CIG 3179d 159
CIG 3191 159
CIG 3197 159
CIG 3202 159
CIG 3204 159
CIG 3205 159
CIG 3206A 159
CIG 3416 388, 390, 416
CIG 3422 283, 386, 387, 388, 391, 456
CIG 3424 390
CIG 3427 388
CIG 3428 388, 390
CIG 3450 332
CIG 3480 283, 456
CIG 3485 283
CIG 3495 283
CIG 3496 283, 288, 296, 456
CIG 3497 283
CIG 3499 283
CIG 3504 283, 456, 457
CIG 3851 158, 159
CIG 3926 284
CIG 3935 447, 461
CIG 3936 446, 462
CIG 3938 457, 469
CIG 3942 447
CIG 3944 451
CIJ 2.36 285
CIJ 2.740–741 198
CIJ 2.743 198
CIJ 2.745 125
CIJ 2.746 125
CIJ 2.749–43 170
CIJ 2.982 419
CIJ 2.983 419
CIJ 2:742.29 170
CIJ 752 300
CIL 1.2.1211 292
CIL 1.717–76 268
CIL 3.550 257
CIL 4.9980 388
CIL 5.4501 288, 456
CIL 5.4504 288
CIL 5.4505 288
CIL 6.31898 288
CIL 6.32323 499
CIL 6.33869 288
CIL 6.38869 288
CIL 6.9489 288, 456
CIL 6.9490 288
CIL 6.9491 288
CIL 6.9492 288
CIL 6.9493 288
CIL 6.9494 288
CIL 6.9669 288
CIL 9.2226 288
CIL 9.5831 430
CIL 9.5832 430
CIL 9.826 288, 456
CIL 10.1624 332, 382, 432, 433
CIL 10.5678 288, 456
CIL 11.1031 288
CIL 11.5835 288
CIL 11.6367 288
CIL 11.741 288, 456
CIL 11.862 288
CIL 12.4480 288, 456
CIL 12.4481 288
CIL 14.4573 291
Clement *Ecl.* 4.1 477
Clement *Paed.* 1.5 424
Clement *Paed.* 1.7 400
Clement *Paed.* 2.8 215
Clement *Recog.* 5.34 196
Clement *Strom.* 2.20 142
Clement *Strom.* 5.6 129
Clement *Strom.* 6.58.1 477
Clement *Strom.* 7.1 477
Col 1:10 370
Col 1:11 309
Col 1:15–18 477
Col 1:7 472
Col 2:13 360
Col 2:19 254
Col 2:3 193
Col 3:4 424
Col 3–4 527
Col 4:12 73
Col 4:12–13 471–72
Col 4:13 49, 426, 429
Col 4:15 472–73
Col 4:16 472, 477
CPJ 1:29 255
Ctesias *Per. Books* 7–11, F9 351
Cyprian *Ep.* 55.9 60
Cyprian *Fort.* 11.76 202
Cyprian *Laps.* 1, 2 203
Cyprian *Laps.* 15–21 62
Cyprian *Pat.* 21 171
Cyprian *Test.* 1.22 424
Cyprian *Test.* 490 210
Cyranides *Cyr.* 1.2.20–26 271
Cyranides *Cyr.* 1.2.6 271
Cyril *Cat.* 4.36 434
Dan 1:12 206–7
Dan 1:12–14 207
Dan 1:2 138
Dan 1:20 207
Dan 1:7 423
Dan 2:22 318
Dan 3:12, 18 207
Dan 5:29 490
Dan 7:13–14 303
Dan 9:23 486
Dan 9:24–26 205
Dan 10:11 486
Dan 10:13–21 72
Dan 10:6 302, 305–7
Dan 12:1 148, 413
Dan 12:11 205
Dan 12:3 129
Demosthenes *Cor.* 54–55, 84, 11 215
Deut 1:3 81
Deut 1:8 88
Deut 3:8–24 218
Deut 30:19 85
Deut 30:6 407
Deut 31:5 200
Deut 31:9–13 95
Deut 32:1 93
Deut 32:29 200
Deut 32:39 183
Deut 33:5 83
Deut 33:8 266
Deut 4:1 88
Deut 4:26 93
Deut 4:4 88
Deut 4:8 219
Deut 5:10 200
Deut 5:15 136
Deut 5:18 314
Deut 5:2–5 82
Deut 7:12–13 200
Deut 7:18 136
Deut 7:23 200

Reference	Page
Deut 8:1–4	88
Deut 8:18–19	136
Deut 8:3, 16	148
Deut 8:9	190
Deut 10:1–5	95
Deut 11:16	219
Deut 11:9	88
Deut 13:1–11	312
Deut 13:16–17	89, 364
Deut 15:1–18	190
Deut 16:20	88
Deut 18–20	88
Deut 19:16–21	317
Deut 21:22–23	90
Deut 22:22	314, 317
Deut 23:14	200
Deut 23:3	207
Deut 23:4	148, 256, 309
Deut 24:14–22	190
Deut 24:3–7	68
Deut 24–26	95
Deut 27:11–26	96
Deut 27–30	87
Deut 28:18	90
Deut 28:9	88
Did. 6:3	312
Diodorus *Hist. Lib.* 15.49.1	109
Diodorus *Hist. Lib.* 16.80.8	427
Diodorus *Hist. Lib.* 17.21.7	329
Diodorus *Hist. Lib.* 37.26	229
Diogenes *Vit. Phil.* 4.31	277
Diogenes *Vit. Phil.* 8.1.33	369, 372
Diogenes *Vit. Phil.* 9.11.106	454
Diogenes *Vit. Phil.* 9.12.116	454
Diogn. 8:9	400
Diogn. 9.2	400
Eccl 7:26	152
Eccl 9:8	372
Edict. Diocl. § 19.28	460
Edict. Diocl. § 21.1–12	457
Edict. Diocl. § 26.16	457
Ep Jer 6:15–7:4	49
Ep Jer 7:24–35	49
Ep. Arist. 188	312
Ep. Arist. 280	218
Ep. Arist. 98	422
Eph 1:1	140
Eph 2:19–22	420
Eph 2:8–9	489
Eph 3:13	208
Eph 4:1	370
Eph 4:7–8	358
Eph 4–6	527
Eph 5:13	492
Eph 5:2	409
Eph 9:1	140
Eph 11:2	140
Epictetus *Diatr.* 3.22.26–27	487
Epictetus *Diatr.* 3.26.3	487
Epiphanius *Pan.* 51.12.1–2	47
Epiphanius *Pan.* 51.33.1–3	301, 313
Esth 6:1	373
Esth 6:6–11	490
Esth 8:15	214
Eumelus *Frag.* 18	350
Euripides *Bacch.* 55, 65	349, 462
Euripides *Bacch.* 112	369, 372
Euripides *Bacch.* 222–23	311
Euripides *Bacch.* 237–38	311
Euripides *Bacch.* 260–61	311
Euripides *Bacch.* 353–54	311
Euripides *Bacch.* 487	311
Euripides *Bacch.* 686–87	311
Euripides *Bacch.* 957–58	311
Euripides *Ion 720*	207
Eusebius *Chron.* 19.551–52	43, 44
Eusebius *Dem. ev.* 2.3.80	424
Eusebius *Hist. eccl.* 1.4.3–4	424
Eusebius *Hist. eccl.* 2.22.5	47
Eusebius *Hist. eccl.* 2.23.11, 18	171
Eusebius *Hist. eccl.* 3.17–20	47, 200
Eusebius *Hist. eccl.* 3.18.1	45
Eusebius *Hist. eccl.* 3.23.1–3	47
Eusebius *Hist. eccl.* 3.23.3–4	43, 44
Eusebius *Hist. eccl.* 3.3.43	47
Eusebius *Hist. eccl.* 3.4.5	127
Eusebius *Hist. eccl.* 3:21; 3.23.1, 6	47
Eusebius *Hist. eccl.* 3.29	142
Eusebius *Hist. eccl.* 4.15.25	173, 194
Eusebius *Hist. eccl.* 4.15.40, 45	173
Eusebius *Hist. eccl.* 4.15.46	175
Eusebius *Hist. eccl.* 4.15.48	301
Eusebius *Hist. eccl.* 4.18.6	127
Eusebius *Hist. eccl.* 4.26.13	355
Eusebius *Hist. eccl.* 4.26.13–14	355
Eusebius *Hist. eccl.* 5.1.16	203
Eusebius *Hist. eccl.* 5.16.12	171
Eusebius *Hist. eccl.* 5.17	311, 398
Eusebius *Hist. eccl.* 5.17.3–4	311
Eusebius *Hist. eccl.* 5.24.5	355
Eusebius *Hist. eccl.* 5.8.5	46
Eusebius *Hist. eccl.* 6.25	434
Eusebius *Hist. eccl.* 7.25.9–10	49
Eustathius *Dion. Perieg.* 915	426
Eustathius *Hom. Od.* 19.247	125
Eutropius *Rom Hist.* 4.20	278
Exod 3:7	189
Exod 5:10	80
Exod 6:7	219, 496
Exod 7:1–2	81
Exod 7:14–25	207
Exod 9:1	80
Exod 10:3	80
Exod 15:20	311
Exod 16:15	263
Exod 16:32	263
Exod 16:4, 7, 15	148
Exod 16:4–36	263
Exod 19:3–8	68
Exod 19:5–25	82
Exod 20:1–17	207
Exod 20:14	314
Exod 20:3–6	218
Exod 21:22–25	317
Exod 22:20	88
Exod 23:22	218
Exod 23:8	487
Exod 24:7–8	96
Exod 25	138
Exod 25:16	95
Exod 25:31–40	147
Exod 26:15–25	418
Exod 27:21–22	147
Exod 28:15–21	265
Exod 28:17–21	266
Exod 28:36–38	422
Exod 28:9–12	266
Exod 30:23	152
Exod 34:11–17	218
Exod 34:6	400
Exod 37	138
Exod 40:20	95
Ezek 3:14	152
Ezek 3:27	94
Ezek 4:6	205
Ezek 11:20	496
Ezek 14:11	496
Ezek 16:12	214
Ezek 16:15–58	257
Ezek 16:32	315
Ezek 21:31	214
Ezek 23:1–49	257
Ezek 23:37	143

INDEX OF SCRIPTURE AND ANCIENT WRITINGS

Reference	Page
Ezek 23:40	76
Ezek 23:42	214
Ezek 27:31	152
Ezek 28:12	214
Ezek 28:13	216
Ezek 31:2–9	146, 508
Ezek 31:8–9	216
Ezek 33:27	316
Ezek 34:18	80
Ezek 36:28	219, 496
Ezek 37:23, 27	496
Ezek 43:7	257
Ezek 48:35	423
Ezek 48:35b	423
Ezra 1:2	180, 244, 302, 356, 399, 474
Ezra 1:7	138
Ezra 4:15	373
Felix *Oct.* 22.5	114
Flaccus *Argo.* 2.342	295
FrgPol. 64.23	55, 196, 209–10, 250, 255, 510
Gal 1:1	132
Gal 1:19	132
Gal 1:6–9	136
Gal 2:9	219, 420
Gal 3:13	147, 489
Gal 3:15	219
Gal 3:2–3	136
Gal 4:19	315
Gal 4:26	421, 422
Gal 6:1	205
Gal 6:15	196
Gal 6:16	407, 408
Galen *Anat. Admin.* 1.2	235
Galen *Cogno.* 9	231
Galen *Comp. Med.* 13.119	455
Galen *Meth. Med.* 2.142	454
Galen *Meth. Med.* 5.4.4	264
Galen *Meth. Med.* 10.1.4, 7	454
Galen *Meth. Med.* 10.791	455
Galen *Prop.* 5.49	231
Galen *San. Tu.* 6.12	454
Galen *San. Tu.* 6.3.7	485
Gen 2:25	487
Gen 2:8, 15	147–48
Gen 2:9	146, 148, 216, 508
Gen 3:1–4	250
Gen 3:22, 24	216
Gen 3:22–23	148
Gen 3:23	147
Gen 3:23–24	146
Gen 3:7	487
Gen 3:7; 21	492
Gen 5:22	370
Gen 6:9	370
Gen 12:7	88
Gen 15:18	88
Gen 15:9–18a	201
Gen 17:1	370
Gen 17:15	273
Gen 17:5	273, 423
Gen 22:1b	476
Gen 24:55	206–7
Gen 27:35	90
Gen 31:7, 41	207
Gen 32:27–28	423
Gen 35:10	273, 423
Gen 41:42	490
Gen 41:45	423
Gen 49:9–10	303
Gen. Rab. 41:8	495
Gen. Rab. 50:4	495
Gk. Apoc. Ezra 6:17	214
Gos. Mary 7.10	144, 262, 377
Gos. Mary 8.16	144
Gos. Thom. 21	366
Gos. Thom. 58	218
Gos. Thom. 103	366
Gos. Thom. 8.21, 24	144
Gos. Thom. 8.21, 24, 63, 65, 96	262
Gos. Thom. 8.63	144
HA Comm. 18–20	469
HA Elag. 17.8.4–5	465
Hab 3:3	400
Hag 1:13	76
Hag 1:2	80
Heb 1:13–14	72
Heb 1:14	72, 357
Heb 1:5	320
Heb 1:7	305
Heb 2:18	205
Heb 2:4	132
Heb 4:12–13	316
Heb 4:13	487
Heb 4:15	400
Heb 6:1	312, 360
Heb 7:26	400
Heb 8:10	219
Heb 8:12	421
Heb 9:14	400
Heb 9:28	414
Heb 10:17	421
Heb 10:25	197
Heb 10:34	192
Heb 10:36	309
Heb 10:37	414
Heb 11:10	422
Heb 11:17	205
Heb 11:37	190
Heb 12:22	422
Heb 12:2–3	410
Heb 12:6	492
Heb 12:6, 7, 10	492
Heb 13:14	422
Heb 13:2	495
Heliodorus *Aeth.* 3.3	267
Hermas *Man.* 3.3	312
Hermas *Man.* 4.1.9	315
Hermas *Sim.* 2.9	374
Hermas *Sim.* 8.2.1	212
Hermas *Sim.* 8.2.1–4	214
Hermas *Sim.* 8.2.3	490
Hermas *Sim.* 8.3.6	212, 214
Hermas *Sim.* 8.6.6	312
Hermas *Vis.* 2.1.3	96
Hermas *Vis.* 2.2.2–3	96
Hermas *Vis.* 2.2.7	218
Hermas *Vis.* 3.8.2	418
Hermas *Vis.* 4.2.5	223
Hermas *Vis.* 4.3.4	223
Herodian *Rom. Hist.* 3.5	121
Herodian *Rom. Hist.* 5.5	121
Herodotus *Hist.* 1.13–14	326
Herodotus *Hist.* 1.14	154, 500
Herodotus *Hist.* 1.14.1	154
Herodotus *Hist.* 1.15	327
Herodotus *Hist.* 1.16.1–2	187
Herodotus *Hist.* 1.26	101
Herodotus *Hist.* 1.34	335
Herodotus *Hist.* 1.50	345
Herodotus *Hist.* 1.53	328
Herodotus *Hist.* 1.7	327
Herodotus *Hist.* 1.80–82	328
Herodotus *Hist.* 1.84	328, 329, 367
Herodotus *Hist.* 1.84.3	326
Herodotus *Hist.* 1.84–86	328
Herodotus *Hist.* 1.86–87	327, 329
Herodotus *Hist.* 1.9	335
Herodotus *Hist.* 1.91	329
Herodotus *Hist.* 1.93	368
Herodotus *Hist.* 1.94	326, 346
Herodotus *Hist.* 2.121	366
Herodotus *Hist.* 2.44	419

Herodotus *Hist.* 2:73	185	*I.Eph.* 2.202–208	111	*I.Eph.* 7.3071	105
Herodotus *Hist.* 4.181.3–4	484	*I.Eph.* 2.212	112–13	*I.Eph.* 7.3217	443
Herodotus *Hist.* 5.102	349, 350, 351, 462	*I.Eph.* 2.233	119	*I.Ias.* 1.108	119
Herodotus *Hist.* 5.99–101	329	*I.Eph.* 2.239	419, 422	*I.Laod.* 4b.9	462
Herodotus *Hist.* 7.138	359	*I.Eph.* 2.240	419, 422	*I.Laod.* 5.36	465
Herodotus *Hist.* 7.30	478	*I.Eph.* 2.252–53	304	*I.Laod.* 8.1	462
Herodotus *Hist.* 7.31	148, 380	*I.Eph.* 2.267–271a	119	*I.Laod.* 9.12	461
Herodotus *Hist.* 86	185	*I.Eph.* 2.274	105	*I.Laod.* 9.6	304
Hesiod *Theog.* 918–20	114	*I.Eph.* 2.282D	120, 158	*I.Laod.* 9.9	461
Hippolytus *Comm. Dan.* 1.13–5	171	*I.Eph.* 2.404	122	*I.Laod.* 11.1–2	440
Hippolytus *Comm. Dan.* 1.9	322	*I.Eph.* 2.422	461	*I.Laod.* 13.1–4	440
Hippolytus *Haer.* 5.12	195	*I.Eph.* 2.425.10	107	*I.Laod.* 135	469
Hippolytus *Haer.* 5.6.4	318	*I.Eph.* 2.428	120	*I.Laod.* 15.1–2	304
Hippolytus *Haer.* 6.30.7	318	*I.Eph.* 2.438	120, 158	*I.Laod.* 15.13	461
Hippolytus *Haer.* 6.38.4	477	*I.Eph.* 2.454	288, 456	*I.Laod.* 15.24	461
Hippolytus *Haer.* 7.24	142	*I.Eph.* 2.547	107, 117	*I.Laod.* 15.3	461
Hippolytus *Haer.* 7.36	259	*I.Eph.* 2.547.1	110	*I.Laod.* 16	445
Hippolytus *Haer.* 7.36.3	142	*I.Eph.* 2.585	107	*I.Laod.* 45	58, 468
Hippolytus *Haer.* 9.19	370	*I.Eph.* 2.586	107	*I.Laod.* 51b.2	490
Hipponax *Frag.* 42	326	*I.Eph.* 3.145	111, 129	*I.Laod.* 53.3	462
Homer *Il.* 2.299–332	238, 250	*I.Eph.* 3.611	120, 158	*I.Laod.* 73	450
Homer *Il.* 2.865	327	*I.Eph.* 3.613A	120, 158	*I.Laod.* 75	450
Homer *Il.* 4.141–42	285, 347, 456	*I.Eph.* 3.636	107	*I.Laod.* 81A	450
Homer *Il.* 5.43	327	*I.Eph.* 3.649	120, 158	*I.Laod.* 83.13	462
Homer *Il.* 8.539	207	*I.Eph.* 3.661	120, 158	*I.Laod.* 85.132	462
Homer *Il.* 11.431	327	*I.Eph.* 3.686	120, 158	*I.Laod.* 85.14	462
Homer *Il.* 12.133	207	*I.Eph.* 3.727	288, 456	*I.Perg.* 2.402.2	461
Homer *Il.* 13.826	207	*I.Eph.* 3.951	103	*I.Perg.* 3.47.7	461
Homer *Il.* 20.385	327	*I.Eph.* 3.961	117, 131	*I.Perg.* 485–88	240
Homer *Il.* 21.470	114	*I.Eph.* 3.985–86	120, 158	*I.Phil.* 1428	58, 396
Homer *Il.* 22.317	322	*I.Eph.* 4.1001.5	472	*I.Phil.* 1430	387
Homer *Od.* 1.145	500	*I.Eph.* 4.1012.4	472	*I.Phil.* 1434	382, 396
Homer *Od.* 1.22	463	*I.Eph.* 4.1058	108	*I.Phil.* 1435	382
Homer *Od.* 6.207–8	495	*I.Eph.* 4.1060	108	*I.Phil.* 1439	382, 387
Horace *Ep.* 1.1.1–3	268	*I.Eph.* 4.1070	109	*I.Phil.* 1452–53	387
Horace *Od.* 1.12.47	323	*I.Eph.* 4.1251	125	*I.Phil.* 1472	58, 396
Horace *Sat.* 1.5.30–31	455, 491	*I.Eph.* 4.1387	288	*I.Phil.* 1484	58, 396
Hos 1:10	496	*I.Eph.* 4.1452.3	111	*I.Phil.* 1490–92	386
Hos 1:2:3	315	*I.Eph.* 4.1457	111	*I.Phil.* 1506	395
Hos 2:22	189	*I.Eph.* 4.1457.4	111	*I.Phil.* 1514	388
Hos 4:1	143, 189, 262, 377, 424	*I.Eph.* 4.1518–19	419	*I.Phil.* 1539	395
Hos 5:4	189, 257	*I.Eph.* 4.1676	125	*I.Phil.* 1539–44	395
Hos 6:10	257	*I.Eph.* 4.1677	125	*I.Phil.* 1540	420
Hos 13:4–5	189	*I.Eph.* 6.2061	105	*I.Phil.* 1542	420
I.Eph. 1.20B	472	*I.Eph.* 6.2212	107, 117, 131	*I.Phil.* 1545–46	394
I.Eph. 1.23	105	*I.Eph.* 6.2441	107	*I.Phil.* 1548	390
I.Eph. 1.24	119	*I.Eph.* 7.1.24	110	*I.Phil.* 1549	390
I.Eph. 1.28.9–10	111	*I.Eph.* 7.1.3017	110	*I.Phil.* 1551	390
I.Eph. 1.29.19–20	111	*I.Eph.* 7.3006	106	*I.Phil.* 1625–26	395
I.Eph. 1a.20.10	461	*I.Eph.* 7.3008	461	*I.Phil.* 1630–31	395
I.Eph. 1a.24B	158	*I.Eph.* 7.3066	105	*I.Phil.* 1634–35	390

I.Phil. 1637	390	I.Thyat. 935	283	IGR 1.130	469
I.Phil.1434	58	I.Thyat. 940	298	IGR 3.228	460
I.Philipp. 2:697	286	I.Thyat. 945	283, 286, 287	IGR 3.309–11	304
I.Sard. 100	420	I.Thyat. 946	277	IGR 3.314	304
I.Sard. 7.1.13, 14	352, 353	I.Thyat. 955	298	IGR 4.1169	283
I.Sard. 7.1.17	350	I.Thyat. 956	277	IGR 4.1205	283
I.Sard. 7.1.181	340	I.Thyat. 960	277	IGR 4.1213	347
I.Sard. 7.1.21	351	I.Thyat. 962	298	IGR 4.1216	283
I.Sard. 7.1.22	348	I.Thyat. 963	298	IGR 4.1226	283
I.Sard. 7.1.221	350	I.Thyat. 965	286, 287	IGR 4.1239	286, 347
I.Sard. 7.1.38	419	I.Thyat. 966	283	IGR 4.1242	299, 347
I.Sard. 7.1.4	351	I.Thyat. 970	298	IGR 4.1244	283
I.Sard. 7.1.45	347, 353	I.Thyat. 972	283, 286, 287, 299	IGR 4.1250	347
I.Sard. 7.1.47–48	348, 349	I.Thyat. 973	277	IGR 4.1252	288, 456
I.Sard. 7.1.50–55	348, 349	I.Thyat. 974	279	IGR 4.1257	297
I.Sard. 7.1.58	349	I.Thyat. 976	297	IGR 4.1259	283, 306
I.Sard. 7.1.77–79	352	I.Thyat. 978	282, 286, 287, 298	IGR 4.1265	347
I.Sard. 7.1.79	352	I.Thyat. 980	286, 287, 298	IGR 4.1278	452, 454
I.Sard. 7.1.8	339, 350	I.Thyat. 983	282	IGR 4.1386	169
I.Sard. 7.1.8.112–15	352	I.Thyat. 986	283	IGR 4.1388	158–59
I.Sard. 7.1.8.50–55	339	I.Thyat. 989	277, 283, 286, 287	IGR 4.1415	158
I.Sard. 7.1.8.91–93	339	I.Thyat. 991	287	IGR 4.1418	158–59
I.Sard. 7.1.9	338, 348	I.Thyat. 995	297	IGR 4.1419A	159
I.Sard. 7.91–93	348	I.Thyat. 995–96	277, 297	IGR 4.1420	159, 169
I.Sard. 8.22	304	I.Thyat. 1002	279, 283	IGR 4.1421	159
I.Sard. 8.99	58, 299	I.Thyat. 1019	283	IGR 4.1425	159
I.Sard. 17	350	I.Thyat. 1029	287	IGR 4.1426	159
I.Sard. 46	287	I.Thyat. 1081	287	IGR 4.1427	285
I.Smyr. 2.1.635	119	I.Thyat. 1098	58, 299	IGR 4.1428	158–59
I.Smyr. 2:102	255	IG II 2.1315	350	IGR 4.1431	169
I.Smyr. 22.4–5	461	IG X 2.1 291	289, 347	IGR 4.1435	169
I.Smyr. 120	369	IG XII 2.109	285	IGR 4.1444	158
I.Smyr. 429.6	255	IG XII 2.271	285	IGR 4.1449	169
I.Smyr. 536–37	453	IG XIV 1063	469	IGR 4.1482	158, 159
I.Smyr. 599.7	461	IGLAM 6263	433	IGR 4.15.14	332
I.Smyr. 637	158, 182	Ignatius Eph. 1:3	127	IGR 4.1506	349
I.Smyr. 643.6–7	461	Ignatius Eph. 4:1	370	IGR 4.1509	347, 353
I.Smyr. 665.2–4	158	Ignatius Eph. 6:2	127, 132, 133	IGR 4.1519	352
I.Smyr. 721	489	Ignatius Eph. 7:1	133	IGR 4.1644	386
I.Smyr. 826	304	Ignatius Eph. 9:1	132, 133	IGR 4.1756	353
I.Thyat. 862	282	Ignatius Magn. 10:1	424	IGR 4.393a	169
I.Thyat. 870A	299	Ignatius Magn. 11:3	313	IGR 4.425	285
I.Thyat. 882–83	277, 297	Ignatius Magn. 12:1	370	IGR 4.541	159
I.Thyat. 894–96	298	Ignatius Magn. 2:1	370	IGR 4.824	119
I.Thyat. 897–900	298	Ignatius Phld. 5	424	IGR 4.845	447, 461
I.Thyat. 902	58, 298, 304	Ignatius Phld. 6.1	195	IGR 4.846	446
I.Thyat. 902; 980	58	Ignatius Phld. 6:1–2	408	IGR 4.848	451
I.Thyat. 914	283	Ignatius Phld. 7:1	316	IGR 4.861	446
I.Thyat. 931	297	Ignatius Pol. 8.2	178	IGR 4.863	284, 457
I.Thyat. 932	297	Ignatius Smyrn. 1.2	194	IGR 4:1209	282
I.Thyat. 933	283	Ignatius Smyrn. 12.2	178	IGR 4:1239	282

IGR 4:1252	283	Isa 19:4	80	Isa 62:2	265, 274, 423
IGR 4:1431.29	170	Isa 20:4	487	Isa 62:3	214
IGR 4:859	469	Isa 20:4–5	487	Isa 65:15	265, 274, 423
IGR 4:863	469	Isa 22:15, 25	80	Isa 65:16	475
IJO 2.146	300	Isa 22:15–25	401	Isa 65:16–18	475
IJO 2.97–98	344, 354	Isa 22:17, 21	416	Isa 65:17	88
IJO 2:187–92	311	Isa 22:18	214	Isa 65:19	400
IJO 2:297–302	300	Isa 22:20	402	Isa 65:6	222
ILS 6572	430	Isa 22:20–22	399	Jas 1:12	212, 214, 217, 219–20, 410
ILS 6573	430	Isa 22:21	214	Jas 1:13	205
ILydiaHoz 1.2	391, 395, 411	Isa 22:22	401, 408	Jas 1:2–3	205
ILydiaHoz, 59–60	390	Isa 22:25	418	Jas 1:2–4	217
IlydiaKP 2.224	395	Isa 24	413	Jas 1:25	217
Imhoof KM 118	433	Isa 28:3, 5	214	Jas 1:3	309
Imhoof KM 28	463	Isa 28:5	214	Jas 1:3–4	217
Imhoof KM 39	465	Isa 33:7	152	Jas 2:15	487
Imhoof Nymphen 411 var	469	Isa 34:1–2	89, 365	Jas 2:17	360
Irenaeus Haer. 1.18.1	477	Isa 36:14	80	Jas 2:2	197
Irenaeus Haer. 1.26.3	142, 259, 507	Isa 36:20	208	Jas 2:5	192–93, 492
Irenaeus Haer. 1.30.15	195	Isa 36:3	401	Jas 4:4	315
Irenaeus Haer. 2.22.1	318	Isa 36:4	80	Jas 5:10–11	217
Irenaeus Haer. 2.22.5	46	Isa 38:15, 17	152	Jas 5:11	220, 309
Irenaeus Haer. 2.32.4	272	Isa 38:5	80	Jas 5:2	459
Irenaeus Haer. 2.33	47, 127	Isa 40:25	400	Jas 5:7–9	414
Irenaeus Haer. 2.49.3	272	Isa 41:17	190	Jas 5:9	494
Irenaeus Haer. 2.6.2	194, 272	Isa 41:4	184	Jdt 2:5	80
Irenaeus Haer. 3.3	47	Isa 42:19–20	487	Jdt 14:7	408
Irenaeus Haer. 3.3.4	46	Isa 43:4	409	Jer 1:11–13	76
Irenaeus Haer. 3.9.1	142	Isa 44:21	136	Jer 2:12	93
Irenaeus Haer. 3:11.1	259	Isa 44:26	76	Jer 2:4	143
Irenaeus Haer. 4.21.3	171	Isa 44:6	184	Jer 2:4–5	94
Irenaeus Haer. 5.17.3	147	Isa 45:14	408	Jer 3:17	423
Irenaeus Haer. 5.30.3	46	Isa 46:8–9	136	Jer 3:2, 9	257
Isa 1.2	93	Isa 48:12	182, 184	Jer 3:6	315
Isa 1:10	143, 262, 377, 424	Isa 49:1	94	Jer 3:9	315
Isa 1:21	143	Isa 49:2	245	Jer 4:18	152
Isa 1:2–20	93	Isa 49:23	408	Jer 7:23	219, 496
Isa 1:25	489	Isa 51:21–23	190	Jer 7:3	80
Isa 1:26	423	Isa 51:4	94	Jer 8:6	312
Isa 4:3	374	Isa 52:13	221	Jer 10:10	400
Isa 5:20	152	Isa 52:14	222	Jer 11:4	219, 496
Isa 7:7	80	Isa 53:11	221	Jer 13:12–14	413
Isa 8:18	316	Isa 53:7	194	Jer 13:18	214
Isa 8:3	311	Isa 54:11	190	Jer 13:27	257
Isa 10:24	80	Isa 54:8	208	Jer 17:10	316
Isa 11:15	89	Isa 55:1	489	Jer 23:6	423
Isa 11:4	245, 322	Isa 55:1–2	489	Jer 24:7	189, 496
Isa 14:12	322, 515	Isa 56:10	487	Jer 26:5	76
Isa 14:24	80	Isa 56:5	274	Jer 27:9	313
Isa 17:3	80	Isa 57:11	136	Jer 29:19	76
Isa 17:6	80	Isa 60:14	408, 423	Jer 29:24–32	49

Index of Scripture and Ancient Writings

Reference	Page	Reference	Page	Reference	Page
Jer 29:4–32	49	John 5:25–27	303	Jos. As. 14:1	322
Jer 30:22	219, 496	John 6:31–33	263	Jos. As. 17:6	418
Jer 30:7	413	John 6:37	264	Josephus *Ag. Ap.* 1.176–83	170
Jer 31:1; 33	496	John 6:39	88, 203	Josephus *Ag. Ap.* 2.215	314
Jer 31:34	190	John 6:44	88	Josephus *Ag. Ap.* 2.6	198
Jer 32:28	496	John 6:50–51	263	Josephus *Ant.* 1.200	495
Jer 33:16	423	John 6:54	88	Josephus *Ant.* 2.312	496
Jer 35:14	76	John 6:69	400	Josephus *Ant.* 3.178	422
Jer 39:18	201	John 7:13	400	Josephus *Ant.* 3.26–32	263
Jer 42:7	206	John 7:18	400	Josephus *Ant.* 4.126–30	256
Jer 51:20	322	John 8:12	370	Josephus *Ant.* 7.347	148
Jer 52:17	148	John 8:33	196	Josephus *Ant.* 8.186	148
Jer 52:19	138, 147	John 8:44	407	Josephus *Ant.* 8.316–59	309
Jerome *Comm. in Ep. Paul*	114	John 8:46	492	Josephus *Ant.* 8.330	309
Jerome *Vir. ill.* 9	46	John 8:51, 52, 55	406	Josephus *Ant.* 8.335	400
Jerome *Vir. ill.* 24	355	John 9:22	404, 406	Josephus *Ant.* 8.337	400
Job 1:2	202	John 9:39	490	Josephus *Ant.* 8.338	400
Job 1:6–12	407	John 9:40–41	487	Josephus *Ant.* 8.343	400
Job 1:8–12	205	John 10:12	134	Josephus *Ant.* 8.347	309
Job 2:1–6	407	John 12:35	370	Josephus *Ant.* 8.402	400
Job 15:6	214	John 12:42	406	Josephus *Ant.* 8.45–49	272
Job 19:2–3	207	John 13:1	410	Josephus *Ant.* 8.77–78	418
Job 19:3	206	John 13:2	202	Josephus *Ant.* 9.108	309
Job 19:9	214	John 13:27	202	Josephus *Ant.* 9.122–23	309
Job 22:25	205	John 13:4, 12	459	Josephus *Ant.* 9.256	400
Job 23:10	205, 488	John 14:1–3	414	Josephus *Ant.* 9.47	309
Job 28:16	266	John 14:23, 24	406	Josephus *Ant.* 10.263	400
Job 29:18	185	John 15:18–16:4	208	Josephus *Ant.* 11.26	79
Job 31:19	487	John 15:20	406	Josephus *Ant.* 11.327	369, 372, 490
Job 31:36	214	John 15:27	132	Josephus *Ant.* 11.331	490
Job 32:10	205	John 16:2	406	Josephus *Ant.* 11.55	400
Job 32:2	214	John 16:28	134	Josephus *Ant.* 12.121	470
Job 38–42:6	76	John 16:30	316	Josephus *Ant.* 12.125	170
Job 40:4	214	John 16:33	145, 208, 320, 417	Josephus *Ant.* 12.147–49	470
Job 45:12	214	John 16:8	492	Josephus *Ant.* 12.147–53	353
Joel 2:1–32	413	John 17:3	400	Josephus *Ant.* 12.250	138
Joel 2:27	219, 496	John 17:33	220	Josephus *Ant.* 12.3.4	437
John 1:1	423	John 17:6	406	Josephus *Ant.* 14.1.3–4	255
John 1:14	304	John 17:8	363	Josephus *Ant.* 14.10.21	109
John 1:18	304	John 18:4	316	Josephus *Ant.* 14.115	196
John 1:2–3	477	John 19:12	202	Josephus *Ant.* 14.150	111
John 1:3	477	John 19:13	249	Josephus *Ant.* 14.153	215
John 1:41–42	273	John 19:14–15	194	Josephus *Ant.* 14.232	354
John 1:42	423	John 19:2, 5	214	Josephus *Ant.* 14.235	354
John 1:49	304	John 19:23–24	459	Josephus *Ant.* 14.240–243	470
John 2:25	316–17	John 19:39	152	Josephus *Ant.* 14.259–261	354
John 3:16	304	John 19:6–7	194	Josephus *Ant.* 14.259–61	354
John 3:20	492	John 20:15	133	Josephus *Ant.* 14.261	354
John 4:29	316	John 20:29	490	Josephus *Ant.* 16.164	300
John 4:3	134	John 21:10	203	Josephus *Ant.* 16.171	354
John 4:39	316	John 21:17	316	Josephus *Ant.* 16.259–261	354

Josephus *Ant.* 17.1.3	255	Justin *Dial.* 30.3	272	Livy *Hist. Rome* 5.13.6	498, 526
Josephus *Ant.* 18.1.1	245	Justin *Dial.* 47.4	199	Livy *Hist. Rome* 7.35	269
Josephus *Ant.* 20.9.5	204	Justin *Dial.* 47.4,15	194	Livy *Hist. Rome* 27.46	269
Josephus *J.W.* 2.1	369, 372	Justin *Dial.* 61.1	477	Livy *Hist. Rome* 33.38.3	166
Josephus *J.W.* 2.123	370	Justin *Dial.* 62.4	477	Livy *Hist. Rome* 34.59.4	166
Josephus *J.W.* 2.138	370	Justin *Dial.* 76.6	272	Livy *Hist. Rome* 35.17.1	166
Josephus *J.W.* 2.398	196	Justin *Dial.* 81	43	Livy *Hist. Rome* 37.37.6, 9	277, 331
Josephus *J.W.* 2.8.1	245	Justin *Dial.* 85	271	Livy *Hist. Rome* 37.37–45	430
Josephus *J.W.* 4.467	148	Justin *Dial.* 85.2	272	Livy *Hist. Rome* 37.44.4	277, 331
Josephus *J.W.* 5.190–91	420	Justin *Dial.* 93	365	Livy *Hist. Rome* 37.8.7	277
Josephus *J.W.* 5.200	420	Justin *Dial.* 93.4	199	Livy *Hist. Rome* 37.8.8	277, 331
Josephus *J.W.* 5.203	420	Justin *Dial.* 95, 96	365	Livy *Hist. Rome* 38.58.9	430
Josephus *J.W.* 5.217	129	Justin *Dial.* 95.4	199	Livy *Hist. Rome* 44.4	277, 331
Josephus *J.W.* 5.235	422	Justin *Dial.* 96.2	199	Livy *Per.* 58.4	430
Josephus *J.W.* 5.413	316	Justin *Dial.* 106.4	322	Livy *Per.* 78	430
Josephus *J.W.* 6.6	148	Justin *Dial.* 108.3	199	Lucian *Char.* 9	326
Josephus *J.W.* 7. 218	471	Justin *Dial.* 116.1	400	Lucian *Dial. meretr.* 9	267
Josephus *J.W.* 7.100–111	470	Justin *Dial.* 123	365	Lucian *Lex.* 8	482
Josephus *J.W.* 7.148	138	Justin *Dial.* 133	365	Lucian *Merc. cond.* 13	326, 367
Josephus *J.W.* 7.43	196	Justin *Dial.* 133.6	199	Lucian *Phar.* 3.209–10	347, 489
Josephus *J.W.* 8.186	372	Justin *Dial.* 135	271	Lucian *Philop.* 22	305
Josephus *Life* 277	300	Justin *Dial.* 137.2	199	Lucretius *Re. Nat.* 2.35	295
Josh 6:21	89, 364	Juvenal *Sat.* 3.171–80	372	Lucretius *Re. Nat.* 6.848–78	484
Josh 10:28	89, 364	Juvenal *Sat.* 10.221	454	Luke 1:11	72
Josh 13:22	148, 256, 309	Juvenal *Sat.* 10.45	372	Luke 1:32	249
Josh 24	68	Juvenal *Sat.* 14.298–300	347	Luke 1:35	400
Josh 24:26	95	Lactantius *Inst.* 2.16	272	Luke 1:52	249
Josh 24:9, 10	309	Lactantius *Inst.* 4.27	272	Luke 1:52–53	492
Jub. 5	136	Lactantius *Phoen.* 11, 20	185	Luke 1:59	273
Jub. 15:31–32	357	Lam 1:4	152	Luke 2	206
Jude 6	72	Lam 2:15	214	Luke 3:8	364
Jude 11	256	Lam 3:64	313	Luke 4:12	205
Jude 23	368	Lam 5:16	214	Luke 4:13	205
Judg 3:16	245	Lev 17–18	319	Luke 4:34	400
Judg 4:4	311	Lev 18:5, 28	484	Luke 5:24	303
Judg 11:14–15	128, 180, 244, 302, 356, 399, 474	Lev 20:10	315, 317	Luke 6:13	132
		Lev 24:19–21	317	Luke 6:14	132
Justin *1 Apol.* 5	203	Lev 26	87	Luke 6:20	193
Justin *1 Apol.* 30.78	203	Lev 26:12	219, 496	Luke 6:5	303
Justin *1 Apol.* 31.5–6	171, 194	Lev 27:19	89, 364	Luke 8:15	309
Justin *1 Apol.* 31.6	406	Lev 28–29	89, 364	Luke 8:31	303
Justin *1 Apol.* 36.36	171	*LIMC* 4.1.378	502	Luke 8:49	77
Justin *1 Apol.* 57.1	203	*LIMC* 4.1.684	502	Luke 8:8	94, 144, 262, 377, 424
Justin *1 Apol.* 63.10	203	*LIMC* 4.1.865	501	Luke 9:1	132
Justin *1 Apol.* 131.2	203	*LIMC* 4.1.866–67	501	Luke 9:22, 26, 44	303
Justin *2 Apol.* 6.6	272	*LIMC* 4.2.213	502	Luke 9:52	72
Justin *Dial.* 2–8	127	*LIMC* 4.2.220	502	Luke 10:20	374
Justin *Dial.* 5	203	*LIMC* 4.2.415, 416	502	Luke 10:27	308
Justin *Dial.* 16	365	*LIMC* 4.2.578	501	Luke 11:19	272
Justin *Dial.* 16.2	194	*LIMC* 4.2.581	501	Luke 11:49	203
Justin *Dial.* 16.4	199	*Lindgren* 1:774	391	Luke 12:16–21	486

Index of Scripture and Ancient Writings

Luke 12:21	193	Marcellus *Comp. Doct.* 2.4.M549	295	*Mart. Carp.* 34	315
Luke 12:33–34	193	Mark 1:13	205	*Mart. Ignat.* 7	203
Luke 12:35–37	496	Mark 1:24	400	*Mart. Pionii* 2.1	55, 175–76, 196, 209
Luke 12:35–38	495	Mark 2:10, 28	303	*Mart. Pionii* 3.3, 4	165
Luke 12:35–40	365	Mark 2:16	495	*Mart. Pionii* 3.6	55, 99, 176, 196
Luke 12:39–40	367	Mark 3:14; 6:7	132	*Mart. Pionii* 4.2	55, 160, 176
Luke 12:9–10	406	Mark 3:16	132	*Mart. Pionii* 4.2, 8	196
Luke 13:10–17	77	Mark 3:17	423	*Mart. Pionii* 4.24	168
Luke 13:14	77	Mark 4:10–12	99	*Mart. Pionii* 4.3	176
Luke 14:15	496	Mark 4:9	99, 144, 262, 377, 424	*Mart. Pionii* 4.4–6	176
Luke 14:35	94, 144, 262, 377, 424	Mark 4:9, 23	99	*Mart. Pionii* 4.8	176
Luke 15:17–18	136	Mark 5:22	77	*Mart. Pionii* 5.2	168
Luke 15:2	495	Mark 5:35–38	77	*Mart. Pionii* 7.2	168
Luke 15:7	364	Mark 7:3f, 8	254	*Mart. Pionii* 8.4	168
Luke 17:22	303	Mark 8:31, 38	303	*Mart. Pionii* 13.1	55, 196
Luke 18:8	303	Mark 8:38	315, 500	*Mart. Pionii* 13.2	198
Luke 19:10	303	Mark 9:1	500	*Mart. Pionii* 14.1	55, 196, 209
Luke 19:35–36	459	Mark 9:2–8	500	*Mart. Pionii* 15.7	166, 169, 183
Luke 21:12	406	Mark 9:3	459	*Mart. Pionii* 21.1	162
Luke 21:19	309	Mark 9:9, 12	303	*Mart. Pionii* 23.1	175
Luke 21:25–28	414	Mark 10:33, 45	303	*Mart. Pol.* 1.13	55, 172, 196, 209, 210, 250, 255, 510
Luke 21:27, 36	303	Mark 11:7–8	459	*Mart. Pol.* 2.4	203
Luke 21:5	266	Mark 12:14	400	*Mart. Pol.* 3.2	173
Luke 22:20	496	Mark 12:30–31	308	*Mart. Pol.* 9.2	207
Luke 22:22	303	Mark 13:13	410	*Mart. Pol.* 9:2–3	406
Luke 22:28–30	500	Mark 13:22	132	*Mart. Pol.* 10.1	207
Luke 22:3	202	Mark 13:24–27	414	*Mart. Pol.* 12.2	55, 173, 196
Luke 22:30	496	Mark 13:25	361	*Mart. Pol.* 12.2–3	194
Luke 22:48	303	Mark 13:26	303	*Mart. Pol.* 12–18	175
Luke 22:69	303	Mark 13:29	494	*Mart. Pol.* 13.1	171
Luke 22:69–70	303	Mark 13:30	414	*Mart. Pol.* 13:1	194
Luke 23:2	202	Mark 13:32	414	*Mart. Pol.* 17.1	203, 215
Luke 23:20–23	194	Mark 13:33–37	495–96	*Mart. Pol.* 17.2–18.1	171
Luke 23:34	459	Mark 13:35	505	*Mart. Pol.* 19.1	172, 398, 411
Luke 24:30–31	497	Mark 13:7–20	413	Martial *Epig.* 1.23, 96	124
Luke 24:47	364	Mark 13:7ff	223	Martial *Epig.* 3.57	124
Luke 24:7	303	Mark 13:9	208, 406	Martial *Epig.* 3.72	124
Lydus *Mens.* 4.58	383, 388	Mark 14:12–14	194	Martial *Epig.* 3.87	124
m. Pir. 'Abot 1:17	479	Mark 14:21, 41, 62	303	Martial *Epig.* 4.46.17	295
m. Pir. 'Abot 3:1	400	Mark 15:17	214	Martial *Epig.* 4.64	130
m. Pir. 'Abot 5:22	262	Mark 15:20, 24	459	Martial *Epig.* 5.64.1–2	483
m. Pir. 'Abot 5:3	207	Mark 15:23	152	Martial *Epig.* 8.7	269
Mal 2:1	76	Mark 15:29	194, 199	Martial *Epig.* 9.33	124
Mal 3:1	76	Mark 16:20	132	Martial *Epig.* 11.47	124
Mal 3:2–3	488	*Mart. Asc. Isa.* 3.11	203	Martial *Epig.* 11.63	124
MAMA 4.260	347	*Mart. Asc. Isa.* 4:16	490	Martial *Epig.* 11.95	124
MAMA 4.279–90	368	*Mart. Asc. Isa.* 5.1	203	Martial *Epig.* 14.103–4	483
MAMA 6.15	495	*Mart. Asc. Isa.* 8.26	214	Martial *Epig.* 14.105	483
MAMA 6.87	463	*Mart. Asc. Isa.* 9:9, 17	490	Martial *Epig.* 14.128	460
Manilius *Astron.* 1.177–78	322	*Mart. Carp.* 1–23	249	Matt 2:11	152
Marcellinus *Hist.* 16.8.8	295	*Mart. Carp.* 27	301		

Matt 2:13–14	407	Matt 24:34	414	*NewDocs* 1:5	313, 496, 498
Matt 3:8, 11	364	Matt 24:36	414	*NewDocs* 1:84	267, 512
Matt 3:9	196	Matt 24:42	361	*NewDocs* 2:201–2	368
Matt 4:1	205	Matt 24:43–44	367	*NewDocs* 2:28	313
Matt 4:3	205	Matt 24:52	505	*NewDocs* 215 n.23	125
Matt 4:3, 6	423	Matt 24:9	134	*NewDocs* 3:116	125
Matt 5:3	193, 492	Matt 25:31	249	*NewDocs* 3:56–57	491
Matt 5:34	249	Matt 25:36	487	*NewDocs* 4.202–209	266, 376
Matt 6:19–21	192	Matt 26:2	303	*NewDocs* 4:113	125
Matt 6:20	193	Matt 26:24	303	*NewDocs* 4:7–10	117, 132
Matt 6:4, 6, 18	316	Matt 26:29	496	*NewDocs* 4:75–76	111
Matt 7:15	133	Matt 26:45	303	Num 5:11–31	314
Matt 8:11	269, 496	Matt 26:63–64	303	Num 6:27	422
Matt 8:29	423	Matt 26:64	303, 414	Num 8	138
Matt 9:10	495	Matt 26:65	459	Num 11:19	206–7
Matt 9:20	459	Matt 27:19	249	Num 14:22	206–7
Matt 9:4	316, 317	Matt 27:22–23	194	Num 14:34	205
Matt 9:6	303, 423	Matt 27:29	214	Num 18:19	495
Matt 10:1–5	132	Matt 27:31, 35	459	Num 21:2	89, 364
Matt 10:17	406	Matt 27:39	194	Num 22:15–16	128, 180, 244, 302, 356,
Matt 10:22	134, 410	Memnon *Hist. Her.* 12.7	277, 429	399, 474	
Matt 10:2–4	132	Menaÿ. 42b	293	Num 22:23, 31	262
Matt 10:33	406	Mic 2:3	80	Num 22:5–25:3	256, 309
Matt 11:15	87, 94, 144, 262, 377, 424	Mic 6:1–8	93	Num 22–24	142, 148, 256
Matt 12:27	272	Mic 6:1f	93	Num 24:17	148, 304, 322
Matt 12:43	87	Mic 6:2	94	Num 24:9, 10	256
Matt 12:8	303	Mic 6:5	136, 256, 309	Num 25:12	219
Matt 12:9	87	*Midr.* 1:1–13	219	Num 25:1–2	142, 143
Matt 13:19	94, 144, 262, 377, 424	*Midr. Rab.* Cant. 4:7	139	Num 25:1–3	142
Matt 16:13, 27–28	303	*Midr. Rab.* Cant. 5:2	404, 494	Num 27:21	266
Matt 16:16	304	*Midr. Rab.* Eccl. 1.9	263	Num 31:16	142, 309
Matt 16:18	273, 402	*Midr. Rab.* Eccl. 4:1	139	Num 31:8	309
Matt 17:2	459	*Midr. Rab.* Exod 33:3	494	Num 31:8, 16	256
Matt 17:9, 12, 22	303	*Midr. Rab.* Lev 30.2	139	Obad 1:1	80
Matt 18:10	72	*Midr. Rab.* Lev 32:8	139	*Odes Sol.* 1:17, 20	215
Matt 19:17	406	*Midr. Rab.* Num 12:13	129	*Odes Sol.* 3:10–11	94, 144, 262, 377, 424
Matt 19:21	193	*Midr. Rab.* Num 13:8	139	*Odes Sol.* 9.6	410
Matt 19:28	249, 500	*Midr. Rab.* Num 15:10	139	*Odes Sol.* 9:11	375
Matt 20:18, 28	303	*Midr. Rab.* Ps 16.12	139	*Odes Sol.* 29:8	320
Matt 20:22–23	45	Mionnet 4.530	393, 395	*Odes Sol.* 42:8, 9, 20	273
Matt 21:7–8	459	Mionnet 4.769	468	*OGIS* 1.211	277
Matt 22:16	400	MM 451	368	*OGIS* 2.308.15	380
Matt 23:16–17	487	Nah 3:4	257	*OGIS* 2.338.7	228, 331, 381
Matt 24	208	Nah 3:5	487	*OGIS* 2.458	270
Matt 24:12–14	135	Neh 4:12	207	*OGIS* 2.514.3–4	158, 182
Matt 24:13	410	Neh 5:18	206	Origen *Cels.* 1.59–60	322
Matt 24:15–31	413	Neh 6:14	311	Origen *Cels.* 1.6, 25, 67	272
Matt 24:22	208	Neh 9:15	263	Origen *Cels.* 3.15	60
Matt 24:29–31	414	Neh 9:6	400	Origen *Cels.* 3.24	272
Matt 24:30	303	Neh 13:1	207	Origen *Cels.* 6.27	171
Matt 24:33	494	Neh 13:2	256, 309	Origen *Cels.* 6.27	203

Origen *Comm. Gen.* 1.1	477	Pausanias *Descr.* 10.11.6	419	Phil 3:20–4:3	374
Origen *Comm. Job.* 1.19	477	PDM 12.6–20	271	Phil 3:4	196
Origen *Comm. Matt.* 16.6	45	*Pesiq. Rab.* 51.4	139	Phil 4:1	214
Origen *Fr. Ps.* 2.2	422	*Pesiq. Rab.* 7.7	139	Phil 4:18	73
Origin *Cels.* 1.24	271	*Pesiq. Rab.* 8.4	139	Philo *Abr.* 103	422
Origin *Cels.* 4.33–34	271	Petronius *Sat.* 65	482	Philo *Abr.* 107–18	495
Origin *Cels.* 5.45	271	PGM 1	498	Philo *Cher.* 17	487
Ovid *Fas.* 4.221–44	350	PGM 1.1–195	500	Philo *Contempl.* 66	369, 372
Ovid *Metam.* 3.251	114	PGM 1.167–77	498	Philo *Fug.* 17	193
Ovid *Metam.* 5.43	528	PGM 1.89–90	414	Philo *Her.* 45.221–25	129
Ovid *Metam.* 6.8–9	293	PGM 3.123–24	414	Philo *Leg.* 1.245	170
Ovid *Metam.* 8.626–78	495	PGM 4.1048	271	Philo *Legat.* 155–58	300
Ovid *Metam.* 11.136–45	327, 489	PGM 4.1057	271	Philo *Legat.* 245	196
Ovid *Metam.* 11.142–45	346	PGM 4.1245	414	Philo *Legat.* 349–67	198
Ovid *Metam.* 15.402	185	PGM 4.1404	305	Philo *Mos.* 1.263–304	256
Ovid *Metam.* 15.41–42	267	PGM 4.1593	414	Philo *Mos.* 2.102–5	129
Ovid *Trist.* 4.8.23–24	269	PGM 4.1840–70	500	Philo *Opif.* 69	316
Ovid *Trist.* 4.8.34	268	PGM 4.1851–67	499	Philo *Plant.* 69	193
P.Oxy. 1.110	496, 498	PGM 4.1924	414	Philo *Praem.* 104	193
P.Oxy. 3.523	496, 498	PGM 4.2037	414	Philo *Prob.* 9	487
P.Oxy. 3693	313	PGM 4.2098	414	Philo *QE* 2.73–81	129
P.Oxy. 4.658	61	PGM 4.236–37	414	Philo *Sacr.* 91–92	92, 476
P.Oxy. 12.1464	61	PGM 4.3045	322	Philo *Sobr.* 56	193
P.Oxy. 13.1755	496, 498	PGM 4.3046–47	316	Philo *Somn.* 1.87	316
P.Oxy. 19.2230	460	PGM 4.3068	322	Philo *Somn.* 1:179	193
P.Oxy. 41.2990	61	PGM 4.937	271	Philo *Spec.* 1.315–17	312, 313
P.Oxy. 42.3035	62	PGM 5.209–10	322	Philo *Spec.* 4.10	366
P.Oxy. 52.3693	498	PGM 6.14	414	Philostratus *Vit. Apoll.* 1.4.7	154, 213
P.Oxy. 58.3929	61	PGM 7.248–49	414	Philostratus *Vit. Apoll.* 1.8.24	154
P.Ryl. 2.189	460	PGM 8.40–41	419	Philostratus *Vit. Apoll.* 3.48	461, 466
Palestina 12	375	PGM 11a.1–40	500	Philostratus *Vit. Apoll.* 4.11	236
Paterculus *C. Rom. Hist.* 2.18	229	PGM 12.14–95	500	Philostratus *Vit. Apoll.* 4.1–4	135
Pausanias *Descr.* 1.10.3–4	227	PGM 12.209	271	Philostratus *Vit. Apoll.* 4.34	235, 250
Pausanias *Descr.* 1.10.5	227	PGM 12.280	271	Philostratus *Vit. Apoll.* 4.7	160
Pausanias *Descr.* 1.9.7	101	PGM 13.763–64	271	Philostratus *Vit. Apoll.* 6.37	326, 347, 489
Pausanias *Descr.* 2.26.7	235, 251	PGM 13.845	271	Philostratus *Vit. Apoll.* 6.42	385
Pausanias *Descr.* 2.27.2	250	PHI 137473	289, 347	Philostratus *Vit. Apoll.* 7:21	204
Pausanias *Descr.* 2.3.6	392	PHI 264344	283	Philostratus *Vit. Apoll.* 8.7.8	102
Pausanias *Descr.* 2.35.5	369, 372	PHI 264363	283	Philostratus *Vit. Soph.* 1.2	495
Pausanias *Descr.* 2.36.9	166	PHI 264408	286	Philostratus *Vit. Soph.* 1.22	249
Pausanias *Descr.* 4.31.8	113, 116	PHI 264416	283	Philostratus *Vit. Soph.* 1.25	113, 158, 182, 245, 427
Pausanias *Descr.* 4.32.1	338, 525	PHI 26443	283		
Pausanias *Descr.* 5.20.6–7	419	PHI 264450	283	Philostratus *Vit. Soph.* 1.25.10	113, 158, 182
Pausanias *Descr.* 6.14.1	162	PHI 264529	299		
Pausanias *Descr.* 7.17.9–12	350	PHI 264573	300	Philostratus *Vit. Soph.* 1.25.2	245
Pausanias *Descr.* 7.2.6	101	PHI 277547	283	Phlm 10	315
Pausanias *Descr.* 7.5.1	154	Phil 2:10–11	409	Pionius *Vit. Polyc.* 1.3	172
Pausanias *Descr.* 7.5.2	154	Phil 2:25	73	Pionius *Vit. Polyc.* 30.4	160
Pausanias *Descr.* 7.5.9	166	Phil 2:9	424	*Pirqe R. El.* 34	221
Pausanias *Descr.* 8.37.4	501	Phil 3:10	188	*Pist. Soph.* 1.17, 19, 33, 42, 43	144, 262
Pausanias *Descr.* 9.31.2	124	Phil 3:20	374, 421	*Pist. Soph.* 2.68, 86, 87	144, 262

Pist. Soph. 3.124, 125	144, 262	Pliny *Nat.* 36.21.95ff	117	Prov 5:4	245
Plato *Resp.* 2.437D	482	Pliny *Nat.* 36.26.45	289	Prov 7:17	152
Plautus *Bacchides 312*	117	Pliny *Nat.* 36.95	420	Prov 8:30	476
Plautus *Curc.* 292–93	482	Plutarch *Ant.* 38.61.2	431	Prov 12:4	214
Plautus *Rud.* 1013–14	482	Plutarch *Ant.* 58.5	232	Prov 14:24	214
Pliny *Ep.* 10.19, 20	204	Plutarch *Ant.* 58.9–59.1	232	Prov 15:18	479
Pliny *Ep.* 10.96	55, 63, 245, 257, 406	Plutarch *Caes.* 49.3f	232	Prov 16:31	214
Pliny *Ep.* 10.97	63	Plutarch *Comp. Phil. Flam.* 3	215	Prov 17:27	479
Pliny *Ep.* 3.9.15	245	Plutarch *Cor.* 3.3	215	Prov 17:6	214
Pliny *Nat.* 2.200	104, 229	Plutarch *De Herod.* 24	329	Prov 24:12	313, 316
Pliny *Nat.* 2.36–38	322	Plutarch *Mor.* 186	267, 512	Prov 27:7	152
Pliny *Nat.* 2.37	322	Plutarch *Mor.* 288	273	Ps 2	194
Pliny *Nat.* 2.86.200	331, 367, 382, 421, 432	Plutarch *Mor.* 348–68	312	Ps 2:8	320
		Plutarch *Mor.* 612d	495	Ps 2:9	320, 321, 322, 516
Pliny *Nat.* 4.12.69	45, 46	Plutarch *Mor.* 755f	238, 250	Ps 16:10	400
Pliny *Nat.* 5.105	429, 431, 462–63	Plutarch *Mor.* 771d	490	Ps 20:4	214
Pliny *Nat.* 5.111	331, 382	Plutarch *Peric.* 100.10	364	Ps 27:4	313
Pliny *Nat.* 5.126	226, 276, 278	Plutarch *Praec. ger. publ.* 807b	249	Ps 28:4	316
Pliny *Nat.* 5.19	293	Plutarch *Quaest. conv.* 5.3	215	Ps 30:5	208
Pliny *Nat.* 5.29	109, 389, 422	Plutarch *Quaest. conv.* 5.7.2	305	Ps 34:7	72
Pliny *Nat.* 5.30	379, 385	Plutarch *Quaest. conv.* 9.5	125	Ps 37:11	88
Pliny *Nat.* 5.31	109, 277	Plutarch *Quaest. rom.* 26.270D–F	372	Ps 44:21	316
Pliny *Nat.* 5.33	278	Plutarch *Sull.* 14.1–7	430	Ps 45:9	152
Pliny *Nat.* 6.201	293	Plutarch *Sull.* 15.1–3	430	Ps 50:4	93
Pliny *Nat.* 7.56.195	285, 347	Pol. *Phil.* 11	177	Ps 62:12	316
Pliny *Nat.* 8.191	460	Pol. *Phil.* 2	177	Ps 64:11f	214
Pliny *Nat.* 8.193	460	Pol. *Phil.* 5:1	370	Ps 64:4	152
Pliny *Nat.* 8.73.190	456–57, 459	Pollux *Onom.* 1.45–49	293	Ps 66:10	489
Pliny *Nat.* 9.60–64	293	Polyaenus *Strat.* 4.9.4	326, 330	Ps 69	194
Pliny *Nat.* 9.61	293–94	Polyaenus *Strat.* 7.16.1	427	Ps 69:28	148, 374
Pliny *Nat.* 10:33.9	169	Polybius *Hist.* 1.66	408	Ps 77:25	263
Pliny *Nat.* 10:5.118	153	Polybius *Hist.* 2.5.5	427	Ps 86:15	400
Pliny *Nat.* 12.3	264	Polybius *Hist.* 21.43	430	Ps 86:2	313
Pliny *Nat.* 13.21	232, 234	Polybius *Hist.* 4.66.7	364	Ps 89:23	321
Pliny *Nat.* 14.12	293	Polybius *Hist.* 5.107	330	Ps 90:4	208
Pliny *Nat.* 14.9	379, 385	Polybius *Hist.* 5.57.5	430	Ps 91:11	72
Pliny *Nat.* 16.79	116	Polybius *Hist.* 6.34	269	Ps 92:12	185
Pliny *Nat.* 25.5.14	348	Polybius *Hist.* 6.37–38	246	Ps 103:4	305
Pliny *Nat.* 26.20	293	Polybius *Hist.* 7.15–17	330	Ps 105:40	263
Pliny *Nat.* 29.3.47	369, 371	Polybius *Hist.* 7.15–18	330, 367	Ps 109	194
Pliny *Nat.* 29.38.117–32	491	Polybius *Hist.* 7.16.6	327, 330	Ps 137	194
Pliny *Nat.* 31.20.29	439, 478	Polybius *Hist.* 8.17–23	330	Ps 146:6	245
Pliny *Nat.* 33.27.114	491	Polybius *Hist.* 10.18	408	Pseud. *Clem.* Rec. 5.34	196
Pliny *Nat.* 33.53.148	228, 331, 381	Polybius *Hist.* 15.1	408	Pseudo-*Galen Introd.* 100.4	454
Pliny *Nat.* 33.66	326, 347	Polybius *Hist.* 18.52.1	166	Pseudo-*Philo L.A.B.* 64.6	372
Pliny *Nat.* 34.108	455	Propertius *Eleg.* 1.14.20	295	Pss 2:7–8	303
Pliny *Nat.* 34.53	101	Propertius *Eleg.* 2.29.26	295	Pss 2:8–9	148
Pliny *Nat.* 35.172	335	Prov 1:9	214	Pss 50:1–15	93
Pliny *Nat.* 35.26.45	291, 296	Prov 3:12	491	Pss 61:1–3	313
Pliny *Nat.* 35.44–45	293	Prov 3:18	216	Pss 89:19–45	303
Pliny *Nat.* 36.21	116	Prov 4:9	214, 216	Pss 89:26–27	303, 305

Index of Scripture and Ancient Writings

Reference	Pages
Pss 89:26–29	219
Pss. 139:1–6	316
Pss. Sol. 2:16	313
Pss. Sol. 2:34–35	316
Pss. Sol. 2:40	309
Pss. Sol. 17:23	321
Pss. Sol. 17:8	313
Rev 1:1	71, 81
Rev 1:10–20	81
Rev 1:11	48, 71, 76, 79, 96
Rev 1:12	138
Rev 1:12–13	188
Rev 1:12–20	81
Rev 1:13	131, 188
Rev 1:1–3, 5	145
Rev 1:14	490
Rev 1:16	73, 75, 244, 245, 254
Rev 1:17	184, 202
Rev 1:17–18	81, 181
Rev 1:18	184, 201, 209
Rev 1:19	71, 96
Rev 1:2	93
Rev 1:20	73-75, 88, 130, 136, 138-39, 188
Rev 1:3	48–49, 76, 79–80, 86, 96, 126, 211, 217, 314
Rev 1:4–5	48
Rev 1:5	94, 221, 255, 303–4, 308–9, 490
Rev 1:6	210, 221, 265
Rev 1:7	414
Rev 1:8	80, 81
Rev 1:9	44–45, 93, 190, 208, 210, 309
Rev 2	52, 73, 79, 81, 87, 93, 137, 145, 147, 153, 180–81, 195, 206, 209, 214, 216–17, 239, 253, 305, 320, 429, 507
Rev 2:1	48, 71, 79, 81, 128, 180, 244, 254, 302, 356, 399, 474
Rev 2:10	54, 85, 90, 193, 201–6, 208–10, 214, 217, 219
Rev 2:11	50, 93, 96, 98–99, 201, 210, 219–21, 223
Rev 2:1–17	128
Rev 2:12	48, 71, 81, 128, 180, 244, 302, 356, 399, 474
Rev 2:13	90, 189, 210, 248, 254, 255
Rev 2:13–15	415
Rev 2:13b	251
Rev 2:14	64, 142, 148, 256, 258, 309, 507, 512
Rev 2:14–15	141
Rev 2:15	64, 258
Rev 2:16	85, 88, 137, 211, 245, 261, 320, 414
Rev 2:17	93, 96, 98–99, 148
Rev 2:18	48, 71, 81, 128, 180, 244, 302, 356, 399, 474
Rev 2:18–29	302
Rev 2:19	189, 210, 308–9, 312, 319
Rev 2:2	189, 205, 362
Rev 2:20–24	141, 256, 257
Rev 2:21	85
Rev 2:22	85
Rev 2:22–23	88, 211, 310
Rev 2:22b	319
Rev 2:2–3	309
Rev 2:23, 24	131
Rev 2:25	137, 366
Rev 2:26	320–22
Rev 2:26–27	148
Rev 2:26–29	220
Rev 2:27	310
Rev 2:28	148
Rev 2:29	50, 93, 96, 98, 99
Rev 2:3	208, 217
Rev 2:4	308, 377, 406, 424, 507, 514
Rev 2:5	85, 88, 137, 211, 258, 320, 414, 492
Rev 2:6	64
Rev 2:7	50, 54, 76, 79, 93–94, 96, 98–99, 143, 147, 216
Rev 2:8	48, 71, 81, 128, 180–81, 184, 210, 217, 222, 244, 302, 356, 399, 474
Rev 2:9	55, 189–90, 193, 195, 198, 205, 209, 211, 216, 221, 318, 407
Rev 2:9–10	178
Rev 3:1	48, 71, 81, 189
Rev 3:10	88, 309
Rev 3:11	137, 211, 214, 261, 366, 414
Rev 3:12	148, 265, 362, 404
Rev 3:13	50, 93, 96, 98–99, 143, 377
Rev 3:14	48, 71, 81, 85, 94, 128, 180, 244, 255, 302, 356, 399, 474
Rev 3:14–22	471
Rev 3:15	189
Rev 3:15, 16	492
Rev 3:15–18	478–79, 483, 519
Rev 3:16	64, 88, 211, 368, 483, 484, 488–93, 500
Rev 3:17	193, 364, 485, 492
Rev 3:18	459, 488–93, 500
Rev 3:19	85
Rev 3:19–20	366
Rev 3:1a	128, 180, 244, 302, 356, 399, 474
Rev 3:20	495
Rev 3:20–21	494
Rev 3:21	214, 481, 500
Rev 3:22	50, 96, 98–99
Rev 3:22–24	216
Rev 3:26	265
Rev 3:3	85, 88, 137, 320, 360–61, 364–65, 488, 492
Rev 3:3, 9	131
Rev 3:3–4	360
Rev 3:3b	211
Rev 3:4	368, 370, 373, 376, 459, 490
Rev 3:5	54, 145, 148, 214, 320, 417, 488
Rev 3:6	50, 96, 98
Rev 3:7	48, 71, 81, 128, 180, 244, 302, 356, 399, 474
Rev 3:8	189, 254
Rev 3:9	55, 195, 203, 485
Rev 4:1	404
Rev 4:10	214, 408
Rev 4:10–11	214
Rev 4:11	370
Rev 4:2–11	249
Rev 4:3	266
Rev 4:4	214, 217, 488, 490
Rev 4:8	80
Rev 5	214
Rev 5:10	88, 195, 221, 265
Rev 5:12	89, 194, 201, 365
Rev 5:13–14	407
Rev 5:14	408
Rev 5:2	370
Rev 5:2, 5	485
Rev 5:4	362
Rev 5:5	90, 145, 194, 303–4, 320, 417
Rev 5:6	89, 194, 201, 216, 365
Rev 5:6, 8	90
Rev 5:8	400
Rev 5:8–13	477
Rev 5:9	195, 490
Rev 5:9–10	221, 404
Rev 6:10	400–1, 407, 413
Rev 6:11	370, 488, 490
Rev 6:2	214, 216
Rev 6:4	245, 364
Rev 6:8	316
Rev 7:13-14	488

Jesus Speaks to Seven of His Churches

Rev 7:13–14	368, 370	Rev 13:7	400	Rev 18:11–19	487
Rev 7:14	89, 201, 208, 360, 365, 413, 490	Rev 13:7–8	207	Rev 18:21–23	421
		Rev 13:8	194, 201, 217, 374–75	Rev 18:3	320
Rev 7:15	420	Rev 13:8, 14	413	Rev 18:3, 9	313
Rev 7:17	89, 365, 502	Rev 13:9	93	Rev 18:6	313
Rev 7:9	195, 370, 373, 488	Rev 14:1	266, 422	Rev 18:8	316
Rev 7:9–10	373	Rev 14:12	201, 210, 308–9, 410	Rev 19:11	264, 373, 400
Rev 7:9–12	249	Rev 14:12–13	90	Rev 19:12	214, 423
Rev 7:9–14	490	Rev 14:12–14	217	Rev 19:13	485
Rev 8:13	361, 413	Rev 14:13	48	Rev 19:14	488
Rev 9:20	361	Rev 14:14	214, 216	Rev 19:15	320
Rev 9:21	312, 313	Rev 14:14–17	414	Rev 19:15, 21	245
Rev 9:7	214	Rev 14:1-5	210	Rev 19:16	81
Rev 10:4	364	Rev 14:15, 17	420	Rev 19:2	313
Rev 10:4, 9	485	Rev 14:4	368	Rev 19:20	408
Rev 11:10	413	Rev 14:5	362	Rev 19:6, 15	80
Rev 11:1–13	139	Rev 14:6	413	Rev 19:8, 14	490
Rev 11:1–2	420	Rev 14:6–9	368	Rev 19:9	48, 270, 496
Rev 11:13	361	Rev 14:8	313, 320	Rev 20:11	490
Rev 11:17	80	Rev 14:9	408	Rev 20:11–12	249
Rev 11:18	477	Rev 15:3	80	Rev 20:11–15	317
Rev 11:2	320	Rev 15:3–4	320, 350	Rev 20:12, 13	313
Rev 11:2, 3	205	Rev 15:4	408	Rev 20:12–13	364
Rev 11:4	138	Rev 15:5–8	420	Rev 20:12–15	87, 376
Rev 11:9	203	Rev 16:1, 17	420	Rev 20:13	316
Rev 12:1	214	Rev 16:10	248	Rev 20:14	222
Rev 12:10	321, 408, 485	Rev 16:11	194	Rev 20:14–15	221
Rev 12:11	89–90, 145, 201, 210, 220, 308, 320, 365, 410, 417	Rev 16:15	361, 365–66, 414, 459, 487, 492	Rev 20:15	362, 374
				Rev 20:3	320
Rev 12:12	93, 413	Rev 16:19	320, 362, 403, 477, 487	Rev 20:4	500
Rev 12:14, 15	250	Rev 16:21	194	Rev 20:4–5	364
Rev 12:17	201, 410	Rev 16:37	273	Rev 20:4–6	207
Rev 12:3	214	Rev 16:5	350	Rev 20:4–6	265
Rev 12:4	136	Rev 16:6	370	Rev 20:6	221, 222
Rev 12:5	320	Rev 16:7, 14	80	Rev 21:1–22:5	88, 477
Rev 12:6	205	Rev 16–20	93	Rev 21:16	106
Rev 12:8	362	Rev 17:1	313	Rev 21:16–18	149, 507
Rev 12:9	250	Rev 17:1–18	71	Rev 21:1–8	207
Rev 12–16	47	Rev 17:12	207	Rev 21:19	54
Rev 13:1	194, 207, 214	Rev 17:12–14	194	Rev 21:2	404, 423
Rev 13:10	210, 308–9, 410	Rev 17:14	89, 145, 210, 320, 365, 417	Rev 21:2, 10	421
Rev 13:10, 14	245	Rev 17:16	207	Rev 21:20	266
Rev 13:13–14	132	Rev 17:2	313	Rev 21:22	80, 420–21
Rev 13:14–15	207	Rev 17:2, 4	313	Rev 21:24	320
Rev 13:17–18	422	Rev 17:2, 8	413	Rev 21:25–26	409
Rev 13:18	207	Rev 17:3	194, 207	Rev 21:27	219
Rev 13:2	247	Rev 17:3–4	487	Rev 21:3	222
Rev 13:2, 7	502	Rev 17:4	266	Rev 21:3, 7	221
Rev 13:4, 8	408	Rev 17:7	207	Rev 21:3–5	249
Rev 13:5	194	Rev 17:8	374–75	Rev 21:4	219
Rev 13:6	194	Rev 18:11–13	107	Rev 21:5	48, 400, 477

Reference	Pages
Rev 21:7	88, 145, 219–20, 222, 305, 320, 321, 374, 417
Rev 21:7–8	219
Rev 21:8	221, 222, 313
Rev 21:9–22:5	71
Rev 22:1, 3	502
Rev 22:10–21	70
Rev 22:12	313, 316, 414
Rev 22:13	184
Rev 22:14	87, 360, 364, 368, 490
Rev 22:1–4	216
Rev 22:15	313
Rev 22:1–5	148
Rev 22:16	75, 79, 96, 304, 322
Rev 22:18	49, 76, 79, 86, 93, 96
Rev 22:18–19	87
Rev 22:2	149
Rev 22:20	75, 414, 477
Rev 22:21	48
Rev 22:25–28	273
Rev 22:3	87, 89, 90, 219, 365, 407, 408
Rev 22:4	266, 422
Rev 22:5	265, 500
Rev 22:6	71, 400, 477
Rev 22:7	87, 93, 414
Rev 22:7, 12, 20	261
Rev 22:8	76, 79
RIC 1.2992	332
RIC 1.37a	304, 323
RIC 1.48	332, 367, 433
Rom 1:4	304
Rom 1:9	477
Rom 2:16	316–17
Rom 2:28–29	196
Rom 2:29	407
Rom 2:4	312
Rom 2:6	313
Rom 3:4	220
Rom 3:8	199
Rom 38	194
Rom 5:3; 15:4	309
Rom 8:17–25	88
Rom 8:2	358
Rom 8:32	193
Rom 8:35–39	410
Rom 10:19–11:32	409
Rom 11:26	409
Rom 11:33	318
Rom 12:6–8	308
Rom 13:11	361
Rom 15:15	136
Rom 15:19	362
Rom 15:26	105
Rom 16:3–16	273
Rom 16:7	132
RPC 1.1329	382
RPC 1.1332	389–90, 393, 396
RPC 1.1334	388
RPC 1.1338	394
RPC 1.2911	433
RPC 1.2988	332
RPC 1.2991	332, 350
RPC 1.398	374
RPC 2.1336	385
RPC 2:942	299
RPC 2893	454
RPC 2893–2895	454
RPC 2894	452
RPC 3.2376	394
RPC 3.3212	387
RPC 9792	465
RPC I 2222	116
RSC 30	116
Ruth 1:13	152
Sappho *Frag.* 96, 98	325
SEG 4.247.2	498
SEG 4.247–61	498
SEG 4.250.2	498
SEG 4.541	285
SEG 6.252	368
SEG 26.1817.80	267
SEG 28	288
SEG 29.1205	350
SEG 31.953	443
SEG 35.1169	304
SEG 35.1174–231	395
SEG 37.886	112–13
SEG 39.851	246
SEG 40.1045	283
SEG 41.1033	283
SEG 42.311	347
SEG 45.1133	246
SEG 45.1524	347
SEG 46.1519	351
SEG 46.1520	351
SEG 46.1521	344
SEG 46.1523	347
SEG 46.1524	287, 344, 347
SEG 46.1528	351
SEG 46.1529	350
SEG 55.2001	443
Seneca *Ep. Mor.* 62:3	193
Seneca *Ep. Mor.* 78.23	483
Seneca *Ep. Mor.* 94.21	136
Seneca *Med.* 99	295
Seneca *Nat. quaest.* 6.1.13	331
Servius *ad Aen.* 10.76	498, 526
Shem. Rab. 2	418
Shem. Rab. 31	218
Sib. Or. 3.271	196
Sib. Or. 3.716–20	408
Sib. Or. 3.725–31	408
Sib. Or. 5.516	322, 515
Sib. Or. 5.527	322
Sib. Or. 5:289	355
Sib. Or. 7.149	263, 514
Sidonius *Ep.* 4.15	499
Sifre Deut 10	139
SIG 3.741	430
SIG 3.867	112–13
SIG 3.883. 26–27	111
SIG 3.973	165
SIG 3.985	391, 395, 411
SIG 3.1003.15–17	111
Sir 6:3	214
Sir 11:11	214
Sir 11:18	214
Sir 16:12, 14	313
Sir 21:3	245
Sir 25:6	214
Sir 35:24	316
Sir 42:18–19	316
Sir 44:17, 20	362
Sir 50:12	214
SNG BnF 1021	389, 396
SNG BnF 1314	381
SNG BnF 924	393, 395
SNG BnF 925	393–94
SNG BnF 951A	393
SNG BnF 97	389
SNG Cop. 337	395
SNG Cop. 379	385
SNG Cop. 442	112, 121
SNG Cop. 502	351
SNG Cop. 515	332, 350
SNG Cop. 549	433
SNG Cop. 555	452, 454
SNG Cop. 583–586	469
SNG Cop. 589–591	469
SNG Cop. 595–97	469
SNG Cop. 598	469
SNG Cop. 599	469
SNG Cop. 600–601	469

Reference	Page(s)
SNG Cop. 620	374
SNG München 391	469
SNG München 419	388
SNG Righetti 1065	389–90, 393
SNG Righetti 582	381
SNG Tübingen 3752	393
SNGvA 2.3058	395
SNGvA 2.3077	390
SNGvA 2.3081	396
SNGvA 2.3820	463
SNGvA 2.3851–3854	469
SNGvA 2.3856–3862	469
SNGvA 2.3858	468–69
SNGvA 2.3863	469
SNGvA 2.8414	469
SNGvA 2.8417	469
SNGvA 2.8418	469
SNGvA 2.8419	469
SNGvA 2.8420	469
Soph. Jes. Chr. 98, 105, 107	144, 262
Sophocles Aj. 131.623	207
Sophocles Phil. 391–95	347
Stabo Geogr. 16.2.23	290
Statius Silv. 4.1.1–4	323, 515
Statius Theb. 4.265	295
Stephanus De Urb. 869	276
Strabo Geogr. 1.3.21	326, 348, 350
Strabo Geogr. 1.3.4	419
Strabo Geogr. 3.2.6	456
Strabo Geogr. 3.5.5–6	419
Strabo Geogr. 5:11.5.4	153
Strabo Geogr. 6.14.1.37	154, 187
Strabo Geogr. 6.14.1.4	151, 154
Strabo Geogr. 6.41	104
Strabo Geogr. 6:12.3.21	153
Strabo Geogr. 6:14.1.15	191
Strabo Geogr. 6:14.1.37	160–61
Strabo Geogr. 8.6.20	123
Strabo Geogr. 8.71	101
Strabo Geogr. 11.4.4	277
Strabo Geogr. 11.493	431
Strabo Geogr. 11.495	431
Strabo Geogr. 11.5.3–4	101
Strabo Geogr. 11.578	431
Strabo Geogr. 12.1.54f	232
Strabo Geogr. 12.8, 16	429
Strabo Geogr. 12.8.16	427–31, 433, 437, 441, 456–57, 459, 461, 490
Strabo Geogr. 12.8.18	278, 380, 382, 385, 405, 421, 432, 518
Strabo Geogr. 12.8.20	161, 453, 487
Strabo Geogr. 13.4	227–28, 276–77, 326, 328, 331–32, 339, 345, 348, 367, 381, 385, 427, 431, 441, 483, 485
Strabo Geogr. 13.4.1	227
Strabo Geogr. 13.4.10	380, 382, 385, 405, 421, 518
Strabo Geogr. 13.4.2	228, 331, 381
Strabo Geogr. 13.626	327
Strabo Geogr. 14.1.15	160
Strabo Geogr. 14.1.2	153
Strabo Geogr. 14.1.21	101
Strabo Geogr. 14.1.23	116
Strabo Geogr. 14.1.24	102, 104
Strabo Geogr. 14.1.37	154, 160–61, 164, 184
Strabo Geogr. 14.1.40	327
Strabo Geogr. 14.2.29	153
Strabo Geogr. 14.38	278
Strabo Geogr. 14.4.1	428
Strabo Geogr. 23.4.4	276
Suetonius Aug. 40.2	270
Suetonius Aug. 42.3	270
Suetonius Cal. 22.3	59
Suetonius Cl. 17.3	372
Suetonius Cl. 24.3	372
Suetonius Dom. 13.2	63
Suetonius Dom. 14.2	385
Suetonius Dom. 3.1	130, 305
Suetonius Dom. 4.5	269
Suetonius Dom. 7.2	385
Suetonius Dom. 8.14.4	372
Suetonius Galb. 11	245
Suetonius Jul. 26.3	443
Suetonius Nero 11	270
Suetonius Nero 16.2	405
Suetonius Tib. 43.1	124
Suetonius Tib. 48.2	278, 331
Suetonius Tib. 8	278, 432, 433
Sus 42	316
T. Ab. 1:2, 5	495
T. Ab.10.9	214
T. Ben. 4.1	212, 217
T. Dan 5.12	217
T. Job 37:6	318
T. Job 40:3	214
T. Jud. 24:1	304, 322
T. Levi 18.11	216
T. Levi 18:10–14	148
T. Levi 18.11	146, 508
T. Levi 18:3	304
T. Levi 8.12–14	266, 514
T. Levi 8.2, 9	212
T. Livi 18:3	322
T. Mos. 8:1	413
Tacitus Ann. 1.17	443
Tacitus Ann. 12.18	408
Tacitus Ann. 14.27.1	433, 461, 486
Tacitus Ann. 15.44	499
Tacitus Ann. 2.47	104, 229, 278, 331, 353, 367, 382, 421, 432
Tacitus Ann. 2.80	111
Tacitus Ann. 3.2	372
Tacitus Ann. 3.63	166
Tacitus Ann. 3.68	245
Tacitus Ann. 3.69	44
Tacitus Ann. 4.15	58
Tacitus Ann. 4.30	45, 46
Tacitus Ann. 4.37	167, 229, 252, 253
Tacitus Ann. 4.37–8	167
Tacitus Ann. 4.55	118, 167, 191, 333, 353, 432, 468
Tacitus Ann. 4.55–56	166, 191
Tacitus Ann. 4.56	167, 432, 448
Tacitus Ann. 4:56	209
Tacitus Ann. 6.1	124
Tacitus Ann. 6:20	185
TAD 20, no. 2 (1973): 17–27	278
TAM V 1.225	395
TAM V 1.85	288, 456
TAM V 1.972	287
TAM V 2.1002	287
TAM V 2.1019	288, 456
TAM V 2.1098	299
TAM V 2.1497	388, 395–96
TAM V 2.1539	411
TAM V 2.932	284
TAM V 2.935	288
TAM V 2.945	288
TAM V 2.965	288
TAM V 2.968	287
TAM V 2.975	287
TAM V 2.978	287
TAM V 2.980	287
TAM V 2.991	288
Teach. Silv. 116.3	316
Tertullian Apol. 7.3	171
Tertullian Cor. 10.9	171
Tertullian Marc. 1.29	142
Tertullian Praescr. 33	142
Tertullian Praescr. 36	45
Tertullian Pud. 19	142

Tertullian *Scorp.* 10.10	194	Wis 5:16	214
Tertullian *Scorp.* 10.6	197	Wis 7:1	316
Tertullian *Scorp.* 9.2	171, 197	Xenophanes *Pol.* 4.173	345
Tg. Isa. 22:14	221	Xenophanes *Pol.* 9.3	326, 346
Tg. Isa. 22:22	402	Xenophon *Anab.* 1.2	428
Tg. Isa. 65.15	221	Xenophon *Anab.* 1.2.6	427
Tg. Jer. 51:39, 57	221	Xenophon *Anab.* 1.2.7	148
Tg. Neof. Deut 33:6	221	Xenophon *Anab.* 1.3.14	148
Tg. Neof. Deut. 33:6	222	Xenophon *Anab.* 1.7	341
Tg. Neof. Deut. 51:39, 57	222	Xenophon *Anab.* 1.8.16	269
Tg. Noef. Deut. 8:16	263	Xenophon *Anab.* 2.4.14, 16	148
Tg. Onq. Deut 33:6	221	Xenophon *Anab.* 6.3.25	269
Tg. Pal. Exod. 40:4	129	Xenophon *Anab.* 7.8.8–22	227
Tg. Ps.-J. Exod. 16:4, 15	263	Xenophon *Cyr.* 7.2.2–4	329, 367
Theophrastus *Char.* 17.8	267	Xenophon *Eph. Tale* 1.1–3	111
Thucydides *Hist.* 3.104	110	Xenophon *Eph. Tale* 1.2–3	111
Thucydides *Hist.* 3.36.3	364	Xenophon *Hell.* 1.5.3	500
Thucydides *Hist.* 7.10	59	Xenophon *Hell.* 3.1.6	227
Tim.Frag. 137	117	Xenophon *Hell.* 3.4.11–24	329
Titus 1:4	315	Xenophon *Mem.* 2.1.30	483
Titus 1:5	127	Zech 1:3	80
Titus 2:13	414	Zech 11:5	486
Titus 2:2	309	Zech 13:9	488–89
Tob 1:17	487	Zech 14:11	89, 364
TP 100.3	165	Zech 2:11	496
Ulpian *Dig.* 1.18.6.8	245	Zech 3:1–2	202
Ulpian *Dig.* 28.3.7	205	Zech 3:1–3	373
Ulpian *Dig.* 48.19.35	204	Zech 3:1–5	368, 407
Ulpian *Dig.* 48.19.8.9	204	Zech 4	129
Ulpian *Dig.* 48.22.6	205	Zech 4:1–10	358
Varro *Rust.* 2.11.6–9	291	Zech 4:2	138
Varro *Ling.* 5.128	501	Zech 4:6–9	139
Varro *Rust.* 2.2.18	291	Zech 6:14	214
Varro *Rust.* 133.9	295	Zech 8:20–23	408
Victorinus *Comm. Apoc.* 10.11	46	Zech 8:3	423
Victorinus *Comm. Apoc.* 17.10	46	Zech 8:8	496
Victorinus *Comm. Apoc.* 2:17	267	Zeph 1:14	152, 413
Virgil *Aen.* 2.67	295		
Virgil *Aen.* 6.782	130		
Vitruvius *Arch.* 10.2.11–12	117		
Vitruvius *Arch.* 2.8.9–10	335		
Vitruvius *Arch.* 3.2.7	117		
Vitruvius *Arch.* 7.13.1–3	295		
Vitruvius *Arch.* 7.13.2–3	289		
Vitruvius *Arch.* 7.4	233		
Vitruvius *Arch.* 7:13	293		
Vitruvius *Arch.* 8.3.1	441, 485		
Vitruvius *Arch.* 8.3.14	456, 459		
Wis 12:10	312		
Wis 14:12	257		
Wis 16:20	263		

www.ingramcontent.com/pod-product-compliance
Lightning Source LLC
Chambersburg PA
CBHW080527300426
44111CB00017B/2635